The SAGE
Handbook of
Conflict Resolution

International Advisory Board

The SAGE
Handbook of
Conflict Resolution

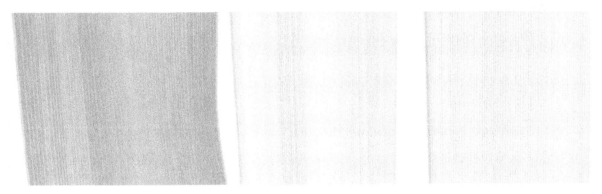

Edited by
Jacob Bercovitch,
Victor Kremenyuk,
and I William Zartman

Los Angeles • London • New Delhi • Singapore • Washington DC

First published 2009

SAGE Publications Ltd
1 Oliver's Yard
55 City Road
London EC1Y 1SP

SAGE Publications Inc.
2455 Teller Road
Thousand Oaks, California 91320

SAGE Publications India Pvt Ltd
B 1/I 1 Mohan Cooperative Industrial Area
Mathura Road
New Delhi 110 044

SAGE Publications Asia-Pacific Pte Ltd
33 Pekin Street #02-01
Far East Square
Singapore 048763

Library of Congress Control Number: 2008921082

British Library Cataloguing in Publication data

A catalogue record for this book is available from the British Library

ISBN 978-1-4129-2192-3

Typeset by CEPHA Imaging Pvt. Ltd., Bangalore, India

Dedication

This book is dedicated to all the Nobel Peace Prize Laureates, in the hopes of furthering greater Conflict Resolution.

2007 – Intergovernmental Panel on Climate Change, Al Gore
2006 – Muhammad Yunus, Grameen Bank
2005 – International Atomic Energy Agency, Mohamed El Baradei
2004 – Wangari Maathai
2003 – Shirin Ebadi
2002 – Jimmy Carter
2001 – United Nations, Kofi Annan
2000 – Kim Dae-jung
1999 – Médecins Sans Frontières
1998 – John Hume, David Trimble
1997 – International Campaign to Ban Landmines, Jody Williams
1996 – Carlos Filipe Ximenes Belo, José Ramos-Horta
1995 – Joseph Rotblat, Pugwash Conferences on Science and World Affairs
1994 – Yasser Arafat, Shimon Peres, Yitzhak Rabin
1993 – Nelson Mandela, F.W. de Klerk
1992 – Rigoberta Menchú Tum
1991 – Aung San Suu Kyi
1990 – Mikhail Gorbachev
1989 – The 14th Dalai Lama
1988 – United Nations Peacekeeping Forces
1987 – Óscar Arias Sánchez
1986 – Elie Wiesel
1985 – International Physicians for the Prevention of Nuclear War
1984 – Desmond Tutu
1983 – Lech Walesa
1982 – Alva Myrdal, Alfonso Garcã Robles
1981 – Office of the United Nations High Commissioner for Refugees
1980 – Adolfo Pérez Esquivel
1979 – Mother Teresa
1978 – Anwar al-Sadat, Menachem Begin
1977 – Amnesty International
1976 – Betty Williams, Mairead Corrigan
1975 – Andrei Sakharov
1974 – Sean MacBride, Eisaku Sato
1973 – Henry Kissinger, Le Duc Tho
1972*
1971 – Willy Brandt
1970 – Norman Borlaug
1969 – International Labour Organization
1968 – René Cassin
1967**
1966*
1965 – United Nations Children's Fund

1964 – Martin Luther King Jr.
1963 – International Committee of the Red Cross, League of Red Cross Societies
1962 – Linus Pauling
1961 – Dag Hammarskjald
1960 – Albert Lutuli
1959 – Philip Noel-Baker
1958 – Georges Pire
1957 – Lester Bowles Pearson
1956**
1955*
1954 – Office of the United Nations High Commissioner for Refugees
1953 – George C. Marshall
1952 – Albert Schweitzer
1951 – Léon Jouhaux
1950 – Ralph Bunche
1949 – Lord Boyd Orr
1948**
1947 – Friends Service Council, American Friends Service Committee
1946 – Emily Greene Balch, John R. Mott
1945 – Cordell Hull
1944 – International Committee of the Red Cross
1939–1943**
1938 – Nansen International Office for Refugees
1937 – Robert Cecil
1936 – Carlos Saavedra Lamas
1935 – Carl von Ossietzky
1934 – Arthur Henderson
1933 – Sir Norman Angell
1932*
1931 – Jane Addams, Nicholas Murray Butler
1930 – Nathan Saderblom
1929 – Frank B. Kellogg
1928*
1927 – Ferdinand Buisson, Ludwig Quidde
1926 – Aristide Briand, Gustav Stresemann
1925 – Sir Austen Chamberlain, Charles G. Dawes
1923–1924*
1922 – Fridtjof Nansen
1921 – Hjalmar Branting, Christian Lange
1920 – Léon Bourgeois
1919 – Woodrow Wilson
1918*
1917 – International Committee of the Red Cross
1914–1916*
1913 – Henri La Fontaine
1912 – Elihu Root
1911 – Tobias Asser, Alfred Fried
1910 – Permanent International Peace Bureau
1909 – Auguste Beernaert, Paul Henri d'Estournelles de Constant
1908 – Klas Pontus Arnoldson, Fredrik Bajer
1907 – Ernesto Teodoro Moneta, Louis Renault
1906 – Theodore Roosevelt
1905 – Bertha von Suttner
1904 – Institute of International Law
1903 – Randal Cremer
1902 – Élie Ducommun, Albert Gobat
1901 – Henry Dunant, Frédéric Passy

The prize money was allocated 1/3 to the Main Fund and 2/3 to the Special Fund of this prize section.

**The prize money was allocated to the Main Fund.*

Contents

Author Biographies

EDITORS

Jacob Bercovitch is professor of International Relations, and Fellow of the Royal Society, at the University of Canterbury in Christchurch, New Zealand. He received his PhD from the London School of Economics. His main research interests are in the areas of international conflict resolution and mediation. He is former vice president of the International Studies Association, and the author or editor of 12 books and about 100 articles on these issues. He has held fellowships from London, Harvard, Georgetown, the US Institute of Peace, and the Hebrew University in Jerusalem. His most recent publication is *Conflict Management, Security and Third Party Intervention in East Asia* (Routledge, 2008).

Victor Kremenyuk is Russian historian and political scientist, professor and Deputy Director of the Institute for US and Canadian studies of the Russian Academy of Sciences. His areas of interest include international relations, conflict studies, risk and crisis control, and international negotiation. He has published almost 250 works in Russian, English, Chinese, Arabic, French, and Swedish. Since 1983, he is associated with IIASA Process of International Negotiation Programme, is editor of the state-of-the-art *International Negotiation: Analysis, Approaches, Issues* (two editions at the Jossey Bass in 1991 and 2002), and is winner of the 2002 Book Award at the CPR Institute for Dispute Resolution (New York) and for several other books. He is also winner of the Soviet National Prize for Science and Technology (1980), and of the Russian government prize for the strategic risk analysis (2004). He was included into the list of leading intellectuals of 2007, compiled by the International Biographical Centre, Cambridge, UK.

I. William Zartman is Jacob Blaustein Professor of Conflict Resolution and International Organization at the Nitze School of Advanced International Studies at Johns Hopkins University. He is the author of *The Practical Negotiator, The 50% Solution, Cowardly Lions: Missed Opportunities to Prevent Deadly Conflict and State Collapse*, and *Ripe for Resolution*, editor of *The Negotiation Process and Positive Sum*, among other books, and co-editor of *Diplomacy Games*, a recent book in the PIN Series. Professor Zartman is a member of the Steering Committee of the (PIN) at (IIASA). He is organizer of the Washington Interest in Negotiations (WIN) Group and was a distinguished fellow at the US Institute of Peace. He received his PhD from Yale University and an honorary doctorate from the Catholic University at Louvain.

CONTRIBUTING AUTHORS

Part I

Louis Kriesberg (PhD, 1953, University of Chicago) is Professor Emeritus of Sociology, Maxwell Professor Emeritus of Social Conflict Studies, and founding director of the Program on the Analysis and Resolution of Conflicts (1986–1994), all at Syracuse University. In addition to over 125 book chapters and articles, his published books include: *Constructive Conflicts* (1998, 2003, 2007), *International Conflict Resolution* (1992), *Timing the De-Escalation of International Conflicts* (co-ed., 1991), *Intractable Conflicts and Their Transformation* (co-ed., 1989), and *Social Conflicts* (1973, 1982). His current research interests include the transformation of violent civil conflicts, alternative American foreign policies, intractable conflicts, and reconciliation.

Christer Jönsson is professor of Political science at Lund University, Sweden. He earned his PhD at Lund University in 1975, and has been visiting professor at Kyung Hee University, Seoul, and Stanford University. His research interests include international negotiation, diplomacy, and the role of transnational networks in international cooperation. He has published numerous books, articles, and book chapters, and is the co-author of *Organizing European Space* (2000) and *Essence of Diplomacy* (2005).

J. David Singer is Professor Emeritus of Political Science at the University of Michigan, Ann Arbor. He holds a BA from Duke University (1946) and a DPhil from New York University (1956). His interests include world politics, war and peace, and quantitative history. He has authored more than twenty books on these issues.

Jack S. Levy (PhD, University of Wisconsin Madison, USA) is Board of Governors' Professor of Political Science at Rutgers University, and Senior Associate at the Saltzman Institute of War and Peace Studies at Columbia University. He is president of the International Studies Association (2007–08) and past president of the Peace Science Society (2005–06). His current research interests include preventive war, balance of power theory, power transition theory, the evolution of war, the militarization of commercial rivalries, applications of prospect theory to international relations, time horizons and discounting, intelligence failure, the causes of World Wars I & II, and qualitative methodology. See www.rci.rutgers.edu/~jacklevy/

Rudolf Avenhaus is professor of Statistics and Operations Research at the University of the Federal Armed Forces Munich, Germany. Prior to his academic appointment in1980, he was research assistant at the Universities of Karlsruhe and Geneva, Research Scholar at the Nuclear Research Center, Karlsruhe, and Lecturer at the University of Mannheim. From 1973 to 1975 and again in 1980, he worked at the International Institute for Applied Systems Analysis (IIASA). Professor Avenhaus has written numerous scientific journal publications, as well as *Material Accountability* (1977), *Safeguards Systems Analysis* (1987), *Compliance Quantified* (together with M. Canty, 1996), *Verifying Treaty Compliance* (ed. with N. Kyriakopoulos, M. Richard and G. Stein, 2006). In 1989 and 1990, he was Chairman of his Faculty, in 1993 and 1994, Vice President, and in 1994, Acting President of his University. Since 1996, he has been a member of the Steering Committee of the Processes of International Negotiations (PIN) Program of IIASA.

Dean G. Pruitt is Distinguished Scholar in Residence at the Institute for Conflict Analysis and Resolution at George Mason University and SUNY Distinguished Professor Emeritus in the

Department of Psychology at the University at Buffalo: State University of New York. He has a PhD from Yale University and taught social psychology at the University of Delaware and the University at Buffalo for 41 years. He has received the Lifetime Achievement Award from the International Association for Conflict Management and the Harold D. Lasswell Award for Distinguished Scientific Contribution to Political Psychology from the International Society of Political Psychology. He is author or co-author of *Negotiation Behavior*, *Negotiation in Social Conflict*, and *Social Conflict: Escalation, Stalemate, and Settlement* (1st, 2nd, and 3rd editions); co-editor of *Mediation Research and Theory* and *Research on the Causes of War*; and author of more than 100 articles and chapters. His areas of interest are social conflict, negotiation, and mediation. He is currently working on case studies of peace processes in ethno-political conflict.

Daniel Druckman is a professor in the Department of Public and International Affairs at George Mason University. He has been the Vernon M. and Minnie I. Lynch Professor of Conflict Resolution at George Mason, where he has coordinated the doctoral program at the Institute for Conflict Analysis and Resolution. He is also a professor at the University of Queensland in Brisbane, Australia, a member of the faculty at Sabanci University in Istanbul, and a visiting professor at National Yunlin University of Science and Technology in Taiwan and at the University of Melbourne in Australia. He received a PhD from Northwestern University and was awarded a best-in-field prize from the American Institutes for Research for his doctoral dissertation. He has published widely on such topics as negotiating behavior, nationalism and group identity, human performance, peacekeeping, political stability, nonverbal communication, and research methodology. He is a board member or associate editor of eight journals and co-edits a new book series on *International Negotiation*. He received the 1995 Otto Klineberg award for Intercultural and International Relations from the Society for the Psychological Analysis of Social Issues for his work on nationalism, a Teaching Excellence award in 1998 from George Mason, an award for the outstanding article published in 2001 from the International Association for Conflict Management (IACM), and the 2006 outstanding book award for *Doing Research: Methods of Inquiry for Conflict Analysis*. He is the recipient of the 2003 Lifetime Achievement award from the IACM.

Tamra Pearson d'Estrée, PhD in Social Psychology, Harvard University, is Henry R. Luce Professor of Conflict Resolution at the University of Denver, and the Director of their Conflict Resolution Institute's Center for Research and Practice. She has also held faculty appointments at the Institute for Conflict Analysis and Resolution (ICAR) at George Mason University, and the Psychology Department at the University of Arizona. Her research interests lie at the intersection of conflict resolution and social psychology, including work on social identity, intergroup relations, and conflict resolution processes, as well as on evaluation research and reflective practice. She is the author, with Bonnie G. Colby, of *Braving the Currents: Evaluating Conflict Resolution in the River Basins of the American West* (Kluwer), as well as several book chapters and articles in various interdisciplinary journals. She has led trainings and facilitated interactive problem-solving workshops in various intercommunal conflict contexts including Israel–Palestine, Ethiopia, and in US intertribal disputes, and she has directed and/or evaluated projects aimed at conflict resolution capacity- and institution-building in Israel–Palestine, Ukraine, and Georgia. She has consulted for UNESCO and UNDP on conflict resolution activities in regional conflicts. She is currently working with community mediation centers in Colorado to develop a common evaluation framework, and directs two externally funded projects partnering the University of Denver with universities abroad to develop their countries' mediation capacities: University of West Indies, Trinidad and Tobago (State Dept-funded); and Tbilisi State University, Georgia (USAID/HED-funded).

Richard Jackson is reader in International Politics at Aberystwyth University, UK. He obtained his PhD in Political Science from the University of Canterbury, New Zealand. He is the founding editor of the journal *Critical Studies on Terrorism*. His current research interests include the discourses of terrorism, international conflict resolution, and the social construction of contemporary war.

Part II

John A. Vasquez is the Thomas B. Mackie Scholar in International Relations at the University of Illinois at Urbana-Champaign. His PhD is from the Maxwell School, Syracuse University. He has published widely on causes of war, territorial disputes, peace research, and international relations theory. His most recent book is *The Steps to War: An Empirical Study* (with Paul D. Senese), Princeton University Press, 2008.

Philippe Le Billon (MBA Paris, PhD Oxford) is assistant professor at the University of British Columbia with the Department of Geography and the Liu Institute for Global Issues. Before joining UBC, he was a research associate with the Overseas Development Institute (ODI) and the International Institute for Strategic Studies (IISS), having previously worked on humanitarian and resource management issues in Angola, Cambodia, Sierra Leone, and the former Yugoslavia.

Gunnar Sjöstedt is senior research fellow at the Swedish Institute of International Affairs and also associate professor of political science at the University of Stockholm. His research work is concerned with processes of international cooperation and consultations in which negotiations represent an important element. He has studied the OECD as a communication system and the external role of the European community, as well as the transformation of the international trade regime incorporated in GATT and its external relations. He is the editor of International *Environmental Negotiations* and the co-editor of *Negotiating International Regimes*, the second and fourth books, respectively, in the PIN series.

Donald Rothchild, who sadly passed away in February 2007, was professor of Political Science at the University of California, Davis. His recent books include authoring *Managing Ethnic Conflict in Africa: Pressures and Incentives for Cooperation* (Brookings, 1997); *Sovereignty as Responsibility: Conflict Management in Africa* (co-author, Brookings, 1996), and co-editing *International Spread of Ethnic Conflict: Fear, Diffusion, and Escalation* (Princeton, 1998); *Ending civil wars: The Implementation of Peace Agreements* (Lynne Rienner, 2002); *Sustainable Peace: Power and Democracy after Civil Wars* (Cornell, 2005); and *Africa–US Relations: Strategic Encounters* (Lynne Rienner, 2006).

S. Ayse Kadayifci-Orellana is currently assistant professor in the field of Peace and Conflict Resolution at the School of International Service at American University, Washington, DC. She is also one of the founding members and the associate director of Salam Institute for Peace and Justice, a non-profit organization for research, education, and practice on issues related to conflict resolution, nonviolence, and development with a focus on bridging differences between Muslim and non-Muslim communities. She received her PhD from American University's School of International Service in Washington, DC in 2002 with a Master's degree in Conflict Analysis from University of Kent in Canterbury, England. Dr Kadayifci-Orellana has authored *Standing on an Isthmus: Islamic Narratives of War and Peace in the Palestinian Territories* and co-authored the edited volume, *Anthology on Islam and Peace and Conflict Resolution in Islam: Precept and Practice*. Her research interests include cultural and religious traditions and conflict resolution,

Islamic approaches to peace and conflict resolution, interfaith dialogue, among others. She has facilitated dialogues and conflict resolution workshops between Israelis and Palestinians, conducted Islamic conflict resolution training workshops to imams and Muslim youth leaders in the United States, organized and participated in interfaith and intra-Muslim dialogues, and organized and participated in the first American Muslim Delegation to Iran (November 2007)

Part III

Michael S. Lund is Senior Specialist for Conflict and Peacebuilding, Management Systems International, Inc. and Consulting Program Manager, Woodrow Wilson International Center for Scholars. He does research and consulting for governments and international organizations. He is author of *Preventing Violent Conflicts: A Strategy for Preventive Diplomacy* (USIP Press, 1996) and numerous book chapters, assessments, and evaluations. He has edited and contributed to several books, including *Critical Connections: Security and Development*, a comparison of seven countries (Lynne Rienner, forthcoming, 2008). His analyses have been commissioned by the US Department of State, CIA, USAID, US Council on Foreign Relations, Carnegie Commission for Preventing Deadly Conflicts, World Bank, United Nations (UNDP, UNDPA), European Commission, OSCE, and many more. Lund worked in the US Congress, federal agencies, and the Urban Institute, and was the founding Director of the Jennings Randolph Fellows Program and a Senior Scholar at the US Institute of Peace. He has a BD from Yale University and a PhD in Political Science from the University of Chicago, and has taught at Cornell, UCLA, the University of Maryland, George Mason University, and Johns Hopkins School of Advanced International Affairs.

Franz Cede is a retired Ambassador, a former legal advisor to the Austrian Ministry for Foreign Affairs and former Austrian Ambassador to Russia, Belgium, and NATO. He is affiliated to the German Society of International Law and Austrian Institute for European Security Policy. He holds a doctorate in Law (University of Innsbruck, 1968), and an MA in International Affairs (School of Advanced International Studies SAIS, Washington, DC, 1972). His main research interests are international law, European affairs, and international security policy.

Harold H. Saunders is president of the International Institute for Sustained Dialogue and has conducted sustained non-official dialogues among people in conflict since ending a 25-year career in foreign affairs in the US government in 1981. From 1974 to 1979, he was intensively involved in the Arab–Israeli peace process, flying on the Kissinger shuttles, and, as Assistant Secretary of State, he was a principal drafter of the Camp David accords in 1978 and a mediator of the Egyptian–Israeli peace treaty. He holds a BA from Princeton and a PhD in American Studies from Yale. He is author of *A Public Peace Process: Sustained Dialogue to Transform Racial and Ethnic Conflicts* (1999) and *Politics is About Relationship: A Blueprint for the Citizens' Century* (2005).

Andrea Bartoli is Drucie French Cumbie Chair of Conflict Analysis and Resolution. He is currently working at the Institute for Conflict Analysis and Resolution, George Mason University. Dr Bartoli completed his Italian dottorato di ricerca (PhD. equivalent) at the University of Milan and his laurea (BA–MA equivalent) at the University of Rome. His main research interest is peacemaking and genocide prevention. Dr Bartoli is studying the emergence of peace in Mozambique. In collaboration with the Dynamical System Teams, he is developing new research methodologies to understand more accurately how peace emerges. He has initiated a series of workshops on the Genocide Prevention Program and on Peacemaking, a project that engages government officials from 192 UN member states on genocide prevention. He has been involved in numerous conflict resolution activities as a member of the Community of St Egidio.

Connie Peck is the principal coordinator of the UNITAR Programme in Peacemaking and Preventive Diplomacy, which she founded in 1993, and which provides advanced training to UN staff and diplomats. Her most recent books are *On Being a Special Representative of the UN Secretary-General*; *Sustainable Peace: The Role of the United Nations and Regional Organizations in Preventing Conflict*; *Increasing the Effectiveness of the International Court of Justice*; and *The United Nations as a Dispute Settlement System: Improving Mechanisms for the Prevention and Resolution of Conflict.*

Part IV

William A. Donohue is currently a Distinguished Professor of Communication at Michigan State University. He received his PhD in 1976 from the Ohio State University in Communication. Bill's work lies primarily in the areas of mediation, crisis negotiation, and counterterrorism. He has worked extensively with several state and federal agencies in both training and research activities related to violence prevention and hostage negotiation. He has authored over 70 publications dealing with various communication and conflict issues and has won several awards for his scholarship from national and international professional associations. Bill is an active member of the International Association for Conflict Management and is currently its president. He is on the editorial board of several journals in the areas of conflict management and communication and serves on the steering committee of the Processes of International Negotiation program that functions within the International Institute for Applied Systems Analysis.

Eytan Gilboa (PhD, Harvard University) is professor and Chair of the Communication Program and Director of the Center for International Communication at Bar-Ilan University. He is also a Visiting Professor of Public Diplomacy at the University of Southern California. His research interests include mass communication aspects of conflict and diplomacy.

David L. Rousseau is associate professor in the Department of Political Science at the University at Albany (SUNY: State University at New York). He holds a PhD from the University of Michigan and an MPP from the Kennedy School of Government at Harvard University. Dr Rousseau is the author of *Democracy and War: Institutions, Norms, and the Evolution of International Conflict* (Stanford University Press, 2005) and *Identifying Threats and Threatening Identities: The Social Construction of Realism and Liberalism* (Stanford University Press, 2006). His research interests include the democratic peace, identity, constructivism, interdependence, weapons of mass destruction, argumentation, and research methodologies.

David Kinsella (PhD, Yale University, 1993) is professor of Political Science in the Hatfield School of Government at Portland State University and Editor-in-Chief of *International Studies Perspectives*, a journal of the International Studies Association. He is co-author of *World Politics: The Menu for Choice*, co-editor of *The Morality of War: A Reader*, and has published widely in scholarly journals. His most recent research has focused on illicit arms trade networks and the implications for violent conflict and arms control.

Fen Osler Hampson is professor and director of the Norman Paterson School of International Affairs, Carleton University. A graduate of the University of Toronto and the London School of

Economics, he received his PhD in political science from Harvard University. He is the author or co-author of eight books on international affairs and the editor/co-editor of 23 other volumes. His most recent books are *Taming Intractable Conflict: Mediation in the Hardest Cases* (with Chester Crocker and Pamela Aall) and *Grasping the Nettle: Analyzing Cases of Intractable Conflict* (co-edited with Crocker and Aall), both published by the United States Institute of Peace Press. His research interests are in the fields of conflict management and international negotiation.

Guy Olivier Faure is professor of Sociology at the Sorbonne University, Paris V, where he teaches 'International Negotiation', 'Conflict Resolution', and 'Strategic Thinking and Action.' He is a member of the editorial board of three major international journals dealing with negotiation theory and practice: *International Negotiation* (Washington), *Negotiation Journal* (Harvard, Cambridge), and *Group Decision and Negotiation* (New York). His major research interests are business and diplomatic negotiations, especially with China, focusing on strategies and cultural issues. He has authored, co-authored, and edited a dozen books and over 50 articles. Among his most recent publications are *How People Negotiate* (Kluwer Academic), *Escalation and Negotiation* (Cambridge University Press) with I. William Zartman, and *La négociation décloisonnée* (Paris, Publibook). Together with the late Jeffrey Z. Rubin, he edited *Culture and Negotiation*, the third volume in the PIN series. His works have been published in 11 different languages.

Paul F. Diehl is Henning Larsen Professor of Political Science and University Distinguished Teacher/Scholar at the University of Illinois at Urbana-Champaign. He received his PhD in Political Science at the University of Michigan in 1983. His areas of expertise include the causes of war, UN peacekeeping, and international law.

Valérie Rosoux has a PhD from the *Université Catholique de Louvain* (UCL), Belgium, in International Relations. She graduated in Political Science and Philosophy. She is a research fellow at the Belgian National Fund for Scientific Research (FNRS) and teaches International Negotiation at UCL. Her main research interest is memory and Conflict Resolution. Her latest publications concern the Franco-German, Franco-Algerian, and Rwandan cases. She is the author of several books and articles about the transformation of relations between former belligerents, the latest of which are "The Figure of the Rescuer in Rwanda", *International Social Science Journal*, no. 189, 2008; "Rwanda : l'impossible 'mémoire nationale'?"; *Ethnologie française*, XXXVII, no. 3, 2007, 409–415; "Human rights and the 'work of memory' in international relations", *International Journal of Human Rights*, vol. 3, no. 2, June 2004, 159–170; and "Memory and International Negotiation: the Franco-German Case", in I.W. Zartman and V. Kremenyuk (ed.), *Peace versus Justice. Negotiating Forward-and Backward-Looking Outcomes* (Lanham: Rowman & Littlefield, 2005, 155–177).

Scott Sigmund Gartner is a professor of Political Science at the University of California, Davis, where he teaches courses on US National Security and International Relations. He received his PhD from the University of Michigan. His two main research topics are the effects of dispute management on peace and conflict (e.g. Gartner and Bercovitch, *International Studies Quarterly*, 2006) and the interactive relationship between war and domestic politics (e.g. Gartner, *American Political Science Review*, 2008). He is author of *Strategic Assessment in War* (Yale University Press, 1999), and co-editor of *The Historical Statistics of the United States* (Cambridge University Press, 2006) and the forthcoming *International Conflict Mediation: New Approaches and Findings* (Routledge).

Cecilia Albin (PhD, SAIS, Johns Hopkins, 1993) is professor of Peace and Conflict Research at Uppsala University, Sweden. Her main research interests include international negotiation, issues of justice and ethics, and international cooperation over global issues. Among her publications are *Justice and Fairness in International Negotiation* (Cambridge, 2001) and *Negotiating International Cooperation: Global Public Goods and Fairness* (Cambridge, 2003).

Kristian Skrede Gleditsch (PhD in Political Science, University of Colorado, Boulder, 1999) is professor in the Department of Government, University of Essex (2005 to date) and Research Associate at the Centre for the Study of Civil War, PRIO (2003 to date). His research interests include conflict and cooperation, democratization, and spatial dimensions of social and political processes. He is the author of *All International Politics is Local: The Diffusion of Conflict, Integration, and Democratization* (University of Michigan Press, 2002). His articles have appeared in *American Journal of Political Science*, *American Political Science Review, Annals of the Association of American Geographers, International Interactions, International Organization, Internasjonal Politikk, International Studies Quarterly, Journal of Conflict Resolution, Journal of Peace Research, Political Analysis,* and *Political Psychology*.

Eileen F. Babbitt is professor of International Conflict Management Practice and Director of the International Negotiation and Conflict Resolution Program at the Fletcher School of Law and Diplomacy at Tufts University. She is also a Faculty Associate of the Program on Negotiation at the Harvard Law School where she co-directs the Project on International Institutions and Conflict Management. Her research interests include identity-based conflicts; co-existence and trust-building in the aftermath of civil war; and the interface between human rights concerns and peace-building. Dr Babbitt holds a Master's Degree in Public Policy from the Kennedy School of Government at Harvard University, and a PhD from MIT.

Paul Meerts graduated in Political Science at the University of Leyden in The Netherlands. His position is with the Netherlands Institute of International Relations "Clingendael". As a member (since 1999) of the PIN Steering Committee, he participates in PIN research on a structural basis with a special focus on issues like the evolution of interstate negotiation, the connection between negotiation and warfare, as well as negotiation processes in the European Union and other multilateral regimes. As trainer (Clingendael) and professor (College of Europe) in Diplomatic Negotiation, he works with diplomats/civil servants and (post-)graduate students around the globe.

CO-AUTHORS

Karin Aggestam is an associate professor in political science and director of Peace and Conflict Studies at Lund University, Sweden. She has published widely in international journals and edited volumes in the fields of negotiation, diplomacy, conflict theory, and the Middle East peace process. She is presently coordinating a large EU project on just and durable peace in the Middle East and Western Balkans within the Seventh Framework Programme.

Molly M. Melin received her PhD in Political Science from the University of California at Davis in 2008. Her research and teaching interests are in the areas of international relations and political methodology, with emphasis on international conflict and conflict management. She is also interested in international organizations and foreign policy decision-making. Her current research focuses on third-party interventions in ongoing international conflicts and the dynamics of conflict expansion.

Brandon Valeriano is an assistant professor at the University of Illinois at Chicago. He completed his PhD at Vanderbilt University in 2003 in the field of International Relations. He has previously taught at Vanderbilt and Texas State University. Dr Valeriano's main research interests are in the causes of war and peace. His book in progress is an exploration of the onset of all interstate rivalries from 1816 to 1992. Other ongoing research looks at classification systems of war, complex rivalries, immigration, and Latino foreign policy issues.

Chester A. Crocker is the James R. Schlesinger Professor of Strategic Studies at Georgetown University where his teaching and research focus on conflict management and regional security issues. He served as chairman of the board of the United States Institute of Peace (1992–2004), and continues as a member of its board. From 1981 to 1989, he was US Assistant Secretary of State for African Affairs. As such, he was the principal diplomatic architect and mediator in the prolonged negotiations among Angola, Cuba, and South Africa that led to Namibia's transition to independence, and to the withdrawal of Cuban forces from Angola. He serves on the boards of ASA Ltd., a NYSE-listed, closed-end fund focused on gold mining; Universal Corporation, Inc., a leading independent trading company in tobacco, agricultural and lumber products; Good Governance Group Ltd; and First Africa Holdings Ltd. He serves on the advisory board of the National Defense University in Washington.

Acknowledgements

As we survey the stacks of massive contributions in front of us, we realize that the book represents what is known about conflict resolution today. It embodies the ideas, insights, and experiences of some of the best scholars and practitioners of the field. Pleased as we are with it, we cannot but be aware of the many debts we have incurred in completing a task of this magnitude. It is a pleasure to acknowledge all the people and organizations who have helped us. Above all, we owe a tremendous debt to all our distinguished colleagues and friends who contributed chapters for this volume, and worked within our guidelines and requests without too many complaints. Their contributions have been truly outstanding, and it was a pleasure to work with such a dedicated and professional group of people. Lucy Robinson and Sage Publications have commissioned us to produce this volume. We are grateful to them for their vote of confidence in us, and their continued support and encouragement.

Eight anonymous reviewers read through our draft proposal and made some very helpful comments. We wish we could thank them individually, but we have no idea who they are, save that they are masters in the field of Conflict Resolution. We owe special thanks to our International Advisory Board, who in faith backed this project before the results came in.

We must pay special thanks to the International Institute of Applied Systems Analysis (IIASA) and its Director Leen Hordijk. In many ways, IIASA was the home of the project, and we doubt that it would have been possible without the Institute's support. Through the PIN project, they hosted all the contributors at a three-day conference at their site in Laxenburg, Austria, in the summer of 2007. The conference was a marvelous opportunity to meet each other in person, share experiences, discuss the strengths of each chapter, and ensure the coherence of the whole enterprise.

We have to single out one particular individual at IIASA, and that is Tanja Huber, the PIN Project Coordinator. From its very inception, Tanja became the indispensable link through which all chapters were channeled, all communications were undertaken, and all arrangements were made. Editing a book of this size when the editors are either traveling constantly or are in three different continents requires a central person with special talents. Tanja had these talents in abundance. We owe Tanja a truly profound debt, and it is a pleasure to be able to acknowledge it here. We also want to thank Isabelle Talpain-Long for keeping the project in order on the Washington side.

Our biggest thanks must go to our families. They did not write any of the chapters, but without their support, understanding, patience, and often forbearance, you, dear reader, would not have held this book in your hands right now. Now that you have opened it, we hope you will read parts, or most of it, and, dare we hope, enjoy the experience.

Jacob Bercovitch, Victor Kremenyuk, and I. William Zartman
Christchurch, Moscow, and Washington, DC

About the Processes of International Negotiation (PIN) Network at the International Institute for Applied Systems Analysis (IIASA)

Since 1988, the PIN Network at IIASA in Laxenburg, Austria, has been conducted by an international Steering Committee of scholars, meeting three times a year to develop and propagate new knowledge about the processes of negotiation. The Committee conducts one to two workshops every year devoted to the current collective publication project and involving scholars from a wide spectrum of countries, in order to tap a broad range of international expertise and to support scholarship on aspects of negotiation. It also offers mini-conferences on international negotiations in order to disseminate and encourage research on the subject. Such "Road Shows" have been held at the Argentine Council for International Relations, Buenos Aires; Beida University, Beijing; the Center for Conflict Resolution, Haifa; the Center for the Study of Contemporary Japanese Culture, Kyoto; the Diplomatic Academy, Tehran; the Netherlands Institute of International Relations, Clingendael, The Hague; the Swedish Institute of International Affairs, Stockholm; the University of Cairo; University Hassan II, Casablanca; the University of Helsinki; and the UN University for Peace, San José, Costa Rica, among others. The PIN Network publishes a semiannual newsletter, *PINPoints,* and sponsors a network of over 4,000 researchers and practitioners in negotiation. The Network has been supported by the William and Flora Hewlett Foundation and the US Institute of Peace. Contact: pin@iiasa.ac.at.

Members of the PIN Steering Committee

Rudolf Avenhaus
The German Armed Forces
    University, Munich

Franz Cede
Austrian Ambassador to Belgium
    and NATO

Guy Olivier Faure
University of Paris V-Sorbonne

Victor Kremenyuk
The Russian Academy of Sciences

Paul Meerts
The Netherlands Institute of
    International Relations, Clingendael

Gunnar Sjöstedt
The Swedish Institute of
    International Affairs

I. William Zartman
The Johns Hopkins University

Mark Anstey
Nelson Mandela University, South Africa

Selected Publications of the PIN Program

Escalation and Negotiation in International Conflicts, I.W. Zartman, G.O. Faure, editors, 2005, Cambridge University Press, Cambridge, UK.

Peace versus Justice: Negotiating Backward- and Forward-Looking Outcomes, I.W. Zartman, V. Kremenyuk, editors, 2005, Rowman & Littlefield Publishers, Inc., Lanham, MD, USA.

Negotiating European Union, P.W. Meerts, F. Cede, editors, 2004, Palgrave Macmillan, Basingstoke, UK.

Getting It Done: Post-Agreement Negotiations and International Regimes, B.I. Spector, I.W. Zartman, editors, 2003, United States Institute of Peace Press, Washington DC, USA.

How People Negotiate: Resolving Disputes in Different Cultures, G.O. Faure, editor, 2003, Kluwer Academic Publishers, Dordrecht, Netherlands.

Professional Cultures in International Negotiation: Bridge or Rift? G. Sjöstedt, editor, 2003, Lexington Books, Lanham, MD, USA.

Containing the Atom: International Negotiations on Nuclear Security and Safety, R. Avenhaus, V.A. Kremenyuk, G. Sjöstedt, editors, 2002, Lexington Books, Lanham, MD, USA.

International Negotiation: Analysis, Approaches, Issues, 2nd Edition, V.A. Kremenyuk, editor, 2002 Jossey-Bass Inc. Publishers, San Francisco, CA, USA.

Preventive Negotiation: Avoiding Conflict Escalation, I.W. Zartman, editor, 2001, Rowman and Littlefield Publishers, Inc., Lanham, MD, USA.

Power and Negotiation, I.W. Zartman, J.Z. Rubin, editors, 2000, The University of Michigan Press, Ann Arbor, MI, USA.

International Economic Negotiation. Models versus Reality, V.A. Kremenyuk, G. Sjöstedt, editors, 2000, Edward Elgar Publishing Limited, Cheltenham, UK.

Negotiating International Regimes: Lessons Learned from the United Nations Conference on Environment and Development (UNCED), B.I. Spector, G. Sjöstedt, I.W. Zartman, editors, 1994, Graham & Trotman Limited, London, UK.

International Multilateral Negotiation: Approaches to the Management of Complexity, I.W. Zartman, editor, 1994, Jossey-Bass Inc. Publishers, San Francisco, CA, USA.

International Environmental Negotiation, G. Sjöstedt, editor, 1993, Sage Publications, Newbury Park, CA, USA.

Culture and Negotiation. The Resolution of Water Disputes, G.O. Faure, J.Z. Rubin, editors, 1993, Sage Publications, Inc., Newbury Park, CA, USA.

Processes of International Negotiations, F. Mautner-Markhof, editor, 1989, Westview Press Inc., Boulder, CO, USA.

Introduction: The Nature of Conflict and Conflict Resolution

Jacob Bercovitch, Victor Kremenyuk, and I. William Zartman

INTRODUCTION

Conflict Resolution is a broad and fast growing academic field that needs to find its place in the world of disciplines. Although it is a relatively young focus of study, having begun to emerge as a specialized field only in the 1950s, when superpower conflict threatened the very existence of humankind, it has rapidly grown into a self-contained, vibrant, interdisciplinary field where theory and practice pace real-world events. Essentially, scholars working on Conflict Resolution study the phenomenon of conflict and analyze ways to bring it under control, bringing their insights and concepts to bear on actual conflicts, be they domestic or international, so as to foster better and more effective relations among states and peoples. Conflict Resolution is about ideas, theories, and methods that can improve our understanding of conflict and our collective practice of reduction in violence and enhancement of political processes for harmonizing interests. In this field, theory and practice are inextricably linked. What we know about conflict affects the way we approach it. Whether the focus is on international, internal or communal conflict, ideas and theories are available to change the way actors approach conflict and seek to resolve it.

Although the systematic study of Conflict Resolution is relatively new, conflicts and wars have long been the subject of research and teaching in such fields as diplomatic history, international relations, history, political science, law, and social psychology. Even disciplines as diverse as economics, business, and operations research and mathematics study different aspects of conflict. Thus, the very history and foundation of Conflict Resolution is one of rich diversity and cross-fertilization. The new field of Conflict Resolution, building on the work of many analysts, diplomats, and practitioners, is today one of the most interdisciplinary of all academic fields.

While each of its components maintains its roots in its own discipline, their contributions to the field of Conflict Resolution is much larger than the sum of its parts. Each contributes its own concepts and answers to the basic question of the field: how best to approach and resolve or manage conflicts? Contributions do not all come at the same time from all sources, and these various spurts of attention drive the field forward into new areas of inquiry, knowledge, and prescriptions. At the same time, the conceptual growth of the field has practical payoffs that keep research and teaching on Conflict Resolution focused on useful and relevant knowledge.

The task for the academic efforts of a volume of this magnitude is to give the reader a general idea of the scope of the field, to identify its useful concepts, and to provide evidence and evaluations. We decided to go much further. We have invited a distinguished group of experts who can not only give a grounded assessment of the state of the art but can also look into the future. Second, the recent evolution of Conflict Resolution provided us with some good lessons for discussion: the end of the Cold War, the management and even resolution of conflicts in Africa, Latin America, the Balkans, and some significant cases of conflict prevention and even transformation in other parts of the world. Third, there is a growing role for new actors, such as transnationals, non-governmental organizations (NGOs), academics and think-tanks, and international organizations (IGOs). Fourth, there is an openness for what 15 years ago was called "new thinking," an attempt to look at old phenomena from a totally new perspective. We have tried to incorporate all these elements in this volume.

This is a particularly propitious time to launch a handbook of knowledge on Conflict Resolution. The bipolar era of the Cold War is over, and the world is balancing between mitigated unipolarism and re-emergent multipolarism. But the current era is not just post-Cold War; it has often been called the Era of Terrorism, in which the globalizing world centred on the West (and the United States)

is met by a countervailing balance-of-power reaction, not only or so much from a group of states but from self-proclaimed representatives of the offended populations, using highly unconventional means of conflict. Both the cause and the means mark a new era of conflict to be resolved. It is therefore time to take stock of the state of our knowledge, sifting what does not pertain from the past era from what is still relevant in the present and future.

The rise in importance of Conflict Resolution as an identified field of inquiry follows the same path of context-relevant scholarship that accounted for the rise of previous paradigms. Just as the patent inadequacies of the inter-war Idealism were shown so clearly by World War II and then the Cold War, giving rise to the school of International Relations dubbed "Realism," in both study and practice, so the failure of Realism to provide guidance for the conflict management policies practiced despite the Cold War hostility and to explain the collapse of the Cold War in the end gave impetus to a new approach that came to bear the name of Conflict Resolution. New elements and patterns of thinking appeared alongside the old patterns. A natural question came to the fore: is it worth destroying each other for the achievement of existing goals? Are there other, more dignified means of solving existing problems? Are we doomed to fight each other for ever? What is more humane: to fight or to talk, even when you hate your opponent? The questions needed answers and Conflict Resolution has tried to fill the gap. It has meant at least two things: to try to resolve what already existed, and to suggest ways to prevent new unnecessary conflicts in the future and, increasingly, to *manage* what cannot be fully resolved.

Conflict Resolution is a vibrant field of enquiry. This is the first thing to understand. One can hardly imagine the current world of policy without it. It is not an abstract theoretical construction but an element of both academic research and practical policy. And it is growing: it is not a sketchy outline of possible strategies but a robust and healthy policy of decision-making. The more it has to show both as an explanation and a guide to practice, the more promising will be the future of Conflict Resolution.

Given these identifying characteristics of the current era, this Handbook adopts the considered assumptions (1) that the new challenges of the post-Cold War era make Conflict Resolution more difficult, but (2) that basic tools developed over past experiences have not changed and are still applicable. Terrorist conflict borrows the causes and grievances of past and local conflicts to anchor itself in local scenes; it makes its principal, specific cause the corruption and inadequacies of local governments and their foreign, globalizing support, and draws on alienated populations for its permissive sea of support. But the tools available to meet its outbursts are both broad and limited, comprising the same array of prevention, management, resolution, and transformation that past experience has developed. If there is something new demanded by the new era, it is the need to put great emphasis on handling structural causes (grievances and alienation) and on pursuing post-conflict reconstruction (peace-building). It is important to extend consideration of peacemaking measures into prevention, before the conflict erupts into violence, and implementation, before conflict re-erupts into violence.

Numerous scholars and researchers have sought to develop an adequate body of knowledge on conflict, in order to guide us in deciding how to reduce it, enhance it, or resolve it. That the quest for knowledge about conflict still continues unabated reflects not so much on the skills and expertise of those involved in it, as it does on the immensity and complexity of the phenomenon to be investigated. Social conflict is, after all, interwoven with the entire fabric as a social system. We may certainly strive to attain knowledge on that, but the process, however long or well-structured, cannot be totally satisfactory. With this in mind, we propose to examine in this chapter the ideas, values, definitions, and approaches in the study of conflict, and to attempt to integrate these in an effort to develop a comprehensive framework of the state of knowledge in this field.

Conflict Resolution as a field of study was most developed in North America and then in Europe. From there, it began to grow and spread. Academic journals, independent centres, university departments, and clusters of scholarship and teaching are now found in every part of the world. The number of scholars and institutions devoted to conflict resolution and making a practical difference to conflicts in places such as the Middle East, South Africa, Northern Ireland, Central America, and East Asia is an impressive testimony to the global commitment to the ideas of conflict resolution and the power of ideas to achieve this objective.

CONFLICT

Conflict, to begin with, refers either to a violent dispute or to an incompatibility of positions, according to Webster. To adopt the first definition is to lose sight of the initial reasons why the dispute arose or came to violence, one of the most important aspects of conflict. The second definition, adopted here, allows analysis to examine the initial sources and incompatibilities of positions, and to explain the process whereby it escalated to or towards violence.

As such, conflict is normal, ubiquitous, and unavoidable. It is an inherent feature of human existence.It is even useful on occasion. It is difficult to conceive of a situation which is conflict-free. Indeed, the very presence of conflict is at the heart of all human societies. This being the case, it is hardly surprising to note that "conflict is a theme that has occupied the thinking of men more than any other, save only God and love" (Rapoport, 1960: 12). The notion that it can be eliminated is idealistic and unreal, in general, although it may be applicable to specific instances. What can be eliminated (even if it should not, in some selected cases) is the violent expression of conflict, in the first definition. Further, in some cases, the possibility of resorting to violence, as threat or coercion, may be a necessary adjunct to de-escalation, and of course it is useless as a threat if its implementation is inconceivable or incredible. That is one of the many fine lines in the subject.

One school of thought identifies it as a *psychological* state of affairs, a particular situation "in which the parties are aware of the incompatibility of potential future positions" (Boulding, 1962: 5). Conflict is thus seen as a situation in which the parties *perceive* goal incompatibility, but do not necessarily engage in behaviour which is mutually incompatible. The idea that conflict refers to a cognitive rather than a behavioural state is supported by Stanger (1956; 1967) and Hammond (1965). Such a conception leads to an examination of attitudes in conflict, hostility, emotional orientations, perceptual conditions and other psychological processes (e.g. cognitive rigidity) which are brought out in a conflict.

Of course, parties can find themselves holding incompatible positions and let it go at that. But once they move from that passive or static position and start expanding efforts to prevail, active conflict begins: escalation is dynamic conflict. The term conflict is derived from the Latin word *confligere* where it means to strike together. This physical sense of two or more bodies moving against each other has been retained by those who offer an empirical definition of conflict. Conflict thus defined refers to overt and coercive behaviour initiated by one contending party against another.

In the physical sense, conflict may be taken to mean "a struggle over values and claims to scarce status, power and resources in which the aims of the opponents are to neutralise, injure or eliminate their rivals" (Coser, 1956: 7). Himes suggests that social conflict "refers to purposeful struggles between collective actors who use social power to defeat or remove opponents and to gain status, power, resources and other scarce values" (1980: 14). Morton Deutsch, whose influence on the discipline has been so seminal, refers to conflict as a situation which manifests itself whenever incompatible *activities* occur (1973: 10, our emphasis).

Mack & Snyder (1957) suggest that the term refers to a range of empirical phenomena which can be identified or characterized by four conditions: the existence of two or more parties, a situation of resource or position scarcity, the presence of behaviour that is designed to hurt or injure the other, and mutually opposed goals. These properties are offered by Mack and Snyder as the necessary empirical conditions for the existence of conflict. These conditions may exist within and among individuals, groups or nations. We can therefore speak of interpersonal, intergroup and international conflict. We can also speak of conflict *within* parties, and conflict *between* parties. We can distinguish between institutionalized and non-institutionalized conflict, conflicts between equal parties and conflicts between asymmetric parties (i.e. subordinate v superordinate). On the basis of these empirical conditions, we can generate quite a large number of possible conflict situations or types of conflicts (see Boulding, 1957; 1962).Let us look at each of these in some detail.

Parties in conflict

One of the key issues in the analysis of any conflict concerns the identity of the parties. The term "parties in conflict" is taken here to mean individuals, groups, organizations, nations, or other systems in conflict. It is an analytical construct referring to those units which initiate a conflict, pursue it, and determine its outcome. If we want to understand conflict situations, we have to know something about the parties in conflict.

Identifying parties in the abstract may be self-evident; identifying them in a particular conflict situation is much more complicated. Parties in conflict normally entail sub-systems or are themselves sub-systems of a larger unit. Parties in conflict may experience intra-party strife, or they may be manipulated by a stronger and much wealthier party. Some conflict parties may act as autonomous units, others may not. Some parties can be identified as wholly rational beings acting in their best interests, others cannot. To compound the analytical problems involved in identifying conflict parties, it must be recognized that an observer may define some units as conflict parties, whereas the participants themselves may not concur. Indeed, the identity of the parties in conflict may very well be an issue which all those involved are likely to contend.

Notwithstanding all these serious conceptual difficulties, as well as the many others which relate to parties' attributes and the degree of symmetry or asymmetry between them, it is useful to distinguish types of parties on several aggregation levels and give conventional names to sets of elements. Thus, the concept of parties in conflict may refer to an entire scale of entities ranging from the individual to the national and international organization. Each aggregation level could denote different conflict parties and different levels of analysis. One possible classification of parties in conflict, or levels of analysis, could include the following social categories: individuals, groups, communities, ethnic groups, nations, states, and regions.

This classification of parties in conflict assumes that there exist significant differences in the degree of organization and differentiation between the various levels. These differences imply that conflict between individuals might differ in some important aspects, from conflict between two nations. Classifying conflict parties on the basis of different structural dimensions suggests that conflict behaviour is not necessarily a continuous process, nor can one type of conflict be subsumed merely as a special case of conflict at a higher or lower level. Each conflict party develops its own means and procedures for dealing with its adversaries and pursuing its conflicts.

The discussion on the nature of parties in conflict may in fact be carried a step further by suggesting a dichotomy between intrasystem conflict and intersystem conflict. This distinction has appeared, in one form or another, in the writings of Coser (1956), Mack and Snyder (1957), and Boulding (1957). It was given its most explicit treatment by Galtung (1965) who developed a four-cell scheme based on the distinctions between individual and collective parties, and intra-system and inter-system conflict. Galtung's scheme can be used in a different form which retains the basic dichotomy but expands upon it by introducing a distinction between equal and unequal parties, and taking into account four, rather than two, main types of conflict parties. Taken together, a systematic party-based classification may be presented in a tabular form with abstract categories and concrete examples.

This classification purports to bring a semblance of order to the discussion of parties in conflict. It can also serve as a reminder, in case it is needed, of just how far we are from having theories to account for the various types of conflict, let alone from a general theory of social conflict. A large number of variables may be used to define, describe and analyse the course and consequences of various conflicts. Of these, the nature of the parties and their structural–organizational locus is perhaps one of the most important.

Issues in conflict

Conflict situations are essentially situations in which parties hold divergent or incompatible goals which motivate their behaviour. These incompatible goals define the range of issues in conflict – they tell us what the conflict is about.

Issues in conflict define the logical structure of a conflict situation. As parties in conflict differ so widely in terms of their values, beliefs and goals, it is to be expected that they will differ with respect to their perception of the issues in conflict. In fact, conflict parties often disagree on the issues in conflict, or on what the conflict is about. One party may see the issues in conflict as pertaining to the right of self-determination, while the other may see them as pertaining to its security and survival. Getting both parties to agree on what the conflict is about, or to think in terms of similar issues, may go a long way towards its successful resolution or management.

Why do parties have such different conceptions of the issues in conflict? Why do they often have opposed "definitions of the situation"? To answer this, we must realize that the parties' response to conflict stimuli is neither mechanistic or rational, nor interchangeable. On receiving a conflict stimulus (e.g. experience of frustration as a result of goal-interference), parties go through a complicated series of steps before they assign meaning to their experience, conceptualize its issues and select a response behaviour. This sequence of steps is affected by the state of each party, its values and needs, its historical experience, competence, context and modes of attribution. As these internal and external dimensions differ so widely between parties, we can perhaps appreciate why there are so many different interpretations of the situation or definitions of the issues in conflict.

As so many factors affect the perceptions – and definitions – of issues in conflict, how can we classify conflict issues? Various categories may be used (e.g. affective v substantive, realistic v non-realistic), but a more satisfactory way would be to define issues in conflict in terms of (a) the parties' evaluation (b) the rewards associated with various issues, and (c) their content.

1. Conflicted evaluations. Broadly speaking, two kinds of issues are at stake in all conflict situations; issues expressing a disagreement over means, and issues expressing disagreement over ends. The former, which we may describe as issues of interest, occur in situations where the parties agree on what they want, but disagree on how to obtain it. The latter, described as issues of value, characterize conflict situations where the parties differ even on what they want, or what is desirable (Aubert, 1963).

When conflict issues are defined in terms of interests, the basic incompatibility between the parties is perceived as differences on the preferred distribution of resources. When they are defined as conflicts of value, the basic incompatibility is perceived in terms of differences in beliefs, ideologies, and cognitive structure. Such differences in the parties' definition, or evaluation, of the issues in conflict, have a significant effect on the process of conflict management. Conflicts over values, or dissensual conflicts, are much less amenable to a compromise solution than conflicts of interests, or consensual conflicts (Druckman & Zechmeister, 1970; 1973). If conflict parties could somehow be persuaded to define their issues on the interests, rather than the values dimension, a meaningful and viable basis for cooperation could be created.

2. Differential rewards. Another way of looking at conflict issues is to ascertain the rewards, or punishments, which can accrue to each party from various possible issues which define the extent of their conflict. Conflict is minimal when conflict issues are defined so as to produce identical or correlated rewards for both parties (e.g. if one party gets more resources, the other party also gets more); it is maximal when the rewards for one party occur at the expense of the other (e.g. what one wins, the other loses). Conflicts of this type, often called zero-sum conflicts (because the parties' rewards also add up to zero), are characteristic of situations where parties are motivated by totally antagonistic interests stemming from each other's claim to *exclusive* position, ownership, or resources. There is only one possible outcome, namely, victory for one party and defeat for the other, and the likelihood of cooperation or compromise is extremely limited indeed.

Conflicts in real life are naturally much more complex than that. Issues are not normally defined in such a dichotomous manner. As most conflict situations contain a mixture of common and antagonistic interests, the issues in contention will not be viewed as a zero-sum situation. When the rewards or costs associated with each issue are not the same for each party, we talk of mixed motive situations or variable-sum conflict. In such situations, the parties may be motivated by (a) the desire to cooperate around the common interests, and (b) the desire to get a more favourable share of the resource, or position that is at the centre of their conflict. Even conflicts which may appear at first sight to be zero-sum (e.g. USA v Soviet Union) contain many common interests (e.g. avoiding a nuclear war) and are over issues with varying degrees of costs and rewards. The rewards associated with different conflict issues thus determine the extent and purity of a conflict, as well as the nature and possibilities of its management.

3. **Contending content.** This seems to be the most common way of analysing issues in conflict. Here we do not concern ourselves with whether conflicts are objective or subjective, nor do we concern ourselves with the extent and intensity of conflict in a relationship. Instead, we simply classify issues in terms of their content. Thus, we can have conflict situations where the issues centre around survival or scarcity. We can have situations where issues pertain to resources (e.g. territory, income), or to interaction norms (e.g. status, prestige, honour). Issues can express a basically intangible incompatability (e.g. a conflict over union recognition), or a basically tangible incompatibility (e.g. how to divide profits between labour and management).

A useful discussion of conflict situations in terms of their issue contents appears in Deutsch (1973), Holsti (1983) and Mitchell (1981). Deutsch describes five basic types of conflict issues: (a) resources, (b) preferences, (c) the nature of relationship, (d) values, and (e) beliefs. Holsti, focusing on international conflict, gives prominence to six types of issues: (a) limited territorial, (b) nature of government, (c) national honour, (d) liberation conflict, (e) imperialism, and (f) national unification. The most useful classification of issue contents appears in Mitchell. He describes five basic types of issues which I merely propose to paraphrase and state more simply as (a) issues of resources, (b) issues of sovereignty, (c) issues of survival, (d) issues of honour, and (e) issues of ideology.

Environment of conflict

The intellectual orientation towards conflict adopted in this book emphasizes the development of a taxonomy to influence the formulation of theories and the designs of empirical research. Such a taxonomy would enable better reference to and consideration of the conflict environment in any analysis of conflict.

A conflict relationship occurs within a specific social context; it affects it, and is in turn affected by it. A conflict may take place in a structured environment in which the parties' behaviour – and the manner by which resources are allocated – are specified or prescribed by norms (e.g. collective bargaining). A structured environment makes available various instrumentalities of conflict management, and determines kinds of behaviour which are considered legitimate or illegitimate. Conflict parties in a structured environment have a shared understanding which encourages appropriate responses, non-coercive strategies and a cooperative perspective.

In a structured environment, conflict management is institutionalized. This suggests that when dissatisfaction expresses itself or when conflict arises, well-supported and generally well-understood procedures for handling can be, and usually are, invoked. Goals, issues and the parties' sense of grievance are channelled by these procedures, and the likelihood of a compromise solution is enhanced considerably.

When a conflict occurs in an unstructured environment (e.g. a revolution), the parties typically believe they are in a zero-sum (i.e. win or lose) relationship. Here the parties lack the formal and informal norms that could provide a sense of community. Consequently, when a conflict becomes manifest, each party's behaviour may be limited only by its own capacity and disposition. Each party considers the other as a threat, and each is prepared to act violently against the other, even if it means injuring or destroying it.

The environment within which the conflict parties exist helps to shape their perceptions of the conflict, their options, responses and possible outcomes (Brickman, 1974). The aspects of a situation may not necessarily be accurately mirrored in the partiers' subjective perceptions. A discussion of the contextual variable with particular reference to the degree of differentiation, social organization, collective identity and nature of social change is, however, absolutely indispensable in developing an integrated approach to the study of conflict. Logical positivism and methodological individualism with their reductive tendencies may have excluded meaningful consideration of the social context. This is an unwarranted exclusion which offers no help in trying to organize the field of social conflict. It must be rectified.

Attitudes in conflict

Conflict is a social phenomenon that is generated and supported by a number of psychological factors. Of these, attitude formation is undoubtedly the most important.

The concept of attitude is one of the most widely used concepts in the social sciences. Broadly speaking, attitudes define the parties' evaluative and response tendencies in social situations. Attitudes are relatively enduring dispositions, having three basic dimensions: (a) the cognitive, (b) the affective, and (c) the behavioural. The cognitive dimension refers to the parties' beliefs and ideas about their environment, the affective dimension refers to the parties' feelings and emotions and the behavioural dimension refers to the specific readiness to respond. Each of these dimensions is affected by, and influences, a conflict situation. The result is that attitudes in conflict are made more negative or extreme, and are so structured as to view the other party in the worst possible light. To understand why this happens and why attitudes in conflict are so resistant to change, we need to know how attitudes are formed or acquired.

Perception is the process by which individuals receive and extract information about their environment. It is a cognitive process which involves reception of stimulus, mental organization and response. The final step in the process – the response – consists of an overt act, or the formation of an attitude. Attitudes are thus determined by each person's perception and conform to his picture, or image, of his environment.

Perception does not just happen randomly, nor can an individual perceive the numerous stimuli which bombard him in the course of his daily life. An individual is not merely a passive recipient of undetected stimuli, he is an active participant in the process. He *selects* stimuli and *organizes* them into patterns and meaningful categories. Selection and organization are crucial in the process of perception. It is precisely because individuals do not merely respond to a stimulus – they interpret, organize and react to it in their own way – that each person may hold a unique perception of the world.

Most of our perceptions seem clear and veridical (i.e. directly given to us). They seem to result from a stimulus in the environment and make up a set of images congruent with that environment. We assume that if we see a person or an object in a certain way, others will perceive it in the same way. The idea that there is such a thing as 'pure perception', or an unmediated and unidirectional stimulus response sequence may have had some appeal to nineteenth-century British empiricists. It is, however, a completely erroneous idea.

People from different cultures, or with different experiences, 'see' the same stimuli differently. What they see may appear veridical, but in reality it is only so because their needs, values, expectations and cognitive processes create the world which they perceive. Vision alone does not account for perception. Mental processes, dispositions and abilities determine the way we see the world and understand it. This is why what we perceive is in a sense exclusively ours. It may or may not be shared by others. If it is, we operate without validated or consensual grounds. Thus, one party in a conflict situation may attribute the causes of its own behaviour to events in the environment over which it has no control, while attributing the causes of the other's behaviour to personality attributes (e.g. inherent aggression) or faults.

Behaviour in conflict

Conflict behaviour occurs in a specific interaction content and is best described as a means by which each party proposes to achieve its goal. As such, it must be clearly understood that conflict behaviour does not necessarily refer to physical violence only. There are other means of achieving a goal, short of injuring or eliminating the adversary. Conflict behaviour is a broad term embracing a wide range of activities ranging from verbal acts (e.g. warnings, threats) to acts of direct physical damage. Conflict behaviour can be defined, as Mitchell (1981a: 122) notes, as any behaviour which occurs within the context of a conflict situation.

As the range of behaviour implied by this definition is so bewilderingly large, some order may be introduced by discussing zones of conflict behaviour. The most obvious distinction is between conflict behaviour that involves violence and coercion, and conflict behaviour that does not. A more useful distinction is that offered by Kriesberg (1982). He suggests that parties in conflict may resort to three basic types of behaviour: (a) persuasion, (b) coercion, and (c) reward (cf. Williams, 1977). All these types of behaviour purport to influence the adversary to change, modify, or abandon a goal, but they all give rise to different kinds of actual conduct.

Persuasion refers to types of conflict behaviour that seek to influence the other party through the use of reasonable arguments, appeals to common interests, and reference to generally accepted values and norms of fairness and equity. Such behaviour is, by definition, verbal only, and its characteristic features include advocacy and the utilization of symbolic means of communication. It is a mode of behaviour which has low costs in both resources and risks. Coercion involves trying to influence the other party through the imposition of unacceptable costs or actual injury. Coercive behaviour takes many forms. It may be threatened (deterrence) or implemented (violence). When implemented, it invariably involves the use of force and the infliction of damage, or destruction, to life or property. Coercive behaviour, whether at the interpersonal or international level, involves negative sanctions, high expenditure

of resources and high costs and sacrifices. The last category of conflict behaviour – reward – refers to promises of positive sanctions and inducements as a strategy of encouraging compliance. Reward, as a conflict behaviour strategy, is based primarily upon positive influence and offers of benefits, and is, not unlike the threat of coercion, totally contingent upon the response of the other party.

What is possible is a channelling of the conflict into political (non-violent) mechanisms for its management. These can appropriately be called regimes, sometimes formal and legally institutionalized, and sometimes informal. In many countries, political opponents for state leadership no longer kill each other to decide succession. They accept (and manipulate) the formal selection/election regime whose rules and regulations provide a winner, but they also engage in an informal regime whose norms provide acceptance of a political solution.

It is also possible in some cases actually to resolve the conflict. The issue over which the parties hold their incompatible positions may be decided, either as part of a general regime affecting those types of issues or as a specific political exercise. Again, there is a specific decision to square the incompatibility and also a longer process of letting it sink in, implementing it, and building on it, like a road repair.

At either end of the process are two other possibilities. To really eliminate the conflict, it can be transformed, replacing incompatibilities with ties of cooperation and interdependence. Even in this case, the transformation may not remove the original incompatibilities, but simply outweigh, bypass or overcome them, leaving the conflict enmeshed in cooperation but still there.

The other end of the process is conflict prevention, the product of the previous three but also their predecessor, making them less necessary. As usual by now, prevention often does not remove the conflict but puts a lid on its escalation. It also can make that escalation unnecessary by providing a resolution before further efforts to prevail become necessary.

A number of points emerge from this rapid epistemological review:

(1) Conflict, the existence of incompatible positions, is normal, ubiquitous, and unavoidable. Escalation is dynamic conflict. Sometimes measures can be taken to eliminate or reduce it; more often measures aim at keeping it from turning violent.

(2) Conflict resolution, as used in the title of this compendium, refers to all four types of action: prevention, management, resolution, and transformation. Again, some will act to remove or decide the conflict, while others will merely work to keep it at a manageable, political level.

(3) Any of these policies involves a specific act directed at the specific conflict, and a longer-term series of moves to implement that decision and to surround it with ties of acceptance. Conflict resolution involves attention to a specific conflict, with its history, emotion, and identity aspects, and also to generalized regimes, formal or informal, to provide behavioral and normative guidelines for "cases like this."

TERMS AND ASSUMPTIONS

Within this field of ongoing debate and investigation, a few terms are the subject of a special debate all of their own. Two such concepts are particularly difficult. There will be no attempt here to decree *ex cathedra* a standard meaning, but rather to indicate the range of the debate and, where possible, the particular meaning used here.

One such term is "success" or the broader area of evaluation. It is literally an endless task to seek a "final" evaluation of the effectiveness of conflict resolution measures, and much mindless energy has gone into demanding or concocting quantitative standards. One measure of "success" is simply the accomplishment of the act – the signature of an agreement, the holding of a series of dialogue meetings, the reduction of hostile acts. This measure, of course, does not take into account subsequent events that may revive the conflict or be its unintended consequences. An extension of the first is to give a time

dimension to the benchmarks – agreements that last more than a week or five years, a time period without renewed conflict. Any such measure is completely arbitrary (as arbitrary as the commonly used measure of 1000 deaths per year as an indication of a conflict worth attention) and although it should be considered as such, it is often difficult to avoid giving it substantive meaning. A third meaning of success could be the point when the conflict resolution action, external or internal, is no longer needed, i.e. when negotiations are ended or dialogue managers are no longer required or peacekeepers can go home or cries for justice are no longer heard. Such a measure adds a substantive element that in itself becomes hard to evaluate. Many of the following chapters will discuss their own problems of measuring success, and no universal definition fits all.

The other notion is the idea of "ethics" in regard to Conflict Resolution. A mediator is a meddler and Conflict Resolution practices seek to reduce violence and attenuate conflict in cases where the parties feel themselves to be completely justified and are often enjoying their efforts. "No gain without pain!" There is not a single author in this collection who does not come from a country which attained its independence or its form of government without violence in an event later celebrated as a national holiday [this was written on the 4th of July!]. An attempt to tone down the French or Russian Revolution, the US Civil War (or War between the States), or the Algerian National Liberation Struggle, among many others, was or would have been roundly denounced by the parties (including often the eventual losers) and would have produced results, if successful, making a profound difference in world events that would evoke varying appreciations today. So Conflict Resolution carries with it a certain presumption, if not arrogance, that its practitioners know better than the conflicting parties. Conflict Resolution requires humility.

On the other hand, parties in a conflict need help. The reduction of violence, and its consequent human, economic and political losses, has a value in and of itself, and often – although not always – the conflicting goals can be attained by other than violent means and can be made compatible with each other. Finally, the parties, either as states or as less sovereign actors, are ultimately in a position to decide whether to resist the pressures and opportunities associated with conflict resolution measures. In the end, conflict resolution, we feel, is a good thing, not an ultimate standard, a battle cry against evil, or an exclusive judgment, but an effort, in its forms of prevention, management, resolution and transformation, that works to the protection and improvement of human life and world conditions.

THE HANDBOOK

The following work is divided for convenience into four sections. The first deals with the history and methods of the study of conflict resolution. Following an opening history of the new field and an appreciation of diplomatic evolution, an overview chapter on methods and approaches leads to presentations on qualitative case study, quantitative analysis, rational choice analysis, experimentation, problem-solving and constructivism. The second section provides an overview of issues and sources of conflict. These are identified as Territory, Resources, Ecology, Ethnicity/Identity, Religion. The third turns to the Methods and Agencies of the practice of Conflict Management, beginning with Prevention, Negotiation, Mediation Arbitration, and Dialogue, and then turning to NGOs and universal and regional IGOs. The fourth section examines new challenges to conflict resolution, new modes of conflict and diverse issues arising within these approaches. These include terrorism, insurgencies, the media, democracy, development, human rights, intractability, culture, peacekeeping, reconciliation, durability, justice, coercion and training. These sections present their subject as the result of an evolution to the current state of the art (and its development). The conclusion continues this dynamic evaluation by presenting emergent problems for theory and practice.

REFERENCES

Boulding, K. 1962. *Conflict and Defense.* New York: Horper & Row.

Coser, L.C. 1956. *The Functions of Social Conflict.* New York: The Free Press.

Deutsch, Morton. 1973. *The Resolution of Conflict.* Princeton, N.J.: Princeton University Press.

Himes, J.S. 1980. *Conflict and Conflict Management.* Athens, G.A.: University of Georgia Press.

Holsti, K. 1983. *International Politics: A Framework for Analysis.* Englewood Cliffs, N.J.: Prentice-Hall.

Kriesberg, L. 1982. *Social Conflicts.* Englewood Cliffs, N.J.: Prentice Hall.

Mack, R.W. and R.C. Synder. 1957. "The Analysis of Social Conflict: Toward an Overview and Synthesis", *Journal of Conflict Resolution,* 1 (2): 212–248.

Mitchell, C.M. 1981. *Peacemaking and the Consuetants Role.* London: Gower Publishing.

Rapoport, A. 1960. *Fights, Games and Debates.* Ann Arbor: University of Michigan Press.

Williams, R.M. 1977. *Mutual Accommodation: Ethnic Conflict and Cooperation.* Minneapolis: Univeristy of Minnesotta Press.

PART I

History and Methods of Study

The Evolution of Conflict Resolution[1]

Louis Kriesberg

INTRODUCTION

Before discussing how the field of contemporary conflict resolution (CR) has evolved and continues to evolve, we must consider different views of its parameters and of the major realms it encompasses. This is needed because consensus about those characteristics is lacking. For some workers in the field, the term refers essentially to a specific kind of work, for example, engaging in mediation in a particular manner. For many other conflict resolvers, it refers to ways of settling or ending conflicts that entail joint efforts to reach mutually acceptable agreements. For still others, conflict resolution is a Weltanschauung that can apply to all stages of conflicts, and encompasses relatively constructive ways of conducting and transforming conflicts and then maintaining secure and equitable relations. A very broad conception of CR is adopted here, which facilitates discussing the changing conceptions of the field as it evolves.

Conflict resolution relates to all domains of conflicts, whether within or between families, organizations, communities, or countries. Workers in the CR field differ in the degree to which they focus on theory, research, or practice, attending to a single domain or to a wide range of arenas. This chapter emphasizes large-scale conflicts, within and among societies, but conflict resolution work in all arenas is recognized.

CR workers often stress that the field incorporates conflict applications as well as academic theorizing and researching. Indeed, the changing interplay among these realms is quite important in the evolution of the field. Therefore, each realm: theory, research, and practice, and their relations are discussed at the outset of this chapter.

Theory building in CR, as in other social science disciplines, varies in range and to the degree that it is inductive or deductive. Some theories refer to limited conflict arenas or to particular conflict stages, while some purport to provide a general understanding of a wide range of conflicts in their entire course; but there is no consensus about any comprehensive theory of social conflicts and their resolution. There is, nevertheless, general agreement that conflicts can be managed better than they often are. This view may entail a vision of a harmonious world or it may entail only the belief that terribly destructive conflicts often can be avoided or at least limited.

Considerable agreement exists about particular conflict processes and empirical generalizations, as noted in this Handbook. Without a comprehensive theory, however, inconsistencies among various generalizations and propositions are not reconciled. Moreover, without a comprehensive theory or theories of a middle range, it is difficult to know under what specific conditions a particular social process or empirical generalization is or is not operative, and difficult to focus the application of such knowledge on practice. On the other hand, the more general and necessarily abstract theories about social conflicts lack the precision needed for reliable applications. Despite these considerations, empirical generalizations and knowledge of relevant conflict processes can be useful guides to effective actions that minimize the destructiveness of conflicts, if used in conjunction with good information about them.

The realm of practice includes actions that particular persons or groups undertake to affect the course of conflicts, applying their understanding of CR methods. For the purposes of this chapter, practice also includes actions taken by persons unwittingly applying CR, such as in the work of many traditional mediators. Because of their relevance to CR theory and research, practice will also include the actions of persons and groups that are inconsistent with good CR principles and methods. The experiences and consequences of acting contrary to CR ideas provide the appropriate comparisons to assess the effectiveness of adhering to conflict resolution ideas. Practice, in this broad sense, provides much of the data for conflict resolution research and theory building. The data may be case studies of peace negotiations or quantitative analyses of mediations or of crises, as discussed in other chapters.

Finally, the realm of research includes the analyses that help test deductive theory and are the bases for inductive theory building. Furthermore, analysis is an integral part of good conflict resolution applications. Every conflict is unique in some ways, but like some other conflicts in certain ways; determining how a conflict is like and unlike other conflicts helps decide what would be appropriate actions. Good analysis of the conflict in which a practitioner is engaged or is considering entering, whether as a partisan or as an intermediary, helps determine which strategy and tactics are likely to be effective. Significantly, research assessing the consequences of various CR methods is now underway and increasing.

PERIODS OF CONFLICT RESOLUTION EVOLUTION

Since humans have always waged conflicts, humans have also always engaged in various ways to end them. Often, one side coercively imposes its will upon the other side, sometimes violently, and thus terminates a conflict. Within every society, however, many other ways of settling fights have long been practiced, including various forms of mediation or adjudication. Even between opposing societies, negotiations have been used throughout history to reach agreements regarding issues of contention between them.

Contemporary CR differs in several ways from many traditional conflict resolution methods. The differences include the CR emphasis upon conflict processes that generate solutions yielding some mutual gains for the opposing sides. In addition, the contemporary CR approach builds on academic research and theorizing, as well as traditional and innovative practices. It tends to stress relying minimally, if at all, on violence in waging and settling conflicts. Finally, it tends to emphasize the role of external intermediaries in the ending of conflicts.

The breadth and diversity of the contemporary CR field is a consequence of the long history of the field and of the many sources of its present-day character. Its contemporary manifestation initially focused on stopping violence but it has broadened greatly to incorporate building the conditions for peace, including post-violence reconciliation, enhancing justice, establishing conflict management systems, and many other issues. Certainly, calls and actions for alternatives to war and other violent conflict have a long history; major exemplary documents, starting from classical Grecian times, are available in Chatfield and Ilukhina (1994). The time between the American and French revolutions and the First World War deserve noting, prior to discussing the more proximate periods. The revolutions of the late 1770s established the importance of popular participation in governance and of fundamental human rights. Many intellectual leaders of that time, particularly in Europe and North America, discussed the processes and procedures to manage differences and to avoid tyrannies. They include Voltaire (1694–1778), Jean Jacques Rousseau (1712–1778), Adam Smith (1723–1790), Thomas Jefferson (1743–1826), and James Madison (1751–1836). The moral and practical issues related to dealing with various kinds of conflicts were widely discussed, emphasizing the importance of reasoning. For example, Immanuel Kant (1724–1804) wrote about perpetual peace resulting from states being constitutional republics and John Stuart Mill (1806–1873) wrote about the value of liberty and the free discussion of ideas.

But the path of progress was not smooth; wars and oppression obviously were not abolished. Many explanations for these social ills and ways to overcome them were put forward, including the influential work of Karl Marx (1818–1883), which emphasized class conflict and its particular capitalist manifestation. Vladimir Ilyich Lenin (1870–1924) elaborated Marxism with his still influential analysis of the relationship between capitalism and imperialism, which generated wars and struggles for radical societal transformations. Many other non-Marxist and more reformist efforts were undertaken to advance justice and oppose war-making, for example, by Jane Adams in the United States.

Finally, during this time, religious thought and practice were also developing in ways that proved relevant to CR. Pacifist sentiments and commitments had long been an element of Christianity and other religions, often expressed by quiet withdrawal from worldly conflicts. During this time, however, various forms of engagement became manifest, for example, in the anti-war reform efforts of the peace societies in North America, Britain, and elsewhere in Europe (Brock 1968).

Mohandas Gandhi, drawing from his Hindu traditions and other influences, developed a powerful strategy of popular civil disobedience, which he called Satyagraha, the search for truth (Bondurant 1965). Gandhi, after his legal studies in London, went to South Africa, where, in the early 1890s, he began experimenting with different nonviolent ways to counter the severe discrimination imposed upon Indians living in South Africa. The nonviolent strategies he developed were influential for the strategies that the African National Congress (ANC) adopted in its struggle against Apartheid.

With this background, we can begin examining four major periods in the evolution of contemporary CR: (1) preliminary developments, 1914–1945, (2) laying the groundwork, 1946–1969, (3) expansion and institutionalization, 1970–1989, and (4) diffusion and differentiation, since 1989. In the last part of this chapter, current issues are discussed.

Preliminary developments, 1914–1945.
The First World War (1914–1918) destroyed many millions of lives and also shattered what seemed to have been illusions of international proletarian solidarity, of global harmony from growing economic interdependence, and of rational political leadership. The revulsion from the war's mass killings was expressed in the growth of pacifist sentiments and organizations, in the Dada art movement, and in political cynicism. Nevertheless, in the United States and in many European countries, peace movement organizations

renewed their efforts to construct institutions to reduce the causes of war and in many cases to foster collective security to stop wars (Cortright 2008). These efforts pressured many governments to establish the League of Nations; but the terms of the Versailles treaty undercut the League. Similarly, public pressures fostered the 1928 Kellogg-Briand Pact to outlaw wars; however, to the consternation of peace movement organizations, the governments failed to take actions consistent with the Pact.

Numerous religious and other nongovernmental groups had mobilized to stop warfare; for example, in December 1914, at a gathering in Cambridge, England, the interfaith Fellowship of Reconciliation (FOR) was organized; and in 1915, the US FOR was founded. In 1919, the International FOR (IFOR) was established to foster reconciliation, nonviolence, and to empower youth to be peacemakers. The IFOR and other groups began to win governmental recognition of the right for individuals to refuse military service, as conscientious objectors. In the United States, these efforts were significantly pursued by members of the Jehovah Witness, and by traditional peace churches, the Brethren, the Mennonites, and the Society of Friends (Quakers).

The worldwide economic depression of the 1930s, the rise of Fascism in Germany and Italy, and the recognition of the totalitarian character of Stalinism in the Soviet Union, however, made these efforts seem inadequate. In any case, in actuality, governments and publics tried to deal with conflicts in conventional ways to advance their narrow interests and relying upon military force. The result was the wars in Spain and in China, culminating in the horrible disasters of World War II.

Many societal developments in the period between the outbreak of World War I and the end of World War II were the precursors for contemporary conflict resolution. They include research and social innovations that pointed to alternative ways of thinking about and conducting conflicts, and ending them. The variety of sources in the emergence of CR resulted in diverse perspectives and concerns

in the field, which produced continuing tensions and disagreements.

Much scholarly research focused on analyzing violent conflict; it included studies of arms races, war frequencies, revolutions, and also peace making, for example, by Quincy Wright (1942), and Pitirim Sorokin (1925). Other research and theorizing examined the bases for conflicts generally, as in the work on psychological and social psychological processes by John Dollard and others (1939).

Non-rational factors were also recognized as important in the outbreak of conflicts. Research on these matters examined scapegoating and other kinds of displaced feelings, susceptibility to propaganda, and the attributes of leaders who manipulated political symbols (Lasswell 1935, 1948). These phenomena were evident in various social movements and their attendant conflicts. For some analysts, the rise of Nazism in Germany exemplified the workings of these factors.

Conflicts with non-rational components may erupt and be exacerbated in varying degrees by generating misunderstandings and unrelated concerns. In some ways, however, the non-rational aspects of many conflicts can make them susceptible to control and solution, if the source of displaced feelings are understood and corrected. The human relations approach to industrial conflict is built on this assumption (Roethlisberger et al. 1939). Other research about industrial organizations stressed the way struggles based on differences of interest could be controlled by norms and structures, if asymmetries in power were not too large. The experience with regulated collective bargaining provided a model for this possibility, as exemplified in the United States, with the establishment of the National Labor Relations Board in 1942. Mary Parker Follett (1942) influentially wrote about negotiations that would produce mutual benefits.

Laying the groundwork, 1946–1969.
Between 1946 and 1969, many developments provided the materials with which contemporary CR was built. Many governmental and nongovernmental actions were undertaken to

prevent future wars by building new transnational institutions and fostering reconciliation between former enemies. Globally, this was evident in the establishment of the United Nations (UN), the United Nations Educational, Scientific, and Cultural Organization (UNESCO), the International Monetary Fund, and the World Bank. Regionally, such efforts were most notable in Europe. A prime example is the European Coal and Steel Community, which was established in 1952 and was the forerunner of the European Union. In 1946, in Caux, Switzerland, a series of conferences began to be held to bring together persons, from countries and communities that had been in intense conflict, for mutual understanding and forgiveness; this nongovernmental endeavor was inspired by Moral Re-Armament (Henderson 1996).

The developments also included numerous wars and crises associated with the global Cold War and the national liberation struggles of the de-colonization process. Those conflicts generated traumas that were a source of more violence, but, if managed well, some offered hope that conflicts could be controlled (Wallensteen 2002). For example, the outbreak of the Cuban Missile Crisis was a frightening warning about the risks of a nuclear war, and its settlement an example of effective negotiation. Also, high-level, non-official, regular meetings of the Pugwash and the Dartmouth conferences, starting in 1957 and 1960, respectively, greatly aided the Soviet-American negotiations about arms control.

Indian independence from Britain was achieved in 1947, following many years of nonviolent resistance, led by Mohandas Gandhi. The Satyagraha campaigns and related negotiations influentially modeled methods of constructive escalation. The strategies of nonviolent action and associated negotiations were further developed in the civil rights struggles in the United States during the 1960s. For many academic analysts, the value of conflicts to bring about desirable social change was evident, but the dangers of failure and counterproductive consequences also became evident.

Many scholarly endeavors during this period helped provide the bases for the evolution of contemporary CR (Stephenson 2008). In the 1950s and 1960s, particularly in the United States, the research and theorizing was intended to contribute to preventing a devastating war, perhaps a nuclear war. Many academics consciously tried to build a broad, interdisciplinary, cooperative endeavor to apply the social sciences so as to overcome that threat. Several clusters of scholars undertook projects with perspectives that differed from the prevailing international relations "realist" approach.

The Center for Advanced Study in the Behavioral Sciences (CASBS), at Stanford, California, played a catalytic role in the emergence of what was to be the contemporary CR field (Harty and Modell 1991). CASBS was designed to foster major new undertakings in the behavioral sciences. In its first year of operation, 1954–55, several scholars were invited who reinforced each other's work related to the emerging field of CR; they included: Herbert Kelman, Kenneth E. Boulding, Anatol Rapoport, Harold Laswell, Ludwig von Bertalanffy, and Stephan Richardson. Kelman brought some issues of the mimeographed newsletter, *The Bulletin of Research Exchange Prevention of War*, which was begun in 1952, under the editorship of Arthur Gladstone. Richardson brought microfilm copies of the then unpublished work of his father, Lewis F. Richardson (1960); is statistical analyses of arms races and wars was influential in stimulating such research.

After their CASBS year, Boulding, Rapoport, and von Bertalanffy returned to the University of Michigan; and joined with many other academics to begin *The Journal of Conflict Resolution* in 1957, as the successor to the *Bulletin.* Then, in 1959, they and others established the Center for Research on Conflict Resolution at the University of Michigan. Robert C. Angell was the first director, succeeded by Boulding.

Scholars at the Center and in other institutions published a variety of works that might contribute to developing a comprehensive inter-disciplinary theoretical analysis of conflicts. Such works were authored by Boulding (1962), Coser (1956), Lentz (1955), and Schelling (1960). Other works focused on particular phases of conflicts, such as those written by Karl Deutsch and associates (1957), about the formation of security communities between countries. Ernest B. Haas (1958) analyzed the European Coal and Steel Community as an example of functionalism, how international cooperation in one functional area can foster increased cooperation and integration in other areas, an idea developed by David Mitrany (1948).

Influential research and theorizing examined the bases for conflicts generally, for example, the work on psychological and social psychological processes (Lewin 1948) and the functions of social conflict (Coser 1956). More specifically, analyses were done about the military industrial complex in the USA and elsewhere (Mills 1956; Pilusik and Hayden 1965; Senghaas 1970).

Numerous research projects were undertaken, varyingly part of a shared endeavor. They included the collection and analyses of quantitative data about interstate wars, notably the Correlates of War project, initiated in 1963, under the leadership of J. David Singer, also at the University of Michigan. The logic of game theory and the experimental research based on it has also contributed to CR, showing how individually rational conduct can be collectively self-defeating (Rapoport 1960, 1966).

Related work was conducted at a few other universities. At Stanford, Robert C. North led a project examining why some international conflicts escalated to wars and others did not. At Northwestern, Richard Snyder analyzed foreign policy decision-making and Harold Guetzkow developed computerized models and human-machine simulations to study and to teach about international behavior. A great variety of work was done by academics in other institutions, including research and theorizing about ways conflicting relations could be overcome and mutually beneficial outcomes achieved, for example, by forming superordinate goals, as discussed by Muzafer

Sherif (1966) and by Graduated Reciprocation in Tension-Reduction (GRIT), as advocated by Charles E. Osgood (1962).

CR centers in Europe took a somewhat different course. Most began and have continued to emphasize peace and conflict research, which often had direct policy relevance. Many centers were not based in colleges or universities, receiving institutional support and research grants from their respective governments and from foundations. The first such center, the International Peace Research Institute (PRIO), was established in Oslo, Norway in 1959, with Johan Galtung as Director for its first ten years. Galtung founded the *Journal of Peace Research* at PRIO in 1964, and in 1969 he was appointed Professor of Conflict and Peace Research at the University of Oslo. His work was highly influential, not only in the Nordic countries, but also throughout the world; for example, his analysis of structural violence was important in the conflict analysis and resolution field in Europe and in the economically underdeveloped world (Galtung 1969).

In Sweden, the Stockholm International Peace Research Institute (SIPRI) began operations in 1966 (see anniversary.sipri.org/book/book_html/intro/introduction). Its establishment followed years of discussion in the Swedish Government and Parliament and Swedish universities and research institutes. Two security issues were matters of high priority: the uncontroversial policy of neutrality and the decision on whether or not to acquire nuclear weapons. Alva Myrdal was Sweden's chief disarmament negotiator and urged the government to produce more information and analyses relevant to disarmament. She and her husband Gunnar Myrdal pushed for the establishment of a research center that would gather such material and make it available. SIPRI was established with governmental support and it began to publish the vitally significant *SIPRI Yearbook of World Armaments and Disarmament*.

In 1968, Swisspeace was founded in Bern, Switzerland to promote independent action-oriented peace research. Also in 1968, the Centre for Intergroup Studies was established in Capetown, South Africa, which became a channel for meetings between meetings of ANC officials and Africaan leaders (van der Merwe 1989).

Some academics began to apply their CR ideas to ongoing conflicts; for example, they conducted problem-solving workshops with officials, or often with non-officials, from countries in conflict. Thus, John W. Burton, in 1965, organized such a productive workshop with representatives from Malaysia, Indonesia, and Singapore. Burton, who had held important offices in the Australian government, including Secretary of External Affairs, had established the Centre for the Analysis of Conflict, at the University of London, in 1963. The workshop was an effort to apply the ideas he and his associates were developing as an alternative to the conventional international relations approach (Fisher 1997).

Finally, we should note the development of professional CR networks in the form of national and international associations. Thus, in 1963, the Peace Science Society (International) was founded with the leadership of Walter Isard. In 1964, the International Peace Research Association was founded in London, having developed from a 1963 meeting in Switzerland, which was organized by the Quaker International Conferences and Seminars.

Expansion and institutionalization, 1970–1989

The years 1970–1989 include three distinctive international environments. Early in the 1970s, the Cold War became more managed, a variety of arms control agreements between the USA and the USSR were reached and détente led to more cultural exchanges between the people of the two countries. Furthermore, steps toward the normalization of US relations with the People's Republic of China were taken. However, at the end of the 1970s, US–Soviet antagonism markedly rose, triggered by the Soviet invasion of Afghanistan and intensified during the first administration of Ronald Reagan. Finally, in 1985, Mikhail Gorbachev was chosen to

lead the Soviet Union, which accelerated the Soviet transformation that resulted in the end of the Cold War in 1989.

Within the United States and many other countries around the world, the civil rights struggle and the women's, student, environmental, anti-Vietnam war, and other social movements reflected and magnified the power of nongovernmental actors. These phenomena appeared to many people to demonstrate that conflict was a way to advance justice and equality, and improve the human condition. Importantly, these struggles also revealed how conflicts could be conducted constructively, often with little violence. The CR field's evolution was affected by these international and national developments, and at times affected them as well.

Interestingly, the period of rapid CR expansion and institutionalization began in the 1970s, at a time when many of the pioneers in CR in the United States had become disappointed with what had been achieved during the 1950s and 1960s (Boulding 1978; Harty and Modell 1991). Many of them felt that too little progress had been made in developing a comprehensive agreed-upon theory of conflicts and their resolution. Moreover, funds to sustain research and professional activities were inadequate, and academic resistance to CR remained strong. All this was exemplified in the 1971 decision by the University of Michigan trustees to close the Center for Research on Conflict Resolution.

The improvement in the fortunes of the CR field in the 1970s and 1980s was spurred by the great increase in a variety of CR practices in the United States. Alternative dispute resolution (ADR) practices quickly expanded, partly as a result of the increase in litigation and court congestion in the 1970s and the increased attraction of non-adversarial ways of handling disputes. Community dispute resolution centers with volunteer mediators were established across the country.

The productive US mediation in the Middle East in the 1970s, by national security adviser and then secretary of state Henry Kissinger and by President Jimmy Carter, raised the visibility and increased the confidence in the potentialities of such undertakings. During the 1970s and 1980s, numerous interactive problem-solving workshops were conducted by John W. Burton, Leonard Doob, Herbert C. Kelman, Edward E. Azar, Ronald J. Fisher, and other academically based persons; the workshops related to conflicts in Northern Ireland, Cyprus, the Middle East, and elsewhere. In addition, NGOs were founded in this period that conducted training, consultations, and workshops relating to large-scale conflicts.

Many professional associations in the social science disciplines established sections related to peace and conflict studies, in response to the escalating war in Vietnam and the intensified Cold War. These have continued and in many cases have incorporated the CR approach as it rose in salience and relevance.

Academic and non-academic books and articles continued to be published along the lines of research and theory begun earlier. Some of these works developed fundamental ideas about the possibilities of waging conflicts constructively, as in the social psychological research (Deutsch 1973). Analyses were also made of the ways that conflicts de-escalated, as well as escalated, and how even seemingly intractable conflicts could become transformed and cooperative relations established (Axelrod 1984; Curle 1971; Kriesberg 1973; Kriesberg, et al. 1989; Sharp 1973).

During this period, the increase in writing about negotiation and mediation is particularly striking, reflecting the expansion of these activities within the now fast-growing field of CR. The book, *Getting to YES*, by Roger Fisher and William Ury (1981), was and remains highly popular and influential, explaining how to negotiate without giving in and moreover how to gain mutual benefits. Many other analyses of the different ways negotiations are done in diverse settings were published, with implications for reaching agreements that strengthen relations between the negotiating sides; (see, for example, Gulliver 1979; Rubin and Brown 1975; Strauss 1978; Zartman

1978; Zartman and Berman 1982). Mediation was also the subject of research and theorizing, often with implications for the effective practice of mediation (Moore 1986). Much research was based on case studies (Kolb 1983; Rubin 1981; Susskind 1987; Touval and Zartman 1985), but quantitative data were also analyzed (Bercovitch 1986).

During the 1970s and 1980s, CR took great strides in becoming institutionalized within colleges and universities, government agencies, and the corporate and nongovernmental world. The William and Flora Hewlett Foundation contributed greatly to this development, expansion, and institutionalization of the field. William Hewlett, the founding chairman of the Foundation, and Roger Heyns, who became its first president in 1977, shared a commitment to develop more constructive ways to resolve conflicts (Kovick 2005). This was evident in the Foundation's support for new decision-making models in regard to environmental issues beginning in 1978 and in joining with the Ford, MacArthur, and other foundations to establish the National Institute of Dispute Resolution in 1981. Then, in 1984, the Foundation launched a remarkable field-building strategy, providing long-term grants in support of CR theory, practice, and infrastructure. Bob Barrett, the first program officer, began to implement the strategy, identifying the persons and organizations to be recruited and awarded grants. The first theory center grant was made in 1984 to the Harvard Program on Negotiation, a consortium of the Massachusetts Institute of Technology, Tufts University, and Harvard University. In the same year, it initiated publication of the *Negotiation Journal*. In 1985, Hewlett grants were made to start centers at the Universities of Hawaii, Michigan, and Minnesota; in 1986, Hewlett-funded centers began at Northwestern, Rutgers, Syracuse, and Wisconsin Universities, and then at George Mason University in 1987. By the end of 1994, 18 centers had begun to be funded. Practitioner organizations in the environment, community, and in many other sectors were also awarded grants. The infrastructure for the field was strengthened, primarily by supporting professional organizations. In 1985, Hewlett began providing funding to the Society for Professionals in Dispute Resolution (SPIDR) and to the National Conference on Peacemaking and Conflict Resolution (NCPCR), and went on to support many other professional CR associations.

The establishment of graduate programs in CR in the 1980s and 1990s was also spurred by the rising demand for training in negotiation and mediation. MA degree programs were instituted in several universities, including the Eastern Mennonite University, the University of Denver, the University of Notre Dame, and Wayne State University. Many universities began to offer educational concentrations in conflict resolution, often issuing certificates in conjunction with PhD or other gradu- ate degrees; this was the case at Cornell University, Fordham University, The Johns Hopkins University School of Advanced International Studies, Syracuse University, and the Universities of Colorado, Hawaii at Manoa, and New Hampshire. A major PhD program in CR was established at George Mason University in 1987; yet since then only two other PhD programs have been instituted in the USA, at Nova Southeastern University and at the University of Massachusetts at Amherst.

Several other kinds of independent centers were also established in the United States, during the 1980s, to carry out a variety of CR applications. In 1982, former US President Jimmy Carter and former First Lady Rosalynn Carter founded the Carter Center, based in Atlanta, Georgia. The Center's activ- ities include mediating conflicts, overseeing elections, and fighting disease worldwide. Also in 1982, Search for Common Ground (SFCG) was founded in Washington, DC, funded by foundations and nongovernmental organizations. It conducts a wide range of activities to transform the way conflicts are waged around the world, from adversarial ways to collaborative problem-solving meth- ods. Significantly, after long Congressional debates and public campaigns, the United States Institute of Peace Act was passed and signed into law by President Ronald Reagan

in 1984. The Institute was opened in 1986, and includes programs of education, of research grants and fellowship awards, and of policy- related meetings and analytical reports.

In Europe, too, many new CR centers were founded, but with somewhat different orientations. Generally designated as peace and conflict research centers, they were more directed at international affairs, more closely related to economic and social development and more linked to government policies, as well as to peace movements in some instances. The international and societal contexts for the European centers were also different than those for the American CR organizations. The 1969 electoral victory of the Social Democratic party (SPD) in West Germany had important CR implications. Under the leadership of Chancellor Willy Brandt, a policy that recognized East German and East European realities was undertaken; this "Ost-Politik" entailed more East–West interactions.

In 1975, after long negotiations, the representatives of the 35 countries in the Conference on Security and Cooperation in Europe (CSCE) signed the Helsinki Accords. The agreement entailed a trade-off between the Soviet Union and the Western countries. The Soviets achieved recognition of the permanence of the border changes following World War II, when the Polish borders were shifted westward, incorporating part of Germany and the Soviet borders were shifted westward incorporating part of Poland. In a kind of exchange, the Soviets agreed to rec- ognize fundamental human rights, including greater freedom for its citizens to leave the Soviet Union.

The new German government moved quickly to help establish independent peace and conflict institutes, for example, the Hessische Stiftung Friedens und Konfliktforschung (HSFK) was founded in Frankfurt in 1970. Additional peace and conflict institutes were established in other European countries, including the Tampere Peace Research Institute, which was founded by the Finnish Parliament in 1969 and opened in 1970. The Danish Parliament established the Copenhagen Peace Research Institute (COPRI) as an independent institute in 1985.

In the early 1970s, peace and conflict chairs and programs began to be established in more European universities; for example, in 1973, the Department of Peace Studies was opened at the University of Bradford in the United Kingdom. In 1971, a university-based center emerged at Uppsala University, in Sweden, which soon began teaching undergraduate students; in 1981, the Dag Hammarskjold Peace Chair was established and after Peter Wallensteen was appointed the chair in 1985, a PhD program was begun in 1986.

The research and theorizing in these European centers were undertaken to have policy implications for nongovernmental as well as governmental actors (Senghaas 1970). The Arbeitsstelle Friedensforschung Bonn (AFB) or Peace Research Information Unit (PRIU) was established in 1984 to provide information about peace research findings in forms that were accessible and relevant to government officials.

The International Institute of Applied Systems Analysis (IIASA) was created in 1973 in Laxenburg, Austria, as an international think-tank to bridge Cold War differences. Subsequently, in the 1980s, the Processes of International Negotiation (PIN) Project was launched at IIASA to develop and propagate knowledge about negotiation (Kremenyuk 1991; Mautner-Markhof 1989; Zartman and Faure 2005). PIN brought together a group of six European scholars and diplomats and two (later one) Americans. It was initially funded by the Carnegie Corporation and then for ten years by the Hewlett Foundation.

The work of peace researchers in Denmark, West Germany, and other European centers significantly contributed to ending the Cold War (Evangelista 1999; Kriesberg 1992). The researchers analyzed the military structures and doctrines of NATO and reported on how the Warsaw Pact Soviet forces were arrayed to ensure that a war, if it came, would be carried forward against the enemy, and not have their forces fall back to fight the war in their homeland. At the same time,

the NATO forces were also structured to quickly advance eastward, to avoid fighting on West European territories. Each side, studying the other side's military preparations, could reasonably believe that the other side was planning an aggressive war (Tiedtke 1980). The peace researchers developed possible ways to construct an alternative military posture, which would be clearly defensive, a non-provocative defense (Komitee für Grundrechte und Democratie1982). They communicated their findings to officials on both sides of the Cold War, and received an interested hearing from Soviet officials, in the Mikhail Gorbachev government. Gorbachev undertook a restructuring of Soviet forces and adopted some of the language of the peace researchers. These developments helped convince the US government and other governments in NATO of the reality of a Soviet transformation.

Institutions providing training in CR methods as well as engaging in mediation and dialogue facilitation continued to be established in other countries in the world. For example, in Kenya, the Nairobi Peace Initiative–Africa (NPI–Africa) was founded in 1984 and conducts such activities in East, Central and West Africa. The increasing CR activities throughout the world are discussed in the next section.

Diffusion and differentiation, 1990–2008.

The world environment was profoundly changed by the ending of the Cold War in 1989 and the dissolution of the Soviet Union in 1991. With the end of the Cold War, the UN was better able to take actions to stop conflicts from escalating destructively, and consequently wars that had been perpetuated as proxy wars were settled. Many other developments contribute to limiting destructive international and domestic conflicts. These include the increasing economic integration of the world and the intensification of global communications. The developments also include the growing adherence to norms protecting human rights, the increasing number of democratic countries, the growing engagement of women in governance, and the increasing attention to feminist perspectives. Finally, transnational social movements and organizations increased in number and level of engagements. All these developments contributed to greater resistance in allowing destructive conflicts to arise and persist (Kriesberg 2007).

Indeed, since 1989, international wars declined in number and magnitude (Eriksson and Wallensteen 2004; Human Security Centre 2005; Marshall and Gurr 2005). Civil wars, after the spike of wars in 1990–1991 associated with the breakup of the Soviet Union, also declined. Since the end of the Cold War, many large-scale conflicts, which had been waged for very many years, were settled by negotiated agreements (Wallensteen 2002). Of course, all destructive conflicts were not ended; some continued and new ones erupted.

The September 11, 2001 attacks carried out by Al Qaeda against the United States and the subsequent wars in Afghanistan and Iraq may seem to have marked the beginning of a new world system in which terrorist attacks, violent repressions, and profound religious and ethnic antagonisms were intensifying and spreading. These new destructive conflicts are, to some degree, the consequence of some of the global developments noted above. Some social groups feel harmed or humiliated by the new developments and, using particular elements of them, fought against other elements. This is illustrated by the increase in religious militancy within Islam, Hinduism, Judaism, and Christianity.

The CR field has been deeply affected by these many developments, but it also impacts on them. The CR field affects the way various conflicts are conducted and contributes to the increase in peaceful accommodations in the 1990s and beyond. The witting and unwitting rejection of the CR approach by leaders of Al Qaeda, and in some ways the response of leaders in President George W. Bush's administration, have exacerbated erupting conflicts, increasing their destructiveness and duration. These complex matters cannot be fully explored in this chapter, but they provide the context for the observations that will be made regarding the ongoing evolution of the CR approach.

Beginning in the 1990s, the practice of CR grew in its established arenas and expanded into new spheres of work. More specialized applications and research activities became evident, for example, in the publication of *International Negotiation* by the Johns Hopkins Washington Interest in Negotiation Group. In addition, external interventions and negotiated agreements increased, ending many protracted international and civil conflicts. Even after violence was stopped or a negotiated agreement was reached, the frequent recurrence of wars made evident the need for external intervention to sustain agreements. Governments and IGOs were not fully prepared and lacked the capacity to manage the multitude of problems that followed the end of hostilities. They increasingly employed nongovernmental organizations to carry out some of the needed work of humanitarian relief, institution building, protection of human rights, and training in conflict resolution skills. The number and scope of NGOs working on such matters grew quickly, many of them applying various CR methods.

Some of the CR methods that had been developed earlier to help prepare adversaries for de-escalating steps began to be employed at the later phases of conflicts as well. These include small workshops, dialogue circles, and training to improve capacities to negotiate and mediate. Such practices helped avert a renewal of vicious fights by fostering accommodations, and even reconciliation at various levels of the antagonistic sides. Government officials have become more attentive to the significance of nongovernmental organizations and grassroots engagement in managing conflicts and in peace-building, matters that have always been important in the CR field.

Concurrent with these applied CR developments, numerous publications described, analyzed, and assessed these applications. An important development, linking theory and applied work, is the assessment of practitioner undertakings. A growing body of empirically grounded assessments of CR applications examine what kinds of interventions, by various groups, have diverse consequences (Anderson and Olson 2003; O'Leary and Bingham 2003).

A growing literature focuses on post-agreement problems and solutions, relating to external intervention and institution building (Paris 2004; Stedman et al. 2002). The role of public engagement and attention to participatory governance has also increased in the CR approach. Another trend is greater attention to conflict prevention and to establishing new systems of participatory governance to minimize unproductive and destructive conflict. These developments are related to the growing view that conflict transformation is central to the field of CR (Botes 2003; Kriesberg 2006; Lederach 1997).

The period since 1989 is characterized by worldwide CR diffusion and great expansion. The diffusion is not in one direction; rather, ideas and practices from each part of the world influence the ideas and practices in other regions. Analyses and reports about CR methods and approaches in diverse cultures increased, for example, in African and Arab societies (Malan 1997; Salem 1997). Moreover, more and more organizations function as transnational units, with members from several countries. For example, the PIN Project, associated with IIASA gave rise in turn to national networks, such as Groupe Français de Négociation (GFN) (Faure et al. 2000 Faure 2005; Zartman and Faure 2005), FinnPIN, and the Negociation Biennale (Dupont 2007), as well as to negotiation courses in as diverse places as the Catholic University of Louvain and Foreman Christian College in Lahore (Kremenyuk 1991; Zartman 2005). The Loccum Academy and the Deutschen Stiftung Friedensforschung have supported CR programs (Hauswedell 2007), and the Bernhein Foundation program at the Free University of Brussels has developed a teaching, research, and publication program (Jaumain and Remacle 2006).

The Internet provides other ways of conducting CR education and training transnationally. TRANSCEND, led by Johan Galtung, is a prime example of such programs (see www.transcend.org). It is a "peace and development network for conflict transformation by peaceful means" and it operates the Transcend Peace University online. The Universitat Oberta de Catalunya, based in Barcelona, also offers graduate degrees in conflict resolution, also online. In addition, some websites provide information about various CR methods and approaches and analyses of specific conflicts. See, for example, www.crinfo.org, The Conflict Resolution Information Source; www.beyond intractability.org, Beyond Intractability; mediate.com, information about resolution, training, and mediation; www.c-r.org, Conciliation Resources; www.incore.ulst.ac.uk/cds, ethnic conflicts; and www.crisisgroup.org, International Crisis Group.

CR educational programs are being established in countries around the world. As of 2007, 88 graduate programs of some kind are active in the United States, but PhD programs remain few (Botes 2004; Polkinghorn et al. 2007). There has been a great increase in certificate programs, associated with Law Schools and graduate degrees in international relations and public administration. CR programs are increasing in many countries. In 2007, there were 12 active programs in England, 4 in Ireland and Northern Ireland, 12 in Canada, and 10 in Australia (Polkinghorn et al. 2007). In Latin America, there are more than 25 certificate mediation training programs, and Master Programs in CR in five countries: Argentina, Colombia, Ecuador, Peru, and Mexico (Femenia 2007).

CR research centers and organizations providing CR services are also increasingly being established in many countries. For example, the African Centre for the Constructive Resolution of Disputes (ACCORD), based in Durban, South Africa, was founded in 1991 and operates throughout Africa. Academic Associates Peace Works (AAPW) was founded in Lagos, Nigeria in 1992 and under the leadership of Judith Asuni, it has conducted very many skills-building workshops as well as mediated conflicts throughout Nigeria.

Beginning in the 1990s, ADR programs spread in Latin America and some countries reformed their legal systems to include mandatory mediation. CR organizations proliferated, offering mediation training and services to help settle private disputes, for example, the Libra Foundation began training mediators in Argentina in1991, the Instituto Peruano de Resoluciòn de Conflictos, Negociaciòn, y Mediaciòn was established in Peru in 1992, and Mediare opened in Brazil in 1997. Publications pertaining to CR increasingly began to appear in many languages, including German, Spanish, and French (Camp 1999, 2001; Eckert and Willems 1992; Six 1990).

The diffusion of the CR approach also takes the form of institutionalizing CR practices, for example, by mandating mediation in disputes of a civil matter. This is the case in Peru and other Latin American countries (Ormachea-Choque 1998). In the United States, state and local governments, as well as the US Government, increasingly mandate the utilization of CR methods in providing services, settling child custody disputes, improving inter-agency relations and in formulating and implementing policy. At the federal level, this is particularly evident in managing conflicts relating to environmental issues; see the Institute for Environmental Conflict Resolution (www.ecr.gov). On August 28, 2004, President George W. Bush released Executive Order 13352, "Facilitation of Cooperative Conservation," to support constructive approaches to resolving conflicts regarding the use, conservation, and restoration of the environment, natural resources, and public lands.

Asia is also a growing locus of CR practices and institutions (Jeong 2006). For example, in South Korea, the increased freedom in the civil society and the decline in the "high context" or "collectivist" character of its culture, which had contributed to conflict avoidance, have helped generate interest in CR training and the adoption of the CR approach. The Korean government has established CR working groups by presidential decree and allocated funding for CR education from elementary to college levels. The Korean government has also established various dispute resolution mechanisms, including ombudsman offices and mediation in cases of divorce. In Japan, CR has been less in demand for domestic issues, but more developed in foreign policy circles and development aid groups.

China has not yet become a locus of significant contemporary conflict resolution activity. It is true that mediation has been an important conflict settlement method in China before Maoist rule and during it. But in the Imperial period, mediation was done by the gentry who decided which side was correct in a dispute and in the period under Mao, mediation committees decided what the ideologically correct outcome was to be. In both periods, the process was closer to arbitration than to mediation, as understood in the conflict resolution field. Subsequently, mediation has continued to be practiced, but in a less doctrinaire manner. There has been a great expansion of the judicial system in recent years, but it is not yet functioning satisfactorily for many people. Access to official procedures is limited and unequal, with local officials who are viewed as the cause of many grievances being seen to have privileged access to the official justice system (Michelson 2007). The socio-politico-cultural conditions are not conducive to the widespread adoption of the contemporary conflict resolution approach. The growing prevalence of protests and demonstrations, however, may increase the attractiveness of the CR approach.

CONTEMPORARY CR ISSUES

Workers in the CR field differ about the directions the field should take. Many of these differences are primarily internal to the field, while some relate to public policy and to relations with other fields. The resulting issues are interrelated, as the following discussion makes evident.

A major internal issue concerns the extent to which CR is and should be a focused discipline or a broad general approach. The vision for many workers in the CR field in the 1950s, of a new interdisciplinary field with a shared research-grounded theory, has not been realized. Some CR workers continue to work toward this vision and some programs and centers are relatively focused on particular matters for investigation and practice, for example, the Program on Negotiation (PON) based in Harvard University, the Dispute Resolution Research Center at Northwestern University, and the Washington Interest in Negotiation Group at the Johns Hopkins University. Others tend to emphasize a wider range of CR matters, for example, The Joan B. Kroc Institute for International Peace Studies at the University of Notre Dame, the Institute of Global Conflict and Cooperation at the University of California, and the Program on the Analysis and Resolution of Conflicts (PARC) at Syracuse University.

A related issue is the relative emphasis on core topics that are crucial in training and education or attention to specialized knowledge and training for particular specialties within the broad CR field. Another contentious issue is the degree to which the field is an area of academic study or is a profession, with the academic work focused on providing training for practitioners. In addition, there are debates about certification and codes of conduct and who might accord them over which domains of practice.

An underlying difference is between CR analysts and practitioners who stress the process that is used in waging and settling conflicts and those who emphasize the goals sought and realized. Thus, in theory and practice about the role of the mediator, some CR workers stress the neutrality of the mediator and the mediator's focus on the process to reach an agreement. However, others argue that a mediator either should avoid mediating when the parties are so unequal that equity is not likely to be achieved or should act in ways that will help the parties reach a just outcome. Some maintain that the way ADR is practiced tends to adversely affect the weaker party, otherwise protected by the equalizing rules and standards of law (Nader 1991). The reliance on the general consensus embodied in the UN declarations and conventions about human rights offers CR analysts and practitioners standards that can help produce equitable and enduring settlements.

An enduring matter of controversy relates to the universality of CR theory and practices (Avruch 1998). Obviously, ways of negotiating, forms of mediation, styles of confrontation, and many other aspects of conducting and settling conflicts vary to some degree among different national cultures, religious traditions, social classes, gender, and many other social groupings (Abu-Nimer 2003; Cohen 1997; Faure 2005). Moreover, within each of these groups, there are sub-groupings and personal variations. The differences between groups are matters of central tendencies, with great overlaps of similarities. More needs to be known about the effects of situational as well as cultural effects and of the ease with which people learn new ways of contending and settling fights.

Another contentious issue relates to the use of violence in waging conflicts. There is widespread agreement among CR analysts and practitioners that violence is wrong, particularly when violence is used to serve internal needs rather than for its effects upon an adversary. They generally agree that it is morally and practically wrong when it is used in an extremely broad and imprecise manner, and when it is not used in conjunction with other means to achieve constructive goals. However, some CR workers oppose any resort to violence in conflicts while others believe various kinds of violence are sometimes necessary and effective in particular circumstances. These differences are becoming more important with increased military interventions to stop destructively escalating domestic and international conflicts and gross violations of human rights. More analysis is needed about how specific violent and nonviolent policies are combined and with what consequences under various conditions.

CR workers also differ in their time perspectives. Frequently, CR analysts stress long-term changes and strategies for conflict transformation, while CR practitioners tend to focus on short-term policies of conflict management. Theoretical work tends to give attention to major factors that affect the course of conflicts, which often do not seem amenable to change by acts of any single person or group. Persons engaged in ameliorating a conflict feel pressures to act with urgency, which dictates short-term considerations; these pressures include fundraising concerns for NGOs and electoral concerns for government officials driven by upcoming elections. More recognition of these different circumstances may help foster useful syntheses of strategies and better sequencing of strategies.

These contentions are manifested in institutions of higher learning among the diverse MA programs, certificate programs, courses, and tracks within university graduate schools, law schools, and other professional schools in the United States and around the world (see www.campusadr. org/Classroom_Building/degreeoprograms. html). PhD programs remain few in number, reflecting the emphasis on training students for applied work, the lack of consensus about CR being a discipline, and the resistance of established disciplines to the entry of a new one.

A major issue relates to the degree and nature of the integration of theory, practice, and research. Each has varied in prominence within the field and all have been regarded as important, in principle. In actuality, however, they have not been well integrated. Research has rarely sought to specify or assess major theoretical premises or propositions. Often, it is largely descriptive of patterns of actions. Recently, more research is being done on assessing practice, but this has been focused on particular interventions and within a short time-frame. Overall, however, much more work is needed to integrate these realms more closely.

Another set of issues pertain primarily to external relations. Funding for CR poses a major concern. The Hewlett Foundation ended its 20-year program of support for the conflict resolution program in December, 2004, and no comparable source for sustaining programs of theory, research, and applications has appeared. Tuition charges help support education and training, service fees help sustain NGOs doing applied work, and government agencies and various foundations provide funds for particular research and service projects. All this keeps the work relevant for immediate use. However, the small scale and short duration of such kinds of funding hamper making the long-term and large-scale research assessments and theory building that are needed for creative new growth and appropriate applications.

Coordination of applied work poses other issues. As more and more intervening governmental and nongovernmental organizations appear at the scene of major conflicts, the relations among them and the impact of their relations expand and demand attention. The engagement of many organizations allows for specialized and complementary programs but also produces problems of competition, redundancy, and confusion. Adversaries may try to co-opt some organizations or exploit differences among them. To enhance the possible benefits and minimize the difficulties, a wide range of measures may be taken, ranging from informal ad hoc exchanges of information, regular meetings among organizations in the field, and having one organization be the "lead" agency.

Finally, issues relating to autonomy and professional independence deserve attention. CR analysts as well as practitioners may tailor their work to satisfy the preferences, as they perceive them, of their funders and clients. This diminishes those goals that in their best judgment they might otherwise advance. These risks are enhanced when tasks are contracted out by autocratic or highly ideological entities. Furthermore, as more NGOs are financially dependent on funding by national governments and international organizations, issues regarding autonomy and co-optation grow (Fisher 2006).

CONCLUSION

The CR field is in continuing evolution. The breadth of interests considered continues to expand both in the range of conflict stages and in the variety of conflicts that are of interest. The field is necessarily becoming more differentiated, with workers in the field specializing in particular kinds and stages of conflicts and particular aspects and methods of conflict resolution.

The CR field is likely to increase in size and societal penetration in the future. The need and the potentiality for growth are great in many regions of the world, notably the Middle East, parts of Asia, and in Western and Central Africa. Furthermore, the need for increased knowledge and application of the CR approach is growing. Intensifying world integration is a source of more and more potentially destructive conflicts, as well as a source of reasons to reduce and contain them. The cost of failing to prevent and stop destructive conflicts is rising and CR can help foster more constructive methods to wage and resolve conflicts. Traditional reliance on coercive impositions with little regard to possible mutual gains and reasonable regard for opponents' concerns is proving to be increasingly maladapted to contemporary global developments.

NOTES

1 I thank the editors of this volume, I. William Zartman, Victor Kremenyuk, and Jacob Bercovitch, for their helpful comments and suggestions. I also want to thank the many persons who commented on earlier versions of this chapter and provided me with information about CR developments in particular places and times, including Nora Femenia, Geraldine Forbes, Ho Won Jeong, Karlheinz Koppe, Marie Pace, Brian Polkinghorn, Peter M. Wallensteen, Hongying Wang, and Honggang Yang.

REFERENCES

Abu-Nimer, Mohammed. 2003. *Nonviolence and Peace Building in Islam: Theory and Practice*. Gainesville, FL: University Press of Florida.

Anderson, Mary B. and Lara Olson. 2003. "Confronting War: Critical Lessons for Peace Practitioners." pp. 1–98. Cambridge, MA: The Collaborative for Development Action, Inc.

Avruch, Kevin. 1998. *Culture and Conflict Resolution*. Washington, DC: United States Institute of Peace Press.

Axelrod, Robert. 1984. *The Evolution of Cooperation*. New York: Basic Books.

Bercovitch, Jacob. 1986. "International Mediation: A Study of Incidence, Strategies and Conditions of Successful Outcomes." *Cooperation and Conflict* 21: 155–168.

Bondurant, Joan V. 1965. *Conquest of Violence: The Gandhian Philosophy of Violence*. Berkeley and Los Angeles: University of California Press.

Botes, Johannes. 2003. "Conflict Transformation: A Debate over Semantics or a Crucial Shift in the Theory and Practice of Peace and Conflict Studies?" *International Journal of Peace Studies* 8 (2): 1–27.

——. 2004. "Graduate Peace & Conflict Studies Programs: Reconsidering Their Problems & Prospects." *Conflict Management in Higher Education Report* 5 (1): 1–10.

Boulding, Kenneth. 1962. *Conflict and Defense*. New York: Harper & Row.

Boulding, Kenneth E. 1978. "Future Directions in Conflict and Peace Studies." *The Journal of Conflict Resolution* 22 (2) June: 342–354.

Brock, Peter. 1968. *Pacifism in the United States: From the Colonial Era to the First World War*. Princeton, NJ: Princeton University Press.

Camp, Eduard Vinyamata. 1999. *Manual de Prevención y Resolución de Conflictos: Conciliación, Mediación, Negociación*. Barcelona: Ariel.

——. 2001. *Conflictología: Teoría y Practica en Resolución de Conflictos*. Barcelona: Ariel.

Chatfield, Charles, and R.M. Ilukhina. 1994. *Peace/mir: An Anthology of Historic Alternatives to War*. Syracuse, NY: Syracuse University Press.

Cohen, Raymond. 1997. *Negotiating Across Cultures*. Washington, DC: US Institute of Peace Press.

Cortright, David. 2008. *Peace: A History of Movements and Ideas*. New York: Cambridge University Press.

Coser, Lewis A. 1956. *The Functions of Social Conflict*. New York: The Free Press.

Curle, Adam. 1971. *Making Peace*. London: Tavistock.

Deutsch, Karl W., Sidney A.Burrell, Robert A. Kann, Maurice Lee Jr., Martin Lichterman, Raymond Lindgren, Francis L. Loewenheim, and Richard W. Van Wagenen. 1957. *Political Community and the North Atlantic Area*. Princeton, NJ: Princeton University Press.

Deutsch, Morton. 1973. *The Resolution of Conflict: Constructive and Destructive Processes*. New Haven, CT: Yale University Press.

Dollard, John, Leonard W. Doob, Neal E. Miller, O. H. Mowrer, and Robert R. Sears. 1939. *Frustration and Aggression*. New Haven: Yale University Press.

Dupont, Christophe (Ed.). 2007. *Transformations du Monde et Négociation Implications, Défis et Opportunitiés*. Paris: Negocia.

Eckert, Roland and Helmut Willems. 1992. *Konfliktintervention: Perspectivenubernahme in gesselschaflichen Ausienandersetzungen*. Opladen: Leske and Budrich.

Eriksson, Mikael and Peter Wallensteen. 2004. "Armed Conflict, 1989–2003." *Journal of Peace Research* 41, 5: 625–636.

Evangelista, Matthew. 1999. *Unarmed Forces: The Transnational Movement to End the Cold War*. Ithaca and London: Cornell University Press.

Faure, Guy Olivier (Ed.). 2005. *La Négociation: Regards sur sa Diversité*. Paris: Publibook.

Faure, Guy Olivier, Mermet L., Touzard H. and Dupont C. 2000. *La Négociation: Situations et Problématiques*. Paris: Dunod.

Femenia, Nora. 2007 January 15. "Personal communication." email.

Fischer, Martina. 2006. "Civil society in Conflict Transformation: Ambivalence, Potentials and Challenges." Berlin: Berghof Research Center for Constructive Conflict Management. 1–33.

Fisher, Roger and William Ury. 1981. *Getting to YES: Negotiating Agreement Without Giving In*. Boston: Houghton Mifflin.

Fisher, Ronald. 1997. *Interactive Conflict Resolution*. Syracuse: Syracuse University Press.

Follett, Mary Parker. 1942. *Dynamic Administration: The Collected Papers of Mary Parker Follett*. New York and London: Harper.

Galtung, Johan. 1969. "Violence, Peace, and Peace Research." *Journal of Peace Research* 3 (3): 168.

Gulliver, P.H. 1979. *Disputes and Negotiations: A Cross-cultural Perspective*. New York: Academic Press.

Haas, Ernst B. 1958. *The Uniting of Europe*. Stanford, CA: Stanford University Press.

Harty, Martha and John Modell. 1991. "The First Conflict Resolution Movement, 1956–1971: An Attempt to Institutionalize Applied Interdisciplinary Social Science." *Journal of Conflict Resolution* 35: 720–758.

Hauswedell, Corinna (Ed.). 2007. *Deeskalation von Gewaltkonflikten seit 1945*. Essen: Klartext.

Henderson, Michael. 1996. *The Forgiveness Factor*. London: Grosvenor Books.

Human Security Centre. 2005. *Human Security Report 2005*. New York: Oxford University Press.

Jaumain, Serge and Remacle Eric (Eds.). 2006. *Mémoire de Guerre et Construction de la Paix*. Frankfort am Main: Peter Lang.

Jeong, Ho-Won. 2006 December 3. "personal communication." email.

Kolb, Deborah M. 1983. *The Mediators*. Cambridge, MA: MIT Press.

Komitee für Grundrechte und Democratie. 1982. *Frieden mit Anderen Waffen*. Reinbeck bei Hamburg: Rowohlt.

Kovick, David. 2005. "The Hewlett Foundation's Conflict Resolution Program: Twenty Years of Field-Building, 1984–2004." Menlo Park, CA: Hewlett Foundation.

Kremenyuk, Victor A. (Ed.). 1991. *International Negotiation: Analysis, Approaches, Issues*. San Francisco and Oxford: Jossey-Bass.

Kriesberg, Louis. 1973. *The Sociology of Social Conflicts*. Englewood Cliffs, NJ: Prentice-Hall.

——. 1992. *International Conflict Resolution: The US-USSR and Middle East Cases*. New Haven: Yale University Press.

——. 2006. "Assessing Past Strategies for Countering Terrorism in Lebanon and by Libya." *Peace and Conflict Studies* 13 (1): 1–20.

——. 2007. "Long Peace or Long War: A Conflict Resolution Perspective." *Negotiation Journal* 20 (1): 97–116.

Kriesberg, Louis, Terrell A. Northrup, and Stuart J. Thorson (Eds.). 1989. *Intractable Conflicts and Their Transformation*. Syracuse: Syracuse University Press.

Lasswell, Harold Dwight. 1935. *World Politics and Personal Insecurity*. New York and London: McGraw-Hill.

——. 1948. *Power and Personality*. New York: Norton.

Leatherman, Janie. 2003. *From Cold War to Democratic Peace*. Syracuse, NY: Syracuse University Press.

Lederach, John Paul. 1997. *Building Peace: Sustainable Reconciliation in Divided Societies*. Washington, DC: United States Institute of Peace Press.

Lentz, Theodore F. 1955. *Towards a Science of Peace: Turning Point in Human Destiny*. New York: Bookman Associates.

Lewin, Kurt. 1948. *Resolving Social Conflicts: Selected Papers on Group Dynamics 1935–1946*. New York: Harper.

Malan, Jannie. 1997. *Conflict Resolution Wisdom from Africa*. Durban, South Africa: African Centre for the Constructive Resolution of Disputes (ACCORD).

Marshall, Monty G. and Ted Robert Gurr. 2005. "Peace and Conflict, 2005." College Park, MD: Center for International Development and Conflict Management, University of Maryland.

Mautner-Markhof, Frances (Ed.). 1989. *Processes of International Negotiations*. Westport, CT: Praeger.

Michelson, Ethan. 2007. "Climbing the Dispute Pagoda: Grievances and Appeals to the Official Justice System in Rural China." *American Sociological Review* 72 (3): 459–485.

Mills, C. Wright. 1956. *The Power Elite*. New York: Oxford University Press.

Mitrany, David. 1948. "The Functional Approach to World Organization." *International Affairs*.

Moore, Christopher W. 1986. *The Mediation Process*. San Francisco: Jossey-Bass.

Nader, Laura. 1991. "Harmony Models and the Construction of Law." pp. 41–59 in *Conflict Resolution: Cross-cultural Perspectives*, edited by Keven Avruch, Peter W. Black, and Joseph A. Scimecca. New York: Greenwood Press.

O'Leary, Rosemary and Lisa Bingham (Eds.). 2003. *The Promise and Performance of Environmental Conflict Resolution*. Washington, DC: Resources for the Future Press.

Ormachea-Choque, Ivan. 1998. *Análisis de la Ley de Conciliación Extrajudicial*. Lima, Peru: Cultural Cuzco.

Osgood, Charles E. 1962. *An Alternative to War or Surrender*. Urbana: University of Illinois Press.

Paris, Roland. 2004. *At War's End: Building Peace After Civil Conflict*. Cambridge, UK: Cambridge University Press.

Pilusik, Marc and Thomas Hayden. 1965. "Is There a Military Industrial Complex Which Prevents Peace?" *Journal of Social Issues* 21 (January): 67–117.

Polkinghorn, Brian, Robert LaChance and Haleigh LaChance. 2007. "A Comprehensive Profile and Trend Forecast of the Conflict Resolution Field in the United States." Center for Conflict Resolution at Salisbury University.

Rapoport, Anatol. 1960. *Fights, Games, and Debates*. Ann Arbor: University of Michigan Press.

———. 1966. *Two-Person Game Theory: The Essential Ideas*. Ann Arbor: University of Michigan Press.

Richardson, Lewis F. 1960. *Statistics of Deadly Quarrels*. Pittsburgh, PA: The Boxwood Press.

Roethlisberger, Fritz Jules, William John Dickson, Harold A. Wright, and Western Electric Company. 1939. *Management and the Worker: An Account of a Research Program Conducted by the Western Electric Company, Hawthorne Works, Chicago*. Cambridge, MA: Harvard University Press.

Rubin, Jeffrey Z. (Ed.). 1981. *Dynamics of Third Party Intervention: Kissinger in the Middle East*. New York: Praeger.

Rubin, Jeffrey Z., and Bert R. Brown. 1975. *The Social Psychology of Bargaining and Negotiation*. New York: Academic Press.

Salem, Paul, (Ed.) 1997. *Conflict Resolution in the Arab World: Selected Essays*. Beirut: American University of Beirut.

Schelling, Thomas C. 1960. *The Strategy of Conflict*. Cambridge, MA: Harvard University Press.

Senghaas, Dieter. 1970. *Friedensforschung und Gesellschaftskritik*. München: C. Hanser.

———. 1972. *Rüstung und Militarismus*. Frankfurt am Main: Suhrkamp.

Sharp, Gene. 1973. *The Politics of Nonviolent Action*. Boston: Porter Sargent.

Sherif, Muzafer. 1966. *In Common Predicament*. Boston: Houghton Mifflin.

Six, Jean-François. 1990. *Le Temps des Médiateurs*. Paris: Seuil.

Sorokin, Pitirim Aleksandrovich. 1925. *The Sociology of Revolution*. Philadelphia and London: J. B. Lippincott.

Stedman, Stephen John, Donald Rothchild, and Elizabeth M. Cousens (Eds.). 2002. *Ending Civil Wars: The Implementation of Peace Agreements*. Boulder and London: Lynne Rienner.

Stephenson, Carolyn M. "Peace Studies, Overview," in Lester Kurtz (ed.), *Encyclopedia of Violence, Peace and Conflict* 2nd Ed. Oxford: Elsevier, 2008.

Strauss, Anselm. 1978. *Negotiations: Varieties, Contexts, Processes, and Social Order*. San Francisco, Washington, and London: Jossey-Bass.

Susskind, Lawrence. 1987. *Breaking the Impasse: Consensual Approaches to Resolving Public Disputes*. New York: Basic Books.

Tiedtke, Stephen. 1980. *Rüstungskontrolle aus sowjetischer Sicht*. Frankfurt: Campus Verlag.

Touval, Saadia and I. William Zartman. 1985. *International Mediation in Theory and Practice*. Boulder, CO: Westview Press.

van der Merwe, Hendrik. 1989. *Pursuing Justice and Peace in South Africa*. London and New York: Routledge.

Wallensteen, Peter. 2002. *Understanding Conflict Resolution: War, Peace and the Global System*. London: Sage.

Wright, Quincy. 1942. *A Study of War*. Chicago: University of Chicago Press.

Zartman, I. William (Ed.). 1978. *The Negotiation Process*. Beverly Hills, CA: Sage.

Zartman, I. William and Guy Olivier Faure (Eds.). 2005. *Escalation and Negotiation in International Conflicts*. Cambridge, UK: Cambridge University Press.

Zartman, I. William and Maureen Berman. 1982. *The Practical Negotiator*. New Haven, CT: Yale University Press.

2

Diplomacy and Conflict Resolution

Christer Jönsson and Karin Aggestam

The words "diplomacy" and "diplomatic" are used for several different meanings. In fact, the words have been characterized as "monstrously imprecise," simultaneously signifying "content, character, method, manner and art" (Marshall, 1990: 7). According to Sir Peter Marshall (1990), at least six related meanings may be distinguished, all of which have a bearing on conflict resolution.

First, "diplomacy" sometimes refers to the *content* of foreign affairs as a whole. Diplomacy then becomes more or less synonymous with foreign policy. Several books and articles portraying the diplomacy of countries X, Y and Z are indicative of this usage. Second, "diplomacy" may connote the *conduct* of foreign policy. The word is then used as a synonym of statecraft. Henry Kissinger's book *Diplomacy* (1994), which draws on his experiences as US Secretary of State, is a case in point. Ostensibly, the broad understanding of diplomacy in terms of foreign policy or statecraft is more common in the United States than in Europe (cf. James, 1993: 92; Sharp, 1999: 37).

A third connotation of diplomacy focuses on the management of international relations by *negotiation*. Thus, the *Oxford English Dictionary* defines diplomacy as "the conduct of international relations by negotiation." Adam Watson (1982: 33) offers a similar definition as "negotiations between political entities which acknowledge each other's independence." In more elaborate terms, G.R. Berridge (1995: 1) characterizes diplomacy as "the conduct of international relations by negotiation rather than by force, propaganda, or recourse to law, and by other peaceful means (such as gathering information or engendering goodwill) which are either directly or indirectly designed to promote negotiation."

Fourth, diplomacy may be understood as the use of diplomats, organized in a *diplomatic service*. This usage is more time-bound, as the organization and professionalization of diplomacy is rather recent. Only in 1626 did Richelieu institute the first foreign ministry, and England established its Foreign Office as late as 1782 (Anderson, 1993: 73–87;

Hamilton and Langhorne, 1995: 71–75). Not until the latter half of the nineteenth century did European governments begin to recruit diplomats on the basis of merit rather than social rank, so that by the outbreak of World War I, diplomacy could be considered a fairly well-established profession (Anderson, 1993: 123; Berridge, 1995: 8).

Fifth, diplomacy, and especially the adjective "diplomatic," often refers to the *manner* in which relations are conducted. To be diplomatic means to use "intelligence and tact," to quote Ernest Satow's (1979: 3) classical formulation. A sixth, related conceptualization is to understand diplomacy more specifically as the art or *skills* of professional diplomats. The craftsmanship of diplomats includes shared norms and rituals as well as a shared language, characterized by courtesy, nonredundancy and constructive ambiguity (cf. Cohen, 1981: 32–5).

To be sure, all these different conceptualizations can be related to conflict resolution. Diplomatic efforts to resolve international conflicts constitute integral parts of the foreign policy and statecraft of the involved states; they invariably include negotiations; they engage professional diplomats, and rely on their mores and skills. When related to conflict resolution, diplomacy is perhaps most commonly understood as diplomatic *practice*. As noted, negotiation is the most prominent practice associated with diplomacy, with mediation as an important subcategory. Negotiation and mediation are subjects of the chapters by Zartman and Bercovitch in this Handbook and will not be treated at length here. Suffice it to point out that the prefix "diplomatic" implies that these and other practices are carried out by diplomats, that is, official representatives of states.

An alternative understanding of diplomacy, which transcends the ambiguity referred to initially, avoids duplication with other chapters and facilitates a discussion of its contributions to conflict resolution, is in terms of a transhistorical, international *institution* (cf. Jönsson and Hall, 2005). Diplomacy, like war, can be seen as a perennial institution, influencing relations between polities throughout history.

DIPLOMACY AND WAR AS INTERNATIONAL INSTITUTIONS

An institutional perspective on diplomacy implies an understanding in terms of a relatively stable collection of social practices consisting of easily recognized *roles* coupled with underlying *norms* and a set of *rules* or conventions defining appropriate behavior for, and governing relations among, occupants of these roles (Young, 1989: 32; cf. March and Olsen, 1998: 948). These norms and rules "prescribe behavioral roles, constrain activity, and shape expectations" (Keohane, 1988: 383). Diplomacy as an institution represents a response to "a common problem of living separately and wanting to do so, while having to conduct relations with others" (Sharp, 1999: 51).

Understood as an ancient, perennial international institution, diplomacy is comparable to, and contemporary with, war. In a sociological or institutional sense, war can be seen as a "social custom utilizing regulated violence in connection with intergroup conflicts." War, like diplomacy, "appears to have originated with permanent societies" (Wright, 1942: 36). Diplomacy and war alike presume that individuals, through language and tradition, are able to identify themselves with the group. And the recorded history of both institutions dates back to the literate civilizations of Mesopotamia and Egypt (Wright, 1942: 38).

Diplomacy is often contrasted with war. Thus, diplomacy has been characterized as "the peaceful conduct of relations amongst political entities" (Hamilton and Langhorne, 1995: 1) or "the art of convincing without using force" (Aron, 1967: 24). Whereas diplomacy is commonly seen as the opposite of war or any use of force, several scholars are reluctant to draw such a clear-cut line. "Diplomacy is among the oldest forms of intervention to limit recourse to war but it has also been its handmaiden"

(Fierke, 2005: 21). Students of contemporary international relations have coined the phrase "coercive diplomacy" to denote the use of threats or limited force to persuade opponents not to change the status quo in their favor or to call off or undo an encroachment (George, 1991; George and Simons, 1994). The concept was used in Thomas Schelling's (1966) pioneering study of the political use of force, in which he distinguished between the unilateral, "undiplomatic" use of force and coercive diplomacy based on the power to hurt. Whereas the success of brute force depends on its use, Schelling argues, the power to hurt is most successful when held in reserve.

> It is the *threat* of damage, or of more damage to come, that can make someone yield or comply. It is *latent* violence that can influence someone's choice – violence that can still be withheld or inflicted, or that a victim believes can be withheld or inflicted. (Schelling, 1966: 3)

Coercive threats are made either to compel or to deter. Compellence refers to attempts to get the opponent to change behavior; deterrence to efforts at stopping actions before they take place. UN threats of military action to Saddam Hussein if he did not remove his troops from Kuwait in 1990, as well as NATO threats to start bombing Serbia if Milosevic did not sign the Rambouillet Accords in 1999, are examples of compellence. Deterrence was prominent during the Cold War, as the United States and NATO as well as the Soviet Union and the Warsaw Pact communicated to each other that military intervention would inflict tremendous pain. The purpose of compelling as well as deterring threats is to convince the opponent that the cost of non-compliance is sufficiently high to elicit compliance (cf. Schelling, 1966: 69–72; Fierke, 2005: 81–82).

Diplomacy, in this view, can be an integral part of armed conflict, insofar as the critical targets are "in the minds of the enemy as much as on the battlefield; the state of the enemy's expectations is as important as the state of his troops; the threat of violence in reserve is more important than the commitment of

force in the field" (Schelling, 1966: 142–3). In other words, several types of interventions can be labeled "diplomatic," insofar as they "involve some form of communication to avoid or limit recourse to force, as well as to realize it" (Fierke, 2005: viii). Thus, in one sense, diplomacy and war can be seen as complementary, "one or the other dominating in turn, without one ever entirely giving way to the other except in the extreme case either of absolute hostility, or of absolute friendship or total federation" (Aron, 1967: 40). Diplomacy is pursued in the shadow of war, and war is waged in the shadow of diplomacy.

In Aghanistan, Iraq and the Middle East, peace and war exist in parallel and contemporary peace operations are simultaneously making war and building peace. Warfare and peacemaking are therefore intimately connected and should be regarded as a continuous process. Various diplomatic practices, such as competitive negotiation and power mediation, illustrate the oscillation between threat and reward strategies, which are used to influence the pay-off structure and incentives toward conflict resolution. Still, the use of threats and escalation is a high-risk strategy. The parties may keep on escalating in the hope that the other side will give in. At the same time, they may find themselves unable to escape escalation. As a consequence, they are likely to end up in a "competitive irrationality" in terms of possible outcomes, such as war (Zartman and Faure, 2005: 10). For instance, the outbreak of hostilities in the Middle East in recent decades has invariably been accompanied by feverish diplomatic activity. Since the breakdown of the Camp David summit in the summer of 2000 and subsequently the peace process, Israelis and Palestinians are locked in a dangerous violent escalation in which the parties are trying to get the other side to yield and back down.

Still, "every war must end" (Iklé, 1971), which again underscores the interface between diplomacy and war. Throughout history, some of the most prominent diplomatic gatherings have been in the wake of devastating wars. If the outbreak of hostilities implies the breakdown of diplomacy, the end of fighting and the final outcome of a war require diplomatic efforts. Moreover, a lot of diplomatic activity takes place in the shadow of potential violence. Crisis management is a prominent example of diplomatic interaction involving perceptions of a dangerously high probability that large-scale violence might break out.

The alternation between diplomacy and violence may also continue in the implementation phase, after a peace agreement has been signed. Most contemporary peace processes suffer from a lack of adherence to signed peace agreements. Spoiler groups, that is, actors actively engaged in violent actions aimed at undermining a peace process, are frequent phenomena and troublesome to deal with since they tend to become veto holders of peace processes. As Kydd and Walter (2002: 264) underline, "extremists are surprisingly successful in bringing down peace processes if they so desire." For instance, only 25 percent of signed peace agreements in civil wars between 1988 and 1998 were implemented due to violence taking place during negotiations. Without any violence, 60 percent of the peace accords were implemented (Kydd & Walter, 2002: 264). The power of spoiler groups tends to increase when political leaders publicly declare and make commitments not to negotiate and make concessions under fire. It is assumed that negotiating while violence continues signals weakness to the other side (Aggestam, 2006). Yet, in practice, diplomats become hostages to spoilers who determine the pace and direction of a peace process (Darby, 2001: 118). This is well illustrated in a comparison between the different negotiation styles of Yitshak Rabin and Ariel Sharon. The peace process in the 1990s was early on beleaguered by terrorist attacks, and yet Rabin declared after every attack in Israel by Hamas and Islamic Jihad that to stop the peace process would be to give in to terror and extremism. Sharon on the contrary argued consistently that he refused to deal with the Palestinian leadership as long as the violence continued, which partly explains why every attempt to negotiate a de-escalation of the conflict failed.

Hence, in recent years, a major challenge for diplomats is how to manage these spoiler groups. International custodians, overseeing implementation of negotiated agreements, have therefore become increasingly common.

In short, if war and diplomacy cannot be seen as mutually exclusive institutions influencing international conflict resolution, diplomatic practices are usually contrasted with the methods of warfare. Normatively, diplomacy is preferable to war; yet states frequently resort to war in resolving their conflicts. This gives rise to two broad questions: How do the norms, rules and practices of diplomacy contribute to conflict resolution? Under what circumstances do states prefer diplomacy to war? In line with our institutional perspective, our primary focus will not be diplomatic practice – such as negotiation and mediation – but the normative foundation guiding diplomatic practice.

DIPLOMATIC NORMS AND PRACTICES FACILITATING CONFLICT RESOLUTION

As an international institution, diplomacy has throughout the ages rested on certain fundamental norms and provided more or less detailed rules of appropriate procedures in the intercourse between states. Some of these norms and rules have remained unchanged over long periods of time; others have changed and evolved in response to changing circumstances. Whereas most of the diplomatic normative framework facilitates conflict resolution, it should be noted that some norms, rules and practices may contribute to interstate conflicts.

Coexistence and reciprocity

Ultimately, diplomacy rests on a norm of coexistence, allowing states "to live and let live." In the words of Garrett Mattingly (1955: 196), "unless people realize that they have to live together, indefinitely, in spite of their differences, diplomats have no place to stand." Acceptance of coexistence reflects the realization on the part of states that they are mutually dependent to a significant degree. Interdependence may be, and is most often, asymmetrical. Yet coexistence implies, if not equality, at least equal rights to participate in international intercourse. The norm of coexistence obviously facilitates conflict resolution, in contrast to notions of exclusion or excommunication, which render interaction with disapproved partners impossible.

Reciprocity appears to be another core normative theme running through all diplomatic practice (Cohen, 2001: 25). Reciprocity implies that exchanges should be of roughly equivalent values. Moreover, reciprocity entails contingency, insofar as actions are conditional on responses from others. Reciprocal behavior returns good for good, ill for ill. The distinction between *specific* and *diffuse* reciprocity is pertinent in this connection. In situations of specific reciprocity, partners exchange items of equivalent value in a delimited time sequence, whereas diffuse reciprocity implies less precise definitions of equivalence and less narrowly bounded time sequences. Diffuse reciprocity implies that the parties do not insist on immediate and exactly equivalent reciprocation of each and every concession, on an appropriate "quid" for every "quo" (Keohane, 1986).

Buyers and sellers of houses or cars practice specific reciprocity; families or groups of close friends rely on diffuse reciprocity. Reciprocity in diplomatic relations falls in between, or oscillates between the two poles. To the extent that diplomatic interaction comes close to the pole of diffuse reciprocity, conflict resolution becomes easier. Conversely, insistence on specific reciprocity often makes it more difficult. The practice of expelling foreign diplomats for espionage or otherwise declaring them *persona non grata* represents one variant of specific reciprocity. When a state expels diplomats from a foreign country, that government is likely to respond in kind by immediately expelling an equivalent number of the initiating state's own diplomats. On the one hand, the anticipation of specific reciprocity may deter states from initiating cycles of uncooperative behavior.

On the other hand, the specific reciprocity triggered by the expulsion of diplomats has often aggravated interstate conflicts.

Successful conflict resolution seems to require at least a semblance of reciprocity. The denouement of the Cuban missile crisis in 1962 is a case in point. In exchange for the Soviet Union's withdrawal of its missiles from Cuba, the United States dismantled its missiles in Turkey (which President Kennedy had previously ordered removed as obsolescent) and pledged not to invade Cuba (which it had no intention to do). As Glenn Snyder and Paul Diesing (1977: 19) noted in their pioneering study of 16 major twentieth-century international crises, it is important "whether the loser is 'driven to the wall' and humiliated or given some face-saving concession that can be presented as a 'compromise'." And all compromises presuppose reciprocity.

Open communication channels and a shared language

Keeping communication channels open is another aspect of diplomacy that facilitates conflict resolution. "Communication is to diplomacy as blood is to the human body. Whenever communication ceases, the body of international politics, the process of diplomacy, is dead, and the result is violent conflict or atrophy" (Tran, 1987: 8). "The pristine form of diplomacy," argues Hedley Bull (1977: 164), "is the transmitting of messages between one independent political community and another." In short, diplomats are messengers and diplomacy involves communication between states. Ever since the first recorded diplomatic exchanges dating back to the third millennium BC in Mesopotamia, rulers have exchanged messengers, who have been the "eyes and ears" and the "mouthpieces" of governments.

Today, the need to communicate is most graphically demonstrated, paradoxically, when diplomatic relations are severed and the parties almost always look for, and find, other ways of communicating (James, 1993: 96). States lacking diplomatic relations may exchange messages through intermediaries. They may also communicate directly. One method builds on the established state practice of entrusting the protection of their interests to the mission of a third state in cases of broken diplomatic relations. Through the creation of "interests sections," consisting of diplomats of the protected state operating under the legal auspices of the protecting state, enemies may permit their own diplomats to remain in states from which they have been legally expelled. In 1977, for instance, the United States created a US interests section in the Swiss embassy in Havana at the same time as Cuba opened its interests section in the Czechoslovak embassy in Washington. Trade missions and other diplomatic fronts with genuine "cover" functions represent alternative "disguised embassies" (Berridge, 1994: 32–58). Ceremonial occasions, such as "working funerals," and the exchange of secret, special envoys are other ways of communicating despite severed diplomatic relations (cf. Berridge, 1993, 1994).

Mediators play a central role in keeping communication channels open, ongoing and undistorted between mistrusting parties who attempt to settle a conflict. In these situations, mediators may for instance act as go-between, facilitate back-channel negotiations, supply additional information and identify common problems that may inhibit deadlocks and enhance communication. As Princen (1992: 8) states, a mediator gathers necessary information and "serves as a regime surrogate in disputes where institutionalization is impractical." For instance, the Norwegian diplomats played a critical role as "communicators" in 1993 between the negotiation sessions, since Israel and the Palestine Liberation Organization (PLO) at the time lacked any direct communication channels.

Most importantly, diplomatic communication is facilitated by a shared language with mutually understood phrases and expressions as well as rules governing the external form of intercourse. The institutionalization of diplomacy has involved the development of a common language with ritualized phrases, which have

allowed cross-cultural communication with a minimum of unnecessary misunderstanding. Courtesy, non-redundancy and constructive ambiguity are prominent features of diplomatic language. Each era appears to have its own set of ritualized phrases that enable diplomatic agents to communicate even unpleasant things with an amount of tact and courtesy. The principle of non-redundancy means that "a diplomatic communication should say neither too much nor too little because every word, nuance of omission will be meticulously studied for any shade of meaning" (Cohen, 1981: 32). Constructive ambiguity avoids premature closure of options. Circumlocution, such as understatements and loaded omissions, permits controversial things to be said in a way understood in the diplomatic community but without needless provocation (Cohen, 1981: 32–4).

We may think of diplomats as "intuitive semioticians," as conscious producers and interpreters of signs. Although semiotics is rarely part of their formal education, diplomats are by training and experience experts at weighing words and gestures with a view to their effect on potential receivers (Jönsson, 1990: 31). We may also be reminded that hermeneutics, the science of interpretation, is explicitly associated with Hermes, the ancient Greek deity of diplomacy (Constantinou, 1996: 35). The shared language and intersubjective structures of meaning and collective understanding among diplomats are significant assets when it comes to conflict resolution limited to the diplomatic community. However, the diplomatic language may render communication between professional diplomats and non-professionals more difficult, as the meanings of diplomatic communications are not immediately obvious to outsiders.

Commitment to peace

Diplomats are commonly described as sharing a commitment to peace or international order. Diplomat-cum-scholar Adam Watson (1982), for example, argues that diplomats throughout history have been guided not only by *raison d'état*, but also by *raison de système*. One author refers to diplomacy as "the angels' game," arguing that diplomats, "regardless of nationality, have an enduring obligation to their guild and to each other to work always toward that most elusive of human objectives – a just, universal, and stable peace" (Macomber, 1997: 26). One may even wonder whether "the idea that diplomats serve peace predates that of serving the prince" (Sharp, 1998: 67). Diplomats are said to be "conscious of world interests superior to immediate national interests" (Nicolson, 1959: xi), and to feel bound by their professional ethic to "act in such a way as to ensure that the functioning of the international state system is sustained and improved" (Freeman, 1997: 139). While this may sound like old-fashioned rhetoric, benefiting the diplomatic guild, outside observers point to the continued representation of ideas.

Secularism and statism were great spurs to the development of diplomacy as a profession, but they did not overwhelm the earlier commitment to peace. Indeed, a shared commitment to peace and saving their respective princes from themselves became hallmarks of the profession, something which diplomats could hold in common to cement their sense of corps and to gain some distance from their political leaderships (Sharp, 1998: 67).

To the extent that diplomatic agents are able to "strike a balance between diplomacy as a means of identifying and fostering 'us' and diplomacy as a means of fostering the latent community of mankind" (Hill, 1991: 99), diplomacy contributes to effective conflict resolution.

Diplomatic immunity

The principle of diplomatic immunity represents another facilitating norm, insofar as it provides for unharmed contacts between diplomats of conflicting states. It is reasonable to assume, as Nicolson (1977: 6) does, that this principle was the first to become established in pre-historic times. Anthropoid apes and savages must at some stage have realized the advantages of negotiating understandings about the limits of hunting territories. With this must have come the realization that these negotiations could never reach a satisfactory conclusion if emissaries were killed and eaten. The inviolability of messengers seems to be an accepted principle among aboriginal peoples (Numelin, 1950: 147–52).

The inviolability of diplomatic agents is seen to be a prerequisite for the establishment of stable relations between polities. "Rooted in necessity, immunity was buttressed by religion, sanctioned by custom, and fortified by reciprocity" (Frey and Frey, 1999: 4). The sanctity of diplomatic messengers in the ancient world implied inviolability. Traditional codes of hospitality may have contributed to the notion of according diplomatic envoys inviolability. The medieval diplomat "represented his sovereign in the sense that he was him or embodied him (literally in some readings) when he presented himself at court" (Sharp, 1998: 61). While such a view is alien to modern thought, today's principle of diplomatic immunity has deep roots in notions of personal representation. The most perennial and robust foundation of diplomatic immunity seems to be functional necessity: the privileges and immunities that diplomatic envoys have enjoyed throughout the ages have simply been seen as necessary to enable diplomats to perform their functions (McClanahan, 1989: 32). Functional necessity rests on the principle of reciprocity: "governments expect that other governments will reciprocate in the extension of immunities to similar categories of diplomatic and non-diplomatic personnel" (Wilson, 1967: 32).

Pacta sunt servanda

The old dictum *pacta sunt servanda*, which has been a cornerstone of diplomacy for ages, increases the likelihood that agreements resolving interstate conflicts will be honored. In the Ancient Near East, treaties invariably ended with summons to the deities of both parties to act as witnesses to the treaty provisions and explicit threats of divine retribution in case of violation. The number of deities assembled as treaty witnesses was often substantial, in some cases approaching one thousand (see Beckman, 1996: 80–1). Oaths were sworn by the gods of both parties, so that each ruler exposed himself to the punishment of both sets of deities should he fail to comply. The practice of uttering religious oaths as part of the ceremony of signing treaty documents is found in early Byzantine diplomacy as well. The Byzantines accepted non-Christian oaths of validation, in a way reminiscent of the Ancient Near East practice of invoking multiple deities as witnesses (Chrysos, 1992: 30). Religious appeals, at a time when gods were considered as real as the material world, had its advantages; "since divine sanction rather than national consent gave ancient international law its obligatory quality, it was in some respects more feared and binding than modern international law" (Cohen and Westbrook, 2000: 230).

DIPLOMATIC NORMS AND PRACTICES COMPLICATING CONFLICT RESOLUTION

Most diplomatic norms and practices facilitate conflict resolution. The principle of reciprocity, as we have seen, may contribute either to the resolution or aggravation of conflict. Other diplomatic norms and practices are more pronouncedly double-edged and may in many cases render conflict resolution more difficult. Examples include precedence, openness, constructive ambiguity, diplomatic recognition and multilateralism.

Precedence

Historically, diplomatic notions of precedence have aggravated conflict resolution and, in several cases, contributed to conflict and violence. Yet this represents a problem that has eventually found a diplomatic solution. Whereas diplomacy has always rested on notions of coexistence and reciprocity, as mentioned above, great importance has been attached to the precedence, or order of importance, of individual rulers and states.

In the Ancient Near East, a standardized and generally accepted arrangement distinguished between "great kings" and "small kings," and in the evolving complex network of relationships with Egypt, rivalries and jealousies among great kings over their standing in Pharaoh's eyes were frequent (Avruch, 2000: 164; Liverani, 2001: 39–41). Disputes over precedence are recorded in ancient Chinese and Byzantine diplomacy as well (cf. Britton, 2004: 95; Shepard, 1992: 61–2).

Early European diplomacy was "full of endless crises caused by intended or unintended slights occurring between ambassadors or their retinues – usually the latter – and also resulting from attempts by ambassadors to gain a higher status in their treatment by the ruler to whom they were accredited, sometimes by seeking to perform highly personal services" (Hamilton and Langhorne, 1995: 65). Especially between France and Spain, there were endless struggles for precedence entailing violence and threats of war (see, for example, Jönsson and Hall, 2005: 54–55).

Conflicts over precedence haunted international conferences as well, entailing long, and not always successful, negotiations concerning the order in which representatives would be seated at the conference table. For instance, the Thirty Years' War was prolonged and the Treaty of Westphalia delayed as a result of quarrels over status and precedence, which reflected the competing principles of hierarchy versus dynastic state equality (Holsti, 1991: 33).

Further disputes could arise regarding the order in which representatives would sign agreements and treaties. Treaty signatures were long ordered according to precedence, which invited controversies. Gradually, however, a new principle emerged, the *alternat*, according to which each representative signed his own copy of the treaty first. While disputed at first, this principle has been institutionalized to the extent that it is still adhered to today. The *alternat* did not solve problems of precedence altogether, as it did not prescribe the order in which other signatures were to follow (Nicolson, 1977: 99–100; Satow, 1979: 24).

When the Holy Roman Empire came to an end in 1806 and France, with a republican rather than monarchical form of government, was no longer in a position to reassert its claims to privileged rank, questions of precedence became less acute (Satow, 1979: 24–5). The Congress of Vienna in 1815 drew up a convention establishing precedence among diplomatic envoys according to the date they have presented their credentials, disregarding precedence among their principals altogether. Thus, the ambassador who has served longest at a post is considered *doyen* or dean. As spokesman of the diplomatic corps, the *doyen* has certain rights and duties as well as an amount of influence (Nicolson, 1977: 226).

The Congress of Aix-la-Chapelle in 1818 established the principle that representatives at conferences sign treaties in alphabetical order (Nicolson, 1954/1998: 45–6). Alphabetization has since become used by most international organizations for avoiding precedence issues in seating representatives. Thus, devices have been found that deprive the precedence issue of its previous controversy and drama and that have become firmly institutionalized. While issues of precedence may still arise, they do not carry the same significance and can be resolved creatively and pragmatically. No longer do precedence issues contribute to conflict or complicate conflict resolution in the way they did in earlier history.

Openness

If precedence as a conflict-generating diplomatic norm has been neutralized and given way to diplomatic practices that facilitate conflict resolution despite status differences, other diplomatic norms and practices are more double-edged. In the last century, the transition from "old" to "new" diplomacy has had important implications on diplomatic norms and conflict resolution. The American President Woodrow Wilson stated after World War I in his Fourteen Points that a new kind of diplomacy based on moral and *democratic principles* was to be developed. Hence, Wilson's well-quoted statement about

"open covenants openly arrived at" became the normative principle of a new and public diplomacy (Eban, 1983: 345). These principles stemmed from a view that old diplomacy, characterized by secrecy, encouraged conspiracies and war. It meant, for instance, that international negotiations should now be pursued openly and in public, without private or secret understandings. These assumptions were strengthened by the growing influence of media and public opinion, which demanded an open and democratic diplomacy. The expectation that diplomatic practice in general would change resulted in an increase of open international conferences, multilateral diplomacy and personal involvement of politicians (Eban, 1985: 10; Watson, 1982: 121). Hence, public diplomacy became an integral principle of any state claiming to be a democracy and the "public's right to know" was not to be disregarded, for instance, concerning information about new policies and official negotiation positions.

At the same time, as Eban (1983: 34) notes, "the hard truth is that the total denial of privacy even in the early stages of a negotiation process has made international agreements harder to obtain than ever in the past history." Hence, there is a built-in tension between publicity and diplomacy. In some circumstances, diplomats may prefer to negotiate privately and thereby limit the publicity surrounding a diplomatic process. In contrast, news media work to expose and scrutinize activities of diplomats and politicians, thereby strengthening the public consciousness that secrecy runs counter to democratic principles (Cohen, 1986: 69). In short, publicity and the need for privacy in diplomacy are clearly two opposing principles that originate from two completely different frames of reference involving the nature of information and who possesses it. Privacy and discreet diplomatic strategies are often critical when pursuing conflict resolution and rapprochement between hostile parties. Tony Armstrong (1993: 138–40) concluded from his analysis of three cases (1972 Basic Treaty between West Germany and East Germany; US normalization with China in the 1970s; and the peace treaty between Israel and Egypt in 1979) that diplomatic initiatives, which successfully reached an agreement, were conducted away from the public, on a high political level, and with few participants involved. In these secret and private negotiations, assurances and commitments were provided, which were essential for the parties to negotiate in "good faith."

Consequently, high media exposure has to a certain extent limited the autonomy and flexibility of diplomats. Particularly in cases with active domestic constituencies with hawkish and opposing views of conflict resolution, concession-making is difficult. Thus, there exists ambivalence among diplomats about the publicity surrounding some of their activities. The bumpy start of the Middle East peace process in the 1990s is a case in point. The bilateral negotiations in Washington were hampered by constant leaks as well as press conferences in which the parties justified their position. Every minute of the negotiation sessions was recorded and usually published in the media. This publicity inhibited flexibility, and the negotiating positions often became so rigid that concessions were impossible. Each delegation sought to signal through the media to its domestic constituency that its official negotiation position had not changed and no concessions had been made (see Ashrawi, 1995; Peres, 1995). For some observers, "the klieg lights" of the media had reduced the talks to public posturing and the talks were likened to a "PR campaign" (Makovsky, 1996: 13; see also Hirschfeld, 1994).

This was one major reason why secret negotiations were sought in Oslo. Yet, the setbacks and problems in conducting secret negotiations were soon discovered by both sides after the signing of the Declaration of Principles (DOP) in 1993. If secrecy was the key to reach an agreement, it was also the key to its undoing. For fear of leaks, never in the entire process of negotiation did the Palestinians review the documents with legal consultants. The Israelis also avoided any involvement of experts, including military

ones. Most importantly, the negotiators did not prepare and mobilize domestic support for the agreement. As Yossi Beilin (1999: 3), one of the architects behind the Oslo channel, poignantly states: "We thought we were absolved of the need to continue molding public understanding, and in this we were wrong. We were also mistaken in that we didn't show the public what we envisaged at the end of the process, and we thereby exposed ourselves to unnecessary accusations and questions."

Constructive ambiguity

Another double-edged principle concerns constructive ambiguity. As discussed earlier, it may facilitate conflict resolution. Yet it may also be obstructive. Constructive ambiguity is often used to overcome deadlocks by avoiding and postponing detailed interpretations until implementation. The basic rationale is that the parties will be committed to a signed agreement, following the dictum of *pacta sunt servanda*. However, such an ambiguity may generate counterproductive results in the long run. Statistics reveal that many cases of negotiated peace agreements suffer from incomplete implementation (Stedman, Rothchild and Cousens, 2002). First, constructive ambiguity may exacerbate an already fragile situation characterized by suspicion and mistrust, and create new grounds for hostilities, as these ambiguities need to be addressed, interpreted and agreed upon. Particularly in identity-based conflicts, where the parties are lacking established rules of engagement and conflict resolution, the use of constructive ambiguity often becomes destructive and counterproductive. Second, a "skeptical scrutiny" of a peace agreement may develop, weakening the support for an agreement significantly (Ross, 1995: 34). This is the reason why diplomats and scholars alike are arguing for the necessity of enforcement mechanisms as well as promoting the idea of acting custodians over peace processes (Stedman, 1997). Custodians have been used, for instance, in Cambodia by the United Nations and in the Northern Ireland peace process by the United Kingdom and Ireland acting as internal custodians.

Recognition

Diplomatic recognition, in terms of accepting other actors as more or less peers and treating them accordingly, is equally essential to personal and international relations. There is, however, one significant difference between the two. Whereas the development of relations precedes reciprocal recognition between individuals, recognition is a prior condition for official relations to develop at the international level. Recognition is a prerequisite for reciprocal exchanges in international relations. From the viewpoint of individual political units, diplomatic recognition represents a "ticket of general admission to the international arena" (Krasner, 1999: 16).

The principles of diplomatic recognition have varied considerably throughout history, ranging from inclusive to highly exclusive. At one extreme, recognition might be, and has been, granted to virtually anyone with some authority and material or moral resources, as was the case in medieval Europe. At the other extreme, only specific actors with certain attributes are recognized, such as sovereign states adhering to the principles of Western civilization. Whereas inclusive recognition patterns would seem to facilitate the resolution of conflicts involving several different types of international actors, exclusive recognition limits the ability of diplomacy to resolve conflicts to those involving a specific kind of recognized actors.

The Treaty of Westphalia in 1648 laid a foundation for the gradual emergence of the territorial, sovereign state. As diplomatic recognition gradually became essential to statehood, other types of political formations were delegitimized. Recognition, in other words, became increasingly exclusive. Eventually, rules of diplomatic recognition were incorporated in international law. Even if international lawyers, diplomats and statesmen today agree that statehood requires a central government that exercises effective control over a defined territory and a permanent population, and has the capacity to enter into relations with other states, there are examples of non-recognition of units that fulfill these criteria as well as recognition of units that do not fulfill them. For instance, in 1988, the Palestine Liberation Organization (PLO) declared the state of Palestine on the basis of the UN partition plan from 1947 that proposes one Jewish and one Arab state. At the time of declaration, the PLO did not control one inch of Palestinian territory, and yet over 100 states recognized the state of Palestine. Hence, the factual conditions many states require for recognition have changed over the years, and ultimately recognition remains a political act.

During the nineteenth century, diplomacy had the character of a European "club," into which other states were admitted only if they were "elected" – that is, recognized – by the other "members." The Congress of Vienna in 1815 established that states would not be regarded as sovereign unless recognized by other powers, primarily the great powers of the day. The Final Act of the Congress listed 39 sovereign states in Europe, much fewer than the number of polities claiming to be sovereign (Holsti, 2004: 128). After 1815, in the Concert of Europe era, members of the Holy Alliance tended to treat revolutionary or republican governments as outlaws to be excluded from the "club" (Malanczuk, 1997: 83). Nor did the European states allow non-European polities into the "club." Despite commercial relations with Asian powers, such as China and Japan, whose rulers were treated as if they were sovereign, none was recognized as a state. Imperialism implied "civilizing" rather than recognizing states (Holsti, 2004: 129).

After World War I, democratic constitutions and guarantees for minority rights were added to the recognition criteria used by the victorious states (Holsti, 2004: 129–30). US President Woodrow Wilson's plea to "make the world safe for democracy" was emblematic of this change, and a prominent case of non-recognition was the US refusal to recognize the Soviet Union until 1934.

After World War II, recognition and non-recognition again became prominent political instruments as a result of three major developments. Most important was the ideological and strategic rivalry of the superpowers, but concomitant processes of decolonization and the proliferation of international organizations also contributed to bringing issues of diplomatic recognition to the forefront (Doxey, 1995: 307).

The most striking manifestations of political use of the recognition tool during the Cold War were the cases of China and the German Democratic Republic. Between 1949 and 1979, successive US administrations refused to recognize the communist government of the People's Republic of China as the legitimate government of China, instead supporting the claim of the nationalist government of Taiwan to represent all China. This entailed preventing the PRC from taking China's seat in the UN Security Council until 1971. Another example was the Hallstein Doctrine of the West German government, denying recognition of any government recognizing the GDR, which was seen as a creation of the Soviet Union in breach of treaties between the allies concerning the administration of Germany after World War II. Only after Chancellor Willy Brandt's *Ostpolitik* led to mutual recognition of the two Germanies in 1972 did Western states recognize the GDR (Doxey, 1995: 308).

Recognition of the new state formations that resulted from the end of the Cold War was relatively unproblematic: neither the reunification of Germany nor the dissolution of the Soviet Union or the "velvet divorce" negotiated by the Czech and Slovak republics raised thorny questions of recognition. However, recent developments seem to have sharpened the political conditions many states require for diplomatic recognition. For instance, in response to the momentous developments after the end of the Cold War, EC member states adopted common guidelines for the recognition of new states in December 1991. Specific requirements include the rule of law, democracy and human rights; guaranteed minority rights; the inviolability of frontiers; acceptance of commitments regarding disarmament and nuclear non-proliferation; and an undertaking to settle by agreement all questions concerning state succession and regional disputes. Recognition of "entities which are the result of aggression" is expressly excluded (Malanczuk, 1997: 89; Cassese, 2001: 50; Doxey, 1995: 312–13). Other criteria for recognition that are used or proposed in today's world are non-dependence on foreign military support and respect for other states' rights (Peterson, 1997: 77–81).

In many contemporary conflicts, diplomacy is stalled because recognition needs to be resolved before any meaningful progress can be made. Non-state actors contest their unrecognized status and governments dispute claims for "proto-political status" (Richmond, 2006: 68). Diplomacy therefore becomes a new "battle ground" where parties are not primarily seeking compromise and conflict resolution, but use these diplomatic processes to gain recognition and international legitimacy. As Oliver Richmond (2006: 66) underlines: "The assumption of a compromise is so often of only secondary concern." This was the reason why it took over two years before any progress was made in the Middle East peace process in the early 1990s. It was only with the mutual recognition between the Israeli government and the PLO that an agreement could be reached in late 1993.

Another example where considerations of recognition delayed conflict resolution is in the prolonged controversy over the shape of the table at the Paris negotiations to end the Vietnam War. To seat the Vietnamese National Liberation Front (Vietcong) at a four-sided table with representatives of the United States, North Vietnam and South Vietnam would have accorded it equal status. Therefore, much time and creativity were spent on finding a configuration that did not imply diplomatic recognition.

As these examples illustrate, problems of recognition may hamper interaction between states and non-state entities in particular. Today, the growing interface between domestic and international conflicts necessitates just this kind of interaction. Diplomats and NGO representatives communicate, share information and negotiate with increasing frequency and in varying contexts to solve global or regional conflicts. Yet mutual suspicion tends to preclude full mutual recognition (cf. Cooper and Hocking, 2000).

Multilateralism and "polylateralism"

Multilateralism entails several constructive innovations in diplomatic practice, but may also complicate conflict resolution. The earliest multilateral forums were high-level congresses called to arrange the terms of peace settlements, such as the Congresses of Osnabrück and Münster resulting in the Peace of Westphalia in 1648. Diplomatic conferences, peacetime meetings of diplomats, were unknown before 1830 (Langhorne, 2004: 284–5) but have since then surged in frequency, significance and complexity. In the middle of the nineteenth century, there were about three international conferences annually, today more than 3000 (Holsti, 2004: 191).

The creation of the League of Nations after World War I and the United Nations after World War II were attempts to create permanent multilateral institutions to prevent and resolve international conflicts and wars. In many ways, multilateralism has increased transparency and new democratic practices of diplomacy. Some even argue that multilateralism provides the best opportunity for successful conflict resolution, since multilateralism is inclusive, subject-focused and sets explicit deadlines for negotiations. As a result of the revolution in mass communication, conference diplomacy may also be viewed as an excellent tool for political leaders to publicly demonstrate their commitment to resolving international crises (Berridge, 2002: 148–49).

Conference diplomacy differs from previous diplomatic forms in several respects, such as the forging of coalitions and groupings, potential leadership roles for the chair and international secretariats assuming important functions. Moreover, diplomatic conferences provide ample room for informal "corridor activity" (cf. Kaufmann, 1996; Walker, 2004).

In global conferences and multilateral forums, NGOs have increasingly been granted presence. The growing participation by a variety of actors has resulted in "polylateralism" as a new mode of diplomatic dialogue besides bilateralism and multilateralism, implying relations between official entities (states, international organizations) and unofficial, non-state entities (Wiseman, 1999). Twenty years ago, NGOs staged protests outside the doors of international organizations and had to gather information from the dustbins of national delegations; today, many of them are involved in preparing global UN conferences and routinely get the floor in plenary meetings. On several global issues, such as environmental protection, trade and human rights, NGOs have become key actors that cannot be bypassed in the search for viable solutions. Two prominent examples of active NGO involvement in diplomatic processes concern the 1997 Ottawa convention banning anti-personnel landmines and the 1998 Rome treaty establishing the International Criminal Court (Cooper and Hocking, 2000: 361–76).

According to Hocking (2004: 92), the diversity and heterogeneity of actors and practices have transformed diplomacy from operating within clearly delineated borders to a "boundary-spanning" activity. For instance, track-one diplomacy may be supplemented with track-two diplomacy, which refers to everything from citizen diplomacy, pre-negotiation, interactive problem solving to back-channel negotiation. Track-two diplomacy is frequently used to resolve deep-rooted and complex identity-based conflicts and conducted by informal intermediaries, such as NGOs, academics and private citizens. They strive to create a non-judgmental, non-coercive and supportive environment for conflict resolution. Without governmental constraints, it is assumed that such a framework will facilitate shared perceptions of fears and needs, which may reframe conflict and generate mutual understanding and ultimately new ideas of conflict resolution (Rothman, 1997).

Yet, multilateralism may also complicate or hinder conflict resolution. For instance, conference diplomacy is often described as a highly complex and unmanageable practice, with too many actors, issues and levels of negotiations. Consequently, a central issue in many multilateral settings is to manage complexity and insecurity. One way to reduce and manage the number of actors and negotiation positions is to form coalitions. However, it is time-consuming to consolidate a joint platform. When a consensus is achieved, it tends to generate inflexibility and rigidity in the negotiation process, since unity within the coalition is prioritized (Leigh-Phippard, 1999: 98–101). Moreover, conference diplomacy is often criticized as a kind of "public appearance diplomacy" where political leaders are more concerned with their public image than with negotiating the issue at stake. For instance, in the early 1990s, a series of conferences on the war in Bosnia were held under public pressures. World leaders convened several times to give a public appearance of concern about the war, but with poor results (Aggestam, 2004: 6).

CHOOSING BETWEEN DIPLOMACY AND WAR

As we outlined initially, in conflict situations, state policy-makers may have recourse to norms and practices of diplomacy, war or a combination of the two institutions. Reliance on law and adjudication, an alternative mode of conflict resolution domestically, is a rare option in international relations. Under what circumstances, then, do policy-makers opt for or against diplomacy?

One obvious answer is that the choice is a result of a rational calculus. The transaction costs of war are vastly greater than those of diplomacy. In comparison to mobilizing armies, the costs of engaging diplomats are negligible. Only when the parties perceive (rightly or wrongly) that the conflict of interest is so deep that it cannot be resolved either by unilateral retreat or by compromise will they resort to war (cf. Snyder and Diesing,

1977: 502). Yet, there might be other, less tangible factors influencing their preferences.

Trust

To rely on diplomacy, policy-makers must have trust in the institution and in diplomats as agents of conflict resolution. This cannot be taken for granted but has varied among states and over time. For instance, the United States distrusted the diplomatic system fashioned and developed in European courts well into the twentieth century. Condemning European power politics and secret diplomacy, the United States minimized its involvement in the diplomatic world. Still, in 1906, there were only nine US embassies abroad, the rest being legations, and up to the end of World War II, fewer than half of the heads of mission were career diplomats (Eban, 1983: 343). Only after World War II did the idea of diplomacy as a valuable institution and an honorable profession rather than a disagreeable necessity take root in the United States. Similarly, after the Russian revolution in 1917, the Soviet government wanted to distance itself from bourgeois diplomacy.

Generally, the level of trust in diplomacy was at a low level after World War I, when the secretiveness of the "old" diplomacy came under heavy criticism, and the entire diplomatic system was held responsible for the failure to prevent the outbreak of war. In the harsh judgment of one observer, "what we now know as diplomacy is nothing more than a convicted fraud, a swindler of mankind, and a traitorous assassin of the morality and progress of the human race" (Hayward, 1916: 255). While much less virulent, lacking trust in diplomacy is discernible in various parts of the world today as well.

Worldview

Whether or not diplomacy is preferred also has to do with the worldview of policy-makers. Fundamentalist, absolutist outlooks tend to preclude diplomacy, which presumes pragmatic, relativist attitudes. For instance, the sixteenth-century religious wars nearly destroyed the European institution of diplomacy. European diplomacy had served what was, in effect, one society with common upper class and dynasty standards and attitudes. The dynastic power struggles were then reduced to a kind of family quarrel within a ruling aristocracy. The intensification of religious strife in the 1560s was a catastrophic interruption, entailing mutual suspicions that the other's embassies were centers of hostile and subversive ideas. In short, whereas successful diplomacy requires that the parties can imagine a mutually satisfactory settlement, a clash of ideological opposites leaves little room for diplomacy (cf. Mattingly, 1955: 195–6).

This negative correlation between absolutist worldviews and reliance on diplomatic means of conflict resolution recurs in more recent history. At the height of the Cold War, the United States and the Soviet Union perceived each other as conspiracies disguised as states to be fought globally as well as at home. "Communism was a virus, a social sickness, a disease of the body politic. Capitalism, bourgeois culture, was a source of contamination, cancer, rot" (Barnet, 1977: 73). For a long time, these attitudes precluded the use of diplomatic means of conflict resolution.

Similar tendencies are observable in the new millennium, when the "war on terror" rules out diplomatic dialog not only between states and organizations labeled as terrorists, but also between states with leaders expressing fundamentalist, absolutist outlooks, such as US President George W. Bush and Iranian President Mahmud Ahmadinejad. Anathematizing each other, they rule out diplomatic dialog as an alternative.

Political will

Political willingness is a key factor in explaining why policy-makers prefer diplomacy or not. In recent years, growing concerns over humanitarian catastrophes, collapsing states and gross human rights abuses have resulted in a number of policy reports, which focus on how diplomatic practices may be refined

and conflicts prevented and resolved. Most of them share the concern that there has to exist a political willingness to achieve effective preventive diplomacy. For instance, the independent international commission on intervention and state sovereignty, which concluded its report in 2001 on the right of humanitarian intervention and responsibility to protect, stressed the necessity of international political will in order to implement their policy recommendations. However, as demonstrated in the case of Darfur, a humanitarian catastrophe can be widely recognized, and yet the international community lacks a political will to act.

According to Dean Pruitt (1997: 239–40), the motivation and cooperative behavior of political leaders are to a large extent determined by the goal of achieving mutual cooperation. Yet, optimism about the other parties' reciprocity is equally important and determines the extent to which this goal will affect behavior. Optimism about a jointly negotiated outcome is necessary since the danger of unilateral conciliatory efforts might be exploited by the opponent and viewed as weak or even treasonous by one's supporter. The turbulent and yet so astonishing transition of South Africa illustrates well the importance of combining diplomatic leadership and political willingness when pursuing conflict resolution. F.W. de Klerk shocked the world by announcing the release of Nelson Mandela and his intention to negotiate in good faith the end of apartheid. Mandela responded with courage by calling for national reconciliation and embracing white leaders with no sign of bitterness (Sisk, 2001: 107).

CONCLUSION

The Westphalian system of sovereign states has engendered exclusive norms of recognition which, on the whole, have been detrimental to the resolution of conflicts involving other actors than recognized states. Today's notions of a globalized world envisage an international society with a diminished role, if not obsolescence, of the state and enhanced roles of other actors, such as NGOs engaged in conflict resolution, private military companies (PMCs), transnational terrorist networks and organized crime. Paradoxically, "the virtually universal recognition of territorial sovereignty as the organizing principle of international politics" goes hand in hand with an equally clear "tendency toward erosion of the exclusivity associated with the traditional notion of territoriality" (Kratochwil, 1986: 27). This raises the question whether diplomacy, understood as an interstate institution, will be able to contribute to the resolution of contemporary and future complex conflicts, involving heterogeneous actors.

To be sure, diplomacy has become a more complex practice, involving many different actors. Yet, it has also shown its resilience and adaptability to new circumstances. For instance, in cases of complex political emergencies, a whole range of diplomatic tools are required and performed by states and non-state actors alike, such as multilateral and bilateral diplomacy, peacekeeping, economic and humanitarian aid to assist civilian reconstruction and peacemaking. Hence, most diplomats recognize the need of multiple tracks of diplomacy. Contemporary terrorism, however, does pose a particular challenge to diplomacy, in the sense that terrorists loathe the diplomatic rules of engagement, such as communication and negotiation. At the same time, the "war on terror" has in many ways produced counterproductive results, which is why varieties of "soft instruments of power," such as prevention, persuasion and coordination of international diplomatic efforts, are suggested as more productive.

In sum, diplomacy remains a vital institution for effective conflict resolution, even in a world where interstate conflicts are not the only – or even the most serious – problems. At the same time, diplomacy offers no panacea, and there are diplomatic norms and practices that are not always conducive to conflict resolution. Diplomacy, in short, is a perennial international institution that can be regarded as a necessary, but not sufficient, condition for successful conflict resolution.

REFERENCES

Aggestam, Karin. (2002) "Quasi-Informal Mediation in the Oslo Channel," in Jacob Bercovitch (ed.), *Studies in International Mediation*. Basingstoke and New York: Palgrave Macmillan.

Aggestam, Karin. (2004) "Two-Track Diplomacy: Negotiations Between Israel and the PLO Through Open and Secret Channels," in Christer Jönsson and Richard Langhorne (eds), *Diplomacy, Volume III*. London: Sage.

Aggestam, Karin. (2006) "Internal and External Dynamics of Spoiling: A Negotiation Approach," in Edward Newman and Oliver Richmond (eds), *Spoilers and Peace Processes: Conflict Settlement and Devious Objectives*. Tokyo: UN University Press.

Anderson, M.S. (1993) *The Rise of Modern Diplomacy 1450–1919*. London and New York: Longman.

Armstrong, Tony. (1993) *Breaking the Ice: Rapprochement Between East and West Germany, The United States and China, and Israel and Egypt*. Washington, DC: United States Institute of Peace Press.

Aron, Raymond. (1967) *Peace and War: A Theory of International Relations*. New York: Praeger.

Aspaturian, Vernon V. (1971) *Process and Power in Soviet Foreign Policy*. Boston: Little, Brown.

Avruch, Kevin. (2000) "Reciprocity, Equality, and Status-Anxiety in the Amarna Letters," in Raymond Cohen and Raymond Westbrook (eds), *Amarna Diplomacy: The Beginnings of International Relations*. Baltimore and London: Johns Hopkins University Press.

Barnet, Richard J. (1977) *The Giants: Russia and America*. New York: Simon and Schuster.

Beckman, Gary M. (1996) *Hittite Diplomatic Texts*. Atlanta, GA: Scholars Press.

Beilin, Yossi. (1999) *Touching Peace: From the Oslo Accord to a Final Agreement*. London: Weidenfeldt & Nicholson.

Berridge, G.R. (1993) "Diplomacy after Death: The Rise of the Working Funeral," *Diplomacy and Statecraft*, 4, 2: 217–34.

Berridge, G.R. (1994) *Talking to the Enemy: How States without 'Diplomatic Relations' Communicate*. New York: St. Martin's Press.

Berridge, G.R. (2002) *Diplomacy: Theory and Practice*. 2nd edn. London: Prentice Hall and Harvester Wheatsheaf.

Britton, Roswell. (2004) "Chinese Interstate Intercourse Before 700 BC," in Christer Jönsson and Richard

Langhorne (eds), *Diplomacy, Volume II*. London: Sage.

Bull, Hedley. (1977) *The Anarchical Society: A Study of Order in World Politics*. London: Macmillan.

Cassese, Antonio. (2001) *International Law*. Oxford: Oxford University Press.

Chrysos, Evangelos. (1992) "Byzantine Diplomacy, AD 300–800: Means and Ends," in Jonathan Shepard and Simon Franklin (eds), *Byzantine Diplomacy*. Aldershot: Variorum.

Cohen, Raymond. (1981) *International Politics: The Rules of the Game*. London and New York: Longman.

Cohen, Raymond. (2001) "The Great Tradition: The Spread of Diplomacy in the Ancient World," *Diplomacy and Statecraft*, 12, 1: 23–38.

Cohen, Raymond and Raymond Westbrook. (2000) "Conclusion: The Beginnings of International Relations," in Raymond Cohen and Raymond Westbrook (eds), *Amarna Diplomacy: The Beginnings of International Relations*. Baltimore and London: Johns Hopkins University Press.

Cohen, Yoel. (1986) *Media Diplomacy: The Foreign Office in the Mass Communication Age*. London: Frank Cass.

Constantinou, Costas M. (1996) *On the Way to Diplomacy*. Minneapolis, MN: University of Minnesota Press.

Cooper, Andrew F. and Brian Hocking. (2000) "Governments, Non-governmental Organisations and the Re-calibration of Diplomacy," *Global Society*, 14, 3: 361–76.

Darby, John. (2001) *The Effects of Violence on Peace Processes*. Washington, DC: United States Institute of Peace Press.

Doxey, Margaret. (1995) "'Something Old, Something New': The Politics of Recognition in Post-Cold-War Europe," *Diplomacy and Statecraft*, 6, 2: 303–22.

Eban, Abba. (1983) *The New Diplomacy: International Affairs in the Modern Age*. New York: Random House.

Eban, Abba. (1985) "Interest and Conscience in Modern Diplomacy," *Fourth Morgenthau Memorial Lecture on Morality & Foreign Policy*. New York: Council on Religion and International Affairs.

Fierke, Karin M. (2005) *Diplomatic Interventions: Conflict and Change in a Globalizing World*. Houndmills: Palgrave Macmillan.

Freeman, Chas W. Jr. (1997) *Arts of Power: Statecraft and Diplomacy*. Washington, DC: United States Institute of Peace Press.

Frey, Linda S. and Marsha L. Frey. (1999) *The History of Diplomatic Immunity*. Columbus, OH: Ohio State University Press.

George, Alexander L. (1991) *Forceful Persuasion: Coercive Diplomacy as an Alternative to War*. Washington, DC: United States Institute of Peace Press.

George, Alexander L. and William E. Simons. (eds) (1994) *The Limits of Coercive Diplomacy*. Boulder, CO: Westview.

Hamilton, Keith and Richard Langhorne. (1995) *The Practice of Diplomacy: Its Evolution, Theory and Administration*. London and New York: Routledge.

Hayward, Charles W. (1916) *What Is Diplomacy?* London: Grant Richards.

Hill, Christopher. (1991) "Diplomacy and the Modern State," in Cornelia Navari (ed.), *The Condition of States*. Milton Keynes and Philadelphia: Open University Press.

Hirschfeld, Yair. (1994) "Dynamics of Israeli-Palestinian Negotiations," in Barry Rubin, Joseph Ginat and Moshe Ma'oz (eds), *From War to Peace: Arab-Israeli Relations 1973–1993*. Brighton: Sussex Academic Press.

Hocking, Brian. (2004) "Diplomacy," in Walter Carlsnaes, Helen Sjursen and Brian White (eds), *Contemporary European Foreign Policy*. London: Sage.

Holsti, Kalevi J. (1991) *Peace and War: Armed Conflicts and International Order 1648–1989*. Cambridge: Cambridge University Press.

Holsti, Kalevi J. (2004) *Taming the Sovereigns: Institutional Change in International Politics*. Cambridge: Cambridge University Press.

Iklé, Fred Charles. (1971) *Every War Must End*. New York: Columbia University Press.

International Commission on Intervention and State Sovereignty. (2001), co-chaired by Gareth Evans and Mohamed Sahnoun, *The Responsibility to Protect*. Ottawa: International Development Research Centre.

James, Alan. (1993) "Diplomacy," *Review of International Studies*, 19, 1: 91–100.

Jönsson, Christer. (1990) *Communication in International Bargaining*. London: Pinter.

Jönsson, Christer and Martin Hall. (2005) *Essence of Diplomacy*. Houndmills: Palgrave Macmillan.

Kaufmann, Johan. (1996) *Conference Diplomacy: An Introductory Analysis*, 3rd revised edn. Houndmills: Macmillan.

Keohane, Robert O. (1986) "Reciprocity in International Relations," *International Organization*, 40, 1: 1–27.

Keohane, Robert O. (1988) "International Institutions: Two Approaches," *International Studies Quarterly*, 32, 4: 379–96.

Kissinger, Henry A. (1994) *Diplomacy*. New York: Simon and Schuster.

Krasner, Stephen D. (1999) *Sovereignty: Organized Hypocrisy*. Princeton, NJ: Princeton University Press.

Kydd, Andrew and Walter, Barbara. (2002) "Sabotaging the Peace: The Politics of Extremist Violence," *International Organization*, 56, 2: 263–96.

Langhorne, Richard. (2004) "The Development of International Conferences, 1648–1830," in Christer Jönsson and Richard Langhorne (eds), *Diplomacy, Volume II*. London: Sage.

Leigh-Phippard, Helen. (1999) "The Influence of Informal Groups in Multilateral Diplomacy," in Jan Melissen (ed.), *Innovation in Diplomatic Practice*. London and New York: Macmillan and St. Martin's Press.

liverani, Mario. (2001) *International Relations in the Ancient Near East, 1600–1100* BC. Houndmills: Palgrave Macmillan.

McClanahan, Grant V. (1989) *Diplomatic Immunity: Principles, Practices, Problems*. London: Hurst & Co.

Macomber, William. (1997) *The Angels' Game: A Commentary on Modern Diplomacy*. Revised edn. Dennisport, MA: Crane Corporation.

Makovsky, David. (1996) *Making Peace with the PLO: The Rabin Government's Road to the Oslo Accord*. Boulder, CO: Westview.

Malanczuk, Peter. (1997) *Akehurst's Modern Introduction to International Law*. 7th revised edn. London and New York: Routledge.

March, James G. and Johan P. Olsen. (1998) "The Institutional Dynamics of International Political Orders," *International Organization*, 52, 4: 943–69.

Marshall, Sir Peter. (1990) *The Dynamics of Diplomacy*. London: The Diplomatic Academy of London.

Mattingly, Garrett. (1955) *Renaissance Diplomacy*. London: Jonathan Cape.

Nicolson, Harold. (1954/1998) *The Evolution of Diplomatic Method*. London: Constable, 1954; reprinted by the Diplomatic Studies Programme, Centre for the Study of Diplomacy, University of Leicester, 1998.

Nicolson, Harold. (1977) *Diplomacy*. 3rd edn. Oxford: Oxford University Press.

Numelin, Ragnar. (1950) *The Beginnings of Diplomacy: A Sociological Study of Inter-tribal and International Relations*. Oxford: Oxford University Press.

Peres, Shimon. (1995) *Battling for Peace: Memoirs*. London: Weidenfeld & Nicolson.

Peterson, M.J. (1997) *Recognition of Governments: Legal Doctrine and State Practice, 1815–1995*. London: Macmillan.

Pruitt, Dean. (1997) "Ripeness Theory and the Oslo Talks," *International Negotiation*, 2, 2: 239–40.

Richmond, Oliver. (2006) "The Linkage between Devious Objectives and Spoiling Behaviour in Peace Processes," in Edward Newman and Oliver Richmond (eds), *Spoilers and Peace Processes: Conflict Settlement and Devious Objectives*. Tokyo: UN University Press.

Ross, Lee. (1995) "Reactive Devaluation in Negotiation and Conflict Resolution," in Kenneth Arrow, Robert H. Mnookin, Lee Ross, Amos Tversky and Robert Wilson (eds), *Barriers to the Negotiated Resolution of Conflict*.

Rothman, Jay. (1997) *Resolving Identity-Based Conflict*. San Francisco: Jossey-Bass.

Satow, Ernest. (1979) *Satow's Guide to Diplomatic Practice*. 5th edn, ed. Lord Gore-Booth. London and New York: Longman.

Schelling, Thomas C. (1966) *Arms and Influence*. New Haven and London: Yale University Press.

Sharp, Paul. (1998) "Who Needs Diplomats? The Problem of Diplomatic Representation," in Jovan Kurbalija (ed.), *Modern Diplomacy*. Malta: Mediterranean Academy of Diplomatic Studies.

Sharp, Paul. (1999) "For Diplomacy: Representation and the Study of International Relations," *International Studies Review*, 1, 1: 33–57.

Shepard, Jonathan. (1992) "Byzantine Diplomacy, AD 800–1204: Means and Ends," in Jonathan Shepard and Simon Franklin (eds), *Byzantine Diplomacy*. Aldershot: Variorum.

Sisk, Timothy. (2001) "Profile: South Africa," in John Darby (ed.), *The Effects of Violence on Peace Processes*. Washington, DC: United States Institute of Peace Press.

Snyder, Glenn H. and Paul Diesing. (1977) *Conflict among Nations: Bargaining, Decision Making, and System Structure in International Crises*. Princeton, NJ: Princeton University Press.

Stedman, Stephen J. (1997) "Spoiler Problems in Peace Processes," *International Security*, 22, 2: 5–53.

Stedman, Stephen J., Donald Rothchild and Elizabeth Cousens. (2002) *Ending Civil Wars*. Boulder, CO: Lynne Rienner.

Tran, Van Dinh. (1987) *Communication and Diplomacy in a Changing World*. Norwood, NJ: Ablex.

Walker, Richard Louis. (1953) *The Multi-State System of Ancient China*. Hamden, CT: Shoe String Press.

Walker, Ronald A. (2004) *Multilateral Conferences: Purposeful International Negotiation*. Houndmills: Palgrave Macmillan.

Watson, Adam. (1982) *Diplomacy: The Dialogue Between States*. London: Eyre Methuen.

Wilson, Clifton E. (1967) *Diplomatic Privileges and Immunities*. Tucson, AZ: University of Arizona Press.

Wiseman, Geoffrey. (1999) "'Polylateralism' and New Modes of Global Dialogue," *Discussion Paper*, No. 59. Leicester: Leicester Diplomatic Studies Programme.

Wright, Quincy. (1942) *A Study of War, Vol. 1*. Chicago: University of Chicago Press.

Young, Oran R. (1989) *International Cooperation: Building Regimes for Natural Resources and the Environment*. Ithaca, NY: Cornell University Press.

Zartman, I. William and Guy Olivier Faure. (2005) "The Dynamics of Escalation and Negotiation," in I. William Zartman and Guy Olivier Faure (eds), *Escalation and Negotiation*. Cambridge: Cambridge University Press.

3

Conflict Resolution in the International System: A Quantitative Approach

J.David Singer and Shahryar Minhas

INTRODUCTION

As pleased as we are to contribute to this project, it may nevertheless be useful to begin with a few caveats. Perhaps the most critical of these is the historical fact that, of the many strategies for conflict resolution over the centuries, war may come close to being the one most frequently used. Normally, we think of conflict resolution as a set of strategies by which disputes between and within nations can be resolved short of war. An interesting historical aside is that when we created the first scientifically oriented peace research institute, those of us at Michigan rapidly endorsed the Kenneth Boulding proposal that we call it the Center for Research on Conflict Resolution. What he had in mind was, first of all, an understanding that conflict – not military or necessarily the violent type – is inherent in all human relationships and was unlikely to disappear from the human condition in the relevant future. Boulding liked to say that

our mission was to "make the world safe for conflict," by which he meant reduce the likelihood that social conflict would regularly erupt into armed combat and war. Thus, our mission was to come to grips with social conflict at the international and other levels of aggregation and discover the tactics and strategies by which the protagonists and potential interveners might find or create ways of ameliorating the severity of these conflicts. Another of our founding fathers was Anatol Rapoport, who early on drew an interesting set of distinctions in his *Fights, Games and Debates* (1960). In his view, a fight was a conflict in which the protagonists would seek to destroy one another, in a game the idea was to outwit and dominate one another, and in a debate the idea was to persuade one another. Little has happened in the half century since to change our view that war continues to be a widely practiced mode of conflict resolution. Surely, we see an increasing reliance on an interesting range of less violent strategies, but we can hardly urge that these strategies have been particularly effective.

This leads us, then, to the somewhat unconventional suspicion that the conflict resolution field has not been especially successful and that may well be because of a failure in our research strategy. As a good many of the contributors to this volume seem to understand, grasping the etiology of conflict at the various levels of social aggregation, from interpersonal to international, must be seen as a prerequisite for greater success in the conflict resolution endeavor. Hence, we offer this chapter as a contribution to the current discussion and will present what we consider to be some of the more relevant findings in the peace science effort to explain interstate armed conflict. To that end, we hope that our chapter will play a useful and catalytic role in engaging the peace science and conflict resolution communities to engage one another in an ambitious integration of empirical findings and theoretical speculations. We will organize our report by differentiating in terms of the level of social aggregation at which we find major contextual correlates of war, then describing some of the behavioral correlates of war, and concluding with some conflict resolution implications emerging from the peace science enterprise.

THE STATE LEVEL OF AGGREGATION

In this section, we consider some of the more interesting and relevant monadic level findings as to what it is that makes states and other social actors especially dispute- and war-prone.

Demographics

We begin with the Bremer, Singer, and Luterbacher (1973) study, in which they examine population, area, and war for the European state system from 1816 to 1965, and find that neither population nor population density are related to the frequency of war. While looking at the impact of population growth and density on involvement in international conflict initiation

and escalation, Tir and Diehl (1998) find that the less developed a state, the more subject it is to population pressures and conflict compared to countries that are more developed and possess a higher level of technology.

Somewhat related is the lateral pressure argument, in which expanded industrialization, along with population growth, will lead states to look abroad for resources, markets, and investment opportunities. As plausible as this may sound, especially *vis-á-vis* the advanced European states in the late nineteenth century, the findings are weak, except for Japan in the early twentieth century (Choucri and North, 1972). Overall, the empirical research in this area finds little evidence for the lateral pressure argument, and this is probably due to the effects of globalization and the opening of commodity markets, which has facilitated access to resources for states across the world.

Economic development and the business cycle

There has also been a fair amount of work trying to solve the war puzzle through investigating possible correlations between economic development and the business cycle with war. One of the earlier studies on the subject was by Richardson (1960), who finds no statistically significant correlation among levels of economic development and 300 deadly quarrels from 1820 to 1945. In a study of a possible association between phases of the business cycle and war initiation, Thompson (1982) examines the experiences of four advanced nations between 1792 and 1973 and concludes that expansion and contraction phases of a capitalist economy are not related to patterns of war initiation.

Domestic stability

Counter to some standard arguments linking domestic instability and interstate conflict, the evidence is mixed as to whether or not there is a correlation. Searching foreign conflict vectors of 128 states over the years 1963 to 1967 for a possible relationship with a factor dimension of domestic turmoil, Vincent (1981) reports a statistically significant correlation between these two dimensions and concludes that the degree of a state's internal stability may be a useful predictor of its degree of foreign conflict behavior. In contrast, Geller (1985) examines a set of domestic and foreign conflict variables for 36 states between 1959 and 1968 and concludes that nations exhibiting high internal stability are more likely to engage in conflictual foreign policies than are nations with much less stability.

A more recent study by Leeds and Davis (1997) compares domestic political vulnerability to international disputes by examining the relationships between economic decline, the electoral cycle, and measures of aggressive international action for 18 advanced industrialized democracies during the period from 1952 to 1988. They found no consistent support for a relationship between constraining domestic political conditions and aggressive international behavior. The conflicting results can be partially attributed to the temporal spans that each study covers; while Geller and Vincent use rather short temporal spans, the study conducted by Leeds and Davis encompasses a somewhat longer period of 36 years.

Government centralization

A study conducted by the Cross-Polity Survey (1963) reports that the stronger the degree of executive leadership, the greater the tendency toward both diplomatic and violent foreign conflict. In a more current and comprehensive study, Enterline (1998a) finds a strong link between autocratization and dispute initiation, and a less powerful relationship between autocratization and war initiation. So far, empirical research on the subject does call attention to the importance that government centralization might have upon interstate conflict, but does not necessarily tell us that centralized regimes are likely to initiate war.

Regime type: democracy and war

While most of the research on the effects of regime type focuses on the dyadic level

of aggregation, it all started with the Cold War acolytes of Immanuel Kant. In 1961, the journal *Industrial Research* conducted a survey among its readers, most of whom agreed that democracies are very peace-loving, while autocracies were more war-prone. The editors asked the COW team whether the historical evidence would support that, and in a rather simple study of the system since 1815, they found this not to be (Small and Singer, 1976). There were no significant differences between the frequencies with which the two regime types either initiated or participated in international wars. They did however find no wars in which there were democracies on both sides, but explained this as a historical–geographical artifact, given that there were very few democracies during that period, and moreover, even fewer were geographically contiguous – the most important of all variables in accounting for dyadic war. Here, continuing on the dyadic level of aggregation, we summarize the extent to which regime type affects the war-proneness of states while controlling for and interacting with other domestic variables, such as regime type.

Nonetheless, the argument that democracies do not go to war with each other has become an often discussed topic in the peace science literature; essentially, its advocates claim that democratic leaders are more influenced by their domestic setting (e.g. opposition parties, constituencies, electoral cycles) at home, which then restrains them from going to war with other democracies. Several studies have tested the relationship between the electoral cycle and interstate conflict in democratic countries; one of these was done by Gaubatz (1991) using COW data for war participation of democratic nations during the period between 1816 and 1980. He finds that the frequency of war *initiation* by democratic states is unrelated to the phase of the election cycle, but he did find that there is a significant tendency for nations to *enter* wars during the earlier – rather than later – phases of the election cycles.

A formal model developed by Bueno de Mesquita, Morrow, Siverson and Smith (1999) highlights the fundamental assumption of the democratic peace model; this is the idea that the highest priority of political leaders is to stay in power. This leads them to conclude that democratic leaders are more cautious about launching wars that they might lose. Adding to the study of the democratic peace argument, Brecher, James, and Wilkenfeld (2000), using data collected by the International Crisis Behavior Project (ICB), find that democracies are more inclined to go "all-out" once a conflict with a non-democratic adversary escalates.

More recently, Huth and Allee (2002), using a political accountability model tested against a data set of 348 territorial disputes for the period from 1919 to 1995, find that electoral cycles and the strength of opposition parties are important in explaining patterns of conflictual and cooperative behavior by democratic states. Specifically, they conclude that the timing of military confrontations by democracies is linked to electoral cycles, in that democratic leaders prefer to offer concessions in periods shortly after national elections. They also discover that other domestic-level variables, such as opposition parties, have an impact on the escalation of military confrontations as well. Using a two-stage probit model on a new data set of all leaders between 1919 and 1992, Chiozza and Goemans (2003) analyze the reciprocal relationship between the probability of losing office and the probability of crisis initiation. Their results show that an increase in the risk of losing office makes leaders less likely to initiate a crisis, also suggesting that democracies overall are less likely to initiate a crisis because of the domestic political insecurity of their leaders.

Leblang and Chen (2003) disaggregate democracies by the details of their respective political system, such as parliamentary versus presidential, rule by a single dominant party versus a coalition government, and phases of the electoral cycle. They seek to explain the variations in war involvement among the established democracies on the basis of major differences in institutions of governance. They find that a country's electoral system turns out to be the most important institutional factor in reducing involvement in war, and that established democracies with

a proportional representation system tend to have significantly less such involvement. Their analysis brings into question the view that divided governments are better at reducing war involvement, and their results indicate no systematic difference between presidential and parliamentary forms of government, nor is there any difference in war involvement when states are governed by a single party or by a coalition of parties. But their analysis does show that a proportional representation system tends to be significantly less likely to engage in foreign belligerence.

Another element to consider is what role the origins of a state play in how conflict-prone a state becomes. Maoz and Abdolali (1989), using COW militarized dispute data for the years between 1816 and 1976, find a positive association between violent or revolutionary state formation/transformation processes and militarized dispute involvement: states formed through non-violent or "evolutionary" means tend to be less conflict-prone in their international behavior. A somewhat related finding by Enterline (1998b) investigates 360 new political regimes and evaluates how a new political regime's institutional type and the political composition of its "geographic neighborhood" influences patterns of "intra-neighborhood militarized conflict." He suggests that the homogeneity of regimes in a certain region, rather than their type, may play an important role in analyzing what makes states more war-prone. However, he argues that more work needs to be done to better understand the role that regime coherency plays in the shaping of interstate conflict.

Major powers

Major powers and their relation to war has been a topic often discussed, and on the monadic level the consensus does hold that there is positive relationship between major powers and conflict initiation, at least relative to minor powers. Using the original (1816–1965) and expanded (1816–1980) COW database, Small and Singer (1976, 1982) demonstrate that major powers are much more likely to engage in war than are minor powers. Bremer (1980), also using COW data, reports that nations that rank high on a composite index of national capability (CINC) are involved in a greater number of wars and initiate wars with greater frequency than do lower ranked states. Elberwein (1982) in a replication of Bremer adds to the finding that more powerful nations tend to use military force more frequently, and that power status alone accounts for over 60 percent of the variance in "joining" ongoing militarized interstate disputes.

Militarization

In terms of militarization and war-prone states, one of the earliest studies was by Feierabend and Feierabend (1969), who report a positive correlation between militarization and foreign conflict for the subset of highly developed states. Similarly, Weede (1970), using the DON database for the period 1955 to 1960 and defining "militarization" by the twin ratios of military personnel to total population and defense expenditures to GNP, notes a positive association between militarization and both verbal and violent foreign conflict behavior.

In examining the rate of change in military expenditure for a possible connection between the frequencies of dispute involvement and initiation, Diehl and Kingston (1987) conclude that military buildups in major powers do not affect a state's tendency to initiate or to become involved in militarized international disputes. Also, Goldsmith (2003) finds that under conditions of economic growth or high levels of wealth, "extra" resources are diverted disproportionately to the military, but he does not find any linkage between military buildup and dispute initiation.

Capabilities and power cycles

Hoping that "power (capability) cycles" will help elucidate the correlation between the capabilities of a state and its involvement in interstate conflict, Doran and Parsons (1980) posit that certain critical points in

a major power's cycle of increasing and decreasing capabilities (relative to the major-power system's capability pool) are likely to be associated with both the onset and the severity, duration, and magnitude of its wars. They maintain that states move through a general, cyclical pattern of capability growth, maturation, and decline. Four critical points on the evolutionary curve of a state are important because they present a disjuncture between a "state's interests and aspirations ... and its actual capability" (Doran, 1983). Due to the shift in direction or rate of capability growth (lower turning point, rising inflection point, upper turning point, declining inflection point), the state must reevaluate its relative position, capability base, and foreign policy goals. He argues that the foreign policy stakes at these critical points are enormous – involving status, security, and power – and are therefore more likely to lead to war involvement. In short, the probability of war involvement increases for states passing through a critical point on the power cycle. For the initial study, capabilities are measured by an index composed of five material indicators, with the population inclusive of all major powers for the years between 1816 and 1975. They conclude that a major power's point on the power cycle is an important determinant of its probability of initiating a war, involvement in war, and of the characteristics of wars in which it engages, and also determine that 90 percent of major powers passing through a critical point on the power cycle are subsequently engaged in war.

To end the capabilities section, we cite one brief study on status quo orientation and its relationship to war; this was done by Geller (1994) who examines 43 rivalry wars between 1816 and 1986. He finds that challengers to the status quo initiate 30 of these, while defenders of the status quo initiate 13 of the preemptive or preventive type.

Environmental degradation

A new front opening in the peace science literature is concerned with the extent to which environmental degradation or resource maldistribution is associated with the onset of state-involved armed conflict. Many analyses test factors like deforestation, land degradation, and scarce supply of freshwater, alone and in combination with high population density, then test what role these factors play in increasing the risk of armed conflict. Professor Lee at American University began a Trade Environment Database (TED) in September 1992, in which he has amassed over 700 case studies that among trade and cultural variables use environmental variables to explain the causes of war. One apparent result from many of his case studies is that armed conflict leads to resource scarcity and that resource scarcity leads to more conflict, thus there might exist something akin to a cyclical trap for nations facing these types of problems. The importance of bi-directional interplay was also stressed by Maxwell and Reuveny (2000), who argue that conflict due to "renewable resource scarcity" could be cyclical, which would then lead to recurring phases of conflict. However, when taking into account economic and political factors, such as level of economic development, Hauge and Ellingsen (1998) find that the environmental scarcity variables do not play a decisive a role in predicting the incidence of armed conflict. Percival and Homer-Dixon (1998), in analyzing the relationship between environmental scarcity and conflict in the case of South Africa, note that environmental scarcity emerges within a political, social, and economic context, and that it "interacts with many of these contextual factors to contribute to violence."

DYADIC LEVEL OF SOCIAL AGGREGATION

Within the peace science community there has been considerable debate as to the usefulness of trying to describe and explain armed conflict at the state level; dissatisfaction with that emphasis has led to a veritable cottage industry of research that reflects the proposition: "It's the dyad, silly, not the monadic." We thus turn now to some of the more promising findings at the dyadic level.

Capability and parity

The first variable deals with the impact of the direction and rate of change in relative capabilities on the likelihood of war at the dyadic level. There are two dominant schools of thought: parity and preponderance. The parity school holds that the more equal two states are in military and industrial capabilities, and thus uncertain as to which can dominate in a confrontation, the less likely they are to risk war against one another as each can successfully deter the other (Waltz, 1979). The preponderance school, on the other hand, holds that the very uncertainty of victory can lead to instability in the dyad, and create temptation on the part of one or another of the parties to strike first, especially as capabilities shift.

Closely related is the so-called "Power Transition" paradigm, in which it is argued that when two major powers are moving toward parity in their capabilities, the likelihood of war will rise (Organski and Kugler, 1980). Another perspective concerns the number of major powers in the system; Deutsch and Singer (1964) state that a bipolar configuration is dangerous and that the number of fairly distinct coalitions or poles decreases the likelihood of war between any two members in the major power subsystem.

Using data for the years 1815 through 1965 to examine both the initiation and escalation of international conflicts, Siverson and Tennefoss (1984) also provide evidence in general support of the basic hypothesis. Their dyadic-level findings suggest support of the balance of power paradigm: few disputes among major powers (presumably more or less equal in capabilities) escalated to military action, whereas a much higher proportion of conflicts initiated by major powers against minor powers escalated to reciprocated military action. However, they also note that approximately 19 percent of the total conflicts involved minor power initiation against stronger states, and that over 25 percent of these escalated to the mutual use of force. Also, in regard to parity on the dyadic level, Mihalka (1976), using COW data for the years between 1816 and 1970, indicate that the probability of a confrontation escalating to the level of military violence was significantly higher when the capability differentials between the disputants were marginal. Mandel (1980) examines interstate border disputes for the years between 1945 and 1974 with Managing Interstate Conflict (MIC) data and reaches a similar conclusion: violent border disputes were more likely to occur under a condition of relative parity in capabilities. Employing a Markov chain analysis of 456 militarized disputes occurring between 1816 and 1986, Geller (1993) finds that power parity and shifts toward parity are approximately twice as likely to be associated with war as is a condition of capability preponderance. Equality of capability or shifts toward equality lead to a situation where both sides can perceive the potential for successful use of force.

Kim (1991) also examines great power wars (COW database 1816–1975) and reports that the probability of war for major power dyads whose capabilities (including alliances) were equal is more than double the probability for dyads whose capabilities were unequal. In an expanded analysis, Kim (1996) examines the interaction of dyadic capability balances, status quo orientation, and alliance relationships among great powers for the period from the Peace of Westphalia in 1648 to 1975. His findings indicate that basic equality in capabilities between great powers and dissatisfied challengers increases the probability of the onset of war. A more up-to-date analysis by Moul (2003) looks at great power disputants between 1816 and 1989 and also finds that approximate parity in capabilities actually encouraged war.

Shifts and transitions in regimes have also been tested for correlations with war on the dyadic level. Houweling and Siccama (1988) provide a re-analysis of the Organski and Kugler power transition test using a more extensive set of nations (all major powers) and

a composite indicator of national capabilities (CINC). They conclude that differential growth rates that result in capability transitions toward parity are strongly associated with the occurrence of major power war.

Continuing the analysis of capability change and the onset of interstate war, a study by Kim and Morrow (1992) reports the absence of any statistically discernible association between war occurrence and the rate of capability change among major power rivals. On the other hand, Huth, Bennett, and Gelpi (1992) report significant effects for capability transitions on dispute initiation patterns (MID Database) among a set of 18 great power rivalries for the period from 1816 to 1975. The findings indicate that a capability "transition" (defined as a military expenditure growth rate differential of 10 percent or more) has a significant and positive impact on the initiation of militarized conflict among great power rivals.

Taking this analysis a step further, Wayman (1996) compares capability shifts in non-rival and rival dyads, and analyzes a set of major power rivalries (COW database) and compares their capability and war patterns with non-rival dyads. He reports that the statistical association between capability shifts and war is stronger among rival states than for non-rivals, and that a capability shift within a rival dyad approximately doubles its probability of war.

Recurring conflicts

Also at the dyadic level, an interesting area of research has been that of recurring conflicts. Gochman and Maoz (1984) report that 76 percent of militarized disputes are followed by another dispute between the same states within a brief period of time. In the same vein, Leng (1983), examining the bargaining behavior of states in rivalry, finds that they become increasingly coercive with successive confrontations, with war regularly resulting, after three such confrontations, in 18 out of the 24 cases. Brecher (1984) notes similarly that protracted conflicts are more likely to escalate to war when they occur in a sequence of recurring confrontations. Huth (1988) suggests that the use of extreme strategies of either "bully" or "conciliation" weakens future efforts at deterrence, and increases the likelihood of war in that dyad. Greico (2001) also undertakes an analysis of recurring conflicts, and comes up with many salient findings. One is that "repetitive military challenges," in which the challenger in a given conflict is in the same role in the next conflict, constitutes the majority of recurrent conflicts. Greico also uses a Cox proportional hazard model of the risk that, after a given conflict, the defender is again challenged by the initial challenger, and his model indicates certain attributes that increase the chances of another challenge. One such attribute is that for those countries who move from military inferiority to parity or superiority, the risk of a re-challenge falls by one-fourth during the first year; another is that a defender experiencing fundamental internal turmoil sustains a level of risk of experiencing a re-challenge that is 350 percent greater than one that is not. He further finds that democratic defenders are 200 percent more likely to experience a re-challenge than a non-democratic defender during the first year post-conflict, and that even after five years, the democratic defender's risk of a re-challenge is 16 percent greater.

Nuclear weapons

Since the bombing of Hiroshima and Nagasaki, most observers have expressed serious concern and alarm at the possibility that nuclear weapons will proliferate. On the other hand, a few observers have argued that the gradual spread of nuclear weapons will promote peace and reinforce international stability, as they assume that nuclear weapons are the agents of equalization and thus the means by which to create a balance of power in the international system. Bueno de Mesquita and Riker (1982), using COW data for 1945–1976, report that disputes involving both nuclear and non-nuclear powers were more likely to escalate to the "intervention" level than

disputes between nuclear-armed states. They conclude that a system in which selective states possess nuclear weapons may be less dangerous than a system with partial possession. Strengthening this proposition was a study by Paul (1994), in which he takes three case studies (i.e. China/United States, 1950; Egypt/Israel, 1973; and Argentina/Britain, 1982) and finds that the possession of nuclear weapons does not appear to inhibit escalatory behavior by non-nuclear opponents. He concludes that nuclear weapons appear to have limited utility in averting conflict between nuclear and non-nuclear states, as there is great difficulty in converting the putative capability of nuclear weapons into actualized power. However, Kraig (1999) challenges the pro-proliferation school for their simplistic treatment of deterrence between developing countries. He finds that "nuclear blackmail" is still a possibility in dyads that experience asymmetric proliferation or in dyads where threat credibility at the nuclear level favors one side; an important caveat is that the nuclear threat has to be credible, and the non-nuclear actor has to believe with a high enough probability that the nuclear actor is willing to use nuclear weapons. Thus, in such a situation, Waltz's conclusions of stability should be looked upon with doubt; for Kraig, even with equal nuclear capability, stability is related to the interrelationships of credibility, conventional strength, and "the dynamics of escalation."

Geller (2003) uses Doran's power cycle conjecture to gain better insights into the global ramifications of a nuclear arms race. He guesses that an arms race between Pakistan and India would trigger China to increase its own nuclear stockpile, which would then force Russia to do the same, and consequently the United States as well. He also asserts that if India's share of the capability pool rises to a level dangerous to China, then China could be moved to a point of international conflict and war on its own power cycle. And some academics, such as Jo and Gartzke (2007), argue that United States "hegemony" has the potential to encourage nuclear proliferation. Before, United States intervention in the third world would have been met with resistance by countries like the Soviet Union, however, the lack of a "nuclear defender" might lead states to proliferate.

Proximity of states

Shifting now to studying the proximity of states and how that might affect war initiation on the dyadic level, Diehl (1985) finds that the probability of dispute escalation to full-scale war is much greater for dyads in which at least one of the states is contiguous to the site of the dispute. Bremer (1992) studies 202,778 non-directional dyad-years for the period between 1816 and 1965, and classifies dyads as either land contiguous, sea contiguous (separated by 150 miles or less of water), or non-contiguous. He concludes that the probability of war increases significantly with the presence of either land or sea contiguity. If the categories of land and sea contiguity are combined, then the probability of war between contiguous states is approximately 35 times greater than the likelihood of war between non-contiguous nations. Lending support to Bremer's findings is Kocs (1995) who also finds that contiguous dyads with an unresolved territorial claim were more than forty times more likely than other dyads to go to war during the 1945–87 period, thus asserting the basic claim that territorial disputes are a very important determinant of war initiation.

Alliances

The standard classification of formal alliances is that of Singer and Small (1966), consisting of defense pacts, non-aggression treaties, and ententes. *Defense pacts* are formal treaties in which each signatory commits to defend its allies in the event of an attack on one of them, non-aggressive neutrality pacts are self-evident, and the entente is merely an understanding to consult. Weede's (1975) analysis of military conflicts among 3321 dyads for 1950 through 1969 shows that common bloc membership (alliance) served to reduce interstate conflict between

members of a dyad. Bremer (1992) similarly concludes that the absence of an alliance (in conjunction with other factors) increases the war-proneness of a dyad. On the other hand, Vasquez (1993) argues that while major powers are more prone to get involved in wars and alliances than minor states, once they have formed an alliance, their probability of going to war increases further. In the case of minor states, he argues that since their capabilities are substantially less than that of majors, alliance initiation on their part is probably an attempt to avoid a future war. Also, Maoz (1997) finds that alliance commitment has a significantly and consistently pacifying effect on conflict outbreak, conflict occurrence, and conflict escalation. However, it is useful to bear in mind (Sabrosky, 1998) that during the period from 1816 to 1992, defense pact commitments were only honored in 30 odd percent of the cases.

Democracy and war

We have already mentioned the analysis of democracy on the monadic level, but a good many scholars agree with Small and Singer (1976) who are quite skeptical. Many also doubt that the empirical findings can be explained by the democratic peace argument, since it neglects a number of other factors. Henderson (1999) argues that "factors including bipolarity, nuclear deterrence, alliance membership, and trade links contributed to the formation of an international security regime among the major power democracies and their minor power democratic allies" thereby explaining the peace as not simply a byproduct of the existence of a certain regime type. There is still considerable scholarly support for the democratic peace argument at the dyadic level, yet the results that have accumulated are complicated and by no means conclusive. Maoz and Abdolali (1989) examine all nation-dyads in the international system for the years between 1816 and 1976, including militarized disputes as well as wars, and report that democratic states are significantly less likely to engage in militarized conflict or war with each other than are dyads with other regime types.

Gleditsch and Hegre (1997) found that if the conventional wisdom holds at the dyadic and national levels, the probability of war in a *politically mixed* dyad must be higher than the probability of war between non-democracies, and the relationship between democracy and war at the system level must be an inverted u-shape, which means that increasing democratization initially produces more war, and the reduction of war starts only at a higher level of democratization. Another study by Remmer (1998) draws upon a data set covering dyadic interactions among Mercosur (Latin American) nations during the 1947–1985 period, and finds a positive relationship between democracy and cooperation.

Like many findings in this area at the dyadic level, the conclusion is that there is only limited support for the hypothesis that democracy promotes cooperation. Despite ambiguous results, many researchers, such as Maoz (1997), Oneal and Russett (1999, 2001) and Ray (2005), continue to assert their belief in a "democratic peace." Essentially, these authors argue that disputes arising between two democratic regimes will likely be resolved as democratic leaders inherently prefer the non-military resolution; however, the argument does come with the caveat that when democratic regimes interact with non-democratic regimes, democratic leaders are more likely to see military force as a method of conflict resolution. Some, such as Gartzke (2007) and Weede (2004), have accepted that democracies are less conflict-prone against other democracies, but they dispute whether or not the finding is a result of democratization or something they term the "capitalist peace." They assert that economic development, free markets, and trade interactions lessen militarized disputes and wars.

Status quo orientation

A recurrent and subordinate theme in the literature has to do with the way in which status quo and revisionist major powers interact with one another. While not a great deal of databased work has centered around this issue, there is the study by Anderson and McKeown (1987) in which they analyze 77 wars (COW database 1816–1980) in terms of capability balances and the degree to which belligerents' "aspirations diverge from actual or expected achievements." Their model also finds that capability balance is associated with war initiation by both challengers and defenders of the status quo for preemptive war initiated by a status quo defender. Huth, Gelpi, and Bennett (1993) report findings for a set of nine major powers (MID database 1816–1984) in "extended and direct immediate deterrence encounters," which suggest the salience of the conventional military balance between challengers and defenders for probabilities of conflict escalation. They conclude that a shift in the military balance "from a three-to-one defender advantage to a three-to-one challenger advantage increases the probability of escalation by approximately 33%."

Trade and economic openness

Trade between nations has often been seen as a method of conflict prevention, and scholars such as Sullivan (1974) examine this statement by looking at the dyadic trade flow of states for evidence of conflict patterns over the brief period 1955–1957. Employing trade data generated by the UN, he reports that trade flows are negatively correlated with dyadic-level verbal conflict and are positively correlated with the percentage of cooperative interactions. An inverse relationship between trade and dyadic level conflict behavior was posited by Gasiorowski and Polachek (1982), who go even further and note that the results of a Granger casualty test indicate that trade reduces conflict.

Another economic indicator that has been studied is the level of economic development and how that relates to war. Bremer (1992) is one scholar who provides evidence regarding dyadic economic development levels and war. Using four variables from the COW material capabilities data set, he constructs two indices reflecting the demographic and economic dimensions of development and then classifies dyads as symmetrically developed, asymmetrically developed, or symmetrically underdeveloped. The multivariate results (for the years between 1816 and 1965) with six additional predictor variables indicate a negative relationship between economic development and war.

Polachek, Robst, and Chang (1999) examined how the gains from trade are affected by foreign aid, tariffs, contiguity, and country size (with foreign aid, and contiguity increasing the gains from trade and tariffs reducing the gains from trade). They rely on the assumption that countries seek to protect their trade gains, and that foreign aid and contiguity will decrease conflict, while tariffs will increase conflict. The contiguity results suggest that conflict between neighboring countries would be greater than observed if not for the mitigating effects of trade. They tested their results against empirical evidence from the Conflict and Peace Data Bank and they found that the results supported their hypotheses.

In contrast, Barbieri (1996) finds that extensive economic interdependence tends to increase the likelihood that dyads will engage in militarized interstate disputes. She finds that peace through trade is most likely to arise among dyads composed of mutually dependent trading partners, but that even then, the relationship between interdependence and conflict appears to be curvilinear, where low to moderate degrees of interdependence reduce the likelihood of dyadic disputes, and extensive economic linkages increase the probability of militarized disputes. Further, she finds that extreme interdependence is most likely to increase the likelihood of conflict.

Adding to Barbieri's criticism of the "capitalist peace" argument are Bennett and Stam (2003) who suggest that there is a short-term tradeoff between economic gains and the likelihood of war. They observe that during periods of sustained economic growth throughout the system, the incidence of war increases remarkably. Across all conflict categories, the increases in risk are generally of similar magnitude, with a 40 to 100 percent increase in the odds of conflict involving force during periods of economic upswing compared to periods of downswing. The "capitalist peace" argument also does not take into account the development of a free-trade system where there is both a multiplicity of buyers and sellers; Brooks (2001) suggests that the ability of a state to substitute for lost trade through another partner might lower the economic costs of conflict associated with trade disruption.

THE REGIONAL AND GLOBAL LEVEL OF AGGREGATION

In a regional level analysis, O'Loughlin and Anselin (1991) indicate that African states interact primarily with their immediate neighbors, and that either conflictual or cooperative behavior "beyond that (contiguous) level is rare and insignificant for the African system as a whole."

On a more global level, Levy (1984) explores a possible linear association between the number of great powers (system size) and war for the extended temporal span of 1495–1975. He reports that the frequency, magnitude, and severity of war in the international system is not related to the number of major powers in the system. This leads to a somewhat related study which examined the impacts of alliance configuration. In "Alliance Aggregation and the Onset of War," Singer and Small (1968) attempted one of the earlier multivariate analyses of the impact of alliance configurations on war and the international system, and found that moving from alliance aggregation to the growth of international intergovernmental organizations, Singer and Wallace (1970) found that the number and size of IGOs had no impact on the incidence of war in the system, whereas the amount of war that ended in a particular half decade showed a strong positive correlation with the amount of new IGOs established in the next half decade.

Gleditsch and Hegre (1997) show that the probability of war in a politically mixed dyad must be higher than the probability of war between two non-democracies, and the relationship between democracy and war at the system level must be parabolic. Thus, increasing democratization initially produces more war, and the reduction of war takes effect only at a higher level of democratization. Crescenzi and Enterline (1999) measure the statistical relationships between democracy, democratization, and war, conducting their analysis on both the regional and global levels. At the global level, they did not find any revealing results, but at some regional levels they found validation of the Gleditsch and Hegre asserted parabolic relationship between the proportion of democracy in a system and the incidence of war. They find that the Middle East and African systems do not conform with the suggested parabolic relationship, while the relationship did find support in the European system. They thus conclude that it might be more fruitful to continue this analysis on an exclusively regional level, given such significant variation between regions.

There is a theoretical school emanating from the Correlates of War project that proposes to examine the impact of "structural clarity" of the system's hierarchies and coalitions and its possible impact on the war-proneness of the international system. Clarity would be a function of the similarities and isomorphism of interstate coalitions resting on trade, alliances, and diplomatic bonds, and the extent to which these configurations are highly similar. Similarly, when we look at hierarchical patterns, high clarity would rest on the extent to which pecking orders in terms of military and industrial capabilities, commercial dominance, and diplomatic prestige should show the same approximate patterns. Despite the plausibility of the argument, almost no systematic empirical results have emerged.

BEHAVIOR AND INTERACTION

Up to this point, we have summarized a fair representation of data-based studies that illustrate how the conflict process culminates in war. What most of these studies lack is the inclusion of variables that are more susceptible to political intervention; most of the investigations discussed so far rest heavily on structural conditions and the characteristics of the states, dyads, and systems out of which these wars arise. The next sets of studies we discuss will deal explicitly with the moves and countermoves taken by policymakers, how successful those decisions have been, and recommendations for alternative strategies in order to resolve conflicts.

Behavioral correlates of war

For example, in the Behavioral Correlates of War project (BCOW), largely under the direction of Russell Leng at Middlesbury, we begin to identify moves, countermoves, and tactics that have tended to play a significant role in the escalation of rivalries and disputes to war. In attempting to address why some disputes culminate in war, Leng and Gochman (1982) propose two factors that can account for differing outcomes: disputes associated with bargaining behavior, and those associated with the attributes of the actors. They define behavioral elements as the manner in which actors interact with one another, whereas attributes at the various levels of social aggregation are meant to signify the context within which disputes unfold. The authors use a bargaining model, and differentiate tactics in extremes: "fight" and "prudence." The "prudence" strategy suggests a situation wherein one side surrenders or accepts a diplomatic compromise before the conflict becomes highly militarized. Their analysis suggests an independent impact of bargaining behavior on dispute outcomes where 83 percent of "fight" decisions resulted in war, while no disputes erupted in war emerging from "prudent" strategies. The policy implications in terms of conflict resolution or prevention is that the use of bullying strategies (i.e. fight strategies which involve militarization and escalating behavior) to deter or coerce an adversary employing a similar strategy is likely to lead to war.

In another study, Leng (1988) attempts to examine the effects of changes in the strategy choices of policymakers from one crisis to the next, and in order to answer this question he constructs four crisis-learning games from a data-based study of bargaining in recurrent crises between evenly matched states. He finds that states unsuccessful in one crisis were likely to use more coercive bargaining strategies in the next crisis. For Leng, the crisis could have been averted if the initial strategy was not what realpolitik reasoning prescribed, but rather if the initial strategy were more cooperative, while subsequent strategies had been tit-for-tat responses. He argues that realpolitik reasoning, which prescribes using a confrontational initial choice, forecloses certain outcomes in later stages of the bargaining game.

In an earlier study, Leng and Walker (1982), with data generated according to the Behavioral Correlates of War coding scheme, randomly select twenty "serious disputes" within the twentieth century. They find that disputants will adopt increasingly coercive bargaining strategies during the confrontation phase of the crisis in the absence of an awareness of the crisis structure. Leng (1993) analyzes the effectiveness of reciprocating influence strategies in militarized interstate crises, and notes that the success of reciprocating strategies in these crises is related to withholding cooperative initiatives until the reciprocating party has demonstrated its resolve. He suggests that the use of reciprocating strategies in defense of the status quo reflects a prudent understanding of the defensive nature of a firm-but-flexible influence strategy, and that the underlying logic of a reciprocating strategy and its relative effectiveness can be seen as well when reciprocating strategies intersect with trial-and-error as well as bullying strategies.

Arms races

Among those studies that should also shed some light on the behavioral phenomena is that of arms races, developing from the early work of Richardson (1960) and Huntington (1958). Perhaps the first data-based treatment going back to the Congress of Vienna was that by Wallace (1979), who finds an extraordinarily strong relationship between countries that are rapidly arming and their disputes escalating to war. Of ninety-nine total dyadic disputes between 1816 and 1965, twenty-eight occurred while both countries were building up their weapons, and twenty-three of those escalated to war. The conclusion was a strong statement that arms races led to wars, but his findings were called into question largely because he disaggregated multilateral wars such as World War I and World War II into dyadic wars. As a matter of fact, Diehl (1985), who did not disaggregate the World Wars, found a positive but somewhat weaker relationship between arms races and wars.

Other analyses have also suggested a positive relationship. In a bivariate logit analysis carried out by Sample (2000), the relationship was statistically significant using one measure of arming, but not so over the whole Correlates of War (COW) period using the other. She observes that there is a militarized dispute occurring in 15 or 16 percent of the dyad years characterized by a mutual military buildup. Her evidence suggests that rapid military buildups do increase the likelihood of war and that military buildups are positively related to the occurrence of a militarized dispute between two countries. The empirical evidence cautions us to be careful as we postulate links between arms race and war, and as Siverson and Diehl (1989) note, "If there is any consensus among arms race studies, it is that some arms races lead to war and some do not."

Bargaining, negotiations, and conflict termination

Moving further along the continuum from explaining armed conflict to reducing or mitigating it, we turn here to a few studies of a quantitative sort that address the amelioration and termination of armed conflict. Studies centered around rational war termination primarily draw from the work of Schelling among others, and they view war and strategic deterrence as an organized coercive process through which opponents attempt to persuade, dissuade, or otherwise manipulate one another, and since war is viewed as an extremely costly process, both sides have incentives to avoid it while conceding as little as possible.

By constructing a laboratory bargaining setting, Boyle and Lawler (1991) set up an experiment in which parties exchange offers and counter-offers on an issue across a number of rounds while also having the option to engage in punitive action against one another. The tactics that the authors provide to the actors are hostile or conciliatory, and the goal for both parties is to maximize their utility through mutual conciliation, but it is difficult for either side to convince the other that they want to achieve the goal of mutual conciliation; thus, the game gets repeated over a number of rounds or only ends with the intervention of third parties (e.g. allies, international institutions). In the absence of credible or trustworthy third parties, the authors conclude that the theory of unilateral initiatives, using conciliatory tactics, offers a way to mitigate the distrust that exists, while punitive or retaliatory action furthers the distrust and mutual antagonism between the actors involved. The results of their experiment indicated that the best combination of tactics was a mix of unilateral initiatives and retaliation, which produced an agreement rate of over 50 percent.

An important question the bargaining literature has recently sought to address is why states would go to war at all considering the heavy costs associated with it. While attempting to answer this question, Garfinkel and Skaperdas (2000) point out that though most armed conflict can be viewed as a result of misperceptions, incomplete information, or even irrationality, it might also be the result of long-term incentives. To do this, they emphasize the link between the present and future conditions, positing that if an actor succeeds against his opponent in the present situation, then the chances of doing so again or being in a better initial condition in the future are enhanced. The authors show how war emerges as an equilibrium outcome in a model that takes those types of considerations into account; thus, the more important the future, the more likely war is to occur. The method of conflict resolution that their model calls for is the creation of long-term commitment devices, in order to avoid war and inhibit competitive arming. These long-term commitment devices necessitate the critical role that enforceable laws, courts, norms, and other institutions of conflict management at both the domestic and international levels could play.

Three rationalist explanations for going to war are given by Filson and Werner (2007), who first state that despite the presence of a potential settlement, both actors might prefer to fight because no actor is able to credibly maintain the terms of the agreement; second, the issue in dispute may not be divisible; third, the actors in the conflict might have differing beliefs that ensure they cannot agree on a mutually acceptable agreement, and will then continue to engage each other in armed conflict until one or both side's resources fall below the minimum necessary resources to continue fighting. They define war as an alternating sequence of negotiations and battles; in war, each actor's objective is to obtain as many benefits as possible while conserving military resources. The amount of resources at each stage depends on who wins each battle. The sequence of battles and negotiations can end when one side's resources fall below the minimum level necessary to continue fighting, although it typically ends sooner than that. Their model also finds that when the costs of war are decreased, the duration of war is likely to increase. In the end, the models they provide are useful for understanding the decisions of actors in the run-up to and the continuation of armed conflict, but they do not provide as much insight into how to resolve a conflict, though their model helps establish under what conditions conflict is terminated. Nevertheless, states have incentives to misrepresent their capabilities in hopes of getting a more favorable settlement, and what is truly needed are constraints on a states' ability to deceive others of its capability, and methods through which the credibility of genuine threats can be increased. Schultz (2001) advises that these types of constraints can be provided by international and domestic institutions as they can increase the costliness of war by exacerbating the problem of credibility, which could then raise doubts about a state's ability to carry out its threats.

Walter (2003), in an analysis of government decision-making, concludes that one of the most common indivisible issues of dispute is territory, but its indivisibility does not rest with the land's strategic importance. Rather, she points out that governments refuse to negotiate with the very first challenger over territory as it is part of a rational strategy to eliminate high long-term costs of multiple future wars. She asserts that a government's decision to negotiate has more to do with the signal the government wishes to send to future challengers than with any specific characteristics of the conflict itself. States do this as part of a rational reputation-building strategy. Consequently, conflict resolution should be looked upon as not only a present condition but an inter-temporal goal, where governments need to redefine issues of dispute in a narrow enough way, such that it allows them to simultaneously negotiate with one challenger, while maintaining a reputation for toughness against all other potential challengers at later stages.

Offering an important challenge to some of the bargaining models presented here is Reiter (2003), who notes that much of it comes from theoretical literature that proposes that armed conflict in and of itself may have positive utility for states. It can be used as a means of furthering national identity or a government's hold on domestic political power through the manifestation of an external enemy, and goes on to say that some forms of this argument are beginning to earn some empirical support. Another critique of this literature is in its practical application, specifically, when attempting to quantify the potential benefits and military resources of actors.

One of the most obvious conclusions from the many studies discussed above is that the most effective way of mitigating armed conflict is for the protagonists in disputes, rivalries, and confrontations to avoid the many moves that show up as tension generating and should be avoided. In this connection, we need to appreciate that while the road to war has more than sufficient exits, they are too infrequently taken. Sometimes they are not well-marked, sometimes they provide a temporary detour but bring us right back onto the original path, sometimes there is just too little certainty as to what lies beyond, and of course there rarely will be police who can not only direct the traffic, but enforce agreements that have been made along the way. If we knew more about the behavioral throughput between background conditions and the onset of hostilities, we should be able to monitor and perhaps discourage conflict-generating tactics and moves.

STATISTICAL FINDINGS AND EARLY WARNING INDICATORS

It is one thing for us to summarize what we know about international disputes and rivalries that culminate in war, but the question is whether this research can be useful in heading off or ameliorating violent conflict in the international system. Perhaps one of the more useful applications would have to do with early warning indicators. By ascertaining the kinds of actors and situations that culminate in war, the peace researcher and the policy community may be alerted to those situations that have historically escalated to war. Especially relevant here is the mandate of the United Nations Charter that encourages the Secretary-General to bring to the attention of the Security Council breaches of the peace and threats to the peace. Those advising national governments need to be much more aware of the second and third order consequences of the policies that they recommend. What might look like an effective influence strategy may well turn out historically to be a consistent stimulus toward conflict escalation. This kind of research suggests the relative virtues of multilateral versus unilateral or regional organization intervention, but so far has not shown us nearly enough.

CONCLUSION

What seems to emerge from our report is, first, that we now have fairly solid evidence as to the characteristics of the states, their rivals, their region, and the global system, and the extent to which these sets of factors help account for the incidence of international war.

As already suggested, that knowledge largely tells us what kinds of structural conditions and behaviors increase the probability of armed conflict. The research priorities that emerge, then, are the need to go into greater empirical detail and perhaps even further disaggregation of the moves and countermoves of states in conflict, as they shuffle beyond the exit ramps that might get them off the road to war. One element here that certainly requires more attention is the kinds of mechanisms that would inhibit excessive reliance on escalatory moves, and would make less costly conciliatory and compromising moves. In this context, we would certainly benefit from an expanded attention to the kinds of institutions, regimes, and norms that could be quite constructive in this regard. One might say that those of us in the conflict resolution enterprise have given insufficient research attention to the possibilities of governance, with particular attention to third party responsibilities. That is, those of us who still – at this late stage – have much confidence in diplomatic bargaining and negotiation in the absence of credible supra-national institutions that can appreciably modify the incentives and disincentives of the protagonists. We need to give greater attention to the possibility that international institutions may hold better promise than currently thought in the prevention or negotiation of armed conflict.

An obvious conclusion from much of the literature introduced in this chapter is that protagonists should not be relied upon to resolve conflicts themselves. At the very least, we should emphasize the need to partially insulate our diplomats from the domestic actors who will initially seek to sabotage efforts toward compromise and conciliation. There will almost always be the internal elements who seek political advantage via charging the incumbents with "giving away the store" or capitulation to "the enemy." One option is for the contending parties to engage professional agents or parties who will negotiate on their behalf (Singer, 1965) and insulate them from the destructive efforts of one's domestic "hawks." Equally important are those increasingly available UN or regional organization peace-making and peace-keeping units, which are sometimes able to intervene before an interstate rivalry gets out of control.

Then there is the early warning role entrusted to the UN Secretary General under Charter. Article 97 encourages him to bring to the Security Council threats to the peace or breaches of the peace, but while the latter are readily recognizable, the former always remain ambiguous and controversial. Thus, we need a major research investigation into the juncture at which a dispute, rivalry, or confrontation approaches the point at which the odds of a peaceful settlement are dangerously low. A number of preliminary studies are assembled in: *Early Warning Indicators in World Politics* (Singer and Wallace, 1979), and *Indicators in World Politics: Timely Assurances and Early Warning Indicators* (Singer and Stoll, 1984).

Thus, the promotion of international organizations on both the global and regional level is needed. In this vein, it should be positive news that the United Nations has seen a six-fold increase since 1998 in the number of soldiers and military observers it deploys around the world, but the onus of peacekeeping operations has not fallen solely on the shoulders of the UN; NATO, the European Union, and the African Union have some 74,000 soldiers trying to restore peace and stability in troubled countries. Even other regional organizations such as MERCOSUR, ASEAN, and the SAARC have begun to shift away from a purely economic focus to one that also focuses on regional stability. As both global and regional organizations begin to grow and take on the tasks of conflict management, it is essential that they give due focus to establishing better norms, institutions, and practices.

These institutions should also use early warning indicators in order to locate where war is most likely to break out. By knowing where war is more likely, regional and global organizations might then be able to provide the exit ramps of war before the paths of the actors are set. This will require not only more research in third-party involvement and its relationship to conflict amelioration but also a better understanding of the early warning indicators of war; as of yet, there has been a promising start made on both these fronts but more needs to be done. For example, recent findings bear out the long ago observation by Morgenthau about how important it is to understand the incentives and constraints under which an adversary is operating. In the Cuban missile crisis, the Americans understood that Khrushchev could not withdraw his missiles from Cuba without a clear American commitment to not invade that island and a less explicit commitment to phase out US missiles in Turkey. On the other hand, in the case of the Iraqi invasion of Kuwait, recent findings show that the USA was relatively unaware of and indifferent to the commitments and constraints under which Sadaam Hussein was operating. Further, recent studies show how the Bush administration made no serious effort to appreciate the consequences of disbanding the Iraqi army and police. Delving into the quantitative literature, we find that the very moves and countermoves that characterize the escalation of international conflict should provide plenty of ammunition for those of us whose preoccupation is with the management and resolution of such conflict.

REFERENCES

Anderson, P.A., & McKeown, Timothy (1987). Changing Aspiration, Limited Attention, and War. *World Politics*, 40, 1–29.

Banks, A., & Textor, R.B. (1963). *A Cross Polity Survey*, Cambridge: MIT Press.

Barbieri, K. (1996). Economic Interdependence: A Path to Peace or a Source of Interstate Conflict?. *Journal of Peace Research*, 33(1), 29–49.

Bennett, D.S., & Stam, A.C. (2003). *The Behavioral Origins of War*. Ann Arbor: University of Michigan Press.

Blomberg, S.B., & Hess, G.D. (2002). The Temporal Links between Conflict and Economic Activity. *Journal of Conflict Resolution*, 46(1), 74–90.

Boyle, E.H., & Lawler, E.J. (1991). Resolving Conflict Through Explicit Bargaining. *Social Forces*, 69(4), 1183–1204.

Brecher, M. (1984). International Crises and Protracted Conflicts. *International Interactions*, 11, 237–297.

Brecher, M., James, P., & Wilkenfeld, J. (2000). Escalation and War in the Twentieth Century: Findings from the International Crisis Behavior Project. In J.A. Vasquez, *What Do We Know About War?* (pp. 37–57). Lanham: Rowman & Littlefield Publishers, Inc.

Bremer, S.A. (1980). National Capabilities and War Proneness. In J. David Singer (ed.), *The Correlates of War: II. Testing Some Realpolitik Models*. New York: The Free Press, pp. 57–82.

Bremer, S.A. (1992). Dangerous Dyads: Conditions Affecting the Likelihood of Interstate War, 1816–1965. *Journal of Conflict Resolution*, 36, 309–341.

Bremer, S.A., Singer, J.D., & Luterbacher, U. (1973). The Population Density and War Proneness of European Nations, 1816–1965. *Comparative Political Studies*, 6, 329–348.

Brooks, S. (2001). "The Globalization of Production and the Changing Benefits of Conquest." Ph.D. diss. Yale University, New Haven, CT.

Bueno de Mesquita, B., & Riker, W. (1982). An Assessment of the Merits of Selective Nuclear Proliferation. *Journal of Conflict Resolution*, 26, 283–306.

Bueno de Mesquita, B., Morrow, J.D., Siverson, R.M., & Smith, A. (1999). An Institutional Explanation of the Democratic Peace. *American Political Science Review*, 93(4), 791–807.

Chiozza, G., & Goemans, H.E. (2003). Peace through Insecurity: Tenure and International Conflict. *The Journal of Conflict Resolution*, 47(4), 443–467.

Choucri, N., & North, R.C. (1972). Dynamics of International Conflict: Some Policy Implications of Population, Resources, and Technology. *World Politics*, 24, 80–122.

Crescenzi, M.J., & Enterline, A.J. (1999). Ripples from the Waves? A Systemic, Time-Series Analysis of Democracy, Democratization, and Interstate War. *Journal of Peace Research*, 36(1), 75–94.

Deutsch, K.W., & Singer, J.D. (1964). Multipolar Power Systems and International Stability. *World Politics*, 16, 390–406.

Diehl, P.F. (1985). Arms Races to War: Testing Some Empirical Linkages. *Sociological Quarterly*, 26, 331–349.

Diehl, P.F., & Kingston, J. (1987). Messenger or Message?: Military Buildups and the Initiation of Conflict. *Journal of Politics*, 49, 801–813.

Doran, C.F. (1983). Power Cycle Theory and the Contemporary State System. In William R. Thompson (ed.), *Contending Approaches to World Systems Analysis*. Beverly Hills: Sage, pp. 165–182.

Doran, C.F. (1985). Power Cycle Theory and Systems Stability. In Paul M. Johnson and William R. Thompson (eds.), *Rhythms in Politics and Economics*. New York: Praeger, pp. 292–312.

Doran, C.F. (1989). "The Discontinuity of Dilemma of Changing Systems Structure: Confronting the Principles of the Power Cycle." Paper presented at the 36th Annual Convention of the International Studies Association, February 21–25, Chicago, Illinois.

Doran, C.F., & Parsons, W. (1980). War and the Cycle of Relative Power. *American Political Science Review*, 80, 1151–1169.

Elberwein, Wolf-Dieter (1982). The Seduction of Power: Serious International Disputes and the Power Status of Nations, 1900–1976. *International Interactions*, 9, 57–74.

Enterline, A. J. (1998a). Regime Changes and Interstate Conflict, 1816–1992. *Political Research Quarterly*, 51(2), 385.

Enterline, A.J. (1998b). Regime Changes, Neighborhoods, and Interstate Conflict, 1816–1992. *Journal of Conflict Resolution*, 42(6), 804–829.

Feierabend, I.K., & Feierabend, R.L. (1969). Level of Development and International Behavior. In R. Butwell (ed.), *Foreign Policy and the Developing Nation*. Lexington: University of Kentucky Press, pp. 135–188.

Filson, D., & Werner, S. (2007). The Dynamics of Bargaining and War. *International Interactions*, 33(1), 31–50.

Garfinkel, M.R., & Skaperdas, S. (2000). Conflict without Misperceptions or Incomplete Information: How the Future Matters. *Journal of Conflict Resolution*, 44, 793–807.

Gartzke, E. (2007). The Capitalist Peace. *American Journal of Political Science*, 51(1): 166–191.

Gasiorowski, M., & Polachek, S. (1982). Conflict and Interdependence: East–West Trade and Linkages in the Era of Detante. *Journal of Conflict Resolution*, 26, 709–728.

Gaubatz, K.T. (1991). Election Cycles and War. *Journal of Conflict Resolution*, 35, 212–224.

Geller, D.S. (1985). *Domestic Favors in Foreign Policy: A Cross-National Statistical Analysis*. Cambridge: Schenkman.

Geller, D.S. (1993). Power Differentials and War in Rival Dyads. *International Studies Quarterly*, 37, 173–193.

Geller, D.S. (1994). "Patterns of War Initiation Among Status Quo Challengers and Defenders." Paper presented at the XIVth World Congress of the International Political Science Association, August 21–25, Berlin, Germany.

Geller, D.S. (2003). Nuclear Weapons and the Indo-Pakistani Conflict: Global Implications of a Regional Power Cycle. *International Political Science Review*, 24(1), 137–150.

Gleditsch, N.P., & Hegre, H. (1997). Peace and Democracy: Three Levels of Analysis. *Journal of Conflict Resolution*, 41, 283.

Gochman, C.S., & Maoz, Z. (1984). Militarized Interstate Disputes, 1816–1976: Procedures, Patterns, and Insights. *Journal of Conflict Resolution*, 28, 585–616.

Goldsmith, B.E. (2003). Bearing the Defense Burden, 1886–1989: Why Spend More?. *Journal of Conflict Resolution*, 47(5), 551–573.

Grieco, J.M. (2001). Repetitive Military Challenges and Recurrent International Conflicts, 1918–1994. *International Studies Quarterly*, 45, 295–316.

Hauge, W., & Ellingsen, T. (1998). Beyond Environmental Scarcity: Causal Pathways to Conflict. *Journal of Peace Research*, 35(3), 299–317.

Henderson, E.A. (1999). Neoidealism and the Democratic Peace. *Journal of Peace Research*, 36(2), 203–231.

Houweling, H., & Siccama, J.G. (1988). Power Transitions as a Cause of War. *Journal of Conflict Resolution*, 32, 87–102.

Huntington, S. (1958). Arms Races: Prerequisites and Results. *Public Policy*, 18, 41–46.

Huth, P.K. (1988). *Extended Deterrence and the Prevention of War*. New Haven, CT: Yale University Press.

Huth, P.K., & Allee, T.L. (2002). Domestic Political Accountability and the Escalation and Settlement of International Disputes. *The Journal of Conflict Resolution*, 46(6), 754–790.

Huth, P.K., & Russett, B. (1993). General Deterrence Between Enduring Rivalries: Testing Three Competing Models. *American Political Science Review*, 87, 61–73.

Huth, P.K., Bennett, S., & Gelpi, C. (1992). System Uncertainty, Risk Propensity, and International Conflict Among the Great Powers. *Journal of Conflict Resolution*, 36, 478–517.

Huth, P.K., Gelpi, C., & Bennett, S. (1993). The Escalation of Great Power Militarized Disputes: Testing Rational Deterrence Theory and Structural Realism. *American Political Science Review*, 87, 609–623.

Jo, Dong-Joon, & Gartzke, E. (2007). Determinants of Nuclear Weapons Proliferation. *Journal of Conflict Resolution*, 51(1), 167–194.

Kim, W. (1991). Alliance Transitions and Great Power War. *American Journal of Political Science*, 35, 833–850.

Kim, W. (1996). Power, Parity, Alliance, and War from 1648 to 1975. In Jack Kugler and Douglas Lemke (eds.), *Parity and War: Evaluations and Extensions of The War Ledger*. Ann Arbor: University of Michigan Press, pp. 93–105.

Kim, W., & Morrow, J.D. (1992). When Do Power Shifts Lead to War? *American Journal of Political Science*, 36, 896–922.

Kocs, S. (1995). Territorial Disputes and Interstate War, 1945–1987. *Journal of Politics*, 57, 159–175.

Kraig, M.R. (1999). Nuclear Deterrence in the Developing World: A Game-Theoretic Treatment. *Journal of Peace Research,* 36(2), 141–167.

Leblang, D., & Steve, C. (2003). Explaining Wars Fought by Established Democracies: Do Institutional Constraints Matter? *Political Research Quarterly*, 56(4), 385–400.

Leeds, B.A., & Davis, D.R. (1997). Domestic Political Vulnerability and International Disputes. *Journal of Conflict Resolution*, 41(6), 814–834.

Leng, R.J. (1983). When Will They Ever Learn? Coercive Bargaining in Recurrent Crises. *Journal of Conflict Resolution*, 27, 379–419.

Leng, R.J. (1988). Crisis Learning Games. *The American Political Science Review*, 82(1), 179–194.

Leng, R.J. (1993). Reciprocating Influence Strategies in Interstate Crisis Bargaining. *Journal of Conflict Resolution*, 37(1), 3–41.

Leng, R.J., & Gochman, C.S. (1982). Dangerous Disputes: A Study of Conflict Behavior and War. *American Journal of Political Science*, 26(4), 664–687.

Leng, R.J., & Walker, S.G. (1982). Comparing Two Studies of Crisis Bargaining: Confronation, Coercion, and Reciprocity. *Journal of Conflict Resolution*, 26(4), 571–591.

Levy, J.S. (1984). Size and Stability in the Modern Great Power System. *International Interactions*, 11, 341–358.

Mandel, R. (1980). Roots of the Modern Interstate Border Dispute. *Journal of Conflict Resolution*, 24, 427–454.

Maoz, Z. (1997). The Controversy over the Democratic Peace: Rearguard Action or Cracks in the Wall?. *International Security,* 22(1), 162–198.

Maoz, Z. (2002). Paradoxical Functions of International Alliances: Security and Other Dilemmas. In John, A. Vasquez and Colin Elman (eds). *Balancing of Power.* Boston: Rowman and Littlefield, pp. 200–221.

Maoz, Z., & Abdolali, N. (1989). Regime Types and International Conflict, 1816–1976. *Journal of Conflict Resolution*, 33, 3–35.

Maxwell, J.W., & Reuveny, R. (2000). Resource Scarcity and Conflict in Developing Countries. *Journal of Peace Research*, 37(3), 301–322.

McKeown, T.J. (1987). Changing Aspirations, Limited Attention, and War. *World Politics*, 40(1), 1–29.

Mihalka, M. (1976). Hostilities in the European System, 1816–1970. *Peace Science Society Papers*, 26, 100–116.

Morgenthau, H.J. (1967). *Politics Among Nations: The Struggle for Power and Peace*, 4th ed. New York: Knopf.

Moul, W. (2003). Power Parity, Preponderance, and War between Great Powers, 1816–1989. *Journal of Conflict Resolution*, 47(4), 468–489.

O'Loughlin, J., & Anselin, L. (1991). Bringing Geography Back to the Study of International Relations: Spatial Dependence and Regional Context in Africa, 1966–1978. *International Interactions*, 17, 29–61.

Oneal, J.R., & Russett, B. (1997). The Classic Liberals were Right: Democracy, Interdependence, and Conflict, 1950–1985. *International Studies Quarterly*, 41, 267–294.

Oneal, J.R., & Russett, B. (1999). The Kantian Peace: The Pacific Benefits of Democracy, Interdependence, and International Organizations. *World Politics*, 52(1), 1–37.

Oneal, J.R., & Russett, B. (2001). "Causes of Peace: Democracy, Interdependence, and International Organizations, 1885–1992." Paper presented at the 2001 Annual Meeting of the American Political Science Association, San Francisco, CA.

Organski, A.F.K., & Kugler, J. (1980). *The War Ledger.* Chicago: University of Chicago Press.

Paul, T.V. (1994). *Asymmetric Conflicts: War Initiation by Weaker Powers.* Cambridge: Cambridge University Press.

Percival, V., & Homer-Dixon, T. (1998). Environmental Scarcity and Violent Conflict: The Case of South Africa. *Journal of Peace Research*, 35(3), 279–298.

Polachek, S.W., Robst, J., & Chang, Y. (1999). Liberalism and Interdependence: Extending the Trade-Conflict Model. *Journal of Peace Research*, 36(4), 405–422.

Ray, J.L. (2005). Constructing Multivariate Analyses (of Dangerous Dyads). *Conflict Management and Peace Science*, 22, 277–292.

Ray, J.L., & Singer, J.D. (1973). Measuring the Concentration of Power in the International System. *Sociological Methods and Research*, 1, 403–437.

Reiter, D. (2003). Exploring the Bargaining Model of War. *Perspectives on Politics*, 1(1), 27–43.

Remmer, K.L. (1998). Does Democracy Promote Interstate Cooperation? Lessons From the Mercosur Region. *International Studies Quarterly*, 42(1), 25–51.

Richardson, L.F. (1960). *Statistics of Deadly Quarrels*. Pittsburgh and Chicago: Boxwood and Quadrangle.

Sabrosky, Alan (1980). Interstate Alliances. Their Reliability and the Expansion of War. In J. David Singer, ed. *The Correlates of War II: Testing some Realpolitik Models*. New York: Free Press.

Schultz, K.A. (2001). Democracy and Coercive Diplomacy. Cambridge: Cambridge University Press.

Senese, P.D. (1996). Geographical Proximity and Issue Salience: Their Effects on the Escalation of Militarized Interstate Conflict. *Conflict Management and Peace Science*, 15, 133–61.

Singer, J.D. (1965). Negotiation by Proxy: A Proposal. *Journal of Conflict Resolution*, 9, 538–541.

Singer, J.D., & Small, M. (1966). National Alliance Commitments and War Involvement, 1815–1945. *Peace Research Society (International) Papers*, 5, 109–140.

Singer, J.D., & Small, M. (1968). Alliance Aggregation and the Onset of War, 1815–1945. In J. David Singer (ed.), *Quantitative International Politics: Insights and Evidence*. New York: Free Press, pp. 247–286.

Singer, J.D., & Small, M. (1972). *The Wages of War, 1816–1965*. New York: John Wiley & Sons.

Singer, J.D., & Wallace, M. (1970). Inter-Governmental Organizations and the Preservation of Peace, 1816–1964: Some Bivariate Relationships. *International Organizations*, 24, 520–547.

Singer, J.D., & Stoll, R.J. (1984). *Quantitative Indicators in World Politics: Timely Assurance and Early Warning*. New York: Praeger.

Siverson, R.M., & Tennefoss, M.R. (1984). Power, Alliance, and the Escalation of International Conflict, 1815–1965. *American Political Science Review*, 78, 1057–1069.

Small, M., & Singer, J.D. (1976). The War Proneness of Democratic Nations, 1816–1965. *Jerusalem Journal of International Relations*, 1, 49–69.

Small, M., & Singer, J.D. (1982). *Resort to Arms: International and Civil War, 1816–1980*, Beverly Hills, CA: Sage.

Sullivan, M. (1974). Escalatory and Non-Escalatory Systems. *American Journal of Political Science*, 18, 549–558.

Thompson, W.R. (1982). Phases of the Business Cycle and the Outbreak of War. *International Studies Quarterly*, 26, 301–311.

Tir, J., & Diehl, P.F. (1998). Demographic Pressure and Interstate Conflict: Linking Population Growth and Density to Militarized Disputes and Wars, 1930–89. *Journal of Peace Research*, 35 (3), 319–339.

Vasquez, J. (1993). *The War Puzzle*. Cambridge: Cambridge University Press.

Vincent, J. (1981). Internal and External Conflict: Some Previous Operational Problems and Some New Findings. *Journal of Politics*, 43, 128–142.

Walter, B. (2003). "Reputation and War: Explaining the Intractability of Territorial Conflict." Unpublished paper.

Waltz, K.N. (1979). *Theory of International Politics*. Reading, MA: Addison-Wesley.

Waltz, K.N. (1981). "The Spread of Nuclear Weapons: More May Be Better." Adelphi Papers, no. 171, London International Institute for Strategic Studies.

Wayman, F.W. (1996). Power Shifts and the Onset of War. In Jack Kugler and Douglas Lemke (eds.), *Parity and War: Evaluations and Extensions of the War Ledger*. Ann Arbor: University of Michigan Press, pp. 145–162.

Weede, E. (1970). Conflict Behavior of Nation-States. *Journal of Peace Research*, 7, 229–237.

Weede, E. (1975). World Order in the Fifties and Sixties: Dependence, Deterrence and Limited Peace. *Peace Science Society Papers*, 24, 49–80.

Weede, E. (2004). The Diffusion of Prosperity and Peace by Globalization. *The Independent Review*, 9(2).

Xiang, J., Xiahong, X., & Keteku, G. (2007). Power: The Missing Link in the Trade Conflict Relationship. *The Journal of Conflict Resolution*, 51, 646–663.

4

Case Studies and Conflict Resolution

Jack S. Levy

Political leaders have engaged in international conflict resolution for millennia, yet it is only relatively recently that scholars have developed explanatory and prescriptive theories about this important phenomenon. World War I generated some preliminary research, but it was Cold War fears and the 1962 Cuban missile crisis in particular that led to the emergence of an academic field of conflict resolution.[1] With the decline in the frequency of interstate war in the six decades since World War II, and with the sharp increase in civil war and "identity wars" between communal groups after the end of the Cold War,[2] the interdisciplinary study of conflict resolution has broadened from a primary focus on interstate conflict resolution to a concern with conflict resolution in intra-state and intra-group conflict.[3]

Scholars have approached the study of conflict resolution through a variety of methodologies, including interactive conflict resolution and simulations, large-n data analyses, formal modeling, and historical case studies. My focus here is on case study analysis,

which has been the subject of intensive methodological discussion and debate during the last decade in political science, sociology, and related disciplines. Indeed, scholars in the social sciences have increasingly come to see case study approaches as a genuine *methodology*, on par with statistical methodology, with standards and rules of inference that good work in the field is expected to satisfy. Thus, a brief review of the current state of the art in case study analysis will serve as a useful guide to conflict resolution theorists working in disciplinary settings that have become increasingly demanding in terms of methodological self-consciousness and sophistication.

Beyond a brief review of the literature on case study methodology, I have a second aim in this chapter: I look more specifically at the question of crisis management, both to illustrate the application of methodological principles and to suggest the kinds of substantive propositions that have emerged from the case study literature. I focus in particular on the two leading crises of the 20th century, the July 1914 crisis and the Cuban missile crisis.

CASE STUDY METHODOLOGY

Given the proliferation of scholarship on case study methodology (Brady and Collier, 2004; George and Bennett, 2005; Zartman, 2005; Goertz, 2006; Bennett and Elman, 2006; Gerring, 2007; Blatter and Blume, 2008), a complete review is not necessary here.[4] I do not deal with the question of the definition of case study and case study method, other than to say that the increasing emphasis on theory has led to the widespread shift away from the definition of a case as a temporally and spatially bounded series of events, to the conception of a case as an *instance* of something else, of a theoretically defined class of events. George and Bennett (2005: 5, 17), building on (George, 1979), define a case as "an instance of a class of events," and a case study as "the detailed examination of an aspect of a historical episode to develop or test historical explanations that may be generalizable to other events." Thus, a standard question for any case study is "what is this a case of?"

The theoretical orientation of contemporary case study research leads to discussions of the various roles of case studies in theory development, and to case selection criteria that advance those theoretical aims. I focus on these issues in the next two sections.

Types of case studies

One can identify several types of case studies, and also a variety of ways of classifying them. Let me suggest the following classification, which is based on the theoretical purpose or function of case studies. It represents a combination of categories proposed by Lijphart (1971) and Eckstein (1975), which have been quite influential.[5] These are ideal types, and in practice many case studies combine several of these aims

(1) *Atheoretical/idiographic* case studies are descriptive studies of individual cases that aim to understand and interpret a single case as an end in itself rather than to develop broader theoretical generalizations. They are fundamentally inductive. The scholar does not use any specific hypotheses or theoretical framework to guide the study. Instead, she lets the facts "speak for themselves," so that the interpretation emerges in a "bottom up" fashion from the case. The study may be guided by implicit theoretical preconceptions – as in fact all empirical studies are to one extent or another – but the point is that such preconceptions are implicit rather than implicit.

(2) *Theory-guided/idiographic* case studies also aim to explain and/or interpret a single case, but that interpretation is explicitly structured by a theory or well-developed conceptual framework that focuses attention on some theoretically specified aspects of reality and neglects others.[6] This is analytic history rather than total history.

As the social sciences have shifted in a more theoretical direction in the last few decades, theory-guided explanations of individual cases – what Van Evera (1997) calls "case explaining" case studies – have replaced atheoretical explanations of individual cases. Even more common and more influential, however, are case studies that are explicitly designed to contribute to the construction and testing of theoretical generalizations about a broader class of behavior.

(3) *Hypothesis generating* case studies have more explicit theoretical purposes. They examine a particular case or perhaps several cases for the purpose of developing more general theoretical propositions, which can then be tested through other methods, including large-n methods. By permitting an intensive examination of individual historical episodes, case studies can contribute to theory development by suggesting additional causal variables, causal mechanisms, and interaction effects. They also help to suggest important contextual variables, thus to identify the scope conditions under which particular theories are valid. These are all important steps in the theory-building process.

The role of case studies in generating hypotheses, and particularly in refining and sharpening them, is enhanced by the close interaction of theory and data in case study analysis (and in some other forms of inquiry as well). The starting point is a theory, which the analyst uses to interpret a case, and evidence from the case is then used to suggest important refinements in the theory, which can then be tested on other cases or perhaps even on other aspects of the same case.[7] The more explicit and precise the theory guiding inquiry – including the selection of the historical case(s) to provide maximum leverage on the theory and the construction of the appropriate case study research design – the more useful the evidence in providing feedback on the theory, and the more efficient the hypothesis-generating process.

A good example is George and Smoke's (1974) analysis of deterrence in American foreign policy, which is organized sequentially in terms of theory specification, application of the theory to historical cases, and reformulation of the theory based on the cases. Another example, involving multiple authors, is Zartman's (1995) collection of comparative case studies on the ending of civil wars. The theoretical lessons generated by the study were the product of an ongoing dialogue between the conceptual framework guiding the project and evidence from specific cases.

(4) *Deviant case studies* focus on empirical anomalies in established theoretical generalizations in order to explain those anomalies and in the process refine the existing theory that failed to predict the anomaly, by identifying omitted variables, interaction effects, or alternative causal paths, or by specifying the scope conditions under which a particular theory is valid. Thus, deviant cases aid in the hypothesis generating function of case studies. A deviant case strategy can be usefully combined with statistical methods, in that some of the most significant deviations from the regression line in a statistical analysis are ideal cases for selection for more thorough examination by case studies.

(5) *Theory-testing case studies.* In addition to their essential role in the explanation of individual historical episodes and a contributory role in the generation of hypotheses, case studies can also be used to test hypotheses and theories. The basic requirements are that the hypotheses to be tested are explicitly stated and expressed in a form that leaves them open to empirical falsification, and, ideally, that the researcher specifies in advance the kinds of evidence that would falsify the hypothesis.[8] Lijphart (1971: 692) suggests the categories of *theory-confirming* and *theory-infirming* case studies. I combine these into a single theory-testing category.

As early work in case study methodology acknowledged (Campbell, 1975; Lijphart, 1971), a potentially serious problem confronting the theory-testing role of case studies is the combination of many variables and a relatively small number of cases – the low N/V ratio. This often makes it difficult if not impossible to attribute changes in the dependent variable to changes in the theoretically specified independent variables and not to the effects of extraneous variables. The problem of how to make causal inferences in small-n research, when the number of variables generally exceeds the number of cases, is a central question in case study methodology.

The comparative method[9] is often defined as a strategy for conducting research of naturally occurring phenomena in a way that aims to control for potential confounding variables through careful case selection and matching rather than through experimental manipulation or partial correlations (Frendreis, 1983: 255). The problem, of course, is finding sufficiently matched cases to justify this inference. I return to this issue, along with a discussion of alternative research designs for theory testing in small-n research, in the next section, after first completing this typology of case studies.

(6) *Plausibility probes.* Many qualitative methodologists have followed Eckstein (1975) in suggesting plausibility probes as a distinct category of case studies. The aim is nomothetic, since presumably what is being

probed is the match between the details of a particular case and some broader theoretical proposition. The design, however, involves something less than a fully fledged test of a theoretical proposition. Plausibility probes, like pilot studies in experimental or survey research, are intermediate steps between hypothesis construction and hypothesis testing. They enable the researcher to refine the hypothesis or theory, or to explore the suitability of a particular case as a vehicle in testing the theory, before engaging in a costly and time-consuming research effort, whether through the massive collection of quantitative data or through extensive fieldwork. While plausibility probes can serve a useful function, they are best conceived of as one stage of a multi-stage research design, of necessity followed by more thorough research based on a more rigorous design.

I have suggested several different objectives of case studies. It is important to be explicit about the specific objective of a specific case study, because different theoretical (or descriptive) purposes require different kinds of case study research designs. If the aim is the idiographic one of explaining a particular case, whether through an inductive analysis or an analysis driven by an explicit theoretical framework, then case selection becomes somewhat less critical, since theoretical imagination becomes more important than establishing scientific control over extraneous variables. A hypothesis-testing case study, however, has a different set of requirements, including a carefully matched set of cases to maximize control over extraneous variables.

Case study designs for theory testing

Variations on Mill's methods

The comparable-cases strategy is closely related to John Stuart Mill's (1875/1970) *method of difference*, which focuses on cases that have different values on the dependent variable and similar values on all but one of the possible causal variables. Since the values of alternative causal variables are constant, they cannot explain the variation in the dependent variable and hence can be eliminated as sources of causation, leaving the one independent variable that co-varies with the dependent variable. Mill's *method of agreement* focuses on cases that are similar on the dependent variable and different on all but one of the possible independent variables. Independent variables that vary across cases do not co-vary with the dependent variable and hence can be eliminated as potential causes. The basic logic of the two designs is the same – to identify patterns of co-variation and to eliminate independent variables that do not co-vary with the dependent variable (Frendreis, 1983).

Przeworski and Tuene's (1970) description of "most different" and "most similar" systems designs (see also Meckstroth, 1975) follows similar inferential logic. A *most different systems* design identifies cases that are different on a wide range of explanatory variables but similar on the dependent variable, while a *most similar systems* design identifies cases that are similar on a wide range of explanatory variables but different on the value of the dependent variable.[10]

As many critics have pointed out, a potentially serious problem in the application of Mill's methods and of most similar and most different systems designs is the difficulty of identifying cases that are truly comparable – identical or different in all respects but one. The less perfectly matched a set of cases, the weaker the causal inferences that can be drawn. Even if well-matched cases can be found, however, another problem remains. Mill's methods work fine for bivariate hypotheses involving a single explanatory variable, if the researcher can find matched cases and if she can assume that measurement error is low. Those methods work well enough for additive models in which there are multiple causes but no interaction effects, though the number of cases required to incorporate sufficient controls may become cumbersome. Mill's methods are much more problematic, however, in situations involving complex causation involving interaction effects, and particularly if there are several different sets of conditions that may lead to the same outcome (Ragin, 1987; Lieberson, 1992).

It is useful to distinguish between cross-case designs and within case designs, and between longitudinal designs and various forms of cross-sectional designs. Longitudinal, within-case comparisons of hypothesized relationships at different points in time within the same case are particularly powerful. They are essentially "most similar" systems designs because the dependent variable of interest changes over time; hypothesized explanatory variables change, but many other variables are constant, including political history, culture, institutions, geography, and other variables that change only slowly (if at all) over time. This facilitates the identification of the small number of variables that vary with the dependent variable of interest.

Good examples of such longitudinal designs include Touval's (1982) study of nine attempts at mediation in the Arab-Israeli conflict and Stedman's (1991) comparative study of mediation in the war in Zimbabwe. One can also combine cross-case and within-case designs, in order to impose more controls. Snyder's (1991) study of imperial overextension, for example, combines comparisons among the behaviors of different states, different individuals within the same state but in different bureaucratic roles, and the same individuals within a given state over time.

Process tracing

Mill's methods and related varieties of matching case selection strategies are basically correlational, and examine whether a particular set of conditions is associated with hypothesized outcomes while holding constant as many other factors as possible. George and Bennett (2005), building on George (1979), refer to within-case comparisons of hypothesized relationships at different points in time within the same case as the "congruence method" and include it within the methodology of structured, focused comparison.

Another approach to within-case analysis, one that is quite common in the practice of case study research but that was often neglected in early efforts to formally describe case study methodology, is *process-tracing* (George, 1979; George and Bennett, 2005). Process tracing follows a different logic than correlational methods. It tries to uncover the intervening causal mechanisms between conditions and outcomes through an intensive analysis of the development of a sequence of events over time.[11] Process tracing is particularly useful for exploring the perceptions, expectations, and political interactions of actors inside the "black box" of decision-making.[12]

Process tracing can be useful for several different theoretical tasks. It is often essential for a complete description and explanation of a particular historical episode. It can also contribute to hypothesis construction. Many propositions about bureaucratic politics, for example, originate in Allison's (1971) intensive study of the Cuban missile crisis. Process tracing can also contribute to the testing of certain theoretical propositions. One of the implications of the democratic peace proposition, for example, is that political leaders differ in their perceptions of democracies and autocracies, and that these differences have a significant impact on behavior. Such perceptions are usually better explored through small-n case study methods than through large-n statistical methods. To take another example, validations of prospect theory propositions on loss aversion and risk behavior, which are central to conflict resolution behavior, require the identification of actors' reference points. Case studies provide the most efficient way of determining reference points.[13]

Crucial case studies[14]

Eckstein (1975: 113–23) suggested that *crucial case studies* can be useful for the purposes of testing certain types of theoretical arguments – where predictions were precise and where measurement error was low. Two important types of crucial case studies are *most-likely* or *least-likely* case research designs. Each implicitly adopts a Bayesian perspective, and basically weights the evidence from a particular case as a function of prior theoretical expectations (McKeown, 1999). If one's theoretical priors suggest that a particular case is quite unlikely to be consistent with a theory's predictions – either because the theory's assumptions and scope conditions are not fully satisfied or because the values of many of the theory's key variables point in the other direction – and if the data supports the hypothesis, the evidence from the case provides a great deal of leverage for increasing our confidence in the validity of the theory. Similarly, if one's theoretical priors suggest that a theory is highly likely to be confirmed, and if the data do not support the theory, that result can be quite damaging to a theory. The logic of least-likely case design is based on the "Sinatra inference" – if I can make it there, I can make it anywhere. Similarly, the logic of most-likely case design is based on the inverse Sinatra inference – if I cannot make it there, I cannot make it anywhere (Levy, 2002: 442).

Allison's (1971) application of his three models of foreign policy decision-making to the Cuban missile crisis provides a good example, though he did not explicitly use the language of most-least-likely case analysis. Allison argued that the conventional wisdom in foreign policy analysis held that politics stopped "at the water's edge," particularly in acute international crises involving serious and immediate threats to vital national interests. As perhaps the most extreme threat to US national security interests, the Cuban missile crisis was a most-likely case for the "rational unity actor model" of foreign policy decision-making, and simultaneously a least-likely case for alternative organizational process and governmental politics models of decision-making. By showing that the evidence contradicted many predictions of the rational unitary actor model but fit many of the predictions of the organizational process and governmental process models, Allison (1971) made a strong argument for the limitations of Model I and the potential applicability of Model II and Model III.[15]

This discussion of most- and least-likely case study research designs, in conjunction with our earlier discussion of the role of case studies in testing hypotheses positing necessary or sufficient conditions, demonstrates that a small number of case studies, and possibly even a single case study, can be quite valuable for the purposes of testing certain types of theoretical propositions, if the theory takes a particular form, and if cases are selected in a way that maximizes leverage on the theory (Dion, 1998). A hypothesis positing a necessary condition for a particular outcome can be severely damaged by a single case in which the condition is absent but the outcome nonetheless occurs, and a hypothesis positing a sufficient condition for a particular outcome can be severely damaged by a single case in which the condition is present but the hypothesized outcome is absent. In addition, a theory can be severely damaged if it can be demonstrated that the theory is invalid in a case where theoretical expectations lead us to think it is an easy case for the theory.

Having briefly surveyed the literature on types of case studies and types of research designs for hypothesis testing, let me turn to the substantive questions of crisis management, a subset of conflict resolution, and explore the contributions of case studies to the development and testing of a theory of crisis management.

CRISIS MANAGEMENT

Crisis management is often defined as an attempt to avoid war while maintaining one's vital interests (George, 1991a).[16] Thus, crisis management has dual objectives, and there is a tension between them. If political leaders make too many concessions in an attempt to avoid war, they may sacrifice vital interests. If they refuse to compromise at all, they risk escalation to war. Crisis management involves a delicate balance between these two objectives.[17]

Scholars began to think seriously about systematizing a theory of crisis management after the Cuban missile crisis. Perhaps the most useful theory is the "provisional theory" provided by George (1991a), who aimed to explain the behavior of actors and to provide a useful guide for policy makers. George identified both political and operational requirements for crisis management. Political requirements include the limitation of objectives pursued in the crisis and the limitation of the means employed on behalf of those objectives. George (1991a: 24) recognized, however, that avoiding war does not always take priority over maintaining or even advancing one's interests, that actors are often willing to go to war to secure or advance their interests, and that not all wars result from a failure of crisis management. He knew that in addition to identifying the strategies most conducive to successful crisis management and the conditions that facilitated those strategies, a theory of crisis management also had to explain when political leaders made no effort to manage a crisis to avoid war. Thus, he emphasized the importance of actors' incentives to avoid war, their opportunities for doing so, and their level of skills.

Even if political leaders on both sides have incentives to avoid war, a peaceful outcome is not guaranteed, and George (1991a: 25) constructed a list of "operational" principles or requirements for successful crisis management. These criteria are somewhat redundant, and I consolidate and reorganize them. The most basic requirements are that political leaders on each side must maintain top-level civilian control of military options, select military actions that advance political objectives, and coordinate military and diplomatic actions. Although George does not explicitly build on Clausewitz (1832/1976), it is clear that Clausewitz's conception of war as fundamentally political runs throughout George's work on crisis management, coercive diplomacy, and deterrence. George repeatedly emphasizes the importance of a political–military strategy, and not a military strategy alone. This involves defining military objectives and setting the appropriate level of acceptable costs and risks as well as making decisions for war, and it also applies to military alerts, deployments,

and low-level actions. At the same time, however, George qualifies his prescriptive theory by emphasizing the potential dangers of micromanagement, which can interfere with military efficiency, prolong warfare, and increase costs. George emphasizes that political leaders must understand the trade-off between political control and military efficiency in order to make the appropriate tradeoffs.

This general emphasis on the control of military force by political leaders for the purposes of advancing the broader political objectives of the state lead George to suggest a number of more specific operational requirements of crisis management. In order for political leaders to be able to tailor their military actions to specific political objectives, they must possess a range of military options commensurate with those objectives. They must select military actions and threats of force that are appropriate to limited crisis objectives. Their military actions should signal their limited objectives and their interest in negotiating a way out of the crisis, and make it clear that they do not seek a military solution or are about to resort to large-scale warfare. Political leaders should create pauses in the tempo of military actions, in order to slow down the momentum of events, reduce the danger of loss of control, and signal their interest in managing crisis to avoid war. They should select diplomatic and military options that leave the opponent a way out of the crisis that is compatible with its fundamental interests. This includes face-saving compromises.

A number of scholars have used George's (1991a) framework in their own case study analyses of crisis management. Here I focus on case studies of the two leading interstate crises of the 20th century: the July 1914 crisis and the Arab-Israeli crisis of 1967 and the Cuban missile crisis of 1962.

July 1914 crisis

In applying George's crisis management framework to the July 1914 crisis, Levy

(1990–91) asked whether the outbreak of war was due to a failure of crisis management or to a more basic conflict of fundamental interests. Employing a modified rational choice framework, he identified four possible outcomes of the crisis initiated by the assassination of Austrian Archduke Ferdinand: a negotiated settlement between Austria and Serbia; a local war in the Balkans between Austria and Serbia; a continental war resulting from the intervention of Russia, Germany, and then France; and a world war resulting from the intervention of Britain. Levy rank-ordered the preferences of each of the European great powers (plus Serbia) over these possible outcomes, argued that they were stable over the course of the crisis, and then noted an interesting puzzle: each of the major actors preferred a negotiated settlement to a world war, yet the outcome of the crisis was a world war.

Levy identified a series of critical decision points in the escalating crisis, and at each of these key points identified the choices available to each of the major actors, the international and domestic constraints on their actions, and the available information. He concluded that nearly all the decisions by each actor at each critical decision point were basically rational given actors' interests and constraints. Moreover, each choice further narrowed the range of choices available at subsequent decision points, increased the costs of failing to match the escalatory actions of other states, and further narrowed the very limited opportunities for actors to manage the crisis to avoid war.

The key actor was Germany, who continued to encourage Austria to initiate a war in the Balkans. Germany hoped would eliminate the ongoing threat to the internal stability of Germany's only great power ally in Europe and precipitate a diplomatic realignment in Europe, thus eliminating the encirclement of Germany by the Franco-Russian alliance at a time that Russian power was growing rapidly. If that diplomatic alignment failed to materialize, Germany was willing to adopt a strategy of preventive war to defeat Russia and its French ally before that

combination grew too strong for Germany by 1917.

Repeated British attempts to manage the crisis, including the famous "Halt-in-Belgrade" proposal, were rejected by German Chancellor Bethmann-Hollweg because he preferred a local war and even a continental war to a negotiated settlement, and because he was reasonably confident that Britain would stand aside in a continental war, or at least stand aside long enough for Germany to achieve an irreversible advantage in the war. This was a critical misperception. Like a modest number of other misperceptions, however, it was not unreasonable given the information available at the time. Britain had not joined the Franco-Russian defensive alliance, made any commitment to intervene in a war on the continent, or made any effort to deter Germany from war against either France or Russia. Even Britain's allies in Paris and St. Petersburg had no idea what Britain might do in the event of war, and British Foreign Secretary Edward Grey himself was not certain if he would be able to secure a vote for military intervention from the Cabinet. Thus, Germany's critical misperception can hardly be described as lacking in any rational basis.

Once German leaders learned (late on July 29) that Britain would probably intervene in the war, they reversed course, tried to hold Austria-Hungary back, and even threatened to abandon its Austrian ally if it did not accept the Halt-in-Belgrade plan. By that time, however, it was too late. After Austrian-Hungarian leaders had taken the politically difficult decisions to issue the ultimatum, declare war, and begin mobilization, they felt they could not reverse course without undermining Austrian credibility, upsetting a coalition of domestic political interests that had been very difficult to construct, and breaking a serious psychological commitment.

The primary explanation for the escalation to war, Levy argues, was not the failure of political leaders to manage the crisis, but the lack of incentives to manage the crisis to begin with, given the structure of power and alliances and the interests of the actors (as they defined them) in place at the onset of the crisis. His case study shows that the actors in 1914 faced a social dilemma, like the Prisoner's Dilemma but involving a number of choices by different actors at different decision points. The structure of the situation in conjunction with actors' preferences induced each actor to make choices that were rational when they were made but that narrowed the range of future choices and led through a process of entrapment in escalating conflict to outcomes all actors would have preferred to avoid.[18]

Cuban missile crisis

George (1991b) used his framework to explain the peaceful outcome of the Cuban missile crisis, which he regarded as a case of highly successful crisis management. After noting the incentives that Kennedy and Khrushchev each had to avoid war, particular given the incalculable costs of escalation, George emphasized the limited nature of Kennedy's objectives – to remove Soviet missiles from Cuba, and not to overthrow the Castro regime or to eliminate Soviet influence from Cuba (as some of his advisors recommended).[19] The means employed, particularly by Kennedy, were also limited.[20] The US blockade strategy avoided the likely escalatory effects of the air strike or invasion options, and it also served as a signal of both resolve and a willingness to find a way out of the crisis. Kennedy tried to create pauses in military movements (refraining from a military response to the Soviet downing of an American U-2 over Cuba, ordering that the blockade be moved in closer to Cuba to delay the time to a naval confrontation), in part because he recognized that the possibility of maintaining presidential control over the crisis would rapidly decline if there was a military incident. Also important was Kennedy's willingness to offer Khrushchev a face-saving way out of the crisis (the no-invasion pledge and eventual withdrawal of US missiles in Turkey).

As for Khrushchev, while many have regarded the initial Soviet decision to place offensive missiles in Cuba as quite risky, George proposed a more nuanced interpretation Building on George and Smoke (1974: 489, 527–30), he introduced an additional dimension by distinguishing between actors' perceptions of the magnitude of the risks and their assessment of the controllability of the risks through the evolution of the crisis.[21] In some (but not all) cases where leaders anticipate that a particular course of action runs high risks later in the crisis, they may nevertheless be willing to embark on that course of action if they are confident that they can manage and control those risks as part of a strategy of limited probes or controlled pressure. There is some evidence in support of the wider validity of this proposition. In their case studies of a number of instances of failures of deterrence, George and Smoke (1974: 527) found that in nearly all their historical cases "the initiator tried to satisfy himself before acting that the risks of the particular option he chose could be calculated and … controlled by him so as to give his choice of action the character of a rationally calculated, acceptable risk."[22]

George (1991b) also examined the bargaining dimensions of the interactions between Kennedy and Khrushchev, and in doing so suggested an interesting line of interpretation and some interesting theoretical propositions that went beyond his "principles of crisis management." He acknowledged the lack of theory or evidence suggesting that there is an optimal combination of coercion, persuasion, compromise, and positive inducements that is likely to lead to successful crisis management, though he argued that coercive or bullying strategies are not optimal under most conditions (Leng, 1993). George stressed, among other things, the importance of the sequencing and timing of different actions. He argued that while Kennedy was quite willing to be conciliatory toward Khrushchev, the president also believed that is was essential to begin with coercive threats and actions at the onset of the crisis, in order to demonstrate his own credibility and reverse any image of weakness in the mind of the adversary. Only then was he willing to discuss concessions.

George basically accepted the rationale behind Kennedy's strategy, and argued that had he begun with a purely diplomatic strategy without coercive threats, he would have reinforced Khrushchev's image of Kennedy as weak, lead to less compromising behavior by Khrushchev. That would have prolonged the crisis and increased the likelihood that it would have escalated to risky military action.

CONCLUSIONS

I had two aims in this chapter on case studies and conflict resolution: to summarize some of the recent literature on case study methodology, and to examine the role of case studies in the development of theory about crisis management. With respect to case study methodology, I suggested a modification in conventional typologies of case studies, and focused on the theoretical purposes for which case studies are designed to serve. I also examined alternative research designs for facilitating use of case studies to test theories. I emphasized that different case study designs are more or less useful depending on the theoretical aims of the study, and that many designs are best conceived as stages in an overall research program. While I accept the conventional wisdom that for many theoretical purposes many cases are better than fewer, as long as the cases all satisfy the theoretical criteria guiding the study, I argued that for the purposes of hypothesis testing as well as hypothesis construction, a small number of cases or even a single case study can be extremely useful. With respect to hypothesis testing, this is particularly true for hypotheses that posit necessary or sufficient conditions or for situations in which cases satisfy "most-likely" or "least-likely" criteria based on theoretical priors.

I then turned to case studies of crisis management, with particular attention to George's (1991a) provisional theory of crisis management and its application to the July 1914 crises and to the Cuban missile crisis.

I argued that World War I provides a useful reminder that crises can escalate to war not only because of the failure of crisis management, but also because the structure of preferences and international and domestic constraints sometimes create few incentives for leaders to try to manage the crisis. I argued that the Cuban missile crisis is a classic case of a crisis that could have escalated out of control but that was successfully managed by political leaders.

NOTES

1 On the evolution of the field, see Kriesberg (1997).

2 On changing patterns of warfare, see Holsti (1996); Human Security Centre (2005); Marshall and Gurr (2005); and Harbom, Högbladh, and Wallensteen (2006).

3 For useful reviews, see Galtung (1965), Zartmann (1985, 1995), Azar and Burton (1986), Burton (1990), Kriesberg (1992), Bercovich (1996), Carnegie Commission (1997), Fisher (1997), Stern and Druckman (2000), Malone and Hampson (2001), and Wallensteen (2002).

4 Case study methods are a subset of qualitative methods, which include interpretive ethnographic studies, archival analysis, elite interviews, macrohistorical analysis, intensive analyses of particular historical episodes, "qualitative comparative analysis" based on Boolean and fuzzy set methods (Ragin 1987, 2000), alternative conceptions of causation (Goertz and Levy, 2007), and a range of other topics. My focus here, following most but not all of the expanding literature on case study methodology in the fields of international relations and comparative politics field (e.g., George and Bennett, 2005: 18–19), is on comparative and case study methods that aim to produce causal explanations and to develop a set of cumulative generalizations about the social world. I exclude postmodern narratives and other qualitative work that rejects the possibility of causal explanation, while incorporating other forms of interpretive or discourse analysis that accepts the goal of causal explanation and the possibility of generalization.

5 Verba (1967) distinguished between configurative and disciplined configurative analyses. Lijphart (1971: 691) distinguished among atheoretical, interpretive, hypothesis-generating, theory-confirming, theory-infirming, and deviant case studies. Eckstein (1975: 96–123) suggested a similar typology: configurative-idiographic, disciplined configurative, heuristic, and crucial-case studies based on most-likely and least-likely designs, and also plausibility probes.

6 Idiographic refers to the aim of inquiry (the explanation of an individual case), and not whether the inquiry is theoretical or not. Theory can be used to structure an idiographic case study (Levy, 2001).

7 The revised hypothesis cannot, however, be tested against the same data that was used to generate the hypothesis to begin with (King, Keohane, and Verba, 1994; George and Bennett, 2005).

8 Critics of case-study research often complain that case studies are so pliable that researchers' can interpret any outcome as consistent with their theoretical argument. One motivation for the growth of qualitative methodology is to eliminate whatever remnants of that research practice still existed. For an example of a case study that begins with a falsifiable interpretation, suggests evidence that would falsify the argument, and in fact uncovers that evidence and concludes that the hypothesized interpretation was false, see Gochal and Levy (2004).

9 After early debates, the literature on case study methodology now equates the comparative method with the analysis of a small number of cases (Collier, 1993: 105).

10 Note that Mill defines agreement or difference in terms of values on the *dependent* variable, whereas Przeworski and Tuene (1970) define similar and different in terms of *explanatory* variables. Thus, Mill's method of agreement is equivalent to a most different systems design, and Mill's method of difference is equivalent to a most similar systems design. Scholars often confuse these different terminologies.

11 The logic of inference is much more similar to what philosophers of history call *genetic explanation* (Gallie,1963; Nagel, 1979: 564–68) than to explanations based on covering-laws and deductive-nomological logic (Hempel, 1942).

12 Experimental methods may be superior for testing many of these hypotheses, but it is often difficult to generalize from highly controlled laboratory settings that cannot fully replicate the stakes and emotions inherent in the world we are trying to explain. This problem of "external validity" has always plagued the application of experimental methods to the study of international relations and conflict resolution.

13 Prospect theory (Kahneman and Tversky, 1979) posits that people "frame" choice problems around a reference point, give more weight to losses than to comparable gains as defined by that reference point, and engage in risk-averse behavior with respect to gains and risk-acceptant behavior with respect to losses. It helps to explain why people fight to keep territory and other things they would not have fought to gain in the first place, why threats are more effective in deterring people from improving their positions than in coercing them to accept losses from their reference point, and why they often take enormous risks to eliminate losses – even at the risk of incurring even greater losses. For applications to international relations, see Levy (2000).

14 I treat crucial case studies as a design that serves the hypothesis-testing function of case studies, rather than as a distinct type of cases studies, which is more common in the literature.

15 Another example of a most-likely case design is Ripsman and Levy's (2007) analysis of the absence of a "preventive war" against Germany in the 1930s. If ever conditions were ripe for preventive action against a rapidly rising and threatening adversary, it was in the mid-to-late 1930s with Hitler's Germany. On preventive war, and how it differs from preemption and other sources of better-now-than-later logic, see Levy (2008).

16 Scholars often define crises as situations involving a threat to basic values, a high probability of involvement in military hostilities, and a finite time for response (Brecher, 1980: 1). Crisis management can also be applied to intra-war crises, where it involves an attempt to avoid war or limit or control the escalation of violence. Although the literature on crisis management focuses on interstate conflicts (Williams, 1976; George, 1991a), it can also be applied to crises involving rebel groups or non-state actors.

17 Thus, I define crisis management in terms of the de-escalation of conflict (Kriesberg, 1992), rather than in terms of the more permanent elimination of the conflict of interests between parties (Burton, 1987: 7–8). See also Stern and Druckman (2000: 44) and Maoz (2004: 17–18).

18 On entrapment, see Brockner and Rubin (1985). For a summary of recent interpretations suggesting that Germany was in fact not so adverse to a world war, see Lieber (2007). If correct, this would further reinforce the argument that the outbreak of World War I was not a failure of crisis management, but undercut the argument about entrapment in an escalating conflict.

19 George (1991b) contrasted Kennedy's behavior with Truman's behavior in the Korean War – escalating both his objectives (unifying the two Koreas by military force) and the means for achieving them (permitting MacArthur to march north toward the Yalu).

20 George (1991b) acknowledged some brinkmanship behavior that violated the "limited means" criterion (such as the anti-submarine warfare activities of the US navy), but noted that it reminded each side of the risks of provoking the other and of an inadvertent escalation, and that it ultimately contributed to de-escalation.

21 George's (1991b) multidimensional conception of risk contrasts with standard treatments in the literature, which generally assume that risk is a uni-dimensional variable and which treats actors in terms of their degree of risk aversion or risk acceptance. For formal decision theorists, risk orientation is simply the shape of the utility function (concave downward for risk aversion, linear for risk neutrality, and convex for

risk acceptance). Prospect theorists posit an S-shaped value function with varying risks as a function of losses and gains (Levy, 2000).

22 The "tried to satisfy himself" phrasing suggests another hypothesis about the psychology of risk – that risk does not shape motivation but is endogenous to it, and that a highly motivated actor will subconsciously adjust its risk assessment (or perhaps consciously, if it wants to convince other decision-makers) so as to justify an action it wants to take.

REFERENCES

Allison, Graham T. (1971) *Essence of Decision*. New York: Little Brown.

Azar, Edward E., and Burton, John W. (eds.) (1986) *International Conflict Resolution: Theory and Practice*. Boulder, CO: Lynne Rienner.

Bennett, Andrew, and Elman, Colin (2006) 'Qualitative Research: Recent Developments in Case Study Methods', *Annual Review of Political Science*, 9: 455–76.

Bercovitch, Jacob (ed.) (1996) *Resolving International Conflicts: The Theory and Practice of Mediation*. Boulder, CO: Lynne Rienner.

Blatter, Joachim, and Till Blume (2008) 'In Search of Co-variance, Causal Mechanisms or Congruence? Towards a Plural Understanding of Case Studies.' *Swiss Political Science Review*, 14 (2): 315–55.

Brady, Henry E., and Collier, David (eds.) (2004) *Rethinking Social Inquiry: Diverse Tools, Shared Standards*. Lanham, MD.: Rowman & Littlefield.

Brecher, Michael (1980) *Decisions in Crisis*. Berkeley: University of California Press.

Brockner, Joel, and Rubin, Jeffrey Z. (1985) *Entrapment in Escalating Conflicts: A Social Psychological Analysis*. New York: Springer-Verlag.

Burton, John W. (1987) *Resolving Deep-rooted Conflicts*. Lanham, MD: University Press of America.

Burton, John W. (1990) *Conflict: Resolution and Prevention*. New York: St. Martin's.

Campbell, Donald. (1975) 'Degrees of Freedom and the Case Study', *Comparative Political Studies*, 8 (2): 178–193.

Carnegie Commission (1997) *Preventing Deadly Conflict: Final Report*. Washington, DC: Carnegie Commission.

Clausewitz, Carl von (1832/1976) *On War*, ed. and trans. by Michael Howard and Peter Paret. Princeton, NJ: Princeton University Press.

Collier, David (1993) 'The Comparative Method', in Ada Finifter (ed.), *Political Science: The State of the Discipline II*. Washington, DC: American Political Science Association. pp. 105–119.

Dion, Douglas (1998) 'Evidence and Inference in the Comparative Case Study', *Comparative Politics*, 30 (2): 127–146.

Eckstein, Harry (1975) 'Case Studies and Theory in Political Science', in Fred Greenstein and Nelson Polsby (eds.), *Handbook of Political Science*, vol. 7. Reading, MA: Addison-Wesley. pp. 79–138.

Fisher, Roger (1997) *Interactive Conflict Resolution*. Syracuse, NY: Syracuse University Press.

Frendreis, John (1983) 'Explanation of Variation and Detection of Covariation: The Purpose and Logic of Comparative Analysis', *Comparative Political Studies*, 16 (2): 255–272.

Gallie, W.B. (1963) 'The Historical Understanding', *History and Theory*, 3 (2): 149–202.

Galtung, Johan (1965) 'Internationalized Conflict Resolution', *Journal of Peace Research*, 2 (4): 348–97.

George, Alexander L. (1979) 'Case Studies and *Theory Development'*, in Paul Lauren (ed.), *Diplomacy: New Approaches in Theory, History, and Policy*. New York: Free Press. pp. 43–68.

George, Alexander L. (1991a) 'A Provisional Theory of Crisis Management', in *Avoiding Inadvertent War: Problems of Crisis Management*. Boulder, CO: Westview. pp. 22–27.

George, Alexander L. (1991b) 'The Cuban Missile Crisis', in George (ed.), *Avoiding Inadvertent War: Problems of Crisis Management*. Boulder, CO: Westview. pp. 222–68.

George, Alexander L., and Bennett, Andrew (2005) *Case Studies and Theory Development in the Social Sciences*. Cambridge, MA: MIT Press.

George, Alexander L., and Smoke, Richard (1974) *Deterrence in American Foreign Policy*. New York: Columbia University Press.

Gerring, John (2007) *Case Study Research*. New York: Cambridge University Press.

Gochal, Joseph R., and Levy, Jack S. (2004) 'Crisis Mismanagement or Conflict of Interests? A Case Study of the Crimean War', in Zeev Maoz, Alex Mintz, T. Clifton Morgan, Glenn Palmer, and Richard J. Stoll (eds.), *Multiple Paths to Knowledge in International Relations: Methodology in the Study of Conflict Management and Conflict Resolution*. Lexington, MA: Lexington Books. pp. 309–42.

Goertz, Gary (2006) *Social Science Concepts*. Princeton: Princeton University Press.

Goertz, Gary, and Levy, Jack S. (eds.) (2007) *Explaining War and Peace: Case Studies and Necessary Condition Counterfactuals*. New York: Routledge.

Harbom, Lotta, Högbladh, Stina, and Wallensteen, Peter (2006) 'Armed Conflict and Peace Agreements', *Journal of Peace Research*, 43 (5): 617–31.

Hempel, Carl G. (1942) 'The Function of General Laws in History', *Journal of Philosophy*, 39: 35–48.

Holsti, Kalevi J. (1996) *The State, War, and the State of War*. New York: Cambridge University Press.

Human Security Centre (2005) *Human Security Report 2005: War and Peace in the 21st Century*. New York: Oxford University Press.

Kahneman, Daniel, and Amos Tversky. (1979) 'Prospect Theory: An Analysis of Decision Under Risk', *Econometrica*, 47 (1): 263–91.

King, Gary, Keohane, Robert, and Verba, Sidney. (1994) *Designing Social Inquiry*. Princeton: Princeton University Press.

Kriesberg, Louis. (1997) 'The Development of the Conflict Resolution Field', in I. William Zartman and J. Lewis Rasmussen (eds.), *Peacemaking in International Conflict*. Washington, DC: United States Institute of Peace. pp. 51–77.

Kriesberg, Louis (1992) *International Conflict Resolution*. New Haven: Yale University Press.

Leng, Russell J. (1993) *Interstate Crisis Behavior, 1816–1980: Realism Versus Reciprocity*. New York: Cambridge University Press.

Levy, Jack S. (1990–91) 'Preferences, Constraints, and Choices in July 1914', *International Security*, 15 (3): 151–186.

Levy, Jack S. (2000) 'The Implications of Framing and Loss Aversion for International Conflict', in Manus I. Midlarsky (ed.), *Handbook of War Studies II*. Ann Arbor: University of Michigan Press. pp. 193–221.

Levy, Jack S. (2001) 'Explaining Events and Testing Theories: History, Political Science, and the Analysis of International Relations', in Colin Elman and Miriam Fendius Elman (eds.), *Bridges and Boundaries*. Cambridge: MIT Press. pp. 39–83.

Levy, Jack S. (2002) 'Qualitative Methods in International Relations', in Michael Brecher and Frank P. Harvey (eds.), *Millennial Reflections on International Studies*. Ann Arbor: University of Michigan Press. pp. 432–54.

Levy, Jack S. (2008) 'Preventive War and Democratic Politics', *International Studies Quarterly*, 52 (1): 1–24.

Lieber, Keir A. (2007) 'The New History of World War I and What It Means for International Relations Theory', *International Security*, 32 (2): 155–191.

Lieberson, Stanley (1992) 'Small Ns and Big Conclusions', in Charles Ragin and Howard Becker (eds.), *What Is a Case?* New York: Cambridge University Press. pp. 105–18.

Lijphart, Arend (1971) 'Comparative Politics and the Comparative Method', *American Political Science Review*, 65 (3): 682–93.

McKeown, Timothy (1999) 'Case Studies and the Statistical World View', *International Organization*, 53(1): 161–190.

Malone, David, and Hampson, Fen Osler (eds.) (2001) *From Reaction to Conflict Prevention: Opportunities for the UN System*. New York: The International Peace Academy.

Maoz, Zeev (2004) 'Conflict Management and Conflict Resolution: A Conceptual and Methodological Introduction', in Zeev Maoz, Alex Mintz, T. Clifton Morgan, Glenn Palmer, and Richard J. Stoll (eds.), *Multiple Paths to Knowledge in International Relations*. Lanham, MD: Lexington Books. pp. 1–32.

Marshall, Monty G., and Gurr, Ted R. (2005). *Peace and Conflict 2005: A Global Survey of Armed Conflicts, Self-Determination Movements, and Democracy*. College Park: Center for International Development and Conflict Management, University of Maryland.

Meckstroth, Theodore (1975) '"Most Different Systems" and "Most Similar Systems": A Study in the Logic of Comparative Inquiry', *Comparative Political Studies*, 8 (2): 133–177.

Mill, John Stuart (1875/1970) *A System of Logic*. London: Longman.

Nagel, Ernest (1979) *The Structure of Science*. Indianapolis: Hackett.

Przeworski, Adam, and Teune, Henry (1970) *The Logic of Comparative Social Inquiry*. New York: Wiley.

Ragin, Charles C. (1987) *The Comparative Method*. Berkeley: University of California Press.

Ragin, Charles C. (2000) *Fuzzy-Set Social Science*. Chicago: University of Chicago Press.

Ripsman, Norrin, and Levy, Jack S. (2007) 'The Preventive War that Never Happened: Britain, France, and the Rise of Germany in the 1930s', *Security Studies*, 16 (1): 32–67.

Snyder, Jack. (1991) *Myths of Empire: Domestic Politics and International Ambition*. Ithaca, NY: Cornell University Press.

Stedman, Stephen J. (1991) *Peacemaking in Civil War: International Mediation in Zimbabwe, 1974–1980*. Boulder, CO: Lynne Rienner.

Stern, Paul C., and Druckman, Daniel (2000) 'Evaluating Interventions in History: The Case of International Conflict Resolution', in Paul C. Stern and Daniel Druckman (eds.), *International Conflict Resolution after the Cold War*. Washington, DC: National Academy Press. pp. 38–99.

Touval, Saadia (1982) *The Peace Brokers: Mediators in the Arab-Israeli Conflict, 1948–1979*. Princeton: Princeton University Press.

Van Evera, Stephen (1997) *Guide to Methods for Students of Political Science*. Ithaca, New York: Cornell University Press.

Verba, Sidney (1967) 'Some Dilemmas in Comparative Research', *World Politics*, 20(1): 111–27.

Wallensteen, Peter (2002) *Understanding Conflict Resolution*. London: Sage.

Williams, Phil (1976) *Crisis Management*. New York: Wiley.

Zartman I. William (1985) *Ripe for Resolution*. New York: Oxford University Press.

Zartman, I. William (1995) *Elusive Peace: Negotiating an End to Civil Wars*. Washington: Brookings Institution.

Zartman, I. William (2005) 'Comparative Case Studies', *International Negotiation*, 10: 3–15.

5

Game Theory as an Approach to Conflict Resolution

Rudolf Avenhaus

INTRODUCTION

There is general consent that game theory provides by its very nature the appropriate tools for the analysis and eventual solution of conflicts of any kind, that is, also as considered here, international conflicts. In fact, there are books dealing with this subject that express this already in their titles. *The Strategy of Conflict*, written by Schelling in 1960, was an early and highly influential book on the subject, *Game Theory as a Theory of Conflict Resolution* was edited in 1974 by Rapoport, another important researcher of those years. *Resolving Conflicts with Mathemetica – Algorithms for Two-person Games*, published by Canty in 2003, demonstrates the use of Mathematica software for analyzing those models which are too complicated for traditional pen and pencil methods.

If one studies the published literature on game theoretic approaches to conflict resolution, there are a large number of contributions written by game theorists which deal with mathematical aspects but present only illustrative examples instead of real applications. One also finds many papers written by political or social scientists who analyze international conflicts with the help of very simple formal models, or by just the use of game theoretical terminology. There are, however, relatively few studies that use genuine and non-trivial formal methods in order to analyze concrete international conflicts. Some of them will be discussed subsequently.

Since game theory as of today is a very large field – the three volumes of the *Handbook of Game Theory* (1994–2002) comprise 2200 pages with thousands of references – we do not attempt here to systematically scan different areas and methods in order to find models of, in and for resolving international conflicts. Also, we do not try to classify international conflicts in order to see if there are analyses which use specific game theoretical methods. (This has been done in some way in 1994 by O'Neill who listed more than 600 references on game theoretic models for peace and war.) Finally, we do not enter into a general discussion of the value of game theoretic models since this has been done extensively on several occasions – see, such as the Journal *International Security* (1999), or Snidal (2005). Nevertheless, there remains a challenge.

Here, we choose the following approach: instead of any kind of systematic procedure, a few case studies are given which are selected in order to demonstrate at the same time the variety of problems as well as methods for their solution. In addition, the case studies are discussed and commented on, such that, with additional references, at least some kind of coverage of the area is given. Of course, there remain gaps both in theory and application, and even more so in the literature.

In this chapter, we do not attempt to present any kind of introduction into game theory itself, since there are so many excellent introductory textbooks, for example, by Myerson (1991), or by Fudenberg and Tirole (1998). We try to answer the question: what is the purpose of game theoretical models of conflicts? In general, they enable the analyst to do the following:

Describe a conflict in terms of a general theory, namely, formulate strategies, payoffs, information, and the like, and interpret the resolution – if there is one – as an application of some general principles covering human action.

Gain insights into apparently strange – we avoid saying irrational - behavior of participants in a conflict and show how such behavior can be understood in terms of an appropriate general theory.

Advise those who are involved in a concrete conflict, if possible, or at least advise retrospectively if a conflict has already been solved, and assess the actual resolution of a conflict in terms of the preferences of the participants and their strategic possibilities.

With respect to the first two purposes, we consider game theory a descriptive theory; for the last, we consider it a normative theory. Our case studies of the past are of a descriptive nature, whereas some of the case studies which deal with not yet solved conflicts, at least to some degree, may be considered normative ones.

CASE STUDIES

The cases and their analyses are chosen such that they are interesting both from the issue and from the method points of view, as already mentioned. They are chosen such that they are not trivial, but can be presented, together with discussion and comments, on a few pages; more extended analyses will also be mentioned.

The case studies will be organized as follows, although too strict a form will be avoided: first, the conflict will be described. Second, the game theoretical model will be presented and analyzed. Third, some comments on the mathematical model will be given and finally, further applications will be discussed.

Even though some attempts will be made to present a coherent description of game theoretical models, game trees, for example, will always be presented vertically from the top down to the end; we also try to maintain the terminology of different authors in order to ease further reading. Thus, we keep the different words of players, actors, protagonists and others for the same subject intentionally in order to maintain the spirit of the different authors' intentions.

First case: Europe 1914

Let us describe the European crisis in 1914 in the words of Snyder and Diesing (1977) who gave a short outline in order to justify their model and a longer one as an annex in their book.

Even though there were at least five or six great power actors involved in that crisis, one gets a rough approximation if one considers Austria-Germany as the actor and Russia-France as another, with England and Italy as uncertainly aligned states, estimates of whose intentions nevertheless affected the payoff structures of the main protagonists. The high degree of solidarity between France and Russia on the one hand and Germany and Austria on the other makes it plausible to consider the pairs as unitary actors.

The immediate crisis precipitate to the outbreak of hostilities was the assassination of the Austrian Archduke Ferdinand. This was merely the most dramatic episode in the long-run or general precipitant, the continual Serb agitation in Bosnia, which, in the opinion of Austrian and German decision makers, threatened to escalate to general Slav revolution throughout the empire and cause its likely dissolution. The Austrian challenge followed: an ultimatum to Serbia that, if accepted, would have turned Serbia into an Austrian protectorate; if not accepted, would serve as a pretext to destroy Serbia by force.

At this stage, there was vacillation and difference of opinion internally in Austria and Germany as to whether the preferable outcome was war or Serbian acceptance of the ultimatum. From the Russian standpoint, the story was altogether different. Russian reputation for resolve was very low due to events in the previous years. If Russia now acquiesced in the destruction of her last client, Serbia, she would have no more influence in the Balkans, the balance of power would turn dangerously against her, and her resolve, reputation and general influence in world politics would be demolished. Russia felt that she had to fight to prevent the loss of Serbia. However, she was willing to make some concessions on the ultimatum to preserve peace, so long as Serbian sovereignty remained intact. France shared these preferences with a different cost: failure to support Russia would mean the defeat and loss of a badly needed ally.

According to this outline, both actors, Austria-Germany (AG) and Russia-France (RF), had two pure strategies, namely to concede or to stay firm, with the following consequences:

- Both concede: Some Serbian apology and humiliation by Austria.
- AG stays firm, RF concedes: A controls Serbia, end of subversion, Empire saved. R humiliated. Loss of all influence in the Balkans.
- AG concedes, RF stays firm: A is humiliated, more Serb agitation, rapid dissolution of the Empire. Serbia and Russian influence in the Balkans is preserved, prestige is restored.
- Both stay firm: War.

In Figure 5.1, this situation is depicted as a *non-cooperative* 2 × 2 *two-person game in normal form*. The pure strategies of AG are given by the two rows, those of RF by the two columns. The payoffs to the two actors are expressed by so-called utilities which are normalized to one for the worst, four for the best outcomes; they represent the evaluation of the consequences of the pairs of strategies to both actors as described above.

A Nash equilibrium (Nash, 1953) of any non-cooperative game is defined as a pair of strategies with the property that, if one actor deviates unilaterally from his equilibrium strategy, he will not increase his payoff. A Nash equilibrium is called a solution of a game if it is unique. In our case, we can easily find the equilibrium with the help of the preference directions. As a result,

RF AG	Concede	Stay firm
Concede	3 2	4 1
Stay firm	1 4	2 3 *

Figure 5.1   Graphical representation of the normal form game describing the European crisis in 1914. AG: Austria Germany. RF: Russia France. Lower-left payoffs are those to AG., upper-right payoffs those to RF. Arrows indicate preference directions, and the asterisk denotes the Nash equilibrium.

the pair of strategies (firm, firm) is the only Nash equilibrium and, therefore, the solution of the game, and the consequence is war.

The model and its solution explain how it could happen, that the crisis ended in war, a result which none of the actors had really wanted or anticipated if one believes the statements of leading politicians of the time. Even though the model oversimplifies the complicated sequence of actions of the involved states, it describes the situation and provides insight into the mechanism and perceived consequences.

It should be noted in passing that Snyder and Diesing did not make explicit use of the Nash equilibrium concept. They described their model as an illustration of the so-called *Prisoners' Dilemma* (*PD*) paradigm. Without repeating the explanation of the origin of this name, we just note that in such a case a solution is obtained which in fact none of the actors wants. In general, one speaks of a PD game if there is a strategy combination which has higher payoffs to both players than those given by the equilibrium; this is not the case here if we take the payoffs as they are. Retrospectively, we estimate the war cost much higher than the actors in 1914 did; thus, in hindsight, we may be led to a PD game in its literal meaning.

Non-cooperative 2 × 2 two-person games in normal form have been widely used for analyses of international conflicts and crises. As in our case, they do not describe the details or the dynamics of such events, but provide principal insight for those who are not trained to work with more complicated mathematical models. Snyder and Diesing (1977) discuss several other conflicts of the past in terms of 2 × 2 games. Recently, Rudnianski and Bestougeff (2007) analyzed the Icelandic fisheries conflict between Iceland and the United Kingdom that way. In particular, the PD game is used frequently to explain why conflicts arose or developed in a way nobody wanted; all kinds of arms races are examples (Brams and Kilgour, 1988; Zagare and Kilgour, 2002; Beetz, 2005).

Second case: cuban missile crisis

Probably the most dangerous confrontation between major powers ever to occur was that between the United States and the Soviet Union in October 1962. This confrontation, in what has come to be known as the Cuban missile crisis, was precipitated by a Soviet attempt to install in Cuba medium-range and intermediate-range nuclear-armed ballistic missiles capable of hitting a large portion of the United States. The description of that crisis as well as the first part of its analysis follow those of Brams (1985 and 1990).

After the presence of such missiles was confirmed on October 14, the United States Central Intelligence Agency estimated that they would be operational in about ten days. A so-called Executive Committee of high-level officials was convened to decide on a course of action for the United States, and the Committee met in secret for six days. Several alternatives were considered, which were eventually narrowed down to the two that will be discussed here.

The most common conception of this crisis is that the two superpowers were on a collision course. *Chicken*, which derives its name from a kind of mad sport in which two drivers race toward each other on a narrow road, would at first blush seem an appropriate model of this conflict. Under this interpretation, each player has the choice between swerving, and avoiding a head-on collision, or continuing on the collision course. As applied to the Cuban missile crisis, with the United States and the Soviet Union the two players, the alternative courses of action and a ranking of the players' outcomes in terms of the game of chicken are shown in Figure 5.2. It is again a non-cooperative 2 × 2 two-person game in normal form.

The goal of the United States was immediate removal of the Soviet missiles, and United States policy makers seriously considered two alternative courses of action to achieve this end. First, a naval blockade, or quarantine as it was euphemistically called, to prevent shipment of further missiles, possibly

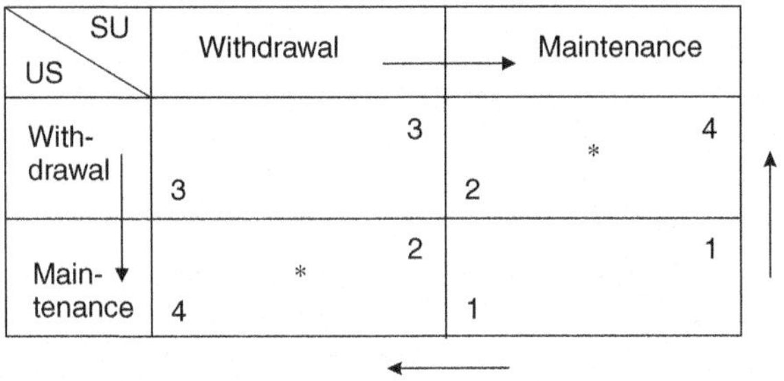

Figure 5.2   Graphical representation of the normal form game describing the Cuban missile crisis in 1962. US: United States; SU: Soviet Union.

followed by stronger action to induce the Soviet Union to withdraw those missiles already installed. Second, a surgical strike to wipe out the missiles already installed, insofar as possible, perhaps followed by an invasion of the island. The choices open to Soviet policy makers were withdrawal of their missiles and maintenance of their missiles.

Needless to say, the strategy choices and probable outcomes as presented in Figure 5.2 provide only a skeletal picture of the crisis as it developed over a period of thirteen days. Both sides considered more than the two alternatives listed above, as well as several variations on each. The Soviets, for example, demanded withdrawal of American missiles from Turkey as a quid pro quo for withdrawal of their missiles from Cuba, a demand publicly ignored by the United States. Furthermore, there is no way to verify that the outcomes given in Figure 5.2 were probable, or valued in a manner consistent with the game of Chicken. For example, if the Soviet Union had viewed an air strike on their missiles as jeopardizing their vital national interests, the crisis may well have ended in nuclear war between the two sides. Still another simplification relates to the assumption that the players choose their actions simultaneously, when in fact a continuous exchange in both words and deeds occurred over those fateful days in October 1962.

Nevertheless, most observers of this crisis believe the two superpowers were on a collision course. Most observers also agree that neither side was eager to take any irreversible step, such as the driver in a game

of Chicken might do by defiantly ripping off his steering wheel in full view of his adversary, thereby foreclosing his alternative of swerving.

Contrary to the game of Figure 5.1, which represented the European 1914 crisis, the game given in Figure 5.2 has two Nash equilibria in pure strategies, as can again be seen immediately by use of the method of preference directions. In fact, there is a third equilibrium in so-called mixed strategies which is not given here. This is the lesson to be learned from this model: because of the existence of several equilibria, each of which was very bad for at least one of the players, the situation was very dangerous.

Although in one sense the United States won by getting the Soviets to withdraw their missiles, Premier Khrushchev at the same time extracted from President Kennedy a promise not to invade Cuba, which seems to indicate that the eventual outcome was a compromise solution of sorts. These results render it plausible to describe the outcome of the crisis in terms of a *Nash bargaining solution* (Nash, 1950) which, surprisingly enough, to our best knowledge, never has been discussed in the literature.

In order to discuss Nash's concept, we present first the area of expected payoffs to both players, with the United States as player 1 and the Soviet Union as player 2 (see Figure 5.3).

According to Figure 5.2, if the United States chooses its first strategy with probability p and its second with 1–p, while the Soviet Union chooses its first strategy with

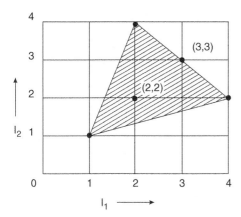

Figure 5.3   Area of expected payoffs to the United States (I_1) and to the Soviet Union (I_2). (2,2) are the guaranteed payoffs, (3,3) is the Nash bargaining solution.

probability q and its second with 1–q, the expected outcomes are:

$$I_1 = p(3q + 2(1 - q)) + (1 - p)(4q + 1 - q)$$
$$I_2 = q(3p + 2(1 - p)) + (1 - q)(4p + 1 - p).$$

If we now take all possible pairs (p, q), with values of p and q between zero and one, we get the shaded area in Figure 5.3 which represents the area of expected payoff pairs (I_1, I_2) to both players. For the sake of illustration, the pairs of payoffs for the four combinations of pure strategies are explicitly marked. Of special importance is the upper right border of the area: along this border, which is called the Pareto frontier, none of the two players can improve his expected payoff without decreasing that of the other one.

Now let us describe Nash's concept. He assumes that both sides talk to each other – which means that we now enter the domain of *cooperative game theory* – and agree on the following six principles on a negotiated outcome of the bargain.

N1. Both players get at least as much as they got if they did not talk to each other.
N2. The outcomes are feasible, that is, they can in fact be obtained under the circumstances given.
N3. The outcomes fall on the Pareto frontier.
N4. If the solution lies in a subset of the area of possible solutions, then it is also a solution in the original set of possible solutions (independence of irrelevant alternatives).
N5. The solution is independent of positive linear transformations of the payoffs.
N6. If the area of possible outcomes is symmetric, then the solution is symmetric.

Given these six assumptions, Nash showed that the bargaining solution is determined by maximizing the product of the two players' expected payoffs minus their guaranteed ones, that is, those payoffs which the players obtained if they did not cooperate.

Now let us come back to our case. Since the area of possible expected payoffs as given by Figure 5.3 is convex, it will not be enlarged by the possibility of cooperation. It should be mentioned in passing that this is a special case; in other cases like the famous *Battle of the Sexes* (see e.g. Luce and Raiffa, 1957), this is not the case for the non-cooperative game, and the first step of the cooperation is to consider an extension of the area of expected payoffs such that it becomes a convex set. As can be seen immediately by looking at Figure 5.2, the guaranteed payoff to both players in case they do not cooperate is two. Therefore, we have to look for the maximum of the product $(I_1 - 2)(I_2 - 2)$ on the Pareto frontier. The result is, as can again be seen easily, the payoff three to both players, and this is just the pair (blockade, withdrawal) of pure strategies of the non-cooperative game, which is not an equilibrium of that game.

In sum, at the beginning of the crisis, the situation may, in a very simple way, be described as a Chicken-type model, which illustrates the danger the world experienced during those days. Later on, however, the two statesmen talked to each other: in responding to a letter from Khrushchev, Kennedy wrote "if you would agree to remove these weapons systems from Cuba…we, on our part, would agree … (a) to remove promptly the quarantine measures now in effect and (b) to give assurances against an invasion of Cuba." Thus, an application of Nash's bargaining concept seems to describe the situation at a later stage of the crisis, of course in a very simplified way, quite well.

In the game theoretical literature, Nash's bargaining solution has a very important role. The assumptions have been carefully discussed and also criticized, in particular assumption N4, and replaced by other assumptions. Also, the concept was extended to more than two players. Contrary to that, so far there have been surprisingly few applications, especially in the field of international relations.

International water disputes have been analyzed in terms of Nash's bargaining concept by Richards and Singh (1997), but they considered only idealized states and disputes. Trade of emission permits in the context of the Kyoto Protocol provisions were discussed this way by Okada (2007). United States–Japan trade negotiations were studied by Hopmann (1996); he describes their results also in terms of Nash's bargaining model, although not quantitatively. There may be different reasons for this deficiency: the approach is not so intuitive as simple normal form games and, therefore, for a long time it was not so well known among political and social scientists, as well as among practitioners.

Third case: nuclear deterrence

During the height of the Cold War, say in the 1970s of the last century, all responsible parties agreed that nuclear war would be an unparalleled disaster, but under which conditions might a government think about the unthinkable? To set the scene, a greatly simplified discussion of some issues is presented, with some modifications drawn from Morrow (1994).

Some rational leaders might consider launching a nuclear first strike if it would disarm the other side, preventing any response, assuming that long-run ecological damage would not impose serious costs on the striking side. But during the Cold War, both the United States and the Soviet Union had nuclear arsenals that made a first strike that disarmed the other side highly improbable. From the mid-1960s on, each side had a secure second-strike capability; that is, both the United States

and the Soviet Union could have responded to any initial nuclear strike with a devastating retaliatory strike, primarily from submarine-based missiles, but also from surviving land-based missiles. First strikes were deterred by this credible threat of retaliation. This case illustrates a general point: neither side will be willing to launch a first strike when an attack will only lead to its own destruction through nuclear retaliation.

This conclusion has a disturbing side-effect: it eliminates the use of nuclear weapons for extended deterrence – the protection of allies from external threats through nuclear threats. For example, during the Cold War, the United States threatened to use strategic nuclear weapons if the Soviet Union invaded Western Europe – but if such a nuclear first strike had led to the devastation of the United States by Soviet nuclear retaliation, the threat of initiating nuclear war to defend Western Europe would not have been credible. For nuclear weapons to have political utility beyond the deterrence of nuclear war, both sides must believe there is some chance that a nuclear war could begin. Otherwise, the threat was hollow.

Schelling (1960) proposed one solution to this problem: the reciprocal fear of a surprise attack. Assume there is some advantage in striking first if nuclear war occurs: the side that strikes first is somewhat less devastated than the other. Both sides can still launch devastating second strikes, but it is better to strike first than second because the first strike takes out some of the other side's missiles. Each side might contemplate a first strike, not because it expected to win by attacking, but rather because it feared that the other side was preparing to attack and it wished to gain the first strike advantage for itself. These fears could build upon one another in a vicious circle, creating the reciprocal fear of a surprise attack. Nuclear war might then be launched, not because either side thought it could win, but because each side feared the other was about to launch an attack.

This argument places several restrictions on possible models. Neither side must know that the other side has committed itself to not attacking when it must decide whether to launch an attack itself. If neither side decides to attack the status quo, the best outcome for both sides should prevail. If a first strike is launched, the other side retaliates, but the side that strikes first suffers less.

Before modeling the conflict as described, let us first consider a hypothetical conflict, where one power (1) decides first whether to launch an attack (A) or to delay it (D), and where in the latter case the other power (2) decides to launch an attack (a) or to delay it (d). This situation is modeled as a *non-cooperative two-person game in extensive form with perfect information* (see Figure 5.4). In such a game, the players know where they are in the game tree whenever they have to make a choice. We will not give a formal definition of extensive form games (see, for example, Myerson, 1991), but explain this type of game with the help of our case.

The payoffs to both powers are zero if both delay, they are $-a_1$ and $-r_2$ if (1) attacks and $-r_1$ and $-a_2$ if (2) attacks with $o < a_i < r_i$ for $i = 1,2$. A simple backward induction shows that (D, d) is the only Nash equilibrium, which means that none of the two powers will launch a first strike.

Now let us turn to the original conflict situation as described before. We model it as a non-cooperative two-person game in

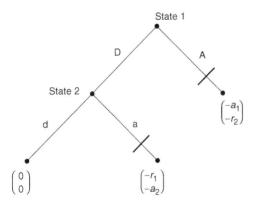

Figure 5.4 Graphical representation of the extensive form game with perfect information describing the superpower conflict. D (d): Delay an attack. A (a): Launch an attack. Crossed alternatives are deleted.

extensive form with *imperfect information* (see Figure 5.5).

The A and a actions are nuclear first strike attacks, and the D and d actions delay the launching of a first strike. The a payoffs are for launching a first strike, and the r payoffs are for receiving such a strike and then retaliating. The difference between the two measures is the first strike advantage. The larger $r - a$ is, the greater the advantage to striking first. If neither side attacks, the status quo holds – the zero payoff. We assume that striking first is preferable to receiving a first strike, but that no nuclear war is preferable to any nuclear war, that is, again $0 < a_i < r_i$ for $i = 1,2$. The chance move and information sets capture the idea that neither player knows whether the other is preparing a first strike when it must decide whether to launch a first strike of its own. Neither player knows whether delaying the strike ends the game at the status quo or gives the other player the opportunity to launch its own strike.

Because of the more complicated information structure of this game, the simple backward induction procedure does not work anymore. Again, we have to take into account so-called mixed strategies, i.e. probability distributions over the pure strategies. Without presenting the solution procedure here, we just give its result. There are three different Nash equilibria.

In the first equilibrium, each side attacks if it wins the draw because each knows that if it does not attack, the other side will attack in turn. This equilibrium describes the reciprocal fear of surprise attack run amok. Each player attacks out of the fear that the other will attack if it does not.

In the second equilibrium, neither side attacks because each knows that the other side will not attack in turn. Here, we have mutual confidence in restraint; neither player launches an attack because they both believe the other player will not launch one.

In the third equilibrium, both sides play mixed strategies, with each side's probability of attacking increasing as the other side's first strike advantage $r - a$ decreases. If the third equilibrium seems bizarre, we remember that

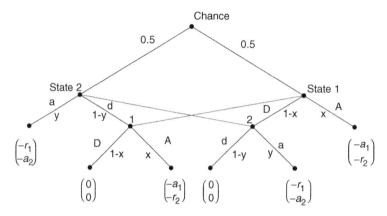

Figure 5.5   Graphical representation of the extensive form game with imperfect information. Dashed lines indicate information sets. x resp. y are probabilities for choosing A resp. a.

each side's probability of attacking is chosen to make the other side indifferent between attacking and not attacking.

Because of our assumptions, the second equilibrium provides the highest payoffs to both players, in other words, it is *payoff-dominant* as compared to the other ones. The second equilibrium leads to the worst payoffs, and the third one is just in between. We see, that even though both parties would be well advised to agree on the second equilibrium, this is not automatically the solution to the game, since no mechanism is foreseen, or, there is no confidence in any kind of agreement, which allows them to take a joint decision for the benefit of both of them.

These results may explain why the situation during the Cold War was so serious. Since there are several equilibria, two of which foresaw the possibility of a first strike, there was a paralyzing uncertainty about the intentions of the other side. On the other side, a first strike did not occur, perhaps since there was a silent agreement on the payoff-dominating equilibrium. Or, with all due care, considerations like these may have had a normative impact on the decision makers of that time.

There are much less analyses of international conflicts using extensive form games than normal form games. The existing ones primarily use those with perfect information. Just to name a few prototypical cases: the

Cuban missile crisis was analyzed that way (e.g. Wagner, 1989; Brams, 1990). Bueno de Mesquita (2002) carefully discussed the Concordat of Worms in 1122, where the so-called Investiture Struggle between the Emperor of the Holy Roman Empire German Nation and the Pope was resolved. Extensive form games with two-sided imperfect information are used by Morrow (1989) and by Zagare and Kilgour (2002) in order to discuss deterrence problems in general.

Fourth case: Greek–Turkish territorial waters conflict

A major conflict confronting Greece and Turkey until today is the breadth of territorial waters in the Aegean Sea. Greece claims that it has the freedom to extend its territorial waters to twelve miles, while Turkey has indicated that a Greek move to extend territorial waters constitutes a casus belli. Currently, both countries apply the six-mile limits, even though several crises have already occurred over the issue. The following description and analysis which has been simplified here is from Güner (2007).

Greece and Turkey are the only littoral states in the Aegean. More than 3000 islands, islets and rocks cover the sea. All, apart from three small islands, belong to Greece with some rocks and islets forming contested sovereignty zones. The 1923 Treaty of Lausanne fixed the extension of the littoral states' territorial waters at three miles. Greece unilaterally declared territorial waters of six miles in 1936 during a détente period between the two states. Turkey responded in 1964 with a similar move, and the current status quo formed: both states maintain six miles of territorial sea.

In accordance with the United Nations Convention on the Law of the Sea (UNCLOS), signed in 1982, which entered into force in 1994, signatory states have the right to establish territorial waters up to twelve miles. Greece, as a signatory state, considers the determination of the breadth of its territorial waters to be a sovereign right. It claims it will extend its territorial waters to twelve miles in the future. A revised status quo, if both littoral states do the same, implies the resolution of the continental shelf issue in favor of Greece and the undersea connection of the Greek mainland with thousands of islands scattered around the Aegean. This constitutes a considerable gain of shelf. While Greece defends the rule of territorial integrity, that the islands and the mainland form an unbreakable whole and cannot be separated from the mainland, Turkey insists that the continental shelf delimitation should be established by drawing an equidistant line between the Greek and Turkish continental land masses and that the Greek islands clustering along the Turkish coast cannot have their own continental shelfs.

Following the ratification of UNCLOS by the Greek parliament in June 1994, the Turkish parliament approved a resolution authorizing the government to use all necessary measures to protect the rights of Turkey should the need arise. The Turkish position stems from Article 300 of UNCLOS, according to which "parties shall fulfil in good faith the obligations assumed under this Convention and shall exercise the rights, jurisdiction and freedoms recognized in this Convention in a manner which would not constitute an abuse of right." The Aegean, according to Turkey, is a semi-enclosed sea and therefore requires the application of particular rules. Turkey insists that a Greek extension of its territorial waters to twelve miles will imply that even maritime transport between Turkish ports would require Greek permission. Turkey considers this to be an abuse of a right. Greece argues exactly the opposite, that is, the Aegean is not a semi-enclosed sea, and that the Turkish declaration of casus belli is against international norms. Greece believes that according to the UN Charter, Article 2, Paragraph 4, its territorial integrity is under threat.

We describe this conflict in terms of a non-cooperative two-person game *of asymmetric incomplete information in extensive form*. In such a game, at least one of the players does not know the other's preferences for every outcome. We take the Greek Government's point of view (see Figure 5.6).

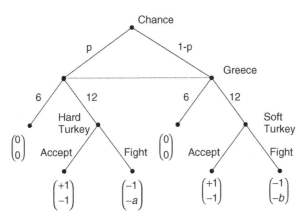

Figure 5.6   Graphical representation of the extensive form game with incomplete information describing the conflict between Greece and Turkey. −b < −1 < −a < 0.

Greece is uncertain as regards to the nature of Turkey: while it knows that in case of an extension of the territorial waters, Turkey will evaluate both alternatives, accepting it or going to war, it knows only with probability p that Turkey will prefer accepting to fighting, and with probability $1 - p$ the other way round.

Following Harsanyi (1967–68), we model this conflict as a *three-person game* with Greece, Hard Turkey and Soft Turkey as the three players. Before presenting its solution, let us consider the two games with *complete* information: in the first one, Greece against Hard Turkey; in the second one, Greece against Soft Turkey (see Figure 5.7).

A simple backward induction shows that in both games war is not an equilibrium strategy: in the first game, Greece backs down; in the second game, Turkey gives in.

Now let us turn to the original model. Both Turkeys will eliminate one of their alternatives, thus, we are led to the simplified game as given by Figure 5.8.

Greece, not knowing which Turkey it is confronted with, chooses limitation with probability x and extension with probability $1 - x$ obtaining the expected payoff $x(2p - 1)$. Since it wants to maximize its expected payoff, the following Nash equilibrium is obtained depending on the value of p: for $p > 0.5$, no extension, and for $p < 0.5$, extension ($p = 0.5$ may be ignored since the value of p can be estimated only very roughly anyhow.) As a result, Greece will extend its territorial waters if it considers Turkey to be soft, and vice versa.

The important lesson here is the following: whereas in case of complete information about

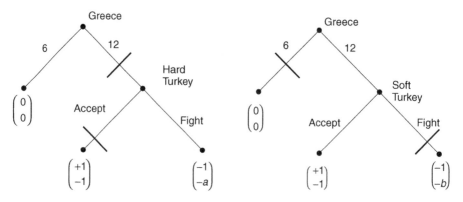

Figure 5.7   Graphical representation of the extensive form games with complete information describing the conflict between Greece and Turkey. Crossed branches are deleted.

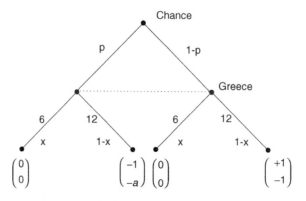

Figure 5.8   Reduced form of the game given in Figure 5.6.

Turkey either being hard or soft, there will be no war, now with probability p (<0.5) there will be war, since Greece assumes Turkey is soft, whereas in fact it is hard. Thus, we get the insight that incomplete information may lead to a result nobody wants, since in that case the payoffs to both actors are worse than those of the status quo.

It should be noted in passing that $p = 0.5$ is the turning point since we assumed −1 to be the payoff against both Turkeys in case of war. The worse Greece's payoff is in case of war against Hard Turkey, compared to that against Soft Turkey, the closer the turning point of p gets to one which means that Greece will extend its territorial waters only if it is very confident that Turkey is soft.

As mentioned, Güner has developed a more complicated model. For example, he took into account in case of war the two alternatives of Greece or Turkey winning the war. He claims that the model can be used as a tool for politicians and diplomats, who are encouraged to make their own estimates of probabilities and payoffs, finding out what the possible consequences of their assumptions are. In this sense, the model may be considered to be of the normative type.

There are not so many applications of games with incomplete information in the area of the resolution of international conflicts. Most of them deal with nuclear conflicts (e.g. Powell, 1997) and deterrence in general (Zagare and Kilgour, 2002).

Fifth case: reorganization of the United Nations Security Council

In the resolution 47/62 of the General Assembly (GA) of the United Nations (UN), entitled question of equitable representation on and increase in the membership of the Security Council (SC) and adopted on 11 December 1996, the member states were invited to submit comments on a possible review of the membership of the Security Council. On the basis of these comments, the ensuing discussion should lead to a reform of the SC with a high consensus of acceptance.

Why is there need for such a reform? The UN was founded in 1945 by the 51 victorious states of the Second World War. The SC consisted of eleven members, five of which were permanent and six of which were elected by the GA. The privilege to have permanent membership including the veto right was reserved for the main victorious powers of the war. The ratio of the number of member states in the SC to the number of member states in the GA was $R = 22\%$.

By 1963, the number of member states had increased to 113. At the same time, their representation in the SC was cut in half to $R = 10\%$. This led to an increase in the number of temporary members in the SC to 10 so that the total number of SC members was then fifteen and the above mentioned ratio was $R = 13\%$. In 1997, the UN had 184 and the ratio has decreased to $R = 13\%$. A large majority of UN member states was in favor of a renewed increase of the SC to guarantee adequate representation. A number of member states suggested further reforms of the UN structure, such as changes in the regional distribution of the SC seats or a weakening or even abolition of the veto right.

A mathematical tool to analyze a given voting system is the Power Index Analysis (PIA). It offers the possibility to calculate the power distribution in a voting system over its members which are the voters. It has to be said that with the PIA, only the formal voting power in the system can be determined. It is assumed that the voters are totally independent of each other. The economic, political, military, social and cultural factors which influence decision making are not taken into account. Nevertheless, power indices are meaningful objects which may serve as a guide for setting up norms or standards when designing or revising a legislative body such as the UNSC. The following analysis is taken from Kerby and Göbeler (1996).

A mathematical abstraction of a voting system is determined by the number of voters and a rule which gives the conditions that must be satisfied for a decision to be passed. For example, in the present SC where all important issues confronting the UN are decided, the voting rule for non-procedural issues says the decision is carried if a coalition of supportive voters forms such that the five permanent members and at least four other members belong to the coalition.

The power of an individual voter in such a voting system is measured in terms of the number of times the voter casts the deciding vote. Suppose the voters cast their votes in some given order. Further, suppose the first voter in this order votes in favor of the decision, then the second voter and so on. A voter casts the deciding vote if the voting rule is not satisfied until he casts his vote. The number of such orderings in which a voter makes the decision in this way divided by the number of all possible orderings of the voters is defined to be the *power index or Shapley value* of this voter. This index was first introduced by Shapley (1953), who also gave it its axiomatic justification.

Here, we will not present the mathematical derivation nor the resulting formula for the power index, but apply it immediately to the SC. A non-permanent member casts the deciding vote in precisely those cases where the five permanent members and exactly three other non-permanent members line up in front of that member and cast their votes in favor of the decision. This leads to a power index of 0.00187 for a non-permanent member and, consequently, since the power indices of all members have to add up to one, to a power index of 0.196 for permanent ones. Thus, each permanent member of the SC has about 100 times more deciding power than a non-permanent member as measured by these indices.

Following the initially mentioned invitation by the UNGA, several proposals for new distributions of the voting power of states in the SC were made, such as by Costa Rica, United States and others. As Kerby and Göbeler showed, they changed only marginally the present voting power since they did not touch the veto right of the present permanent members, nor did they increase their number. They also showed, realistically

assuming that a complete abolition of the veto right was – and obviously still is – not possible, that a weakening of the veto right, would lead to a much better distribution: if, for example, two vetoes would be needed in order that some decision is not taken, then the voting power of the permanent SC members would be reduced by a factor of eight; if three vetoes would be needed, by a factor of 32 and so on.

Despite the urgent need and several attempts in recent years, the UNSC has not yet been reformed, and if it will be reformed, Power Index Analysis will not play a decisive role. It can, however, quickly show, as demonstrated by Kerby and Göbeler, if some new suggestion leads to a significantly better balance of voting power of states in the SC or not.

There are other measures for voting power, for example, the so-called Banzaf-Coleman index, which cannot, however, be justified game theoretically, therefore, we do not discuss this index here. Also, it should be mentioned that the Shapley value can be related to Nash's bargaining scheme (see Ordeshook, 1986), which means that we are on safe theoretical ground.

Power index analysis has been widely used to analyze the power distribution in parliaments and other legislative bodies, that is, for descriptive purposes. There are not so many cases like the one discussed above where it is – as mentioned at least in principle – used to discuss new schemes. Avenhaus (2002) has analyzed the power distribution in a future committee of the five littoral states of the Caspian Sea, if votes are distributed according to some geographically determined scale, such as smoothed lengths of coasts of the states.

FURTHER APPROACHES AND CHALLENGES

There are further game theoretic concepts which provide valuable insight into international conflicts and their resolution; some of them could eventually be used for normative purposes. A few of them are presented subsequently, together with applications if existing.

In all game theoretic concepts discussed so far, the payoffs to the players were scalar utilities, that is, they were characterized by one single quantity for each possible outcome. Since this is in most cases a gross simplification, games with *vector-valued payoffs* have been developed. Usually these games have many equilibria and therefore they are less suited for practical use, even though just because of that fact they may describe the conflict more realistically. There are not many applications. Wierzbicki (1990) has studied fishery conflicts this way. Avenhaus and Krieger (2007) analyzed the Rambouillet negotiations of the Kosovo conflict (2007), and Avenhaus and Huber (2007) recently studied the conflict about Iran's nuclear program with the help of vector-valued payoffs.

Sequential bargaining models like those by Stahl (1972) and Rubinstein (1981) look very attractive for the study of international conflicts since they take into account the dynamics of the problem (even though the solution does not). There are, however, to our best knowledge so far no applications in the area considered here.

Fair division procedures are another wide field of game theoretic research, and by definition they serve normative purposes (although in serious conflicts they will at best provide some guidelines for political action). Raiffa (1982) discusses in detail the application of such a procedure to the Panama conflict in 1974, and Massoud (2000) has applied the so-called Adjusted Winner procedure to the conflict between Israelis and Palestinians.

Finally, there is the very large area of cooperative game theory dealing with *coalitions* which, however, is mathematically demanding. This may be the reason why there are so many fewer applications than one would expect. For the purpose of illustration, the very elaborate work of Okada (2003) on CO_2 emission trading in the framework of the Kyoto Protocol is mentioned.

In the future, what are the challenges of the game theoretical approach to international conflict resolution that need to be met? Some of them, which are of a more technical nature, have already been mentioned above. Quite generally, as also demonstrated by our case studies, only relatively simple models have been used or developed in the field considered here. In other areas, like economics or, very specially, the verification of treaties and agreements, the art of using sophisticated game theoretic models is more advanced, and one might learn from this experience.

The simple models generally used in political science, together with the dearth of introductory textbooks on game theory dealing seriously with real-world applications, have led to a considerable degree of misperception (see, for example, *International Security*, 1999). This misperception is perhaps best characterized by the question: "what can all of these graphs and equations tell us that can't be expressed just as well in simple language?" We hope that the case studies presented here help to answer this question and make it clear that it is simply not possible to understand or appreciate such a paradoxical situation as the prisoners' dilemma without resorting to the formalism of noncooperative game theory. Nor can one understand the consequences of incomplete or imperfect information in conflict situations without this formalism. It will certainly remain a challenge to convey this message to the political science community as a whole.

More importantly, however, is another challenge which Raiffa formulated in 1991 for the Processes of International Negotiations (PIN) Program of the International Institute for Applied Systems Analysis (IIASA).

Regrettably, a lot of profound theorizing by economists, mathematicians, philosophers, and game theorists on topics related to negotiation analysis has had little or no impact on practice. An important question for the PIN Project to answer will be why this is so. An important reason is clearly the lack of effective communication and dissemination of theoretical research results. Such communication could be improved if there were more intermediaries who are comfortable in both worlds and who could act as inventive go-betweens to facilitate the transfer of information that shows how theory can influence practice and how practice can influence the research agendas of theorists. The information must flow in both directions; many practitioners have developed valid, extremely useful, and often profound insights and analyses, which should help to guide the agendas of researchers in this field.

We think that Raiffa's 1991 diagnosis and proposed therapy, applied to the more general field of resolving international conflicts, holds true today.

REFERENCES

Aumann, Robert J. and Sergiu Hart (Eds) (2002) *Handbook of Game Theory*, Volumes I, II, III. North Holland Publishers, Amsterdam,.

Avenhaus, Rudolf, Negotiation Power in the Caspian Sea Council (2002). *PINPoints* 197, The International Institute for Applied Systems Analysis (IIASA).

Avenhaus, Rudolf and Thomas Krieger (2007) Formal Methods for Forecasting Outcomes of Negotiations on Interstate Conflicts. In: *Diplomacy Games – Formal Models and International Negotiations*, by Rudolf Avenhaus and I. William Zartman (Eds). Springer Publisher, Berlin.

Avenhaus, Rudolf, and Reiner K. Huber (2007) A Game Theoretical Analysis of the Conflict about Iran's Nuclear Program. *PINPoints* 28, 13–15. The International Institute for Applied Systems Analysis (IIASA).

Beetz, Jürgen, Spieltheoretische Analyse von Rüstungswettläufen (2005) PhD Dissertation, University of the Armed Forces, Munich, Germany.

Brams, Steven J. (1985) *Superpower Games – Applying Game Theory to Superpower Conflict* . Yale University Press, New Haven and London.

Brams, Steven J. (1990) *Negotiation Games – Applying Game Theory to Bargaining and Arbitration*. Routledge, New York and London.

Brams, Steven and D. Marc Kilgour (1988) *Game Theory and National Security*. Basil Blackwell, New York.

Bueno de Mesquita, Bruce (2002) *Predicting Politics*. The Ohio State University Press, Columbus, Ohio.

Canty, Morton J. (2003) *Resolving Conflicts with Mathematica – Algorithms for Two-Person Games*. Academic Press, Amsterdam.

Fudenberg, Drew, and Jean Tirole (1998) *Game Theory*. The MIT Press, Cambridge, MA.

Güner, Serdar (2007) Greek–Turkish Territorial Waters Game. In *Diplomacy Games – Formal Models and International Negotiations*, by Rudolf Avenhaus and I. William Zartman (Eds). Springer Publisher, Berlin.

Harsanyi, John C. (1967–68) Games with Incomplete Information Played by Baesian Players. *Management Science* 14, (Series A), 159–182, 320–334, 486–502.

Hopmann, P. Terrence (1996) *The Negotiation Process and the Resolution of Internal Conflicts*. University of South Carolina Press, Columbia, SC.

International Security (1999), Vol. 23.

Kerby, William and Frank Göbeler (1996) The Distribution of Voting Power in the UN. A Power Index Analysis of some Proposals for a Reform of the UN Security Council. *Nova J. Math. Game Theory Algebra* 6 (1), 55–63.

Luce, Duncan R. and Howard Raiffa (1957) *Games and Decisions – Introduction and Critical Survey*. John Wiley and Sons, New York.

Massoud, Tansa George (2000) Fair Division, Adjusted Winner Procedure (AW) and the Israeli–Palestinian Conflict. *Journal of Conflict Resolution* 44, 333–358.

Morrow, James D. (1989) Capabilities, Uncertainty, and Resolve: A Limited Information Model of Crisis Bargaining. *American Journal of Political Science* 33, 941–972.

Morrow, James D. (1994) *Game Theory for Political Scientists*. Princeton University Press, Princeton, NJ.

Myerson, Roger B. (1991) *Game Theory – Analysis of Conflict*. Harvard University Press, Cambridge, Ma.

Nash, John F. (1950) The Bargaining Problem. *Econometrica* 18, 155–162.

Nash, John F. (1953) Two-Person Cooperative Games. *Econometrica* 21, 128–140.

Okada, Akira (2003) A Market Game Analysis of International CO_2 Emission Trading. Evaluating Initial Allocation Rules. In: *International Frameworks and Technological Strategies to Prevent Climate Change*, by Takamitsu Sawa (Ed.). Springer Publisher, Tokyo.

Okada, Akira (2007) International Negotiations on Climate Change: A Noncooperative Game Analysis of the Kyoto Protocol. In: *Diplomacy Games – Formal Models and International Negotiation*, by Rudolf Avenhaus and I.William Zartman (Eds). Springer Publisher, Berlin.

O'Neill, Barry (1994) Game Theory Models on Peace and War. In: *Handbook of Game Theory*, by Robert J. Aumann and Sergiu Hart (Eds), Vol. 2, North Holland Publishers, Amsterdam.

Ordeshook, Peter C. (1986) *Game Theory and Political Theory – An Introduction*. Cambridge University Press, Cambridge, Ma.

Powell, Robert (1997) Nuclear Brinkmanship with Two-sided Incomplete Information. *American Political Science Review* 82, 155–178.

Raiffa, Howard (1982) *The Art and Science of Negotiation.* Harvard University Press, Cambridge, MA.

Raiffa, Howard (1991) Contributions of Applied Systems Analysis to International Negtiation. In: *International Negotiation – Analysis, Approaches, Issues*, by Victor Kremenyuk (Ed.). Jossey Bass, San Francisco, CA.

Rapoport, Anatol (Ed.) (1974) *Game Theory as a Theory of Conflict Resolution.* D. Reidel Publishing Company, Dordrecht, Holland.

Richards, Alan and Nirvikar Singh (1997) Two Level Negotiations in Bargaining over Water. In: *Game Theoretical Applications to Economics and Operations Research*, by Thandavarayan Parthasarathy, Bhaskar Dutta, J.A.M. Potters, T.E.S. Raghavan, Debray Ray and Amartya Sen (Eds). Kluwer Academic Publishers, Boston, MA.

Rubinstein, Ariel (1981) Perfect Equilibrium in a Bargaining Model. *Econometrica* 50, 97–110.

Rudnianski, Michel and Helene Bestougeff (2007) Bridging Games and Diplomacy. In: *Diplomacy Games – Formal Models and International Negotiations*, by Rudolf Avenhaus and I. William Zartman (Eds). Springer Publisher, Berlin.

Schelling, Thomas (1960/1979) *The Strategy of Conflict.* Harvard University Press, Cambridge, MA.

Shapley, Lloyd S. (1953) A Value for N-Person Games. *Annals of Mathematics Study* 28, 307–317.

Snidal, Duncan (2005) Rational Choice and International Relations. In: *Handbook of International Relations*, by Walter Carlsnaes, Thomas Risse and Beth A. Simmons (Eds). Sage, London.

Snyder, Glenn H. and Paul Diesing (1977) *Conflict among Nations – Bargaining, Decision Making and System Structure in International Crises.* Princeton University Press, Princeton, NJ.

Stahl, Ingo (1972) *Bargaining Theory.* Economic Research Institute, Stockholm, Sweden.

Wagner, Robert H. (1989) Uncertainty, Rational Learning, and Bargaining in the Cuban Missile Crisis. In: *Models of Strategic Choice in Politics*, by Peter C. Ordeshook (Ed.). The University of Michigan Press, Ann Arbor, MI.

Wierzbicki, Andrej, P. (1990) Multiple Criteria Solutions in Noncooperative Game Theory. Part ii: An example of fishery game. Discussion paper No. 285, Kyoto Institute of Economic Research, Kyoto University, Japan.

Zagare, Frank C. and D. Marc Kilgour (2002) *Perfect Deterrence.* Cambridge University Press, Cambridge, UK.

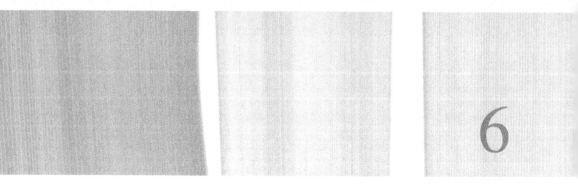

Experimental Research on Social Conflict

Dean G. Pruitt

Experiments are a quantitative method for examining the relationships between one or more independent (antecedent) variables and one or more dependent (consequent) variables. They differ from correlational studies in that the researcher manipulates at least one of the independent variables rather than measuring all of the variables. Most experiments are designed to develop and test theoretical propositions, but applied experiments are also sometimes performed with the aim of evaluating a proposed government policy or a new agency strategy in a realistic or simulated setting.

There are many advantages of doing experiments on social conflict, and the method has often been used in the study of social dilemmas, negotiation, and some kinds of third party interventions. However, students of other conflict phenomena have usually not adopted this method. That is partly because of a lack of training (McDermott, 2006), partly because there are no ready experimental paradigms that fit their theoretical problems, and partly because of a questionable belief that experiments – especially if done in the laboratory – lack external validity. Hence, experiments are a promising but underutilized method.

The chapter will begin with a description of two experiments that manipulated the independent variable in different ways. It will then turn to the advantages and disadvantages of doing experiments as opposed to correlational studies and of doing experiments in the laboratory rather than the field. External validity and the narrowness of current experimental paradigms will next be discussed. The final section will review some experimental findings on social conflict.

EXAMPLES OF EXPERIMENTS

'Manipulation' means actively varying the states of a variable. There are two methods of manipulation: (a) assigning different states of the variable to different participants and (b) assigning different states to the same participant at different times.

Assignment to different participants is illustrated by an experiment that was designed to test the hypothesis that emotions that compete with anger will inhibit aggression by people who have been provoked (Baron, 1976). The study took place at a busy intersection. Periodically, a car driven by a male confederate (assistant of the experimenter) drove up to the intersection just as the traffic light was turning red and remained stopped for a period of time after the light turned green. If a car driven by a male driver pulled up behind the stopped car, the driver of that car (the participant) was unknowingly assigned at random to one of the four conditions (states of the independent variable) shown in the columns of Table 6.1.

There were three competing-emotion conditions. In the *empathy* condition, an attractive female confederate on crutches crossed the street in front of the participant's car. In the *amusement* condition, the same confederate was dressed as a clown. In the *mild sexual arousal* condition, she wore skimpy clothes. To determine how these conditions affected aggression, they were compared with a fourth *control* condition in which no competing emotion was aroused. The female confederate crossed the street in ordinary conservative clothing.

In experiments, the dependent variable(s) are free to vary and are measured to see how they are affected by the independent variable(s). In the experiment just described, aggression was assumed to have occurred if the participant honked his horn. Two measures of aggression were employed: (a) A qualitative measure: whether the horn was honked or not. The first row in Table 6.1 shows the proportion of participants who honked their horns in each of the four conditions; (b) A quantitative measure: the latency of honking (the time elapsed between the light turning green and the honk if it occurred). A slower

honk was assumed to be less aggressive. The second row shows the mean (average) latency in the four conditions.

Comparison of the proportions in the first row shows that there were fewer aggressive participants in the competing-emotion conditions than in the control condition, supporting the hypothesis. Comparison of the means in the second row shows that honking came later in the competing-emotion conditions, again supporting the hypothesis. Both results were statistically significant, which means that the probability of their occurring by chance was less than .05.[1]

This study, like most experiments, involved replication, that is, the assignment of several participants to each condition. Replication is necessary because participants differ from one another in their circumstances and personal qualities, causing variation in the dependent variable(s) over and above that produced by the manipulation of the independent variable(s). Because of replication, we look at proportions and means rather than the scores of individual participants.

The other type of manipulation, assigning the states of a variable to the same participant at different times, is illustrated by a national opinion survey study in which participants were asked two questions: 'how long their friendship would be disrupted if a friend of theirs got into a fist fight with them' and how long it would be disrupted if their friend 'called them a liar and a coward' (Nisbett and Cohen, 1996: 31). Southern white Americans reported that the insult (the liar-coward statement) would disrupt their friendship for a considerably longer time than a fist fight; but Midwestern white Americans did not differ in their answers to the two questions. The authors interpreted these findings, in conjunction with results of other

Table 6.1 Aggression as a function of emotions that compete with anger.

| | Experimental Condition | | | |
	Empathy	Amusement	Mild Sexual Arousal	Control
Proportion of drivers honking	0.57	0.50	0.47	0.89
Latency of honking (in seconds)	10.73	11.94	12.16	7.99

Source: Adapted from Baron (1976)

studies, as evidence that there is a culture of honor in the South in which insults elicit an unusually high level of aggression.

The reader may have noted that there were two independent variables in the latter experiment: the fist-fight versus insult variable, which was manipulated, and the Southern versus Midwestern variable which was measured by asking respondents where they lived. The dependent variable was the degree of reported disruption in the friendship. Experiments in which there are two or more independent variables are said to employ *factorial designs*. This one employed a 2×2 factorial design, with two types of annoyance from the friend and two regions of the country. Larger factorial designs are also found – for instance, 2×3, 3×4, and $2 \times 2 \times 2$.

Factorial designs allow us to study how independent variables interact in their effect on dependent variables. Two independent variables interact if one of these variables has a different effect depending on the level of the other variable. For example, in the study just described, the impact of the insult variable on the disruption in the relationship was greater for the Southerners than for the Northerners.

ADVANTAGES AND DISADVANTAGES OF EXPERIMENTATION

As mentioned earlier, the alternative to doing an experiment is to do a correlational (also called observational) study, in which all the variables are measured. For example, consider the hypothesis tested in the horn-honking experiment described above, that emotions competing with anger will inhibit aggression by people who have been provoked. How might it have been tested in a correlational study? The researcher (Robert Baron) might have asked participants to remember the most recent incident in which they were frustrated or provoked by another person. To measure the independent variable, he might have asked them about additional experiences they were having at the same time and classified these experiences into those that would produce competing emotions and those

that would not. To measure the dependent variable, he might have asked them how they reacted to the provocation and graded the aggressiveness of that reaction on a scale from 1 to 7. The hypothesis would have been supported if aggressiveness had been lower when competing emotions were present than when they were absent.

There are both advantages and disadvantages of doing experiments rather than correlational studies. This means that both kinds of study have their place in research on social conflict, depending on the circumstances and the goals of the research.

Advantages of experimentation

There are at least five advantages of doing experiments. Some are so compelling that serious consideration should be given to using this method in most research.

Creating novel conditions

One advantage is that experiments allow the study of conditions that do not ordinarily occur. For example, in the hypothetical correlational study just described, it might be hard to find people who were experiencing competing emotions at the time they were frustrated or provoked. But Baron easily produced such emotions in his experiment. Similarly, experiments are necessary to test the effectiveness of conflict resolution techniques that are not yet in use. Thus, Conlon, et al. (2002) evaluated arb-med, a novel kind of third-party procedure in which an arbitrator makes a sealed decision about a controversy, which then goes into mediation. If the mediation fails, the arbitrator's decision is opened and becomes binding on the disputants. In an experiment involving a simulated merger negotiation between two companies, this procedure was compared with med-arb, a common procedure in which arbitration occurs only if mediation fails. Arb-med turned out to be superior, with more disputants settling in the mediation phase and settlements involving larger joint benefit.

Establishing cause and effect

The second advantage is that experiments make it easier to distinguish cause and effect among the variables in the study. For example, in the hypothetical correlational study just described, there could have been ambiguity about the causal direction between the two variables that were measured. A result supporting the hypothesis could have been due to the *impact of competing emotions on aggression*. But it also could have been due to the *impact of aggression on memories about competing emotions*. In other words, heavy anger and aggression might have caused participants to lose sight of other concurrent experiences, including competing emotions. Ambiguity about causal direction was not a problem in the horn-honking experiment, because the presence or absence of competing emotions was produced by the researcher and hence could not have been influenced by the participants' levels of aggression.

The following is a broader statement of the advantage of experiments over correlational studies for assessing cause and effect: when a study of any kind shows a relationship (covariation) between two variables, X and Y, there are four possible explanations: (1) X (or an associated variable) influences (has a causal impact on) Y; (2) Y influences X; (3) some third common factor, Z, influences both X and Y, producing a 'spurious' relationship between them; (4) the relationship between X and Y is due to chance. Statistical tests of significance allow us to rule out explanation 4 at an acceptable level of confidence. Beyond that, it is a matter of reasoning, weighing the *plausibility* of each of the other three explanations. If the study is an experiment and X is a manipulated variable, we can rule out explanations 2 and 3, by arguing that the investigator is the source of variation in X and hence neither Y nor Z can have influenced X. This reasoning leaves explanation 1 as the only plausible account – that the relationship was produced by X (or an associated variable) having a causal impact on Y.

In correlational studies, it is sometimes possible to explore cause and effect by means of path analysis or causal modeling, but these methods seldom allow watertight conclusions. Only experiments definitively sort out cause and effect.

Reducing confounding

Another important advantage of experiments is that they allow purification of independent variables by reducing the amount of confounding. When we manipulate or measure a variable, X, we are always inadvertently manipulating or measuring a number of other 'confounded' variables (A, B, C, D, E, etc.) that covary with X. If an X–Y relationship is shown in our data, it could be due to a causal relationship between one of these confounded variables and Y rather than between X and Y. Variables such as X can be manipulated with much more precision than they can be measured. Hence, the number of confounded variables is greatly reduced in most experiments, and it is easier to pinpoint the precise source of any changes that are found in the dependent variable(s).

This purification can be seen in the horn-honking study. The researcher held constant across the four conditions many variables that might otherwise have been confounded with the intended variable. Thus, the procedure was exactly the same and the same intersection and confederates were used in all four conditions. Furthermore, he randomly assigned participants to conditions, making it unlikely that the conditions would differ in the type of participant assigned to them. Confounds of this kind are much greater in correlational studies, where circumstances and participant characteristics often differ substantially across conditions.

Experiments are never completely successful in eliminating confounds. For example, in the amusement condition of the horn-honking study, though participants did laugh at the clown garb, it is possible that other psychological states produced the low level of aggression. Examples are surprise, disbelief, and psychological distancing, all plausible confounds of amusement. The solution to this residual problem of confounding is to do further experiments in which the variable(s) in question are manipulated in other ways that involve different confounds (Carnevale and De Dreu, 2005; McDermott, 2006).

Controlling for random variation

Another great advantage of experimentation is that it is possible to treat all participants in a given condition exactly the same way. This reduces random variation – differences between participants in the way they behave in a given condition – increasing the chances of reaching statistical significance if one is testing a valid hypothesis. Random variation is typically much greater in correlational studies, which means that a much larger number of participants must be used to reach statistical significance.

Assessing process

In experiments, as opposed to correlational studies, researchers are usually closer to the process that generated the relationship between the independent and dependent variables. This means that it is usually easier for them to map out that process.

Attention to process is illustrated by a laboratory experiment performed by Cohen et al. (1996) to test another version of the culture-of-honor hypothesis, that Southern men who are insulted will exhibit more dominance than men from other parts of the country. Participants were white college students from the South and the North. The events in the experiment occurred in the following order: first, the participant was asked to fill out a questionnaire and take it to a table at the end of a long, narrow hall. As he went down the hall, he had to brush by a male confederate who was working at a filing cabinet. In the *insult* condition, the confederate slammed in the filing drawer, bumped the participant, and called him an 'asshole'. In the *control* condition, the confederate did nothing.

Two measures of dominance were then taken for all participants. First, as the participant continued back down the hall, another confederate, a 250-pound male, came around a corner and walked rapidly toward the participant in what amounted to a game of chicken. Dominance was measured by how close the participant came to the confederate before swerving. Then the participant shook hands with a third male confederate who had seen him being bumped and was supposed to evaluate him. The second measure of dominance was the firmness of this handshake. As hypothesized, Southerners who had been insulted swerved later in the game of chicken and shook hands more firmly than in the control condition, but the insult did not affect how the Northerners behaved.

Three process measures were used in this and a comparable experiment. At the end of the experiment, participants were asked to guess what the third confederate thought of them on various dimensions. The insult caused Southerners to report that they looked weak and cowardly, but it did not have the same effect on Northerners. This suggests that the insult may have caused the Southerners to feel that their masculine reputation had been damaged and, hence, that dominance was necessary to repair this damage. In addition, saliva samples were gathered from the participants at the beginning and end of the experiment. Chemical assays showed sharply increased levels of cortisol and testosterone in the insulted Southerners but not in the control Southerners or the two groups of Northerners. The cortisol results mean that the insulted Southerners were experiencing an unusual level of stress, and the testosterone results mean that their hormones were preparing them for dominance or aggressive behavior. These three process findings give us insight into the psychological and physiological mechanisms linking the independent and dependent variables.

Advantages of correlational studies

Some variables are very difficult or impossible to manipulate and hence must be examined by means of correlational studies, for example, the behavior of the heavenly bodies or of nation states. If we want to do experiments on these phenomena, we are forced to employ simulations, which are always simplifications of the real thing (see next). It is also not possible to manipulate participant character-istics, such as sex, age, and race. In addition, there are ethical objections to manipulating some variables. Even if we were able to create serious marital quarrels to see how they affect the offspring, we should not try to do so. To stay within ethical boundaries, we must measure such variables.

Correlational designs must also be used when one wants to look at the interrelations among a large number of variables, since only a few variables can be manipulated in an experiment. A case in point is a survey study done in several Crimean towns and villages by Korostelina (2005). This involved one depen-dent variable – readiness for conflict on behalf of one's ethnic group – and *six* measured independent variables: ethnicity (Crimean Tatar vs. Russian), salience of ethnic identity, salience of national (Ukranian) identity, belief that the national identity should be Ukranian, belief in a multicultural national identity, and belief that national identity consists of civic obligations. The investigator found that salient ethnic identity predicted high readiness for conflict and salient national identity predicted low readiness for conflict. There were also some complex interactions among her independent variables; for example, she found that, 'possession of a salient national identity and of the ethnic concept of national identity strengthens the influence of salient ethnic identity on conflict readiness among Russians and weakens it among Crimean Tatars' (p. 103).

In theory, Korostelina could have manip-ulated her five psychological variables (the salience and belief variables) in a clever experiment.[2] But in practice, this would have been difficult, as it would have required run-ning participants in at least 32 experimental conditions (a $2 \times 2 \times 2 \times 2 \times 2$ factorial design).[3]

A third advantage of correlational designs is that they allow us to examine the impact of one independent variable on another, a result that is not possible if these variables are manipulated. For example, Korostelina found that ethnic identity was stronger in Crimean Tatars than that in Russians.

A fourth advantage of correlational studies is that they can be used to evaluate the strength of the relationship between an independent and a dependent variable (Carnevale and De Dreu, 2005). This is not possible when the independent variable is manipulated, because good experimental design requires augmenting the strength and potency of the manipulated variables and reducing variation in the measured variables. This allows us to reach statistical significance if our variables are related to each other, but unnaturally magnifies the strength of that relationship. Experiments are for finding out *whether* variables are related to each other, not for determining the *extent* of that relationship.

LABORATORY VS. FIELD EXPERIMENTS

Laboratory experiments take place in artificial settings constructed by the investigator, while field experiments (see Pruitt, 2005a) take place in naturally occurring settings. Cohen's study of insult and dominance behavior is an example of a laboratory experiment, while Baron's horn-honking study is an example of a field experiment. Both studies involved elaborate hoaxes, in which the participant had no idea he was in an experiment at the point where the critical variable was being manipulated. (In the Baron study, he had no idea he was in an experiment at all.) There are other types of laboratory and field experiments.

Other types of laboratory experiments

Some laboratory experiments involve sim-ulations, in which the participant is asked to play a role that exists in real life. For example, the author and one of his students (Ben Yoav and Pruitt, 1984) performed a study in which male undergraduates were asked to play the roles of buyer and seller in a wholesale market, setting the prices of three appliances. Each party knew the profit to his firm associated with each of the possible prices, and some combinations of prices were worth far more than others to the two parties collectively. Two variables were manipulated in a 2 x 2 factorial design: (a) accountability to the owner of one's company, a role played by another participant. At the end of the experiment, under high accountability, the owner would write an evaluation of the negotiator and decide how to divide a sum of money between himself and the negotiator. Under low accountability, neither of these events would take place; (b) expectation of cooperative future interaction (ECFI) with the opposing negotiator. Participants were told there would be a second study after this one was finished. In the high ECFI condition, they were told that the two negotiators were going to work together on a common goal. In the low ECFI condition, they were told that they would work individually.

The main dependent variable was joint benefit – the amount of money made by the two parties collectively. Joint benefit was considerably higher in the high accountability-high ECFI condition than in the other conditions. This may have been because the participants in that condition were under the cross-pressures of trying to serve the interests of the owner and maintaining the good will of the other negotiator. If so, it should be possible to generalize this result to other situations where negotiators are under such cross-pressures.

The experiment just described involved *active* simulation, in which participants were required to take actions in response to conditions they were facing. Much more elaborate active simulations are sometimes used, involving many more features of a real situation, for example, simulations of international situations (Wilkenfeld, 2005). Other researchers use *passive* simulation, where participants fill out a questionnaire as if they were in a particular role. For example, Rothbart and Hallmark (1988) had participants read about a conflict between two hypothetical countries, their own and a rival. They then rated a series of tactics as to how effective they would be if used against the rival and against their own country.

Most participants thought that coercive tactics would be most effective when used against the rival and conciliatory tactics would be most effective when used against their own country.

Whether elaborate or uncomplicated, simulations always simplify reality by eliminating many features of the settings they are trying to portray. Even more simplified are the *experimental games* used by some experimenters, in which participants are given a set of choices and a list of outcomes that depend on the decisions they and the other participant(s) make. The outcomes are usually monetary and, in research by experimental economists, may be quite sizable (Croson, 2005), so as to focus the participants' attention on the incentives and away from 'extraneous' issues.

Some of the most interesting experimental games involve resource dilemmas where individuals in a group must make decisions that affect their own and the group's welfare. The dilemma inheres in the fact that decisions that help oneself tend to hurt the group as a whole, which means that one's own welfare may eventually be hurt. One variety of resource dilemma is the *commons* dilemma in which the group members withdraw resources from a common pool, which is slowly replenished. If people take too much, the pool disappears and everyone is hurt. In a study of this kind, where the resources withdrawn from a computer-administered pool were converted into money, Allison and Messick (1985) found that larger groups withdrew resources at a faster rate than smaller groups and ended up with less money. Another variety of social dilemma is the *public goods* dilemma, where individuals must decide how much to contribute to a common pool of resources that benefits all of them. In these situations, there is a temptation to become a 'free rider' and retain one's own resources while letting others contribute to the common pool. But if enough people do so, the pool disappears, hurting everyone. Again, members of larger groups contribute less than members of smaller groups, resulting in smaller long-run benefits (Yamagishi, 1992).

Other types of field experiments

Examples have already been given of two types of field experiments: elaborate hoaxes in natural settings (like the horn-honking study) and parallel questions in surveys (like the study of how long a friendship would be disrupted by an insult). A third type involves trying out a new government policy in a pilot project or a new kind of treatment in a clinic or mediation agency.

An example of the latter kind of experiment was performed by the author and his students at a community mediation center (McGillicuddy, et al. 1987). Our aim was to assess the impact of med-arb on the process of mediation. Cases that came from City Court were randomly assigned to two conditions: med-arb, in which the mediator became an arbitrator if agreement was not reached, and straight mediation, in which it was not clear what would happen if agreement was not reached. Two observers sat in the room during the mediation and content-analyzed what was said. The results showed that the disputants behaved more constructively under med-arb than under straight mediation, making fewer hostile comments and invidious comparisons and proposing more new alternatives for dealing with the issues.[4] Other data suggest a possible explanation for the impact of med-arb, that the disputants feared binding arbitration because they would lose control over part of their life; hence, they were especially keen on settling their dispute.

Advantages of doing laboratory experiments

Laboratory experiments are much more common than field experiments in research on social conflict. There are two main reasons for this: greater control and a wider range of available manipulations and measures (Aronson, et al. 1998).

Control

Laboratory settings usually allow more control over the elements of research than do field settings. This makes it easier to conduct good experiments, for example, to randomize assignment of participants to conditions. Randomization is easy to do in the laboratory but hard to do in public service agencies, because the agency usually insists on deciding who will go into what condition. In the med-arb study, we were lucky that the mediation center allowed us to randomize assignment to the three conditions. But at the end of the study, the director of this center told us that she would never again allow a randomization study because it was too disruptive for her staff.

Greater control also makes it possible to create more precise manipulations in the laboratory, holding more variables constant between conditions and thus reducing the number of confounds and alternative interpretations of the results. Holding variables constant also reduces random error, making it easier to reach statistical significance.

Range of manipulations and measures

Another reason for doing laboratory experiments is that they allow a wider range of manipulations and measures than do field experiments. Investigators are king in the laboratory and, within ethical limits, can do almost anything they want – create almost any condition and measure almost any effect.

There are many more constraints in field settings. Constraints are especially severe when field experimenters stage elaborate hoaxes in which they try to disguise the fact that participants are in a study so as to encourage normal behavior. This produces three kinds of constraints: (1) In order to avoid detection, investigators must impose conditions that would plausibly be encountered in everyday life. (2) Because they cannot solicit informed consent, they are limited to producing innocuous conditions that do not stress the participants. (3) They are limited to measurements that are available in natural settings. We saw the latter limitation in the horn-honking study, where horn honking was the only available measure of aggression. This measure is ambiguous, because horn honking can be a way to communicate with the driver of the next car as well as a form of aggression.

Experimenters who use social service agencies are also constrained because they must stick to conditions that can be justified as part of the agency's mission. For example, the conditions in our med-arb experiment (McGillicuddy, et al. 1987) were part of the mediation center's ordinary program. Most of the other procedures we might have studied would have bent their program too far out of shape. Another constraint was that we could not tape-record the mediation sessions for fear that the recordings could be subpoenaed by the court. This meant that we could not check the accuracy of our content analysis or go back with new measures after the fact.

Advantages of doing field experiments

If laboratory experiments provide more control and flexibility, why should anyone do a field experiment? One reason is that some conditions and variables can only be realistically produced in the field. Thus, one must move to the field in order to study whether arrest or counseling is more effective at stopping men from abusing their wives. Sherman and Berk (1984) did such an experiment and found only half as much recidivism over a six-month period (10% vs. 19%) in men who were sent to jail rather than counseled. Likewise, Emery and his colleagues (Emery, et al. 2001) could not have used laboratory methods to study whether mediation, as opposed to litigation, of divorce custody produced a different relationship between children and the nonresidential spouse.

It is also easier to study long-term effects in the field, because laboratory effects are usually too weak to persist very long. The Emery study is a good example. They found that, 'in comparison with families who litigated custody, nonresidential parents who mediated were more involved in multiple areas of their children's lives, maintained more contact with their children, and had a greater influence in co-parenting 12 years

after the resolution of their custody disputes' (Emery, et al. 2001: p. 323).

Motivational and emotional impact

Disputants usually experience stronger passions – such as frustration, anger, and the desire for revenge – in the field than in the laboratory, because they are dealing with issues that are more important to them (Barry, et al. 2004). This means that effects that are produced by such passions are likely to be strengthened as we move from the laboratory to the field, an advantage in research on conflict.

Our med-arb study (McGillicuddy, et al. 1987) is an example of an effect that was strengthened by moving into the field. Before doing the field experiment, we ran some participants in a laboratory negotiation task. A mediator, who could become an arbitrator in the med-arb condition but not in the straight mediation condition, helped them with the negotiation. This laboratory experiment yielded only weak trends in the direction later taken by the results of our field experiment. This is probably because the issues faced in the laboratory were less motivating and emotion-producing than those faced in the field. Hence, the participants in the med-arb condition were less anxious about losing control over the decision making and hence less motivated to reach agreement during mediation.

EXTERNAL VALIDITY

A common criticism of laboratory experiments is that it is hard to generalize their results to real-life settings – the so-called issue of 'external validity'. Laboratory settings seem so simplified and rarified that there are doubts about whether people behave the same way in practical settings. There is no simple answer to this criticism. Sometimes there is a good match between a laboratory setting and a practical setting and sometimes there is not. The critical issue is not whether the two settings *look alike* but whether the *same processes* intervene between the independent variable(s) and the dependent variable(s) and hence whether the laboratory has captured the conditions that allow these processes to go forward.

In defense of the laboratory, a number of generality studies have found similar results in the field as in the laboratory. For example, the two culture-of-honor studies discussed earlier produced nearly identical results (aggression and dominance are two sides of the same coin), and the same mechanism was probably at work in both settings – Southerners, compared to Northerners, had a stronger feeling of being 'put down' by an insult and hence a stronger need to take action to rescue their dignity.[5] Similarly, Anderson and Bushman (1997) showed that eight well-known laboratory findings about aggression were also supported in field settings.

Yet there are also cases where field results do not match those obtained in the laboratory. For example, our laboratory findings about the impact of med-arb were a pale copy of those obtained in the field. As mentioned earlier, this is probably because med-arb produced stronger emotions in the field than in the laboratory.

It is important to note that collecting data in the field is no panacea for the problem of external validity, because variables often relate to each other differently in different field settings. Consider, for example, Sherman and Berk's (1984) study of recidivism in wife abuse. Can the finding that a jail sentence is superior to counseling be generalized to other kinds of assault or to recidivism in juvenile delinquency? Again, the issue is whether similar mechanisms are at work in the research setting and the setting to which we wish to generalize, and hence whether the critical conditions are the same.

To be absolutely certain that one can generalize from a research setting (laboratory or field) to a practical setting, one needs to do generality studies in that precise practical setting. But this is often not feasible, and it is important to be able to make educated guesses on the basis of the research findings on hand. The best way to make educated guesses is to identify the critical mechanisms

and variables that produced our research findings and to reason clearly about whether they also obtain in the setting to which we wish to generalize. This means that we must generalize over the 'bridge of theory'[6] …and laboratory experiments are a good way to develop and test theory.

THE NARROWNESS OF CURRENT LABORATORY PARADIGMS

In my experience, the biggest problem with laboratory research on social conflict is not its lack of external validity but the *narrowness* of current laboratory paradigms – the limited set of manipulations, tasks, and measures now available for studying conflict. This narrowness leaves many questions unasked and fails to explore countless mechanisms that exist in real life. Most of these questions and mechanisms could be examined in the laboratory, but researchers seldom do so because they rely too much on techniques that were used in the past.

A case in point is the dominant tradition of laboratory research on negotiation (Gelfand and Brett, 2004; Neale and Bazerman, 1991; Thompson, 2006). This research has focused for about 50 years on direct interaction between negotiators who are trying to reach a singular agreement. Yet that is only one corner of the entire negotiation process. We know from writers who use case materials (for example, Druckman, 1986; Hampson, 1996; Pruitt, 2005b; Zartman and Berman, 1982) that negotiation is a much more complex affair. Complex circumstances determine whether parties are willing to go into negotiation. Pre-negotiation preparations – which may involve direct meetings between the parties or communication through chains of intermediaries – are often more extensive than the actual negotiation itself. Intermediaries often continue to be active during formal negotiation, along with secret side-bar talks between the parties, and such events may be at the heart of the action. When negotiations are between nations or other organizations, complex communication processes *within* each side precede the development of positions and concessions. Negotiated agreements often have a multi-level feature, starting with a broad statement of agreed principles and ending, sometimes years later, with a detailed plan for the implementation of these principles. The post-negotiation period, in which agreements can succeed or fail, is another critical phase of the negotiation process. Laboratory researchers have almost totally ignored these important issues because they are still grinding in the same methodological groove.

What this means is that the challenge for laboratory research on social conflict is to build new experimental paradigms that capture a broader set of processes than those currently under study.

EXPERIMENTAL FINDINGS

What do we learn from experimental research that is useful for understanding or coping with social conflict? There is no way to summarize the vast corpus of experimental findings in the brief space available here, so only a few highlights will be mentioned.

Social dilemmas

Social dilemmas are dyadic or group settings in which one is tempted to be non-cooperative at the expense of the other(s), but if the other(s) are also non-cooperative, one is worse off than if everyone cooperated (see Weber and Messick, 2004). In short, they are variants of the prisoners' dilemma. Resource dilemmas of the kind described earlier are one form of social dilemma. Arms races and other kinds of security dilemmas are another.

Experimental research reveals a number of ways to enhance the likelihood of cooperation in such situations. One approach is to encourage communication among the parties in the dilemma (Deutsch, 1973; Kerr and Kaufman-Gilliland, 1994). Communication fosters coordination, which is sometimes the main problem. A second approach is to encourage interdependence among the

parties, such that each party perceives that the other party(ies) can provide it considerable rewards in exchange for cooperation (Pruitt, 1967). A third approach is for one or more parties to employ a tit-for-tat strategy, in which they begin by cooperating and then match the other parties' cooperation or non-cooperation (Axelrod, 1984; Komorita and Esser, 1975). Tit-for-tat provides rewards for cooperation and punishment for non-cooperation. In larger groups, tit-for-tat only works if a number of parties enact it at the same time (Komorita, et al. 1992). A fourth approach is to encourage attraction (Yamagishi and Sato, 1986), perceived similarity (McNeel and Reid, 1975), or perceived common group identity (Brewer and Kramer, 1986) among the parties. These emotions and perceptions foster generosity and trust that others will reciprocate one's cooperative actions. A fifth approach is to break a large group into smaller parts since, as was mentioned earlier, there is more cooperation in smaller groups (Allison and Messick, 1985; Yamagishi, 1992).

When trust is low and the parties are locked into a vicious circle of non-cooperation, it is sometimes possible for one of them to break out of this circle and take a dramatic unilateral conciliatory initiative. An example of such an initiative is Egyptian President Anwar Sadat's flight to Jerusalem in 1977, which came soon after a war between Egypt and Israel and paved the way to peace between these countries. Laboratory studies have shown that this tactic is most successful when the actor announces a series of initiatives ahead of time (Lindskold and Aronoff, 1980) and carries them out as announced (Lindskold, et al. 1976). There is also evidence that unilateral initiatives are especially effective when the actor is of equal or greater strength than the target (Lindskold and Aronoff, 1980).

Negotiation

Negotiation is a genteel form of conflict that transforms issues into words. Words allow the development of solutions to complex problems, though there is no guarantee of success. Most of the experimental research on negotiation has looked at the two-party case.

Getting the other party to concede

Some of this research yields advice about how to get the other party to concede. The more the other concedes, the more likely it is that agreement will be reached and the larger will be one's outcomes. Setting high aspirations, making an ambitious initial offer, and conceding slowly at first tend to diminish the other's expectations and encourage the other to concede (Huber and Neale, 1986). These effects are especially large if one makes the very first offer, before the other has a chance to state his or her demands (Galinsky and Mussweiler, 2001). However, there is usually a limit to how far one can pull the other toward one's preferred solution, hence more substantial concessions may eventually be needed to ensure that agreement is reached (Esser and Komorita, 1975). This slow–fast pattern elicits more concessions from the other party than a fast–slow pattern, in which one concedes a lot at first and then slows down (Benton, et al. 1972). Indeed, substantial early concessions tend to give the other party false hopes that can lead to failure to reach agreement (Bartos, 1974).

Positional commitments, in which one indicates that one has reached the limit of concession making, are also useful in pulling the other party in one's direction (Chertkoff and Baird, 1971). But this is also a hazardous tactic because there is usually a limit to how far the other can concede. Hence, experienced negotiators tend to delay positional commitments until they have a good idea about the other party's limit (Kelley, 1966). Another approach to persuading the other to concede is to exhibit anger, which tends to make the other think that one cannot concede very far (van Kleef, et al. 2004).

Finding integrative agreements

In most negotiations, there is the possibility of reaching integrative agreements – of adopting creative options that yield good outcomes to both sides. But such agreements are often hard to find in comparison to simple compromises, in which both parties move toward each other on an obvious dimension. Hence, they require effortful problem solving. Integrative agreements provide a number of benefits in comparison to compromises: they are more popular with the parties, more likely to be complied with, and more beneficial to the relationship between the parties (Pruitt and Carnevale, 1993). In addition, when aspirations are high on both sides, they are the only way to reach agreement (Pruitt and Lewis, 1975).

How to increase the likelihood of integrative agreements? One way is for one or both sides to take a firm but concerned approach to the negotiation, adopting high aspirations for oneself but at the same time seeking an agreement that will satisfy the other party's needs (De Dreu, et al. 2000). Managers can foster such a negotiation style in their subordinates by holding them accountable for the outcome of the negotiation while encouraging them to develop a positive relationship with the other negotiator (Ben Yoav et al. 1984). Another approach is to seek information about the other party's priorities and the interests underlying his or her positions, and to provide such information about one's own priorities and interests (Thompson, 1991). Such information allows one or both parties to locate mutually beneficial options. A third approach is to seek post-settlement settlements – the parties continue negotiating after they have reached agreement, with the understanding that the original agreement holds if nothing better is found. This procedure often yields a more integrative agreement in the second round of negotiation than in the first (Bazerman, et al. 1987).

Features of the negotiation setting also affect the likelihood of finding integrative agreements. High time pressure tends to defeat integrative bargaining because it takes time and effort to find mutually beneficial options (Yukl, et al., 1976). Face-to-face negotiation tends to produce more problem solving than message-only negotiation (McGinn and Croson, 2004).

Third-party intervention

Third parties are often important in preventing and coping with conflict. For example, research on aggression reveals many ways in which third parties can reduce the likelihood that frustrated or insulted people will retaliate against those who annoyed them. The horn-honking experiment described earlier suggests that third parties can encourage emotions that compete with anger, for example, by amusing the frustrated individual (Baron, 1976). They can remove angry people from settings that would remind them of aggression (for example, a televised prize fight) (Berkowitz and LePage, 1967) and from aggressive individuals who would otherwise serve as models (Bandura, 1973). Other conditions that encourage frustrated people to aggress include unpleasantly hot or cold surroundings (Baron and Bell, 1975; Berkowitz, et al. 1981), autonomic arousal (for example, by exercise) (Zillmann, et al. 1972), and the necessity of a quick response (Yovetich and Rusbult, 1994). Third parties can attempt to remove such conditions. Another approach is to try to persuade people that the annoyance they experienced was unintentional or justified and hence that retaliation is inappropriate (Ferguson and Rule, 1983).

When conflicts are mild, third parties can help to reduce tensions by encouraging pleasant interaction between the disputants (Pruitt and Kim, 2004). If the disputants are groups and the contact is between individual group members, intergroup tensions will only be reduced if each individual sees the other as a typical member of the other's group (Wilder, 1984). These generalizations do not extend to severe conflicts, where interaction between the disputants tends to be worse than useless, often generating angry and insulting interchanges that intensify the conflict (Rubin, 1980; Sherif and Sherif, 1969).

Third parties can also help disputants to develop superordinate goals – common aims that require cooperation between the groups (Sherif and Sherif, 1969), such as defeating a common enemy. Having and working on such goals enhances unity between the parties in numerous ways (Pruitt and Kim, 2004). However, if superordinate goals are not achieved (for example, if the common enemy wins), unity is likely to disintegrate and the prior conflict will reassert itself (Worchel and Norvell, 1980).

Furthermore, third parties can attempt to diminish ingroup identity in members of groups that are in conflict. This can be done by enhancing identity with a larger entity that embraces both groups, for example, the nation to which both belong (Korostelina, 2005). Another way to diminish ingroup identity is to construct 'cross-cutting' groups that contain members of both of the conflicting parties (Vanbeselaere, 1991).

Mediation involves third-party efforts to help disputants reach their own agreements. There is a large literature on mediation and how to do it, but relatively little of this literature is based on experimental research (Herrman, 2006; Kressel, et al. 1989; Pruitt and Kim, 2004). We know from experimentation that mediator bias in favor of the other disputant reduces receptivity to mediation (Welton and Pruitt, 1987). However, disputants are less troubled by a mediator's closeness to the other side before the start of mediation than by a mediator's support of the other side's position during mediation (Wittmer, et al. 1991). As mentioned earlier, mediation tends to be more successful if the disputants understand that failure to reach agreement will lead to binding arbitration (Conlon, et al. 2002; McGillicuddy, et al. 1987).

Some experimental literature provides advice about mediator behavior. For example, mediators should try to put the disputants in a good mood, as this makes them more cooperative and more creative (Carnevale and Isen, 1986; Forgas, 1998). Mediators should also try to reframe the task and the issues. If disputants see their task as dealing with a 'partner' or 'arranging an exchange', they are more likely to reach a mutually favorable agreement than if they see it as dealing with a 'competitor' or arranging a 'business transaction' (Batson and Moran, 1999; Burnham, et al. 2000). Reframing the options under consideration as various forms of 'gain' rather than various forms of 'loss' also makes it easier for disputants to make concessions (Bazerman, et al. 1985). Another useful tactic is for the mediator to present as his or her own proposal a position that is acceptable to the other party but would be rejected if put forward by that party because of reactive devaluation (Ross and Stillinger, 1991).

Mediation need not always involve a human being. A number of computer programs have been developed to advise negotiators who are having trouble reaching agreement (Pruitt and Carnevale, 1993). One of these programs, the electronic mediator, asks the parties a number of questions about the dispute and then offers some advice. The developers of this program (Druckman, et al. 2004) have evaluated it in three experiments involving a simulated international negotiation. More agreements and more integrative agreements were reached when the program was accessed by the two sides jointly than when it was accessed by the two sides separately; and the latter condition produced more agreements than were reached in the absence of the program. Clearly, the electronic mediator was a success.

These are only a few of the many experimental findings on social conflict. For a fuller account, see Pruitt (1998).

NOTES

1 There was also a second control condition in which nobody crossed the street in front of the participant's car. The results for this condition closely resembled those for the control condition shown in Table 6.1.

2 Salience of political identity was manipulated in an experiment by Gaffié (2006), who found that identity as 'left' versus 'right' had a larger effect on attitude toward delinquents when it was made more salient by having the participant contrast these two orientations on a number of dimensions.

3 Difficult but not impossible. Appelbaum, et al. (2006) report an experiment on political attitudes in

which several independent variables were manipulated across survey participants.

4 There was also a med-arb(diff) condition, in which a different person conducted the mediation and the arbitration. This condition was intermediate between the other two conditions on these measures.

5 Note that the laboratory experiment did a better job of pinpointing this mechanism than did the field experiment. As mentioned earlier, this is often the case.

6 The phrase comes from Morton Deutsch (private communication).

REFERENCES

Allison, Scott T. and Messick, David M. (1985) 'Effects of experience on performance in a replenishable resource trap', *Journal of Personality and Social Psychology*, 49: 941–8.

Anderson, Craig A. and Bushman, Brad J. (1997) 'External validity of "trivial" experiments: The case of laboratory aggression', *Review of General Psychology*, 1: 19–41.

Applebaum, Lauren D., Lennon, Mary C. and Aber, J. Lawrence (2006) 'The influence of the belief in a just world on American attitudes toward anti-poverty policy', *Political Psychology*, 27: 387–402.

Aronson, Elliot, Wilson, Timothy D. and Brewer, Marilynn B. (1998) 'Experimentation in social psychology', In Daniel T. Gilbert, Susan T. Fiske and Gardner Lindzey (eds), *The Handbook of Social Psychology*, 4th ed. New York: McGraw-Hill. Vol. 1, pp. 99–142.

Axelrod, Robert (1984) *The Evolution of Cooperation*. New York: Basic Books.

Bandura, Albert (1973) *Aggression: A Social Learning Analysis*. Englewood Cliffs, NJ: Prentice-Hall.

Baron, Robert A. and Bell, Paul A. (1975) 'Aggression and heat: Mediating effects of prior provocation and exposure to an aggressive model', *Journal of Personality and Social Psychology*, 31: 825–32.

Baron, Robert A. (1976) 'The reduction of human aggression: A field study of the influence of incompatible reactions', *Journal of Applied Social Psychology*, 6: 260–74.

Barry, Bruce, Fulmer, Ingrid S. and Van Kleef, Gerben A. (2004) 'I laughed, I cried, I settled: The role of emotion in negotiation', In Michele J. Gelfand and Jeanne M. Brett (eds), *The Handbook of Negotiation and Culture*. Stanford, CA: Stanford University Press. pp. 258–279.

Bartos, Otomar J. (1974) *Process and Outcome in Negotiation*. New York: Columbia University Press.

Batson, C. Daniel and Moran, Tecia (1999) 'Empathy-induced altruism in a prisoner's dilemma', *European Journal of Social Psychology*, 29: 909–24.

Bazerman, Max H., Magliozzi, Thomas and Neale, Margaret A. (1985) 'Integrative bargaining in a competitive market', *Organizational Behavior and Human Decision Processes*, 35: 294–313.

Bazerman, Max H., Russ, Lee E. and Yakura, Elaine (1987) 'Post-settlement settlements in dyadic negotiations: The need for renegotiation in complex environments', *Negotiation Journal*, 3: 283–97.

Ben Yoav, Orly and Pruitt, Dean G. (1984) 'Accountability to constituents: A two-edged sword', *Organizational Behavior and Human Performance*, 34: 283–95.

Benton, Alan A., Kelley, Harold H. and Liebling, Barry (1972) 'Effects of extremity of offers and concession rate on the outcomes of bargaining', *Journal of Personality and Social Psychology*, 24: 73–83.

Berkowitz, Leonard and LePage, Anthony (1967) 'Weapons as aggression-eliciting stimuli', *Journal of Personality and Social Psychology*, 7: 202–7.

Berkowitz, Leonard, Cochran, Susan T. and Embree, Marlowe C. (1981) 'Physical pain and the goal of aversively stimulated aggression', *Journal of Personality and Social Psychology*, 40: 687–700.

Brewer, Marilynn B. and Kramer, Roderick M. (1986) 'Choice behavior in social dilemmas: Effects of social identity, group size, and decision framing', *Journal of Personality and Social Psychology*, 50: 543–9.

Burnham, Terence, McCabe, Kevin and Smith, Vernon L. (2000) 'Friend-or-foe intentionality priming in an extensive form trust game', *Journal of Economic Behavior and Organization*, 43: 57–73.

Carnevale, Peter J. and De Dreu, Carsten K.W. (2005) 'Laboratory experiments on social conflict', *International Negotiation*, 10: 51–65.

Carnevale, Peter J. and Isen, Alice M. (1986) 'The influence of positive affect and visual access on the discovery of integrative solutions in bilateral negotiation', *Organizational Behavior and Human Decision Processes*, 37: 1–13.

Chertkoff, Jerome M. and Baird, Suzanne L. (1971) 'Applicability of the big-lie technique and the last clear choice doctrine to bargaining', *Journal of Personality and Social Psychology*, 20: 298–303.

Cohen, Dov, Nisbett, Richard J., Bowdle, Brian F. and Schwarz, Norbert (1996) 'Insult, aggression, and the Southern culture of honor: An "experimental ethnography"', *Journal of Personality and Social Psychology*, 70: 945–60.

Conlon, Donald E., Moon, Henry and Ng, K. Yee (2002) 'Putting the cart before the horse: The unexpected benefits of arbitrating before mediating', *Journal of Applied Psychology*, 87: 978–84.

Croson, Rachel (2005) 'The method of experimental economics', *International Negotiation*, 10: 131–48.

De Dreu, Carsten K.W., Weingart, Laurie R. and Kwon, Seungwoo (2000) 'Influence of social motives on integrative negotiation: A meta-analytic review and test of two theories', *Journal of Personality and Social Psychology*, 78: 889–905.

Deutsch, Morton (1973) *The Resolution of Conflict: Constructive and Destructive Processes.* New Haven, CT: Yale University Press.

Druckman, Daniel (1986) 'Stages, turning points, and crisis: Negotiating military base rights, Spain and the United States', *Journal of Conflict Resolution*, 30: 327–60.

Druckman, Daniel, Druckman, James N. and Arai, Tatsushi (2004) 'e-mediation: Evaluating the impacts of an electronic mediator on negotiation behavior', *Group Decision and Negotiation*, 13: 481–511.

Emery, Robert E., Laumann-Billings, Lisa, Waldron, Mary C., Sbarra, David A. and Dillon, Peter (2001) 'Child custody mediation and litigation: Custody, contact, and coparenting 12 years after initial dispute resolution', *Journal of Consulting and Clinical Psychology*, 69: 323–32.

Esser, James K. and Komorita, Samuel (1975) 'Reciprocity and concession making in bargaining', *Journal of Personality and Social Psychology*, 31: 864–72.

Ferguson, Tamara J. and Rule, Brendan G. (1983) 'An attributional perspective on anger and aggression', In Russell G. Geen and Edward Donnerstein (eds), *Aggression: Theoretical and Empirical Reviews.* New York: Academic Press. Vol. 1, pp. 41–74.

Forgas, Joseph P. (1998) 'On feeling good and getting your way: Mood effects on negotiator cognition and bargaining strategies', *Journal of Personality and Social Psychology*, 74: 565–77.

Gaffié, Bernard (2006) 'Effect of political positioning on explanations of delinquency: The experimental study of social differentiation and representation', *Political Psychology*, 27: 403–22.

Galinsky, Adam D. and Mussweiler, Thomas (2001) 'First offers as anchors: The role of perspective taking and negotiator focus', *Journal of Personality and Social Psychology*, 81, 657–69.

Gelfand, Michele J. and Brett, Jeanne M. (eds) (2004) *The Handbook of Negotiation and Culture.* Stanford, CA: Stanford University Press.

Hampson, Fen O. (1996) *Nurturing Peace: Why Peace Settlements Succeed or Fail.* Washington: United States Institute of Peace.

Herrman, Margaret S. (ed.) (2006) *The Blackwell Handbook of Mediation.* Malden, MA: Blackwell.

Huber, Vandra L. and Neale, Margaret A. (1986) 'Effects of cognitive heuristics and goals on negotiator performance and subsequent goal setting', *Organizational*

Behavior and Human Decision Processes, 38: 342–365.

Kelley, Harold H. (1966) 'A classroom study of the dilemmas in interpersonal negotiations', In Kathleen Archibald (ed.), *Strategic Interaction and Conflict*. Berkeley, CA: Institute of International Studies. pp.49–73.

Kerr, Norbert L. and Kaufman-Gilliland, Cynthia M. (1994) 'Communication, commitment, and cooperation in social dilemmas', *Journal of Personality and Social Psychology*, 66: 513–29.

Komorita, Samuel S. and Esser, James K. (1975) 'Frequency of reciprocated concessions in bargaining', *Journal of Personality and Social Psychology*, 32: 699–705.

Komorita, Samuel S., Parks, Craig D. and Hulbert, Lorne G. (1992) 'Reciprocity and the induction of cooperation in social dilemmas', *Journal of Personality and Social Psychology*, 62: 607–17.

Korostelina, Karina (2005) *Readiness to Fight in Crimea: How It Interrelates with National and Ethnic Identities*. Unpublished manuscript.

Kressel, Kenneth, Pruitt, Dean G. and Associates (1989) *Mediation Research*. San Francisco: Jossey-Bass.

Lindskold, Svenn and Aronoff, Jonathan K. (1980) 'Conciliatory strategies and relative power', *Journal of Experimental Social Psychology*, 16: 187–96.

Lindskold, Svenn, Bennett, Russell and Wayner, Marc (1976) 'Retaliation level as a foundation for subsequent conciliation', *Behavioral Science*, 21: 13–18.

McDermott, Rose (2006) 'Editors' introduction' [to the special issue on experiments in political psychology], *Political Psychology*, 27: 247–58.

McGillicuddy, Neal B., Welton, Gary L. and Pruitt, Dean G. (1987) 'Third party intervention: A field experiment comparing three different models', *Journal of Personality and Social Psychology*, 53: 104–12.

McGinn, Kathleen L. and Croson, Rachel (2004) 'What do communication media mean for negotiators? A question of social awareness', In Michele J. Gelfand and Jeanne M. Brett (eds), *The Handbook of Negotiation and Culture*. Stanford, CA: Stanford University Press. pp. 334–49.

McNeel, Steven P. and Reid, Edward C. (1975) 'Attitude similarity, social goals, and cooperation', *Journal of Conflict Resolution*, 19: 665–81.

Neale, Margaret A. and Bazerman, Max H. (1991) *Negotiator Cognition and Rationality*. New York: Free Press.

Nisbett, Richard E. and Cohen, Dov (1996) *Culture of Honor: The Psychology of Violence in the South*. Boulder, CO: Westview.

Pruitt, Dean G. (1967) 'Reward structure and cooperation: The decomposed prisoner's dilemma game', *Journal of Personality and Social Psychology*, 7: 21–27.

Pruitt, Dean G. (1998) 'Social conflict', In Donald T. Gilbert, Susan T. Fiske and Gardner Lindzey (eds), *Handbook of Social Psychology*, 4th edn. New York: McGraw-Hill. Vol. 2, pp. 470–503.

Pruitt, Dean G. (2005a) 'Field experiments on social conflict', *International Negotiation*, 10: 33–49.

Pruitt, Dean G. (2005b) *Whither Ripeness Theory?* Working Paper #25, Institute for Conflict Analysis and Resolution, George Mason University, Fairfax, VA. Web address: www.gmu.edu/departments/ICAR/wp_25_pruitt.pdf

Pruitt, Dean G. and Carnevale, Peter J. (1993) *Negotiation in Social Conflict*. Buckingham, England: Open University Press and Pacific Grove, CA: Brooks/Cole.

Pruitt, Dean G. and Kim, Sung Hee (2004) *Social Conflict: Escalation, Stalemate, and Settlement*, 3rd edn. New York: McGraw-Hill.

Pruitt, Dean G. and Lewis, Steven A. (1975) 'Development of integrative solutions in bilateral negotiation', *Journal of Personality and Social Psychology*, 31: 621–33.

Ross, Lee and Stillinger, Constance (1991) 'Barriers to conflict resolution', *Negotiation Journal*, 7: 389–404.

Rothbart, Myron and Hallmark, William (1988) 'Ingroup-outgroup differences in the perceived efficacy of coercion and conciliation in resolving social conflict', *Journal of Personality and Social Psychology*, 55: 248–57.

Rubin, Jeffrey Z. (1980) 'Experimental research on third-party intervention in conflict: Toward some generalizations', *Psychological Bulletin*, 87: 379–91.

Sherman, Lawrence W. and Berk, Richard A. (1984) 'The specific deterrent effects of arrest for domestic assault', *American Sociological Review*, 49: 261–72.

Sherif, Muzafar and Sherif, Carolyn W. (1969) *Social Psychology*. New York: Harper and Row.

Thompson, Leigh L. (1991) 'Information exchange in negotiation', *Journal of Experimental Social Psychology*, 27: 161–79.

Thompson, Leigh L. (ed.) (2006) *Negotiation Theory and Research*. New York: Psychology Press.

Vanbeselaere, Norbert (1991) 'The different effects of simple and crossed categorization: A result of the category differentiation process or of differential category salience?', In Wolfgang Stroebe and Miles Hewstone (eds), *European Review of Social Psychology*. Chichester, England: Wiley. Vol. 2, pp. 247–79.

van Kleef, Gerben A., De Dreu, Carsten K.W. and Manstead, Anthony S.R. (2004) 'The interpersonal effects of anger and happiness in negotiations',

Journal of Personality and Social Psychology, 86: 57–76.

Weber, J. Mark and Messick, David M. (2004). 'Conflicting interests in social life: Understanding social dilemma dynamics', In Michele J. Gelfand and Jeanne M. Brett (eds), *The Handbook of Negotiation and Culture*. Stanford, CA: Stanford University Press. pp. 374–94.

Welton, Gary L. and Pruitt, Dean G. (1987) 'The mediation process: The effects of mediator bias and disputant power', *Personality and Social Psychology Bulletin*, 13: 123–33.

Wilder, David A. (1984) 'Intergroup contact: The typical member and the except to the rule', *Journal of Experimental Social Psychology*, 20: 177–94.

Wilkenfeld, Jonathan (2005) 'Reflections on simulation and experimentation in the study of negotiation', *International Negotiation*, 9: 429–39.

Wittmer, Jerry M., Carnevale, Peter J. and Walker, Michael E. (1991) 'General alignment and overt support in biased mediation', *Journal of Conflict Resolution*, 35: 594–610.

Worchel, Steven and Norvell, Nancy (1980) 'Effect of perceived environmental conditions during coopera-tion on intergroup attraction', *Journal of Personality and Social Psychology*, 38: 764–72.

Yamagishi, Toshio (1992) 'Group size and the provision of a sanctioning system in a social dilemma', In Wulin B.G. Liebrand, David M. Messick and Henk A.M. Wilke (eds), *Social Dilemmas*. Oxford: Pergamon. pp. 267–87.

Yamagishi, Toshio and Sato, Kaori (1986) 'Motivational bases of the public goods problem', *Journal of Personality and Social Psychology*, 50: 67–73.

Yovetich, Nancy A. and Rusbult, Caryl E. (1994) 'Accommodative behavior in close relationships: Exploring transformation of motivation', *Journal of Experimental Social Psychology*, 30: 138–64.

Yukl, Gary A., Malone, Michael P., Hayslip, Bert and Pamin, Thomas A. (1976) 'The effects of time pressure and issue settlement order on integrative bargaining', *Sociometry*, 39: 277–81.

Zartman, I. William and Berman, Maureen R. (1982) *The Practical Negotiator*. New Haven, CT: Yale University Press.

Zillmann, Dolf, Katcher, Aaron H. and Milavsky, Barry (1972) 'Excitation transfer from physical exercise to subsequent aggressive behavior', *Journal of Experimental Social Psychology*, 8: 247–59.

7

Doing Conflict Research Through a Multi-Method Lens

Daniel Druckman

There is a noticeable trend in the social sciences toward doing multi-method research. This trend is particularly evident in the more inter-disciplinary fields such as conflict management and resolution (Maoz et al., 2004; Druckman, 2005). The widespread desire among conflict scholars to embrace this approach is due in large part to the complexity of the problems confronting them as well as to the overlap with several other fields, each emphasizing a particular mode of inquiry. A full understanding of protracted conflicts depends on the insights gained from both comparative and case-specific research. Comparative methods have been developed and fine-tuned by political scientists working with aggregate data sets and by psychologists conducting replicated laboratory experiments. Case research has evolved from largely descriptive to analytical studies as political scientists, sociologists, and anthropologists have recognized the need for more theory-based research on particular cases or regions. Both these research traditions are highlighted in this chapter. An attempt is made to survey the scope of methods used by conflict scholars along with examples of projects that illustrate the application. A goal of the chapter is to convey the value of using multiple, complementary methods for exploration.

Recognizing the value of both the general and the specific, conflict analysts have addressed several issues concerning the foundations for doing research. One issue is the philosophical divide between positivism and constructivism. The former aligns more closely with traditional scientific approaches to knowledge accumulation; the latter are rooted in more subjective phenomenological approaches to understanding.[1] Another issue is a preference for either quantitative or qualitative methods of exploration. Although part of this tension resides in comfort with numbers or words, the more fundamental difference is between whether an investigator seeks the generality that comes from using a common yardstick for measurement or the depth of understanding that can emerge from a more nuanced study of a group or culture. A third distinction is between etic and emic approaches. For "etics," a particular case of conflict is seen as an instance of a large class of conflict processes. For "emics," a conflict is a unique event to be understood within its own contexts. Heated debates have turned on these sticking points. However, by considering each of these preferences as a particular aspect of doing research, the dualities break down and the seeds for a multi-method approach are sown.

Many of the examples of research projects discussed show how both features of the divide inform the research process. Many conflict investigators collect data from the vantage points of object and subject. Observed behaviors or events are complemented by interviews that reveal perceptions, interpretations, and perspectives. Data collected in an aggregate form for statistical analysis are complemented by interpretations of the way a process plays out in sampled cases. A good deal of my own research travels between case and comparative analysis. For example, the concept of turning points in negotiation was discovered in single-case studies – using quantitative (Druckman, 1986) and qualitative (Druckman et al., 1991) methods of analysis. The concept was verified in a comparative, qualitative analysis of 34 cases (Druckman, 2001). These projects illustrate the mix of small-n (one or few cases) and large-N (many cases) approaches to research as well as combining quantitative with qualitative analyses. They also call attention to strengths and limitations of each of the methods, a theme that will be developed in the sections to follow.

A variety of methodologies used in studies of conflict are discussed in this chapter. Many of these studies rely primarily on a particular methodological approach, which is usually an experiment, survey, or case study. A few more recent studies have combined two or more methods in the investigation. Both the single- and multiple-method approaches are discussed in the sections to follow. I begin with published examples of simulation experiments followed by modeling, surveys, case studies (single, time series, comparative), content analysis, and evaluation research.

Each section includes a brief review of the strengths and weaknesses of the approach. Then, I proceed to give examples of the way that multiple methods are used together in several research projects. In these studies, the particular strengths of the different methods complement one another. This theme is carried forward in a concluding section. The discussion shows how the multi-method strategy has evolved to deal with the challenge of "compensating for weaknesses" in single-method studies of conflict.

DOING EXPERIMENTS

A considerable amount of our knowledge about negotiation, mediation, and other small-group conflict processes come from laboratory experiments. Spurred on by the path-breaking experiments conducted on levels of aspiration by Siegel and Fouraker (1960) and on the development of social norms and trust by Deutsch and Krauss (1962), negotiation researchers have found this approach useful for isolating important variables. (See Rubin and Brown, 1975, for a review of the early experimental studies on bargaining.) Examples are self–other orientations, distributive or problem-solving approaches, pre-negotiation experience, time pressure, constraints on representations, the role played by values and interests, alternative power configurations, alternatives to negotiated agreements, and task framing. With regard to mediation, we have learned about effects of different mediator approaches, the timing and functions of mediation, and the use of electronic aids in performing diagnoses and analyses of conflicts. (See Carnevale and De Dreu, 2006, for a recent review of laboratory findings.). In addition to constructing and refining theories, the experimental findings have been used in training contexts for developing negotiating skills (e.g. Druckman, 2006). Few researchers would deny that these studies have made important contributions. At the same time, few would claim that the laboratory findings encompass the complexities of many real-world conflicts.

For methodologists, this is the trade-off between internal and external validity. I now turn to a discussion of this issue.

Experiments have the distinct advantage of allowing researchers to infer causation with some degree of confidence. Referred to as internal validity, this is due essentially to three features of experimental design: random assignment of experimental subjects to conditions (groups, treatments), control by the experimenter over independent (or causal) variables, and replication of the experiments many times. Random assignment assures comparability of the groups (experimental and control conditions) being compared. Control groups decrease the chances that alternative (uncontrolled) variables explain the findings. Replication allows a researcher to assess variability or to judge whether the same finding re-occurs in repeated administrations of the experiment. These features also enable a researcher to use statistical tests in order to discover relationships between independent and dependent variables and to ascertain whether the relationships are due largely to chance.

On the flip side of these advantages are problems that result from the very features essential to inferring causation. Highly controlled and compressed-time situations, needed to increase confidence in causal inference, create artificial settings. The more controls instituted to reduce the plausibility of alternative explanations – or to increase internal validity – the less the experimental setting resembles other situations. The relatively homogeneous populations used in most experiments combined with contrived tasks and limited time periods pose threats to generalizability or external validity. The interesting challenge for researchers is to conduct studies in realistic settings (field or simulation) while retaining the analytical advantages of experimentation. This challenge calls for balancing the two validities in the design of studies. Examples of several balancing strategies are offered in the paragraphs to follow.

Three strategies are comparing laboratory with field data, designing realistic laboratory simulations, and conducting randomized experiments in field settings. The comparison strategy is illustrated by the work of Hopmann and Walcott (1977) and Beriker and Druckman (1996). The former investigators explored the relationship between external stress and negotiating behavior in two settings, a simulation of the Partial Nuclear Test Ban Treaty of 1963 and in the actual negotiations. Convergences were found between the experimental and field results, indicating that stresses were dysfunctional for the negotiations: high stress produced greater hostility, harder bargaining strategies, and fewer agreements than low stress. The experimental findings showed that a high-stress condition produced significantly fewer solutions than both a low-stress and neutral condition. This kind of controlled comparison is a strength of experiments; unlike the actual talks, the simulation provided for variation in outcomes. The comparison showed that low stress does not improve outcomes, but high stress hinders attempts to reach agreements.

A similar type of comparison was made in the Beriker and Druckman study of the Lausanne peace conference in 1922–1923. An additional condition created for the simulation provided insights not likely to be obtained from an analysis of the actual talks. Negotiators in a weak power-symmetry condition were more satisfied with the outcome, achieved faster resolutions, disagreed less often, and made fewer competitive statements during the discussions than those in the other conditions. These studies illustrate an advantage of experiments: they allow for exploration of new conditions not present in the setting being simulated. Further, similarities found between the simulation and field bolster support for the external validity of the laboratory simulation.

The realistic simulation strategy is illustrated by my study of situational levers. An attempt was made in that study to create "packages" of variables for each of four phases of a multilateral conference over environmental issues: pre-negotiation planning, setting-the-stage, the give-and-take, and the endgame. The variables were drawn from a well-known framework of factors that influence negotiating processes (see Sawyer and Guetzkow, 1965). Hypotheses about flexible (or inflexible) negotiating behavior were evaluated by gearing the variables in the direction of more or less flexibility. Many of the hypotheses were confirmed. More importantly, however, the study shows how complexity can be incorporated in simulations. Comparisons were also made between different kinds of role-players in the simulation, scientists, and diplomats. Correspondences between the findings from these samples contribute further to the external validity of the experiment (see Druckman, 1993).

An example of the randomized field experiment strategy is the study by McGillicuddy et al. (1987). This is a rare example of a field study that randomly assigned 36 disputant pairs and mediators to one of three experimental conditions: mediation without arbitration, mediators become arbitrators if the dispute is not settled (med/arb same), and a new party is appointed to be an arbitrator if the dispute is not settled (med/arb different). Strong differences were found between the conditions on process but not outcomes. The med/arb same condition disputants were less hostile, made more new proposals and more concessions, agreed more often with the other disputant, and were more satisfied with the outcome than disputants in the other two third-party configurations. The cooperative motivation shown by disputants in this condition may have been an attempt to discourage the mediator from arbitrating the competing claims. However, subject morality posed a threat to the internal validity of the experiment: 68% of the participants dropped out of the study before it was concluded. By showing that the distribution of dropouts was random across the three conditions, the threat to validity was not serious. This study is a good example of increasing the relevance of findings for real-world settings while retaining the analytical advantages of classical experimental designs. (See Pruitt, 2005b, for a review of field experiments on social conflict.)[2]

MODELING CONFLICT PROCESSES

For some conflict processes, it is possible to specify relationships between variables with precision. These specifications may take the form of models that are often evaluated with experiments. They may also depict outcomes that would have resulted if the conditions had been different. This is referred to as counterfactual analysis (see Sprinz and Wolinsky-Nahmias, 2004, pp. 369–371). Examples are solution concepts for two-person games, coalition formation, concessions in negotiation, and transition rates in conflict processes. Each of these examples is described in this section.

The most popular solution concept for two-person games is the Nash equilibrium. The simplicity and elegance of this concept derives from the property that it minimizes the losses incurred by game players. It is a social norm in the sense that all players prefer this outcome to any alternative. It is calculated as the outcome that maximizes the product of the preferences of the two parties. Along with other solution concepts (see Avenhaus and Zartman, 2007; Guner and Druckman, 2000), this idea covers a wide range of choice situations where a person must decide between making an offer or remaining silent, voting for one candidate or another, or intervening versus standing aside. It has the feature of providing a parsimonious explanation for social behavior such as bystander apathy. (See Osborne, 2004, for this and other examples.) These concepts come to life in the sequence of players' choices in different types of game structures.

An old problem for students of politics is the decision to form a party coalition. And, perhaps the oldest idea about how to do this is the minimum winning coalition (Riker, 1962): this is a coalition consisting of only those parties needed to win. Further work extended this idea by adding policy positions to the model. Referred to as a minimum connected winning coalition, this model has been shown to be a better predictor of coalitions in some parliamentary systems (Axelrod, 1970). A more detailed version of the connected coalition was developed by dividing policies into their weighted parts, such as the relative importance of ideological and material values. This enlarged model was shown to predict coalition choices in laboratory simulations (Krause et al., 1975). Other modifications to the general formulation were introduced in order to account for decisions made by parties that challenge political regimes. The modifications consisted of dividing interests into two parts, asset complementarity and legitimacy as well as substituting a measure of "social comfort" for ideology. This model provided useful estimates of the likelihood that various alternative coalitions would form and challenge the incumbent regime.

Another type of model was developed for capturing the exchanges that occur during a negotiation leading toward an agreement or impasse. The model consists of three parameters, the tendency to reciprocate, the tendency to make unilateral concessions or to initiate reciprocation, and the level of friendly feelings. It is evaluated by varying the values of these parameters and observing the timing and type of agreement reached. Using computer simulation, Bartos (1995) evaluated the relative merits of a concession exchange (distributive) and an informative search (integrative) approach to bargaining. This was done by having the computer generate a series or path of demands that each type of party (a distributive or integrative bargainer) would make. He concluded that the concession exchange process is faster, but the information search process may be more productive because it can increase the chances of getting an agreement.

Many conflicts and negotiations pass through phases of antagonistic and coopera-tive behavior. A key challenge is to identify the transitions that occur between these phases. This challenge has been addressed by a form of modeling that captures the dynamics of conflict, referred to as stochastic processes. The models attempt to define the parameters that influence rates of transition from one state to another. Two parameters were highlighted by Coleman (1973): the transition rate at the time of an initiating event and the rate of decline. These parameters

capture two processes. One refers to decay in rates of change as a function of time in a particular state: The longer a negotiation process remains in a state of cooperation, the lower the probability that it will move to a state of competition between the parties. The longer parties remain in a state, the less they attend to cues that may signal change in either process or relationship. The other process refers to the effects of a terminating event such as a deadline. When faced with an end-state, transitions increase over time in a systematic fashion. Data showing that rates of transition slow down with time from an initiating event – such as a cooperative move after a period of hostility – and speed up with time to a terminating event have implications for interventions aimed at moving parties out of antagonistic spirals.

A number of other formal models of conflict processes have been shown to be useful. These include negotiation support systems, game and decision-theoretic formulations, and system dynamics. For summaries and examples of application, the reader is referred to the book edited by Avenhaus and Zartman (2007). Vallacher and Nowak (2007) offer an interesting new approach to modeling social–psychological processes and mechanisms with implications for resolving intractable conflicts. Referred to as a dynamical systems model, this approach is useful for capturing both gradual and sudden changes that are likely to occur in the course of an unfolding conflict (Coleman et al., 2005). A related form of modeling is developed by Gabbay (2007). His non-linear approach to modeling captures the internal dynamics of small-group decision making with implications for the occurrence of turning points in complex international negotiations.

Another recent modeling approach has been found to provide insights into factors that drive conflict-resolving processes. Referred to as machine learning, this approach uses decision-tree algorithms to sort through a variety of coded variables hypothesized to influence outcomes. It was shown to provide added value to statistical approaches, particu-larly with regard to contingent relationships among variables. The path-like features of the decision trees and the "if-then" feature of the association rules can reveal hidden structures in the data. For example, Druckman et al. (2006) found that enlarged joint benefits occur when friendly parties discuss only a few issues or when they discuss many issues in an asymmetrical power structure. The authors considered this finding to be a refinement over those obtained with multidimensional scaling techniques. For discussions of a variety of other computer-aided methods for conflict analysis, see the chapters in Trappl (2006).

COLLECTING AND ANALYZING SURVEY DATA

Survey research has played a less prominent role in the study of conflict processes. Two possible reasons are that survey data are often difficult to collect and sample surveys can be expensive to conduct. For many conflict zones, population registries are not available, respondents are difficult to contact, and attributions about the researcher's intent lead to suspicions about how the data will be used. But, even when lists are available and respondents are eager to be of assistance, the costs can be prohibitive. Most probability samples require large numbers of respondents, many of whom must speak through interpreters. Without substantial support, surveys – unlike many of the other approaches discussed in this chapter – are difficult to implement. With proper support, surveys can provide valuable insights into the way people think about their group identities and the implications of those attachments for the course of a conflict and its settlement. A good example of this kind of survey is the recent study by Burn (2006).

Burn implemented a survey of citizens in two countries, Kyrgyzstan and Kazakhstan. Her team conducted face-to-face interviews with 753 citizens drawn from the most recent (1999) census in each country. Although these were not probability samples – in the sense that each citizen had the same chance of being chosen – a careful attempt was made

to represent the demographic breakdown of groups. This was done by matching sample percentages with those in the population. For example, the census and sample breakdowns for ethnic groups in Kazakhstan was Kazakh (58% vs. 53%); Russian (23% vs. 22%); Uzbek (6 % vs. 13%); and other (13% vs. 11%). Representative samples have the advantage of ensuring that the key categories are included in the survey in proportion to the population; they have the disadvantage of over- or under-representing respondents from certain categories. The proportional representation approach to sampling used by Burn was a strength of the study. Not only did this sampling approach enable her to examine impacts of the varied group identities in each society, it also shed light on important theoretical questions about factors that facilitate or impede transitions to democracy.

The survey methodology used by Burn enabled her to compare groups and to assess relationships between the theoretically relevant concepts. One set of hypotheses compared the strength of clan identities among various demographic categories. For example, she hypothesized that clan identity will be stronger in rural than in urban areas. People living in urban areas have more opportunities to identify with other groups. Another set of hypotheses examined relationships among variables. For example, strong clan identity is correlated with greater tolerance for authoritarian leaders; it is also correlated with less support for democratic institutions. Each of the variables was defined by indicators that could easily be represented by survey questions. For example, salience of clan identity was measured by answers to three questions – willingness to financially support clan members, voting preferences for clan members, and preferential treatment of clan members (compared to non-clan members). The survey questions on clan identity captured several aspects of identity including commitment, spread, durability, and salience. These were the intervening variables in a framework that connected clan expectations, roles, and behavior to political institutions. The survey data provided evidence about the constraining and facilitating roles played by group identities in the transition of political systems.

Surveys are useful for gathering information about defined populations. For some issues, all members of the population can be interviewed. An example is Birkhoff's (2001) study of mediators' perspectives on power. She mailed surveys to each of the members of the Society for Professionals in Dispute Resolution (SPIDR), which were considered to be a population of professional mediators. Although her return rate was only 37%, she was able to show that this "sample" represented the membership on key demographic variables. In this study, the "sample" was defined by the returns rather than by random selection from population lists. The responses to her questions suggested an interesting taxonomy of the varied meanings of power in practice. Other research questions that would benefit from surveys include the extent of polarization on values within societies, the spread and durability of group or national identity, and changes in perceptions of relationships with other societies following such interventions as problem-solving workshops. Panel (repeated) surveys would be particularly useful for gauging changes in attitudes through time. Conducting surveys in conjunction with other methodologies may be useful for linking micro- (small-group interactions) with macro-level (societal trends) processes.

PERFORMING CASE STUDIES

Case studies come in several forms, ranging from the single case to a large number of cases used for making comparisons. In my earlier work, I distinguished among four approaches: the enhanced case study, time-series analysis, focused case comparisons, and aggregate or large-N case comparisons. (See Druckman [2002; 2005] for a comparison of features of these approaches.). Each approach has both strengths and weaknesses. The issues are depth (enhanced case study) versus breadth (time series and aggregate methods), control

for internal validity (focused comparison) versus robust sampling for external validity (aggregate), and cross-sectional (aggregate) versus longitudinal analyses (time series). Used together, the weaknesses of one approach – for example, limited sampling of the focused comparison method – can be offset by the strengths of another, for example, representative sampling for comparative case studies. I will return to this issue in the final section on multi-methods. Studies that illustrate each type of case-based approach are discussed in this section.

Enhanced case studies. This research approach consists of viewing a case through the lens of a theoretical framework. Key concepts are used to interpret the way a conflict process unfolds or how it is resolved. Many published analyses of negotiation and mediation use this approach: examples are Haskel's (1974) use of the concept of power symmetry/asymmetry to understand Scandinavian market negotiations, Winham's (1977) emphasis on issue complexity as the primary challenge in multilateral trade talks, and the studies by Cameron and Tomlin (2000) and Druckman et al., (1991) on turning points in NAFTA and the INF talks respectively. The books edited by Rubin (1981), Zartman, (1994), and Cohen and Westbrook (2000) provide examples of how particular cases – Kissinger's shuttle diplomacy, European Community talks, Bronze-Age diplomacy with Egyptian pharaohs – can be viewed from a variety of theoretical perspectives, such as game, decision, coalition, or leadership theories. The evaluations of various theory-derived hypotheses about choices made in the Crimean (Gochal and Levy, 2004) and Vietnam (Walker, 2004) wars are good examples of enhanced case studies on successful and failed strategies to manage conflict.

My 1995 study with Green (Druckman and Green, 1995) on negotiations between the Philippines Aquino regime and the National Democratic Front shows the relevance of the concept of "ripeness" for decisions to negotiate and "formula" for opportunities discovered or squandered during the process of negotiating. Further insights into that negotiating process came from superimposing concepts from the literature on the sociology of conflict, particularly with regard to the interplay between values and interests, onto the unfolding discussions. (See also the other case studies of internal conflict in Zartman, 1995.) These enhanced case studies call attention to the relevance of theory for capturing the essential processes of complex cases. They do not, however, provide sound explanations for relationships among variables in the conflict setting, process, or outcome. Explanatory goals are addressed by the comparative methods to be discussed in the sections to follow.

Time-series analysis. This approach to analysis captures the dynamics of conflict processes. It consists of a family of techniques that analyzes a sequence of events that occur over a relatively long period of time in the context of one or more cases. The techniques include experimental before–after comparisons, correlation/regression analyses of trends, probability forecasting, and qualitative process tracing. An example of each of these applications is provided in this section.

Before and after comparisons of trends are illustrated by our study of mediation during the conflict over Nagorno-Karabakh (Mooradian and Druckman, 1999). Nearly 4000 events from 1990–1995 were coded on a six-step scale ranging from significant action toward peace ($+3$) to significant violence directed at an adversary (-3). A time-series of monthly violence scores was compared six months before and six months after each of the six mediations; none of the comparisons were statistically significant. A significant change did occur, however, between the months preceding and following the period of intensive combat between April 1993 and February 1994. These results lend support to the hypothesis that a mutually hurting stalemate is a condition for getting warring parties to the table to negotiate a cease fire. Since then, the violence has subsided although

the issues that gave rise to the conflict have not been resolved. (See also Druckman, 2002, for the distinction between settlements and resolutions of conflicts.)

Another attempt to explore the effects of mediation on violence is the study by Schrodt and Gerner (2004). Using various indices of cooperation and competition, they examined ten cases of mediated dyadic conflicts. For each conflict, they cross-correlated mediator behavior with the level of violence over time. This technique is useful for examining long-term, time-delayed effects of interventions. Of particular interest is their finding about the sticks-or-carrots issue: Is mediation more or less effective when mediators use rewards (including side payments) or coercive measures such as sanctions? Their technically sophisticated machine-coding approach to analysis produced a complex, contingent finding: violence was reduced when mediation was accompanied by both coercive measures and by cooperative incentives directed at the weaker party in the dyad.

Probability forecasting with Bayesian techniques is illustrated by asking whether a peace agreement will hold through time. Probabilities can be estimated from historical data showing that agreements hold for at least five years in one third of the cases examined. The question is whether this is sufficient information for projecting the longevity of future agreements. The Bayesian answer is that other factors, referred to as conditional probabilities, must also be taken into account. Examples of these factors are spoilers, schisms between parties, regime continuity, international pressure, and availability of arms. Probabilities for each factor can be provided by expert panels. For example, the experts agree that international pressure to sustain an agreement results in a .7 probability that the agreement will hold and a .2 chance that it will fall apart. When these estimated probabilities are inserted into the Bayesian formula (see Frei and Ruloff, 1989), the result is a revised estimate of longevity. This estimate is regarded as an update from the historical record. In this example, longevity is increased from .33 (based only on the record) to .63 (when pressures are taken into account). However, when all of the factors are included together, the revised probability of .30 is virtually the same as the historical probability of .33. This is because the factors have offsetting effects, some favoring, and others hindering the durability of agreements.

Qualitative time-series often takes the form of process tracing. This consists of searching an historical record of events for evidence about whether an hypothesized process did or did not occur. An example is the paths developed from cases of negotiation in my study of turning points (Druckman, 2001). Focusing on departures in trends, I traced the relationship between causes, referred to as precipitants, and consequences following the occurrence of a departure, known as a turning point. Paths were traced for each of three types of negotiations, those over security issues, environmental concerns, and trade matters. The case-specific paths were combined by discovering the most frequent precipitant (inside or outside the negotiation), departure (abrupt or non-abrupt), and consequence (escalatory or de-escalatory). A particularly interesting finding is that outside factors were needed for departures in the security while inside factors (either new ideas or procedures) were usually the cause of change for the environmental and trade cases. An explanation for this difference is that security negotiators are more averse to risk than their counterparts in the other areas.

An interesting application of this three-part framework is Dougherty's (2006) study of social movements in Northern Ireland. Her detailed historical traces of the school integration movement provided insights into the factors that precipitate the transformation of social conflicts. The link between collective action and transformation was shown to turn on the development of a critical mass of key members of the movement. Other examples of the tracing of conflict dynamics are Carstarphen's (2003) analysis of dialogues about prejudice among small groups of men from different backgrounds and Pruitt's (2005b) chain analysis of two cases, the Northern Ireland peace process and the talks between Israel and the PLO in Oslo.

Focused case comparisons. Another enhancement to the traditional case study is the structured, focused case comparison. Similar to the enhanced case study discussed earlier, the focused comparison uses theory to guide case selection and analysis. Unlike the single-case study, a focused comparison consists of a matching of similar cases. It is an attempt to impose the logic of experimentation on a small number of cases. (See Faure's 1994 discussion of the Most Similar Systems Design [MSSD].) One of the early examples of application is Putnam's (1993) comparison of a northern and southern Italian province in terms of a number of performance indicators. The provinces were similar in most aspects of their political systems. They differed only in terms of economic development, with the north outpacing the south, and the development of a civic culture. These were the independent variables in the focused comparison. If, as Putnam argued, the provinces differed only on economic and civic development, then either or both of these variables can be used as an explanation for differences in performance. Using partial correlation, he showed that civic culture was the better explanation: When levels of civic culture were controlled, economic development made little difference in performance. These results produced an interesting debate about alternative explanations (see Tarrow, 1996). Indeed, it is the suggestive implications of focused comparisons that contribute to the refinement of theory. Further examples of the approach come from studies on conflict management.

One of these studies is Allen Nan's (1999) analysis of coordination among conflict-resolving organizations. The research focused on processes of complementarity and coordination among NGOs in three former Soviet republics: Abkhasia, South Ossetia, and Transdniestria. These cases were matched on types of disputing parties, interests, time, and power. A key difference however was whether they initiated a process of long-term unofficial facilitated joint analysis among negotiators (LUFJAAN) of the contending groups: only Abkhasia did not entertain this process. The cases differed also on the key dependent variable progress toward a cease fire. Progress occurred in South Ossetia and Transdniestra, but not in Abkhasia. Because the cases were carefully matched on other variables, she inferred that there was a relationship between the LUFJAAN process (the independent variable) and the reduction of violence toward a cease-fire agreement (the dependent variable).

Additional coding of the South Ossetia negotiations by Irmer (2003) revealed that the process consisted of more problem solving than competitive bargaining statements, leading to comprehensive (rather than partial) outcomes. Further analyses showed that trust between the negotiators increased through the course of the talks. These effects may have resulted from the long-term facilitation process used in this case as documented by Allen Nan. Considered together, the two studies illustrate the value of combining methods, MSSD and statement coding.

Another small-n case-study approach emphasizes differences rather than similarities between cases. Referred to by Faure (1994) as the Most Different Systems Design (MDSD), this approach is useful for developing typologies. An example is Weiss' (2002) study of mediator sequencing strategies. Three cases of peace processes were used as exemplars of alternative sequencing approaches: gradualism (Mozambique), boulder in the road (El Salvador), and committee (Angola). Content analyses of the negotiation process in each case confirmed the approach used and identified a number of factors that distinguished among them, for example, type of most contentious issue, type of reasoning, trust building, and ripeness in the process. These factors were used to construct a profile for each of the three types of mediator sequencing strategies.

Another MDSD study, conducted by Druckman and Lyons (2005), compared Mozambique with Nagorno Karabakh. The different profiles for these cases resembled the distinction – made by Galtung (1969) – between negative (Nagorno Karabakh) and positive (Mozambique) peace. Additional coding showed that the cases differed also on various indicators of distributive (competitive) and integrative (problem-solving) bargaining. Further insights about these cases emerge when we consider findings obtained in other, related studies. Concerning Mozambique, the gradualist mediation strategy discovered by Weiss may have encouraged problem-solving and forward-looking rhetoric coded by Druckman and Lyons (2005) and by Irmer (2003). Concerning Nagorno Karabakh, the 1994 war between Armenia and Azerbaijan (see Mooradian and Druckman, 1999) may have led to the distributive bargaining process and partial, cease fire outcome also coded by Irmer (2003). The larger picture for these cases emerges from studies that employed several methodologies – MDSD, content analysis, and interrupted time series. I will return to the topic of complementary methods in the sections to follow.

Aggregate case comparisons. Comparative case studies are also performed across a large number of different cases. Referred to as the method of concomitant variation (Faure, 1994), large-N case studies are another form of MDSD. Unlike the controlled comparisons discussed in the previous section, these studies consist of sampling of cases from a larger universe. When carefully done, the sampling increases confidence in the generality (or external validity) of the findings. Random sampling of cases from a defined universe reduces the possibility of selection biases (or self-selection) which pose the dilemma of alternative explanations for findings (see Sprinz and Wolinsky-Nahmias, 2004, pp. 368–369). The large number of cases also increases the scope of the comparisons and permits the use of statistical techniques for evaluating relationships among variables. This tradition of case-based research in international relations can be traced to McClelland's (1976) analyses of the World Events Interaction Survey. In anthropology, this tradition has been strongly influenced by Murdock's (1957) World Ethnographic Sample and by Whiting and Child's (1953) cross-culture analyses of child training. It has been refined by Naroll (1962) and by the authors in Naroll and Cohen's (1973) handbook. Building on these foundations, the method has gained popularity in research on conflict management.

Parallel aggregate case research streams have been developed by Bercovitch and collaborators on international mediation and by Druckman and associates on negotiation. The former have compiled a useful data set of 333 international conflicts since 1945. A variety of coded features include information about the parties, the conflict, and the conflict management agents. Guided by a conceptual framework that connects these categories, the authors have identified conditions influencing mediation success. Their statistical analyses make evident contingent relationships between independent (concerning the dispute, the parties, the mediation process, and the mediator) and dependent (mediation success) variables. For example, short conflicts with few fatalities are more amenable to mediation than other kinds of disputes; conflicts involving parties with the same amount of power are more likely to be successfully mediated than conflicts between parties that differ in power or available resources (Bercovitch and Trappl, 2006). Further aggregate analyses of mediation showed that third parties were more likely to be used in complex (many issues) negotiations (Druckman, 1997).

The large-n analyses of international negotiations have also produced a number of interesting findings. A key dimension that ran through 23 negotiation cases was whether the talks were bilateral or multilateral. More treaties result from talks with a smaller number of parties (Druckman, 1997). In an analysis of 30 cases of negotiation sampled from a listing of 176 cases in the Pew Case Studies in International Affairs, Druckman et al., (1999) found that the cases were distinguished in terms of a well-known typology

of negotiation proposed by Iklé (1964): profiles of features differed depending on whether the talks were primarily distributive, integrative, normalizing, extension, or side effects. Another analysis examined turning points that occurred in 34 cases, distinguished in terms of issue area – security, trade, or environmental. The most frequently occurring trigger for the security cases was an external event, such as third-party assistance; triggers of turning points were from within the talks (as substantive or procedural decisions) in the trade and environmental cases.

These differences highlight the risk-averse approaches taken by negotiators in the area of security (Druckman, 2001). Risk aversion is also highlighted in the Ember and Ember (1992) study of resource security and warfare in 186 societies (using the Human Relations Area Files). They showed that fear of others and of nature were the strongest predictors of war. Specifically, fear of the future rather than current problems of scarcity appeared to be the primary motive for war. Warfare was used for plundering resources in order to protect against an uncertain future.

Interesting findings about conflict have been obtained also from a number of other aggregate case studies. Diehl et al., (1998) multidimensional scaling of expert judgments showed that different types of peacekeeping missions clustered around two dimensions, roles and processes. Peacekeepers in some missions played primary roles (e.g. collective enforcement, state/nation building). In other missions (e.g. election supervision, arms control verification), they are third parties. Missions characterized primarily by distributive processes include collective enforcement, sanctions enforcement, and pacification. Those where integrative or problem-solving processes are emphasized include election supervision, nation building, and observation. These findings contribute to the development of taxonomies with implications for training.

Compelling findings about the factors that lead to the initiation (but not the duration) of ethnic conflict within societies were reported by Gurr and his colleagues (2005).

Their sophisticated statistical analyses produced a probability (odds ratio) ordering of various drivers of internal conflict: state-led discrimination, ethnic diversity, regime type, spillover or neighborhood effects, recency of ethnic wars, and youth bulge. Similar factors were shown to drive conflict in predominantly Muslim societies. This study is notable for the careful analyses performed as well as the policy implications derived. Factionalism, more than regime type, led to a larger risk of ethnic conflict. This suggests the strategy of institutionalizing political participation in a manner that cuts across communal lines with policies aimed at easing discrimination against minorities. Another implication from the findings concerns transitions to democracy. The authors suggest that attempts to democratize autocratic regimes in Muslim countries increase the short-term risks of political instability. This would seem to be a result of the persisting influence of under-development and being in "bad neighborhoods."

Another recent aggregate case analysis with policy implications was performed by Downs and Stedman (2002). They were interested in the factors that influenced the successful implementation of peace agreements negotiated during the early 1990s. Specifically, they examined the relative impact on the implementation outcome of the difficulty of the conflict environment and the willingness of other states to intervene in the conflict. A difficulty index was constructed as an aggregate score of eight measured factors: for example, the number of warring parties, hostile neighboring states, number of soldiers, wars of secession. A willingness index was composed of three factors – major or regional power interest, resource commitment, and acceptance of risk to soldiers. These indices were regressed on an implementation outcome judged as a success, partial success, or failure. The difficulty index was a stronger predictor of outcomes than the willingness index: a partial correlation of $-.66$ between difficulty and outcome actually increases to $-.76$ when willingness is controlled; the correlation between willingness and outcomes

is .33. The key factors in the conflict environment were the existence of a spoiler, the presence of disposable resources, and a neighboring state hostile to the agreement.

Taking the Downs-Stedman analyses a step further, Druckman and Albin (2008) included the extent to which each of these cases included principles of distributive justice in the text of the agreement: each document was coded for the number of principles included – equality, proportionality, compensation, need. They found that justice moderated the relationship between difficulty and the implementation outcome: the more justice principles included in the agreement, the less severe the effects of difficult environments. Justice principles can offset the negative effects of the conflict environment; they can also reinforce the positive effects of an environment that is more conducive to peace. These findings were bolstered by the results of complementary qualitative (focused comparisons) analyses and will be re-visited in the section below on multi-method research.

The four case-study approaches entail somewhat different data requirements. For enhanced case studies, detailed descriptive information is needed. Event chronologies must be developed for both qualitative and quantitative time series. Comparable units must be constructed for matched-cases in focused comparisons and generic codes (e.g. cooperation–competition scales) are essential for aggregate analyses. These data and measurement requirements turn on the availability (and quality) of information. Often, the information comes from archival sources such as the Pew Case Studies in International Affairs (1999). Missing from most archival documentation, including the Pew cases, is a common framework that organizes the diverse case material for analysis. This shortcoming was noted by the authors in the special issue on data sets edited by Telhami (2002). They recognized the value of conceptual frameworks that capture processes, dynamics, structures, relationships, and issue areas for analyses of negotiation in particular but also for studies of conflict management more generally. Such frameworks should guide (primary analysis) rather than follow (secondary analysis) data collection. With the advent of web-based technologies, case researchers can access information directly from conflict actors, even before settlements or resolutions have occurred, reducing their reliance on secondary analyses of information gathered at an earlier time for other purposes (Druckman, 2002). The discussion of documentation continues in the next section.

ANALYZING DOCUMENTS

Documents are important sources of material about conflict and conflict-resolving approaches. Often they are the primary source of information about a conflict that occurred in the past. They come in many forms including speeches given by leaders or group representatives, conversations held between negotiators, and events or activities observed by scholar-researchers. The quality of the documentation varies with the extent to which it captures what was actually said or presented: transcripts of speeches or conversations are more valuable for analysis than documents based on observers' judgment of what occurred. Both types of documentation, first and second-person, have been used for qualitative and quantitative content analyses of relationships between conflict processes and outcomes, as well as for assessing the impacts from interventions on the course of a conflict. The content analysis studies discussed in this section provide examples of applications on several topics.

An important contribution of content analysis is to the comparative analysis of conflict processes. Comparison is facilitated when the same categories are used to code conversations among disputing parties or their representatives in different negotiations. Recorded conversations between negotiators were the material used for coding labor – management disputes (Landsberger, 1955), religious conflict (McGrath and Julian, 1963), industrial wage negotiations (Stephenson et al., 1977), arms control talks (Bonham,

1971; Jensen, 1984), base rights negotiations (Druckman, 1986), and a variety of laboratory simulations (Zechmeister and Druckman, 1973; Pruitt and Lewis, 1977; Beriker and Druckman, 1996). Many of the coding systems used in these studies evolved from Bales' (1950) interaction process analysis. The changes reflect differences between problem-solving and negotiation groups, particularly with regard to the mixed-motive (cooperative and conflictual) features of negotiation. These features are captured in the popular coding system known as bargaining process analysis (BPA). A sampling of findings from these studies follows.

The BPA system has been used to evaluate a number of hypotheses in a variety of cases. Hopmann's (1978) analysis of the Conference on Security and Cooperation in Europe showed that threat potential (how much a country stands to lose by no agreement) influenced the outcome (portion of the text authored by each member state). Exercising their right to use a veto over the agenda, the more powerful parties effectively prevented unfavorable decisions from being made. They acted together to preserve their joint interest in domination over their blocs and the nonaligned states. On the other hand, countries with low threat potential (Yugoslavia, Romania, France) became somewhat influential by acting together on the basis of their common interest to change the prevailing structures.

Further evidence for super-power dominance – or structural asymmetry – comes from King's (1979) study of the UN Special Session on Disarmament and from a study of the Mutual and Balanced Force Reduction talks discussed by Druckman and Hopmann (2002). Both these studies provided content-analysis evidence for a "bilateral condominium" between US and Soviet negotiators: they were more responsive to each other than to any of their allies. Many of these BPA studies were included in a multi-case analysis of responsiveness by Druckman and Harris (1990). These researchers found that a particular model, referred to as comparative reciprocity, best captured the way that bargainers responded to each other. Bargainers responded to each other's moves in similar ways across a variety of types of security talks: different parties, issues, time periods, and length. This study demonstrates the value of content analysis for creating data points in a time series used for comparative analyses.

The BPA system has also been used to compare processes in historical negotiations with those that take place in a laboratory simulation of those talks. The study by Beriker and Druckman (1996) compared the way bargainers reached agreements in the peace talks at Lausanne following WWI with student-role players of those diplomats. Content analysis of the Turkish-language transcripts of the official talks and the taped conversations of the laboratory bargainers produced several interesting findings. For example, the enhanced competitiveness of the Turkish delegates on issues in which they were part of a coalition (compared to issues when they were a single party facing a coalition) was reproduced in the simulation. An additional finding from the laboratory was that more agreements occurred when equally weak parties (Turkey and Greece) negotiated. In another BPA comparison of a real-world and simulated case, Ozcelik (2004) found similar differences between asymmetrical and symmetrical power configurations in the UN Framework Convention of Climate Change and a simulation of those talks. Using a different coding system – messages coded for hostility and attacks on the motives of the other side – Bonham (1971) demonstrated that the experimentally induced differences between parties about the relative importance of two disarmament issues resulted in greater negative affect and hostility, fewer concessions, less reciprocation, and fewer agreements in a simulation of the 1955 trilateral (USA, Soviet Union, United Kingdom) UN Disarmament Subcommittee. These studies illustrate a contribution of content analysis to simulation validity.

As is apparent from the studies reviewed above, content analysis has made many contributions to our understanding of negotiation

processes. This may be due, in large part, to the quality of public documentation available for many cases. It is also due to the efforts that have been made to develop reliable and valid coding systems tailored to this kind of interaction. Add to this the care that has been taken to insure a systematic procedure, and the ingredients for a successful study are in place. (See Druckman, 2005, Chapter 9 for a checklist of steps in performing content analysis.) However, valuable contributions can be made with less precise documentation. An example is the study by Irmer (2003) on comparative peace processes. Instead of coding words or sentences, she developed scales to capture such dimensions as distributive or integrative bargaining processes. The scales were better suited to the more interpretive material available on these cases. Strong relationships between processes and outcomes across 30 cases were demonstrated. Another contribution comes from researchers who have developed more complex approaches to coding. These include Roberts' (1997) semantic text analysis, Donohue and Roberto's (1993) negotiated order approach, and the various forms taken by narrative or discourse analysis (Riessman, 1993). Each of these approaches is intended to capture more nuanced communication from the text with an eye on deeper meaning. They are also suited to the concepts that emanate from more complex theories of communication.

EVALUATING INTERVENTIONS

Conflict management is both a theoretical and an applied field. Many of the methods reviewed to this point in the chapter are suited to addressing theoretical issues or debates. They also consist of tools that can be used to evaluate interventions designed to settle or resolve conflicts. Several tools – both quantitative and qualitative applications – are often combined in the course of an evaluation project. The interventions include a variety of conflict domains and conflict resolution approaches: for example, formal and informal mediation, facilitation and interactive conflict resolution, peace-keeping missions, peace-building programs, transformative and structural interventions, and humanitarian programs implemented by non-governmental organizations. In this section, I discuss the challenges of evaluating interventions and provide examples of how evaluation projects are done.

A first challenge is to answer the question: What is being evaluated? An intervention can be a single, well-defined treatment such as an electronic mediation delivered at the time of a negotiation impasse. It can also consist of a family of procedures such as a peacekeeping mission. The former type of intervention is easier to evaluate; comparisons with a no-treatment control group facilitate causal inference. The latter presents the larger challenge of ascertaining the contributions of different parts of the package. Another distinction is between case-specific and generic evaluations. Programs designed for implementation in specific schools, communities, or regions are evaluated in the context of those institutions or organizations. Administrators and policy makers are concerned about local impacts: Does it work? Much of the peer-mediation literature consists of program-specific evaluations. A more theoretical approach to evaluation is taken by those investigators (and practitioners) interested in types of interventions. The concern here is with generality: Does the approach of interactive conflict resolution work? This question is addressed with accumulated cases in a comparative research design. The single, well-defined intervention facilitates attempts to infer causation between the administration of the intervention and its impact on processes or outcomes.

A second challenge asks about effectiveness. This includes addressing the summative (impact) question: Did it work? It also includes the formative question: How did it work? Summative evaluations turn on the distinction between short- and long-term impacts. A reduction in violence or stabilization may last only as long as the peacekeeping forces remain in the country. School violence may erupt again sometime after the peer mediation programs have ended. This reversal calls attention to the need to monitor situations for some time after the intervention. They raise questions about whether to return or to alter the approach taken by the initial mission or program. Formative evaluations ask about the reasons for success or failure of interventions. Alternative explanations for outcomes often emerge. For example, an increased number of court cases investigating corrupt practices suggest that the rule of law has been restored. They may also suggest that the level of corruption remains high despite the efforts of the peace-building team. School peer-mediation programs may reduce violence because of the climate created by their implementation rather than the specific techniques used. Explaining the reason for observed impacts is important. It helps evaluators understand why impacts occur and to re-consider the way their interventions are delivered.

A third challenge refers to the dynamics of interventions. The popularity of a contingency approach to conflict analysis is based on the observation that situations and perceptions change. Intervention may have different effects at different stages of a resolution process. Negotiation research has shown that situational influences change from one stage of the talks to another (Druckman, 1993). At different stages, particular aspects of the situation seem to cause the way a negotiation (or conflict) process moves – often abruptly – from a sequence of escalatory moves to de-escalation (Zartman, 2000). These observations call attention to the idea that interventions may be moving targets analyzed with interrupted time-series research designs (see the section above on time-series analysis). The dynamics challenge is met when the evaluation produces time and situation-specific effects for the interventions. An added bonus would be a comparison to no-intervention "controls."

These challenges raise issues about the value of evaluations. They are practical concerns for the client or sponsoring organization. They are also research concerns for the evaluator who is keen on making a more lasting contribution to the field. The practical concerns include a clear definition of the intervention or program being evaluated, identification of the stakeholders and their interests, developing both summative and formative indicators, assembling a team with an appropriate division of labor, providing briefings and draft reports that are sensitive to the political environment in which the evaluation is conducted, and insuring that the recommendations are implemented. Clarity in defining the intervention is also a concern for researchers. But, in addition, sampling, control groups (including a matched "treatment"– no treatment comparison), and monitoring effects over time for assessing change are important considerations.

A layer of complexity is added to evaluations when interventions conducted at a micro-level (interactions among disputants) are evaluated for impact at a macro-level (societal changes). This problem is illustrated by evaluations of problem-solving workshops, where assessments of attitude change at a micro-level are linked to assessments of public opinion at a macro-level (Rouhana, 2000). A question of interest is whether changes in workshops surface in larger changes in their respective populations. A technical challenge is to insure proper time lags to infer causality: long enough to allow for transfer from the workshops to the societies but not so long as to put other influences on societal opinions into play. A number of the research methods discussed in the sections above can be used together in a complementary fashion: for example, pre/post-test comparisons for attitude changes at the micro-level, sample surveys for public opinion assessment, time series for monitoring changes in public attitudes, and Bayesian techniques for updating probability estimates based on changes in situations or the introduction of new interventions.

Evaluations can be performed in a variety of ways. Useful recommendations can be made from the application of less-rigorous approaches to research design. One of these approaches is referred to

as action research. Like other forms of evaluation research, this approach seeks to provide recommendations (action plans) for organization or community change. Unlike evaluation research, it promotes close collaboration between investigators and organization/community members in all phases of the research process. The participants in the research do not simply provide information to the researchers; they influence the direction taken by the project by designing the change, observing what happens following the change, reflecting on these processes and consequences, and planning further action (Kemmis and Wilkinson, 1998). The emphasis of these activities on process places action research in the realm of formative evaluation. The central role played by the consumers of the project and its products renders this approach different than other formative evaluations. Although there is considerable flexibility in the way an action project is implemented, most are guided by a sequence of tasks discussed by Bassey (1998), Robson (2002), and Druckman (2005).

Senehi's (2002) idea of constructive storytelling resonates with the connection between social change and conflict intervention. Stories are regarded as being accessible, fluid, vivid, and powerful forms of expression that can bring disputants together; but they can also be divisive. By incorporating storytelling activities into action research projects, participants may acquire insights that compel them to take action. Another application of the action-research approach to resolving conflicts has been made by Rothman (1997) in an Israeli training context. (See also Ross and Rothman, 1999, for a perspective on both action and evaluation research.). Although not made explicit by its practitioners, the goals and procedures used for implementing problem-solving workshops may be considered as action research. An emphasis on social change is reflected in the shared goal of contributing to the resolution of resolving bitter conflicts between participants' countries. The idea of involving workshop members in – or at least being transparent about – all phases of the activities is intended to enhance their desire for change, reduce divisions among them, and encourage them to promote change in their societies. Lacking, however, in these and many of the other action research projects is evidence on effectiveness from the standpoint of both formative and summative criteria.

Other forms of applied research on conflict come under the rubric of research consulting. This refers to projects driven by problems defined by clients. The analytical consultants on many of these projects are asked to perform a variety of roles. For example, four roles were implemented on a recent consulting project. The problem consisted of development of a framework for organizing the various parts of complex inter-governmental negotiations. The role of advisor turned into that of bridge-builder (between the consulting/policy and academic communities) as the lead investigator sought input from academic specialists familiar with frameworks and with specific cases. The tasks involved theoretical knowledge and technical skills. The former was needed to identify key features of negotiation and to organize them into a framework that connected them in space and through time. The latter role involved reliability testing, refinement, developing weighting procedures, and performing analyses. The product was transmitted to the client in the form of a report that emphasized applications of the framework to familiar cases of negotiation. Training in a variety of methodological approaches goes a long way toward producing a useful product. It is also useful for making contributions to theory in the field of conflict analysis. I turn next to a discussion of the value of multi-method research.

RESEARCH CONDUCTED THROUGH A MULTI-METHOD LENS

It is clear from the discussion that a variety of methodological approaches have been used to analyze conflict. Only a few of these studies have employed several methods. Researchers in this field have not, for the most part, taken advantage of the complementarities that exist among the various approaches to doing research. This is evident as well in the chapters written for the Maoz et al. (2004) book on different methodological approaches to the study of mediation and conflict management. Each author illuminates the value of a particular approach used to address research questions in the field. The approaches include game theory, simulation, large-N statistical analyses, and historical case studies.[3] In his concluding essay, Stoll (2004) describes the strengths and weaknesses of each approach but laments the state-of-the-art by noting that: "Research that relies on any one approach is usually inferior to research that makes use of several methods" (2004, 360). He adds "that it is a rare situation where one method is so superior that the others can safely be ignored" (2004, 360). Several multi-method studies are discussed in this section.

A multi-method design trades the weaknesses of one approach for the strengths of another as these are described in this chapter and by Stoll (2004): for example, the breadth of a random-sample survey for the depth of a detailed case study. When the different approaches are used together in sequence, a more complete picture of the conflict or resolution process is achieved. This can be illustrated by two studies of peace agreements: our study of relationships between principles of justice and the durability of agreements negotiated during the late 1980s and early 1990s (Druckman and Albin, 2008) and Irmer and Druckman (2007) study of the relationship between the processes and outcomes of a variety of peace agreements.

The justice and durability study combined an aggregate analysis of 16 peace agreements with a focused comparison of selected cases. The former analysis produced a statistical model of the role played by justice in implementing the agreements: justice principles moderated the relationship between the conflict environment and implementation success. The latter analysis showed that many principles of justice increased the chances of success in difficult conflict environments.

Few justice principles in an agreement decreased the chances of complete success in less difficult environments.

The qualitative results bolster the quantitative findings: both show that justice principles play a moderating role, first in the form of a statistical path model and then as a 2 × 2 matrix of difficulty (high or low) by justice principles (many or few). Both analyses illuminate the value of control: partial correlations were used in the aggregate analysis, while case selection (the combinations of high-low, few-many of the two variables) created independent variables in the focused comparison. The complementarity is between the more robust analysis of a variety of cases and a more controlled analysis of cases selected on the theoretical variables of interest.

Irmer and Druckman's study is novel in the way it uses methods to build a logical argument that bolsters explanation. The analyses proceed in sequence from initial quantitative work to later qualitative inquiries. After constructing process and outcome indicators and assembling a data set of 26 cases, the investigator calculated a correlation among the process and outcome indices. An average correlation of .82 indicates a very strong relationship. Not considered in the analysis, however, were the effects of context: the strong association between process and outcome may be accounted for by correlated context variables. Thus, a second step consisted of controlling for context by calculating partial correlations. These correlations remained strong, indicating that process rather than context accounted for the outcomes. The next question asked was whether this relationship was causal. By tracing the process in each of four cases (not part of the aggregate data set), they showed that outcomes – as comprehensive, partial, or deadlock – were indeed caused by the coded processes. A final step in the sequence entailed an attempt to discover a mechanism that could explain the causal relationship. Referred to as a plausibility probe, the analysis showed that the development of trust through phases of the talks appeared to provide a plausible

explanation. The mode of inquiry used in this study – designated as A (association), C (causation), E (explanation) – may be considered a model for research on negotiation and peace processes.

This study provides an example of moving beyond the use of single methods. It addresses the internal validity of statistical relationships. Earlier multi-method analyses of negotiation addressed issues of external validity. These include Hopmann and Walcott's (1977) pioneering effort to combine simulation and content analysis of transcripts in seeking to understand the behavior of arms-control negotiators. They also include the simulation/case study analyses by Beriker and Druckman (1996) on multilateral post-WWI peace talks and by Ozcelik (2004) on multilateral environmental regime talks. Similarly, my research on turning points and models of responsiveness, discussed earlier, shows how findings obtained from single-case studies can be generalized by conducting statistical analyses of many cases.

Another example of combined methods comes from a study on mediating international crises. Wilkenfeld and his colleagues (2003) explored the same research questions with two methods: the International Crisis Behavior events data set and an experimental simulation based on the Ecuador/Peru border dispute of 1981. The historical events data analyses showed that mediated crises were usually characterized by compromise among the disputants, more likely to end in agreement, and indicated a tendency toward long-term tension reduction. The simulation findings confirmed these findings while also adding other results: mediation leads to crises of shorter duration and to greater satisfaction with the outcome. In addition, the simulation data revealed that a manipulative mediation style produced more benefits from crisis termination than a facilitation style.

These findings illuminate several advantages of a multi-method approach. One concerns the validity of results: confirmation with another method increases confidence in the results. Another concerns additional discoveries: new findings extend our understanding of mediation impacts. And, a third advantage is the opportunity to explore questions that cannot be addressed with events data: information on crisis duration and on mediator style were obtained from the laboratory study. Going further, the laboratory allows for imaginative construction of conditions that did not occur in the case but have theoretical relevance as illustrated by this study and that conducted by Beriker and Druckman (1996). (See Sprinz and Wolinsky-Nahmias, 2004, for more on counter-factual analysis.)

These studies illuminate the value of multi-method research on negotiation. Conceivably, this topic is suited to these sorts of complex analyses. One reason is that there is a treasure trove of well-documented cases for content analysis. Another is that the processes in many of these cases are relatively easy to simulate. And, a third reason is that the literature is well developed in terms of theories, models, and empirical research. For these reasons, among others, we have learned much about processes and strategies of negotiation. Among the remaining research challenges are connecting negotiation to the sources of conflict that gave rise to the issues and to the aftermath of the implementing phase where relationships between disputing parties undergo change. These problems would also benefit from studies that view them through a multi-method lens.

CONCLUSION

The multi-method approach taken in this chapter was inspired by the innovative approach to research developed half a century ago by Campbell. The Campbell and Fiske (1959) idea of a multi-method multi-trait matrix was a major departure from the way that psychologists did research. The idea that methods can contribute to findings and their interpretation was novel. It challenged the prevailing positivist assumptions about the way that empirical research was

to be performed. Continuing along these lines, Campbell trumpeted the value of quasi-experimentation. First, with his colleague Stanley (Campbell and Stanley, 1963), he provided a foundation for field experimentation by showing that valid findings can be obtained even when the hallowed assumption of random assignment is not satisfied. Then, with Cook (Cook and Campbell, 1979), he further developed the statistical tools for inferring causality from field data. Cook (1985) took the gauntlet from Campbell and proposed a philosophical departure for social science referred to as "post-positivist critical multiplism." The strategy that was being advanced by these pioneers was that of "triangulation." According to Stern and Druckman, this refers to "multiple data sources and multiple modes of analysis to correct the characteristic sources of error and bias in each and to help analysis converge on results that can be accepted with reasonable confidence" (2000: 60). This approach to research is also gaining momentum in international relations (Sprinz and Wolinsky-Nahmias, 2004) and conflict analysis (Maoz et al., 2004; Druckman, 2005).

The variety of examples discussed in this chapter illustrate pluralism in research on problems of conflict and conflict resolution. Although pluralism is more evident *between* studies, there is a discernable trend in the direction of using several methods *within* studies. Increasingly, conflict researchers are becoming aware of the advantages of compensating for the weaknesses in a particular method by adding another approach to data collection and analysis.[4] The multi-method lens may be best understood in terms of the tradeoffs between methods.

The age-old challenge of bridging internal with external validity has become the joint plight of the experimental and field researcher. For the experimentalist, a turn toward simulation with its emphasis on scenario design has provided a way of addressing issues of context (external validity) without forfeiting the analytical advantages of laboratory controls. For the field researcher, a turn toward focused comparisons has provided a way of introducing "controls" (internal validity) into case study designs without forfeiting the advantages of the context provided by field or archival research. Teaming up by conducting simulations and doing focused comparisons, the experimentalist and field researcher can accomplish their joint goal of developing and testing theory-inspired ideas in relevant settings. Going still further, the team can address the problem of counterfactuals by creating hypothetical laboratory scenarios of unrealized pasts or futures. They can also probe more deeply – in the form of an enhanced case study – into particular conflict processes by selecting a case from the focused comparison for more detailed examination of conflict cycles and third-party interventions.

Although this dual-method strategy would bridge internal and external validity challenges, weaknesses remain. Neither approach includes a random sampling design. Without random – or representative – sampling, results are subject to the possibility of selection bias. This means that experimental and case findings may be limited to the particular subjects and cases chosen. The challenge is to define a universe from which subjects are chosen and cases are selected. Nor do the approaches explicitly analyze data collected over time. This entails more data points in a repeated-measures experimental design or a time series of events that are documented for a defined period. The "data points" can also be stages in a process-tracing design or sequential interviews of stakeholders in a formative evaluation design. The importance of these data, whether coded numerically or categorically, is that they capture change, which is an essential feature of conflict. Change is also important in the applied world of conflict practitioners. Placing the experiments and case studies in an evaluation or action research context would create another bridge, between the research and applied communities. Proceeding in sequence from one method to another satisfies the checklist of weaknesses to be addressed by a research project. It also pushes the investigative envelop

in the direction of more holistic research programs.

NOTES

1 Because of space limitations, this chapter does not review the valuable contributions made by constructivist researchers to methods for studying conflict. Studies on discourse analysis and grounded theory are particularly relevant. The interested reader should consult Cheldelin et al. (2008, Chapter 2) for a review of studies in this tradition. On discourse analysis, Winslade and Monk (2000) discuss their approach to the theory and practice of narrative mediation. On the rationale and application of grounded theory, see Strauss and Corbin (1990).

2 Perhaps the earliest attempt to perform a field experiment on conflict resolution is the popular robbers cave study performed by Sherif and his colleagues (1961). Their demonstration of the positive impact of a superordinate goal has captured the popular imagination. The problem with the study is that it was a non-replicated demonstration experiment. The value of the study is that it stimulated a debate during the cold war about alternative strategies for reducing tensions as well as considerable research on the topic. (See Johnson and Lewicki [1969] for an example of earlier research; see Brown and Wade [2006] for a recent study on the concept. The research shows both positive and negative impacts of superordinate goals on resolving conflicts.)

3 Despite the differences in methodological approach, the various studies in this volume converge on the general conclusion that there are no assurances that international mediation will lead to better outcomes or a successful conclusion of negotiations. The effects of mediation are contingent on a variety of factors in the situation as well as the broader context of the conflict (see, in particular, the chapter by Bercovitch and Regan, 2004).

4 The idea of methodological pluralism differs from cumulation in research. A key difference is that pluralism is based on methods variance, while cumulation depends to a large extent on methods invariance. The former emphasizes robustness, while the latter "adds up" results obtained from replicated studies. These different aims are also reflected in technical approaches to doing research: complementary methods that address the same research question versus effect sizes calculated with meta-analytic techniques. Both approaches are concerned with the issue of generality but approach that issue from different angles. Just as replicated findings provide evidence for general effects, similar results from different methods also provide evidence for generality. However, the multi-method approach allows for the possibility of contingent findings. A number of multi-method studies illustrate both

types of findings (e.g. Wilkenfeld et al., 2003). The meaning of cumulation in an age of methodological pluralism is an issue that merits more attention. It is relevant to the debate over internal versus external validity.

REFERENCES

Allen Nan, S. (1999). *Complementarity and coordination of conflict resolution efforts in the conflicts over Abkhazia, South Ossetia, and Transdniestria.* Unpublished doctoral dissertation, George Mason University, Fairfax, VA.

Avenhaus, R. and Zartman, I.W. (Eds.) (2007). *Diplomacy Games: Formal Models of International Negotiation.* Berlin Heidelberg: Springer.

Axelrod, R. (1970). *Conflict of Interest: A Theory of Divergent Goals with Applications to Politics.* Chicago: Markham.

Bales, R.F. (1950). *Interaction Process Analysis.* Reading, MA: Addison-Wesley.

Bartos, O.J. (1995). Modeling distributive and integrative negotiations. *Annals of the American Academy of Political and Social Science,* 542, 48–60.

Bassey, M. (1998). Action research for improving educational practice. In R. Halsall (Ed.) *Teacher Research and School Improvement: Opening Doors from the Inside.* Buckingham, England: Open University Press.

Bercovitch, J. and Regan, P.M. (2004). Mediation and international conflict management: A review and analysis. In Z. Maoz, A. Mintz, T.C. Morgan, G. Palmer, and R.J. Stoll (Eds.) *Multiple Paths to Knowledge in International Relations.* Lanham, MD: Lexington Books.

Bercovitch, J. and Trappl, R. (2006). Machine learning methods for better understanding, resolving, and preventing international conflict. In R. Trappl (Ed.) *Programming for Peace: Computer-aided Methods for International Conflict Resolution and Prevention.* Dordrecht, The Netherlands: Springer.

Beriker, N. and Druckman, D. (1996). Simulating the Lausanne peace negotiations, 1922–23. *Simulation & Gaming,* 27, 162–183.

Birkhoff, J.E. (2001). *Mediators' perspectives on power: A window into a profession?* Unpublished doctoral dissertation, George Mason University, Frairfax, VA.

Bonham, M.M. (1971). Simulating disarmament negotiations. *Journal of Conflict Resolution,* 15, 299–318.

Brown, R. and Wade, G. (2006). Superordinate goals and intergroup behaviour: The effect of role ambiguity and status on intergroup attitudes and task performance. *European Journal of Social Psychology,* 17, 131–142.

Burn, M. (2006). *Loyalty and order: Clan identity and political preference in Kyrgyzstan and Kazakhstan, 2005.* Unpublished doctoral dissertation, George Mason University, Fairfax, VA.

Cameron, M. and Tomlin, B. (2000). *The Making of NAFTA: How the Deal Was Done.* Ithaca, NY: Cornell University Press.

Campbell, D.T. and Fiske, D.W. (1959). Convergent and discriminant validation by the multitrait-multimethod matrix. *Psychological Bulletin,* 59, 81–105.

Campbell, D.T. and Stanley, J.C. (1963). *Experimental and quasi-experimental designs for research.* Boston: Houghton-Mifflin.

Carnevale, P. and De Dreu, C.K.W. (2006). Laboratory experiments on social conflict. In P. Carnevale and C.K.W. De Dreu (Eds.) *Methods of Negotiation Research.* Leiden, The Netherlands: Martinus Nijhoff Publishers.

Carstarphen, N. (2003). *Shift happens: Transformations during small group interventions in protracted social conflicts.* Unpublished doctoral dissertation, George Mason University, Fairfax, VA.

Cheldelin, S., Druckman, D., and Fast, L. (2008). *Conflict: From Analysis to Action, 2nd Edn.* London: Continuum.

Cohen, R. and Westbrook, R. (2000). (Eds.) *Amarna Diplomacy: The Beginnings of International Relations.* Baltimore, MD: Johns Hopkins University Press.

Coleman, J.S. (1973). *The Mathematics of Collective Action.* Chicago: Aldine.

Coleman, P.T., Vallacher, R., Nowak, A., and Ngoc, L.B. (2005). Intractable conflict as an attractor: Presenting a dynamical model of conflict escalation and intractability. Paper presented at the 18th Annual conference of the International Association of Conflict Management, Seville, Spain.

Cook, T.D. (1985). Post-positivist critical multiplism. In R.L. Shotland and M.M. Mark (Eds.) *Social science and social policy.* Beverly Hills, CA: Sage.

Cook, T.D. and Campbell, D.T. (1979). *Quasi-experimentation.* Boston: Houghton-Mifflin.

Deutsch, M. and Krauss, R.M. (1962). Studies of interpersonal bargaining. *Journal of Conflict Resolution,* 6, 52–76.

Diehl, P., Druckman, D., and Wall, J. (1998). International peacekeeping and conflict resolution: A taxonomic analysis with implications. *Journal of Conflict Resolution,* 42, 33–55.

Donohue, W.A. and Roberto, A.J. (1993). Relational development as negotiated order in hostage negotiations. *Human Communication Research,* 20, 175–198.

Dougherty, J. (2006). *The Critical Mass of Social Change: Northern Ireland Integrated Education.*

Unpublished doctoral dissertation, George Mason University, Fairfax, VA.

Downs, G. and Stedman, S.J. (2002). Evaluation issues in peace implementation. In S. Stedman, D. Rothchild, and E. Cousens. (Eds.) *Ending Civil Wars: The Implementation of Peace Agreements.* Boulder, Colorado and London: Lynne Rienner Publishers.

Druckman, D. (1986). Stages, turning points, and crises: Negotiating military base rights, Spain and the United States. *Journal of Conflict Resolution*, 30, 327–360.

Druckman, D. (1993). The situational levers of negotiating flexibility. *Journal of Conflict Resolution*, 37, 236–276.

Druckman, D. (1997). Dimensions of international negotiations: Structures, processes, and outcomes. *Group Decision and Negotiation*, 6, 395–420.

Druckman, D. (2001). Turning points in international negotiation: A comparative analysis. *Journal of Conflict Resolution*, 45, 519–544.

Druckman, D. (2002). Case-based research on international negotiation: Approaches and data sets. *International Negotiation*, 7, 17–37.

Druckman, D. (2005). *Doing Research: Methods of Inquiry for Conflict Analysis.* Thousand Oaks, CA: Sage.

Druckman, D. (2006). A marathon exercise. In A.K. Schneider and C. Honeyman (Eds.) *The Negotiator's Fieldbook: The Desk Reference for the Experienced Negotiator.* Washington, DC: American Bar Association.

Druckman, D. and Albin, C. (2008). Distributive justice and the durability of negotiated agreements. Occasional Paper No. 10, Australian Centre for Peace and Conflict Studies, University of Queensland, Brisbane, Australia (see www.uq.edu.au/acpacs).

Druckman, D. and Green, J. (1995). Playing two games: Internal negotiations in the Philippines. In I.W. Zartman (Ed.) *Elusive Peace: Negotiating an End to Civil Wars.* Washington, DC: Brookings.

Druckman, D. with Hopmann, T.P. (2002). Content analysis. In V.A. Kremenyuk (Ed.) *International Negotiation: Analysis, Approaches, Issues.* San Francisco: Jossey-Bass.

Druckman, D. and Lyons, T. (2005). Negotiation processes and post-settlement relations: Comparing Nagorno Karabakh with Mozambique. In I.W. Zartman and V.A. Kremenyuk (Eds.) *Peace vs. Justice: Negotiating Forward- and Backward-Looking Outcomes.* Lanham, MD: Rowman & Littlefield.

Druckman, D. and Harris, R. (1990). Alternative models of responsiveness in international negotiation. *Journal of Conflict Resolution*, 34, 234–251.

Druckman, D., Harris, R., and Furnkranz, J. (2006). Modeling international negotiation: Statistical and machine learning applications. In R. Trappl (Ed.) *Programming for Peace: Computer-aided Methods for International Conflict Resolution and Prevention.* Dordrecht, The Netherlands: Springer.

Druckman, D., Husbands, J.L. and Johnston, K. (1991). Turning points in the INF negotiations. *Negotiation Journal*, 7, 55–67.

Druckman, D., Martin, J. Allen Nan, S.and Yagcioglu, D. (1999). Dimensions of international negotiation: A test of Iklé's typology. *Group Decision and Negotiation*, 8, 89–108.

Ember, C.R. and Ember, M. (1992). Resource unpredictability, mistrust, and war: A cross-cultural study. *Journal of Conflict Resolution*, 36, 242–262.

Faure, A.M. (1994). Some methodological problems in comparative politics. *Journal of Comparative Politics*, 6, 307–322.

Frei, D. and Ruloff, D. (1989). *Handbook of Foreign Policy Analysis.* Dordrecht, The Netherlands: Martinus Nijhoff.

Gabbay, M. (2007). A dynamical systems model of small group decision making. In R. Avenhaus and I.W. Zartman (Eds.) *Diplomacy Games: Formal Models and International Negotiations.* Berlin Heidelberg: Springer.

Galtung, J. (1969). Violence, peace and peace research. *Journal of Peace Research*, 6, 167–191.

Gochal, J.R. and Levy, J.S. (2004). Crisis management or conflict of interests? A case study of the Crimean war. In Z. Maoz, A. Mintz, T.C. Morgan, G. Palmer, and R.J. Stoll (Eds.) *Multiple Paths to Knowledge in International Relations.* Lanham, MD: Lexington Books.

Guner, S. and Druckman, D. (2000). Identification of a princess under incomplete information: An Amarna story. *Theory and Decision*, 48, 383–410.

Gurr, T.R., Woodward, M. and Marshall, M.G. (2005). Forecasting instability: Are ethnic wars and Muslim countries different? Paper presented at the annual meeting of the American Political Science Association, Washington, DC.

Haskel, B. (1974). Disparities, strategies, and opportunity costs. *International Studies Quarterly*, 18, 3–30.

Hopmann, P.T. (1978). Asymmetrical bargaining in the conference on security and cooperation in Europe. *International Organization*, 32, 141–177.

Hopmann, P.T. and Walcott, C. (1977). The impact of external stresses and tensions on negotiation. In D. Druckman (Ed.) *Negotiations: Social–Psychological Perspectives.* Beverly Hills, CA: Sage.

Ikle, F.C. (1964). *How Nations Negotiate.* New York: Harper & Row.

Jensen, L. (1984). Negotiating strategic arms control, 1969–1979. *Journal of Conflict Resolution,* 28, 535–559.

Johnson, D.W. and Lewicki, R. (1969). The initiation of superordinate goals. *The Journal of Applied Behavioral Science,* 5, 9–24.

Kemmis, S. and Wilkinson, M. (1998). Participatory action research and the study of practice. In B. Atweh, S. Kemmis, and P. Weeks (Eds.) *Action Research in Practice: Partnerships for Social Justice in Education.* London: Routledge.

King, T.D. (1979). Bargaining in the United Nation's Special Session on Disarmament. Paper presented at the American Political Science Association, Washington, DC.

Krause, R.M., Druckman, D., Rozelle, R., and Mahoney, R. (1975). Components of value and representation in coalition formation. *Journal of Peace Science,* 1, 141–158.

Landsberger, H.A. (1955). Interaction process analysis of the mediation of labor management disputes. *Journal of Abnormal and Social Psychology,* 51, 552–558.

Maoz, Z., Mintz, A., Morgan, T.C., Palmer, G. and Stoll, R.J. (Eds.) (2004). *Multiple Paths to Knowledge in International Relations.* Lanham, MD: Lexington Books.

McClelland, C.A. (1976). *World event interaction survey code book (ICRSR 5211).* Ann Arbor, MI: Inter-University Consortium for Political and Social Research.

McGillicuddy, N.B., Welton, G.L., and Pruitt, D.G. (1987). Third-party intervention: A field experiment comparing three different models. *Journal of Personality and Social Psychology,* 53, 104–112.

McGrath, J.E. and Julian, J.W. (1963). Interaction process and task outcome in experimentally created negotiation groups. *Journal of Psychological Studies,* 14, 117–138.

Murdock, G.P. (1957). World ethnographic sample. *American Anthropologist,* 59: 664–687.

Naroll, R. (1962). *Data Quality Control: A New Research Technique.* New York: Free Press.

Naroll, R. and Cohen, R. (Eds.) (1973). *A Handbook of Method in Cultural Anthropology.* New York: Columbia University Press.

Osborne, M.J. (2004). *An Introduction to Game Theory.* New York: Oxford University Press.

Pew Case Studies in International Affairs (1999). *The ISD Compendium of Case Study Abstracts and Indexes.* Washington, DC: Institute for the Study of Diplomacy, Edmund A. Walsh School of Foreign Service, Georgetown University.

Pruitt, D.G. (2005a). Escalation, readiness for negotiation, and third-party functions. In I.W. Zartman and G.O. Faure (Eds.) *Escalation and Negotiation.* Cambridge, England: Cambridge University Press.

Pruitt, D.G. (2005b). Field experiments on social conflict. In P. Carnevale and C.K.W. De Dreu (Eds.) *Methods of Negotiation Research.* Leiden, The Netherlands: Martinus Nijhoff Publishers.

Pruitt, D.G. and Lewis, S.A. (1977). The psychology of integrative bargaining. In D. Druckman (Ed.) *Negotiations: Social–Psychological Perspectives.* Beverly Hills, CA: Sage.

Putnam, R. (1993). *Making Democracy Work: Civic Traditions in Modern Italy.* Princeton, NJ: Princeton University Press.

Riessman, C.K. (1993). *Narrative Analysis.* Newbury Park, CA: Sage.

Riker, W.H. (1962). *The Theory of Political Coalitions.* New Haven, CT: Yale University Press.

Robson, C. (2002). *Real World Research: A Resource for Social Scientists and Practitioner-Researchers, 2nd edn.* Oxford, UK: Blackwell.

Ross, M.H. and Rothman, J. (Eds.) (1999). *Theory and Practice in Ethnic Conflict Management: Conceptualizing Success and Failure.* London: Macmillan.

Rothman, J. (1997). Action evaluation and conflict resolution training. *International Negotiation,* 2, 451–470.

Rouhana, N.N. (2000). Interactive conflict resolution: Theoretical and methodological issues. In P.C. Stern and D. Druckman (Eds.) *International Conflict Resolution after the Cold War.* Washington, DC: National Academy Press.

Rubin, J.Z. (Ed.) (1981). *Dynamics of third-party intervention: Kissinger in the Middle East.* New York: Praeger.

Rubin, J.Z. and Brown, B.R. (1975). *The social psychology of bargaining and negotiation.* New York: Academic Press.

Sawyer, J. and Guetzkow, H. (1965). Bargaining and negotiation in international relations. In H.C. Kelman (Ed.) *International Behavior: A Social–Psychological Analysis.* New York: Holt, Rinehart, and Winston.

Schrodt, P.A. and Gerner, D.J. (2004). An event data analysis of third-party mediation in the Middle East and Balkins. *Journal of Conflict Resolution,* 48, 310–330.

Senehi, J. (2002). Constructive storytelling: A peace process. *Peace and Conflict Studies,* 9, 41–63.

Sherif, M., Harvey, O.J., White, B.J., Hood, W.R., and Sherif, C.W. (1961). *Intergroup Conflict and Cooperation: Robbers Cave Experiment.* Norman, OK: University of Oklahoma Book Exchange.

Siegel, S. and Fouraker, L.E. (1960). *Bargaining and Group Decision Making: Experiments in Bilateral Monopoly.* New York: McGraw-Hill.

Sprinz, D.F. and Wolinsky-Nahmias, Y. (Eds.) (2004). *Models, Numbers & Cases: Methods for Studying International Relations*. Ann Arbor, MI: University of Michigan Press.

Stephenson, G.M., Kniveton, B.F., and Morley, I.E. (1977). Interaction process analysis of an industrial wage negotiation. *Journal of Occupational Psychology*, 50, 231–241.

Stern, P.C. and Druckman, D. (2000). Evaluating interventions in history: The case of conflict resolution. *International Studies Review*, 2, 33–63.

Stoll, M.J. (2004). Conclusion: Multiple paths to knowledge? Integrating methodology and substance in the study of conflict management and conflict resolution. In Z. Maoz, A. Mintz, T.C. Morgan, G. Palmer, and R.J. Stoll (Eds.) *Multiple Paths to Knowledge in International Relations*. Lanham, MD: Lexington Books.

Strauss, A. and Corbin, J. (1990). *Basics of qualitative research: Grounded theory procedures and techniques*. Newbury Park, CA: Sage.

Tarrow, S. (1996). Making social science work across space and time. A critical reflection on Robert Putnam's *Making Democracy Work. American Political Science Review*, 90, 389–397.

Telhami, S. (Ed.) (2002). Establishing a data set on intrastate and international negotiation and mediation. Special issue, *International Negotiation*, 7 (1).

Trappl, R. (Ed.) (2006). *Programming for Peace: Computer-aided Methods for International Conflict Resolution and Prevention*. Dordrecht, The Netherlands: Springer.

Walker, S.G. (2004). The management and resolution of international conflict in a "single" case: American and North Vietnamese exchanges during the Vietnam war. In Z. Maoz, A. Mintz, T.C. Morgan, G. Palmer, and R.J. Stoll (Eds.) *Multiple Paths to Knowledge in International Relations*. Lanham, MD: Lexington Books.

Weiss, J.N. (2002). *Which way forward: Mediator sequencing strategies in intractable communal conflicts*. Unpublished doctoral dissertation, George Mason University, Fairfax, VA.

Whiting, J.W.M. and Child, I.L. (1953). *Child Training and Personality: A Cross-Cultural Study*. New Haven, CT: Yale University Press.

Wilkenfeld, J., Young, K., Asal, V., and Quinn, D. (2003). Mediating international crises: Cross-national and experimental perspectives. *Journal of Conflict Resolution*, 47, 279–301.

Winslade, J. and Monk, G.(2000). *Narrative Mediation: A New Approach to Conflict Resolution*. San Francisco: Jossey-Bass.

Zartman, I.W. (Ed.) (1994). *International Multilateral Negotiation: Approaches to the Management of Complexity*. San Francisco: Jossey-Bass.

Zartman, I.W. (Ed.) (1995). *Elusive Peace: Negotiating an End to Civil Wars*. Washington, DC: The Brookings Institution.

Zartman, I.W. (2000). Ripeness: The hurting stalemate and beyond. In P.C. Stern and D. Druckman (Eds) *International Conflict Resolution after the Cold War*. Washington, DC: National Academy Press.

Zechmeister, K. and Druckman, D. (1973). Determinants of resolving a conflict of interest: A simulation of political decision making. *Journal of Conflict Resolution*, 17: 63–88.

8

Problem-Solving Approaches

Tamra Pearson d'Estrée[1]

INTRODUCTION AND DEFINITIONS

Problem solving, when referring to conflict resolution approaches, has come to have more than one meaning as a term of art. These meanings are not unrelated conceptually, but as the term is used differently in different subsets of the field, it will be reviewed separately here also. In both cases, *problem-solving approaches* refer to specific intervention methodologies, with their own strategies, tactics, and assumptions.

First, in the work of intergroup and international conflict resolution, *problem-solving approaches* have come to mean off-the-record, face-to-face meetings between members of adversarial groups, where a third party facilitates participants working through a structured agenda that asks participants to consider the concerns of all parties participating, the shape of possible solutions, and the constraints faced by all parties participating to accepting the varying possible solutions. Underlying this approach is a goal of addressing basic human needs, with the assumption that frustrated basic human needs is the source of serious conflicts. The confidential nature of such meetings is meant to allow for more candid discussions and more creativity in the generation of new options and makes it more politically possible for influentials to attend. Joint action steps are often devised. Such an approach is typically, but not always, used specifically with influentials in order to maximize the impact of new insights and solutions.

By contrast, in the area of mediation more generally, *problem-solving approaches* have come to be applied to the style and school of mediation that stresses a focus on identifying underlying interests and reaching integrative agreements. This is contrasted by authors such as Bush and Folger (1994/2004) with other mediation approaches such as *transformative approaches,* where the emphasis is not on reaching an agreement, but rather on changing the participants and their way of relating. Though the notion of problem solving in mediation is very old, applying this term to refer to a certain school of mediation is relatively recent.

The use of problem solving as a frame for the task in a negotiation has an even longer history, and thus will be useful for setting the context for these approaches. Across the spectrum of human cultures, one finds multiple means for conflict management (Gulliver, 1979; Moore, 2003; Nader & Todd, 1978). Within this spectrum, two methods are of particular usefulness to contrast: adjudication and negotiation. These two forms of conflict management may be more or less formal, and more or less institutionalized, but the primary difference between them is the locus of the decision making (or problem solving, in this context), which in turn influences both the nature of the relationship and the interaction between the parties (Gulliver, 1979). In adjudication, the parties are supplicants to an authority figure who makes the decision; in some variants such as arbitration, the parties choose to give this authority over to a third party. However, in negotiation, or its variant of mediated negotiations (mediation), the parties retain the role of decision maker. Though one party may have more power or influence than the other party, a negotiation still requires mutual influence and the accession of both parties, thus each party must attempt to influence the other. The negotiation process requires parties to communicate, to learn how to influence each other, and to develop some level of collusion and coordination.

Negotiation assumes interdependence, thus parties must influence the other to achieve their own goals. Influencing the other in a negotiation can run the spectrum from persuasion to coercion. Problem solving in negotiation, whether in interpersonal or international, suggests a framing of the task from one where one forces one's solution or decision, to a task where "two heads are better than one" and the parties solve the problem together. The dynamic of the struggle for dominance, of the need to "win," may still play a role; however, the joint responsibility for solving a problem becomes the primary focus.

PROBLEM SOLVING AS STRATEGY

Problem solving is a strategy for achieving a goal. When that goal is to resolve conflict, a "problem-solving approach" operates in several ways: to change the focus of the disputants (e.g. "separate the people from the problem," Fisher & Ury, 1981), to change the framing of the problem and the associated incentives and goals (cooperation vs. competition, Deutsch, 1973), and to change the interaction from escalatory to de-escalatory (Burton, 1969; Kelman, 1986). Problem solving has been investigated in several ways, with complementary results: it can be explored as an individual task, as a group task, and as an alternative frame for a task initially seen as competitive.

Individual problem solving

Interest in the problem solving of individuals goes back at least as far as Aristotle, through many subsequent philosophers, and emerging as a significant area of research in modern psychology. A *problem* is conceived of as any situation where "an organism has a goal but lacks a clear or well-learned route to the goal" (Dominowski & Bourne, 1994). *Problem solving* captures that process by which the organism arrives at behavior that is effective in achieving its goal. This process is one engaged in by many organisms besides humans, and some would argue by computers as well. In the next section, we will consider groups as problem-solving entities.

Two issues drive the consideration of problem solving: mental representation and mental computation (Dominowski & Bourne, 1994). In other words, how are the external world and its contingencies represented internally, and how are these representations changed, augmented, and acted upon? While some consider trial and error to be one form of working toward a problem solution (Van Gundy, 1988), Hunt (1994) suggests that "problem solving occurs when we understand the external world by exploring an internal mental model of that world, instead of poking around in the external world directly" (p. 216).

Many writers credit a sea change in thinking and research on problem solving to Newell, Shaw, and Simon's (1958) proposal that computer programs be used as models for human thought. With both humans and computers, reasoning involves the manipulation of the internal world, though differences in representation between humans and computers may mean that the transformations also differ (Hunt, 1994). Newell and Simon's (1972) basic model for problem solving suggested assessment of the problem space with nodes and links between them, and then the development of a strategy for moving from node to node in order to eliminate the gap between the current state and the goal state.

Subsequent research indicated that though this may characterize the process used by those who do not know clearly how to solve a problem, those with domain expertise have been found to proceed differently. Experts rely on schemata, which follow upon a sophisticated analysis of situations. "Schemata...are socially acquired ways of dealing with problems [and] provide an orderly way to shift attention from one aspect of a problem to another" (Hunt, 1994, p. 227). Experts short-circuit the search process by applying previously learned rules.

In sum, one fundamental aspect of problem solving involves gathering information to better understand the problem space, and manipulating that information so that it invokes and creatively combines already-learned solutions and strategies for action.

Group problem solving

It is not a huge leap to see how one might use a group to increase information available for problem solving. After all, schemata used to streamline or short-circuit the search process are themselves often socially constructed and transmitted.

Early work on group problem solving identified the benefits of utilizing groups to produce more efficient solutions (Brown, 1986; Burnstein, 1982; Hackman, 1990; Osborn, 1957; Paulus et al., 2001). More people meant more information available to set the problem and formulate a strategy for solving it. Differences among group members could actually promote more effective problem solving, in that more diverse information was available for creative solutions

(Ghiselli & Lodahl, 1958; Hoffman, 1959; Hoffman & Maier, 1961; Maier, 1958). Since a dominant individual could interfere with the free expression of differing options (Maier & Hoffman, 1960, 1961), authority figures were encouraged to refrain from expressing their ideas in a work group, at least until subordinates had a chance to be heard (Maier, 1952). Some (Hoffman et al., 1962) even go so far as to encourage increased commitment to points of view so that conflict can be generated and thus encourage creative problem solving. Here, producing the conditions for creative problem solving to improve the quality of group solutions to a problem actually involves encouraging difference.

Influence from new insights into human problem solving more generally have led to enhanced models for problem solving in groups. As in individual problem solving, group problem solving can benefit from a structure to the approach. While routine problems can be solved via standard operating procedures, and more uncertain problems can draw on heuristics and past experience, the most complex, uncertain, and ambiguous a problem is, the more likely custom-made solutions will be needed (Van Gundy, 1988). Problem solving provides the structure needed to solve ill-structured problems. In groups, this typically involves techniques for both analyzing and refining the problem, and for generating ideas for solutions. For example, redefinition methods provide new perspective on problems, while analytic methods break down the problem into its elements in order that interrelationships can be identified.

Group problem solving has multiple stages. Simon (1977) proposed a three-stage process: *intelligence*, where a problem is recognized and then further defined through information gathering, *design*, where problem solutions are generated, and finally, *choice*, when options are selected and implemented. Similar tripartite stages exist throughout this literature. Most problem-solving conflict resolution processes have been structured to include similar stages. Wallas (1926) proposed four stages to the creative process: preparation, incubation, illumination, and verification;

however, Van Gundy (1988) cautions that in group techniques that push for the quick generation of a large number of ideas, incubation is often sacrificed. Another well-known line of research (Janis, 1982) has documented the problems associated with social pressures that truncate the processes defining the problem and generating options, labeling this distortion of group problem solving, "groupthink."

Group problem solving and conflict: cooperation vs. competition

As outlined earlier, groups can provide more information and work creatively to solve problems. Whether parties actually work together or instead they work at cross purposes is primarily a function of the situation, as parties perceive it is defined. Morton Deutsch early on identified patterns of cooperative and competitive contexts that were both mutually exclusive and self-reinforcing. In other words, cooperative behavior led to further cooperation, while competitive behavior led to further competition. This reciprocity rule was captured in his process model first as his "crude law of social relations," namely that "the characteristic processes and effects *elicited by* a given type of social relationship...tend also to *elicit* that type of social relationship" (Deutsch, 1973, p. 365, italics added).

Deutsch's theories on cooperation and competition were linked to goals. Parties pursue goals through engaging in activities, and when activities of parties are incompatible, a conflict exists. According to Deutsch, conflict behavior can be predicted by the relationship that one perceives between one's own goals and those of another party. If one perceives incompatible activities (conflict) but a positive relation between one's own goals and those of another, in that the goals are only reachable if the parties work together (positive interdependence), then cooperative behavior will result. If one perceives incompatible activities and a negative relationship between the goals, in that one can only achieve one's own goals if the other party does not achieve theirs (negative interdependence), then competitive behavior will result.

Cooperative behaviors include readiness to be helpful; shared, open communication; trusting and friendly attitudes; perceptions of similarity; awareness and emphasis on common interests and values; confidence in one's own ideas and the value others see in them; coordination of effort and division of labor; and an emphasis on enhancing mutual power, sometimes through enhancing the other. Competitive behaviors include tactics of coercion, threat, or deception; poor or deceptive communication; suspicious and hostile attitudes; mistrust; duplication of effort; minimizing similarity; awareness and emphasis on differing interests and deemphasizing common interests and values; and an emphasis on increasing the power difference and therefore the need to accumulate power to oneself (Deutsch, 1973; 2000).

It is helpful to distinguish between cooperative and competitive behaviors on the one hand, and the context that produces them on the other. Some might call such contexts "cooperative or competitive contexts" because of the behaviors they elicit, while others prefer a cleaner conceptual separation, particularly for research purposes (Van deVliert & Janssen, 2001). Cooperative or competitive behaviors arise from cognitive and affective responses to certain perceived goal linkages (Van deVliert & Janssen, 2001). "Positive goal linkages foster the willingness to allow someone else's actions to be substituted for one's own (substitutability), the development of positive attitudes toward each other (positive cathexis), and the readiness to be influenced positively by one another (inducibility), which subsequently results in cooperative behavior" (p. 278). Contrariwise, perceived negative goal linkages result in no substitutability, negative attitudes, and an unwillingness to be influenced by the other, which produces competitive behavior.

Most situations are actually a mix of both positive and negative goal linkages: so-called mixed motive situations (Deutsch, 1973: Lax & Sebenius, 1986; Schelling, 1960).

Rather than propose that either competition or cooperation will dominate depending on the relative strengths of the perceived goal linkages, most propose a mixture in the resulting process (Deutsch, 2000; Van de Vliert & Janssen, 2001). In other words, conflicts are typically mixes of cooperative and competitive processes, and "the course of the conflict will be determined by the nature of the mixture" (Deutsch, 2000, p. 14).

Problem solving in negotiation: integrative vs. distributive

Problem solving is the process of closing the gap between what exists and what is desired: the process of reaching a goal. If the task of achieving this goal is defined as a group task, then in addition to the cognitive and motivational factors of individual problem solvers, the problem solving will be influenced by group dynamics. Group problem solving can both be more creative, and subject to negative group influences such as groupthink noted above. In addition to the information processing of the individuals involved, factors such as the confluence or divergence of the goals of group members, alternative agendas, leadership, and conformity processes will all influence the capabilities and form of groups engaging in problem solving.

One of the challenges of group problem solving is for the members to perceive that they are indeed one group attempting to solve a problem together, rather than two or more groups competing for their definition of the problem and/or the solution to triumph. This challenge, of framing (or reframing) the problem as a joint problem to be solved together rather than as a competition between parties for domination of their own solution, captures the essence of problem solving in conflict resolution.

The roots to this notion of joint problem solving, joint gains, and creating value, so critical to modern processes of conflict resolution, reach back to several sources. Many within the field of alternative dispute resolution trace the notion of integrative solutions to the 1920s and the work of Mary

Parker Follett (Davis, 1989; Graham, 1996; Menkel-Meadow, 2000). Though developed perhaps more prominently in the work of Walton and McKersie (1965) and others (Blake & Mouton, 1964; Fisher & Ury, 1981; Pruitt & Rubin, 1986), Follett framed three ways to handle conflict: domination, compromise, and integration. She made a point of distinguishing the last two: conflict could be constructive, and did not necessarily require parties to give up or give in on things most important to them. Parties could increase the likelihood of integrative solutions "by bringing differences out into the open, facing the conflicts and underlying desires, evaluating and re-valuing desires and preferences when the other parties' desires are made known, and looking for solutions in which the 'interests may fit into each other'" (Menkel-Meadow, 2000). Her examples of integration have now become classic stories for teaching and training in integrative bargaining: of the two library patrons negotiating over opening a window, where one wanted fresh air and the other wanted to avoid a draft, and of two sisters and the last orange, where one wanted the flesh and the other needed the peel. In each case, what appears to be distributive problems where only one can be satisfied, become problems that can be solved creatively once underlying desires are known.

Trained as a political scientist, Follett applied the notions of democratic governance to improve the functioning of groups in organizations. She "was interested in how groups, using principles of democratic governance, could work together and produce better outcomes than hierarchically produced orders" (Menkel-Meadow, 2000, p. 7). In this, she foreshadows the seminal work of Kurt Lewin and colleagues (Lewin et al., 1939) on democratic vs. autocratic leadership and group functioning, as well as the work on creative group problem solving discussed above.

In sum, problem solving in a conflict resolution context, or frankly, in any context involving more than one individual, adds additional complexities. In addition to identifying or setting the problem, and then developing a plan for moving from the current state to the desired state, problem solving with more than one person layers on additional agendas and motives, concerns over leadership, perceptions about the other's goals, and norms about behavior in the perceived context. Though informationally "two heads may be better than one," the jump to more than one problem solver layers on perceptions about each others' goals that result in strategies that are either cooperative or competitive, integrative or distributive, dominating or democratic. In order to move the perceived primary task away from the "social" task of dominating or "winning" over others, to the "instrumental" task of achieving a joint goal, then these other dynamics must be managed. Problem-solving approaches attempt to harness the positive dynamics of group interaction (increased information, diversity of knowledge, creativity) while managing the negative dynamics of group interaction (inclinations toward competition and domination which reduce the group's creative and problem-solving capacities) in order to produce both efficient problem solutions and the motivation to implement them jointly.

Prescriptions resulting from research

While the research reviewed above has been descriptive and explanatory (Van de Vliert & Janssen, 2001), the following prescriptions can be inferred to inform better conflict resolution practice. Based on the research reviewed, processes should be structured so as to:

- change "concern" for the other
- change perceptions of the other's goals
- change perception of the structure of the task – from fixed-sum to variable-sum
- change goal orientation – from maximizing individual outcomes to maximizing joint outcomes
- improve the accuracy of perception of the other's priorities
- improve perception of the compatibility of interests.

Several works build on these strategies to outline and prescribe processes to achieve more constructive solutions to conflict (Fisher & Ury, 1981; Mnookin et al., 2000; Moore, 2003; Pruitt & Rubin, 1986).

PROBLEM-SOLVING APPROACHES IN INTERNATIONAL CONFLICT: NEGOTIATIONS

Conflict management has long been a topic in the study of international relations, arguably going back at least as far as the Greeks (Thucydides, 500 BC). Bercovitch (1996) traces mediation at least as far back as the Bible, Homer's *Illiad*, and Sophocles' *Ajax*.

To trace the exploration of problem solving in international conflict, Hopmann (1995) argues one should begin with the first systematic theorizing about international negotiations reflected in Thomas Schelling's (1960) *Strategy of Conflict*, Anatol Rapaport's (1960) *Fights, Games, and Debates*, and Fred Charles Iklé's (1964) *How Nations Negotiate*. These authors all shared a grounding in mixed motive, or non zero sum, games, where both cooperative and competitive options are available to parties. Their work was in turn influenced by game theory as developed by von Neumann and Morgenstern, Nash, and Luce and Raiffa. Though the mixed-motive games described in the works of these authors revealed the choice of cooperative or competitive options, Hopmann (1995) maintains that these authors diverged in their emphasis, with some highlighting competitive aspects, including the need to protect oneself from exploitation (as in the prisoner's dilemma game), and others highlighting cooperative efforts where value is created through enlarging joint interests.

Hopmann (1995) notes that Rapaport went beyond game theory to point out that game theory, while encouraging new thinking about conflict, also leads to impasses where it is theoretically insufficient to deal with certain types of conflict situations. "These impasses set up tensions in the minds of people who care. They must therefore look around for other frameworks into which conflict situations can be cast" (Rapaport, 1960, p. 242). Rapaport thus added a concept he called "debate," to capture when parties aim for understanding and attempt to identify possible mutual gains.

Rapaport's expansion of game theory to include "debate" contributed to the development of an alternative paradigm of problem solving in international negotiations (Hopmann, 1995). Though parallel developments in labor negotiations such as the aforementioned work of Walton and McKersie were noted, "integrative" bargaining and problem solving did not become a distinctive area of study in international negotiations until about 1980. Hopmann credits the development of this paradigm within international negotiations to the influence of Fisher and Ury (1981) (interests rather than positions), Zartman and Berman (1982) (diagnosis, formula, detail), and the work of Burton (1987) and Kelman (Rouhana & Kelman, 1994) (who address basic needs and identity through informal interactions; discussed in more detail later).

Hopmann argues that the contrast between the bargaining and problem-solving paradigms of international negotiations parallels the contrast between realism and liberalism, the two primary paradigms of international relations (Hopmann, 1995). In particular, realism's emphasis on the importance of relative gains over adversaries contrasts with liberalism's emphasis on absolute gains even if others benefit as well or even more, and the accompanying search for joint gains and positive sum solutions.

When is problem solving used in international negotiations? When do absolute gains become the focus more than relative advantage? Hopmann indicates that, besides "purely rational calculation," negotiation behavior will depend on two factors: (1) the "orientation" and larger world view of the individual decision maker, and (2) the dynamic of the interaction process operating to produce mutual cooperation, exploitation of one by the other, or mutual competition.

Regarding decision maker's orientation, Hopmann argues that some individuals are intolerant of ambiguity, see the world as competitive, and are thus motivated to win in most contexts. Such individuals may pursue a competitive strategy even in contexts where an equally competitive opponent may mean they both fall, as in the dilemma encapsulated in the Prisoner's Dilemma game (Luce & Raiffa, 1957). To these individuals, it matters less what is gained or lost, as long as they come out ahead of their opponent. Social psychological research supports the prevalence of this behavior (Tajfel, 1978) although finding it to be produced as much or more by the situation than by individual proclivities. By contrast, other individuals may view the world differently. "They may be more tolerant of ambiguity, more cognitively complex, and more willing to cooperate with others to achieve collective benefits" (p. 36) over time. Their strategy may be to forego short-term gains in favor of long-term gains through a cooperative relationship.

How might its use be made more likely? How might dynamics be shaped to be most likely to produce stable cooperation? Can even the decision maker's initial orientations and assumptions about human nature (or at least about the other party) be altered?

PROBLEM-SOLVING APPROACHES IN INTERNATIONAL CONFLICT: INTERACTIVE CONFLICT RESOLUTION

Nature of protracted intergroup conflict

In addition to the fundamental reconceptualization of the problem and the task inherent to all problem-solving approaches, new thinking was occurring regarding the nature of international and intercommunal conflict that suggested what then must have seemed like radical and unorthodox approaches to intervention. John Burton, an international relations specialist and former Australian diplomat, argued against the effectiveness of traditional power approaches. In light of the emerging "pluralist" alternative to the "realist" view of the international system, he and his colleagues crafted a new forum to incubate security, with a long-term view and a problem-solving approach.

Important new work was appearing on the nature of international conflict. Azar's (1980, 1983) early quantitative work on international conflicts underlined their true nature: since World War II, most had occurred in the developing world, with most of them ethnic rather than strategic, but exacerbated by superpower rivalries played out on their stage. Azar felt that the focus of international relations was misplaced, neglecting the two-thirds of states that were small, destitute, underdeveloped, and potentially split by both ethnic alliances and by international machinations. Rather, Azar felt it critical to focus on "protracted social conflicts," which he considered to be "hostile interactions which extend over long periods of time with sporadic outbreaks of open warfare fluctuating in frequency and intensity" (Azar et al., 1978).

According to Azar and colleagues, protracted social conflicts (PSCs) are a mixture of socioethnic and interstate elements that defy traditional settlement methods, and generate escalating perceptions and behaviors. Because crises are managed to restore the status quo and keep conflict at only a moderate intensity, the conflicts take on an inertial or even "frozen" quality, lacking any resolution despite repeated attempts at settlement.

Fisher (1997, p. 80) further summarizes Azar's (Azar et al., 1978) insights:

First, strong equilibrating forces will operate to undermine attempts at settlement, partly because of vested interests, but also because the unpredictable nature of a possible termination threatens personal, social, and national identities. Because the struggles for recognition and acceptance, which are a major part of the conflict, cannot be won or lost through typical PSC behavior, the approach of gradualism in conflict resolution and peacebuilding is necessary. Meanwhile the appalling absorptive capacity of PSCs is demonstrated through the enormous human and material resources that are consumed by the conflict. Finally, the protractedness of the conflict will be reinforced by the tendency of decision makers to use the conflict as

an excuse for inaction on pressing problems, such as the place of ethnic minorities, the distribution of income and services, and societal mobility. Such inaction may be excused as caution, indecision, or as cunning, but the outcome is that fundamental needs for development are ignored in the face of the conflict.

Azar and Farah (1981) added that PSCs involve deep-seated religious, racial and ethnic animosities that set these conflicts apart from those not involving group identities and the rights asserted and sought through these. Similarly, Lederach (1997) asserts that because some states do not meet the needs of all its citizens, people find security and identity in narrower groups that are more familiar, historical, and controllable, focusing on group rights rather than individual rights. The process by which identity narrows, often leading to breakdowns in central authority, is rooted in long-standing mutual distrust, hatred, fear, and often historical injury, and reinforced by recent violence (Lederach, 1997).

However, ethnicity is not the sole causative factor in these conflicts. Azar and Farah (1981) highlight the role played by structural inequalities and political power differences, particularly when these in turn result in differential distribution of rewards among groups in the society. These differentials typically are reinforced through unequal international connections, meaning that uneven and unequal development benefits will actually further exacerbate differences. One group dominates over others, thereby linking discrimination and victimization to group identity. Group identity and hatred frames all interactions and attributions, and passes from one generation to the next through socialization.

While Azar felt the protracted nature of these conflicts stems from unintegrated social and political systems and unintegrated development, he traced causation back to basic human needs, as had Burton (earlier). "The real source of conflict is the denial of those human needs that are common to all and whose pursuit is an ontological drive in all" (Azar, 1985), especially "*security, distinctive identity, social recognition of identity,* and *effective participation*" in processes that determine the conditions of security of identity" (p. 60). When these are denied, people will rise up and risk much to respond to what may be perceived as an existential threat. For a more recent treatment on the expression of the needs of identity, security, recognition of identity, and effective participation in calls for, or defense of, "voice," see d'Estrée (2005).

Burton's theory development proceeded inductively, drawing on insights gained from controlled communication and problem-solving workshops, and from interaction with colleagues such as Azar and Kelman. As noted, Burton felt that what he labeled "deep-rooted conflict" came from fundamental, underlying, basic human needs that were not negotiable or suppressible. However, these needs were common to all, and an appropriately facilitated analytical discussion could allow for this to be discovered by the parties themselves, as well as the means to constructively address these needs. The theoretical underpinnings for these problem-solving approaches are discussed below.

Principles of interactive problem-solving approaches in intergroup conflict resolution

Goals, objectives, and assumptions

Based on the aforementioned nature of deep-rooted, protracted conflict, traditional conflict management strategies fall short of achieving stable peace. As noted above, innovators drew on diverse areas of thinking to frame a new approach. This new approach has been called by several names, including "Track Two diplomacy" (Diamond & McDonald, 1991; Montville, 1987), "problem-solving workshops" (Kelman, 1972), "problem-solving forums" (Azar, 1990), "collaborative analytical problem-solving" (Mitchell & Banks, 1996), "interactive conflict resolution" (Fisher, 1997), "third-party consultation" (Fisher, 1983), or "informal mediation" (Kelman, 1992). Though several have contributed to the general paradigm of interactive problem solving, its essence can

be gleaned from the common themes across the writings of its primary framers.

The essence of interactive problem solving can be summarized as:

- Bringing the primary, interdependent parties together to solve it themselves (likely with third-party facilitation).
- A focus on addressing human needs (since their neglect has led to the conflict becoming protracted).

This is done through the intentional and skilled use of processes, facilitated by a third party, that are designed to foster the following process objectives: changing communication, "analyzing the conflict" (sometimes contrasted but paired with problem solving), changing stereotypes and enemy images, changing options available and developing new ideas for solutions, changing one's perceptions of change, both in the other and in the relationship, connecting the individual with his or her system and yet internalizing change, and finally, transforming the inter-group/intersocietal relationship.

Basic design elements

Interactive problem solving has assumptions that address both thinking processes and sociopolitical processes. Like all problem-solving models, it assumes that a problem-solving process involves moving through a systematic, constructive thinking process to reach a desired goal state. And like group problem solving models, it assumes "two heads are better than one," that benefits come from putting together those who have divergent views, experiences, and expertise. In fact, interactive problem solving in a conflict context assumes that both heads *must* participate because the nature of conflict comes from parties that are interdependent and intertwined. Therefore, if parties are interdependent, the system is served by both parties benefiting to some degree and neither party losing, that is, with a "win-win" or integrative solution. This third assumption stems from problem-solving approaches in negotiation.

Two additional assumptions are added when considering the problem-solving approaches used in an intergroup conflict context. First, because the sources of protracted intergroup conflict are linked to unmet human needs, addressing human needs such as identity and security must be the focus of the problem solving. Second, because protracted intergroup conflict engages the whole society rather than just elites, problem-solving approaches operate at multiple levels to change the intersocietal relationship. Nonetheless, because they are fundamentally problem solving in approach, the central task of such a process remains achieving a humane and responsive solution.

As interactive problem solving evolved as a particular process methodology, these assumptions drove the choices that led to certain standardizing in format, participants, agenda, and process. Variations reflect perhaps differing emphases and differing interpretations of theory, yet the core of this model remains basically the same.

Topic and communication.

For many of the original developers of international interactive problem-solving approaches, the impetus was to find an alternative to the way traditional international relations are conducted (Burton, 1969; Kelman & Cohen, 1976; Montville, 1987; Saunders, 2001). Rather than focus on power considerations or questions of rights, problem-solving approaches focus on underlying human needs. To focus a meeting on human needs requires conscious structuring of meeting agendas and controlling of communication. Burton (1987, 1990) proposes that without a third party and the proper setting, the traditional interaction between conflicting parties would mean that parties would see what they expect to see and likely lapse into bargaining or adversarial interaction. Kelman (1992) suggests that typical conflict norms call for defending rights, posturing for negotiations, and speaking "for the record"; third-party facilitation is necessary to produce a different kind of interaction: one where parties are encouraged to talk to each other rather than constituencies or third parties, one where they actually listen to each other, not to score debating points but to

"penetrate each other's perspective," and, finally, one where an analytic focus can be sustained and understanding of the other party's concerns and constraints can be gained to allow for true problem solving of inventive solutions.

In any meeting, rules of procedure influence both process and outcome. Problem-solving processes use informal ground rules or guidelines to shape interaction. For example, privacy and confidentiality allows participants to express and explore new and sometimes controversial ideas without the stifling influence of an external audience or an official record. Meetings are consciously unofficial, for similar reasons. Other common ground rules include: a "no fault" principle, not because parties are equally at fault, but to shift the discussions from assigning blame to exploring causes (Kelman, 1992); and commitment to attend all sessions of a workshop (Babbitt & d'Estrée, 1996). Participants are consciously seated in their groups during the interaction so as not to distort or lose the intergroup nature of the interaction; this is not a classic contact effort (Pettigrew, 1998) where interpersonal interaction is stressed and friendships are the goal. Kelman felt that although it was necessary to build working trust, it "must not be allowed to turn into excessive camaraderie transcending the conflict, lest the participants lose their credibility and their potential political influence once they return to their home communities" (1992, p. 77). Burton went so far as to house the groups separately. Though others did not agree with this extreme separation, Burton felt that participants should not interact apart from across the table in front of the third-party panel, both to ensure that all concerned can share in each communication or interpretation, and to make sure that "the participants do not alter significantly their own value systems and perceptions of the nature of the conflict as a result of the group dynamics and friendships which develop during the process. When they 'reenter' their own society they will have a problem conveying any new ideas to decision-makers in a convincing way if this happens" (p. 201).

He felt that participants had to be able to sell new options, not on the basis of some changed interpersonal perception or personal relationship, but because of the merits of those options.

Burton also felt that such control of interaction was necessary to prevent parties from prematurely jumping to the preparation of proposals. Though this procedure might be standard in other conflict resolution processes – in fact, in negotiation and mediation theories, parties are encouraged to develop a "single text" to focus on (Fisher & Ury, 1981; Moore, 2003) – it must come only after participants have spent the time and hard work learning to understand each other's needs and constraints. Analysis allows goals, tactics, interests, values, and needs to be clarified first so that possible outcomes can be formed based on this analysis.

Participants.

Interactive problem solving is meant to be part of a larger strategy to build a working relationship between parties severed by long-term conflict so that official negotiations might be supported and official solutions might ultimately be put into place. Therefore, the choice of who to bring together for interactive problem solving is to be made with an eye to both official impact and broad societal impact. John Burton and Christopher Mitchell both felt the highest levels of government should be involved, at least potentially in the identification of participants to attend in an unofficial capacity (Burton, 1987; Mitchell & Banks, 1996).

Others, such as Herbert Kelman, made an argument for involving influentials expressly not in government positions, on the grounds that the flexible thinking required for creative problem solving could not be done by those restricted by official policy lines. Montville (1987) labels this a "second-track" approach. In his theory of peacebuilding, Lederach (1997) proposes a multitiered approach that includes a middle level of influentials able to build cross-cutting professional networks, working out of the media glare, who are best situated to both represent broader societal concerns and to influence official leadership.

Setting.

Recall above that in order to generate creative problem solving in groups, one needed both divergent views and also the norms that allowed for their expression. Establishing a forum that allows for such activity requires attention to both the topic and agenda, but also to the context of the meeting. Context should allow for free expression of ideas, and exploration of new and unusual ways of tackling problems. Many suggest that, like with other forms of activity designed to shift thinking or allow for new ways of thinking such as corporate retreats, a setting apart from daily pressures and standard roles is critical. Two primary sorts of settings have been used: an academic setting or a retreat setting.

Retreat settings are designed to remove distractions and encourage reflection. Their typical luxurious or at least idyllic quality allows participants the "space" to meet each other in a neutral context, to think differently, and to interact differently. Academic settings provide logical places to think analytically and creatively, with fairly strong norms encouraging the consideration of alternative viewpoints (Kelman, 1992). They also provide a place to which opposing groups can be brought with less resistance or suspicion, as universities play host to many divergent groups regularly.

Time frame and timing.

Probably one of the more variable aspects of problem-solving approaches is the time frame set aside for interaction between the parties. Burton's original meetings lasted 7–10 days. Kelman's primary problem-solving workshop model was designed around a long weekend, about the longest amount of time influentials could get away for a chance at unofficial brainstorming and interaction. The interaction would be preceded by uninational preworkshop meetings with the third party on separate evenings to allow participants from the same group to meet each other before meeting those from the adversary group, to familiarize participants with the agenda and ground rules, and to allow for uninational venting with a third-party audience before interacting with the adversary. Rouhana and Kelman (1994) later expanded the workshops to a "continuing" format, meeting with roughly the same group of influential participants over the course of months or years. In many ways, these came to resemble Saunders' (2001) model of "sustained dialogue."

In contrast to theories of negotiation and mediation that suggest conflict can best be settled when it is "ripe" (Touval & Zartman; see Chapter 16 in this volume), work on interactive problem solving suggests such meetings can be fruitful in generating input to decision making and in changing relationships at many different points in a conflict's development. Kelman describes interactive problem solving as designed for prenegotiation, before parties are willing to engage in official settlement processes, but as useful also during negotiations to open up creative options for particularly difficult issues, or in post negotiations, to clarify implementation. Mitchell and Banks (1996) outline how problem-solving workshops are most effective if begun before conflict lines have hardened; these workshops can continue to support official negotiations.

Third party.   The role of the third party is primarily to facilitate analysis (Burton, 1990). While traditional mediators can be expected to suggest reasonable compromises, this is not appropriate in problem-solving, as the issues to be focused on are not ones which can be compromised: identity, security, recognition, etc. Though goals cannot be compromised, the means to reach these goals can be modified; in fact, the third party convenes the meeting in order for participants to discover new, mutually agreeable options for meeting these needs and goals.

Mitchell and Banks (1996) argue that traditional third-party intervention adds on to the parties' goals an additional goal of stopping the violence, which may settle the conflict, though typically favoring the goals of one party over other parties. This asymmetric settlement will not endure. Mitchell and Banks consider violence as a problem where because the parties have begun it, only the

parties themselves can really stop it; external efforts cannot be relied upon. They argue that what is needed is "assistance of a nonforcible kind" (p. 5).

Facilitating the analysis needed (Burton, 1990) and the interaction that will be constructive (Kelman, 1986) requires special skills. Third-party members should be "impartial, knowledgeable, and skilled scholar-practitioner[s] with the expertise to facilitate...direct discussion of contentious issues" (Fisher, 1997, p. 145). Typically, they are chosen to form a "panel" of 3–8 members that will convene the meetings and facilitate the process. Opinions vary on whether panel members are better to have little direct knowledge of the conflict in question (Burton, 1990a), or whether they should represent a "balanced" third party that reflects the identities of the parties in conflict while advocating a new and constructive joint process (Kelman, 1986).

The third party plays an essential role, providing a context in which the parties can come together, and serving as "a repository of trust" (Kelman, 1992) for parties who cannot trust each other. The third party establishes a framework and ground rules, proposes a broad agenda, and moves the discussion forward. It may contribute content observations around interpretations and implications of what has been said, process observations about parallels between workshop dynamics and larger conflict dynamics, and theoretical inputs helpful for conflict analysis (Kelman, 1992). Insights from other conflicts may be shared as well (Burton, 1990; Mitchell & Banks, 1996).

Agenda.   The agenda is designed to encourage analysis, re-perception of the conflict and reality checking, increased mutual understanding of underlying needs and concerns as well as political constraints, and the generation of new options in light of this new information. In this way it parallels the classic problem-solving steps described throughout this chapter. A fairly traditional Kelman-type workshop would begin with introductions and ground rules, proceed to identification of each participant's sense of the range of views in their community and how they might situate themselves in this, a sense of the current situation, a deeper discussion of political and psychological concerns ("needs and fears" – Kelman, 1992), the shape of solutions that might address all primary parties' concerns, constraints to implementing such solutions, and ways to overcome constraints and support each other. Ideas for concrete, joint actions may also be attempted (Kelman, 1992; see Babbitt & d'Estrée, 1996, for a sample agenda).

Examples of interactive problem-solving interventions

In keeping with their original aims, interactive problem-solving workshops have been used in the most visibly protracted conflicts of the current age: Cyprus, Sri Lanka, Northern Ireland, the Middle East, the Horn of Africa. These are contexts of high social inequality, where political participation is frustrated, identity cleavages channel energy and resources, and violence operates close to the surface when values are threatened.

Former Australian diplomat John Burton and his colleagues at University College London organized the first workshop in the mid-1960s, hoping both to influence the state of the conflict between Indonesia, Malaysia, and Singapore, and to make a point to international relations colleagues that another model of international conflict analysis could be useful and practical (Fisher, 1997). Unofficial, but officially sanctioned, delegates met for sessions in London that allowed for the examination of assumptions, the analysis of the conflict, and a consideration of new options. The exercise re-established diplomatic relations and has been credited with developing the framework and understanding that then appeared in the 1966 Manila Peace Agreement (Fisher, 1997).

Soon thereafter, Burton's group became involved in the Cyprus conflict, hosting representatives from the Turkish and Greek communities during an impasse in official UN brokered negotiations, which then resumed after these discussions (Mitchell, 1981).

Drawing on the work of both Burton and social psychologist Leonard Doob (Doob et al., 1969), social psychologist Herbert Kelman began to apply the approach to the Israeli–Palestinian conflict. Working with colleague Stephen Cohen, they piloted and then refined the methodology (Kelman & Cohen, 1986). Over several decades, Kelman and colleagues organized more than thirty workshops with influential Palestinian and Israeli participants (Babbitt & d'Estrée, 1996; Kelman, 1986, 1995, 2000; Kelman & Cohen, 1986; Rouhana & Kelman, 1994). Begun as prenegotiation work, attempting to create the conditions for official negotiations between Israelis and Palestinians, these meetings fed insights into the Madrid negotiations, and paved the way for both the Oslo back channel process and the official accords signed in 1993 (Kelman, 1995, 1997a, 1998; Rothman, 1993).

After early work on a Kelman workshop, political scientist Edward Azar joined with Cohen to arrange a series of problem-solving discussions on the Egypt–Israel conflict in the late 1970s. Cohen and Azar (1981) combined insights from these workshops with document analysis and detailed interviews with decision makers to inform a social–psychological description and evaluation of the peace process. Fisher (1997) points out the postnegotiation design, in that "this workshop was the first unofficial meeting between influential Egyptians and Israelis in the wake of the Camp David Accords designed to consider the full range of issues stemming from the agreement. In other words, the workshop focused on issues that had to be addressed to build a peaceful and enduring relationship between the two societies, with the peace treaty serving as the legal framework" (p. 81).

Edward Azar joined with John Burton to host several problem-solving initiatives. After the Falklands/Malvinas conflict between Argentina and England led to military confrontation in 1982, three forums were held, generating a set of principles to inform the official negotiations. Meetings were also arranged during 1984 to address the Lebanese civil war; these meetings helped establish a network that developed the 1988 National Covenant Document that was incorporated into the 1989 Taif Accords (Fisher, 1997). Problem-solving meetings on the Sri Lankan conflict were also held in 1985–1987.

Other colleagues of these innovators have used variants of the problem-solving workshop with influentials in other conflict contexts. Many of these are reviewed by Fisher (1997). These include Cyprus (Broome, 1997; Fisher, 1991, 1992), the US–Soviet relationship (Chufrin & Saunders, 1993), Tajikistan (Slim & Saunders, 1996), the Arab–Israeli conflict (Hicks et al., 1994), and the Hopi–Navajo conflict (d'Estrée, 1999). Problem-solving meetings with influentials have also occurred in conflicts in Curaçao (Hare et al., 1977), Cambodia (1991), and Afghanistan (1993). Many of these initiatives have used other models of interaction such as sustained dialogue (Saunders, 2001; see Chapter 19 in this volume) and decision seminars (Lasswell, 1966), and meet the core components of interactive problem solving outlined above in varying degrees. It is to be expected that the degree to which these initiatives deviate from the core components of the interactive problem-solving model, they would be expected to produce different results. For example, not using influentials as participants may decrease the immediate policy impact, while not including a focus on basic human needs, while still constructive, may not produce insights into long-term solutions.

Theoretical/research support

Like many forms of intervention, problem-solving approaches began as an attempt by thoughtful people to improve the way that things were done, in this case, the way that representatives from nations resolved conflict. The best intervention is a pairing of thoughtful action and reflection, so that action might be continually fine-tuned. Schön (1983) called this "reflection-in-action," and considered it the hallmark of the true professional. Kelman (1992) wrote of problem-solving approaches as a form of "action research." Many of the leaders in problem solving have taken the time to reflect on the implicit and explicit theoretical base that informs their work.

Burton (1969, 1990) considered the source of persistent intergroup conflict to be the result of frustration of basic human needs. Burton felt it was critical for conflict analysis to distinguish both conceptually and practically between interests, which are negotiable, and needs, which are non-negotiable. He felt that identity needs underlay most intractable conflicts, so that until these identity needs were addressed, conflict would recur. Clarity was also needed to separate out actual needs from the tactics used to meet those needs, which themselves could be altered. The role of the third party in problem solving was to facilitate the parties in a process where they might develop insight into underlying needs and how to constructively meet them in an interdependent relationship.

Burton's Human Needs Theory suggests that human motivations (and particularly political objectives) fall into three categories: those that are universal and required for development, those tied to a particular culture, and those that are transitory and linked to aspirations. In the first category are needs. Needs had drawn interest from many quarters in the time period Burton was framing his theory. Drawing on the work of Maslow (1970), Sites (1973), and others, Burton highlighted the universal motivations for not only food and shelter, but also needs related to growth and development, such as identity, autonomy, and consistency in response. "Human needs in individuals and identity groups who are engaged in ethnic and identity struggles are of this fundamental character" (1990a, p. 36). Needs will be pursued by all means available: socially sanctioned ones first, but outside the legal norms of society if necessary. Burton takes pains to underline how meeting such needs may lead individuals or groups to "behaviors that cannot be controlled to fit the requirements of particular societies" (p. 37).

Burton contrasts needs, which are primordial and universal,[2] with values, which are the preferences and priorities held by particular social communities. Values are acquired, and their defense may themselves be important to the needs of personal security and identity, particularly in conditions of oppression, underprivilege, or isolation. Burton considers it to be values that have divided many multiethnic and multicommunal societies, such as Northern Ireland and Lebanon. Over generations, values can change, but only in a context of security. More typically, separate customs and lifestyles are used as reasons for discrimination, and also as ways to defend an identity from the results of discrimination.

Finally, Burton considers interests to be "the occupational, social, political and economic aspirations of the individual, and of identity groups of individuals within a social system" (1990a, p. 38). He considers interests to be more narrowly defined than a term covering all motivations; instead, he considers them to relate primarily to material gain or to role occupancy. The dynamic is typically competitive, as they are often framed as zero-sum, though this framing can be altered (see Problem Solving in Negotiation, above). An important feature of interests is that they are negotiable; they can be traded off.

Separating interests from needs and values becomes important in both conflict analysis and in considering processes of resolution. Burton asserts that too often these are conflated, leading to a lack of awareness that needs and values are not for trading. "Great powers have not yet come to terms with their failures to control by military force, because they have as yet little understanding that there are human needs that are not for trading and cannot be suppressed" (p. 40). The insight into the distinction between these types of motivations he traces back directly to analysis occurring in facilitated conflict resolution processes (Azar & Burton, 1986; Burton, 1979, 1984). Though interests can be traded off, suggesting processes whereby effective packages can be negotiated, processes that lead to the identification of needs in turn

can help to highlight the universal, shared nature of these needs. Once parties discover that they have goals in common, such as Cyprus or Lebanon as an independent state, the groundwork is laid for finding ways to satisfy parties' needs.

Another important conceptual distinction Burton draws is between needs and the satisfiers sought to meet those needs, also described by him as "goals" vs. "tactics." Often, the tactics chosen to satisfy a goal or need end up being mistaken as the goal itself. For example, an international dispute over territory may at its root be about security or autonomy or identity. He cites the example of Israel holding the Golan Heights, first occupied by Israel as a means of defense, where the holding of the Heights in turn became a goal in itself. This confusing of tactics and goals in politics leads to impasses, because tactics may erroneously become non-negotiable.

Burton's theory leads to two other essential points. First, though Burton considers traditional power theories to be correct in hypothesizing conflict over scarce resources, they fail "in assuming that human behavior was determined mainly or solely by material benefits, and that the source of conflicts was over competition for scarce resources" (1990a, p. 46). In his estimation, behavior is more often oriented toward the deeper concerns of identity and autonomy. Second, he considers valued relationships to also be a basic human need, or at least a satisfier of recognition and identity needs. Valued relationships provide a constraint on negative behaviors, and impetus for conforming behaviors. "A conflict is not resolved merely by reaching agreement between those who appear to be the parties to the dispute. There is a wider social dimension to be taken into account: the establishment of an environment that promotes and institutionalizes valued relationships" (p. 47). One could go so far as to say that needs are not satisfied apart from valued relationships, so that a long-term approach to resolution of necessity must address the intergroup relationship. This theme is further echoed in the writings of subsequent theorists

(Crocker et al., 1999; Kelman, 1999, 2005; Lederach, 1997; Saunders, 2001).

According to Burton, though humans may use aggression to pursue individual development, they also have conscious and creative resources: the ability to make choices, anticipate events, and cost consequences, and also the ability to deliberately alter environments and social structures. The role of conflict resolution and a third party is then the provision of opportunities for analysis and the use of these conscious and creative resources.

The most effective conflict resolution in such contexts is problem solving, which is inherently analytical. Burton (1990a) outlines four distinctive characteristics of problem solving. First, the solution is not an end-product; it establishes another set of relationships. These relationship themselves may produce new problems. It is an ongoing process. Second, problem solving requires a change in conceptualization of a problem. Third, problem solving deals with a problem in its total environment – political, economic, and social – which is continually evolving. Fourth, sources and origins must be considered in order to be effective, rather than focusing on immediate causal factors.

Burton considers that conflict resolution must be the result of parties engaging in their own study of their own patterns of behaviors "in an intimate and analytical interaction in which there can be detailed checking." He sought a setting whereby the protagonists could check on their mutual perceptions and on the relevance of their tactics and their associated consequences, as well as to explore new options once re-perception and reassessment had begun. It was, in the classic sense of problem solving described earlier, an opportunity to gather additional new information, to reassess the problem space, and from there to generate options.

The hypothesis that Burton puts forth, then, is that "once the relationships have been analyzed satisfactorily, once each side is accurately informed of the perceptions of the other, of alternative means of attaining values and goals, and of costs of pursuing present

policies, possible outcomes are revealed that might be acceptable to all parties" (p. 205).

When Kelman was first exposed to Burton's approach, he made the observation immediately that it was social–psychological in orientation. Social–psychological assumptions undergird the workshop structure, process, and content (Kelman, 1992).

Kelman (1997b) later linked the conceptual undergirding for interactive problem solving more explicitly to a social–psychological analysis of international conflict itself. Though many disciplines and schools of thought contribute lenses through which to analyze international conflict, a social–psychological analysis can offer additional unique and complementary insights. First, international conflict can be seen as a process driven by collective needs and fears, rather than purely by the rational calculations of national interest by decision makers. Second, as noted earlier, international conflict is not merely intergovernmental but intersocietal. Third, this intersocietal nature means that there are multiple avenues for mutual influence, and multiple forms that influence can take beyond coercion. Finally, conflict is an interactive process with an escalatory, self-perpetuating dynamic such that without determined and deliberate intervention, the natural interaction between parties will likely only increase hostility, distrust, and a sense of grievance.

According to Kelman (1997b), conflict interaction is characterized by the following social–psychological processes that produce escalation and perpetuation, particularly in deep-rooted identity conflicts. These processes are both normative (social) and perceptual (cognitive), securing the conflict and making change difficult.

First, Kelman argues that public opinion on conflict issues is influenced by collective moods, both transitory and those more pervasive, that support escalatory actions and make rapprochement difficult. Transitory collective moods such as determination or wariness linked to recent events can either support or hinder a leader's pursuit of peaceful policies. Pervasive and enduring skepticism produced by historical experiences make change seem dangerous. Second, leaders gain deeper support for policies by mobilizing group loyalties than by making rational appeals. Groups invoke loyalty because they address core psychological needs for self-protection and for self-transcendence (Kelman, 1969; Smith & Berg, 1987). Group loyalty processes such as the stifling of dissent, the influence of militant elements, and the way loyalty is measured create barriers to the search for new alternatives. Third, the nature of decision making in conflict and crisis means that decision makers limit the search for options and go with dominant responses, which are likely to be aggressive. Groupthink (Janis, 1982) means that the consensus is not questioned and members are unlikely to offer criticism or to explore alternatives thoroughly. Fourth, norms in long-standing conflicts support zero-sum framing of any negotiation, where the way to gain is to make the other lose. These perceptions and norms make thinking about the interests, needs, or fears of the other party unlikely, precluding effective negotiations. Fifth, structural and psychological commitments to maintaining the conflict – either for professional survival, psychological investment, or to avoid a less than satisfactory resolution – make changes toward conflict resolution fraught with risk. Finally, perceptual processes such as the formation of enemy images, and these images' resistance to contradictory information result in self-fulfilling prophecies and a resistance to see or consider change.

Such processes result in parties underestimating "the degree to which change has taken place and further change is possible," and also results in behaviors that make change in the relationship less likely. However, this same lens that has helped identify barriers can suggest ways to overcome them:

To overcome these barriers requires the promotion of a different kind of interaction, one that is capable of reversing this conflict dynamic. At the micro-level, problem-solving workshops...can contribute to this objective by encouraging the parties to penetrate each other's perspective, to differentiate their image of the enemy, to develop

a de-escalatory language and ideas for mutual reassurance, and to engage in joint problem solving designed to generate ideas for resolving the conflict that are responsive to the fundamental needs and fears of both sides. At the macro-level, reversal of the conflict dynamic depends on the establishment of a new discourse among the parties, characterized by a shift in emphasis from power politics and threat of coercion to mutual responsiveness, reciprocity, and openness to a new relationship. (Kelman, 1997b, p. 233)

Fisher (1972, 1997) considers problem-solving approaches to be a form of third-party consultation, and outlines the theoretical basis for this class of intervention. His model of conflict resolution as third-party consultation particularly focuses on the essential role of the third party. In Fisher's (1972) search to improve international negotiation, he found the most significant need to be not so much for more models of effective negotiation, but for better understanding of the contributing role of attitudinal and relationship challenges that hamper parties from effectively addressing the conflict themselves.

In addition to Burton, Fisher draws primarily on the work of Walton (1969), and Blake et al. (1964) to formulate his model. Walton (1969) coined the term "third-party consultation" to refer to his work with corporate executives caught in dysfunctional conflicts. His approach, now standard in organizational development, involves "productive confrontation." Such a dialogue of parties directly discussing the difficult issues between them involves strategic functions of an experienced and skilled third party, such as encouraging positive motivation to attempt to reduce the conflict, improving the communication, pacing the phases, influencing the choice of context for the interaction, etc. Blake and Mouton (1961) and colleagues (1964) also offer procedures for intervening into conflicted intergroup relations in organizations, including procedures for mutually analyzing the conflict and for engaging in joint problem solving. As described above under Problem Solving in Negotiation, the essential focus of their work was on reframing perceived zero-sum or "win–lose" approaches to integrative, "win–win" strategies. Blake and Mouton (1984) propose problem-solving methods where the parties themselves diagnose the conflict and work to restore respect and trust.

Fisher builds on these theorists to propose his model of the third party, including specifications for the third-party tactics and procedures, helping relationship, identity, role, and functions, as well as situation and objectives. Fisher is probably most known for his various writings on the role, or appropriate behaviors, for the third party in problem solving (Fisher & Keasley, 1988, 1991), where he has gone to lengths to distinguish the facilitative and diagnostic role in problem solving from other third-party roles, such as those in arbitration and mediation. He has also gone farther than most to document both the strategies – such as improving openness, increasing communication accuracy – and tactics – such as summarizing, stopping repetitive interactions – that are used by the third-party consultant.

Chataway (2004) reviewed both experimental research that informed interactive problem-solving approaches and also research that had been done on the workshops themselves. She reviewed the social–psychological research supporting what she considered to be the essential design features of the Kelman approach to interactive problem solving: confidential dialogue, facilitated discussion of underlying needs and fears, and joint problem solving by the parties themselves with a nonevaluative facilitator. Dialogue that is confidential rather than nonconfidential seems to permit more reevaluation of stereotypes and more openness to ideas, especially among participants who are politically accountable (Pruitt, 1995; Tetlock, 1992). During confidential dialogue, fears and aspirations that drive aggressive behavior can be clarified while information is shared (Ross & Ward, 1995). Discussing needs and fears that motivate conflict behavior leads to increased perspective-taking, as well as increased self-understanding, and results in more changes in subsequent thinking and behavior (Greenberg et al., 1993; Izard, 1993). Parties to a dispute

who have engaged in joint problem solving have a higher commitment to a solution which they have had a direct hand in crafting (Petty et al., 1994; Stephenson & Wicklund, 1983) and show less favoritism toward their own group (Aronson et al., 1978).

Chataway also summarizes research supporting another key feature: using influential participants to promote the transfer of new ideas into policy and public opinion. Work on minority influence in groups (Bray et al., 1982; Tindale et al., 1990) has found that those most able to influence others when espousing alternative ideas are those who enjoy general societal respect, have reputations as competent contributors, and are articulate and confident in presenting new positive norms.

Confidentiality requirements and a reluctance to inject research protocol requirements into workshop interaction has made direct research on workshops difficult (d'Estrée et al., 2001). Direct research on interactive problem-solving workshops has fallen into three categories (Chataway, 2004): unobtrusive research on workshop interaction, research on simulated workshops, and evaluation of workshop products.

According to Chataway, the unobtrusive research on workshop interaction, mostly unpublished, has shed light on workshop phases and reentry preparation, interaction patterns, and the process by which participants learn to shape effective gestures of reassurance. In addition, d'Estrée and Babbitt (1998) sought to examine whether or not gender had an impact on the values discussed. Upon comparing interaction during an all-female Israeli–Palestinian workshop with a mixed male and female workshop that had occurred two weeks earlier, they found the workshops to be roughly equivalent in discussion of rights, but the all-female workshop to contain significantly more discussion of responsibilities as well. Facilitators noted more frequent use of personal experience and a sense of honesty.

To determine short-term changes in attitudes and behaviors of participants after a workshop, researchers have resorted to comparative simulations, typically comparing participants in simulated interactive problem-solving workshops with simulations of other interventions into intergroup conflict such as negotiations. Cross and Rosenthal (1999) increased realism through inviting Israeli and Jewish–American students together in pairs with Arab and Arab–American students to discuss the issue of Jerusalem. Groups were assigned to one of three conditions – distributive bargaining, integrative bargaining, and interactive problem solving – and subsequent attitudinal outcomes were examined. The interactive problem-solving condition produced the most positive attitude change toward the other, as well as the largest decreases in divisiveness, pessimistic attitudes toward the conflict, and the belief that the two sides' positions, interests, and needs were incompatible. Cross and Rosenthal concluded that the focus on reaching an agreement, characterizing both distributive and integrative bargaining, may have made it more difficult to obtain other attitudinal outcomes such as understanding and acknowledging the other's perspective, recognition, and empathy.

Chataway considers the third research category of workshop products to be "evidence of IPSW influence on the long-term attitudes and behaviors of participants, and on the intersocietal atmosphere and policymaking" (2004, p. 221). Various scholars have argued for a stage model of intervention, where at polarized stages of the conflict, generating concrete suggestions may be counterproductive, and energy is best spent building relationships across conflict lines that lay the basis for official negotiations. Once official negotiations have begun, unofficial diplomacy efforts such as interactive problem-solving may take a heightened task focus as well (Carnevale et al., 1989; Cross & Rosenthal, 1999; Keashley & Fisher, 1996; Lund, 1996). Outputs from these two stages may look very different.

One of the more significant revisions of the model seemed to come with the extension of the meeting to a series of meetings over months or years, particularly in the case of Kelman's Israeli–Palestinian workshops. This "continuing workshop" (Rouhana & Kelman, 1994) was better able to support and reinforce changed attitudes and relationships, and also increase direct impact on policymaking. The participants continued contact with each other and the third party outside of the workshops. Four became involved in the official negotiations; the group reconstituted with replacement members became a policy working group, wrestling in advance of the negotiations with some of the most contentious issues.

Enduring and potentially impactful products from these efforts include writings reflecting new ideas and options. In the Israeli–Palestinian workshops of Kelman and colleagues, writings by participants of continuing workshops, as well as by Kelman himself (1987) contributed to the pool of policy options and helped to disseminate better understanding. Using criteria from hermeneutic approaches to psychology, Chataway (2004) proposes that in terms of both quality of interpretation and of coherence, Kelman's writings were ahead of their time, while noting that some (Rouhana & Korper, 1996) consider that workshop products were not adequately reflexive, noting how differences in resources, experiences, and power might play a role.

In the d'Estrée and Babbitt (1998) study noted above, follow-up interviews with participants in an all-female Israeli–Palestinian problem-solving workshop found that participants could identify new understanding, respect, and acceptance of the other's perspective, but could not point to specific changes in their political behavior as a result of one particular workshop.

d'Estrée and colleagues, using evaluation methodologies to track the impact of workshops, have highlighted the importance of the changes that take place at the level of local institutions to which participants return (d'Estrée, 2006; d'Estrée et al., 2001). Though documenting changes in the relationship between two large communities and linking it back to workshop experiences may be a daunting research task, more immediate and no less important change occurs at lower levels as participants diffuse their new learning. Participants provide leadership for change in numerous ways, including (d'Estrée, 2006): civilizing the political debate, convening new meetings or creating new organizations, adding a cross-community element to existing organizations or programs, forming new organizational linkages, initiating new projects, developing more regional and/or cross-community projects, coordinating with (and therefore influencing) existing institutions (e.g. law enforcement, education), speaking for the cause of peace with new input and enhanced authority, educating one's own community about the political impacts of actions and policies, beginning or facilitating joint administration of resources or services, exchanging models across organizations for enhanced social change, influencing those setting policy (through position papers, etc.), influencing one's own community's extremist groups and others that are creating negative "facts on the ground," linking with other organizations for advice and support, and using networks and contacts to diffuse tension in times of crisis.

Evaluation and critiques of interactive intergroup problem-solving approaches

Interactive problem-solving approaches have been controversial from the beginning. Burton developed the approach to challenge traditional ways of thinking about international conflict and its resolution, and so invited critiques from the start. Over the years, as these intervention methods have evolved, questions have been raised that have in turn stimulated responses and sometimes revisions. The primary challenges that have been raised are relevance and effectiveness.

One of the earliest critiques of the first problem-solving workshops of Burton and his colleagues at University College London was by Ronald Yalem (1971). Yalem felt Burton's "controlled communication" to be "primarily a social–psychological device for altering the attitudes and perceptions of the representatives of states in conflict, so that on the basis of reduced hostility and tension they may be able to come together for serious and productive negotiations" (p. 263). He had several criticisms. One was its supposed emphasis on the subjective aspects of conflict, to the exclusion of "objective clashes over concrete interests." He was also concerned that there were no reports of how controlled communication had actually affected the outcome of a conflict, and concerned that the reports he had seen, because of secrecy, could not reveal details of even the states involved, thus hampering social science methods. It had been done on few cases. Success was inferred from analogy, rather than by testing directly. He questioned the centrality of communication as a cause of interstate conflict, and the effectiveness of using participants that were other than the primary decision makers. He acknowledged that the method might deliver new insights and build trust, but considered it supplemental to traditional methods of conflict resolution.

Mitchell (1973), at that time one of Burton's colleagues at the Centre for the Analysis of Conflict, acknowledged the importance of several of Yalem's concerns, but countered many of the points he had raised. Their discussion in the literature foreshadowed many of the issues that continue to be raised regarding problem-solving approaches as well as related intergroup relations interventions. He divides Yalem's concerns into two categories: practical, and theoretical. One practical problem that Yalem raises that continues to make scholarship on actual workshops difficult to this day, is the challenge to social science research methodology posed by the requisite confidentiality of the whole affair. As Mitchell summarizes it, "…had secrecy not been guaranteed no exercise would have occurred. The choice has thus been to operate within the limitations of guaranteed secrecy, as the alternative was not to operate at all." (p. 124). As with other case analysis – individuals, organizations, and the like – it is possible to draw insights from single cases for a particular class or type.

Mitchell also rebuts the criticism for using "subordinate officials," arguing that while such officials may be subordinate to heads of state, they are sufficiently close and trusted to insure that new insights will be passed back to leaders. Indeed, as argued elsewhere, their presence in a nonofficial capacity is what provides leeway to explore behind and beyond officially stated positions. Mitchell reiterates that controlled communication is not meant to be a substitute for traditional negotiation, rather to supplement or prepare parties for such negotiation (Mitchell, 1973).

However, Mitchell supports Yalem's concerns on the practical problem of participants retaining new insights and changes in attitudes once they return to their normal environment, where they are likely to be pressured to return to former patterns of thinking and acting. This concern dogs all such exercises in intergroup relationship change, dubbed by some "the reentry problem." Doob (1970) found that in problem-solving groups, a shift in attitudes and positions back toward those previously held can be observed even toward the end of the exercise itself, *before* participants returned to their environments, as if in preparation for reentry. Mitchell adds a concern, that of the potential danger to participants once they return home with changed perceptions: "...in which types of conflict might there be a personal risk, in career terms or even (in extreme cases) to life and limb?" (p. 126). Subsequent contributors to this method have attempted to address reentry concerns by keeping the exercise focused on intergroup interaction, as well as tied in to real group constraints, which can act as brakes to unrealistic and nonpragmatic shifts (Kelman, 1986). He also acknowledges the difficulty of assessing the actual degree to which insights from workshops are input into relevant decision making processes, though stressing the visible difference in interaction patterns witnessed in workshops themselves.

Mitchell (1973) considers Yalem's theoretical critiques to be twofold: first, the degree of subjectivity of conflict, and second, the validity of utilizing findings from other fields to support the application of problem-solving techniques to situations of international conflict. On the first debate, Mitchell presents what is still one of the most eloquent arguments in the field. It is worth reading in the original, but essentially his points are that when conflict researchers argue for subjective factors, they mean "more than that violent conflict behavior occurs because individuals, human groups, or nations misperceive the situation and their adversaries" (p. 127). Though false evaluation and false impressions, such as of goals, clearly play a role, a "fuzz" of misperceptions arises also from the dynamic of all leaders having to speak to multiple audiences. Leadership groups cannot easily demonstrate to each other that their goals have modified, or were incorrectly ascribed. "As the conflict proceeds over time, and meaningful communication becomes less, it becomes progressively more difficult for the leaders of one side to assess the actual long-term goals, the fundamental fears, the existing level of hostility, and the interpretation of the situation held by their opponents" (p. 127). As Burton observed, few opportunities exist for reality-testing, an important part both of conflict de-escalation and of constructive negotiations.

Other ways in which the conflict may be subjective, and thus subject to influence through exercises in controlled communication and problem solving: (1) the conflict may be over values that are not in limited supply, such as security or increased national wealth, that may more effectively be addressed jointly, even though initially the dispute may appear to be an "objective" one over territory; (2) groups pursue multiple goals simultaneously, and no group goal has immutable value, so that preference orderings can change; (3) parties can develop greater awareness of sacrifices required to obtain goals in conflict, resulting in a reassessment of costs. Thus, "while a conflict may be objective at a particular *point* in time, changes in the parties' objectives, preferences, evaluations, and calculations that occur over a *period* of time render it a changeable and hence an intensely subjective phenomenon" (p. 128). The point is not that all goals are subjective and changeable, but that some are more changeable than others. This supports the use of such methods even in the face of "objective" and structural conflict.

Mitchell rejects Yalem's concerns about analogical reasoning, chalking them up to differences in assumptions about to what degree one can transfer reasoning in one field or domain to another. Mitchell argues that not only is it appropriate to build on evidence from small group dynamics and social psychology regarding likely effects of meetings, such as problem-solving workshops on individual participants' perceptions, but it is also appropriate to draw from one level of human political behavior to transfer to another.

Mitchell (1973) reiterates that any discussion of the efficacy of controlled communication or problem solving must explore two quite separate sets of issues: its effectiveness in changing participants' attitudes and perceptions, and the conditions best suited for this, as well as the separate issue of the effectiveness of workshop initiatives for actually bringing about a change in the pattern of conflict interaction and the relations between parties to the conflict. These issues resurface in subsequent critiques.

Bercovitch (1986) considers the interactive problem-solving approach as a form of mediation and notes its shortcomings in this light. He notes that increasing communication may actually be detrimental to the progress of negotiations because it can increase areas of disagreement. He questions the problem-solving workshop approach's relevance and effectiveness, in its focus on analysis as the answer to resolution and in its interpersonal approach, and he proposes that its approach "provides no way of relating... to the actual policy making process" (p. 45).

Kelman (1992) responds to Bercovitch's critiques, by first reasserting that such approaches are not mediation, except in perhaps the broadest of senses. He argues, like Fisher and Keashley (1988), that the two differ in both objectives and methods, and thus interactive problem solving should not be evaluated as mediated negotiation. More specifically, he counters that interactive

problem solving does not attempt to increase communication *per se*, but rather to foster a particular form of communication conducive to a certain kind of learning. It is also not based only on analysis: "Analysis is only one aspect of the interaction process that we try to encourage in workshops, and workshops themselves are seen as only one input into a multifaceted process of conflict resolution." (p. 68) Kelman argues that considering the use of interpersonal interaction as a weakness is puzzling, since most diplomacy is conducted through interpersonal interaction. Participants do not interact with the same official capacity, but it is this difference that allows for the generation and consideration of new options. Kelman reemphasizes that the interpersonal is important only insofar as it impacts or reflects the relationship between the communities. Kelman does take Bercovitch's point that this approach, as with many others, needs to be better tailored to differences in conflict intensity. The interaction in the literature between Bercovitch, Kelman, and Fisher and Keashley helped to clarify the particular niche and role that interactive problem-solving approaches sought to play in the larger array of conflict resolution approaches.

Rouhana and Korper (1996) raise important critiques regarding the role that asymmetries of power may play both in the dynamics of conflict and in the workshop in particular.

Fisher (1997) reviews evaluation efforts within the broader interactive conflict resolution (ICR) field. He notes that while micro processes such as individual change have been easier to assess, seeking to measure the impact of ICR workshops on the larger negotiation or political process has been more difficult. He catalogued several more well-known published examples of the application of the interactive problem-solving workshop approach to various international and intercommunal conflicts. Beyond the basic contributions of increased understanding and changed attitudes, he found that certain practitioners reported considerable contributions to peace processes, including tension reduction initiatives, principles for settlement, and plans for peacebuilding activities.

However, the effects reported are rarely a result of systematic evaluation or comparative case analysis. As Fisher (1997) claims, "...very few studies assess transfer effects back to the parties, the wider relationship and the conflict, and the few that do offer only anecdotal impressions as opposed to more systematic follow-up procedures and evidence. Although descriptive methods are useful for initially documenting the approach, they are not adequate for testing theoretical linkages or making inferences about effectiveness" (pp. 210–211). Theory development, where it exists at all, is not grounded in systematic empirical comparisons.

After reviewing earlier efforts at evaluation, d'Estrée and colleagues (2000) identified two commonly voiced concerns regarding evaluation and assessment of interactive problem-solving and peacebuilding interventions more generally: (1) uncertainty about how to link immediate or short-term micro-level changes (e.g. in participant attitudes) to long-term changes in structures – changes that often represent what are considered to be "making peace," and (2) uncertainty about which criteria to apply, that is, how "success" is defined – through a universally accepted set of criteria, or ones that vary depending on context, purpose, actors. Like many fields of intervention, the field of interactive conflict resolution had lacked a common conceptual framework for making case comparisons and documenting changes over time. Their framework provided four overarching categories of criteria, each containing goals of interactive problem solving and thus criteria for success (d'Estrée, 2006; d'Estrée et al., 2000, 2001):

- Changes in thinking (new learning, attitude change, integrative framing, problem solving, better communication, and new language)
- Changes in relations (empathy, improvements in relational climate, better communication and new language, validation reconceptualization of identity, security in coexistence)
- Foundation for transfer – occurs in room, but focus is out of room (artifacts/drafts, structures for implementation, perceptions of possibility,

empowerment, new leadership, problem solving, influential participants)
- Foundation for outcome/implementation – out of room (networks, reforms in political structures, new political inputs and processes, increased capacity for jointly facing future challenges).

This framework has been applied in a limited number of cases in its original form (d'Estrée, 2006). Subsequent attempts to enhance research and evaluation on problem-solving approaches (Church & Shouldice, 2002, 2003; Çuhadar-Gürkaynak, 2006; Çuhadar-Gürkaynak et al., forthcoming) have built upon and modified these earlier frameworks.

In her 2004 review of research-supporting, interactive, problem-solving approaches, Chataway also outlines further revisions research would suggest. Because new attitudes gained toward others through such interventions often regress back over time (Cook & Flay, 1978), analytical interventions need to be paired with emotional and behavioral interventions (Tesser & Shaffer, 1990), as well as follow-up that reinforces exposure to the new attitudes (Petty et al., 1995). She argues that with a primary focus on rational discussion, coupled with a lack of explicit attention to behavioral and emotional realms, most interactive problem-solving workshops may reduce their impact on participants. She does not review approaches which are considered to focus more on emotion, such as those of Volkan and colleagues (1991a, 1991b).

Chataway also points out that the research on minority influence shows enhanced influence if participants work together and can support each other after a workshop (Tindale et al., 1990). Speaking out is enhanced when a minority view is spoken by more than one person. She suggests that workshops should be structured so as to enhance the likelihood that participants will be subsequently in regular contact and have the opportunity to discuss the workshop ideas, either through follow-up contact activities or because participants were chosen because of already having a structure for contact.

Remaining issues and future research

One recent discussion in the literature involves the integration of official negotiations and problem-solving approaches. One can certainly take a problem-solving approach to any negotiation, including international negotiations, and thus focus more on the joint task of reaching a solution rather than "winning" over the other. However, debate exists in the field as to whether or not problem solving in its more specific forms such as problem-solving workshops, as framed above, should be considered as integral to international negotiations or as a parallel and complementary process.

Kelman himself seems to be of two minds on this. In earlier works, he discusses problem solving as a prenegotiation process, as supplemental to current negotiations, and as useful postnegotiation to work out implementation challenges. However, in later works (1996, 1999), he adds the notion that interactive problem solving can be seen as a metaphor for how negotiations *themselves* should be conducted. Fisher (1997; Fisher & Keashley, 1991, 1996) sees the role of these processes as complementary. By contrast, Stein (1999) takes pains to explain why she thinks that the original framing of the role of interactive problem solving should be preserved.

Other issues seem to recur across the decades of work on problem-solving approaches. These are issues of the work's relevance to the larger conflict systems, the challenges of research, and the dilemmas and risks of participant reentry back into the conflict system.

Relevance. Relevance operates at many levels. Do the workshop interactions actually produce changes (new insights, changed attitudes, alternative behaviors) that are important and reliable? Do these changes persist in people's lives long enough to potentially influence the larger society? Do these new insights then influence the larger society in some form? Is this in enough of a way that then policies and actions

of states change? Though evidence exists for the first question, arguing for at least relevance to changing conflict relationships at the level of changing individuals, as one proceeds up the ladder, the evidence is less clearly identifiable. This is partly an insolvable epistemological conundrum, both because of the multidetermined nature of complex phenomena and due to the research issues outlined below. However, if changes in individuals are not in fact linked to changes in societies, the exercise as relevant to the behavior of states can be called into question.

Relevance is also determined by the method's validity. If the enterprise is not producing a realistic reflection of dynamics in the actual conflict, or subject to biases such as those outlined by Rouhana and Korper above, its usefulness may be limited.

Research. Research and evaluation are necessary components to improving the method, and for continuing to modify it to match changing environmental conditions. Research on any phenomenon still embedded in the complexity of its context is difficult. However, research on problem-solving approaches has two additional challenges. First, the promise of confidentiality made to participants that both allows them to come and protects the process from other influences makes reliable research challenging. Second, researchers in the physical and social sciences have long known about the impact the research process has on the phenomenon itself (e.g. the Hawthorne effect first documented by Mayo, 1933). Things appear differently because of the process of being watched. Scholar-practitioners using problem-solving approaches have been reluctant to risk impacting the workshop interaction in order to achieve research objectives; thus, researchers have tended to rely on noninvasive and/or interpretive methods, which in turn offer less reliable and more speculative research results.

Reentry. Once attitudes and perceptions change, and new learning takes place, participants may have trouble fitting back in with old behaviors and old social networks.

The pressure to "belong" to one's group(s) may include maintaining old attitudes and approaches, threatening the integration and maintenance of changed attitudes and behaviors. Or one may find oneself marginalized and outcast if one's new attitudes and behaviors are perceived as threatening to the group. This phenomenon is common to all social change interventions, whether it be drug or alcohol rehabilitation, gender sensitivity training, or ethnic conflict interventions.

Concerns about so-called reentry effects have been raised not only by critics of problem solving (Yalem, 1971), but also by its designers (Burton, 1987, 1990; Doob, 1970; Mitchell, 1973; Mitchell & Banks, 1996). Practitioners have been challenged to envision frameworks that would better support participants returning to their societies (Chataway, 2004). Only then can those with new understanding and new insights be best positioned to bring their problem-solving gifts to their weary communities.

NOTES

1 The author would like to acknowledge the research assistance of Dennis Barbour, Christina Farnsworth, and Sara Noel.

2 Avruch and Black (1993) challenge this assumed universality of basic human needs.

REFERENCES

Aronson, E., Blaney, N., Stephan, C., Sikes, J., & Snapp, M. (1978). *The jigsaw classroom*. Beverly Hills, CA: Sage.

Avruch, K., & Black, P.W. (1993). Conflict resolution in intercultural settings: Problems and prospects. In D.J.D. Sandole & H. van der Merwe (Eds.), *Conflict resolution theory and practice* (pp. 131–145). Manchester, UK: Manchester University Press.

Azar, E.E. (1980). The Conflict and Peace Resarch Data Bank (COBDAB) project. *Journal of Conflict Resolution*, 23, 143–152.

Azar, E.E. (1983). The theory of protracted social conflict and the challenge of tranforming conflict situations. *Monograph Series in World Affairs*, 20 (No. M2), 81–99.

Azar, E.E. (1985). Protracted international conflicts: Ten propositions. *International Interactions*, 12, 59–70.

Azar, E.E. (1990). *The management of protracted social conflict*. Hampshire, UK: Dartmouth.

Azar, E.E., & Burton, J.W. (Eds.). (1986). *International conflict resolution: Theory and practice*. Brighton, UK: Wheatsheaf.

Azar, E.E., & Farah, N. (1981). The structure of inequalities and protracted social conflict: A theoretical framework. *International Interactions*, 7, 317–335.

Azar, E.E., Jureidini, P., & McLaurin, R. (1978). Protracted social conflict: Theory and practice in the Middle East. *Journal of Palestine Studies*, 8(1), 41–60.

Babbitt, E., & d'Estrée, T.P. (1996). An Israeli-Palestinian women's workshop: Application of the problem-solving approach. In C. Crocker (Ed.), *Managing global chaos: Sources of and responses to international conflict* (pp. 521–529). Washington, DC: US Institute of Peace.

Bercovitch, J. (1986). A case study of mediation as a method of international conflict resolution: The Camp David experience. *Review of International Studies*, 12, 43–65.

Berkovitch, J. (1996). Introduction: Thinking about mediation. In J. Berkovitch (Ed.), *Resolving international conflicts: The theory and practice of mediation* (pp. 1–9). Boulder, CO: Lynne Rienner.

Blake, R.R., & Mouton, J.S. (1961). *Group dynamics: Key to decision making*. Houston, TX: Gulf.

Blake, R.R., & Mouton, J.S. (1964). *The managerial grid*. Houston, TX: Gulf.

Blake, R.R., & Mouton, J.S. (1984). *Solving costly organizational conflicts*. San Francisco: Jossey-Bass.

Blake, R.R., Shepard, H.A., & Mouton, J.S. (1964). *Managing intergroup conflict in industry*. Houston, TX: Gulf.

Bray, R.M., Johnston, D., & Chilstrom, J.T. (1982). Social influence by group members with minority opinions: A comparison of Hollander and Moscovici. *Journal of Personality and Social Psychology*, 43, 78–88.

Broome, B.J. (1997). Designing a collective approach to peace: Interactive design and problem-solving workshops with Greek-Cypriot and Turkish-Cypriot communities in Cyprus. *International Negotiation*, 2, 381–407.

Brown, R. (1986). *Social psychology: The second edition*. New York: Free Press.

Burnstein, E. (1982). Persuasion as argument processing. In H. Braendstetter, J.H. Davis & G. Stocker-Kreichgauer (Eds.), *Group decision making* (pp. 103–124). London: Academic Press.

Burton, J.W. (1969). *Conflict and communication: The use of controlled communication in international relations*. London: Macmillan.

Burton, J.W. (1979). *Deviance, terrorism, and war: The process of solving unsolved social and political problems*. New York: St Martin's Press.

Burton, J.W. (1984). *Global conflict: The domestic sources of international conflict*. Brighton, UK: Wheatsheaf.

Burton, J.W. (1987). *Resolving deep-rooted conflict: A handbook*. Lanham, MD: University Press of America.

Burton, J.W. (1990a). *Conflict: Resolution and provention*. New York: St Martin's Press.

Burton, J.W. (Ed.). (1990b). *Conflict: Human needs theory*. New York: St Martin's Press.

Bush, R.A.B., & Folger, J.P. (1994/2004). *The promise of mediation*. New York: Jossey-Bass.

Carnevale, P., Lim, R., & McLaughlin, M. (1989). Contingent mediator behavior and effectiveness. In K. Kressel & D. G. Pruitt (Eds.), *Mediation research: The process and effectiveness of third party intervention* (pp. 213–240). San Francisco: Jossey-Bass.

Chataway, C. (2004). Assessing the social-psychological support for Kelman's interactive problem-solving workshops. In A. Eagly, R. M. Baron & V. L. Hamilton (Eds.), *The social psychology of group identity and social conflict: Theory, application and practice*. Washington, DC: American Psychological Association.

Chufrin, G.I., & Saunders, H.H. (1993). A public peace process. *Negotiation Journal*, 9, 155–177.

Church, C., & Shouldice, J. (2002). *Evaluation of conflict resolution interventions: Framing the state of play*. Londonderry: INCORE, University of Ulster.

Church, C., & Shouldice, J. (2003). *Evalution of conflict resolution interventions part II: Emerging practice and theory*. Londonderry: INCORE, University of Ulster.

Cohen, S.P., & E. Azar (1981). From war to peace: The transition between Egypt and Israel. *Journal of Conflict Resolution*, 25, 87–114.

Cook, T.D., & Flay, B.R. (1978). The persistence of experimentally induced attitude change. In L. Berkowitz (Ed.), *Advances in experimental social psychology* (Vol. 11, pp. 1–57). San Diego, CA: Academic Press.

Crocker, C., Hampson, F., & Aall, P. (1999). *Herding cats: Multiparty mediation in a complex world*. Washington, DC: US Institute of Peace.

Cross, S., & Rosenthal, R. (1999). Three models of conflict resolution: Effects on intergroup expectancies and attitudes. *Journal of Social Issues*, 55, 561–580.

Çuhadar-Gürkaynak, E. (2006). Expanding the d'Estrée et al. evaluation framework: Empirical evidence from Israeli-Palestinian workshops 1991–2000. Annual International Studies Association Convention, San Diego, CA.

Çuhadar-Gürkaynak, E., Dayton, B., & Paffenholz, T. (forthcoming). Evaluation in conflict resolution and peacebuilding. In S. Byrne, D.J.D. Sandole, I. Sandole-Staroste & J. Senehi (Eds.), *A handbook of conflict analysis and resolution*. London and New York: Routledge.

d'Estrée, T.P. (1999). The Hopi-Navajo land dispute: Official and unofficial interventions. In M. H. Ross & J. Rothman (Eds.), *Theory and practice in ethnic conflict management: Conceptualizing success and failure*. London: Macmillan.

d'Estrée, T.P. (2005). The role of voice in conflict deescalation and resolution. In F.M. & C.E. Stout (Eds.), *The psychology of resolving global conflicts: From war to peace*. New York: Praeger.

d'Estrée, T.P. (2006). Identifying the impact of interactive conflict resolution: How political influentials create frameworks for peace. In T. Gärling, Backenroth-Ohsako & B. Ekehammar (Eds.), *Diplomacy and psychology: Prevention of armed conflicts after the cold war* (pp. 226–253). Singapore: Marshall Cavendish.

d'Estrée, T.P., & Babbitt, E. (1998). Women and the art of peacemaking: Data from Israeli-Palestinian interactive problem-solving workshops. *Political Psychology*, 19, 185–209.

d'Estrée, T.P., Fast, L.A., Weiss, J.N., & Jakobsen, M.S. (2001). Changing the debate about "success" in conflict resolution efforts. *Negotiation Journal*, 17(2), 101–113.

d'Estrée, T.P., Weiss, J., Jakobsen, M.S., Fast, L., & Funk, N. (2000). *A framework for evaluating intergroup interactive conflict resolution*. George Mason University.

Davis, A.M. (1989). An interview with Mary Parker Follett. *Negotiation Journal*, 5, 223–237.

Deutsch, M. (1973). *The resolution of conflict: Constructive and destructive processes*. New Haven, CT: Yale University Press.

Deutsch, M. (2000). Cooperation and competition. In M. Deutsch & P.T. Coleman (Eds.), *The handbook of conflict resolution* (pp. 21–40). San Francisco: Jossey-Bass.

Diamond, L., & McDonald, J.W. (1991). *Multi-track diplomacy: A systems guide and analysis*. Grinnell, Iowa: Iowa Peace Institute.

Dominowski, R.L., & Bourne, L.E. (1994). History of research on thinking and problem solving. In R.J. Stermberg (Ed.), *Thinking and problem solving* (2nd edn). San Diego: Academic Press.

Doob, L.W. (Ed.). (1970). *Resolving conflict in Africa: The Fermeda workshop*. New Haven, CT: Yale University Press.

Doob, L.W., Foltz, W.J., & Stevens, R.B. (1969). The Fermeda workshop: A different approach to border conflicts in eastern Africa. *Journal of Psychology*, 73, 249–266.

Fisher, R.J. (1972). Third party consultation: A method for the study and resolution of conflict. *Journal of Conflict Resolution*, 16(1), 67–94.

Fisher, R., & Ury, W. (1981). *Getting to yes: Negotiating agreement without giving in*. New York: Houghton Mifflin.

Fisher, R.J. (1983). Third-party consultation as a method of conflict resolution. *Journal of Conflict Resolution*, 27: 301–34.

Fisher, R.J. (1991). *Conflict analysis workshop on Cyprus: Final workshop report*. Ottawa: Canadian Institute for International Peace and Security.

Fisher, R.J. (1992). *Peacebuilding for Cyprus: Report on a conflict analysis workshop, June 1991*. Ottawa: Canadian Institute for International Peace and Security.

Fisher, R.J. (1997). *Interactive conflict resolution*. Syracuse, NY: Syracuse University Press.

Fisher, R.J., & Keashley, L. (1988). Third party interventions in intergroup conflict: Consultation is not mediation. *Negotiation Journal*, 4, 381–391.

Fisher, R.J., & Keashley, L. (1991). The potential complementarity of mediation and consultation within a contingency model of third party intervention. *Journal of Peace Research*, 28(1), 29–42.

Fisher, R.J., & Keashley, L. (1996). A contingency perspective on conflict interventions: Theoretical and practical considerations. In J. Berkovitch (Ed.), *Resolving international conflicts*. Boulder: Lynne Reinner.

Ghiselli, E.E., & Lodahl, T.M. (1958). Patterns of managerial traits and group effectiveness. *Journal of Abnormal and Social Psychology*, 57, 61–66.

Graham, P. (Ed.). (1996). *Mary Parker Follett, prophet of management: A celebration of writings from the 1920s*. Cambridge, MA: Harvard Business School.

Greenberg, L.S., Rice, L.N., & Elliott, R. (1993). *Facilitating emotional change: The moment-by-moment process*. New York: Guilford Press.

Gulliver, P.H. (1979). *Dispute and negotiations*. New York: Academic Press.

Hackman, J.R. (Ed.). (1990). *Groups that work (and those that don't): Creating conditions for effective teamwork*. San Francisco: Jossey-Bass.

Hare, A.P., Carney, F., & Ovsiew, F. (1977). Youth responds to crisis: Curaçao. In A.P. Hare & H.H. Blumberg (Eds.), *Liberation without violence* (pp. 220–238). London: Rex Collings.

Hicks, D., O'Doherty, P., Steiner, P., Taylor, W., & Trigeorgis, M. (1994). Addressing intergroup conflict by integrating and realigning identity: An Arab-Israeli workshop. In M. Ettin, J. Fidler, & B. Cohen (Eds.), *Group development and political evolution*

(pp. 279–302). Madison, Conn.: International Univ. Press.

Hoffman, L.R. (1959). Homogeneity of personality and its effect on group problem-solving. *Journal of Abnormal and Social Psychology*, 58, 27–32.

Hoffman, L.R., Harburg, E., & Maier, N.R.F. (1962). Differences and disagreement as factors in creative group problem solving. *Journal of Abnormal and Social Psychology*, 64(3), 206–214.

Hoffman, L.R., & Maier, N.R.F. (1961). Quality and acceptance of problem solutions by members of homogeneous and heterogeneous groups. *Journal of Abnormal and Social Psychology*, 62, 401–407.

Hopmann, T.P. (1995). Two paradigms of negotiation: Bargaining and problem solving. *Annals of the American Academy of Political and Social Science*, 542, *Flexibility in International Negotiation and Mediation*, 24–47.

Hunt, E. (1994). Problem solving. In R.J. Sternberg (Ed.), *Thinking and problem solving* (pp. 215–232). San Diego: Academic Press.

Iklé, F.C. (1964). *How nations negotiate*. New York: Frederick A. Praeger.

Izard, C. (1993). Four systems for emotion activation: Cognitive and noncognitive processes. *Psychological Review*, 100, 68–90.

Janis, I.L. (1982). *Groupthink* (2nd edn). Boston: Houghton-Mifflin.

Keashley, L., & Fisher, R.J. (1996). A contingency perspective on conflict interventions: Theoretical and practical considerations. In J. Bercovitch (Ed.), *Resolving international conflicts* (pp. 235–262). London: Lynne Rienner.

Kelman, H.C. (1969). Patterns of personal involvement in the national system: A social–sychological analysis of political legitimacy. In J.N. Rosenau (Ed.), *International politics and foreign policy: A reader in research and theory* (Revised edn). New York: Free Press.

Kelman, H.C. (1972). The problem solving workshop in conflict resolution. In R. L. Merritt (Ed.), *Communication in international politics*. University of Illinois Press.

Kelman, H.C. (1986). Interactive problem solving: A social-psychological approach to conflict resolution. In W. Klassen (Ed.), *Dialogue: Toward interfaith understanding*. Tantur, Jerusalem: Ecumenical Institute for Theological Research.

Kelman, H.C. (1987). The political psychology of the Israeli-Palestinian conflict: How can we overcome the barriers to a negotiated solution? *Political Psychology*, 8, 347–363.

Kelman, H.C. (1992). Informal mediation by the scholar practitioner. In J. Bercovitch & J. Rubin (Eds.), *Mediation in international relations: Multiple approaches to conflict management* (pp. 64–96). New York: St Martin's Press.

Kelman, H.C. (1995). Contributions of an unofficial conflict resolution effort to the Israeli-Palestinian breakthrough. *Negotiation Journal*, 11(1), 19–27.

Kelman, H.C. (1996). Negotiation as interactive problem solving. International Negotiation. *Journal of Theory and Practice*, 1(1), 99–123.

Kelman, H.C. (1997a). Group processes in the resolution of international conflicts: Experiences from the Israeli-Palestinian conflict. *American Psychologist*, 52(3), 212–220.

Kelman, H.C. (1997b). Social-psychological dimensions of international conflict. In I.W. Zartman, & J.L. Rasmussen (Eds.), *Peacemaking in international conflict: Methods and techniques* (pp. 191–237). Washington, DC: United States Institute of Peace.

Kelman, H.C. (1998). Social-psychological contributions to peacemaking and peacebuilding in the Middle East. *Applied Psychology: An International Review*, 47, 5–28.

Kelman, H.C. (1999). Interactive problem solving as a metaphor for international conflict resolution: Lessons for the policy process. *Peace and Conflict: Journal of Peace Psychology*, 5(3), 201–218.

Kelman, H.C. (2000). The role of the scholar-practitioner in international conflict resolution. *International Studies Perspectives*, 1, 273–288.

Kelman, H.C. (2005). Building trust among enemies: The central challenge for international conflict resolution. *International Journal of Intercultural Relations*, 29, 639–650.

Kelman, H.C., & Cohen, S.P. (1976). The problem-solving workshop: A social-psychological contribution to the resolution of international conflict. *Journal of Peace Research*, 13, 79–90.

Kelman, H.C., & Cohen, S.P. (1986). Resolution of international conflict: An interactional approach. In S. Worchel, & W.G. Austin (Eds.), *Psychology of intergroup relations* (2nd edn). Chicago: Nelson-Hall.

Lasswell, H. (1966). Conflict and leadership: The process of decision and the nature of authority. In A. de Reuck, & J. Knight (Eds.), *Conflict in society: a CIBA Foundations Volume*. J. and A. Churchill Ltd.

Lax, D., & Sebenius, J. (1986). The manager as negotiator: bargaining for cooperation and competitive gain.

Lederach, J.P. (1997). *Building peace: Sustainable reconciliation in divided societies*. Washington, DC: US Institute of Peace Press.

Lewin, K., Lippett, R., & White, R. (1939). Patterns of aggressive behavior in experimentally created "social climates." *Journal of Social Psychology*, 10, 271–299.

Luce, R.D., & Raiffa, H. (1957). *Games and decisions*. New York: John Wiley.

Lund, M.S. (1996). *Preventing violent conflicts*. Washington, DC: United States Institute of Peace Press.

Maier, N.R.F. (1952). *Principles of human relations*. New York: Wiley.

Maier, N.R.F. (1958). *The appraisal interview: Objectives, methods and skills*. New York: Wiley.

Maier, N.R.F., & Hoffman, L.R. (1960). Quality of first and second solutions in group problem solving. *Journal of Applied Psychology*, 44, 278–283.

Maier, N.R.F., & Hoffman, L.R. (1961). Organization and creative problem solving. *Journal of Applied Psychology*, 45, 277–280.

Maslow, A.H. (1970). *Motivation and personality* (2nd edn). New York: Harper and Row.

Mayo, E. (1933). *The human problems of an industrial civilization*. New York: MacMillan.

Menkel-Meadow, C. (2000). Mothers and fathers of invention: The intellectual founders of ADR. *Ohio State Journal on Dispute Resolution*, 16(1), 1–37.

Mitchell, C.R. (1973). Conflict resolution and controlled communication: Some further comments. *Journal of Peace Research*, 10(1/2), 123–132.

Mitchell, C.R. (1981). *Peacemaking and the consultant's role*. Westmead, UK: Gower.

Mitchell, C.R., & Banks, M. (1996). *Handbook of conflict resolution: The analytical problem-solving approach*. London: Pinter.

Mnookin, R.H., Peppet, S.R., & Tulumello, A.S. (2000). *Beyond winning: Negotiating to create value in deals and disputes*. Cambridge, MA: Bellknap/Harvard.

Montville, J.V. (1987). The arrow and the olive branch: The case for track two diplomacy. In J.W. McDonald & D.B. Bendahmane (Eds.), *Conflict resolution: track two diplomacy (pp. 5–20)*. Washington, DC: Foreign Service Institute, US Department of State.

Moore, C. (2003). *The Mediation Process* (3rd edn.). New York: Jossey-Bass.

Nader, L., & Todd, H. (1978). *The disputing process: law in ten societies*. New York: Columbia University Press.

Newell, A., Shaw, J.C., & Simon, H.A. (1958). Elements of a theory of human problem solving. *Psychological Review*, 65(3), 151–166.

Newell, A., & Simon, H.A. (1972). *Human problem solving*. Englewood Cliffs, NJ: Prentice-Hall.

Osborn, A.E. (1957). *Applied imagination* (1st edn.). New York: Scribner's.

Paulus, P.B., Larey, T.S., & Dzindolet, M.T. (2001). Creativity in groups and teams. In M.E. Turner (Ed.), *Groups at work: Theory and research* (pp. 319–338). Mahwah, NJ: Lawrence Erlbaum.

Pettigrew, T.F. (1998). Intergroup contact theory. *Annual Review of Psychology*, 49, 65–85.

Petty, R., Haugtvedt, C.P., & Smith, S.M. (1995). Elaboration as a determinant of attitude strength.

In R.E. Petty & J.A. Krosnick (Eds.), *Attitude strength: Antecedents and consequences* (pp. 93–130). Mahwah, NJ: Erlbaum.

Petty, R., Priester, J., & Wegener, D. (1994). Cognitive processes in attitude change. In R. Wyer, & T. Srull (Eds.), *Handbook of social cognition* (Vol. 2, pp. 69–142). Mahway, NJ: Erlbaum.

Pruitt, D.G. (1995). Process and outcome in community mediation. *Negotiation Journal*, 11, 365–377.

Pruitt, D.G., & Rubin, J.Z. (1986). *Social conflict: Escalation, stalemate, and settlement*. New York: McGraw-Hill.

Rapaport, A. (1960). *Fights, games, and debates*. Ann Arbor: University of Michigan.

Ross, L., & Ward, A. (1995). Psychological barriers to dispute resolution. In M.P. Zanna (Ed.), *Advances in experimental social psychology* (Vol. 27, pp. 255–304). San Diego, CA: Academic Press.

Rothman, J. (1993, September 14). Unofficial talks yielded mideast peace. Philadelphia Inquirer.

Rouhana, N.N., & Kelman, H.C. (1994). Promoting joint thinking in international conflict: An Israeli-Palestinian continuing workshop. *Journal of Social Issues*, 50(Spring), 157–178.

Rouhana, N.N., & Korper, S. (1996). Dealing with the dilemmas posed by power asymmetry in intergroup conflict. *Negotiation Journal*, 12, 353–366.

Saunders, H.H. (2001). *A public peace process: sustained dialogue to transform racial and ethnic conflict*. New York: Palgrave.

Schelling, T. (1960). *The strategy of conflict*. Cambridge, MA: Harvard University Press.

Schön, D.A. (1983). *The reflective practitioner*. New York: Basic Books.

Simon, H.A. (1977). *The new science of management decision*. Englewood Cliffs, NJ: Prentice-hall.

Sites, P. (1973). *Control: The basis of social order*. New York: Dunellen.

Slim, R.M., & Saunders, H.H. (1996). Managing conflict in divided societies: Lessons from Tajikistan. *Negotiation Journal*, 12, 31–46.

Smith, K.K., & Berg, D.N. (1987). *Paradoxes of group life*. New York: Jossey-Bass.

Stein, J.G. (1999). Problem solving as metaphor: negotiation and identity conflict. *Peace and Conflict: Journal of Peace Psychology*, 5(3), 225–235.

Stephenson, B., & Wicklund, R. (1983). Self-directed attention and taking the other's perspective. *Journal of Experimental and Social Psychology*, 19, 58–77.

Tajfel, H. (1978). *Differentiation between social groups: studies in the social psychology of intergroup relations*. London: Academic Press.

Tajfel, H. (1981b). *Human groups and social categories: studies in social psychology*. Cambridge: Cambridge University Press.

Tesser, A., & Shaffer, D. (1990). Attitudes and attitude change. *Annual Review of Psychology*, 41, 479–523.

Tetlock, P.E. (1992). The impact of accountability on judgment and choice: Toward a social contingency model. In M. Zanna (Ed.), *Advances in Experimental Social Psychology* (Vol. 25, pp. 331–376). San Diego, CA: Academic Press.

Tindale, R.S., Davis, J.H., Vollrath, D.A., Nagao, D.H., & Hinsz, V.B. (1990). Asymmetrical social influence in freely interating groups: A test of three models. *Journal of Personality and Social Psychology*, 58, 438–449.

Van deVliert, E., & Janssen, O. (2001). Description, explanation, and prescription of intragroup conflict behaviors. In M.E. Turner (Ed.), *Groups at work: Theory and research*. Mahwah, NJ: Lawrence Erlbaum.

Van Gundy, A.B. (1988). *Techniques of structured problem solving* (2nd ed.). New York: Van Nostrand Reinhold.

Volkan, V.D., Julius, D.A., & Montville, J.V. (Eds.). (1991a). The psychodynamics of international relationships. Volume I: Concepts and theories. Lexington, Mass.: Lexington Books.

Volkan, V.D., Julius, D.A., & Montville, J.V. (Eds.). (1991b). *The psychodynamics of international relationships. Volume II: Unofficial diplomacy at work*. Lexington, Mass.: Lexington Books.

Wallas, G. (1926). *The art of thought*. New York: Harcourt.

Walton, R.E. (1969). *Interpersonal peacemaking: Confrontations and third party consultation*. Reading, MA: Addison-Wesley.

Walton, R.E., & McKersie, R.B. (1965). *A behavioral theory of labor negotiations: An analysis of a social interaction system*. New York: McGraw-Hill.

Yalem, R.J. (1971). Controlled communications an conflict resolution. *Journal of Peace Research*, 8(3/4), 263–272.

Zartman, I.W., & Berman, M.R. (1982). *The practical negotiator*. New Haven, CT: Yale University Press.

9

Constructivism and Conflict Resolution

Richard Jackson

Constructivism is a social theory rather than a substantive theory of international politics. Broadly speaking, constructivists are concerned with the way agents and structures co-constitute each other, the socially constructed nature of actors and their identities and interests, and the importance of ideational, normative and discursive factors in the shaping of international political reality. Constructivist approaches are unique in that they occupy a middle ground between rationalist/positivist and idealist/interpretive approaches to the study of international politics (Adler, 1997), thereby offering the possibility of a more holistic, multi-dimensional understanding of processes such as war, conflict and conflict resolution.

Constructivism offers insights for conflict analysis and conflict resolution at the international level because it draws attention to a range of factors and processes that are frequently missing from the rationalist and structurally based explanations of neo-realism and neo-liberalism, including: the historically contingent and mutually constitutive nature of the structures and agents of international conflict; the socially constructed nature of identities, interests and structures; the role of discursive factors, such as political language, ideas, norms, knowledge, symbols, history and culture, in the initiation and reproduction of conflict; and the key role played by elites and other conflict agents in constructing and manipulating group identities, among others.

Together with neo-realism and neo-liberalism, constructivism is now a well-established and widely accepted approach within international relations (IR). However, it has yet to make a significant impact on the study of international conflict and conflict resolution which continues to be dominated by rational choice and structurally based quantitative approaches. In spite of its under utilization, constructivism is the most well-suited of all the main IR approaches to understanding conflict and conflict resolution, not least because it focuses on many of the same issues and shares a similar positive approach to the agency of actors. That is, just like conflict resolution, constructivism is concerned with the beliefs, attitudes and perceptions of parties in conflict, the normative structures that regulate conflict behaviour, the formation of regimes, the communicative–discursive strategies adopted by intermediaries in conflict, the role of language, memory and narratives in reconciliation and the actions that individuals and groups can take to shape their lives and resolve their conflicts – among others (see the Introduction to this volume).

The chapter begins with a brief overview of constructivism – its origins, types, shared assumptions and ontology, and its methodological approaches. The second section reviews a number of constructivist studies on interstate and intrastate conflict; it argues that constructivism can make a genuine contribution to conflict analysis, particularly in terms of the ideational and discursive basis of political violence. The third section assesses some of the implications of a constructivist account of war and conflict for conflict resolution, while the final section attempts to provide an evaluation of constructivism and make some suggestions regarding a future research agenda.

Two important caveats are needed at the outset. First, constructivism is an approach to social research – a theoretical lens and a set of conceptual tools – and not a substantive theory in itself. In this sense, and similar to case study, experimental and game theoretic approaches (see Levy, Pruitt and Avenhaus in this volume), constructivism does not have anything specific to say about war, conflict or conflict resolution; anything that can be said about conflict resolution can only be inferred from the broader theory and research findings of particular constructivist studies.

Second, a great many of the insights drawn from constructivism are not necessarily original when placed in the context of the wider conflict resolution field. The constructivist emphasis on agents and structures, the role of identity and the importance of language and discourse, for example, were concerns of early peace studies' scholars like Kenneth Boulding, Johan Galtung, John Burton, Edward Azar, Herb Kelman and others. The importance of constructivism lies mainly in its potential contribution to

the international conflict management subfield, which has tended for the most part to adopt neo-realist and neo-liberal approaches and has ignored much of the research emanating from peace studies (Ramsbotham, Woodhouse and Miall, 2005). Constructivist research is particularly useful for the way in which it both theorizes some of these central concepts more completely into social theory, and the way it explores the micro-physics of their practice in actual cases. In sum, constructivism provides a complementary and confirmative approach to the broader field of conflict resolution, rather than a novel or rival approach.

CONSTRUCTIVISM

Constructivism is one of three main approaches to the study of international relations. Neo-realism, the most influential approach in IR, is founded on a number of core beliefs and assumptions, including, among others: states are the primary actors in international politics; the international system is fundamentally anarchic, providing no central authority for enforcing rules, upholding norms or protecting the interests of the larger global community; the structural condition of anarchy is the main determinant of both national interests and state behaviour, which is oriented towards survival and maximizing power; states are self-interested, rational actors who favour self-help over cooperation; and state actions aimed at ensuring survival create a permanent security dilemma. Neo-realism employs rationalist and positivist approaches to the study of international politics, and purports to provide an accurate description of international 'reality'. From a neo-realist perspective, war and conflict is an inevitable consequence of structural anarchy and the consequent struggle for security and power that states engage in. More importantly, neo-realists argue that the anarchical nature of the state system precludes the possibility of genuine conflict resolution or transformation; in a world of self-maximizing states, effective conflict *management*, often through the use of power mediation or peace enforcement, is the optimal achievable condition.

A second influential approach within IR is neo-liberalism. It shares many of neo-realism's core assumptions about the actors, issues, structures and power arrangements of the international system, but tends to focus on questions of interstate cooperation, institutions, regimes and political economy, rather than issues of security and conflict. Often called neo-liberal institutionalism, it argues that international institutions, regimes and the shared interests and mutual interdependence of states under globalization can mitigate the effects of anarchy, allow states to achieve absolute gains in security and create the basis for real peace and prosperity. Consequently, neo-liberal institutionalists seek to both understand and encourage multilateral cooperation, the persistence of international and regional institutions, the establishment of international law, global governance, regimes and norms, the creation of security communities, the use of cosmopolitan peacekeeping and the extension of the democratic peace, among others. Importantly, the sub-field of international conflict management has roots in both the neo-liberal and the neo-realist traditions.

Constructivism has emerged recently as a widely accepted alternative approach to both neo-realism and neo-liberalism; three main developments were crucial to its rise (see Adler, 2003; Barnett, 2005; Price and Reus-Smit, 1998). First, beginning in the 1980s, a debate started between critical scholars and the dominant neo-realists and neo-liberalists which opened up the space for an alternative constructivist research agenda. Drawing from critical and sociological theory, scholars such as John Ruggie (1983), Richard Ashley (1984), Alexander Wendt (1987), Friedrich Kratochwil (1989) and Nicholas Onuf (1989) presented a powerful critique of neo-realism and neo-liberalism, in part by demonstrating the effects of normative structures and ideational factors on world politics. The admission by leading neo-realists and neo-liberals, most notably Robert Keohane (1989),

that such criticisms were valid but needed to be backed up by testable theories and empirical research, led to a proliferation of constructivist-oriented studies.

The 'constructivist turn' in international relations was given further impetus by the collapse of the Soviet Union and the end of the Cold War, which occurred without any significant shift in the distribution of capabilities in the international system and largely through domestic political transformation, in part due to the impact of so-called 'norm entrepreneurs' like Mikhail Gorbachev. This seriously undermined the explanatory power of neo-realism and neo-liberalism which had failed to predict, and had no real basis for understanding, such as revolutionary transformations in the international system (Kratochwil, 1993). In this way, international change provided a catalyst for theoretical change.

Since then, constructivism has developed in a number of different directions, depending upon the specific theoretical traditions drawn upon, the central focus of the research and the main methodological approaches employed by the researcher. As a consequence of these fault-lines, there is now an increasing variety of labels for constructivist scholarship, including: conventional, modernist, post-modern, thick, thin, narrative, strong, systemic and holistic – among others (Adler, 1997: 335–6; Barnett, 2005: 258). Arguably the most important division is between modernist and post-modernist forms (Price and Reus-Smit, 1998: 267–8; Smith, 2004: 501). The principle differences between post-modern constructivism and other constructivist approaches is one of analytical focus and methodology: post-modernists tend to focus closely on the relationship between knowledge and power and employ forms of genealogical, predicate, narrative and deconstructive analysis influenced by the Foucaultian theoretical tradition (see for example, Campbell, 1992, 1993, 1998). However, in practice it is often difficult to distinguish between different types of constructivism and with the decline of high epistemological debate in favour of analytical engagement and empirical research, such differences have waned in importance.

Despite the heterogeneity of constructivist forms, they all share a number of concepts, assumptions and ontological commitments that collectively amount to a distinctive analytical approach within IR. First, constructivism's core observation, and arguably its most important contribution, is the social construction of reality. Rooted in earlier sociological theory, this notion has a number of related elements, including the claim that the perceptions, identities and interests of individuals and groups are socially and culturally constructed, rather than existing outside of or prior to society, as individualist and rationalist approaches like neo-realism assume. Related to this, constructivists point to the existence of social facts; unlike brute facts such as gravity or oceans which exist independently of human agreement, social facts are wholly dependent on human agreement. Money, terrorism, sovereignty, anarchy and conflict, for example, are all social constructions that only exist so long as human agreement exists (Barnett, 2005: 259). Importantly, when social facts are treated as objective facts, such as neo-realism's understanding of anarchy, they become a constraint on behaviour and thereby function as conditioning structures. The existence of social facts, in turn, draws attention to the inter-subjective nature of reality; that is, individuals and groups recreate and maintain these structures through their shared beliefs, practices and interactions (Checkel, 1998: 326). Critically, the observation of the socially constructed nature of reality provides a lens through which to understand political change – such as the changes brought about by conflict resolution (see below).

Second, constructivists hold to a particular view of the agency–structure problem. Taking a mediative position, they argue that agents and structures are inter-dependent and co-constitutive (Adler, 1997: 325–6). That is, agents produce structures through their beliefs, actions and interactions, while structures produce agents by helping to shape their identities and interests. In other words, based on a form of holism, constructivism views the agency–structure relationship as a dynamic, continuous and contingent process. Such a conception is important because it brings human agency back into political analysis; it recognizes that agents have some autonomy and their beliefs, practices and interactions help to construct, reproduce and transform existing structures (Barnett, 2005: 259). This is a contrasting position to the structural determinism of neo-realism, for example.

A third constructivist commitment is to ideas, language, symbols and other discursive processes as constitutive – of identities, interests, beliefs and perceptions, which in turn construct powerful normative structures. A form of idealism, constructivism does not reject the existence of material reality. Instead, it recognizes that the meaning of material realities and their effects on human behaviour and social organization is dependent upon and constructed through the use of language, ideas, symbols and the like. Simply put, language allows individuals to construct and give meaning to material and social reality. For example, while a drought produces a number of observable material effects, the notions of 'humanitarian disaster' and 'humanitarian relief' are socially constructed through shared language and ideas related to assessments of the number, location and nature of victims, the role of nature, the appropriate response of the authorities and the like.

Importantly, constructivists argue that language and discourse has a 'causal' effect on social action in that discourses function to define issues and problems, confer normative and political authority on certain responses, create actors authorized to speak, silence and exclude alternative forms of action and construct and endorse a certain kind of widely accepted common sense (Milliken, 1999: 229). In these ways, some courses of action are enabled and made possible, while others are excluded and disqualified (Laffey and Weldes, 1997; Yee, 1996). In addition, discourses do not exist independently of society, but are a kind of structure that is actualized through regular use by people; they are a 'structure of meaning-in-use' (Milliken, 1999: 231). Obviously, ideas and language are historically and culturally contingent, which helps to explain historical and contextual differences in political practices and social realities in ways that rationalist and structural accounts often cannot.

Fourth, constructivists share an understanding of the importance of normative structures, and in particular, of the way they construct categories of meaning, constitute identities and interests and define standards of appropriate behaviour (Howard, 2004; Ruggie, 1997). While some of the rules and norms of international politics are regulative, many are constitutive in the sense that they create the very possibilities of behaviour. For example, while the rules of the World Trade Organization regulate trade, the rules of sovereignty not only regulate state interactions but also make possible the very idea of the sovereign state and help to construct its interests (Barnett, 2005: 255). Moreover, rules and norms provide interpretive frameworks and define what counts as appropriate behaviour for different situations, thereby normalizing some forms of behaviour over others (Checkel, 1998). At the same time, normative structures are not so determining that they eliminate the possibility of critical self-reflection and the possibility of structural transformation. At times, agents such as norm entrepreneurs attempt to construct new norms and rules that may alter the very structure itself.

Lastly, in terms of social science, constructivists reject the narrow logic of traditional social scientific explanation based on linear notions of cause and effect and adopt a more interpretive 'logic of understanding' (Milliken, 1999). That is, they subscribe to a broader notion of social causality that takes reasons as causes, in the sense that norms and rules structure or constitute – that is, 'cause' – the things that people do (Adler, 1997: 329). Constructivists also argue that understanding the structure, which is an antecedent condition to action, does important explanatory work.

Thus, constructivism provides a particular sort of explanatory theory which rejects the search for laws in favour of contingent generalizations which ask the question, 'how possible?', rather than simply 'why?' (Alkopher, 2005; Price and Reus-Smit, 1998). Consequently, constructivists employ a variety of methods in their research, including: ethnographic and interpretive techniques; discursive and genealogical methods; historical and comparative approaches; and large-n quantitative studies and computer simulations.

CONSTRUCTIVISM AND CONFLICT ANALYSIS

An evaluation of constructivism and conflict resolution begins with the fundamental issue of conflict analysis; without an effective diagnosis of the nature and causes of conflict, conflict resolution is likely to be ad hoc, ineffectual or even counter-productive. Conflict analysis has emerged as its own important sub-field within conflict resolution, and it is here that constructivism makes arguably its most useful contribution. On the basis of a constructivist understanding of conflict, it is then possible to draw some conclusions about constructivist approaches to conflict resolution.

However, it is important to recognize that there are relatively few self-consciously constructivist studies which focus directly on war and conflict, although there are a growing number of studies on related issues, such as: national security and the decision to use force (Campbell, 1993; Katzenstein, 1996; Williams, 1998); the construction of national security threats (Campbell, 1992; Howard, 2004; Weldes, 1996, 1999); securitization and critical security studies (Buzan, Waever and de Wilde, 1998); national security cultures (Gusterson, 1998); military doctrine (Kier, 1997); military strategy (Johnson, 1995); war proneness (Ross, 1993); and the social construction of genocide (Bauer, 2001; Browning, 2001). In part, this is due to the tendency of many constructivists to concentrate on the impact of positive norms and ideas in international politics. Nonetheless, it is a cause for concern that war and violence, a key concern of IR, is accorded a relatively low priority in the broader constructivist research agenda (Adler, 1997: 346–7; Checkel, 1998: 339). This situation is particularly surprising given that like any other social institution, war is a social construction and would therefore appear to be an ideal subject for constructivist research.

Despite the relative dearth of explicitly constructivist studies, it is possible to sketch out a constructivist framework for studying and understanding war and conflict and a set of supporting findings on many of its key elements. Constructivist research on conflict aims broadly to uncover the constitutive nature of norms, ideas and other discursive elements in making the social practices of war and conflict possible in specific historical contexts and in general (Alkopher, 2005: 716), and to elaborate on the relationship between the structures, agents and deliberative agentic action of conflict. Based on the findings of existing studies – some of which are explicitly constructivist in design, others which are not but nonetheless adopt broadly constructivist assumptions – and drawing upon wider constructivist theory, it is possible to identify three broad elements in the social construction of conflict: the construction and manipulation of identity; the co-constitution of structures and agents; and the construction of society-wide conflict discourses. As noted above, while these findings are not necessarily novel in the context of earlier peace studies research, they do challenge the narrow focus of much IR-based conflict analysis and open up space for considering alternative kinds of questions about the nature and 'causes' of war to those posed by neo-realism and neo-liberalism.

The construction of identity

Like other approaches within the conflict resolution field, constructivists argue that identity – individual, group or national – is critical in the construction of war and conflict for a number of obvious reasons.

In the first instance, war and conflict require a clearly identifiable enemy 'other' against whom to struggle. Moreover, the practicalities of generating the necessary legitimacy and consensus to launch a war, mobilizing the necessary resources from society, and motivating individuals to kill in battle, necessitates the social existence of a negative, and importantly, deeply threatening, 'other'. In addition, identity – of both 'self' and 'other' – plays a central role in defining and structuring both interests and norms of behaviour, a notion that challenges rationalist accounts of international politics. More prosaically, constructivists would point out that the vast majority of conflicts since the end of the Cold War have, in fact, been fought over issues related to ethnic and national identity.

The important point that constructivists make is that identities are not pre-existing, prior to society and culture, or fixed; rather, they are context-dependent, highly malleable and continuously evolving in response to external events and processes, such as immigration and globalization. Identity is never settled or essential, but is made and re-made everyday through a vast array of discursive processes and social practices, including war and conflict, and its content is liable to change – even if discursive practices make it seem as if identities are fixed and immutable. Constructivists draw attention to the key roles played in this process by different types of political and cultural elites, and the importance of history, myth, culture, symbols, ideology, religion, political practice and nationalism in the constitution and maintenance of identity. In addition, constructivists demonstrate how violence and conflict itself acts as a discursive structure which constructs identity in particular kinds of ways. In some cases, violence may be deliberately constructed as 'ethnic' or 'communal' violence by elites in order to obscure its origins in other kinds of material or political struggles, but this construction nonetheless has lasting effects on the identities of the conflicting parties.

Constructivism draws on sociological and anthropological theory to highlight how identity is, in fact, predicated on an external 'other' which in turn constructs a series of subject positions within a broader narrative, usually based on dichotomous categories such as friend/enemy, civilized/savage, peaceful/violent and the like. There is a great deal of research, for example, which demonstrates how the identity of the civilized, peaceful Western 'self' has been constructed historically in opposition to a savage, violent Eastern 'other' (Hurd, 2003; Said, 1978). Constructivists also demonstrate that exclusionary identities are embedded in the practices and ideas of sovereignty and international politics. The very notion of citizenship of a nation-state is meaningless without the category of non-citizen or alien. It is, therefore, an inherently exclusionary identity that crucially makes political violence possible; without such identity categories, political violence would be impossible.

Critically, constructivist research does not support the view that difference is sufficient on its own to initiate war (Fearon and Laitin, 2000: 859–60). There are, after all, literally thousands of ethnic groups divided among hundreds of states, but relatively few identity-based wars. Instead, constructivists argue that two other conditions are necessary for constructing conflict: first, a particular kind of identity construction which plays on fear, threat, hatred, victimhood and dehumanization of the 'other'; and second, the presence of elites committed to organizing the discursive and material instruments of war. Without these two factors, identity differences may result in sporadic outbreaks of violence during long periods of accommodation and co-existence, but not in full-scale war.

In sum, a constructivist account of conflict starts with an analysis of the nature and purposes of identity construction; it suggests that understanding how groups and nations conceive of themselves and others, and how elites instrumentalize particular kinds of identity, goes a long way towards explaining how violent conflict is initiated and reproduced. This argument is in no way novel to the broader conflict resolution field, but it does challenge the rationalist

neo-realist and neo-liberal approaches which dominate much of the international conflict management sub-field.

There is a growing body of case research which broadly fits into a constructivist framework which illuminates the central role of identity in international conflict (Bowman, 1994, 2003; Brass, 1997; Campbell, 1998; Fearon and Laitin, 2000; Jackson, 2004; Kapferer, 1988; Kaufman, 2001; Lemarchand, 1994; Mertus, 1999; Prunier, 1995; Wilmer, 2002; Woodward, 1995). This research demonstrates that elites play a key role in deliberately constructing hostile identities between ethnic groups, often reversing decades of peaceful co-existence and inclusive political identities. In each case, ethno-nationalist elites reconstructed existing group identities into hostile, dehumanized and threatening oppositions, defining their group's interests in zero-sum ethnic terms. Importantly, much of this research shows that the initial violence at the start of the conflict has the intended effect of constructing opposing identities in evermore antagonistic and rigid ways (Fearon and Laitin, 2000: 846), and that the apotheosis of inter-ethnic hatred comes after the violence has got under way. The construction of such deeply threatening and dehumanized forms of identity, and its intensification through acts of violence, goes some way to explaining the disturbing level of atrocity and human rights abuses visible in many of these conflicts. These studies also confirm earlier anthropological and post-colonial research which demonstrates the central role that colonialism played in constructing hostile identities to begin with (see Prunier, 1995).

Interestingly, constructivist research demonstrates that violent identity construction processes are not confined to intrastate conflicts. Roxanne Doty (1993), for example, has demonstrated how the discursive construction of Philippine national identity as underdeveloped, unstable, childlike and vulnerable (to Soviet control), subject-positioned next to the United States' identity as responsible, enlightened and paternal, enabled US counter-insurgency in that country in the 1950s. Her later research on British colonial policy towards Kenya uncovered similar discursive processes in relation to African 'natives' (Doty, 1996). Similarly, Jutta Weldes (1999) found that identity construction and subject-positioning in relation to Cuba and the Soviet Union were critical elements in aggressive US decision-making during the Cuban missile crisis. More recently, discursive studies on the war on terror (Croft, 2006; Jackson, 2005) have revealed the way in which American national identity is constructed and positioned in direct opposition to an evil, threatening, Islamic, terrorist 'other', and how notions of identity provide cultural–political legitimation for US leadership of the global counter-terrorist campaign. The point is that without the existence, maintenance and manipulation of certain kinds of identities, conflict and war would be impossible; identity therefore, functions as a necessary 'causal' condition for violent conflict.

Structures and agents

In terms of the structures and agents of conflict, constructivists take as their point of departure the observation that similar structural conditions often produce different conflict outcomes. Stuart Kaufman (2001), for example, notes that despite similar structural conditions in the aftermath of the collapse of the Soviet Union, only 6 of the 15 former republics experienced sustained civil war, and while the break-up of Czechoslovakia was peaceful, the break-up of Yugoslavia was extremely violent. Similarly, Jackson (2004) raises the point that while virtually all African states share the same debilitating structural features of poverty, corruption, instability, ethnic division and the like, only a few experience sustained violent conflict and only for certain periods of time. A key limitation of many of the structural correlation-based studies that dominate IR scholarship, therefore, is that they cannot explain why societies which possess all the features highly correlated with the outbreak of conflict do not experience war or why

war erupts at particular times and not others.

The answer to this apparent puzzle according to constructivists is that social, economic, political, cultural and normative structures are insufficient on their own to cause conflict; agents are required to transform the latent structures of conflict into the manifestation of violence. On the other hand, certain agents may desire to construct conflict (such as white supremacists wishing to trigger a race war), but lack the necessary structural conditions to enable them to achieve their goals. In this sense, structures and agents are inter-dependent and co-constitutive in the construction of conflict.

One important way that structures and agents interact in violence construction is that political elites use the grievances generated by existing structural conditions – such as poverty, unemployment, discrimination, corruption and state incapacity – to inflame and manipulate identities and perceptions of threat and victimhood, thereby laying the foundation for legitimizing violent retaliation (Kapferer, 1988). At the same time, these structural conditions provide the human raw material for initiating and sustaining organized violence: large numbers of unemployed, lumpen youth who can be recruited from slums and jails. In a number of conflicts during the 1990s, such elements were organized into armed gangs and irregular fighting units and it was these elements who committed much of the violence directed against civilians in Rwanda, the Balkans, Sierra Leone and elsewhere (see Abdullah, 1998; Woodward, 1995).

The value of this approach is that it provides important clues as to why conflicts break out at particular junctures: it takes a coincidence of enabling structures and purposeful actors to provide the necessary conditions to spark a war. In the case of Yugoslavia, for example, it was the combination of severe economic crisis, social and political instability and the actions of Milosevic and his nationalists that created the conditions which made war possible. One without the other – the absence of debilitating structural conditions or a determined nationalist leadership – would have likely resulted in sporadic disturbances and isolated acts of violence rather than the sustained and widespread warfare that was seen.

Central to the process of violent conflict construction is the role of conflict agents, typically described as 'conflict entrepreneurs' or 'ethnic entrepreneurs' (Lemarchand, 1994). These actors are usually elites – political, military, religious or cultural and local or national. The point is that while individuals in society strategically construct identity boundaries on a daily basis, and while some may desire to engage in violence against an 'other', it takes the political power of elites to materially and discursively organize and construct a society-wide conflict or war. The reasons why elites would deliberately construct hostile identities and conflict revolve around the desire to gain, maintain or increase their hold on political power, the need to eliminate or neutralize sources of opposition, the desire to defend boundaries or the pursuit of material gain through the control and exploitation of economic resources (Fearon and Laitin, 2000).

A number of studies (Alkopher, 2005; Jackson, 2004; Kaufman, 2001; Wilmer, 2002) reveal that in violent conflict, actors attempt to achieve similar sets of goals across different cultural contexts and historical periods. In an organized and concerted effort to construct the necessary conditions for conflict, elites attempt to deconstruct existing social norms of tolerance, non-violence and peaceful co-existence, put in place new norms of 'other'-directed violence, reconstruct group identities into clearly defined dichotomies, enforce group unity and cooperation in the nationalist project, redefine group interests in zero-sum terms, establish a pervading sense of threat and victimhood, censor and de-legitimize alternative non-violent discourses, militarize society and physically organize the means and tools of war. Elites do this by attempting to exert direct control over authoritative discursive sites in society, such as political institutions, the media, education, religion and other cultural processes, and the means of coercion, such

as the security services and the military. Typically, key posts across all social institutions are filled with individuals willing to promote the entrepreneur's political agenda. Usually, after a few years of organizing and when the conditions are 'ripe' for conflict, it is not uncommon to see violent provocations used as a trigger to launch all-out war.

In this sense, constructivists argue that war is always a social construction requiring deliberative action by individuals and groups and extensive social cooperation and organization between different groups and individuals. It is a form of deliberative politics made possible by particular kinds of discourses and social practices. They would argue, therefore, that key weaknesses of rationalist and structurally based quantitative approaches are that they fail to fully examine or account for the role of agents and agency in deliberately constructing war and conflict and the political struggles that this entails. Without a framework that includes a clearly defined notion of human agency, the resultant understanding of conflict processes will necessarily be limited. Moreover, they would argue that effective conflict analysis requires in-depth, qualitative, case-specific knowledge, preferably gathered through ethnographic methods, rather than the necessarily simplified and generalized data that tends to characterize much quantitative research.

The discourses of conflict

Constructivist approaches to war and conflict also focus closely on the key role played by ideational and discursive factors, such as myths, narratives, histories, symbols, beliefs, ideologies and discourses. They suggest that the initiation of war requires the construction (by agents) of a vast and powerful cultural complex – a society-wide conflict discourse – that makes war possible by rendering it conceivable, legitimate and reasonable; it involves the construction of a new common sense. Importantly, such conflict discourses draw upon a mix of existing discursive and normative structures, such as national myths, political symbols, cultural norms, popular narratives, historical memory and newly introduced discursive elements deriving from recent events and processes, such as immigration or terrorist attacks, for example. Historically contingent on the discursive opportunity structures of particular societies, conflict discourses may entail substantial reinvention of tradition and history, or simply the mobilization of existing cultural material. In this process, symbols, ideas and discourses are deployed instrumentally by elites as a kind of 'symbolic technology' (Laffey and Weldes, 1997) in the effort to create a dominant 'regime of truth' or 'grid of intelligibility' for large numbers of people (Milliken, 1999: 230).

Critical to this process is the role played by existing normative structures which function to construct identities and interests; such structures can be either pacifist or conflictual (Alkopher, 2005: 720; Jabri, 1996). The ideas and practices of sovereignty and anarchy (Wendt, 1992), for example, both internationally and domestically, encourage actors to define their identities, interests, perceptions and behaviours in ways that provoke self-perpetuating security dilemmas. Similarly, the normative structures imposed by the ideas and practices of citizenship create exclusionary and oppositional identities easily manipulated to encourage conflict. From this perspective, it can be seen that conflict discourses do not emerge from a vacuum, nor do they operate in only one direction from the elite to the masses. Rather, conflict discourses are embedded in the normative and discursive structures of society and everyday reality and both draw upon and reflect the cultural and historical context in which they operate; they combine and recombine extant cultural materials and linguistic resources (Milliken, 1999: 239; see also Laffey and Weldes, 1997). At the same time, individuals construct and reconstruct identities and identity boundaries through their everyday practices and behaviour 'on the ground', as it were. Ontologically, this suggests that conflict is not a breakdown in essentially peaceful social systems or a temporary abnormality, but is instead rooted in the structures, practices and conditions of social existence (Duffield, 1998).

A growing number of studies (Alkopher, 2005; Bowman, 1994; Brass, 1997; Campbell, 1993, 1998; Jabri, 1996; Jackson, 2004; Kapferer, 1988; Kaufman, 2001; Weldes, 1999; Weldes et al., 1999; Woodward, 1995) reveal some of the main elements of conflict discourses. These include: the construction of exclusionary and oppositional identities; the invention, reinvention or manipulation of grievance and a sense of victimhood; the construction or exaggeration of a pervading sense of threat and danger to the nation or community; the stereotyping and dehumanization of the enemy 'other'; and the legitimization of organized pre-emptive and defensive political violence. The role of the media is crucial in this process, which is why conflict entrepreneurs go to extreme lengths to influence or control media sources. In Serbia, for example, in the lead-up to the war, the official Milosevic-dominated press started to publish stories about Albanian Muslims raping Serbian women, the expulsion of Serbian families by Albanian officials, and the desecration of orthodox monasteries in Kosova, creating a widespread sense of threat (Bowman, 1994). In relation to Croatia, the Serb media revived memories of the Ustasha regime, which appeared to be reincarnated in the declarations and symbols of the new Croat government. Newspapers and bookshops filled with stories illustrating the history of the 'Croatian' attempt to exterminate the 'Serbs'. At the same time, in Croatia and Slovenia, the media published pictures of thousands of allegedly Slovene and Croat victims of partisan reprisals from World War II.

Importantly, Vivienne Jabri (1996) demonstrates the role of cultural–political notions of just war and militarist values and practices in reproducing war as a social continuity, particularly in Western societies. The existence and dominance of such narratives in society provide a potent discursive resource for elites wishing to mobilize for war against other states. Jabri also draws attention to the ways in which war (re)constructs individual and national identity. The prevalence and potency of 'good war' and 'just war' narratives referring to World War II in the dominant discourse of the war on terror (Croft, 2006; Jackson, 2005) are a current example of this process. Interestingly, Tal Alkopher's (2005) study reveals that similar kinds of ideas and institutions – particularly the potent, religiously imbued notion of 'just war' – made the social practices of the Crusades possible. Similarly, Stuart Kaufman's (2001) analysis of 'symbolic politics' in the former Soviet Union draws attention to the ways in which local symbols and myths are imbued with potent meanings and manipulated by political leaders pursuing nationalist aims.

In short, constructivist accounts of conflict fill an important gap in many rationalist and quantitative studies by revealing the necessary ideational and discursive conditions that permit the construction of war and political violence; such 'variables' are rarely included in rationalist studies. Mapping such processes require interpretive rather than quantitative methodologies, as much of the relevant discourse falls outside of rational choice analyses. In addition, constructivist analyses add depth and detail to existing peace studies research by exploring the micro-physics of discourse construction and manipulation. Combining all these elements – the concurrent presence of conflict structures and purposive agents, the manipulation of oppositional identities, and the construction of powerful society-wide discourses – furnishes a comprehensive and richly textured understanding of conflict, which in turn is a necessary initial step in conceptualizing conflict resolution.

CONSTRUCTIVISM AND CONFLICT RESOLUTION

Constructivism is limited in what it can say directly about conflict resolution for two main reasons. First, because it is an approach to social research rather than a substantive theory of politics or society, constructivism contains no direct theory of conflict or its resolution. Second, with few notable exceptions

(see, for example, Carnegie Commission on Preventing Deadly Conflict, 1997; Duffield, 2001; Paris, 2004), there are to date only a handful of constructivist-oriented studies that focus directly on processes or instances of conflict resolution and even fewer which locate themselves directly within a constructivist framework; most constructivist research has so far focused on norms, with a lesser amount focusing on war and conflict. Nonetheless, extrapolating from constructivist theory and existing constructivist findings into the social construction of war and conflict in particular, a number of important implications for the theory and practice of conflict resolution and conflict transformation can be discerned. At the very least, revealing the mechanisms by which agents and structures construct and reproduce conflict discourses provides important clues for conflict resolution practitioners about how to counteract, deconstruct and ultimately transform such discourses and patterns of behaviour.

The first broad implication of a constructivist understanding of conflict is that to be effective, conflict resolution efforts must be characterized by holism. In other words, constructivist approaches would emphasize the necessity for both structural and discursive transformation to bring about lasting conflict resolution. They would suggest that the two are inter-dependent, and while conflicts may initially be ended through discursive strategies in which actors reconstruct their interests and identities by employing a new political language, for example, without subsequent alteration in the precipitating structural conditions, the potential for further outbreaks of conflict will remain – particularly if economic deprivation or political injustice allows new conflict entrepreneurs to promote conflict discourses.

More specifically, a constructivist approach would confirm the long-standing assertion that conflict resolution must focus upon dealing with both overt violence and 'structural' and 'cultural violence' (Galtung, 1990), and must aim at achieving 'positive peace' not merely 'negative peace'. A focus on holism also recognizes the importance of engaging with all levels of society, in the mode of John Paul Lederach's notion of the 'peace pyramid' (Lederach, 1997). That is, for the purposes of building positive peace and genuine conflict transformation, the reconstruction of peaceful discourses and non-hostile identities must occur at the level of civil society, as well as local and national leadership. In turn, this confirms the important role that non-official and citizen-based diplomacy can play in conflict resolution activities (Diamond and McDonald, 1996; see also Bartoli in this volume).

A second set of implications for conflict resolution flows from constructivist concep-tions of the role of ideational and discursive factors in the social construction of conflict, namely, the importance of discursive-based forms of conflict resolution, such as dialog-ical conflict resolution, interactive conflict resolution, analytical problem-solving, peace-building, peace education, reconciliation and truth-telling and transitional justice (see D'Estree, Meerts, Saunders, Tamra, Rosoux and Albin in this volume). The emergent field of discursive conflict transformation, in particular, aims to deconstruct violent discourse and foster non-violent discourses by undermining hegemonic discourses and generating a common language through dia-logical exchange (Ramsbotham, Woodhouse and Miall, 2005: 288–301; Jabri, 1996). Similarly, reconciliation, truth-telling and transitional justice approaches aim in part to re-write an authoritative shared national history and counter historical distortions, educate society, break down stereotypes and hostile identities, construct a common vision of a shared future, deconstruct and de-legitimize a culture of impunity for human rights abuses and initiate a national dialogue on reconciliation (Hayner, 1994; Popkin and Roht-Arriaza, 1995; Rosoux and Albin in this volume). More prosaically, mediators in conflict should focus a large part of their efforts on helping the par-ties to adopt new ways of speaking and thinking about each other and about the conflict. All of these functions and activities

are vitally important for reconstructing the discursive and ideational structures that underpin violence and conflict.

A third implication of constructivist approaches to conflict lies in the area of early warning and preventive diplomacy. To date, early warning systems have focused largely on monitoring the structural correlates of conflict, such as economic crises, famines and food shortages, social breakdown, de-stabilizing political events, human rights abuses, corruption and the like (see Lund in this volume). The limitation of such systems is that a great many countries possess all the structural conditions normally associated with war, but do not necessarily present an imminent risk of conflict. A constructivist understanding of conflict suggests that a careful monitoring of particular kinds of agents – ethnic entrepreneurs and nationalist elites, for example – and particular kinds of discourses by these agents – identity-based, ethno-nationalist or conflict-oriented discourses – must be added to the monitoring of the relevant structural conditions if a more accurate picture is to be maintained. Specifically, attention needs to be given to the use of symbolic politics and threat narratives in national and local political discourse, as well as identity manipulation, the creation of victimhood, stereotyping, justification of violence and the like. When these discursive processes begin to manifest and gain significant social acceptance, the international community – the United Nations, NGOs and other states and organizations – needs to intervene with appropriate discursive strategies designed to counter and deconstruct such discourses. The work of the NGO, *Search for Common Ground*, is instructive in this regard. This organization has worked in several conflict-ridden countries, such as Burundi, Macedonia and Angola, producing television programmes, songs, radio programmes and publications aimed at countering stereotypes, encouraging cooperation and building inter-communal understanding – exactly the kind of activities called for to counter violence-generating nationalist discourses

(Brown, 1996; Mearsheimer, 1990; Van Evera, 1994).

In conjunction with outside intermediaries attempting to re-mould conflict discourses and normative structures, the strengthening of the society's internal sites of opposition and non-violent discursive formation must also be supported. Peace groups, genuinely democratic and inclusive political organizations, independent universities and tolerance-promoting religious groups are just some of the sites where discursive struggle against violence takes place. In Serbia in early 1991, right before the outbreak of war, there were still many sites of struggle and protest. Thousands of students and members of the political opposition took to the streets in opposition to the emerging discourses of hate, singing 'give peace a chance'. Unfortunately, they received little outside support and were quickly crushed by the security forces. The international community, instead of taking a hands-off approach until it is too late or supporting dubious political factions for strategic reasons, needs to consider lending greater support to those groups and social movements promoting tolerance, genuine democracy and human rights values.

In the end, however, the political challenge of taking discursive approaches seriously and incorporating them into contemporary diplomatic practices is formidable, particularly given the dominance of neo-realist thinking and practice within international relations more generally and international conflict management more specifically. However, a constructivist understanding of international politics suggests that change is always possible and through different forms of discursive struggle by 'peace entrepreneurs' (Goodhand and Hulme, 1999), new attitudes and practices towards conflict resolution are possible.

EVALUATION AND FUTURE CONFLICT RESOLUTION RESEARCH AGENDA

The central limitation of the constructivist approach is that, unlike critical theory or peace studies, it does not furnish an ethical–normative foundation for peaceful conflict resolution and transformation – it is has no in-built commitment to any specific notion of emancipation, for example. It does not offer a method for choosing between different interpretations or visions of political reality; it is not a theory of politics as such (Adler, 1997: 323). Thus, in its analysis of war and conflict, it does not provide any *a priori* normative–political basis for privileging peaceful over violent conflict resolution, although it is often a subtext of constructivist research and there are some studies on issues related to conflict resolution, such as studies on arms control (Adler, 1992; Price, 1995, 1997) and liberal peace-building (Paris, 2004). It is in this sense that it remains firmly a social theory – a method of social inquiry – rather than a substantive theory of international politics. Moreover, it remains an explanatory rather than a predictive approach to the study of social action; rooted in a 'logic of understanding' rather than a 'logic of causality', it aims to build contingent generalizations rather than to generate specific predications – although prediction based on the past patterns of behaviour and normative structures of a particular case is certainly possible. In addition, it is a framework designed primarily for the study of international conflict; most of its core concepts and analytical tools are oriented to the world of international politics. In this sense, it is an IR-based approach that does not easily speak to other social levels and domains. Finally, as noted, a major weakness of constructivism is that it simply has not yet produced a significant body of research into conflict and conflict resolution.

Nevertheless, constructivism provides an insightful approach to the study of war and conflict, particularly in comparison to other IR approaches and to neo-realist and neo-liberal-based forms of international conflict management. In particular, the constructivist insistence on holism and the co-constitution of agents and structures, the importance of agency, the centrality of identity as constitutive of interests and the key role of ideational and discursive factors in international politics, has the potential to open up alternative kinds of questions, suggest new avenues of research and enrich current research on war.

Constructivism is also important for the way it challenges dominant models and understandings of conflict itself, the central phenomenological focus of the field. In the first instance, dominant positivistic conceptions see conflict as largely external to daily life and political activity, as abnormal, irrational and pathological – as essentially the breakdown in normally peaceful social systems (David, 1997). In contrast, constructivist ontology suggests that conflict is integral to society and political life, and that

> [i]f we wish to examine conflict we must begin by analysing what is normal. Or at least, those long-term and embedded social processes that define the conditions of everyday life. The purpose and reasons for conflict are located in these processes. From this perspective, political violence is not different, apart or irrational in relation to the way we live: it is an expression of its inner logic. (Duffield, 1998: 67)

This view of conflict not only opens up new space for research into the causes of conflict (within everyday discourse and individual lifestyles, for example), but also presages an ethical engagement with those elements of society which construct and reproduce the conditions for conflict and war, such as militarism, imperialism, just-war narratives, cultural stereotyping, national myths, exclusionary identities and such like. Constructivism also challenges dominant models which view conflict and conflict resolution processes as developing in linear, observable and sequenced patterns or stages, a view seemingly inherent to positivist approaches. Instead, constructivist approaches would highlight the unique context-specific human agency at the heart of conflict processes, and draw attention to the malleable nature of the ideational and discursive structures which make conflict possible.

Related to this, constructivism is important for drawing attention to the role of the conflict resolution field itself as a constitutive agent.

Not only are a great many conflict resolution scholars also practitioners, but the knowledge produced by the field also impacts on actual political practice in a number of ways (see Duffield, 2001; Ramsbotham, Woodhouse and Miall, 2005). From this perspective, conflict resolution functions as an important discursive structure that co-constitutes the practices of conflict management and resolution – in the same way that IR as a knowledge-producing field is implicated in the actual practices of international politics (Smith, 2004). Apart from opening up new kinds of research questions, this observation calls for a critical reflexivity on the part of conflict resolution scholars and a sensitivity to the uses to which the knowledge it produces is put. In particular, it should sensitize scholars to the danger that in some cases, conflict resolution can function as a tool of hegemonic control by insisting that oppressed groups pursue non-violent strategies in the face of violent oppression by stronger parties (Ramsbotham, Woodhouse and Miall, 2005).

A future research agenda

Notwithstanding the obvious strengths of constructivist scholarship, there is clearly a great deal more work to be done before a constructivist theory of war, conflict and conflict resolution with its own *a priori* content can be articulated. An assessment of existing research suggests that there are a number of areas where further research would be beneficial. Of course, new research will always throw up other questions and issues that will in turn require its own research.

First, there is an urgent need for further case studies of specific conflicts, both to strengthen initial findings about the social and political construction of war and to provide the basis for much needed comparative analysis (Fearon and Laitin, 2000). To date, constructivist studies of war have generally tended to cluster around conflicts from the 1990s, such as the Balkans conflict, Rwanda, the former Soviet republics and Sierra Leone. Constructivist studies of earlier conflicts like the Korean and Vietnam wars, the Falklands/Malvinas conflict and the Iran–Iraq war, as well as more recent conflicts like the USA–Iraq war, are needed to provide the basis for comparison and the eventual construction of a middle range constructivist theory of conflict.

Further research also needs to focus on different kinds of conflict, social levels, types of actors and conflict processes. At the most fundamental level, further constructivist research is needed comparing the social construction of war within and between states, and the ways in which the normative and material structures of the international system impinge on conflict processes in ways different to the social construction of intrastate conflict. Added to this, further studies on the social construction of different kinds of conflict, such as terrorism, communal conflict, industrial conflict, organizational conflict and the like, are needed to provide other points of comparison.

Questions of identity in conflict are particularly salient to constructivist approaches and further research is required in this important area. Greater empirical research and more case studies are needed to explain a number of puzzles: how exactly are identities constructed, maintained and mobilized for conflict as a particular kind of political project? In what ways exactly does conflict alter, reinforce, undermine or change identities in more antagonistic and rigid ways? How do both material and ideational factors construct hostile identities? In addition, there is the highly sensitive question of cultural factors in the construction of hostile identities and war (Fearon and Laitin, 2000: 864). Key questions include: are particular cultures, such as martial cultures, more prone to conflict construction due to the kinds of narratives, myths, identities and histories they contain? What kinds of cultural materials and linguistic resources work in constructing conflict discourses? Clearly, such research needs to be handled sensitively and with an appreciation of the symbolic and representational structures

within Western culture that reproduce war (Jabri, 1996).

Further research is also needed on the micro-physics of the processes of conflict construction, in particular, what might be termed 'the cognitive microfoundations' of the social construction of reality (Checkel, 1998: 344; see also Fearon and Laitin, 2000: 850). A number of questions would seem critical here: what exact discursive strategies do conflict entrepreneurs and norm entrepreneurs employ in the construction of conflict, and do they do so fully conscious of the likely effects of their interventions? How do conflict entrepreneurs choose particular strategies, and how do they identify the kinds of discursive opportunity structures needed to construct conflict? Are the discursive strategies of conflict entrepreneurs generic across geographical and temporal contexts, or are they always context-specific? By what micro-processes do individuals come to accept and inculcate the discourses and norms of entrepreneurs? Why do publics follow leaders down paths that clearly serve elite interests rather than public interests?

Finally, and perhaps most crucially, further research is needed to understand how violent conflicts end or evolve into less destructive forms. There are to date very few studies which map out in a systematic way exactly how conflict discourses collapse, evolve and lose their power to construct violence. In part, there are interesting possibilities for exploring the well-known concept of conflict 'ripeness' (see Zartman in this volume) from within a discursive framework: how exactly are violent discourses de-legitimized during war, and how do ideas of dialogue and conflict resolution come to be seen as possible or desirable at a given moment? How do ideas and discourses evolve and change during war, and who are the key agents in change processes and what kinds of action do they engage in? This last question points to the critical role played by 'peace entrepreneurs' (Goodhand and Hulme, 1999). Further research is needed to capture the dynamics and functions of such actors.

CONCLUSION

Constructivist approaches to conflict confirm genuine reasons for optimism about the possibilities of conflict transformation: if war and conflict are socially constructed by human beings and maintained through inter-subjective meanings and actions, then they can also be deconstructed and transformed through similar kinds of processes and actions. This chapter has attempted to show some of the ways in which constructivist approaches to war, conflict and conflict resolution can contribute to, and complement, present understandings of these important phenomena. However, notwithstanding the obvious potentialities of constructivist theories and methods, it remains an approach to social research that has generated a number of useful findings rather than any substantive theory of political action (Fearon and Laitin, 2000: 847–8). It has also been argued that constructivist research in conflict adds little that is new or unique; rather, it is largely confirmatory of a great deal of existing research, particularly from the peace studies sub-field.

The primary contributions of constructivism are, first, to challenge the dominant views of conflict and conflict resolution within the IR-based international conflict management sub-field – to provide an alternative ontology and set of analytical tools through which to generate new questions and understandings of conflict processes at the international level. Second, constructivism can add more elaborate social theory and greater empirical detail about the micro-physics of the social construction of conflict to existing research. Lastly, constructivism challenges the broader conflict resolution field to exhibit a greater critical reflexivity and sensitivity to the interaction of theory and practice and uses to which conflict resolution knowledge is put. For all these reasons, constructivism should be viewed as a welcome addition to the existing heterogeneity of methodologies and approaches of the broader conflict resolution field, and its key insights should be utilized in the evaluation of research findings, particularly in terms of international conflict.

REFERENCES

Abdullah, Ibrahim 1998. "Bush Path to Destruction: The Origin and Character of the Revolutionary United Front/Sierra Leone", *Journal of Modern African Studies*. 36(2): 203–35.

Adler, Emanuel 1992. "The Emergence of Cooperation: National Epistemic Communities and the International Evolution of the Idea of Nuclear Arms Control", *International Organization*. 46: 101–45.

Adler, Emanuel 1997. "Seizing the Middle Ground: Constructivism in World Politics", *European Journal of International Relations*. 3(3): 319–63.

Adler, Emanuel 2003. "Constructivism", in Walter Carlsnaes, Beth Simmons, and Thomas Risse, eds., *Handbook of International Relations*. Thousand Oaks: Sage.

Alkopher, Tal Dingott 2005. "The Social (and Religious) Meanings that Constitute War: The Crusades as Realpolitik vs. Socialpolitik", *International Studies Quarterly*. 49: 715–37.

Ashley, Richard 1984. "The Poverty of Neo-Realism", *International Organization*. 38(2): 225–86.

Barnett, Michael 2005. "Social Constructivism", in John Baylis and Steve Smith, eds., *The Globalization of World Politics: An Introduction to International Relations*. Oxford: Oxford University Press, 251–70.

Bauer, Yehuda 2001. *Rethinking the Holocaust*. New Haven, NH: Yale University Press.

Bowman, Glenn 1994. "Xenophobia, Fantasy and the Nation: The Logic of Ethnic Violence in Former Yugoslavia", in Victoria Goddard, Joseph Llobera and Chris Shore, eds., *Anthropology of Europe: Identity and Boundaries in Conflict*. London: Berg, 143–71.

Bowman, Glenn 2003. "Constitutive Violence and Rhetoric of Identity: A Comparative Study of Nationalist Movements in the Israeli-Occupied Territories and Former Yugoslavia", *Social Anthropology*. XI(3): 37–58.

Brass, Paul 1997. *Theft of an Idol: Text and Context in the Representation of Collective Violence*. Princeton, NJ: Princeton University Press.

Brown, Michael 1996. "The Causes and Regional Dimensions of Internal Conflict", in Michael Brown, ed., *The International Dimensions of Internal Conflict*. Cambridge, MA: MIT Press.

Browning, Christopher 2001. *Ordinary Men: Reserve Battalion 101 and the Final Solution in Poland*. London: Penguin.

Buzan, Barry, Ole, Waever and Jaape de Wilde 1998. *Security: A New Framework for Analysis*. Boulder, CO: Lynne Rienner.

Campbell, David 1992. *Writing Security: United States Foreign Policy and the Politics of Identity*. Minneapolis: University of Minnesota Press.

Campbell, David 1993. *Politics Without Principle: Sovereignty, Ethics and the Narratives of the Gulf War*. Boulder, CO: Lynne Rienner.

Campbell, David 1998. *National Deconstruction: Violence, Identity and Justice in Bosnia*. Minneapolis: University of Minnesota Press.

Carnegie Commission on Preventing Deadly Conflict 1997. *Preventing Deadly Conflict: Final Report*, Carnegie Corporation, New York, available at: www.wilsoncenter.org/subsites/ccpdc/pubs/rept97/finfr.htm

Checkel, Jeffrey 1998. "The Constructivist Turn in International Relations Theory", *World Politics*. 50(2): 324–48.

Croft, Stuart 2006. *Culture, Crisis and America's War on Terror*. Cambridge: Cambridge University Press.

David, Steven 1997. "Internal War: Causes and Cures", *World Politics*. 49(4): 552–76.

Diamond, Louise and John McDonald 1996. *Multi-Track Diplomacy: A Systems Approach to Peace*. West Hartford, CT: Kumarian Press.

Doty, Roxanne 1993. "Foreign Policy as Social Construction: A Post-Positivist Analysis of U.S. Counterinsurgency Policy in the Philippines", *International Studies Quarterly*. 37: 297–320.

Doty, Roxanne 1996. *Imperial Encounters*. Minneapolis: University of Minnesota Press.

Duffield, Mark 1998. "Post-Modern Conflict: Warlords, Post-Adjustment States and Private Protection", *Civil Wars*. 1(1): 65–102.

Duffield, Mark 2001. *Global Governance and the New Wars: The Merging of Development and Security*. London and New York: Zed Books.

Fearon, James and David Laitin 2000. "Violence and the Social Construction of Ethnic Identity", *International Organization*. 54(4): 845–77.

Galtung, Johan 1990. "Cultural Violence", *Journal of Peace Research*. 27(3): 291–305.

Goodhand, Jonathan and David Hulme 1999. "From Wars to Complex Political Emergencies: Understanding Conflict and Peace-Building in the New World Order", *Third World Quarterly*. 20(1): 13–26.

Gusterson, Hugh 1998. *Nuclear Rites: A Weapons Laboratory at the End of the Cold War*. Berkeley, CA: University of California Press.

Hayner, Priscilla 1994. "Fifteen Truth Commissions – 1974 to 1994: A Comparative Study", *Human Rights Quarterly*. 16: 597–655.

Howard, Peter 2004. "Why Not Invade North Korea? Threats, Language Games, and U.S. Foreign Policy", *International Studies Quarterly*. 48: 805–28.

Hurd, Elizabeth 2003. "Appropriating Islam: The Islamic Other in the Consolidation of Western Modernity", *Critique: Critical Middle Eastern Studies*. 12(1): 25–41.

Jabri, Vivienne 1996. *Discourses on Violence: Conflict Analysis Reconsidered*. Manchester: Manchester University Press.

Jackson, Richard 2004. "The Social Construction of Internal War", in Richard Jackson, ed., *(Re)Constructing Cultures of Violence and Peace*. New York: Rodopi, 61–77.

Jackson, Richard 2005. *Writing the War on Terrorism: Language, Politics and Counterterrorism*. Manchester: Manchester University Press.

Johnson, Alastair 1995. *Cultural Realism: Strategic Culture and Grand Strategy in Chinese History*. Princeton, NJ: Princeton University Press.

Kapferer, Bruce 1988. *Legends of People/Myths of State: Violence, Intolerance, and Political Culture in Sri Lanka and Australia*. Washington, DC: Smithsonian Institution Press.

Katzenstein, Peter, ed., 1996. *The Culture of National Security: Norms and Identity in World Politics*. New York: Columbia University Press.

Kaufman, Stuart 2001. *Modern Hatreds: The Symbolic Politics of Ethnic War*. London: Cornell University Press.

Keohane, Robert 1989. *International Institutions and State Power*. Boulder, CO: Westview Press.

Kier, Elizabeth 1997. *Imagining War: French and British Military Doctrine Between the Wars*. Princeton, NJ: Princeton University Press.

Kratochwil, Frederich 1989. *Rules, Norms, and Decisions*. Cambridge: Cambridge University Press.

Kratochwil, Frederich 1993. "The Embarrassment of Changes: Neo-Realism as the Science of *Realpolitik* without Politics", *Review of International Studies*. 19(1): 63–80.

Laffey, Mark and Jutta Weldes 1997. "Beyond Belief: Ideas and Symbolic Technologies in the Study of International Relations", *European Journal of International Relations*. 3(2): 193–237.

Lederach, John Paul 1997. *Building Peace: Reconciliation in Divided Societies*. Washington, DC: United States Institute of Peace Press.

Lemarchand, Rene 1994. *Burundi: Ethnocide as Discourse and Practice*. Washington, DC: Woodrow Wilson Center Press.

Mearsheimer, John 1990. "Back to the Future: Instability in Europe after the Cold War", *International Security*. 15(4): 5–56.

Mertus, Julie 1999. *Kosovo: How Myths and Truths Started a War*. Berkeley, CA: University of California Press.

Milliken, Jennifer 1999. "The Study of Discourse in International Relations: A Critique of Research and Methods", *European Journal of International Relations*. 5(2): 225–54.

Onuf, Nicholas 1989. *A World of our Making: Rules and Rule in Social Theory and International Relations*. Columbia, SC: University of South Carolina Press.

Paris, Roland 2004. *At War's End: Building Peace after Civil Conflict*. Cambridge: Cambridge University Press.

Popkin, Margaret and Naomi Roht-Arriaza 1995. "Truth as Justice: Investigatory Commissions in Latin America", *Law and Social Inquiry*. 20(1): 79–116.

Price, Richard 1995. "A Genealogy of the Chemical Weapons Taboo", *International Organization*. 49(1): 73–104.

Price, Richard 1997. *The Chemical Weapons Taboo*. Ithaca: Cornell University Press.

Price, Richard and Christian Reus-Smit 1998. "Dangerous Liaisons? Critical International Theory and Constructivism", *European Journal of International Relations*. 4(3): 259–94.

Prunier, Gerard 1995. *The Rwanda Crisis: History of a Genocide*. New York: Columbia University Press.

Ramsbotham, Oliver, Tom Woodhouse and Hugh Miall 2005. *Contemporary Conflict Resolution*. 2nd Edition, Cambridge: Polity Press.

Ross, Marc 1993. *The Culture of Conflict: Interpretations and Interests in Comparative Perspective*. New Haven: Yale University Press.

Ruggie, John 1983. "Continuity and Transformation in the World Polity: Toward a Neo-realist Synthesis", *World Politics*. 35(2): 261–85.

Ruggie, John 1997. "The Past as Prologue? Interests, Identity, and American Foreign Policy", *International Security*. 21: 89–125.

Said, Edward 1978. *Orientalism*. London: Penguin.

Smith, Steve 2004. "Singing Our World into Existence: International Relations Theory and September 11", *International Studies Quarterly*. 48: 499–515.

Van Evera, Stephen 1994. "Hypotheses on Nationalism and War", *International Security*. 18(4): 5–39.

Weldes, Jutta 1996. "Constructing National Interests", *European Journal of International Relations*. 2(3): 275–318.

Weldes, Jutta 1999. *Constructing National Interests: The United States and the Cuban Missile Crisis*. London: University of Minnesota Press.

Weldes, Jutta, Mark Laffey, Hugh Gusterson and Raymond Duvall, eds., 1999. *Cultures of Insecurity: States, Communities and the Production of Danger*. London: University of Minneapolis Press.

Wendt, Alexander 1987. "The Agent-Structure Problem in International Relations", *International Organization*. 41(3): 335–70.

Wendt, Alexander 1992. "Anarchy is What States Make of It: The Social Construction of Power Politics", *International Organization*. 46: 391–425.

Williams, Michael 1998. "Identity and the Politics of Security", *European Journal of International Relations*. 4(2): 204–25.

Wilmer, Franke 2002. *The Social Construction of Man, the State, and War: Identity, Conflict, and Violence in the Former Yugoslavia*. New York: Routledge.

Woodward, Susan 1995. *Balkan Tragedy: Chaos and Dissolution After the Cold War*. Washington, DC: Brookings Institution.

Yee, Albert 1996. "The Causal Effects of Ideas on Politics", *International Organization*. 50(1): 69–108.

PART II

Issues and Sources of Conflict

10

Territory as a Source of Conflict and a Road to Peace[1]

John A. Vasquez and Brandon Valeriano

Diplomats have long seen that territory is a persistent source of conflict, but what has not been known is that once neighbors settle their territorial disputes, they can have long periods of peace and prosperity, even if new salient issues arise. In this way, territory is a key both to war and to peace. This chapter will review the major findings on territory within the international relations field and discuss its implications for conflict resolution. Emphasis is placed on interstate war because this is where most of the research has occurred. Although there are implications for intrastate and civil war, more research in this area is needed before the conclusions here could be confidently applied to that area.

INTELLECTUAL BACKGROUND

Territorial issues have often been a focus of diplomatic efforts in the international community. A fairly large body of international law exists dealing with boundary disputes. Similarly, territorial disagreements have been at the center of the efforts of international

institutions—such as the International Court of Justice and boundary disputes. Despite such efforts, territorial disputes have been quite intractable. Even when they pose no danger of war, these issues can linger for years as did the El Chamizal dispute between the USA and Mexico (see Lamborn and Mumme, 1988). More ominously, when they fester for decades without going to war, they can (as in the Falklands/Malvinas dispute) suddenly erupt into a war (see Kacowicz, 1994: Ch. 7). Until recently, however, international relations scholars have not placed any special theoretical significance on territory as a fundamental cause of conflict or war. Realist theory has consistently seen all issues, including territorial issues, as reducible to the issue of power (Morgenthau, 1960: 27). It is the struggle for power within an anarchic system, not any specific issue that *causes* war. Territory may be a motive for war, but it is its role as a source of power that is crucial for realists.

While realist approaches have dominated much of international relations (IR) theory, this is not to say that theories of conflict focusing on territory as a unique source of conflict have not been constructed. Many of these have looked at territory through biological and evolutionary lenses (see Ardrey, 1966), but these have usually been dismissed in political science as overly deterministic. As the social sciences have become more influenced by post-modernism and constructivism, such approaches have fallen even further out of favor, while such seemly biological concepts, like territoriality, have been reconceptualized in constructivist terms (Sack, 1986; Blanchard, 2005). Consequently, the extent to which territory is of causal significance has sometimes been underestimated.

In recent years, this has changed. First, advances in the life sciences, including ethology and neuroscience, have made political scientists argue that their theories cannot ignore the insights and research of these disciplines in explaining human behavior and decision making (Masters, 1989; Rosen, 2005). Within international relations, most scholars who take work in the life sciences seriously adopt a non-deterministic approach, like Vasquez (1993), who in his territorial explanation of war argues that humans are both genetically predisposed to certain behaviors (like territorial conflict) but are also able to change behavior in response to ideas (what Somit, 1990: 569 calls "soft-wired" as opposed to "hard-wired").

New research in evolutionary psychology and on the biological and neuro-psychological basis of territoriality has added to our understanding of where territoriality comes from (see Alcock and O'Neill, 1987; Buss, 1995). While this work is often grounded in socio-biological assumptions, its findings still must be dealt with. Related to this perspective is the issue of crimes of passion and how they may be associated with territory. Even though research on individuals may not apply to collectivities, one of the more relevant insights of this work is that the emotional/biological response to territorial questions is conditioned by our evolutionary past (Simmons, 1998). Since collectivities, do seem to respond to territorial issues in

a manner that is often in excess of a strict cost/benefit analysis, this literature may give us some clues as to why.

A second and more influential reason for the change in attitude has been the release of a new data set on militarized interstate disputes from 1816–1992 by the Correlates of War project (Jones et al., 1996) that includes data on territorial disputes and has led to a surge of quantitative research on territory and war. This has produced some important findings that show that territorial disputes are highly war-prone.

One of the puzzles raised by this research is why territorial issues can be so intractable when on the surface it appears that territory is both tangible and divisible. Some answers place great emphasis on reputation effects (Walter, 2003). Reputation is certainly a component, but in and of itself it is too narrow an emphasis to provide a complete answer, and it overlooks other processes that can be useful for conflict resolution. Quite some time ago, Mansbach and Vasquez (1981: 234–250) pointed out that conflict and cooperation consists of three separate but interrelated dimensions— opinion (agreement–disagreement), behavior (positive and negative acts, e.g. carrots and sticks), and psychological attitude (friendship–hostility). They hypothesize that over time, persistent disagreement leads to an over-reliance on negative acts and coercion. These acts instead of changing the issue position of the other side engender psychological hostility, which in turn encourages disagreement.

Such a vicious circle directly affects the way issues are framed. A conflict spiral can transform concrete and tangible stakes, such as territory, by infusing them with symbolic and even transcendent qualities. Symbolic stakes are more intractable because giving in implies giving in on all the other stakes they represent or, at minimum, setting a precedent that will lead to a slippery slope of losses (here is where a reputation effect is most relevant). Transcendent stakes involve a further and different transformation. Here, the conflict process makes the stake representative of very salient (typically moral) values, like freedom, honor, and identity.

Infusing concrete stakes with symbolic and transcendent qualities makes them intangible and difficult to divide. Territory often becomes infused with these qualities in the conflict process. For Serbs, the land at Kosovo Polje is not just the earth with a certain mineral content; it is where the battle of Kosovo took place in 1389. It is representative of their soul, their history, their destiny (White, 2000: Ch. 6; see also Newman, 2006).

As stakes become more symbolic and transcendent, they encourage disagreement, which in turn leads to more negative coercive acts, which then leads to more hostility. At the same time, a shift to more symbolic and transcendent stakes leads the contending actors to make certain kinds of proposals for the disposition of an issue. In brief, symbolic and transcendent stakes lead actors basically to make zero-sum proposals for settling the issue. Proposals of this type give one side all the benefits and make the other bear all the costs. This is because such stakes tend to be intangible and cannot be divided, thereby encouraging proposals of the winner-take-all type.[2]

The above analysis should make it clear that it is not conflicts that are intractable, but issues that are intractable. Theory and research will be more productive if we think in terms of *intractable issues*, rather than intractable conflicts. What makes some conflicts difficult to resolve is that the underlying issue has certain characteristics, like its being intangible or over territory that has been infused with symbolic qualities. These in turn lead to zero-sum proposals which hamper negotiations.

TERRITORY AND CONFLICT: EMPIRICAL PATTERNS

As a field, international relations has relied on theory to identify the conditions under which conflict resolution is most apt to be successful (Zartman, 1989) and the kinds of

techniques that can be implemented to deal with specific problems (Pruitt and Rubin, 1986; Kriesberg, Northrup et al., 1989; Burton, 1990). Empirical research on specific cases of success and failure (Bercovitch and Jackson, 1997) have also been analyzed to delineate certain patterns that can be useful for understanding the dynamics of conflict and its resolution, management or settlement (Bercovitch and Diehl, 1997; Zartman and Rasmussen, 1997).[3] In the last decade, there has been a great deal of systematic research on territorial disputes which has given us a much more complete picture of the role of territory in bringing about conflict that leads to war. In this section, we outline the principal patterns that have been delineated by this research.

Conflict at the most basic level involves disagreement, and disagreement is inherent in social behavior. Not all disagreements need end in violence, however. Most practitioners of conflict resolution become concerned when disagreements are handled with the use of militarized force. Crossing this threshold puts the conflict into a different category, one where the risk of war has suddenly increased, even though most interstate attempts to handle issues through the use of force do not escalate to war. Thanks to the Correlates of War project, we now have a fairly complete record of all instances of the threat or use of force between legally recognized nation-states from 1816–2001. Such instances are called militarized interstate disputes (MIDs).

Using MIDs as the dependent variable, it has been found that states with territorial disagreements are more apt to have a MID than states without territorial disagreements (Senese and Vasquez, 2003). Territorial disagreements appear to be special kinds of issues in that their presence encourages the use of militarized force.

A second factor that is related to the threat or use of force between states is whether they are neighbors. States that are contiguous (by land or within 150 miles of water) are more apt to have a MID than non-contiguous states (Senese, 2005).

It is reasonable to assume, as the territorial explanation of war would expect, that disputes between neighbors involve territory, although this hypothesis has not been fully tested. What tests we do have consistently show that neighbors fight not because they are contiguous and have frequent interactions, but because they have territorial disputes (Hensel, 2000; Vasquez, 2001; Ben-Yehuda, 2004; Senese, 2005). This means that territory is more important than contiguity in terms of the onset of war.

Once territorial disputes emerge between two states, whether they are neighbors or not, they are more apt to recur (Hensel, 1994). We also know that states that have territorial disputes are likely to become enduring rivals (have six or more MIDs within a 20-year period) (Vasquez and Leskiw, 2001).[4] From research on rivalry and protracted conflict, we know that disputes that recur between the same two states have a greater risk of escalating to war (Goertz and Diehl, 1992a; Brecher and Wilkenfeld, 1997; Diehl and Goertz, 2000). Since territorial disputes recur, we would expect that they would have a higher probability of going to war than other types of disputes.

In fact, the major finding we have in conflict studies is that territorial disputes have a greater probability of ending up in war than other types of disputes, specifically regime and policy disputes. This was one of the first findings on territory and war using the MID data and it has been confirmed in several studies. The simplest and most straightforward test is in Vasquez and Henehan (2001: 128). They find that territorial disputes have the highest probability of going to war in the 1816–1992 period (.091) compared to regime disputes (.078) and policy disputes (.033). A comparison of the conditional probabilities with the overall base probability of war, which is .058, shows that territorial and regime disputes are significantly more apt to escalate to war than expected by chance and that policy disputes have a significantly lower likelihood of going to war than the base.

Vasquez and Henehan (2001: 134–135) also test this hypothesis controlling for historical era (1816–1945, 1946–1992) and whether the two states in a dispute are both major states (e.g. Germany, UK), both minor, or major–minor. These controls generally reconfirm the findings. The only exceptions are that under certain circumstances, regime disputes have a higher probability of war when both sides are minor states or when the dispute occurs in the post-1945 period. Nevertheless, territorial disputes account for most war escalations— 53 of 97 (54.6%) compared to only 9 of 97 (9.3%) for regime disputes for the entire 1816–1992 period (Vasquez and Henehan, 2001: 131).

Note, however, that territorial disputes are not necessary conditions for war, but only increase the probability of war when they are present. Other issues can also give rise to war. Vasquez and Henehan (2001: 131) show that 31 of the 97 (32%) war escalations arise from policy disputes. Territory is responsible for only one category of war, albeit the most frequent.[5] In work seeking to classify types of wars, Valeriano and Vasquez (2005) find that territorial wars account for the majority of wars occurring from 1816– 1997. Looking at multilateral wars, they get even stronger results in that 20 of the 28 (71.4%) multilateral wars can be classified as territorial wars.

The hypothesis that territorial disputes between nation-states are highly prone to war has been tested by numerous scholars in different ways and using different data sets. The earliest published studies were by Senese (1996) and Hensel (1996), both of whom group policy, regime, and other disputes into a single non-territorial category. Senese (1996) finds that territorial MIDs are more prone to having fatalities than non-territorial disputes regardless of whether they go to war or not. He infers that there is something about territorial disputes that makes decision makers willing to sacrifice lives rather than give in to demands. Similarly, Hensel (1996) shows that not only are territorial MIDs more prone to fatalities, but they incur the highest fatalities (note: a war by definition must produce at least 1000 battle deaths). Ben-Yehuda (2004) using International Crisis Behavior (ICB) project data also finds that crises involving territorial issues are more war-prone than other types of crises.

One of the criticisms of the above sort of studies is that they may be prone to selection bias, that is, that it is not territorial MIDs that bring about war, but the factors which bring about territorial MIDs in the first place that make for war. Several sophisticated analyses have tested for this possibility and none of them have found selection effects operating in the MID data (Senese and Vasquez, 2003; Senese, 2005; Rasler and Thompson, 2006). What the above studies find is that while territorial claims or contiguity may increase the probability of a MID arising, it is the presence of a territorial MID (and not territorial claims or contiguity) that make war likely.

All of this research suggests that conflict resolution should make the settlement of territorial disputes a focus of its efforts, since territorial disputes are highly war-prone and account for most interstate wars and rivalries. But where does one begin and are all territorial disputes alike?

One optimistic set of findings, which is also consistent with the territorial explanation of war, is that it is not territorial disputes that greatly increase the probability of war, but how they are handled and whether they lead to a rivalry. Recent work (Valeriano, 2003; Rasler and Thompson, 2006) has shown that rivalry and the timing of events prior to and during a territorial dispute are critical for the escalation to war and termination of outstanding territorial claims. This view challenges the conventional wisdom that territorial disputes in and of themselves lead to militarized action and warfare. Rather, territorial issues lead to rivalry, which then leads to intense disputes and war. It follows that settling a territorial issue is not simply demarking a border (say in Kashmir), but resolving all the other questions, like the symbolic and transcendent value of the territory, which are endemic to a rivalry. Unless the rivalry relationship is addressed, the vicious circle of conflict to which rivalries are prone will not be broken and

the territorial dispute is unlikely to be settled.

Rivalry (Diehl and Goertz, 2000; Thompson, 2001) is an essential variable because issues at stake within such a relationship fester and repeat. Rivalry is a situation of historic animosity where any and all issues at stake between the disputants take on a serious and deadly tone. One state would slash its own nose in order to deny a benefit to its rival. It is during these situations that territory becomes dangerous and war-prone. One state may take a portion of territory and settle the question for the time being, but if the rivalry persists, that territorial issue will repeat and reemerge even decades later.

The timing of events during a territorial disagreement is crucial to the outcome of settlement efforts. Rasler and Thompson (2006) find that war is unlikely over a territorial issue in the absence of an ongoing strategic rivalry. Valeriano (2003) finds that war and enduring rivalry are unlikely without territorial issues and power politics tactics such as alliances, simultaneous disputes, grand strategy development, and arms races occurring prior to the onset of rivalry.

Senese and Vasquez (2005) show that as states resort to various forms of power politics to get the other side to accept its territorial demands, the probability of war progressively increases. Trying to deal with territorial issues by seeking outside allies, building up one's military, or engaging in repeated militarized confrontations produces a security dilemma that makes the other side respond in kind. The research shows that each time one of these practices is employed, there is a concomitant increase in the probability of war (ranging from around .50 to .90 for 1816–1945). During the Cold War, alliances and arms races are not a significant factor, but this may be a function primarily of the impact of nuclear weapons which acted as a restraint on superpower competition (Senese and Vasquez, 2005). How territorial disputes are handled once they arise makes a big difference in the probability of war and provides an opening for effective conflict resolution intervention and points out the importance of timing.

These findings raise the question of what distinguishes the territorial disputes that go to war from those that do not. One answer to that question (as exemplified by the above research) is in terms of process—it is the process by which actors handle territorial issues that distinguish those that go to war from those that do not. One such key factor is whether territorial MIDs recur.[6]

Another and equally plausible answer as to why certain territorial disputes are more war-prone is that it is something intrinsic to the issue itself—its salience or the type of territory under question. Goertz and Diehl (1992b) measure the area of the territory and the size of its population to get at the importance of the territory in question. Hensel (2001) adds to the salience measure, indicators of economic resources, homeland vs. colonial territory, ethnic identity, and mainland vs. offshore territory. He finds some evidence that salience is important not only for predicting war, but also the probability of peaceful settlement. From his perspective, salience forces leaders "to do something" and that can be either engaging in nonviolent practices (like negotiations or mediation) or going to war. Hensel (2001: 83) rightly regards these as substitutable means. The pressure "to do something" may also account for why intangible territorial issues have more peaceful settlements than tangible territorial issues, even though intangible territorial issues have a higher probability of going to war and having MIDs.

Huth (1996) and Huth and Allee (2002) classify territorial claims according to type— ethnic (including bordering minorities of the same ethnic group), strategic, and economic. They find that ethnic and strategic territorial claims are highly conflict-prone—in terms of escalation and war. Conversely, they find that territorial claims associated with economic resources are prone to peaceful resolution, especially if they involve developing countries. Here, joint ventures and the need for capital can provide incentives to resolve the issue. Further refinement of typologies that look at the substantive nature of territorial issues (e.g. border adjustments vs. core

territory, etc.) is an area that might prove productive for matching the right conflict resolution techniques with the relevant type of issue.

One factor that has long been a characteristic that is seen as making it more difficult to settle an issue is the number of actors involved. Multiple actors are seen as making negotiations and compromise more difficult. Brecher and Wilkenfeld (1997) provide some evidence (using ICB data) for this with regard to international crises—showing that multiparty crises are more prone to escalation and the use of violence. Petersen, et al. (2004) show the same is true of multiparty MIDs in terms of their having an increased probability of going to war. Of interest is that they demonstrate that this relationship is especially true of multiparty territorial disputes. Similarly, Valeriano and Vasquez (2005) find that most multiparty wars arise out of territorial disputes rather than regime or policy questions.

The research on territorial disputes has shown that it is an important source of conflict and that it is also a key factor (if not *the* factor) in the outbreak of interstate war. Since it is such an important factor, it is essential that territory be the focus of attention for war avoidance and reduction, but the territorial explanation of war is more optimistic than that. It maintains that among neighbors, territory is so important that once this issue is settled, it can lead to long periods of peace, even if other salient issues arise. This hypothesis is one of the major testable differences between the territorial explanation of war and realism, which sees war as inherent in the struggle for power. We turn now to research relevant to this claim about the relationship between territory and peace.

TERRITORY AND PEACE: EMPIRICAL PATTERNS

Vasquez (1993: 146) has stated: "If the territorial divisions among neighbors are not challenged but accepted as legitimate, peaceful relations can govern. Most borders once satisfactorily settled remain so for long periods of time."

Is it the case that once a border is mutually accepted that peace can reign?[7]

The earliest systematic evidence we have on this is from Kocs (1995). Examining all contiguous states from 1945–1987, he finds that war is not very likely if neighbors accept their border and have no territorial claim against one another. War is about 40 times more likely to break out between contiguous states if they are involved in a territorial disagreement that has never been resolved (Kocs, 1995: 172). Kocs' evidence is indirect in that acceptance of a border is based on the absence of a territorial claim and not some direct measure of border legitimacy.

Gibler (1996, 1997) has two studies that show that settling a territorial dispute is related to peace between states. Gibler's (1996) first study is done in the context of work on alliances that shows that certain types of alliances are followed by war within five years (Levy, 1981). One type that is not is an alliance made to cement a territorial settlement. Only 1 of 27 territorial settlement treaties is followed by a war of any kind (Gibler, 1996). In a more systematic study, Gibler (1997) shows that alliances that settle territorial disputes also have a pacifying effect on interstate rivalry, which, as noted earlier, is very prone to war.

Using recently collected data on all territorial claims made between states from 1816 through 2001 for the Western Hemisphere and Western Europe, Hensel (2006) finds support for the proposition that if territorial claims are settled (either violently or non-violently), then there is a decreased probability of subsequent MIDs. Overall, he finds that once a territorial claim has been settled, the probability of a subsequent MID goes down significantly below the probability of having an MID when a territorial claim is present (Hensel, 2006: 15). This finding supports the hypothesis that settling territorial claims between neighbors will result in a significant reduction of all militarized conflict, not just war. In addition, the reduction in conflict is

over any issue and not just a reduction in territorial MIDs (Hensel, 2006: 1).

How can territory have this peaceful and even transformative effect on relations between neighbors? The reason is that once borders are accepted; they can fulfill their role in the modern global system as international institutions. Borders, as Simmons (2006: 253–259) points out, are not just sites of contention, but international institutions that provide a number of mutual benefits (see also Blanchard, 2005).

Borders are international institutions in that they are a set of practices that allocate physical space according to a constructed understanding of reality. Borders divide space and allocate sovereignty, which gives a host of rights to certain individuals and groups and not to others. Borders say, in effect, that in one space such and such can be done and in this other space, these other rules apply. This is what it means to own the land and to have sovereignty over it. Borders can have a tremendous impact on identity, ways of life, and so forth (see Sahlins, 1989).

Simmons (2006) focuses on the economic benefits derived from borders as institutions, which are considerable. Accepted boundaries provide a demarcation of sovereignty and recognition of one another's laws and regulations regarding property rights, investment, and trade. When boundaries are not accepted, it is difficult to engage in extensive economic interaction because uncertainty is so high. Uncertainty undermines the normal stability of expectations about the future on which contracts are based. This can be most easily seen with regard to property rights and direct investment. When borders are in contention, there is a lack of consensus on the applicability of basic ground rules in certain geographical spaces.

In contrast, acceptance of boundaries allows parties to see where sovereignty lies and what laws apply. Stable borders embody an institution that allocates certain legal competencies as well as embodying a set of mutual understandings about rules and norms that apply with regard to what the border means and who can do what on each side of the border. In fact, many scholars (Goff, 2000; Simmons, 2006) conclude that, in spite of theories suggesting the decline of the state, borders remain an important factor in international politics. Henrikson (2000) suggests that "good neighborhood" or bon voisinage treaties should be concluded to force states to accept the territorial boundary lines and encourage cooperation.

Economic interaction and trade, in particular, takes place in the context of a variety of rules and practices reflecting legal standards. These reduce transaction costs and thereby increase profits, but mostly they reduce financial risk. Borders help identify who owns what. In doing so they delegitimize theft through conquest. Working borders reduce risk and fear, making trade a viable substitution for conquest (Rosecrance, 1986; Bueno de Mesquita et al., 2003: Ch. 9; Gartzke and Rohner, 2006). Simmons (2006) uses a gravity model of trade to try to estimate the value of trade lost because of a territorial dispute. She points out that the acceptance of a line of demarcation will permit this trade, which would normally exist, to flow. In many ways, what is important is not where the demarcation line is drawn, but simply that it is drawn.

The benefits of borders as institutions for non-economic matters can be even greater. Constructivists have shown that borders serve a number of functions (Blanchard, 2005). Of special importance are the identity and constitutive functions. With the norm of nationalism and self-determination, territory has become a way to ground identity. Another function of borders is to delimit what constitutes the state (Blanchard, 2005: 691–692). The constitutive function originates with national sovereignty and is institutionalized in the Peace of Westphalia and international law. International law recognizes that states, and usually states alone, have political sovereignty over a specific piece of territory.

Mutual acceptance of a border and the existing territorial distribution permits actors to reap the benefits of both of these functions. Contesting the border interrupts the smooth functioning of the border, making for great uncertainty. This can be seen in the way a border serves to institutionalize a way of life. When borders are accepted, normal interaction and politics come to the forefront. This opens up new possibilities, especially along the borderlands. For Diez (2004: 137), when borders are stable, they are more apt to become porous; what seems to be occurring in this process is that the border "as division" is replaced with the border as "a reference point" that brings people (legal equals) together across a number of stable cross-border interactions. In contrast, contesting borders reinforces them as a focal point of conflict, insecurity, and uncertainty.[8]

A dramatic case for how this process occurs is Western Europe. For centuries, Western Europe's borders have been contested and fought over in numerous wars. One of the great lessons for peace research is how this war-torn region becomes a security community in the Deutschian sense.[9] The Schumann plan was based on a theory of peace (Mitrany, 1943) that sees economic integration as a foundation that will spill over to produce political integration and peace. It is this theoretical approach that was used to guide much of European integration, and it is clearly antithetical to realist international relations theory. As such, the ensuing West European peace poses an anomaly for the realist paradigm, in that it is a non-realist theory associated with a set of policies that brings about peace in a war-torn region that had been dominated by realist practices of power politics.

While economic integration is a key, one of the things that distinguish the post-1945 economic integration of Western Europe from the economic interdependence and trade of pre-1914 Europe is that the former is built on a firm acceptance of borders. While the acceptance of borders was not the centerpiece of Europe's Common Market, but a side-effect, from the perspective of the territorial explanation of war, it was a side-effect that made a crucial difference. In this sense, one of the most important (and overlooked) historical events of our time that produces peace is the acceptance in 1990 of the

German–Polish border by the unified German government.

With the creation of the European Union and its enlargement, acceptance of borders has become a keystone in its strategy for peace. The demand that new states settle their territorial disputes as a price for admission will provide a test of the peace proposition within the territorial explanation of war. It predicts that mutually acceptable borders among these states will give rise to long periods of peace between neighbors. This would be expected to be particularly the case in the context of the European Union, which provides an economic and political structure for institutionalizing borders in a fashion that quickly provides benefits (see Diez et al., 2006).

This conceptual analysis, buttressed by case evidence, supports the general proposition that once territorial disputes are settled, they set neighbors on a road to peace. More importantly, it points to why and how peace occurs. From the perspective of the territorial explanation of war, peace does not involve the disappearance of borders, as some who take a globalization perspective argue (Ruggie, 1993), but their acceptance and desecuritization. Borders are a foundation upon which peace can be built. Globalization involves not so much a removal of borders but an acceptance of them and a set of economic agreements that make them more porous and interactive.

If territory is in fact a key to peace, then there should be some observable trace of this in the historical record. One way to test this notion is to observe periods of peace and see if, in fact, they are associated with the absence (or a reduction in the probability) of war for territorial disputes.[10] Henehan and Vasquez (2006: 290, Table 11.4) provide evidence to this effect. They use Wallensteen's (1984) identification of periods of peace among the major states from 1816 to 1976 (with an update through 1991) to see if in these peaceful periods, territorial disputes are less prevalent.

They find that there are few territorial MIDs (in absolute numbers) in these periods of relative major state peace—1 in 1816–1848, 4 in 1871–1895, 0 in 1919–1932, and 11 in 1963–1991. Interestingly, during the early League of Nations period, territorial disputes are kept completely off the agenda. More systematically, there are 16 territorial disputes during the 101 "relatively peaceful years" (.16 per year) compared to 61 territorial disputes during the 73 "relatively war-prone years" (.84 per year).

This statistical evidence implies that there is something about these periods that reduces the number and danger of territorial disputes. Two hypotheses are suggested. One is the hypothesis that guides Wallensteen's (1984) study—that peace is associated with major states attempting to establish a common set of rules of the game to guide their behavior (and thereby govern the system). The second is the hypothesis under discussion here—the acceptance of borders. These two hypotheses, however, are not unrelated. For example, in the Congress of Vienna, borders were fixed and at the same time a set of informal rules of the game regulating major state interactions were adopted.

Another body of evidence that peace is associated with the absence of territorial disputes comes from the democratic peace. It is known that democratic dyads (pairs of states) rarely go to war against each other. Is this because they tend not to have territorial disputes? Mitchell and Prins (1999) are the first to explore this question. They find that democratic dyads mostly have maritime disputes and not territorial MIDs. James et al. (2006) go a step further and argue that territorial disputes can wash out the effects of the democratic peace. Gibler (2007) provides even more evidence that the absence of territorial disputes might be a major reason for the democratic peace. He finds that democratic dyads have few territorial issues, have settled borders with their democratic neighbors, and do not fight each other. He argues that democratic states tend not to fight each other because they have settled their borders. These three studies add to the evidence that peace reigns in the absence of territorial disputes. Further detail on this process is provided by Allee and Huth (2006) who show that democracies tend to use legal settlements as domestic political cover in their attempts to deescalate territorial disputes and are successful at resolving these (between like-minded democracies) before any threat of force is used (see also Huth and Allee, 2002).

While the research on territory and peace is not as extensive nor as robust as the findings on territory and war, it consistently shows that resolving or settling territorial issues can be a road to peace for neighbors. Neighbors who have settled outstanding territorial claims, regardless of whether they have settled them violently or non-violently, have a much lower probability of militarized conflict (a MID) on any issue than neighbors with a claim, which means they are much less likely to go to war or experience rivalry. The findings imply that states need not be trapped in a vicious circle of power politics, conflict, and war. They are at peace and move on to making the border work for them, as outlined by Simmons (2006) and Diez (2004), and not against them.

IMPLICATIONS FOR CONFLICT RESOLUTION

The above review supports the claim that territory is a key to war and to peace. Learning how to manage, settle, or resolve territorial issues will not eliminate all war, but it will do much to reduce a certain class of wars, especially among neighbors. In this concluding section, we outline some of the implications of the research on territory for the theory and practice of conflict resolution. The implications must be seen as initial suggestions that conflict resolution theorists and practitioners will need to adapt to specific circumstances, since most research does not suggest how one should apply these findings to ongoing conflicts.

An important contribution of the empirical research is that it tells us where we should focus our energies. Interstate war is most apt to occur between neighbors and its source is most likely to be territorial. Therefore, we

should focus on either keeping such issues off the agenda or reducing their salience or intangibility. Attaining this goal will make for peaceful relations between neighbors over the long term. While territorial conflict between neighbors is not uncommon, the empirical research on territory and peace tells us that once borders are accepted, neighbors need not be at high risk of war. Settling or resolving territorial issues between neighbors can have a high and long-term payoff.

A second contribution of the empirical research is that it makes it clear that territorial disputes do not inevitably end in war; it all depends on how they are handled.

A diplomacy of peace must know the difference between practices that increase the risk of war and those that reduce it. Current research on the steps to war suggests that mediators or other outside parties should encourage disputants to avoid making outside alliances or building up their military, which increase threat perceptions. Forming an outside alliance is not going to make one more secure, but will only provoke a counter-alliance. Avoiding alliances will nip this vicious circle in the bud, but avoiding alliances will not be easy because the presence of salient territorial disputes will make states feel the need for outside support. The same security dilemma operates with military buildups. In addition, trying to settle the issue unilaterally through militarized confrontation is going to lead to a sense of rivalry. Each of these factors can be seen as taking the parties along a realist road to war.

Nevertheless, there are many exits off the road to war.[11] If one has a territorial dispute, then one should avoid making outside alliances. If one has already made an alliance after a territorial dispute, war might still be prevented by not building up one's military and engaging in arms races. Lastly, a number of crisis management and even crisis prevention techniques can be employed to break a pattern of repeated militarized confrontations, as was learned in the Cold War (George, 1983; see also Axelrod's (1984) analysis of tit-for-tat strategies). Failing to break a pattern of recurring territorial disputes is the best guarantee of a war. War often arises between neighbors because it is a unilateral way of imposing one's preferred outcome.

A third contribution of the empirical research on territory is to highlight the importance of prevailing norms for the transfer of territory. The modern global system has always had certain norms for the transfer of territory. In the early years, territory was seen as the personal property of monarchs, and it could be transferred through the rules of dynastic succession (including marriage) (Luard, 1986: 101, 110). Since the mid-nineteenth century, nationalism and self-determination has been the dominant norm.

Agreement on norms makes it easier to settle a territorial dispute peacefully. Kacowicz (1994: 75–76, 82, 86) provides some statistical evidence that agreement on norms leads to a peaceful transfer of territory about 80% of the time; whereas disagreement over norms leads to a failure to settle the dispute peacefully about 80% of the time. Indeed, it seems the more stringent the norms, the less likely wars. As Luard (1986: 87) points out, many past wars arose because loopholes or ambiguities within the rules for dynastic succession provided an opportunity for territorial expansion. The lesson here is clear—tighten loopholes and reduce ambiguity. When this is done, it becomes more difficult to claim that one has a legitimate resort to arms. More importantly, however, such norms provide a reasoned basis for expanding common ground and producing a solution that will sell at home.

In this sense, the growth in the body of international law for adjudicating boundary claims is a great asset and provides a separate (legal) decision game that works with norms for transferring territory. As with norms, a main consequence of international law is that it provides a procedure for determining who should win (or who should get what). Like all decision games, it provides an authoritative allocation of value(s). Agreement on a procedure has two obvious advantages: it provides a way of ending the issue, which may be important if the territory is salient, and it is a procedure that is considerably

less costly than war (and more legitimate in today's international society).

Opting for a binding procedure to determine who wins may also be a way for a leader to avoid the domestic costs associated with the continuation of the issue or the possibility of losing territory. Simmons (1999) shows that leaders are more apt to use arbitration to deal with territorial issues in a highly contentious domestic environment to avoid costs associated with a settlement.

For high salience territorial issues, losing in one decision game often means the actor shifts to another strategy and a new game. Similarly, when the status quo state drags on negotiations for years and sometimes decades, as Britain did with Argentina over the Falklands/Malvinas, it risks a sudden shift to the war game by the revisionist state when an opportune moment arises. Kacowicz (1994: 169, 173) argues that British abandonment of accommodative strategies during the negotiations "in favor of a prolongation of the status quo" led Argentina to shift to a coercive game, which of course backfired. Hensel (2001) also finds a link between the failure to reach a settlement through negotiation and a shift to war.

How can one settle or resolve such issues? There seem to be two main obstacles to reaching an agreement. The first is domestic opposition and the second involves emotional attachments that make the issue intangible and difficult to divide. Each of these are areas where conflict resolution efforts have played a role in the past. Overcoming these obstacles greatly increases the likelihood of success.

Sometimes, even when leaders agree on a solution, domestic opposition or the opposition of relevant non-state actors can overturn an agreement. This has been a perennial problem in the Middle East. It must be remembered that someone must stand for peace at the highest levels, if peace is to be attained. Often, leaders who are hardliners or who have been a successful military leader in the past (see Chiozza and Choi, 2003) are more able to push through an agreement, mostly because they are able to control hard-line constituencies. This was certainly the case, respectively, with Nixon in recognizing "Red China" and with de Gaulle in Algeria. One cannot always count on such leaders emerging, however. For conflict resolution to be successful, it often boils down to a question of agenda politics where the right leaders appear at the right moment, often in the context of a hurting stalemate (Zartman, 1989). Kingdon's (1995) model of agenda politics is relevant here.

In the absence of such a concatenation of factors, it is necessary to either impose an agreement externally or think in terms of more long-term processes that will transform the domestic political environment of one or both sides. The external imposition of an agreement is what "great power" diplomacy (e.g. in the Concert of Europe) was all about. When major states are reluctant or unable to impose solutions, then efforts must focus on the long-term process of changing the actor's issue positions. One long-term solution is to bargain in the context of gaining on another issue that is more salient. This is an unlikely scenario for territorial disputes like Kashmir or Palestine, but issue linkages can play a role in smaller territorial disputes that are visible mostly to those in the border region.

Another alternative is to try to drain the emotional foundation of the issue that leads to hard-line constituencies in the first place, either by letting the issue lie dormant or by taking a more active role in reframing the issue. When issues that have little tangible value are highly conflictive, as when governments fight over land that has little economic value (as Walter, 2003 finds), the most likely reason is that these issues are commanding emotional attention. Conflict resolution theorists and practitioners have tried to deal with this problem by reframing and reconceptualizing such issues. Instead of treating them as zero sum, they have tried to show how certain solutions can make the issue contention more of a positive sum game or at least not totally zero sum. The art of conflict resolution is to generate a solution that transforms the issue in this manner.[12]

The prospect of each side winning something significant reduces hostility.

In ethnic disputes, a simple solution is to separate or partition the territory along ethnic lines when this is possible and both sides accept the nationalism norm. Plebiscites supervised by international organizations provide a procedure for implementing the nationalism norm. Autonomous regional governments follow the same logic. Tir (2006: Chs 4, 6) finds that territorial transfers are sometimes successful conflict management techniques, especially if the partition does not divide members of the same ethnic group or punish the loser too harshly, but at other times partition can be problematic.

More often than not, ethnic groups are too intermingled for partition to work. Here, one may want to take Burton's (1990) approach, which emphasizes the importance of meeting mutual needs. With ethnicity, this approach would emphasize tolerance of different ways of life and permitting a multilayered use of the same space to practice different cultures. Identity is seen as not zero sum because one's "Spanishness" should not diminish another's "Basqueness" and vice versa. In fact, a tolerance and a granting of space, but not necessarily territory, to each identity are likely to increase mutual security. There may still be other issues, such as social integration, prohibitions on intermarriage, and so forth, but the issue is stripped of its territorial content. Extreme mingling of ethnic groups have led some to emphasize human rights' guarantees to practice one's identity, and this may work even in non-democratic societies, if human rights are not interpreted so broadly that this effort is seen as one of trying to change the form of government.

An important foundation of this solution is what might be called "deterritorializing" the issue. In this case, ethnicity or identity is not tied to owning a particular piece of territory. Instead, the legal structure permits identity to be practiced non-exclusively anywhere (or exclusively in a certain space or time; for example, in special buildings or on certain days).[13] Separating specific issues from territory can lead to less conflict because the variable that produces violence is not ethnicity, but territory.

This still leaves the problem of the symbolic quality of territorial issues. Here, territory resists settlement because one piece of territory stands for several other' territories. One way of dealing with this problem is to delink the stakes. This tack has proven partially successful in the Middle East where the question of Sinai was separated from the question of the Golan Heights and the West Bank/Gaza. Such an approach has the advantage of reducing the number of actors needed to reach agreement, and not holding the solution hostage to the most hard-line group in the coalition and the most intractable territorial stake in the broader issue.

Part of draining territory of its emotional content and making it less of an intangible stake requires dealing with the sense of rivalry that has made the issue take on these characteristics. The current state of knowledge in the field suggests researchers should not focus their conflict management and resolution techniques solely on specific territorial issues in the hope of ending the conflict entirely. It is important that conflict resolution efforts deal with territorial issues in the context of the larger rivalry in which they are embedded; thereby changing the underlying relationship which has framed the issue so that it is intangible and infused with symbolic and transcendent qualities. Dealing with rivalry also helps reduce the influence of domestic hardliners that stir up historic animosity and make issues difficult to settle between states. By recognizing that their collective mutual interest in conflict resolution will produce benefits (especially economic benefits) that are greater than the benefits of continuing the rivalry, a pair of states can make progress toward ending one of the main sources of disagreement and conflict.

CONCLUSION

We have argued and presented evidence to show that territory is a key to war and a key to peace. There is considerable evidence that the presence of territorial issues and disputes increase the probability of war and conflict. No matter what data set or method used, the results always show support for this important finding. What also seems to be clear is that not all territorial issues are equally prone to war. It seems that states rarely go to war over tangible territorial issues and territory disputed solely for economic reasons; rather, they fight when the territory under question is infused with intangible qualities or is tied to ethnic factions.

How territorial issues are handled once they arise is a crucial variable. If they are handled in a power politics manner, they are apt to repeat and promote rivalry. The first step to ending territorial disputes might be managing the tactics leaders employ to deal with these issues. This will help set the stage for the stable acceptance of borders as an institution, which can provide significant economic benefits to both sides of the dispute.

Peace seems to lie with the settlement of territorial disputes. Recent research has shown that once territorial disputes are settled, neighbors and neighborhoods can have long periods of peace. Future research should focus on concrete examples of how territorial disputes can be resolved and how those disputes can be defused of their transcendent and symbolic qualities. The task for conflict resolution is to apply its insights and practical wisdom to settling the ongoing territorial disputes that still wrack so much of the world. Such an emphasis is apt to have the highest payoffs.

NOTES

1 Our thanks to the editors, Peter Wallensteen, and the participants in the Sage "Confllict Resolution" Conference held in Laxenburg, Austria, June 30–July 2, 2007 for their comments and suggestions.

2 See Dzurek (2005) for a useful effort to create a taxonomy that evaluates the symbolic and tangible values of territory.

3 We use the distinction common in the conflict resolution literature between settlement, which refers to a termination of the issue regardless of the means

employed (i.e. including imposition of an agreement, as in Second World War) and resolution, which refers to a mutual satisfaction with the agreement and one that meets some if not all of the underlying needs related to the conflict.

4 This finding is correlational in nature, while we think that territorial disputes lead to rivalry, there are some cases, like Algeria-Morocco, where the rivalry leads to territorial disputes.

5 Territorial issues also play an important role in civil wars, see Toft (2003), Walter (2003).

6 A key area for future research is what domestic factors make territorial disputes recur.

7 Note this proposition does not mean that it is impossible for wars to occur because of other issues, but simply that between neighbors the probability of war in the absence of territorial disputes is greatly reduced. The pacifying effect of accepting borders between neighbors is much greater than among non-neighbors. Indeed, one possible non-territorial source of wars between neighbors is from contagion effects. This can be seen in the First World War and the Second World War where Germany attacks Belgium in the absence of a territorial dispute between them.

8 Diez (2004) treats the borders in Nordic areas, including the highly autonomous Aland Islands (within Finland), as the paradigmatic case of how territorial conflicts that threaten war at one point can become peaceful and stable at another, and quite porous.

9 For Deutsch (Deutsch, Burrell et al., 1957) a security community is one where the states do not believe that war between them is possible.

10 Such a test implies that the absence or low frequency of territorial disputes is almost a necessary condition for peace. While the territorial explanation of war says that war can arise out of other issues, territorial issues are seen as having a high probability of escalating to war. Because of this, removing them as a source of conflict and war should result in a visible effect in periods of peace, even though it is not going to be a universal effect. Treating the absence of territorial disputes as a sufficient condition of peace would involve a different sort of research, one more like that of Vasquez and Henehan (2001) already reported on above.

11 We take this phrase from J. David Singer, who has used in conversations in meetings.

12 One way of doing this is to get individuals (outside of government) to meet and come up with possible solutions. This is sometimes done at higher levels in Track Two diplomacy (Montville, 1987). Kelman (1982) has pioneered a more than twenty-year effort to hold unofficial problem-solving workshops between Arabs and Israelis. Such workshops help individuals and groups reframe the issue.

13 Thus, old "blue laws" in the US did not permit most businesses to be open or liquor to be sold on Sunday, a day of worship under the dominant Christian identity.

REFERENCES

Alcock, John and Kevin M. O'Neill (1987) 'Territory Preferences and Intensity of Competition in the Grey Hairstreak and the Tarantula Hawk Wasp', *American Midland Naturalist* 118(1): 128–138.

Allee, Todd L. and Paul Huth (2006) 'The Pursuit of Legal Settlements in Territorial Disputes', *Conflict Management and Peace Science* 23(4): 285–307.

Ardrey, Robert (1966) *The Territorial Imperative*. New York: Atheneum.

Axelrod, Robert (1984). *The Evolution of Cooperation*. New York: Basic Books.

Ben-Yehuda, Hemda (2004) 'Territoriality and War in International Crises: Theory and Findings, 1918–2001', *International Studies Review* 6(4): 85–105.

Bercovitch, Jacob and Paul F. Diehl (1997) 'Conflict Management of Enduring Rivalries: The Frequency, Timing, and Short-Term Impact of Mediation', *International Interactions* 22(4): 299–320.

Bercovitch, Jacob and Richard Jackson (1997) *International Conflict: A Chronological Encyclopedia of Conflicts and Their Management, 1945–1995*. Washington, DC: CQ Press.

Blanchard, Jean-Marc (2005) 'Linking Border Disputes and War: An Institutional-Statist-Theory', *Geopolitics* 10(4): 688–711.

Brecher, Michael and Jonathan Wilkenfeld (1997) *A Study of Crisis*. Ann Arbor: The University of Michigan Press.

Bueno de Mesquita, Bruce, Alastair Smith, Randolph M. Siverson, and James D. Morrow (2003) *The Logic of Political Survival*. Cambridge, MA: MIT Press.

Burton, John W. (1990) *Conflict: Resolution and Provention*. New York: St. Martin's Press.

Buss, David M. (1995) 'Evolutionary Psychology: A New Paradigm for Psychological Science', *Psychological Inquiry* 6(1): 1–30.

Chiozza, Giacomo and Ajin Choi (2003) 'Guess Who Did What: Political Leaders and the Management of Territorial Disputes, 1950–1990', *Journal of Conflict Resolution* 47(3): 251–278.

Deutsch, Karl W., Sidney Burrell, et al. (1957) *Political Community and the North Atlantic Area: International Organization in the Light of Historical Experience*. Princeton: Princeton University Press.

Diehl, Paul F. and Gary Goertz (2000) *War and Peace in International Rivalry*. Ann Arbor: University of Michigan Press.

Diez, Thomas (2004) 'The Subversion of Borders', in Stefano Guzzini and Dietrich Jung (eds.), *Contemporary Security Analysis and Copenhagen Peace Research*. London: Routledge. pp. 128–140.

Diez, Thomas, Stephan Stetter, and Mathias Albert (2006) 'The European Union and Border Conflicts: The Transformative Power of Integration', *International Organization* 60(3): 563–593.

Dzurek, Daniel (2005) 'What Makes Territory Important: Tangible and Intangible Dimensions', *GeoJournal* 68(4): 63–274.

Gartzke, Erik and Dominic Rohner (2006) 'To Conquer or Compel: Economic Development and Interstate Conflict', paper presented at the International Studies Association Annual Meeting.

George, Alexander L. (1983) *Managing U.S.-Soviet Rivalry: Problems of Crisis Prevention*. Boulder: Westview Press.

Gibler, Douglas (1996) 'Alliances That Never Balance: The Territorial Settlement Treaty', *Conflict Management and Peace Science* 15(1): 75–97.

Gibler, Douglas (1997) 'Control the Issues, Control the Conflict: The Effects of Alliances That Settle Territorial Issues on Interstate Rivalries', *International Interactions* 22(4): 341–368.

Gibler, Douglas M. (2007) 'Bordering on Peace: Democracy, Territorial Issues, and Conflict', *International Studies Quarterly*.

Goertz, G. and Paul Diehl (1992a) 'The Empirical Importance of Enduring Rivalries', *International Interactions* 18(2): 151–163.

Goertz, Gary and Paul F. Diehl (1992b) *Territorial Changes and International Conflict*. London: Routledge.

Goff, Patricia M. (2000) 'Invisible Borders: Economic Liberalization and National Identity', *International Studies Quarterly* 44(4): 533–562.

Henehan, Marie T. and John A. Vasquez (2006) 'The Changing Probability of War, 1816–1992', in Raimo Vayrynen (ed.), *The Waning of Major War*. London, Frank Cass. pp. 280–299.

Henrikson, Alan K. (2000) 'Facing across Borders: The Diplomacy of Bon Voisinage', *International Political Science Review* 21(2): 121–147.

Hensel, Paul R. (1994) 'One Thing Leads to Another: Recurrent Militarized Disputes in Latin America, 1816–1986', *Journal of Peace Research* 31(3): 281–98.

Hensel, Paul R. (1996) 'Charting a Course to Conflict: Territorial Issues and Interstate Conflict, 1816–1992', *Conflict Management and Peace Science* 15(1): 43–73.

Hensel, Paul R. (2000) 'Territory: Theory and Evidence on Geography and Conflict', in John A. Vasquez (ed.), *What Do We Know about War?* Lanham: Rowman & Littlefield. pp. 57–84.

Hensel, Paul R. (2001) 'Contentious Issues and World Politics: The Management of Territorial Claims in the Americas, 1816–1992', *International Studies Quarterly* 45(1): 81–109.

Hensel, Paul R. (2006) 'Territorial Claims and Armed Conflict between Neighbors', paper presented to the Lineae Terrarum International Borders Conference, El Paso, TX.

Huth, Paul (1996) *Standing Your Ground: Territorial Disputes and International Conflict*. Ann Arbor: University of Michigan Press.

Huth, Paul K. and Todd L. Allee (2002) *The Democratic Peace and Territorial Conflict in the Twentieth Century*. Cambridge: Cambridge University Press.

James, Patrick, Johann Park, and Seung-Whan Choi. (2006) 'Democracy and Conflict Management: Territorial Claims in the Western Hemisphere Revisited', *International Studies Quarterly* 50(4): 803–818.

Jones, Daniel, Stuart Bremer, and J. David Singer (1996) 'Militarized Interstate Disputes, 1816–1992: Rationale, Coding Rules, and Empirical Patterns', *Conflict Management and Peace Science* 15(2): 163–213.

Kacowicz, Arie M. (1994) *Peaceful Territorial Change*. Columbia, SC: University of South Carolina Press.

Kelman, Herbert (1982) 'Creating Conditions for Israeli-Palestinian Negotiations', *Journal of Conflict Resolution* 26(1): 39–75.

Kingdon, John W. (1995) *Agendas, Alternatives and Public Policies*. New York: Harper Collins.

Kocs, Stephen (1995) 'Territorial Disputes and Interstate War, 1945–1987', *Journal of Politics* 57(1): 159–175.

Kriesberg, Louis, Terrell A. Northrup, et al. (1989) *Intractable Conflicts and Their Transformation*. Syracuse: Syracuse University Press.

Lamborn, Alan C. and Stephen P. Mumme (1988) *Statecraft, Domestic Politics, and Foreign Policy Making: The El Chamizal Dispute*. Boulder: Westview Press.

Levy, Jack S. (1981) 'Alliance Formation and War Behavior: An Analysis of the Great Powers, 1495–1975', *Journal of Conflict Resolution* 25(4): 581–613.

Luard, Evan. (1986) *War in International Security*. New Haven: Yale University Press.

Mansbach, Richard W. and John A. Vasquez (1981) *In Search of Theory: A New Paradigm for Global Politics*. New York: Columbia University Press.

Masters, Rodger D. (1989) *The Nature of Politics*. New Haven: Yale University Press.

Mitchell, Sara McLaughlin and Brandon Prins (1999) 'Beyond Territorial Contiguity: Issues at Stake in Democratic Militarized Interstate Disputes', *International Studies Quarterly* 43(1): 169–183.

Mitrany, David (1943) *A Working Peace System: An Argument for the Functional Development of International Organization*. Chicago: University of Chicago Press.

Montville, Joseph, ed. (1987) *The Arrow and the Olive Branch: A Case for Track Two Diplomacy*. Washington, DC: Foreign Service Institute, US Department of State.

Morgenthau, Hans J. (1960) *Politics among Nations*. 3rd edition. New York: Knopf.

Newman, David (2006) 'The Resilience of Territorial Conflict in an Era of Globalization', in Miles Kahler and Barbara F. Walter (eds.), *Territoriality and Conflict in an Era of Globalization*. Cambridge: Cambridge University Press. pp. 85–110.

Petersen, Karen K., John Vasquez and Yija Wang (2004) 'Disputes and the Probability of War, 1816–1992', *Conflict Management and Peace Science* 21: 85–100.

Pruitt, Dean and Jeffrey Rubin (1986) *Social Conflict: Escalation, Stalemate and Settlement*. New York: Random House.

Rasler, Karen and William Thompson (2006) 'Contested Territory, Strategic Rivalries, and Conflict Escalation', *International Studies Quarterly* 50(1): 145–167.

Rosecrance, Richard N. (1986) *The Rise of the Trading State: Commerce and Conquest in the Modern World*. New York: Basic Books.

Rosen, Stephen P. (2005) *War and Human Nature*. Princeton: Princeton University Press.

Ruggie, John Gerard (1993) 'Territoriality and Beyond: Problematizing Modernity in International Relations', *International Organization* 47(1): 139–174.

Sack, Robert David (1986) *Human Territoriality: Its Theory and History*. Cambridge: Cambridge University Press.

Sahlins, Peter (1989) *Boundaries: The Making of France and Spain in the Pyrenees*. Berkeley: University of California Press.

Senese, Paul D. (1996) 'Geographical Proximity and Issue Salience: Their Effects on the Escalation of Militarized Interstate Conflict', *Conflict Management and Peace Science* 15 (2): 133–161.

Senese, Paul D. (2005) 'Territory, Contiguity, and International Conflict: Assessing a New Joint Explanation', *American Journal of Political Science* 49(4): 769–779.

Senese, Paul D. and John Vasquez (2003) 'A Unified Explanation of Territorial Conflict: Testing the Impact of Sampling Bias', *International Studies Quarterly* 47(3): 275–298.

Senese, Paul D. and John Vasquez (2005) 'Assessing the Steps to War', *British Journal of Political Science* 35(4): 607–633.

Simmons, Annette (1998) *Territorial Games: Understanding and Ending Turf Wars at Work*. New York: AMACOM.

Simmons, Beth A. (1999) 'See You in "Court"? The Appeal to Quasi-Judicial Legal Processes in the Settlement of Territorial Disputes', in Paul F. Diehl (ed.), *A Road Map to War: Territorial Dimensions of International Conflict*. Nashville: Vanderbilt University Press. pp. 205–237.

Simmons, Beth A. (2006) 'Trade and Territorial Conflict in Latin America: International Borders as Institutions', in Miles Kahler and Barbara Walter (eds.), *Territoriality and Conflict in an Era of Globalization*. Cambridge: Cambridge University Press. pp. 251–287.

Somit, Albert (1990) 'Humans, Chips and Bonobos. The Biological Bases of Aggression, War, and Peacemaking', *Journal of Conflict Resolution* 34(3): 553–582.

Thompson, William (2001) 'Identifying Rivals and Rivalries in World Politics', *International Studies Quarterly* 45(4): 557–586.

Tir, Jaroslav (2006) *Redrawing the Map to Promote Peace*. Lanham: Lexington.

Toft, Monica (2003) *The Geography of Ethnic Violence: Identity, Interests, and the Indivisibility of Territory*. Princeton: Princeton University Press.

Valeriano, Brandon (2003) 'Steps to Rivalry: Power Politics and Rivalry Formation', PhD dissertation, Vanderbilt University.

Valeriano, Brandon and John Vasquez (2005) 'Mapping the Spread of War: Classifying Complex Wars', paper presented to the Peace Science Society (International) Annual Meeting, Iowa City, Iowa.

Vasquez, John A. (1993) *The War Puzzle*. Cambridge: Cambridge University Press.

Vasquez, John A. (2001) 'Mapping the Probability of War and Analyzing the Possibility of Peace', *Conflict Management and Peace Science* 18(2): 145–174.

Vasquez, John and Marie T. Henehan (2001) 'Territorial Disputes and the Probability of War, 1816–1992', *Journal of Peace Research* 38(2): 123–138.

Vasquez, John and Christopher S. Leskiw (2001) 'The Origins and War-proneness of International Rivalries', *Annual Review of Political Science* 4: 295–316.

Wallensteen, Peter (1984) 'Universalism vs. Particularism: On the Limits of Major Power Order', *Journal of Peace Research* 21(3): 243–257.

Walter, Barbara F. (2003) 'Explaining the Intractability of Territorial Conflict', *International Studies Review* 5(4): 137–153.

White, George W. (2000) *Nationalism and Territory: Constructing Group Identity in Southeastern Europe.* Lanham: Rowman and Littlefield.

Zartman, I. William (1989) *Ripe for Resolution: Conflict and Intervention in Africa.* New York: Oxford University Press.

Zartman, I. William and J. Lewis Rasmussen (1997) *Peacemaking in International Conflict: Methods and Techniques.* Washington, DC: United States Institute of Peace Press.

Economic and Resource
Causes of Conflicts

Philippe Le Billon

Conflicts have complex causes rooted in history, domestic governance, economic circumstances, and international relations. The resolution of any conflict must therefore attend to its specifics and the context in which a settlement is to be reached. This chapter reviews economic and resource-related causes of conflicts. The end of the Cold War marked a decline in the number of armed conflicts, after a steady rise since the Second World War (Human Security Report, 2005). Prior to the 1990s, the economic agenda for conflict resolution mostly consisted of resolving the inequities of colonialism and ending domestic and internationalized struggles over the spoils of independence. Curtailing foreign financial support by Cold War sponsors and regional powers such as South Africa and Libya was a major challenge left unaddressed by a paralyzed international system. Since the early 1990s, the economic dimensions of conflicts have been rethought. Globalization, transition from socialist regimes, the commercialization of war, and the rise of 'warlordism', 'terrorism' and 'humanitarian interventions' have renewed

economic perspectives on conflicts (Duffield, 1994; Chingono, 1996; Jean and Rufin, 1996; Keen, 1998; Kaldor, 1999; Reno, 1999; Berdal and Malone, 2000).[1] Economically focused responses flourished, such as economic sanction regimes, often with mixed results (Nitzschke and Studdard, 2005). The first section of this chapter discusses major possible economic causes of conflict, such as poverty and inequality. The second examines three perspectives linking resources and conflicts.

ECONOMIC CAUSES OF CONFLICTS

There is a broad consensus that poverty constitutes the leading risk factor for conflicts, especially for civil wars (Flanigan and Fogelman, 1971; Fearon and Laitin, 2003; Collier and Hoeffler, 2004).[2] But whose poverty matters, and why, remain debated. Since the end of the Second World War, most deadly conflicts have been fought in low-income countries, especially in the form of civil wars. Based on conflict statistics between 1946 and 1999, moving from a GDP per capita of $250 to $600 reduces the risk of conflict for a country from 15% to 7% (Humphreys and Varshney, 2003). Above $5000, the risk is reduced to less than 1%. This is not to say that rich countries are not *involved* in conflicts. In fact, France, Great Britain and the USA are among the 'top ten' countries most frequently at war since 1946. Unlike poor countries, however, conflict rarely occurs on their territory. Transnational terrorism provides a major exception to this pattern, but this case seems mostly limited to countries more directly involved in military interventions abroad. Overall, higher levels of economic developments of a country reduce the number of terrorist incidents inside it and its trading partners (Li and Schaub, 2004). In contrast, lower levels of economic development in terrorists' home country, and poverty among terrorists, are not significantly related to terrorism (Kruger and Malečková, 2003; Abadie, 2004; Testas, 2004; Piazza, 2006). At a country level, wealth reduces the likelihood of conflict at home but is no guarantee for peace, especially among major powers with a history of overseas military intervention. This leads to several major questions: how do wealth and poverty relate to conflict? What is the relative importance of income levels, variations in growth rates and income inequalities within and between countries?

Two major complementary paradigms relate wealth or poverty to conflict. The first is that wealth represents the outcome of relations between production and exchange activities over predation and conflict ones (Hirshleifer, 2001). Low-income countries are trapped in poverty because predatory activities overwhelm productive ones. Not only are predatory activities costly for production, but wealth accumulated through predation rarely ends up staying in poor countries. Violent technologies of predation, unequal distribution of productive resources at the interpersonal level, and individual rather than collective modes of protection against predation, also increase the ratio of predation to production and its social costs (Grossman,

1998). Poverty could be interpreted as a coping mechanism to avoid predation and conflict (Colson, 1974). As discussed below, the structure of the economy may aggravate this pattern and lock resource dependent countries into a poverty and conflict trap. The second paradigm is that poverty reflects the absence of institutions capable of promoting the accumulation of wealth through 'controlled' violence. Much of the literature stresses the importance of institutions for economic performances (North, 1991, Acemoglu et al., 2001), most notably institutions protecting private property. If critics recognize in the violence of private property rights a tool of dispossession (Blomley, 2003), others see it as a necessary ingredient of prosperity (Bates, 2001; Bates et al., 2002). What matters, from a conflict perspective, is the capacity of institutions to avoid an *escalation* of violence, one which would qualify violence as 'armed conflict'.[3]

Whose poverty matters is closely related to inequality, itself interpreted as a main cause of rebellion since at least the Enlightenment and revolutions of the late 18th century (Tocqueville, 2000 [1835]). Karl Marx expanded on the impact of inequalities on the rebellion of the industrial working class, which he associated with market crises (Boswell and Dixon, 1993). Dependency theorists, among others, linked modernization and more recently globalization with increased inequalities causing conflicts (Hobsbawm, 1959; Wolfe, 1969; Galtung, 1971; Russell, 1974; Paige, 1975; Muller, 1985). Ted Robert Gurr's concept of relative deprivation linking economic disparities and political violence initiated a systematic analysis of the role of inequality in conflicts (Gurr, 1970). Much of the early qualitative and quantitative studies of inequalities and conflicts supported the relative deprivation arguments (Russett, 1964; Muller and Seligson, 1989; Timberlake and Williams, 1987; Boswell and Dixon, 1990). The limits of these studies were exposed by Lichbach (1989), and later studies using new data sets found no significant cross-national relationship between inequality and war onset

(Fearon and Laitin, 2003; Collier and Hoeffler, 2004).

At the core of the inequality and conflict debate lie definitions of inequalities and their application to individuals or groups. Among economists, Sen (1992) has expanded the realm of inequalities from economic assets to welfare, rights and liberties. Drawing from a major study on the social and economic causes of Complex Humanitarian Emergencies, Frances Stewart (1998: 1) identified horizontal inequalities (between social groups as opposed to vertical inequality between individuals within society) as 'the fundamental source of organized conflict'. Empirical testing supported the 'horizontal inequality' argument in the case of Nepal for conflict intensity (Murshed and Gates, 2005), and for cross-national panels for social polarization and horizontal social inequality, but not inter-individual inequalities and combined ethnic and socio-economic polarization for conflict onset (Østby, 2008). Several studies have also indirectly informed the debate on inequality and conflicts. One is that forced recruitment appears as common practice within many contemporary conflicts, as found in the case of Sierra Leone (Humphreys and Weinstein, 2006), and that inequalities understood in terms of motivation for conflict onset and intensity may be misplaced. Rather, inequalities would be reflected in the likelihood of forced recruitment. Another, deriving from the study of inequalities and crime in Colombia, suggest that criminal activities are mostly conducted by people from households with per capita income below 80% of the mean (Bourguignon et al., 2003). This suggests that inequality among the poorest may matter more than inequality within the upper and middle classes.

Building on his findings linking resource dependence to conflict onset, Collier (2000) later stressed that economic opportunity (rather than greed as a motivational factor) is a major factor in the escalation of violence. His findings were supported by analyses emphasizing the economic benefits derived from conflicts (Keen, 1998), although not in terms of initial funding of rebellions by resources (Ross, 2004a). Beyond the feasibility argument of rebellion, Weinstein (2007) also demonstrated the negative impacts that economic opportunities independent of local population support had on the organization and behaviour of rebel groups.

If poverty is associated with armed conflicts, economic growth should be the solution. At the aggregate level, unprecedented economic growth in the 20th century did not prevent it from being the most deadly in history. There is good evidence, however, to show that growth reduces the risk of conflict, but can indirectly create greater vulnerability to conflict due to negative economic shocks. Major interstate conflicts, such as the Second World War, often took place following protracted economic recessions.[4] Low rates of economic growth are also robustly correlated with civil war onsets (Fearon and Laitin, 2003; Collier and Hoeffler, 2004; Hegre and Sambanis, 2006). The direction of the relationship between growth collapse and conflicts is difficult to determine, however, since they can mutually influence each other. Measures of rainfall variation as an instrumental variable for economic growth in 41 African countries between 1981 and 1999 suggest that growth collapse increases the risk of conflict (Miguel et al., 2004). Findings also suggest that the impact of growth shocks is not mitigated by higher income levels, stronger democracy or higher ethnic diversity.

The mode of economic development, through which growth is achieved, is also important. The liberal peace theory, drawing from Montesquieu (1949 [1759]) and Kant (1939 [1795]), argues that commerce is pacifying and economically interdependent countries would be less likely to go to war (Angell, 1911). The two world wars cast much doubt about this argument (Carr, 1940; Morgenthau, 1948). Most statistical studies have since confirmed that trade reduces the risk of conflict onset (Polachek, 1980; Oneal and Russett, 1999).[5] Yet, the probability of conflict increases when increases in trade unilaterally increase the dependence of the smaller economy in the dyad (Russet and Oneal, 2001).

Furthermore, not all traded goods achieve a similar dampening effect. This effect could work through the different effects of economic trade sectors on poverty and inequality, with agricultural goods promoting higher levels of poverty and inequality than manufactured goods (Gissinger and Gleditsch, 1999). More generally, trade in primary commodities more easily appropriable by force have a weaker dampening effect on conflict risk than most manufactured goods (Dorussen, 2006). If trade reduces inequalities, foreign direct investment (FDI) increases them (Gissinger and Gleditsch, 1999). Critics of the argument that trade between two countries promotes peace also point out that whereas trade ties help to achieve negotiated settlements to conflicts, this does not spare them from being more likely to experience wars (Barbieri, 2002). Whereas those who are heavily trade dependent may be less likely to engage in conflicts, economically strong states in the system are more likely to do so.

Studies of the economic causes of conflicts have reached a consensus that war is more likely in poorer countries, and that the incidence of wars among the poorest countries results from a two-way causality. First, the high costs of conflict increase poverty. This is particularly true if hostilities are taking place on their territory. In the case of interstate wars, poorer countries are more likely to bear the brunt of hostilities than their richer opponent. Since conflicts are often chronic, over time, conflict-affected countries become poorer. Countries spared by conflicts on the contrary should see their income level increase, at least with respect to the conflict factor. Second, poverty weakens the capacity of the state to resolve conflict and curtail an escalation of violence. Poverty alone and in itself, however, does not provide an explanation for conflicts. Poverty is correlated with other factors affecting the likelihood of conflict, such as low levels of education, the absence of a middle class, and weak democracies, factors which have been associated with higher risks of conflict onset. The impacts of inequality and patterns of economic growth are also important to take

into account (Nafziger and Auvinen, 2002). These have been better addressed through clearer definitions, improved methodologies, and broader linkages with other sources of conflicts. The importance of chronic versus transient poverty (Goodhand, 2003), horizontal versus vertical inequalities (Stewart, 1998) and government policies and economic structure are now better understood. No single narrative can reflect the individual circumstances of a conflict, but a general pattern for economic causes of conflicts include poor countries facing growth collapse in the context of group-based inequalities. As discussed in the following section, resources may be prone to set such a context, and to provide means, motivations and rewards for conflicts.

RESOURCES AND CAUSES OF CONFLICTS

Links between resources and conflicts are often popularized through the concept of 'resource war'. Mediatized in the late 1970s as a metaphor describing renewed tensions between the USA and the Soviet Union over the control of fuel and minerals in disputed 'peripheries', such as the Middle East and Southern Africa (Russett, 1981), the term refers to conflicts revolving over the 'pursuit or possession of critical materials' (Klare, 2001, 25). 'Critical' resources have mostly included water and petroleum, but also diamonds, timber or fisheries. Generally referring to interstate conflicts, the term is also applied to describe the struggles of local populations against large-scale resource exploitation projects, and neoliberal reforms in the control of resources and public utilities (Gedicks, 1993; Perreault, 2006).

The term of resource wars often implies an exclusive analytical focus on resources, and asserts a direct link between conflicts and resources. Such narrow engagement overlooks the multidimensionality of conflicts and resources. First, the term 'resource war' reduces conflicts to a single factor, and thereby risks oversimplification, as in the case of 'ethnic war'. Second, it risks missing the political dimensions of resources by focusing on the economic (exchange) or utilitarian (use) value of resources. As such, the term may underplay the influence of resource sectors in the making of places, political systems and social movements involved in conflicts. The mere presence of resources should also not be simply understood for the current or future stakes that they represent. Rather, the influence of a resource in conflicts needs to be understood in historical terms. The significance of oil in contemporary conflicts in Iraq, for example, should be situated within their historical context, such as coercive British colonialism in the early 20th century (Atarodi, 2003). Conflicts over resources are often played in a 'repeated game', with conflicts being waged over the long term and the 'conflict's history being invoked and reworked to make moral claims in the present' (Turner, 2004: 878). Studies of so-called 'resource wars' should thus bring in a detailed historical and geographical contextualization. Given that many of the narratives of 'resource wars' are about future conflicts over 'increasingly scarce resources', studies of (future) resource wars should also engage with the deconstruction of particular geographies of vulnerability, threat and insecurity (Dalby, 2002). This section discusses three perspectives on 'resource wars': geopolitical, political economy and political ecology – including their main arguments and methodologies.

Geopolitical perspectives

Classical geopolitical perspectives have most frequently linked the concept of 'resource war' to interstate conflicts over the supply of 'strategic resources', giving way to a narrow and militaristic notion of 'resource security' (and in particular 'energy security'). Western geopolitical thinking about resources has been dominated by the equation of trade, war and power, at the core of which were overseas resources and maritime navigation, with resources providing some of the means and motives of early European power expansion,

and being the focus of interstate rivalry and strategic denial of access. During the mercantilist period of the 15th century, trade and war became intimately linked to protect or interdict the accumulation of the 'world's riches', mostly in the form of bullion, enabled by progresses in maritime transport and upon which power was perceived to be determined (Lesser, 1989). Since sea power itself rested on access to timber, naval timber supply became a major preoccupation for major European powers from the 17th century onwards; a situation comparable to the case of oil in the 20th century. With growing industrialization and increasing dependence on imported materials during the 19th century, Western powers intensified their control over raw materials, leading to (along with many other factors e.g. political ideologies) an imperialist 'scramble' over much of the rest of the world (Choucri and North, 1974). The significance of imported resources, and most notably oil, during the First and Second World Wars reinforced the idea of resource vulnerability among European powers.

Strategic thinking about resources during the Cold War continued to focus on the vulnerability arising from resource supply dependence and the potential for international conflicts resulting from competition over access to key resources (Westing, 1988). Emphasis was placed on concepts of 'resource security' (through strategic reserves and alliances with producing countries), and a military 'balance of power' between the US and Soviet blocks. The decolonization process, 1956 Suez crisis, 1973 Arab oil embargo, and 1979 Iranian revolution also contributed to an increase in focus of Western strategic concerns (as well as resource businesses) on domestic and regional political stability and alliances (Russett, 1981). Beyond the Cold War, such security of 'resource supply' continues to inform governmental and corporate decisions in the management of several minerals, particularly concerning high-tech and radioactive materials, even if oil stands largely alone in terms of global strategic importance (Anderson and Anderson, 1998).

By the 1970s, broader geopolitical conceptualizations of security had started to incorporate issues such as population growth, environmental degradation and social inequalities in poor countries (Brown, 1977; Ullman, 1983). The ensuing concept of 'environmental security' came about to reflect ideas of global interdependence, illustrated through the debates on global warming, environmental 'limits to growth', and the political instability caused by environmental scarcity in the South. The concept, however, was decried as representing a skewed and controversial 'securitization' of environmental issues, occasionally casting the blame on the poor, calling for 'military' and 'international development' solutions and constructing biased identities and narratives of endangerment (Dalby, 2002).

As further attention was devoted to the internal mechanisms of wars at the end of the Cold War, a view emerged that a new and violent scramble for resources amongst local warlords, regional hegemons and international powers was becoming a major feature of contemporary conflicts (Annan, 1998; Reno, 1999; Klare, 2001). A popular understanding of future 'resource wars' is that a combination of population and economic growth leading to a relentless expansion in the demand for raw materials, expected resource shortages and contested resource ownership might stimulate further armed conflicts (Klare, 2001). Asia's growing mass consumerism and energy demand, for example, are of specific concern for the militarized control of the South China Sea (especially the Spratly Islands), Caspian region, Gulf of Guinea and the Middle East. While the role of oil or diamonds in several civil wars in Africa had already drawn renewed attention to resource-funded conflicts, the US-led invasion of Iraq in 2003 put the concept of 'resource war' at the forefront of global antiwar activism.

Like the Cold War, the 'war on terror' conducted by the Bush junior administration has rearticulated security threats and strategies along corporate interests. In this case, it has aimed at regimes opposing the USA, which are also reluctant to open their oil and gas fields to Western companies (i.e. Iraq, Iran, Venezuela). Akin to the Cold War, interventions have been framed upon the conflation of concepts of freedom and security. Debates on oil and the United States' security agenda have significantly shifted as a result of the '9/11' attacks in the US, however. If on one side, those opposing US military interventionism have argued that the 'war on terror' provided one more convenient cover for a renewed 'imperialist oil grab' in the region; on the other, links between oil and terrorism pointed at problems of authoritarian (and warmongering) governance in several oil-producing countries. As the 'war on terror' became justified as a war of liberation against oil-funded dictatorial regimes, the USA portrayed its foreign policy as shifting from ensuring a free flow of oil from the Middle East to the world market, to delivering 'freedom' to local populations in oil-producing regions through democracy and market reforms (Le Billon and El Khatib, 2004). Nowhere was this geopolitical construct more blatant (and tragically wrong-headed) than in the US-led invasion of Iraq in 2003. This broadens geopolitical explanations of territorial control of Iraq by US military forces for the sake of oil control to a geo-economic war seeking 'to control the global political economy within which the disposition of oil resources will be organized... a war for the fruition of ... US globalism' (Smith 2003, 265).

Critical geopoliticians also point out that the stereotyping of resource exporting countries plays an important role in 'essentializing' places and actors supposedly involved in 'resource wars'. Drawing on simplistic representations of 'resource geography', the regions at war often become caricatured through the concept of resource war, brushing aside issues of scale and the multiplicity of distinct spaces and places. As each particular region becomes caricatured through its dominant resource sector, other aspects of conflict get brushed aside. Narratives of 'blood diamonds' fuelling the war in Sierra Leone during the 1990s, for example, overlooked agrarian issues (Richards, 2005). Geopolitical perspectives also often assert to provide a 'big picture' of the future of international tensions over 'strategic' resources, thereby informing and reflecting dominant geostrategic policies and world-views. Yet, as suggested above, such classical perspectives have often reflected Manichean constructs of places and identities, and biased conceptions of security. Given contemporary geopolitical narratives of 'war on terror', 'clash of civilizations' and 'empire', there remains much need for critical approaches to geopolitical interpretations and forecasting of 'resource wars' (Dalby, 2004).

Political economy perspectives

The second set of perspectives originate from political science and development economics studies, and are based on the assumption that the significance of resources in wars is largely rooted in questions of resource scarcity, abundance or dependence (de Soysa, 2002). Until relatively recently, the orthodoxy was that the likelihood of conflict increases as resources become more scarce (Homer-Dixon, 1999). According to this 'resource scarcity' argument, widening the scope of the (international) security agenda to include environmental breakdown and livelihood resource access could help provide a basis for peace (Myers, 1993; Conca and Dabelko, 2002). Some of this work has received potent critiques for their methodological approach (Gleditsch, 1998), neo-Malthusian assumptions and essentializing character (Peluso and Watts, 2001), and for naturalising an environment-insecurity nexus in the South exonerating (northern-led) modernity and development (Dalby, 2002).

Moving beyond scarcity and finding primary commodity export dependence to constitute 'the strongest single driver of the risk of conflict', Collier (2000, 101) argued that 'the true cause of much civil war is not the loud discourse of grievance but the silent force of greed' (see also de Soysa, 2002). In response to the controversy and broad media coverage surrounding this statement, numerous studies have tested its validity and interpretation. Debates in this regard have focused on the selection of variables (primary commodity exports as a share of Gross Domestic Product, resource production or resource stock per capita), the specificities of the models, the robustness of findings, as well as the validity of quantitative approaches (Cramer, 2002; Marchal and Messiant, 2002; Ross, 2004b; Ron, 2005).

Overall, war onset does not seem to be robustly related to the broad category of 'primary commodities', at least defined in terms of export dependence. By distinguishing between different types of commodities and types of conflicts, however, patterns appear to emerge (Humphreys, 2005; Ross, 2006). Oil wealth seems to increase the likelihood of civil war (Fearon, 2005), especially onshore compared to off-shore oil (Lujala, 2004; Ross, 2006), while 'contraband' goods such as gemstones, drugs and narcotics do not increase the likelihood of conflict onset (with the exception of alluvial diamonds in relation to ethnic conflicts and for the 1990s, Lujala et al., 2005), but prolong conflicts (Fearon, 2004). Agricultural commodity production would increase the risk of conflict (Humphreys 2005), but like timber remains relatively undertested.

To explain potential relations between resources and wars, political economy perspectives have articulated three main arguments about resources: an *institutional weakening effect* increasing vulnerability to conflict; a *motivational effect* increasing the risk of armed conflict and an *opportunity effect* associated with resources financing belligerents (see Table 11.1). The first relates to the idea of 'resource curse', according to which resource wealth results in economic and political underperformance as resource rents distort the economy and states rely on them rather than on broad taxation. Auty (2001; 2004), Ross (2004a,b) and Le Billon (2001; 2005) have focused on economic collapse and political instability associated with the resource curse. Demonstrating the impact of political and economic dependence on resource rents, Verwimp (2003)

Table 11.1 Mechanisms linking resource wealth and armed conflicts[6]

Resource dependence weakening of states and society organization
Weak state mechanism
- Poor taxation/representation (government fiscally autonomous from population).
- Authoritarianism and corruption.
- Weak tax handle (resource sectors hard to tax due to the ease of illegal activities and poor bureaucratic control capacity).

Weak socio-economic linkages
- Low socio-professional diversification, social cohesion and regional integration.

Resource wealth and exploitation motivating armed conflict
Grievance mechanisms
- High income inequality.
- High economic vulnerability to growth collapse.
- Grievances over socio-cultural-environmental 'externalities'.
- Grievances over unfair revenue distribution.

Greedy rebel mechanisms
- 'Economic violence' by domestic groups.
- Greater rewards for state capture.
- Greater rewards for secessionism.

Greedy outsiders' mechanisms
- High (future) profits.
- Strategic leverage on competitors through resource supply control.

Resource revenues financing hostilities
- Higher viability of armed hostilities (resources financing the weaker party, but also covering for war-related budgetary expenditure).

demonstrates how the Habyarimana regime in Rwanda switched from buying political loyalty through coffee revenue redistribution to holding onto power through massive repression following the late 1980s collapse of the international coffee price. Arguing that industrial exploitation provided the state with more secure fiscal revenues than artisanal exploitation, Snyder and Bhavnani (2005) emphasise that the 'tax handle' characterizing the resource sector can contribute to political (in)stability. Jones Luong and Weinthal (2006) have focused on resource ownership and suggested that private ownership appears to reduce the risk of 'resource curse' and hence potentially the incidence of 'resource wars'.

The second argument is that resources motivate rebellion because of high potential gains (resource revenues) and low opportunity costs (prevalent poverty and lack of revenue alternative in many low-income and resource-dependent countries). Most prominently, Collier (2000) argued that impoverished youth fought in the hope of gaining access to resource revenues.

Although the prospect of 'loot' has long been used to recruit and motivate fighters, many contemporary armed groups forcedly recruit fighters, especially among children and youth, questioning the whole motivational aspect. Furthermore, youth (often forcedly) integrated into rebels movements, such as the Revolutionary United Front in Sierra Leone, more frequently reported social justice, including economic equity, than individual rewards as motivational factor, with 'conflict diamonds' themselves inaccessible to foot soldiers and petty rewards provided by the movement on a relatively egalitarian basis (Peters and Richards, 1998). As Weinstein (2007) notes, however, economically motivated leaders appear to take over the control of armed groups over ideological ones in 'resource rich' contexts.

The third argument relates to the escalating, worsening and prolonging effects of resources on armed conflicts, and has received broader empirical support. Access to resource revenues ensures that more arms can be purchased, and conflicts can thus escalate. There is little evidence that resource revenues fund rebellions in their initial phase of escalation, at least in most recent cases of civil war involving financing by resources, but more evidence in terms of conflict prolongation (Ross, 2004a, b). Overall, the influence of resource revenue access on the escalation and prolongation of conflicts depends in large part on which side benefits from such access: if the weaker party benefits, then prolongation and possibly escalation is likely; if the stronger party benefits, a more rapid escalation towards its military victory is more probable. As argued by Keen (1998), however, profitable conflict stalemates are also frequent, whereby access to resource revenues by both parties appear to take precedence over military victory or conflict settlement objectives. Weinstein (2007) also found that resource contexts allowing for the financial autonomy of armed groups from the local population results in worse human rights abuses.

Political ecology perspectives

The third set of perspectives draws from political ecology and geography. It emphasizes contextualization, multidimensional power relations, and a broad characterization of resources and their mode of production, circulation and consumption. Through attention to historical context, identities, power relations and forms of violence, political ecology approaches recognize the chronic and multiscalar character of many resource-related conflicts, beyond narrow definitions of conflict onset, duration and intensity (Dunn, 2001; Le Billon, 2001; Peluso and Watts, 2001; Korf and Funfgeld, 2006). A first contribution of political ecology is a reconceptualization of resource scarcity, abundance and dependence, notably through attention given to uneven resource distribution and commodity production and circulation (Peluso and Watts, 2001). A second is a greater sensitivity to the materiality, commodity characteristics, and spatiality of resources. Locating conflicts and resources more precisely at the subnational level, through spatial analyses using new subnational data and GIS, allows for

a better specification of models used in large N-studies (Buhaug and Lujala, 2005; Buhaug and Rød, 2006). As suggested by a study of land conflict in the Eastern Brazilian Amazon, such analyses have to be complemented by detailed and historically grounded case studies, including at the micro-scale (Simmons, 2004). Broader spatial characteristics of resources, both physical and social, also influence their accessibility by belligerents (Le Billon, 2001), along with other resource characteristics such as legality (e.g. narcotics versus legal cash crops), transportability (e.g. weight/volume ratio) and 'obstructability' (Ross, 2003). The argument is that the characteristics of resource sectors provide a context for political mobilization as well as for the motivations, strategies, capabilities and behaviour of belligerents (Le Billon, 2005). Empirical testing of some of these hypotheses through quantitative studies suggest that long-standing rebellions tend to be associated with more easily accessed resources, such as alluvial or secondary diamonds (Lujala et al., 2005) or 'contraband goods' (Fearon, 2004); and separatist conflicts with nonfuel mineral revenues (Ross, 2006).

A fourth contribution has been recognition of a broader range of violence than geopolitical and political perspectives, and broader connections. Peluso and Watts (2001, 5) call not only for understanding conflicts as 'globally' contextualized by history, power relations and material transformation taking place at a diversity of scales, but also for multiple forms of violence to be acknowledged in relation to resources. Beyond the coercive use of physical force to control or access resources, such studies engage with broader understandings of violence, such as Galtung's (1990) notions of physical, cultural and structural violence, or multiscalar forms of social, economic and political violence (McIlwaine, 1999). Narrower definitions, as noted above, can overlook long histories of single-sided 'repressive' violence by the state, or protracted high levels of 'criminal' violence in the postconflict period (Pearce, 1998). Political ecology perspectives seek to be attentive to the social construction of resources and their connections with violence (Le Billon, 2006). This implies analyses of commodification (i.e. how 'things' become resources or commodities defined by their exchange value), and fetishization (i.e. how imaginative aspects of resource production and consumption affect power relations). Commodity chain analysis and ethnographic accounts have been able to provide more nuanced accounts, and bridge site-specificity and multiscalar interconnections between resources and wars (Nordstrom, 2004). By following resources, connections are made and actors, their motivations and power relations are more easily identified; thereby allowing for some degree of accountability beyond the immediate perpetrators of physical violence. This helps to identify responsibilities, regulatory spaces (and absence thereof), and illicit (i.e. socially unacceptable) and illegal (i.e. legally banned) social practices (van Schendel and Abraham, 2005). Human rights organizations, such as Global Witness, as well as 'expert panels' from the United Nations, have successfully taken this approach to publicly expose resource businesses and politicians implicated in the financing of war crimes. One of the purposes of commodity chain analysis is to bridge or fold scales in order to counter the 'localism' present in many narratives of contemporary armed conflicts. By showing the connections between 'killing fields' and 'shopping malls', commodity chain analysis moves from one scale to the other; broadening understandings of 'local' forms of violence away from the most physically direct consequences capturing the interest of the media, and recasting them within much broader processes of global commodity circulation and consumption.

To sum up, mainstream geopolitical perspectives on resources have clearly put a priority on the resource supply security of wealthy nations, to the point of calling for military invasions abroad or resource autarky at home. There is little doubt that resource supply is a major concern of 'realpolitiks', but geopolitical narratives have often been blinded by seductive (and sometimes dubious) supply and demand statistics, articulated by an oversimplified geographic understanding of power relations and representations of potential 'flash points'. Critical geopolitical perspectives have rightly denounced such narratives, pointing to the vested interests involved and built-in prejudices, and calling for greater contextual sensitivity and nuance towards power relations between firms, communities and authorities.

Studies from political economy perspectives have strived to find general patterns in the conditions and processes linking resources and conflicts, and for methodological rigueur through mostly quantitative studies. The methodological approach taken by these studies has often limited the scope of their historical engagement, the form of violence studied and the possible variables that could factor for the processes hypothezised. These studies have yielded major insights into the significance of resource dependence for conflict risks, and patterns of conflicts relating to particular types of resources and mode of exploitation and regulation. Finally, political ecology perspectives have emphasized contextualisation and multiscalar relations, pointing also to the specific material and social dimensions of resources. Most political studies have continued a fruitful tradition of fine-grained and historically grounded analysis of largely individual case studies with a focus on nuanced analyses of power relations. Significant findings have been gained on the importance of the historical, institutional and material context of 'resource wars'. Certain resources have been found to increase vulnerability to certain types of conflict or to prolong conflicts. Bridging and renewing conceptual and methodological approaches drawn from these three perspectives could yield yet further insights on the economic and resource causes of conflicts.

CONCLUSION

Reviewing economic and resource causes of conflict is at risk of being conceptually 'reductionist', especially so when considering the importance of politics and identity in the causes of conflict (Arnson and Zartman, 2005). A narrow understanding of economic and resource dimensions, focused on econometric indicators or the exchange or use value of resources and their physical location, is likely to obscure important factors and underlying causes. Based on most of the available literature, poverty alleviation is an essential ingredient in reducing conflicts. Doing so in a way that addresses group-based inequalities is also important, even if debates about linkages with conflicts remain debated. A strong growth rate thus appears as one of the best avenues to avoid conflicts, especially with respect to the long-term security of the poorest countries. This is where attention should be mostly devoted.

Economic growth can nevertheless prove a double-edged sword, especially when pursued through resource exploitation that often provides one of the main export-driven growth options for poor countries. The ways through which growth is achieved may be as important as growth per se, at least if broad definitions of conflict and violence are applied. Furthermore, growth effective in terms of conflict preventions should not be prone to collapse. High inequalities and negative shocks present major risks, and particularly so if they are articulated along pre-existing social fault lines. This has important implications as a large proportion of the world has been experiencing high growth rates since the latter part of the 20th century, most notably in Asia. Sharp economic recessions and a backlash against economic globalization represent in this regard major challenges to peace and security. As discussed above, this finding is also relevant for resource dependent economies, which are particularly prone to growth collapse. Overall, the major policy implications of the current literature are that economic development efforts should focus on the poorest countries; income equalization schemes contribute to peace and reduce violence, especially if targeting the most economically disenfranchised groups; and precautionary principles should apply

to growth policies to reduce the risk of negative shocks, especially in the resource sectors.

NOTES

1 For a review of the literature on the political economy of war for that period, see Le Billon, 2000; Humphreys, 2002.

2 The leading political argument of 'democratic peace', for example, does not stand to the test of poverty: democracy does not shield poor countries from the scourge of war (Mousseau et al., 2001).

3 The main definition of armed conflicts used in quantitative studies is 'a contested incompatibility that concerns government and/or territory where the use of armed force between two parties, of which at least one is the government of a state, results in at least 25 battle-related deaths' (UCDP/PRIO, 2006). A higher threshold of 1000 battle-related deaths is also used. A human rights or human security perspective would assert that conflicts and violence at the micro-scale is also significant.

4 The global growth collapse of the 1930s was largely defined by inadequate monetary policies, free trade restrictions, and capital repatriation (Crafts, 2000). Its impact was aggravated by the historical context set by the First World War. Arguments that war onset by major powers is precipitated by brief economic downturn, however, have been rejected by Thompson (1982).

5 Early quantitative studies of wars found no evidence that commerce creates bonds pacifying nations, but observed that sharp declines in trade set the economic context of the Second World War (Richardson, 1960a, b).

6 Adapted from (Humphreys, 2005).

REFERENCES

Abadie, A. (2004) Poverty, Political Freedom, and the Roots of Terrorism. NBER Working Paper No. W10859.

Acemoglu, D., J.A. Robinson and S. Johnson (2001) 'The colonial origins of comparative development: An empirical investigation', *American Economic Review*, 91: 1369–1401.

Anderson, E.W. and L.D. Anderson (1998) *Strategic Minerals: Resource Geopolitics and Global Geo-economics*. Chichester: Wiley.

Angell, N. (1911) *The Great Illusion: A Study of the Relation of Military Power in Nations to Their Economic and Social Advantage*. Toronto: McClelland and Goodchild.

Annan, K. (1998) *The Causes of Conflict and the Promotion of Durable Peace and Sustainable Development in Africa*. New York: United Nations.

Arnson, C.J. and I.W. Zartman (eds) (2005) *Rethinking the Economics of War: The Intersection of Need, Creed, and Greed*. Baltimore, MD: John Hopkins University Press.

Atarodi, H. (2003) *Great Powers, Oil and the Kurds in Mosul: Southern Kurdistan/Northern Iraq, 1910–1925*. Lanham, MD: University Press of America.

Auty, R.M. (ed.) (2001) *Resource Abundance and Economic Development*. Oxford: Oxford University Press.

Auty, R.M. (2004) 'Natural resources and civil strife: A two-stage process', *Geopolitics*, 9(1): 29–49.

Barbieri, K. (2002) *The Liberal Illusion. Does Trade Promote Peace?* University of Michigan Press.

Bates, R.H. (2001) *Prosperity and Violence. The Political Economy of Development*. New York: Norton.

Bates, R.H., A. Greif and S. Singh (2002) 'Organizing violence', *Journal of Conflict Resolution*, 46(5): 599–628.

Berdal, M. and D. Malone (eds) (2000) *Greed and Grievance: Economic Agendas in Civil Wars*. Boulder and London: Lynne Rienner.

Blomley, N. (2003) 'Law, property, and the geography of violence: The frontier, the survey, and the grid', *Annals of the Association of American Geographers*, 93(1): 121–141.

Boswell, T. and W.J. Dixon (1990) 'Dependency and rebellion: A cross-national analysis', *American Sociological Review*, 55(4): 540–559.

Boswell, T. and W.J. Dixon (1993) 'Marx's theory of rebellion: A cross–national analysis of class exploitation, economic development, and violent revolt', *American Sociological Review*, 58(5): 681–702.

Bourguignon, F., F. Sanchez and J. Nuñez (2003) 'A structural model of crime and inequality in Colombia', *Journal of the European Economic Association*, 1(2–3): 440–449.

Brown, L.R. (1977) *Redefining National Security*. Washington, DC: Worldwatch Institute.

Buhaug, H. and P. Lujala (2005) 'Accounting for scale: Measuring geography in quantitative studies of civil war', *Political Geography*, 24: 399–418.

Buhaug, H. and J.K. Rød (2006) 'Local determinants of African civil wars, 1970–2001', *Political Geography*, 25: 315–335.

Carr, E.H. (1940) *The Twenty Years' Crisis, 1919–1939: An Introduction to the Study of International Relations*. London: Macmillan.

Chingono, M. (1996) *The State, Violence and Development: The Political Economy of War in Mozambique 1975–1992*. Aldershot: Avebury.

Choucri, N. and R.C. North (1974) *Nations in Conflict: National Growth and International Violence*. San Francisco, CA: Freeman.

Collier, P. (2000) 'Doing well out of war: An economic perspective'. In M. Berdal and D. Malone (eds) *Greed and Grievance: Economic Agendas in Civil War*. Boulder, CO: Lynne Rienner.

Collier, P. and A. Hoeffler (2004) 'Greed and grievance in civil war', *Oxford Economic Papers*, 56(4): 563–595.

Colson, E. (1974) *Tradition and Contract: The Problem of Order*. Chicago, IL: Aldone.

Conca, K. and G. Dabelko (eds) (2002) *Environmental Peacemaking*. Baltimore and Washington, DC: The Woodrow Wilson Center Press and Johns Hopkins University Press.

Crafts, N. (2000) Globalization and Growth in the Twentieth Century. IMF Working Paper 00/44, March. Washington, DC: International Monetary Fund.

Cramer, C. (2002) 'Homo Economicus goes to war: Methodological individualism, rational choice, and the political economy of war', *World Development*, 30: 1845–64.

Dalby, S. (2002) *Environmental Security*. Chicago, IL: University of Minnesota Press.

Dalby, S. (2004) 'Ecological politics, violence, and the theme of Empire', *Global Environmental Politics*, 4(2): 1–11.

de Soysa, I. (2002) 'Ecoviolence: Shrinking pie or honey pot?', *Global Environmental Politics*, 2(4): 1–36.

Dodds, K. (2003) 'Licensed to stereotype: Popular geopolitics, James Bond and the spectre of Balkanism', *Geopolitics*, 8: 125–156.

Dorussen, H. (2006) 'Heterogeneous trade interests and conflict', *Journal of Conflict Resolution*, 50(1): 87–107.

Duffield, M. (1994) 'The political economy of internal war: Asset transfer, complex emergencies and international aid'. In J. Macrae and A. Zwi (eds) *War and Hunger: Rethinking International Responses to Complex Emergencies* (pp. 50–69). London: Zed Books.

Dunn, K. (2001) 'Identity, space and the political economy of conflict in Central Africa', *Geopolitics*, 6(2): 51–78.

Fearon, J.D. (2004) 'Why do some civil wars last so much longer than others?', *Journal of Peace Research*, 41: 275–303.

Fearon, J.D. (2005) 'Primary commodity exports and civil war', *Journal of Conflict Resolution*, 49(4): 483–507.

Fearon, J. and D. Laitin (2003) 'Ethnicity, insurgency, and civil war', *American Political Science Review*, 88(3): 577–592.

Flanigan, W.H. and E. Fogelman (1971) 'Patterns of political science in comparative historical perspective', *Comparative Politics*, 3(1): 1–20.

Galtung, J. (1971) 'A structural theory of imperialism', *Journal of Peace Research*, 8(2): 81–117.

Galtung, J. (1990) 'Cultural violence', *Journal of Peace Research*, 27(3): 291–305.

Gedicks, A. (1993) *The New Resource Wars. Native and Environmental Struggles Against Multinational Corporations*. Cambridge: South End Press.

Gissinger, R. and N.P. Gleditsch (1999) 'Globalization and conflict: Welfare distribution, and political unrest', *Journal of World-Systems Research*, 5(2): 327–365.

Gleditsch, N.P. (1998) 'Armed conflict and the environment: A critique of the literature', *Journal of Peace Research*, 35(3): 381–400.

Goodhand, J. (2003) 'Enduring disorder and persistent poverty: A review of the linkages between war and chronic poverty', *World Development*, 31(3): 629–646.

Grossman, H.I. (1998) 'Producers and predators', *Pacific Economic Review*, 3(3): 169–187.

Gurr, T.R. (1970) *Why Men Rebel*. Princeton, NJ: Princeton University Press.

Hegre, H. and N. Sambanis (2006) 'Sensitivity analysis of empirical results on civil war onset', *Journal of Conflict Resolution*, 50(4): 508–535.

Hirshleifer, J. (2001) *The Dark Side of the Force: Economic Foundations of Conflict Theory*. Cambridge: Cambridge University Press.

Hobsbawm, E.J. (1959) *Primitive Rebels*. New York: Norton.

Hoeffler, A. and P. Collier (2006) 'The political economy of secession'. In H. Hannum and E.F. Babbitt (eds) *Negotiating Self-Determination*. Lanham, MD: Lexington Books.

Homer-Dixon, T.F. (1999) *Environment, Scarcity and Violence*. Princeton, NJ: Princeton University Press.

Human Security Report (2005). *War and Peace in the 21st Century*. Oxford: Oxford University Press.

Humphreys, M. (2002) Economics and Violent Conflict. Harvard University. (www.idrc.ca/uploads/user-S/10588054981Humphreys_Essay.pdf, accessed on 3 September 2007).

Humphreys, M. (2005) 'Natural resources, conflict, and conflict resolution: Uncovering the mechanisms', *Journal of Conflict Resolution*, 49(4): 508–537.

Humphreys, M. and Varshney (2003) Violent Conflict and the Millennium Development Goals: Diagnosis and Recommendations. Prepared for the meeting of the Millennium Development Goals Poverty Task Force Workshop, Bangkok, June 2004.

At www.columbia.edu/~mh2245/papers1/HV.pdf (accessed 29 August 2007).

Humphreys, M. and J.M. Weinstein (2006) 'Handling and manhandling civilians in civil war', *American Political Science Review*, 100(3): 429–447.

Jean, F. and J.-C. Rufin (eds) (1996) *Economie des Guerres Civiles*. Paris: Hachette.

Jones Luong, P. and E. Weinthal (2006) 'Rethinking the resource curse: Ownership structure, institutional capacity, and domestic constraints', *Annual Review of Political Science*, 9(1): 241–263.

Kaldor, M. (1999) *New and Old Wars: Organized Violence in a Global Era*. Cambridge: Polity Press.

Kant, I. (1939 [1795]) *Perpetual Peace*. New York: Columbia University Press.

Keen, D. (1998) *Economic Functions of Violence in Civil Wars*. Adelphi Paper 320. Oxford: Oxford University Press.

Klare, M.T. (2001) *Resource Wars: The Changing Landscape of Global Conflict*. New York: Henry Holt.

Korf, B. and H. Funfgeld (2006) 'War and the commons: Assessing the changing politics of violence, access and entitlements in Sri Lanka', *Political Geography*, 37: 391–403.

Kruger, A.B. and J. Malečková (2003) 'Education, poverty, and terrorism: Is there a causal connection?', *Journal of Economic Perspectives*, 17(4): 119–44.

Le Billon, P. (2000) The Political Economy of War: An Annotated Bibliography. London: HPG report 1. Overseas Development Institute.

Le Billon, P. (2001) 'The political ecology of war: natural resources and armed conflicts', *Political Geography*, 20(5): 561–584.

Le Billon, P. (2005) *Fuelling War: Natural Resources and Armed Conflicts*. Adelphi Paper 373. London: Routledge.

Le Billon, P. (2006) 'Fatal transactions: Conflict diamonds and the (anti)terrorist consumer', *Antipode*, 38(6): 778–801.

Le Billon, P. and F. El Khatib (2004). 'From free oil to 'freedom oil': Terrorism, war and US geopolitics in the Persian Gulf', *Geopolitics*, 9(1): 109–137.

Lesser, I.O. (1989) *Resources and Strategy*. Basingstoke: Macmillan.

Li, Q. and D. Schaub (2004) 'Economic globalization and transnational terrorist incidents: A pooled time series analysis', *Journal of Conflict Resolution*, 48(2): 230–258.

Lichbach, M.I. (1989) 'An evaluation of "does inequality breed political conflict?" studies', *World Politics*, 41: 431–470.

Lujala, P. (2004) *The Spoils of Nature: Oil, Diamonds, and Civil War*. Norwegian University of Science and Technology, unpublished manuscript.

Lujala, P., N.P. Gleditsch and E. Gilmore (2005) 'A diamond curse?: Civil war and a lootable resource', *Journal of Conflict Resolution*, 49: 538–62.

Marchal, R. and C. Messiant (2002) 'De l'avidité des rebelles. L'analyse économique de la guerre civile selon Paul Collier', *Critique Internationale* , 16 : 58–69.

McIlwaine, C. (1999) 'Geography and development: Violence and crime as development issues', *Progress in Human Geography*, 23(3): 453–464.

Miguel, E., S. Satyanath and E. Sergenti (2004) 'Economic shocks and civil conflict: An instrumental variables approach', *Journal of Political Economy*, 112: 725–753.

Montesquieu, Charles de (1949 [1759]) *The Spirit of Laws*. New York: Haffner.

Morgenthau, H. (1948) *Politics Among Nations: The Struggle for Power and Peace*. New York: Knopf.

Mousseau, M., H. Hegre and J.R. ONeal (2001) 'How the Wealth of Nations Conditions the Liberal Peace', *European Journal of International Relations*, 9(2): 277–314.

Muller, E.N. (1985). 'Income inequality, regime repressiveness, and political violence', *American Sociological Review*, 50(1): 47–61.

Muller, E.N. and M.A. Seligson (1987) 'Inequality and insurgency', *American Political Science Review*, 82(2): 425–451.

Murshed, M. S. and S. Gates (2005) 'Spatial-horizontal inequality and the Maoist insurgency in Nepal', *Review of Development Economics*, 9(1): 121–134.

Myers, N. (1993) *Ultimate Security: The Environmental Basis of Political Stability*. New York: W.W. Norton.

Nafziger, E.W. and J. Auvinen (2002) 'Economic development, inequality, war, and state violence', *World Development*, 30(2): 153–163.

Nitzschke, H. and K. Studdard, K. (2005) 'The legacies of war economies: Challenges and options for peacemaking and peacebuilding', *International Peacekeeping*, 12(2): 222 – 239.

Nordstrom, C. (2004) *Shadows of War: Violence, Power, and International Profiteering in the 21st Century*. Berkeley, CA: University of California Press.

North, D.C. (1991) 'Institutions', *Journal of Economic Perspectives*, 5(1): 97–112.

Oneal, J.R. and B. Russet (1999) 'Assessing the liberal peace with alternative specifications: Trade still reduces conflict', *Journal of Peace Research*, 36(4): 423–32.

Østby, G. (2008) 'Polarization, horizontal inequalities and violent civil conflict', *Journal of Peace Research*, 45(2): 143–162.

Paige, J.M. (1975) *Agrarian Revolution*. New York: Free Press.

Pearce, J. (1998) 'From civil war to civil society: Has the end of the Cold War brought peace to Central America?', *International Affairs*, 74: 587–615.

Peluso, N.L. and Watts, M. (2001) *Violent Environments*. Ithaca, NY: Cornell University Press.

Perreault, T. (2006) 'From the Guerra del Agua to the Guerra del Gas: Resource governance, popular protest and social justice in Bolivia', *Antipode*, 38(1): 150–172.

Peters, K. and P. Richards (1998) '"Why we fight": Voices of youth combatants in Sierra Leone', *Africa*, 68(2): 183–210.

Piazza, J.A. (2006) 'Rooted in poverty?: Terrorism, poor economic development, and social cleavages', *Terrorism and Political Violence*, 18(1): 159–77.

Polachek, S.W. (1980) 'Conflict and trade', *Journal of Conflict Resolution*, 24(1): 55–78.

Reno, W. (1999) *Warlord Politics and African States*. Boulder, CO: Lynne Rienner.

Richards, P. (2005) 'To fight or to farm? Agrarian dimensions of the Mano River conflicts (Liberia and Sierra Leone)', *African Affairs*, 104: 517–590.

Richardson, L.W. (1960a) *Arms and Insecurity: A Mathematical Study of the Causes and Origins of War*. Edited by Rashevsky, N. and E. Trucco. Pittsburgh, PA: Boxwood Press.

Richardson, L.W. (1960b) *Statistics of Deadly Quarrels, 1809–1949*. Edited by Wright, Q. and C.C. Lienau. Pittsburgh, PA: Boxwood Press.

Ron, J. (2005) 'Paradigm in distress? Primary commodities and civil war', *Journal of Conflict Resolution*, 49(4): 443–450.

Ross, M.L. (2003) 'Oil, drugs, and diamonds: The varying roles of natural resources in civil war'. In K. Ballentine and J. Sherman (eds) *The Political Economy of Armed Conflict: Beyond Greed and Grievances* (pp. 47–70). Boulder, CO: Lynne Rienner.

Ross, M.L. (2004a) 'How does natural resource wealth influence civil war? Evidence from 13 Cases', *International Organization*, 58(1): 35–67.

Ross, M.L. (2004b) 'What do we know about natural resources and civil wars?', *Journal of Peace Research*, 41(3): 337–356.

Ross, M.L. (2006) 'A closer look at oil, diamonds, and civil war', *Annual Review of Political Science*, 9: 265–300.

Russell, D.E.H. (1974) *Rebellion, Revolution, and Armed Force: A Comparative Study of Fifteen Countries with Special Emphasis on Cuba and South Africa*. New York: Academic Press.

Russett, B.M. (1964) 'Inequality and instability: The relation of land tenure to politics', *World Politics*, 16(3): 442–454.

Russett, B.M. (1981) 'Security and the resources scramble: Will 1984 be like 1914?', *International Affairs*, 58(1): 42–58.

Russett, B.M. and J.R. Oneal (2001) *Triangulating Peace: Democracy, Interdependence, and International Organization*. New York: Norton.

Sen, A. (1992) *Inequality Reexamined*. New York: Clarendon.

Simmons, C.S. (2004) 'The political economy of land conflict in the Eastern Brazilian Amazon', *Annals of the Association of American Geographers*, 94(1): 183–206.

Smith, N. (2003) *The Endgame of Globalization*. London: Routledge.

Snyder, R. and R. Bhavnani (2005) 'Diamonds, blood, and taxes. A revenue-centred framework for explaining political order', *Journal of Conflict Resolution*, 49(4): 563–597.

Stewart, F. (1998) The Root Causes of Conflict: Some Conclusions. Working Paper Number 16. Oxford: Queen Elizabeth House. (www3.qeh.ox.ac.uk/RePEc/qeh/qehwps/qehwps16.pdf, accessed on 4 September 2007)

Testas, A. (2004) 'Determinants of terrorism in the Muslim world: An empirical cross-sectional analysis', *Terrorism and Political Violence*, 16(2): 253–273.

Thompson, W.R. (1982) 'Phases of business cycle and the outbreak of war', *International Studies Quarterly*, 26(2): 301–311.

Timberlake, M. and K.R. Williams (1987) 'Structural position in the world system, inequality, and political instability', *Journal of Political and Military Sociology*, 15(1): 1–15.

Tocqueville, A. de (2000 [1835]) *Democracy in America*. Chicago: Chicago University Press.

Turner, M.D. (2004) 'Political ecology and the moral dimensions of "resource conflict": The case of farmer-herder conflicts in the Sahel', *Political Geography*, 23: 863–889.

UCDP/PRIO (2006) Armed Conflict Dataset Codebook. At www.prio.no/cwp/armedconflict/current/Codebook_v4–2006b.pdf (accessed 29 August 2007).

Ullman, R.H. (1983) 'Redefining security', *International Security*, 8(1): 129–153.

Van Schendel, W. and I. Abraham (2005) *Illicit Flows and Criminal Things: States, Borders, and the Other Side of Globalization*. Bloomington, IN: Indiana University Press.

Verwimp, P. (2003) 'The political economy of coffee, dictatorship, and genocide', *European Journal of Political Economy*, 19(2): 161–181.

Weinstein, J. (2007) *Inside Rebellion: The Politics of Insurgent Violence*. Cambridge: Cambridge University Press.

Westing, A. (ed.) (1988) *Global Resources and International Conflict: Environmental Factors in Strategy Policy and Action*. Oxford: Oxford University Press.

Wolfe, E.R. (1969) *Peasant Wars of the Twentieth Century*. New York: Harper and Row.

12

Resolving Ecological Conflicts: Typical and Special Circumstances

Gunnar Sjöstedt

Environmental issues are of mounting importance in international politics. The present worldwide great concern with climate warming is a stark manifestation of this development. Ultimately coping with environmental problems is a struggle against nature. Successful abatement requires some sort of intervention in an ecological system. In order to, say, slow down or eliminate climate warming, stop the depletion of the ozone layer in the atmosphere, or avoid damage of groundwater resources, instrumental technology has to be developed and applied. If policy makers do not have access to the necessary technical means to struggle with nature successfully, their political intentions and declarations to stop environmental degradation are futile.

However, ecological conflict may also represent a struggle of man against man. Environmental problems are to a large extent anthropogenic. They are created by important human activities like industrial production, agriculture, mining, transportation or the heating of buildings. Ecological damage in one country is often caused by activities and emissions in another country. For example, "acid rain" in Scandinavia has to a high degree been the result of emissions of sulphur in, for example, Poland and Britain. Environmental issues typically contain an important distributive element pertaining to both positive and negative values. Pollution is a negative side effect when positive economic and social values are produced. In many cases, environmental issues contain the seed of conflict. The main question addressed in this chapter is whether governments and other international actors perform in a special way when they participate in the resolution of ecological conflicts. Does ecological conflict resolution have any typical and special features differing from conflicts in other issue areas?

This chapter proposes that the resolution of ecological clashes tends to have a distinctive character because environmental issues have special features conditioning how international actors perform in a conflict. The principal aim is to assess what the conditioning factors of ecological conflicts are (Sjöstedt, 1993). The ultimate objective is to clarify how special properties of environmental issues and ecological conflicts affect conflict resolution. Issue characteristics do not only have an impact on the motivation and preferences of conflicting parties. Other issue features than perceived values may also influence how conflicting parties perform and interact in international negotiation or other forms of conflict resolution. In some cases, the difficulty of simply understanding an environmental issue may call for the participation of scientists in the process. This development gives a somewhat different character to the process of conflict resolution than traditional diplomatic interaction (Kjellén, 2007). For example, the construction of consensual knowledge becomes more important in an inter-scientist dialogue.

Negotiation on environmental issues has a number of typical or special properties that have been highlighted in the literature. One example is the tendency of environmental issues to attract the attention of NGOs and other transnational actors as well as the public opinion (Susskind et al., 2002). The approach of this chapter is to analyze and assess how such general characteristics of environmental issues may, firstly, color ecological conflicts and, secondly, constrain the performance of international actors in this type of context. The ultimate question addressed here is whether environmental issues have characteristics constraining how nations choose to *fight* or *talk* in an ecological conflict.

CHARACTERIZATION OF ENVIRONMENTAL ISSUES

An *international ecological conflict* is at hand when actors representing at least two different nations have diverging positions on an environmental issue and at least one of them also takes action to protect or promote its

interests in that connection. A conflict between two or more countries does not exist in the absence of conflict performance even if, say, a scholarly analysis convincingly demonstrates that the parties involved have opposing interests regarding an international environmental issue. Actions manifesting conflict may be of many different kinds ranging from a military operation to the submission of a scientific argument in an international institution such as the Inter-Governmental Panel on Climate Change (IPCC).

The negative consequences of an *environmental issue* are often highlighted because they include the distribution, or redistribution, of scarce and vital natural resources. For example, many analysts have pointed to Israel's shortage of water as a fundamental factor in the Israel-Syria peace negotiations. Twenty-five percent of Israel's water supply depends on access to the Golan Heights. This predicament helps explain why Israel, since its 1967 occupation of the Golan Heights, has claimed this territory as its own (New York Sun, 2007).

According to a UN Environmental Program report, ecological degradation and desertification influence conflict in Darfur. The Sudanese government's manipulation and appropriation of such scarce resources as land, water, and especially oil exacerbate conflict-inciting tensions. For example, in eastern Sudan, Khartoum diverted limited water from grazing land to commercial irrigation, leading to fighting in the region (New York Times, 2007).

Entirely natural phenomena like an eruption of a volcano may have disastrous consequences for the environment and the people living around it, such as the destruction of buildings and cultivated land. However, often, an environmental problem is caused, or significantly influenced, by human activities like, say, the generation and disposal of hazardous waste, transportation of goods and people, agriculture, or war. For example, freons and halons are released from human activities, rise to the stratosphere and destroy the ozone layer, filtering ultraviolet radiation from the sun which, in turn, causes skin cancer and other undesirable effects (Benedick, 1990). In order to cope with such anthropogenic effects, states and other types of actors need to influence each other to reduce hazardous emissions sufficiently. This interdependence may generate agreement and joint action but may also lead to conflict.

In this chapter, no *a priori* distinction is made between *dispute* and *conflict*. The understanding of what a conflict represents is held very open within the constraints of the wide conflict definition used here. In a particular situation, the stakes of an ecological conflict may be relatively small but in some cases they may also be of extreme magnitude. Conflict intensity may be low, moderate, or very high. Conflicting parties may in some cases be satisfied to use normal and not particularly costly policy measures to have their way, but in other ecological conflicts, they may conceivably be willing to take substantial risks and mobilize huge resources for this purpose. Hence, it is a purely empirical question as to how intensive an ecological conflict may become and what instruments and power resources conflicting parties will rely on in order to try to have their way.

In several respects, ecological conflicts may have a great variation. The number of conflicting parties may differ dramatically with important consequences for conflict resolution. The differences between Denmark and Sweden concerning the Swedish nuclear power plant at Barsebäck are an example of an ecological conflict with minimum scope: a bilateral situation (Löfstedt, 1998). In contrast, the negotiation on climate change has a global scope with thousands of participants of different types; governments, non-governmental organizations, scientists, and business organizations, performing different roles. Between these two extremes, many cases of ecological conflict involve few, several or many parties in a pluri-lateral situation like a negotiation between littoral states on an environmental protocol in a river convention (Thompson, 2006).

Ecological conflicts: A basic typology

It is frequently hard to delimit an ecological conflict because its environmental issue component is linked to other issues. Desertification is allegedly associated with a number of severe and violent conflicts in the Third World. One may, however, argue that desertification as such, the geographical expansion of a desert, does not cause conflict among nations but that the effects of such a development may generate discord between individuals, tribes or nations. One contingency is that people are forced to leave their homes because their farmland or grazing areas are overrun by an expanding desert. Flows of refugees crossing national borders ultimately following from desertification may cause disturbances and sometimes inter-governmental conflict. Pollution in a river may be perceived by people because it is indicated by the color or the unpleasant odor of the water. These immediate manifestations of pollution in an inland waterway or lake are not likely to cause serious international conflict but diminished fresh water resources due to the deterioration of water quality may have such an effect.

Environmental damage is typically linked to loss of natural resources of such economic and social importance that it is prone to generate conflict amongst stakeholders. Consequently, numerous authors do not distinguish between ecological and resource conflicts. In their view, international ecological conflicts occur because they have distributional effects on the supply of scarce natural resources.

The degree to which the environmental component of an ecological conflict is linked to other contentious issues is important to note. From this point of view, it is meaningful to distinguish between three types of ecological conflict: *"pure" ecological conflicts, embedded ecological conflicts,* and *embracing ecological conflicts.*

"Pure" ecological conflicts are dominated by one particular environmental issue. Other issues may be involved but have a limited significance. An environmental issue in a

"pure" ecological conflict tends to represent *risk* rather than *crisis*. Policy makers and other actors (e.g. diplomats) engaged in international conflict resolution activities do not have to address various associated acute problems like, for example, ethnic or religious confrontations, economic distribution issues or the effects of uncontrolled migration flows.

One example of a pure risk-driven environmental conflict is the dispute between Austria and the Czech Republic regarding the Czech nuclear power plant at Temelin not far from the Austrian border. The essence of this conflict is straightforward. Austria wants to have the Temelin nuclear plant closed down in order to avoid the risk of a nuclear accident, whereas the Czech Republic needs its production of electric power for both welfare and security reasons.

The stand of the Austrian government on the Temelin power plant was fully consistent with the general nuclear energy policy that had been developed in Austria in the 1970s. A 1978 referendum rejected the start of operation of a newly constructed nuclear power plant at Zwentendorf. As a result, the Austrian Parliament prohibited the use of nuclear energy in the country. The anti-nuclear opinion in Austria was further reinforced by the Chernobyl disaster in 1986 and soon also targeted the Soviet type nuclear reactors under construction at Temelin in the Czech Republic only 100 kilometers from the Austrian border. The Czech government rejected the Austrian demand that the Temelin reactors should be closed and simply refused to engage themselves in formal negotiations on this topic.

However, in reality, the Czech government agreed to participate in an informal dialogue with the Austrians that was carried out at a medium political level with an important participation of technical experts. The logic of these consultations became a stepwise Czech acceptance of Austrian requirements for specific technical modifications of the Temelin reactors. Scientific and technical knowledge were hence of principal instruments in the Austrian–Czech diplomatic exchanges that were increasingly constrained by public opinion in Austria.

The Temelin case exhibits important properties of environmental issues representing a pure ecological conflict that are negotiated in the United Nations and other international institutions. In one sense, these "pure" environmental conflicts are not exceptional cases. The 1972 UN Conference on the Human Environment (the Stockholm conference) initiated a political process which created a large constellation of separate international treaties, each of which refers to a very specific environmental issue like, for example, depletion of the ozone layer in the atmosphere. Disputes about the establishment of these accords represent examples of a "pure" ecological conflict. These confrontations have usually been peaceful: the parties involved have not found it instrumental to use military force in order to defend or promote their special interests. Rather, such violent resolution methods have hitherto been unthinkable in pure ecological conflicts.

A second category is *embedded ecological conflicts*. Many disputed environmental issues are strongly linked to other topics that are addressed in a process of conflict resolution. Pollution in a river, say, the Jordan, the Nile or the Rhine, or an international lake like the Caspian Sea, is a good case of illustration. In these cases, the authorities in riparian states have been concerned with water pollution but have embedded this problem in a larger agenda including an alignment of important issues such as natural resources (fish), national security, human health, and transportation of goods and people.

In embedded ecological conflicts, the impact of the environmental issue is hard to determine and assess. Other issues may have generated the conflict at hand and may also have had stronger influence than an environmental problem on how the related process of conflict resolution evolves.

An *embracing ecological conflict* also encompasses other topics than an environmental issue. However, in contrast to an *embedded ecological conflict,* the environmental issue dominates and embraces the other issues. The UN negotiations on climate change illustrate this contingency. These talks have a clear focus on the climate issue which has been carefully constructed in the process. The climate issue is, in turn, a row of other issue areas representing either sources or effects of climate warming, e.g. energy, land use, industrial production, and transportation.

Institutionalization of environmental issues into permanent issue areas has by now become a permanent feature. Most environmental issues have attained their institutionalized form in the period after the 1972 Stockholm Conference on the Human Environment and have been defined in an international treaty that has usually been developed stepwise by means of recursive negotiation.

There are hundreds of bilateral, regional and global international environmental treaties, many of which are considerably institutionalized (MacCaffrey, et al. 1998). Table 12.1 below gives examples of treaties and international regimes containing institutionalized issue definitions (Mitchell, 2003). The table gives some idea of the varied character of the institutionalized system of environmental issues that has been established in the last few decades such as hazardous waste, biological diversity,

depletion of the ozone layer, or long-range air pollution in a particular geographical region.

Table 12.1 also recalls that some environmental issue areas have a global reach whereas others pertain to a relatively small group of nations. Quite different types of environmental problems are covered by the conventions referred to in Table 12.1 which reflects the existing high degree of fragmentation of the overall environmental policy area. In the period after the 1972 Stockholm Conference on the Human Environment, issue fragmentation has in different ways facilitated the resolution of environmental conflicts, especially when it addresses institutionalized issues and unfolds in an international institution like an organization in the United Nations family.

The system of fragmented issue areas contributes to facilitate the resolution of ecological conflicts in at least three ways:

(i) issue complexity has been reduced to an acceptable level because each individual issue has been narrowly delimited;

(ii) the norms and consensual knowledge in which the environmental issue definitions are embedded give authoritative guidance to regime building and conflict resolution. For example, if an authoritative definition and

Table 12.1   Selected international environmental agreements including institutionalized issue definitions

- "**Basel Convention**" – Basel Convention on the Control of Transboundary Movements of Hazardous Wastes and Their Disposal
- "**CBD**" – Convention on Biological Diversity
- "**CCAMLR**" - Convention on the Conservation of Antarctic Marine Living Resources
- "**CCSBT**" - Convention for the Conservation of Southern Bluefin Tuna
- "**CITES**" – Convention on the International Trade in Endangered Species of Wild Fauna and Flora
- "**CLC**" – Convention on Civil Liability for Oil Pollution Damage
- "**FCCC**" – United Nations Framework Convention on Climate Change
- "**LRTAP**" – Geneva Convention on Long-Range Transboundary Air Pollution
- "**Montreal Protocol**" – Montreal Protocol on Substances that Deplete the Ozone Layer
- "**OSPAR Convention**" – Convention for the Protection of the Marine Environment of the North-East Atlantic
- "**Paris Convention**" – Paris Convention on Third Party Liability in the Field of Nuclear Energy
- "**Stockholm Convention**" – Stockholm Convention on Persistent Organic Pollutants
- "**UNCCD**" – United Nations Convention to Combat Desertification
- "**UNCLOS**" – United Nations Convention on the Law of the Sea
- "**UNFCCC**" – United Nations Framework Convention on Climate Change
- "**Vienna Convention**" – Convention for the Protection of the Ozone Layer
- "**Wetlands Convention**" – Convention on Wetlands of International Importance especially as Waterfowl Habitat.

description states that an ecological problem area state is due to emissions of certain hazardous emissions, then it is implied that these emissions should be phased out;

(iii) The fragmented issue structure has created a considerable number of acknowledged focal points for international negotiation.

International ecological conflicts may also concern a multitude of topics (Mitchell, 2003). There are considerable dissimilarities between issues like, say, hazardous waste, biodiversity or climate change. Nevertheless, this chapter argues that environmental issues tend to share a number of general features contributing to condition how an ecological conflict emerges, develops and is likely to be resolved.

Issue impact on conflict resolution: A general outlook

Different issues can be expected to have a dissimilar impact on conflicts and conflict resolution when their general and typical characteristics diverge. For example, a contentious territorial issue is likely to drive conflicting parties in another direction than a problematic trade issue concerning non-tariff barriers in the World Trade Organization, WTO. There are numerous cases where governments have responded with military force in a territorial conflict, an option which is not likely to be used in a conflict about trade liberalization.

The parties to an ecological conflict are concerned with the values underlying the environmental issue, for example, those of access to fresh water in a conflict concerning water pollution. Obviously, it makes a difference if the values at stake are of great or moderate significance. The greater the magnitude of the values at stake, the more energy and resources is a government, or any other type of actor involved, willing to invest in action meant to defend its interests in the conflict.

However, other generalized issue properties than values may also affect ecological conflict resolution, although in different ways. The degree of *distributiveness* of the stakes related to a particular issue is a case in point.

Jerusalem as an issue in the Middle East negotiations is a well-known illustration of the problem of non-distributive issue.[1] The fact that conflicting parties have considered Jerusalem to be an indivisible value has significantly impeded Middle East peace negotiations (Albin, 1997). Thus, the very small degree of distributiveness of the Jerusalem issue has represented a serious obstacle for a productive exchange of concessions and compromises. In contrast, the high degree of distributiveness characterizing the tariff issue has been a significant facilitating factor in the international trade talks under GATT and in WTO (Kremenyuk & Sjöstedt, 2000). From a technical negotiation point of view, bargaining on detail for a final tariff agreement has been uncomplicated. Negotiation parties have been able to make offers and requests with great precision.

Non-tariff barriers to trade (NTBs), which cannot easily be quantified, have been much more difficult to cope with. "Tariffication" has sometimes been used as a method of attaining a higher degree of distributiveness of this issue. The estimated protection effect of an NTB has been transformed into a tariff which has thereafter been put on the negotiation table.

Environmental issues share a number of other general features at the side of *the degree of distributiveness* that tend to color an ecological conflict and the way it is addressed and handled by the parties involved when they try to cope with it:

(1) Their special trans-boundary character;
(2) Their high issue complexity;
(3) Their tendency to draw in a complex combination of participants;
(4) Their distribution of negative rather than positive values;
(5) Their special uncertainty problems;
(6) Their propensity to be framed as either crisis or risk;
(7) Their propensity to become securitized;

(1) Their *trans-boundary character* is the fundamental reason why environmental issues generate ecological conflicts involving two

or more countries. An environmental issue is trans-boundary and potentially contentious because it concerns more than one country, but to a different degree, in different ways and for different reasons. For example, air pollutants may harm a number of nations other than the country emitting them. Therefore, the scope of nations' involvement in an environmental issue may vary from a bilateral situation to global engagement. For example, the possibility that an accident may happen in the Swedish nuclear plant at Barsebäck is not immediately a world issue, but is considered to represent an unacceptable environmental risk in the Danish capital Copenhagen which is situated only a few miles away (Löfstedt, 1996, 2005). The Danish government has demanded that the nuclear reactors in Barsebäck be closed down and has thus created a bilateral environmental dispute with Sweden. Thus, the Barsebäck reactors embody a clear case of a bilateral ecological conflict.

The deterioration of water pollution in the Mediterranean Sea has engaged all riparian states in a process of collaboration and regime building in order to cope with this problem jointly (Haas, 1990). This is a pluri-party situation of mixed conflict and cooperation.

Global problems like climate warming or the depletion of the ozone layer in the atmosphere affect all nations and all people in some way or other. As a result, global negotiations have been conducted in these issue areas for two decades or longer (Benedick, 1990).

Issues in a conflict are not given by nature. They are constructions by the parties involved, although like the shadows in Plato's cave, they reflect a physical reality.[2]

This includes the perception of a trans-boundary dimension of an environmental issue. Essentially, issues have a trans-boundary dimension for two reasons. Either two or more countries directly share an environmental problem like water pollution in an inland waterway, or governments need to cooperate in order to develop effective methods to stop local environmental degradation as in the case of threatened biodiversity (Jen, 1999).

However, there is not necessarily a perfect fit between the construction of trans-boundary issues in international contexts and the reality that they represent. For example, acidification of Scandinavian lakes existed as a noteworthy, real, domestic environmental problem long before its trans-boundary dimension was fully acknowledged in the negotiations on long-range air pollution in Europe (Björkbom, 1999). Governments and other international actors have a considerable latitude to delimit and define trans-boundary issues. Still, the real world trans-boundary character of an environmental issue represents constraints in this regard.

The trans-boundary dimension of an environmental issue can be conceived of as a package of relations of interdependence linking two or more countries. These couplings emerge when emissions of pollutants or hazardous waste, originating in one country, cross borders and cause environmental harm in another nation. How such interdependence packages with a conflict potential present themselves in a particular situation may have a considerable impact on how an ecological quarrel is structured and develops over time.

Some critical and recurrent characteristics of interdependence packages can be expected to have a certain predictable impact on an ecological conflict. An upstream/downstream model helps to describe an important part of the trans-boundary dimension of ecological conflicts.

The relative upstream/downstream position of a country has a noteworthy influence on how it takes a stand in an ecological conflict (Wolf, 1993; Furlong and Gleditsch, 2006). Dispute over water pollution in a river is both a concrete example and a model for the interpretation of this type of conditioned positioning.

Generally, downstream countries are more strongly victimized by the polluted water than upstream countries. As the river flows from its inland sources to the sea, it cumulates pollutants and waste from all riparian nations. For example, in the case of the Rhine, its flowing water has become more polluted when it reaches downstream Netherlands than it was in upstream Switzerland. Consequently, a downstream state typically has a greater incentive than upstream countries to cope with water pollution in collaboration with other riparian states. A downstream position also gives rise to a strong willingness to mobilize available power resources in a regime-building negotiation.

In a conflict involving riparian countries, upstream states have a power advantage because they have relatively more physical control of the pollution of a river than downstream nations. It also has a greater control of its own environmental predicament. For example, Tibet/China can reduce the water available from the Indus to downstream Pakistan by means of dam constructions, whereas Pakistan has no capacity to stop water flows going to Tibet/China.

An upstream position also gives more environment-specific power than a down-stream position because it has more environ-mental policy options.[3] Land-based sources polluting the river within the national borders are located on its own territory. Therefore, the government of the extreme upstream country is less dependent on collaboration with other nations along the river as it controls so much stronger policy instruments. Domestic environmental policy measures to abate river pollution are likely to be much more effective than in downstream nations. The government of the extreme downstream country has less environment-specific power as it has more constrained decision autonomy with regard to the pollution problem: no satisfactory solution is possible without assistance from upstream countries. This skewed distribution of the need for mutual cooperation means asymmetrical interdependence which gives power leverage to the least dependent party, the upstream country.

The problem of acid rain due to long-range air pollution in Europe illustrates the upstream/downstream syndrome applied to a wider environmental context than a river. To some extent, all European states are damaged by certain pollutants (e.g. sulphur) that have originated in some other country. But some states are more injured than

others because they have a more marked downstream position. With regard to long-range air pollution, Europe can be pictured as a trading system with upstream countries representing net exporters and downstream countries being net importers of pollutants. Net importers have been more concerned with reducing sulphur emissions in Europe than net exporters. How trans-boundary air pollution is generated also systematically influences how this issue is addressed in an ecological conflict.

It is particularly important to distinguish between two principal type situations. One contingency is represented by a conflict concerning a nuclear plant located close to an international border. If a nuclear accident occurs, the decision makers in a downstream country on the other side of the border can trace radioactive clouds back to a single emission point in the upstream country, giving a conflict with other countries a sharp focal point.

The structure of the conflict becomes quite dissimilar when many countries involved in an ecological conflict are both culprits and victims at the same time although to a varying degree and there are a multitude of emission sources. In such a multi-source situation, the allocation of responsibility for environmental damage becomes an extremely complicated and extensive part of conflict resolution. The case of the negotiations on long-range air pollution in Europe is a good illustration. In order to attain a fair understanding of who polluted who and to what degree, it was necessary to construct extremely complex computer models and use their results as input into the negotiation (the RAINS model and measurements of critical loads) (Björkbom, 1999).

(2) *High issue complexities* are a charac-teristic to deal with in international conflict resolution because they are difficult to analyze and assess and are furthermore characterized by a base of scarce and deficient knowl-edge/information. Recall that environmental issues are relatively new on the political agenda in individual nations as well as interna-tionally. In the early 1960s, special ministries

or national central agencies for environmental issues were exceptional, although environmental degradation and destruction caused by human activities is certainly not a new phenomenon. After conquering Carthage, the Roman general Scipio Africanus had salt spread over the cultivated land around the city in order to prevent people from living in the area. Over the centuries, shipbuilding led to large-scale deforestation around the Mediterranean Sea which in turn led to dire environmental consequences. Nevertheless, many of the environmental issues that are currently on the agenda of international politics are relatively new constructions that have been developed since the 1960s onward and particularly since the 1972 UN Conference on the Human Environment. The Stockholm Conference initiated an intensive period of regime building in the environmental area. In many cases, these regime-building processes were hampered by the lack of adequate issue knowledge needed for both effective problem solving and binding commitments.

Typically, environmental issues are pluridimensional in the sense that they contain several different layers of necessary knowledge/information that are inter-linked in a complex manner. The negotiated issue of climate change offers a good illustration. The bottom layer of this issue construction consists of knowledge/information about a number of greenhouse gases emitted from an enormous number of many types of sources located around the earth. This layer of issue knowledge describes the contents and volume of these emissions of greenhouse gases; their origin, their magnitude and the formation of long-term concentrations in the atmosphere (IPCC assessment reports).

Knowledge/information pertaining to the second layer of the issue construction concerns the immediate effects of expanding concentrations of greenhouse gases in the atmosphere/ climate warming: what increases of the temperature of the atmosphere are expected, and how fast this change will occur (IPCC assessment reports)?

The third layer, finally, refers to the consequences of climate warming and the fourth to counter-measures for the purpose of slowing/stopping climate warming and its consequences, or to adapting to them (IPCC assessment reports).

This multi-layer structure of required knowledge/information is one manifestation of the complexity characterizing environmental issues when they are addressed in processes of conflict resolution. Issue linkages exemplify another important complexity dimension. Many environmental issues are not completely independent from one another, although they have been treated separately in the context of fairly autonomous international regimes. For example, the issue area of climate change has strong links to several other institutionalized issue areas, for example, *depletion of the ozone layer in the atmosphere* and *desertification*. Ozone which is addressed in a separate institutional context for the purpose of stopping the depletion of the ozone layer is also one of the substances contributing to the warming of the atmosphere. Another example: halted climate warming would contribute to reducing desertification which also pertains to another regime than that of climate change.

Separation of issues and issue areas have in certain ways created more favorable conditions for regime building and conflict resolution in the area of environmental politics. Issue fragmentation has created a row of focal points which has contributed to significantly facilitating international environmental negotiation and regime building. However, reinforced issue linkages between numerous environmental issues have seemingly decreased the effectiveness of a regime-building strategy which is based on continued distinct fragmentation of issues. The strong recommendation of the 2002 Johannesburg Ministerial Conference (UNCSD) to pronounce sustainable development to be a guiding principle for international regime building and cooperation generally is one important indication.

Environmental issues are also often closely linked to issues belonging to policy areas outside the environmental sector, not least as a consequence of the UN norm of sustainable development. Water pollution is a good illustration. Water in a river represents a multitude of stakes for people and governments of riparian countries due to its many functions. Some rivers supply drinking water and are an irreplaceable irrigation source. Transport of goods and people take place along rivers and across lakes. Inland waterways contain biological resources, notably in the form of fish. Some rivers have a political meaning by representing a natural border between nations. In Europe, great rivers like the Rhine and the Danube have had this role at least since Roman times.

Linkages between water pollution and other different issues often make it difficult – even impossible – to tackle environmental issues separately. For example, in many cases, water pollution needs to be addressed as an element of a larger issue – water resources – which, in turn, is coupled with still other issues like, say, migration and national security.

Issue complexity may lead to an asymmetrical distribution of knowledge/information with the effect that awareness and understanding of a disputed issue varies considerably across stakeholders impeding joint perception, the construction of consensual knowledge and effective problem solving in a process of conflict resolution. This situation may, however, become counter-balanced by the effects of special institutions and procedures that have been established in order to bring scientific knowledge/information into the process.

(3) *The tendency to involve a complex combination of participants in conflict resolution* is a characteristic generated by the complexity of environmental issues. In any non-military conflict between states, governments and their selected representatives in foreign ministries make up the core of the participants. Such traditional diplomatic encounters may occur also in ecological conflicts. But traditional diplomacy is often not sufficiently instrumental when states quarrel over environmental issues. Because they are technically complex, there is a strong demand for a variety of scientific expertise, which has drawn scientific advisors into

the processes of conflict resolution. Often, invited scientists and other experts perform a very active role in conflict resolution, for example, in special working groups (Kjellén, 2007). The climate talks offer a good illustration.

When international conflicts erupt around environmental issues, they often tend to attract the attention of environmental NGOs, the public opinion and the media (Betsill and Corell, 2001). Environment represents one of the issue areas where the extent, as well as intensity, of NGO participation has been the greatest. At the present time, a considerable number of NGOs are drawn into international policy processes outside the environmental sector. This is a relatively new situation in many multilateral trade talks, for example, in the World Trade Organization. However, the situation was quite different under the predecessor organization of WTO. During the GATT (General Agreement on Tariffs and Trade) period ending in 1994, only a few international governmental organizations and practically no NGOs were given access to the multilateral trade negotiations as members or observers. In contrast, the participation of NGOs in the climate talks and other environmental negotiations has been extensive for decades and particularly after the United Nations Conference on Environment and Development (UNCED) in 1992.

The mobilization of different kinds of actors into environmental negotiations has affected this type of conflict resolution in various significant ways. Firstly, the transparency of the negotiations has increased. Thereby, the room for maneuver for secret deals has decreased. Public opinion and lobbying groups have attained better possibilities to supervise and influence international negotiations. Increased actor complexity has contributed to make multilateral environmental negotiations more cumbersome. The process has become more protracted and it has become more difficult to reach a final agreement.

Some environmental issues have been regarded as abstract and distant by the general public such as, for example, biodiversity. However, some environmental issues like the risk of an accident occurring in a nuclear power plant have stirred up strong reactions by large parts of a country's population, green parties or militant environmental non-governmental organizations (NGOs). Such reactions, or other demonstrations by "green" actors, have often been reported under large headlines in the media and have sometimes had a strong influence on political decisions. A prime example is represented by nuclear policies in Austria, Germany and Sweden. In Austria, nuclear power was banned altogether although reactors had been constructed. A national referendum has prohibited the expansion of the Swedish nuclear problem and the German nuclear policy is strongly constrained by the "green" opinion.

Opinion building and lobbying by green groups may emerge as an influential force in some ecological conflicts complicating conflict resolution in various ways. For example, the central decision makers in a country importing an environmental problem may be forced to take a hard stand against the nation exporting it. This may, in turn, lead to other complicating developments like conflict escalation and less room for pragmatic compromises.

(4) *The distribution of negative rather than positive values* is a concern for the parties in an ecological conflict. Positive values are often related to natural resources (e.g. fresh water) that will be preserved by the abatement of an environmental problem (e.g. pollution). Negative values are represented by abatement costs. However, abatement as such is related to a structure of only negative values. Environmental deterioration or destruction is perceived as a cost that has to be offset by another cost generated by the measures that are applied in order to achieve abatement.

Thus, parties to ecological conflicts typically quarrel or fight about the distribution of negative values and the tradeoff between environmental destruction costs and environmental abatement costs (Sjöstedt, 1993). This predicament can be expected to influence how conflicting parties act in a negotiation or other type of conflict resolution. Prospect theory suggests that parties perform differently when

they are confronted with expected gains and losses respectively (Kahneman and Tversky, 1979). They tend to be more sensitive to losses than to gains. This represents a hindrance as compared to processes of conflict resolution which, like trade talks in WTO, ultimately strive to distribute positive values. The special uncertainty problems that also characterize ecological conflicts contribute to increasing the significance of this obstacle still further.

(5) *Pluri-layered uncertainty problems* plague environmental issues. Some ecological conflicts erupt because the parties involved become aware of the seriousness of an environmental problem. Negotiation on long-range air pollution in Europe took off when dead and dying forests activated the German government (Bäckstrand, 2001). The visual observation of actual holes in the ozone layer situated in the stratosphere convinced governments around the world that joint action was necessary to cope with this problem. Often, an environmental crisis due to new environmental awareness has been an important precondition for negotiation, conflict resolution and regime building.

Three dimensions of climate warming need to be considered simultaneously in international negotiations. One focus is set on emissions of CO_2 and other greenhouse gases into the atmosphere. These releases build up concentrations of greenhouse gases in the atmosphere which will then raise the average atmospheric temperature in the future. In turn, the higher temperature is expected to cause various harmful or disastrous effects such as, for example, storms, floods or desertification (Luterbacher and Sprintz, 2001).

All these three layers of the complex structure of the issue of climate change (emissions, concentration, warming and harmful consequences), as well as the causal relationships between them, are characterized by problematic uncertainty. Scientists can only roughly estimate current emissions of greenhouse gases into the atmosphere and they are still more uncertain about the volume of future releases. Some nations are more problematic than others. There is agreement within the scientific community that larger concentrations of greenhouse gases will warm the atmosphere but there are different views of how large this increase will be. Many researchers have described possible negative effects of climate warming but there is no comprehensive and certain appraisal of what its total costs will be this year, next year or further in the future (IPCC assessment reports). The effects of possible approaches to slow down or stop climate warming are also uncertain. For example, scientists cannot predict with reasonable certainty what positive effects will follow from a 20% global reduction of greenhouse gas emissions.

The special uncertainty problems related to environmental issues have a variety of consequences for conflict resolution. Many of these effects follow one of two different tracks.

One track tends to involuntarily slow down the process or even prevent its successful conclusion. The high degree of perceived uncertainty regarding both environmental problems and possible problem solutions can be expected to make the parties more reluctant to make costly and binding commitments, for example, to make considerable cuts of emissions of hazardous substances coming from important human activities like agriculture, transports or industrial production of goods. Uncertainty impedes parties from making reliable assessments of the relationship between the costs of climate warming and of climate policy measures respectively.

Another track calls for more effective management of the uncertainty problems. The usual strategy to attain this objective is to bring more scientific knowledge/information into the process. This development may in itself have consequences for a process of conflict resolution. For example, special procedures or organizational bodies may have to be created in order to make the accumulation of scientific knowledge instrumental and adequate. Scientists may have to be invited to participate in the conflict resolution process that otherwise would have been completely dominated by diplomats

and top policy makers. The involvement of scientists may contribute to frame the risk discourse used in the process which in turn may have an impact on how conflicting parties interact.

(6) *Issue frames highlighting either crisis or risk* underlie environmental conflicts. Environmental issues in a potential or actual ecological conflict reflect a physical reality but are still constructions by the conflicting parties. An issue construction related to a given real world phenomenon (say, emissions of certain pollutants) may take on different forms and contents depending on the circumstances at hand and the interests of leading actors. Issue framing, pre-negotiation and agenda setting represent strategic stages in a process of conflict resolution (Bercovitch, 1991; Elgström and Strömvik, 2005). However, policy makers tend to choose between two main frames when they address international, environmental issues. One is *crisis* and the other is *risk*.

An environmental issue is likely to be framed as a crisis when actual and considerable damages are occurring at the present time, driving a number of stakeholders to put this topic on a joint agenda (Boin, et al. 2005). The 1987 catastrophic accident in the Chernobyl nuclear power plant was immediately framed as a crisis in the Soviet Union itself as well as in numerous neighboring countries. Clouds of radioactive particles were blown toward Western and Northwestern Europe, contaminating large areas of land.

Ensuing inter-governmental talks about Chernobyl essentially focused on two topics. In the short term, discussions concerned the actual development of the Chernobyl disaster and its immediate consequences in neighboring countries around the Soviet Union (The Case of the Chernobyl Nuclear Accident, 2002). Chernobyl also affected the ongoing negotiation in IAEA on nuclear safety very strongly. These talks had been stalled and without result for several years. The Chernobyl accident happened in May 1987. Already in the autumn the same year, a treaty on nuclear safety was negotiated during a few brief months (Sjöstedt, 1993).

In contrast, the issue of a nuclear accident at the Swedish nuclear plant at Barsebäck has been framed as a risk (Löfstedt, 1996). No disaster has actually happened but some parties think it may transpire in the future. This is a risk that people in neighboring Copenhagen are not willing to take. In the informal and relatively non-transparent discussion about Barsebäck, the Danish side wants the Swedish government to establish a concrete plan for the closure of this nuclear plant.

The distinction between a crisis and a risk perspective on an international environmental issue is important because the two approaches will probably lead to distinctly dissimilar patterns of interaction in an ecological conflict.

A crisis situation puts high values at stake and requires swift action, while at the same time, parties typically lack essential information about the situation (Boin et al., 2005). There is a need for creative and innovative policy measures to reach constructive agreements between states. The high values at stake in an ecological crisis represent a strong motivation for most or all parties to do something about the rapidly deteriorating situation. The trans-boundary dimension calls for joint state action but is also a potential source of conflict. The high, or extreme, stakes involved may incite conflicting parties to prioritize their own separate interests over common interests. Uncertainty regarding the environmental issue that has provoked the ecological crisis may also obstruct effective collaboration because parties make different risk assessments.

Climate change is a prime example of an environmental issue in international negotiation that from the start was framed as a risk. Some experts and opinion builders argue that negative effects of climate warming have already occurred, for example, in the form of stronger hurricanes and more rainfalls in recent years. The mainstream of the international scientific community believes that more damaging consequences of climate warming will occur in 40–50 years when the average temperature of the atmosphere is expected to have risen between two and three degrees Celsius or even more, unless powerful counter-measures are implemented. A large number of scientific investigations support this assessment while admitting that it has some degree of uncertainty. It is not possible to determine with certainty how large amounts of greenhouse gases will be emitted into the atmosphere in the coming decades, exactly what the harmful effects will be and how they will be distributed around the world. Neither can it be predicted with certainty exactly what alternative counter-measures will accomplish. Nor can it be foreseen with certainty exactly how costly each such approach will be.

In a conflict related to an environmental crisis, a main problem is the need for immediate action which may lead to miscalculations and mistakes (Robinson, 1996). In a risk scenario, a principal problem is instead diverging risk perceptions amongst conflicting parties in combination with relatively poor instruments for risk communication (Linneroth et al., 2001). As a result, parties will often find it difficult to attain a common understanding of the problem concerned and develop a joint solution to the environmental problem on the table. Particularly, environmental issues are typically characterized by a high degree of uncertainty impeding costly commitments.

In numerous cases, the countries involved in an ecological conflict have not been able – or willing – to engage themselves in a project of environmental problem solving conceived of as risk management until a crisis situation emerges. Long-range air pollution in Europe is one example. Pictures in German newspapers of dead forests damaged by acidification represented a turning point in these talks.

(7) *Securitization of environmental issues* occasionally appears by all, or some, of the stakeholders in an ecological conflict including national governments. In many, and probably most cases, environmental issues have been treated in the context of "normal" politics in both national and international affairs. But when securitized, the environmental issue takes on a new character (Eriksson, 2002; Balzacq, 2005).

The main reason for the securitization of environmental issues is their representation of values of extreme importance generally pertaining to scarce natural resources (Homer-Dixon, 1999; Dolatyar and Gray, 2000). For example, pollution in inland waterways may drastically reduce the quality and quantity of available fresh water resources in a region, thereby causing serious health problems and perhaps making living conditions unsupportable. Likewise, desertification diminishes available water resources in a region, hence threatening cultivated land, cattle and other animals and may lead to losses of human life. In recent decades, such developments have occurred in Sudan and other parts of the Sahel area. More frequent and stronger storms due to climate warming will kill people, destroy their houses and property, as well as public and private infrastructure not least in coastal areas. Rising sea levels will have similar effects. Melting glaciers will cause both inundations and water scarcity in downstream countries.

Securization may contribute to intensify an ecological conflict and also to change the performance of the parties when they strive to cope with a conflict, for example, increase their willingness to take risks by resorting to a unilateral strategy. How large risks are governments willing to take in an ecological crisis? Are they ready to go to war? A common opinion is that detrimental environmental effects do not lead directly to violent conflict, although they may contribute to intensifying a conflict regarding other issues such as territory, ethnicity or the distribution of natural resources (Homer-Dixon, 1991). On the other hand, the awareness of the risk for violent confrontation may strongly increase the incentives for the parties to the ecological conflict to search for a cooperative resolution approach.

Fight or talk? special and typical features in the resolution of environmental conflicts

The ultimate question addressed in this chapter is if, and how, ecological conflicts have certain typical features distinguishing them as a separate category. The chapter has proposed that if such typical features exist, they are to some extent conditioned by typical and special attributes of environmental issues: trans-boundary, complexity, stakeholders, negative values, uncertainty, securitization, crisis or risk, and institutionalization in international regimes. One could also add their tendency to mobilize NGOs and public opinion.

Some of these environmental issue characteristics seem to influence the basic approach governments choose to defend their interests in an ecological conflict, particularly whether they prefer to *fight* – to use military force – or whether they prefer to *talk*, to negotiate and prioritize problem solving.

Fighting in ecological conflicts has occurred in some international ecological conflicts. Some analysts warn that ecological conflicts will grow more serious in the future and increase the risk for military confrontation. Others argue that the support for this proposition is weak for both methodological and empirical reasons. They contend that there is no single known example of a conflict on an environmental issue which has directly driven two or more nations to start a war. The implication is that fighting is not likely to take place in *pure ecological conflicts*, to use a categorization introduced at the beginning of this chapter. Neither can fighting be expected to occur in *embracing ecological conflicts* like the negotiations on climate change or ozone depletion.

However, it is also pointed out in the literature that ecological issues have recurrently been associated with military confrontations in the Third World although they have not represented a single or even clear cause of war. The typical situation seems to be an *embedded ecological conflict*, in which the environmental element has interacted with other factors like ethnicity, political/ideological difference or an unequal distribution of natural resources (Libiszewski, 1992; Carius et al., 1997; Homer-Dixon, 1999).

The civil war in southern Sudan (Darfur) is one example of such an embedded ecological conflict (Johnson, 2003). War between the North and the South in Sudan has occurred repeatedly for centuries and is part of the colonial legacy. The conflict has an important ethnic/cultural dimension expressed by the differences between Arab/Muslims in the North and African/Christians in the South. Oil in the South and water in the Nile have represented critical bones of contention between the North and the South. Internal large flows of refugees and across its borders to neighboring countries have contributed to worsen and further internationalize the civil war in Sudan.

Some ecological problems have also played an important role in the conflict about Darfur. *Climate change, desertification* and the *environmental destruction* caused by the exploitation of oil resources have decreased the area of habitable land and other resources, notably water, to an extent that they cannot sustain the population living in the area. This situation has caused starvation, flows of refugees and also intensified the conflict about the increasingly scarce land where people can live and survive.

It is, hence, argued that environmental degradation represents an important background factor in the Darfur conflict, as well as in other military confrontations in the Third World. Environmental damage is significant because it contributes to create, or sustain, conditions which increase the risk for military confrontations. Allegedly, environmental factors have had a similar role in other Third World embedded ecological conflicts. A recurrent scenario is that environmental degradation causes or reinforces the depletion of a natural resource which is of critical importance in the geographical area where the embedded ecological conflict unfolds. In turn, this resource depletion is one of the factors causing, reinforcing or sustaining the use of military means or other instruments of force in an embedded ecological conflict.

However, when an embedded ecological conflict leads to military confrontations, the parties involved are not likely to focus on the environmental dimension. Environmental issues will remain background factors.

A couple of special properties of environmental issues may affect a militarized ecological conflict. For example, if in an embedded ecological conflict, an environmental issue which is strongly linked to a scarce natural resource such as fresh water is *securitized* or is *framed as a crisis,* it may conceivably reinforce or sustain the causes of violent approaches to conflict resolution.

However, if an embedded ecological conflict evolves into international or civil war between conflicting parties, the special or typical features of environmental issues are not likely to influence how the military operations are conducted by the conflicting parties. They are concerned with more immediate issues like the direct control of land, water and people.

In recent decades, military conflicts with an ecological component have exclusively taken place in the developing world and often in extremely poor countries like Congo and Sudan. Such international or civil wars have not confronted well-trained armies equipped with sophisticated weapons systems. Often, primitive weapons have been employed with brutality not only in battles but also against civilian populations in order to drive them away from the land they live on. In the process, horrendous atrocities have been committed and large migration flows have been generated. Thousands and sometimes millions of refugees have fled out of the war zone and into neighboring countries. Due to weak or failed states, conflict resolution has been cumbersome and has in many cases required far-reaching conciliation measures.

"Talking" in ecological conflicts represents the normal approach to the resolution of ecological conflicts; dialogue and negotiation (Sjöstedt, 1993; Susskind et al., 2002). The dominance of peaceful conflict resolution is total amongst industrialized countries. Pure and embracing ecological conflicts have up till now excluded military confrontations regardless of what countries have been involved.

The absence of violence in ecological conflicts that are not embedded in other types of conflict concerning, say, national security, territory or ethnicity is due to both instrumental and normative factors pertaining to the general characteristics of environmental issues. *Issue complexity* is a basic instrumental conditioning factor. Even if the transboundary nature of an environmental problem like pollution in the atmosphere, in the ocean or in inland waterways is obvious, it has often been unclear exactly how problem causes and problem effects are distributed between the nations involved. Although the transboundary character of many environmental issues has been a necessary condition for the emergence of an international ecological conflict, its close association with issue complexity has created a need for common international problem solving enabling joint abatement. The effective solution of most trans-boundary environmental conflicts precludes unilateral action in order to cope with this problem. Voluntary cooperation between exporters and importers of pollution is usually necessary because all nations are typically both exporting and importing pollution.

Conflict resolution efforts are much more concentrated on environmental issues in *pure* and *embracing ecological conflicts* than in *embedded ecological conflicts*. Accordingly, the impact of the special and typical features of environmental issues has a stronger impact in these two cases. In this sense, conflict resolution in the form of dialogue or negotiation tends to be colored by the characteristics of the environmental issue addressed to a much higher extent than in an embedded ecological conflict where the impact can be expected to be nil.

Peaceful resolution of an ecological conflict may unfold in a bilateral setting. One case of illustration is the location of a nuclear power plant in border areas like in the cases of the Temelin (Austria/Czech Republic) and Barsebäck (Denmark/Sweden) nuclear power plants.

These two cases indicate that bilateral conflict resolution amongst industrialized countries regarding a sensitive environmental issue, like the risk for a nuclear accident, tends to have a low transparency. The negotiation on the Temelin reactors points to at least two basic reasons why the parties to a bilateral environmental negotiation, in this case the governments of Austria and the Czech Republic respectively, want to conduct the dialogue under a veil of secrecy. They both wish to avoid opinion building against their preferred line of action. One party (in the example, the Czech Republic) is requested by the other side to undertake measures to reduce the negotiated environmental problem (in the example, to close down the nuclear power plant). The two governments want low transparency in order to conceal possible necessary concessions to the other side. This predicament is not unusual in international negotiations but is particularly pronounced when environmental issues are addressed. A reason is that NGOs and other opinion builders have so far had easier and more extensive access to international decision processes in the environmental issue area than in most other policy sectors.

The recurrent properties of environmental issues have a tendency to color the peaceful resolution of ecological conflicts. This influence is diffuse and complex. Different issue properties tend to have a somewhat dissimilar impact on the process of conflict resolution. Furthermore, the effects of individual properties of environmental issues tend to vary as the process of international negotiation evolves stagewise from *pre-negotiation* to *agenda setting* and *issue clarification* through *negotiation on formula* and *detail* to *agreement* and *post-negotiation*.[4] *Implementation* of an agreement may also be included in the process of conflict resolution, particularly if it is part of a recursive, multilateral negotiation. Implementation may follow after, or unfold parallel to, post-negotiation (Zartman, 1994; Kremenyuk, 2002). For example, post-negotiation may start because of implementation difficulties or problems that emerge as a consequence of successful implementation.

Pre-negotiation in a process of ecological conflict resolution has typically unfolded at a high political level (Pantev, 1998). However, in many cases, these inter-governmental consultations have followed discussions amongst scientists that may have been going on for years. The key driver in the initiation of the pre-negotiation has been awareness of top decision makers of a common environmental problem and some of its key characteristics, its trans-boundary dimension, the high or extreme stakes involved, an emerging crisis situation, diverging interests in some leading nations and tendencies of issue securitization in some states. Awareness has been the result of the inter-play of various factors, especially build-up of issue knowledge in the international scientific community in combination with dramatic media reports.

Agenda setting and issue clarification in any multilateral talks has strategic meaning because the outcome of this process stage conditions ensuing activities in the negotiation and ultimately the agreement that will be attained in the process. In multilateral environmental negotiation, agenda setting is particularly important and not least the element which is here referred to as *issue clarification*. One reason is the combination of dense *international interdependence*, *extreme complexity* and high degree of *uncertainty* typifying important environmental issues, such as climate change, ozone depletion or biodiversity.

In contrast to, say, tariffs or territory, environmental issues are relatively new on the agenda of international politics. In combination with high issue complexity and uncertainty, this state of affairs has meant that negotiating parties have found it necessary to allocate large resources to both individual and joint knowledge building in order to elucidate the ecological issue addressed. *Issue clarification* has become a crucial element of agenda setting. In all negotiations, the parties obviously need sufficient knowledge and updated information about questions that have been put on the negotiation and hence also the entire table. This knowledge/information affects the performance of the actors involved and hence indirectly has an impact on the whole negotiation process. However,

knowledge and knowledge builders have a somewhat different role and impact in a typical environmental negotiation, a process of conflict resolution, than in talks in many other issue areas. The UN negotiation on climate change is a helpful case of illustration (UNFCCC, 2002).

The climate talks cover highly contentious issues. For example, there is the deep divergence between the United States and the European Union concerning the future of the Kyoto Protocol and the difference between the OECD member states and developing countries regarding binding commitments to reduce emissions of greenhouse gases into the atmosphere. However, the climate talks are driven by the joint interest of negotiating parties to cope with climate warming and the disastrous consequences that it is expected to engender unless effective counter-measures are undertaken. The resolution of conflict is subordinated to joint problem solving.

The conflict between negotiating parties concerns primarily what policy instruments should be employed to arrest climate warming (e.g. market instruments or regulations); and how abatement costs (e.g. emission reductions) should be distributed between nations. National positions depend on a solid and accurate basis of scientific knowledge enabling policy makers and negotiators to fully understand climate change; its causes, its manifestations, its consequences as well as the costs and benefits of mitigation and adaptation. Control of knowledge and information has a central part in the power game of nations which is embedded in the climate negotiation. This situation is similar in other environmental talks although the climate talks represent an extreme case indicated by a special institution, the Inter-governmental Panel on Climate Change (IPCC), with the primary task of building and disseminating knowledge/information (Skodvin, 2000). The output of this process has been consensual knowledge which has functioned as an important driver in the climate talks. Consensual knowledge has not only served as a common frame of reference for negotiating parties (Rothstein, 1984). It has also identified their specified common interests early in the climate talks, as well as in other environmental negotiations, beginning already in the agenda setting phase of the process. Common interests are implied by the definition and description of the environmental problem which has brought about an international negotiation. For example, in the negotiation on long-range air pollution in Europe, the scientific description of acid rain implied a joint interest of all European nations to eliminate its causes, and sulphur emissions into the atmosphere. Although governments had differing views of the problem of acid rain as such, major conflict in this area concerned the measures to cope with it in coordinated national policies (Bäckstrand, 2001). A principal bone of contention has been the distribution of emission reductions. As seen from the perspective of conflict resolution, a special feature of environmental negotiations has been that negotiating parties specify their separate interests following agreement on joint interests and general common goals.

The agenda setting stage of environmental negotiations is dominated by *knowledge diplomacy* (Haas, 1996). In this phase of the talks, the capacity to contribute to the framing of issues and the construction of consensual knowledge represents a principal avenue to influence over other parties or over the whole process.

Multilateral environmental negotiations have typically been recursive building up an international agreement stepwise. The institutionalization of issue constructions following from this recursive progress has gradually narrowed down the room of maneuver in agenda setting and issue clarification as the process of negotiation has unfolded.

Bargaining on formula and detail is a significant part of multilateral negotiation that has been described as "the management of complexity" (Zartman, 1994). The transition from agenda setting to negotiation on formula represents a particularly critical stage in this management process. A formula

is necessary to make the issues at stake negotiable during the remaining stages of the negotiation (Skodvin, 1999). In environmental negotiations with their comparatively complex issues, formula construction has been relatively demanding as compared to other issue areas. Scientific knowledge, and sometimes scientific models, have been necessary tools to develop a formula that is both politically and technically feasible (Amann, 2007).

Multilateral negotiations put a premium on the ability to find integrative solutions by defining situations in ways that include and are responsive to the perspectives and needs of all the parties. Verbal persuasion replaces bargaining from strength, and consensus supplements compromise. Nevertheless, international environmental negotiation is partly colored by ecological conflict and is a power game in which parties strive to promote and defend their interests. For this purpose, they may employ various types of influencing methods. They may, for example, resort to political pressure or sanctions in order to get concessions from another party. However, knowledge diplomacy conditioned by issue complexity represents a major avenue to effective influence in environmental negotiations embedding ecological conflicts.

In some cases and under some conditions, smaller states with little military power are able to cope with this situation. The negotiations on long-range air pollution in Europe exhibit a good example (Larsson, 1996). In its initial stages, these talks were driven by two Scandinavian countries, Norway and Sweden, against an opposition including all major West European nations. The main explanation is that these small states had built up a superior knowledge about acidification and other aspects of long-range air pollution because they were the first serious victims. However, usually sophisticated issue knowledge needed for effective diplomacy in ecological conflicts is highly asymmetrically distributed amongst conflicting parties in a pattern that is favorable to larger and technologically highly developed countries.

Poor and less developed countries are not able to pursue effective knowledge diplomacy and for this reason they have difficulties in defending their interests. A large Third World coalition of states like the Group of 77 may have a certain veto power which, however, is strongly limited and has often been circumvented by counter-strategies of the more advanced nations, such as the 1997 Kyoto Protocol annexed to the UN Framework Convention on Climate Change (UNFCCC). A small victory of developing countries was that they were able to avoid binding commitments to reduce emission of greenhouse gases although they became part of the Kyoto Protocol. But developing countries were not able to stop industrialized countries from signing and putting the Kyoto Protocol into operation.

Other issue characteristics than *high complexity* also constrain conflict resolution in international environmental negotiation. The special *uncertainty* problems of environmental issues and their propensity to be framed as *risk* is likely to affect the negotiation process negatively, particularly when negotiation parties begin to consider costly and binding commitments. One reason is that a government is not able to make a trustworthy assessment of the ratio of current costs (say emission reductions) and future benefits (say the utility of stabilized greenhouse gas concentrations in the atmosphere) caused by an international agreement such as an amended Kyoto Protocol. The lack of comparatively certain cost/benefit assessments results in a lack of enthusiasm to accept a costly undertaking in order to cope with climate warming. This is the position that the United States and other nations have taken with regard to the Kyoto Protocol.

In contrast, *institutionalization* of issues and procedures for negotiation and conflict resolution has in many cases contributed to facilitating talks on environmental issues. Institutionalization may be regarded as one face of a learning process in which negotiation parties gradually develop more effective methods for both problem solving and exchange of concessions.

NOTES

1 An issue is the whole problem area addressed in a process of conflict resolution. The stakes represent the contested elements of the issue.

2 Issue construction may mean that the actors concerned accept an issue established by others or by themselves in earlier confrontations.

3 Of course, there are important exceptions to this general proposition. For example, the upstream country may be poorer and less developed than downstream nations. It may not have the capability and the resources to deal with its own pollution and for that reason has a great incentive to cooperate with downstream nations in order to attain more capacity and resources.

4 Recall that *post-negotiation* may lead to a new round of *pre-negotiation* which, in turn, initiates a whole new loop of conflict resolution, for example, a new COP meeting in the climate talks (Spector and Zartman, 2003).

REFERENCES

Albin, C. (1997). "Securing the peace of Jerusalem. On the politics of unifying and dividing". *Review of International Studies,* 21 (2).

Amann, M. (2007). "Some lessons from the use of the RAINS model in international negotiation" in Avenhaus, R. & Zartman, W. (eds). *Diplomacy games: Formal models and international negotiations.* Berlin: Springer.

Bäckstrand, K. (2001). *What can nature withstand? Science, politics and discourses in transboundary air pollution.* Lund: Lund Political Studies.

Balzacq, T. (2005). "The three faces of securitization: Agency, audience and context". *European Journal of International Relations,* 11 (2).

Benedick, R. (1998). *Ozone diplomacy: New directions in safeguarding the planet.* Cambridge (Mass.): Harvard University Press.

Bercovitch, J. (1991). "International negotiation and conflict management: the importance of prenegotiation". *The Jerusalem Journal of International Relations,* 13: 1.

Betsill, M. & Corell, E. (2001). "NGO influence in international environmental negotiations. A framework of analysis". *Global Environmental Politics,* 1: 4. Massachusets Institute of Technology.

Björkbom, L. (1999). "Negotiation over transboundary air pollution: The case of Europe". *International Negotiation.*

Boin, A., t Hart, P. Stern, E. and Sundelius, B. (2005). *The politics of crisis management: Public leadership under pressure.* Cambridge: Cambridge University Press.

Bryant, R. (1998). "Power, knowledge and political ecology in the third world: A review". *Progress in Physical Geography*, 22 (1). OBS MÅSTE FÖRAS IN.

Caspian Environmental Program. National report of the Republic of Kazakhstan. (1998). Minister of Ecology and National Resources of the Republic of Kazakhstan.

Dolatyar, M. and Gray, T. (2000). "The politics of water scarcity in the Middle East". *Environmental Politics*, 9 (3).

Elgström, O. and Strömvik, M. (2005)."Setting the global trade agenda: The European Union and the launch of the Doha Round" in Elgström, O. & Jönsson, Ch. (eds). *European Union negotiations: Processes, networks and institutions*. New York: Routledge.

Eriksson, J. (2001). *Threat politics: New perspectives on security, risk and crisis management*. Aldershot: Ashgate Publishing.

Haas, P. (1990). *Saving the Mediterranean*. New York: Columbia University Press.

Haas, P. (1996). (ed.). *Knowledge, power and international policy coordination*. Colombia: South Carolina University Press.

Homer-Dixon, T. (1991). "On the threshold. Environmental changes as causes of acute conflict". *International Security*, 16 (2).

Homer-Dixon, T. (1999). *Environment, Scarcity and Violence*. Princeton: Princeton University Press.

IPCC assessment reports

Jen, S. (1999). "The convention on the conservation of European wildlife and natural habitats: Procedures of application in practice". *Journal of International Wildlife Law & Policy*, 2: 2.

Johnson, D. (2003). "The root causes of Sudan's civil wars". *African Studies Quarterly*, 7 (1), Spring.

Kahneman, D. and Tversky A. (1979). "Prospect theory. An analysis of decisions under risk". *Econometrica*, XLVII.

Kjellén, B. (2007). *A new diplomacy for sustainable development: The challenge of global change*. London: Routledge.

Kremenyuk, V. (2002). (ed.). *International negotiation: Analysis, approaches, issues*. San Francisco: Jossey-Bass Publishers.

Larsson, P. (1996). *International Environmental Regime Negotiations: A Study of the LRIAP-Convention Negotiations*. Lund: Scripta Academica Lundensia.

Linneroth, R., Löfstedt, R. and Sjöstedt, G. (2001). (eds). *Transboundary Risk Management*. London: Earthscan.

Löfstedt, R. (1996). "Risk communication: The Barsebäck nuclear plant case". *Energy Pol*, 24.

Löfstedt, R. (2005). *Risk management in the post-trust society*. London: Palgrave Macmillan.

Luterbacher, U. and Sprintz, D. (2001). *International relations and global climate change*. Cambridge: The MIT Press.

Mitchell, R. (2003). "International environmental agreements: A survey of their features, formation and effects". *Annual Review of Environment and Resources*, 28.

New York Sun. (2007). "Water or war". August 1.

New York Times. (2007). July 22.

Pantev, P. (1998). *Prenegotiations. The theory and how to apply to Balkan issues*. Research Study No. 6, Institute for Security and International Studies, Sofia.

Robinson, P. (1996). *The politics of international crisis escalation: Decision making under pressure*. Tauris Publishers.

Rothstein, R. (1984). "Consensual knowledge and international collaboration: Some lessons from the commodity negotiations". *International Organization*, 38 (4).

Saunders, H. (1987). *The peace process. The importance of prenegotiation approaches*. (Unpublished manuscript). Washington, DC: Brooking Institution.

Sebenius, J. (1984). *Negotiating the law of the sea: Lessons in the art of reaching agreement*. Cambridge: Harvard University Press.

Sjöstedt, G. (1993). (ed.). *International environmental negotiation*. San Francisco: Sage Publications.

Sjöstedt, G. (2003). (ed.). *Professional cultures in international negotiation: Bridge or rift?* Lexington Books: New York.

Skodvin, T. (1999). *Making climate change negotiable. The development of the global warming pollution index*. Working paper 1999: 9. Oslo: Cicero.

Skodvin, Tora, (2000). "Revised rules of procedure for the IPCC process". *Climatic Change*, 46 (4): pp. 409–415.

Suliman, M. (1999). (ed.). *Ecology, politics and violent conflict*. London: Zed Books.

Susskind, L., Moomaw, W. and Gallagher K. (2002). (eds). *Transboundary environmental negotiation: New approaches to global cooperation*. San Francisco: Jossey-Bass Publishers.

Tang, P. and Kets, W. (2003). *Globalization: Risks and benefits*. The Hague: Netherlands Bureau of Economic Policy Analysis.

The Case of the Chernobyl Nuclear Accident: A Strategy for Recovery. (2002). A Report commissioned by UNDP and UNICEF and sponsored by UN-OCHA and WTO.

Thompson, A. (2006). "Management under anarchy: The international politics of climate change". *Climate Change*, 78 (1).

UNFCCC. (2002). *A guide to the climate change convention process.* Bonn: Climate Change Secretariat.

Wolf, A. (1993). "Criteria for equitable allocations: The heart of international water conflict". *Natural Resources Journal*, 33: 3.

Zartman, W. (1994). *International multilateral negotiation: Approaches to the management of complexity.* San Francisco: Jossey-Bass Publishers.

13

Ethnicity, Negotiation, and Conflict Management

Donald Rothchild

If, as is commonly asserted, ethnic entre-preneurs manipulate ethnic identities to advance their economic and political self-interests, then it is important to ask why the members of the ethnic group allow themselves to be maneuvered from above. Why do the followers follow, and what does that say about the genuineness of ethnic ties? I accept the existence of a cleavage between ethnic elites and members in terms of their basic concerns. However, I contend that elites can manage their memberships because they tap into something genuine: a deep desire for inclusion in the identity group, an uncertainty that the state will prove a reliable and effective protector, and a fear that the balance of forces among groups will shift decisively to the disadvantage of their community. Thus, political leaders can play the ethnic card not only because they champion the material and nonmaterial concerns of their group mem-bership, but also because the members have genuine uncertainties about their security and the security of their children. In an attempt to cope with these uncertainties, I will dis-cuss five institutional arrangements: reserved seats in the legislature, proportional repre-sentation, transethnic electoral requirements in presidential elections, ethnic federalism, and inclusive power-sharing arrangements – valued by exposed minorities for their ability to protect the security and well-being of vulnerable groups.

The problem that must be addressed, then, is how and to what extent can the state reassure its power minorities about their safety and economic well-being in the years ahead? And to what extent, when state norms collapse and civil wars take place, can international mediators take up the slack and facilitate commitment to peace agreements, overcoming basic insecurities among weaker parties about the intentions of ruling state elites?

ETHNICITY AND ETHNIC GROUP

In some cases, it is the ethnic commu-nity that proves most successful in uniting many of society's members for some of life's primary purposes: cultural fulfillment, belongingness, social intercourse, psychological security, and physical survival. Ethnicity, as used in this context, refers to a subjective perception of common origins, historical memories, interpersonal ties, and aspirations. Ethnicity, or a sense of peoplehood, has its foundation in combined remembrances of past experience and in common inspirations, values, norms, and expectations. The accuracy of these beliefs and remembrances is less significant to creating an overarching sense of affinity than is the ability of a people to symbolize their closeness to each other.

Ethnicity as a subjective basis for collective consciousness becomes relevant to the political process when it spurs group formation and underpins political organization. A group mythology, observes Stuart Kaufman (2006, 52), "must exist before a politician can manipulate it." In its capacity to stimulate awareness and a sense of fellowship among the potential members of a group, the psychological dimension of ethnicity complements and buttresses the political dimension of interest-oriented action. Thus, a sense of peoplehood—often linked to other potentially mobilizable bases of identity such as language, religion, tribe, caste, or clan—can be instrumental to group formation and participation in the political process (Posner 2005). Nevertheless, initiative on the part of elite members remains critically important for the promotion and defense of group interests and security. Success in building a sense of community often remains a precondition for effective political initiatives by a group spokesperson. Ethnicity acts as a connector around which group members can mobilize and compete effectively for state power, economic resources, governmental and parastatal positions, contracts, awards, and protection.

Where ethnic identity is in essence "a subjective self-concept or social role" (Young 1976, 65), the ethnic group is a culturally based social organization. The notion of a group suggests organized activities by people linked by a consciousness of a special identity who jointly seek to maximize their collective political, economic, and social interests.

Ethnic groups persist in modern times, Robert Bates notes (1983, 161), because they have proved effective in extracting "goods and services from the modern sector and thereby satisfy[ing] the demands of their members." In this respect, ethnic groups have an important functional role to play, being managed by ethnic entrepreneurs who rally the call for an increased share of state-controlled resources to benefit both group and his or her own interests (Arnson 2005, 9–11). When groups feel threatened, moreover, their memberships can coalesce to protect themselves and safeguard the future of generations to come. The ethnic group engages in ongoing social interactions with state elites and with the elites of other cultural and social groups to advance their group's (as well as their own) interests. "To the extent that actors use ethnic identities to categorize themselves and others for purposes of interaction," Fredrik Barth comments (1969, 13–14), "They form ethnic groups in this organizational sense." The ethnic group joins the subjective dimension of peoplehood with the articulation of objective interests. It operates socially in a relationship governed largely by formal and informal rules of interaction that are recurrent and predictable. In practice, the ethnic group acts as other political interest groups do, using influence, concessions, alliances, and threats, and in the way that these groups make claims upon the state. Although it seems reasonable to include the ethnically inspired grouping under the broader category of political interest groups, it is important not to overlook an important difference: most political interest groups can terminate their existence by enacting an appropriate resolution, but the ethnic group, which seeks to advance the common concerns of its members, cannot end its existence so simply. Its operating procedures may resemble those of other interest groups, but its character, which is an expression of group autonomy and distinctiveness, does not.

Several characteristics of ethnic groups have important implications for the activities of these groups in the political arena— their fluidity, their lack of homogeneity and cohesiveness, and their espousal of the common (or indivisible) interests of its membership. With respect to the fluidity of these identity groups, it is inaccurate to characterize them as having a fixed, centuries-old, primordial consciousness. Among such African groups as the Yoruba and Igbo of Nigeria, the Kikuyu and Luhya of Kenya, and the Karamojong of Uganda, the initial affinities were based on coresidence in a region and on similarities of culture, traditions, and legal and economic practices. Aidan Southall (1970: 33), writing about the Luhya, notes that this group is a striking example of a named entity that was first identified as a "tribe" during the colonial era "and must in this sense necessarily be considered a product" of colonial rule.

Thus, an awareness of the ethnic group as a distinct entity in relation to other identity groups is, in many instances, a relatively recent phenomenon (Forrest 2004, 28). It reflects competition with other interests for political power, status, and scarce state resources. The struggle among Nigeria's political parties, based largely on the country's ethno-regions, for control of the political center during the First Republic was described in the *Report of the Political Bureau* (1987, 25) as "extremely vicious and combative; no tricks or methods, however dubious, were regarded as inappropriate." With respect to perceived threats to group security, René Lemarchand (1994, 27) points to "collective fears of the future" in Burundi as a source of political mobilization along ethnic lines (Lake and Rothchild 1998, 8). The emergence of Hutu consciousness in Burundi points up the importance of local security and economic resources as sources of contention. In Burundi, as a side-effect of Tutsi repression in 1972, a sense of shared fate emerged, uniting the Hutu of the north-center with the Hutu of the south-Imbo, a process described by one observer as "enforced ethnicity" (Weinstein 1972, 27). The Hutu and Tutsi use the same language and institutions and often resemble each other in appearance. Belgian colonial rule did much to foster a sense of distinctness, and its influence eventually led to the emergence of a consciousness

of separate identities that gained political expression in collective competition and conflict. The origins of a people may indeed be imaginary, as many social scientists contend; however, as political memory interacts with the experiences in the present, new socially constructed identities emerge and become the basis of a consciousness that can prove constructive or destructive (Anderson 1983; Vail 1989).

The relatively recent origins of many ethnic groups point to another characteristic—the groups' lack of homogeneity and cohesiveness. Although ethnic groups differ from other economic and social interests in the diffuseness of the obligations placed upon their memberships, they all allow for the emergence of multiple identities and internal interests (Barrows 1976, 162; Marenin 1981, 27). The control that group elites exercise over members is frequently insufficient to prevent the emergence of diverse concerns and commitments. The individual member, variously involved in a host of dissimilar social and economic roles, develops crosscutting ties of religion, language, socioeconomic class, subregion, and social cause that modify the exclusivity of primary group obligations. As Lewis Coser (1956, 76–79) observes, such an interdependence of group identities and affiliations can have a stabilizing effect because it avoids the division of a society along a single line, thereby creating a polarized situation. The presence of intraethnic cleavages also creates important possibilities for protecting minority groups. Thus, when framing constitutions in a pluralistic society, political scientists may advocate a power-dividing (or multiple majorities) strategy rather than a power-sharing strategy in the hope that cross-ethnic alliances may emerge in the legislature to defend the civil rights of all citizens. When crosscutting interests are shared by the minority as well as a faction of the majority in the legislature, "subgroups within the ethnic majority are more likely to jump to the defense of the rights of ethnic minorities to defend the rights they share in common" (Roeder and Rothchild 2005, 342).

The ethnic group, as a culturally based social organization, interacts with other ethnic, economic, and social interest groups to promote the salient interests (political power, status, resources, and protection) of both the elite and the membership. In a process that can be likened to a two-level game, leaders must negotiate a common position within the group before engaging in a meaningful bargaining encounter with ethnic patrons at the top of the system (Putnam 1988). No matter how successful these coalition-building efforts may be, intragroup cleavages along the lines of ethnicity, region, ideology, and socioeconomic class are likely to persist. These cleavages allow political entrepreneurs an opportunity to interact with rival factions on a separate track rather than compel them to negotiate with the ethnic collectivity as a whole.

In addition to class cleavages, the political behavior of African ethnic groups since independence reveals a persistence of subethnic schisms along the lines of age-set, clan, and regional cleavages. Zartman (1980, 87) points to "evipolitical" (i.e. time of life or age) groups as important bearers of demand within as well as between ethnic units. These people band together "either because their individual action is insufficient or because their demand is for a collective good shared with others" (1980, 88). Recent statistical data indicate that these age-set differences are quite significant in terms of views held by older Russians toward other groups in their midst (Bahry et al. 2005, 527, Table 3).

Although the relations among the leaders of the major ethnic groups (the Shona and Ndebele) are important to an understanding of Zimbabwe's politics, a comprehensive picture of the political process must also include negotiations and conflicts among such Shona subethnicities as the Manyika, Karanga, and Zezuru. Similarly, Kenya's interethnic conflicts are not simply an exchange of political goods at the top; for example, predominantly Kikuyu Central Province is divided into the three rival districts of Muranga, Nyeri, and Kiambu, and generational differences remain strong.

Kenya's other major ethnic groups—the Luo, Luhya, Kamba, and Kalenjin—are also torn by divided interests and leaderships and are not, as is so commonly assumed, internally united (Gertzel 1970, 17).

Clan politics are also highly significant in Somalia, which is divided into six clan-families and many subclans. During President Siad Barre's rule, the powerful Mijerteyn clan felt disadvantaged in relation to Barre's own Marehan clan and his mother's clan, the Ogaden. "The more [Barre's] political foes voiced their opposition," Anna Simons writes (1995, 51), "the more he relied on people he knew he could trust—namely his relatives— and the more he rewarded his relatives the more distrust this sowed within the population at large." Following Barre's overthrow in January 1991, General Mohamed Farah Aidid, the military commander of the United Somali Congress (USC), fought a series of engagements with several Darod factions in the area between Mogadishu and Kismayu and in the central part of the country. Bitter battles also broke out within the Hawiye-based USC for control of Mogadishu itself. These ongoing encounters pitted Aidid's Habir Gedir subclan against Ali Mahdi Mohamed's Abgal subclan. With no Somali state to enforce the peace, there was no effective institution in place to manage the conflict. The result was an unstable balance of subclan power in Mogadishu (Hirsch and Oakley 1995, 10–16; Menkhaus and Lyons 1993, 2–4).

This internal diversity has a significant effect on the process of intergroup bargaining. Rather than a simple exchange relationship between homogeneous unitary actors, group differences require a more complicated bi-level process of negotiations, both within the heterogeneous ethnic group at the local and regional levels and among the ethnic patrons and central leaders at the top. In this two-level encounter, the political entrepreneur faces double jeopardy. A Kalenjin leader in Kenya must forge a united position among diverse representatives of the Kipsigis, Marakwet, Nandi, Pokot, Elgeyo, Tugen, and others before dealing with the leaders of important ethnic interests (the Kikuyu, Luo,

Embu, Meru, Masai, Luhya, Mijikenda) at the political center. Similarly, a Somali leader must reconcile the differences among the many clans and subclans in his own country before entering into exchange relationships with his counterparts in Kenya or Ethiopia. It is this bi-level aspect of negotiations that so often frustrates state leaders, as they seek to bargain with ethnic patrons who may not be able to maintain a united front within their own constituency.

Finally, class and ethnicity are both viewed as situational variables, fluid and changing in the circumstances of contemporary Africa. Both are products of the state, which must respond, to some extent, to their various demands for public resources. Certainly, these socially constructed groups rest upon different attributes and types of behavior. Yet, in practice, they often overlap and become intertwined with each other. The appeals of ethnic elites, patron-client ties, articulation of interests, language, and occupational patterns are not static and are indeed influenced by the new political and economic developments in the postindependence environment. The effect of these realignments is to shape and give meaning to both class and ethnic attachments. Hence, class and ethnicity, rather than being interpreted as fixed, rigid, and exclusive categories, can more accurately be viewed in terms of the political, economic, and social contexts in which the various groups interact and attempt to achieve their collective purposes.

In light of this overlapping, the issue of which, if any, of these variables is salient at any particular time is largely determined by the setting in which it operates. As Nelson Kasfir (1983, 6) observes: "Class and ethnicity, as well as regionalism or religion, are organizing principles of social action that may act alone, may reinforce, or may work against each other, depending on the social situation." Ethnic and class leaders can make various appeals to gain support for their claims upon the state. Which identity is salient in a particular conflict situation often depends on the symbols used by political elites to mobilize their supporters (Giliomee 1989, 49).

THE ROLE OF THE ETHNIC INTERMEDIARY IN THE POLITICAL PROCESS

Keeping in mind that ethnicity, language, subregion, and socioeconomic class can all overlap in various contexts, I will nonetheless focus upon the way that political elites make use of ethnicity to advance their own self-interests, as well as those of their ethnic constituents. Ethnic leaders who maintain close ties with the mostly urban ruling elite have interests and lifestyles that diverge from those of their constituents. Because rural clients depend heavily on their representatives to put forward their claims to those in positions of power, they have little choice but to give their patrons wide discretion in the way they advance their demands at the political center. The effect is to create a gap between the ethnic constituency's demands for change and the political entrepreneur's selection and shaping of these demands before channeling them to high-level decision-makers (Rothchild 1983: 184). The ethnic entrepreneur has considerable, but not total, latitude in determining which demands to present. If an entrepreneur's choice of claims masks his or her class privileges without taking adequate account of client concerns, that person may well find it difficult to maintain constituent support at election time (Hyden and Leys 1972, 401).

Ethnic entrepreneurs make use of the classic tactics of interest group representatives the world over when pressing their claims for security and material resources upon subregional or central authorities. These ethnic elites vary enormously in terms of influence, access, and types of relationship with state officials and other interest group representatives. They are active in all types of political regime situations: democratic or polyarchical, elite power sharing, and hegemonic. Ethnic spokespersons operate for the most part out of public view and use a variety of formal and informal channels—contacts with politicians and bureaucrats, support for sympathetic parties and candidates, pressure on legislators, logrolling, alliances, and threats of noncooperation and noncompliance—to influence decision-making elites to act positively on their demands. Thus, ethnicity, like socioeconomic class, has proved to be a state-linked category that involves various claims by ethnic intermediaries for state-controlled political and economic resources.

Elites can manipulate ethnic symbols and mobilize their communities for political action precisely because the ethnic group is a base around which the communal membership can unite to attempt to secure satisfaction for their human needs. The ethnic group is indeed a recent social construct, but it has nonetheless developed into a meaningful contemporary vehicle for organizing group members and competing for scarce state-controlled resources. On this, Alex de Waal (1994, 3–4) says: "To argue that the [ethnic groups] thus manufactured are artificial is to miss the point.... it is impossible to interpret recent events without recourse to [ethnic] labels, and they are the labels used by the people themselves." Ethnic group participation in the dynamic struggle over power and scarce resources reflects the political imperatives of the times and cannot be wished away by the exhortations of rulers. As Abner Cohen (1969, 190) states: African ethnicity is "basically a political and not a cultural phenomenon, and it operates within contemporary political contexts and is not an archaic survival arrangement carried over into the present by conservative people." Whether mythical or real, then, as long as political elites can manipulate ethnic loyalties to promote collective purposes, such groups can be expected to play significant roles in advancing what are perceived to be the particular interests of the patrons and the common interests of their memberships.

SHAPING STATE–ETHNIC RELATIONS

The representation and advancement of ethnic group objectives in the political process takes various forms and involves continuing negotiations not only with the state but also with spokespersons for other ethnic groups. State regimes vary enormously in terms of the access and participation they allow ethnic patrons in representing the concerns of their clients at the political center and the subregions. Although ethnicity certainly plays a role in such important political institutions as national elections, power-sharing coalitions, federalism, and resource allocation, state elites generally remained circumspect regarding the ability of ethnic groups in these institutions to have an important influence on political outcomes Zartman 1990.

National elections. Because ethnic groups "are often characterized by relatively dense social networks" (Fearon and Laitin 1996, 719), as well as common political and economic interests, it is unsurprising that national electoral outcomes, particularly in spatially divided societies, display an ethnic factor at work. Accordingly, Donald Horowitz (1985, 86, 194) likens many elections to a "census" and describes this census as "related to the fear of extinction." In this census, numbers may be decisive in terms of state recruitments and allocations, motivating group members to combine behind their leaders to have maximum leverage on the policy process. The effects of this imperative to unite appeared in Ghana's elections in the 1990s, for example. As the Rawlings regime recognized the need to establish a new, firm, support coalition, it moved cautiously and deliberately toward opening the political system. Partial democratization moved ahead in 1992 as multiple parties and leaders emerged to campaign for the presidency. The head of state, Jerry John Rawlings, had a distinct advantage in the electoral process, as he was able to use state resources to outspend his opponents and win a clear majority of over 58 percent of the votes cast in the country as a whole. But this overall victory should not obscure the existence of extensive subregional support for the three leading candidates. Rawlings won 93 percent of the vote in the Ewe-speaking Volta region; over 60 percent in the Akan-speaking Western, Central, Eastern, and Brong Ahafo regions; over 50 percent in the Mole/Dagbani-speaking regions; and 53 percent in Greater Accra. Meanwhile, former president Hilla Limann won 37 percent in the Mole/Dagbani-speaking Upper East region and 33 percent in the Upper West regions, and opposition leader Adu Boahen secured 61 percent in the Akan-speaking Ashanti region. A somewhat similar ethno-regional breakdown appeared in the follow-up 1996 presidential election, with J.A. Kuffuor winning 66 percent of the Ashanti region vote and Rawlings gaining 95 percent support in the Volta region and over 60 percent in the Brong Ahafo, Northern, Upper East, and Upper West regions. As Horowitz (1985, 342) contends, in these electoral contests, "party competition in [a partially] ethnic party system [occurred] within ethnic groups but not across ethnic group lines." Ethnic solidarity remained reasonably firm, particularly in the Ashanti and Volta regions, reflecting a communalistic urge in what were perceived by the voters to be highly competitive situations. In this context of ethnic uncertainty, losing in a competitive election was regarded as no small matter. Following the 1992 election, I witnessed angry demonstrations in the Ashanti capital city of Kumasi, leading to the imposition of a dusk-to-dawn curfew.

The majoritarian dynamic at work in the Ghana elections has been a cause of considerable uncertainty in minority circles, because weaker parties fear being shut out of the government, limiting their access to a fair share of state allocations. Losing in elections is perceived in zero-sum terms as a defeat for communal interests. This fear has caused party officials in some instances to cross the aisle to join the dominant coalition. It has also led to efforts to design electoral institutions to promote the inclusion of all main ethnic interests in the ruling coalition.

Elites have displayed considerable ability to design alternative electoral procedures, including reserved seats in the legislature for minority representation, two-house legislatures, the appointment of the best losing candidates (in the minority communities), proportional representation systems, and broad-based procedures for electing presidents. The latter is exemplified by the crafting of Nigeria's 1979 federal constitution, where those writing the basic law provided that a candidate for president would be elected when that person had a majority of the total votes and one-fourth of the votes cast in two-thirds of the states (Constitution of the Federal Republic of Nigeria 1979, 125). The effect of this procedure was to allay the worst fears of minorities over the possibility of exclusion and to encourage the selection of moderate candidates with broad national appeal.

Power-sharing coalitions. Wide-ranging national coalitions formed on the basis of ethnic interests are frequently used when leaders want to reassure weaker groups about their security and well-being. This practice becomes particularly evident after civil wars, for power-sharing institutions hold out the prospect of inclusion of all major groups in the decision-making process after a peace agreement is signed (Rothchild 2005, 248). In principle, inclusion is seen as empowering minority groups, enabling them to protect their vital interests from within the government. In many weak state situations, where resources are tight and investment capital and job opportunities remain in short supply, gaining access to the state becomes a source of intense competition; having ethnic representation at the state level is perceived as critical to ensure a fair share of allocations. Barbara Walter's (2002, 80) data indicate that when a peace treaty includes provisions for power sharing in the national executive, 38 percent of the combatants are more likely to accept the accord. Thus, when a government caught up in a mutually hurting stalemate takes steps to negotiate on the possibility of a coalition regime at the political center, it provides an incentive to the weaker party to reach a compromise solution (Zartman 1989).

Ethnic power-sharing arrangements have been particularly common in Africa with respect to inclusive decision-making institutions (e.g. in the executive branch) after civil wars (Roeder and Rothchild 2005; Sisk 1996). In negotiating these collaborative institutions, state elites absorb the costs of including a sometimes recalcitrant opponent in the government in order to preserve the unity of the country, while the former insurgent party yields its claims to central state control or full autonomy to secure the legitimacy and resources that come from inclusion in the government. In either case, the bargain remains fragile, for suspicion and insecurity continue to be widespread, commonly accepted norms are weak, and party members may resist the terms of the settlement. This uncertainty can lead to tensions within the ruling coalition and possibly to the emergence of hard-line challengers or outbidders (extremist politicians who take hard-line positions and attempt to outflank moderate politicians within their own community) (Horowitz 1985) in the parties making up the grand coalition.

Three general patterns have materialized from this effort by mediators and others to use power-sharing institutions in Africa's post-civil-war circumstances. First, external mediation resulted in unsteady power-sharing arrangements in the Democratic Republic of the Congo (DRC), Burundi, and Liberia where, in the transition period, the ethnic intermediaries managed to maintain their collaborative institutions, but the procedures and working relations did not meet expectations. In the DRC, the power-sharing arrangement was marred by the continuance of a lack of trust on the part of conflicting political elites. Not only did the Sun City agreement of 2002 leave out important parties such as Etienne Tshisekedi's Union pour la Démocratie et le Progrès Social and the former rebel group, the Rassemblement Congolais pour la Démocratie (RCD-Goma), led by Azarias Ruberwa, but a continuing lack of confidence among the elites prevailed. As one political observer put it, the "leaders themselves do not have trust in each other; as ... power-sharing is conceived in [a] zero-sum game perspective" (Majavu 2003). Burundi's National Forces for Liberation continued to attack the country's military units, and leaders of the Tutsi-led National Union for Progress (UPRONA) expressed strong dissatisfaction with the percentage of seats reserved for

their representatives in the National Assembly (Rothchild 2005, 252–253).

During Liberia's transition to democratic rule, menacing rifts developed among the factional elites in the power-sharing cabinet as well as within Liberians United for Reconciliation and Democracy (LURD), the former rebel group. Fearing a weakening of unity within LURD's ranks arising from participation in the grand coalition, some LURD members sought for a time to undermine the transitional cabinet they were a part of in an effort to keep their militia intact for possible future deployment ("Liberia: Silencing the Guns" 2004, 2). On one occasion, as strains within the cabinet and within LURD approached the breaking point, the UN Secretary-General's special adviser, Jacques Paul Klein, and the US ambassador, John Blaney, stepped into the conflict in an effort to shore up Interim President Gyude Bryant's authority ("Liberia: LURD Rift" 2004, 15608); also, Bryant himself interceded in the leadership crisis within LURD ranks to encourage an easing of tensions. In these three cases of unsteady political coalitions at the political center, the power-sharing agreement survived the transition period but nonetheless revealed potentially dangerous cleavages among ethno-regional and ethno-militia interests.

Second, state ethno-regional bargaining resulted in an asymmetrical pattern when one set of Sudanese negotiators reached an agreement (including a protocol on power sharing) but the others failed to move toward a decisive outcome. The consequence was an incomplete peace process, with the continuing possibility that the unsuccessful negotiations in one subregion will have a destabilizing effect on the other. This pattern remains in contemporary Sudan, for negotiators succeeded in negotiating a Comprehensive Peace Agreement ending the north-south conflict in January 2005, but the negotiations in Abuja over Darfur in 2007 remained largely deadlocked. Certainly, the Darfur conflict is distinct in key respects from the prolonged fighting between northern and southern forces. The Darfur conflict is relatively recent in origin, appears in part to be racially inspired, and lacks the religious overtones associated with the Islamic government's relations with the partly Christian south. Even so, the link in the minds of many local and foreign observers between the two conflicts creates uncertainties in the minds of southerners about the commitment of the Sudanese regime to their peace settlement. The international ramification of continued fighting in Darfur adds to this general uncertainty. As Nelson Kasfir (2005, 201) notes: "It remains to be seen whether Western countries, which made promises contingent on a successful agreement, will respond to internal public revulsion by introducing new demands to settle the war in Darfur [before normalizing relations], thereby risking resumption of the civil war in the south." Clearly, asymmetrical bargaining outcomes can fester and have destabilizing implications.

Third, when tensions run high within an elite coalition, especially after a civil war, power-sharing systems have sometimes proven unworkable, with highly destructive consequences. In Rwanda, the negotiation of the power-sharing arrangement sharpened perceptions of ethnic threat, hastening the process of societal breakdown. The externally mediated 1993 Arusha accords were seemingly balanced in their provisions, for they distributed cabinet positions equally between the predominantly Hutu Movement Révolutionnaire National pour le Développement (MRND) and the Tutsi-led Rwanda Patriotic Front (RPF) (the politically moderate Hutu parties receiving an additional number of seats). Nevertheless, as the hard-line Hutu groups perceived a possible alliance emerging between the RPF and the Hutu moderates, they recognized the imminent possibility of a change in the balance of political forces that would be disadvantageous to their security and well-being (Khadiagala 2002, 469). The effects of this shift in the power balance, and particularly the exclusion of the Hutu extremists in the Coalition pour la Défense de la République under the Arusha accords, was highly destabilizing. By pushing well beyond what the hard-line Hutu leaders felt was

acceptable, the power-sharing arrangement exacerbated conflict to a dangerous level, ultimately leading to their fateful decision to launch the 1994 genocide (Jones 2001, 95).

In Côte d'Ivoire, provisions to balance recruitment of cabinet members also created conflict. The Marcoussis agreement, negotiated in France in January 2003 between President Laurent Gbagbo and rebel spokesmen, sought to advance peace by providing for shared power between the president (Gbagbo, a southerner) and the prime minister (Seydou Diarra, a northern Muslim) as well as between southerners and northerners in the government of national reconciliation. Under the agreement, the cabinet included two government ministers from Gbagbo's Ivorian Popular Front, two from former president Henri Konan Bedie's Democratic Party, two from former prime minister Alassane Ouattara's Rally of the Republicans, and two from the rebel forces. Rebel leaders demanded that northerners be appointed to the key ministries of defense and interior, raising concerns in southern circles regarding security. Thus, rather than promoting an easing of tensions, the peace agreement heightened uncertainty, triggering rioting against French interests in the south for their alleged bias in favor of the northerners. In the months that followed, rebel resentment over Gbagbo's unwillingness to give effective power to prime minister Diarra led to several boycotts of cabinet meetings. In September 2003, the rebels, now renamed the New Forces, suspended the participation of their members in the government, only joining again in December in response to international pressure. Another walkout occurred in March 2004, highlighting the lack of trust between the parties.

Thus, although a shaky power-sharing regime survived in Liberia and Burundi during the transition period, power-sharing regimes in Côte d'Ivoire and Rwanda could not guarantee stable relationships and effective governance. Paradoxically, what seems to be a logical means of overcoming deep suspicions in multiethnic societies has all too often caused increasing ethnic tensions in African countries undergoing a transition to stable regimes.

Federalism.   Executive power sharing seeks to promote ethnic cooperation through inclusive decision-making, but federalism attempts to achieve ethnic peace by means of partitioned decision-making. Federalism, a form of constitutional government that distributes the functions and power of the state among various tiers of government, with each competent in a limited sphere of activities (Wheare 1963, 10), has enormous appeal because it can be designed to take account of ethnic pluralism, but it is a highly complex regime type, requiring the maintenance of a balanced relationship between the center and the regions. As recent data indicate, negotiating parties have not realized genuine federalism as part of a civil war settlement; of the 55 agreements that ended civil wars since 1945 (either by military victory or negotiations), there were no cases of full political decentralization and only nine cases of semi-federalism (Lake and Rothchild 2005, 112–114). In Africa's major experiences with political decentralization (in Ethiopia and Nigeria, but also in Libya, Cameroon, Tanzania, the Mali Federation, and colonial federations in West Equatorial, and Central Africa), the centralizing dynamics were consistent with this finding.

In Ethiopia, the government of President Meles Zenawi adopted ethnic federalism in an effort to reverse the repressive political centralization policies of both the Haile Selassie and Derg regimes and to gain support (Keller and Smith 2005, 266; Mengisteab 1997, 120–121). The 1994 Constitution recognized the right of every "nation" to self-determination (including self-governance, cultural autonomy, and secession) and provided for a ten-state federal arrangement based largely on national identities. The nations were given formal legislative, executive, and judicial powers over a wide range of responsibilities, excluding such central responsibilities as defense, foreign affairs, and economic policy. In light of the dependence of the states on the central government for financial backing, however,

what emerged was a political structure that was politically decentralized in principle but relatively centralized in practice.

A highly centralized form of federalism also marked the Nigerian experience. The colonial federal structure, based on the country's three dominant groups (the Hausa-Fulani in the north, the Yoruba in the west, and the Igbo in the east) may have been necessary to enlarge and consolidate the Nigerian state, but it established an unstable conflict management system (Rothchild 1997a, 41). As independence took hold, the political parties competed intensely for inclusion in the central government, as well as for a favored share of centrally controlled resources. While competition marked party relationships at the political center in the 1960 period, with the predominantly Yoruba Action Group feeling left out of the ruling coalition, the country underwent a series of crises: the undermining of the central coalition, the violence and declaration of a state of emergency in the western region, the dispute over the federal census, the treason trial of Action Group leader Chief Obafemi Awolowo, the boycotts of the 1964 federal election in the eastern and mid-western regions, and the western election crisis of 1965–1966. These unsettling events ultimately set the stage for two military coups. The first occurred in January 1966, when young army officers seized state power and turned governmental authority over to Major-General John Aguiyi-Ironsi. Ironsi proceeded on a unitarist course, abolishing the old regions and uniting the civil services under a single Public Service Commission. The second coup, in July 1966, represented a reaction to the first, accepting the need for some form of federalism as the basis for Nigerian unity. The second coup also led to the death of many Eastern soldiers and massacres of Igbos living in the north. In this situation of increasing regional distrust and polarization, the head of the Federal Military Government, General Yakubu Gowon, reinstated the federal system and, despairing of a political solution to the growing regional rifts, went on to declare a state of emergency and to redivide the country into a twelve-state federation.

The Eastern leader, General C. Odumegwu Ojukwu, rejected the twelve-state decree and proclaimed his region, now renamed Biafra, a sovereign state, ushering in the Nigerian civil war (1967–1970).

Central government action ultimately proved decisive, and a centralized form of federalism survived in Nigeria in the period that followed. A number of features stand out in this evolutionary political process: the tripling in the number of states from the time of the Gowon decree (often creating new ethnic majorities and minorities); the change in the presidential electoral system to require broad-based ethno-regional support for the winning candidate in an effort to encourage unity and moderation; the adoption of the "federal character" principle in appointments to the cabinet, and shifting decrees on the allocation of revenues to the center, regions, and local governments. The dramatic increase in oil revenues in the 1970s and 1980s and the new emphasis in the revenue-allocation formulas on equity and population (as opposed to derivation) created an incentive to form additional states (Bach 1997, 336). Accordingly, the number of states increased over time from 12 to 36, satisfying local elite demands for status and resources—but at a heavy cost in terms of effective governance and aggregate expenditures. The 1979 Constitution gave each state at least one cabinet-level minister, making the cabinet broadly inclusive but reducing central government decisiveness (Constitution of the Federal Republic of Nigeria 1979, 135(3)). Thus, inclusive and partitioned decision-making coincided in Nigeria, resulting in a centralized power-sharing structure that offered weak leadership to a country in need of effective central direction and coordination (Roeder and Rothchild 2005). In Nigeria, Rotimi Suberu (2001, 7) notes, "The dynamics of Nigeria's federalism have had less to do with the geographical dispersal of development from a central capital to regional jurisdictions than with plain, and increasingly fierce, interethnic struggles for centrally controlled resources and rewards."

Resource allocation. Finally, the ethnic principle was evident in Africa in the way that central revenues were allocated to the local districts and regions. Uneven rates of subregional modernization, often resulting from differential colonial development policies and unequal contacts with the outside world, produced wide gaps in social and economic opportunities in postcolonial states. In Zambia, for example, opportunities in provinces with rail lines (the so-called line of rail provinces) and those without (the so-called nonline of rail provinces) were manifestly unequal, and efforts by the government of President Kenneth Kaunda to overcome these differences met with limited success. Despite adopting reallocative policies in Zambia's first development plan, the government actually spent more money on the development of the relatively advantaged line of rail provinces than was allotted to them under the plan, and less was distributed to the relatively disadvantaged nonline of rail provinces than provided for—an outcome largely explained by the latter's inability to absorb the funds (Rothchild 1972: 238). Such regional disparities cause considerable ethno-regional grievance in the relatively disadvantaged areas. If subregional elites begin to feel gravely disadvantaged, as in the Delta Region of Nigeria or among Africans in Darfur, Sudan, their latent sense of grievance contributes to violent opposition.

Unsurprisingly, the relatively disadvantaged subregions have the highest expectations of central government financial support. Surveys on local governance conducted by the Department of Political Science at the University of Ghana at Legon in 1973 indicated a clear preference on the part of respondents in the relatively disadvantaged northern and Upper regions for dependence on central government largesse than was the case in the relatively advantaged western and Ashanti regions and Greater Accra. A significant number of northern and Upper respondents supported the central government initiative, seeing it as more efficient and financially capable than local council action, but those in the relatively advantaged areas contended that local councils did most of the development and were closer to the needs of their constituents (Rothchild 1979, 138–141).

Because most African states are unitary in nature and relatively centralized, their central governments have considerable discretion in determining distributional policies. Nigeria and Ethiopia, although ostensibly federal states, also display substantial central fiscal dominance over their subregions. Variances were evident among Africa's unitary and federal states regarding distributional priorities, with changing emphases on such principles as need and derivation in evidence; however, what seems clear is the primacy of the central government in setting policies on allocations to the subregions.

FROM CONSTRUCTIVE TO DESTRUCTIVE CONFLICT

Thus far we have focused on intrastate ethnic conflicts, in which largely reasonable demands are channeled to state leaders according to the rules of the game. In fact, most of Africa's ethnic conflicts began as reasonable demands from an aggrieved group. Negotiable conflicts remain manageable partly because what are contested are divisible resources and partly because elites and group members embrace pragmatic perceptions of each other's intentions. Above all, group leaders and their memberships feel relatively secure regarding their lives, civil liberties, properties, and cultural practices. Only as the various ethnic interests come to feel reasonably confident that the state regards them as honorable members of society and will protect their physical and cultural security can they lower their guard and coexist with others within the same borders. Struggles over principles become struggles over issues and can be managed through an ongoing bargaining encounter. Such a bargaining encounter is facilitated by a number of factors: in particular, a stable state environment, an inclusionary ideology, a broad sharing of economic opportunities, readily available

information about an opponent's intentions, wide acceptance of resolving differences through bargaining, and the beliefs that the negotiating parties have the capacity and goodwill to deliver on their agreements and the state has the ability to enforce its basic rules.

Ethnic-related conflicts gain in intensity and become less negotiable, however, as the state weakens, exclusionary ideologies gain widespread public support, and competition over scarce resources (land, commercial opportunities, state distributions, government positions) increases. As groups feel threatened physically, culturally, or economically, and as political elites engage in dangerous "outbidding" tactics, intergroup relations become polarized, and bargaining becomes more problematic. Previously agreed-upon commitments come into question, and grave doubts arise about the enforcement of agreements (Lake and Rothchild 1998, 13–17). These problems are exacerbated in conditions of state weakness because the absence of an effective central enforcer means that groups or elements within these groups must fend for themselves in an increasingly dangerous political environment. Paul Collier and his associates (2003, 83; also Goldstone et al. 2000, ix) observe that, "The typical country reaching the end of a civil war faces around a 44 percent risk of returning to conflict within five years." Negative memories and lack of confidence in the intentions of adversaries, then, can produce a spiral effect. When this uncertainty combines with the problem of unreliable information, these processes can reinforce each other and lead to new tensions and possibly to intergroup violence.

Thus, the nature of constructive and destructive ethnic transactions is largely explained by the strategic interactions of elites and their perceptions of their interests, not the existence of ethnic pluralism as such or the presence of ancient hatreds. When ethnic elites place general interests above the particular interests of their own and those of their group, disputes remain negotiable; however, when political leaders manipulate the ambitions and uncertainties of their followers regarding their safety and well-being, then they create a political environment in which suspicion and fear promote zero-sum thinking and efforts, whether nonviolent or violent, to promote special group interests. The descent into parochialism becomes especially dangerous when the state is marked by a low level of legitimacy or a single ethnic group gains dominance over the state and pursues discriminatory policies. Jack A. Goldstone and his associates (2000, ix) find that in multiethnic countries "where certain ethnic minorities are subjected to significant political or economic discrimination, the odds of a new ethnic war were more than *ten times* as high" as the norm.

It is important to stress that strategic interactions among group leaders are not static in nature but can be affected by changes in the balance of power and the way that ambitious or insecure politicians respond to these shifts. They can be particularly dangerous in soft state situations, where elites feel excluded from power and threatened by the ruling state elite, causing them to withdraw from the bargaining process and to seek protection by building up their military capacity. Such a pullback entails a weakening or breaking of linkages and, with it, an isolation that prevents leaders from obtaining reliable information about the intentions of adversaries. The result can be further polarization and distrust that complicates credible commitment to agreements. If polarization deepens and the middle ground disappears (Kuper 1977), the ethnic strongmen may come to see negotiations as doomed to failure and pursue other means—repression or violent action—to achieve their objectives. In that case, sporadic violence gives way to organized collective violence. In the worst cases, the conflict can escalate into genocide or prolonged war.

CONCLUSION: PREVENTING BARGAINING FAILURE

By now, it should be apparent that when a number of conditions are present—pragmatic perceptions, high information, an ability on the part of elites to hold their ethnic coalition together and deliver on their commitments, and a relatively strong state—the context may be favorable for managing conflict through interethnic bargaining and cooperation. However, the best-case scenario does not always exist, and private interest, uncertainty, hostile memories and perceptions, and elite manipulation can work at cross-purposes with effective bargaining. As Horowitz (1985: 565) observes, "Although some form of regularized interethnic bargaining may be essential, this may require precisely the kind of pragmatism that is lacking among ethnic groups that see their vital interests threatened by other groups." Such ethnic pragmatism is not only essential between groups but also within groups and requires a precarious process whereby ethnic negotiators bargain simultaneously at these two levels (Putnam 1988).

In these circumstances, what steps can state or international actors take to reduce the intensity of conflict and to maintain regularized patterns of intergroup relations? It seems too optimistic to expect magnanimity (although it was evident in Nigeria after the civil war), and to remain neutral and let the ethnic fires burn themselves out (as in Rwanda) seems cynical, even irresponsible. It is essential in these situations to take preventive action, encouraging the building of effective institutions, interceding diplomatically by structuring incentives to promote intergroup reciprocity and political exchange, and, at times, intervening with military force. Institutions, Douglass North (1990, 3) writes, "Are the rules of the game in a society or, more formally, are the humanly devised constraints that shape human interaction?" Institutions, which largely reflect the values, social history, and political culture of a society, cannot be viewed as a panacea for deeply divided states. The Weimar constitution, in many respects a liberal and well-conceived basic law, did not prove sufficiently durable to survive the Nazi onslaught. However, when institutions gain legitimacy in the eyes of the community at large, they can then encourage joint problem solving and a sense of interdependence.

Within the state, various rules and regulations have been put into effect that, if implemented impartially, can build minority confidence in the intentions of the state by ensuring protection or restructuring political or economic opportunities. Interethnic negotiations, whether direct or indirect, may have important implications for reducing ethnic fears about the future by producing agreements on such issues as inclusive recruitment, proportional subregional allocations, affirmative action programs, ethnic balance in university scholarships, group protection, the location of industries on a countrywide basis, and election procedures that promote ethnic coalitions. However, because many of these measures represent concessions by the majority to the minority, they may not survive a change of leadership or a grave economic downturn in the country at large. The commitment problem still has not been resolved. One set of rulers may not regard themselves as bound by the arrangements negotiated at an earlier time; they may therefore take advantage of their majority position to reinterpret or dismantle the tenuous protections of the past (as happened in Kenya and South Africa).

What, then, can the main institutional arrangements highly prized by vulnerable minorities—reserved seats in the legislature, proportional representation, transethnic electoral requirements in presidential elections, ethnic federalism, and inclusive power-sharing arrangements—be expected to achieve with respect to protecting vulnerable peoples? Representatives of weaker groups may view these arrangements as structuring relations to put their representatives at the center of the decision-making process. Where polyarchical regimes exist and majorities acquiesce, reserved seats and electoral requirements can offer a basis for a limited inclusion. Furthermore, their numbers often allow the representatives of weaker parties only a limited influence in political process, and less powerful groups can be compromised by the selection of spokespeople who lack authentic group credentials.

With respect to proportional representation, it may have little cross-ethnic impact where populations are territorially concentrated. In Namibia, where the South-West Africa People's Organization won over two-thirds of the seats in the first two parliamentary elections, proportional representation failed, according to Joel Barkan (1998, 61), "to provide sufficient minority representation to block constitutional changes that could be injurious to minority interests. ... Rather, it is the self-restraint of the majority government of President Sam Nujoma, along with international pressure, that has been responsible for the protection of minority interests."

Instead of relying on proportional representation, weaker parties often focus on the institutions of federalism and executive power sharing as the primary protections of their security and well-being over time. They do so precisely because these institutions are firmly embedded in the constitution and represent guarantees of partitioned or inclusive participation in the decision-making process (Roeder and Rothchild 2005: 31–34). In principle, federalism spreads state power between the central governments and the subregions, each being guaranteed separate responsibilities in its own right. As a consequence, the basic law often gives local elites an important say over social and cultural matters affecting minority ethnic communities. In practice, however, central authorities remain in a strong position to influence the decisions made at the subregional level, mainly because of the political center's fiscal dominance. Federal practices in such African states as Nigeria and Ethiopia clearly reflect this central fiscal dominance, resulting in a political system that is more politically decentralized in principle than in practice (Lake and Rothchild 2005). As Rotimi Suberu (2001: 76) puts it, "The [Nigerian] federal government controls a disproportionate share of federally collected revenues to the chagrin of the states and localities whose independent revenue sources have remained grossly inadequate."

Efforts to achieve inclusive decision-making have been employed widely in

Africa, especially during the transition period following civil wars. In such countries as South Africa, Namibia, Mozambique, DRC, Côte d'Ivoire, Liberia, Burundi, and Sudan, provision for power-sharing institutions can be reassuring to weaker parties whose spokespersons are therefore included in the inner sanctums of government (Rothchild 2005). Recent statistical evidence indicates that power-sharing institutions do play a role in encouraging adversaries to negotiate agreements after civil wars (Hoddie and Hartzell 2005, 102–103). In the long-run, however, as the agreement on peace becomes a less urgent matter to the majority party, commitment to the spirit of the power-sharing arrangement declines, and cabinet members from the weaker parties often lose positions or receive less critical assignments. Given the insecurities of the post-civil-war political environment, it may prove difficult to maintain a balance of power between ethnic groups, and the opposition parties may lack the capacity to prevent a centralization of power. In such situations, power dividing (or a multiple-majorities strategy), not power sharing, may prove a more effective long-term means of protecting weaker parties. Because power dividing avoids the rigidity of assigning cabinet seats to specific groups and institutionalizes a separation of power among branches of government elected on different, albeit majority, bases, it opens up the possibility that majority and minority factions may join forces by voting together in a particular chamber and protect the society from abuses of civil rights. "In ethnically divided societies," Philip Roeder (2005, 62) writes, "by dividing any ethnic majority among multiple crosscutting majorities and minorities, the power-dividing strategy seeks to foster through politics the development of dispersed rather than cumulative cleavages." Unlike the other institutions discussed above, a power-dividing strategy seeks to protect weaker interests by checking power with power. Clearly, there can be no certainty that the cleavages within majorities will develop and provide the necessary protective shield, but it appears the best available mechanism for

safeguarding minority groups in an insecure setting.

If none of the protections of minority safety can be viewed as reliable guarantees within the state, it becomes necessary, by default, to look to external actors to conciliate and mediate conflict; stabilize peace agreements; provide monitoring, peacekeeping, and oversight services; exert pressures and incentives; and, as a last resort, intervene militarily, alone or as part of a multilateral force. When internal bargaining between the state and insurgents or among ethnic interests within the state leads to frail agreement or proves inconclusive, weaker parties look outside their borders for a rescuer, one that will overcome the dilemmas of information and commitment and, in the worst cases, halt the spiraling into an ethnic security dilemma (Posen 1993; Rothchild 2000). International actors have played useful roles in facilitating the management of conflict in Angola, Mozambique, Zimbabwe, Namibia, Sudan, Burundi, Côte d'Ivoire, Liberia, and elsewhere (Rothchild 1997b; Zartman 1989; Stedman, Rothchild, and Cousens 2002). At times, however, external interventions have proved too provocative or too limited and slow to have a positive effect. As Romeo Dallaire, the former UN force commander in Rwanda, said about the 6000-strong African Union (AU) force in Darfur, "There is concern among the people around here as to the full effectiveness of the AU. [But] if you do not give them sufficient resources then you are setting them up" (quoted in McDoom 2005). Clearly, if stable relations are to be restored in Darfur in 2006, there is a need for greater logistical and communications support, increased UN military involvement, and a more robust mandate. Unfortunately, this situation is not atypical of possible international initiatives and raises questions about the political will of international actors to make a critical difference in protecting beleaguered minorities.

In sum, ethnic groups do have a common, overarching interest in establishing and maintaining regular and predictable patterns of relationships among themselves. For the most part, they do, in fact, engage in these ongoing encounters. At times, majorities, seeking to hold their countries together, act with a degree of generosity toward minority citizens around them. Yet as competition and conflict ensue, some political elites may seize the opportunity to manipulate the security concerns of their ethnic followers in part, at least, to advance their private interests. Even then, state institutions may be sufficiently resilient to contain the rising tensions. However, should the balance of power between the groups shift, it may trigger violent encounters, often sporadic but later organized and deadly. By default, it falls to international actors to intercede in the escalating encounter to prevent the point of no return (Deng et al. 1995; Evans & Sahnoun 2001). The problem of our times is that the international community is insufficiently organized and prepared for the trajectory of ethnic conflict to move toward its logical end of mass killing and warfare. In such events, the international community cannot afford to stand aside and be indifferent. Rather, it must globalize its response and develop the necessary procedures for effective conflict prevention and management.

REFERENCES

Anderson, Benedict. 1983. *Imagined Communities: Reflections on the Origins and Spread of Nationalism*. London: Verso.

Arnson, Cynthia J. 2005. "The Political Economy of War: Situating the Debate." In *Rethinking the Economics of War: The Intersection of Need, Creed, and Greed*. Edited by Cynthia J. Arnson and I. William Zartman. Washington, DC: Woodrow Wilson Center Press and Baltimore: Johns Hopkins University Press, p. 22.

Bach, Daniel C. 1997. "Indigeneity, Ethnicity, and Federalism." In *Transition Without End: Nigerian Politics and Civil Society under Babangida*. Edited by Larry Diamond, Anthony Kirk-Greene, and Oyeleye Oyediran. Boulder: Lynne Rienner, pp. 333–349.

Bahry, Donna, Mikhail Kosolapov, Polina Kozyreva, and Rick K. Wilson. 2005. "Ethnicity and Trust: Evidence from Russia." *American Political Science Review* 99, no. 4 (November), pp. 521–532.

Barkan, Joel D. 1998. "Rethinking the Applicability of Proportional Representation for Africa." In *Elections and Conflict Management in Africa*. Edited by Timothy D. Sisk and Andrew Reynolds. Washington, DC: US Institute of Peace Press.

Barrows, Walter L. 1976. "Ethnic Diversity and Political Instability in Black Africa." *Comparative Political Studies* 9, no. 2 (July), pp. 139–170.

Barth, Fredrik, ed. 1969. *Ethnic Groups and Boundaries*. Boston: Little, Brown.

Bates, Robert H. 1983. "Modernization, Ethnic Competition, and the Rationality of Politics in Contemporary Africa." In *State Versus Ethnic Claims: African Policy Dilemmas*. Edited by Donald Rothchild and Victor A. Olorunsola. Boulder: Westview, pp. 152–171.

Cohen, Abner. 1969. *Custom and Politics in Urban Africa*. Berkeley: University of California Press.

Collier, Paul et al. 2003. *Breaking the Conflict Trap: Civil War and Development Policy*. Washington, DC: World Bank and Oxford University Press.

Constitution of the Federal Republic of Nigeria. 1979. Lagos: Federal Ministry of Information.

Coser, Lewis A. 1956. *The Functions of Social Conflict*. New York: Free Press.

Deng, Francis, Mimaro, Sadikiel, Lyons, Terrence, Rothcild, Donald & Zartman, I William. *Sovereignty as Responsiblity: Conflict Management in Africa*. Washington: Brookings.

Evans, Gareth & Sahnoun, Mohamed, eds., *The responsobility to Protect*. Ottawa: International Commission on Intervention and State Sovereignty.

Fearon, James D. and David D. Laitin. 1996. "Explaining Interethnic Cooperation." *American Political Science Review* 90, no. 4 (December), pp. 715–735.

Forrest, Joshua B. 2004. *Subnationalism in Africa: Ethnicity, Alliances, and Politics*. Boulder: Lynne Rienner.

Gertzel, Cherry. 1970. *The Politics of Independent Kenya, 1963–1968*. London: Heinemann.

Giliomee, Hermann. 1989. "The Beginning of Afrikaner Ethnic Consciousness, 1850–1915." In *The Creation of Tribalism in Southern Africa*. Edited by Leroy Vail. Berkeley: University of California Press, pp. 21–54.

Goldstone, Jack A. et al. 2000. *State Failure Task Force Report: Phase III Findings*. McLean, VA: Science Applications International Corporation, www.cidem.umd.edu/inscr/stfail

Hirsch, John L. and Robert B. Oakley. 1995. *Somalia and Operation Restore Hope*. Washington, DC: US Institute of Peace Press.

Hoddie, Matthew and Caroline Hartzell. 2005. "Power Sharing in Peace Settlements: Initiating the Transition from Civil War." In *Sustainable Peace: Power and Democracy after Civil Wars*. Edited by Philip G. Roeder and Donald Rothchild. Ithaca: Cornell University Press, pp. 83–106.

Horowitz, Donald L. 1985. *Ethnic Groups in Conflict*. Berkeley: University of California Press.

Hyden, Goran and Colin Leys. 1972. "Elections and Politics in Single-Party Systems: The Case of Kenya and Tanzania." *British Journal of Political Science* 2, no. 4 (October), pp. 389–420.

Ignatieff, Michael. 1993. *Blood and Belonging: Journeys into the New Nationalism*. New York: Noonday Press.

Jones, Bruce D. 2001. *Peacemaking in Rwanda: The Dynamics of Failure*. Boulder: Lynne Rienner.

Kasfir, Nelson. 1983. "Relating Class to State in Africa." *Journal of Commonwealth and Comparative Politics* 21, no. 3 (November), pp. 1–20.

———. 2005. "Sudan's Darfur: Is It Genocide?" *Current History* 104, no. 682 (May), pp. 195–202.

Kaufman, Stuart J. 2006. "Symbolic Politics or Rational Choice? Testing Theories of Extreme Ethnic Violence." *International Security* 30, no. 4 (Spring), pp. 45–86.

Keller, Edmond J. and Lahra Smith. 2005. "Obstacles to Implementing Territorial Decentralization: The First Decade of Ethiopian Federalism." In *Sustainable Peace: Power and Democracy after Civil Wars*. Edited by Philip G. Roeder and Donald Rothchild. Ithaca: Cornell University Press, pp: 265–291.

Khadiagala, Gilbert M. 2002. "Implementing the Arusha Peace Agreement on Rwanda." In *Ending Civil Wars: The Implementation of Peace Agreements*. Edited by Stephen John Stedman, Donald Rothchild, and Elizabeth M. Cousens. Boulder: Lynne Rienner, pp. 463–498.

Kuper, Leo. 1977. *The Pity Of It All: Polarization of Racial and Ethnic Relations*. Minneapolis: University of Minnesota Press.

Lake, David A. and Donald Rothchild, eds. 1998. *The International Spread of Ethnic Conflict: Fear, Diffusion, and Escalation*. Princeton: Princeton University Press.

———. 2005. "Territorial Decentralization and Civil War Settlements." In *Sustainable Peace: Power and Democracy after Civil Wars*. Edited by Philip G. Roeder and Donald Rothchild. Ithaca: Cornell University Press, pp. 109–132.

Lemarchand, René. 1994. *Burundi: Ethnocide as Discourse and Practice*. Cambridge: Cambridge University Press.

"Liberia: LURD Rift." 2004. *Africa Research Bulletin* 41, no. 1, pp. 15608–15609.

"Liberia: Silencing the Guns." 2004. *Africa Confidential* 45, no. 3, pp. 1–2.

MacIver, R.M. 1948. *The Web of Government*. New York: MacMillan.

Majavu, Mandisi. 2003. "The Failure of an African Political Leadership." Interview with Professor Wamba dia Wamba (18 July), www.globalpolicy.org/security/issues/congo/2003/ 0718failure.htm

Marenin, Otwin. 1981. "Essence and Empiricism in African Politics." *Journal of Modern African Studies* 19, no. 1 (March), pp. 1–30.

McDoom, Opheera. 2005. "AU Darfur Force Needs Stronger Mandate—Dallaire." *Sudanese Online* (November 15), www.sudaneseonline.com/enews2005/nov15–08522.shtml 11/15/2005

Mengisteab, Kidane. 1997. "New Approaches to State Building in Africa: The Case of Ethiopia's Ethnic-Based Federalism." *African Studies Review* 40, no. 3 (December), pp. 111–132.

Menkhaus, Ken and Terrence Lyons. 1993. "What Are the Lessons to Be Learned from Somalia?" *CSIS Africa Notes*, no. 144 (January).

North, Douglass C. 1990. *Institutions, Institutional Change, and Economic Performance*. Cambridge, UK: Cambridge University Press.

Posen, Barry R. 1993. "The Security Dilemma and Ethnic Conflict." In *Ethnic Conflict and International Security*. Edited by Michael E. Brown. Princeton: Princeton University Press, pp. 103–124.

Posner, Daniel N. 2005. *Institutions and Ethnic Politics in Africa*. Cambridge, UK: Cambridge University Press.

Putnam, Robert D. 1988. "Diplomacy and Domestic Politics: The Logic of Two-Level Games." *International Organization* 42, no. 3 (Summer), pp. 427–460.

Report of the Political Bureau. 1987. Lagos: Federal Republic of Nigeria (March).

Roeder, Philip G. 2005. "Power Dividing as an Alternative to Ethnic Power Sharing." In *Sustainable Peace: Power and Democracy after Civil Wars*. Edited by Philip G. Roeder and Donald Rothchild. Ithaca: Cornell University Press, pp. 51–82.

Roeder, Philip G. and Donald Rothchild, eds. 2005. *Sustainable Peace: Power and Democracy after Civil Wars*. Ithaca: Cornell University Press.

———. 2005. "Conclusion: Nation-State Stewardship and the Alternatives to Power Sharing." In *Sustainable Peace: Power and Democracy after Civil Wars*. Ithaca: Cornell University Press, pp. 319–346.

Rothchild, Donald. 1972. "Rural-Urban Inequities and Resourced Allocation in Zambia." *Journal of Commonwealth Political Studies* 10, no. 3 (November), pp. 222–242.

———. 1979. "Comparative Public Demand and Expectation Patterns: The Ghana Experience." *African Studies Review* 22, no. 1 (April), pp. 127–147.

———. 1983. "Collective Demands for Improved Distributions." In *State Versus Ethnic Claims: African*

Policy Dilemmas. Edited by Donald Rothchild and Victor A. Olorunsola. Boulder: Westview.

———. 1997a. "Unofficial Mediation and the Nigeria-Biafra War." *Nationalism and Ethnic Politics* 3, no. 3 (Autumn), pp. 37–65.

———. 1997b. *Managing Ethnic Conflict in Africa: Pressures and Incentives for Cooperation*. Washington, DC: Brookings Institution Press.

———. 2000. "Ethnic Fears and Security Dilemmas: Managing Uncertainty in Africa." In *Being Useful: Policy Relevance and International Relations Theory*. Edited by Miroslav Nincic and Joseph Lepgold. Ann Arbor: University of Michigan Press, pp. 237–266.

———. 2005. "Reassuring Weaker Parties after Civil Wars: The Benefits and Costs of Executive Power-sharing Systems in Africa." *Ethnopolitics* 4, no. 3 (September), pp. 247–267.

Simons, Anna. 1995. *Networks of Dissolution: Somalia Undone*. Boulder: Westview.

Sisk, Timothy D. 1996. *Power Sharing and International Mediation in Ethnic Conflicts*. Washington, DC: US Institute of Peace Press.

Southall, Aidan W. 1970. "The Illusion of Tribe." *Journal of Asian and African Studies* 5, nos. 1–2 (January–April), pp. 28–50.

Stedman, Stephen John, Donald Rothchild, and Elizabeth M. Cousens, eds. 2002. *Ending Civil Wars: The Implementation of Peace Agreements*. Boulder: Lynne Rienner.

Suberu, Rotimi T. 2001. *Federalism and Ethnic Conflict in Nigeria*. Washington, DC: US Institute of Peace Press.

Vail, Leroy, ed. 1989. *The Creation of Tribalism in Southern Africa*. Berkeley: University of California Press.

Waal, Alex de. 1994. "The Genocidal State: Hutu Extremism and the Origins of the 'Final Solution' in Rwanda." *The Times Literary Supplement,* n. 4761, July 1, pp. 3–4.

Walter, Barbara F. 2002. *Committing to Peace: The Successful Settlement of Civil Wars*. Princeton: Princeton University Press.

Weinstein, Warren. 1972. "Conflict and Confrontation in Central Africa: The Revolt in Burundi, 1972." *Africa Today* 19, no. 4 (Fall), pp. 17–37.

Wheare, K.C. 1963. *Federal Government*. London: Oxford University Press.

Young, Crawford. 1976. *The Politics of Cultural Pluralism*. Madison: University of Wisconsin Press.

Zartman, I. William. 1980. "Toward a Theory of Elite Circulation." In *Elites in the Middle East*. New York: Praeger, pp. 84–115.

———. 1989. *Ripe for Resolution: Conflict and Intervention in Africa*. New York: Oxford University Press.

———. 1990. "Negotiations and Prenegotiations in Ethnic Conflicts: The Beginning, the Middle and the Ends," In Joseph Montville, ed., *Conflict and Peacemaking in Multiethenic Societies*. Boston: Lexington, reprinted in Zartman, *Negotiation and Conflict Management: Essays on Theory and Practice*. London: Routledge, 2008.

14

Ethno-Religious Conflicts: Exploring the Role of Religion in Conflict Resolution

S.Ayse Kadayifci-Orellana

INTRODUCTION

Since time immemorial, political and religious leaders have exploited the unique power of religion to justify violence and to mobilize populations to kill and be killed. Even though the main reasons and issues may not be of religious character, religion plays a significant role at times of conflict especially when different religious systems encounter each other because religion, as a system of beliefs and practices relating to the sacred, and uniting its adherents in a community, has a powerful hold on people's way of thinking, acting and perception of interests (Kadayifci-Orellana 2003: 26). Then again, religious traditions that are used to legitimize violence and war have also been sources of inspiration for establishing peace and resolving conflicts over the centuries. Still, the field of conflict resolution failed to pay sufficient attention to the critical role religion plays in conflicts until recently. However,

in the majority of conflicts today (e.g. Israel–Palestine, India–Pakistan; Sri Lanka; Iraq, Nigeria among others), religion has been employed by political and religious leaders to justify violence, intolerance and hatred. At the same time, religious actors and faith-based organizations (e.g. Quakers, Mennonites, St Egidio Community, Interfaith Mediation Center in Nigeria among others) are becoming more involved in conflict resolution, mediation and interfaith dialogues to transform the conflictual relations between parties (see, e.g. Little 2007).

This revival of religiously motivated violent conflicts and mounting involvement of religious actors to resolve them have made it inevitable for the field to take a deeper look into the dynamics of these conflicts and to develop effective approaches to deal with them. It is increasingly becoming evident that to resolve these conflicts effectively and establish a sustainable and long-lasting peace, conflict resolution approaches must take into consideration the religio-cultural traditions of the communities involved. For that reason, emerging literature in the peace and conflict resolution field is emphasizing the importance of understanding the power of religion to mobilize parties for war or for peace (Abu-Nimer 2003; Appleby 2000; Augsburger 1992; Avruch 1998; Gopin 2000; Johnston 1996; Kadayifci-Orellana 2003; 2006; Sampson 1997; Sampson and Lederach 2000; Smock 1995, 2002) and the role religious actors can play to resolve these conflicts (Abu Nimer and Kadayifci-Orellana 2005; Little 2007; USIP 2001, 2003).

This chapter attempts to look into the uncanny relationship between religion and violent conflict. More specifically, this chapter will offer a definition of ethno-religious conflicts and identify some of their characteristics and the unique role religion plays therein, discuss religion both as a source of conflict and a resource for its resolution, explore some of the contributions faith-based actors can make; and consider specific conflict resolution tools that may be employed to resolve them.

CHARACTERISTICS OF ETHNO-RELIGIOUS CONFLICTS

In this study, "ethno-religious conflicts" refer to those conflicts which involve parties that are defined along religious lines, societies where religion is an integral aspect of social and cultural life and where religious institutions represent a significant portion of the community and possess moral legitimacy as well as the capacity to reach and mobilize adherents throughout the community. A combination of characteristics distinguishes ethno-religious conflicts from other kinds of conflicts. These include the following:

1. Centrality of identity issues: As noted above, the majority of the conflicts today are identity conflicts, where the parties define themselves along ethno-religious lines. Identity is related to a description of who one is and how one fits into social groups and society overall and is closely tied with culture

and religion. Various theories have been developed to understand the development and functions of identity (Burton 1990; Kelman 1990; Mitchell 1990; Seul 1999). A wider social recognition of identity – that is the way people and/or groups see, understand and define themselves – and effective participation in social, economic and political processes are recognized today as basic needs of all humanity (Azar 1986; Burton 1990; Kelman 1998; Mitchell 1990). Denial of that identity may lead to a sense of victimization and also to conflict (Burton 1990; Kelman 1990; Rupesinghe 1988: 45). "Identity conflicts are deeply rooted in the underlying human needs and values that together constitute people's social identities" (Rothman 1997: 6). One crucial aspect of identity conflict is that it incorporates psychological, physical, and social dimensions, since identity is an intrinsic element of the "self," and a perceived threat to "self" or to a sense of security based on a distinctive identity usually overrides rational thought and reason (Kadayifci-Orellana forthcoming: 19). Oppression and discrimination of one or more religious groups cause frustration of identity needs, which leads to ethno-religious conflicts and religion, as a core component of identity, serves to separate sharp distinctions between parties during ethno-religious conflicts.

2. Intra-state conflicts: Ethno-religious identity conflicts are usually intra-state conflicts involving people from different religious and/or cultural traditions that live close to each other, or have been put together within the artificial state boundaries. As Lederach (1998: 8) points out, today most current wars (e.g. Iraq, ex-Yugoslavia, Sri Lanka) are intra-state affairs, and they are deep-rooted. As such, they have a long history of mistrust and conflict, which feeds negative enemy images and stereotypes. Also, this means that in the aftermath of the conflict, parties will continue to live close to each other either as neighbors, or as fellow citizens. Therefore, merely resolving the conflict, that is identifying and addressing the underlying reason of the conflict such as needs deprivation,

is not enough. There is also a need to reconcile parties by transforming negative images into positive ones and establishing structures to address conflict before it escalates into violence.

3. Civilian casualties:
The majority of the victims of ethno-religious conflicts tend to be civilians as parties increasingly employ unconventional methods and weapons (such as suicide bombings, ethnic cleansing, etc.). Indeed, Wallensteen and Sollenberg (1996) note that the intensity of these intra-state conflicts and casualties caused by them have been so high that the first post-Cold War decade has been the bloodiest since the advent of nuclear weapons. Therefore, communities involved in these kinds of conflicts often suffer deep collective traumas and injuries and develop deep-rooted and hard-to-transform, negative images of each other.

4. Intractability:
Conflicts that are based on ethno-religious identity are usually much more complicated and harder to resolve than those conflicts over resources. These conflicts tend to resist conflict resolution attempts and endure for long periods of time. In order to capture the unique features of these conflicts, new concepts such as "enduring", "intractable" and "protracted" conflicts have been introduced (Azar 1986: 9; Bercovitch and Kadayifci-Orellana 2002; Diehl, 1985; Gochman and Zeev 1984; Goertz and Diehl 1992; 1993; 1995).[1] Therefore, they require special efforts if they are to be accurately defined, adequately analyzed, and effectively resolved (Fisher 2001: 307).

5. Centrality of religion and religious institutions:
Another distinguishing characteristic of these conflicts is that religion is one of the central identifying characteristics of communities, and religious institutions represent a significant portion of the population possessing moral legitimacy as well as the capacity to reach and mobilize adherents throughout the community. Often, religious feelings can mobilize people faster than other elements of their identity because religion

touches upon deep levels of identity (Abu Nimer 2001; Seul 1999). David Little (1991) argues that religious beliefs play an active and prominent part in defining group identity and in picking out and legitimating particular ethnic and national objectives, because of the human need to "elevate given political and economic arrangements in reference to sacred or cosmic standards" (Little 1991: xx). As such, religion and religious institutions play a central role in ethno-religious conflicts.

6. Use of religious language, texts and images:
As noted by Rothman (1997: 11), identity conflicts are connected to more abstract and interpretive dynamics of history, psychology, culture, values and beliefs of identity groups. During ethno-religious conflicts, religious beliefs, sacred texts, and images are often used and abused to incite hatred and depict enemy images. These beliefs, texts and images serve as lenses through which history and events are interpreted from. Various verses or stories may be interpreted to depict the enemy as 'evil,' 'satanic,' or 'demonic,' making reconciliation extremely difficult. As words of God, or transcendent guidelines, sacred texts provide a degree of truth and certainty for the believers and may have the power to inform attitudes and behaviors of its followers. As a powerful source of legitimation and justification, religious texts, images and language are often used in ethno-religious conflicts.

7. Impact of colonization:
Many of the communities plagued with ethno-religious conflicts are traumatized with the impact of colonization and imperialism. Historically, in order to control and rule the local communities, colonizers have resorted to 'divide and rule' strategy and set up political systems that favored certain ethno-religious communities that were sympathetic to them. This created bitterness and hostilities among the ethno-religious communities. Today, many of these communities are lagging behind the West in material, technical and scientific terms. Most of them suffer from extreme poverty

and economic deprivation and the pressure of globalizing economic structures (Kadayifci-Orellana forthcoming: 22). The common sentiment is that the colonizers, who have exploited and continue to exploit their natural resources, are responsible for this situation of deprivation. This also fuels resentment, and often leads to scapegoating outsiders and/or ethno-religious other, and facilitates constructing enemy images.

8. Crisis of legitimacy: Additionally, many of these societies are faced with a crisis of legitimacy which facilitates attacks on the socio-political legitimacy and economic performance of incumbent governments especially with religious ideologies (Haynes 1994; Juergensmeyer 1993; Sahliyeh 1990). In this context, it becomes easier for religious leaders to use their moral legitimacy to incite violence and hatred and both political and religious leaders do not hesitate to employ religious objects such as sacred texts, symbols, imagery, myths, hymns and so on. to invoke various emotions such as heroism, chivalry, bravery, vengeance, among others. These religious objects, together with other cultural and linguistic constructs, are frequently used to perpetuate a cultural violence, contributing to the continuation of the conflict.

RELIGION AS A SOURCE OF VIOLENCE

As Weber noted in his *Sociology of Religion* (1963), religion is a concept hard to define. Still, one definition suggests that religion is a system of beliefs and practices relating to the sacred (Kadayifci-Orellana 2006). Religious traditions are vast and complex bodies of wisdom built over many generations and their foundational sources, such as holy texts, oral traditions and so on. interpret and express the experiences of the sacred that lead to the formation of the religious community. (Appleby 2000: 16). The sacred manifests itself as the ultimate reality, the source of existence of all in the universe, invokes awe and compels human spirit, drawing it beyond the ordinary range of imagination and desire

(Appleby 2000: 28). Rudolph Otto recognizes that "numinous quality of the sacred is the deepest and most fundamental quality in…strong and sincerely felt religious emotion" (cited in Appleby 2000: 28). Religion, as a human response to this reality perceived as sacred informs the way people think, act and perceive their interests (Kadayifci-Orellana 2002: 81). Religious feelings, then, can mobilize people faster than other elements of their identity.

Many political and religious leaders have not vacillated to use this inimitable power of religion to mobilize the population towards their set goals. Especially, at times of violent conflict, which involves sacrificing human and financial resources, continuation of the conflict requires deep commitment and a belief in the righteousness of the cause. To provide support for their policies, leaders often employ sacred texts, religious myths and images to invoke emotions such as heroism, chivalry or vengence, perpetuating a culture of violence. Defined by Johan Galtung as those religious, ideological or linguistic symbols that legitimize direct or structural violence (Galtung 1990: 291), cultural violence contributes to the continuation of the conflict by teaching, preaching or condoning those acts that dehumanize the opponent. Religion as a critical component of identity, which influences individual attitudes and behaviors, and as a powerful source of legitimizing violent conflict, is often abused to promulgate cultural violence.

Various reasons for employing religious rhetoric, myths and symbolism to legitimize policies and to mobilize the population towards certain political ends, including war, have been identified (Gopin 2002; Kadayifci-Orellana 2006). As spiritual beings, human beings struggle with questions regarding existence, life and death, suffering, injustice and the meaning thereof. Rodney Stark and William Bainbridge (1985: 366) observe that people generally have a coherent, over-reaching, and articulated "Weltanschauung" worldview, perspective, a frame of reference, value orientation, or meaning system that is often based on a religion. Religion addresses some of the most profound existential issues of human life, such as "freedom/inevitability, fear/security, right/wrong, sacred /profane" among others, because it is "a powerful constituent of cultural norms and values" and "embodies and elaborates upon its highest morals, ethical principles and ideals of social harmony" (Said and Funk 2002: 37–38). Religious traditions construct a cosmic universe that is bigger than both the community and the individual, offer a language and symbolism through which human beings interpret reality as well as get comfort for trauma and injuries (Kadayifci-Orellana 2002: 88). Religious ideology conceives of the world in coherent manageable ways, and offers explanations for worldly events. This view is supported by Clifford Geertz (1973) who argues that people find religion necessary to interpret the world around them, especially when bad things happen.

Religious traditions also hold reservoirs of meaning that shape identities, incorporate powerful myths, rituals and symbols that give expression to collective needs and desires. Myths and rituals play an important role in the symbolic dimension of conflicts. Rituals are powerful means of communication, in which followers of a religion connect to their spiritual sources and observe their values and beliefs (Abu-Nimer 2003: 18). Rituals communicate myths, symbols and metaphors that allow for multiple interpretations. They offer alternative ways of communicating difficult issues and emotions such as anger, frustration and suffering among others, as well as creating a space in which people can release emotions and trauma. Rituals can nurture commitment of social values and goals in times of crisis (Schirch 2005).

Myths, on the other hand, provide contents to religious tradition and identity. For example, myths of origin explain the beginnings of the group in cosmological terms and locate the group in the origin of the universe. Robert Luyster (1966) states that religious significance of an event is revealed only in its associated symbols and myths, for it is only through these that the mind apprehends what it has seen and attempts

to express its meaning. Myths translate complex problems into manageable cognitive structures and make them comprehensible to the human mind. During times of conflict, myths become tools to make sense of human atrocities, to 'explain' the reasons and sources of the conflict to the people in a 'clear' way. They provide a deeper meaning to what is happening to the community. These myths may also be utilized to draw the borderlines of what is considered legitimate and what is considered illegitimate. Based on these limits, they render various acts (which would otherwise be considered illegitimate) legitimate.

Religious discourse is powerful because it claims to be the *Truth*. Theologically, *Truth* is defined in terms of the absolute, the complete and the changeless, whereas modern/scientific conception of truth is one that is logically or empirically verifiable (Dicenso 1990: xiii). Although it is not possible to prove the truth of religious claims scientifically and that religion seems to be beyond the realm of reason and rationality, religious discourse makes perfect sense to the community of the faithful as it explains why things are the way they are. Because of its claim to hold the *Truth*, religious discourse rejects all other worldviews and explanations. This exclusionist aspect of religious discourse delineates sharp and difficult-to-overcome lines between the in-group (us/we) and out-group (them) (Kadayifci-Orellana 2006). Informing the formation of individual and group identity, these lines are drawn even sharper at times of conflict.

Religion addresses the need for a sense of social, geographical, cosmological, temporal or metaphysical locatedness (Seul 1999: 558) and religious norms and values are often at the core of one's identity. "Religious meaning systems define the contours of the broadest possible range of relationships – to self, to others near and distant, to friendly and unfriendly, to the nonhuman world, to the universe, to God or that which one considers ultimately real or true" (Seul 1999: 558). For instance, religious beliefs such as the doctrine of chosenness may define borders of relationships and cultivate a sense of belonging, brotherly love and affirmation, often leading to sacralization of group identities (e.g. Ummah, sangha, ecclesia, etc.). As a result, religious traditions may serve to stabilize individual or group identity, provide predictability and continuity and safeguard order through objectification of religious order (Mol 1976). They may also become a force of control that is internalized in individual consciousness, a tool for social control (Cristi 2001: 77, 79).

For these reasons, religious ideology plays a profound role in the molding of social structures and provides the authority that gives social and political order its justification (Kadayifci-Orellana forthcoming: 251). Therefore, religion may act as a legitimizing force both for governments and those who oppose them (Kokosolakis 1985: 371; see also Cristi 2001 and Kadayifci-Orellana 2002). It also defines what is proper individual behavior by providing believers with a moral framework that guides their actions, thus affecting the behavior and actions of individuals (Juergensmeyer 1993: 30–31). Consequently, moral and spiritual forces of religion encourage people to act and change.

Violent conflicts entail significant human suffering as they involve destruction of lives, and the social, economic, political and cultural fabric of the society. Because of the high risks involved, continuation of these conflicts requires the conviction of the individuals in the legitimacy of the narrative that justifies the conflict. Understanding how religious beliefs and convictions influence attitudes and behavior, especially at times of violent conflict, is critical for the conflict resolution field to comprehend the dynamics of mass mobilization towards war or peace and to understand why people take up arms to kill and be killed. More specifically, conflict resolution scholars need to understand how the process of interpretation impacts on the human decision-making process to act in particular ways, as well as its impact on social mobilization and legitimation of discourses of war or peace.

DYNAMICS OF RELIGION AS A SOURCE OF VIOLENCE

It is important to note, however, that religious traditions are not unified but virtually all religious traditions contain a variety of interpretations in regards to war and peace. These interpretations range from justifying violence to promoting nonviolence. For instance, similar to other religious traditions, there are different Islamic interpretations on when war is permitted. These range from nonviolent Islamic interpretations that refuse use of violence under any circumstance a defensive Islamic interpretation of war that allows Muslims to use violence only when attacked, or an offensive Islamic interpretation of war that permits Muslims to use violence to bring non-Muslim communities under Muslim control (see Kadayifci-Orellana 2003, 2006, and forthcoming).

Multiple interpretations within a single religious tradition are facilitated by the fact that religious traditions are recorded in sacred texts, such as the Bible, Torah, Quran, Mishna and so on which are written down in a distant time, usually in a language that is different from the ones used by the current communities. These texts are often filled with ambiguities and contradicting statements, posing a major challenge for interpretation. Although sacred texts, as the direct word of God, are considered by the believers to be universal, timeless truths, they still have to go though human interpretation because religious experience is filtered through human perception and is interpreted within the symbolic frames of myth and ritual (Appleby 2000: 29). Furthermore, life is dynamic and conditions, problems, needs and questions change constantly over time. As living traditions, religious traditions adapt to their environments in order to address contemporary needs and they can do that without eroding continuity with the sacred because the past is capacious (Appleby 2000: 33). Therefore, the way religious texts are understood and acted upon during a violent conflict always involves a tension between the fixed text, the word of God and the sense arrived at by applying it at the concrete moment of interpretation in preaching, which is influenced by the social, political, economic and cultural contexts.

There are a variety of possible reasons as to why people choose one religious response to a conflict over another. Some of these explanations are related to cognitive and emotional needs that may be met by particular religious imagery, symbolism and text. Complexity of the process is aptly captured by Gopin (2000: 11) who states that the way sacred texts are used to foster peace or promote violence and destruction "... seems to depend on the complex ways in which the psychological and sociological circumstances and the economic and cultural constructs of a particular group interact with the ceaseless human drive to hermeneutically develop religious meaning systems, texts, rituals, symbols and laws. Especially under extreme conditions, such as at times of war, religious texts are interpreted through deep fears and concerns. At such times, various verses, ideas or spiritual images may meet the cognitive and emotional needs of the individual (Gopin 2000: 11).

Accordingly, the turbulent relations with the enemy impact on the way texts are understood. Various tales, sagas and myths are selected to support interpretation of the religious tradition that legitimizes war, and constructs negative enemy images. In this process, religious actors simplify religious myths, dehistoricize religious texts, and construct a story in which all time, place and difference are represented as meaningful parts of a divine project (Kadayifci-Orellana 2003: 28). With the aid of religious imagery and vocabulary, various sagas, myths and tales, with which the population is familiar, past, present and future are linked in the minds of the population (Kadayifci-Orellana 2002: 357). Religious objects provide cosmology, history and eschatology of the war and simplify the world into good and evil. This simplification distinguishes the faithful one, who is on the side of God, thus good and pure, from the *other*, who is against God, thus evil, therefore must be eliminated. Religious imagery provides the faithful with hope of victory as well as other-worldly rewards, such as eternal bliss in heaven.

For instance, in Sri Lanka, Sinhalese Buddhists have justified the use of violence against the Hindu Tamils by reinterpreting the Buddhist chronicles of Ashoka that date back 2300 years (see Bartholomeusz 2002). Buddhist monks interpreted the conversation that took place between eight Buddhist monks and King Arjuna, who, after bloody war, had doubts about the moral value of his actions. According to the records, eight Buddhist monks reassure Arjuna that he, in fact, killed only one and a half souls (a monk and a novice), and that the rest do not count as souls since they were not Buddhists, and that it was all right to kill the unbelievers. This conversation is used in the modern day conflict to justify killing thousands of Tamils in the name of Buddhism. By reinterpretation of these chronicles, Buddhist monks represent the other, the Hindu Tamils, as unworthy souls as they do not belong to the group, the Buddhist. Various monks in Sri Lanka today interpret the Buddhist texts through the lenses of turbulent relations with the Hindu Tamils and employ this particular conversation, which is not part of Buddhist texts in Buddhist countries other than Sri Lanka, as a key to construct the theology of the *other* in their understanding of Buddhism.

Political, social, economic and cultural factors also shape the way individuals view their conflict, perceive their enemies and their options regarding the conflict as they form their understanding in search of religious/ cultural values and texts to make sense of their lives, sufferings and ways to deal with them. Historical events that influence the experience and interpretive process of the individuals may generate attention on a particular problem, win credibility for a movement's frame (e.g. liberation of the land), encourage new organizations to join a movement (e.g. Hamas and Islamic Jihad), or serve as a model of success that foment expectations among constituents of future movement victories (see Klandermans 1992: 92–93,

77–92; Klandermans 1988: 185). Significant events (e.g. invasions, wars, upheavals, peace agreements etc.) disrupt the operative systems of ideas, beliefs, values, roles and institutional practices in a given society (Sahlins 1991: 44). In return, these events change the way in which social actors think about the meaning and importance they assign to modes of actions and the rules that govern interaction, groups and their discourses, symbols and rituals (Ellingson 1997). Social motivations and personal experiences also play a critical role in determining affiliations with a group that espouses a certain interpretation of religious texts.

In the process of legitimization of an interpretation, various religious myths are interpreted and reinterpreted to justify violence and construct negative enemy images. Past wars and victories are interpreted from the perspective of the religious tradition, and are employed to recreate the history of the people. By locating these victories and wars in the collective memory of the population, religious and political actors engage the population into the politics of interpretation (Kadayifci-Orellana forthcoming: 180). By retelling these religious myths, sagas and stories, they rewrite the history and shape the spaces (e.g. national homeland) and events (e.g. wars, victories, massacres etc.) that constitute the basis of religious identity. Such stories create the imaginative boundaries that contain the identity of the people and influence self-interpretations and modes of exclusion and inclusion (see Kadayifci-Orellana forthcoming), of self–other. These narratives reconfigure the imagination of the population within which the actions have meaning and thus become the contexts for action, such as defending the nation through war or suicide attacks.

For example, in the West Bank and Gaza, suicide attacks are made possible through Hamas's interpretation of the martyrdom myth (see Kadayifci-Orellana forthcoming). The myth of martyrdom and the symbol of 'the martyr' represent the utmost act of devotion to God in the Islamic tradition. As a powerful mythic construct, it gives meaning not only to

one's existence, but more importantly, to one's death (Gopin 2002: 31–32). Suicide, on the other hand, is one of the gravest sins according to Islam. Nevertheless, by reinterpreting the myth of martyrdom to include suicide attacks, Hamas leadership invokes the myth of the ultimate form of sacrifice for God, for justice, and for one's own people (see Kadayifci-Orellana forthcoming). From the perspective of the Palestinians, Israel is one of the world's strongest armies which is also supported by the world's only super power, whereas they lack a legitimate state and have no army. In this unequal war, suicide bombs become the ultimate weapons as each individual turns himself into a weapon (Kadayifci-Orellana forthcoming). Furthermore, this weapon is easier to hide or transport and is much cheaper. These factors facilitate the reinterpretation of the Islamic martyrdom myth and make suicide attacks acceptable to various groups. Such an interpretation endows Palestinians with the sense that they are not powerless or subservient, but can do something about the situation, and sap the Israeli morale, thus obliterate their psychology. Besides, by lending meaning and dignity to these actions in their minds, the myth of martyrdom provides comfort and paramount means of coping with suffering and loss, especially to the families of these individuals who undertake suicide actions (Kadayifci-Orellana 2003: 30).

Again, in ex-Yugoslavia, Bosnian genocide was religiously motivated and justified on religious grounds by the Orthadox Serb nationalists by identifying Bosnians with the Ottoman army that killed the Serbian King in the 14th century and captured Serbia. This particular battle and the myth of the fallen Serbian King drew the imaginative boundaries that contained the identities of the parties, their self-interpretations and modes of inclusion/exclusion (Serbian Christians, defending themselves against infidel Muslim Bosnians/Ottomans). Sells (1996: 123) captures this dynamic in his analysis of this myth as follows:

Religious symbols...myths of origin (pure Serb race), symbols of passion (Lazar [the Serbian King who died during the war against the Ottomans]), eschatological longings (resurrection of Lazar) were used by religious nationalists to create a reduplicating Milos Obilic (the assassin of Sultan Murat [the Ottoman Sultan that was killed during the war]), avenging himself on the Christ killer, the race traitor, the alien, and ironically, the falsely accused "fundamentalist" next door.

Additionally, in many conflict situations, one can observe multiple groups attempting to mobilize the population towards their political and strategic narratives. For example, offensive religious interpretations might be competing with nonviolent religious interpretations that aim to find a peaceful solution to the conflict. Again, secular/nationalist narratives might compete with these religious narratives as well. Particularly, when there is no official army but clandestine military groups, guerillas and so on every individual becomes a potential soldier in the path of "liberation." In this case, different leaderships try to recruit the population into their camp. Who is more successful is then measured in terms of their ability to mobilize the population towards their objectives. This process becomes especially important in legitimization of their leadership policies. As Kelman states, "[l]eaders need assurance that the public is prepared to accept the costs and risks that their policies will inevitably entail" (Kelman 1997: 215). In this process, the critical factor is the *population* (Shapiro 1989: 74; see also Kadayifci-Orellana forthcoming: 30).

Population as a political and economic resource is a fairly novel idea. In this aspect, population implies that people of a community become a major actor in an economic and political problem. Population also implies that people become conscious of their abilities and roles in the political and economic spheres of social life, and not simply subjects of a government (Shapiro 1989: 74). As Foucault wrote, "[t]his privileging of the population as a major actor and identity in the modern nation-state provides much of impetus and legitimization for conflict and war" (Foucault 1978: 25). In other words, "citizens have to be encouraged to support

the strategic understanding among competing states and be willing to mobilize for war (offer their bodies) and support that mobilization (offer their political acquiescence)" (Foucault 1978: 25).

When that is the case, each of these groups need to provide overall frames of meaning within the historical, cultural and religious context of their society. In order to get the support of their population, leaders use symbols that can evoke strong emotional reaction, and according to Kelman, the use of these symbols—which are developed in the early and continuing socialization process— "translates into automatic endorsement of the policies and actions that the leadership defines as necessary" (Kelman 1997: 215). Especially when there is not a single well-defined leadership but a number of groups that are competing for that position, this process becomes more complicated. All of these groups attempt to use various national or religious resources for symbols to evoke the emotions of their populations.

At times, violent or politically coercive aspects of a particular religious response may not be as important as other benefits received from a particular institution. For instance, research in the West Bank observes that most Hamas supporters in the West Bank, including non-Muslims, emphasize the effectiveness and the quality of the services provided by the institutions (such as medical centers, educational and charity institutions) that were affiliated with Hamas rather than the violent and coercive aspects of the organization (see Kadayifci-Orellana forthcoming). These individuals stated that Hamas was the only group that was doing work to alleviate the suffering of the Palestinian people (Kadayifci-Orellana forthcoming). Therefore, the struggle for legitimacy is often carried to these institutional sites, where their arguments and interpretations are introduced to and disseminated among the population. It is at these institutional sites that different perspectives and interpretations compete for legitimacy, and insert themselves as the *Truth*. Again, at these sites, manifold relations of power permeate, characterize and constitute the social body (see Kadayifci-Orellana forthcoming: 41).

Individuals, such as religious or political leaders, who are recognized as having legitimacy to craft new arguments and adopt pre-existing ones, then arrange these arguments in various combinations to pursue their goals. These goals or expected outcomes might include alternative conceptions of what the debate is about (e.g. liberation and struggle against an enemy), what the potential consequences are, contesting ideologies (e.g. religious states, nationalism, secularism or Marxism) or the meaning of categories that underline different interpretations (e.g. jihad, martyrdom etc.), challenging or reinforcing collective beliefs and discrediting rival speakers' arguments by aligning them with illegitimate ideologies or social groups or constructing rivals as public enemies. These narrators might reject solutions (e.g. peace agreement or cease-fire), change goals or rework their arguments when they contradict or fail to resonate with their audiences. Failure to do so may undermine the legitimacy of their position or impair their capacity to mobilize their audiences (Ellingson 1997: 272).

The meaning-making process is not a static but a dynamic one in which the narrators compete with other narrators in the same discursive field for legitimacy. As stated by Ellingson, "[m]eaning is thus constructed through the ongoing process of contestation within a discursive field as speakers jockey to gain legitimacy for their position, the support of targeted audiences, and the opportunity to implement their solutions" (1997). In this process, when the expected outcomes are not reached, and new events occur, and when the solutions fail, the audiences may alter their interests and beliefs, change the meaning of various actions and identify new ways to achieve their goals and look for ways to achieve them. As Ellingson states, under these conditions (1997: 272–273):

[a]s the horizons change, some solutions may be rejected and some diagnoses judged incorrect, while others are accorded greater authority. Speakers respond to the event and altered horizons by reworking their discourses, jettisoning arguments that are untenable, adopting those of their rivals, or crafting new ones that incorporate the event…as the ground from which to asses the viability and legitimacy of old and new arguments to make them more resonant with their audiences' new horizons of expectations and to help speakers compete more effectively within the field of debate.

Religious interpretations do not emerge in a void but develop from pre-existing fields of possibilities, which new interpretations can realign and reconfigure. A field of possibilities is constituted by various historical, social, political and cultural contexts in which the past, the present and an image of a future is constructed. These interpretations operate in a material world, against and in relation to prior and contemporary interpretations, and social, political and economic material forces. Within their religio-cultural structure, religious interpretations that incite violence or peace become effective and they constitute and reproduce systems of power and authority in which they coordinate the actions of the individuals. Within this context, the constellation of power relations and leaders enables a certain narrative to emerge as the dominant one at a particular period.

Power is not static but mobile and flows from one place to another very quickly. Relations of power are immanent in all types of relationships such as economic process, knowledge relationships and so on (Foucault 1978: 86–87). Power is first found and constituted at micro-levels (such as work places, prisons, churches, mosques, schools, hospitals etc.) and later incorporated and developed into larger institutional structures. In this process, power moves around and through different groups (e.g. the government, religious groups etc.), events, institutions and individuals. Furthermore, the way people understand the world, develop values and aspirations and the way they react to events are constituted out of various technologies of power. Hence, individuals are strongly influenced by the power of institutions, such as universities, mosques, churches, synagogues or medical agencies.

At a time when access to nuclear technology and weapons of mass destruction is easier than ever, ethno-religious conflicts present a gruesome challenge to the scholars and practitioners of conflict resolution. As a starting point, understanding the dynamics of religiously motivated conflicts requires an in-depth study of the sources of legitimacy, institutional sites and relevant religious objects (texts, myths, symbols etc) of the communities involved. A second step would be to identify ways in which these religious traditions can be employed to transform the conflictual relations into peaceful ones. The next section will discuss how religious traditions can be part of the solution to the problem of ethno-religious conflicts.

RELIGIOUS SOURCES OF CONFLICT RESOLUTION AND PEACE BUILDING

Aptly recognized by Scott Appleby, "the dreadful record of religiously inspired violence and intolerance withstanding, history paints a more complicated picture of religious identity" (Appleby 2000: 5). Indeed, virtually all religious traditions incorporate ideals of peace and promise peace as the outcome of their application. They all embody a rich variety of cultural and moral resources, which configure the basis of personal and communal values that prevent conflicts. For instance, Christianity has been an inspiration for the civil rights movement of Martin Luther King, Gandhi's nonviolent resistance was influenced by Hinduism and Ghaffar Khan of Pathans constructed a nonviolent army based on the Islamic principles of peacebuilding, forgiveness, patience, and compassion (see Johansen 1997; Kadayifci-Orellana 2006), whereas the Dalai Lama's nonviolent resistance is strongly based on his understanding of Buddhism and the Buddhist values such as compassion.

As noted before, because religious traditions form the basis of legitimacy of these conflicts, transforming ethno-religious conflicts into peaceful relations requires replacing the cultural violence with a cultural peace by tapping into religio-cultural symbols, values, myths and images that promote reconciliation,

coexistence and peace. Transforming the culture of violence and resolving ethno-religious conflicts and building peace demands first an understanding of how religious traditions and identities contribute to a culture of violence. Second, it requires transforming the conflictual relationship based on violence and hatred by engaging religious leaders and other faith-based actors in peace building efforts, and highlighting religious values, traditions, texts and myths that focus on justice, tolerance, coexistence and peace.

Defined "as a range of activities performed by religious actors for the purpose of resolving and transforming deadly conflict with the goal of building social, religious and political institutions characterized by an ethos of tolerance and nonviolence" (Little and Appleby 2004: 5), religious peacebuilding can contribute and has contributed to effective resolution of ethno-religious conflicts. Bringing in religious resources may bring social, moral and spiritual resources to the peace-building process, and can inspire a sense of engagement and commitment both to peace and to the transformation of a conflictual relationship into a peaceful one (Abu Nimer 2001: 686). Religious rituals (e.g. cleansing ceremonies) and values and principles (forgiveness, patience, mercy, accountability or predestination, etc.) may facilitate managing and healing deep injuries and traumas, which is essential to the transformation of relationships between opponents. They can bring in legitimacy to the reconciliation process and encourage engaging with the 'opponent.' Religious involvement in peacemaking initiatives can also prepare and equip conflict resolution practitioners and diplomats for much more proactive roles in transforming the conflict. Also, as Abu-Nimer notes, "framing the interventions within a religious context and deriving tools from a religious narrative have made it possible for interveners to gain access and increase their potential impact on the parties" (Abu-Nimer 2001: 686). Thus, engaging in religious peace-building can provide a spiritual basis for transformation and compensate for the mechanistic and instrumental conflict resolution models.

Indeed, religious traditions incorporate a vast and established repertoires of values, principles and mechanisms that emphasize harmony, reconciliation and peaceful coexistence. These values and principles include, but are not limited to, love for God's creation, compassion, mercy, patience, forgiveness and justice. These values and principles can provide a moral framework, inform attitudes and guide action towards resolving conflicts. For example, emphasizing the belief that every one is created in the image of God may be a useful tool for rehumanizing the opponent, and the religious call for attonement may encourage self-criticism, leading to acceptance of responsibility and asking forgiveness, which is key to any reconciliation process. Values of compassion and mercy connote that a true believer cannot be insensitive to suffering of other beings (physical, economic, psychological or emotional), nor can s/he be cruel to any creature. Thus, they may discourage torture, inflicting suffering or willfully hurting another human being.

In addition to these values, religious traditions provide vocabulary, images and myths —exemplars to serve as positive symbols and examples of peace. Many religious traditions incorporate rituals of healing of trauma and injuries, forgiveness, reconciliation and peace making. For example, *Enemy Way* rituals in Africa, which emphasize purification and atonement after being involved in violence, and symbolize rebirth, have facilitated reintegration of child soldiers, and others who have been captured and/or raped by rebels into their communities (Baines 2005; Ross 2004). Again, after the Bali bombings, the Hindu community in Bali performed religious rituals to purify the stained earth ("Pemerayasita Durmanggala") in accordance with the Balinese Hindu belief. According to this belief, the actual place of bloodshed must be restored with blessings and many Hindus offered prayer, fruit, holy water and flower petals to restore harmony (Head 2002).

Additionally, religious traditions incorporate historical examples and myths that emphasize reconciliation, tolerance, compassion and forgiveness among others.

For instance, three Abrahamic Faiths—Judaism, Christianity and Islam—share the family myth of Abraham, who is recognized as the father of these traditions. These religious traditions, via myths and stories, emphasize the importance of reconciliation among the children of Abraham (Gopin 2002). Another example is the myth of Able and Cain in the Islamic tradition. According to this myth, when his brother attempted to kill him, Able responds, "if you stretch your hand to slay me, it is not me to stretch my hand against you to slay you for I fear Allah (…)" (Quran 2: 28). This myth has been emphasized by various Islamic nonviolent activists such as Jawdat Said to argue that Islam calls for a nonviolent response even when one is faced with violence (Kadayifci-Orellana 2002).

Constructive myths such as these can be powerful sources of inspiration to engage in conflict resolution and reconciliation processes for the community of the faithful. Therefore, identifying these myths as well as values and also rituals of reconciliation and peace making can become effective conflict resolution strategies for practitioners in the field. Gopin supports this argument by stating that "a close study of the sacred texts, traditions, symbols and myths that emerge in conflict situations may contribute to theoretical approaches to conflict analysis by providing a useful frame of reference for conflict resolution workshops and interfaith dialogue groups, and by creating a bridge to the unique cultural expression of a particular conflict" (Gopin 2000: 15). Religious peace building, then, could become a major tool for training, empowering and motivating religiously oriented people towards peace.

CHARACTERISTICS OF RELIGIOUSLY MOTIVATED CONFLICT RESOLUTION

Although religiously motivated conflict resolution approaches are quite similar to the secular ones (USIP 2001) and they utilize secular theories, approaches and methods, certain aspects separate them from secular approaches. Based on Mohammed Abu

Nimer's (2002) categorization, five characteristics that distinguish religiously motivated conflict resolution from secular ones can be identified. These are:

1. Spirituality:
Even though religion and spirituality do not always correspond, religious peace building aims to focus on spiritual aspects of human existence. Spiritual identities include belief and value systems, which in turn, often influence perceptions and attitudes. As Sacks also notes, because religion tracks the deepest connections between self, the other and the universe, it is sensitive to transformation (Sacks 2002: 136). Religious conflict resolution approaches acknowledge that human beings are spiritual beings and incorporate spirituality into the processes. As such, recognizing the emotional, psychological and spiritual needs of the parties, they aim to address a combination of material as well as spiritual needs of the parties. Combined with empathy, spirituality aims to foster interconnectedness between the participants and invoke the divine within them.

2. Religious values and vocabulary:
Religious conflict resolution approaches integrate religious values and vocabulary such as forgiveness, holding on to truth, personal accountability, love, patience, justice, compassion and mercy among others. During dialogue meetings, conflict resolution workshops or mediation processes, religious myths and stories are invoked to emphasize the importance of justice, peace and reconciliation among others. These values and texts inspire and provide guidance to the participants, especially when difficult issues are being discussed, and remind the participants of the greater good and divine purpose of these efforts.

3. Sacred texts:
Religious conflict resolution approaches bring in sacred texts such as verses from the Holy Books, religious myths and images to inspire participants to become agents of change and to take up the challenge to listen to the opponent with an open heart and open mind. These texts provide a level of "certainty" and "truth" (Abu Nimer 2002: 19), a divine voice. They can assist overcoming deadlocks, and provide prophetic examples of peace making. Therefore, they can be a source of comfort, guidance, and inspiration and bring a new perspective to the process.

4. Rituals:
Religious conflict resolution approaches incorporate various religious rituals to communicate difficult feelings, to create a sense of connectedness and to transform relationships. Believers connect to their religious tradition and observe their values and beliefs through rituals (Abu Nimer 2002: 18). As symbolic acts, rituals are powerful means of communication. They can effectively communicate complex feelings and emotions in symbolic ways. Especially at difficult moments during the conflict resolution processes, prayers, meditation or other rituals can be quite effective to overcome deadlocks or to re-engage the participants with the peace process by reminding the participants of the greater good that they are aiming at, and inspiring them with heroic or prophetic examples. Experiencing each others' rituals can also help develop a better understanding of the religious tradition of the 'other' and help recognize and overcome stereotypes and prejudices.

5. Involvement of faith-based actors:
Another distinguishing characteristic of religious peace building is the involvement of faith-based actors in the process. Defined as those organizations, institutions and individuals who are motivated and inspired by their spiritual, religious traditions, principles and values to undertake peace work (Bercovitch and Kadayifci-Orellana forthcoming), these faith-based or religious actors uphold, extend and defend norms and precepts of their religious traditions (Appleby 2000: 8). As Cynthia Sampson observes, "a growing number of religious actors of many sorts–laypersons, individual religious leaders, denominational structures, *ad hoc* commissions and delegations and interdenominational and multireligious bodies–have been involved in a range of

peace-building efforts over the past decades" (Sampson 1997: 273–274). Many of these initiatives take place in addition to and in conjunction with other efforts such as official mediation, problem-solving workshops or negotiations. In addition to developing a better understanding of how religious traditions can contribute to resolving conflicts and framing their interventions within a religious context when appropriate, conflict resolution scholars and practitioners should engage religious leaders and faith-based organizations in conflict resolution processes. Yet, until quite recently, there has been a rift between secular conflict resolution scholars and practitioners and religious actors. Both groups have their distinctive strengths and could make important contributions. It would be invaluable if both groups could work in a synergy to resolve ethno-religious identity conflicts.

POTENTIAL CONFLICT RESOLUTION ROLES FOR FAITH-BASED ACTORS

There are various specific roles religious leaders or faith-based actors can play in resolving ethno-religious conflicts (see USIP 2001; 2003). Based on the categorization developed by Cynthia Sampson (1997), these can be identified as advocacy, mediation, observation, education and interfaith dialogue (see Curle 1971 and Sampson 1997). For example, as advocates, they may be catalysts for empowering the weaker party, restructuring relationship and transforming unjust social structures (Sampson 1997: 279). As intermediaries, they may be effective in bringing parties together to resolve the conflict and transform the conflictual relationships. As observers during such elections, ceasefires and so on they may be effective in preventing violence and transforming the conflict dynamics (Sampson 1997: 280). As educators, they may work towards conflict transformation by reaching out to the community through sermons, training seminars and other social activities, and as facilitators and pioneers of interfaith dialogue, they may bring

together parties across religious and sectarian lines to develop a better understanding of each other's perspectives (Kadayifci-Orellana 2007). Faith-based actors can also be involved in humanitarian relief and development work to relieve suffering of communities inflicted with conflict, or provide conflict resolution training (USIP 2001: 3–7; 2003: 6).

Unique qualities of religious leaders and faith-based organizations

There are many benefits involved in including religion and religious actors in conflict resolution processes. These benefits are derived from the unique qualities religious leaders have (for more information, see Bercovitch and Kadayifci forthcoming). Three major distinctive qualities of these actors include:

1. Legitimacy and credibility:
Willingness, commitment to peace and motivation are critical for resolving conflicts and building peace (Bercovitch and Kadayifci-Orellana 2002). Third parties or individuals who have credibility and legitimacy in the eyes of the parties are often better situated to bring about willingness and commitment to the peace process and to change the attitudes and behaviors of the parties. Religious leaders usually have greater legitimacy and credibility in communities where religion plays an important role in the society. In many of the communities inflicted with ethno-religious identity conflicts, like Pakistan, Afghanistan, Palestine, Sierra Leone and Iraq among others, traditional religious leaders are highly respected and recognized as legitimate moral and spiritual guides. Due to this legitimacy, religious leaders and faith-based institutions often have a unique advantage to resolve conflicts.

Religious leaders derive this legitimacy from the religio-cultural tradition of their societies, which is what Weber (1978) called "subjective sources of legitimacy." This legitimacy equips religious leaders with the sole authority to interpret religious texts. Although conflict resolution scholars and practitioners can tap into various religious sources of conflict resolution, only religious leaders, who are recognized as an authority, can interpret religious texts legitimately.

Additionally, as people of faith and God, religious leaders are usually perceived to be more even-handed and trustworthy, as they are considered to be working only to please God. Thus, they have stronger moral/spiritual legitimacy than secular leaders, especially in communities where corruption and bribery has been a problem. They are very respected and listened to in their communities, thus they can influence the opinions of their followers.

Additionally, many religious actors have been working within these communities for long periods of time and have a credible record of work and commitment. Thus, as insider-partial interveners and as middle-range leaders (Wehr and Lederach 1991), who know the history and the traditions as well as the needs (both physical and emotional) of the parties, they are often better equipped to reach out to the people both at grass-roots and top leadership levels, to mobilize them, to rehumanize the *other* using religious values and to motivate them to work towards peace. Because of this unique leverage they have to reconcile among conflicting parties and rehumanize the opponents, they are often more effective agents of conflict transformation. Especially "when a moral message serves to mobilize mass action, or when the moral messenger backs its words with effective leadership of its own, the religious actor can become a significant catalyst for change" (Sampson 1997: 281).

2. Resources to heal trauma and injuries:

At times of conflict, parties may commit gross violations of human rights and excessive violence. Consequently, communities involved in conflict are traumatized and have deep injuries. Painful memories of conflict, loss of loved ones and injuries suffered cause deep emotional and psychological stress (see also Gopin 2002: 95–100). In order to establish a sustainable peace, there is need to heal these injuries and trauma. Especially during ethno-religious conflicts, where parties live

very close to each other and share a long history of violence and conflict, these injuries and traumas can be quite deep, thus hard to heal. Religious texts and images provide the faithful with a sense of meaning to suffering, death and destitution. Religious beliefs such as belief in destiny, divine justice and rewards could help people overcome grief and give them tools to cope with loss and suffering. Religious values such as forgiveness, patience and reconciliation may help them reconcile with catastrophic events, and let go of pain and hurt. Religious leaders often know their communities well and have a better sense of their physical, psychological and spiritual needs. Consequently, they can provide the appropriate emotional, psychological and spiritual support and resources for healing trauma and injuries. Religious leaders, with their knowledge of the tradition and training in empathy among others, can help individuals and groups to refocus on these values, images and beliefs and thus may effectively help them overcome their suffering and pain.

3. Financial, institutional and human resources available to them:

Another key aspect of religious actors is the financial, institutional and human resources available to them. It is quite often the case that when a peace agreement is signed, funding organizations and states shift their resources to other areas which they consider more urgent because conflict resolution and peace building processes are costly. However, resolving conflicts and building sustainable peace requires long-term commitment and financial, institutional and human resources to support that commitment. Faith-based groups such as St Egidio Community, Mennonites Islamic Relief Services among others have well-established regional and global networks which they can draw upon for institutional, financial and human resources.

Religious leaders also have a broad community base through their congregations or mother institutions, which provide a wide pool to draft committed and unwavering staff that can devote the necessary time to mediation, reconciliation or peace education as part of service to God. These leaders have access to community members through mosques/churches/temples, community centers and educational institutions, such as Bible/Quranic schools. Through sermons, lectures, and education, they can reach out to a large number of people, both at grass-roots level and at the level of top leadership as their status is recognized at both levels. For that reason, at times, they can be more effective than secular institutions with less financial, institutional and human resources.

Contributions of religious leaders and faithbased actors

Based on these qualities, religious actors may make unique contributions to conflict resolution. Some of these contributions include the following (see also Abu Nimer and Kadayifci-Orellana 2005; Bouta et al. 2005):

1. Altering behaviors, attitudes, negative stereotypes and mind frames: As stated earlier, one of the key requirements for transforming ethno-religious identity conflicts is altering the behaviors, attitudes, negative stereotypes and mind frames of the parties. When religious traditions inform the worldviews and attitudes of the parties, religious leaders can employ sacred texts, images and examples to rehumanize the *other,* and invoke compassion, mercy and forgiveness, as well as encourage them to recognize wrong doings and ask for forgiveness. Through these religious objects, religious actors can contribute to the willingness to resolve the conflict and to altering negative mind frames and stereotyping through their speeches, sermons and education.

2. Healing trauma and injuries: As mentioned above, ethno-religious identity conflicts of our time often take place between communities that live in close proximity. These communities usually have a long history of violence and gross violations of human rights. During these conflicts, civilians suffer disproportionately, fostering bitter feelings towards the *other.* Without addressing the suffering and the pain, and without healing trauma and injuries caused by these conflicts, it is virtually impossible to repair the relationship between the parties. Religious actors, with the spiritual, psychological, emotional and textual resources they have, are in a unique position to address such suffering and heal traumas and injuries. For that reason, their involvement in conflict resolution processes can make a contribution by helping parties heal.

3. Contributing to more effective dissemination of ideas such as democracy, human rights, justice and development: It is becoming widely recognized today that the absence of democratic values, human rights principles, institutions that promote social and economic justice and sustainable development leads to structural violence (Galtung 1990). In ethnically or religiously divided societies, the presence of structural violence can be especially volatile, as it can be a fertile ground for the dynamics of cultural violence to lead to direct violence. For that reason, democratic values, principles of pluralism and human rights as well as institutions that ensure social and economic justice and sustainable development need to be woven into the fabric of these societies in order to prevent and resolve ethno-religious conflicts. Again, in societies where religion plays a key role in defining identities and influencing behaviors and actions of the individuals, religious actors, who have legitimacy and credibility, can effectively encourage these values and principles within their religious contexts and through their areas of influence; they can disseminate them among large segments of the population more effectively than secular organizations.

4. Drafting committed people from a wide pool due to their broad community base: Resolving complex conflicts such as ethno-religious identity conflict requires the involvement of all segments of the communities involved and a large number of unwavering people committed to peace. However, peace work is often dangerous as

it may involve interacting with paramilitaries, rebels or insurgents. This interaction may be perceived as suspicious, therefore a threat, by the government authorities. Moreover, talking to the *enemy* may incite accusations as traitors and threaten the lives of these actors. In addition to the physical dangers involved, peace making involves time and finances, which are scarce. Therefore, finding committed people, who are willing to risk their lives and livelihood is not always easy. On the other hand, religious actors, such as the Mennonites for example, view peace making as a religious calling. Through their international and local connections, these actors can draft committed people to do peace work for the sake of God.

5. Challenging traditional structures: In many of the societies experiencing ethno-religious conflicts, there are traditional structures that discriminate against certain segments of the societies (such as religious other, women etc.). These traditional structures facilitate the institutionalization of structural violence, and when coupled with cultural violence, they often lead to direct violence. In societies where religion plays an important role, these structures are justified though religious traditions. When that is the case, religious actors, who have the legitimate authority to interpret the religious texts, can challenge these structures more effectively than secular ones. Therefore, religious actors can be effective agents of change to replace these structures with more inclusive ones.

6. Reaching out to the government, effecting policies, and reaching out to grass-roots: Involving all segments of the society is key to resolving ethno-religious conflicts and establishing sustainable peace. This means that both an official peace agreement between governments and changing the mind frame of the population at the grass-roots level is necessary. As pointed out by Lederach (1998), middle-range leaders who are connected to both top-level leadership and the grass-roots level can effectively contribute to conflict resolution. Religious actors fit into the

description of middle-range leaders offered by Lederach. Often, they have legitimacy in the eyes of both the government and the public in general. Their involvement has the potential to motivate the ordinary people to pressure their political leaders to adopt a political settlement to resolve the conflict, because they can mobilize and motivate their communities to change their behavior and attitudes much more effectively then secular actors. Although these religious leaders or actors cannot resolve the conflict alone, they can significantly contribute to the official and other secular mediation and settlement efforts. Their involvement may motivate parties to negotiate, as was the case with Sierra Leone (Turay n.d.), or may open a rehumanizing window, as was the case with the Quakers in Nicaragua (Nichols 1994; Sampson 1994). Therefore, they can effectively communicate with and influence both groups, and bridge gaps between them.

7. Mediating between conflicting parties: Increasingly, religious actors are intervening in conflict situations as mediators, and not without success (see Bercovitch and Kadayifci-Orellana forthcoming). For example, Pope John Paul II was able to successfully mediate the hundred-year-old conflict between Chile and Argentina during the Beagle Channel conflict (Garrett 1985). The Vatican was the only mediator both governments could agree to, as it possessed moral power and in these two Catholic nations, the public opinion was profoundly affected by the Pope's moral authority (Laudy 2000: 317). In addition to the moral legitimacy religious leaders have, they are often connected to the parties in some way. Therefore, they do not fit into the traditional mediator identity that is an impartial outsider. On the contrary, these religious leaders tend to be either from within the communities themselves or know the parties, their history and value systems well. Wehr and Lederach (1991) observe that in various communities, such as Central America, those actors who are respected by the parties and have a vested interest in the outcome may be more effective peace makers. Key to the effectiveness of these "Insider-Partial" mediators (Wehr and Lederach 1991: 87) is the trust and credibility they have among their communities. Religious actors, as insider-partial mediators thus, can become effective mediators or facilitators to resolve ethno-religious conflicts.

CONCLUSION

As this chapter is discussed, unique qualities of ethno-religious conflicts distinguish them from other forms of conflicts and present a major challenge to the field of conflict resolution. One of the central characteristics of these conflicts is the use of religious beliefs, myths, symbols and images to justify violence and dehumanization of the opponent. Yet as this chapter argued, religious traditions, with their unique empowering and transforming power, can also be employed to legitimize peace and positive images of the other especially where religion is a critical aspect of conflict dynamics. This chapter also argued that to effectively resolve these conflicts, scholars and practitioners should study the sources of legitimacy, contextual, textual and institutional contexts of each community, in order to understand how they contribute to the perpetuation of violence and construction of negative images of the *other*. They should also develop tools and methods to understand the meaning making processes of religiously motivated groups and individuals. More specifically, they should address the critical events that are interpreted to justify violence and analyze how these catastrophic events are perceived, remembered or interpreted by the population as well as perceptions of injustice that lead people to invoke texts that promote violence or nonviolence. Additionally, they should identify negative myths that have provided the basis for violence, and how these myths have been manipulated should be analyzed thoroughly (see Gopin 2002). This should be accompanied by the identification of those myths that call for justice and promote nonviolence. These "positive" myths can be woven into the fabric of narratives

of peace to mobilize people towards reconciliation and coexistence through the active involvement of religious actors (Kadayifci-Orellana forthcoming: 313). These myths should also be supported with religious texts and images.

Also, scholars and practitioners should identify those religious and cultural values that promote peace and coexistence and include them in conflict resolution models in order to facilitate reconciliation between communities. These values should be put into practice by engaging religious leaders that are committed to peace and the nonviolent pursuit of justice and must be supported by religious texts and myths. Likewise, since institutions play a major role in the legitimization of the conflict and mobilization of society, those institutions that uphold nonviolent values and are committed to justice should be identified and empowered. In that line, scholars and practitioners should first identify institutional sites that could contribute to peace building and reconciliation; following that, they should develop strategies to empower these institutions financially, technically and also by providing the necessary training (see Kadayifci-Orellana forthcoming). One way to do that would be to open channels through which these institutions could connect to a wider network of peace-building initiatives across the social, political and economic spectrum. In addition to training and working with these actors and institutions towards preparing them for dialogue with the other, they should also encourage them to reach out to their communities to change the attitudes, mind frames and negative enemy images through lectures, sermons and rituals. Only through such holistic and inclusive approaches can the sources and dynamics of these conflicts be understood and appropriate strategies be developed to effectively resolve them.

NOTES

1 Edward Azar first drew attention to the special features of long-standing conflicts, and termed them protracted conflicts.

REFERENCES

Abu Nimer, Mohammed (2001) "Conflict Resolution, Culture, and Religion: Toward a Training Model of Interreligious Peacebuilding," *Peace Research,* 38 (6), 685–704.

Abu Nimer, Mohammed (2002) "The Miracles of Transformation Through Interfaith Dialogue: Are You a Believer?" in David R. Smock ed. *Interfaith Dialogue and Peacebuilding.* Washington, DC: United States Institute of Peace Press.

Abu-Nimer, Mohammed (2003) *Nonviolence and Peacebuilding in Islam.* Florida: University Press of Florida.

Abu-Nimer, Mohammed and S. Ayse Kadayifci-Orellana (2005) *"Muslim Peace Building Actors Report in Africa and the Balkans."* Washington, DC: Salam Institute.

Appleby, Scott (1994) *Religious Fundamentalism and Global Conflict.* New York: Foreign Policy Association Headline Series no. 301.

Appleby, Scott (2000) *The Ambivalence of the Sacred: Religon, Violence and Reconciliation.* Lanham, MD: Rowman and Littlefield.

Augsburger, D.W. (1992) *Conflict Mediation Across Cultures.* Louisville, KY: Westminster/John Knox Press.

Avruch, Kevin (1998) *Culture and Conflict Resolution.* Washington, DC: United States Institute of Peace Press.

Azar, Edward (1986) "Protracted International Conflict: Ten Propositions," in Edward Azar and John W. Burton eds. *International Conflict Resolution.* London: Wheatsheaf Books.

Bartholomeusz, Tessa (2002) *In Defense of Dharma: Just War Ideology in Buddhist Sri Lanka.* London: RoutledgeCurzon.

Bercovitch, Jacob and S. Ayse Kadayifci-Orellana (2002) "Conflict Management and Israeli-Palestinian Conflict: The Importance of Capturing the 'Right Moment'," *Asia-Pacific Review,* 9 (2), 113–129.

Bouta, Tsjeard, Mohammed Abu-Nimer with S. Ayse Kadayifci-Orellana (2005) "Faith-Based Peace-Building: Mapping and Analysis of Christian, Muslim and Multi-Faith Actors," Netherlands Institute of International Relations 'Clingendael' in cooperation with Salam Institute for Peace and Justice, December, Washington, DC.

Burton, John ed. (1990) *Conflict: Human Needs Theory.* New York: St Martin's Press.

Cristi, Marcela (2001) *From Civil to Political Religion: The Intersection of Culture, Religion and Politics.* Waterloo, Ontario: Wilfrid Laurier University Press.

Curle, Adam (1971) *Making Peace.* London: Tavistock Publications, 279–290.

Dicenso, James (1990) *Hermeneutics and the Disclosure of Truth: A Study on the Work of Heidegger, Gadamer, and Ricoeur.* Charlottesville, VA: University Press of Virginia.

Diehl, Paul (1985) "Contiguity and Military Escalation in Major Power Rivalries," *Journal of Politics,* 47 (4), 12-3–1211.

Ellingson, Stephen (1997) "Understanding the Dialectic of Discourse and Collective Action: Public Debate and Rioting in Antebellum Cincinnati," in Dough McAdam and David A. Snow eds. *Social Movements: Readings on Their Emergence, Mobilization and Dynamics.* Los Angeles, CA: Roxbury Publishing Company.

Fisher, R.J. (2001) *"Cyprus: The Failure of Mediation and the Escalation of an Identity-Based Conflict to an Adversarial Impasse,"* Journal of Peace Research, 38 (3) 307–326.

Foucault, Michel (1978) *History of Sexuality: An Introduction, Volume I.* New York: Vintage Books.

Galtung, J. (1990) "Cultural Violence," *Journal of Peace Research,* 27 (3) 291–305.

Galtung, Johan (1996) "Violence, Peace and Peace Research," *Journal of Peace Research,* 6 (3), 167–191.

Garrett, James L. (1985) "Beagle Channel Dispute: Confrontation and Negotiation in the Southern Cone," *Journal of InterAmerican Studies and World Affairs,* 27 (3, Autumn), 81–109.

Geertz, Clifford (1973) "Religion as a Cultural System," in M. Banton ed. *Anthropological Approaches to the Study of Religion and Interpretation of Culture.* New York: Basic Books.

Gochman, Charles and Maoz Zeev (1984) "Militarized Interstate Disputes, 1816–1976 Procedures, Patterns, and Insights," *Journal of Conflict Resolution,* 18 (4), 586–615.

Goertz, Gary and Paul F. Diehl (1992) "The Empirical Importance of Enduring Rivalries," *International Interactions,* 18 (1), 1–11.

Goertz, Gary and Paul F. Diehl (1993) "Enduring Rivalries, Theoretical Constructs and Empirical Patterns," *International Studies Quarterly,* 37 (2), 147–171.

Goertz, Gary and Paul F. Diehl (1995) "The Initiation and Termination of Enduring Rivalries: The Impact of Political Shocks," *American Journal of Political Science,* 39: 30–52.

Gopin, Marc (2000) *Between Eden and Armageddon: The Future of World Religions, Violence, and Peacemaking.* New York: Oxford University Press.

Gopin, Marc (2002) *Holy War Holy Peace.* New York: Oxford University Press.

Haynes, Jeff (1994**)** *Religion in Third World Politics.* Boulder, CO: Lynne Rienner.

Head, Jonathan (2002) Bali Ritual to Purge Blast Site, BBC (November 15) news.bbc.co.uk/2/hi/asia-pacific/2478801.stm (retrieved August 10, 2007)

Johansen, Robert C. (1997) "Radical Islam and Nonviolence: A Case Study of Religious Empowerment and Constraint Among Pashtuns," *Journal of Peace Research,* 34 (1), 53–71.

Johnston, Douglas M. (1996) "Religion and Conflict Resolution." Paper presented at Fletcher Forum of World Affairs, Winter/Spring.

Juergensmeyer, Mark (1986). *Fighting Fair: A Nonviolent Strategy for Resolving Everyday Conflicts.* San Francisco, CA: Harper and Row.

Juergensmeyer, Mark (1993) *The New Cold War?* Berkeley, CA: University of California Press.

Juergensmeyer, Mark (2000) *Terror in the Mind of God: The Global Rise of Religious Violence.* Berkeley and Los Angeles, CA: University of California Press.

Kadayifci-Orellana, S. Ayse (2002) "Standing on an Isthmus: Islamic Narratives of War and Peace in Palestine." Doctoral dissertation, Washington, DC: School of International Service, American University at Washington, DC.

Kadayifci-Orellana, S. Ayse (2003) "Religion, Violence and the Islamic Tradition of Nonviolence," *Turkish Yearbook of International Relations,* 34.

Kadayifci-Orellana, S. Ayse (2006) "Islamic Tradition of Nonviolence: A Hermeneutical Approach," in Daniel Rothbart and Karina Korostelina eds. *Identity, Morality, and Threat: Towards a Theory of Identity-based Conflict,* New York: Lexington Books.

Kadayifci-Orellana, S. Ayse (2007) "Interfaith Dialogue and Peace Making." Paper presented at Solidarity and Stewardship: Interfaith Approaches to Global Challenges, June 4–5, Al Akhawayn University, Ifrane, Morocco.

Kadayifci-Orellana, S. Ayse (forthcoming) *Standing on an Isthmus: Islamic Narratives of War and Peace in West Bank and Gaza.* New York: Lexington Books.

Kelman, Herbert C. (1990) "Applying a Human Needs Perspective to the Practice of Conflict Resolution: The Israeli-Palestinian Conflict," in John Burton ed. *Conflict: Human Needs Theory.* New York: St Martin's Press, 283–297.

Kelman, Herbert C. (1996) "The Interactive Problem-Solving Approach," in C.A. Crocker, F.O. Hampson and P. Aall. eds. *Managing Global Chaos: Sources of and Responses to International Conflict.* Washington, DC: United States Institute of Peace Press, 501–519.

Kelman. Herbers (1997) "Social-Psychological Dimensions of International Conflict," in I. William Zartman and J. Lewis Rasmussen eds. *Peacemaking in International Conflict: Methods and Techniques.* Washington, DC: United States Institute of Peace Press, 191–238.

Kelman, Herbert (1998) "The Place of Ethnic Identity in the Development of Personal Identity: A Challenge for the Jewish Family," in Peter Y. Medding ed. *Coping with Life and Death: Jewish Families in the Twentieth Century.* Oxford: Oxford University Press, 3–26.

Klandermans, B. (1988) "The Formation and Mobilization of Consensus," *International Social Movement Research, vol. 1.* Greenwich: CT JAI Press pp. 173–196.

Klandermans, Bert (1992) "The Social Construction of Protest and Multiorganizational Fields," in A.D. Morris and C. McClurg eds. *Frontiers of Social Movement Theory.* New Haven, CT: Yale University Press, 77–103.

Klandermans, Bert, H. Kreisi and S. Tarrow eds. (1988) "The Formation and Mobilization of Consensus," *International Social Movement Research,* vol. I. Greenwich, CT: JAI Press, 77–92.

Kokosolakis, Nikos (1985) "Legitimation, Power and Religion in Modern Society," *Sociological Analysis,* 46 (4), 367–376.

Laudy, Mark (2000) "The Vatican Mediation of the Beagle Channel Dispute: Crisis Intervention and Forum Building," in Melanie C. Greenberg, John H. Barton, and Margaret E. McGuinness eds. *Words over War: Mediation and Arbitration to Prevent Deadly Conflict.* Carnegie Commission on Preventing Deadly Conflict. Lanham, MD: Rowman and Littlefield, 293–320.

Lederach, Jean Paul (1998) *Building Peace: Sustainable Reconciliation in Divided Society.* Washington, DC: United States Institute of Peace Press.

Little, David (1991) *Ukraine: The Legacy of Intolerance.* Washington, DC: United States Institute of Peace Press.

Little, David ed. (2007) *Peacemakers in Action: Profiles of Religion and Conflict Resolution.* New York: Cambridge University Press.

Little, David and Scott Appleby (2004) "A Moment of Opportunity? The Promise of Religious Peacebuilding in an Era of Religious and Ethnic Conflict," in Harold Coward and Gordon S. Smith eds. *Religion and Peacebuilding.* Albany, NY: State University of New York Press.

Luyster, Robert (1966) "The Study of Myth: Two Approaches," *Journal of Bible and Religion,* 34 (3, July): 235–243.

Mitchell, Christopher (1990) "Necessitous Man and Conflict Resolution: More Basic Questions About Basic Human Needs Theory," in John Burton ed.

Conflict: Human Needs Theory. New York: St Martin's Press, 149–174.

Mol, Hans (1976) *Identity and the Sacred: A Sketch for a New Social-Scientific Theory of Religion.* Oxford: Basil Blackwell.

Nichols, Bruce (1994) "Religious Conciliation Between Sandanistas and the East Coast Indians of Nicaragua," in Douglas Johnston and Cynthia Sampson eds. *Religion, the Missing Dimension of Statecraft.* New York: Oxford University Press, 64–87.

Ross, Will (2004) Forgiveness for Uganda's Former Rebels, BBC (October 25) news.bbc.co.uk/2/hi/pro grammes/ from_our_own_correspondent/3951277. stm (retrieved August 12, 2007)

Rothman, Jay (1997) *Resolving Identity-Based Conflict in Nations, Organizations, and Communities.* San Francisco, CA: Jossey-Bass.

Rupesinghe, Kumar (1988) *Civil Wars, Civil Peace: An Introduction to Conflict Resolution.* London: Pluto Press.

Sacks, Jonathon (2002) *The Dignity of Difference: How to Avoid the Clash of Civilizations.* New York: Continuum Books.

Sahlins, M. (1991) "The Return of the Event, Again: With Reflections on the Beginnings of the Great Fijian War of 1843 to 1855 between the Kingdoms of Bau and Rewa," in Aletta Biersack ed. *Clio in Oceania: Toward a Historical Anthology.* Washington, DC: Smithsonian, 37–100.

Sahliyeh, E. (1990) *Religious Resurgence and Politics in the Contemporary World.* New York: State University of New York Press.

Said, Abdul Aziz and Nathan C. Funk (2002) "The Role of Faith in Cross-Cultural Conflict Resolution," *Peace and Conflict Studies,* 9 (1, May), 37–50.

Sampson, Cynthia (1994) "To Make Real the Bond Between Us All: Quaker Conciliation During the Nigerian Civil War," in Douglas Johnston and Cynthia Sampson eds. *Religion, the Missing Dimension of Statecraft.* New York: Oxford University Press, 88–118.

Sampson, Cynthia (1997) "Religion and Peace Build-ing," in W. Zartman and L. Rasmussen eds. *Peacemaking in International Conflict: Methods and Techniques.* Washington, DC: United States Institute of Peace Press.

Sampson, Cynthia and John Paul Lederach ed. (2000) *From the Ground Up: Mennonite Contributions to International Peacebuilding.* Oxford: Oxford Univer-sity Press.

Schirch, Lisa (2005) *Ritual and Symbol in Peacebuilding.* Bloomfield, CT: Kumarian Press.

Sells, Michael (1996) *The Bridge Betrayed: Religions and Genocide in Bosnia.* Berkeley, CA: University of California Press.

Seul, Jeffrey R. (1999) "Is the Way of God Religion, Identity, and Intergroup Conflict?" *Journal of Peace Research,* 36 (5, Sep.), 553–569.

Shapiro, Michael J. (1989) "Representing World Politics: The Sport/War Intertext," in James Der Derian and Michael J. Shapiro eds. *International/ Intertextual Relations: Postmodern Readings of World Politics.* New York: Lexington Books, 69–96.

Smock, David (1995) *Perspectives on Pacifism: Christian, Jewish, and Muslim Views on Nonviolence and International Conflict.* Washington, DC: United States Institute of Peace Press.

Smock, David R. ed. (2002) *Interfaith Dialogue and Peacebuilding.* Washington, DC: United States Institute of Peace Press.

Stark, Rodney and William Bainbridge (1985) *The Future of Religion: Secularism, Revivalism, and Cult Formation.* Berkeley: University of California Press.

Turay, Thomas Mark (n.d.) Civil Society and Peace-building: The Role of the Inter-Religious Council of Sierra Leone at www.c-r.org/our-work/accord/sierra-leone/inter-religious-council.php (retrieved August 12, 2007)

USIP (2001) Faith-based NGOs and International Peacebuilding, Special Report No. 76, October 22, Washington, DC.

USIP (2003) Can Faith-Based NGOs Advance Inter-faith Reconciliation? The Case of Bosnia and Herzegovina, Special Report No. 103, March, Washington, DC.

Wallensteen, Peter and Margareta Sollenberg (1996) "After the Cold War: Emerging Patterns of Armed Conflict, 1989–1994," *Journal of Peace Research,* 32 (3), 345–360.

Weber, Max (1963) *Sociology of Religion.* Boston, MA: Beacon Press.

Weber, Max (1978) *Economy and Society.* In Guenther Roth and Claus Wittich eds. Berkeley, CA: University of California Press.

Wehr, Paul and John Paul Lederach (1991) "Mediating Conflict in Central America," Journal of Peace Research, 28 (1), Special Issue on International Mediation (February): 85–98.

Methods of Managing Conflict

15

Conflict Prevention: Theory in Pursuit of Policy and Practice

Michael S. Lund

AN IDEA WHOSE TIME HAS COME AND GONE?

The world seems to be getting more dangerous. Terrorism and the 'war on terrorism' are straining relations between Muslims and the West. Despite interstate wars being in decline, five attacks by a state on another have occurred in the new century. Competition for oil and other essential natural resources makes inter-state wars over territory, viewed as a thing of the past (John Mueller, 1989), more imaginable. Confrontations over nuclear weapons have arisen with North Korea and Iran. Longstanding arms control regimes are unraveling. Further intra-state conflicts could erupt, as closed regimes face violent oppositions; fledgling democracies destabilize; and post-conflict countries fall back into war (Gurr and Marshall, 2005). Trends such as environmental degradation, climate change, population growth, chronic poverty, globalization, and increasing inequality risk future conflicts (e.g., CNA, 2007).

Facing such threats, governments and international bodies could be pursuing how to prevent escalation of emerging tensions into wars, thus avoiding the immense human suffering and problems that wars always cause, both for the countries involved and the rest of the world.[1] Compared to the huge costs of war, the costs of preventing it are dramatically less.[2] Many people are convinced the horrific human costs of the current Iraq War were avoidable. Statistical research on third-party diplomacy also supports the belief that acting before high levels of conflict intensity is better than trying to end them (Miall, 1992: 126; Berkovitch, 1986, 1991, 1993).[3] To try to head off more future conflicts seems possible, moreover, for armed conflict has declined since the end of the Cold War, in part because of an 'extraordinary upsurge of activism by the international community that has been directed to conflict prevention, peacemaking, and peacebuilding' (Human Security Report, 2005: 155).[4] Indeed, conflict prevention is now official policy in the UN, the EU, the G-8, and many states (Moolak, 2005: G-8). It has been tried in places where the risk of conflict was present but they were averted, such as South Africa, Macedonia, the Baltics, Crimea, and the South China Sea.[5] In short, prevention is not simply a high ideal, but a prudent option that sometimes works (cf. Jentelson, 1996; Zartman, 2001: 305f; Miall, 2007: 7,16,17).

Given the evidence that inaction is wasteful and preventive labors can bear fruit, international actors could be collecting and applying what has been learned from recent experience to manage the tensions around the world from which future conflicts will emerge: mitigating sources of terrorism and extremism; averting genocides and other mass atrocities; buttressing fragile governments; reducing weapons of mass destruction; alleviating competition over oil and water; and defusing inter-state rivalries such as China–Taiwan and among the major powers. Yet these actors show little interest in building on recent accomplishments to reduce the current risks (e.g., the deterioration of Zimbabwe and possible renewed war between Ethiopia and Eritrea).[6] Why this apparent gap exists between the promise of conflict prevention and its more deliberate pursuit is the puzzle this chapter seeks to unravel.[7] The following sections seek to get beyond conventional answers by examining three facets of conflict prevention that define its current status: concepts, activities, and impacts. The conclusion sums up the state of the art and offers ideas to advance it.

WHAT IS CONFLICT PREVENTION? A DISTINCT PERSPECTIVE

As the idea has come into vogue, 'conflict prevention' and synonyms such as 'preventive diplomacy' and 'crisis prevention' are bandied about more loosely. New government units and non-governmental organizations have sprung up that tout the term in their logos. To be *au courant*, established organizations add it to mission statements. But though 'conflict prevention' may now be heard more often than the previously dominant 'conflict resolution,' it is not clear whether the activities carried out under this new rubric are actually new. Despite the ambiguity due to the idea's rise to fame, however, close analysts have hammered

out a core definition. Knowledge can cumulate when people use the same terms for inquiry.

Conflict prevention applies to peaceful situations where substantial physical violence is possible, based on typical indicators of rising hostilities. Everyday spates where no blood is spilled, or public controversies that get so rancorous that social groups stop communicating are socially unhealthy, but much less grievous than states or groups about to kill each other with deadly weapons.[8] A coup d'etat is less grave than the genocide of hundreds of thousands of people.[9] Though thus narrowed to conflicts with potentially wide lethality (hereafter 'conflicts' for short), specialists' definitions have varied in two main respects: a) the stage or phase during the emergence of violence when prevention comes into play; and b) its methods of engagement, which are geared to the differing drivers of potential conflicts that preventive efforts address.[10]

Moments for prevention

Conflict prevention has been distinguished from other approaches to conflict mainly by *when* it comes into play during a conflict, not *how* it is done. When UN Secretary General Hammerskjold first coined 'preventive diplomacy' in 1960, he had in mind the UN keeping superpower proxy wars in third-world countries from escalating into global confrontations. When the end of the Cold War brought unexpected intra-state wars such as in Yugoslavia, UN Secretary General Boutros-Ghali extended Hammerskjold's term in an upstream direction to mean not simply keeping regional conflicts from going global, but from starting in the first place (UN, 1992). This conceptual breakthrough shifted the moment for taking action back to stages when non-violent disputes were emerging but had not escalated into significant violence or armed conflict.

Just how far back in the etiology of conflicts might preventive action go to work? Leaving the pre-violent period open to a possible infinite regress might extend it to to causes as primordial as original sin or as dispersed as child-rearing practices, thus dooming the concept to impracticality.[11] To mark a beginning point when pre-emptive actions first become practicable, Peck (1995) usefully delineated early and late prevention. The former seeks to improve the relationship of parties or states that are not actively fighting but deeply estranged. Left unaddressed, such latent animosities might revert to the use of force as soon as a crisis arose.[12] Late prevention pertains to when fighting among specific parties appears imminent.

Boutros-Ghali also extended conflict prevention downstream to actions to keep violent conflicts from spreading to more places. But because such 'horizontal' escalation seemed to go beyond averting the rise to violence ('vertical' escalation) and thus to include containing open warfare, some analysts worried that it implied suppressing physical violence at any subsequent stage in an armed conflict. This would conflate it too easily with actions in the middle of wars (even though Boutros-Ghali offered the separate term 'peacemaking' for those). Bringing prevention into the realm of active wars would eclipse its proactive nature behind the conventional interventions that occur late in conflicts, for which terms like conflict management, peace enforcement or peacekeeping were more fitting. This merging would vitiate the pre-emptive uniqueness of prevention compared to those other concepts (cf. Lund, 1996). It would forego the opportunity to test the central premise that had animated this new post-Cold War notion: that acting before violent conflicts fully breaks out is likely to be more effective than acting on a war in progress. To think of prevention as occurring while wars are already waging not only disregards most people's connotation of 'prevention,' but would relegate the international community to remediating costly war after costly war in a perpetual game of catch-up, foregoing the chance to ever get ahead of the game. While some analysts continued to apply prevention to any subsequent level of violent conflict (Leatherman et al. 1999), most now confine it to actions to avoid the

eruption of social and political disputes into substantial violence, keeping the emphasis squarely on stages before, rather than during violent conflicts.

In particular, the focus of this chapter is 'primary prevention' of prospective new or 'virgin' conflicts, where a peaceful equilibrium has prevailed for some years, but fundamental social and/or global forces are producing new controversies, tensions and disputes.[13] However, imperative later interventions are for minimizing loss of life, they are less humane and likely more difficult because the antagonists are organized, armed, and deeply invested in destroying each other.[14] Graph 15.1 locates this particular moment in conditions of unstable peace and distinguishes it from actions at other conflict stages.

Methods of prevention

Notions of prevention have also varied with regard to the means of engagement, but here too a consensus has emerged. The tools used depend on which causes of conflict are targeted, and thus which providers of tools get involved. Boutros-Ghali listed early warning, mediation, confidence-building measures, fact-finding, preventive deployment, and peace zones. But subsequent UN policy papers of the 1990s (e.g., 'Agenda for Development') greatly expanded preventive measures to a panoply of policies that address the institutional, socio-economic, and global environment within which conflicting actors operate – as diverse as humanitarian aid, arms control, social welfare, military deployment, and media.[15] It can now involve almost any policy sector, whether labeled conflict prevention or not. Recent UN usage of 'preventive action' (e.g., Rubin, 2004) is better suited to this range of potentially useful modalities.

Direct and structural instruments
To classify its array of methods, intercessory initiatives aimed at particular actors in manifest conflicts are distinguished from efforts to shape underlying socio-economic

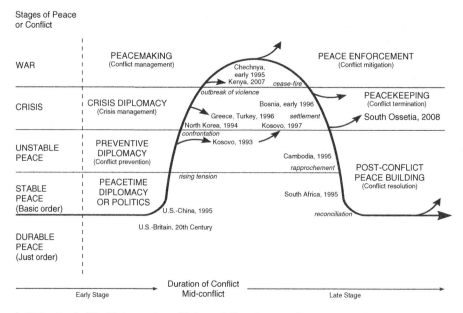

Graph 15.1   Basic life-history of conflicts and the phases of engagement

conditions and political institutions and processes. The former 'direct,' 'operational,' or 'light' prevention (Miall, 2004) is more time-sensitive and actor- or event-focused – for example, diplomatic demarches, mediation, training in non-violence, or military deterrence – and seeks to keep divisive expressions of manifest conflicts from escalating, and thus it targets specific parties and the issues between them.[16] Integral also is 'structural' or 'deep' prevention, meaning actions or policies that address deeper societal conditions that generate conflicts between interests and/or the institutional, procedural and policy deficits or capacities that determine whether competing interests are channeled and mutually adjusted peacefully. These more basic factors make up the environment within which contending actors operate and thus policies toward them can create constraints or opportunities that shape what the actors do. Diverse examples are reducing gross regional disparities in living standards, reforming exploitative agricultural policies, and building effective governing institutions.[17] These structural targets make prevention more than simply

avoiding violence, or 'negative peace,' but rather aspiring to positive peace. In pragmatic terms, it means being able to meet the inevitable arrival of disruptive social and global forces with the ability to bring about change peaceably (cf. Miall, 2007). In recent years, for example, it conflict prevention has been integral to the larger post-Cold War agenda of creating peaceful democratic states out of societies in transition from authoritarianism and patrimonialism (Lund, 2006).

Accordingly, the actors that may be involved in prevention have expanded from official emissaries to a host of third-party governmental and non-governmental actors in social, economic, cultural, and other agencies, such as within the UN system; international financial institutions; regional organizations; and major governments through bi-lateral development and security assistance. Nor is it limited to the governmental world but may include NGOs, the private business sector through trade, finance, and private investment (Ouellete), even celebrities. Preferably, prevention starts through the efforts of the government and other actors in the countries where violent conflicts might emerge. Secretary General Annan deemed this multi-tooled, multi-actored, multi-leveled concept a 'culture of prevention.'[18]

Ad hoc and A priori instruments

A less recognized expansion of prevention extends it 'up' from actions directed at specific countries facing imminent conflicts (*ad hoc* prevention) to include global- and regional-level legal conventions or other normative standards, such as in human rights and democracy. These regimes seek to influence entire categories of countries or agents, where violations might contribute to conflicts although no signs of conflict have yet appeared (*a priori* prevention). Whereas the former actions are hands-on ways (either direct or structural) to respond to country-specific risk factors, the latter are generic international principles agreed on by global and regional organizations as guideposts that whole classes of states are expected to stay within. There are two varieties: a) supra-national normative regimes, such as human rights conventions, and b) international regulations of goods that may fuel or ease conflict such as arms, diamonds, and other trade. Examples of a priori direct prevention are the International Criminal Court and War Crimes Tribunals for Yugoslavia and Rwanda, which are believed effective in deterring future crimes against humanity, not just prosecuting those who have already committed them; the OAS's proscribing of military or executive coups as threats to democracy; and international regulation of arms transfers. Adherence to international standards and rules before any violations occur is conflict prevention where such violations could lead to violent repression, resistance, and conflict.[19] This socializing of governments in international expectations has been applied most vigorously in eastern and southern Europe (e.g., Schneider and Weitzman, 1996; 15), where the EU, NATO, OSCE, and Council of Europe uphold similar standards. Analogous compacts are being tried through NEPAD, the USA's partnership for African Development.

To illustrate the wide range of possible methods for conflict prevention, Table 15.1 lists illustrative possible prevention instruments under these cross-cutting categories.[20]

Despite this variety of moments and methods for prevention, a core concept has emerged. Not a specific instrument, conflict prevention is a distinctly pro-active *stance* that, in principle, many actors could take to respond to unstable, potentially violent situations before violence becomes the way tensions and disputes are pursued. Not a single technique, it is a *disposition* toward incipient stages of conflict that may draw upon a repertoire of responses that would help to keep tensions and disputes from escalating into significant violence and armed force, to strengthen capabilities of parties to resolve issues peacefully, and to progressively reduce the underlying problems that produce serious disputes.[21] The challenges this expansive notion poses for timeliness, coherence, and efficacy are discussed in later sections.

Conflict prevention, management, resolution, transformation

In the context of the school of conflict resolution that emerged in the 1970s, this post-Cold War concept marked new conceptual ground. Differing stages and intervention tools for conflict were implicit but not theoretically central concepts, and the terms in that field still tend to be used interchangeably for any stage. Founders such as Boulding envisioned a global network of 'social data stations' to monitor and warn about emerging conflicts, but in the Cold War context of the time, conflict resolution came to mean addressing already-tense international crises, or active internal wars, rather than keeping them from starting in the first place.[22] Another founder sought to greatly deepen the causes of conflict to include "basic human needs" (e.g., Burton). Yet, the chief instruments the field has promoted are confined to inter-active techniques such as problem-solving workshops or other direct intercession, all of which engage small groups representing parties already tied up in manifest conflicts. Structural and a priori prevention have placed

Table 15.1   Taxonomy of illustrative conflict prevention instruments

	A Priori Measures (Generic norms and regimes for classes of countries)	Ad Hoc Measures ('Hands on' actions targeted to particular places and times)
Structural Measures (Address basic societal, institutional and policy factors affecting conflict/peace)	Standards for human rights, good governance Environmental regimes World Trade Organization negotiations OAS and AU's protocols on protecting democracy International organization membership or affiliations	Economic reforms and assistance Enterprise promotion Natural resource management Decentralization, federalism Long-term observer missions Group assimilation policies Aid for elections, legislatures Human rights and conflict resolution education Aid for police and judiciary Executive power-sharing Security sector reform
Direct Measures (Address more immediate behaviors affecting conflict/peace)	International Criminal Court War Crimes Tribunals Special Rapporteurs for Human Rights Arms control treaties Global regulation of illegal trade (e.g., Kimberly Process for 'conflict diamonds') EU Lome and Cotonou processes on democracy, governance, and human rights	Human rights capacity-building Inter-group dialogue, reconciliation Conditional budget support Fact-finding missions Arms embargoes 'Peace radio' Good offices, facilitation, track-two diplomacy 'Muscular' mediation Preventive deployment Economic sanctions Threat of force Rapid reaction forces

this micro-focus within the macro-focus of the larger processes of nation and state-building, in which interactive techniques are only one among a much larger set of instruments.

Prevention by other names

Table 15.1 reveals also that many de facto direct, structural and generic preventive instruments may not be recognized as such because they operate under aliases. Historically, the Congress of Vienna, League of Nations, the United Nations system of agencies, Marshall Plan, European Union, and NATO and other security alliances were all established to reduce the potential for future inter-state or intra-state conflicts and are thus fundamentally preventive (Lund, 1996a, 1997). During the Cold War, détente and co-existence, arms control treaties, and the CSCE sought to keep the tense superpower relationship from erupting into conventional or nuclear war. Since the Cold War, many

other policies and institutions encourage peaceful management of disputes, such democracy-building and as rule of law programs, nuclear non-proliferation, and regional organizations.[23] Whether any of these tools explicitly bear the term conflict prevention is immaterial, as long as features are built into them that perform prevention effectively. Conflict prevention is also at stake in current debates over current potential crises, such as Iran's nuclear plans, although those words are not used (Ignatius, 2006). All in all, one answer to our question of why it seems that prevention is not tried more often is that it may actually be operating, but under other labels.

WHAT IS BEING DONE? A WELL-KEPT SECRET

The examples so far show that conflict prevention is neither hypothetical nor new.

Although Darfur, the Russia–Georgia conflict, and other unaverted conflicts reflect a frequent failure to act when violence is growing, significant effort has been devoted to preventive action and capacity-building, especially since the ending of the Cold War.

1. Early warning and advocacy

From Quincy Wright to Paul Collier, leagues of social scientists have identified causes of inter-state and intra-state conflict. Databases track the global trends and locuses of conflicts (SIPRI, Human Security Report, 2005) and assess the prospects for conflict or peace in particular countries (e.g., the former Conflict Prevention Network). Some country risk indicators and early warning systems are university-based and open-sourced (e.g., CIDCM, CIFP), and some provide political risk assessments commercially. Helped by the connectivity of the Internet, NGOs issue periodic alerts to official bodies and the public, with recommended responses (e.g., International Crisis Group, Human Rights Watch, International Alert, the former Forum for Early Warning and Early Response [FEWER]). Intergovernmental and bi-lateral agencies have set up in-house systems (UN, OSCE, USAID, CIA, ECOWAS, IGAD). More recently, USAID outlined a 'fragile states' strategy including a 'watch list' to identify priority countries for attention. In short, what one book foresaw as an 'emerging global watch' seems to be gradually taking concrete shape (Ramcharan, 1991).

Conflict prevention defined above has been taken up by several successive non-governmental programs,[24] and was studied and promoted by the Carnegie Commission. In public advocacy, the Global Partnership for Prevention of Armed Conflict (GPPAC) is seeking to capacitate NGOs for early warning and peacebuilding. Efforts are being made to sensitize private corporations to the impacts their commercial activities may have on conflicts, negatively or positively (Wenger and Möckli, 1991). A recent initiative, ENOUGH, is seeking to garner public support for action in Darfur and other African mass atrocities.[25]

Though such efforts to rouse public support for preventive action are useful in the long run, they depend on media coverage of remote events and a distracted public that is touched only by highly emotive material (cf. Kristoff, 2007), and so are prone to belated responses, not pro-active ones. Preventive action has to become largely a full-time professional and governmental endeavor.

Policy agenda

Since the 1990s, more and more intra-state conflicts have burdened the UN and other organizations' humanitarian caseload, the number of UN peacekeeping missions has far exceeded all previous ones since the UN was founded, and the financial costs in post-conflict countries have mounted. As over and over, new conflicts caused human suffering and diplomatic and peacekeeping travail, world leaders and organizations were increasingly swayed by the appealing argument that it would be more humane and cost-effective to try to keep as many bloody and devastating wars as possible from occurring at all. Conflict prevention came specially to the fore after the embarrassing failures by the UN, the USA, and others to stem the massive genocide in Rwanda in 1994. Numerous conferences on particular wars or peacekeeping issues solemnly concluded that what really ought to have happened was more vigorous effort at the outset to avoid such conflicts from occurring in the first place.

Conflict prevention entered the official policy statements of the USA and other major governments, the UN, the EU, and many regional bodies. The title of the 1999 annual report on all the activities of the UN system summed them up as 'Preventing War and Disaster.' Conflict prevention was the topic of two UN Security Council discussions in 2000 and 2001; a priority urged in July, 2000 by the G–8 Okinawa Summit; and the focus of major reports of the UN Secretary General in June, 2001 and 2006. Since 9/11, the notion that failed states breed extremism and conflict added to this impetus under the rubric of preventing state failures, and the

UN has sought to promote more pro-active attention on conflict and other global threats (e.g., UN High Level Panel Report on Global Threats).

Initiatives on the ground

Prevention has gone considerably beyond exhortation and policy into actual efforts in specific countries. Though little-publicized, direct and structural activities have been applied in such diverse places threatened by conflict as Slovakia, Indonesia, and Guyana. These activities range from bi-lateral and regional high-level diplomacy (e.g., by ECOWAS) to NGO projects in peace building at the local level, such as dialogues, peace radio, and inter-ethnic community development programs, to mention a few. The UNDP local community development program in southern Krygyzstan was explicitly entitled 'preventive development.' Again, many programs in potential conflict settings are intended as conflict-preventive but not so labeled, like the UN good offices' efforts with the Myanmar regime, and the World Bank offer in 2000 to help fund land reform in Zimbabwe as its political crisis over land worsened.[26]

Institutional capacity-building

Ongoing response mechanisms have been set up to trigger actions automatically based on risk criteria, at least in principle. The UN Secretariat, the European Commission, and inter-governmental, regional, and sub-regional bodies have staffed small units to watch for early warning signs and consider preventive responses. At UN headquarters, the Secretariat's 'Interagency Framework Team for Coordinating Early Warning and Information Analysis' identifies countries at risk of conflict and applicable UN preventive measures. In addition to the most active regional mechanisms of the OSCE and OAS, all African sub-regional organizations have agreed to prevention mechanisms (e.g., AU; ECOWAS; IGAD; SADC; ECCAS). Although many are not fully operational,[27] some have been used to respond to threatening situations, such as in Congo-Brazzaville and Guinea-Bissau.

Ahead of foreign and defense ministries, major development agencies have taken the lead in intra-state conflict prevention. Countless training workshops have been carried out by the UN for staff and donor implementing partners.[28] NGOs and universities offer institutes for training in conflict analysis and 'peace and conflict impacts assessment.' Conflict and peace-building units exist in all major development agencies including the World Bank. These agencies have supported numerous assessments of the conflict drivers and peace capacities in particular countries. While they have funded unofficial diplomatic initiatives, such as in Georgia, Uganda, Senegal, and the DRC, their preventive efforts have been shifting from specially dedicated activities such as dialogues to 'mainstreaming' conflict and peace-building criteria into all development sectors, such as agriculture, health, education, economic growth, environment, youth, democracy- and state-building, civil society building, as well as security sector professionalism, and into the full programming cycle from assessment through design, monitoring, and evaluation. USAID's Office of Conflict Mitigation and Management is producing practical 'toolkits' that provide lessons learned about how to address typical sources of conflicts arising from issues such as water, minerals, forests, land, youth, human rights, and livelihoods (e.g., CMM). Consultants are tasked with doing assessments of programs for their effects specifically on conflicts and peace (e.g., Lund and Wanchek, 2005) and how they might be improved or at least 'do no harm' by inadvertently exacerbating risk factors (Anderson, 1999). A host of practical analytical tools have been developed for these assessments and formulating appropriate program designs,[29] published in practical guides. These present the typical sources of conflicts, how to assess the impacts of programs on conflict, and how they might be improved. The UN and some donor and multi-lateral organizations are also trying to incorporate conflict-sensitive development into country-wide development strategies such as PRSPs and the UN's CCA and DAF.

Changing norms

New international norms appear to be emerging, albeit slowly and tacitly, that affirm an international obligation to respond to potential eruptions of violence, especially genocide. As successive bloody wars have hit the headlines, one no longer hears that they are inevitable 'tragedies' resulting from 'age-old hatreds.' Instead, concerns are voiced that the calamity could have been avoided, and about what went wrong and who is responsible. UN Secretary General Annan and US President Clinton both acknowledged that they could have acted more vigorously to halt the 1994 Rwanda genocide. Parliamentary public inquiries were held in France and Belgium on the roles that their governments may have played in neglecting or worsening the genocide, and in the Netherlands about the roles of their forces under the UN during the atrocities at Sbrenica. In 2001, the International Commission on Intervention and State Sovereignty asserted a 'responsibility to protect' (R2P) ordinary people who are at risk of crisis or conflict.[30] This duty rests first with sovereign governments about their own citizens, but if states are unwilling or unable, the responsibility to intervene to protect those in harm's way devolves to the international community.[31] R2P may become a critical impetus for conflict prevention, for the Commission argued that the duty to protect also 'implies an accompanying responsibility to prevent' such threats (ICISS, 2001: 19).

Governments in potentially conflict-prone countries often object to this trend as undue interference in their domestic affairs, especially as it implies possible military intervention. But the more that late and possibly non-consensual armed interventions are justified and necessary to halt atrocities, the more acceptable earlier and consensual preventive engagement may become as an alternative. Moreover, the norm of outside responsibility for avoiding threats to citizens is gaining some hold in such countries as well. The African Union now includes a fifteen-member Peace and Security Council that if authorized by the Assembly can deploy military force in a member state in the event of genocide, war crimes and crimes against humanity. Though such authority to stop an humanitarian calamity or genocide is very late prevention, this moves upstream in the conflict cycle the point at which involvement is considered legitimate without a government's consent.[32]

In sum, conflict prevention is now more common. In addition to these explicit efforts, much of it is hidden in plain sight under other rubrics such as nuclear arms control, democratization, non-violent regime change, people power, power-sharing, conditional aid, and counter-terrorism. Though such activities can contribute to preventing conflict, they are taken for granted and not registered in the conflict prevention column. Media tend to report on wars, not how peace is maintained much of the time.[33] The failures to prevent in Bosnia, Rwanda, and Kosovo are widely reported, the successes in Albania (Tripodi) and Romania (Mihailescu) go unnoticed. This lack of awareness outside professional circles of advances and achievements may deflate the preventive enterprise, perpetuating unwarranted pessimism regarding its value. So another part of the answer to our question as to why conflict prevention is disregarded is that lack of awareness of what is actually being done keeps it off the table of actions that could be taken in current potential conflict situations. If one does not believe an activity exists, one does not consider it an option or devote resources to it.[34]

Obstacles

Despite incremental progress in pro-activism, international actors often fail to apply vigorous measures to unraveling societies when they are first significantly threatened by social turmoil, state breakdown, gross human rights violations, and violence. In one study to ascertain the most active third parties in the early stages of recent conflicts, the U.N. and the USA led other third parties, but the responses occurred at late stages of crisis or actual war and in salient arenas such as the Middle East

(Moller and Svensson, 2007: 17). U.S.foreign policy debates constantly dwell only on the narrow question of how "tough" to be toward enemies and whether to go to intervene militarily here or there, thus totally ignoring the options available before such adversaries are created and crisis points are reached. Although humanitarian and development aid have increased, resources earmarked for conflict prevention, with the exception of a few dedicated funds, have not.

Dispersion of wills

The conventional explanation of why major international organizations do not respond to potential conflicts is a 'lack of political will.' But this is vague and does not explain how it can be that preventive actions sometimes *are* taken. While it may be assumed that Western publics are opposed to the use of force abroad to stop genocide or humanitarian crises, it is not clear they would balk at strengthening the capacity to avert crises and avoid later costs. (Jentleson, 1996: 14). Public opinion is also not the final arbiter, for political leaders can circumvent or influence it. Several recent prevention decisions have been taken quietly with little or no wider consultations (Lund, 1999). In 2002–3, the USA's handwringing throughout the 1990s about humanitarian interventions and disdain for nation-building were quickly swept aside with regard to Iraq by White House arguments justifying the more drastic and costly choice of preventive war and forceful regime change.[35]

More often, the problem may be that there is an *excess* of political wills. The major powers and international community are present extensively in most developing countries, including those vulnerable to conflict. This presence takes many forms such as diplomatic missions, cultural activities, health and education and infrastructure development, trade and commerce, military assistance, as well as efforts to promote democracy, human rights, and civil society. But this multitude of activities building schools, training nurses, assisting elections, digging wells, teaching good business practices, you name

it, is pursuing a variety of differing policy goals that are not necessarily supportive of conflict prevention. If many actors are already engaged in conflict-prone places, often in sizeable numbers, the problem is not what is commonly depicted as receiving an early warning from some remote country and then pressuring international actors to rush to it before a crisis erupts. International actors are *already there*. Yet each mission is expending energy and resources in many dispersed directions other than preventing violent conflicts. An effective prevention system does not operate in potential conflict areas because *everyone is busily pursuing other mandates*. While some of these conflict-blind activities may help, some enable or worsen conflicts.

Even the most prevention-relevant activities listed above are too segmented. Early warning and conflict indicators come up through separate reporting channels and program desks, such as for human rights, humanitarian aid, and development, arriving at differing definitions of local problems and interpretations of conflict causes. This information is not synthesized to reveal possible overlap and complementarity. For example, genocide prevention is advocated as if it is a separate problem from intra-state conflict. But most genocides by far occur during wars (Harff, 2003), and wars are hard to stop, so the best way to prevent genocide is to prevent the wars in which they usually arise.

Clash of professions

Lying behind the problem of disparate wills are differing values and paradigms of separate disciplines and professions such as conflict resolution, peace studies, human rights, economic development, political development, and security studies. Contradictions arise over the often-inescapable need to make tradeoffs between these fields' desirable but competing goals. The prevailing Western liberal model often assumes that the democracy, human rights, rule of law, free markets, and economic growth are all compatible with one another and with peace. But in many situations, such compatibility does not hold, yet there is no common understanding or procedure for prioritizing goals at differing stages of conflict.

These value conflicts reflect differing worldviews of diverse professionals regarding how to conflict. Diplomatic, military, and security communities often ignore the need to address underlying, longer-term factors that contribute to conflicts, as they pursue predominantly elite-oriented and state-centered approaches to already armed conflicts. On the other hand, development agencies and NGOs generally fail to recognize the need for sufficient diplomatic clout or other forms of power to confront the immediate drivers of intra-state conflicts, such as political leaders who can mobilize popular followings and armed groups. On their part, the human rights community often takes a legal-juridical approach to exposing violations of human rights principles and punishing the guilty – justice over peace – whereas the conflict resolution school emphasizes stopping violence, strengthening human relationships and achieving reconciliation.[36] But these philosophical differences lead the various fields to elevate one value above others and pursue differing policy goals, thus frustrating the achievement of effective overall prevention strategies. All good things do not necessarily go together. Empirically speaking, one kind of leverage without others may have serious limits or cause harm (see the following section). What is required is recognition that no one value necessarily can be achieved absolutely; compromises need to strike balances between competing values in differing circumstances.

These dissonances may be getting more crossfield attention, however. Procedurally, efforts to achieve policy coherence are being made by country-level coordinators such as the UN Secretary General's special representatives and UNDP resident representatives. Whole-of-government efforts are reflected in such entities as the US State Department's new Coordinator for Reconstruction and Stabilization. Inter-agency harmonization is being attempted by the UN's Peacebuilding Commission, at least for post-conflict countries.[37] Some development agencies are funding non-official diplomacy initiatives that are intended to influence domestic power politics, while the notion of 'soft power' encourages diplomats and military officials to explore the utility of development and other non-coercive policies. In sum, another part of the lack of sufficient proactive response is the dispersion of international activities and goals already in countries threatened by violence. The problem is not deploying them anew. A downside of the expansive notion of prevention is that these various activities are pursued with no procedures for galvanizing them into concerted prevention strategies. Alternatively, a considerable multiplier effect would be achieved if the multiple efforts in a given country were each made more 'conflict-smart,' for their aggregate impact would be more potent. Conflict prevention might be largely a matter of re-engineering the many diplomatic, development and other programs that already operate in developing countries so that they serve conflict prevention objectives more directly and in a more concerted way (Lund, 1998a).

WHAT KINDS OF PREVENTION ARE EFFECTIVE? GETTING AHEAD OF THE CURVE

Much extant research looks at failure: countries that faced potential violent conflict, and where no preventive effort was tried or opportunities were missed (e.g., Zartman, 2005). However, the simple antidote to 'act early' has given way to a deeper concern about getting those actions right. This is because misapplied preventive efforts, even if timely, may be worse than taking no action at all. (cf. Lund, 1998a). Thus, the growing research on 'success' – preventive actions that were tried and no escalation occurred – is especially policy relevant. Instruments in the potential prevention toolbox are not *ipso facto* effective, for that hinges on which is applied when, where, and how.

Basic ingredients

The first wave of this research looked mainly at preventive diplomacy (direct prevention), and thus relatively late stages of confrontation (e.g., Miall, 1992; Manuera, 1994; Lund, 1996). It suggests convergence around elements that appear to be associated with effective avoidance of violence:[38]

1. Act at an early stage (Miall, 1992: 198)., that is before a triggering event (Wallensteen, 1998: 15), "early, early, early" (Jentleson, 2000: 337).
2. Be swift and decisive, not equivocal and vacillating (Wallensteen; Jentleson, 2000: 343; Hamburg, 2002: 146; Harff, 2006: 6).
3. Use talented, influential international diplomats who command local respect (Jentleson, 2000: 336; Miall, 1992: 193).
4. Convince the parties that the third parties are committed to a peaceful and fair solution, and oppose the use of force by any side (Jentleson, 2000: 341).
5. Use a combination of responses, such as carrots and sticks, implemented more or less coherently (Hamburg, 2002: 146–47; Wallensteen, 1998: 15; Jentleson, 2000: 336; Leatherman, 1999: 182–94; Zartman, 2005: 14; Byman, 2002: 217).
6. Provide support and reinforcement to moderate leaders and coalitions that display non-violent and cooperative behavior Zartman, 2000: 310.
7. Build local networks that address the various drivers of the conflict, but avoid obvious favoritism and imbalances (Wallensteen: 15; Jentleson, 2000: 336; Hamburg, 2002: 147; Leatherman, 1999: 199).
8. If necessary to deter actors from using violence, use credible threat of the use of force or other penalties such as targeted sanctions (Jentleson, 2000; Zartman, 2005: 202).
9. Neutralize potential external supporters of one side or the other, such as neighboring countries with kin groups to those in a conflict (Miall, 2000; Hamburg, 2002: 147).
10. Work through legitimate local institutions to build them up (Wallensteen: 15).
11. Involve regional organizations or regional powers, but don't necessarily act entirely through them (Wallensteen: 15) Jentleson: 339; Miall: 198).
12. Involve major powers that can provide credible guarantees, but use UN or other multi-lateral channels to ensure legitimacy

(Jentleson: 337; Wallensteen: 15; Hamburg, 2002: 147; Leatherman et al. 1999: 216; Zartman, 2005: 13).

The studies also find that certain local and regional conditions significantly enhance the chances of success (e.g., Miall):[39]

1. Domestic leaders who are relatively secure and feel a self-interest in stability, and thus are open to third parties facilitating or mediating emerging disputes.
2. Major factions that show some mutual ability to manage societal disputes and carry out public policies that benefit all communities.
3. Accommodative policies and procedures such as voting systems and opportunities for political participation that blunt the impact of grievances felt by one side or the other.
4. Relations between major political groups that have been peaceful in the recent past.
5. One side is not much more powerful than another.
6. Weak group solidarity or political mobilization within one of the protagonists, such that they cannot mobilize beyond a certain level.
7. The country is small and relatively dependent on the international community economically, politically, and militarily.

Toward a theory of prevention: timing and sequencing

While very useful, these findings do not reveal the utility of particular instruments at different stages. It is widely accepted that different interventions are needed at different moments (e.g., Lund, 1996: 191; Rothchild CAII, 1996: 44). As indicated, it is also believed that several kinds of instruments are needed. But such a multi-pronged strategy cannot mean everyone doing everything in every stage and place. More is not necessarily better. Consequently, the leading current research question being urged for the field is which *mixes* of differing instruments are most effective in which stages of conflict and contexts, other things being equal (e.g., Miall, 1992; Nicolaides, 1996; Harff, 2005).[40] Case-studies and 'large n' quantitative studies have begun to mine recent experience (e.g., Rubin,

1998, 2004; Nicolaides; Rowsbotham and Miall; Leatherman et al.,)[41] to get at this issue. Differing levels of analysis, typologies, and cases have impeded the task of cumulating and verifying findings, and many are partly deductive rather than empirical (e.g., Lund, 1997; Leatherman; Kriesberg, 2003: Rothchild, 2003: 45). Nevertheless, gathering up what extant findings and grounded reasoning suggest so far can provide useful heuristic guidelines for policymakers about which combinations of instruments to apply to the early stages of conflict.[42]

To explore the available evidence, we examine below what research suggests are most useful of the basic types of prevention at each of three distinguishable early phases of conflicts. These phases lie in the realm of unstable peace between a peaceful equilibrium where conflicts are managed predictably, on the one hand, and tensions are beginning to escalate into confrontation, significant violence or organized armed conflict, on the other (cf. e.g., Mitchell, 1981; 2006; Lund, 1996; Lund, 1997; Kriesberg, 2003; Ramsbotham and Miall, 2005).[43] To frame the following discussion, we pose here a familiar assumption that "soft" measures must be followed by "hard" ones, the more a conflict escalates – e.g., diplomacy must precede the use of force. The UN Charter envisions that the procedures in Chapter Six for peaceful settlements of disputes may have to be followed by the more coercive measures in Chapter Seven of sanctions and peace enforcement. Others subscribe to this graduated 'ladder of prevention' (Eliasson). Similarly, regarding interactive conflict resolution methods, the contingency model hypothesizes that the greater the intensity of conflict, the more that non-assertive techniques of facilitation must give way to the directive techniques of mediation, arbitration and adjudication (Fisher and Keashly, 1991).

Latent conflicts

These arise when exogenous or endogenous changes are generating underlying but unacknowledged strains among societal groups but they have yet to mobilize to express their interests.[44]

A priori instruments: structural and direct

As described earlier, one prominent a priori instrument involves global and regional organizations promulgating standards or regulations backed by incentives in order to encourage present or prospective member states to respect human rights, adopt democratic procedures, settle disputes peacefully with their own minorities and neighboring states, or submit to restrictions on terms of trade (e.g., Lund, OECD-DAC, 1998; Jentleson, 2000: 338; Hamburg, 2002: 147; Cortright, 269–72).[45] The evident effectiveness of this instrument in reducing potential causes of conflict seems to derive from the conditional incentives offered to leaders who have already subscribed to particular norms, at least nominally, and are already in power *before* particular conflicts ensue, thus avoiding the difficulties of intervening where parties have already violated the norms and become entrenched in opposed positions on specific disputes. When agreeing to them, a regime's future stakes are not immediately apparent, compliance can be voluntary, there is time to adjust a country's policies, and individual actors cannot argue they are being singled out. If the penalties for violations are significant, 'the sunk costs borne by the parties ... are not so overwhelming as to dwarf the public good provided by the institution' (Nicolaides: 60, 46–48). A possible negative side-effect occurs if the benefits of incorporating some states into international organizations and excluding their neighbors intensifies tensions between 'ins' and 'outs' (Bonvicini, 1996; 9; Shambaugh, 1996).[46]

Ad hoc structural instruments

Vigorous structural measures can help specific governments to alleviate underlying socioeconomic sources of conflicts or institutional and policy deficits that keep countries from addressing those problems meaningfully and peacefully. When in the 1980s, international lending institutions began to pressure developing countries to privatize para-statals, reduce public spending, remove price subsidies, stabilize monetary systems, and liberalize trade regulations (Muscat, 2002: 196), the rationale was not solely economic productivity and growth, but political stability, an implicit theory of peace. In fact, considerable large 'n' research suggests that economic liberalization such as free trade policies are highly correlated with lower levels of poverty, and that development correlates with lower levels of conflict (e.g., Hegre et al., 2002; Goldstone et al., 2003). Failing to enact reforms, on the other hand, is likely to deepen poverty and inequities that increase the chances for upheaval.

However, critics argue that structural adjustment measures can increase political instability and thus risk of conflict, especially in the poorest countries by reducing income and increasing competition among prospective losers and gainers during de-statalization. In this view, globalization increases vulnerability to complex humanitarian emergencies by liberalizing trade, increasing capital mobility, raising debt, lowering commodity export prices, and reducing foreign direct investment (e.g., Rapley, 2009). In countries with governments run by ethnic minorities such as Sri Lanka, for example, elites can hold onto their position by securing access to privatized industries. If other minorities are shut out, the economic inequality, or at least its perception, produces inter-group resentment and tensions (Chua, 2003).

This debate revolves in part around differing time frames. To derive the ingredients of peace from ahistorical econometric methods that pinpoint the highest correlations among indicators in large numbers of countries ex post facto is not to understand how these correlations came into being over time and the ways that the variables actually behaved and interacted within particular countries.[47] Though austerity measures may provoke violent protests in the short run, the evidence of political instability is mixed and context-specific (Muscat, 1995). Such adjustment policies may not create fundamental threats to regimes (Bienen, 1986). In fact, early policies

toward natural resources, trade access, diversification, corruption, price shocks, and ethnic quotas can boost growth (Collier, 125–40).[48] Whether such policies mitigate or worsen conflict also depends on how these international and domestic policies are designed, introduced, and implemented.[49] Social safety-net programs can be used to compensate groups that are especially hard-hit by short-term effects of economic austerity.[50] In any case, normal policies of international lending institutions applied automatically without tailoring them to each country context may be especially destabilizing in the poorest and least capable states.[51] In short, economic reform may have better chances of success at this stage, than when politics are more polarized, but they need to be conflict-sensitive and accompanied by compensatory measures.

As against such conditional aid,[52] donors also provide outright aid such as in health and education to alleviate social needs and thus encourage economic activity. Such support programs are believed to have stabilizing effects because they can create new markets and increase social interaction (Cortright, 1997; Collier, 134). A drawback is that such assistance is implemented through divisible projects and programs, so benefit allocations may reflect the differential access of a society's ethnic groups, causing 'horizontal inequities' (Stewart,), especially where prebendal or patronage mechanisms distribute resources and life chances as is common in Africa. When the competitive pressures of democratization arise, ruling parties have especially strong incentives to use social and economic programs to win and reward supporters. Thus, conflict-blind aid intended to alleviate poverty may actually privilege certain and identity groups and intensify inter-group rivalries (Graham, 1994).[53] Donors often find that even well-intentioned support may visibly affect the relative position of politically significant groups in a society and thus exacerbate the sources of conflict (Collier, 138). Where there are politicized ethnic divisions, aid programs may contribute more to conflict than do macro-economic reforms because they are more or less 'lumpy.'[54] Implementing programs through multi-group and locally–run mechanisms may help to avoid obvious partiality and bridge such cleavages (e.g., Anderson).[55]

Both economic reform and outright aid are less likely to provoke conflict if developing societies have *institutions* that manage the social strains and inequalities that globalization can cause (Rodrik, 1997). As many donors concluded that structural adjustment could not work unless bolstered by effective governance (Stokke, 1995: 26), the latter became another entry point for structural conflict prevention. International agencies now widely subscribe to the view that democracy-building is an effective way to achieve domestic stability.[56] Again, the evidence arises from strong cross-sectional statistical associations in a large number of countries between democracy and peace between and within nations (e.g., Russett, 1993). At the stage of latent conflict, such support for building institutions that can regulate emerging social conflicts is promising (Nicolaides: 53). Some countries like Indonesia though ethnically fragmented have taken genuine steps toward popular democracy and maintained relative stability.

However, views that any steps toward more democracy are gains for conflict reduction (e.g., Diamond, 1996: 40–8) do not recognize that democratization also risks destabilization. Studies of actual dynamics of change in particular countries find that the risk of conflict often rises during periods when authoritarian systems are shifting to more pluralistic structures (e.g., Mansfield and Snyder, 1995a,b).[57] Alternatively, transitioning polities may remain 'partial' or 'illiberal' democracies (Ottaway, 2003; Zakaria, 1997) in which the regime's hold on power is not challenged, political and civil rights are abridged, and representation occurs through informal power-sharing within cliques. If such autocratic or oligarchic regimes ('anocracies') continue to resist meaningful democratic reform, they could simply stagnate economically as well as politically, inviting state breakdown and violent conflict.

At the same time, it is unclear whether such regimes necessarily lead to stagnation and violent conflict or can evolve gradually toward more openness and stability. Informal power-sharing among less than fully accountable political leaders, though falling short of formal democracy in a Western sense, does not lead inevitably to conflict.[58] In fact, intra-elite co-optative bargains, though less than ideal by Western standards, may be a pre-requisite for political stability and thus eventual development (e.g., Rothchild, 2004, Byman). So once again, the likelihood of conflict may be determined more by whether governments make accommodative adjustments, such as allowing for some political activity (cf. Cramer and Weeks, 2002: 41f).[59] Positive discrimination programs to increase access of minorities to government jobs and services can co-opt group resentments (Rothchild, 2004: 47). These diverging scenarios make the current national politics in authoritarian countries such as Saudi Arabia, Uzbekistan, and Egypt, and more pluralistic but weak systems like Kyrgyzstan and Azerbaijan, crucial focuses for early warning and conflict prevention.[60]

Appropriately, especially since 9/11, analysts have looked increasingly to 'supply-side' programs that support institutions of the state to make governments more effective from the inside. Several analysts argue that before representative democracies can function effectively, basic institutions of the state need to operate effectively.[61] Fragile and failed states need to have effective ministries, local authorities, and judiciaries delivering health, education, roads, sanitation, and justice.[62] State strengthening includes professionalizing a country's security forces, both to restrain them from abusing its citizens and enable them to provide security.[63] National laws also need to provide guarantees such as property rights (Kapstein, 2004), enforce policies governing the economy, establish regulatory agencies such as for banking and trade, and respect civil and political rights and criminal laws through courts,[64] including protections for minorities and other limits on arbitrary power: 'constitutional liberalism' (Zakaria, 2003).[65]

On a broader plane, much research has weighed the utility for preventing ethnic conflicts of constitutional engineering that allocates political authority through differing options: unitary systems versus federalism, autonomy or partition; presidential versus parliamentary systems, and proportional versus plural electoral rules (see e.g., Horowitz; Wimmer, 2004). Federalism is often presented as a possible means of conflict resolution or prevention, for devolving policymaking can shield minorities and be more responsive to regional or local interests. But decentralization has both calmed and divided societies (Siegle and O'Mahony, 2007). Proportional representation and winner-take-all voting helped in South Africa and not in Northern Ireland. Again, how such differing arrangements affect the risk of conflict in a given country depends on other particular factors, such as the political relationship between contending identity groups and the politics of change.

In sum, all such economic, political and constitutional structural changes envision ultimate states of affairs that, if attained, would undoubtedly reduce conflicts significantly. But the challenge is *getting to* these endpoints without destructive conflict. In the short run, reforms such as structural adjustment and majoritarian elections are not always feasible, and can be counterproductive if applied too quickly or with insufficient attention to a country's balance of power, political economy, and potential for backlash and deeper polarization. Liberalizations that fragment power have to be balanced by stabilization that consolidates it (cf. Paris, 2001), such as state and societal institutions with authority to reconcile competing interests and force compromises. Many ideal liberal-internationalist solutions set aside the difficulties and pitfalls of getting reforms adopted and do not calculate the risk of destabilization in view of the capacities of differing societies for peaceful change.[66] Merely prescribing ultimate ideals is as useful as a doctor advising an obese patient with heart trouble to 'lose weight.'[67]

Ad hoc direct instruments

Structural policies do not necessarily engage the specific stakeholders in emerging national conflicts, although they require consent or at least toleration by host governments where they are applied. Critical to their adoption and implementation are the processes and channels through which governing elites make decisions about them, steps that affect the prospects for social conflict. This reality thus calls for direct forms of preventive engagement even at this stage of latent conflict.[68] But despite the frequent obeisance expressed to the idea of engendering 'local ownership,' structural programs often treat the leaders in a country not as active agents of change but automatons who respond to incentives and disincentives in some Pavlovian stimulus–response international experiment.

Obviously, direct prevention is premature if no conscious sense of a serious prospective harm or opportunity is present (Berkovitch; Nicolaides 1996: 52). Where societies see no serious problem that needs fixing, it is hard for third-party would-be preventors to explain why they are needed. Pointing to a conflict of interests might actually destabilize the situation (Kemp: 50ff).[69] Or, if no aggrieved parties have stepped forward, it is unclear whom one can talk to. But once underlying problems are beginning to surface as contentious issues, direct engagement fostered by trusted third parties is best carried out *within* existing institutions and ruling processes, thus giving standing regimes the chance to respond in ways that do not immediately threaten their status while allowing them to address emerging problems. State elites acting early on to deal with structural conditions can be effective prevention (Rothchild, 2003: 46). Whether or not governments have accepted inter-national standards through agreements they have signed, they may take umbrage at criticism and dismiss outside pressure. But fact-finding missions from institutions such as the UN can overcome resistance, especially if complemented with direct support that addresses the deficiencies (Rothchild, 2003: 46–7). As it is better to foster compliance than rely only on ex poste condemnations of deviations (Nicolaides, 1996: 54), multilateral organizations have also moved from simply promulgating and pressing standards on a government to hands-on assistance. The Office of the UN High Commissioner on Human Rights, for example, has shifted from simply monitoring human rights to helping governments comply, through creating national institutions that build human rights capacity. A related approach is the Lome consultations the EU holds with governments in Africa, the Caribbean, and the Pacific for incrementally establishing democratic institutions, thus allowing for flexibility regarding which countries are expected to meet which benchmarks by when.

Manifest limited conflict

The stakes of conflict increase when wider forces of change elicit awareness of conflicting interests and energize affected groups, issues come into the open, and potentially diverging positions are decided upon and voiced (Miall, 2007). Accepted forms of protests may be underway as well as irregular acts, including violence. The aim is both to prevent confrontations that escalate, hardening of positions and polarization, rising fears, and mutual defensive measures that create security dilemmas and to find bases for cooperation. For some, this is the most strategic moment for prevention, as the tasks of earlier and more basic structural prevention are seen as too demanding and complex (Ottaway and Mair, 2004). Some rawness of sores of discontent may be needed to expect positive change to occur (cf. Stedman, 1995). Structural measures continue to be useful – but now, less for alleviating the underlying sources of the conflict than as 'purchase' (Rothchild, 2003), to 'sweeten' an agreement, that purveyors of direct prevention can use tactically.

Direct measures thus become more essential. Opposed groups often have little inclination to initiate mutual engagement, at least until they fail to achieve their objectives unilaterally through first trying coercive or violent means. Still, some may seek outside help at this early stage more often than may be realized (Nicolaides, 1996: 49), as when the Barre regime was under challenge by various clans. Direct methods through which third parties can intervene peacefully include the classic array of official and non-official interactive methods. All these are intended to get parties in closer contact and communication for more accurate information about mutual interests and needs, dispel ignorance and fear, and expose them to more options, possibly leading to agreements (e.g., Rothchild, 2003: 46; Zartman and Rasmussen, 1997).[70]

One direct approach uses non-binding interactions such as various types of conflict transformation workshops that precede, follow or operate under or alongside official 'track one' diplomacy or political processes (Fisher, 2005; cf. Ropers, 2005). Rather than take up substantive issues to seek settlements through adversarial, judgmental approaches, these gentler methods or 'soft mediation' (Nicolaides, 1996: 51) create a non-threatening milieu to simply facilitate inter-party communication, thus expecting to elicit more committed participation and pave the way to locally decided and 'owned' accommodations (e.g., Zartman and Rasmussen). One study found that extensive mutual communication rather than hard bargaining has been more effective (Bercovitch, 1998: 243). In 2003, for example, UNDP and Guyanese leaders agreed to a whole series of governmental and civil society dialogues that resulted in the country's first ever non-violent elections in 2006. Success may depend greatly on whether they are spearheaded by prominent outsiders who command respect (Lund and Myers, 2007). Yet, even if a small society and government is immersed in workshops, if improved relationships are not translated into legal and policy changes that institutionalize and uphold agreed rules even on stormy days, the usual political styles can return (Lund and Myers, 2006). It is difficult to instill new habits unless they are embedded in locally run institutions (Nicolaides, 51). A point is reached when the question is whether a body politic adopts such habits on its own without third-party therapy. Such non-formal methods are not intended as alternatives to tougher approaches, but complementary (Fisher, in Zartman and Rasmussen, 1997: 241).

A innovative hybrid of a priori, ad hoc, structural and direct engagement that lies between non-formal facilitation and formal mediation is the work of the OSCE High Commissioner on National Minorities (HCNM), an office mandated to become proactively engaged in ethnic disputes arising in the 1990s. The first able incumbent and his successors have made innumerable visits to Eastern Europe and newly independent states to meet with leaders and minority groups. They facilitate dialogues, recommend policy remedies to chief executives and parliaments, and show how OSCE norms may apply, including drafting model legislation. Only very rarely have they publicly pressured the parties, but crucial to the success that many analysts judge this innovation has often had in reducing divisive tensions and eliciting accommodation is the eventual reward for good behavior of economic aid and membership in the EU, NATO, and other Western bodies (e.g., Hopmann, Mychajlyszyn).

Still, leaders in conflict-vulnerable societies and weak states are often disinclined to compromise and/or they affirm positions and agreements they cannot enforce (Nicolaides, 1996: 52). If their recalcitrance breaks off communication or thwarts opportunities for joint problem-solving, third parties may need to get more directive by engaging parties in 'muscular mediation' or formal negotiations with teeth (e.g., Jakobsen, 1996: 24), such as proferred aid or 'coercive diplomacy,' such as threats to cut off aid (Rothchild, 2002: 48f), impose economic sanctions, or use force (e.g., George, 1994: 199).

Military measures can also be used for direct prevention, but not yet in the form of a threat or actual use of force. The usual foreign policy debate over 'force versus diplomacy' tends to pertain to high levels of confrontation. But before that stage,

the overlooked but promising instrument of preventive deployment (Nicolaides, 44f) can act as a deterrent by inter-positioning forces even before any hostile actions have occurred. The only clear example has been UNPREDEP, the UN force that posted 1100 troops along Macedonia's border with Albania and Serbia from 1992 until 1999. Though its firepower could not withstand a Yugoslav army attack, UNPREDEP created a tripwire that would likely trigger more forceful responses. Its removal in 1999 was followed two years later by an insurgency that originated in border areas UNPREDEP had once patrolled (Lund, 2005). As significant, it had a calming effect on domestic inter-ethnic relations (Lund, 1997).[71] Similarly, peace zones secured militarily can contain actual or potential conflict by cordoning off specified areas, with or without the consent of a government (Nicolaides 45), such as in Northern Iraq under Hussein.[72]

Escalating violent conflicts

Positions are hardening, relationships breaking off, parties disengaging. Irregular expressions of grievances grow into wider violence, foretelling possible organized conflict. Major hostilities look imminent. The aim is to avoid an irrevocable spiral.

To pre-empt increasing intransigence, invoking and enforcing a priori norms might still be effective. Less than totally punitive measures can activate those in the country who support peaceful resolution. But using coercive diplomacy in the absence of a clear pattern of overt violence or gross violations of norms may be seen as unfair and illegitimate (Nicolaides, 1996: 44) because it presumes actions would occur for which the evidence is equivocal. Another mistaken reflex is to try to address the supposed 'root' causes of a conflict such as ethnic or religious differences, economic disparities, or lack of democracy, as if they mainly now drive the violence. But such ad hoc structural measures are less and less useful as well as feasible, when it is the violence that drives violence. What is most urgent is to halt the spiral through potent political and military direct prevention.[73]

The tougher tools of formal diplomacy, though difficult, may arrive at short-term settlements to buy time such as ceasefires (Nicolaides, 1996: 52; Rothchild, 2002: 54; Heldt, 8). These are more likely to be effective to the extent a strong mediator or team is skillful in instilling the parties with an urgent sense of the costs that can come from further bloodshed (Rothchild, 2002: 55). They also work better if accompanied by potential rewards that buy off the parties and help them fulfill an agreement, including the offer of development aid (Cortright, 1998, Rothchild, 2002), and/or punishments that pressure them to agree. Where there is asymmetry in power between the parties, measures to strengthen the power of the weaker party may budge the stronger.

Where the parties remain obdurate, coercive diplomacy such as sanctions or threat of force may be needed to reverse undesired actions or compel desired actions. Threats of the use of force were used when, for example, Presidents Bush and Clinton issued several warnings to President Milosevic not to support any armed activity in Kosovo as he had in Bosnia. Such threats are more likely to be effective if issued before possible escalations of hostile actions occurs, or if they follow immediately upon initial manifestations of violence (Nicolaides, 44–5), not ex post facto. Threatening to expel a state from an international organization is less effective once significant investment in a violent course has occurred. The more that the conflicting parties inflict physical harm on each other, they cannot just back down the ladder they climbed up, for mutual hurt and increasing fear remain (Mitchell, 2005; cf. Rothchild, 2002: 51). By the same token, indictment by a war crimes tribunal is not likely to prevent the perpetrator continuing to fight, and can be counter-productive, once they are named and being hunted down, as they have no incentive to refrain from fighting, unless some provision allows amnesty. If sanctions are actually used, they must be comprehensive to be effective (Jentleson, 2000: 337). But such coercive

diplomacy is less applicable when the threat is a breakdown of a state since the source of the problem is hard to target (Nicolaides, 42). Similarly, non-targeted sanctions have been widely criticized as having considerable negative side-effects for the general population while benefitting well-positioned elites.

One of the few joined debates in this scattered literature pertains to this stage: when are conflicts 'ripe for prevention?' Some analysts believe it more propitious to act before the outbreak of any significant violence. Violence 'crosses a Rubicon' from which it is very difficult to return (Jentleson, 2000), creating huge challenges for intervenors (cf. Edmead, 1971 cited in Berkovitch, 1996: 251). Others believe that some initial fighting that gets nowhere, a 'soft stalemate,' is needed before parties will no longer be tempted to try violence to see if it gets them gains (Berkovitch, 1996: 251). Thwarted violence or blocked confrontation are thus needed to soften parties up to compromise.[74]

Third-party willingness to use force can also influence the calculations of actors regarding their use of force. Much discourse in conflict prevention assumes military force to be antithetical to peace. Some NGOs that first stepped up to undertake conflict resolution responsibilities in threatened countries tend to oppose any form of force ideologically, or to downplay the role of any coercion in favor of non-coercive methods and policies such as diplomacy and, lately, development assistance. But some analysts suggest that sticks as well as carrots need to be exerted more or less simultaneously – with flexibility shown regarding what quotients of each are applied in specific situations (Jentleson, 2000; Byman, 2002: 219). '...while coercion rarely is sufficient for prevention, it often is necessary' (Jentleson, 2000: 5). Deterrence through the threat of using force may often be a pre-requisite for effective negotiations and, by implication, structural initiatives. Threats of force can encourage allies within a country to spring up. Still, threat of force must be made clear and credible by clearly conveying a concrete demand and the certainty that non-compliance will be punished

(Jakobsen, 1996: 3), such as through possessing capabilities and having domestic and international backing that can be sustained. They also need to be targeted precisely at specific actors who might otherwise escalate their actions, be potentially more costly to the parties than their persevering, identify the proscribed behaviors, and be accompanied by realistic alternative solutions (Nicolaides, 42–4).[75] The chances increase if the balance of power favors the threat sponsor and the value to the targeted actor of ignoring the threat is greater than the costs of compliance (Jakobsen, 1996: 3–5).[76]

Alternatively, if the threat of force is not backed up with credible force when there is non-compliance, they run the risk of encouraging aggression by calling the bluff of the international actors (Nicolaides, 45).[77] A lack of follow-through or half-hearted measures can embolden their target (Nicolaides, 1996: 42–3) if that party comes to believe that the threat is empty. Empty threats toward Bosnian Serbs had adverse effects when the latter did not follow through in protecting safe areas such as in Sbrenica (Jakobsen, 1996: 24).[78]

Actual use of force may be needed to limit emerging violence such as being visited upon a threatened minority group (Nicolaides, 42). Several argue that timely introduction of a relatively small force in Rwanda in May of 1994 would have stopped Hutu extremists from continuing to carry out their plans to kill thousands of Tutsi and Hutu moderates (Feil, 1998; Feil (1998) cited in Jentleson, 2000: 16; cf. Melander, 10f.). But this has been questioned (Kuperman, 2000). The tactical question is what amount is sufficient to restrain or reverse the undesired behavior.[79]

If violence does cease, security guarantees are in place and diplomatic processes are in play, neither freezing of the violence nor diplomatic agreement is sufficient by itself to move the actors to tackle the abiding political and socio-economic problems that occasion a conflict. For these, assistance is also needed for programs in institution building and development, now that they can operate in an environment that is basically stable and not constantly threatened by violence.

All in all, this quick review supports the notion that differing kinds of interventions are needed at particular settings and stages of conflict, and in certain combinations of hard, soft, and other kinds of measures. However, they complicate the simple sequencing that is often presumed: that the greater the hostilities in a conflict, the more that coercive measures are needed.

If one looks at the whole early period, the research does support a general picture in which increasingly coercive measures are needed to the degree a conflict escalates. However, the emerging literature qualifies that simple formula and adds altogether new elements to the equation. Before societal strains become salient, a priori regimes whose specific implications are unforeseeable but hold out attractive incentives can socialize leaders into international expectations. If enforced and resourced, these standards can foster structural and institutional changes that make more likely the peaceful management of transitional stresses from economic reform and democratization. But such liberalization needs to be accompanied by compensatory measures. Democratization needs incremental steps for effecting peaceful transition such as power-sharing arrangements, accompanied by conditional material aid for implementing changes. As political and policy disputes over such changes inevitably arise, sympathetic international envoys or missions with significant authority can usefully enter the picture, much earlier than usual, to midwife their resolution – playing 'good cop' by persuading incumbent leaders to inaugurate changes before they lose control. During such potentially unstable periods – contrary to the assumed sequence whereby military power is a last resort following the exhaustion of diplomatic efforts – security assurance may be essential for undergirding the ensuing domestic political negotiations. Where regimes choose to resist openings and move to repress them violently, firm coercive sanctions and credible threat of military force can deter them, and actual use of effective deadly force can halt their extremes. In short, the conventional scenario (derived perhaps from a Cold War crisis paradigm in which sovereignty is supreme and engagement comes late in the form of diplomacy or military action) does not sufficiently factor in structural measures, hands-on institutional support and positive incentives, and deterrent military measures. Regrettably, however, as useful as all these research findings may be as guidelines to action, they are not followed because decisionmakers do not have such lessons at their fingertips.[80]

NEXT STEPS: TAPPING THE POTENTIAL

To answer the puzzle this chapter first posed, conflict prevention is still a relatively marginal international concern for several reasons: a plurality of possible instruments and agents; its de facto operation under other names, lack of conceptual closure about stages and types of interventions; a lack of confidence due in part to dim awareness of the actual extent of recent capacity building and effective actions on the ground; dispersed activism globally and in a given country by diverse professions and overstretched governmental and non-governmental international organizations; and scattered research agendas and findings, yielding little usable guidance for would-be preventors. Yet, pro-active responses to head off potential conflicts are happening, and prima facie evidence suggests that combined with certain conducive factors, they can be effective. To tap the unfulfilled potential of conflict prevention, this state of the art could be advanced through three steps:

1. Consolidate what is known.   Lack of sufficient knowledge does not excuse why more frequent and effective responses to incipient conflicts are not undertaken. Policymakers tend to ignore the useful knowledge that already exists. Professionals need to gain access to top officials to present promising options and evidence of their results. The main problem is not epistemological but organizational. We need not wait until social

scientists have found the universally highest correlations among the limited set of variables already most plausibly known as relevant before we continue as in the previous section to gather, synthesize, and disseminate the existing findings among policymakers and field practitioners. Enough is known to produce heuristic guidance, for even the most verified conclusions are cannot be implemented mechanically in any particular conflict setting, but used as action-hypotheses to be combined with astute political judgments. A structured framework could pull together the preventive instruments available with guidelines about which are likely to be most feasible and productive in what conditions.

2. Focus the knowledge on emerging conflicts.   Conflicts do not emerge in Washington, New York or Brussels, but in particular developing countries at specific times. To have practical value, any gathered policy wisdom needs to be applied on the ground in real time. Many currently early-warning-identified poor societies and weak states (e.g., Papua, Kyrygystan, Guinea) would benefit from pro-active and concerted efforts that apply peaceful policies to avoid escalation to crises and violent conflicts. The country level is where the diverse agendas and tools are most clearly juxtaposed and concretely reconciled. This requires organizing consultations through which key actors (USG, UN, EU, regionals, governments, NGOs) can jointly assess the country situations and devise and implement diagnosis-driven targeted strategies, both at the field and desk officer level. Such processes would (a) apply conflict-sensitive indicators to identify systematically the most important short- and long-term risks in a country that are affecting the prospects for escalating conflict as well as its capacities for peaceful management of conflict; (b) identify what actions each actor can contribute within the strategy; and (c) consult the lessons learned from actual experience with various combinations of instruments.[81] To harness their global influence, leading actors such as the USA and other governments, the EU, and the World Bank, in cooperation with agencies in the UN system, could convene these multi-lateral country consultations to develop jointly formulated, analytically based, multi-faceted strategies. The processes could be linked to existing country-specific development planning procedures such as the PRSP and CAS, but should also involve diplomatic and military agencies as well as inside stakeholders.

3. Conduct more basic prevention research.

Though would-be preventors need not be inhibited by overly fastidious methodological standards, existing findings must be treated as preliminary hypotheses that research needs to test further.[82] More rigorous and comprehensive policy research is still needed to establish what types of preventive actions at both a priori and ad hoc levels, in what combinations, are likely to have what positive or negative effects in different stages of conflicts and contexts.[83] Promising structural and direct instruments have received little if any research, such as positive incentives to governments to encourage compliance with accepted international norms, special envoys with preventive mandates such as the HCNM, institutional support for strengthening equitable state service-provision, and preventive deployment.[84]

NOTES

1 Describing civil wars as 'development in reverse,' Collier lists the costs for the countries in conflict as military and civilian deaths, disease (HIV/AIDS, malaria), physical destruction, population displacement, high military expenditures, capital outflows, policy and political breakdown, psychological trauma, and landmines. The costs to other nations during and after conflicts include refugees, humanitarian aid, reconstruction aid, disease, increased military expenditures and tasks such as peacekeeping, reduced economic growth, illicit drugs, and international terrorism (Collier, 2003). Africa's two dozen internal wars in 23 countries from 1990–2005 are calculated to have cost $18 billion a year, which could have gone to HIV/AIDS and other disease protection, education, health, and water infrastructure. 'Africa Wars Costs Billions,' a report by Oxfam can be found at www.cnn.com/2007/WORLD/africa/10/11/africa.billions.ap/index.html.

2 Estimates have been made of the costs of interventions in recent wars compared with the costs if preventive action had been taken, and of the actual costs of preventive action taken in vulnerable societies that did not break out into wars compared with the estimated costs had war occurred. All showed huge possible savings. Prevention was significantly cheaper in all cases, with the ratios of prevention to war ranging from 1–1.3 to 1–479, an average of 1–59 (Brown and Rosecrance, 1999). In an estimate of Macedonia, the actual cost of UNPREDEP was $255 million, or 0.02% of the estimated cost of $15 billion for a two-year conflict (Thayer: 62). Chalmers finds all 12 of the retrospective and prospective conflict prevention packages that were estimated for the Balkans, Afghanistan past and future, Rwanda, Sudan, and Uzbekistan to be cost-effective (Chalmers, 2005: 6f.).

3 'High fatalities encourage further hostility and contentious behavior, and these diminish the likelihood of mediation effectiveness (just as they diminish the chances of an agreement in negotiations) (see Pruitt, 1981). Dispute complexity, which in any event is associated with lengthy, protracted conflicts and higher fatalities, also appears to be incompatible with successful mediation. … dispute duration also has a strong inverse relationship with successful mediation, but only when it combines with fatalities and complexity' (Bercovitch, 1993: 688–689). The parties discover more and more grievances against each other, and more parties may join the fray.

4 The report claims that 'whatever conflict prevention policies were being attempted in this period were a dismal failure…[because] there were *twice as many* conflict onsets in the 1990s as in the 1980s… the rate of new conflict onsets between 2000 and 2005 has remained higher than it was in the 1970s and 1980s' (Human Security Center, 2006: 4). Yet, although each war since the end of the Cold War could be considered failed prevention, to reach such a conclusion requires factoring in all the situations with a high risk of conflict that did not break out due to various preventive efforts. This is an especially turbulent period. On the surprisingly low number of ethnic conflicts occurring as the Soviet Union broke apart, see Fearon and Laitin, 1996 who attribute the result to local self-regulating mechanisms (cf. Wallensteen and Moller, 2003: 15f, 19.).

5 One study counts 47 disputes since the end of the Cold War that had a history or likelihood of conflict but where third parties took action and no armed conflicts ensued in the following year (Wallensteen and Moller, 2003: 27).

6 In contrast, governments and institutes devote immense resources to learning how to avoid relapse into war in post-conflict situations (e.g., Stedman, 1995; Dobbins, Doyle and Sambanis, 2000). Yet all that work could be characterized as glorified ambulance-chasing, for it comes into play only after

wars have wreaked great damage. The imbalanced attention to post-conflict situations has been fed by the widely cited belief that the existence of future conflicts is one of the strongest predictors of future wars. Yet the empirical basis of that claim has shifted downward from 40 to 50 percent to around 23 percent (Suhrke and Samset, 1996). Even accepting the upper estimate, over 50 percent of wars are not preceded by earlier ones. Were prevention done more often, the market for the chapters in this volume on post-conflict peacekeeping, reconciliation, intractable conflicts, and civil war would shrink considerably.

7 Though some insights here may apply to potential inter-state conflicts, the chapter focuses on intra-state wars such as civil wars, insurgencies, uprisings, major inter-communal conflicts, genocides, politicides, and revolutions, and indirectly to fragile and failing states. Intra-state conflict may cause state failure (e.g., Somalia) or be caused by it (e.g., Zaire), and either phenomenon may occur without the other, (e.g., Colombia, Zimbabwe).

8 'Violence prevention' may be more apt, but that evokes trying to break up a gang rumble, nasty fight on the playground, or spousal dispute. For less harmful conflicts below the threshold of collective violence, 'dispute resolution' may be more fitting. The Carnegie Commission adopted 'preventing deadly conflict' (Carnegie Commission on Preventing Deadly Conflict, 1997), which helpfully implies that the conflicts of concern might cause widespread bodily harm. This chapter does not cover the growing research on violent localized conflicts, such as pastoralist massacres and ethnic riots (see e.g., Horowitz, 1985).

9 'Conflict prevention' is actually a misnomer, for it implies avoidance of all conflict. If the classic definition of conflict is any real or perceived incompatibility between interests, not all conflicts are harmful and should be prevented. Conflict is normal in social and international relations and, as in the competition in politics, business, science, and the arts, is encouraged for society's benefit (cf. Kriesberg, 2003). What is to be prevented is not any conflict, but *destructive* and *violent* forms: wars between and within countries, oppression, inter-communal bloody quarrels – where few redeeming consequences can be imagined and productive alternatives exist.

10 We use 'engagement' to not conjure up the military connotations of 'intervention,' although military activities may be one method used (see below).

11 There was also concern about Boutros-Ghali's peculiar implication that disputes could or should be prevented from arising, for some can be constructive as long as they are conducted non-violently.

12 Some conflict theory makes room for addressing latent conflicts, and thus not restricting conflict to observable groups that are conscious of mutual incompatibilities (cf. Dahrendorf, 1959).

13 Of course, wars not prevented but ending can break out again. Though mid-conflict stages might be relegated to other terms, the violence pre-emption in prevention logically also entails keeping recently terminated wars from *re*-erupting (although Boutros-Ghali had designated this phase 'post-conflict peacebuilding'). Thus, prevention also is applied to avoiding post-conflict relapse. Because action at such a moment would come only after many lives have been lost, it is a fall-back option when earlier 'primary prevention' has failed. Such 'secondary prevention' in post-conflict countries has a vast literature and is addressed in several other chapters.

14 This focus still allows for deterrent or containment actions to protect a country that is threatened by the spillover of an already violent conflict in a neighboring country, as well as the cordoning off of localities within a country where war rages elsewhere within its borders.

15 Analysts since have demarcated several basic entry points for engagement in conflicts that are virtually parallel: lack of *resources*, lack of *protection* from violence, lack of *solutions*, lack of a *process*, and lack of *trust* (Lund, 1996: 140–43), conflicting actors' *behaviors*; the *relationships* between conflicting actors; the *capacities* of peaceful actors and processes; and the social and economic *environment* that affects conflicting actors and peace processes (Uvin, 2002); *structural* transformation; change in the *players* or personnel who have influence; *issue* transformation, or *personal* transformations of leading figures (cf. Miall 1992, 2008: 5).

16 Clearly, prevention cannot ignore 'the crystallizing agent...the personally motivated political actor who sees a described situation as vulnerable to his blandishments and ready for conflict...loose tinder lying around only excites pyromaniacs, it does not create them; they must pass by and see the opportunity' (Zartman, 1998: 1f).

17 Actually, Dag Hammerskjold had mentioned economic development programs as among possible tools for 'preventive diplomacy.' Such instruments of structural prevention could also be called preventive peacebuilding. This facet of prevention can address either manifest or latent incompatibility of interests.

18 Whether these various measures and actors are actually effective is a separate issue, however. That depends on their timing, design, targeting and other factors, discussed in a subsequent section.

19 Systemic and targeted measures may be combined in the same institutions, such as seen in the efforts of the OSCE's High Commissioner on National Minorities to assist particular countries to meet the OSCE's general standards for human rights and governance, and in the OAS's automatic mechanism for dispatching an emissary to member countries where democratic institutions appear to be under threat.

20 This descriptive taxonomy draws from Nicolaides (1996), Lund (1996), and Rubin (2004). As seen, these forms may convey various degrees of positive incentives and negative disincentives, such as coercion, persuasion, support (e.g., Ball, 1992; Rothchild, 2002; Moller et al.).

21 Some argue that trying to trace the effects on conflicts of systemic and structural instruments is causally too indirect (e.g., Ottaway). But this ignores the extensive conflict research on their indirect sources and narrows the goals of prevention to negative peace. To focus only on highly time-sensitive measures also would narrow prevention to the acts of outside third-party intervenors and divert it from examining the benefits or harms that flow from many current international policies at the global level, such as trade policies.

22 Differing stages of conflict, such as emergence, escalation, de-escalation, (re)construction, and reconciliation, have since been adopted as an organizing framework by more recent conflict textbooks (e.g., Kriesberg, 2003; Miall et al., 1999; 2004).

23 An illustration of unacknowledged preventive action is found in a prestigious journal in which leading American scholars of ethics and international relations discussed how to deal with violations of human rights. While the articles mainly deal with the mid-conflict option of military interventions to save people from imminent slaughter and the largely ex post facto option of war crimes tribunals, a few passages imply that pro-active responses try to prevent gross human rights violations and conflicts such as genocide *before* they occur. Yet these passages never use the term conflict prevention or a synonym, treating the idea under rubrics such as the OSCE, democratization, a NGO culture of human rights, and transnational networks (*Daedalus*, Winter 2003).

24 The NGO, International Alert, had called attention to the need for conflict prevention in the 1980s and early 1990s, but the first post-Cold War project exclusively focused on it may have been the Preventive Diplomacy Initiative at the US Institute of Peace (USIP) in 1994–95, which grew out of a USIP/US State Department Study Group on Preventive Diplomacy in 1993–94. The subject was subsequently taken up by the Carnegie Commission on Preventing Deadly Conflict until 1999, the Center for Preventive Action at the Council of Foreign Relations from about 1995, the EU's Conflict Prevention Network of the Stiftung Wissenschaft und Politik from 1996 to 2001, and since then, the International Peace Academy, the Woodrow Wilson International Center, and the Center for International Cooperation at New York University.

25 An earlier World Federalist project sought to generate broad-based interest in prevention through its grass-roots members.

26 There are often good reasons not to label such activities as conflict prevention, for that can cause alarm, and instead, to use euphemisms such as national reconciliation and social cohesion.

27 Even ASEAN has addressed conflict prevention informally through the Asian Regional Forum, though under the rubric of inter-state military confidence building measures.

28 Week-long training workshops by the UN Staff College since 1998 have 'graduated' over 1800 staff from all major UN agencies, each of whom have been introduced to early warning, conflict, and preventive responses.

29 Other donor agencies (UNDP; DFID; USAID; SIDA; CIDA; the Dutch Cooperation Ministry and most other major multi-lateral and bi-lateral agencies) have also carried out country conflict assessments through conflict offices that provide technical assistance to country missions. Trends are surveyed by Leonhardt (2000a, 2000b). Early examples of such an analytical tool are Lund et al. (1997) prepared for USAID; Lund (1999) for country desk officers of the European Commission, and Lund (2000) for the UN Framework Team. For a recent example and overview, see Clingendael (2005).

30 The UNSG 2000 report on prevention of armed conflict argued that the first responsibility for preventing conflict lies with the country itself. Similarly, analysts have proposed the concept of 'responsible sovereignty,' which implies state obligation and accountability to its own citizens in a way that is potentially enforceable by the international community. In this view, states have the right to sovereignty only in so far as they are willing and able to fulfill their responsibility to their own citizens by upholding their human rights and fulfill other basic needs.

31 Leaving the door open to possible intervention does not justify intervention by a state into another using just any altruistic rationale, such as loose claims that a regime has oppressed its people and they deserve democracy.

32 If R2P gains more acceptance, it would reinforce the shift occurring in the balance between the rights of sovereign states and the human rights of individuals. Article 2(4) in the UN Charter upholding non-intervention was intended mainly to protect states from military aggression by other states. But subsequent to the Charter, international conventions such as the UN Declaration of Human Rights established rights for individuals such as against torture and suppression of free speech their governments. The tension between these principles also occurs when large numbers of people are threatened by massive suffering, yet their own governments are unable to either prevent it or protect them from it. Since a responsibility thus exists for the international community to uphold individual human rights, the two sets of rights clash if sovereign governments are directly responsible for creating conflicts by carrying out massacres or oppressing their own people.

In fact, many more people have been killed in recent decades by their own governments than by other governments.

33 Another unheralded example is the OAS Secretary-General's recent efforts to mediate disputes between the government and opposition in Venezuela. Not simply an *ad hoc* discretionary mission, his action was required by a procedure the OAS adopted in 1991 that automatically activates a diplomatic response to possible threats to democracy in member states. In June, 1991, the OAS General Assembly adopted Resolution 1080, which bound the Secretary General and Permanent Council to immediate action in the event of a 'sudden or irregular interruption of the democratic political institutional process or of the legitimate exercise of power by the democratically elected government' of any of the OAS member states (OAS, 1991). Such threats trigger the agency's automatic and immediate response. The following year, the OAS was allowed to suspend a member state should its democratic government be overthrown by force (OAS, 1992). In 1995, Executive Order 95–6 created more specialized agencies to support democratic institutions, oversee elections, and promote dialogue (OAS, 1995). The mechanism also has been used to address attempted executive coups in Guatemala, Peru, and Venezuela.

34 In this light, the conclusion that 'conflict prevention is still more an aspiration rather than an established practice' (Human Security Report, 16) is glib and likely uninformed by how much preventive action actually has occurred.

35 Notwithstanding that the attacks on 9/11 provided a rationale for military actions against Afghanistan and Iraq, the extent to which the US public has accepted the lost lives and other sacrifices of the Iraq war, even under the subsequent rationale of establishing democracy, suggests that the power of the presidential 'bully pulpit' for promoting foreign engagement was previously underestimated or underutilized.

36 An illuminating discussion of how such contending approaches lead to different action prescriptions is found in Rubin, 2002, pp. 161–166. The tension between conflict resolution and human rights reflects a classic value conflict between peace, in the sense of avoiding violence, and justice (USIP, 2006). This antinomy is usually discussed in connection with mid- or post-conflict situations. As seen recently in northern Uganda, seeking to bring perpetrators of crimes against humanity to justice might prolong a war if the violators can only avoid prosecution by continuing to fight. Where perpetrators have already committed egregious human rights violations, insisting they be brought to justice could be incompatible with conflict termination, because doing the first may delay or block the second. The pursuit of justice by enforcing human rights can often conflict with peace (in the sense of cessation of violence) where

powerful parties have to be accommodated if they are to be induced to desist from further human rights violations. A similar value conflict can arise between stability and political justice, in the sense of democracy, where authoritarian regimes face possible rapid transitions to more liberal systems and thus violent conflict is a risk (Lund, 2006). In essence, these are conflicts between negative and positive peace, the present and the future. The challenge is to understand how power is distributed and find an appropriate balance between staying engaged with offenders in an effort to transform them, while not enabling further oppression.

37 Precedents for closer consultations across development sectors exist in the aforementioned UN's Common Country Assessments (CCA) and Development Assistance Framework (UNDAF) and the World Bank's Poverty Reduction Strategy Process (PRSP). But so far, these latter rarely build in as explicit criteria for the reduction of a country's conflict sources and strengthening of its peace capacities.

38 This research concerns the strategic question of which basic types of actions have what effects, not how to implement a particular tool. We also set aside which actors use which tools where (see Moller et al., 2007). The focus here is also more substantive than the widespread truisms that urge certain general attitudes and practices in preventive planning and implementation, such as: do an analysis of the situation; be flexible, engender local ownership; develop clear, comprehensive, and coherent policies; and involve women and youth (e.g., OECD-DAC, 2001). These generic reminders to practitioners are applicable to almost any international conflict or development activity, but offer nothing specific about what types of activities have what effects in what circumstances.

39 For example, in Estonia's 'success' story, where many of the international ingredients above were present, several local and regional factors also help to explain why the language and citizenship disputes between its Russian speaking population and ethnic Estonians did not escalate to violence. Russian identity never solidified despite conditions of exclusion. Russian elites were accommodated by the electoral system and the formation of ethnically polarized parties inhibited extremism. Electoral data show that Russian-speakers supported a range of Estonian parties, especially left-wing parties and the Centre Party, which showed willingness to cooperate with Russian speakers. Many Russians weren't registered to vote in the 1992 elections and after the 1995 elections, internal problems between Russian party leaders made them ineffective for a few years. This system tended to discourage politicians from resorting to ethnic stereotyping and public denigration of other groups. Meanwhile, political volatility in Russia distracted Moscow's attention from the 'near abroad' (Khrychikov and Miall, 1992: 204).

40 The most useful findings would be conditional generalizations in the form: 'If A (action), then B (impact), under x, y, and z (limiting conditions)' (cf. George, 1993: 120–125; Moller et al., 17f).

41 Some conflict-sensitive evaluations of individual programs and projects can also be useful as proxies for generic types of instruments (e.g., Lund, 2004, 2006).

42 Also useful for producing testable hypotheses would be generic theory in inter-group and international conflict, such as on the social psychology of conflict, techniques such as GRIT, escalation dynamics, the logic of collective action (mobilization), and cooperation theory. See Miall, 2007: 19–84.

43 The notion that conflicts go through certain stages and reflect overall cycles has been questioned (e.g., Berghof, 2006; Leatherman et al., 2000). True, like the shaded hues on a color wheel, distinctions among stages are not sharp. Nor are the phases completely objective. Movement through them is neither deterministic nor always uni-directional (e.g., Lund, 1996; Miall, 2007; Kriesberg, 2003: 370), and conflict indicators are not one-dimensional and uni-layered. Nevertheless, most analysts agree that conflicts reflect great variations in intensity and 'have a beginning, middle, and end' (Kriesberg, 2003: 22). While some conflicts are the unfinished business or re-configurations of previous conflicts, and so-called 'intractable' conflicts rise and fall over long periods of time, all conflicts are not simply episodes of previous conflicts. Where long periods with peaceful equilibriums set in, the subsequent conflicts are new. Thus, the notion of a life-cycle and phases is very useful.

44 As discussed above, conflict prevention includes efforts to address the underlying sources of latent conflicts. One of the most critical focuses for inquiry is how formal or implicit social contracts that have achieved some stabilizing equilibrium begin to unravel due to internal and external pressures. In particular, the post-independence years of new nations involve severe pressures and constraints that test their elites' political skills for establishing legitimate and effective states (e.g., Ayoob). It is also useful to put the recent intra-state conflicts into a historical perspective by recognizing that they thus existing formal or implicit social contracts are unraveling equilibrium.

45 In return for compliance, concrete benefits may be offered such as membership and aid and trade favors. Violations are subject to sanction such as exclusion from privileges or the organization (KN 48). Thus, countries need to be monitored to detect discrepancies so potential violations can be forestalled or penalties imposed for violations. Countries are periodically assessed for their progress in qualifying, and provisional arrangements mark their status and establish schedules for conformance (Nicolaides, 47).

46 Exits from such organizations or their disintegration have been followed by use of force, even among former alliance members. Countries of Central and Eastern Europe and Taiwan entering international organizations have been seen as threats by rival states (Russia, the ROC, and PRC respectively), thus possibly increasing the risk of conflicts. This may abate to the extent that 'outs' are brought into the organization (Shambaugh, 1996).

47 See Sambanis (2003), Lund (2006) and Uvin (2005).

48 These different conclusions have to do in part with differing research methods, country contexts, varied degrees of adjustment policy, difficulties in obtaining data on impacts, and other factors (Cramer and Weeks, 2002: 44f).

49 Structural adjustment and stabilization policies may elicit conflict depending on whether governments are sufficiently inclusive and accommodative such as by allowing political activity, the extent they are done, whether they are transparent, the sharpness of divisions in society, and other policies (cf. Cramer and Weeks, 2002: 41f). For example, exporting of agricultural goods is more conducive to poverty and inequality and thus potential political instability, than is exporting manufacturing goods (Gissinger and Gleditsch, 1999; Collier, 126). In Yugoslavia, the debt crisis, decline in terms of trade, and global credit tightening in the 1980s, forced austerity and low living standards, but instead of adjusting, its leaders fell back onto ethnic nationalist appeals that weakened state authority and invited inter-republic conflict (Nafziger, 2002: 14, drawing on Woodward, 1995).

50 Social safety nets in Zambia and Chile were found not only to reduce poverty and increase political support for economic adjustment programs (Graham). In that way, they may help as well to maintain governmental legitimacy and political stability.

51 Among the recommendations to the World Bank, IMF, and WTO are less dependence of the poorest countries on them and their rules rather than other sources; and special policies regarding bi-lateral and multi-lateral transfers and agreements affecting trade, banking services, currency rates, and aid, such as for agriculture. These would cushion external price shocks and improve foreign investment, debt rescheduling, and capital movements (Nafziger, 2002: 5). There should be less concern about inflation rates and budget deficits, and more about building regulatory systems and economic institutions (Nafziger, 2002: 15). Domestic growth strategies need to stabilize prices and exchange rates and spending, create appropriate economic institutions, improving the ability of the state to collect taxes and provide basic services, agrarian reform and land redistribution, and securing property rights. Due attention is also needed to their effects on the poor, minorities, rural and working people, and women and children (Nafziger, 2002: 5).

52 Compliance to structural adjustment policies were often presented as a condition for budget support.

53 Aid allocations in Kenya and Sri Lanka from the 1970s to the 1990s reveal strong evidence that donor toleration of or participation in the practice of allocating benefits according to ethnic, tribal, and regional criteria helped to fuel later inter-communal conflict (Cohen 1999, Herring).

54 Donors may go along with such practices to soften the blow of economic adjustment, keep a working relationship with governments, or show results (Herring), but thus perpetuating group competition can fuel hostilities, especially when the economy declines. Aid in Kenya after President Moi's governing coalition came to power in 1978 shows how the geographic allocation of local development projects and monies as well as implementation choices such as awarding consulting and construction contracts, were largely shaped by the government's desire to expand and buttress the emerging Kalenjin-led coalition by rewarding past supporters and recruiting new members (Cohen). Because program aid was grafted onto a largely unreformed one-party state, it became subject to inter-ethnic patronage politics, and as multi-party political competition intensified, it indirectly contributed to the tribal strife later in the Rift Valley.

55 Although it deals with a mid-conflict situation, an illuminating example was established in Sri Lanka, where a donor financed irrigation project deliberately delegated to both Tamil and Singhalese farmers allocation decisions and encouraged selection of their leaders on non-political grounds. Apparently, this kept the ethnic strife that was waging more widely in that country from spilling over into at least that project area (Uphoff).

56 However, the widely used terms such as 'governance,' 'democracy,' 'rule of law' and, more recently, 'state-building,' are such broad rubrics, they are not concrete enough to delineate specific institutions and alternative choices that might produce differing results. 'Demand-side' democracy promotion programs, for example, seek to make governments more accessible and accountable to their citizens. Thus, development programs may aid *representative* processes like elections and parties to expand access to government decision-making *by* the people, as well as help finance *executive and judicial service* functions that governments perform through public administration, courts and other regulatory functions, and security forces, to improve government services *for* the people.

57 Full-fledged democracies and autocracies are both the most politically stable. But partial democracies, and weak full democracies, are the most unstable systems, even more so than strong quasi-democracies (Goldstone et al., 2003). They have an irregular, non-institutionalized pattern of political competition that tends to cause executive leaders to be constantly imperiled by rival leaders, and encourage elites to maintain themselves in power despite the existence of democratic procedures. One growing form in the developing world are 'anocracies.' If autocracy and democracy are placed at the opposite ends of a continuum, an anocratic regime possesses a mixture of democratic and autocratic features in the middle of that continuum. Anocracy may apply to an autocracy where electoral and competitive features are in place and to a democracy where existing procedural democratic features are undermined (Gurr, 1974: 487; Mansfield and Snyder, 1995: 9).

58 The pace of overall change in many post-Soviet states toward consolidating democracy had slowed significantly by 1998, prompting questions whether they were in transition at all but instead '... represent relatively stable new political and economic arrangements that are neither free market nor socialist' (Karatnycky: 2–4) – notwithstanding the fact that a few years later, three on the post-Soviet list – Serbia in 2000, Georgia in 2003, and Ukraine in 2005 – experienced non-violent transitions from their first post-Cold War regimes to more liberal governments. Patrimonial, corporatist regimes can survive for long periods through currency stability, restraining the growth of the state sector, maintaining balanced budgets, and allowing export-drive growth (Karatnycky: 7, 9) Serbia in 2000, Georgia in 2003, and Ukraine in 2005 – experienced non-violent transitions from their first post-Cold War regimes to more liberal governments.

59 Although oligarchical regimes may tend to adopt policies that favor their bases of support, not all elite-dominated regimes have opposed reforms and thus encouraged conflict, and fuller democracies are not always more inclusive. In Malaysia and Mauritius, governments led by political elites have made explicit decisions to work together in policy coalitions that addressed potential imbalances among ethnic groups, deliberately enacting redistributive policies that ameliorated inequities and pre-empted the emergence of inter-group resentments. A crucial question seems to be whether 'crony capitalism, monopolism, and corruption within such systems' as in the former Soviet Union will thwart sustained growth and provoke economic crises, and even then, whether they will open up to emerging interests that bring democracy peacefully, or instead, repressive measures will restrict human rights and democracy and plunge them into instability and civil conflict (Karatnycky).

60 At the local level, development tools such as participatory community development projects, which are ostensibly aimed at producing useful material benefits such as improved local infrastructure, are increasingly being used by donor agencies as ways to create social capital and capacities for conflict management. Through creating capable local civil

society leaders and organizations, they are thought to provide a yeast that over time may produce a middle class and professional ranks that help to develop a country and transform authoritarian societies. These programs may operate under the radar of a government or be tolerated as long as they do not stimulate activities that are seen by elites to threaten the status quo. But as such, they can be effective in regard to localized conflicts, such as over water or ethnic tensions, and thus as possible safety-valves, but not as leverage directly or in the short term on the national-level conflicts that have been typical of the post-Cold War period (Lund and Wanchek, 2004).

61 'An effective and legitimate state is essential not only to promote economic development but also for democratic governance' (De Zeeuw and Kumar, 2006). Before moving toward mass democratic participation, strong political institutions are necessary (Mansfield and Snyder, Zakaria).

62 This argument resonates with Fukuyama's helpful distinction between the *scope* of the state, or the extent it plays roles in the society and the economy, and its *strength* in carrying out whatever broad or limited roles it has (Fukuyama).

63 Security sector reform includes national or local bodies mandated to use deadly force; adjudicatory institutions, civilian management and oversight bodies.

64 While economic growth encourages the emergence of democratic institutions, the specific mechanism through which this occurs is not clear. Democratic politics do not spring spontaneously from creating opportunities for markets to operate, or if established, these institutions will not last without laws protecting individual rights. This is because most of the developing societies into which markets are introduced are governed by ethnic, clan, or other group loyalties that determine how public as well as private goods are distributed.

65 It remains unclear whether the object of such strengthening of the rule of law is institutional attributes or cultural values, how change toward the rule of law occurs, the effects of the changes, and what forms of assistance are most effective (Carothers, 2006).

66 Similarly: '...rather than a one-size fits all approach in foreign policies and aid strategies that presses for the same liberalizing reforms everywhere, individual countries need to be differentiated according to their capacity to absorb disruptive shifts in unregulated power and consequent instability without violent conflict. A more balanced, holistic, contextualized approach to fostering desirable change needs to be applied. Clearly, moves toward democratization and other reforms can themselves often be among the adaptive mechanisms that help ensure a peaceful transition in particular settings. But the overarching and overriding policy goal perhaps should not be simply democracy or human rights or markets,

at any cost. It should rather be *peaceful transition* toward, ultimately, more democratic, or at least legitimate and effective governments, increasingly more productive economies, and more humane societies' (Lund, 2001).

67 Another structural approach to domestic instability, not taken up here, works through ideological campaigns and other programs to engender social solidarity and cohesion by eroding the bases for divisive group identities (e.g., Byman, 2002: 100–25). Similarly, the concept of social capital has been advocated as a useful focus for conflict prevention and resolution (Morfitt, 2002). Instruments such as truth and reconciliation commissions, for example, are promoted as ways to prevent future conflict by balancing the yearning for justice with the need of societies to move on. But...'while socialization can be a powerful tool when used in combination with appropriate resources and coercive incentives, socialization alone is a weak reed' (Leatherman: 188). Little rigorous research has been done on whether such instruments actually achieve reconciliation.

68 What applies to implementing development also applies to prevention: '...political will and indigenous leadership are essential for sustainable policy reform and implementation. No amount of external donor pressures or resources, by themselves, can produce sustained reform. It takes ownership, both of the policy change to be implemented and of any capacity building efforts intended to enhance implementation. Unless someone or some group in the country where policy reform is being pursued feels that the changes are something that it wants to see happen, externally initiated change efforts...are likely to fail. Such individual or groups serve as "policy champions" or "policy entrepreneurs"' (Brinkerhoff and Crosby, 2002: 6).

69 'Preventive mediation is more effective when it is initiated early, but not before the parties' positions and interests have crystallized. It is impossible to guide the parties toward a settlement, facilitate discussion of issues, or structure the interactions until the full implications of a conflict, and the options related to it, are well understood by those involved. Early intervention should never become premature intervention' Bercovitch (1996).

70 Official forms include conciliation, good offices, mediation, negotiation, arbitration, and adjudication. Non-official forms are facilitation, dialogue, track-two diplomacy, pre-negotiations, problem-solving workshops, and leadership training. Subsequent chapters reflect the extensive study of these well-known methods, but mainly when applied at mid- or post-conflict stages as in official peace processes. Little explicit attention has been paid to which intercessory methods may apply best at incipient stages of conflicts (e.g., see Greenberg; Zartman). 'The question that scholars need to ask is the extent to which mediation practice and

negotiations theory need to be adapted when the ultimate goal is preventing deadly conflict inside states…' (Nicolaides, 49–50).

71 It was deemed effective to a great extent because almost one-third of its 1100 troops were American.

72 Similarly, analysts have argued that small military protective corps can help to prevent escalation of violent conflict by protecting multi-ethnic governments that are under threat, as was needed in Burundi in 1993 and 1994, thus enabling them to function so as to prove their utility and legitimacy (Lund et al., 1997).

73 A critique frequently raised against the idea that prevention effectiveness can ever be demonstrated appears to pertain mainly to this stage of late and direct prevention. Despite the claimed successes, a widely uttered conventional wisdom claims it is not possible epistemologically to assess whether preventive action has made a difference. The argument is that there is no way to tell whether such efforts are effective because one cannot know whether the conflict in question would have otherwise escalated without them and so did not because of them. Since no violent conflict erupted, it cannot be assumed that it would have occurred if the preventive action was not applied. But combining conflict research, evaluation methods, and process-tracing can increase the plausibility of such arguments.

The critique is more telling when it comes to knowing whether specific violent acts would have occurred at a given moment if a given action of direct prevention was not taken. Analysts would not even try to claim success except where typical warning signs of violent conflicts are not actually present that have been gathered from extensive conflict research. Still, in such contexts, specific violent acts cannot be precisely predicted because they could occur or be withheld at the highly uncertain discretion of specific would-be perpetrators of violent acts. Targeted actors need to have intended to take the action that the preventive action identified as unacceptable but then cease doing so, but not for other reasons besides the preventive action, such as running out of resources. To establish that such perpetrators refrained from violence because of a given preventive action requires getting inside their heads to see how they interpreted their immediate circumstances and whether the preventive action or other factors played a part in their decision not to act violently. However, where actual acts of violence have begun to occur, analysis can show through process-tracing plausible causal link between its leading agents and their actions and the measures taken. In cases like Rwanda in May, 1994, the comparison between the capacity of direct military measures applied compared to the efficacy of a killing machine and its forces may not be definitive but it is not impossible to do. If low-level violence broke out, it

could be demonstrated how it was actually contained and kept from escalating due to the constraints of a deterrent force. Other plausible linkages can be argued regarding the influence on specific actors of other direct diplomatic or other actions taken toward them.

The objection is less daunting when applied to structural preventive measures because they deal with the proximate processes, behavior-conditioning factors, and deeper societal conditions that indirectly influence the probability of violent acts. Where such signs are present but violent conflict has not broken out, a host of institutions, processes, and incentives and disincentives may also be in place that preserve relationships and communication among disputing parties and otherwise shape the environment of incentives and disincentives in which actors make choices whether they will act in violent or restrained ways. If potentially violent conditions are present, and it can be shown that well-targeted, timed, and proportional preventive actions are directed at them that empirical research suggests have affected these particular conflict factors in like cases, the prima facie evidence makes it possible to infer with greater confidence that the actions are likely to have had some impact in lowering the relative *probability* of violence, especially if indicators such as level of hostilities or peaceful interaction between protagonists also show change following the intervention.

To expect definitive proof of such impact would be like going to the doctor after signs of possible heart trouble and dismissing his professional recommendation that you quit smoking, simply because the statistical link between cigarettes and heart disease does not always occur in every individual case, and so might not apply to you. Though technically correct, most prudent people would honor the professional's advice.

74 The notion is analogous to the 'mutual hurting stalemate' noted at levels of armed conflict as conducive to war termination, but this deadlock arises at lower levels of hostility based on a shared sense that a greater harm to them looms. What is at issue is how readily a point of sufficient mutual anxiety is reached even before the parties spill each other's blood. A substantial difference would seem to exist between stalemates after many people have been killed, than in, for example, a stalled but physically benign altercation such as in trade, environmental, boundary, arms control, and labor negotiations (e.g., Zartman, 2001: 4, 202; cf. Heldt, 8). Is some early threshold of bloodshed reached when it becomes qualitatively more difficult to dissuade the parties from avoiding a vortex of violence that becomes significantly harder to halt? Is such a threshold exceeded as well where low-intensity violence, even though it periodically subsides, as in the Israeli-Palestinian conflict? In any case, to the extent such moments come late in an increasingly violent on and off again conflict, the less the action

is preventive, and the more it is management and termination.

75 Six major threats of the use of force were issued by the USA and its European allies to try to stop the fighting in Bosnia, but all failed until a bombing campaign against the Bosnian Serbs in 1995.

76 In Bosnia, deadlines were not issued, public controversy arose in the West over the possible use of airstrikes, publics were unwilling to provide ground troops, and the Bosnian Serbs were more motivated to pursue force than the allies (Jakobsen, 1996: 22–3). Because the Western powers did not see Bosnia as in their vital interests, they were not as willing to commit ground troops to stop the killing as the Serbs were willing to suffer the possible consequences of what were unconvincing threats of force (p. 25).

77 International actors must be prepared to apply either carrots or sticks to induce desired responses by the parties. The threatened must not be able to use force except at very high cost. If these elements are not present, the best fall-back option is not half-hearted coercion but seeking out opportunities to bring the parties into consultation that rely on persuasion.

78 Kuperman makes a related argument from the cases of Bosnia, Rwanda and Kosovo that a form of 'moral hazard' occurs when minorities that are weaker militarily than majorities but seek secession or autonomy provoke the majorities so that the latter retaliate. This repression prompts the international community to come to the minority's aid, and a local conflict thus becomes internationalized (Kuperman, n.d.; 2008). A similar hypothesis with regard to the possible role of well-intentioned international policies in fostering the onset of some conflicts is that '…a certain pattern has characterized the international responses to pre-genocide Rwanda, 1993–94; Burundi, 1993; Kosovo, 1992–98; and East Timor, 1999, and possibly other cases. The international community's sympathetic political championing of an ethnic minority's rights, such as through honoring unofficial referendums and denouncing the human rights violations of their oppressors, may tend to polarize the local political relations further by demonizing the perpetrators, and thus help to catalyze violence. The forces of violent backlash in those settings may be encouraged to pre-empt militarily the impending threat of political change, but the international community is not prepared to deter that reaction. Ostensible violence *prevention* can become violence *precipitation*, if well-intentioned advocacy of human rights promotion, provision of humanitarian aid, or other international measures are advanced on behalf of a vulnerable group, but actually puts them at greater risk by tempting the more powerful and better-armed forces of reaction to strike while they can pre-empt the forces of change, because adequate international provision is not made to protect their victims' (Lund, 1999).

79 Such forces will be more feasible as well as effective to the extent they have the approval of the government of the host country. Introducing such stabilization forces without such acquiesence may provoke violence instead, as was threatened when the OAU discussed sending a multi-lateral force into Burundi in 1998.

80 'The shift that needs to be consolidated is multifold: toward an increasingly insider approach to conflict prevention; toward earlier mediation; and toward bottom-up approaches aimed at societies as a whole.' (Nicolaides 1996: 50).

81 NGOs such as FEWER, International Alert, and the International Project on Peace and Prosperity (IPPP) have acted as informal hosts and conveners of multi-actor consultations in countries such as southern Georgia, Kenya and Guinea-Bissau. UNDP country consultation projects are also catalyzing concerted preventive initiatives in threatened countries such as Fiji and Guyana. Given sufficient training over time in conflict assessments and conflict-sensitive programming, these processes might garner more discretion for the country level to decide on appropriate prevention decisions and strategies. The stovepipe structure of most development organizations has to be altered by giving more analytical power, policy authority, flexibility, and implementation resources to country missions and cross-agency bodies at regional and country levels, which is where necessary value tradeoffs as well as tactical decisions need to be made.

82 One key research question is how significant such the local and other non-intervention conducive factors must be for prevention to succeed. Many of these factors tend to be present in the more successful cases in Europe. So what is unclear is how effective or limited external intervention can be in the absence of such favorable endogenous environments, such as in Africa and Asia.

83 Such as through the new Uppsala MILC database on direct prevention measures vis-à-vis minor armed conflicts (Moller et al., 2007; Heldt, 2007).

84 These analyses need to be organized around distinct intervention categories and the levels and contexts in which they operate in order to cumulate knowledge and be subject to further testing and refinement. A consistent framework for presenting the lessons is needed to provide comparable profiles of different instruments. The categories most fruitful for comparative policy research should correspond to concrete, observable, alternative activities that correspond to choices that policymakers can actually make, and not remain abstractions. But they also cannot be based simply on descriptive, sectoral goals or program labels, which may prove analytically barren. Research designs also need a typology of contexts into which interventions are introduced, such as the level of hostilities, power balances of contending parties

(symmetric or asymmetric conflicts), and the degree of support. Although every individual application of a generic instrument encounters a unique combination of circumstances, it is possible to identify types of conditions whose variations seem to be most important in producing differing impacts, so as to apply findings to analogous situations.

REFERENCES

Allen-Nan, Susan. (2003) *Intervention Coordination*.Washington, DC: Alliance for Conflict Transformation.

Anderson, Mary. (1999) *Do No Harm: How Aid Can Support Peace–Or War*. Boulder, CO: Lynne Rienner.

Annan, Kofi A. (2002) *Prevention of Armed Conflict: Report of the Secretary-General*. New York, NY: United Nations Press.

Ayoob, Mohammed. (1996) 'State Making, State Breaking and State Failure,' in Crocker, Chester and Hampson, Fen (eds.), *Managing Global Chaos*. Washington, DC: US Institute of Peace.

Ball, Nicole. (1992) *Pressing for Peace: Can Aid Induce Reform?* Washington, DC: Overseas Development Council.

Bienen, Henry S., and Gersovitz, Mark. (1986) 'Consumer Subsidy Cuts, Violence, and Political Stability,' *Comparative Politics*, 19(1, October): 25–44.

Boutros, Boutros-Ghali. (1994) *Building Peace and Development 1994. Report on the Work of the Organization from the Forty-eighth to the Forty-ninth Session of the General Assembly*. New York, NY: United Nations.

Brown, Michael and Rosecrance, Richard. (1999) *The Costs of Conflict: Prevention and Cure in the Global Area*. Lanham, MD: Rowman and Littlefield.

Bush, Kenneth. (2003) 'Hands-On PCIA' (Federation of Canadian Municipalities) [www.peacebuild.ca].

Bussmann, Marget and Schneider, Gerald. (2007) 'When Globalization Discontent Turns Violent: Foreign Economic Liberalization and Internal War,' *International Studies Quarterly*, 51: 1, 79.

Byman, Daniel L. (2002) *Keeping the Peace: Lasting Solutions to Ethnic Conflicts*. Baltimore, MD: Johns Hopkins University Press.

Carment, David and James, Patrick. (eds.) (1998) *Peace in the Midst of Wars: Preventing and Managing International Ethnic Conflicts*. Columbia, SC: University of South Carolina Press.

Carment, David and Schnabel, Albrecht. (2004) *Conflict Prevention from Rhetoric to Reality, Volume I: Organizations and Institutions*. Lanham, MD: Lexington Books.

Carnegie Commission on Preventing Deadly Conflict. (1997) *Preventing Deadly Conflict*. Washington, DC: Carnegie Commission.

Chopra, Jarat. (ed.) (1998) *The Politics of Peace-Maintenance*. Boulder, CO: Lynne Rienner.

Chua, Amy. (2003) *World on Fire: How Exporting Free Market Democracy Breeds Ethnic Hatred and Global Instability*. New York, NY: Doubleday.

Cohen, J. (1999) *Conflict Prevention in the OSCE: An Assessment of Capacities*. The Hague, Netherlands: Netherlands Institute of International Relations.

Collier, Paul and Dehn, Jan. (2001) *Aid, Shocks, and Growth*. Washington, DC: World Bank, Development Research Group.

Collier, Paul. (2003) *Breaking the Conflict Trap: Civil War and Development Policy*. Washington, DC: World Bank.

Commission on Weak States and US National Security. (2004) *On the Brink: Weak States and US National Security*. Washington, DC: Center for Global Development.

Cortright, David. (ed.) (1997) *The Price of Peace: The Role of Incentives in International Conflict Prevention*. Lanham, MD: Rowman and Littlefield.

CPR Unit. (2002) 'The Conflict Analysis Framework (CAF): Identifying Conflict-related Obstacles to Development,' *CPR Dissemination Notes*, No. 5, October. Washington, DC: World Bank.

Crocker, Chester. (2003) 'Engaging Failed States,' *Foreign Affairs* September/October: 32–44.

Dahrendorf, Ralf. (1959) *Class and Class Conflict in Industrial Society*. Stanford, CA: Stanford University Press.

Davies, John L., and Gurr, Ted Robert. (eds.) (1998) *Preventive Measures*. Lanham, MD: Rowman and Littlefield.

De Nevers, Renee. (1999) 'Slovakia,' in Michael E. Brown and Richard N. Rosecrance (eds.), *The Costs of Conflict: Prevention and Cure in the Global Arena*. Lanham, MD: Rowman and Littlefield.

Doyle, Michael W. (1997) *Ways of War and Peace: Realism, Liberalism, and Socialism*. New York, NY: Norton.

Doyle, Michael W., and Sambanis, Nicholas. (2000) 'International Peacebuilding: A Theoretical and Quantitative Analysis,' *American Political Science Review*, 94: 779.

Dwan, Renata. (2001) 'Armed Conflict Prevention, Management and Resolution,' in *SIPRI Yearbook 2001: Armaments, Disarmament and International Security*. New York, NY: Oxford University Press.

Esman, Milton J. (1998) 'Can Foreign Aid Moderate Ethnic Conflict?' *Peaceworks*, No. 13. Washington, DC: US Institute of Peace.

Evans, Gareth and Sahnoun, Mohamed. (2001) *The Responsibility to Protect*. Ottawa, Ontario: International Development Research Centre.

Fearon, J.D., and Laitin, D. (1996) 'Explaining Interethnic Cooperation,' *American Political Science Review*, 90(4): 715–735.

FEWER, International Alert, and Saferworld. (2003) *Conflict-sensitive Approaches to Development, Humanitarian Assistance and Peacebuilding: Tools for Peace and Conflict Impact Assessment*. London.

Fisher, Ronald J. (1989) *The Social Psychology of Intergroup and International Conflict Resolution*. New York, NY: Springer-Verlag.

Gaigals, Cynthia, and Leonhardt, Manuela. (2001) *Conflict-sensitive Approaches to Development*. London, England: International Alert.

Galama, Anneka and van Tongren, Paul (eds.) (2002) *Towards Better Peacebuilding Practice: On Lessons Learned, Evaluation Practices and Aid and Conflict*. Utrecht, Netherlands: European Centre for Conflict Prevention.

George, Alexander. (1993) *Bridging the Gap: Theory and Practice in Foreign Policy*. Washington, DC: US Institute of Peace.

Gissinger, Ranveig and Gleditsch, Nils Petter. (1999) 'Globalization and Conflict: Welfare, Distribution, and Political Unrest,' *Journal of World Systems Research*, V(2): 327–365.

Gleditsch, Nils Petter. (1998) 'Armed Conflict and the Environment: A Critique of the Literature,' *Journal of Peace Research*, 35(3).

Gleditsch, Nils Petter, *et al.* (2002) 'Armed Conflict 1946–2001: A New Data Set,' *Journal of Peace Research*, 39(5).

Goldstone, Jack, *et al.* (2003) 'Beyond Democracy,' paper submitted to Combat Political Violence Competition, February.

Goodhand, Jonathan. (2001) *Conflict Assessments. A Synthesis Report: Kyrgystan, Moldova, Nepal, and Sri Lanka*. London, England: Centre for Defense Studies.

Greenberg Melanie, John H. Barton, and Margaret E. McGuinness (eds.), *Words Over War*. Lanham, MD: Rowman & Littlefield.

Gurr, Ted Robert. (1974) 'Persistence and Change in Political Systems, 1800–1971,' *American Political Science Review*, 68(4): 1487.

Gurr, Ted Robert. (2000) 'Ethnic Warfare on the Wane,' *Foreign Affairs*, 79(3).

Gurr, Ted Robert, Marshall, Monty, G., and Khosla, Deepa. (2000) *Peace and Conflict 2001*. College Park, MD: University of Maryland Press.

Gurr, Ted Robert and Marshall, Monty G. (2003) *Peace and Conflict 2003: A Global Survey of Armed Conflicts, Self-Determination Movements, and Democracy*. College Park, MD: Integrated Network for Societal Conflict Research, Center for International Development and Conflict Research, University of Maryland.

Hamburg, David A. (2002) *No More Killing Fields: Preventing Deadly Conflict*. Lanham, MD: Rowman and Littlefield.

Hampson, Fen Osler. (1996) *Nurturing Peace: Why Peace Settlements Succeed or Fail*. Washington, DC: United States Institute of Peace.

Hampson, Fen Osler and Malone, David M. (2002) *From Reaction to Conflict Prevention: Opportunities for the UN System*. Boulder, CO: Lynne Rienner.

Harff, Barbara. (1998) 'Early Warning of Humanitarian Crises: Sequential Models and the Role of Accelerators,' in John L. Davies and Ted Robert Gurr (eds.), *Preventive Measures: Building Risk Assessment and Crisis Early Warning Systems*. Lanham, MD: Rowman and Littlefield.

Harff, Barbara. (2003) 'No Lessons Learned from the Holocaust? Assessing Risks of Genocide and Political Mass Murder since 1955,' *American Political Science Review*, 97(1): 57–73.

Harff, Barbara. (2005) 'Humanitarian Intervention,' in Martin Griffiths (ed.), *Encyclopedia of International Relations and Global Politics*. New York, NY: Routledge, pp. 376–385.

Harff, Barbara. (2006) 'Risk Assessment and Early Warning of Genocide: Some Guidelines for the Office of the Special Adviser to the UN Secretary-General on the Prevention of Genocide,' posted on www.unausa.org, January.

Hartzel, Caroline A. (1999) 'Explaining the Stability of Negotiated Settlements to Intrastate Wars,' *The Journal of Conflict Resolution*, 43: 3–22.

Hegre, Havard, Gleditsch, Nils Petter, and Ranveig Gissinger (2002) 'Globalization and Internal Conflict,' paper presented at the Midwest Political Science Association annual conference, Chicago.

Horowitz, Donald L. (1985) *Ethnic Groups in Conflict*. Berkeley, CA: University of California Press.

Human Security Centre. (2005) *Human Security Report*. New York, NY and Oxford, England: Oxford University Press.

Human Security Centre. (2006) *Human Security Brief*. New York, NY and Oxford, England: Oxford University Press.

International Commission on Intervention and State Sovereignty. (2001) *The Responsibility to Protect*. Ottawa: International Development Research Centre.

Jentleson, Bruce W. (1999) 'Preventive Diplomacy: Analytical Conclusions and Policy Lessons,' in Bruce W. Jentleson (ed.), *Opportunities Missed,*

Opportunities Seized. Lanham, MD: Rowman and Littlefield.

Jentleson, Bruce W. (2001) 'Preventive Statecraft: A Realist Strategy for the Post-Cold War Era,' in Chester A. Crocker, Fen Osler Hampson, and Pamela Aall (eds.), *Turbulent Peace: The Challenges of Managing International Conflict*. Washington, DC: United States Institute of Peace, pp. 249–264.

Kriesberg, Louis. (2003) *Constructive Conflicts: From Escalation to Resolution*, 2nd edn. Lanham, MD: Rowman and Littlefield.

Kuper, Leo. (1985) *The Prevention of Genocide*. New Haven, CT: Yale University Press.

Kuperman, Alan. (n.d.) 'Moral Hazard: How and Why Humanitarian Intervention Promotes Armed Rebellion,' Armed Groups Project website.

Leatherman, Janie, DeMars, William, Gaffney, Patrick D., and Väyrynen, Raimo. (1999.) *Breaking the Cycles of Violence: Conflict Prevention in Intra-state Crises*. West Hartford, CT: Kumarian Press.

Leonhardt, Manuela. (2000a) 'Towards a Unified Methodology: Reframing PCIA,' in Michael Lund and Guenola Rasamoelina (eds.), *The Impact of Conflict Prevention Policy: Cases, Measures, Assessments*. Conflict Prevention Network, Baden-Baden, Germany: Nomos.

Leonhardt, Manuela. (2000b) *Conflict Impact Assessment of EU Development Cooperation with ACP Countries: A Review of Literature and Practice*. London: International Alert – Saferworld.

Leonhardt, Manuela. (2002) 'Improving Capacities and Procedures for Formulating and Implementing Effective Conflict Prevention Strategies – An Overview of Recent Donor Initiatives,' in Michael Lund and Guenola Rasamoelina (eds.), *The Impact of Conflict Prevention Policy: Cases, Measures, Assessments*. Yearbook 2000 of the Conflict Prevention Network, Baden-Baden, Germany: Nomos.

Levy, Jack. (1996) 'Contending Theories of International Conflict,' in Chester Crocker and Fen Hampson (eds.), *Managing Global Chaos*. Washington, DC: US Institute of Peace.

Lund, Michael. (1995) 'Underrating Preventive Diplomacy,' *Foreign Affairs*, July/August.

Lund, Michael S. (1996) *Preventing Violent Conflict*. Washington, DC: US Institute of Peace.

Lund, Michael S. (1998a) 'Not Only When, But How: From Early Warning to Rolling Prevention,' in Peter Wallensteen (ed.), *Preventing Violent Conflict: Past Record and Future Challenge*. Uppsala, Sweden: Uppsala University, Department of Peace and Conflict Research.

Lund, Michael S. (1998b) "Impacts of Development Aid as Incentives or Disincentives in Reducing Internal and Interstate Conflicts: A Review of Findings from Documented Experience." Unpublished report to the Development Assistance Committee Task Force on Peace, Conflict And Development, OECD.

Lund, Michael S. (1998c) 'Developing Conflict Prevention and Peacebuilding Strategies from Recent Experience in Europe,' in Gianni Bonvicini, Ettore Greco, Bernard von Plate, and Reinhardt Rummel (eds.), *Preventing Violent Conflict: Issues from the Baltics and the Caucasus*. Baden-Baden: Nomos.

Lund, Michael S. (1999) 'Preventive Diplomacy for Macedonia, 1992–1997: Containment becomes Nationbuilding,' and other chapters in Bruce Jentleson (ed.), *Preventive Diplomacy in the Post Cold War World: Opportunities Missed, Opportunities Seized and Lessons to Be Learned*. Lanham, MD: Rowman and Littlefield.

Lund, Michael S. (2000) *UN Preventive Measure: A Prototype Manual for Practitioners in Potential Conflict Situations*. New York: UN Framework Team.

Lund, Michael S. (2001) 'Why Are Some Ethnic Disputes Settled Peacefully, While Others Become Violent? Comparing Slovakia, Macedonia, and Kosovo,' in Hayward Alker, *et al.* (eds.), *Journeys through Conflict*. Lanham, MD: Rowman and Littlefield.

Lund, Michael S. (2002) 'From Lessons to Action,' in Fen Hampson and David Malone (eds.), *From Reaction to Prevention: Opportunities for the UN System in the New Millennium*. A Project of the International Peace Academy. Boulder, CO: Lynne Rienner.

Lund, Michael S. (2003) *What Kind of Peace is Being Built? Assessing Post-Conflict Peacebuilding, Charting Future Directions*. Ottawa: International Development Research Centre.

Lund, Michael S. (2004) *The Effectiveness of Local Participatory Community Development in Managing Conflicts: Local Democracy-building, Social Capital and Peace*. Washington, DC: Management Systems International, Inc.

Lund, Michael S. (2005) 'Greed and Grievance Diverted: Why Macedonia Has Avoided Interethnic Civil War,' Case-study for Yale/World Bank.

Lund, Michael S. and John Predergast (1997) *Preventing and Mitigating Violent Conflicts: A Guide for Practitioners*. Washington, DC: Creative Associates International, Inc. (www.caii-dc.com/ghai)

Lund, Michael S., Barnett, Rubin and Hara, Fabienne. (1998) 'Learning from Burundi's Failed Democratic Transition, 1993–1996: Did International Initiatives Match the Problem?' in Barnett Rubin (ed.), *Cases and Strategies of Preventive Action*. New York, NY: Century Foundation Press.

Lund, Michael S. and Andreas Mehler. (1999) *Peacebuilding and Conflict Prevention in Developing*

Countries. Conflict Prevention Network, Stiftung and Wissenschaft und Politik.

Lund, Michael S. and Larry Beyna (2000) *Impacts of Civil Society Projects on Conflict.* Greater Horn of Africa Project. Washington, DC: Management Systems International, Inc.

Mack, Andrew. (2002) 'Civil War: Academic Research and Policy Community,' *Journal of Peace Research*, 39(5).

Mansfield, Edward D. and Snyder, Jack. (1995a) 'Democratization and War,' *Foreign Affairs*, May/June.

Mansfield, Edward D. and Snyder, Jack. (1995b) 'Democratization and the Danger of War,' *International Security*, 20(1): 9.

Marshall, Katherine. (1998) 'Emerging from Conflict: The Role of International Development Finance Institutions,' in Gianni Bonvicini, Ettore Greco, Berbard von Plate and Reinhardt Rummel (eds.), *Preventing Violent Conflict: Issues from the Baltics and the Caucasus.* Baden-Baden: Nomos.

Marshall, Monty and Gurr, Ted Robert. (2003) *Peace and Conflict: 2003.* Center for International Development and Conflict Management (CIDCM).

Miall, Hugh. (1992) *The Peacemakers: Peaceful Settlement of Disputes since 1945.* New York, NY: St Martin's Press.

Miall, Hugh, *et al.* (1999) *Contemporary Conflict Resolution.* Cambridge, England: Polity Press.

Morfit, Michael. (2002) 'Rebuilding Social Capital: A Framework for Assistance in Post-Conflict Societies,' in *Developing Alternatives: Beyond Chaos, Development After Conflict*, 8(1). Washington DC: Development Alternatives, Inc.

Mueller, John. (1989) *Retreat from Doomsday: The Obsolescence of Major War.* New York: Basic Books.

Munuera, Gabriel. (1994) *Preventing Armed Conflict in Europe: Lessons from Recent Experience.* Paris, France: Institute for Security Studies.

Muscat, Robert J. (2002) *Investing in Peace: How Development Aid Can Prevent or Promote Conflict* Armonk, New York: M.E. Sharpe, Inc.

Nelson, Joan M. and Eglinton, Stephanie J. (1993) *Global Goals, Contentious Means: Issues of Multiple Aid Conditionality.* Washington, DC: Overseas Development Council.

Nicolaides, Kalypso. (1996) 'International Preventive Action: Developing a Strategic Framework,' in Robert I. Rotberg (ed.), *Vigilance and Vengeance: NGO's Preventing Ethnic Conflict in Divided Societies.* Washington, DC: Brookings Institution Press.

OECD. (2001) *The DAC Guidelines: Helping Prevent Violent Conflict.* Paris, France: OECD.

Paris, Roland. (2001) 'Human Security: Paradigm Shift or Hot Air?' *International Security*, 26(2): 87.

Peck, Connie. (1989) 'An Integrative Model for Understanding and Managing Conflict,' *Interdisciplinary Peace Research*, 1(1).

Peck, Connie. (1998) *Sustainable Peace: The Role of the UN and Regional Organizations in Preventing Conflict.* Lanham, MD: Rowman and Littlefield.

Ramcharan, B.G. (1991) *The International Law and Practice of Early Warning and Preventive Diplomacy: The Emerging Global Watch.* Dordrecht, The Netherlands: Marinus Nijhoff.

Regan, Patrick M. (2002) 'Third-party Interventions and the Duration of Interstate Conflicts,' *Journal of Conflict Resolution*, 46(1): 55.

Reilly, Ben. (1999) 'Voting is Good, Except When It Guarantees War,' *Washington Post*, October 17, p. B2.

Reinecke, Wolfgang H. (1996) 'Can International Financial Institutions Prevent Internal Violence?: The Sources of Ethno-National Conflict in Transitional Societies,' in Abram Chayes and Antonia Handler Chayes (eds.), *Preventing Conflict in the Post-Soviet World.* Washington, DC: The Brookings Institution.

Rodrik, Dani. (1997) 'Globalization, Social Conflict, and Economic Growth.' Kennedy School of Government.

Ropers, Norbert. (1995) *Peaceful Intervention.* Berlin, Germany: Berghoff Research Center for Constructive Conflict Management.

Rothchild, Donald. (2002) 'Third Party Incentives,' in Stephen John Stedman, Donald Rothchild, and Elizabeth M. Cousens (eds.), *Ending Civil Wars: The Success and Failure of Negotiated Settlements in Civil War.* Lanham, MD: Lynne Rienner.

Rubin, Barnett R. (1998) *Cases and Strategies of Preventive Action.* New York, NY: Century Foundation Press.

Rubin, Barnett. (2004) *Blood on the Doorstep: The Politics of Preventive Action.* New York: The Century Foundation Press.

Sambanis, Nicholas. (2003) 'Using Case Studies to Expand the Theory of Civil War.' *Social Development Papers: Conflict Prevention and Reconstruction*, CPR Working Paper, No. 5. Washington, DC: World Bank.

Schnabel, Albrecht and Carment, David. (2004) *Conflict Prevention from Rhetoric to Reality, Volume II: Opportunities and Innovations.* Lanham, MD: Lexington Books.

Schwank, Nicolas and Rohloff, Christoph. (2001) 'War is Over-Conflict Continues? Conditions for Stable Conflict Outcomes,' paper presented at the Uppsala Conflict Data Conference, Uppsala, Sweden.

Sherriff, Andrew and Karuru, Njeri. (2000) *Methodology for Conflict Sensitive Planning for NGO, INGO and Donor Operations in Kenya.* London: International Alert, Centre for Conflict Research.

Stedman, Stephen J. (1995) 'Alchemy for a New World Order: Overselling "Preventive Diplomacy",' *Foreign Affairs*, 75(3): 14–20.

Stedman, Stephen John, Rothchild, Donald and Cousens, Elizabeth M. (eds.) (2002) *Ending Civil Wars: The Success and Failure of Negotiated Settlements in Civil War*. Lanham, MD: Lynne Rienner.

Stevenson, Jonathan. (2000) *Preventing Conflict: The Role of the Bretton Woods Institutions*. New York, NY: Oxford University Press.

Stockholm International Peace Research Institute and Swedish Institute for International Affairs. (2000) *Preventing Violent Conflict: The Search for Political Will, Strategies and Effective Tools*. Stockholm, Sweden.

Stremlau, John and Sagasti, Francisco R. (1998) *Preventing Deadly Conflict: Does the World Bank Have a Role?* Washington, DC: Carnegie Commission on Preventing Deadly Conflict.

Suhrke, Astri. (1996) 'Environmental Change, Migration and Conflict: A Lethal Feedback Dynamic?' in Chester Crocker, Fen Hampson, and Pamela Aall (eds.), *Managing Global Chaos*. Washington, DC: US Institue of Peace.

Swedish Ministry for Foreign Affairs. (1999) *Preventing Violent Conflict: A Swedish Action Plan*. Stockholm, Sweden.

United Nations. (1992) *Agenda for Peace*. New York: UN Secretary-General.

United States Commission on National Security. (1999) *New World Coming: American Security in the 21st Century*. Phase I Report on the Emerging Global Security Environment for the First Quarter of the *21st* Century.

USAID. (2004) *Steering Youth from Violent Conflict: A Toolkit for Programming*. Washington, DC: Conflict Mitigation and Management Unit.

Uvin, Peter. (2002) 'The Development/Peacebuilding Nexus: A Typology and History of Changing Paradigms,' in *Journal of Peacebuilding and Development*, 11(1).

Wallensteen, Peter. (1998) 'Preventive Security: Direct and Structural Prevention of Violent Conflicts,' in Peter Wallensteen (ed.), *Preventing Violent Conflict: Past Record and Future Challenges*. Uppsala, Sweden: Uppsala University, Department of Peace and Conflict Research.

Walter, Barbara F. (1997) 'Designing Transitions from Violent Civil War.' Policy paper no.31. San Diego, CA: Institute on Global Conflict and Cooperation, University of California.

Weitsman, Patricia A. and Schneider, Gerald (eds.) (1997) *Enforcing Cooperation: Risky States and Intergovernmental Management of Conflict*. New York: St Martin's Press.

Wenger, Andreas and Möckli, Daniel (eds.), Conflict Prevention: The Untapped Potential of the Business Sector Wood, Bernard. (2001) *Development Dimensions of Conflict Prevention and Peacebuilding*. Ottawa, Canada: Bernard Wood and Associates. (Second draft.)

Woodward, Susan. (1995) *Balkan Tragedy: Chaos and Dissolution after the Cold War*. Washington, DC: Brookings Institution.

WWIC (Woodrow Wilson International Center for Scholars). (2002) 'Preventing the Next Wave of Conflict: Understanding Non-traditional Threats to Global Security.' Working Group Papers.

Zartman, I. William (ed.) (1995) *Collapsed States: The Disintegration and Restoration of Legitimate Authority*. Boulder, CO: Lynne Rienner.

Zartman, I. William (ed.) (2001) *Preventive Negotiation*. Lanham, MD: Rowman and Littlefield.

16

Conflict Resolution
and Negotiation

I. William Zartman

Negotiation, the process of combining conflicting positions into a joint agreement, is synonymous with conflict resolution, and is the most common (although not the only) way of preventing, managing, resolving, and transforming conflicts. Indeed, there is little negotiation that does not have to do with conflict resolution. If one adopts a rational choice definition of war or violent conflict as bargaining failure (Fearon 1995; Reiter 2003), then successful bargaining or negotiation is the means of preventing or resolving violent conflict.

Such an understanding requires a return to the antecedent notion of conflict. Conflict arises from incompatible positions; it is ubiquitous, and not especially troublesome—worthy of resolution—in its static phase (Coser 1956; Aron 1957; Bernard 1957; Schelling 1960; Powelson 1972; Pruitt & Kim 2004). But when conflict becomes active and the parties take measures to make their particular position prevail, it does become troublesome; thus, escalation is the active form of conflict (Smoke 1977; Zartman &

Faure 2005). It may block agreement that would permit cooperation to resolve a problem, or it may continue to rise to the point of violence. Conflict continues to escalate until one of three outcomes are reached: victory of one side, painful stalemate forcing the parties to consider deescalation, and stable stalemate. Thus, negotiation as conflict resolution may be used to *prevent* conflict from escalating or from turning violent; it may be used to *manage* conflict—that is deescalate the means of its pursuit from violence to politics; or it may be the means to actually *resolve* the basic incompatibilities of positions or to *transform* them into cooperative relationships.

Since World War II, negotiation to produce a peace agreement has accounted for only about a sixth of the inter- and intrastate conflicts terminated and an eighth of those temporarily managed in a ceasefire, together accounting for something less than the number terminated by victory of one side over the other. Fully a quarter of those conflicts terminated by a conflict-resolving peace

Table 16.1   Conflict outcomes over time, 1946–2005

	Victory	Peace Accord	Ceasefire	Other	Total Ended	Ongoing
1946–50	17	3	0	9	29	41
1951–55	6	4	1	4	15	27
1956–60	8	5	1	9	23	36
1961–65	11	4	4	6	25	47
1966–70	11	3	3	10	27	47
1971–75	11	4	4	7	26	51
1976–80	11	1	1	4	17	52
1981–85	9	1	1	10	21	59
1986–90	12	4	4	22	42	79
1991–95	14	14	12	30	70	96
1996–2000	6	7	10	21	44	75
2001–05	4	7	6	16	33	66
All episodes	120	57	47	148	372	

Source: Kreutz 2006

agreement during this period occurred in the immediate aftermath of the Cold War and another quarter in the decade since then. An equal number were terminated by a simple conflict-managing ceasefire during the same period.

These distinctions are all subsumed under the label of conflict resolution as used in this volume but they break down into two very distinct negotiation subtypes (Zartman 2007). Negotiating can be used to deal with *conflict* in the more common sense of reducing violence, either by deescalating violent conflict or by preventing impending violence from occurring: peace-making, peace enforcement, and part of peace-building, in UN Secretary-General Boutros Boutros Ghali's (1994) operative distinctions. But it is also used in building *cooperation*, to reduce incompatibilities in positions even where no violence is involved, for conflict prevention or conflict transformation. Cooperative negotiations contain conflicts too or else there would be no need for negotiation, but they are not impelled by impending prospects of violence (Taylor 1987; Stein 1990; Stein & Pauly 1993; Zartman & Touval 2008). In addition, cooperative negotiations are most frequently multi- (or pluri-) lateral and only recently have been subject to systematic analysis, whereas bilateral negotiations have been the subject of most advanced theorization. While one might object that the

two types are irreconcilably different and only the case of violent conflict resolution need be considered here, they are integrally tied together by the fact that untreated problems of cooperation may turn violent or may give rise to secondary violence. In addition, negotiation analysis is often equally relevant to cooperative and (violent) conflict negotiations, even though at times the distinction becomes analytically important and will be highlighted below at those junctures. Other distinctions in the type of conflict, between intrastate and interstate, may also have an impact that will be noted where relevant.

Given the relation of negotiation to conflict resolution, this chapter will focus on the ways in which negotiation is studied, in order to bring out current advances in the conceptualization of the subject and to highlight salient questions and areas where further advances are needed (Jönsson 2000; Telhami 2002; Carnevale & deDreu 2004). To do so, it will use as a framework the categorization of analytical frameworks into structural, strategic, processual, and behavioral (Zartman 1988; Hopmann 1996; Kremenyuk 2003). The following review will especially emphasize the practical value of conceptual findings for the better achievement of conflict resolution, in the belief that the purpose of theory is to inform understanding and improve practice.

Within the definition as the process of combining conflicting positions into a joint agreement, negotiation has certain characteristics that distinguish it from the two other basic types of decision-making, voting (coalition) and adjudication (hierarchy) (Zartman 1978; Lewicki et al. 2003, 4–6). It operates under a decision rule of unanimity, with a three-fold choice: yes, no, or continue negotiating (Ikle 1964). It creates a positive-sum outcome, in that no party would agree to the outcome unless it feels itself to be better off than without an agreement (its security point). Thus, negotiation involves an exchange of goods rather than a unilateral victory: negotiation is giving something to get something, so it involves moves by both/all sides, although not necessarily to an equal degree. It can be conducted in one of three ways: concession, compensation, and construction (reframing). Power in the process lies not in numbers or in authority but in alternatives (security point, again) and in persuasion.

The negotiation process operates under a loose bundle of norms that can be termed the Ethos of Equality. Like any norm, this ethos is not absolute, but it does underlie the conduct of negotiation around the world (Faure 2002). It begins with the formal structural equality of the parties, based on the fact that each has a veto over any agreement; therefore, the parties need to grant each other recognition with equal standing in the negotiations. From this, it extends to the behavioral setting that facilitates exchanges through the courtesy of symmetry that each party gives the other, even if the encounter is asymmetrical in other terms. The ethos also covers the process, where requitement—the sense that concessions will be reciprocated—is expected. While the overarching principles of any agreement, or formula, are the primary subject of any negotiation, they always refer to some mutually agreed notion of justice, the basis of which is equality or equalizing, whatever the specific referent (Zartman et al. 1996; Korm 1998). Neglected or ignored though they may be in any particular negotiation, these elements of the ethos of equality have

their influence both for the smooth conduct and for the breakdown of negotiations.

But first, the question of Why negotiate? needs to be addressed, before discussing the question, How negotiate? While parties—states, groups or individuals—generally prefer to resolve their problems unilaterally, where they can be in control of decisions and do not have to bend to other parties' interests, they find they have to involve others when resolution of the problem or conflict is beyond their unilateral means. Resolution may mean ending a conflict with another party or overcoming a problem that needs the participation of another party; it may mean ending a costly situation or creating a beneficial one. However, since there are a number of ways to provide social decisions with their own decision rules, including voting and hierarchy, parties resort to negotiation when there is no authoritative hierarchy and no decision rule of division. Those conditions describe the anarchy of the international relations system and the informality of personal relations. In addition, parties turn to negotiation when they want a sense of ownership over the outcome, which neither voting nor hierarchy provides (at least in the same measure).

Between the inability unilaterally to end (i.e. win) the conflict or solve the problem and the decision to negotiate (and then to agree on the terms created) bi- or multilaterally lies a large area of indecision, dominated primarily by the cost of alternatives, above all the cost of continued conflict or unsolved problems. The cost/benefit value of what a party can obtain without negotiating has many names, including security point, best/worst alternative to a negotiated agreement (BATNA/WATNA), reservation price, threat point, and others, and is the most important reference point in understanding and conducting a negotiation (Pillar 1983). It is the source of relative power and determines whether a party can play it tough or soft in negotiating (tough, if the security point is close to the expected outcome; soft, if the gap is great and there is much benefit to gain or much loss to be protected) (Kahneman & Tversky 1979;

Zartman 2006). If the estimated gap between the two is too small, parties are likely to let the unresolved conflict or problem continue, and may even bog down in an S^5 situation (soft, stable, self-serving stalemate).

STRUCTURE

Structural approaches explain outcomes of negotiation by examining the distribution of the parties' means of attaining them, frequently referred to as power.[1] Power can be thought of as exercises or measures of contingent gratification and deprivation that a party attaches to negotiating offers and security points in order to change their value, the elements which provide an ability of the parties to move each other in an intended direction (Dahl 1951; Zartman & Rubin 2000). Yet very little is known about the relative merits and moments of gratification (promises) vs deprivation (threats), or about the dynamics associated with security points, other than that they are important, in analysis and in practice. Where continued conflict is the parties' shared security point, the parties in negotiation seek to provide a better alternative (gratification) or to make continuing conflict more costly (deprivation) (Zeuthen 1930; Jönsson 1981; Zartman and Touval 2007). The use of deprivation (coercion) is generally associated with distributive or zero-sum bargaining, and of gratification (benefits) with integrative or positive-sum bargaining (Hopmann 1996, 2001; Wagner 2007). It is likely that both are necessary, a fact often forgotten.

When the parties are not able to change each other's calculus to provide a jointly acceptable alternative to violence, they may require the services of a mediator (Wall, Stark & Sandifer 2001). Mediation is considered here to be a subset of negotiation, an activity made necessary by the inability of the conflicting parties to overcome their conflict and produce a joint agreement on their own; it is, however, such an important subset, with its own characteristics provided by the presence of a third party, that it

deserves a separate treatment, fully presented in the next chapter by Jacob Bercovitch. Mediation turns the dyadic relation between the parties into a triad, in which the third angle serves to facilitate negotiation between the other two by overcoming the obstacles which keep them from negotiating directly. Power at the hands of a mediator is (for some unknown reason) termed leverage and it comes in limited amounts and forms, all of them ultimately dependent on the parties' need for a settlement (again in comparison to their security point). The forms of leverage, in general order of availability, are persuasion, limitation (closing alternatives), extraction (getting one party to articulate a solution attractive to the other), termination (mediator's threat to leave), and again (but least available) gratification and deprivation. Assistant Secretary of State Chester Crocker (1992) made sure that his mediation was "the only game in town," urged the parties to "make an offer," and threatened to end mediation on occasion, but had little to offer in the way of carrots and sticks, and was left above all with the power of persuasion, comparing an agreement to the cost of continued conflict. Similar arguments can be wielded by the parties themselves.

Structure refers primarily to the relative position of perceived power of the parties. It is known that a *sense* of equality, or symmetry, is beneficial to the efficient and effective achievement of results, and negotiators are well advised to cultivate that sense so they can move from tending the atmospherics to resolving the problem. But, in fact, symmetry is nonexistent in the real world; even close equals are never sure of their relative position and parties base their perceptions on different aspects of power. All negotiations are asymmetrical, to a greater or lesser degree; there is no absolute equality in the real world, equality between parties, and parties that are nearly or presumptively equal will spend much of their time protecting that equality or seeking to overturn it in their favor. While symmetry has long been thought to be the most favorable situation for efficient and effective negotiations, both social psychology and political science have recently shown that its real-world equivalent, near-symmetry (small asymmetry), is the least productive structure because the parties will spend most of their time and effort in position politics, seeking to maintain or upset (and therefore counter-maintain) the near-symmetry (Hornstein 1965; Vitz & Kite 1970; Hammerstein & Parker 1982; Pruitt & Carnevale 1993; Zartman & Rubin 2000). Asymmetrical parties know their roles and goals and seek absolute gains, whereas rivals at any level of the totem pole contest each other's position and seek relative gains at the other's expense (Powell 1991).

Weaker parties have a potential array of means at their disposal to reduce the degree of asymmetry, by borrowing power from third parties, opponents, context, and process (Zartman & Rubin 2000). Whether the conflict is interstate or intrastate, parties weaker in power also tend to overcome their power deficit by emphasizing commitment. Smaller parties tend to concentrate on a single issue whereas larger parties are burdened by many issues and are easily distracted; the latter focus on setting the formula for a solution at the beginning of the negotiations, leaving the smaller partner to win back initial losses in the detail phase (Crump and Zartman 2003). In intrastate conflicts, the government has the structural advantage but the conditions and tactics are the same, as the rebellion emphasizes commitment and concentrates on recognition— formal symmetry—as its goal and the key to its equality (Zartman 1995). The role of imperfect information in conflict decisions between asymmetrical parties is currently the subject of a surge of rational choice literature, but it ignores negotiations, assuming bargaining failure instead of exploring it.

Weaker parties also have other elements outside the power structure that can compensate for their weaker position. One, already noted, is commitment, the determination to overcome odds. Since power is sometimes characterized as "resources + skill + will," commitment emphasizes the last element over the first. Commitment also returns the

negotiation setting to its formal equality, in which each party holds a veto. The other element, which often underlies commitment, is justice. Even when outgunned, parties may hold out because they hold their cause to be just, and negotiators have been known to turn down deals offered by stronger parties because they were judged unjust. Mexicans offered a fair market price for their gas by the USA rejected the deal because they were not getting a price they considered just by rather extraneous criteria and so lost any income at all (Odell 2000), and despite repeated painful impasses. India and Pakistan reject a salient solution (along the Line of Control) for the Kashmir dispute because both consider it unjust.

Power structures also operate within institutional structures, which can have important effects on power relations. Much of the work in this approach has been done on multilateral, cooperative negotiations rather than on violent conflicts. States institutionalize their relations into international regimes, informal and formal, in order to reduce transaction costs, and such regimes both expand and limit their negotiating possibilities (Hasenclever, Mayer & Rittberger 1997; Jönsson and Talberg 1998; Spector & Zartman 2003). Regimes provide information, monitor progress, expand linkages, establish agendas, and generally reduce uncertainties and regulate expectations; but they also limit options and strategies (Odell 2005). In this, they tend to equalize member parties and reduce asymmetries. Multilateral bargaining (and analysis) also depends largely on the formation of temporary, informal institutions such as party and issue coalitions, involving some very distinct strategies, typologies, and negotiations (Hampson 1994; Zartman 1994, 2006; Sebenius 1996; Bottom et al. 2000; Nalikar 2003; Crump & Zartman 2003; Odell 2005).

Since institutions have their own rules, relations and constraints, drawn in turn from their own internal structures and from their relative positions toward each other, they can have an important impact on negotiators' capabilities. The European Union, for example, is essentially an institutionalized negotiating system where outcomes are strongly affected by the paths the process is required to take, although it has only rarely been analyzed as such (Meerts & Cede 2003; Elgström & Jönsson 2005). An enormous field of inquiry is opened by other institutionalized negotiation fora, from the UN Security Council and the World Trade Organization (WTO) (and other agencies) (Odell 2006) to regional organizations (Rothchild 1997) to national legislatures, constituting a rich subject for negotiation analysis of conflict resolution, much the same way as behavioral analysis overtook judicial studies or socioeconomic analysis electoral studies.

Another form of structural analysis that has developed some insights in regard to cooperative negotiations concerns the negotiatory relation between the negotiations and their domestic constituencies in two-level games. The approach has not been used as much as possible in regard to either interstate or intrastate conflicts (Druckman 1978; Evans, Jacobson & Putnam 1993; Putnam 1998). The idea that negotiating parties need also negotiate with their home constituencies and reach an agreement on the domestic level that corresponds to the parameters of an agreement on the inter-party level is as applicable to conflict negotiations as to cooperation. It opens up a window of enormous complexity, however, when relating to intrastate civil wars, where the internal politics of rebel movements are often inchoate at best. For that very reason, analysis would be useful, even if difficult.

STRATEGY

Contrasted with structural analysis' focus on means as the explanatory concept, strategic analysis uses the rational choice of ends as its terms of analysis, as portrayed in game theory and other rational choice approaches. Unfortunately, the rational choice work on negotiation has literally fled from the subject through its assumptions as well as its analysis. As Fearon (1995, p 390) posits, "There should

exist a set of negotiated agreements that have greater utility for both sides than the gamble of war…So to explain…war,…why might states fail either to locate or to agree on an outcome in this range …?" The subsequent work in the intervening decade then focuses on bargaining failures without looking at the bargaining process itself and explaining its outcomes.

Yet the basic presentations of Prisoners' Dilemma (PDG) and the lesser-used Chicken Dilemma Games (CDG) launched a whole body of literature on negotiation. In these meta-games, both power and process were explicitly excluded, the outcome being explained by the values assigned to various outcomes (Nash 1950, 1953; Powell 2002; Avenhaus & Zartman 2007). Again, the analysis showed that for parties caught in a perceived PDG situation, the determinate outcome or Nash equilibrium is not to negotiate, lest their concession leave them open to be zapped by the other party. As a result, the challenge of negotiation is to find ways of building trust that would establish requitement, the sense that concessions will be reciprocated. The best known device is to establish a reputation in order to "teach requitement" by opening "soft" with a concession and playing Tit-for-Tat thereafter (Cross 1969; Bartos 1978; Axelrod 1984; Brams 1990). The analysis coincided with the introduction of GRIT (Gradual Reciprocation in Tension Reduction) strategy by Charles Osgood (1962) during the Cold War. If it had questionable application during the Cold War, Tit for Tat could be seen in as diverse negotiations as those later on in South Africa and Macedonia. Other ways of establishing trust include making public commitments, negotiating with institutional frameworks, signing enforceable contracts, and employing a mediator (Schelling 1960).

Although it has limited direct use for portraying situations of negotiation, PDG is a cartoon portrayal of many situations of international conflict that long defy negotiation, as discussed by Avenhaus in this volume. Its popularity was doubtless enhanced by its accurate depiction of the Cold War in general

("Better dead than Red"), although by that fact it inhibited or hid real possibilities of East–West negotiation (Kanet & Kolodziej 1991). Another situation captured by PDG has been the Arab–Israeli conflict, but here the delicate process of getting around the dilemma by establishing trust and requitement is well exemplified in the tactics leading to and through the Oslo Agreement of 1993 (Pruitt 1996), subsequently abandoned. PDG also accurately captures such territorial conflicts as the Indo-Pakistani conflict over Kashmir and the Morocco–Algeria conflict over the Western Sahara, among others. There is a huge literature on the role of mediators as a crutch of trust to permit negotiation, covered in the following chapter by Bercovitch.

Another important way of escaping the inhibitions of the PDG is to change the game, through a reevaluation of the end values. One important change is to a CDG, wherein the worst outcome is deadlock (mutual defection or security point) rather than being zapped by the opponent ("Better Red than dead"). Here there is no determinate outcome but two Nash equilibria favoring each party, respectively, creating a coordination rather than a collaboration problem (Snyder & Diesing 1977; Stein 1983 Wagner 1999). But CDG like PDG is a situation of perceived symmetry, so another change in the game would be to introduce asymmetry and thus power. This represents the tactic used by the USA under President Kennedy to end the Cuban Missile standoff (1962) and by President Reagan to end the Cold War in 1989 (Brams 1985).

The study of end value asymmetry has given rise to a large literature sometimes termed negotiation analysis or models for negotiation which seeks to obviate the lengthy and inefficient process of negotiation by indicating fair outcomes based on end values assigned by the parties (Young 1994; Raiffa with Richardson & Metcalfe 2003; Brams & Taylor 1996). While such a procedure might be of use in arbitration-type situations of a CDG, where any end of conflict is preferable to continuing conflict but where the parties are satisfied by a division deemed fair, it

is unlikely to be welcomed in situations of sharp conflict over indivisibles or over non-tradables, situations where process ownership is important, or situations where the stakes include high political commitment, in other words, most intrastate and many interstate conflicts. In this as in other types of formal modeling for and of negotiation, the analysis removed from real world relevance by its absence of process, often based on Rubenstein's (1982) take-it-or-leave-it games that avoid Ikle's (1964) basic three-fold choice (yes, no, keep on talking) as the essence of negotiation.

The task of assigning end values and rankings is often difficult enough but a more precise analysis requires identification of cardinal values for outcomes, which tends toward the impossible, at least in non-monetary cases of conflict. An additional complication has been introduced by a significant reinterpretation of end values, termed prospect theory (Farnham 1992; Tversky & Kahneman 1995; MacDermott 2007). Prospect theory indicates that losses are more highly valued than gains, that parties are more risk-taking over losses and risk-averse over gains, and that the referent frames that parties use determine the comparative value of ends. These considerations make end-based analysis much less reliable while introducing tactical elements that are crucial to effective negotiation.

Another way of analyzing negotiation using game theoretic concepts is to focus on the strategies of the parties, their "general plan[s] of action containing instructions as to what to do in every contingency" (Shubik 1964, p. 13) or "the overall orientation adopted by an actor to achieve his goal," as defined by Faure in his chapter. Most strategies in conflict resolution are mixed and therefore hard to capture in rigorous analysis, but they lie between the two poles of distributive or value-taking and integrative or value-making, departures from the usual minimax strategy (Lax & Sebenius 1986). Research on these strategies has primarily been on cooperative multilateral negotiations, where the differences often appear clearly: minilateral interest-based coalitions conglomerate their way into larger aggregations bargaining for future gains, maximizing positive-sum outcomes and using promises and predictions as exercises of power, whereas maxilateral or hegemon-based coalition accrete their way to dominance, using threats and warnings, trading security for support, avoiding losses rather than focusing on gains (Chasek 1997; Baç 2000, 2001; Crump & Zartman 2003; daConceição-Heldt 2006; Narlikar & Odell 2006; Odell 2006). However, in conflict-type negotiations, Richard Holbrooke tended toward the distributive pole at Dayton, whereas George Mitchell mediated integratively at Belfast (Curran et al. 2004); non-mediated examples, especially of integrative strategies, are harder to find.

PROCESS

Negotiation is a process, and its outcome can be best explained—and hence obtained—by process analysis: "Where you get is a function of how you get there," as Henry Kissinger was to have said. "How you get there," however, is in turn a function of two processes, the conflict process and the negotiation process. The conflict process leads to a decision to negotiate when the conflict is ripe. The ensuing negotiation process then goes through a succession of stages, whose proper accomplishment makes for a coherent agreement that maximizes the payoffs for the parties involved.

Active conflict or escalation typically contains sets of steps to negotiation. One begins with a stage of petition (or diplomacy, in interstate conflicts), where grievances are broadly felt as Needs and the aggrieved party seeks to negotiate redress, recognizing the government's authority. The protest moves on to consolidation, where the rebellion turns inward to build its own solidarity and unity; often using identity or Creed to articulate the grievances and to build support; negotiation is unlikely and antithetical to the rebellion's focus at this stage. Only when consolidation is completed can the

rebellion turn to confrontation, in combat and diplomacy (although the two work against each other) (Stedman 1991; Zartman 1995, 2006). However, at this stage, if victory or negotiation do not take place, the rebellion often turns inward, using its means as ends, and enters a phase of Greed that is much less amenable to negotiation (Collier et al. 2003; Arnson & Zartman 2005).

Parties consider positively the notion of conflict resolution through direct or mediated negotiation when they perceive the conditions of *ripeness* (Touval 1982; Touval & Zartman 1985; Zartman 1982, 1989, 1995, 2000; Gregg 2001). Ripeness occurs when the parties feel that they can no longer expect to win the conflict through escalation (or simply holding out) at an acceptable cost and that there is a possibility of a jointly acceptable solution. These two conditions, termed a Mutually Hurting Stalemate (MHS) and a Way Out (WO), are perceptional and subjective, although they generally have an objective referent. Ripeness is a necessary but insufficient condition for negotiations to begin; it has to be seized and acted upon. In order to reach a successful conclusion, the elements need to be reversed: the parties need to turn the WO into a Mutually Enticing Opportunity complementing the push factor of the MHS with a pull factor that draws the parties to a conclusion (Mitchell 1995; Pruitt & Olczak 1995; Ohlson 1998).

Ripeness was found in the mediated negotiations that resolved the South West African conflict in 1988 (Crocker 1992) and the Salvadoran conflict in 1989 (deSoto 1992) and in the direct negotiation in South Africa in 1990–94 (Sisk 1995). It was carried through to a minimal outcome (agreeing formula) in Nagorno Karabagh (Mooradian & Druckman 2003) and to more or less resolving formulas in Dayton in 1993 (Holbrooke 1998), in the Israeli disengagements (Rubin 1982) and the Israeli–Egyptian Washington Treaty (1979). Ripeness was absent in the failed Carter mediation between Eritrea and Ethiopia in 1990 (Ottaway 1995) and Clinton mediation between Palestine and Israel in 2000 (Enderlin 2002), and was present but not seized in

Liberia in 1990 or Lebanon in 1976 (Zartman 2005).

Once it has become a perceived option by the parties, either directly or through the help of a mediator, negotiation typically goes through its own process involving a number of stages and turning points (Zartman & Berman 1982; Bendahmane & McDonald 1986; Druckman 1986, 2001; Hopmann 1996). These may overlap and parties may backtrack; their passage maybe explicit or implicit; but their functions need to be observed or else the negotiations will fail or produce an incoherent result.

The first stage is *diagnosis*, without which the parties cannot get the most out of the negotiations for themselves and at the same time find terms of agreement that are acceptable to the other party. Parties need to answer such questions as: What are my real interests in this conflict, as opposed to stated positions (Fisher & Ury 1985)? What is my security point? What is this conflict like? How were other similar conflicts handled? And then similar questions need to be ascertained from the other side's point of view. Parties must also—separately or jointly—establish such preparatory elements as: parties to be included and issues to be covered in negotiation, risks and costs incurred in negotiating, support for resolving rather then pursuing the conflict, and preliminary contacts (Stein 1995).

Parties and issues are some of the most difficult prenegotiation problems. While agreeing that negotiations among both sides' moderates only are likely to leave the mass of the rebellion outside the agreement, scholarship and practice are still out on whether to include diehard spoilers in the hopes of carrying them along in the momentum of the negotiations or to leave them out in marginalized isolation (Stedman 2001; Zahar 2007). Inside they may wreck the talks, and outside they may torpedo the results, the critical variable being the weight that they command within the rebellion. Whether the hardline *akazu* and the Committee for the Defense of the Republic (CDR) should have been included in the Arusha negotiations on Rwanda in 1993 is a question that will be long debated and

never answered (Jones 2001; Leader 2001). But the absence of the IRA on one side and the DUP and the UKUP on the other made the Good Friday Agreement possible in 1998 (Curran & Sebenius 2003). In between, excluded parties at the Arusha negotiations on Burundi after 2000 were gradually brought in as the agreement evolved. Similarly, the question of what issues to include without breaking the back of an agreeable agenda is also crucial; it is unlikely that the Jerusalem question could have been included at Oslo or the Kosovo question at Dayton, but the decision to put off a resolution of Brcko at Dayton (1994) and of the Panguna mine at Arawa (2001) were the keys to the last lock on the Bosnian and Bougainville agreements.

Although diplomats may assume that such preparation is natural to negotiation, it is frequently neglected. A comparison of President Carter's (1979) and President Clinton's (2000) preparation for their Camp David Mideast negotiations goes far to explain the relative success of the first and the failure of the second. Rebel groups often need training in negotiation, beginning with the diagnosis phase, as the painful experiences of Renamo in Mozambique leading up to the 1990 negotiations, the Tamil Tigers in Sri Lanka leading up to the 2005 ceasefire, and the Lord's Resistance Army in Uganda leading up to the 2006 negotiations all show, among others.

The second phase is one of *formulation*. Negotiators do not immediately start establishing a meeting point from fixed positions; implicitly or explicitly, they first establish a formula for their agreement, consisting of a common definition of the problem and its solution (emerging directly from the diagnosis components), a common sense of justice, and/or an agreed set of terms of trade. This set of principles serves as the basis for the subsequent allocation of details. Establishing a satisfying formula is the key to a subsequent agreement, and if it is not done, the resolution of the conflict will be slower, less coherent, and less satisfactory (Narlikar & Odell 2006). There are two different types of formulas: a minimal agreeing formula that ends or suspends the violence without touching the basic conflict issues, and a resolving formula that takes on the more difficult challenge of managing both the original issues, the complications that have arisen during the conflict, and mechanism for dealing with old conflict that may reemerge and new conflicts that may arise. The distinction raises a major dilemma in negotiated conflict resolution: should peace be achieved, even if through a minimal agreeing formula that may leave issues unresolved and grievances unaddressed, or should negotiation focus on the achievement of a final resolving formula, even if the search prolongs the violence and killing that come with the struggle for justice (Zartman & Kremenyuk 2005)? Rather than find an answer in the absolute, the optimal strategy involves sequencing, focusing first on conflict management and the reduction of violence and then turning to the search for the ingredients of a just, resolving formula, recognizing that conflict management both undermines and promises conflict resolution since it reduces pressure for a solution (a less hurting stalemate) but also implies subsequent attention to underlying causes lest they return to bring back the conflict.

The notion of justice, which enters the negotiation process through its formula, is important both in understanding the process and in tying negotiation analysis to other elements of social science and diplomatic practice. While some have held that there is a single overarching notion of justice governing negotiated outcomes (Rawls 1971; Barry 1986) and others have held that justice has no place at all in negotiation, it has been found that justice is an important element in the search for a formula but that the particular version of justice to be applied is negotiated between the parties before they can move on to the disposition of specific items in dispute (Gauthier 1986; Elster 1992; Zartman et al. 1996; Albin 2001, 2003).

Formulas abound. The Arab–Israeli disputes were handled on the basis of the UNSCR 242 formula of "Peace for security" in the Israeli–Egyptian Washington Treaty (1979),

the Israeli Jordan Treaty (1995), and the Oslo Accords (1993), and were not managed or resolved with Syria or Palestine because the formula was not applied. The formula may provide one (or a mixture) of three ways by which conflicting positions are combined into a joint agreement: concession, compensation, and construction.

Concession involves mutual movement from initial positions on a single item to a meeting point somewhere in the middle. It is initiated by the establishment of a range where the potential positions of the parties overlap, termed the bargaining range or zone of possible agreement (ZOPA), absence of which agreement is not possible (Pillar 1983). Pioneering work by economists introduced process analysis in the early twentieth century, but, while theoretically elegant, it was hampered by two assumptions: fixed initial positions and constant concession rates (Edgeworth 1881; Zeuthen 1930). Concession behavior occurs most frequently toward the end of the negotiation process, often in the form of split-the-difference, after a general framework has been established (see below) (Tracy 1987). Camp David (1979), for example, cannot be understood by analyzing the parties' movement from given numbers of Israeli settlements or predetermined definitions of Palestinian autonomy to a compromise figure somewhere in the middle. But the Caricom proposal for resolution of the Haitian conflict in 2004 or the Zairean conflict in 1996 did involve concessions from opposite positions favoring removal of the president vs those favoring his maintenance in power, with the middle point—maintenance in position but with power diverted to the prime minister—the basis of the compromise, adopted in the Zairean case and finally rejected in Haiti. In the prolonged negotiation over Aceh, mediator Martti Ahrtissari successfully proposed self-government as the midpoint resulting from concessions from Indonesia's discredited autonomy and the Acehnese independence (Kingsbury 2006). Concession is conceptually zero-sum, although the outcome of the negotiation becomes positive-sum when compared to the security point of continued conflict.

Compensation overcomes the zero-sum problem by bringing in other items as a trade-off. It is expressed in the penetrating insight of the Homans (1961, p 62) Maxim: "The more the items at stake can be divided into goods valued more by one party than they cost to the other and goods valued more by the other party than they cost to the first, the greater the chances of successful outcome," and also in the Nash (1950) Point. Compensation not only underscores the importance of establishing terms of trade as a key to successful negotiation but also reminds negotiators not to leave unclaimed value on the table (Lax & Sebenius 1982).

In the South West African negotiations (1981–88), South Africa insisted on the withdrawal of Cuban troops from Angola, whose presence justified South African troops in South West Africa, whereas Angola (and the South West African People's Organization [SWAPO]) insisted on the withdrawal of the South African Defense Force (SADF) from South West Africa, whose presence justified Angolan troops in Angola. Negotiations looking for a midpoint between zero and 50,000 for either troops would have been meaningless, but using each proposal as compensation for agreement on the other, as the US mediator got the parties to do, produced a highly positive-sum agreement with relatively balanced terms and Namibian independence as well. Similarly, in the famous Cuban Missile negotiations (1972), Soviet missile evacuation was bought by a US pledge not to invade, compensating an action with a promise that was deemed a fair set of terms of trade by the parties.

Construction,[2] sometimes termed integration or problem-solving, refers to the reframing of the conflict or its solution in such a way that an outcome beneficial to both sides can be envisaged. There are many conflicts where Homans Maxim—and all the more so, a concession strategy— simply cannot be made to apply, and where a redefinition of the conflict is necessary to make a solution. In the Peru–Ecuador border

dispute, decades of competing territorial claims produced only war, a real bargaining failure, but redefinition of the problem as one of mutual development made a cooperative settlement possible (1998). In Ulster, the redefinition of the conflict by the mediator into three strands—intra-Ulster, Ulster–Eire, Eire–UK—took it out of a distributive, zero-sum confrontation.

While these three forms are ideal types, they are starting points for variations that make negotiations possible. They indicate that sharing in a coveted payoff, bringing in new values to make a larger pie, and redefining the problem to bring out all parties' interests in a solution are approaches that negotiators need to take to find jointly acceptable solutions. Present-day understanding of process is in terms of stages gained in realism by overcoming the two limiting assumptions at the cost of quantitative theoretical elegance.

BEHAVIOR

Behavioral analysis uses the negotiator as the analytical variable, and in so doing faces serious conceptual challenges that it has not yet fully worked out. The approach is doubtless the oldest and most persistent, for it prevails today at the hands of many diplomats who feel that they alone know how to negotiate, in nontransmissible ways. However, at that level, it becomes totally idiosyncratic. To serve as a basis for analysis, the approach must group individuals into meaningful behavioral categories.

The basic dichotomy of the previous century between Shopkeepers and Warriors (Nicolson 1939) has been repeated in many forms, notably as Softliners and Hardliners (Snyder & Diesing 1975) and Doves and Hawks. While intuitively attractive, it is far too manichean a division, to the point where even the Hawks–Doves added Owls to complete their world. The most recent and more complex attempt divides personalities into five categories—competitor, avoider, accommodator, collaborator/problem-solver, and compromiser (or shark, turtle, teddy bear, owl, and fox, in another formulation) (Thomas & Killman 1974), which have in turn been correlated as appropriate strategies (and hence not personalities at all) for situations of transaction, tacit cooperation, relationships, and balanced concerns, with the compromiser/fox a jack-of-all-conflicts (Shell 1999).[3]

Personalities are often key to the resolution or nonresolution of conflict by negotiation, but their categorization still remains elusive. One can analyze the crucial role of Nelson Mandela and Frederik de Klerk in making a resolution of the South Africa conflict (Sisk 1995; Zartman 1995), and of Menachem Begin, Anwar Sadat, and Jimmy Carter in Camp David I and Ehud Barak, Yasir Arafat, and Bill Clinton at Camp David II, but putting these distinct personalities into meaningful typologies has not yet been accomplished.

Collective personality, in the form of culture, constitutes another focus of negotiation research for conflict resolution, as discussed in the chapter by Faure in this work. A surge of studies on national negotiating styles has produced a better understanding of how nations negotiate (Janosik 1987; Graham & Sano 1989; McDonald 1996; Lebedeva & Kremenyuk 1997; Schecter 1998; Snyder 1999; Solomon 1999; Diamant 2000; Blaker et al. 2002; Smyser 2003; Wittes 2005), but at the risk of stereotyping, thus reducing the creativity that is the key to successful negotiation. More work is needed to find the appropriate collectivity to which the term "culture" can be applied and to identify negotiating traits that are crosscultural compared to those that are intrinsic (and to explain their presence by some other variable than a tautological use of "culture"). Thus, culture is a delicate variable on which to hang an analysis of process and outcomes, yet undeniably it matters. Analysts

are still looking for the best way to handle it (Cohen 1997; Faure & Rubin 1997; Avruch 1998.) One way is to look at crosscutting variables of the same sort that run across national boundaries. Work on professional culture has only begun, showing that such commonalities do matter too, although not definitively (Sjöstedt 2003). The "which when why?" question still poses its challenge.

CONFLICT TYPES

The study of negotiation has made enormous strides since it became a field of research less than a half century ago (Schelling 1960; Ikle 1964; Walton & McKersie 1965). In this, it has kept up with the need for negotiated conflict resolution, as intrastate conflicts persist (after a rise and then a drop in the 1990s, after the Cold War restraints and supports were withdrawn) even though interstate conflicts have declined (Wallensteen 2007).

Negotiation can count many successes in Conflict Resolution to its credit in the same period, more or less resolving intrastate conflicts (in addition to decolonization conflicts) in Mozambique (1992), Aceh (2005), Sudan (2005), Senegal (2006), Liberia (1997 and 2003), Sierra Leone (1999), Bosnia (1994), Kosovo (1999), Congo (1999), Bougainville (2001), among others. It also provided either agreeing or resolving formulas to end interstate conflicts through the Middle East Peace Process in the Israeli–Syrian Disengagements (1977), Israeli–Egyptian Treaty (1979), the Oslo Agreements (1993), and the Israeli–Jordanian Treaty (1995); the Geneva Agreements on Afghanistan (1988), the Ethiopian–Eritrean Agreements (1991 and 2000); the Brazzaville Agreement on

Table 16.2 Outcome and type of conflict, 1946–2005

	Victory	Peace Accord	Ceasefire	Other	Total Ended	Ongoing
Extrastate	4	8	0	9	21	0
Interstate	13	9	19	21	62	0
Intrastate	103	40	28	118	289	31
All Conflicts	120	57	47	148	372	31

Source: Kreutz 2006; see also Pfetsch & Rohloff 2000

Table 16.3 Outcome and regions, 1946–2005

	Victory	Peace Accord	Ceasefire	Other	Total Ended	Ongoing
Europe	10	7	9	12	38	2
Middle East	18	4	8	22	52	5
Asia	25	16	17	64	122	15
Africa	38	23	12	44	117	7
America	29	7	1	6	43	2
All Regions	120	57	47	148	372	31

Source: Kreutz 2006

Namibia (1988); the Peru–Ecuador Border Agreement (1999); the Tashkent (1966) and Simla (1972) Agreements on Kashmir, not to speak of the agreements in the construction of Europe, among others.

And it has led to the establishment of a growing web of international regimes, beginning with the security regime in the UN itself (1945), and going on to the Convention on the Law of the Sea (UNCLOS) (1982), the General Agreement on Trade and Tariffs (GATT) (1947) and then the World Trade Organization (WTO) (1995), the Ozone Treaty (1994) and Framework Convention on Climate Change (1995), the Convention/Organization on Security and Cooperation in Europe (C/OSCE) (1975/1992), and a myriad of other regimes. Each of these types has its dynamics and analyses.

There has been less analysis of interstate conflict negotiations, because there have been fewer interstate wars in the postwar and especially post-Cold War period. Parties to interstate conflicts enjoy formal equality as states, and usually in the post-World War II era their existence is not in question in the conflict; they will continue to exist when the war is over and the conflict is only one of their concerns. That said, their levels of power and commitment may vary greatly, leading to a greater or lesser degree of asymmetry. Much of the work that has been done on negotiating interstate conflicts focuses on territoriality, as discussed in the chapter by Vasquez, and on asymmetry, which is also an angle used by research on war itself. Studies of war asked why weak states attack, attributing the decision to imperfect information (Paul 1994); studies

of negotiation ask how weak states can win something, and often a lot, attributing the result to strategies of borrowing power and of phasing, as already discussed (Zartman & Rubin 2003). Negotiations to end interstate wars, whether mediated or direct, generally tend to be conflict-driven and depend on the elements of ripeness to be perceived before they can begin; thereafter they tend to stop at agreeing formulas, sometimes surprisingly long-lasting, rather then being able to reach into the basic issues to come up with a resolving formula for agreement.

Intrastate conflict negotiations are characteristically asymmetrical, both informally in regard to power and formally in regard to status. In the first, the rebellion opposes its commitment to state power and its fixation on the conflict—an existential struggle to—the state's many other problems; in the second, it seeks recognition as spokesman for its cause, denying the state legitimacy as national authority, and status as an equal. Recognition is necessary for negotiation; negotiation confers recognition. This situation constitutes the major obstacle to substantive negotiating, and once it is overcome, the parties can begin discussing the range of issues lying between integration and independence or takeover. A whole range of intermediate solutions— various forms of autonomy, executive, and legislative power-sharing, elections—is available for the negotiating, but the biggest obstacle is generally the absence of trust. The longer negotiations drag on, the greater the number of additional issues, including wounds and hatreds, that encumber the agenda: the longer it lasts, the harder it is to end, and so the still longer it lasts.

Intrastate conflicts frequently involve identity issues that are highly impervious to negotiation. Such issues require constructive formulas, since concession and compensation are ill suited to deal with the problem.

In interstate cooperation, the path to prevention through the establishment of standards and institutions is entirely a matter of negotiation, as is the matter of maintaining and adjusting such regimes (Hasenclever et al. 1997; Chesterman, Ignatief & Thakur 2005). As in conflict negotiations, parties are formally equal but have different weights in power and, in addition, different roles in the negotiation. As a result, the challenge is one of managing complexity, involving largely the creation of coalitions of parties and of issues (Dupont 1994; Hampson 1995; Sebenius 1996). Negotiations to create regimes are problem-solving negotiations, designed to economize on transaction costs by setting up standard procedures for handling recurrent problems.

NEW CHALLENGES

As scholarship has come face to face with the growing number of cases in reality, and as it has focused increasing attention on the negotiation process itself, it has spread out in new directions. Indeed, what is termed negotiation is in fact (or in concept) three sets of negotiations: negotiations to negotiate, negotiations to end conflict (violent or not), and negotiations to implement the agreement. All of these invite further work. One is the matter of what happens before formal negotiations begin, as in negotiability (Dupont 2006), diagnosis (Zartman and Berman 1982), prenegotiation (Stein 1997), ripening (Haas 1990; Zartman 2008), escalation (Zartman & Faure 2005), entry (Crocker et al. 1999; Maundi et al. 2006), etc. While ripeness theory provides an important key to the decision to negotiate, it is dependent on perception, a condition the parties often cannot achieve alone or together. Much negotiation is usually required by a mediator and within the parties themselves to come to the subject realization of the need and opportunity to negotiate. Conflict itself is the preparation for its own resolution; how can this preparation be accelerated more economically, and the costs of conflict reduced? The important work already done on these topics does not exhaust the subject; to the contrary, it only opens it to further research.

In the analysis of the process itself, the strategic situation demanding coordination, as in CDG or the Battle of the Sexes where there are two Nash equilibria and the challenge becomes the choice or combination between them, as opposed to the PDG challenge of collaboration, poses a major problem for analysis and practice, as Avenhaus discusses in his chapter on game theory. Since many situations do not fall under Homans Maxim or have a Nash Point where compensation and trade-offs are possible, the challenge of concession or construction is mighty.

The other of the processes calling for further study has to do with closure, a topic on which there is essentially nothing. When is enough and when can one side ask for a little more without breaking down the process? The question is crucial to the judgment of whether the parties did the most they could or whether they left unclaimed gains on the table. Do the negotiations in question end on an agreeing formula or a resolving formula, and how can the one lead to the other?

The third direction concerns what happens after successful negotiations, as in implementation, postagreement negotiations (Spector & Zartman 2003), reconstruction, durability (Licklider 1995; Walter 2002; Fortna 2004a, 2004b), fully discussed in the chapter by Gartner and Mellin in this volume. More than the previous subject area, these topics are open-ended and so hard to subject to bounded inquiry. In fact, one of the problems plaguing durability studies is, How long does an agreement have to have lasted (meaning?) to be judged durable? A challenging implication of postagreement negotiations is, How constraining is a regime if renegotiation is a normal part of its nature?

Indeed, some have indicated that negotiation should not be regarded as a process with an end but rather as the beginning of a process of continuing cooperation (Thuderoz 2003). This may be a cultural question: Americans like their negotiations to end with a solid agreement and go home, whereas other cultures (not necessarily Asian) and particularly students of social negotiations see negotiation as merely opening a door. In any case, the viewpoint would be a useful addition to conflict resolution approaches, where parties not only conduct forward-looking negotiations to take care of future possible conflict but where they also seek to build mechanisms for transforming relationships (Zartman & Kremenyuk 2005).

Probably the most challenging issue of the time concerns the profound change in negotiation brought on by a changing nature of the parties. Negotiation with armed bands, terrorists, antiglobalist movements, among others, are not the neat two-party negotiations that current analysis so often assumes. Not only does it involve internal politics (as do all negotiations) but the other party frequently does not exist as a corporate body. There is no leader who can make a decision and hold an agreement, and no delegates who represent the central organization. Furthermore, the "party" frequently does not know what it wants: its actions call for attention, express protest, look to millennial outcomes, and expect conversion and surrender from the other side (or eternal war), as in Uganda and Sri Lanka in current conflicts. Finally, these "parties" usually do not know how to negotiate and often have to be taken aside and given training, as in Darfur, Mozambique, and Sri Lanka in recent conflicts. Negotiating with or between amorphous parties needs entirely different models to capture its process, in concept and in reality.

There is still much life left to live in the old practice and its relatively new analysis.

NOTES

1 Other elements can be structured too, of course, such as number of parties, locations, array of issues, and even evaluation of outcomes discussed in the following section. Most of these can be included within the general category of power structures, the element to which they all contribute.

2 The term was used by Mary Follett 1942, p. 147, cited in Walton & McKersie 1965, p. 128.

3 For a similar categorization of strategies, see Pruitt & Kim 2004.

REFERENCES

Albin, Cecilia 2001. *Justice and Fairness in International Negotiation.* Cambridge

—— 2003. "Negotiating International Cooperation: Global Goods and Fairness." *Review of International Studies,* XXIX 3: 368–385.

Aron, Raymond 1957. "Conflict and War from the Viewpoint of Historical Sociology," in International Sociological Association, ed., *The Nature of Conflict.* UNESCO.

Avenhaus, Rudolf & Zartman, I William, eds. 2007. *Diplomatic Games: The Use of Formal Models in, of, and for Negotiation.* Springer.

Avruch, Kevin 1998. *Culture and Conflict Resolution.* USIP.

Axelrod, Robert 1984. *The Evolution of Cooperation.* Basic Books.

Baç, Mehmet 2000. "A Note on Efficient Signaling of Bargaining Power," *International Journal of Game Theory* XXIX 1: 119–126.

—— 2001. "On Creating and Claiming Value in Negotiations," *Group Decision and Negotiation* X 2: 237–251.

Barry, Brian 1986. *Theories of Justice.* University of California Press.

Bartos, Ottomar 1978. "A Simple Model of Negotiation," in Zartman, ed., 1978.

Bendahmane, Diane & McDonald, John, eds., *Perspectives in Negotiation.* US Government Printing Office.

Bernard, Jessie 1957. "The Sociological Study of Conflict," in International Sociological Association, ed., *The Nature of Conflict.* UNESCO.

Blaker, Michael, Giarra, Paul, & Vogel, Ezra 2002. *Case Studies in Japanese Negotiating Behavior.* USIP.

Bottom, William, Holloway, James, McClury, Scott & Miller, Gary 2000. "Negotiating a Coalition," *Journal of Conflict Resolution* XXXXIV 2: 147–169.

Brams, Steven J. 1990. *Negotiation Games: Applying Game Theory to Bargaining and Arbitration.* Routledge.

—— & Taylor, Alan D. 1996. *Fair Division.* Cambridge University Press.

Carnevale, Peter & deDreu, Carsten, eds. 2006. *Methods of Negotiation Research.* Nijhoff (also appeared as *International Negotiation* IX 3 (2004) and X 1 (2005)).

Chasek, Pamela 1997. "A Comparative Analysis of Multilateral Environmental Negotiations," *Group Decision and Negotiation* VI 4: 437–61.

Chesterman, S., Ignatief, M. & Thakur, R., eds., 2005. *Making States Work: State Failure and the Crisis of Governance.* UNU Press.

Cogan, Charles 2003. *French Negotiating Behavior.* USIP.

Cohen, Raymond 1997. *Negotiating Across Cultures.* USIP.

Coser, Lewis 1956. *The Functions of Social Conflict.* Free Press.

Crocker, Chester A. 1992. *High Noon in South Africa.* Norton.

Cross, John G. 1969. *The Economics of Bargaining.* Basic.

Crump, Larry & Zartman, I. William, eds., 2003. *Multilateral Negotiation and Complexity,* a special issue of *International Negotiation* VIII 1.

Curran, Daniel & Sebenius, James, 2003. "The Mediator as a Coalition Builder," *International Negotiation* VIII 1: 111–147.

——, ——& Watkins, Michael, 2004. "Two Paths to Peace: Contrasting George Mitchell in Northern Ireland and Richard Holbrooke in Bosnia-Herzegovina," *Negotiation Journal* XX 4: 513–538.

daConceição-Heldt, Eugenia 2006. "Integrative and Distributive Bargaining Situations in the European Union," *Negotiation Journal* XXII 2: 145–166.

Dahl, Robert 1951.

DeSoto, Alvaro 1992. "Ending Violent Conflict in El Salvador," in Chester A. Crocker, Fen Osler Hampson and Pamela Aall, eds., *Herding Cats: Multiparty Mediation in a Complex World.* USIP.

Diamant. Niel 2000. "Conflict and Conflict Resolution in China," and Wall, James, Blum, Michael & Jin, Dengjian, "Response," *Journal of Conflict Resolution* XXXXIV 4: 523–551.

Druckman, Daniel 1978. "Boundary Role Conflict," in I. William Zartman, ed., .

—— 1986. "Stages, Turning Points and Crises," in *Journal of Conflict Resolution* XXX 2: 327–360.

—— 2001. "Turning Points in International Negotiation: A Comparative Analysis," *Journal of Conflict Resolution* XXXV 4: 519–544.

Edgeworth, Francis 1881. *Mathematical Physics.* Kegan Paul.

Elgström, Ole and Christer Jönsson, eds., 2005. *European Union Negotiations: Processes, Networks and Institutions.* Routledge.

Elster, John 1992. *Local Justice.* Russel Sage.

Enderlin, Charles 2002. *Le rêve brisé.* Fayard.

Evans, Peter, Jacobson, Harold & Putnam, Robert, eds., 1993. *Double-Edged Diplomacy: International Bargaining and Domestic Politics.* University of California.

Farnham, Barbara, ed., 1992. *Avoiding Losses/Taking Risks: Prospect Theory and International Conflict.* University of Michigan.

Fearon, James 1995. "Rationalist Explanations of War," *International Organization* IL 3: 379–414.

Fisher, Roger & Ury, William 1985. *Getting to Yes.*

Follett, Mary 1942. *Dynamic Administration.* Harper & Row.

Fortna, Page 2004a. "International Intervention and the Duration of Peace after Civil War," *International Studies Quarterly* IIL 2: 269–292.

—— 2004b. *Peace Time: Cease-Fire Agreements and the Durability of Peace.* Princeton.

Gauthier, David 1986. *Morals by Agreement.* Oxford.

Graham, John & Sano, Yoshihiro 1989. *Smart Bargaining.* Sano Publishing.

Gregg, J. Michael 2001. "Moment of Opportunity: Recognizing Conditions of Ripeness in International Mediation between Enduring Rivals," *Journal of Conflict Resolution* VL 6: 691–718.

Hammerstein, P. & Parker, G. A. 1982. "The asymmetric war of attrition," *Journal of Theoretical Biology* IVC 4: 647–682.

Hampson, Fen Osler 1994. *Multilateral Negotiations.* The Johns Hopkins University.

Hasenclever, Abdreas, Mayer, Peter & Rittberger, Volker 1997. *Theories of International Regimes.* Cambridge.

Holbrooke, Richard 1996. *To End a War.*

Holl Lute, Jane, ed. 1997. *Preventing Deadly Conflict.* Carnegie Corporation.

Hopmann, P. Terrence 1996. *The Negotiation Process and the Resolution of International Conflicts.* University of South Carolina.

—— 2001. "Bargaining and Problem-Solving," in Chester A. Crocker, Fen O. Hampson & Pamela Aall, eds., *Turbulent Peace: The Challenges of Managing International Conflict.* USIP.

Hornstein, H. A. 1965. "Effects of different magnitude of threat upon interpersonal bargaining," *Journal of Experimental Psychology* I 3: 282–293.

Human Security Centre. 2005. *Human Security Report 2005.* New York: Oxford.

Ikle, Fred Charles. 1964. *How Nations Negotiate.* Harper & Row.

Janosik, Robert 1987. "Rethinking the Culture-Negotiation Link," *Negotiation Journal* III 3: 385–396.

Jones, Bruce D. 2001. *Peacemaking in Rwanda: The Dynamics of Failure.* Lynne Riener.

Jönsson, Christer 1981. "Bargaining Power: Notes on an Elusive Concept," *Cooperation and Conflict* XVI 2: 249–257.

——— 2000. "Bargaining, Negotiation and Diplomacy," in Walter Carlsnaes, Thomas Risse & Beth Simmons, eds., *Handbook of International Relations*. Sage.

Kahneman, Daniel & Tversky, Amos 1979. "Prospect Theory: An Analysis of Decision under Risk," *Econometrica* IIIL 2: 263–292.

Kanet, Roger & Kolodziej, Edward, eds., 1991. *Cold War as Cooperation*. Macmillan.

Kingsbury, Damien 2006. *Peace in Aceh*. Equinox.

Kremenyuk, Victor, ed., 2003. *International Negotiation*. Jossey-Bass, 2nd ed.

Kreutz, Joakim 2006. "How Wars End," Uppsala Conflict Data Program, www.pcr.uu.se/publications/UCDP_pub_Kreutz_how_conflicts_end061013.pdf

Leader, Joyce 2001. *Rwanda's Struggle for Democracy and Peace*. Fund for Peace.

Lebedeva, Marina & Kremenyuk, Victor 1997. "Negotiations in the former Soviet Union," *International Negotiation* I 3: 351–364, 409–421.

Licklider, Roy 1995. "The Consequences of Negotiated Settlement in Civil Wars 1945–1993," *American Political Science Review* XIC 3: 681–690.

MacDermott, Rose 2007. "Prospect Theory and Negotiation Risks," in Rudolf Avenhaus and Gunnar Sjösted, eds., *Negotiating Risks*. Springer.

McDonald, John, ed. 1996. *Defining a US Negotiating Style*. Special issue of *International Negotiation* I 2.

Meerts, Paul & Cede, Franz 2003. *Negotiating European Union*. Palgrave.

Mitchell, Christopher 1995. "The Right Moment," *Paradigms: The Kent Journal of International Relations* IX 2: 35–52.

Mooradian & Druckman, Daniel 2003. "Hurting Stalemate or Mediation? The Conflict over Nagorno-Karabakh," *Journal of Peace Research* XXXVI 6: 709–727.

Narlikar, Amrita 2003. *International Trade and Developing Countries: Coalitions in the GATT and WTO*. Routledge.

——— & Odell, John 2006. "Negotiating International Institutions," Paper presented to the International Studies Association, San Diego.

Nash, John 1950. "The Bargaining Problem," *Econometrica* XVIII 2: 155–162.

——— 1953. "Two-Person Cooperative Game," *Econometrica* XXI 2: 128–140.

Nicolson, Harold 1939. *Diplomacy*. Oxford.

Odell, John 2000. *Negotiating the World Economy*. Cornell University Press.

——— ed. 2006. *Negotiating Trade: Developing Countries in the WTO and NAFTA*. Cambridge.

Osgood, Charles 1962. *An Alternative to War or Surrender*. University of Illinois Press.

Ottaway, Marina 1995. "Eritrea and Ethiopia: Negotiations in a Transitional Conflict," in Zartman, ed., *Elusive Peace*.

Paul, T. V. 1994. *Asymmetric Conflicts: War Initiation by Weaker Powers*. Cambridge.

Pfetsch, Frank & Rohloff, Christoph 2000. *National and International Conflicts, 1945–1995: New empirical and theoretical approaches*. Routledge.

Pillar, Paul 1983. *Negotiating Peace*. Princeton.

Powell, Robert 1991. "Absolute and Relative Gains in IR Theory," *American Political Science Review* LXXXV 4: 1303–1320.

——— 2002. "Bargaining Theory and International Conflict," *Annual Review of Political Science* 5: 1–30.

Powelson, John 1972. *Institution of Economic Growth: A Theory of Conflict Management in Developing Countries*. Princeton.

Pruitt, Dean G, ed., 1997. *Lessons Learned from the Middle East Peace Process*. Special issue of *International Negotiation* II 2.

——— and Kim, Sung-Hee 2004. *Social Conflict: Escalation, Stalemate and Settlement*. McGraw-Hill.

——— & Carnevale, Peter 1993. *Negotiation in Social Conflict*. Brooks/Cole.

Putnam, Robert 1988. "Diplomacy and Domestic Politics: The Logic of Two-Level Games," *International Organization* XXII 3: 428–460.

Raiffa, Howard with Richardson, John & Metcalfe, David 2003. *Negotiation Analysis: The Science and A of Collaborative Decision-Making*. Harvard.

Rawls, John. 1971. *A Theory of Justice*. Harvard.

Rothchild, Donald 1997. *Managing Ethnic Conflict in Africa*. Brookings.

Rubenstein, A. 1982. "Perfect Equilibrium in a Bargaining Model," *Econometrica* L 1: 97–110.

Schecter, Jerrold 1998. *Russian Negotiating Behavior*. USIP.

Sebenius, James 1996. *Negotiating the Law of the Sea*. Harvard.

Shell, G. Richard 1999. *Bargaining for Advantage*. Penguin.

Shubik, Martin, ed. 1964. *Game Theory and Related Approaches to Social Behavior*. Wiley.

Smoke, Richard 1977. *War: Controlling Escalation*. Harvard.

Smyser, W. R. 2003. *How Germans Negotiate*. USIP.

Snyder, Scott 1999. *Negotiating on the Edge: North Korean Negotiating Behavior*. USIP.

Snyder, Richard and Diesing, Paul 1975. *Conflict among Nations*. Princeton.

Solomon, Richard 1999. *Chinese Negotiating Behavior*. USIP.

Spector, Bertram I. & Zartman, I. William, eds., 2003. *Getting It Done: Post-Agreement Negotiations and International Regimes.* USIP.

Stein, Arthur 1983

—— 1990. *Why National Cooperate* . Cornell University Press.

Stein, Janice, ed. 1995. *Getting to the Table.* The Johns Hopkins University Press.

—— & Pauly, Louis, eds. 1993. *Choosing to Cooperate: How States Avoid Loss.* The Johns Hopkins University Press.

Taylor, Michael 1987. *The Possibility of Cooperation.* Cambridge.

Telhami, Shibley, ed. 2002. *Establishing a Data Set on Intrastate and International Negotiation and Mediation,* special issue of *International Negotiation* VII 1.

Thomas, Kenneth & Killman, Ralph 1974. "Developing a Forced-Choice Measure of Conflict-Handling Behavior," *Educational and Psychological Measurement* XXXVII: 309–325.

Tracy, Brian 1978. "The Spanish Base Negotiations," in Zartman, ed.,

Tversky, Amos & Kahneman, Daniel. 1986. "Rational Choice and the Framing of Decisions," *Journal of Business* IL 4, pt 2: S251–278.

Vitz, P. C. and Kite, W. R. 1970. "Factors affecting conflict and negotiation within an alliance," *Journal of Experimental Social Psychology* V 3: 233–247.

Wagner, Lynn 2007. *Problem-Solving and Convergent Bargaining: An Analysis of Negotiation Processes and their Outcomes.* Nijhoff.

Wagner, R. Harrison 1999. "Bargaining and Conflict Resolution," paper presented to the International Studies Association in Washington.

Wall, James A., Stark, John B., & Standlifer, Rhetta 2001. "Mediation: A Current Review of Theory Development," *Journal of Conflict Resolution* VL 2: 370–390.

Wallensteen, Peter 2007. *Understanding Conflict Resolution.* Sage.

Walter, Barbara 2002. *Committing to Peace.* Princeton University Press.

Walton, Richard and McKersie, Robert 1965. *A Behavioral Theory of Labor Negotiations.* McGraw-Hill.

Werner, Suzanne 1999. "The Precarious Nature of Peace," *American Journal of Political Science* XXXXIII 3: 912–934.

Young, Oran 1968. *The Politics of Force.* Princeton.

Zartman, I. William 1988. "Common Elements in the Analysis of the Negotiation Process," *Negotiation Journal* IV 1: 31–44 (January).

—— 1989. *Ripe for Resolution.* Oxford.

—— 2000. "Ripeness: The Hurting Stalemate and Beyond," in Paul Stern and Daniel Druckman, eds., *International Conflict Resolution after the Cold War.* National Academy Press.

—— 2005. *Cowardly Lions: Missed Opportunities to Prevent Deadly Conflict and State Collapse.* Lynne Rienner.

—— 2006. "Multilateral Negotiations," in *Encyclopedia on Life Support Systems (EOLSS).* UNESCO.

—— 2008. *Handbook for Mediators: Ripening.* USIP/SAIS.

——, ed. 1978. *The Negotiation Process.* Sage, also appearing as a special issue of *Journal of Conflict Resolution* XXI 4 (1977).

——, ed. 1994. *International Multilateral Negotiations.* Jossey-Bass.

——, ed. 1995. *Elusive Peace: Negotiating to End Civil Wars.* Brookings.

——, ed. 2007. *Peacemaking in International* Conflict, 2nd edn. USIP.

—— & Rubin, Jeffrey Z, eds. 2000. *Power and Negotiation.* University of Michigan.

—— & Faure, Guy Olivier, eds. 2005. *Escalation and International Negotiation.* Cambridge.

—— & Touval, Saadia 2007. "Mediation before and after 9/11," in Chester Crocker, Fen Hampson & Pamela Aall, eds., *Unleashing the Dogs of War.* USIP.

—— & ——, eds. 2008. *Cooperation: Gains and Pains of Multilateralism.* In press.

Zeuthen, Frederik 1930. *Problem of Monopoly and Economic Warfare.* Routledge and Kegan Paul.

17

Mediation and Conflict Resolution

Jacob Bercovitch

INTRODUCTION

In all societies, irrespective of their location or level of organization, there is a need to deal with and manage conflicts. Although conflicts have many potential benefits, they can also be destructive and entail high costs for all concerned. Hence, there is a need to manage conflicts to ensure they do not become destructive and costly. Conflicts can, of course, be managed violently, where the parties pursue their differences through violence and coercion, but we are mostly interested in non-violent ways of managing conflicts. The available methods of peaceful settlement of international conflicts are numerous and varied. They are listed in Article 33 of the United Nations (UN) Charter, which requests the "parties to any dispute, the continuance of which is likely to endanger the maintenance of international peace and security, shall, first of all, seek a solution by negotiation, inquiry, mediation, conciliation, arbitration, judicial settlement, resort to regional agencies or arrangements, or other peaceful means of their choice."

The UN Charter recognizes in essence the existence of three basic methods for the peaceful management of international conflicts. These are: (a) direct negotiation among the conflicting parties; (b) various forms of mediation, good offices, and conciliation; and (c) binding methods of third-party intervention (e.g. arbitration and adjudication). Each of these methods has its own characteristics, strengths, and disadvantages, and each may be suited to different conflicts. Here, I wish to explore mediation, understand its unique features, show how it works, appreciate who can undertake mediation activities and the problems mediators typically encounter, and assess how mediation can contribute to resolving conflicts and preventing their escalation in the new international environment.

Mediation is practiced by numerous and diverse actors, ranging from individuals through states to international and non-governmental organizations. When successful, mediation may "soften up" the parties, promote diplomacy, and be instrumental in achieving a cessation of hostilities, a peace agreement, or a full settlement of a conflict.

Notwithstanding mediation's importance and pervasiveness, research on its characteristics and effects has suffered from compartmentalization, with little interaction between scholars from different fields, let alone scholars employing different methodologies. I hope this chapter will help bridge some of these chasms by drawing on an extensive theoretical literature, and highlighting ideas derived from large-scale, longitudinal studies. I hope to place mediation within a broader context, and to suggest "best practices" in mediation. I will do so by examining mediation in terms of three broad issues; firstly, a discussion of definitions, features and characteristics of mediation, then a discussion of mediation performance and factors that affect it, and finally, a discussion of how to evaluate mediation outcomes. These are the three most researched areas in the field of mediation, and I propose to summarize them below.

MEDIATION: DEFINITIONS AND APPROACHES

Definitions

For many years, the study of mediation has suffered from conceptual imprecision and a startling lack of information. Practitioners of mediation, formal or informal, in the domestic or international arena were keen to sustain its image as a mysterious practice, akin to some art form, taking place behind closed doors; scholars of mediation, on the other hand, did not think their field of study was susceptible to a systematic analysis. In short, neither group believed that it could discern any pattern of behavior in mediation's various forms, or that any generalizations could be made about the practice in general.

The prevalent agnosticism toward analysis and the desire to maintain the intuitive mystique of mediation are best exemplified in the observations of two noted American practitioners. Arthur Meyer, commenting on the role of mediators, notes that "the task of the mediator is not an easy one. The sea that he sails is only roughly charted, and its changing contours are not clearly discernible. He has no science of navigation, no fund inherited from the experience of others. He is a solitary artist recognizing at most a few guiding stars, and depending on his personal powers of divination" (Meyer 1960, 160). William Simkin, an equally respected practitioner of mediation, comments in a slightly less prosaic but no less emphatic fashion that "the variables are so many that it would be an exercise in futility to describe typical mediator behavior with respect to sequence, timing or the use or non-use of the various functions theoretically available" (Simkin 1971, 118).

Etymologically, mediation comes from the Latin root to halve, but different definitions of mediation purport to (a) capture the gist of what mediators do or hope to achieve; (b) distinguish between mediation and related processes of third-party intervention (i.e. arbitration); and (c) describe mediators' attributes. It is worth looking at a few definitions of mediation and assessing their implications.

Focusing on what mediators hope to achieve and how they may go about achieving it, Oran Young offers a definition of mediation as "any action taken by an actor that is not a direct party to the crisis, that is designed to reduce or remove one or more of the problems of the bargaining relationship, and therefore to facilitate the termination of the crisis itself" (Young 1967, 34). In much the same vein, Chris Mitchell defines mediation as any "intermediary activity . . . undertaken by a third party with the primary intention of achieving some compromise settlement of the issues at stake between the parties, or at least ending disruptive conflict behavior" (Mitchell 1981, 287). And in a somewhat more detailed fashion, Blake and Mouton define mediation as a process involving "the intervention of a third party who first investigates and defines the problem and then usually approaches each group separately with recommendations designed to provide a mutually acceptable solution" (Blake and Mouton 1985, 15).

Other definitions are less outcome-oriented and focus on the act of the intervention itself.

Ann Douglas defines mediation as "a form of peacemaking in which an outsider to a dispute intervenes on his own or accepts the invitation of disputing parties to assist them in reaching agreement" (Douglas 1957, 70). Moore defines it as "an extension and elaboration of the negotiation process. Mediation involves the intervention of an acceptable, impartial, and neutral third party who has no authoritative decision-making power to assist contending parties in voluntarily reaching their own mutually acceptable settlement" (Moore 1986, 6). And Linda Singer defines it as a "form of third-party assistance [that] involves an outsider to the dispute who lacks the power to make decisions for the parties" (Singer 1990, 20).

Still other definitions focus on neutrality and impartiality as the distinguishing features of mediation. Bingham defines mediation as the "assistance of a 'neutral' third party to a negotiation" (Bingham 1985, 5). Folberg and Taylor see mediation "as the process by which the participants, together with the assistance of a neutral person or persons, systematically isolate disputed issues in order to develop options, consider alternatives, and reach a consensual settlement that will accommodate their needs" (Folberg and Taylor 1984, 7). Moore draws attention to the process of mediation and the neutrality of a mediator in the following definition: "the intervention into a dispute or negotiation by an acceptable, impartial and neutral third party who has no authoritative decision-making power to assist disputing parties in voluntarily reaching their own mutually acceptable settlement of issues in dispute" (Moore 1986, 14). Finally, Spencer and Yang see mediation as "the assistance of a third party not involved in the dispute, who may be of a unique status that gives him or her certain authority with the disputants; or perhaps an outsider who may be regarded by them as a suitably neutral go-between" (Spencer and Yang 1993, 195).

These definitions (and they are but a sample) exemplify the enormous scope of mediation. Mediation may take place in conflicts between states, within states, between groups of states, organizations,

and between individuals. Mediators enter a conflict to help those involved achieve a better outcome than they would be able to achieve by themselves. Once involved in a conflict, mediators may use a wide variety of behaviors to achieve this objective. Some mediators make suggestions for a settlement, others refrain from doing so. Some mediators are interested in achieving a compromise, others are not. We should also note that some mediators may be neutral, others are decidedly not. Former Secretary of State Henry Kissinger in the Middle East, Presidents Carter and Clinton at Camp David, former British and Russian Foreign Secretaries Robin Cook and Yevgeny Primakov or Ambassador Holbrooke all mediating in Kosovo, Colin Powell and Condoleezza Rice shuttling to and fro in the Middle East, or the Chinese in North Korea, as well as many other mediators, may or may not have been neutral in mediating their different conflicts, but that was hardly the most notable feature of their performance.

Some may consider this quibbling over definitions or aspects of neutrality to be a futile exercise in semantic sophistry. It is most emphatically not so. The myriad of possible mediators and the range of mediation roles and strategies are so wide as to defeat many attempts to understand, as we seek to do here, the "essence" of mediation. In the absence of a generally accepted definition, there is a tendency to identify mediation with one particular role (e.g. a go-between) or a single strategy (e.g. offering proposals). This does not help us to understand the reality of international mediation. Assigning an exclusive role or strategy to one kind of mediation overlooks the dynamics of the process. It is also detrimental to the search for common and divergent dimensions of mediation in international and other social contexts, and the effort to draw general lessons from mediation experience.

The reality of international mediation is that of a complex and dynamic interaction between mediators who have resources and an interest in the conflict or its outcome, and the protagonists or their representatives. The most helpful approach to mediation links it to a related approach to conflict, that of negotiation, but at the same time emphasizes its unique features and conditions. The parameters of such an approach were established by Carl Stevens and Thomas Schelling. Stevens (1963, 123) states that "mediation, like other social phenomena, is susceptible to systematic analysis. The key to analysis is in recognizing that where mediation is employed it is an integral part of the bargaining process.... [A]n analysis of mediation is not possible except in the context of general analysis of bargaining negotiations." In a similar vein, Schelling (1960, 22) notes that a mediator "is probably best viewed as an element in the communication arrangements, or as a third party with a payoff structure of his own."

In any given conflict, mediators may change, their role may be redefined, issues may alter, indeed even the parties involved in the conflict may and often do change. A comprehensive definition seems to be a primary requisite for understanding this complex reality. The following broad definition provides suitable criteria for inclusion (and exclusion) and serves as a basis for identifying differences and similarities. Mediation is here defined as a process of conflict management, related to but distinct from the parties' own negotiations, where those in conflict seek the assistance of, or accept an offer of help from, an outsider (whether an individual, an organization, a group, or a state) to change their perceptions or behavior, and to do so without resorting to physical force or invoking the authority of law.

This may be a broad definition, but it is one that can be generally and widely applied. It forces us to recognize, as surely we must, that any mediation situation comprises (a) parties in conflict, (b) a mediator, (c) a process of mediation, and (d) the context of mediation. All these elements are important in mediation. Together they determine its nature, quality, and effectiveness, as well as why some mediation efforts succeed while others fail.

Mediation is, at least structurally, the continuation of negotiations by other means.

Mediation differs from other accommodative strategies such as negotiation (which is dyadic rather than triadic in structure) and arbitration (which has a strong binding character). What mediators do, can do, or are permitted to do in their efforts to resolve a conflict may depend, to some extent, on who they are and what resources and competencies they can bring to bear. Ultimately, though, their efforts depend on who the parties are, the context of the conflict, what is at stake, and the nature of their interaction. "Mediation," as Stulberg so rightly notes, "is a procedure predicated upon the process of negotiation" (Stulberg 1981, 87). Mediation is, above all, adaptive and responsive. It extends the process of negotiation to reflect different parties, different possibilities, and a different situation. To assume otherwise is to mistake wishful thinking for reality.

Characteristics of mediation

What, then, are the main features or characteristics of mediation across levels? A number of these may be listed below:

- Mediation is an extension and continuation of peaceful conflict management.
- Mediation involves the intervention of an outsider—an individual, a group, or an organization, with values, resources, and interests of their own—into a conflict between two or more states or other actors.
- Mediation is a non-coercive, non-violent and, ultimately, non-binding form of intervention.
- Mediators enter a conflict, whether internal or international, in order to affect it, change it, resolve it, modify it, or influence it in some way.
- Mediators bring with them, consciously or otherwise, ideas, knowledge, resources, and interests of their own or of the group or organization they represent. Mediators often have their own assumptions and agendas about the conflict in question.
- Mediation is a voluntary form of conflict management. The actors involved retain control over the outcome (if not always over the process) of their conflict, as well as the freedom to accept or reject mediation or mediators' proposals.
- Mediation usually operates on an *ad hoc* basis only (i.e., a particular mediation effort or series

of efforts are undertaken by one or more actors, and then mediation ceases with or without an agreement).

Approaches in the study of mediation

The literature on international mediation has attracted many scholars and reflects a great diversity in terms of approaches and perspectives (see Kolb and Rubin 1991). All these approaches—and there is a seemingly endless variety of them—range from purely scholarly studies to policy implications to the reflections of mediators themselves, and to studies suggesting that academics should act as third parties in mediation efforts. Different scholars categorize studies of mediation under different categories. For instance, Wall and Lynn (1993) differentiates "general theories," "context-specific theories" and "extended context theories." Sometimes these approaches offer implications for practical involvement, while at other times they focus on descriptions and theory development. The following can be identified as the three main traditions in the study of international mediation:

(1) The first group of studies is essentially pre-scriptive and is devoted to offering advice on what constitutes good conflict management in real-world situations (e.g. Fisher and Ury 1981). These studies, mostly developed by scholars associated with the Program on Negotiation at Harvard University, generate books and manuals on how mediators and negotiators should behave, what constitutes good negotiation or mediation, and how conflicts—serious or otherwise—can be resolved.

(2) Some studies of mediation in a variety of contexts are based on theoretical notions and the participation of academic practitioners in a variety of actual conflicts, with the aim of testing ideas and developing a generic theory for the resolution of social conflicts. These studies use a variety of interaction and problem-solving techniques to combine political action with scientific experimentation and thus contribute to the development of a set of rules that can address all (not just international) conflicts. Some of this research (Burton 1969, 1972, 1984;

Doob 1971; Fisher 1983; Kelman 1992; Walton 1969) has generated valuable insights, but much of it is still in a pioneering phase.

(3) The third set of studies is based on actual descriptions and empirical examinations of mediation cases. These studies seek to develop theories and to offer general guidelines through: (a) the detailed description of a particular case of international mediation (e.g. Ott 1972; Rubin 1981); (b) laboratory and experimental approaches to mediation (e.g. Bartunek et al. 1975; Rubin 1980) to discover how parties and mediators behave in controlled circumstances; and (c) a contingency framework that relies on large-scale systematic studies. This approach draws on numerous cases of international mediation to formulate and test propositions about effective mediation and to assess the conditions under which mediation can be made to work better (e.g. Bercovitch and Rubin 1992; Touval and Zartman 1985). The contingency approach has its roots in the social-psychological theories of negotiation as developed by Sawyer and Guetzkow (1965) and modified by Druckman (1977). This is the approach that I believe can yield the most significant insights and policy advice on mediation.

The contingency approach provides a framework that permits a systematic analysis of the underlying structures and conditions that shape conflict events, and complex relationships of the conflict management process. It takes into consideration the individual influences of personal, role, situational, goal, interactional and outcome variables (Bercovitch 1984, 2000; Fisher and Keashley 1991; Gochman 1993; Keashley and Fisher 1996) as well as their interactive effects within the context, process, and outcome of conflict management (Bercovitch 2000). The contingency approach makes it clear that the choice of a particular form of mediation is rarely random. The choice of mediation is rarely random. It is affected by the characteristics of the dispute, the nature of the social environment and the identity of a mediator, the characteristics of the dispute, and the nature of the social environment amongst others (Assefa 1987). Mediation is a rational, political process, representing a strategic engagement between parties and a mediator, which, under some conditions, may stop violence and hostilities or even facilitate a peace agreement and a transformation of the conflict. What the contingency framework allows us to do is disentangle some conditions from the myriad of factors that may affect conflict management and study these in a systematic manner.

RATIONALE AND MOTIVES OF MEDIATION

An essential question that must be posed at this juncture concerns the motives for mediation. The process is time consuming, involves risks and uncertainty and may, and often does, result in failure. Besides, not every actor can afford or has the credibility and time to mediate. So, why mediate? Why would parties in conflict be prepared to relinquish control over aspects of their conflict management experience, and why, come to that, would a third party be willing to intervene in a serious conflict that has defied many attempts at resolution? There are, I believe, a number of compelling reasons for initiating and undertaking a serious mediation effort.

As an instrument of diplomacy and foreign policy, mediation has become almost as common as conflict itself. It is carried out daily by such disparate actors as private individuals; government officials; religious figures; regional, nongovernmental, and international organizations; ad hoc groupings, or states of all sizes. Each of these mediators brings to the mediation situation its own interests, perceptions, and resources. Each of them may adopt behavior that ranges from the very passive, through the facilitative, to the highly active. The form and character of mediation in a particular international conflict are determined by the context of both the international system and the conflict itself (Bercovitch and Jackson 2001; Kolb 1989a, 1989b; Touval 1985), the issues, the parties involved, and the identity of the mediator. The importance of this reciprocal influence can hardly be overemphasized.

As a form of conflict management, mediation is more appropriate in some conflicts than others. Broadly speaking when (a) a conflict is long, drawn out, or complex; (b) the parties' own conflict-management efforts have reached an impasse; (c) neither party is prepared to countenance further costs or loss of life; and (d) both parties are prepared to cooperate, tacitly or openly, to break their stalemate, mediation may be the preferred choice of conflict management. Even when these conditions prevail, we must wonder why parties in a conflict would accept an outsider or third party, and why an outside third party would become involved in other conflicts, when neither the course of that conflict, nor its outcome, are at all certain.

These are important yet often neglected questions that touch upon the motivation for mediation, and I believe motivation is fast becoming a crucial theme in the mediation literature. It is worth thinking about this issue in terms of mediator's motivations and parties' motivations (on this, see Zartman and Touval 2007).

Mediator motivation

Different mediators have different motives to intervene in a conflict. When the mediator is an unofficial individual (e.g. Adam Curle in the Nigeria–Biafra conflict in 1967–1970, or President Carter in North Korea in 1994), the motives for initiating mediation may include a desire to (a) be instrumental in changing the course of a long-standing or escalating conflict; (b) gain access to major political leaders and open channels of communication; (c) put into practice a set of ideas on conflict management; and (d) spread one's own ideas and thus enhance personal stature and professional status. The presence of one or more of these motives (which may be conscious or subconscious) in an opportune situation provides a very strong rationale for an individual to initiate unofficial mediation (on mediators' motives and dilemmas, see Terris and Maoz 2005).

Where a mediator is an official representative of a government or an organization, as is often the case, another set of motives may prevail. Such persons initiate mediation because (a) they have a clear mandate to intervene in disputes (e.g. the Charters of the Arab League, the African Union, and the Organization of American States each contain an explicit clause mandating that their members seek mediation in regional disputes); (b) they may want to do something about a conflict whose continuance could adversely affect their own political interests; (c) they may be directly requested by one or both parties to mediate; (d) they may wish to preserve intact a structure of which they are a part (e.g. the frequent mediation attempts by the United States in disputes between Greece and Turkey, two valued NATO member-states); or (e) they may see mediation as a way of extending and enhancing their own influence by becoming indispensable to the parties in conflict or by gaining the gratitude (and presumably the political goodwill) of one or both protagonists (e.g. the frequent efforts by the United States to mediate the Arab–Israeli conflict).

Mediators are political actors; they engage in mediation and expend resources because they expect to resolve a conflict and gain something from it (see Greig 2005). For many actors, mediation is a policy instrument through which they can pursue some of their interests without arousing too much opposition (Touval 1992a). The relationship between a mediator and disputants is thus never entirely devoid of political interest. To overlook this aspect is to miss an important element in the dynamics of mediation.

Parties' motivation

Adversaries in conflict have a number of motives for desiring mediation: (a) mediation may actually help them reduce the risks of an escalating conflict and get them closer to a settlement; (b) each party may embrace mediation in the expectation that the mediator will actually nudge or influence the other party; (c) both parties may see mediation as a public expression of their commitment to an international norm of peaceful conflict

management; (d) they may want an outsider to take much of the blame should their efforts fail; or (e) they may desire mediation because a mediator can be used to monitor, verify, and guarantee any eventual agreement. One way or another, parties in conflict— and a mediator—have pretty compelling reasons for accepting, initiating, or desiring mediation.

Whether we are studying ethnic, internal, or international conflict, we should resist the tendency to think of mediation as a totally exogenous input, as a unique role or a distinct humanitarian response to conflict in which a well-meaning actor, motivated only by altruism, is keen to resolve a conflict. A mediator, through the very act of mediating, becomes an actor in a conflictual relationship. This relationship involves interests, costs, and potential rewards and exemplifies certain roles and strategies. A mediator's role, at any one time, is part of this broad interaction. To be effective, mediators' roles must reflect and be congruent with that interaction. This is how mediation should be seen, studied, and considered in international relations.

WHAT DO MEDIATORS DO WHEN THEY MEDIATE?

What is it that mediators do when they intervene in a conflict? Like many questions about mediation, the answer to this one is far from simple or obvious. We must clarify what we mean by mediation behavior, and how best to interpret it. There are various ways in which mediator activities can be identified and accounted for. Much of the early debate about mediation behavior was confused and ambiguous (Burton and Dukes 1990, 26). Traditional research and explanations of mediators' activities were shrouded in terms such as "neutrality," "voluntary," "concessions," and "impartiality," which describe the expectations associated with the practice of mediation, but obscure any understanding of its processes.

Alternatively, mediator activities were organized conceptually to describe mediator behavior in terms of various preordained roles and tactics (Gulliver 1979) or phases (Folberg and Taylor 1984; Mitchell 1981; Moore 1986) that govern mediator intervention behavior. While these may be interesting classifications, they bring us no closer to understanding the underlying dynamics of the mediation process and the reality of the changing nature of a conflict (Bercovitch 1992, 103).

In essence, the practice of mediation revolves around the choice of strategic behaviors that mediators believe will facilitate the type of outcome they seek to achieve in the conflict management process. A mediator may be less reactive and more practical and systematic in his/her behavior than previously thought. That is, mediators may be seen as skilled practitioners of a learned craft. A mediator's behavior is dependent on the perceived role or purpose, and the resources and the techniques available to him/her within the specific dispute context. Mediation behavior can thus be understood as an overall plan or approach to conflict management to achieve a specific end: the settlement of the dispute, the stopping of violence and destruction, or the overall resolution of the conflict.

As such, mediation is not an "art" that is highly idiosyncratic, based on intuitive insights, and resistant to systematic analysis (Meyer 1960); it is rather a coherent and planned activity. Consequently, it is possible to explain and understand a mediator's behavior in terms of the identification and conceptualization of various roles, tactics, processes, and strategies which can be exercised in the practice of mediation.

Mediation strategies

The most useful way of describing and interpreting mediator behavior is to conceptualize their activities in terms of broad strategies. While the analysis of the roles and stages of mediator behavior provide perfectly valid and feasible explanations of single cases, the categorization of mediation behavior into broad strategies is the most practical and useful option when studying a large

number of conflicts. This approach provides a simple yet logical structure within which the extensive inventory of mediator behavior can be organized and understood.

For our purposes, the most useful taxonomy of mediator behavior that can be applied to international mediation analysis is based on the identification of three fundamental mediator strategies along a continuum ranging from low to high intervention. These are: (a) communication-facilitation, (b) procedural, and (c) directive strategies (discussions of these can be found in Bercovitch 1992; Bercovitch and Wells 1993; and Bercovitch et al. 1991). These strategies are based on assumptions derived from Sheppard's (1984) taxonomy of mediator behavior that focuses on the content, process and procedural aspects of conflict management.

(1) *Communication-facilitation strategies* describe mediator behavior at the low end of the intervention spectrum. Here, a mediator typically adopts a fairly passive role, channeling information to the parties, facilitating cooperation but exhibiting little control over the more formal process or substance of mediation. Norway's mediation role in the Oslo agreement between Israel and the PLO of 1993 exemplifies this approach.

(2) *Procedural strategies* enable a mediator to exert a more formal control over the mediation process with respect to the environment of the mediation. Here a mediator may determine structural aspects of the meetings, control constituency influences, media publicity, the distribution of information, and the situation powers of the parties' resources and communication processes. New Zealand's efforts in the Bougainville conflict in 1995, where it brought both parties to a military camp in New Zealand, exemplify this form of mediation.

(3) *Directive strategies* are the most powerful form of intervention. Here, a mediator affects the content and substance of the bargaining process by providing incentives for the parties to negotiate or by issuing ultimatums. Directive strategies deal directly with and aim to change the way issues are framed, and the behavior associated with them. Richard Holbrooke's efforts at Dayton are typical of this approach.

Although mediators have a wide array of tactical choices at their disposal, there is no suggestion here that they may use any of the strategies they wish with its associated tactics in any conflict they intervene. Clearly, there are some conflicts that will show greater amenability to some forms of mediation behavior, and of course there will be mediators who will feel more comfortable with, or have the resources and determination to implement, one strategy rather than another. Analyzing which strategies and which tactics work in which conflicts has been a dominant, if inconclusive, theme of mediation research (for an interesting example of this research, see Beardsley et al. 2005).

Can we, in any way, link strategies to outcomes? Few studies attempt to assess the effectiveness of different strategies. Those that do so have found that the strategies at each end of the intervention spectrum appear to dominate actual mediator intervention in international conflicts (Bercovitch and Houston 1996). Further analyses of mediation revealed that while communication-facilitation strategies are the most frequently utilized by international mediators, directive strategies appear to be the most successful (e.g. Bercovitch and Houston 1996; Gartner and Bercovitch 2006; Wilkenfeld et al. 2003).

The choice of a strategy in any situation is clearly affected, *inter alia*, by the nature of the relationship between the parties, the context of the conflict, and their historical experience. Mediators adapt their style of intervention to meet the requirements of the situation, and we think that certain styles or strategies of mediation will be generally more effective in certain situations. An intense conflict with high fatalities may require more intense interventions than a low-level conflict (see Hiltrop 1985, 1989; Rubin 1980). The costs of no agreement in the former are dangerously high. If a mediator is involved in such a conflict, they will use any stick or carrot at their disposal to nudge the parties toward a zone of agreement. However, given the entrenched and intense nature of the conflict, it is more than likely that the most that can be

achieved is a partial cessation of violence. In a low-intensity conflict, disputants are likely to view those same sticks and carrots as overbearing and too directive in nature – making them less effective, despite the likely lower stakes involved.

Factors affecting the choice of a strategy

A number of factors affect the choice of a mediation strategy and its potential for success. Amongst the most important factors are the following:

(1) *The intensity of a conflict* is recognized as a major factor affecting the nature of conflict management, and any evolving pattern of mediation. But how exactly does the intensity of a conflict influence the implementation of a particular mediation strategy? Conflict intensity usually refers to such factors as the severity of conflict, the level of hostilities, the number of fatalities, the level of anger and intensity of feeling, the types of issues at stake, and the strength of the parties' negative perceptions (Kressel and Pruitt 1989). When conflict intensity is low, Rubin (1980, 389) suggests that the parties are concerned with "mending their own fences" and do not want third-party intrusion. Low-intensity conflicts can usually be dealt with by the parties themselves. If the parties can not do so, a mediator will come in as a catalyst for negotiations. In contrast to that, in high-intensity, dangerous conflicts, a primary task is to prevent further escalation, and to achieve this, mediators may adopt more active forms of intervention. High-intensity conflicts are associated with higher levels of mediation involvement (see Bercovitch and Gartner 2006).

(2) *The type of issues in conflict* may be examined to identify the "essence" of a conflict. Intuitively, we would expect this to be an influential factor in a mediator's choice of strategy, as issues represent the focus of what separates the parties, and what the conflict is all about. But what exactly are issues in conflict, and how can we identify them and conceptualize their presence? Conflicts can, in the first instance, be internal or interstate. When they are internal, they are often focused on issues such as identity, autonomy, and ethnicity. These are

subjective and emotional issues often including fear, resentment, and distrust that are hard to negotiate over, and harder still to mediate. The best that a mediator may do in such contexts is to resort to communication strategies that build the confidence and trust of the parties, and give them an incentive to pursue peaceful conflict management. In contrast, conflicts over issues such as security, resources, and defense, involve more concrete issues that are easier to work with. Here, a mediator may press for concessions on tangible issues to achieve a conflict termination or resolution. Each type of issue in conflict elicits a different form of mediator behavior.

(3) *The internal characteristics of the parties* enable us to examine how each party's political and economic structure affects the process of conflict management and mediation. Parties with similar political systems or social structures (ethnic, cultural, or religious groups organizing society) may be more amenable to serious, active mediation. Parties, on the other hand, with different political, economic, or social systems may be more likely to distrust each other. They may have less in common and perceive the other as a threat to their identity and legitimacy. Actors from different political systems may also possess different norms, protocols, and processes for conflict management. In this case, a mediator may be required to engage in communication strategies, establish channels of communication, educate the parties in the skills of negotiation, and help them clarify the situation.

(4) *The previous relationship and experience of the parties* can be examined to gauge how past experiences of conflict and conflict management affect current behavior and determine choice of mediation strategy. Any social relationship is affected by previous experiences between the same parties. Similarly, any current conflict management is affected by previous conflict management efforts and any learning which may have taken place (on the role of learning in conflict management, see Leng 2000). The past does indeed cast a shadow on the present. Repeated mediation efforts by the same mediator may establish some norms of interaction and to a large extent determine what each party may expect and how it should behave. In an environment of risk and uncertainty, mediators may use information from previous efforts, or build on any rapport they may have had with the parties. Here, I want to suggest that previous conflict experience and mediation may exert a strong influence on the choice of a current strategy. Previous mediation efforts can establish norms and a certain rapport between the parties, and these can affect their current disposition and behavior. There is an element of reinforcement and learning occasioned by previous experience of mediation which influences how mediation is currently conducted. Past conflict management behavior is a pretty good indicator of current and future behavior. Although conflict management is not a linear process, there is certainly an element of learning at work here, and this element affects the choice of a mediation strategy.

(5) *Mediator identity and rank* describe the official position of a mediator. These will clearly affect the choice of a strategy. At the most basic level, some mediators have the potential to utilize resources, use leverage and influence; others can rely only on their legitimacy or reputation. Who the mediator is determines to a large extent what a mediator can do. Mediators' use of a strategy is not random; it is the result of many complex factors. One of these factors relates to the official position and status of different mediators. Some have the full range of resources, and thus the full range of strategies available to them. Others (individual mediators, NGOs) can only use communication strategies as they simply do not have access to expensive resources. Who a mediator is determines what a mediator can do, and which strategies are used.

(6) *The initiation and timing of mediation intervention.* While mediation is ultimately a voluntary process, it may be initiated, that is, suggested, appealed for, or offered, by either the disputants, the mediator, or various other concerned parties. The perceived need or justification for mediation is influenced by the disputants' and mediator understanding of what the role of the mediator should be in managing the conflict. The mandate of the intervener and the legitimacy and authority of mediator behavior are to some extent determined by who initiates the mediation process (Kaufman and Duncan 1992), and the timing of intervention in terms of the conflict phases and the state of the parties' current negotiations.

These factors may determine the acceptability of a specific mediator, and the role, bounds, and expectations within which a mediator may act to manage the conflict, and the type of strategies employed (Kolb 1983; Raiffa 1982). The initiation of mediation, and choice and acceptance of a mediator, are largely dependent on the parties', the mediator's, or other third parties' perceptions of the resources and skills a mediator may have on offer, their expectations of how the outcome of the dispute may be influenced by the intervention of a specific mediator, and the level of commitment and urgency of the parties to achieving a settlement.

(7) *The mediation environment.* An important dimension which may influence mediation behavior and choice of strategies is the mediation environment. The choice of mediation environment may be determined by the demands of the parties, their powers, resources and goals, and their willingness to negotiate, by the extent of constituency and media pressures, or it may be the product of a mediator's strategy to control a particular conflict situation. In turn, the specific environment in which mediation takes place may determine the type of behavior a mediator employs. As such, the mediation environment, with the various opportunities and constraints that it provides, may be a powerful factor in understanding the dynamics of mediation behavior. An ideal mediation environment will support rather than hinder parties' conflict management efforts and interactions, and provide the mediator with opportunities to manage and control the whole process (Touval 1982).

The structure imposed on mediation by the environment provides opportunities for both parties and the mediator to be empowered and manage their conflict competently and productively, and to avoid or mend any dysfunctional behavior that may regress the parties' mediation efforts. The physical context of the mediation event establishes the bounds that dictate, and perhaps constrain, the ability of the parties and the mediator to express their status, authority, power, leverage, and assertiveness within mediation and how their efforts are represented to the external constituencies, media, and international audiences. A mediation environment may also determine the situational powers of the participants, their proximity, and social interactions. Clearly, a party's legitimacy, standing, and integrity are integral characteristics that must be protected and maintained if mediation is to be successful (Rubin and Brown 1975) and are dependent on the nature and urgency of the dispute being managed.

Mediation behavior and choice of strategies cannot be foreordained, nor can these be prescribed in advance. They are part of the overall structure of a mediation event and context. Mediators choose strategies that are available, feasible, permissible, and likely to achieve a desired outcome. Mediation behavior is adaptable; it reflects, to a large extent, the context in which it takes place. I have highlighted some of the important contextual dimensions which may have an impact on mediation behavior and outcomes. We ignore these dimensions at our peril.

THE NOTION OF SUCCESS IN MEDIATION

How do we know that mediation has been successful or not? How can we evaluate its impact? Was the Dayton Agreement a success? And if so, why? Was the Oslo Agreement a success? Are we looking only for a change effected as a result of mediation, or for a specific kind of change? And how do we assess change in the context of social relations? There will be as many answers to these questions as there are commentators. And yet, we have to be able to answer this most fundamental of questions. Too often, it seems success or failure are assumed, postulated, or defined on a case by case basis, and usually in an arbitrary and poorly reasoned manner. Furthermore, the indicators utilized by those attempting to define success or failure are so diverse as to be almost unworkable. We need to engage in a more comprehensive discussion of what is success, what is a failure, and how to recognize them (for a fuller discussion of these, see Bercovitch 2006).

Because international mediation is not a uniform practice, it seems futile to draw up one set of criteria to cover all possible constructs of success. Individual mediators, for instance, may adopt communication-facilitating strategies, and be more concerned with the quality of interaction and the creation of a better environment for conflict management. Mediating states, on the other hand, may seek to achieve more than just a change in interactions; they would like to see a real change in behavior. Different objectives give rise to different meanings of success in mediation. Here, I wish to suggest two broad criteria, subjective and objective, to assess the effects and consequences of mediation in international conflicts.

Subjective criteria

Subjective criteria refer to the parties' or the mediator's perception (and, to some extent, that of other relevant external actors) that the goals of mediation have been achieved, or that a desired change has taken place. Using this perspective, we can suggest that mediation has been successful when the parties feel, or express, satisfaction with the process or outcome of mediation, or when the outcome is seen as fair, efficient, or effective (Susskind and Cruickshank 1987).

Fairness is an intangible abstraction. One cannot define fairness so stringently that it will not still be interpreted differently by different people, much like success itself. However, we do recognize that whatever it may be, fairness suggests to most people an even-handedness of procedure and equitability of outcome, and that is clearly indicative of some conception of "success." Sheppard (1984) presents a number of concrete indicators of fairness that serve to assuage concerns regarding the threat of abstraction. Levels of process neutrality, disputant control, equitability, consistency of results and consistency with accepted norms are all relatively easily observed. Susskind and Cruikshank (1987) meanwhile present similar indicators of fairness (e.g. improvement of procedure and institution of precedent, access to information and opportunity for expression) which provide reasonably concrete conceptions of fairness.

However, while there are certain observable indices of fairness, both Sheppard (1984) and Susskind and Cruikshank (1987) talk about the importance of "perceived fairness" in proceedings. Indicators of fairness mean little to parties in conflict if they themselves do not think the proceedings are fair. This "perception of unfairness," justified or not, is often more crucial than any concrete measures of success. Hence, while such indicators may emphasize balanced procedures, or even equitable solutions, if parties to it don't perceive these as fair, it is unlikely that any resulting outcome will be seen as a "success."

In some respects, participant satisfaction seems like a better indicator of success. If parties in mediation are satisfied with the process or outcome, they are more likely to perceive it as a success and, as Sheppard indicates (1984), more likely to be committed to it. This in turn produces other relevant dimensions of success, such as stability, more likely to be achieved. Shepherd identifies a number of measurable indicators, both as regards process (privacy, level of involvement) and outcome (benefit, commitment).

However, as with fairness, parties' satisfaction is largely a perceptual and very personal quality. Satisfaction is often deemed an almost emotional response to the achievement of a goal or attainment of some requirement. Clearly, the sorts of goals taken into an event by those involved in conflict are personal in nature, and formed by the specific configuration of their personality, environment, values, expectations, etc. This is neither unexpected nor unusual. Satisfaction is both a very personal and very subjective quality, but it does not mean mediators should abandon their quest to achieve outcomes that "satisfy" the parties. Outcomes that are "satisfactory" are more likely to be longer lasting, and least likely to be breached by repeated conflict.

Another possible indication of mediation success is the quality of effectiveness. Effectiveness is a measure of results achieved, or change brought about, of new forms of behavior agreed to. Successful mediation is about achieving some change. For a mediation effort to be deemed successful, it must have some (positive) impact, or *effect* on the conflict. The kind of change I am talking about relates to moving from violent to non-violent behavior, signing of an agreement, accepting a ceasefire or a settlement, agreeing to a UN peacekeeping force, or any such measures. If any of these has occurred as a result of mediation, mediation may be said to have been effective, and thus successful. Effectiveness allows us to observe what has changed after a mediator has entered a conflict. It is to a large extent much less subject to perceptual disagreements and more easily observable and measurable.

The fourth subjective criterion, efficiency, is primarily focused on the procedural and temporal dimension of conflict management. Efficiency addresses such issues as the cost of conflict management, resources devoted to it, timeliness and disruptiveness of the undertaking. In some respects, this may seem extraneous. If a mediation episode is effective in other ways, does efficiency matter? Once again, it must be stressed that conflict and its management does not tend to occur in a vacuum. Costs racked up in order to accrue benefits may be such that those benefits lose their sheen. Susskind and Cruikshank give efficiency the most weight. They suggest that "fairness is not enough. A fair agreement is not acceptable if it takes an inordinately long time to achieve or if it costs several times what it should have" (Susskind and Cruickshank, 1987, p. 27). An agreement may not be all that elegant, but if it is achieved within a reasonably short time without entangling too many people in it, there is much to be said for it.

Fairness of mediation, satisfaction with its performance, or improvement in the overall climate of the parties' relationship cannot be easily demonstrated, but they are undoubtedly consequences of successful mediation. They are subjective because they depend on the perceptions of the parties in conflict. Even if a conflict remains unresolved, mediation— in any guise—can do much to change the way the disputants feel about each other and

lead, however indirectly, to both a long-term improvement in the parties' relationship and a resolution of the conflict. We would all describe these efforts as successful, even if we are not quite certain how to demonstrate the correlates of such success.

Objective criteria

Objective criteria in the study of mediation offer a totally different perspective. Objective criteria rely on substantive indicators that can be demonstrated empirically. Usually such criteria involve observations of change and judgments about the extent of change as evidence of the success or failure of mediation. Thus, one can consider a particular mediation successful when violence has abated, fatalities reduced, conflict intensity lessened, or a cessation of violent behavior and the opening of some dialogue between the parties were achieved. Or, one can call mediation successful when a formal and binding agreement that settles the conflict's issues has been signed. These are tangible changes one may observe and whose significance one may evaluate.

Thinking of the relationship between mediation and objective criteria of success is a relatively straightforward task. Here, success can be gauged in terms of months both parties observe a ceasefire, reduced number of fatalities following mediation, acceptance of UN peacekeeping force, or any other measures which demonstrably affect the extent and seriousness of a conflict. On the face of it, objective criteria seem to offer a perfectly valid way to assess the impact, consequences, and effectiveness of international mediation.

However, it would be unwise to rely solely on objective criteria. Different mediators, and indeed different parties in conflict, have different goals in mind when they enter conflict management. Changing behavior could well be only one amongst many other objectives. Some international mediators may focus on the substance of interactions; others may focus on its climate, setting, and decision-making norms. These goals cannot always be evaluated easily. Mediation should ideally be evaluated in terms of the criteria that are significant to each of the participants in the process. Thus, the questions of whether or not mediation works, or how best to evaluate it, can only be answered by finding out as much as we can about each party's goals and objectives, as well as learning to ascertain when positive change had taken place. There are just too many conceptual problems with the issue of evaluation, and it seems that, on this question at least, our theoretical ambitions must be tempered by the constraints of a complex reality.

CONCLUSION

Until ten or fifteen years ago, scholarly attempts to comprehend the nature and sources of human conflict in general, and the manner of its resolution in particular, were all too few in number and rather marginal in character. This situation has changed considerably. International conflict and conflict management have become subjects for systematic analysis. Scholarly tracts and practitioners' reflections have helped to institutionalize the field and enhance the individual and collective capacity to manage conflicts. The risks, costs, and tragedies of conflicts in the later part of our century have finally forced us to search for better ways to resolve them. The traditional reliance on power or avoidance are as far from being optimal ways of dealing with conflict as they are outdated. Negotiation and mediation are at last beginning to emerge as the most appropriate responses to conflict in its myriad forms and to the challenge of building a more peaceful world. Negotiation and mediation do not just happen. They are social roles subject to many influences; and, like other roles, they can be learned and improved.

The shared quest for learning the principles and practices of mediation can make sense only if it is conducted within some kind of an intellectual framework, one that can explain the logic and reasoning behind this method of conflict management, in which the mediator is neither directly part of a conflict nor totally removed from it. This chapter has sought to provide a way of thinking about mediation, its structure, its context and its consequences.

The approach taken here embodies my conviction that mediation is an aspect of the broader process of conflict management, in which all parties have interests and are prepared to expend resources to achieve these, and that mediation involves the intertwining of interests, resources, and positions in an attempt to influence outcomes. This relationship is critical for analyzing the dynamics of conflict and assessing the prospects of successful mediation. I have tried to unravel many aspects of this relationship and point out their influence on mediation. I do not assume that my analysis is exhaustive, but I believe that the presentation here adequately integrates many findings that have a bearing on conflict resolution and provides answers to the basic question of mediation research, namely when one should mediate and how. To assume that all conflicts can be mediated really ignores the basic structure and logic of the supply and demand of mediation.

The end of the Cold War and the emergence of an ever-increasing number of ethnic and internal conflicts provide many opportunities for a significant expansion in the use of mediation as an instrument of conflict resolution. The old techniques of power and deterrence seem increasingly less relevant to deal with the problems and conflicts confronting us until the end of the century and perhaps beyond. Mediation may well offer the most coherent and effective response to these issues. To ensure that it can also be successful, we need to develop a better understanding of the process and offer consistent guidelines to the many actors involved in mediation. This effort is still in its infancy, and many different fields and disciplines can contribute to its development. In this chapter, I have tried to take a few tentative steps in that direction. The challenge confronting us all is to recognize the diversity, strengths, and limitations of mediation, and then use its most effective range of tools where appropriate. Given the amount of destruction resulting from today's conflicts and tomorrow's potential crises, this is one challenge we cannot afford to ignore.

REFERENCES

Assefa, Hiskias. 1987. *Mediation of Civil Wars: Approaches and Strategies*. Boulder, CO: Westview Press.

Azar, E.E. 1990. *The Management of Protracted Conflict: Theory and Cases*. Aldershot, UK: Dartmouth.

Bartunek, Jean M., Alan A. Benton, and Christopher B. Keys. 1975. "Third Party Intervention and the Behavior of Group Representatives." *Journal of Conflict Resolution* 19 (3): 532–57.

Beardsley, Kyle, David Quinn, and Jonathan Wilkenfeld. 2005 "Mediation Styles and Crisis Outcomes." *Journal of Conflict Resolution* 50 (1): 58–86.

Bercovitch, Jacob. 1984. *Social Conflicts and Third Parties: Strategies of Conflict Resolution*. Boulder, CO: Westview Press.

———. 1986. "International Mediation: A Study of Incidence, Strategies and Conditions of Successful Outcomes." *Cooperation and Conflict* 21 (3): 155–68.

———. 1989. "International Dispute Mediation." In *Mediation Research, The Process and Effectiveness of Third-Party Intervention*, ed. Kenneth Kressel and Dean G. Pruitt. San Francisco: Jossey-Bass, 284–99.

———. 1992. "Mediation and Mediation Strategies in International Relations", *Negotiation Journal* 8 (3): 99–112.

———. 1996. "Understanding Mediation's Role in Preventive Diplomacy." *Negotiation Journal* 12 (3): 241–59.

——— 2006. "Mediation Success or Failure: The Search for the Elusive Criteria." *Cardozo Journal of Conflict Resolution* 7: 601–15.

Bercovitch, Jacob and Allison Houston. 1993. "Influence of Mediator Characteristics and Behavior on the Success of Mediation in International Relations." *International Journal of Conflict Management* 4 (October): 297–321.

———. 1996. "The Study of International Mediation: Theoretical Issues and Emperical Evidence." In Jacob Bercovitch (ed.) *Resolving International Conflicts*. Boulder, CO: Lynne Rienner. pp. 11–35.

———. 2000 "Why Do They Do It Like This? An Analysis of the Factors Influencing Mediation Behavior in International Conflicts." *Journal of Conflict Resolution* 44: 170–202.

Bercovitch J., and R. Jackson. 2001. "Negotiation or Mediation?: An Exploration of Factors Affecting the Choice of Conflict Management in International Conflict.' *Negotiation Journal* 17 (1): 59–77.

Bercovitch, Jacob, and Jeffrey Langley. 1993. "The Nature of the Dispute and the Effectiveness of International Mediation." *Journal of Conflict Resolution* 37 (4): 670–91.

Bercovitch, Jacob, and Jeffrey Z. Rubin. 1992. *Mediation in International Relations*. New York: St Martin's Press.

Bercovitch, Jacob and Richard Wells. 1993. "Evaluating Mediation Strategies: A Theoretical and Empirical Analysis." *Peace and Change* 18 (1): 3–25.

Bercovitch, J., and G. Schneider. 2000. "Who Mediates? Political Economy of International Conflict Management." *Journal of Peace Research* 37 (2): 145–65.

Bercovitch, Jacob, and Scott Gartner. 2006. "Is there Madness in the Method of Mediation: Research into the Conditions of Effective Mediation." *International Interactions* 32: 329–54.

Bercovitch, Jacob, Theodore Anagnoson and Donnette Wille. 1991. "Some Conceptual Issues and Empirical Trends in the Study of Successful Mediation in International Relations." *Journal of Peace Research* 28 (1): 7–18.

Bingham, Gail. 1985. *Resolving Environmental Disputes*. Washington, DC: The Conservation Foundation.

Blake, Robert A., and Jane Srygley Mouton. 1985. *Solving Costly Organizational Conflicts*. San Francisco: Jossey-Bass.

Boutros-Ghali, Boutros. 1995. *An Agenda for Peace*. New York: United Nations.

Burton, John W. 1969. *Conflict and Communication*. London: Macmillan.

———. 1972. "The Resolution of Conflict." *International Studies Quarterly* 16 (March): 5–29.

———. 1984. *Global Conflict*. Brighton, Sussex: Wheatsheaf Books.

Brecher, M. 1993. *Crises in World Politics: Theory and Reality*. Oxford: Perganion Press.

Burton, J., and F. Dukes. 1990. *Conflict: Readings in Management and Resolution*. New York: St Martin's Press.

Butterworth, Robert L. 1976. *Managing Interstate Disputes, 1945–1974*. Pittsburgh: University of Pittsburgh Press.

Carnevale, Peter. 1986. "Strategic Choice in Mediation." *Negotiation Journal* 2 (1): 41–56.

Carnevale, Peter, and Richard Pegnetter. 1985. "The Selection of Mediation Tactics in Public Sector Disputes: A Contingency Analysis." *Journal of Social Issues* 41 (2): 65–81.

Ciamant, N.J. 2000. "Conflict and Conflict Resolution in China: Beyond Mediation-Centered

Approaches." *Journal of Conflict Resolution* 44 (4): 523–46.

Diehl, P.F. 1992. "What are They Fighting For? The Importance of Issues in International Conflict." *Journal of Peace Research* 29: 333–44.

Doob, Leonard W. 1971. *Resolving Conflict in Africa.* New Haven: Yale University Press.

Douglas, Ann. 1957. "The Peaceful Settlement of Industrial and Intergroup Disputes." *Journal of Conflict Resolution* 1 (March): 69–81.

Druckman, Daniel (ed.) 1977. *Negotiations: A Social-Psychological Analysis.* Beverley Hills, CA: Sage Publications.

Elangoven, A.R. 1995. "Managerial Third Party Dispute Intervention: A Perspective Model of Strategy Selection." *Academy of Managerial Review* 20: 800–30.

Fisher, Ronald J. 1983. "Third-Party Consultation as a Method of Intergroup Conflict Resolution." *Journal of Conflict Resolution* 27 (2): 301–44.

Fisher, Roger, and William Ury. 1981. *Getting to Yes.* Boston: Houghton Mifflin.

Fisher R., and J. Keashley 1991. "The Potential Complementarity of Mediation and Consultation within a Contingency Model of Third-Party Intervention." *Journal of Peace Research* 28 (1): 29–42.

Folberg, Jay, and Alison Taylor. 1984. *Mediation.* San Francisco: Jossey-Bass.

Gartner, Scott, and Jacob Bercovitch. 2006. "Overcoming Obstacles to Peace: The Contribution of Mediation to Short-Lived Conflict Settlements." *International Studies Quarterly* 50 (4): 819–40.

Gochman, C.S. 1993. "The Evolution of Disputes." *International Interactions* 19: 49–76.

Grebe, S. 1994. "Building on Structured Mediation: An Integrated Model for Global Mediation of Separation and Divorce." *Mediation Quarterly* 12 (1): 15–35.

Greig, J.M. 2001. "Moments of Opportunity: Recognizing Conditions of Ripeness for International Mediation Between Enduring Rivals." *Journal of Conflict Resolution* 45 (6): 691–718.

Greig, J. Michael. 2005. "Stepping into the Fray: When do Mediators Mediate?" *American Journal of Political Science* 49 (2): 249–66.

Gulliver, P.H. 1979. *Disputes and Negotiations.* New York: Academic Press.

Haas, Richard N. 1990. *Conflicts Unending.* New Haven: Yale University Press.

Hiltrop, Jean M. 1989. "Factors Affected with Successful Labor Mediation." In *Mediation Research, The Process and Effectiveness of Third-Party Intervention,* ed. Kenneth Kressel and Dean G. Pruitt. San Francisco: Jossey-Bass.

Holsti, Kalevi J. 1983. *International Politics: A Framework for Analysis.* 4th ed. Englewood Cliffs, NJ: Prentice-Hall.

Jabri, Vivienne. 1990. *Mediating Conflict: Decision Making and Western Intervention* in *Namibia.* Manchester: Manchester University Press.

Jackson, R. 2000. "Dangers of Regionalizing International Conflict Management: The African Experience." *Political Science* 52 (1): 41–60.

——. 2000. "Successful Negotiation in International Violent Conflict." *Journal of Peace Research* 37 (3): 323–43.

Keashley, L., and R.J. Fisher. 1996. "A Contingency Perspective on Conflict Interventions: Theoretical and Practical Considerations." In *Resolving International Conflicts: Theory and Practice of Mediation,* ed. J. Bercocitch. Boulder, CO: Lynne Reinner, 235–62.

Kleiboer, M. 1996. "Understanding the Success and Failure of International Mediation." *Journal of Conflict Resolution* 40 (2): 360–89.

Kelman, Herbert C. 1992. "Informal Mediation by the Scholar/Practitioner." In *Mediation in International Relations,* ed. Jacob Bercovitch and Jeffrey Z. Rubin. New York: St Martin's Press.

Kohan, T.A., and T. Jick. 1978. "The Public Sector Mediation Process. A Theory and Empirical Examination." *Journal of Conflict Resolution* 22: 209–40.

Kolb, Deborah M. 1983. "Strategy and Tactics of Mediation." *Human Relations* 36 (3): 247–68.

——. 1989a. "How Existing Procedures Shape Alternatives: The Case of Grievance Mediation." *Journal of Dispute Resolution* 59–87.

——. 1989b. "Labor Mediators, Managers, and Ombudsmen: Roles Mediators Play in Different Contexts." In *Mediation Research,* ed. K Kressel and D.G. Pruitt. San Fransisco: Jossey-Bass, 91–114.

Kolb, Deborah M., and Jeffrey Z. Rubin. 1991. "Mediation through a Disciplinary Prism." *Research on Negotiation in Organizations* 3: 231–57.

Kozan, M.K. 1997. "Culture and Conflict Management: A Theoretical Framework." *International Journal of Conflict Management* 8 (4): 338–60.

Kozan, M.K., and C. Ergin. 1999. "The Influence of Intra-Cultural Value Differences on Conflict Management Practices." *International Journal of Conflict Management* 10 (3): 249–67.

Kriesberg, L. 1982. *Social Conflicts.* 2nd edition. Englewood Cliffs, NJ: Prentice Hall.

Kressel, Kenneth. 1972. *Labor Mediation: An Exploratory Survey.* New York: Association of Labor Mediation Agencies.

Kressel, Kenneth, and Dean G. Pruitt, eds. 1989. *Mediation Research. The Process and Effectiveness of Third-Party Intervention.* San Francisco: Jossey-Bass.

Laure, J.H. 1990. "The Emergence and Institution-alization of Third Party Roles in Conflict." In *Conflict: Readings in Management and Resolution*, ed. J. Burton and F. Dukes. New York: St Martin's Press.

Leng, Russel. (2000). *Bargaining and Learning in Recurring Crises*. Ann Arbor: University of Michigan Press.

Lewicki, R.J, and J. Litterer. 1985. *Negotiation*. Homewood, IL: Richard D. Irwin.

Meyer, Arthur. 1960. "Functions of the Mediator in Collective Bargaining." *Industrial and Labour Relations Review* 13 (June): 159–65.

Mitchell, Christopher R. 1981. *The Structure of International Conflict*. London: Macmillan.

Mohammed O. Maundi, I. William Zartman, Gilbert M. Khadiagala and Kwaku Nuamah. 2006. *Getting In: Mediators Entry into the Settlement of African Conflicts*. Washington, DC: United States Institute of Peace Press.

Moore, Christopher W. 1986. *The Mediation Process: Practical Strategies for Resolving Conflict*. San Francisco: Jossey-Bass.

Northedge, Fred S., and Michael D. Donelan. 1971. *International Disputes: The Political Aspects*. London: Europa Publications.

Ott, Mervin C. 1972. "Mediation as a Method of Conflict Resolution." *International Organization* 26 (4): 595–618.

Pearson, J., and N. Thoennes. 1984. "A Preliminary Portrait of Client Reactions to Three Court Mediation Programs." *Mediation Quarterly* 1: 21–40.

Princen, Thomas. 1992. *Intermediaries in International Conflict*. Princeton: Princeton University Press.

Raiffa, Howard. 1982. *The Art and Science of Negotiation*. Cambridge, MA: Harvard University Press.

Regan, P.M., and A.C. Stam. 2000. "In the Nick of Time: Conflict Management, Mediation Timing, and the Duration of Interstate Disputes." *International Studies Quarterly* 44 (2): 239–60.

Roehl, J.A., and R.F. Cook. 1985. "Issues in Mediation: Rhetoric and Reality Revisited." *Journal of Social Issues* 41: 161–78.

Rubin, Jeffrey Z. 1980. "Experimental Research on Third-Party Intervention in Conflict." *Psychological Bulletin* 87 (2): 379–91.

——. 1992. "International Mediation in Context." In *Mediation in International Relations*, ed. Jacob Bercovitch and Jeffrey Z. Rubin. New York: St Martin's Press.

——. ed. 1981. *Dynamics of Third-Party Intervention: Kissinger in the Middle East*. New York: Praeger.

Rubin, J.Z. and B.R. Brown. 1975. The social Psychology of Bargaining and Negotiation. New York: Academic Press.

Sawyer, J. and H. Guetzkow. 1965. "Bargaining and Negotiations in International Relations." In Herbert C. Kelman (ed.) *International Behavior: A Social-Psychological Analysis*. New York: Holt, Rinehart & Winston. pp. 466–520.

Schelling, Thomas. C. 1960. *The Strategy of Conflict*. Cambridge, MA: Harvard University Press.

Sheppard, B.H. 1984. "Third Party Conflict Intervention: A Procedural Framework." *Research in Organization Behavior* 6: 141–90.

Simkin, William E. 1971. *Mediation and the Dynamics of Collective Bargaining*. Washington, DC: Bureau of National Affairs.

Singer, Linda R. 1990. *Settling Disputes: Conflict Resolution in Business, Families, and the Legal System*. Boulder, CO: Westview Press.

Slim, Randa. 1992. "Small-State Mediation in International Relations: The Algerian Mediation of the Iranian Hostage Crisis." In *Mediation in International Relations*, ed. Jacob Bercovitch and Jeffrey Z. Rubin. New York: St Martin's Press.

Spencer, Doyle E., and Huang Yang. 1993. "Lessons from the Field of Intra-National Conflict Resolution." *Notre Dame Law Review* 67: 1495–512.

Stein, Janice Gross. 1985. "Structure, Strategies and Tactics of Mediation." *Negotiation Journal* 1 (4): 331–47.

Stevens, Carl M. 1963. *Strategy and Collective Bargaining Negotiations*. New York: McGraw Hill.

Stulberg, Joseph B. 1981. "The Theory and Practice of Mediation: A Reply to Professor Susskind." *Vermont Law Review* 6: 85–117.

——. 1987. *Taking Charge/Managing Conflict*. Lexington, MA: D.C. Heath.

Susskind, Lawrence, and Jeffrey Cruickshank. 1987. *Breaking the Impasses: Consensual Approaches to Resolving Public Disputes*. New York: Basic Books.

Terris, Lesley, and Zeev Maoz. (2005). "Rational Mediation; A Theory and a Test." *Journal of Peace Research* 42 (5): 563–83.

Touval, S. 1982. The Peace Brokers: Mediators in the Arab-Israeli Conflict, 1948–1979. Princeton, N.J.: Princeton University Press.

Touval, Saadia. 1992a. "The Superpowers as Mediators." In *Mediation in International Relations*, ed. Jacob Bercovitch and Jeffrey Z. Rubin. New York: St Martin's Press.

——. 1992b. "Gaining Entry to Mediation in Communal Strife." In *The Internationalization of Communal Strife*, ed. Manus I. Midlarsky. London: Routledge.

———. 1985. "Context of Mediation." *Negotiation Journal* 1: 373–78.

Touval, Saadia, and I. William Zartman. 1985. "Mediation in Theory." In *International Mediation in Theory and Practice*, ed. Saadia Touval and I. William Zartman. Boulder, CO: Westview Press.

Vasquez, J.A. 1983. *The Power of Power Politics: A Critique*. London : Francis Pinter.

Wall, James A., Jr. 1981. "Mediation: An Analysis, Review and Proposed Research." *Journal of Conflict Resolution* 25 (1): 157–80.

Wall, J.A., and Ann Lynn. 1993. "Mediation: A Current Review." *Journal of Conflict Resolution* 37 (1): 160–94.

Wall, J.A., John B. Stark, and R.L. Standifer. 2001. *Journal of Conflict Resolution* 45 (3): 370–91.

Wallensteen, Peter, and Karin Axell. 1993. "Armed Conflict at the End of the Cold War, 1989–1992." *Journal of Peace Research* 30 (3): 331–46.

Wallensteen, Peter, and Margareta Sollenberg. 1995. "After the Cold War: Emerging Patterns of Armed Conflict, 1989–1994." *Journal of Peace Research* 32 (3): 345–60.

Walton, Richard E. 1969. *Interpersonal Peacemaking: Confrontations and Third-Party Consultation*. Reading, MA: Addison-Wesley.

Wilkenfeld, Jonathan et al. (2003). "Mediating International Crises: Cross National and Experimental Perspectives', *Journal of Conflict Resolution* 47 (3): 279–301.

Yarrow, C.H. 1978. *Quaker Experiences in International Conciliation*. New Haven: Yale University Press.

Young, Oran R. 1967. *The Intermediaries: Third Parties in International Crises*. Princeton: Princeton University Press.

Zacher, Mark W. 1979. *International Conflicts and Collective Security, 1946–1977*. New York: Praeger.

Zartman, I. William. 1985. *Ripe for Resolution: Conflict and Intervention in Africa*. 2nd edn. New York: Oxford.

Zartman, I. William and Saadia Touval. 2007. "International Mediation." In *Leashing the Dogs of War*, ed. Chester Crocker, Fen Hampson and Pamela Aall Washington, DC: United States Institute of Peace Press, 437–454.

18

The Settlement of International Disputes by Legal Means – Arbitration and Judicial Settlement

Franz Cede

INTRODUCTION

It is fitting to include a chapter on arbitration and adjudication in a handbook on conflict resolution, as Article 33 paragraph 1 of the Charter of the United Nations (Simma, 2002) lists explicitly arbitration (Touval and Zartman, 1985) and judicial settlement (Merrills, 2005) among the peaceful means of settling international disputes. Both schemes are techniques for resolving disputes by referring them to a neutral judicial body for a binding legal decision. Compared to the other modes of peaceful dispute settlement mentioned by Article 33 paragraph 1 of the UN Charter, for instance, negotiation, enquiry, mediation, conciliation, or resort to regional agencies or arrangements, the referral of a dispute to a court entails stringent conditions

for the parties to a dispute. Whereas the aforementioned diplomatic means (Berridge, 2005 and Satow, 1917) allow for a large degree of flexibility and liberty to tackle the contentious issue, without too many formal constraints of law and court procedures, the submission of a case to a tribunal often puts a straitjacket on the parties which they will accept for compelling reasons only. Once a case is pending before a court, the parties to the dispute in question are no longer the sole masters of the game. Even though arbitration leaves more ambit for the parties to influence the proceedings than a case submitted to an independent court, quite obviously the involvement of a third party, be it an arbitration tribunal or a fully fledged court, will always remove the decisive control of the situation from the parties. It will automatically subject the solution to the strict rules of international law as applied and interpreted, not by either party but by an independent body.

In the history of international relations (Wendt, 1999), both arbitration and judicial settlement are relatively recent phenomena, appearing only at an advanced stage of development and integration of the international community of states. This state of affairs is not surprising given the fact that until the beginning of the twentieth century, the concept of the sovereign State dominated the international system. The very idea of a State ceding the authority for settling a legal dispute to a third party institution was alien to the concept of absolute State sovereignty. In principle, within the domestic context, courts and tribunals took their authority from the State and generally exercised their jurisdiction over physical persons. It required a momentous paradigm shift to gradually introduce the scheme of adjudication to the international sphere. The growing integration of the international community and the progressive development of international law gained momentum in the course of the twentieth century and furthered the concept of peaceful conflict resolution by legal means. In a system of absolute State sovereignty, the handing over of a legal case to an international court would have been quite unthinkable. Gradually, however, states accepted the concept of international jurisdiction by independent courts and further accepted the idea that they too could be taken to court and put on trial.

Before attempting to define the similar but different concepts of arbitration and judicial settlement, it seems appropriate to draw attention to yet another aspect of conflict resolution by international courts.

As indicated above, originally the judicial settlement of conflicts concerned states only. They were considered the primary subjects of international law which, under certain conditions, could choose to submit a case to international adjudication. In addition to the competence of international courts to pass judgements in legal disputes between states, a new kind of international court and jurisdiction emerged.

Following the two world wars of the twentieth century, a new concept of international criminal courts made its appearance and developed successfully. It was the indictment and judgement of war criminals as exemplified by the Tokyo[1] and Nuremberg[2] tribunals that served as a model for the elaboration of a whole body of international criminal law which culminated in the adoption of the Statute of the International Criminal Court (ICC) (Zimmermann, Tomuschat and Oellers-Frahm, 2006) in 1999. The advancement of international criminal jurisdiction marks a further step in the development of peaceful settlement of disputes by legal means.

In contrast to the traditional scheme of adjudication involving states or other subjects of international law, the very concept of international criminal jurisdiction addresses itself primarily to physical persons. The main argument in favour of including international criminal jurisdiction into the modes of peaceful settlement of disputes stresses the peacemaking role of international penal courts which, by trying persons guilty of international crimes, render justice which in turn is a prerequisite for rebuilding a shattered society.

Reconciliation in regions that were torn by wars or fratricidal ethnic conflicts (e.g. the Balkans, Rwanda) can only proceed successfully if the perpetrators of the most serious crimes related to these conflicts are brought to justice. The re-establishment of peace and stability in a crisis region therefore requires an effective system of criminal justice.

In this regard, the exceptional case of Iraq is worth mentioning. After the downfall of Saddam Hussein, the question of bringing to justice the key figures of his criminal regime had to be resolved. For the particular reasons prevailing in the aftermath of the Iraqi regime, the decision was taken to bring these criminals before a national Iraqi court rather than resorting to an international criminal tribunal.

The innovative element of the concept of international criminal justice or of human rights courts is the fact that the conventional scheme of adjudication and judicial settlement of legal conflicts between states (horizontal jurisdiction) is now complemented by judicial institutions, rules, and procedures that involve individuals (vertical jurisdiction). Both systems thus play a crucial role in contributing to 'peace through justice'. It is for this reason that vertical jurisdictions (criminal courts, human rights courts) are given appropriate consideration in this chapter. It may be questioned whether international human rights courts also belong within the ambit of arbitration and judicial settlement of disputes. However, if one takes a broader view embracing the conviction that "peace begins at home", it makes sense to briefly deal with the international human rights courts which so far have remained a regional phenomenon.

Both court judgements and arbitration awards are rendered on the basis of consent by the parties accepting the jurisdiction of the judicial institution. Such consent can be expressed with regard to a specific case or generally with regard to certain future cases. Often a treaty contains a clause providing for the establishment of a body entrusted with the judicial settlement of all legal disputes arising from the implementation or interpretation of that very treaty. It follows from such an arrangement that the scope of judicial competence of the legal body established is limited to the treaty, or if so agreed, to certain elements of it. Arbitration clauses can be found both in bilateral and multilateral treaties. Whereas in the bilateral context, the two parties to the arbitration proceedings are identified from the outset, this is not necessarily the case in a multilateral context. Multilateral agreements generally provide for dispute settlement clauses concerning the interpretation or application of their provisions. One cannot foresee in advance which party of the multilateral agreement might possibly be involved in a legal dispute over the obligations stemming from the treaty.

Of paramount importance in any decision by the parties to resort to either judicial settlement or arbitration is the preparedness to accept and to implement the ruling of the independent body whose judgement is based on international law. This implies the definition of the dispute in terms of law which is not always easy, as the parties to a dispute usually take different, if not opposing, views on the legal issues at stake.

In summing up, one can retain the following salient features with regard to arbitration and adjudication as means of peaceful dispute settlement:

- Both methods require the consent of the parties to accept the judgement of an independent judicial institution on the dispute which divides them.
- The acceptance of a court's jurisdiction can be expressed by the parties either ad hoc with regard to a specific dispute, or in general and in advance with regard to certain kinds of disputes (e.g. arbitration clauses in treaties, Statute of ICJ Article 36).
- Whereas arbitration leaves more room for influence by the parties on the composition of the tribunal chosen and on the precise scope of its jurisdiction, an institutionalized court, such as the ICJ, imposes stricter conditions on the parties.
- Judicial settlement by an independent international tribunal means accepting the norms of international law as the basis of the judgement. In referring a case to a court, the parties admit that the dispute concerned will be judged as 'a legal dispute'.
- Vertical jurisdictions (e.g. ICC, human rights courts) dealing with individuals represent new forms of dispute settlement methods by legal means. Although they concern primarily individuals, the acceptance of such vertical jurisdiction is also expressed by states on the basis of international agreements. The function of International Criminal or Human Rights courts contributes to the establishment of peaceful international relations and stable domestic conditions, insofar as they ensure respect for human rights and criminal justice. These vertical jurisdictions can be seen as agents of an emerging international public order. In a broader perspective, they can also be considered as legal instruments of the resolution of international disputes.

JUDICIAL SETTLEMENT

Institutions linked to the UN

1. The International Court of Justice (ICJ)

The forerunner of the ICJ was the Permanent Court of International Justice (PCIJ)[3], formally inaugurated in 1922 at The Hague. The PCIJ was the first truly international court. It was established as the juridical organ of the League of Nations and played a significant role during its existence in acting in 29 cases of litigation and in providing 27 legal opinions. The PCIJ terminated its activities in 1940 after the outbreak of the Second World War. It ceased to exist when the league was formally dissolved in 1946. In spite of its contribution to the recognition of international law, the PCIJ was hampered by the limited membership of the League of Nations, preventing the Court from becoming a truly global institution.

Although there exists no legal continuity between the PCIJ and its successor institution, the ICJ, the founding fathers of the UN essentially used the model of the PCIJ for the newly created world court. Its seat is also at The Hague. With minor adjustments, the Statute of the PCIJ and its rules of procedure were taken over as the institutional basis of the ICJ. The Charter lists the ICJ among the principal organs of the UN (Article 7, paragraph 1) (Simma, 2002) and stipulates that its statute forms an integral part of the Charter. Thereby, it is guaranteed that any state admitted as a member of the UN automatically becomes a contracting party to the statute of the ICJ. In keeping with the principle of universality, the Charter enables even states which are not members of the UN to become a party to the Statute of the (Article 93, paragraph 2, UN Charter) (Simma, 2002). With the attainment of nearly universal membership of the UN, however, this provision has lost its previous relevance in the meantime. The ICJ has thus truly become a world court whose great legal authority and jurisdiction is universally recognized.

The main function of the ICJ clearly consists of passing judgements in cases of litigation submitted to it by states. This core function of the Court serves to settle legal disputes, thereby helping to eliminate conflicts of an international dimension. Pursuant to the UN Charter (Article 94, paragraph 1), each member of the UN is obliged to comply with the decisions of the Court in any case to which it is a party. The obligation to honour the Court's decisions enhances the authority of its jurisdiction. In cases in which a party fails to comply with the decision of the ICJ, the other party may seize the SC to take appropriate action (Article 94, paragraph 2, UN Charter). In practice, the latter provision has little relevance, since with few exceptions, states generally do comply with the Court's judgements. In addition to its jurisdiction in cases of litigation, the ICJ is also competent to give advisory opinions. The UN General Assembly, the Secretary General, the Security Council and other organs of the UN or specialized agencies of the UN family may request an advisory opinion of the ICJ on any legal question (Article 96). When all requirements are met, the request for an advisory opinion of the World Court provides an alternative method for finding a legal solution to differences of opinion on important issues. Although advisory opinions do not have a binding effect, they are usually respected given the high legal authority of the Court.

The role of the ICJ (Rosenne, 2006) in clarifying and promoting international law cannot be overestimated. The ICJ is composed of 15 independent judges each from a different country, who are elected through a complicated procedure, for a term of nine years by the General Assembly and the Security Council of the UN. Under certain conditions, judges may be re-elected (Article 13 of the Statute) (Zimmermann, Tomuschat and Oellers-Frahm, 2006). Regardless of their nationality, the judges are elected from among persons of high moral character who possess the qualifications required in their respective countries for appointment to the highest judicial offices, or are jurisconsults of recognized competence in international law (Article 2 of the Statute) (Zimmermann, Tomuschat and

Oellers-Frahm, 2006). According to Article 9 of the Statute, the judges shall represent the main forms of civilization and the principal legal systems of the world. There is an unwritten custom that among the judges of the ICJ, there is always one national of each of the five permanent member states of the UN Security Council. Exceptionally, when a party to a dispute brought before the Court is not represented among the judges, it may appoint an ad hoc member of the Court (judex ad hoc).

The jurisdiction of the ICJ requires the consent of the states which are parties to a dispute. Only states may bring a case of litigation to the Court. The competence of the ICJ presupposes that the state parties have in one way or another expressed their acceptance of the jurisdiction of the ICJ for that particular case. Pursuant to Article 36, paragraph 2 of the Statute, 'the States parties (to the Statute) may at any time declare that they recognize as compulsory ipso facto and without special agreement, in relation to any other State accepting the same obligation, the jurisdiction of the Court'. This 'optional clause' is the legal basis for all unilateral declarations made by states to accept the jurisdiction of the ICJ on the basis of reciprocity. As of 13 March, 2007, 66 states have made such declarations.

Another way of establishing the competence of the ICJ to exercise its jurisdiction is to include a 'compromissory clause' in an international agreement. To date, more than 300 bilateral or multilateral treaties provide such clauses stipulating the jurisdiction of the ICJ.

The acceptance of an international body's jurisdiction always implies giving up a piece of sovereignty. In general, states have a tendency to limit the scope of jurisdictional powers to be transferred to the ICJ. One restriction provided by the Statute itself is the principle of reciprocity (acceptance of the Court's jurisdiction only when the other party accepts the same obligation). A second limitation is the time element also provided for by the Statute (Article 36, paragraph 3) (Zimmermann, Tomuschat

and Oellers-Frahm, 2006) allowing the acceptance of the Court's competence for a certain period of time only. An analysis of the various declarations under the optional clause of the Statute, however, shows that states have not shied away from further restricting the court's jurisdiction. The USA, for instance, in its declaration of acceptance of the competence of the ICJ, dated 14 August, 1946, in accordance with the aforementioned optional clause, made a proviso to the effect that the declaration shall not apply, inter alia, 'to disputes with regard to matters which are essentially within the domestic jurisdiction of the United States of America as determined by the United States of America'. The US reservation, known as the 'Connally-Amendment', is very far reaching as it leaves it to the USA to decide whether it considers a matter to fall under its domestic jurisdiction or not.

In 1985, in the course of the 'Nicaragua case' (1984 ICJ 392), the USA withdrew its declaration of acceptance of the compulsory jurisdiction of the ICJ. The USA has not yet re-accepted the compulsory jurisdiction of the Court.

The ICJ bases its decisions on what is generally referred to as the classic canon of the sources of international law. Article 38, paragraph—(Zimmermann, Tomuschat and Oellers-Frahms, 2006) of the Statute cites four materials which are applied by the Court:

- international conventions
- international custom as evidence of a general practice accepted as law
- the general principles of law recognized by civilized nations
- as subsidiary means for the determination of rules of law – judicial decisions and teachings of the most highly qualified publicists of the various nations.

It has happened several times that a state, party to a legal dispute, contested the competence of the ICJ. That state usually challenged the Court's jurisdiction with the argument that its previous acceptance of the compulsory jurisdiction did not comprise the particular type of dispute under consideration, or that there was a lack of reciprocity in the sense that the applicant state had not so consented.

In such situations, the Court usually proceeds in examining whether it has jurisdiction in the relevant case and determines the scope of consent by the parties to the dispute. In case the Court determines that it has jurisdiction, it examines the merits of the case irrespective of the dissenting opinion of the respondent state. In expanding its powers over the long period of its judicial activities, the ICJ, in certain cases, imposed 'provisional measures' aimed at avoiding tensions between the parties or at preserving specific rights.

Assessing the work of the ICJ since its establishment in 1946, one is surprised by the low number of judgements rendered and advisory opinions given over such a lengthy existence. During the period 1946–2007, the ICJ passed 92 judgements on disputes and gave 25 advisory opinions. However, it would be wrong to measure the importance of the Court solely by the number of its decisions and advisory opinions. The range of disputes dealt with by the ICJ is quite impressive, covering a broad spectrum of legal issues (e.g. territorial and border issues, the non-use of force, diplomatic relations, asylum questions, nationality, economic rights, etc). While a number of cases were of minor importance, some others had great significance for the development of international law. The ICJ has greatly influenced the codification of the law of the sea, the international law of treaties and the law of the environment. The precedents set by the ICJ are usually cited as important points of reference influencing the legal positions of all states, irrespective of whether they were a party to the relevant dispute or not. In that manner, the impact of the Court's jurisdiction, even though it is binding only for the parties to the dispute concerned, goes well beyond the individual case in question.

2. The International Criminal Court (ICC)

The Nuremberg and Tokyo trials held shortly after World War II to bring to justice the German and Japanese perpetrators of the most serious war crimes and crimes against humanity gave an important impetus to the idea of an international criminal court. Earlier attempts had failed to create such a global judicial body in the context of the negotiations on the Genocide Convention in 1948 and the Convention against Apartheid in 1973. During the Cold War, the project of an international criminal court had to be shelved as there was not sufficient support for such a new institution. The movement for the concept of an ICC gained momentum only recently under the backdrop of the horrific crimes committed during the conflict in the former Yugoslavia and the ethnically motivated massacres in Rwanda. These developments then led the Security Council of the UN to create two ad hoc tribunals (International Criminal Tribunal for the former Yugoslavia in 1993, and International Criminal Tribunal for Rwanda in 1994). The establishment of these two ad hoc tribunals underlined the need for a permanent international criminal court. Obviously, the creation of ad hoc tribunals did not provide an alternative for the establishment of an international criminal court. The time was finally ripe for taking on the task of creating such an international institution. It then took years of negotiations before the UN General Assembly convened a conference in Rome in 1998 mandated with the finalization of an international treaty establishing the ICC. As a result, on 17 July, 1998 the Rome Conference adopted the Statute of the permanent International Criminal Court (Triffterer, 1999). The Statute entered into force on July 1, 2002 after 60 States had ratified it, thereby bringing the ICC into legal existence.

The ICC is an independent institution whose seat is at The Hague. Unlike the ICJ, the ICC is not an organ of the United Nations although it is closely linked to the World Organization. As of January 2007, 104 states have become a party to the Statute. Further, 41 states have signed but not yet ratified the Rome treaty. The USA has changed its position towards the ICC. On 31 December, 2000, President Clinton unexpectedly signed the Rome Statute but on 6 May, 2002, the Bush administration 'nullified' the US signature, thus showing that the USA is not yet prepared to transfer criminal jurisdiction to an international institution.

The ICC is composed of 18 independent judges, each from a different country, who are nationals of state parties to the Rome Statute. The description of their qualifications is similar to that of the members of the ICJ. The judges are elected by state parties for a term of up to nine years.

Of central importance is the jurisdiction of the ICC.

Article 5 of the Rome Statute lists four crimes referred to as the 'most serious crimes of concern to the international community as a whole' to fall under the jurisdiction of the ICC:

- the crime of genocide
- crimes against humanity
- war crimes
- the crime of aggression.

With the exception of aggression, the Statute gives a definition for each of these crimes. At the Rome conference, no agreement could be reached on a definition of aggression or on the inclusion of additional crimes for which the ICC should exercise its jurisdiction. Before and during the conference, several attempts failed to submit terrorism, drug trafficking and other illegal activities to the jurisdiction of the ICC.

In order to keep the momentum aimed at enlarging the scope of jurisdiction of the ICC, Article 123 of the Rome Statute provides for a review clause. It is foreseen that in 2009, a review conference shall be convened to reconsider and possibly enlarge the list of crimes contained in Article 5. The main task of the upcoming conference will be to find an acceptable definition of the crime of aggression to be added to the list of crimes under the jurisdiction of the ICC.

As to the Court's territorial jurisdiction, the Rome Conference settled on a compromise. Instead of establishing the competence strictly on the basis of the principle of universality, the jurisdiction of the ICC can be exercised only under the following conditions:

- when the person accused of committing a crime is a national of a state party to the Statute (or in case the person's state has accepted the jurisdiction of the ICC)
- when the alleged crime was committed on the territory of a state party (or if the state on whose territory the crime was committed has accepted the jurisdiction of the ICC)
- in case a situation is referred to the Court by the UN Security Council.

The latter condition shows the close relationship between the ICC and the UN. The Court's jurisdiction is also confined by temporal restrictions. It cannot prosecute crimes committed prior to the date on which the Rome Statute entered into force (1 July, 2002). With regard to states becoming parties to the Rome Statute after that date, the ICC has the right to exercise its jurisdiction only relating to crimes committed after the date of entry into force of the Statute for the relevant states.

The ICC acts on the basis of complementarity, that is, the ICC is a court of last resort in cases in which national criminal courts have failed to investigate or prosecute cases where the ICC has jurisdiction. The organs of the ICC are: the Presidency, the Judicial Divisions, the Office of the Prosecutor and the Registrar.

The Court may be seized in three ways. A situation can be referred to it either by a state party to the Statute, by the UN Security Council or by the Prosecutor (proprio motu).

A survey of the cases brought before the ICC to date reveal over 1700 communications about alleged crimes in 139 countries. Most of them, however, have been inadmissible as they were found to be outside the Court's jurisdiction. Three situations (Uganda, Democratic Republic of Congo, Darfur) became the subject of investigation by the Court's prosecutor.

It cannot be denied that the ICC suffers from the lack of acceptance of the Statute by major states, notably the USA, Russia, and China.

The limited membership considerably weakens the concept of a truly universal criminal jurisdiction. On the other hand, with all its failings, the recent establishment of the ICC undeniably marks the beginning of a universal system of criminal justice. Clearly, the current state of affairs is not the end of the story. The hope may be expressed that the upcoming review conference will be another milestone in the development of such a scheme.

3. Ad hoc criminal tribunals

As mentioned above, two international tribunals preceded the creation of the ICC. Both the International Tribunal for the Former Yugoslavia (ICTY)[4] and the International Tribunal for Rwanda (ICTR)[5] were established by resolutions of the UN Security Council as a reaction to the bloody conflicts on the territory of the former Yugoslavia and in Rwanda where the most serious crimes against humanity, war crimes and acts of genocide had been committed. The scale and gravity of the criminal acts perpetrated during these two conflicts led to the belief of the international community that the persons guilty of such serious offences should under no circumstances go unpunished. Bringing the perpetrators to justice was considered as a necessary precondition for the reconciliation process in the regions afflicted and as a key element for the re-establishment of the rule of law. Based on this conviction, the swift adoption of the relevant Security Council resolutions did not cause any major problems.

The ICTY and the ICTR resemble each other to a great extent. Both judicial institutions have the mandate to prosecute and punish persons guilty of serious offences (genocide, war crimes or crimes against humanity). From an organizational point of view, there are also striking similarities between the two bodies. They operate in trial chambers, each composed of a certain number of judges. They are both endowed with an office of the prosecutor charged with the investigation of the case, for instance, the collection of evidence concerning the persons accused, and with the prosecution of

all cases before the tribunal. They also have a registry which manages the administration of the respective tribunal.

4. The International Tribunal for the Law of the Sea (ITLOS)

On 28 July, 1996, the United Nations Convention on the Law of the Sea (UNCLOS) entered into force. This Convention established a legal framework to regulate the ocean, its uses and resources. Part XV of the Convention creates a comprehensive system for the settlement of disputes that might arise with respect to the interpretation and application of the Convention. States are required to settle such disputes by peaceful means, as prescribed by the UN Charter. Within this system, the International Tribunal of the Law of the Sea (ITLOS) occupies a central place. In addition, two arbitral courts were constituted in accordance with Annexes VII and VIII of the Convention. The mechanism of the UNCLOS is characterized by the attempt to set up a mandatory scheme by which state parties to the Convention are obliged to settle their disputes by legal means, resorting either to the ITLOS, the ICJ or, if applicable, to one of the arbitral courts established under the system.

The ITLOS, established in Hamburg, is an independent judicial body mandated to adjudicate disputes arising out of the interpretation and application of the UNCLOS. It consists of 21 judges from various countries. The ITLOS is organized in three primary bodies: the chamber of summary procedure, the chamber for fisheries disputes and the chamber for marine environment disputes. Additional chambers may be established to deal with specific matters (e.g. disputes over seabed mining). An analysis of the activities of the ITLOS shows a mixed record. When measured by the number of decisions rendered, it has to be said that, since its creation, the Tribunal has delivered only very few judgements. On the other hand, it assumes an increasingly important function in cases of litigation, either by imposing provisional measures or by ordering the prompt release of vessels.

Regional Human Rights Courts

The European Court of Human Rights (ECHR)

The ECHR[6] is to be considered a unique institution on the global scale because it enables citizens of the countries having signed and ratified the European Convention on Human Rights to bring complaints against their own state before the court. The ECHR was established in the framework of the Council of Europe, a regional organization with a special vocation in the field of human rights, democracy and the rule of law. The ECHR is competent to pass judgement on purported violations of the rights enshrined in the said convention. Its judgements generally state whether a human rights violation occurred in a particular case. Within the framework of the European Convention on Human Rights, the court also has the competence to deal with complaints filed by a state against another state on the argument that the latter has violated the rights guaranteed in the convention. However, when compared to the cases submitted by individual plaintiffs, these 'state complaints' play only a minor role in the jurisdiction of the ECHR.

The ECHR has its seat in Strasbourg, France, where the headquarters of the Council of Europe are located. The court consists of 40 members, a number that is equal to that of the state parties to the European Convention on Human Rights. The judges are elected by the Parliamentary Assembly of the Council of Europe on the basis of proposals submitted by governments. The judges are elected for a renewable mandate of eight years. The court is organized in four sections and consists of several chambers, each composed of seven judges. The judiciary function is primarily performed by the chambers. An overall assessment of the activities of the ECHR shows an impressive record of success. Over the years, the Court, by passing judgements on individual complaints by citizens against their own state, has developed a rich body of jurisprudence, which in turn has exercised an important influence on the respective legislation and administrative practice of

the states concerned. As an international instance of last resort, the ECHR has also significantly contributed to standard setting in the field of human rights and, more generally, to the promotion of the rule of law in the vast area under its jurisdiction, now stretching from the Atlantic to the Pacific Ocean. It is noteworthy that, before a state is admitted to the Council of Europe, it must accept the human rights regime of the European Convention on Human Rights. In other words, accession to the Convention and its additional protocols is considered a precondition for membership in the Council of Europe. Accession to the Convention thus implies the acceptance of stringent obligations. The state in question is obliged to honor the human rights provisions enshrined in the convention as well as to accept the jurisdiction of the ECHR. In this way, the countries in transition in Europe that joined the Council of Europe were all committed to the system of human rights protection under the convention. However, this positive development expanding the geographic area of application of the European Convention on Human Rights to Vladivostok in the East has led to a dramatic increase in 'Eastern European cases' brought before the Court. As of January 2007, the ECHR is overburdened with about 90,000 pending cases, 50,000 of which were registered in 2006 only. Unless a fundamental reform of the procedures of the ECHR making them leaner and more efficient can be realized, there is a real danger that the Court will virtually collapse under the weight of its unfinished business.

The Inter-American Court of Human Rights

The American Convention on Human Rights, signed in 1969, established a catalogue of human rights and fundamental freedoms and created a control system to monitor the implementation of its obligations by the contracting states. The Convention which entered into force in 1978 provides for two control mechanisms: the Inter-American Commission on Human Rights and the Inter-American Court of Human Rights. The latter body, consisting of seven judges, has been sometimes compared to the European Court of Human Rights. A closer look at its competence, however, reveals that it does not possess jurisdiction with regard to complaints by individuals against their own state. The Inter-American Court of Human Rights is only competent to mediate disputes in human rights matters and to give advisory opinions upon request, either by a contracting party to the Convention or by a member state of the Organization of American States (OAS). Without having jurisdiction in cases of complaints by individuals, the monitoring instruments of the Inter-American Human Rights system are definitely weaker than the European Court of Human Rights.

Regional integration and adjudication

The European Court of Justice (ECJ)

Within the framework of the European integration, the ECJ (Kennedy, 2006) constitutes the judicial body which makes sure that EU legislation is interpreted and applied in the same way in all EU member states. The Court was set up in 1952 by the European treaty establishing the European Coal and Steel Community (ECSC). Over time, it has acquired a number of important new competences. By upholding community law, the ECJ has the power to give legal judgements on cases brought before it. Its core function consists in settling legal disputes between EU member states, EU institutions, businesses and individuals.

The Court is composed of 27 judges, so that the legal systems of all member states are adequately represented. The judges must qualify for appointment to the highest judicial office in their respective countries and are appointed on the basis of an agreement between the governments of the EU member states. The renewable term of office of the judges is six years.

The bulk of the judicial function is performed in the Grand Chamber of 13 judges or in chambers of three or five judges. In addition to the judges, eight magistrates,

the so-called 'advocates general' assist the ECJ in shaping its decisions. They present their reasoned opinion to the court in public hearings and prepare the deliberations of the judges in a given case.

In 1989, the 'Court of First Instance'[7] was created as a subsidiary body of the ECJ. The main task of this court is to pass judgements on certain types of cases, for instance, all actions brought by private individuals, companies or some organizations. The 'Court of First Instance' is also competent to give judgements on cases relating to competition law.

The most common cases brought before the ECJ are (1) actions for failure to fulfil an obligation of a member state under EU law; (2) actions for annulment of a particular EU law on the argument that it is illegal; (3) actions for failure to act in certain cases where an EU institution fails to make decisions and, last but not least; (4) references under the preliminary ruling procedure. If, under this procedure, a national court of a member state is in doubt about the validity or interpretation of an EU law it may, or sometimes must, resort to the ECJ for advice (preliminary ruling). In this way, the Court ensures that the national courts do not interpret EU law differently or give rulings which deviate from the case law of the ECJ.

The importance of the ECJ in advancing EU law is such that it has sometimes been described as the 'engine of community law'. Member states are obliged to submit all legal disputes on the interpretation and application of community law to the ECJ. They must not seek legal redress in such disputes before another international tribunal.

ARBITRATION

Parallel to the development of adjudication, the concept of arbitration made its way forward with significant success. A number of bilateral agreements provided for arbitration as a means to settle legal disputes. Prominent among those agreements is the Jay Treaty of 1794, concluded by the USA and Great Britain which instituted arbitral tribunals to define the border between the USA and the then British territories in North America. No textbook of international law can ignore the famous 'Alabama case'[8] as an example of the settlement by arbitration of a serious legal dispute between the USA and Great Britain in the wake of the US civil war (1861–1865).

On the eve of the 20th century, the concept of international arbitration enjoyed a renaissance when the two Hague peace conferences sought to establish a new institution in the form of a 'Permanent Court of Arbitration' (PCA)[9].

However, a closer look at the PCA reveals the weak character of this institution. It is neither a court nor an arbitral tribunal. Rather, it can be described as a roster of persons which states are free to choose as arbitrators if they wish to set up an arbitral procedure.

The PCA has never played an important role and was overshadowed first by the Permanent International Court and later by the ICJ. Repeated efforts to revive the PCA have so far been unsuccessful.

On the other hand, one can observe that arbitration as a peaceful means to settle legal disputes has asserted its position quite vigorously both in the inter-state relationship and in the context of disputes involving states and private companies.

In recognition of the continued value of arbitration for the settlement of disputes, the UN General Assembly in 1958 adopted a resolution recommending to states a set of Model Rules of Arbitral Procedure as proposed by the International Law Commission. In a similar vein, the UN Commission of International Trade Law (UNCITRAL)[10] drew up arbitration rules primarily for use of private companies. This renewed interest in the instrument of arbitration for the settlement of international disputes has to do with the high degree of adaptability of arbitration procedures to the needs and requirements of the parties to the dispute in question. Another factor which makes arbitration attractive, in particular for businesses, is the expediency of the procedures which sets it apart from the more stringent rules applied by international courts in cases of litigation.

Usually, arbitration is less expensive for the parties than litigation. For these reasons, the Paris based International Court of Arbitration, established within the framework of the International Chamber of Commerce, has become a great success story and is now the world's leading institution for resolving international commercial and business disputes. Since its foundation, the Court has handled 14,000 cases involving parties from all over the world. The vitality of modern arbitration techniques is also evidenced by the International Centre for the Settlement of Investment Disputes (ICSID)[11], which, under the aegis of the World Bank, provides a very professional and efficient facility.

In short, it can be said that arbitration is alive and well, even though its focus has shifted significantly from the domain of inter-state relations to the area of international business and finance.

ASSESSMENT OF ARBITRATION AND JUDICIAL SETTLEMENT IN THE PRESENT CONTEXT OF INTERNATIONAL RELATIONS

Compliance with the norms of international law by state and non-state actors represents an indispensable prerequisite of an international system governed by the rule of law. In a civilized world, disputes between states and other actors must be settled peacefully. The obvious first choice for resolving an international dispute appears to be the method of negotiation. At first sight, talking to each other on the substance of the dispute and seeking a settlement in direct talks with the other party or parties seems to be the best avenue for eliminating the bone of contention.

In the absence or failure of a negotiated settlement of dispute procedure, the question arises as to which extent current international law prescribes an obligation to resort to a specific method such as arbitration or adjudication. The Charter of the United Nations (Article 33) does not provide for such an obligation. Rather, the Charter leaves it for the parties to the dispute to choose among a whole array of peaceful means of conflict resolution. The Charter explicitly lists negotiation, enquiry, mediation, conciliation, arbitration, judicial settlement, resort to regional agencies or arrangements, or other peaceful means of their own choice. However, in a given case, the parties are rarely free to pick one or the other method of peaceful conflict resolution as Article 33 of the UN Charter suggests. International actors are usually bound by a dense network of treaties which often contain clauses prescribing strict rules and procedures for governing the settlement of disputes arising out of the treaty. Arbitration and adjudication figure prominently in such clauses.

Once a party has consented to submit a dispute to a court or to arbitration, it has to reckon with the possibility that the other party which has accepted the same obligation actually activates the legal procedure in question. This fact alone induces states to honor their international obligations and has, as such, a positive effect.

The relevance of adjudication and arbitration is growing with the development of an international system based on international law. The pros and cons of adjudication versus arbitration have been briefly alluded to. Both methods present risks and opportunities. They entail the risk of losing. It lies in the nature of things that a judicial body has to take a decision which is adverse to one or the other party. On the other hand, when referring a case to a judicial body, at the end of the day, the parties will have the benefit of an authoritative judgement that terminates the legal quarrel that divides them. Even for the party which has lost the case before an international tribunal, the advantage of a definitive settlement of the dispute through a court judgement or an arbitral award may be higher than the alternative, that is, an endless continuation of the conflict in question.

All things considered, a strong case can be made in favor of strengthening adjudication and arbitration as legal techniques for the peaceful settlement of international disputes.

A CLOSER LOOK AT SOME SPECIFIC QUESTIONS

1. The role of law in conflict resolution

Dealing with the various methods of dispute settlement by legal means, in particular, arbitration and judicial settlement, raises the more general question of the 'law factor' in conflict resolution. The broad picture shows that there is no simple answer to this question. Sometimes, political considerations prevail over the respect for international law. On the other hand, it would be wrong to underestimate the influence of legal rules on the actual behavior of international actors. In determining its conduct, no member of the international community can afford to openly defy the authority of international law. Therefore, states and other subjects of international law always seek to legitimize their behavior on the basis of international law. This being said, there is no denying that powerful states, in pursuing their policy goals, are less prone to observe the obligations of international law as they have other means at their disposal to win the day. Weaker states do not have the same clout and, therefore, depend to a much greater extent on the observance of law by all members of the international system. In disputes, they have a tendency to resort to legal settlement methods because judicial proceedings provide a better way to equalize the parties than negotiations. To some extent, the saying that negotiations weaken the weak does not only apply to domestic but also to international disputes.

What motivates great and powerful states to subject themselves to judicial settlement procedures if they can win a dispute by other than legal means?

There are several reasons which may convince a great power to choose a legal method for settling a specific dispute. To a certain degree, each state, great or small, is interested in a functioning system based on law and endowed with impartial judicial institutions. These institutions with their body of case law provide a measure of predictability which is in the general interest. International law as the basis for the jurisdiction of international courts can be considered as the lowest common denominator on which the parties to a dispute may agree. Against this backdrop, powerful states may conclude in specific cases that the best option for them is to refer the settlement of the dispute to a legal body even if they have other instruments at their disposal. To illustrate this point, the Iran–USA Claims Tribunal, mentioned above, may be cited. Under the then prevailing circumstances, the establishment of the claims tribunal offered to both sides the best possible mechanism to settle many outstanding financial and property issues. The USA considered the tribunal as an acceptable substitute for lengthy negotiations with Iran, a country with which diplomatic relations had been severed. Another striking example going in a different direction shows the limits of legal settlement procedures.

In the Nicaragua case (1984 ICJ 392), brought before the ICJ in 1984, the USA was charged by Nicaragua that US support of the contras and other activities directed against the Sandinista regime violated international law. In the course of the proceedings, the USA protested the Court's decision that it had jurisdiction over Nicaragua's claim against the USA and that the matter was admissible and appropriate for judicial consideration.

In consequence, in October 1985, the USA terminated its acceptance of the Court's compulsory jurisdiction under the optional clause, to take effect one year from that date. The lesson to be drawn from the first example (USA–Iranian claims tribunal) is to show that under certain circumstances, even for a big power, the use of a legal instrument may be the most convenient method to settle unresolved issues. The claims at stake were differences over property rights, most of them falling within the purview of private or business law. When, on the contrary, an acerbic dispute erupts with profound political connotations involving a great power and a small country (in the example of the Nicaragua case), the chances are slim that it can be settled by means of a court decision.

2. Conflicts of legal systems

It cannot be overlooked that the search for a conflict resolution by legal means may be hampered by possible inconsistencies between different national legislations or between national and international legal systems.

A serious complication impeding the smooth administration of justice consists in the possible conflict of legal systems. There may be differences of opinion on the question of what legislation applies and of what courts are competent to pass a judgement in a particular case. The controversy about the applicability of law and the competence of courts has the potential to exacerbate the tensions about the substance of the dispute in question.

The example of the Helms-Burton Act of 1996[12] may be given. This US federal law strengthens and continues the US embargo against Cuba. The act extended the territorial application of the initial US embargo to apply to foreign companies trading with Cuba. The Helms-Burton Act was condemned by the European Union which introduced a Council Regulation (binding all EU member states), declaring the extra-territorial provisions of this US law to be unenforceable within the EU, and permitting recovery of any damages under it.

A recent controversy about the Helms-Burton Act involved the former Austrian Bank, BAWAG, which was recently taken over by Cerberus, a US fund. When the CEO of BAWAG announced in a public statement that, in compliance with the provisions of the said US legislation, the bank now owned by a US company, had to close about 100 accounts of Cuban citizens, a conflict of legal systems broke out. The Austrian Foreign Minister stated that 'administrative criminal proceedings' would be introduced against BAWAG in accordance with the relevant Austrian law that implements the aforementioned EU regulation. In Brussels too, tempers were high, as BAWAG was told that it could face EU penalties for having violated the said regulation. At the end of the day, BAWAG caved in and announced it would continue doing business with its Cuban clients. The predicament stemming from a classic conflict of law was finally resolved out of court. Rather, it was managed through direct talk between the CEO of BAWAG and the US authorities.

3. The winning principle

It is true that adjudication and arbitration belong to those schemes of conflict resolution which, unlike negotiation, usually lead to an outcome considered by one party as a victory and a defeat by the other. In vertical jurisdictions, a similar pattern appears. A person accused of having committed crimes will claim victory if the court dealing with the matter decides to let him free. The winning principle is immanent in judicial decisions, although in many cases the judgements leave ample room for ambivalent interpretations allowing each side to save its face and claim victory.

Powerful states are rarely willing to accept the jurisdiction of an international court if there is a serious risk that the winning principle would play in favor of the adversary camp. Sometimes, however, they cannot prevent the court from dealing with a matter whose outcome is likely to be unpleasant for them.

A case in point may be cited. In December 1994, the UN General Assembly requested an advisory opinion from the ICJ on the question of whether the threat or use of nuclear weapons would be forbidden by international law. The USA voted against the relevant GA resolution but was unable to impede its adoption by a majority of UN member states. As a consequence, the ICJ was seized irrespective of the negative vote cast by the US representative in the General Assembly. The Court then gave an advisory opinion on the present question.

The gist of its findings is a masterpiece of ambiguity and therefore deserves to be quoted in full (1996 ICJ 226):

' It follows from the above-mentioned requirements that the threat or use of nuclear weapons would generally be contrary to the rules of international law applicable in armed conflicts, and in particular the principles and rules of international humanitarian law.

However, in view of the current state of international law, and of the elements of fact at its disposal, the Court cannot conclude definitively whether the threat or use of nuclear weapons would be lawful or unlawful in an extreme circumstance of self-defence, in which the very survival of a State would be at stake'.[13]

This opinion is like a sphinx leaving it to the reader to stress either the argument in the first or the second paragraph. The question arises whether such pronouncements of the world's highest judicial authority do indeed contribute to the settlement of a legal dispute. Critics have questioned the usefulness of legal opinions of this kind. On the other hand, one has to admit that the ICJ's proceedings on this most sensitive legal and political issue had an overall positive effect. To those states which supported the request to seize the ICJ by way of a request for an advisory opinion, the very fact that the Court had to deal with it was seen as a victory (winning principle). The proceedings served as an outlet for their concern about nuclear weapons and their use. The examination by the Court also channelled the debate into the domain of international law, thereby setting the parameters of the contentious issue in a legal framework. In spite of the ambivalent conclusions of the legal opinion, it had a pacifying effect insofar as it de-escalated a nasty political and legal conflict which had been poisoning inter-state relations for many years.

One of the lessons to be drawn from this case is certainly the perception that international judicial bodies can make a contribution to conflict resolution in many different ways. While the parties are usually seeking a 'yes or no' answer to their question brought before the court, the reply may turn out to be 'maybe' or 'yes and no'. These more subtle outcomes make it all the more difficult to apply the winning principle without differentiation. The present case concerning the legality of nuclear weapons clearly shows that an authoritative pronouncement by an international judicial body has the capacity to reduce tensions and contribute to the settlement of a conflict even though no party to the dispute can claim full victory.

In rendering a most ambiguous legal opinion, the ICJ has done little to clarify the precise law on the matter but it has allowed each side to save its face, highlighting those parts of the legal opinion which support its own position. At the same time, the dispute could be put to rest and the parties were able to strike the issue from their political agenda. In sum, the court acted in this case as a conflict manager rather than as the authority passing a clear cut judgement on what is right or wrong.

4. The effect of criminal courts on conflict resolution

As has been pointed out above, international criminal courts are considered as indispensable instruments to re-establish peace and to foster reconciliation in the wake of international or domestic armed conflicts. However, the record of these courts in the relatively brief period since their creation shows a mixed picture. It is not possible to give a clear-cut positive assessment of the impact of criminal courts on the process of conflict resolution. To assert that international criminal courts are necessary to re-establish justice after war is one thing. However, showing how and to what extent they are actually making a decisive contribution to the peace consolidation process appears to be much more difficult. In Iraq, for instance, the trial of Saddam Hussein and his execution were considered by many observers as botched. Some critics even went as far as to say that this trial did not have a positive effect on the efforts aimed at stabilizing the situation in Iraq but, on the contrary, that it had rather exacerbated tensions between the various factions in the country. In the context of the conflict in the former Yugoslavia, international justice was also put to the test. When the former Yugoslav leader Milosevic was indicted by the ICTY with more than 60 separate charges, a number of experts of criminal law criticized the lack of focus of the indictment which, in their view, had avoided straightforward proceedings.

They were also critical about the long duration of the proceedings that dragged on for more than four years and Mr Milosevic died before a verdict could be given. So it is too early to tell whether in the final analysis the ICTY has exerted a positive influence in stabilizing the Balkans regions.

In spite of the criticisms levelled against them, it is undeniable that the ad hoc criminal tribunals have also accomplished significant successes. Their jurisprudence has undoubtedly contributed to the development of international criminal law and given a decisive impetus to the creation of the ICC. On the question of whether the two ad hoc tribunals, as some critics say, have exacerbated tensions rather than promoted reconciliation in the conflict areas concerned, one should not put into doubt the impartiality and the legal authority of the judges who were appointed members of these special courts. It can be said that the ICTY and the ICTR have carried out their mandate with a keen sense of impartiality. There is just no alternative to a neutral international institution when it comes to shifting from impunity to accountability in the wake of an armed conflict. It is hard to imagine that the existing national courts in the region would have been inclined to prosecute and try the perpetrators of the serious crimes committed during the armed conflict. This aspect alone justifies the judicial activities of the two special tribunals.

5. A burning case leading to the creation of a special tribunal

It is tempting to briefly discuss a particularly hot issue to shed some light on its legal dimensions and to examine whether adjudication can indeed be a means for the settlement of a burning case. A closer look at the reaction of the international community to the killing of the former Lebanese Prime Minister Hariri, murdered on 14 February 2005 in a terrorist bomb attack in Beyrouth, provides an excellent opportunity to study the difficult relationship between crime, politics, and law in a dramatic conflict situation. After lengthy consultations on 30 May, 2007, the UN Security Council adopted resolution

1757 (2007) whereby a 'Special Tribunal for Lebanon'[14] was established to prosecute the persons responsible for the attack of 14 February 2005 resulting in the death of former PM Hariri. The Security Council adopted the present resolution under Chapter VII of the UN Charter, thereby re-affirming that the Hariri murder and its consequences were considered as a threat to international peace and security. The decision of the SC to create a special Criminal Tribunal for Lebanon to try the perpetrators of this criminal act is noteworthy in many respects. The main driving forces behind the creation of this tribunal were France and the USA, two states which have their own reservations with regard to the concept of a universal criminal jurisdiction as realized in the ICC. At the same time, they were the proponents of the special Lebanon tribunal which provides at least some hope that the killing of former PM Hariri will not go unpunished. Bringing justice back to Lebanon obviously is an endeavour which cannot be left to Lebanese courts. Therefore, an international tribunal appears to offer the only chance to indict and prosecute those who are guilty of having killed ex-PM Hariri. The very fact that no permanent member of the SC has vetoed the decision to establish the Lebanon tribunal sends a strong warning to Syria, suspected of having instigated the Hariri murder.

In the debates of the SC preceding the adoption of the said resolution, several states criticized the fact that the new tribunal was imposed on Lebanon and that it infringed upon the principle of non-intervention into domestic affairs as enshrined in Article 2 (7) of the UN Charter. The proponents of the Lebanon tribunal then pointed to the relevant request by the PM of Lebanon of 13 December 2005 asking inter alia for the establishment of an international tribunal to try all those who are found responsible for this terrorist crime. The states supporting the project of the tribunal also stressed the need for the Security Council to pass this particular resolution under Chapter VII of the Charter, thus creating binding international obligations. The pre-emptive effect of the

Lebanon tribunal was also underlined by its proponents. The practical implementation of the SC resolution creating the Lebanon tribunal still raises enormous challenges indeed. It is hard to see how the various enemy factions in Lebanon will find a minimal consensus to put the tribunal on track. Without any co-operation of the main Lebanese groups, this judicial body simply will not work.

Critics of the Lebanon tribunal assert that it weakens the very idea of a universal system of criminal justice as embodied in the ICC. By establishing one international criminal court after the other (on ex-Yugoslavia, Rwanda and Lebanon), the Security Council reduces the global scheme. However, when discussing the need for the establishment of an international Lebanon tribunal, one has to bear in mind that the ICC has no competence to deal with the case of the Hariri murder.

In view of the particular circumstances of the Lebanese conflict, which in many respects presents the features of a civil war, the establishment of a special court through a UN Security Council resolution provides the sole prospect for bringing justice in a burning case. Without such outlook, the prospects for the process of reconciliation in Lebanon would look even dimmer.

6. Implementation of court decisions and orders

It goes without saying that the impact of judicial decisions varies to the degree to which they are heeded by the parties. The very concept of international jurisdiction would be undermined if the judgements of the courts were ignored by the parties to the dispute. If court decisions were systematically disregarded by the contestant parties, the conclusion would be that adjudication and arbitration had no significant influence on conflict resolution. However, the conduct of the international actors shows that, generally speaking, court decisions and arbitral awards are not ignored. There may be some cases of disregard for court decisions but these are the exceptions rather than the rule. This state of affairs underlines the important role of adjudication and arbitration in the international system.

Various mechanisms exist to ensure that the parties fulfil the obligations deriving from the judicial decision in question.

A particularly effective leverage to persuade the parties to comply with court decisions is provided by Article 171 of the Treaty on the European Community. In cases of non-compliance of a judgement by a member state, this provision enables the European Court of Justice to impose a penalty. Within the framework of the European Convention on Human Rights, the Committee of Ministers of the Council of Europe is given the authority to supervise the execution of the judgements of the European Court of Human Rights and may take appropriate action in cases of non-compliance. In the UN context, reference was already made to Article 94 of the Charter which enjoins member states of the UN to comply with the decisions of the ICJ in any case to which they are a party. In case of non-compliance of any party with the obligations incumbent upon it under a judgement, the other party may have recourse to the Security Council, which may, if it deems necessary, make recommendations or decide upon measures to be taken to give effect to the judgement.

Although the stick of sanctions is seldom used to enforce the implementations of international court decisions, its existence alone puts pressure on the parties to act in compliance with the relevant obligations. The fact that the competence of international courts to institute proceedings in a particular case requires the prior consent of the parties concerned also means that they have accepted the possibility that they may lose a case and that they are obliged to honour the stipulations of the judgement in cases to which they are a party. This way, the acceptance of international jurisdiction exerts a 'civilizing' influence on the conduct of international actors in the sense that they have to reckon with the possibility of losing a case and to bear the negative consequences thereof.

The prospect of losing, together with the obligation to heed a possibly irksome judgement, constitutes in itself an important factor in framing the behavior of international actors. States are thereby induced to act in compliance with international law, otherwise they run the risk of being sued before the court whose jurisdiction they have accepted. Once the court judgement is pronounced, the parties are obliged to implement it faithfully. Otherwise, they would expose themselves to international criticism for being in breach of international law on the substance of the case and for not complying with the relevant court decision.

Furthermore, they would face the negative consequences of the sanction mechanisms whenever they apply.

NOTES

1 The International Military Tribunal for the Far East convened on 3 May, 1946 and adjourned on 12 November, 1948.

2 The Nuremberg Trials are a series of trials that were held from 1945 to 1949. The best known trial is the Trial of the Major War Criminal before the International Military Tribunal, which was held from 20 November 1945 until the 1 October, 1946.

3 The ICJ as the successor of the PCIJ is the principal judicial organ of the United Nations: see also the UN Charter, Arts 92–96 and www.icj-cij.org/pcij/index.php?p1=9

4 The International Criminal Tribunal for the former Yugoslavia was established by Resolution 827 of the United Nations Security Council adopted on 25 May, 1993.

5 The International Criminal Tribunal for Rwanda was created on 8 November, 1994 by the United Nations Security Council and is located in Arusha, Tanzania.

6 The European Court of Human Rights was established as a permanent court on 1 November, 1998 and is located in Strasbourg.

7 See curia.europa.eu/en/instit/presentationfr/index_tpi.htm

8 Moore, History and Digest of the International Arbitrations to which the United States has been a party (I. Bd, 1898, 495).

9 See www.pca-cpa.org/

10 Establishing the United Nations Commission on International Trade Law was formally decided with the Resolution 2205 by the General Assembly on 17 December, 1966. It was designed as a body of member and observer states under the auspices of the United Nations.

11 The International Centre for the Settlement of Investment Disputes was founded as an institution of the World Bank Group in 1966.

12 Helms-Burton Act, Pub.L. 104–114, 110 Stat. 785, 22 U.S.C.§ 6021–6091, See also: www.law.cornell.edu/uscode/html/uscode22/usc_sec_22_00006021—-000-.html

13 Legality of the Threat or Use of Nuclear Weapons. ICJ Reports 1996, Advisory Opinion, Dispositive Paragraph 2E.

14 The Special Tribunal for Lebanon was proposed and approved by the United Nations and was established on 30 May, 2007 as an International Criminal Court. See also the United Nations Security Council Resolution 1757 (2007).

REFERENCES

Berridge, G. R. (ed.) (2005) Diplomacy: Theory & Practice, 3rd edn, Palgrave, Basingstoke.

Kennedy, Tom (2006) The European Court of Justice. In: Peterson, John and Shackleton, Michael (eds). The Institutions of the European Union. Oxford University Press. p. 125.

Merrills, J. G. (2005) International Dispute Settlement, 4th edn.

Rosenne, S. (2006) The Law and Practice of the International Court 1920–2005, Vols. I-IV, 5th edn.

Satow, Sir Ernest (1917) A Guide to Diplomatic Practice. Longmans, Green & Co., London & New York.

Simma, Bruno (ed.) (2002) The Charter of the United Nations: A Commentary. 2nd edn.

Touval and Zartman, W. (eds) (1985) International Mediation in Theory and Practice. United Nations Codification Division. 1992 Handbook on the peaceful settlement of disputes between states.

Triffterer, O. (1999) Commentary on the Rome Statute of the International Criminal Court.

Wendt, Alexander (1999) Social Theory of International Politics. Cambridge.

Zimmermann, Andreas, Tomuschat, Christian and Oellers-Frahm, Karin (eds) (2006) The Statute of the International Court of Justice: A Commentary. Oxford.

CASES CITED

Legality of the Threat or Use of Nuclear Weapons. (Advisory Opinion), 1996 ICJ 226.

Nicaragua: Military and Paramilitary Activities in and against Nicaragua (Nicaragua v. United States of America), 1984 ICJ 392.

Please note: all conventions and legislation cited are available on the internet.

19

Dialogue as a Process for Transforming Relationships

Harold H. Saunders

Focusing on dialogue's role in conflict resolution, I begin with three propositions as elaborated on in the following text.

First, dialogue is a distinctive way of communicating that is the essence of relationship. It is a broadly applicable, probing way of talking – and listening – different in its emphasis from negotiation, mediation, debate, legal argument, diplomatic exchange, declaiming, or normal conversation. It can be important to most instruments of conflict resolution, but it is not automatically so. In a variety of social, political, and economic situations, it can make interaction more constructive, but it requires moving to a deeper level of interaction. Given the many cultures where political, social, and economic exchanges are habitually confrontational and divisive, aspiring to a "culture of dialogue" – a different way of relating – would be a contribution of incalculable value to the peaceful resolution of difference, to productive lives, and to democratic practice. Dialogue as a distinct way of communicating is worthy of study, teaching, and practice in its own right, but to stop there would be to overlook its full value in the resolution of conflict.

Second, when sustained, practiced as a rigorous, carefully designed *process*, and placed in the context of deep-rooted conflict, dialogue can become a systematic instrument for transforming conflictual, dysfunctional, or destructive relationships. It enables participants to surface causes of problems, issues, and suppressed or violent conflict so they can be dealt with collaboratively. Sometimes citizens will generate their own dialogue to address conflict themselves; in other situations, such dialogue may pave the way for instruments such as mediation or negotiation. We have called dialogue as a process "sustained dialogue" to distinguish it as a process for conflict resolution from the basic way of communicating, which it incorporates. Its defining characteristic is not just that it is sustained over time but that it primarily and systematically focuses on the relationships that cause particular problems and conflicts.

There is no clear line between dialogue as communication and dialogue as process.

The first is essential to the second, but the second has characteristics of its own. If there is any way of distinguishing between them, it probably lies in the nature and depth of the conflict being addressed and in the appropriateness of the instrument for dealing with it. Some groups, even when holding sharply different views, are able to talk or negotiate with each other – or they can be helped to communicate more productively. In deep-rooted conflict, historic grievances, anger, and bitterness can be so deep that parties often cannot talk civilly or constructively with their adversary – much less listen seriously to others' different views of the conflict. There is initially no capacity for empathy. As a South African said, "Until people discharge their anger, they can't think straight." In such deep-rooted conflict, a *process* of dialogue can play a critical role in breaking stalemates and moving conflict toward resolution.

Third, using dialogue fully as a process for transforming relationship and legitimizing it as an instrument for conflict resolution requires a shift in the paradigm for the study and practice of politics. That is a shift from primary focus on states, governments, and political institutions and on power as coercion and control to focus, in addition, on citizens outside government as political actors and on power as the capacity to influence – not control – the course of events. It is a shift from what has been called the "realist paradigm" or "politics is about power" to what is being called the "relational paradigm."

It is essential to note at this early point that cultures around the world have their own rich traditions and practices of dialogue. Perhaps we in the West are more in need of help in recovering our traditions of dialogue than those in Africa, in the East, or in our own indigenous cultures. A prominent US scholar has described American culture as "the argument culture" much in need of dialogue as the antidote (Tannen, 1998). Even in cultures with a strong tradition of dialogue, the practice of politics can be vicious and unproductive. Although I write as a US citizen, I hope those

in other traditions may join in a dialogue about dialogue.

Two points, then, are inherent in the concept of dialogue as an instrument in conflict resolution: (1) Dialogue most obviously differs as a way of talking and listening from negotiation, mediation, debate, legal argument, and everyday conversation. Dialogue as a way of communicating – a way of relating – is a skill and an art worthy of analysis and teaching in its own right; (2) Less obviously, dialogue sustained over time and rigorously practiced as a process offers a deepening spiral of opportunities to probe, analyze, and even transform relationships in fundamental ways. When sustained, it can be conceptualized and taught as a carefully defined process for transforming conflictual relationships. The first point is broadly accepted and taught. The second is more slowly but steadily gaining recognition.

DIALOGUE: A DIFFERENT MODE OF COMMUNICATING AND RELATING

What is dialogue? Hear the voices of those who have been prominent in addressing that question.

William Isaacs, lecturer at the Sloan School of Management at the Massachusetts Institute of Technology and president of DIAlogos, a consulting and leadership education firm, says in his book *Dialogue and the Art of Thinking Together* – an "approach to communicating in business and in life":

> Writing a book about dialogue is in some respects a contradiction in terms. *Dialogue*, as I define it here, is about a shared inquiry, a way of thinking and reflecting together. It is not something you do *to* another person. It is something you do *with* people. Indeed, a large part of learning this has to do with learning to shift your attitudes about relationships with others, so that we gradually give up the effort to make them understand us, and come to a greater understanding of ourselves and each other (Isaacs, 1999: 9).

Daniel Yankelovich, one of the leading analysts of how citizens come to public judgment in the United States, says in *The Magic of Dialogue:*

In philosopher Martin Buber's classic work *I and Thou*, Buber suggests that in authentic dialogue something far deeper than ordinary conversation goes on. The I-Thou interaction implies a genuine openness of each to the concerns of the other. In such dialogue, "I" do not, while talking with you, selectively tune out views with which I disagree, nor do I busy myself marshaling arguments to rebut you while only half attending to what you have to say, nor do I seek to reinforce my own prejudices. Instead, I fully 'take in' your viewpoint, engaging with it in the deepest sense of the term. You do likewise. Each of us internalizes the views of the other to enhance our mutual understanding.

To Buber we owe the stunning insight that, apart from its obvious practical value (most problem solving demands mutual understanding), dialogue expresses an essential aspect of the human spirit. Buber knew that dialogue is a way of being. … In dialogue, we penetrate behind the polite superficialities and defenses in which we habitually armor ourselves. We listen and respond to one another with an authenticity that forges a bond between us.

In this sense, dialogue is a process of successful relationship building (Yankelovich, 1999: 14–15).

David Bohm, a British physicist and philosopher, who late in life turned his attention to the role of dialogue in human relationships, defines dialogue by contrasting it with other ways of talking:

Contrast dialogue with the word 'discussion' which has the same root as 'percussion' and 'concussion.' It really means to break things up. It emphasizes the idea of analysis, where there may be many points of view, and where everybody is presenting a different one—analyzing and breaking up. Discussion is almost like a ping-pong game, where people are batting the ideas back and forth and the object of the game is to win or to get points for yourself (Bohm, 1996: 6–7).

In dialogue, by contrast, minds open to take in new ideas and perspectives, modify earlier assumptions, and rethink judgments. Again, David Bohm says:

… consider a dialogue…when one person says something, the other person does not in general respond with exactly the same meaning as that seen by the first person. Rather, the meanings are only

similar and not identical. Thus, when the second person replies, the first person sees a *difference* between what he meant to say and what the other person understood. On considering this difference, he may then be able to see something new, which is relevant both to his own views and to those of the other person. And so it can go back and forth, with the continual emergence of a new content that is common to both participants. Thus in a dialogue, each person does not attempt to *make common* certain ideas or items of information that are already known to him. Rather, it may be said that the two people are making something *in common,* i.e. creating something new together (Bohm, 1996: 2).

Harold Saunders in *A Public Peace Process: Sustained Dialogue to Transform Racial and Ethnic Conflicts* writes:

Dialogue is a process of genuine *interaction* through which human beings listen to each other deeply enough to be changed by what they learn. Each makes a serious effort to take others' concerns into her or his own picture even when disagreement persists. No participant gives up her or his identity, but each recognizes enough of the other's valid human claims that he or she will act differently toward the other (Saunders, 1999: 82).

In debate, one's purpose is to make one's viewpoint prevail, so one listens to other positions only to identify shortcomings in the argument so as to attack them. In dialogue, one's purpose is quite different – to listen to others' views while suspending judgment, recognizing that others' views may deepen one's own thinking and that two sides together may move more deeply toward common ground. Debate entrenches narrow views while dialogue opens minds to new and better approaches.

The aim of negotiation and mediation is a formal, written agreement. The objective of dialogue is a changed relationship. "The currency of negotiation is defining and satisfying material interests through specific jointly agreed arrangements. The outcome of dialogue is to create new human and political capacities to solve problems. Negotiation requires parties who are ready to reach agreement. Dialogue can be made fruitful by involving parties who are not yet ready for negotiation but do not want a destructive relationship to continue. Negotiation deals with goods that can be divided, shared, or defined in tangible ways. Dialogue may change relationships in ways that create new grounds for mutual respect and collaboration" (Saunders, 1999: 85).

Useful handbooks are written and training workshops conducted to convey the philosophy, the art, and the practice of dialogue in communities. One such is *The Little Book of Dialogue for Difficult Subjects* by David Campt and Lisa Schirch, one of a series of short books on various aspects of conflict transformation published by the Center for Justice and Peacebuilding at Eastern Mennonite University (Schirch and Campt, 2007).

They address the role of dialogue organizer, dialogue designer, and dialogue facilitator. They treat the importance of presenting the purpose of a dialogue in a way that makes it relevant to the community; the need to recruit diverse participants so that all significant facets of a problem will be introduced into the dialogue; and the value of thinking through in advance how to create not just a physical space but a relational space in which participants will feel safe in opening up their deeper feelings. They stress the need to establish ground rules to govern interactions in the dialogue; to design opening questions that will decrease anxiety among participants as they introduce themselves and enhance the sense that this is a space where all will be fairly heard – both majority and minority or both sides of a conflict; to design follow-up questions to encourage sharing of experiences and perceptions and to explore differences and commonalities; and eventually perhaps to explore possible action once relationships have begun to change through the dialogue. "Building relationships across lines of division and increasing understanding of a situation can help people see what needs to be done to address the issue and find ways to work together" (Schirch and Campt, 2007: 55). They also devote a chapter to key tasks of the facilitator in pressing participants to deeper and deeper levels of probing the meaning of interactions. They outline the

phases through which a dialogue process might evolve.

The differences between uses and users of dialogue reflect how deeply they need or choose to go in dealing with the problem or conflict they face. They reflect the nature of the conflict faced. One user may need to go no further than to help a group faced with a divisive issue to step back, get angry thoughts off their chests, recover mutual respect, and gain some perspective and composure so they can talk through the issue in a calmer and more constructive way. Another user may be faced with groups who harbor decades if not centuries of anger, pain, and grievance toward each other, have been killing each other, have occupied the other's land, have desecrated historic and personal shrines or monuments. Still another may face people who do not act violently toward each other but who are nevertheless so deeply alienated from one another that, though they may work together in mutual civility within formal structures, deeply rooted resentment, even anger or hatred, blocks willing collaboration outside formal social or economic structures that require it.

While distinctions between the two users will inevitably blur, it seems fair to say that somewhere along the path, some users cross a vague line. On the near side of the line, the user is primarily working among people who can talk reasonably together to improve communication in ways that will reduce tension and enable the parties to perform necessary tasks together. This might or might not be called conflict resolution. On the farther side of the line, the user will find people in such deeply conflictual relationships that they are barely able to look at each other, much less talk together constructively or at least people who viscerally resent and mistrust each other. They will be able to do so only when they clear their minds of anger and learn to listen to each other with some empathy – a capacity that may take a long time, patience, and work to develop.

In the first case, the challenge is to improve the quality of communication. In the second, the challenge is to begin transforming relationships that are the cause of destructively suppressed or openly deadly conflict. More subtly in the second case, a conflict may not be so obvious on the surface, but it is intense and deep-rooted enough to block genuine collaboration even though a civil veneer may hide seething feelings underneath.

The latter case may be exemplified by race relations in many communities in the United States where citizens of different racial and ethnic backgrounds work together each day, but each night they go home to their own neighborhoods, social groups, and cultures and rarely interact. They may be exemplified by racial, ethnic, or religious differences that separate people in regions all over the world. As the leader of a US organization formed in the 1970s said in the early 1990s: "Our organization was formed in the 1970s to improve race relations in this [southern] city. We have worked together and have done a lot of good work to improve interactions in this community. But underneath, I'm not sure how much fundamental relations have changed. I guess we have pursued a strategy of, 'Do it but don't talk about it'."

What distinguishes dialogue as a process for conflict resolution is the space and encouragement it provides to talk deeply over time about dangerously divisive elements in a relationship. These elements may be carefully hidden in order to permit civil relations without removing deeply embedded grievance that blocks willing collaboration, or they may lead to open violence.

However deeply the user may feel the need to go in probing the roots of conflict, whether subterranean or violent, it is important to recognize the profound philosophical bond between dialogue and relationship.

A systematic, intentional effort to transform relationship is a significant factor in defining a dialogue process as an instrument in conflict resolution. Dialogue itself is at the heart of relationship. As Martin Buber has told us, dialogue is the medium through which relationship is experienced. Dialogue creates a common body of knowledge – not only knowledge of *what* the other thinks but of

why the other thinks that way. To quote Bohm again:

> [We] realize what is on each other's minds without coming to any conclusions or judgments.... We...weigh...the question a little, ponder it a little, feel it out.... If we can see what all of our opinions mean, then we are sharing a common content, even if we don't agree entirely.... Accordingly, a different kind of consciousness is possible among us, a *participatory* consciousness.... We would be taking part and communicating and creating a common meaning.... Society is based on shared meanings, which constitute the culture (1996: 20–21, 26, 28).

In dialogue, thought and communication are often at the tacit level; fundamental change will come at that level.

A CONCEPT OF RELATIONSHIP

If one claims that dialogue as a process to change relationships fundamentally is distinguished from other instruments of conflict resolution by its focus on relationship rather than focusing primarily on problem-solving, one needs to be precise in defining relationship. For working purposes, a concept of relationship was conceptualized from experience in a sustained dialogue in the 1980s (Voorhees, 2002). This concept holds that one can understand relationship as comprising five components:

1. *identity* – both the familiar physical characteristics and the life experience that has brought a person to the current moment.
2. *interests* – both the tangible interests that a person may pursue and the less tangible concerns that capture what a person really cares about.
3. *power* – defined not only in the traditional way as coercion and control but more broadly as the shared capacity to influence the course of events.
4. *perceptions* and misperceptions—stereotypes.
5. *patterns of interaction* that characterize how parties habitually deal with each other.

The mix of these elements is continuously changing within each individual or group and between individuals and groups (Saunders, 1999: 33–44; 2005: 60–81).

This concept can be both an analytical and an operational tool. One can observe two or more parties interacting – either in a life situation or in dialogue – and develop a picture of the dynamics of their relationships by sorting and analyzing observations under these headings. Beyond that, it is also an operational tool. It is possible to get inside each of the components of relationship through dialogue and change it. For instance, one's core identity is not likely to change, but our identities grow every day through experience, and seeing ourselves through others' eyes can cause our identities to develop. Antagonists can find common interests. Individuals can find that they need each other in order to achieve their interests – a recognition of the limits of their own power. Stereotypes can change through unfolding contacts. Patterns of interaction can change through interaction itself.

I would posit that it is working with such a concept of relationship that (1) gives rigor and substance to dialogue as a defined conflict resolution process for dealing with deeply hostile and dysfunctional interactions and (2) distinguishes dialogue as a change process over time from the valuable uses of dialogue in more malleable situations.

THE GENESIS: DIALOGUE IN CONFLICT RESOLUTION

Placing the origins of dialogue as an instrument of conflict resolution in both of its modes – as communication and as a process to transform relationships – in historical context can enrich our understanding of this complex instrument. It can illuminate its many facets and uses.

To begin, we need to recall the steady proliferation of "protracted conflict between identity groups" (Fisher, 1997: xi) that characterized the accelerating decline and termination of colonial empires after World War II, especially in the 1960s. As these conflicts began to replace the great state-to-state conflicts of previous eras, old ways of defining and dealing with conflict

proved inadequate. Practitioners began experimenting with innovative approaches. The work of two pioneers set the stage.

John Burton left a distinguished career as a senior Australian diplomat and, in the early 1960s, assumed leadership of a department of international relations in the Faculty of Laws at University College London. As Ronald Fisher records in his path-breaking 1997 analysis of the field, *Interactive Conflict Resolution,* from an unpublished introspection by Burton: "His diplomatic experience had convinced him of the need for an alternative to the power approach that dominated international affairs" in the mid-1960s. "… his unconventional thinking about international relations was at odds with the prevalent, traditional perspectives of most of the academic leaders in the field. The traditional approach … emphasized interactions among sovereign states who pursue their national interests by exercising economic and military power through the formation of alliances, the use of deterrence, and at times, adherence to international law. Security is attained through the threat or use of force, and inevitable conflict is managed through compromise or suppression. Burton was developing his thinking toward a new 'pluralist' paradigm – *the world security perspective* – which emphasized the values and relationships of multiple actors in the global system" (Fisher, 1997: 22–29).

Burton was challenged by traditional scholars to demonstrate that his way of thinking could make a difference. Calling on his former diplomatic relationships and with the permission of the British prime minister, he invited to London for "academic talks" about their conflict representatives of all sides of a violent conflict that had erupted around establishment of a Malaysian confederation which the British had formed as they withdrew from colonial status. Six meetings were held over seven months, beginning in December 1965.

The meetings began with each participant sharing his view of the conflict and with an academic panel offering their analyses.

The meetings proceeded with no formal agenda, no academic papers, and no agreed statement at the end. Through these free-flowing dialogues, participants were able to explore dimensions of the conflict that would not normally be on the agenda of negotiations – for instance, the role of minority groups in influencing policies. They were able to imagine solutions to problems that were very close to those that ultimately found their ways into a peace agreement. Burton and his colleagues felt that the unconventional dialogue demonstrated the value of the approach and of the emerging thinking about conflict behind it. To pursue this exploration, they formed the Centre for the Analysis of Conflict. They held further explorations of other conflicts, most notably Cyprus, but academic responsibilities and lack of adequate funding limited their activities in those early years.

Burton began calling this approach "controlled communication." That phrase soon gave way to "problem-solving procedure." Almost immediately, Burton emphasized that this approach was in no way intended to replace formal negotiation but rather to precede or supplement it. The phrases that would be used later to capture this role are *prenegotiation* and *circumnegotiation* (Saunders, 1996). This presentation of the approach was also used to counter early criticism that the kind of group that Burton had gathered did not necessarily have the power to shape policy – a criticism that practitioners deal with to this day (Fisher, 1997: 22–29).

One of the Americans whom Burton included in his early experimental dialogues was Herbert Kelman, professor of social ethics in the Department of Psychology at Harvard University, who committed himself to applying the knowledge of social science to the analysis and resolution of conflict. In 1971, with fellow faculty member Stephen Cohen, Kelman first used what he called a "problem-solving workshop" as part of a graduate seminar on social psychology and international relations. Over some two decades following that first experiment, Kelman developed the method of the workshop to take the form of a carefully prepared three-day workshop preceded by systematic preworkshop meetings with each group of participants. He gradually enlarged its scope to the point where participants were highly influential members of their societies. Starting more broadly with Arabs and Israelis, he later focused on specific Israeli–Palestinian meetings. Through these decades, the list of those participants became formidable, including many who later became key figures in society, in government, and in negotiating teams.

These meetings were dialogues facilitated by at least two, often more, social scientists and an occasional former diplomat. They focused on bringing to the surface underlying human issues that often blocked progress in negotiations without ever appearing on formal negotiating agendas and then on talking through possible ways of dealing with them. The workshop was simultaneously a laboratory for deepening knowledge of the causes of conflict, engaging participants in recognizing and coming to terms with them, and considering their political and diplomatic implications. For most of the first twenty years, these workshops were one-time events in the sense that participants were mostly different each time. They did not constitute a continuing *process*. At the end of the 1980s, he began a series of continuing workshops with essentially the same participants to produce papers on issues important to the negotiations.

The problem-solving workshops of Burton, Kelman, and their respective associates – among them Edward Azar, Christopher Mitchell, Nadim Rouhana – solidly established systematic dialogue around deep-rooted conflict facilitated by scholar-practitioners as a carefully defined and meticulously practiced instrument of conflict resolution. Their analysis, reflection, and writing from their experience has produced a significant body of valuable literature and has undoubtedly influenced the thinking and action of many participants who later played direct roles in policy-making and negotiation.

CONCEPTUAL INNOVATIONS

Integral to the development of this body of practice and later developments from it were three conceptual innovations. The first – broadening the definition of conflict – was explicit in Burton's work from the start. Kelman's roots in social psychology deepened and broadened it. Following from the first, the second was also articulated by Burton as he challenged the traditional paradigm in the academic study of international relations – a change still not fully accepted. The third – the concept of a continuous political process as an instrument of change in its own right – originated in the 1970s outside the academic fields of international relations and conflict resolution and has been slower to gain explicit academic recognition.

Broadening the definition of conflict

The first innovation was broadening the definition of conflict to recognize the basic human needs that may lie at the roots of conflict as well as the physical interests over which governments and groups differ, fight, and negotiate. For instance, John Burton beginning in the mid-1960s recognized that some problems and conflicts are not ready for formal negotiation. People, for instance, do not negotiate over their identity. In such cases, dialogue provided necessary space for talking around and talking through these problems to understand often unspoken causes before attempting to devise ways of dealing with a conflict. This talk often permitted participants to redefine problems in terms of unmet human needs. This approach made it important to focus on the mode of communication that came to be referred to as dialogue rather than on the familiar language and exchanges of negotiation and diplomacy because dialogue opened the door to broader exchanges that revealed the deeper human causes of conflict.

Burton, like psychologist A. H. Maslow in the 1940s, referred to basic human needs such as physiological (food), safety, love, affection, belongingness, self-respect and the esteem of others that grows from capacity and achievement, and self-actualization (self-fulfillment). As a former diplomat turned scholar, Burton brought attention to those needs in contrast to the exclusive focus of scholars in international relations on material interests as causes of conflict (Saunders, 2005: 6).

Burton distinguished what he came to call *deep-rooted conflicts* from disputes over tangible interests that could be negotiated or differences that could be talked through. He later firmly insisted that *conflict resolution* refer to the former and *dispute settlement* to the latter (Burton, 1987, 1990a, 1990b). Edward Azar used the phrase *protracted social conflict* to denote mostly intra-state conflicts, the primary sources of which lay in denial of basic human needs, assaults on identity, and social injustice (Azar, 1983).

"It follows," observes Ronald Fisher in his 1997 book on this early experimental thinking, "that the central unit of analysis in protracted social conflict is the *identity group*, defined in ethnic, racial, religious, linguistic, or other terms, for it is through the identity group that compelling human needs are expressed in social and often political terms ... conflicts arise when identity groups perceive that they are oppressed and victimized through a denial of recognition, security, equity, and political participation" (Fisher, 1997: 5).

Broadening the political paradigm

The second conceptual development followed from the first – a refocusing of the paradigm for the study and practice of international relations. As the definition of conflict was enlarged to deal with its human dimensions, it became apparent to some practitioners that a state-centered or a government-centered paradigm for the study and practice of politics was not large enough to include dialogue among citizens outside government as a serious instrument of conflict resolution.

As I have noted earlier, John Burton as a former senior Australian diplomat recognized that the traditional paradigm for the analysis and conduct of international relations was no longer large enough to take account of the broadening range of conflicts. He proposed what he called the "pluralist paradigm." The point was simply that conflict was no longer primarily an affair of governments – that it engaged people at all levels of society. This was apparent in his first workshop on the conflict surrounding Malaysia, in which guerrilla movements played a significant role. Much later in the 1990s when the lid of Soviet control was removed from so many situations, we came to speak colloquially of "ethnic" conflict, usually referring to violent intra-state conflicts in which a minority group challenged government, or such groups fought each other in conflicts that were beyond the reach of governments and, often, the conventional instruments of conflict resolution. Ultimately, those conflicts gave birth to the concept of the "failed state."

Articulation of a new paradigm in the United States came later, perhaps because most of the early innovative work in dialogue as conflict resolution was based in disciplines related to social psychology and psychoanalysis rather than to international relations. Significant academic work in international relations beginning in the 1970s recognized the proliferation of nonstate actors such as multinational corporations (Keohane and Nye, 1977) and the increasing permeability of international borders (Brown, 1972). Only when Harold Saunders became involved in nonofficial dialogue in the 1980s – like Burton bringing diplomatic experience to this work – did a practitioner in dialogue feel the importance of a paradigm shift in international relations. "Having worked for five US presidents and with other world leaders," he says, "I was convinced that the conceptual lenses that a leader or a citizen uses to give meaning to events will determine how he or she acts. The only lasting way to change fundamental policy and behavior is to change those conceptual lenses" (Saunders, 1999: xv). His experience in the Arab–Israeli peace process of the 1970s led him eventually to his "relational paradigm," positing "a cumulative, multilevel, open-ended process of continuous interaction engaging significant clusters of citizens in and out of government and the relationships they form to solve public problems in whole bodies politic across permeable borders" (Saunders, 2005: 7–8). It was increasingly recognized that conflict must often be dealt with at different levels of society where needs went unmet and that such a challenge could only be met by innovative instruments.

A continuous political process

The third conceptual innovation was the idea of a continuous political process to change a political environment or to transform relationships – an idea that warranted attention in its own right as an instrument of change. This concept had its roots in the Arab–Israeli peace process after the 1973 Arab–Israeli War.

The US government under three presidents and three secretaries of state launched an intensive mediation lasting through six years, 1974–1979. It began by producing Egyptian–Israeli then Israeli–Syrian disengagement agreements in January and May 1974. The strategy was that a sequence of cumulative agreements, each building from the last, could emerge from and contribute to a powerful political process that could change the political environment and make further agreements possible. Ultimately, after a second Egyptian–Israeli disengagement agreement – "Sinai II" – in September 1975, the fourth and fifth in this sequence were the Camp David Accords of 1978 and the Egyptian–Israeli Peace Treaty of 1979. This process was conducted through a diplomatic innovation that journalists called "shuttle diplomacy" because, at the beginning, the secretary of state and his team flew back and forth between capitals daily during a mediation, steadily putting together the elements of agreements through what we today might call a "virtual" dialogue between parties who for political reasons initially would not meet face to face.

This idea of a continuous political process began broadening thinking to include not just human needs as causes of conflict but also to ask what role they play in influencing an evolving *process of interaction* among groups in conflict and how that interaction might be changed. It has been difficult for many in the field to get their minds around the idea of focusing on the process of interaction itself – instead of focusing only on the actors – but that interaction is the essence of relationship. At the beginning of the twenty-first century, practitioners deal with relationship intuitively, but scholars in politics and international relations have not widely accepted the idea. On the other hand, it came naturally to psychoanalyst Vamik Volkan, who in the late 1970s began conducting what he called psycho-political dialogues that systematically probed the deeper needs that drive a destructive interaction. He later wrote extensively about large group identity and the process of interaction and about interventions to change those patterns of interaction.

The importance and political impact of this insight was dramatized by Egyptian President Anwar al-Sadat's dramatic visit to Jerusalem in November 1977. Declaring that "a psychological barrier" between Egyptians and Israelis "constitut[ed] 70 per cent of the whole problem" (Sadat, 1991), Sadat through a political act transformed the political environment by addressing the historically rooted Jewish feeling of exclusion and the perception that no Arab country would accept Israel as a state in the Middle East. At that moment, the negotiating position he presented was not acceptable to the Israeli government. The change in public perception of the possibility of peace, however, opened the door in the ongoing political process to a change in relationship that permitted negotiation of the Egyptian–Israeli peace treaty. Conceptually, it dramatized that the nature of the overall relationship – the process of interaction itself – is worthy of analysis in its own right.

In fact, that insight is embedded in the phrase "peace process" itself. Those flying on the diplomatic "shuttle" missions of Secretary of State Henry Kissinger in early 1974 began calling what they were doing the "negotiating process" because they were intent on building momentum by mediating one agreement on top of another in a cumulative process. When they realized that each agreement was changing the political environment by enhancing a sense of the possibility of peace in the minds of people, they began using the term "peace process" to capture the multilevel character of the change that was taking place. In each case, the idea of a cumulative, open-ended continuous process was the instrument of change.

Three lessons emerged for those involved in the peace process: first was the power of a continuous political process to change relationships; second was the importance of the human dimension of conflict; and third was the recognition of the multilevel character of deep-rooted human conflict between bodies politic – the way it permeated life at all levels of a body politic and the fact that it shaped the identities of the conflicting parties. Nothing could have underscored these points more vividly than President Sadat's visit to Jerusalem.

The next laboratory that contributed to the idea of dialogue as a process rather than as a workshop or a meeting was the Regional Conflicts Task Force of the Dartmouth Conference – the longest continuous bilateral series of meetings between American and Soviet citizens, which had begun in 1960. In 1981 at the thirteenth plenary, the Conference leadership decided to establish two task forces to meet between plenaries to probe the question: what happened to *détente* – the intensive diplomatic effort in the 1970s to improve the Soviet–US relationship? Harold Saunders, who had by then left government, was asked to be the US co-chair of the task force to study Soviet–US interactions in regional conflicts – those conflicts in which the superpowers competed through proxies. Evgeny Primakov – later foreign minister and then prime minister of the new Russia after 1991 – was the Soviet cochair.

Meeting every six months throughout the 1980s, they learned that bringing the same group back together at semiannual intervals created four opportunities: (1) They were able to create a cumulative agenda with questions left unanswered at the end of one meeting forming the agenda for the next. (2) They developed a common body of knowledge. It was not just knowledge of the other's formal positions but an understanding of why those positions were important – what needs they met. (3) They learned to talk analytically together rather than polemically. (4) Later, in 1992–1993, they learned to work together.

By 1991, looking back over 18 meetings, it was possible to discern a pattern through which dialogue evolved when more or less the same participants came back together repeatedly. Saunders began writing about a staged process. In 1993, he and the Russian cochair of the Regional Conflicts Task Force – Gennady Chufrin, who had succeeded Primakov in 1989 – first published a description of Sustained Dialogue as a five-stage process (Chufrin and Saunders, 1993). Eventually, those five stages took the following shape:

Stage One, "Deciding to Engage": the period when initiators begin a "dialogue about dialogue" or citizens talk among themselves about a serious problem and ultimately decide to take the risk of talking with the adversary.

Stage Two, "Mapping and Naming Problems and Relationships": when participants and their moderators first sit together, they will engage in a period – perhaps lasting over several meetings – in which they will vent their grievances, their anger, their positions, their perspectives. Though often a disorderly exchange, it is important for the participants to be heard and for the moderators to begin getting a sense of the dynamics of the relationships involved. This stage ends when dialogue participants come together around a problem that they feel they must work on together. At this point, the quality of the talk changes palpably from talking *at* each other to talking *with* each other about a problem they agree affects them all.

Stage Three, "Probing Problems and Relationships to Choose a Direction": the moderators' style will shift from permissiveness to be sure everyone is fully heard to a somewhat more directive approach to help the group focus their analysis and probe beneath the surface

for the problems and relationships behind the problems. Participants will inevitably begin talking about what they might do to deal with the problem and deliberating among possible approaches. They identify ways of entering conflictual relationships to change them. At some point – again, perhaps, after a prolonged period which may include time between meetings when they reflect and talk with others – they will reach not a detailed plan of action but a sense of direction in which they might consider moving.

Stage Four, "Scenario Building – Experiencing a Changing Relationship": participants have identified the relationships that must be changed to address the real causes of the conflict. Now they begin to consider what steps can accomplish that purpose, who can take those steps, and how the actors can move in a complex of mutually reinforcing interactive steps that can build momentum around a multilevel process of change. They list the main obstacles to change, remembering that these can be feelings as well as practical factors; list steps to overcome each obstacle; list who can take those steps. Finally, they arrange steps and actors so they reinforce each other, draw in new actors, and build momentum.

Stage Five, "Acting Together to Make Change Happen": once participants have developed a tentative scenario of actions, they must decide whether and how to take that scenario into the larger community to engage others (Saunders, 1999: Chap. 6).

In laying out the five-stage process, the authors underscored that they were not proposing a linear process but rather a progression of experiences in which the tasks gradually evolved. It was expected that participants' minds would wash back and forth over the stages as they rethought earlier judgments in light of new interactions, revisited premises in light of new insights, or tackled new aspects of a problem. This was also seen as a framework flexible enough to be adapted to different cultural traditions and problems.

The first test of the newly conceptualized five-stage process began in March 1993 when three Americans and three Russians from the Dartmouth Conference Regional Conflicts

Task Force began a dialogue process at the height of the civil war that had broken out after independence in the former Soviet republic of Tajikistan. Participants represented most of the principal factions in the civil war. Five meetings were held in 1993, six in 1994, six in 1995 and 36 in all by the tenth anniversary in 2003. That experience not only tested successfully the usefulness of the five-stage conceptualization but also demonstrated that conceptualization of the dialogue process made possible its transfer from one conflict to another.

DISTINCTIONS: SUSTAINED DIALOGUE'S NICHE

Distinctions among approaches within the larger field of conflict resolution and especially within this subfield of interactive conflict resolution are difficult to draw sharply because each approach includes elements of others in almost infinite variations and emphases. Nevertheless, it seems necessary to venture some thoughts, at least for the sake of sharpening our thinking about what each of us is doing and where we are going.

We have said that dialogue as a sustained process for transforming conflictual relationships occupies a niche distinguished by (1) its primary focus on relationships that cause conflict rather than mainly on issues that can be negotiated or talked through; (2) its working within a carefully defined concept of relationship; and (3) an unfolding process that creates space for participants to spend time probing, then gradually developing their relationships, and perhaps even moving together toward reinforcing actions.

A more subtle distinction needs to be mentioned for further thought. How a third party in dialogue plays its role should reflect the spirit of dialogue. Again, the lines between approaches cannot be sharply defined, but some distinctions can be suggested.

Idealistically, one might argue that there should be no third party since dialogue is an intensely interpersonal experience. In fact, in the Dartmouth Conference and the Kettering Foundation's USA–China Dialogue, there has been no third party. The comoderators – one from each side – choose the participants, agree on the approach, derive the agenda from experience in the dialogue, and chair the meetings. Evgeny Primakov, Soviet co-chair of the Dartmouth Conference Regional Conflicts Task Force stated the principle of a cumulative agenda when he said, "We will start the next meeting where this one ended." Questions left unanswered at the end of one meeting could be pondered between meetings and form the agenda for the next. The agenda emerged primarily from the dialogue, sometimes with moderators sharpening the focus.

Realistically, we recognize that a third party is more often than not needed in hot conflicts to create the space for dialogue and to provide a substantive and procedural framework within which the dialogue takes place. Exactly how the third party plays that role, however, opens the door to nuances of difference. It is worth considering this additional question: Where in the dialogue process is the dynamic of interaction centered?

At one end of a spectrum are groups – such as many problem-solving workshops – in which the agenda grows out of the facilitating team's experience, and the facilitation pursues that agenda pretty much along lines it determines, obviously adapting in response to developments in the meetings.

At the other end of the spectrum are dialogues – such as the sustained dialogues – in which moderating teams attempt to create a space where participants from conflicting parties are treated in a way designed to encourage generation of the agenda for their dialogue out of their own interactions. The second stage of the sustained dialogue process is explicitly designed to get out into the open the deeper dynamics of relationships between participants before the parties even address practical issues systematically. This interaction explicitly allows for the discharge of anger and grievance: (1) to clear minds for more analytical talk and (2) to surface the underlying elements of relationships.

The philosophy behind this second approach was reflected in the statement of purpose from within the Dartmouth Conference Regional Conflicts Task Force as it began the Inter-Tajik Dialogue. In essence, we said: We will not attempt to mediate an agreement among the multiple parties in the civil war. Our purpose is to create a space in which to *see whether* a group can form within the dynamics of the civil war that can learn to design a peace process for their own country. The agenda will be generated – and therefore owned – by participants in the dialogue. It is they who understand most fully the dynamics of their conflict and must learn how to engage them in the interest of peace.

This distinction between dialogue directed by facilitators and dialogue generated primarily by participants in a space created either by themselves or by a third party is an important one.

Finally, because in the United States, "dialogue and deliberation" are increasingly linked, a word needs to be said about the distinctions and similarities between them. Dialogue, as we have said, is a way of communicating, listening, and relating that can be the essence of constructive relationship. Although deliberation may well build on dialogic communication, it is particularly a way of deciding. Those deliberating will define a problem, frame their choices for dealing with the problem, and then weigh the potential positive and negative consequences of each approach on the path toward setting a direction for dealing with the problem.

Whereas sustained dialogue is appropriate in situations where conflictual or dysfunctional relationships prevent collaboration, deliberation is for situations in which involved people from most backgrounds and viewpoints are able to talk productively. In a sustained dialogue, participants will be talking more deliberatively when they settle down to more analytical talk in the third stage of dialogue, but their focus will still differ in that their interest will fall on changing the relationships that cause the problems rather than primarily on technical solutions.

A SUMMARY REFLECTION ON THE FORMATIVE PERIOD

Looking back on this period when the foundations for dialogue as a process for conflict transformation were laid, Ronald Fisher in his 1996 study of this new field summarized: "The past thirty years have seen the development and proliferation of small-group discussion methods for analyzing social conflict and creating alternative directions toward management and resolution." He continued:

> I have recently identified this scholarly and professional field as *interactive conflict resolution* to emphasize that effective and constructive face-to-face interaction among representatives of the parties themselves is required to understand and resolve complex intercommunal and international conflicts. In a focused manner, interactive conflict resolution (ICR) is defined as involving small-group, problem-solving discussions between unofficial representatives of identity groups or states engaged in destructive conflict that are facilitated by an impartial third party of social scientist-practitioners.
>
> … The method also takes a social psychological approach by asserting that relationship issues (misperceptions, unmet basic needs, and so on) must be addressed and that the conflict will be resolved only by mutually acceptable solutions that are developed through joint interaction. … 'Conflict resolution' therefore is not seen as a single or time-limited outcome, but as a complex process of de-escalation and reconciliation that develops over time to the point where new qualities and mechanisms exist in the relationship to allow for the constructive resolution of disputes (Fisher, 1997: 7–8).

JUDGING ACHIEVEMENTS AND LIMITS

Judging a process of dialogue to transform relationship must start with a framework for analyzing how change takes place. For this author, that framework is the multilevel peace process, recognizing the continuous *inter*action among four levels of a polity – government, business, a collection of boundary-spanning civil society groups, and the grass roots.

For a sustained dialogue group assembled as a microcosm of parties to a larger conflict, three questions apply: (1) Have participants in the dialogue group transformed their own relationships and learned together how that experience might be built on to influence the larger arena of conflict? (2) Have they been able to influence official peacemaking? (3) Have they contributed to preparing the larger body of citizens outside government to accept possibly painful compromises and to participate in actions that can contribute to postconflict reconciliation and peace-building?

In evaluating a process of sustained dialogue, one must start by recognizing its particular character. As Harold Saunders writes:

> Sustained Dialogue itself – like the peace process of which it is a part – is an open-ended political process. One cannot know at the beginning exactly what the dialogue will produce; the agenda, goals and specific steps must come out of the interaction of the participants. Each time the group takes a concrete step forward, new goals will emerge; achievements may become possible that were not possible before. The progression of goals and achievements can be judged only as the dialogue unfolds. So evaluation becomes part of the process (Saunders, 1999: 221).

As it happened, the initial statement of an objective for the Inter-Tajik Dialogue – to *see whether* a dialogue group can form from within a civil war that can learn to design a peace process for their conflict – was sufficiently specific yet also open-ended to leave it to participants to set their own goals as they went along. In the course of ten years, they set at least four successive goals for themselves as the situation evolved. That seemed to justify the thought that dialogue must – and can – generate its own objectives that can be assessed over time without requiring that they be stated at the outset. At the same time, it calls attention to the need for dialogue groups to be self-conscious at transitional moments about setting new goals for themselves.

In their third three-day meeting in August 1993, participants agreed (1) to work on starting a negotiation between government and opposition. Over the next seven months, they played a significant role in the decisions by government and opposition to join UN-mediated peace talks. When negotiations began in April 1994, they decided (2) not to interfere in the negotiations but to concentrate on designing a political process of national reconciliation for the people of Tajikistan. When a peace treaty was signed in June 1997, they committed themselves (3) to help make democracy work. In 2000, they registered their own nongovernmental organization, the Public Committee for Democratic Processes which (4) defined four tracks in the public arena on which they would work.

During the negotiation, three dialogue participants were members of the negotiating teams while remaining in the dialogue. Five participated in the National Reconciliation Commission – an institution created by the peace treaty to implement the treaty. At the end of many meetings, they produced a joint memorandum on an issue of current importance. Options in one of these memos provided the design for the National Reconciliation Committee.

In short, participants moved from interpersonal hostility to working constructively together. From the dialogue base, they worked in both the policy and the public arenas. One became vice foreign minister. A national dialogue reconstituted in 2006 includes officials from the president's office and leaders in business, banking, journalism, and nongovernmental organizations.

In another experience with conflict in the former Soviet Union, the Dartmouth Conference Regional Conflicts Task Force in 2001 began a dialogue among participants from Armenia, Azerbaijan, and Nagorno Karabakh. The parties to their conflict had signed a ceasefire ending a war in 1994, but post-war negotiations had stalemated. In their eleventh meeting, participants agreed on a paper called "Framework for a Peace Process." They invited American and Russian cochairs to visit their three capitals for public meetings on the "Framework," to give it visibility, but they have been unable to influence the course of official negotiations which are exclusively in the hands of the two presidents who feel constrained by strong public feelings and have done little to lead their publics toward a peace agreement and reconciliation. In short, participants in the dialogue changed, but they are confronted with a harshly unreceptive political environment.

An Arab–American–European dialogue met nine times in 2004–2007. These meetings were organized to address the conflict between the Muslim Arab countries, Western Europe, and the United States. Constructive – though sometimes bitter – dialogue deepened understanding within the group of the roots of behavior and fear on both sides of the relationship, but participants found themselves asking whether they could continue in the absence of concrete "products" or change. They faced the seeming impossibility of any one group's affecting such a complex of relationships and oppressive governments in any finite period as well as uncertainty of funding for the same reasons.

In a very different venue, students on high school and university campuses in the United States are drawn to sustained dialogue because they are deeply disturbed by self-segregation, "racialization" of student climate, or marginalization of minority groups on their campuses. In dialogue, students clearly deepen their understanding of difference and transform personal relationships, but they are frustrated in the short term by their inability to see change in their "student racial climate" or in the social structures on their campuses. Dialogue has succeeded in changing them as individuals – just as many of their courses might – and in generating many worthwhile projects but not yet in producing dramatic systemic change. The fact is, nevertheless, that they have created "public spaces" for this work where none such existed before. The questions are what will constitute a critical mass for change or when will a racial event happen that will be demonstrably handled by students from a sustained dialogue base?

Do these experiences demonstrate limitations of dialogue as a process, or could one say that they simply reveal a need to allow time for development and to be realistic in defining objectives precisely, recognizing what can and cannot be accomplished in a short-term time frame? This question captures the challenges in this field for the next decade.

REFERENCES

Azar, Edward E. 1983. "The Theory of Protracted Social Conflict and the Challenge of Transforming Conflict Situations," *Monograph Series in World Affairs.* M2: 20.

Bohm, David, ed. Lee Nichol 1996. *On Dialogue.* London and NY: Routledge.

Brown, Lester R. 1972. *World without Borders.* NY: Random House.

Burton, John W. 1965. *International Relations: A General Theory.* London: Cambridge University Press.

Burton, John W. 1987. *Resolving Deep-Rooted Conflict: A Handbook.* Lanham, MD: University Press of America.

Burton, John W., ed. 1990a. *Conflict: Resolution and Provention.* NY: St Martin's Press.

Burton, John W. 1990b. *Conflict: Human Needs Theory.* NY: St Martin's Press.

Chufrin, Gennady I. and Saunders, Harold H. 1993. "A Public Peace Process," *Negotiation Journal.* Vol. 9, No. 2.

Fisher, Ronald J. 1997. *Interactive Conflict Resolution.* Syracuse, NY: Syracuse University Press.

Burton, John W. 1968. *Systems, States, Diplomacy and Rules.* London: Cambridge University Press.

Isaacs, William. 1999. *Dialogue and the Art of Thinking Together: A Pioneering Approach to Communicating in Business and in Life.* NY: Doubleday: A Currency Book.

Keohane, Robert O., and Nye, Joseph S. 1977. *Power and Interdependence: World Politics in Transition.* Boston: Little, Brown and Company.

Sadat, Anwar al-. 1991. Speech to the Israeli Knesset, November 20, 1977. In Saunders, Harold H., *The Other Walls: The Arab-Israeli Peace Process in a Global Perspective*, 2nd edn. Princeton, NJ: Princeton University Press.

Saunders, Harold H. 1996. "Prenegotiation and Circumnegotiation: Arenas of the Peace Process." In Crocker, Chester A. and Hampson, Fen Osler with Pamela Aall, *Managing Global Chaos: Sources and Responses to International Conflict.* Washington, DC: United States Institute of Peace Press.

Saunders, Harold H. 1999. *A Public Peace Process: Sustained Dialogue to Transform Racial and Ethnic Conflicts.* NY: St Martin's Press.

Saunders, Harold H. 2005. *Politics Is about Relationship: A Blueprint for the Citizens' Century.* NY: Palgrave Macmillan, p. 6.

Schirch, Lisa and Campt, David. *The Little Book of Dialogue for Difficult Subjects: A Practical Hands-on Guide (The Little Books of Justice and Peacebuilding).* Intercourse, PA: Good Books, 2007.

Tannen, Deborah. 1998. *The Argument Culture: Moving from Debate to Dialogue.* NY: Random House.

Voorhees, James. 2002. *Dialogue Sustained: The Multilevel Peace Process and the Dartmouth Conference.* Dayton, OH and Washington, DC: Kettering Foundation and US Institute of Peace Press. pp. 148–159, 171–185, 190–194, 203–207, 211–217, 237–250, 262–268, 291–326, 363–393.

Yankelovich, Daniel. 1999. *The Magic of Dialogue: Transforming Conflict into Cooperation.* NY: Simon & Schuster.

20

NGOs and Conflict Resolution

Andrea Bartoli

INTRODUCTION: TOWARD A THEORY OF DIRECT INVOLVEMENT OF NGOs IN THE MEDIATION OF PEACE PROCESSES

In March 2007, after the signature of the peace agreement in Ouagadougou, President Laurent Gbagbo of Côte d'Ivoire, in his "C'est la victoire du peuple" address to the nation, said: 'Je remercie la Communauté Sant'Egidio, pour son action discrète mais efficace auprès des uns et des autres durant les discussions.'

Almost 15 years after the first recognized success of a nongovernmental organization (NGO) in facilitating the conclusion of a mediation process in Mozambique, the Community of Sant'Egidio – one of the most well-known international nongovernmental agencies operating in the area of conflict resolution – was again singled out as a contributor to a crucial international agreement.

While there is significant literature on NGOs as an expression of civil society, and while the roles and responsibilities of NGOs in the humanitarian and development sectors have attracted considerable attention (Anderson 1996, 1999), the specific functions

of NGOs in conflict resolution are often overlooked (Aall 1996). Certainly, there is abundant literature on conflict resolution processes involving civil society actors, including academia, think tanks, activist organizations, etc. (Arthur 1999; Cooper & Berdal 1993; Crocker et al. 1999). However, this chapter intentionally limits its scope to relatively rare but significant experiences of direct mediation by NGOs and the evolution of and trends relating to those processes. This section does not focus on techniques, such as interactive problem-solving workshops (Fisher 1997; Kelman 1996) or facilitated dialogues (Bohm 2004; Roberts 2002). Rather than look at NGOs through the prism of multitrack diplomacy (Diamond & McDonald 1996; McDonald 1991, 2003; Notter & McDonald 1996), this chapter analyzes a number of the still relatively rare cases of Track 1 processes in which state actors, international organizations, and nonstate actors claiming political space and recognition, used the mediation services of some NGOs.

The main theoretical thrust of this chapter is that, since the end of the Cold War, NGOs' role in international conflict resolution has become an established and important feature of a negotiations system that is adapting to the extraordinary challenges of state failures, state formation, and state cooperation (Hampson et al. 1999; Hume 1994). The four NGOs to be presented all emerged as relevant actors in the last 20 years as a response to a need for the mediation of internationally relevant conflict without the burdens and constraints of national interests and international organizations. The rise of these NGOs also responded to the vacuum left by states unable or unwilling to provide the services necessary to engage all actors involved in a given conflict in a constructive peace process (Bartoli 1999). According to this working hypothesis, NGOs devoted to conflict resolution – especially those actively pursuing mediation – came to exist because they were needed, and were kept alive by a marginal but significant stream of requests from actors lacking the political stability of an established nation-state (Jones 2002; Zartman 1995). A second hypothesis is that the use of NGOs in conflict resolution reveals a certain "maturity" of the state. Far from signaling an erosion of state power, a state that chooses to involve NGOs demonstrates its confidence: it can engage in a process of transformation using a plurality of actors according to its interests and goals (Akashi 1995–96; Ramsbotham et al. 2005; Rubin 2002).

While the strength of NGOs lies – with good reason – in their independence and impartiality, and their ability to access states while not actually being states, the degree of contact between states and NGOs varies greatly (Ropers 2001; Stephenson 2005). If we imagined a continuum, with on one end those NGOs completely independent from states and, on the other, those completely identified with them, we would see that even the four cases presented in this chapter occupy different positions on the spectrum. For example, the Conflict Management Initiative is closer to states and to their structures while the Community of Sant'Egidio is less intimately associated with them. This indicator also provides some orientation in identifying a particular

NGO's strategy. As illustrated by Bercovitch, mediation behavior can follow different paths (Bercovitch 1991, 1996).

Communication-facilitation: a strategy in which the mediator simply facilitates the process of conflict resolution, which is fundamentally driven by the involved parties themselves; refrains from intrusive techniques; offers physical space for meetings; and opens channels of communication.

Procedural: a strategy characterized by a mediator's substantive contributions to the peace process by not only convening and setting the agenda, but also influencing the outcome by making suggestions and conceiving of an effective process.

Directive: usually identified by the tendency of mediators to use their own power to broker an agreement that, while possibly being the best of all possible outcomes, is achieved by a certain degree of pressure leveled by the mediator.

An NGO's decision to follow a specific style of mediation is likely contingent upon its cultural milieu (Avruch 1998) and its level of access to the specific direct power of one or more states (Crocker et al. 1999). NGOs' access differs enormously, not only from case to case but also from period to period. All four organizations studied are operating in a rapidly changing environment, and while all have a meaningful degree of access to political leverage, the extent of that access will vary dramatically, depending especially on the cyclical redistribution of power in democratic states (think of the different kind of influence of former President Jimmy Carter depending on his relationship with those who succeeded him at the White House). However, it must be noted that the traditional distinction of mediators as individuals, states, and organizations is somewhat challenged by the emergence of organizations that are deeply connected with one founding figure (namely Carter and Martti Ahtisaari). These dynamics, on the one hand, allow for an expansion of the effectiveness of the individual engaging in mediation efforts and the potential for results that would be unimaginable otherwise; on the other hand, these organizations must also demonstrate their capacity to endure beyond the service of that particular individual (Princen 1992). It remains to be seen whether this will be the case.

This is why NGOs should be considered not only in terms of their relation to the state but also, and more fundamentally, as an important part of the larger notion of civil society (Matthews 2001). As such, NGOs contribute to the fabric that comprises the very polity of a country and of the international community. This chapter focuses exclusively on well-reputed NGOs that have actually performed mediation in the international arena and does not take into account a number of other members of civil society that contribute greatly to conflict resolution. From the information gathering and distribution of the International Crisis Group to the polling services offered by the University of Liverpool, the network of WANEP and the highly specialized media programming of Search for Common Ground, the activities indirectly related to conflict resolution are numerous. In order to offer a deeper appreciation of a very specific contribution that NGOs have made through mediation, this chapter will intentionally be limited to the cases in which the following criteria apply:

- Capacity – [follow on]
- the organization is established and recognized as able to provide mediation services.

  - Track record – [follow on]
  - the organization has a track record of mediation services.
  - Evaluation – [follow on]
  - the organization has been subject to independent evaluation of its mediation services.

Methodologically, the chapter will draw upon material produced by the NGOs themselves as a tribute to self-representation (Charmaz 1995; Glaser & Strauss 1967) and a contribution to further research, as well as interviews with representatives of the NGOs to ensure up-to-date information. While acknowledging the importance of NGOs in international affairs in general (already identified by Antonio Donini more

than a decade ago) (Donini 1996), the chapter does not focus on humanitarian and development NGOs, or their indirect, and at times negative, involvement in conflict (brilliantly addressed by others, including Anderson 1996; Goodhand 2006; Minear 2002; and Uvin 1998). Rather, it emphasizes the role that NGOs have played as mediators, facilitators, or in other capacities intentionally linked to conflict resolution strategies and practices. Currently, there is no study that, having access to firsthand sources, has attempted to offer a coherent interpretative framework in this area.

The examples of direct involvement in peace processes that best correspond to the above mentioned criteria are: the Community of Sant'Egidio,[1] the Carter Center,[2] the Center for Humanitarian Dialogue,[3] and the Crisis Management Initiative.[4] The choice of these entities among the many that are actively working in the vast (and ambiguous) area of conflict resolution and peace-building is the product of a series of qualitative interviews in which knowledgeable observers were asked to identify the organizations that best fulfilled the three criteria of capacity, track record, and evaluation.

It is clear that the distinction between those who had been directly and intentionally involved in mediation and others is somewhat arbitrary. Organizations such as the Community of Sant'Egidio, which has more than 50,000 members, contribute greatly to societal processes of transformation as well as to mediation. Conversely, NGOs such as ACCORD[5] played a significant role in actual peace processes in the region in addition to performing grassroots cultural work. For a more comprehensive view of the contributions of NGOs (especially in the area of prevention), the reader is invited to use the well-documented and extraordinarily well-connected site of the Global Partnership for the Prevention of Armed Conflict (GPPAC)[6], whose secretariat is run by the European Center for Conflict Prevention (ECCP).[7]

The distinction is introduced to address a more theoretical argument about the "specificity" of the contribution of nonstate actors in political processes that result in the emergence of sustained peace (Aall 1996; Crocker et al. 1999). In particular, NGOs play a very important connecting role by allowing the daring notion of a peace process to be circulated, explored, and eventually actualized. These transformative (and in many cases very unsettling and challenging) steps require a high degree of alignment in order to be successful (Curle 1986; Kriesberg 1992; Lederach 1995). It is the opinion of the author that the most constructive contributions of NGOs to conflict resolution internationally emerge when synergies with all other relevant actors in the environment are sought and successfully maintained (Bartoli 1999). While NGOs have different mandates, internal cultures, and ways of operating, it is important to identify – as much as possible – functional patterns that maximize positive impact (Coleman 2003). NGOs help states and international organizations to address in particular the problem of legitimacy. In many of the situations in which NGOs have been present, the armed factions were not equal: state actors confronting various formations were often relieved at the possibility of using mediation services that were international enough to offer guarantees but unofficial enough to not be invasive (Lund 1996; Morozzo Della Rocca 2003; Steiner 2004). In a moment of crisis for the state, the availability of NGOs' mediation services has often been perceived as a positive contribution to the evolution of that particular political structure. Precisely because they are not an expression of the state system, NGOs have been able to offer what was needed to effectively manage political transitions resulting from conflict (Princen 1992).

One curious (and almost unexpected) consequence of the involvement of NGOs in mediation is that it can lead to a clearer comprehension of the mediation process itself, and therefore to a more accurate understanding of how the process works. Of the four areas identified by Secretary General Boutros Boutros-Ghali (1992) in his Agenda for Peace (prevention, peace-making,

peace-keeping, peace-building), the second area (peace-making) is the least theoretically developed and often remains limited to biographical sketches, anecdotes, and individual cases (Jeong 2000). This chapter contends that NGOs, together with states and international organizations, could greatly contribute to an accurate understanding of how mediation work is actually done in the realm of peace-making, the conditions for success, and the relevant criteria for evaluation (Bercovitch 1989, 1996).

Considering the particular role of NGOs as mediators, it is helpful to refer to the sources of power available to them and to reflect on the comparative advantages they might have. Using the categorization of reward power, coercive power, expert power, legitimate power, referent power, and informational power (Rubin 1992[8]), it is clear that NGOs' access to these resources is uneven. In particular, their most striking deficit is in coercive power; NGOs lack the capacity to force action by parties, which significantly affects the decision-making process (Griffiths 2005). However, this lack of coercive capacity might actually explain why, under certain circumstances, parties in a conflict might prefer the use of services provided by an NGO rather than a more powerful actor. A "weak" mediation (that is to say, a process that does not impose a solution) might actually help the parties remain genuinely engaged in the process, thus paradoxically paving the way to a "stronger" process in which greater buy-in of the parties leads to lasting results (Hume 1994). Obviously, a mediation that is "weak" in terms of its capacity to coerce isn't necessarily weak in terms of its reward, expert, legitimate, referent, and informational powers. Different actors have different strengths, but there is no doubt that all of them have an impressive capacity to mobilize political capital that parties can use in their attempt to explore the possibilities of a peaceful solution to a conflict. Personal relationships, as well as good framing capacity – network and access as well as precedents and scenarios – are all elements of a strategy that is always new and yet contains recurrent elements (Morozzo Della Rocca 2003).

As it is explained in the literature, the mediation process is a form of assisted negotiation (Bercovitch 1996). The parties are in charge of the decision-making and the selection of the mediators, which is a significant element of the process (D'Amico & Rubinstein 1999). Why are NGOs a reasonable choice? Because they allow mediation among asymmetric parties, helping to bridge the legitimacy gap that separates state and nonstate actors (Bartoli 1999). As it is clear in the case of Mozambique (and confirmed in many other cases), it is at times advantageous for parties in a conflict to consider the mediation services of an NGO that has a strong enough international reputation that it can offer guarantees to the nonstate actor in need of international recognition, but is not so official as to infringe on state sovereignty (Riccardi 1999). Also, the dedication of NGOs with longer-term investment strategies can result in more fruitful results, as opposed to those achievable by official actors with short operation timetables (Matthews 2001).

Considering the three categories of power identified by Kenneth Boulding: destructive, productive and integrative (Boulding 1989), NGOs clearly have their greatest strength in the third. They are able to help parties, not through a series of threats and rewards, but rather through a relational process of transformation that assists the parties in re-framing their own political relations and the conditions of their polity as well as their recognition by the international community (Arnson & Whitfield 2005). Sociologically, it is helpful to note that in recent years, extraordinary growth has been observed in the availability of individuals holding important public political roles in their respective countries and/or in international organizations to conflict prevention, resolution, and peace-building activities. One reason for this sudden growth is the accession of new democracies to a rotation in the distribution of power that allows for many former presidents and prime ministers to remain politically active after leaving office.

Former US President Jimmy Carter and Former Finnish President Martti Ahtisaari are outstanding examples of how the talents of a proven politician can serve the international system in creative ways through an NGO. There are other cases of the phenomenon not mentioned in this chapter but that have the potential to offer similar outcomes. We can identify the Club de Madrid,[9] the Assembly of the Parliament of Cultures in Istanbul,[10] the Forum 2000,[11] the Peres Centre for Peace,[12] Global Panel,[13] and the Global Leadership Foundation, among others.

DIRECT INVOLVEMENT IN PEACE PROCESSES: THE COMMUNITY OF SANT'EGIDIO

Note: This section is built upon open-source material and interviews with actors directly involved in the NGO. As much as possible, we have tried to allow for self-representation as a criterion of inclusion.

Founded in Rome, Italy, in 1968, the Community of Sant'Egidio is a religious organization whose members are not paid and whose work on peace is more the result of a serendipitous series of events than a clearly stated choice enshrined in a mission statement. While the Carter Center, the Center for Humanitarian Dialogue and the Crisis Management Initiative clearly have conflict resolution as a central focus of their work, the self-representation of the Community of Sant'Egidio – as it appears in published materials and as shared by many of its members – is actually spiritual in nature, referring to concepts such as prayer, communicating the Gospel, solidarity with the poor, and ecumenism. It is only in the last item in their list of principles that we find a reference to peace-work: dialogue. The Community of Sant'Egidio further explains that dialogue is "recommended by Vatican II as a way of peace and co-operation among the religions, and also a way of life and as a means of resolving conflicts" (Riccardi 1999).

Started in Rome by the initiative of a young student, Andrea Riccardi, the Community of Sant'Egidio took its current name in 1973 and became involved in peace work as a response to the needs of a dear friend of the community, Jaime Goncalves. Goncalves had been appointed bishop of Beira, Mozambique, after the military coup in Lisbon which allowed the Vatican to establish native, Mozambican bishops rather than Portuguese ones (Morozzo Della Rocca 2003). While the internal war that pitted Mozambique's RENAMO (Resistencia National de Moçambique) resistance movement against the official government of the FRELIMO (Frente de Liberaçao de Moçambique) party started soon after the independence of the country (Abrahamsson & Nilsson 1995), the Community of Sant'Egidio was involved in a long process aimed at reconstructing conditions for full religious freedom in the country. For more than 10 years, the primary focus of the Community's work in Mozambique was facilitating a constructive dialogue between the FRELIMO government, the local Catholic church and the Holy See. This effort reached its climax with the visit of Mozambican President Samora Machel to the Vatican, the visit of Pope John Paul II to Mozambique, and the establishment of diplomatic relations between the two countries. When, in the late 1980s, it became clear that more had to be done to bring peace to a country ravaged by war, the Community of Sant'Egidio could count on a well-established set of relationships both in Mozambique and in Europe to engage in this work (Bartoli 2005).

Mozambique is now at peace, united and independent. This achievement is a first for a country that was created by Portuguese colonialism and had never simultaneously experienced peace, independence and unity. These conditions emerged with the signing of the General Agreement for Peace in Rome 1992, which was the first agreement ever to be mediated by a team put together by an international NGO such as the Community of Sant'Egidio (United Nations 1995). Mozambique has now successfully completed two more election cycles and

the newly elected president, His Excellency Emilio Guebuza, was the chief negotiator of the FRELIMO government (Hume 1994). The level of violence in the country is relatively low (especially compared to other countries in the region) as are its chances of resuming internal war (SwissPeace 2007).

Mozambique's transformation has been extraordinary. After a 30-year war of independence and a 16-year civil war that claimed one million lives and resulted in 4.5 million refugees and internally displaced people (out of a population of 12 million in the early 1990s), Mozambique now features a multiparty democracy where political violence is not a threat (Synge 1997). Clearly, this picture cannot be replicated for Sudan, Rwanda, Burundi, Congo, Angola, or for other African countries on the verge of significant violent conflict, such as Ivory Coast, Ethiopia, or Togo. The difference, this chapter argues, has mainly to do with the capacity of relevant actors to generate a political process able to represent people's interests, memories and needs (Bartoli & Coleman 2003), which are not properly represented in conflict (Gurr 2000). In Mozambique, actors kept the possibility of peace alive and offered spaces in which the possibility of peace could be evaluated. They allowed Mozambique to move away from the narrow-mindedness of violence to the more generative possibilities of sustained interaction as defined by a participatory system (Fisher 1997, 2005).

Truly a pluralistic society, Mozambique fought its wars in political and military terms, rather than in terms of religion. A great first contribution of the local religious communities was to refrain from attempting to follow a hegemonic path or condoning violence through religious terms. Religious communities were on the forefront of the effort to represent the victims of the conflict, their interests, and their needs, thus paving the way for new political arrangements that brought the conflict to an end (Bartoli 2001).

The community of Sant'Egidio was involved in other peace processes after Mozambique. Experiences include Algeria,

Guatemala, Albania, Kosovo, Burundi, Togo, Casamance, and most recently, the Democratic Republic of the Congo, Sudan, Northern Uganda, and Ivory Coast. What emerges from these cases is that the community is able to offer direct connections to non-state actors, especially violent ones, that find themselves without proper connectivity to the international system. As the UN Undersecretary General for political affairs Sir Kieran Prendergast said, referring to the contacts that one officer of the community, Dr. Fabio Riccardi, had maintained with the Lord's Resistance Army in northern Uganda: "Sant'Egidio can speak with those, we can't." One interesting feature of Sant'Egidio's peculiar organizational structure is that, largely because the organization is rooted in religion, no one is paid for the services they provide. Composed of professionals, scholars, and regular citizens doing regular jobs and leading in regular environments, members of the community of Sant'Egidio offer their services without requesting pay. This arrangement allows the community to be involved in relational processes of trust-building that may come to fruition in a full-fledged, well-developed peace process or in less successful yet extraordinarily bold attempts to build peace in war-torn societies (Giro 1998).

The community of Sant'Egidio is able to maximize connectivity by engaging actors in a series of exchanges in which the immediate and successful response to a particular need becomes part of the larger strategy of engagement. For instance, an extraordinary meeting of socialist, nationalist, and Islamist leaders from Algeria, all gathered in a Catholic convent – the Sant'Egidio quarters in the heart of Rome – was an exceptional result of years of friendship built with all sectors of Algerian society (Impagliazzo & Giro 1997). The same is true in cases from Guatemala to Lebanon and from Togo to Sudan.

A third element of Sant'Egidio's success is its ability to navigate political processes by wisely deciding when and how to participate, and when to refrain from participating (Ury 2007). This element is less an expression

of Sant'Egidio's NGO status than it is the product of almost 40 years of uninterrupted commitment to world affairs. One of the most well-known cases of the Sant'Egidio community's decision not to be involved in the political process was its refusal to host a national dialogue unexpectedly offered by the former president of the Democratic Republic of the Congo, Laurent Kabila. Kabila had not consulted with the community and announced his initiative on the radio, communicating only later to the community's mediators that the event would have taken place in Sant'Egidio headquarters according to procedures that were determined by him alone. Considering this unacceptable, the community declined to support the president's overture. Their decision won them significant political capital with Kabila's opponents and laid the foundations for constructive engagement with them in subsequent initiatives (Bartoli 2005).

Connectivity, per se, is not sufficient unless it is sustainable and nourished by a bold vision. The community of Sant'Egidio seems to have the three elements aligned in an effort to seek the possible emergence of peace in very different contexts while always inquiring with all relevant actors about how this emergence could occur. Sant'Egidio in the past 15 years has become, in the words of African statesman Julius Nyerere, "a house for Africa," the place where leaders involved in conflict can explore the possibilities of peaceful settlements in an environment that fosters confidentiality and creativity. Because of its track record, Sant'Egidio doesn't need to seek areas of intervention to add to the list of possible engagements, nor does it need to decide between them. In a sort of automatic selection, actors in immediate contact with Sant'Egidio express their interest for peaceful solutions by approaching the community and exploring these alternatives with senior mediators of the community (Giro 1998).

As is already clear in the case of Mozambique, the Community of Sant'Egidio rates as one actor in a complex system that can facilitate a process with internal coherence through strict discipline and a resolved orientation. While based on the assumption that peace is always possible, the community members involved in political processes tend to check this general assumption against the real conditions on the ground (Hume 1994). Significant to the understanding of what NGOs in general can contribute to conflict resolution processes is the observation that the organizations' intelligence-gathering processes frequently run parallel to the ones available to state actors. To the surprise of many Western diplomats, the community of Sant'Egidio negotiators are frequently very well-informed through their personal connections with all involved actors and relevant observers. As a Catholic organization, Sant'Egidio has been able to successfully and effectively partner with bishops, missionaries, and local communities around the world. The loosely centralized structure of the Catholic Church that allows, in the words of John Paul Lederach, "both verticality and horizontality," is the setting in which the Community of Sant'Egidio develops highly detailed reports from areas of conflict (Lederach 1997).

In contrast to other peace-building NGOs, the community of Sant'Egidio has accumulated significant political capital related to its capacity to accurately understand recent events in light of decades-long patterns. This advantage is largely due to Sant'Egidio's 40-year commitment to peace work, and to the continuity of the personnel working on specific areas (due to the fact that no one is paid and therefore there is no need for turnover). We can compare this information-gathering process to the one established by the International Crisis Group, which sends expatriates to an area of conflict to establish a network that will eventually produce relevant reporting that can be disseminated through the ICG central office in Brussels to decision-makers around the world. In contrast, the Community of Sant'Egidio relies on already established networks of local actors. These local actors speak the language, know the culture, belong to the polity affected by the

conflict, and have been connected with the peace work of the negotiators for a long time, both in their own country and in Rome, giving Sant'Egidio a significant advantage. The aim of the information gathering and analysis performed is not public disclosure, but rather the facilitation of the peace process itself and the creation of loops of confidence strengthened by the confidentiality of the conversations (well documented in the book edited by Ronald J. Fisher 2005). The first peace process ever facilitated by the Community of Sant'Egidio in Mozambique was successful exactly because of the confidentiality of the conversations and its mode of information gathering and verification (Hume 1994).

The Community of Sant'Egidio seems to believe that, although final agreements must have a very public dimension and be welcomed by societies affected by conflict, the preparation for a successful agreement requires carefully maintained confidentiality. When the community of Sant'Egidio team, led by don Matteo Maria Zuppi, was exploring possible processes in Burundi, it was doing so without publicly acknowledging the conversation. Yet, the parties who were not necessarily ready for a serious commitment to the process decided to leak the information to the press and therefore negatively affected the outcome of the conversations.

The Community of Sant'Egidio's experience in Mozambique, as well as all of the other initiatives to date, rests on the assumptions and practice of effective coordination with all relevant actors. However, what was observed during the Mozambique peace process was that there is great variation in actors' perception of what is relevant in the peace process. It was determined that the Portuguese government wanted to play a primary role in the Mozambique peace process and was actively undermining the leadership in that effort. However, the parties themselves, both FRELIMO and RENAMO, did not appreciate having a former colonial power leading a political process that had such a huge impact on the newly independent country and its structure (Hume 1994). While the Portuguese government perceived the Community of Sant'Egidio as a weak mediator, the parties perceived the community as a strong actor capable of asserting the prerogatives of a peace process that had its own endogenous dynamics. An interesting point on a more general and theoretical level is that all mediation efforts suffer the challenges of alternatives that are constantly promoted by some actors in the system who are trying to maximize their gains by manipulating the process (Crocker et al. 1999). However, these challenges should not be viewed as an aberration. They are the normal expression of a lively political process in which a multiplicity of actors participates. It can be said that successful peace processes require effective coordination with all relevant actors. Obviously, coordination doesn't mean consensus or even full disclosure; rather, it means shared goals and open communication (Donini 1996). (See www.santegidio.org/en/index.html)

DIRECT INVOLVEMENT IN PEACE PROCESSES: THE CARTER CENTER

Note: This section is built upon open-source material and interviews with actors directly involved in the NGO.

Former US President Jimmy Carter and former First Lady Rosalynn Carter established the Carter Center in 1982. The Center is self-described as being "committed to advancing human rights and alleviating unnecessary human suffering." To this end, the Carter Center employs a full-time staff dedicated to programs including human rights, democracy, conflict resolution, and health. The health program, in particular, differentiates the Carter Center from other NGOs involved in conflict resolution, and is committed to combating disease throughout the developing world. Unlike the Community of Sant'Egidio, which relies on volunteer members of the Community to conduct its peace processes, the Carter Center has access to a large pool of interns who are willing to work without

salaries. The Center's agenda is guided by five principles:

1. Emphasize action and results. Based on careful research and analysis, it is prepared to take timely action on important and pressing issues.
2. Do not duplicate the effective efforts of others.
3. Address difficult problems and recognize the possibility of failure as an acceptable risk.
4. Remain nonpartisan and act as a neutral in dispute resolution activities.
5. Believe that people can improve their lives when provided with the necessary skills, knowledge, and access to resources.

The Carter Center collaborates with other organizations, public and private, in carrying out its mission. Considered to be free of political or partisan positions, nongovernmental organizations such as the Carter Center have been able to gain access, build relationships, and offer mediation services in situations where more formal diplomacy has not been immediately welcomed (Diamond & McDonald 1996). War-torn countries also may be more receptive to organizations such as the Carter Center that have already provided them with humanitarian or development assistance. With President Carter's involvement, the Center can operate at a level above other nongovernmental organizations, working directly with heads of state. Its role in brokering peace agreements falls between countries' official diplomacy and unofficial peace-building efforts. The Center coordinates its work with government and nongovernmental organizations to avoid duplication of efforts or contradictory plans (Van Tongeren 2001).

Early on, the Carter Center developed criteria for its engagement in violent conflict. In particular, it established that three conditions had to be met in order to develop a full intervention. The first condition was that conflict parties must explicitly and directly request the intervention. While explorations were conducted in many situations, only when all relevant parties involved explicitly requested a more active role for the Carter Center was engagement initiated. The second criterion for engagement was that the Carter Center must be able to identify a clear role for it to play in the engagement. Due to the international respect afforded former President Carter, and the esteem in which the Carter Center is held, it became obvious that appeals for assistance would be made to the Center regardless of its ability to deliver niche services. The last criterion for engagement was monetary. Before engaging in peace-building activities, the Carter Center verified that an appropriate financial investment was available to make its initiatives sustained and viable.

Among the most notable experiences of the Carter Center, the following are clearly relevant to this study: Korea (starting in 1993), Yugoslavia (1994), Burundi (1991), Haiti (1994), Uganda (2002), Sudan (1990), and Liberia (1992). Each case would require an in-depth analysis, but it is helpful to note that in several of these cases the contribution of the Carter Center has lasted due to the effects that its initiatives produced in the larger system. For example, in Burundi, where the peace process is coming to a positive conclusion after years of very difficult negotiations, the Carter Center was able to initiate a trend that led to constructive steps. While not carrying out a direct mediation effort for the whole 15-year period, the Center's framework of a political dialogue as a venue for the emergence of a lasting solution was established in early encounters. Similarly, in all other contexts, from Korea to Liberia, long-term transformation of the political landscape can be associated with early interventions of the Center (Zartman 2001).

The Carter Center plays an important role in the monitoring of elections worldwide (Lindberg 2006; Santa Cruz 2005). It was this role that led to the Center's prolonged engagement in Venezuela beginning in 1998. The election-monitoring delegation was led by President Carter, whose trust-building work at that time would prove invaluable in future conflict resolution initiatives. In 2002, The Carter Center joined the Organization of American States and the UN Development Program to begin a

formal process to help resolve Venezuela's political crisis. This tripartite working group initiated talks between Venezuelan President Hugo Chavez's government and opposition groups consisting of the business community, religious foundations, and guilds, which were organizing strikes and large street protests (Ahmed & Potter 2006). The Carter Center's plan was to combine high-level mediation activities with an attempt to energize positive grassroots involvement (DeMars 2005). After consultation with William Ury of Harvard University, the Center instituted a strategy of exploring the nexus between government supporters and opposition members. Ury's "Third Side" methodology was instructive in helping to identify the actors in the nexus, who hailed from diverse backgrounds including government, civil society, academia, the business community, and religious institutions, and who were dedicated to nonviolent processes (Ury 2000).

Contrary to media images of popular street violence, it became clear that the nonviolent members of the process were in the majority (Sharp 2005). The real challenge was to insist that the parties continue discussions about the conflict (Johnson et al. 2000) rather than support the alternative of widespread violence in the streets. As the nexus gained media attention, there was a general disapproval among the populace toward those seeking violence as a means of polity. Rather than swimming against the "flow," practitioners from the Center realized they had identified the "flow" and were in agreement in preferring non-violent processes, regardless of the outcomes. Another important factor in the Venezuelan process was that those who wanted to use violence knew they were running a huge risk of backlash by resorting to violence (Bartoli & Coleman 2003). There was little prior history in Venezuela of armed mass violence as an acceptable form of discourse.

The credibility of third-party interveners became a key issue in the Venezuelan conflict (Arnson & Whitfield 2005). After the coup attempt against President Chavez, the United States was demonized and the OAS was viewed as too close to the

American government. But President Carter's previous involvement in election monitoring that brought Chavez to power created trust and credibility that extended from the government to the opposition and onward to the business elite. They respected the manner in which Carter and his Center professionally and impartially conducted business. At that time, there were very few people who had the capacity or credibility to engage in conflict resolution in Venezuela. It was this process of trust-building that strongly reinforced the Center's already formidable status in the minds of the relevant actors. (See www. cartercenter.org)

DIRECT INVOLVEMENT IN PEACE PROCESSES: THE CENTER FOR HUMANITARIAN DIALOGUE

Note: This chapter is built upon open-source material and interviews with actors directly involved in the NGO.

Emerging out of the world of the humanitarian concerns, expressed faithfully by the International Committee of the Red Cross (ICRC) and the humanitarian movement that followed its lead, the Center for Humanitarian Dialogue (HD or "the Center") is a more recent attempt to constructively engage the international system by offering a variety of services that would complement the activities of traditional state actors and international organizations (Anderson 1996). Similarly to the ICRC, HD is a private *humanitarian* institution located in Geneva. The self-representation of the Center speaks of "an independent and impartial organization whose motivation is to reduce human suffering in war." Furthermore, the organization believes that "preventing and resolving armed conflicts is the surest means of doing so" (Schnabel & Carment 2004). Principles of independence and impartiality refer to the humanitarian background of the organization, though it has also leveraged privileged relationships with many governments, especially Switzerland and Norway (Hampson & Malone 2002).

The Center is active in many countries, always promoting and facilitating dialogue among belligerents, conducting research and bringing forward policy recommendations.

The Center was established in 1999 as a Swiss foundation intended to explore new concepts of humanitarian dialogue, in which discreet discussions could take place among those who could have a practical impact on humanitarian policy and practice. Early engagements in Aceh, Indonesia, led to an expansion of the organization's mandate to include mediation and conflict prevention activities (Martin 2006). The Center found its comparative advantage in its ability to remain a small, impartial, and independent NGO focusing on bringing to the table senior-level diplomats and leaders of armed groups to resolve their differences peacefully, while discreetly managing these processes. The Center identified three areas in which it sought to proactively engage violent conflict: through direct mediation, providing negotiation and technical expertise to facilitate dialogue, and supporting other facilitators in ongoing peace processes (Martin 2006).

Unlike the Carter Center and the Crisis Management Initiative, which utilize internationally known, former heads of state as a key element in obtaining legitimacy, the Center for Humanitarian Dialogue has established its position through long-term, rigorous, and continuous engagements on the ground, cultivating and developing its reputation with relevant actors (Edwards & Hulme 1996). This commitment to long-term investment, as well as the preeminence of confidentiality, has allowed the Center to politically engage conflict in a proactive manner – something the humanitarian movement from which it grew has struggled with due to issues of neutrality (Griffiths 2005). This relational strategy has proven successful. Since 1999, the Center has been involved in peace-building activities, including mediation, in Asia, Africa, Latin America, the Balkans, and the Middle East, and developed humanitarian ceasefire agreements in Darfur and "cessation of hostility" agreements in Aceh. Due to the confidentiality of many of the Center's initiatives, it is difficult to ascertain the full effect of the Center's contributions to peace.

The Center employs a full-time staff dedicated to programs including mediation and policy research and analysis. Policy research is conducted to inform the Center's staff of important themes related to conflict resolution processes and to identify and horizontally disseminate policy recommendations to the wider conflict resolution community. The Policy Program addresses four major themes: conflict mediation, civilian protection, justice and peace-building, and arms and security issues. This self-described "investment in academically relevant knowledge" illustrates an attempt by the Center to understand the relevant processes related to conflict, rather than simply "do" them. This investment is resulting in an interesting blend of academically sound and politically relevant observations of mediation experiences worldwide. Recognizing that the quality and quantity of the data in the area of mediation is still insufficient, the Center has engaged in a series of attempts to tweak available data sets to allow the mediation experience to be more fully observed, described, and understood.

The Center for Humanitarian Dialogue became involved in the Aceh, Indonesia, conflict in 1999 when it initiated dialogue between the Indonesian Government and the leadership of the Free Aceh Movement (GAM). Observing states began to take notice of the Center's engagement and important linkages were formed, adding to the Center's credibility. Although seen by some as a "weak" mediator, actors were quick to recognize the formidable connections that the Center for Humanitarian Dialogue brought to the mediation. The notion of power is interesting in this context as it was the Center's perceived access to power, rather than actual power it possessed, that lent credibility to its initiative (Akashi 1995–96). Similar to the Community of Sant'Egidio in Mozambique, armed groups perceive the relationship between the NGO and the more powerful state as their access point. Sant'Egidio's linkages with the Vatican and the HD's linkages to the United Nations and the US State Department, perceived or legitimate, exemplified this power connection in the eyes of the actors. (See www.hdcentre.org)

DIRECT INVOLVEMENT IN PEACE PROCESSES: THE CRISIS MANAGEMENT INITIATIVE (CMI)

Note: This chapter is built upon open-source material and will be followed by an interview with CMI founder Martti Ahtisaari.

The Crisis Management Initiative was founded in 2002 by former President of Finland, Martti Ahtisaari, as an organization that works to strengthen the capacity of the international community in crisis management and conflict resolution by using traditional settings and innovative strategies of engagement (Balachandra et al. 2005). Similar to the Carter Center, CMI is able to operate at a level above other nongovernmental organizations due to the formidable political capital Mr Ahtisaari built during his tenure as president. He continues to be very active in the international scene, especially in the Balkans where he is leading efforts to clarify the final status for Kosovo.

CMI's work is divided into two categories: Crisis Management and Conflict Resolution programs and the Martti Ahtisaari Rapid Reaction Facility. Recognizing that, in an era of globalization, distant threats are just as serious as more locally defined ones, CMI's conflict resolution program focuses on previously established networks, particularly within civil society and regional organizations, to monitor potentially violent conflicts and strengthen and facilitate networks of actors committed to peace-building (DeMars 2005). This implicit acknowledgement of the preeminence of prevention colors all CMI initiatives and is illustrated through partnerships with the European Union and NGOs engaged in conflict resolution and peace-building (Weiner 1998).

Speaking about the field of crisis management, Ahtisaari says the EU has taken the frontrunner's role, particularly in the development of a comprehensive crisis management system. An important dialogue has commenced on how to better utilize NGO experience and expertise in the work of multilateral and regional organizations. During the past several years, the European Union has contributed, through its civilian crisis management tools, to solving conflicts and assisting war-torn societies in building sustainable peace and democracy (Reychler & Paffenholz 2001). At the same time, NGOs have carried out similar tasks. Therefore, there is a tangible need to achieve greater conceptual coherence between the overall strategy and goals of civilian crisis management efforts of the EU and nongovernmental organizations.

President Ahtisaari explains that civilian crisis management policies and practices are currently being developed and debated among many stakeholders. The traditional approach towards civilian crisis management emphasized issues such as police training, border control, and peace monitoring. At the same time, there seemed to be a growing need for broader peace-building strategies that treat the development of societies in a comprehensive manner. In these post-conflict development efforts, the role of local civil society is pivotal. Civil society forms a large, diverse, and fragmented body of organizations. NGOs vary from the very large or strong to the extremely small or weak in all aspects, including legitimacy, reliability, aims, roles, staff, financial resources, capacity, and geographical reach (Van Tongeren 2001).

The roles of civil society actors in civilian crisis management cover the broad spectrum of engagement in early warning, prevention, mediation, monitoring, civilian peacekeeping, and reconciliation. While civil society roles and the actors performing them are numerous and diverse, they typically share a common approach that is community-based or "bottom-up." It follows that civil society organizations often have unique access to the "ground truth" and are well placed to monitor and potentially mobilize public support.

Furthermore, NGOs can provide informal mediation between participants (Merikallio 2006). They use mediation techniques, such as problem-solving workshops in which participants are encouraged to look beyond territorial, legal, or military issues and instead focus on issues such as the fears and insecurities, misperceptions and misunderstandings that underpin conflict. This work can be vital in encouraging parties to adopt a more compromising approach prior to the beginning of formal negotiations.

Ahtisaari envisions a greater role for research in peace-making and peace-keeping and believes it is currently under-utilized in the process. Academic institutions and think tanks can generate high-quality and policy-relevant analysis on the root causes of crises and develop innovative frameworks for crisis resolution and for overcoming broader instability (Kriesberg, in this volume). They can also gather and distribute information and expertise within existing crisis management field operations.

There is much uncertainty about the actual added value and effectiveness of NGOs and civil society actors in peace-building and peace mediation, according to Ahtisaari. He recognizes that NGOs are able to fulfill a variety of conflict management roles by serving as early warning monitors of impending conflict; channels of communication; mediators or facilitators of official or unofficial negotiations; promoters of the process of reconciliation through grassroots engagements; and those who strengthen civil society in the postconflict environment to nurture the culture of peace (Ahmed & Potter 2006). NGOs can also, through their experience, contribute to innovative conflict management and resolution strategies (Fitzduff & Church 2004). Local NGOs can be instrumental in addressing the escalation of violence and emergence of war, and they can mobilize political will for peace while developing options and strategies for response by strengthening constituencies for peace (Committee for Conflict Transformation Support 2001).

However, Ahtisaari understands there are also limits to the involvement of NGOs

(Jordan & Van Tuijl 2006). An oft-cited criticism is that civil society actors sometimes start processes that are beyond their skills and abilities. They may also be too small, too isolated or lack the capacity to work with each other. The legitimacy of NGOs as actors is sometimes questioned as well, which hampers their involvement (DeMars 2005). The fact that civil society organizations may be perceived as powerless by many parties to a conflict may increase their attractiveness to the antagonists: if the attempt to open the dialogue fails, the parties lose little by way of reputation or potential inducements to settle (Fox & Brown 1998).

Ahtisaari sees a growing potential for previously untapped sectors of society to be engaged in peace-making and peace-building, including the business sector. There is a growing acknowledgement that although they are often bound up with conflict dynamics, local business actors in conflict-prone countries can also have an interest in securing peace. To date, this complex relationship between local business and conflict has not been well understood. For donors and development agencies, there is much to be learned from sharing experiences on how to integrate a role for the private sector around peace-building and growth in an immediate post-conflict environment (Goodhand 2006). In these situations, there are real opportunities for changes in policies and institutions that affect the private sector, and experience is showing that there is a role for the domestic private sector in crisis prevention and growth.

The most prominent activity of mediation undertaken by CMI was in Aceh where President Ahtisaari offered the effective formula of "self-government" as a way to frame the parameters of a solution amenable to all parties. The Aceh peace process can serve as a good example of both cooperation between the first and second tracks of diplomacy and of the cooperation between European and Asian countries in crisis management (Mendelson & Glenn 2002).

President Ahtisaari acted as facilitator during the negotiation phase of the Aceh peace process. In January 2005, the government

of Indonesia and the Free Aceh Movement (Gerakan Aceh Merdeka or GAM) met in Helsinki to discuss the conflict, which had lasted for almost 30 years. The December 2004 tsunami had devastated Aceh just a month earlier. The government and GAM decided to stop fighting and work towards building a fair and democratic society. The conflict ended, as the negotiating parties promised, and peace has brought hope and the possibility for a new life for the Achenese people (Merikallio 2006).

With so many peace processes failing in the negotiation phase, President Ahtisaari was often asked how CMI was able to facilitate acceptance on the Helsinki agreement during such a short negotiation process. He identified six primary reasons for the success of the negotiation process:

1. The political will of the parties.
2. The skills and resolve of the negotiators in both delegations.
3. Serendipitous timing.
4. The posttsunami environment, which brought about heightened international attention on Aceh and a sense of urgency to resolve the conflict.
5. A multitrack process: the flexibility of the NGO facilitator combined with the leverage of the regional organizations and key states. CMI's networks in the EU and with other NGOs and research organizations were invaluable. Also key was the support of the Finnish Government from the beginning.
6. The well-functioning monitoring mechanisms provided by the EU and the five ASEAN countries.

According to Ahtisaari, it was crucial that the peace agreement was followed by a credible international monitoring mission that ensured both parties would implement their obligations (Paris 2004). The Aceh Monitoring Mission has become one of the key components of the implementation of the agreement and has shown that Asia and Europe can successfully act together in crisis management. Early on in the negotiations, Ahtisaari realized that regional organizations – specifically the EU and ASEAN – could have a significant role in the process. It was equally evident that the organizations could only have this role collaboratively, possibly with support of countries like Norway and Switzerland. Their combined efforts provided the expertise, cultural knowledge and credibility that were needed for the assignment.

The Aceh Monitoring Mission is so far the best and most concrete example of cooperation between Europe and Asia in the field of peace-building and crisis management, according to Ahtisaari. First and foremost, the Mission has had an indispensably important role in monitoring the implementation of the Aceh Peace Accord and thereby consolidating the process within its first vital months (Hampson 1996). This was the very purpose of the mission. Ahtisaari believes this was not, by any means, the only important outcome that the monitoring cooperation has generated. This Europe–Asia teamwork has proven the strength of the regional approach, highlighting the growing potential of cooperation between Europe and Asia in other areas and providing valuable lessons that can be utilized in other civilian crisis management operations.

CONCLUSION

This chapter addresses the impact of NGOs on conflict resolution and peace-building at the international level, through the lens of direct peace-making. The summation of the Cold War instituted a shift at the end of the 20th century, with nonstate actors playing an increasingly significant role in the mediation, management, and resolution of intra-state violent conflict (Ahmed & Potter 2006; DeMars 2005). International observers have recognized this shift, and we have seen the engagement of NGOs affecting conflict dynamics in the past, as well as the present. This trend will certainly continue and likely increase in the future. Researchers now have enough examples of NGO intervention to understand that this trend developed in a post-Cold War environment in which the UN system needed to more effectively handle political transitions and the challenges of global change. Credible, trustworthy NGOs

provided a service to UN member states by offering a sort of change management system. Yet, questions of accountability and effectiveness were raised and concerns over coordination were expressed (Edwards & Hulme 1996; Fox & Brown 1998; Goodhand 2006; Jordan & Van Tuijl 2006; Mendelson & Glenn 2002).

It has been noted that successful mediators engage properly in an intractable conflict setting through analysis at ripe moments and coordinating with others while serving with commitment, resources, persistence, and experience (Bercovich 2002). It has also been observed that success is highly dependent on the participation in the process of recognized and legitimate leaders and on the capacity of the process to include all relevant actors to avoid the emergence of spoilers (Stedman 2002). The involvement of major powers must be constructive and the outcome of the mediation must not run counter to the prevailing interests of these powerful actors. The NGOs examined in this chapter have been able to positively respond to all these criteria for success, creating, as previously stated, a new set of possibilities for states both in conflict and involved in peace processes.

NGO involvement in international conflicts emerged primarily due to the connectivity capabilities of these organizations, which could offer a comparative relational advantage to UN member states that employed their services (DeMars 2005). The unparalleled access of certain organizations (such as Sant'Egidio in Mozambique) allows for dialogue with all stakeholders, including politicians, technocrats, media, and civil society, as well as nonstate opposition movements (Bartoli 1999, 2005). NGOs can facilitate this by creating chains between actors who normally would not communicate. A conflict resolution system is always about managing change, and the connectivity created by NGO involvement creates conditions for change that would not be possible otherwise. NGOs also provide a bridge between the formal and informal dimensions of politics, while providing inclusive legitimacy (Riccardi 1999). Conflict occurs due to a breakdown in the polity, creating a system in which certain actors don't have access to political legitimacy. NGOs add legitimacy through inclusion of all actors in the political process, while not being bound by the constraints of the political system. Because this process of NGO involvement in conflict resolution has already happened, there is now a track record that allows us to examine specific engagements. Conflict dynamics in Burundi, Mozambique, and Ivory Coast reflected the relevant role of NGOs in the management of the relationships between state and nonstate actors. The role of NGOs in these conflicts expanded the range of choices for the various actors so that both state and non-state actors had access to opportunities they otherwise would not have had (Morozzo Della Rocca 2003).

This chapter contends that, for NGOs to be successful in engaging conflict at the state and international level, four conditions must be met. First, the NGO must be credible in its claims. Reputation is extremely important, as evidenced by the Carter Center's initiatives in Venezuela as well as Sant'Egidio's recent work in Ivory Coast. Second, each of the successful NGOs we have discussed places a high value on confidentiality. A confidential, rather than public, process takes precedence in each of the NGOs' operating procedures. Third, an NGO must be able to work effectively with state actors. This condition is met through legitimacy. Some level of legitimacy allows states to work with the NGO in a quasi-diplomatic relationship. The last condition is the NGOs' capacity. Linked similarly to the first condition, the NGO must be able to deliver. When revisiting each of the three NGOs directly involved in peace processes, we see that none of them comes from a pacifist background. Rather, these NGOs emerged from a political milieu in which there is no timidity regarding power. The use of force is reframed not as an aberration, but as something that is against the interest of the parties themselves. Each NGO seems to be able to offer some form of principled politics, upholding the ideal of politics framed in the UN charter

(Akashi, 1995–96). These organizations work to reduce the relevance of violence.

The growth of NGO involvement in mediation and peace processes has also presented unforeseen challenges. One of the areas of greatest concern in literature dedicated to NGOs and their role in conflict resolution is accountability. Another area of concern emerges out of the attempt of some governments to "use" the NGO framework to hide their direct involvement. An interesting development in the growth of nonstate actors is the tension created by this exploitation of the NGO model. The difference between genuinely independent and impartial NGOs and state-sponsored ones is not always clear. This is why some observers have proposed the establishment of an "NGO rating system" that would do for global civil society what independent credit rating agencies do for the global financial system (Edwards & Hulme 1996; Fox & Brown 1998; Goodhand 2006; Jordan & Van Tuijl 2006; Mendelson & Glenn 2002).

Another area of concern is that, together with actors who have achieved the legitimacy necessary to conduct high-level, discreet peace-building work, there is an undisciplined offering of services by a plethora of other actors—NGOs, states, and international organizations—who seek to gain recognition in the field (Van Tongeren 2001). The prestige that is afforded to state and non-state actors who are perceived as successful in mediation and peace-building creates a positive incentive to intervene. The general trend of a growing number of actors who are willing to spend time and resources for meaningful peace-making activities is to be saluted as an important development. However, at times, this proliferation creates *de facto* competition and may disincentivize attempts at horizontal dissemination of information and best practices. This hesitancy to share information is further complicated by the confidentiality concerns that make actors effective interveners, in that they comply with the prudent use of information. Our interviews with practitioners revealed internal debates and institutional concerns involving the ethics of information sharing. State and nonstate interveners run the risk of having their motivations for engagement questioned when so much international clout is at stake. One practitioner interviewed played on the Cold War era "arms race" theme by likening the current state of international mediation to a "peace race" in which honest-broker nations are realizing the enormous respect gained through their initiatives and thus actively seek more involvement in peace-building. Obviously this trend, which is positive *per se*, must be carefully and constructively managed (Aall 1996).

The ultimate efficacy of NGOs operating in conflict resolution capacities must be balanced by the awareness that no process can be successfully accomplished by an individual entity operating alone. What the NGO process facilitates is the creation of a framework for continuity, while bringing together more people to work on a particular conflict resolution or peace-building project. All of the NGOs examined in this chapter have an explicit orientation towards conflict resolution. More importantly, when evaluating efficacy, each organization has a meaningful track record in facilitating contacts, dialogue, and agreements between state and nonstate actors (Edwards & Hulme 1996). The four organizations have demonstrated ongoing relational investment in several countries well before an actual, full-fledged initiative starts up. Another important aspect of the NGOs we have evaluated is that all maintain ongoing, constructive relationships with governments and international organizations, and that the UN system, in particular, has dealt with these NGOs frequently and constructively.

Although we have focused our attention on NGOs with direct involvement in peace processes, the impact of NGOs involved in indirect peace processes has also been significant. While the Community of Sant'Egidio, the Carter Center, the Center for Humanitarian Dialogue, and the Crisis Management Initiative are engaged in quite specific work – namely, state-level, Track 1 diplomacy being done by NGOs – there are thousands of other global NGOs engaged in

excellent work, particularly at the societal level. Organizations such as Search for Common Ground,[14] International Alert,[15] the West African Network for Peace building (WANEP),[16] and The African Centre for the Constructive Resolution of Disputes (ACCORD),[17] have taken leading roles in conflict resolution and peace-building at the societal level. At the same time, the Global Partnership for the Prevention of Armed Conflict (GPPAC)[18] and the European Center for Conflict Prevention (ECCP)[19] seek to address the interface between civil society and governments. Acting as a conduit between conflicted parties and international policy makers, the International Crisis Group[20] has identified its own niche in the field of conflict resolution and peace-building through independent monitoring of conflict zones and the provision of timely policy advice to international decision makers best positioned to act.

Practitioners debate the role NGOs will play in future international peace-building efforts, but agree that the current trend of NGO involvement will continue in the context of the economically developing world. Some practitioners believe that UN member states will seek to engage their resources most heavily in conflicts that are perceived as more strategically important to their individual interests, while passing authority for other engagements to regional and subregional organizations. Other practitioners disagree that strategic and nonstrategic involvement of UN states is an issue, but acknowledge NGO shortcomings. NGOs will continue to play an active role as conveners and mediators in peace-building efforts, but as one practitioner pointed out, NGOs will never possess the ability to implement agreements (Hampson 1996). States will continue to bring clout to the peace agreements, but the post-agreement phase offers a niche for different NGO engagement, both in support of the peace process through monitoring and with further facilitation in parallel to the more traditional work of development and post-conflict reconstruction. One practitioner said a key issue is that the international focus is always on the agreement, while what comes after the agreement is what matters most. Implementation of agreements often involves more mediation than that involved in getting to the actual agreement (Bercovitch, in this volume).

Fifteen years beyond Sant'Egidio's successful engagement in the Mozambique peace process, NGOs continue to play prominent roles in conflict resolution and peace-building. Sant'Egidio broke new ground in Mozambique by "inventing" an option for Track 1 diplomacy that was previously only informally or occasionally available to official actors. More is to come in terms of NGO contributions to international conflict resolution. Three important developments have occurred since the end of the Cold War that will ensure the continued prominence of NGO involvement in peace processes: the proliferation of activist governments seeking to be involved in international peace-building initiatives, the proliferation of NGOs, and the growing number of credible and legitimate former heads of democratic states who are willingly engaging in peace-building work. This growth will offer much to the marketplace of ideas, presenting options unthinkable only 15 years ago. Such a diverse convening of thought has failed to exist in the past, but the careful management of this new marketplace may provide dynamic possibilities for the mediation and resolution of future violent conflicts.

NOTES

1 www.santegidio.org/en/index.html
2 www.cartercenter.org/
3 www.hdcentre.org/
4 www.ahtisaari.fi/
5 www.accord.org.za/web/home.htm
6 www.gppac.org/
7 www.conflict-prevention.net/
8 Jeffrey Rubin identified reward power when the mediator has something to offer to the parties, such as side payments in exchange for changes in behavior; coercive power that relies on threats and sanctions to carry those threats out, again with the intention of changing the behavior of parties; expert power that is based on the mediator's greater knowledge

and experience of certain issues; legitimate power that is based on certain rights and legally sanctioned authority under international law; referent power that is based on the desire of the parties to the conflict to maintain a valued relationship with the mediator; informational power that works on the content of the information conveyed as in the case of a go-between or message carrier.

9 www.clubmadrid.org/cmadrid/index.php?id=1
10 www.parliamentofcultures.org
11 www.forum2000.cz/
12 www.peres-center.org/
13 globalpanel.net/
14 www.sfcg.org/
15 www.international-alert.org/
16 www.wanep.org/
17 www.accord.org.za/web/home.htm
18 www.gppac.net/
19 www.conflict-prevention.net/
20 www.crisisgroup.org/

REFERENCES

Aall, Pamela. 1996. "Nongovernmental Organizations and Peacemaking." In *Managing Global Chaos: Sources of and Responses to International Conflict.* (eds.) Chester A. Crocker, Fen Osler Hampson, & Pamela Aall. Washington, DC: United States Institute of Peace Press.

Abrahamsson, Hans & Nilsson, Anders. 1995. *Mozambique, the Troubled Transition: From Socialist Construction to Free Market Capitalism.* London: Zed Books.

Adresse a la Nation de S.E.M. Laurent Gbagbo Apres la Signature de L'Accord de Paix de Ouagadougou, "C'est la Victoire du Peuple." November 3, 2007. Posted at http://www.santegidio.org/news/rassegna/2007/0311_004685_FR.htm

Ahmed, Shamima & Potter, David. 2006. *NGOs in International Politics.* Bloomfield: Kumarian Press.

Akashi, Yasushi. 1995–96. "The Limits of UN Diplomacy and the Future of Conflict Mediation." *Survival.* 37: (4). Winter. pp. 83–98.

Anderson, Mary B. 1996. "Humanitarian NGOs in Conflict Intervention." In *Managing Global Chaos: Sources of and Responses to International Conflict.* (eds.) Chester A. Crocker, Fen Osler Hampson, & Pamela Aall. Washington, DC: United Institute of Peace Press.

Anderson, Mary B. 1999. *Do No Harm: How Aid Can Support Peace or War.* Boulder: Lynne Rienner.

Arnson, Cynthia J. & Whitfield, Teresa. 2005. "Third Parties and Intractable Conflicts." In *Grasping the Nettle: Analyzing Cases of Intractable Conflict.* (eds.)

Chester A. Crocker, Fen Osler Hampson, & Pamela Aall. Washington, DC: United States Institute of Peace Press. pp. 231–268.

Arthur, Paul. 1999. "Multiparty Mediation in Northern Ireland." In *Herding Cats: Multiparty Mediation in a Complex World*. (eds.) Chester A. Crocker, Fen Osler Hampson, & Pamela Aall. Washington, DC: United States of Institute Peace Press.

Avruch, Kevin. 1998. *Culture & Conflict Resolution*. Washington, DC: United States Institute of Peace Press.

Balachandra, Lakshmi, Barrett, Frank J., Bellman, Howard, Fisher, Colin, & Susskind, Lawrence. 2005. "Improvisation and Mediation: Balancing Acts." *Negotiation Journal*. 21: (4). October. pp. 425–434.

Bartoli, Andrea. 1999. "Mediating Peace in Mozambique: The Role of the Community of Sant'Egidio." In *Herding Cats: Multiparty Mediation in a Complex World*. (eds.) Chester A. Crocker, Fen Osler Hampson, & Pamela Aall. Washington, DC: United States Institute of Peace Press. pp. 245–274.

Bartoli, Andrea. 2001. "Forgiveness and Reconciliation in the Mozambique Peace Process." In *Forgiveness and Reconciliation: Religion, Public Policy & Conflict Transformation*. (eds.) Raymond G. Helmick, & Rodney L. Petersen. Philadelphia: Templeton Foundation Press.

Bartoli, Andrea. 2005. "Learning from the Mozambique Peace Process: The Role of the Community of Sant'Egidio." In *Paving the Way: Contributions of Interactive Conflict Resolution to Peacemaking*. (ed.) Ronald J. Fisher. Lanham: Lexington Books.

Bartoli, Andrea & Coleman, Peter T. 2003. "Dealing with Extremists." In *Beyond Intractability*. (eds.) Guy Burgess, & Heidi Burgess. Boulder: Conflict Research Consortium, University of Colorado.

Bercovitch, Jacob. 1989. "International Dispute Mediation: A Comparative Empirical Analysis." In *Mediation Research: The Process and Effectiveness of Third Party Intervention*. (eds.) Kenneth Kressel, & Dean Pruitt. San Francisco: Jossey-Bass.

Bercovitch, Jacob. 1991. "International Mediation and Dispute Settlement: Evaluating the Conditions for Successful Mediation." *Negotiation Journal*. 7: (1). January. pp. 17–30.

Bercovitch, Jacob. (ed.) 1996. *Resolving International Conflicts: The Theory and Practice of Mediation*. Boulder: Lynne Rienner.

Bercovitch, Jacob. (ed.) 2002. *Studies in International Mediation: Essays in Honor of Jeffrey Z. Rubin*. New York: Palgrave Macmillan.

Bohm, David. 2004. *On Dialogue*. New York: Routledge.

Boulding, Kenneth E. 1989. *Three Faces of Power*. Newbury Park: Sage Publications.

Boutros-Ghali, Boutros. 1992. *An Agenda for Peace: Preventive Diplomacy, Peacemaking, and Peacekeeping*. New York: United Nations.

Charmaz, Kathy. 1995. "Grounded Theory." In *Rethinking Methods in Psychology*. (eds.) Jonathan A. Smith, Rom Harreì, & Luk Van Langenhove. Thousand Oaks: Sage Publications.

Coleman, Peter T. 2003. "Characteristics of Protracted, Intractable Conflict: Towards the Development of a Meta-framework I." *Peace and Conflict: Journal of Peace Psychology*. 9: (1). pp. 1–37.

Committee for Conflict Transformation Support. 2001. "The Role of NGOs, Local and International, in Post-War Peacebuilding." *CCTS Newsletter*. (15). Winter.

Cooper, Robert & Berdal, Mats. 1993. "Outside Intervention in Ethnic Conflicts." *Survival*. 35: (1). pp. 118–142.

Crocker, Chester A., Hampson, Fen Osler, & Aall, Pamela (eds.) 1999. *Herding Cats: Multiparty Mediation in a Complex World*. Washington, DC: United States Institute of Peace Press.

Curle, Adam. 1986. *In the Middle: Non-official Mediation in Violent Situations*. Berg: St Matins Press.

D'Amico, Lynne C. & Rubinstein, Robert A. 1999. "Cultural Considerations When 'Setting' the Negotiation Table." *Negotiation Journal*. 15: (4). October. pp. 389–395.

DeMars, William E. 2005. *NGOs and Transnational Networks: Wild Cards in World Politics*. Ann Arbor: Pluto Press.

Diamond, Louise & McDonald, John. 1996. *Multi-Track Diplomacy: A Systems Approach to Peace*. 3rd edn. West Hartford: Kumarian Press.

Donini, Antonio. 1996. *The Policies of Mercy: UN Coordination in Afghanistan, Mozambique, and Rwanda*. Providence: The Watson Institute.

Edwards, Michael & Hulme, David. (eds.) 1996. *Beyond the Magic Bullet: NGO Performance and Accountability in the Post-Cold War World*. West Hartford: Kumarian Press.

Fisher, Ronald J. 1997. *Interactive Conflict Resolution*. Syracuse: Syracuse University Press.

Fisher, Ronald J. (ed.) 2005. *Paving the Way: Contributions of Interactive Conflict Resolution to Peacemaking*. Lanham: Lexington Books.

Fitzduff, Mari & Church, Cheyanne. (eds.) 2004. *NGOs at the Table: Strategies for Influencing Policy in Areas of Conflict*. Lanham: Rowman & Littlefield.

Fox, Jonathan A. & Brown, L. David. (eds.) 1998. *The Struggle for Accountability: The World Bank, NGOs, and Grassroots Movements*. Cambridge: MIT Press.

Giro, Mario. 1998. "The Community of Sant'Egidio and its Peacemaking Activities." *International Spectator*. 33: (3). July–September. pp. 85–100.

Glaser, Barney G. & Strauss, Anselm L. 1967. *The Discovery of Grounded Theory: Strategies for Qualitative Research.* London: Weidenfeld and Nicolson.

Goodhand, Jonathan. 2006. *Aiding Peace?: The Role of NGOs in Armed Conflict.* Boulder: Lynne Rienner.

Griffiths, Martin. 2005. "Talking of Peace in a Time of Terror: United Nations Mediation and Collective Security." *Centre for Humanitarian Dialogue.* 6. March.

Gurr, Ted Robert. 2000. *Peoples Versus States: Minorities at Risk in the New Century.* Washington, DC: United States Institute of Peace Press.

Hampson, Fen Osler. 1996. *Nurturing Peace: Why Peace Settlements Succeed or Fail.* Washington, DC: United States Institute of Peace Press.

Hampson, Fen Osler, Crocker, Chester A., & Aall, Pamela. 1999. "Multiparty Mediation and the Conflict Cycle." In *Herding Cats: Multiparty Mediation in a Complex World.* (eds.) Chester A. Crocker, Fen Osler Hampson, & Pamela Aall. Washington, DC: United States Insitute of Peace Press.

Hampson, Fen Osler & Malone, David M. 2002. *From Reaction to Conflict Prevention: Opportunities for the UN System.* Boulder: Lynne Reinner.

Hume, Cameron R. 1994. *Ending Mozambique's War: The Role of Mediation and Good Offices.* Washington, DC: United States Institute of Peace Press.

Impagliazzo, Marco & Giro, Mario. 1997. *Algeria in ostaggio: tra esercito e fondamentalismo, stroria di una pace difficile.* Milano: Guerini.

Jeong, Ho-Won. 2000. *Peace and Conflict Studies: An Introduction.* Aldershot: Ashgate.

Johnson, David W., Johnson, Roger T., & Smith, Karl A. 2000. "Constructive Controversy: The Power of Intellectual Conflict." *Change.* 32: (1). pp. 28–37.

Jones, Bruce D. 2002. "The Challenges of Strategic Coordination." In *Ending Civil Wars: The Implementation of Peace Agreements.* (eds.) Stephen John Stedman, Donald S. Rothchild, & Elizabeth M. Cousens. Boulder: Lynne Reinner.

Jordan, Lisa & Van Tuijl, Peter. (eds.) 2006. *NGO Accountability: Politics, Principles and Innovations.* Sterling: Earthscan.

Kelman, Herbert C. 1996. "The Interactive Problem-Solving Approach." In *Managing Global Chaos: Sources of and Responses to International Conflict.* (eds.) Chester A. Crocker, Fen Osler Hampson, & Pamela Aall. Washington, DC: United States Institute of Peace Press. pp. 501–520.

Kriesberg, Louis. 1992. *International Conflict Resolution: The US-USSR and Middle East Cases.* New Haven: Yale University Press.

Lederach, John Paul. 1995. *Preparing for Peace: Conflict Transformation Across Cultures.* Syracuse: Syracuse University Press.

Lederach, John Paul. 1997. *Building Peace: Sustainable Reconciliation in Divided Societies.* Washington, DC: United States Institute of Peace Press.

Lindberg, Staffan I. 2006. *Democracy and Elections in Africa.* Baltimore: The Johns Hopkins University Press.

Lund, Michael S. 1996. *Preventing Violent Conflicts: A Strategy for Preventive Diplomacy.* Washington, DC: United States Institute of Peace Press.

Martin, Harriet. 2006. *Kings of Peace, Pawns of War: The Untold Story of Peace-making.* London: Continuum.

Matthews, Dylan. 2001. *War Prevention Works: 50 Stories of People Resolving Conflict.* Oxford: Oxford Research Group.

McDonald, John W. 1991. "Further Exploration of Track Two Diplomacy." In *Timing the De-Escalation of International Conflicts.* (eds.) Louis Kreisberg, & Stuart J. Thorson. Syracuse: Syracuse University Press. pp. 201–220.

McDonald, John W. 2003. "Multi-Track Diplomacy." In *Beyond Intractability.* (eds.) Guy Burgess, & Heidi Burgess. Boulder: Conflict Research Consortium, University of Colorado.

Mendelson, Sarah E. & Glenn, John K. (eds.) 2002. *The Power and Limits of NGOs: A Critical Look at Building Democracy in Eastern Europe and Eurasia.* New York: Columbia University Press.

Merikallio, Katri. 2006. *Making Peace. Ahtisaari and Aceh.* Helsinki, Finland: WS Bookwell Oy.

Minear, Larry. 2002. *The Humanitarian Enterprise. Discoveries and Dilemmas.* Bloomfield: Kumarian Press.

Morozzo Della Rocca, Roberto. 2003. *Mozambique: Achieving Peace in Africa.* Washington, DC: Georgetown University Press.

Notter, James & McDonald, John. 1996. "Track Two Diplomacy: Nongovernmental Strategies for Peace." *US Foreign Policy Agenda.* 1: (19). December.

Paris, Roland. 2004. *At War's End: Building Peace After Civil Conflict.* Cambridge: Cambridge University Press.

Princen, Thomas. 1992. *Intermediaries in International Conflict.* Princeton: Princeton University Press.

Ramsbotham, Oliver, Woodhouse, Tom, & Miall, Hugh. 2005. *Contemporary Conflict Resolution: The Prevention, Management and Transformation of Deadly Conflicts.* 2nd edn. Malden: Polity Press.

Reychler, Luc & Paffenholz, Thania. (eds.) 2001. *Peacebuilding: A Field Guide.* Boulder: Lynne Reinner.

Riccardi, Andrea. 1999. *Sant'Egidio: Rome and the World.* London: St Paulus.

Roberts, Nancy C. (ed.) 2002. *The Transformative Power of Dialogue.* Boston: JAI Press.

Ropers, Norbert. 2001. "Enhancing the Quality of NGO Work in Peacebuilding." In *Peacebuilding: A Field*

Guide. (eds.) Luc Reychler, & Thania Paffenholz. Boulder: Lynne Reinner.

Rubin, Barnett R. 2002. *Blood on the Doorstep: The Politics of Preventive Action.* New York: Century Foundation Press.

Rubin, Jeffrey Z. 1992. "International Mediation in Context." In *Mediation in International Relations.* (eds.) Jacob Bercovitch, & Jeffrey Z. Rubin. New York: St Martin's Press.

Santa Cruz, Arturo. 2005. *International Election Monitoring, Sovereignty, and the Western Hemisphere Idea: The Emergence of an International Norm.* New York: Routledge.

Schnabel, Albrecht & Carment, David. (eds.) 2004. *Conflict Prevention from Rhetoric to Reality.* Vol. 1 & 2. Lanham: Lexington Books.

Sharp, Gene. 2005. *Waging Nonviolent Struggle: 20th Century Practice and 21st Century Potential.* Boston: Extending Horizons Books.

Stedman, Stephen John. 2002. "Introduction." In *Ending Civil Wars: the Implementation of Peace Agreements.* (eds.) Stephen John Stedman, Donald S. Rothchild, & Elizabeth M. Cousens. Boulder: Lynne Rienner.

Steiner, Barry H. 2004. *Collective Preventive Diplomacy: A Study in International Conflict Management.* Albany: State University of New York Press.

Stephenson, Carolyn. 2005. "Nongovernmental Organizations (NGOs)." In *Beyond Intractability.* (eds.) Guy Burgess, & Heidi Burgess. Boulder: Conflict Research Consortium, University of Colorado.

SwissPeace. 2007. *FAST Update Mozambique No. 3: Trends in Conflict and Cooperation May – June 2007.* www.reliefweb.int/rw/rwb.nsf/db900sid/AMMF-75FDCS?OpenDocument

Synge, Richard. 1997. *Mozambique: UN Peacekeeping in Action.* Washington, DC: United States Institute of Peace Press.

United Nations. 1995. "The United Nations and Mozambique 1992–1995." *UN Blue Book Series.* 5.

Ury, William. 2000. *The Third Side: Why We Fight and How We Can Stop.* New York: Penguin Books.

Ury, William. 2007. *The Power of a Positive No: How to Say No and Still Get to Yes.* New York: Bantam Books.

Uvin, Peter. 1998. *Aiding Violence: The Development Enterprise in Rwanda.* West Hartford: Kumarian Press.

Van Tongeren, Paul J.M. 2001. "Coordination and Codes of Conduct: The Challenge of Coordination and Networking." In *Peacebuilding: A Field Guide.* (eds.) Luc Reychler, & Thania Paffenholz. Boulder: Lynne Reinner.

Weiner, Eugene. (ed.) 1998. *The Handbook of Interethnic Coexistence.* New York: Continuum.

Zartman, I. William (ed.) 1995. *Elusive Peace: Negotiating an End to Civil Wars.* Washington, DC: Brookings Institution Press.

Zartman, I. William. 2001. "The Timing of Peace Initiatives: Hurting Stalemates and Ripe Moments." *The Global Review of Ethnopolitics.* 1: (1). September. pp. 8–18.

21

United Nations Mediation Experience: Practical Lessons for Conflict Resolution

Connie Peck[1]

Since its inception in 1945, much of the effort of the United Nations has been aimed at the 'maintenance of peace and security' and the 'pacific settlement of disputes' – objectives set out in the UN Charter. This chapter will briefly discuss the UN's methodology in the area of conflict resolution within the context of the typology on different approaches to dispute resolution outlined by Ury, Brett and Goldberg (1988). It will then focus more specifically on the UN's interest-based approach and suggest some of the lessons that can be learned for conflict resolution and peacemaking from UN experience.

THE UNITED NATIONS AS A DISPUTE SETTLEMENT SYSTEM

Indeed, the three main approaches to dispute settlement outlined by Ury and his colleagues – power-based, rights-based and interest-based – are all embodied in different parts of the United Nations, as discussed in greater detail elsewhere (Peck, 1991, 1994, 1998). The Security Council represents the UN's power-based approach; the International Court of Justice, its right-based approach; and the Secretary-General and his Representatives, its interest-based approach.[2]

Of course, other parts of the UN system also help to avoid or resolve disputes by establishing norms, standards and rules to guide the interaction of member states with one another as well as with their own populations. The General Assembly, the Economic and Social Council, the Human Rights Council, the Conference on Disarmament, the World Trade Organization and many other fora offer an opportunity for member states of the organization to dialogue and eventually come to agreement on a whole range of topics which help avoid international disputes and/or set forth rules for helping to resolve them when they do occur. The multilateral negotiations in such fora are often intense as multiple parties with different interests try to agree. These organizations are not 'talking shops' as is sometimes claimed; their decisions have a profound impact on both inter- and intra-state relations.

Other parts of the UN system also engage in negotiation and mediation in order to carry out their mandates. For example, humanitarian organizations, such as the World Food Programme, the High Commissioner for Refugees, the United Nations Fund for Children and many others have to negotiate humanitarian access in conflict situations in order to deliver humanitarian assistance to those suffering from the conflict.

However, the three parts of the UN which deal most directly with conflict resolution *per se* are discussed briefly below.

The UN's power-based approach

The Security Council is the UN organ most directly charged by the Charter with the responsibility for maintaining peace and security. Its 15 members[3] meet regularly to discuss trouble spots around the world, to receive input and reports from member states, as well as from the UN system, and from regional and non-governmental organizations and to make decisions about what action should be undertaken. Its actions are negotiated among its members, then voted on and announced in the form of Security Council Resolutions which have the force of international law. The Council can also issue letters or Presidential statements, or establish a Security Council Mission to see a situation firsthand and make recommendations directly to the parties. The Council can take action under Chapter VI of the UN Charter with the consent of the member state involved or under Chapter VII in which consent is not required. The Council can also refer the situation to a regional organization under Chapter VIII.

During the Cold War, the Security Council's ability to take action was constrained by the veto power of its permanent members which was used as part of their Cold War struggle. Since then, however, the veto has been used less frequently and informal consultations,

especially among the permanent members, have allowed the Council to become much more active. Even so, the Council's actions (and sometimes inaction) are not always welcomed. A large number of members feel that the Council is not representative of the UN's membership as a whole and debate is ongoing about the need for Security Council reform, with numerous formulas proposed. There is also widespread concern that the permanent members of the Council too frequently pursue their own geopolitical interests rather than those of the membership as a whole, resulting in different standards being applied to different situations. The Council's greater use in recent years of Chapter VII measures, such as peace enforcement, sanctions or arms embargoes, are also a cause for concern to some. Thus, members are often reluctant to relinquish control over the process and outcome of their disputes to a Security Council with such powerful instruments.

Moreover, even in cases where the Council has tried to act as a kind of arbiter (rather than as an enforcer, bringing parties to the Council chambers for discussion), parties tend to respond by engaging in adversarial debate rather than problem solving. This mutual recrimination and positional arguing by each side to convince the Council of the 'rightness' of its case and the 'wrongness' of the other side tends to further harden positions and inflame the situation. When Council members are forced to declare their sympathies, support for one or both sides can widen the dispute or encourage hostilities. But in spite of these issues, the Security Council's regular monitoring of a large number of conflict situations and actions to try to manage them have undoubtedly had an overall beneficial effect on international peace and security over the years and kept many situations from deteriorating further.

Of all the power-based instruments available to the Council, the most successful has been the use of peacekeeping operations, which were not mentioned in the UN Charter, but were an afterthought proposed by Dag Hammarskjold. Since then, they have become a major instrument for maintaining peace or for restoring peace once a comprehensive peace settlement has been agreed upon by the parties. At the time of this writing, there are 97,924 personnel in the field in 18 peace operations led by the Department of Peacekeeping Operations on four continents (DPKO, 2006).

Peacekeeping missions vary greatly in their mandate, size and structure – ranging from unarmed military observers creating a thin blue line dividing the parties, such as in Cyprus, to large multidimensional peacekeeping forces, such as in Liberia, Sierra Leone or the Democratic Republic of the Congo. In recent years, peacekeeping forces have even been given an executive mandate, where for a limited period, the mission has become the virtual governing body in the country, such as in Cambodia, East Timor and Kosovo. The use of peacekeeping has evolved greatly since its inception and is now being used more extensively than ever before.[4]

Some peacekeeping missions are deployed under Chapter VI where peacekeepers are typically lightly armed, and others under Chapter VII where forces are more heavily armed with more robust rules of engagement about how and when force can be used. Thus, peacekeeping operations can encompass varying degrees of power, but the mere presence of a peacekeeping mission is a source of both power and influence. The supervision, monitoring and reporting functions of the peacekeeping troops and military observers (whether unarmed, lightly armed or heavily armed); civilian police; human rights monitors; civil or political affairs officers and election monitors all exert a wide range of implicit and explicit positive and negative leverage on the leadership of the conflicting parties, their constituents and on the population at large.

Of course, not all peacekeeping missions have been entirely successful and many lessons have been learned from these situations. However, in others, significant progress has been made (to cite a few examples, Angola, Burundi, Cambodia, Cyprus, the Democratic Republic of the Congo,

East Timor, Eastern Slovenia, El Salvador, Ethiopia–Eritrea, Georgia, Guatemala, Haiti, Lebanon, Liberia, Mozambique, Namibia, Sierra Leone and Tajikistan). In recent years, the UN has sought to learn the lessons from the experience of all these missions and to make the necessary reforms within the Department of Peacekeeping Operations to try to ensure that mistakes are not repeated. Nonetheless, the sheer complexity of multidimensional peacekeeping missions which have to operate in an ever-changing conflict environment cannot be underestimated.

The UN's rights-based approaches

Apart from the Security Council, the other UN organ directly charged with the peaceful settlement of disputes is the International Court of Justice (ICJ) located in The Hague. As the principal judicial organ of the UN, it was designed to hear contentious cases between sovereign states and to provide advisory opinions to the authorized organs of the UN. Although the ICJ has been involved in the resolution of a number of conflicts between states over the years, it has not proved to be as useful as the framers of the UN Charter hoped it would be for a number of reasons. One of these is because its statute limits it to disputes between states whereas most conflicts in recent years have been within states (Wallensteen, 2002). The other problem is that, like the UN's other peaceful methods for the settlement of disputes, recourse to the Court is largely voluntary (Peck and Lee, 1997). States can accept its jurisdiction in three ways. The first is through the 'optional clause' of the Court's statute (Article 36 [2]). This allows member states to declare that they recognize the compulsory jurisdiction of the Court, although they can also exempt certain areas from jurisdiction. The second is through the consent of a state to take a dispute to the court as part of a special agreement or compromise (Article 36 [1]). A final avenue is through compromisory clauses in treaty agreements, which stipulate that any dispute arising therefrom must be referred to the Court (Article 36[1]).

Thus, the Court has suffered from much the same problem faced by the Security Council. On the whole, member states have been reluctant to relinquish decision-making control to a third party. One hundred and ninty-one states are parties to the Statute of the Court but only 66 of them have accepted the compulsory jurisdiction of the Court and most of those have introduced reservations. Of even greater concern, only one of the five permanent members of the Security Council (the United Kingdom) has currently endorsed the optional clause for compulsory jurisdiction.

Use of the Court has, nonetheless, grown significantly in recent years and it has been successful in resolving disputes, most commonly territorial disputes between neighboring states over land or maritime boundaries; the treatment of nationals; or cases concerning the use of force by one state against another. In 2005, it rendered a judgment in 10 cases (Jiuyong, 2005).

The UN's interest-based approach

The Secretary-General and his Representatives embody the interest-based approach of the organization. When a preventive diplomacy, peacemaking, peacekeeping or peace-building mission is established, the Secretary-General appoints a Representative of the Secretary-General (also sometimes called Special Representative, Personal Representative, Envoy or Special Adviser) to head up the new peace mission. The size of preventive diplomacy, peacemaking and peace-building missions is usually quite small, whereas peacekeeping missions can be quite large; but in all cases, the Representative is the person on the ground responsible for the actual negotiation and mediation *in situ* with the conflicting parties.

In the case of peacemaking (obtaining a peace settlement after a situation has degenerated into armed conflict) or preventive diplomacy (before it reaches that stage), the Representative reports to the Secretary-General through the Department of Political Affairs. The UN has been involved in peacemaking (sometimes called 'good offices') in a range of situations (e.g. Afghanistan, Angola, Bougainville, Colombia, Cyprus, East Timor, El Salvador, the Former Yugoslavia, Guatemala, Georgia, Haiti, the Iran–Iraq War, Nicaragua, Tajikistan and Western Sahara) with varying degrees of success. As well, the organization sometimes plays a supportive role in situations where peacemaking is undertaken by regional or sub-regional organizations or other third parties (for example, in Burundi, Cambodia, the Democratic Republic of the Congo and Somalia). Even in peacekeeping missions, Representatives are constantly required to use negotiation and mediation to implement the comprehensive peace agreements which have been agreed and to overcome the many obstacles which present themselves during the implementation process. In the latter case, they report to the Secretary-General through the Department of Peacekeeping Operations.

Recently, it has been more widely acknowledged that building sustainable peace in a post-conflict situation requires a much longer-term engagement by the UN and peace-building missions, which stay on in a country after the peacekeeping mission has left, have been established. Once again, Representatives of the Secretary-General are appointed to head up these peace-building missions and to negotiate with the parties on the ground, as well as with the donor community and with the UN Country Team to ensure that the situation receives what is needed to secure the right conditions for a sustainable peace. A new Peace-building Commission has now been established, composed of selected member states, with a Peace-building Support Office in the Secretariat to support its work and to ensure that more attention is given to this vital area.

LESSONS FROM UN EXPERIENCE FOR THE PRE-MEDIATION PROCESS

This chapter will now explore the use of negotiation and mediation by the Secretary-General and his Representatives to assist warring parties in finding (and subsequently implementing) comprehensive settlements to their conflicts and the lessons which can be learned from this experience for conflict resolution practice. Much of this information derives from a five-year study by the author, known as the 'UNITAR Programme for Briefing and Debriefing Special and Personal Representatives and Envoys of the Secretary-General' which has involved: (1) in-depth interviews with current and past Representatives of the Secretary-General (RSGs); (2) the preparation of two editions of a book for in-house UN use only (entitled *On Being a Special Representative of the Secretary-General*), as well as a set of edited DVD interviews – intended for briefing new RSGs and (3) a regular seminar for all current RSGs and senior headquarters staff (of which there have been three to date). The objectives of the study have been to preserve and pass on the valuable lessons and experience of RSGs and to ensure that these are used to refine and enhance future practice. Of course, this knowledge and advice is also of considerable use to our general understanding of conflict resolution and, therefore, is described here in brief.

Although different RSGs take different approaches to their third party role, some of the practical advice from their experience is presented below. Since many of the concepts referred to by RSGs come from the wider conflict resolution literature, the scholars who developed these concepts are also cited in the notes and the references.

Helping to ripen a situation

Some Representatives argue that UN involvement can help to 'ripen' a situation[5] and, therefore, that peacemaking assistance should be offered more proactively. 'When the UN becomes involved, it brings hope,' observes Vendrell (2002). He proposes that, where possible, the parties should be persuaded to accept a modest role for the Secretary-General's Representative as a facilitator or observer and then, when a window of opportunity opens, he/she will be well placed to assist. The UN

presence in Afghanistan prior to September 11, for example, gave it an advantage in being able to organize the talks in Bonn to form the new Afghan government following the defeat of the Taliban. Similarly in 1997, the UN began facilitating talks between Indonesia and Portugal over East Timor at a time when the chances of an agreement seemed unlikely. In January 1999, however, the new President of Indonesia made the startling announcement that East Timor would be offered regional autonomy and, if this was not accepted by its people, then Indonesia would consider releasing East Timor. As Marker (the Personal Representative of the Secretary-General who was facilitating the UN talks) notes, when this window of opportunity opened, 'we were right there and ready' (2001).

In Guatemala, the UN helped to ripen the situation by bringing civil society into the process (for example, trade unions, peasant groups, indigenous groups and human rights groups). This brought a greater element of balance into a situation where the guerrillas were very weak and also allowed more space for NGOs to develop. As well, it brought about a discussion in the media about how to end the conflict. Finally, the kind of proposals that the Secretary-General's Representative was putting forward 'created a dynamic within Guatemalan ruling circles, particularly within the army, that brought about power struggles and purges and, on the whole, resulted in the more moderate elements in the army, who were keener on negotiations, coming to the fore' (Vendrell, 2002).

Dealing with pre-conditions

One common problem that RSGs face occurs when one or both parties demand that certain requirements must be met *before* negotiations can begin. Such pre-conditions are often set by hard-line leaders or in response to hard-line constituents to block negotiations. By setting a pre-condition that one knows the other party is unwilling to accept, one appears willing to negotiate, while shifting blame to the other side for the blockage.

In internal conflicts, the most common pre-condition is a demand by the government for the guerrillas to disarm or sign a cease-fire agreement before negotiations. Guerrilla groups, however, frequently believe that only armed pressure will force concessions from the government, so they are usually unwilling to comply. 'In most cases, such a demand is a non-starter,' comments de Soto. 'War-time negotiations can actually be easier than peace-time negotiations, mostly because of the external pressure that can be brought to bear' (2001). Indeed, de Soto's mediation efforts in El Salvador offer a successful example of this.

Third parties can also make it clear to the parties that substantive pre-conditions are not acceptable. In the negotiations in Burundi, Dinka explained to guerrilla groups the distinction between substantive pre-conditions which had to be the subject of negotiation versus confidence-building pre-conditions which could be agreed to in order to build confidence. 'If the rebels say to me: "We don't want the president to call us rebels; we are an armed group, but we're not rebels!" I can go to the president and say, "When you speak on the radio, please don't call them rebels" – because that is not going to change anything.' By contrast, Dinka makes it clear that substantive issues are what have to be negotiated and no party should be asked to make a concession on such issues before the negotiations begin (2001).

Confidence-building measures

Egeland (2001) points out that, 'Parties often don't know which tools are available to them. They know how to fight, but they don't know how to make peace. They need to be educated in what confidence-building measures they can undertake and what tools the international community can provide.' In some cases, it may be useful to go through a pre-negotiation phase, where the objective is not agreement but merely low-key facilitation of dialogue and confidence-building. 'If you go too fast,' he warns 'you may end up with total rejection of the process.'

To facilitate confidence-building in Colombia, Egeland organized a joint tour by the two negotiating teams – the FARC and the government – to Stockholm and Oslo where seminars were held on human rights, international humanitarian law, experiences from other peace processes, democratic governance, rule of law and transparent governance. As well, the teams were taken on a joint European tour 'to expose them to something different than the vicious cycle they were living in their own country.' This helped to develop relationships between the parties and also established a positive relationship between the parties and the Secretary-General's Representative (2001).

In an attempt to make progress in the Georgia–Abkhazia conflict, a series of conferences were organized to discuss concrete confidence-building measures, such as the exchange of refugees and displaced persons; information sharing among law enforcement organs to prevent crime; cooperation in the field of mass media; economic exchanges in areas such as wineries and joint meetings between parliamentarians, journalists, NGOs, and directors of libraries. In the latter case, for example, the Director of the Georgian National Library agreed to search for books and materials among Georgian holdings to replace the loss of the Abkhaz archives destroyed during the war (Boden, 2001).

An interesting variation on confidence-building measures was used by de Soto at the beginning of the negotiations in El Salvador, when President Christiani was criticized by his constituents for offering a dialogue process with the guerrillas, who had refused to renounce hostilities. Knowing the guerrillas did not want to make a gesture to the government, de Soto took the unusual step of suggesting to the FMLN that it make confidence-building gestures to the Secretary-General (who was intervening for the first time in a good offices role in Latin America). The confidence-building measures adopted in response included the cessation of attacks against businesses, civilian targets and the banning of certain types of land mines, allowing the president to say to his constituents that something had been achieved by entering negotiations (2001).

The UN can also build confidence through its own actions. In both Guatemala and El Salvador, UN human rights monitors were deployed during the peacemaking process. Arnault comments that the deployment of the human rights verification mission created, within the URNG constituency, the sense that the peace process was bringing something tangible. 'Yesterday an army colonel could do anything and now there was an office of MINUGUA in the area, staffed with five police observers and five human rights monitors' (2001).

The need for a single mediator

RSGs were unanimous in agreeing that, for peacemaking to be effective, it must be led by a single mediator. Ould-Abdallah recalls that at one point in the Great Lakes Region there were twelve Representatives from regional organizations, member states, NGOs and the UN. 'Such a proliferation of intermediaries can, of course, engender considerable confusion regarding the role of the international community and create numerous opportunities for extremists to play one intermediary off against another.' In such cases, he advises that a 'lead actor' must be established (2000: 131). In Cyprus, where the UN has a mandate from the Security Council, de Soto (2004) met the other envoys and told them that the Secretary-General viewed them as his friends in the process and sources of advice and support. However, he also explained the importance of maintaining the unity and integrity of the UN's efforts and asked them to consult with him before coming to the island or having contact with the parties.

Deciding who to include in the process

Another issue which can be contentious is who to include in the process. Most RSGs urge that *all* major parties who are stakeholders in the situation should be included and warn that those left outside the talks will have a greater

motivation to act as spoilers.[6] 'Leaving a warring party out of a negotiation is a recipe for failure,' comments de Soto. 'It is essential to have the major protagonists in a conflict at the table, absent which you can't expect them to comply with whatever agreements emerge' (2001).

Tubman describes why the peace process for Somalia, organized by Djibouti in 2000 and dubbed the Arta process, didn't succeed:

> Arta was based on the premise that the warlords had been a problem and that although they were welcome there, the idea was that you would deal with civil society, with the clans, and they would get together and hold the answer to what was needed in Somalia. The warlords would be left out. When the government was formed, those who were left out were free to be co-opted into other arrangements. Ethiopia, which was also largely left out of the Arta process, wasn't happy with the results of Arta, and they reached out to those unhappy warlords and formed them into a group that began to offer a parallel political dispensation to the Transitional National Government. As a result, the people who initiated the next process – IGAD – felt that all stakeholders should be invited into the next peace process. (2003)

Ould-Abdallah (2001), however, warns against including extremists, since they can disrupt an already shaky political environment. By contrast, Vendrell (2002) argues that including an extremist group usually depends on the power of that group. 'The question,' he maintains, 'is not so much whether you have extremist groups at the table, but whether you accede to their demands which are contrary to the objectives and principles of the UN Charter.'

One means for overcoming the problem of extremists is to include a broader-based group of positive, influential actors, such as religious leaders, elders or scholars. Sahnoun (2003) proposes that these individuals should be given visibility, especially when the negotiations meet with success.

Another issue is the involvement of women. Security Council Resolution 1325 (2000) calls for 'an increase in the participation of women at decision-making levels in conflict resolution and peace processes.'

The UNIFEM book, *Women at the Peace Table*, argues that:

> It is predominately male leaders of the fighting parties who are negotiating an end to war and laying the foundation for peace. The justification often given is that the peace table must bring together those who have taken up arms because it is up to them to stop the conflict ... The process of reconstructing a society emerging from war requires the equal contribution of men and women. Ensuring women's participation in such negotiations enhances the legitimacy of the process by making it more democratic and responsive to the priorities of all sectors of the affected population ... In this sense, the peace table becomes a platform for transforming institutions and structures, and opening the door to greater social justice. (Anderlini, 2000: 5)

Other RSGs argue, however, that including too many parties makes agreement less likely. 'Most mediators,' comments Vendrell (2002) 'would look askance at the idea of having civil society (for example, the exile groups or the refugees) represented at the table, because it makes the negotiations totally unmanageable. But civil society will argue, "Why should only those with the guns be negotiating?".'

To overcome this problem in Guatemala, the UN mediation process established an Assembly of Civil Society in 1994, with representatives from a range of civil society groups. While the Assembly did not participate directly in the negotiations between the government and the guerrillas, it was able to input views and, even more importantly, it had the right to review and pass judgement on all agreements reached in the bilateral talks. Its judgement was not binding, but it did exert pressure on the main parties to take into consideration a broader range of interests (Arnault, 2001).

Dealing with decision-makers

Dealing directly with the decision-makers is vital to any peacemaking process. 'It is often a mistake,' advises Egeland, 'to seek contact with those who share your opinions because it's easier to deal with them. If you do that, you end up with a deal that can't be realized,

because those you dealt with have no clout on their respective sides.' He proposes that mediators should try to have the leaders at the table or at least those who can make decisions (2001).

In the 1990–91 El Salvador talks, the government's Dialogue Commission did not have full capacity to make decisions, so de Soto often found himself flying on an urgent basis to San Salvador to deal directly with President Christiani or phoning him from wherever the negotiations were being held. De Soto also travelled to Cuba, Nicaragua and Mexico to meet directly with the commanders of the FMLN (2001).

Agreeing on a venue

Settling on a venue for peace talks may also create problems, since the location can have symbolic meaning for the parties. Typically, governments want to hold talks inside the country, but opposition groups may fear for their security or be concerned about listening devices. In cases where a Group of Friends of the Secretary-General exists (which will be discussed later), the talks can take place in the country of one or more of the friends. More generally, Vendrell (2002) proposes that one should not choose a venue that is identified with either side or too distant. Good communication facilities are important, as is the consent of the host country, since it is usually asked to pay for the local costs. Finally, he recommends that one doesn't want a place 'where the government will try to poke its nose into the negotiations.' His modus operandi is to prepare a list of countries that he believes would be suitable and to individually ask the parties where they would *not* be willing to go. By the time he proposes a venue, he has discussed this thoroughly with all sides.

In Tajikistan, Merrem and his staff found themselves carrying out framework talks in December, 1996 in freezing temperatures at the mountain fortress of Commander Masood in order to overcome the fact that the President wanted talks in Dushanbe and Nuri wanted them at his own base in northern

Afghanistan (Merrem, 2002). In 1997 in the DRC, when Kabila's forces were marching on Kinshasa, Sahnoun and Mandela negotiated with Mobutu and Kabila on a ship provided by South Africa, anchored off the coast of Angola in order to avoid bloodshed (Sahnoun, 2003).

Establishing a framework for negotiations

Most UN mediators stress the importance of trying to obtain a framework agreement as a first step in the negotiation process. Such an agreement commits the parties to a process of negotiation and sets out how the process will be structured and what procedural rules will guide the talks. Framework agreements usually outline: who the parties will be; who the mediator will be; what format the talks will take and the need for high-level representatives from the parties who have the capacity to take decisions. A framework agreement also usually contains a commitment by the parties not to abandon the process unilaterally, as well as rules about who can talk to the media under what conditions. Even when it is not possible to negotiate a framework agreement, the mediator can 'frame' the talks by providing an opening statement which sets out procedural rules for the negotiation and seeks informal agreement on these.

LESSONS ABOUT MEDIATION FROM UN PEACEMAKING EXPERIENCE

Once the above hurdles have been surmounted and the facilitation/mediation process begins, there are a number of other challenges to be faced.

Identifying issues and agreeing on an agenda

Developing an agenda of key issues can be problematic since each party may want to include issues that the other does not wish to consider. 'It's important,' notes Sahnoun, 'that the agenda addresses all of the important grievances. Both sides must see that their legitimate fears are taken care of, but formulated in such a way that they can be accepted by the other side, so that neither party will see in the formulation any kind of provocation' (2003). RSGs generally recommend that agenda items should be framed in a neutral manner, for example, 'constitutional issues' rather than 'constitutional reform' (de Soto, 2001; Vendrell, 2002).

Ordering the agenda can also be problematic. Some RSGs suggests that mediators should begin with the issue on which they think progress is most likely, to give a sense that the negotiations are progressing. Also because agenda items are usually linked, they propose that parties should be warned that issues will not necessarily be negotiated in a sequential manner and that it may be necessary to alternate back and forth between issues. Certain items inevitably come at the end of the process, for example, return of refugees or demobilization, disarmament and reintegration of ex-combatants. In some cases, the mediator may wish to put issues on the agenda that the parties may not think of themselves, such as human rights or verification (Arnault, 2001; de Soto, 2001; Vendrell, 2002).

Bargaining over positions versus reconciling interests

Broadly speaking, two methods of negotiation can be identified. The parties themselves typically view negotiations as a *bargaining* process,[7] which merely transforms their existing power struggle from the military arena to the negotiating table. In such a process, each party advances positions (or advocated solutions) and argues for the acceptance of its positions and against the other party's solution – in pursuit of winning at the bargaining table what they were unable to win on the battlefield. If left unaided by an intermediary, parties tend to employ a range of coercive tactics to force the other side to make concessions. These may include recitation of past grievances, angry recriminations, threats, ultimatums and walk-outs. If unchecked, such tactics can backfire – causing the other party to react in kind, and bringing the whole process to a standstill.

The second approach to mediation, adopted by most RSGs involved in peacemaking, is to attempt to transform the process into a forum for problem solving, in which the objective is to search for innovative solutions which address each side's key interests in order to try to reconcile or bridge differing concerns. The main features that distinguish this more promising approach are:

- an in-depth understanding by the mediator of parties' core interests and concerns which must be addressed to achieve a sustainable settlement;
- the interposition of the RSG as a third party – who, in effect, becomes the negotiating partner for each side – and who, through shuttle or proximity talks, probes interests and explores innovative options with both parties. This allows each party to have a constructive partner as its interlocutor and overcomes the difficulty of parties having to deal directly with those with whom they have a bitter adversarial relationship;
- the use of international standards, practices and models which provide objective criteria upon which agreements can be based;
- an exploration with the parties of innovative options for addressing key interests that move beyond each side's positions and identify new possibilities that may not have been considered before, but which might be gradually pieced together into mutually acceptable agreements. These can be built from ideas presented by the parties themselves, the mediator, experts and civil society or they may be derived from international standards, models and best practices. After a series of consultations with the parties, the ideas are gradually refined until agreement is reached;
- the gradual building of confidence and subsequent improvement of the atmosphere between the parties which comes from sequential successes in reaching agreement; and
- the encouragement and support of influential member states (such as Friends of the Secretary-General) and other actors (such as donors or international financial institutions) which can nudge reluctant parties towards accommodation and agreement.

In facilitating the peace talks on Bougainville from 1999 to 2001, Sinclair defines how he transformed the process from one of arguing over positions to exploring options based on interests:

> In any process of negotiation, it can be important to have an initial period of general exchange of views between the two sides – but if you have too much of it, it can *become* the negotiation. When that happens, you're not doing anything to close the gap between the parties' positions, and if it's allowed to go on unchecked, it can degenerate into a trading of complaints and slogans, with political positions being advanced and insisted upon. When this started to happen in the Bougainville negotiations, I tried to steer the exchanges to a different level. Instead of articulating general positions, I proposed: "Why don't we go to the level of identifying interests? Beyond saying what you would like, let us identify why you would like to have this. What interests are you seeking to protect by putting this position forward? What fears are you trying to guard against by articulating this position?" After that, the nature of the discussions changed noticeably. The two sides became specific, more open, and gave themselves more space to find solutions or agreements. (2001)

Understanding parties' interests and finding solutions that satisfy interests

UN mediators agree that, to be an effective mediator, good listening skills are required in order to understand parties' interests and motivations.[8] This involves trying to see the situation from the parties' perspective – as they themselves see it. Sahnoun (2003) points out that 'When you listen, you create trust. Being listened to creates a psychological catharsis. It is important to ask questions – to go deeper into their thinking, into their views, into their apprehensions, into the way they came to these positions. That is absolutely fundamental.'

Arnault comments that the mediator must have empathy. 'You must be able to relate completely, totally and without reservation with each party's agenda. You must understand what they want, why they want it and why they want it so much.' He observes that the parties may hold positions or have committed acts that the mediator disagrees with but he advises:

> You still have the duty to understand what lies behind this behaviour and to understand where all their mistrust and suspicion comes from. To do this, you have to spend a great deal of time with them. I spent days and nights talking and talking and talking with the two parties. In French we say, *entrer dans les vues de quelqu'un*. It doesn't mean that you share their views – but that you understand them. You get into their shoes. You don't have to stay there, but at least you know what it's like. But doing that imposes a discipline of being simultaneously empathetic with contradictory views. (2001)

Along these same lines, de Soto explains his own approach:

> Going into any negotiation, a mediator should make it his business – as quickly as possible – to try to find out what interests, concerns, fears, aspirations, dreams and nightmares led to setting those positions. If you can identify interests, rather than positions, you're already a long way in the direction of finding the key to the solution of the conflict, especially if you do this with both sides. It's only by identifying the underlying interests and the institutional problems that are frequently attached to them that you can go beyond a glorified cease-fire to build peace that will be durable because you have identified the causes. Identifying interests – going beyond positions – involves finding out the source of grievances. Frequently, these may be exclusionary policies based upon exclusionary institutions. They may be economic, in order to entrench the interests of a certain sector of society; they may be simply for the preservation of the status quo; sometimes they are of an ethnic character. But these are the problems that have to be addressed. (2001)

RSGs also stress the importance of good background research. 'You're negotiating with people and they have to be analyzed,' observes de Mistura. 'You have to study their culture, their background, their motivations, their connections, their tactics and strategies and what they have done so far. In real estate, the experts say the secret is "location, location, location"; in negotiations, it's "homework, homework, homework"' (2004).

Finding proposals that address the parties' core interests requires creativity. In the negotiations over autonomy for Bougainville,

Sinclair was able to help the parties invent new options to address their most important interests. Regarding the police, for example, it was agreed that Bougainville would have its own police force with its own head who would be appointed by a commission that would include Bougainvilleans, as well as the commissioner of police in Port Moresby. The standards of policing were to be the same for both. 'This was a very creative solution,' concludes Sinclair, 'that met the concerns of the national government that the institution of the police not be fractured, and the concerns of the Bougainvilleans that the police arrangements would not be a constant reminder of the atrocities they suffered at the hands of the police during the crisis' (2001).

Finding the best balance between direct and indirect talks

When faced with the problem of how to structure the peace process, RSGs face two choices – whether to bring the parties face-to-face in direct talks or whether to see the parties one at a time in indirect talks, such as shuttle diplomacy or proximity talks. In the former, the mediator shuttles back and forth between parties that are not in close physical proximity, but this puts considerable strain on the mediator. So many prefer proximity talks, with parties located near one another, for example, in a university setting, a hotel or at UN headquarters.

In transforming a bargaining process into a problem-solving one, how negotiations are structured can make a big difference to the outcome. Except in formal conference diplomacy, RSGs, as a rule, tend to favor proximity talks over plenary sessions, where parties meet face-to-face, especially early in the negotiation. As Arnault explains:

> Plenaries are confrontational. They are there to outline your principled stand on an issue. It's very difficult to make concessions in plenary. Plenaries are a good way to commit parties to a certain position. If that's what you want, a plenary is the ideal setting. If you want exactly the opposite – if you don't want parties to be wed to a specific

position and if you are going to ask them to move away from this position – the last thing you want is a plenary, because once they've become wed to a position in front of the other party, they simply cannot abandon it without losing face. The major advantage of proximity talks is that you replace something which is not a dialogue, that is, the two parties talking at each other, with something that is a real dialogue, which is you talking to each of the parties. Essentially, what you do is to renounce the dialogue between the two parties and establish the only thing that can work at this particular point in time, which is a dialogue between you and each of them separately – and that can last quite a long time. (2001)

Voicing a similar view, Vendrell (2002) notes that the problem with face-to-face talks is that 'the parties tend to speak for propaganda purposes, so they reiterate their well-known positions all the time for the sake of the other party. They love to remind the other side of what they did wrong and what their own position is. As a result, you waste a lot of time.'

Indirect talks also make it easier for the mediator to make a proposal, since the parties do not know the source of the ideas. In a plenary setting, a proposal offered by the other side is frequently rejected and, if the mediator endorses it, he/she may be accused of siding with the party that made the proposal. For this reason, Vendrell is opposed to the parties exchanging proposals in writing, arguing that it is more efficacious to ask them to present their proposals to the UN team which can then structure ideas to address the interests of all parties (2002).

Another suggestion for advancing the process is to make use of the multiplicity of possible formats. As Arnault (2001) explains: 'One way to achieve progress is to constantly change the format in search of the easiest path. On the same day, I might move from a closed meeting with the two leaders, to a mid-sized meeting, to a large-sized one and then come back to a mid-sized meeting.' Jumping from one format to another, he argues, can sometimes build consensus.

Technical teams can also be used to advance the process and go beyond agreed-upon principles to flesh out details. Towards the

end of the Cyprus talks in 2003–2004, there were 12 working groups with up to 300 Greek and Turkish Cypriot lawyers and other experts, 'working at breakneck pace, around the clock.' They drafted the biggest peace agreement ever produced which was over 6000 pages. Regrettably, however, after this major effort by the UN, the agreement was ultimately rejected by the Greek Cypriot public in a referendum held on April 24, 2004 (de Soto, 2004).

Balancing asymmetrical power between parties[9]

Since parties are seldom equal in power, this can also present problems for UN facilitators. Egeland (2001) warns that, 'One often has to deal with asymmetric parties – usually it is a strong government and a weak insurgency, but it can be a weak government and a strong insurgency. This asymmetry can lead to a moral dilemma, because if one side is strong, the agreement may end up more favorable to the strong party.'

Vendrell (2002) suggests that it is inappropriate for mediators who have the objectives of the UN in mind to appease the strong and put pressure on the weak. 'If you have no objective, you will pressure the weak because you don't care about the outcome as long as the two sides agree. But if you end up with an agreement that's not just, this outcome probably won't last very long.' Building coalitions with civil society or international and national NGOs or bringing in Friends of the Secretary-General can be used to support a weak party. He further argues that it is important for the mediator to realize that there is rarely equidistance between the parties and that one cannot ask the two sides to make an equal number of concessions. 'When one side has three cards in its hand and the other has fifty, you can't agree with the latter if they say, "If I give up three cards, the other side should give up three as well."' He concludes that it is, therefore, often the stronger side that will have to make more concessions, especially in the beginning.

The mediator can also make the stronger party aware of the long-term negative consequences of certain actions. 'Leaders should be made to feel responsible,' advises Sahnoun. 'One should always stress the effects of the continuing crisis on society – the destruction of institutions, of infrastructure, and the hardship for the people. Sometimes it may even be important to tell them that, if they continue to behave as they are, they might one day be brought before an international court.' He suggests that it is also helpful to highlight factors, such as how the people of the region feel or the possibility of an adverse reaction from the governments of neighboring countries (2003).

Drawing on international norms, standards and models

Another useful strategy employed by RSGs is to bring existing norms, standards or practices into the process to serve as models.[10] 'A very important technique is what I call "technification",' says Arnault. 'In other words, bringing issues down to a technical level and having technical arbitration.' In Guatemala, he called in experts from UN agencies, the World Bank and the IMF to provide such input. For example, experts from the ILO who had devised the Convention on Indigenous Rights were called upon to explain that existing international standards must form the basis of all indigenous policies (2001).

Using a single negotiating text

Several RSGs advocate use of a single negotiating text[11] where, after extensive consultation, the mediator presents a draft text to both parties who, after study, are invited to suggest changes. The mediator then revises the draft and once again presents it for further comments until, in an iterative manner, the text evolves into something that all sides can accept. In Guatemala, Arnault constructed the text from four sources: (1) the interests of the government; (2) the interests of the guerrillas; (3) the interests of the Assembly of Civil Society and (4) expressions of international norms and best practices. But he cautions against prematurely trying to sell a text to the parties:

> The worst mistake you can make is to try to sell the parties something for which they have developed no sense of ownership. You have to walk them from where they are to the final product. Usually, I started by having a dialogue with one side. I looked at their position on a particular issue and tried to get more clarity on their concerns. Then I began engaging them, not based on the other party's position, which would have been rejected – but rather in the light of the positions and interests of civil society and the international community. Once I had something that seemed acceptable, I turned to the other party. But, of course, by then I already had the benefit of what I had heard from the first, so I was better able to build their concerns into the discussion. So, basically, what you try to do is to weave their concerns into yours, yours into theirs, and you end up having two separate negotiations where the parties rarely confront one another's positions directly; they basically raise their concerns to ideas you present and you try to incorporate these. (2001)

Introducing new ideas

RSGs often found it useful to introduce new ideas into the process.[12] In El Salvador, de Soto introduced the concept of the Truth and Reconciliation Commission, as well as the Ad Hoc Commission to Evaluate the Officer Corps of the Armed Forces. He took the notion even further by organizing brainstorming meetings to generate new ideas. In trying to formulate the human rights agreement, he brought together a group of human rights specialists, Salvadorans and personnel from the UN Centre for Human Rights for a brainstorming session. Many of the ideas that they produced subsequently became part of the human rights agreement (2001).

In the Bougainville negotiations, Sinclair tried to encourage the parties to come up with new ideas of their own, but when they were unable to do so, he proposed his own: 'The two delegations were in the same building, but they were not even looking at each other, because the feelings on the referendum were so strong.' To move the process forward,

Sinclair presented a paper outlining his own ideas on the issue. 'The moment I saw the two delegations starting to communicate,' he recalls, 'I realized we had something in this document. We had to do some refining, some finessing, but basically we were on our way to breaking the log jam on the question of the referendum.' The following day, the Loloata Understanding on the Question of a Referendum was signed (2001).

Sometimes, simply the introduction of new terminology can make a difference, as in East Timor where for years, the Indonesian government had rejected the term 'referendum.' It was, however, prepared to accept the new terminology of a 'popular consultation' which basically embodied the same concept of one person, one vote, with only the Timorese voting (Marker, 2003).

Eschewing artificial deadlines

Several RSGs cautioned against setting artificial deadlines.[13] De Soto offers a distinction between natural (or real) deadlines, imposed by the calendar and artificial deadlines, imposed by the mediator and cautions against imposing the latter. Real deadlines 'can and should be grasped and manipulated by a mediator to prod a negotiation along and pry concessions from recalcitrant parties,' he advises. 'But let the mediator beware of conjuring up deadlines not anchored in reality. Calls to settle by a given date "or else" frequently put the mediator's credibility at risk' – since they usually do not work (1999: 382).

Dealing with the media

Although RSGs involved in peacekeeping and peace-building typically find the media helpful, those engaged in peacemaking do not. Egeland (2001) notes that facilitators are 'dealing with vulnerable compromises or ideas that might become agreements further down the road and that would certainly be very controversial among the hawks on either side – if they were known.' For this reason, mediators want as little media attention as

possible until an agreement has been reached and the parties have had an opportunity to discuss it with their constituents. 'I've seen so many agreements crumble,' he cautions, 'because they were revealed at an early stage – shot down by chauvinist public opinion or groups.' But not talking to the press can also become an issue. When approached by the media, Egeland revealed with whom he met, what general issues were discussed and tried to give a positive message of having had good talks, without going into much substance.

Similarly, in describing how he dealt with the media in the tripartite talks with the UN in Indonesia and Portugal over the status of East Timor, Marker (2001) notes, 'We kept a very low profile. We more or less took Trappist vows. The media were a little unhappy about that, but we were very circumspect in what we said – never anything individually, always together with one or both governments.'

Indeed, LeMoyne (2005) describes how the process can go wrong if there is too much media exposure. In Colombia, the government and the guerrillas negotiated in front of the cameras during the entire period and 'turned the process into a media show. That was very damaging and was exploited repeatedly by one side or the other, as well as by the media. It was like a soap opera. It undercut the seriousness of the effort.'

To avoid this kind of scenario, most RSGs try to obtain a procedural agreement from the outset on dealing with the media. Vendrell, for example, asked the parties to agree that the Representative of the Secretary-General would be the *only* person to speak to the media (2002). Arnault (2001) proposed a rule that the parties could talk to the press about their own concerns, but could not comment on the other parties' positions.

The need for patience and persistence

Virtually all RSGs stressed the need for patience and persistence. 'The crucial thing is to stick with the parties, to keep faith with the process,' says Stephen. 'Optimism is a vital thing. You have to look for ways forward that give hope – in every situation' (2001). 'There are valid reasons why you want to rush the parties into something that allows the end of the war,' notes Arnault. 'But if the agreement is to survive, if it is good, legitimate, politically accurate, based on a great deal of mutual confidence and has addressed all major issues – that will require time' (2001).

RSGs also mention that parties need to be helped to understand that they cannot obtain everything they aspire to. 'A peace agreement will always be controversial,' concludes Egeland, 'because both sides have to give up something. Leaders have to accept that by agreeing on a practical although less than perfect deal, they may lose some public support, but history will show that they were heroes of peace who took the courageous decisions' (2001).

Using the Secretary-General's authority

In some cases, RSGs found it useful to call upon the authority of the Secretary-General. In Cyprus, de Soto (2004) used the Secretary-General's authority extensively. He invited the parties to meetings with Annan in New York, Paris, Copenhagen, The Hague, and Burgenstock, as well as in Cyprus itself. At these meetings, the Secretary-General used his own powers of persuasion, building on de Soto's work. He sometimes even read statements prepared by de Soto and his team to outline parameters of the process. On a number of occasions, the Secretary-General hosted working dinners and lunches for the leaders. 'A United Nations good officer, however qualified he may be as a Representative, can never aspire to the kind of authority that the Secretary-General personally carries,' concludes de Soto.

Unravelling the linkage between issues

Because issues in a negotiation are usually linked in complex ways,[14] many UN peace-makers adopt the rule of 'nothing is agreed

until everything is agreed.' This is to ensure that, although peace agreements addressing different agenda items are negotiated and signed one by one, they are then set aside until the full agenda has been dealt with and a comprehensive settlement is in place. At that time, a commitment is made to implement the full set of agreements according to a schedule that is included in the agreement.

Establishing public commitment

Public signing of peace agreements can provide a significant finale to years of negotiating and help to establish a public commitment to peace. De Soto (2001) recalls that the final ceremony for the signing of the El Salvador peace accord was held at Chapultepec Castle in Mexico City on January 16, 1992, before 10 heads of government, including those of all the Central American countries and the Friends of the Secretary-General, as well as the Secretary-General. The opening line of Boutros-Ghali's speech was: 'The long night of El Salvador is drawing to an end.' 'Until then, President Christiani had refused to meet with the guerrillas, but after a remarkable speech, he came down from the stage and embraced the guerrilla delegation members, one by one,' recounts de Soto, 'and he had tears in his eyes.'

Support from Friends of the Secretary-General

Another issue of importance to UN mediation is the support of the organization's member states. In certain situations, this relationship has been formalized by the creation of a Group of Friends of the Secretary-General, which can provide resources, ideas and diplomatic assistance and show the parties and their constituencies that there is international support for the peace effort.

RSGs agree that the choice of friends is crucial. 'It's best to choose countries that have no stake in the outcome,' argues de Soto, 'and to express the strong expectation that those countries who will become entitled to the lofty title of "Friends of the Secretary-General" will behave as such' (2001). Problems are more likely to arise when friends are self-appointed or where one of the friends has strong bilateral interests vis-à-vis one or more of the parties. This is illustrated by the Group of Friends established for Georgia/Abkhazia, where, as Whitfield notes, the Western states were staunchly opposed to the aspirations of the Abkhaz, whereas Russia, which was both a friend and 'facilitator' of the process, saw itself as the Abkhaz protector. Whitfield concludes that members of a Friends Group need to have conflict resolution as their uppermost goal. 'Situations in which individual Friends have a greater interest in the stability or continuing existence of one or other of the parties of the conflict, or their own influence within the conflict arena, than in the resolution of the conflict itself will be complicated by these national priorities' (2005: 13).

Working with regional and sub-regional organizations

In a growing number of situations, the UN has worked closely with regional and sub-regional organizations when they take the initiative in a peace process. For example, Dinka describes the role he played in the Arusha process, where first Julius Nyerere and then Nelson Mandela served as the regional mediators. 'Our role was to attend their meetings and listen and then to go talk to the people that were causing the most difficulty, trying to get them on board, trying to come up with compromise formulations.' He notes that this was effective because the parties trusted the UN to be an honest broker. Dinka then liaised with Nyerere's or Mandela's team to propose new ideas and formulations. 'Once you decide to play this kind of role,' he advises, 'the whole sub-region begins to trust you. But the moment you show some kind of indication that you want to take over the driver's seat, then the entire sub-region turns against you' (2001).

Stephen and Tubman played a similar role in two successive sub-regional peace processes for Somalia – the first sponsored by Djibouti, the second by Kenya. Stephen (2001) comments: 'My role was to accompany the process. I gradually developed a role as a kind of facilitator between the process and the international community's norms.' He worked, for example, to ensure that women and minority groups were adequately represented and had a meaningful role (2001). In the second peace process, Tubman acted as a go-between, exploring issues, interests and options with the parties and communicating these to the Kenyan Special Envoy in charge of the talks (2003).

Another interesting example of close cooperation is the partnership of the UN and the African Union in an initiative known as the International Conference on the Great Lakes Region, where Fall, an RSG for the UN, has worked closely with the Special Envoy of the Chairperson of the AU Commission. After wide consultation with the leaders and civil society of countries in the region, a regional framework and process was established to adopt and implement a Stability, Security and Development Pact to address four thematic issues: (1) peace and security; (2) democracy and good governance; (3) economic development and regional integration and (4) humanitarian and social issues. At the first summit, the Dar-es-Salaam Declaration on Peace, Security, Democracy, and Development in the Great Lake Region was signed in the presence of the UN Secretary-General and the Chairperson of the African Union Commission. A second summit is planned to endorse a plan of action which will constitute the Security, Stability and Development Pact for the region (Report of the Secretary-General, 2006).

LESSONS FOR PEACE AGREEMENTS

A number of lessons also emerge from UN experience regarding substantive aspects of peace agreements that are likely to lead to successful implementation.

Resolution of all major issues with sufficient detail and specificity

'To be effective,' argues Vendrell, 'a peace agreement has to deal with the causes of conflict. It has to either address the causes directly or establish a new system and institutions that will enable these causes to be dealt with over time' (2002). Moreover, peace agreements that are more complete are easier to implement, since more of the issues in contention have been worked out and agreed to ahead of time, leaving less to be decided during implementation. 'Lack of specificity in a peace agreement,' argues Ajello, 'is a recipe for endless discussions and disputes during the implementation phase' (1999: 640). He suggests that the additional time required to make a peace agreement more specific during the mediation phase is worthwhile and creates a more solid base for the implementation process (2001). As Legwaila (2001) notes, the UN Mission in Ethiopia/Eritrea, for which he was responsible, suffered from a lack of specificity in the agreement (brokered by the USA and the OAU) about the boundaries of the Temporary Security Zone, which resulted in endless problems for the mission.

Agreement on how power will be shared

How power is to be shared is also crucial. Careful consideration should be given to finding a model that fits each situation. Based on her experience in Angola, Anstee advises that an election in a post-conflict situation 'should never be based on a "winner takes all" formula. The losers must also have a stake in the future stability and prosperity of the country through a judicious system of power-sharing' (1996: 607). Hampson recommends that a settlement must, at a minimum, 'establish a level playing field and allow equal and fair access to the political process by formerly excluded groups. Everybody must have a sense that they can participate and that political life is not zero sum. The new rules about political competition must also be seen as fair and just' (1996: 218).

Acceptability to the majority of constituents

A peace agreement should also be acceptable to the majority of constituents. Although the peace process in Guatemala involved a special role for civil society, the private sector was not part of the process and this led to problems in implementation when the Constitutional Amendment required to carry out the provisions in the peace accords was defeated in a referendum (Arnault, 2001). As mentioned earlier, this highlights the importance of having all major stakeholders involved, in some way, in the process.

Clear guidelines about implementation priorities and timetables

Peace agreements also need to contain clear guidelines about implementation priorities and realistic implementation timetables. A common problem is that timetables are too ambitious and when deadlines are missed, 'the parties begin to doubt each other's political will to comply with the settlement' (Arnault, 2001). Agreements should spell out how the implementation schedules for different issues interlock with one another, because they often involve 'reciprocal concessions.' As de Soto (2001) explains: 'If the demobilization of guerrillas is contingent upon their receiving – immediately upon hand-over of their weapons – some sort of financial assistance, you had better be sure that you know if and when that assistance can and will be delivered.'

A lead role for the UN in implementation

Most RSGs agree that, in cases where the UN is expected to have a role in implementation, it should broker the peace agreement or have sufficient input to ensure that it is, indeed, implementable. 'Many of the problems encountered in Angola,' laments Anstee, 'were rooted in the nature of the Bicesse Accords, in the negotiation of which the UN played no role. The thesis that the main responsibility for implementing the Accords must be vested in the two parties in the conflict presupposed a Boy Scout's code of honour in circumstances hardly conducive to the evolution of the Boy Scout spirit.' She recommends that the UN should 'never accept any role in the implementation of a peace accord unless the organization has been fully involved in the negotiation of its terms and its mandate' (1996: 532–533).

An implementation mechanism for resolving disputes

Finally, peace agreements should contain an effective mechanism to manage the inevitable disagreements that arise in implementation. 'A strong political structure should be established to manage the peace process,' says Ajello. In Mozambique, the Supervision and Monitoring Commission was composed of the two parties, as well as representatives of the OAU, France, Italy, Germany, Portugal, the United Kingdom and the United States and chaired by Ajello, as the Special Representative of the Secretary-General. He sums up the benefits of this approach:

> This relationship allowed the international community to speak with a single voice and this support and unity of intent produced two important results. The first was that the parties' perception of my role changed dramatically. I was subsequently viewed by the two parties, not as the delegate of a bureaucracy in New York, but as a representative of the international community. (2001)

A wide variety of mechanisms have been effectively established in subsequent peace missions to carry out similar functions.

NEGOTIATION/MEDIATION DURING IMPLEMENTATION

Implementing peace agreements also requires an ongoing process of negotiation and mediation during the peacekeeping phase. RSGs who head up these missions (with the help of the various mission components) carry out constant negotiations – with the parties themselves, with the local population and with the international community – in order to move towards realization of the objectives of the peace agreement. As Hampson notes: 'The demand for mediators does not end once a deal is reached because negotiations between the parties typically do not end. The terms of a settlement are constantly being renegotiated during its implementation and new problems can emerge that have the potential, if left unresolved, to jeopardize the peace process' (1996: 227). Stedman, Rothchild and Cousens (2002) highlight the dangers of failing to satisfactorily implement peace agreements. They note that the breakdown of the Bicesse agreement in Angola in 1993 led to 350,000 deaths and the failure of the Arusha agreement in Rwanda in 1994 to 800,000 deaths.

Although it is beyond the scope of this chapter to describe the multitude of mediation efforts undertaken by RSGs during implementation, Steiner's experience on arrival in Kosovo offers a good example. When he arrived in February, 2002, the elections had been held the previous November but it had been impossible to form a coalition government because of disputes over the distribution of power among the parties. After bilateral discussions with the party leaders, he invited all of the players to a dinner at his residence in Pristina where he presented them with a draft text based on his previous discussions. Rooms were available for bilateral talks between the parties and between the RSG and the parties, and UN staff were positioned in the neighboring rooms for immediate translation into English, Albanian and Serbian. After hours of talks, at three o'clock in the morning, Steiner was able to give a press conference to the reporters who were camped outside his residence, announcing an agreement on the formation of a new government. After further negotiations on who would get what ministry, a couple of days later, the agreement went to parliament for confirmation. Although the constitution foresaw consecutive steps for voting on the president, the prime minister and the rest of the government, there was insufficient trust among the parties to proceed in this sequential manner. To overcome this, Steiner suggested that there should be just one vote to simultaneously elect the president, the prime minister and to confirm who would head each ministry. In the end, he notes, 'the Serbs got their minority posts. The biggest party got what it wanted, the post of president; the second biggest party got the post of prime minister and the various ministries were distributed. There was the normal political bickering but, in the end, people could live with the arrangement' (2003).

Ajello (2001) reminds implementers that understanding the interests of the parties is as important in implementation as it is in mediating the peace agreement. 'If you analyze all the elements, you should be able to say, 'These are the vital interests of these people. If we address these, we have a good chance of being able to solve the problems.' Finally, Hampson notes that:

> Peacemaking and peace-building are a nurturing process … negotiated settlements are unlikely to endure if left unattended; they must be cultivated by skilful, committed people able to manage the problems that inevitably arise as the terms of a settlement negotiated at a given point in time are translated over time into action. By entrenching their roles and remaining fully engaged, third parties can help settlements take root (1996: 217).

Indeed, the capacity of the United Nations to follow through its peacemaking efforts with the deployment of peacekeeping and peace-building missions to assist in implementation of a peace agreement is one of the comparative advantages the organization has over other entities. Further, RSGs are able to harness assistance and leverage from UN agencies, program and funds, as well as from member states to provide help and incentives for parties to follow through on their commitments. The UN mediator, however, differs from other mediators, as he/she must operate entirely within the framework of the UN Charter and the body of human rights laws and general principles and practices that emanate from it. As de Soto (2001) explains, the parties need to know that the United Nations has behind it

'a certain institutional backing, but also that a certain threshold has to be passed and certain standards must be met.'

CONCLUSION

Most UN peacemaking to date has been carried out by a few individuals who were often proactive in their approach and offered their services (sometimes in a modest way initially) to parties who ultimately accepted the assistance and asked for more, as confidence was established. The need to support and strengthen the UN's heretofore modest peacemaking efforts with adequate resources and greater political support was acknowledged at the 2005 World Summit of Heads of State and of Government in the subsequent resolution adopted by the General Assembly which endorsed a greater role for the Secretary-General in this regard: 'Recognizing the important role of the good offices of the Secretary-General, including in the mediation of disputes, we support the Secretary-General's efforts to strengthen his capacity in this area' (2005: 21). Efforts are now under way to do this, with some strengthening of the Department of Political Affairs and the creation of a small Mediation Support Unit in the department. Equally important, however, is the need for mediation and facilitation at the stage of preventive diplomacy before disputes escalate into violent conflict. Although there has been considerable discussion on this topic within UN circles, the capacity and political will for a truly effective conflict resolution approach at the prevention stage has not yet fully materialized. Nonetheless, the knowledge and skills gained from conflict resolution during the peacemaking, peacekeeping and peace-building stages can also be applied to conflict prevention, whenever the political will to do so can be marshalled, among member states and within the UN secretariat. Only then will the United Nations come closer to achieving the objective stated in its Charter: 'to save succeeding generations from the scourge of war.'

NOTES

1 The author wishes to thank the donors who made this project possible: The Department for International Development of the United Kingdom, the Department for Foreign Affairs and International Trade of Canada, the Ministry for Foreign Affairs of Sweden and the Federal Department of Foreign Affairs of Switzerland. It should also be noted that the opinions expressed in this chapter are those of the author and the Representatives she interviewed and do not necessarily reflect those of the United Nations Institute for Training and Research or any other part of the UN system.

2 Ury and his colleagues refer to the use of these approaches by the parties themselves but in this chapter, they are used to refer to third-party approaches.

3 The Security Council is composed of five permanent members who have the power of the veto (China, France, the Russian Federation, the United Kingdom and the United States) and ten non-permanent members who are elected for two-year terms.

4 Readers who wish for more information can consult the Department of Peacekeeping Operations website which is: un.org/Depts/dpko/dpko.

5 I. William Zartman was the first to discuss the concept of "ripeness" in his book *Ripe for Resolution: Conflict and Intervention in Africa* (1985). He has since expanded the concept further in his chapter 'Ripeness: The Hurting Stalemate and Beyond' (2000).

6 Stephen John Stedman first discussed the problem of 'spoilers' in his article 'Spoiler Problems in Peace Processes' published in *International Security* (1997). It has been further elaborated in his book with Donald Rothchild and Elizabeth M. Cousens, *Ending Civil Wars: The Implementation of Peace Agreements* (2002).

7 Bargaining behaviors were operationalized by Charles E. Walcott and P. Terrence Hopmann in a coding system called Bargaining Process Analysis in their chapter 'Interaction Analysis and Bargaining Behavior' in the book by Robert T. Golembiewski (1978). The distinction between bargaining and problem solving has since been further elaborated in P. Terrence Hopmann's own book, *The Negotiation Process and the Resolution of International Conflicts* (1996) and in his chapter 'Bargaining and Problem Solving' in Chester A. Crocker, Fen Osler Hampson and Pamela Aall's edited book, *Turbulent Peace: The Challenges of Managing International Conflict* (2001). See also Terrence P. Hopmann 'Two Paradigms of Negotiation Bargaining and Problem Solving' (1995).

8 The concept of interests was first articulated by Roger Fisher and William Ury in their book, *Getting to Yes: Negotiating Agreement Without Giving In* (1981) where they define interests as "each side's needs, desires, concerns and fears" (see page 42).

They have been further elaborated in Dean Pruitt and Jeffrey Z. Rubin's book *Social Conflict: Escalation, Stalemate, and Settlement* (1986). See also I. William Zartman and Jeffrey Z. Rubin, *Power and Negotiation* (2002).

9 Paul George Swingle discusses power asymmetry in his book, *The Management of Power* (1976). Habeeb also discusses this in his book *Power and Tactics in International Negotiation: How Weak Nations Bargain with Strong Nations* (1988).

10 Roger Fisher and William Ury discuss the use of objective criteria as an important tool in negotiation in their book *Getting to Yes: Negotiating Agreement Without Giving In* (1981). As well, the importance of drawing upon norms is discussed by Michael Barnett and Martha Finnemore in their book *Rules for the World: International Organizations in Global Politics* (2004), as well as by Martha Finnemore in *National Interests in International Society* (1996) and Audie Klotz in *Norms in International Relations: The Struggle Against Apartheid (1996)*.

11 The use of a single negotiating text is mentioned by Roger Fisher and William Ury in their book *Getting to Yes: Negotiating Agreements Without Giving In* (1981) and its practical use explored by James K. Sebenius in *Negotiating the Law of the Sea* (1984) and by William B. Quandt in *Camp David: Peacemaking and Politics* (1986).

12 Roger Fisher and William Ury discuss the importance of "option generation" and new ideas in negotiation and Christopher W. Moore discusses the importance of the mediator offering new ideas in the mediation process in his book, *The Mediation Process: Practical Strategies for Resolving Conflict* (1996).

13 For a discussion of deadlines in mediation processes, see Christopher W. Moore, *The Mediation Process: Practical Strategies for Resolving Conflict* (1996).

14 James K. Sebenius discusses issues related to packaging and separating issues in his article "Negotiation Arithmetic: Adding and Subtracting Issues and Parties" which appeared in *International Organization* (1983).

REFERENCES

Ajello, Aldo (1999) 'Mozambique: Implementation of the 1992 Peace Agreement', in Chester A. Crocker, Fen O. Hampson, and Pamela Aall (eds.) *Herding Cats: Multiparty Mediation in a Complex World*. Washington, DC: United States Institute of Peace Press, pp. 615–642.

Ajello, Aldo (2001) Interview by Connie Peck as part of the UNITAR Programme for Briefing and Debriefing Special and Personal Representatives and Envoys of the Secretary-General, Geneva, Switzerland.

Anderlini, Sanam N. (2000) *Women at the Peace Table: Making a Difference*. New York: United Nations Development Fund for Women.

Anstee, Margaret J. (1996) *Orphan of the Cold War: The Inside Story of the Collapse of the Angolan Peace Process, 1992–93*. London: St Martin's Press.

Arnault, Jean (2001) Interview by Connie Peck as part of the UNITAR Programme for Briefing and Debriefing Special and Personal Representatives and Envoys of the Secretary-General, Geneva, Switzerland.

Barnett, Michael and Finnemore, Martha (2004) *Rules for the World: International Organizations in Global Politics*. Ithaca, New York: Cornell University Press.

Boden, Dieter (2001) Interview by Connie Peck as part of the UNITAR Programme for Briefing and Debriefing Special and Personal Representatives and Envoys of the Secretary-General, Geneva, Switzerland.

de Mistura, Staffan (2004) Interview by Connie Peck as part of the UNITAR Programme for Briefing and Debriefing Special and Personal Representatives and Envoys of the Secretary-General, Geneva, Switzerland.

Department of Peacekeeping Operations (DPKO) (2006) 'Surge Fact Sheet', prepared by the DPKO External Relations, November 1.

de Soto, Alvaro (1999) 'Ending Violent Conflict in El Salvador', in Chester A. Crocker, Fen O. Hampson, and Pamela Aall (eds.) *Herding Cats: Multiparty Mediation in a Complex World*. Washington, DC: United States Institute of Peace Press, pp. 345–385.

de Soto, Alvaro (2001) Interview by Connie Peck as part of the UNITAR Programme for Briefing and Debriefing Special and Personal Representatives and Envoys of the Secretary-General, Geneva, Switzerland.

de Soto, Alvaro (2004) Second interview by Connie Peck as part of the UNITAR Programme for Briefing and Debriefing Special and Personal Representatives and Envoys of the Secretary-General, Geneva, Switzerland.

Dinka, Berhanu (2001) Interview by Connie Peck as part of the UNITAR Programme for Briefing and Debriefing Special and Personal Representatives and Envoys of the Secretary-General, Geneva, Switzerland.

Egeland, Jan (2001) Interview by Connie Peck as part of the UNITAR Programme for Briefing and Debriefing Special and Personal Representatives and Envoys of the Secretary-General, Geneva, Switzerland.

Finnemore, Martha (1996) *National Interests in International Society*. Ithaca, New York: Cornell University Press.

Fisher, Roger and Ury, William (1981) *Getting to Yes: Negotiating Agreements Without Giving In*. London: Arrow Books, Ltd.

General Assembly (2005) Resolution adopted by the General Assembly 60/1. 2005 World Summit Outcome A/RES/60/1, 24 October 2008.

Habeeb, W. M. (1988) *Power and Tactics in International Negotiation: How Weak Nations Bargain with Strong Nations*. Baltimore, Maryland: Johns Hopkins University Press.

Hampson, Fen O. (1996) *Nurturing Peace: Why Peace Settlements Succeed or Fail*. Washington, DC: United States Institute of Peace Press.

Hopmann, P. Terrence (1995) 'Two Paradigms of Negotiation: Bargaining and Problem-Solving', *Annals of the American Academy of Political and Social Science*, 542, 24–47.

Hopmann, P. Terrence (1996) *The Negotiation Process and the Resolution of International Conflicts*. Columbia, South Carolina: University of South Carolina Press.

Hopmann, P. Terrence (2001) 'Bargaining and Problem Solving: Two Perspectives on International Negotiation', in Chester A. Crocker, Fen O. Hampson and Pamela Aall (eds.) *Turbulent Peace: The Challenges of Managing International Conflict*. Washington, DC: United State Institute of Peace Press.

Jiuyong, Shi (2005) Speech by H.E. Judge Shi Jiuyong, President of the International Court of Justice, to the General Assembly of the United Nations, October 27.

Klotz, Audie (1996) *Norms in International Relations: The Struggle Against Apartheid*. Ithaca, New York: Cornell University Press.

Legwaila, Joseph L. (2001) Interview by Connie Peck as part of the UNITAR Programme for Briefing and Debriefing Special and Personal Representatives and Envoys of the Secretary-General, Geneva, Switzerland.

LeMoyne, James (2005) Interview by Connie Peck as part of the UNITAR Programme for Briefing and Debriefing Special and Personal Representatives and Envoys of the Secretary-General, Geneva, Switzerland.

Marker, Jamsheed (2001) Interview by Connie Peck as part of the UNITAR Programme for Briefing and Debriefing Special and Personal Representatives and Envoys of the Secretary-General, Geneva, Switzerland.

Marker, Jamsheed (2003) *East Timor: A Memoir of the Negotiations for Independence*. London: McFarland and Company.

Merrem, Gerd (2002) Interview by Connie Peck as part of the UNITAR Programme for Briefing and Debriefing Special and Personal Representatives and Envoys of the Secretary-General, Geneva, Switzerland.

Moore, Christopher W. (1996) *The Mediation Process: Practical Strategies for Resolving Conflict*. San Francisco, California: Jossey-Bass.

Ould-Abdallah, Ahmedou (2000) *Burundi on the Brink, 1993–95: A UN Special Envoy Reflects on Preventive Diplomacy.* Washington, DC: United States Institute of Peace Press.

Ould-Abdallah, Ahmedou (2001) Interview by Connie Peck as part of the UNITAR Programme for Briefing and Debriefing Special and Personal Representatives and Envoys of the Secretary-General, Geneva, Switzerland.

Peck, Connie (1991) 'Designing More Cost-Effective Methods for Resolving International Disputes', in Mara R. Bustelo and Philip Alston (eds.) *Whose New World Order: What Role for the United Nations.* Canberra, Australia: The Federation Press.

Peck, Connie (1994) *The United Nations as a Dispute Settlement System: Improving Mechanisms for the Prevention and Resolution of Conflict.* The Hague: Kluwer Law International.

Peck, Connie (1998) *Sustainable Peace: The Role of the UN and Regional Organizations in Preventing Conflict.* Lanham, Maryland: Rowman and Littlefield.

Peck, Connie and Lee, Roy S. (eds.) (1997) *Increasing the Effectiveness of the International Court of Justice.* The Hague: Martinus Nijhoff.

Pruitt, Dean and Rubin, Jeffrey Z. (1986) *Social Conflict: Escalation, Stalemate, and Settlement.* New York: Random House.

Quandt, William B. (1986) *Camp David: Peacemaking and Politics.* Washington, DC: The Brookings Institution.

Report of the Secretary-General on the Preparations for the International Conference on the Great Lakes Region (2006) (S/2006/46).

Resolution adopted by the General Assembly: 2005 World Summit Outcome (2005) October 24 (A/RES/60/1).

Sahnoun, Mohamed (2003) Interview by Connie Peck as part of the UNITAR Programme for Briefing and Debriefing Special and Personal Representatives and Envoys of the Secretary-General, Geneva, Switzerland.

Sebenius, James K. (1983) 'Negotiation Arithmetic: Adding and Subtracting Issues and Parties', *International Organization,* 37 (2), 281–316.

Sebenius, James K. (1984) *Negotiating the Law of the Sea.* Cambridge, Massachusetts: Harvard University Press.

Security Council Resolution 1325 (2000) Adopted by the Security Council 4213th Meeting on October 31 (S/RES/1325).

Sinclair, Noel (2001) Interview by Connie Peck as part of the UNITAR Programme for Briefing and Debriefing Special and Personal Representatives and Envoys of the Secretary-General, Geneva, Switzerland.

Stedman, Stephen J. (1997) 'Spoilers in Peace Processes', *International Security,* 22 (2), 5–53.

Stedman, Stephen J., Rothchild, Donald and Cousens, Elizabeth M. (2002) *Ending Civil Wars: The Implementation of Peace Agreements.* Boulder, Colorado: Lynne Rienner.

Steiner, Michael (2003) Interview by Connie Peck as part of the UNITAR Programme for Briefing and Debriefing Special and Personal Representatives and Envoys of the Secretary-General, Geneva, Switzerland.

Stephen, David (2001) Interview by Connie Peck as part of the UNITAR Programme for Briefing and Debriefing Special and Personal Representatives and Envoys of the Secretary-General, Geneva, Switzerland.

Swingle, Paul George (1976) *The Management of Power.* Hoboken, New Jersey: John Wiley and Sons.

Tubman, Winston (2003) Interview by Connie Peck as part of the UNITAR Programme for Briefing and Debriefing Special and Personal Representatives and Envoys of the Secretary-General, Geneva, Switzerland.

Ury, William L., Brett, Jeanne M. and Goldberg, Stephen B. (1988*) Getting Disputes Resolved: Designing Systems to Cut the Costs of Conflict.* San Francisco, California: Jossey-Bass.

Vendrell, Francesc (2002) Interview by Connie Peck as part of the UNITAR Programme for Briefing and Debriefing Special and Personal Representatives and Envoys of the Secretary-General, Geneva, Switzerland.

Walcott, Charles and Hopmann, P. Terrence (1978) 'Interaction Analysis and Bargaining Behavior', in Robert T. Golembiewski (ed.) *The Small Group in Political Science: The Last Two Decades of Development.* Athens, Georgia: University of Georgia Press.

Wallensteen, Peter (2002) *Understanding Conflict Resolution: War, Peace and the Global System.* Thousand Oaks, California: Sage Publications.

Whitfield, Teresa (2005) 'A Crowded Field: Groups of Friends, the United Nations and the Resolution of Conflict', New York: Occasional Paper of the Center on International Cooperation.

Zartman, I. William (1985) *Ripe for Resolution: Conflict and Intervention in Africa.* Oxford: Oxford University Press.

Zartman, I William (2000) 'Ripeness: The Hurting Stalemate and Beyond', in Paul C. Stern and Daniel Druckman (eds.) *International Conflict Resolution: After the Cold War.* Washington, DC: National Academies Press.

Zartman, I. William and Rubin, Jeffrey Z. (2002) *Power and Negotiation.* Ann Arbour: University of Michigan Press.

PART IV

Current Features and Dilemmas in the Study of Conflict Resolution

22

Terrorism and Conflict Resolution

William A. Donohue

DEFINING TERRORISM AND CONFLICT RESOLUTION

Terrorism is both a political and security challenge. From a security perspective, many terrorist groups are diffusely organized and function largely outside of normal diplomatic channels, making them difficult to confront with conventional military resources. Yet, vast resources are committed daily to improving security capabilities to both prevent future attacks and eliminate terrorist groups. Politically, governments struggle to develop strategies for managing dispute resolution with terrorist organizations. According to Hayes (1988), Hayes, et al. (2003) and Harik (2004), there are many occasions in which governments and others engage in conflict resolution strategies with terrorists including amnesties, treatment of arrested terrorists, negotiations during terrorist events and campaigns, negotiations in larger political contexts, bargaining about types and targets of action and the effects of other policies on terrorism. Since most of these dispute resolution efforts focus on negotiation (both direct and indirect), the purpose of this chapter is to reveal what we know about the broad issue of the terrorist negotiation process and examine how it can be managed effectively.

In a thoughtful piece exploring the mind of the terrorist, Victoroff (2005) provides a compelling review of terrorism definitions. He concludes that terrorism is aggression against innocents, aimed largely at influencing a target audience to achieve essentially political goals. In a refinement of this view, Hayes et al. (2003) further divide terrorists into absolute and traditional forms. The absolute types are not willing to enter into political discourse. Their demands are immediate, unconditional, and universal, often using suicide attacks to draw attention to their issues. In contrast are traditional terrorists who focus on more specific ethnic and ideological causes, such as changing a specific political structure in a particular location. Zartman (2003) prefers the term "contingent" as opposed to "traditional" terrorists since they are distinguished by seeking to accomplish more specific instrumental goals.

This distinction suggests that there are two general approaches to the issue of dispute resolution with terrorists. For absolute terrorists, the leaders are generally hidden, unknown, and tangible goals are unclear, making direct negotiations infeasible.

Yet, Hayes et al. (2003) contend that those who oppose terrorism have instead opted to engage in a broader set of dispute resolution strategies. These efforts include negotiating with state supporters of terrorism to eliminate their involvement, isolating the violent actors by, for example, negotiating with agencies that control their finances, and negotiating with nations to fight these terrorist groups through cooperation among intelligence services, incentives for cooperation and so on. While these broad political efforts fall within the general framework of dispute resolution, the focus of this chapter is on managing the terrorist threat through the use of more direct negotiations with contingent terrorist groups.

Perhaps the most common form of dispute resolution with contingent terrorist groups is hostage negotiation. Terrorists might grab a set of innocents by hijacking a plane or capturing athletes in a hotel to draw attention to political issues. In Hayes' (2002) review of terrorist negotiation strategies, based on the analysis of several data sets across a number of studies, some clear trends emerge. First, in hostage events, governments negotiate extensively with terrorists. In these situations, they are more likely to make concessions in external events (outside their geographical boundaries) but to reject them in internal events. Governments also tend to reject demands for prisoner releases more than demands for ransom, publicity, or asylum and safe passage. And, when governments wholly or partially comply with terrorist demands, hostage safety improves, regardless of terrorist demands or the type of event.

Other studies summarized by Hayes (2002) also provide important strategic insights about negotiating with terrorists. For example, governments that make major substantive concessions under threat are likely to experience more terrorism than governments who hold a firm policy about incident management and demonstrate resolve over time. However, making minor concessions for food, safe surrender and even safe passage are not associated with increases in terrorism. In spite of these trends, terrorists remain optimists and assume governments will make major concessions which explains a great deal of their persistence. In addition, research finds that terrorists adapt quickly by changing targets and the types of their attacks on the basis of demonstrated government will and capacity to defeat them.

What sustain such groups are beliefs and attitudes that form the terrorists' identity which is driven largely by ideology (Crenshaw, 1988; Hoffman, 1999). A terrorist's ideological perspective provides a set of beliefs about the external world that not only foster an identity around commitment to a cause, but also shape expectations about the rewards of terrorism and dictate the extent to which the terrorists' goals are dependent on the cooperation of the authorities.

Although every terrorist has an individual identity, researchers have identified three major ideological perspectives (Hoffman, 1999; Post, et al. 2002; Victoroff, 2005). The *nationalist–separatist* seeks to establish a geographically separate political state based on either ethnic or political criteria (e.g. Provisional Irish Republican Army, Popular Front for the Liberation of Palestine). These terrorists are often accountable to a developed criminal organization and are both trained and experienced in the terrorist role. The ideology itself is generally an extreme example of the beliefs and backgrounds of the immediate social group, such that these communities treat the role of terrorist with respect and importance (Silke, 2003). However, because the community's beliefs also dictate the legitimacy of the terrorism, violence is typically planned, only used as necessary, and more likely to be directed away from harming innocents.

The *social revolutionist* uses terrorism as a way of drawing attention and applying pressure on the authorities to promise changes in social or economic order (e.g. Hezbollah). These terrorists necessarily possess a degree of interdependence with the authorities because their goals focus on fighting for improvement or change in a system of which they are already part. By using the threat of killing hostages as a bargaining tool, these terrorists expect to force authorities to compromise on a position or make concessions in support of their cause. However, since one of their aims is to gain support for the revolution, they are likely to avoid levels of aggression that would serve to reduce the public's sympathy (Wilson, 2000).

Radically different from the two secular groups is *religious fundamentalist* terrorism, which is viewed as a "sacramental act" carried out in fulfillment of some theological order (Hoffman, 1999). While the focus of secular terrorists is on using terrorism to change some aspect of the current political or social order, the religious terrorist seeks to cause damage directly to a society (e.g. al-Qaida). Their role is one of an extreme martyr figure who, in making an honorable sacrifice, would expect to receive both social recognition and rewards in the afterlife (Silke, 2003). This set of goals means that religious terrorists have a clear out-group mentality and are likely to show little interdependence with authorities or hostages. They consider themselves as being at "total war," such that greater use of violence is not only morally justified but a necessary expedient for the attainment of their goals (Hoffman, 1999).

A useful way of uncovering the roots of these organizations is detailed in Wagner's (2006) article examining the peace psychology of terrorism. He argues that terrorism stems from four categories of motives or needs including: (1) adverse physical circumstances such as hunger, sickness or family deprivation; (2) security and the unrealistic fear of an exaggerated danger; (3) self-determination or the ability to make one's own decision about life, liberty and the pursuit of happiness; and (4) social respect, or the acknowledgment of the value of the group's social identity or ethnic and religious membership. A terrorist group may use any or all of these motives in sustaining and growing their membership. For example, Reich's (1998) description of the structure and function of Hezbollah makes it clear that this organization sustains its Shi'ite-dominated orientation by appealing to all of these needs. They are organized to deal with adverse physical circumstances, provide for the security of their followers, defend their rights to self-determination and promote respect for their Shi'ite religious roots. Indeed, Hezbollah's official policy is to establish a Muslim caliphate to promote its Islamic values.

THE PROCESS OF CONFRONTING TERRORIST-RELATED CONFLICT

Given these trends in understanding both the types of strategies that appear to work best in dealing with terrorists and their complex web of motives, how can they be confronted from a process perspective in direct talks as in a hostage or kidnapping negotiation? To address this issue, it might be best to take a step back and make a distinction between crisis and normative bargaining. In an earlier essay, Donohue, et al. (1991) make a distinction between crisis and normative bargaining to better understand the general frames that are used to confront the hostage negotiation event. The idea is that crisis bargaining centers on relationship and expressive issues. The disputants begin the interaction in the context of mistrust driven largely by their contrasting identities. The religious fundamentalist terrorists are interacting with police who are fundamentally antagonists. In addition, they are likely to not share cultural values or native languages. These differences also breed dislike, making it difficult to exchange positive relational cues.

Beginning with these relational challenges, the terrorist-police exchange aimed at conflict resolution must first address the relational issues to relieve the crisis and allow the individuals to focus on substantive issues. Once this transition occurs, and individuals have established some kind of working relationship with sufficient levels of trust and affiliation to continue, bargaining becomes more normative and focused on substantive issues capable of resolving the situation. Rogan, Hammer and Van Zandt (1997) make a similar distinction in their communication-based negotiation model between instrumental, relational and identity concerns in a negotiation. These issues are all intertwined, but when they become more balanced, individuals can concentrate on moving toward a negotiated settlement. Situations that stay in crisis have little chance of productive movement since relational and identity concerns dominate. In fact, most of the recommendations that appear in the Rogan et al. (1997) volume concentrate on how to achieve this transition from a crisis to a normative bargaining mode.

Achieving this transition to normative bargaining, particularly with terrorist groups, can be conceptualized as a challenge in removing a number of the paradoxes disputants face in the course of conflict resolution. This chapter will now detail these paradoxes and then use the 40-day siege of the Church of Nativity in Bethlehem (Cristal, 2006) to illustrate how the negotiators managed these paradoxes to make the transition to normative bargaining to resolve the siege.

Paradox and crisis bargaining

The crisis context is organized around a set of interlinked paradoxes, each of which must be addressed for conflict resolution to be successful in a terrorist negotiation event. The first paradox that must be addressed and that underlies the entire conflict event is termed the **competitive paradox**. In a set of papers, Donohue and colleagues (Donohue, Kaufmann, Smith & Ramesh, 1991; Donohue, Ramesh & Borchgrevink, 1991; Donohue, 1998; Donohue & Hoobler, 2002) outlined a theory to account for the dynamic evolution of relationships in conflict. Based on Strauss's (1978) Negotiated Order Theory, Relational Order Theory contends that negotiators continuously create and tacitly negotiate relational limits that serve to constrain the substantive negotiation process. The two main relational parameters or limits that communicators negotiate while they interact are affiliation and interdependence based on the consensus of a variety of papers focusing on the core parameters defining interpersonal relationships (Burgoon &

Hale, 1984). The issue of interdependence focuses on the extent to which parties can influence or exert behavioral control over one another in the context of the relationship between them. Affiliation focuses on expressions of warmth, friendliness, intimacy, respect, trust, and cooperation (see Winter, 1991 for a review).

The competitive paradox is a product of high interdependence a low affiliation. Disputants send unaffiliative and disapproving messages in the context of relational dependence. That is, to defeat their rival, parties must increase interdependence to pull their opponent closer by initiating communication or aggression while also pushing the opponent away through a show of negative affiliation by being unfriendly and untrusting. When parties are in this condition, they communicate very directly while showing signs of negative affect (Donohue & Roberto, 1993). This paradox is disabling if it is not recognized and addressed, because the focus moves away from the obligation to mutually exchange information and proposals to create a better future and more toward asserting individual rights aimed at achieving one's own goals while the obligations to share proposals and ideas, which is the essence of conflict resolution.

Because the emphasis is on asserting rights and resisting obligations, the communication carries almost a moral imperative and authority with it. Parties must resist with all their resources because key, central and defining rights have been violated. This is the kind of communication that Winter (1991) observed during the first few exchanges between leaders dealing with the Cuban Missile Crisis of 1962. The United States certainly asserted its right to enforce the Monroe Doctrine that seeks to prevent non-Western-Hemisphere powers from establishing military dominance in the Western Hemisphere. Yet, as letters from Khrushchev became more conciliatory, the United States altered its focus away from rights and more toward specific substantive issues. The parties moved away from aggression temporarily by agreeing to reduce their interdependence.

Managing the competitive paradox can be accomplished by either increasing affiliation or decreasing interdependence. As the above example suggests, Khrushchev increased affiliation (ever so slightly) which Kennedy interpreted as a cleverly hidden olive branch, which gave Kennedy the opening. In crisis negotiation situations, parties typically begin interaction by moving deeper into the competitive paradox by, for example, restating positions and even using threats as a way of asserting rights and making demands while calling in obligations from the other.

As the interaction evolves, parties committed to forging an agreement look for ways to resolve the paradox by increasing expressions of affiliation or decreasing interdependence. In a recent paper, Taylor and Thomas (2005) examined the linguistic style of hostage takers and hostage negotiators along three dimensions: structural features of language (word count, articles, negations, tense, propositions), social affect (negative and positive emotion, relational references) and cognitive contributions (causation, insight, discrepancy, certainty and exclusivity). The hostage takers in these transcripts ranged from criminals caught in the act to domestic disputes to mentally impaired individuals. The authors found that the hostage negotiator and hostage taker in the successful (a negotiated outcome) condition were synchronous on all but four of the 18 categories across these language choices. In the unsuccessful condition (the situation was resolved tactically), the parties were synchronous on only two parameters.

Further, when the data were analyzed on a turn-by-turn basis, the hostage negotiator in the negotiation condition drove the frame choices whereas in the tactical condition, the hostage taker drove the frame choices. In other words, collaboratively resolved negotiations were characterized by more frame coordination and the use of more collaborative frames with fewer transitions between frames (Donohue & Taylor, 2006). In comparison to unsuccessful negotiations, the dialogue of successful negotiations involved greater coordination of turn taking, reciprocation of

positive affect, a focus on the present rather than the past, and a focus on alternatives rather than on competition.

Within the context of the competitive paradox, there are more specific kinds of relational paradoxes that hostage negotiators must also confront as they learn to deal with hostage takers. In a classic book on policing, Muir (1977) describes the kinds of coercive relationships that often emerge in the course of police work. Coercive relationships, or controlling others through threats to harm, precipitate extortionate transactions in which parties seek their ends through the use of threats which often take the form of hostages and ransoms. Muir argues that extortionate transactions are organized around a series of paradoxes, and that reconstructing these transactions requires managing the paradoxes. Muir's first example is the **Paradox of Dispossession**, or the less one has, the less one has to lose. The idea in this paradox is that the hostage taker is simultaneously powerful and powerless. The hostage taker's power derives from taking something of value from the hostage, but this is an act of a desperately powerless person who must take hostages as a last resort to gain power. If the hostage taker is dispossessed or has the sense that he or she is detached from those things which are valued (even life itself) or has nothing to lose, then the negotiator loses any leverage over the hostage taker. The goal of the negotiator is to find something that the hostage taker values that the negotiator can ultimately control to balance power. This balance is essential in moving from a crisis to a normative bargaining context. When both parties value something, they can bargain in good faith to claim it.

Secondly, the **Paradox of Detachment** holds that parties are both attached and detached simultaneously to one another and to the situation. They are attached in the sense that they must co-confront a difficult negotiation session, but they are detached in the sense that each party moves back and forth within a frame of indifference. By communicating indifference, the victim can become less valuable to the hostage taker.

However, some victims become attached to hostage takers (Stockholm syndrome), thereby increasing their attachment to the situation and their desire to take sides in the conflict. Police might even encourage attachment to improve the hostage's chance for survival, resulting from greater personal attachment between the hostage taker and the hostage. The police are somewhat insulated from the situation and experience occasional indifference to various members of the hostage incident, depending on their level of professional commitment to the lives of the victims and perpetrators and their ability to focus on the lives of the individuals as opposed to other priorities, such as resolving the situation because it is becoming expensive or too public. Finally, the hostage taker can be, and often is, indifferent to survival. Many hostage takers try to communicate detachment and dispossession as a means of appearing more reckless and therefore more powerful.

Ultimately, the police must learn to maintain sufficient levels of attachment among all parties to move from crisis to normative bargaining. When the hostage taker is attached and values something that the negotiator can control, and the negotiator is attached and focused on managing the hostage taker's problem and the victim and hostage taker are somewhat personally attached to one another, then the bargaining can proceed in good faith. During a prolonged negotiation, managing these values is difficult given the restricted lines of communication and the many sources of interference that may impact on the sense of detachment such as direct communication with family members, for example, or overt signs of threat from police that might cause the hostage taker to become less attached and more desperate.

The **Paradox of Face** focuses on the broad issue of identity, and often in a hostage situation, the narrower issue of threat. Parties vacillate between communicating both toughness and flexibility and often must do so simultaneously. The professional police identity is rooted in a desire to be both firm and tough, while being tempered with an ability to be understanding and fair. The hostage

taker's identity is rooted in being perceived as a credible threat to secure a desired outcome, although not so much of a threat that the police are likely to take tactical action to preserve the lives of the hostages. The hostage taker must strike a balance between being tough, but reasonable so that negotiation appears more viable as a strategy than tactical action. The hostage's face can shift between being a helpless victim, to a hostage taker supporter or even an overt detractor.

Of particular interest in managing this paradox is interpreting threats. In a classic work on threats, Shelling (1956) indicates that for threats to be credible, they must be specific and perceived as within the willingness and capability of the threatener. This threat then binds it to the identity of the threatener and becomes part of their face. In an empirical test of coercive power and concession making in bilateral negotiation, de Dreu (1995) found that balanced power produced fewer threats and demands than unequal power. This result suggests that the role of the police is to manage this paradox by seeking to balance identity issues in such a way as to make threats less necessary so the parties can shift to more of a normative bargaining context and resolve the situation appropriately.

Finally, Muir (1977) identifies the **Paradox of Irrationality** which focuses on the issue of emotional involvement. In Muir's terms, the more delirious the threatener, the more serious is the threat, and the more delirious the victim, the less serious is the threat. If the hostage taker is too emotional, he or she may become irrational and incapable of managing the scene or bargaining in any kind of normative manner. Or, if the hostage taker exhibits no emotion or involvement, then it might be a warning sign of detachment which again removes the possibility of normative bargaining. In his chapter on emotion and emotional expression in crisis bargaining, Rogan et al. (1997) make the point that it is vital to both understand the kinds of emotional expressions hostage takers are communicating and be able to respond appropriately to them. Muir would argue that the real challenge is to manage the opposing forces of irrationality that intertwine between the hostage taker, hostage negotiator and the victim. Not only must the police be able to read the hostage taker's emotions, but they must also understand their own emotional conditions. Police can act irrationally when the hostage taker confronts their face or threatens a hostage in some manner. As situations wear on, police might become too emotionally invested in terminating the situation and less invested in concentrating on the welfare of the hostages. Thus, the issue focuses again on the problem of balance. Are the hostage negotiators able to balance the complex set of emotional issues presented by themselves, the hostage takers and the victims?

Clearly, any negotiation can devolve into an extortionate abyss in which parties simply try to overwhelm one another with coercive force. That's what war is all about. The declaration of war is an admission that the ability to balance these four paradoxes within the competitive paradox has failed. In a world where all-out war aimed at defeating an enemy into submission is quickly disappearing, the need to understand and manage the extortionate transaction becomes even more imperative. Toward this end, it might be useful to use the example of the Forty Day Siege of the Church of Nativity that occurred in April and May 2002 between the Palestinians and Israelis (Cristal, 2006). This chapter now turns to a description of that event and an examination of how the paradoxes were resolved in this crisis.

The Church of Nativity example

The wave of violence triggered by the failure of the Camp David accords in 2000 ultimately resulted in the Israeli Defense Force (IDF) occupying Bethlehem in 2002, which was essentially a Palestinian-held city. This effort resulted in many Palestinians, wanted by the IDF for terrorist activities, taking refuge in the Church of Nativity in Bethlehem built over the traditional birthplace of Christ. Rather than take the church by force which would have precipitated an international incident, the IDF decided to use negotiations to relieve the crisis. The standoff began on April 2 and ended with a series of political negotiations on May 10.

There were three main groups caught in the church at the beginning of the siege: members of the Tanzim which is the armed wing of Fateh, commanders of the Palestinian Security Forces who were wanted by Israel for conducting and supporting terrorist activities, and a group of Hamas fighters. The Israeli negotiators pursued three main strategies in working through the crisis. They first sought to undermine the Palestinian's safe zone or sense of security in their military training and orientation. The goal was to change their focus to being on their personal circumstances rather than on their military orientation. Second, they sought to restructure responsibility for all local players by creating a set of procedural rules for how the negotiations were going to occur. Third, the Israelis sought to create a legitimate resolution to the crisis through a negotiation process. They were first committed to negotiation rather than to a tactical conclusion of the crisis.

The negotiations began with an initial exchange of positions which identified key gaps in positions, but more importantly, established a respectful relationship between the parties resulting in a sense that problem solving was possible and likely. The next set of sessions worked to make some procedural decisions such as dividing the people in the church into four different categories and a decision to treat each group differently. This agreement focused on a few of the Palestinians working toward the first goal of reshaping the safe zone for the core group that Israel wanted to focus on. This allowed the Israelis in subsequent negotiations to focus on the individual circumstances of each member of the targeted group regarding their individual status, essentially accomplishing their second negotiation goal. From that point, the negotiations proceeded successfully to resolve the crisis, despite some setbacks both inside the church and external to the immediate situation.

This negotiation is an excellent example of how resolving paradoxes was essential in moving the negotiations forward. The competitive paradox that develops from a lack of affiliation was managed by initial communications that established mutual respect among the parties. A sense of integrity developed that served the parties well as they moved along. As these relational parameters developed, the parties were able to move away from a crisis bargaining orientation and resolve the paradoxes associated with the extortionate transaction. Regarding the paradox of dispossession, the move to divide the Palestinians into different groups was important to insure that most of the individuals inside the church did not feel dispossessed. Clearly, each person, regardless of the group they were in, valued their freedom and the fact that groups were perceived differently kept the focus on the future and the resolution of the crisis.

The paradox of detachment was also addressed skillfully. The key in resolving this crisis is to get the parties involved in the bargaining process. The more they are involved, the less they are detached from the constructive resolution of the situation. The early bargaining to divide groups, and subsequent negotiation sessions that kept everyone involved, were key in resolving this paradox. Similarly, the Israeli team remained active in the sessions by reviewing all details of the events regularly to insure that they remained committed to a negotiated settlement. All signs pointed toward negotiation despite the setbacks.

The third paradox focusing on face was very skillfully managed by the Israeli team. Recall that this paradox focuses on managing the identity issue as it relates to the individuals' desire to appear both firm and flexible. This paradox was very skillfully addressed by shifting the identity of the Palestinians from their military roles to their personal situations. By dividing the church inhabitants into groups and treating each individual separately to discuss their specific future fate, it removed the need to maintain the group military identity and all the power and threat issues that attend this identity. In fact, the face of the Palestinians was

foremost in the minds of the Israeli negotiators as they worked through each phase of the negotiations.

The fourth paradox deals with the potential for irrationality. Again, early on, the Israelis established a very business-like approach to the negotiations. An organization was established, rules were developed and followed, and the development of normative bargaining proceeded effectively, even in the face of various impediments that emerged in the course of the discussions. More importantly, the Israeli negotiators maintained their composure during the 28-day siege which further improved their ability to make the transition to normative bargaining.

In contrast to the Church of Nativity example are the negotiations between the Russian forces and the Chechen in the Moscow theater hostage crisis that took place on October 23, 2002. Dolnik and Pilch (2006) provide an account of the incident based on a compilation of various sources. Since this incident was handled very differently than the Church of Nativity negotiations, it serves as a useful contrast in learning how the management of the extortionate paradoxes influenced the outcome of the event.

The Moscow theater hostage crisis example

While Dolnik and Pilch (2006) provide a thorough account of the Russian and Chechen standoff at the Moscow Theater in 2002, it will be useful to provide a brief description of the event to provide an effective contrast with the Nativity Church negotiations. The siege by the Chechens of the Dubrovka Theater in the heart of Moscow followed two other hostage incidents perpetrated by the Chechens in an attempt to draw attention to their goal of breaking away from the Russian state. The prior incidents resulted in some hostage deaths following the primary tactic of the Russians to storm the scenes rather than engage in negotiations. At the Dubrovka Theatre, the Chechens stormed the building in the middle of a crowded performance taking hundreds of hostages and planting several explosives throughout the building in anticipation of a Russian rescue attempt. The siege occurred after months of planning and meticulous preparation by the Chechens.

Once the negotiations began, the Chechens articulated a primary, but vague demand of Russian withdrawal from Chechen soil. Several Russian negotiators and intermediaries carried on these negotiations which lasted about two days. Many of the hostages were released in the course of these negotiations, which were often tense as the Chechens made two ultimatum threats to kill hostages if interim demands were not met. In the end, the Russians lost patience with the negotiations and stormed the buildings to release gas in an attempt to chemically subdue the Chechens and the hostages. Unfortunately, the dose of gas was lethal and killed all but two of the remaining hostages and a handful of Chechens.

Dolnik and Pilch (2006) provide an excellent review of some of the key mistakes made by the Russians in handling the incident. It seems best to review these errors in the context of the paradoxes to see how the process used by the Russians failed to generally relieve the paradoxes constructively. For example, the competitive paradox remained problematic since the Russians failed to develop any kind of working relationship with the Chechen hostage takers. In contrast to the Israelis, the Russians did not appear to be focused heavily on resolving the situation primarily by negotiation. They probably focused more on resolving the situation tactically, consistent with past practice. As a result, they did not have a consistent negotiation orientation that allowed them to develop an open line of communication capable of rendering some kind of affiliative relationship.

Second, the paradox of detachment was a particularly difficult challenge in this negotiation. The professional nature of the takeover by the Chechens made it clear that they were both powerful and powerless at the same time. They maintained extensive control over the scene in a very careful manner. To balance power and resolve the conflict, the Russians needed to increase the Chechen

dependence on negotiation. They needed to develop a rich and consistent dialogue that explored each avenue for a resolution that saved the lives of the hostages. The lack of interest in substantive negotiations is evidenced by the number of mediaries that intervened in the dispute for the Russians. A committed approach to negotiation would have made a much more consistent path to giving power to the dialogue, and there's ample evidence that the Chechens wanted to talk.

The paradox of dispossession focuses on creating value. Since the Chechens were willing to sacrifice themselves for attention to their cause, it is important to insure that they wanted to live and wanted the hostages to live, as well. Without extensive communication and building this sense of value by reframing their perspectives, it is difficult to successfully deal with this paradox. Indeed, the impatience of the Russians is in stark contrast to the Israelis who exhibited a great deal of patience in managing their siege. Perhaps it is even useful to view this paradox from the Russian perspective. An interesting question is whether they were detached from the safety of the hostages given their primary focus on tactical intervention. At any rate, the Russians clearly failed to deal with the detachment issue, keeping the interaction at a crisis level in an extortionate framework.

The paradox of face focuses on identity. Where the Israelis successfully transformed the identity from soldier to individual person considering personal preferences, the Russians never moved the dialogue toward that objective. The Chechens were treated as one with little focus on individuals further reinforcing the paradox. Perhaps the lack of time the Russians had to deal with the dispute intervened here, as well. They did not seem interested in taking the time needed to transform face and identify strategies that could be used to help both sides manage face costs.

The final paradox is most interesting in this case. Irrationality played a significant role in this negotiation. In particular, the lack of any consistent negotiation strategy, and several important negotiation blunders insured that both parties remained fairly irrational during the entire event. The Russian offer to allow the Chechens to leave the scene in exchange for the hostages angered the Chechens, and was duplicated a few hours later which further drove the negotiation into irrationality. The Russians were similarly challenged since they also became progressively irrational as the event evolved. In reaction to international pressure, and the general policy of quick resolution, the Russians viewed time as more important than successful resolution. Perhaps because the Russians were detached from the lives of the hostages, they were willing to act on their impulses to storm the theater.

It is clear that the Israeli game plan in dealing with the Palestinian siege focused on reliving the crisis bargaining framework to move more constructively toward normative bargaining. The Russians functioned without an apparent negotiation game plan which resulted in the unnecessary loss of life. Perhaps the next step in this process is to review the phases of hostage negotiation to further understand the process of dispute resolution with terrorists.

Managing the Paradox

The question is, how can police place themselves in a position to manage these various paradoxes and transform the conflict from a crisis bargaining (Donohue & Roberto, 1993) to a normative bargaining situation? The general idea is that in the initial stages of a crisis event, the focus of the communication is not on the exchange of proposals to resolve the substantive issues dividing parties, but on managing the peripheral issues associated with the paradoxes and managing the crisis itself. Once these issues have been addressed, then parties can settle into a more normative bargaining mode that allows for exchanging proposals and building agreements. While Faure (2006) provides a very useful analysis of the 1979 hostage case at the US Embassy in Teheran using Zartman's three-phase model of pre-negotiation, formula and details, this

chapter will offer a refinement of that model that addresses the key process issues identified above.

Containment   The first step in managing a hostage scene is containing the hostage takers in a fixed location (Donohue, et al. 1991). This is a pre-negotiation activity. The hostage negotiation team must be satisfied that they have eliminated routes into and away from the scene while also minimizing the ability of the hostage takers to contact third parties. Containment is essential to eliminate escape options to insure that negotiation is the only way out of the situation for the hostage takers. It also ensures that the hostage takers are not playing the crowd or talking to audiences with a different point of view (Cambria et al., 2002). The disastrous consequences of not containing an incident are made transparent by incidents in which well-intentioned members of the public are harmed or killed (McMains & Mullins, 2001).

In an era of modern electronics, communication containment is very difficult. The hostage takers can learn about police activities from TV news coverage or use a cell phone to communicate with an outsider. In many bargaining contexts, the availability of information from third parties can dramatically shift the balance of power and undermine even the most persuasively crafted position. Yet, negotiators and scholars outside of the hostage context continue to focus on events at the negotiation table, with only cursory recognition of the "negotiations" that occur away from the table. Thus, it is important for negotiators and scene commanders to think broadly about the scene to help them manage the perceived value of issues while trying to gain influence and power (see Donohue & Hoobler, 2002; Donohue & Taylor, 2004).

Containment also has a positive effect on individuals' engagement and cooperation within an interaction. Negotiators typically show more interdependence, are more likely to reciprocate cooperation, and ultimately achieve higher joint outcomes than negotiators who have alternative options

(Donohue & Taylor, 2004; Giebels, et al. 2000). Police negotiators often refer to this as creating a "we-are-in-it-together" environment, whose rationale centers on the fact that it is more difficult for an individual to withdraw from the negotiating process when they perceive themselves as having a role in the interaction and as having ownership (i.e. a stake) in the negotiation's success. Such engagement with the hostage taker is critical to successfully managing a high-stress, protracted interaction.

Beyond helping to influence a hostage taker's behavior, containment also plays an important role in police negotiator efforts to present information persuasively. Containment not only allows negotiators to limit a hostage taker's knowledge of what might be available, but it also allows them to distort the value of the alternatives. For example, police negotiators will often remonstrate at length about the difficulty of providing something to the hostage taker. This approach draws on the scarcity principle (Cialdini, 2001, p. 203), which is to view a resulting offer or concession as considerably more attractive when it is presented as a rare event. Similarly, police negotiators will always try to break down any substantive considerations into their constituent parts. For example, this is rather than talk about providing fixed sandwiches (and whether the police negotiator and hostage taker have common preferences in condiments), what the bread should be (and the problems with certain vegetables in the sandwich), what drink should be included, whether or not there should be any side orders and so on. This process also facilitates relationship building as both parties are problem solving and having a communication success.

In summary, police negotiators rely on containment to limit the influence of unpredictable outside factors and to allow for some control of how information is fed to the other party. The impact of not containing these factors is very apparent in the high-stakes, uncertain environment of hostage taking, where a mismatch between what negotiators say and what others do or say can critically reshape the conflict, as the end of the Branch Davidian siege at Waco unfortunately testifies (Wright, 2003). The lesson here, then, is to remember that negotiations are often shaped away from the table, and that individuals' perceptions and beliefs while at the table may be crafted to be very different from the reality away from the table, but only if the negotiation is successfully contained.

Relational development After police have successfully contained the hostage takers, they are free to initiate negotiations. Establishing communication can be difficult if the hostage taker does not have access to a phone or other modes of communication. However, the police must establish a channel that allows for the free exchange of information. Once a channel has been established, the negotiator must begin communicating with the hostage taker who is leading the hostage-taking effort. The hostage negotiators are usually part of a tactical team and must ultimately serve the interests of that team with all members working together to free the hostages. The negotiation team often consists of at least three roles: a speaker who cannot make decisions but establishes communication with the hostage taker, a strategist who interacts with the speaker to help guide the interaction and a psychologist who can comment on the mental capacities of the hostage taker.

Once communication has been established, the first task in managing the crisis is to simply establish a relationship with the hostage taker. Initially, the hostage negotiator allows the hostage taker to maintain control of the communication, playing a one-down role, as a means of reducing perceived resistance and avoiding a power struggle. The key transformation is moving from a highly distributive, competitive mode to a more collaborative orientation focusing on underlying psychological issues. When collaborating, the fundamental, underlying basis of the conflict becomes exposed, and personal needs (tied to self-concept) emerge, allowing mutually fulfilling outcomes to emerge in turn.

An example might serve to illustrate these points. In an airline hijacking in the early 1970s in the USA, a passenger hijacked an airplane bound for Atlanta by packing dynamite under his coat. When negotiations began, he shared demands for many items such as money, fuel to get to Cuba and so on. As the interactions unfolded, the police negotiator learned that the hostage taker hijacked the plane to demonstrate his manhood to his partner, with whom he had fought the night before. This personal opening became a turning point from cooperation (sharing demands and information) to collaboration, in which underlying issues were explored. The resolution called for the hijacker to release the passengers in exchange for a phone to call his partner. The passengers were released, and the phone call was made. (Unfortunately, in this instance, the hijacker committed suicide while on the phone).

Both cooperation and competition present paradoxical relational challenges to negotiators. A cooperative relationship is paradoxical because parties like and trust one another, but resist the kind of engagement that would expose them extensively. They are pushing the other away while also pulling them closer. Similarly, a competitive relationship is also paradoxical, since parties do not like and trust one another, but they are highly engaged. They are pulling the other closer in order to defeat or in other ways harm them.

In the opening movements of a hostage negotiation, very competitive relationships tend to dominate. The police negotiator tries to slowly but deliberately shift away from this approach into more of a time-out period characterized by exchanging preliminary information, and moving hostage takers away from demands and threats. Parties explore roles and engage in a great deal of small talk. The goal of the police negotiator is to build sufficient trust to move toward a more cooperative relationship. These preliminary discussions often center on such substantive issues as food, heat, light and logistics as a means of moving the hostage taker into a more cooperative orientation. Once a collaborative orientation

starts to emerge, then more substantive issues and demands can be explored. If that trust can be established through relatively minor exchanges of food for hostages, for example, then more important demands can follow – but not too rapidly. Thus, police negotiators are keenly aware of how to manage the relational perspectives of hostage takers to build the foundation that allows certain issues and demands to emerge. Without this foundation, executing the substantive goals becomes quite difficult.

Issue development Substantively, hostage negotiation revolves around the interplay between demands and issues that both sides must manage. Hostage takers, often suffering from a psychological disorder or fanatical commitment, have little difficulty articulating their demands. They may want specific, concrete items like money or freedom for political prisoners, or they may make more nebulous demands for revenge. However, while clear on these substantive issues, hostage takers do often have difficulty articulating the underlying issues that brought them to this precipice. For hostage negotiators, their demands revolve around freeing the hostages, but the process of executing this goal is often driven by various issues that can be difficult to sort through, such as staff fatigue, overtime costs for maintaining the scene and police jurisdictional and publicity issues.

Most negotiation research recognizes the importance of "expanding the pie" and searching for optimal solutions. However, negotiators and negotiation theory have traditionally viewed this integrative strategy as relating to substantive issues. For police negotiators, however, issue exploration comes second to emotional exploration. Recent estimates suggest that nearly 80% of all hostage situations are emotion- or relationship-driven (Vecchi, et al. 2005). For this reason, police negotiators have learned to work quickly to understand and negotiate around expressive aspects of the situation. They seek to reduce the tensions and perceived threats of the context, and they focus early efforts on developing trust and identifying face-saving strategies (Donohue, et al. 1991; Taylor, 2002).

What is unique about this perspective is not the recognition that emotive factors play a role in negotiation, since this is now recognized across many disciplines (Barry, 1999). The unique aspect of this perspective is the way in which emotive concerns are viewed. In many traditional negotiation contexts, relational and identity dynamics continue to be viewed as mediating factors that help or hinder efforts to work towards a substantive agreement. The traditional view is to conceptualize emotion as something that needs to be dealt with before considering instrumental issues (McMains & Mullins, 2001), or as something that informs understanding of instrumental positions (Van Kleef, et al. 2004). In contrast, for the police negotiator, it is as important, if not more important, to search the emotional pie and address emotions as negotiation issues in their own right.

To illustrate this shift in perspective, consider a hypothetical organizational take-over and efforts by the potential buyer to identify what is likely to persuade the organization's board. In all likelihood, a tra-ditional buyer would seek to determine the board's perception of the organization's value by gleaning information about costs and overheads, the value of subsidiary assets, whether money can be saved in staffing and so on. However, a police negotiator would ask whether members of the board are concerned for the well-being of their employees, are worried about their personal reputation after the take-over, have a desire to retain influence on the board and so on. By asking these kinds of emotive questions, a negotiator begins to uncover what might persuade the board members to accept less attractive offers than would rationally be the case when dealing with instrumental factors.

Expanding the emotional pie involves two main processes. The first is that police nego-tiators work proactively to manage a hostage taker's anxieties (Miron & Goldstein, 1979; Noesner & Webster, 1997). Rather than rush to deal with instrumental aspects

of the negotiation, police negotiators use techniques such as mirroring, self-disclosure, and paraphrasing (Hammer & Rogan, 1997; Noesner & Webster, 1997; Vecchi et al., 2005) to show their interest in the hostage taker's emotive concerns. Coupled with supportive feedback and non-assumptive questions such as "I've not been in your position, but I guess you must be feeling very lonely," their efforts to show interest allow the hostage taker to express their concerns while simultaneously venting their emotions. Police negotiators do not try to counter emotionality with rational debate, which is generally ineffective in high-pressure scenarios (Vecchi et al., 2005). Instead, they accept that emotion itself is an important issue of the negotiation, which must be continuously monitored, explored and addressed.

The second is that police negotiators work to identify the hostage taker's main underlying problem or driver. At any one time, a hostage taker will communicate about one particular concern or issue, ranging from concerns about personal identity, to concerns about relational issues such as trust and power, through to concerns about substantive issues (Taylor, 2002; Taylor & Donald, 2004). Police negotiators listen carefully to the hostage taker's dialogue, identify the underlying problem and then address it by matching the framing of their message to the hostage taker's framing. For example, it is not useful to be making substantive offers when the hostage taker's real concern is for his personal identity and the shame the incident will bring to his family. By focusing on an inappropriate frame, a negotiator is in danger of making the hostage taker feel misunderstood or unvalued, which may lead to further conflict and heightened emotions. By interpreting the focus of dialogue, negotiators may also act proactively to identify under-explored issues that will expand the emotional pie. For example, by tracking changes in dialogue, it is possible to gauge how much time has been spent discussing various identity, relational and substantive issues. If negotiations come to a standstill, they are able to review the motivational focus of previous dialogue and move to an issue that has yet to be covered. Much of police negotiators' efforts to resolve hostage crises rely on their ability to explore and understand the emotional drivers of the hostage taker. Far from being hindrances or mediating issues in the interaction, emotions are defining points of bargaining that often determine how the interaction unfolds.

Proposal development and scene resolution

Once the issues have been developed, the hostage negotiator can begin to work toward proposal development and scene resolution. The hostage negotiator may propose solutions that allow the hostage taker to address their underlying issues which will then lead to the surrender sequence and scene resolution. The surrender sequence is very risky for several reasons. The hostage taker becomes very powerless in contrast to the bulk of the negotiations in which the perpetrator had significant bargaining power while holding the hostages. At the surrender, the person's power comes only in being able to cause problems in the final surrender. In addition, the police are anxious that the sequence goes smoothly and no one behaves precipitously to create any sudden surprises that might disrupt the flow. These sequences must be slow, carefully negotiated, very specific, well organized and executed with disciplined officers who can make the process controlled and deliberate.

Factors impacting negotiation with terrorist groups

To be successful in bargaining with terrorists, the police negotiators must also understand the factors that impact how parties approach the negotiation process. First is the issue of **power complementarity**. Terrorists are inherently constrained in their ability to control the negotiation process and attain their desired outcomes by virtue of being contained by police. The response of many terrorists is to adopt a one-down position and threaten or actually use violence to generate fear, coercion or intimidation in

an effort to realign the balance in power (Russell, et al. 1979). If the negotiations can be transformed so that the parties are able to bargain over substantive proposals, then the inherent dangers associated with the one-down power complementarity become less relevant. However, if the interaction remains in a crisis mode and parties have difficulty transforming the negotiations, then the one-up party often withdraws affiliation in favor of more aggression (Alexandroff, 1979). Thus, managing the one-down role is important in building toward more productive outcomes.

Second is the **prominence of identity**. As indicated above, central to the beliefs and attitudes that form the terrorists' identity is an ideology (Crenshaw, 1988; Hoffman, 1999). Understanding the terrorist's ideology provides clues concerning the kinds of paradoxes that might dominate the terrorist negotiation process. For example, a religious fundamentalist driven terrorist might be willing to sacrifice his life to achieve his objectives in the incident. This condition suggests that the paradox of detachment might be particularly problematic for negotiators to address. Also, the fanaticism could dig the negotiations deeper into the paradox of irrationality in which emotion begins to dominate the interaction.

The third issue is **individual bias** from situational, task and frame perspectives. The one-down role effect appears most likely to emerge when a number of individual biases start to develop. For example, when negotiators define the task as revolving around a single issue, they remove options for more collaborative tradeoffs and more nuanced views of the conflict. Also, more aggressive strategies emerge when individuals perceive that violent means of addressing the issues are socially sanctioned, and they enter the conflict with a fixed sum bias and a negative frame. As noted by Corsi (1981), the propensity for these dynamics to emerge will vary across the types of terrorist incidents, since each type differs in terms of its setting, the available possibilities, and the way in which the interaction is played out.

To examine the impact of these effects, Donohue and Taylor (2004) conducted an analysis of 186 descriptive accounts of terrorist incidents collected from the chronologies compiled by Mickolus and his colleagues (Mickolus, 1980, 1993; Mickolus, et al. 1989; Mickolus & Simmons, 1997). The accounts selected contained sufficient descriptive material to enable a coding of behaviors that occurred during the incidents as well as a coding of the way in which the incident ended. A hundred of these accounts were aerial hijackings in which the perpetrators took control of an airplane or helicopter for a sustained period of time. The remaining 86 accounts were barricade-siege incidents in which the perpetrators took control of a public building (e.g. embassy) or a private location (e.g. bank). The selected incidents took place between 1968 and 1991, and were located in over 50 different countries. The incidents were reportedly committed by both autonomous perpetrators and perpetrators affiliating themselves with known terrorist organizations including the Black Panther Party, Islamic Jihad, the Irish Republican Army and the Popular Front for the Liberation of Palestine. These affiliations allowed the incidents to be grouped according to whether they were associated with a nationalist–separatist, social revolutionary or religious fundamentalist ideology (Post et al., 2002).

A content analysis of the descriptive accounts revealed a number of variables that reflected overt power moves and affiliative acts within the terrorist incidents. These behaviors were identified through a grounded approach to categorizing descriptions in which the coding scheme was continually expanded and refined until it effectively reflected the behavior of both terrorists and authorities (Glaser & Strauss, 1967; Holsti, 1969; Krippendorff, 1980).

The data generally provide support for the three-key dimensions of the one-down effect in the context of terrorist negotiation that include power complementarity, the prominence of identity that can magnify the role effect, and the impact of the situation on individual biases that affect the degree and type of behavior. Specifically, the data revealed that terrorists who responded to their one-down role by making excessive demands were more likely to achieve a negotiated outcome. Although this contrasted with our expectations that making excessive demands may have perpetuated a crisis bargaining frame, the demands served to escalate the level of dialogue which ultimately served to transform the interaction and overcome the power discrepancy.

Regarding the prominence of role identity, when compared to nationalist–separatists and social revolutionaries, the terrorists with a religious ideology typically used more aggressive strategies. This use was pervasive across the different kinds of aggressive strategies, which is consistent with the idea that these terrorists aim to maximize fear and threat rather than use these dynamics to achieve some other goal. Religious terrorists engaged in very little affiliative behavior compared to nationalist–separatists and social revolutionaries. This unwillingness to engage in normative interaction illustrates the religious terrorist's lack of interdependence with the system they are attacking and their determination to achieve a set of goals without giving consideration to alternatives (Silke, 2003). These findings suggest that identity plays a significant role in the evolution of terrorist negotiations and, consequently, that it is important to understand the cultural and social background of those terrorists authorities engage in negotiation.

However, it is important to note that there were some important variations across the hijacker and barricade-siege roles. Compared to barricade-siege incidents, hijackers typically used more overt aggression as a means of shifting power, tended not to negotiate or use threats to the hostages as a way of gaining leverage in the incident or negotiation, and were less likely to make concessions, presumably because they were less prepared to engage in any form of bargaining to obtain a certain outcome. The focus of aerial hijacks was on overt aggression to maximize the threat of the situation and force the authorities into capitulating. In contrast, the barricade-siege incidents focused on more indirect attempts to change the power structure combined with normative bargaining for a resolution.

Perhaps the most significant implication of these findings is that in extreme circumstances, the role effect takes some interesting twists. In less extreme conditions, such as buyer–seller negotiations, the one-down effect generally reveals more conciliatory behavior from the higher-power party. The higher-power party experiments with reaching out to propose more negotiated options while focusing on the substantive nature of the conflict. However, in the current findings, when the lower-power party (i.e. the terrorist) engaged in extreme aggression, the higher-powered authorities quickly reciprocated with tactical attempts to resolve the dispute.

Thus, the profile of the more high-risk terrorist negotiation is one in which the perpetrators are religious extremists, they make references to their one-down, low-power role, they focus on a single issue and they repeat information about their identity. The question at this point is how to approach these individuals given the general framework proposed in this chapter. The final section now turns to the task of integrating the perspectives offered here to create a comprehensive strategy for conflict resolution with terrorists.

SUMMARY

This chapter approaches the process of conflict resolution with terrorists from a language frame perspective, focusing both on the kinds of relational challenges and the paradoxes that they present. These challenges are best addressed by using a process capable of first working through relational issues and then dealing with substantive issues. The terrorist profile that presents the most difficult challenge in working through this process involves religious fundamentalist groups who are very identity-driven and fixated on power and

single issues. Developing a relationship with these kinds of individuals requires listening to the language that the terrorists are using to conceptualize their plight. Once a relationship begins to develop, then the negotiation team can start to move toward managing the issues and resolving the situation. The contrast between the Israeli negotiations with the Palestinians in the Church of Nativity and the Russian negotiations with the Chechens in the Moscow theater illustrates how a failure to manage the process and develop a functional relationship can cost lives. Negotiating in a crisis situation is never an easy task, but it is important to think strategically through a model and this chapter seeks to provide that option while also addressing the more global issues of how to manage terrorism more broadly.

REFERENCES

Alexandroff, A. (1979). *Symmetry in international relations*. Ithaca, NY: Cornell University Press.

Barry, Bruce. (1999). The tactical use of emotion in negotiation. In Robert J. Bies, Roy J. Lewicki, & Blair C. Sheppard (Eds.), *Research on negotiation in organizations, Vol. 7*. Stamford, CT: JAI Press.

Burgoon, Judee K., & Hale, Jerold L. (1984). The fundamental topoi of relational communication. *Communication Monographs, 51*, 193–214.

Cambria, Jack, DeFilippo, Richard J., Louden, Robert J., & McGowen, Hugh. (2002). Negotiation under extreme pressure: The "mouth marines" and the hostage takers. *Negotiation Journal, 18*, 331–343.

Cialdini, Robert B. (2001). *Influence: Science and practice*. Boston, MA: Allyn and Bacon.

Corsi, Jerome R. (1981). Terrorism as a desperate game: Fear, bargaining, and communication in the terrorist event. *Journal of Conflict Resolution, 25*, 47–85.

Crenshaw, Martha. (1988). The subjective reality of the terrorist: Ideological and psychological factors in terrorism. In Robert O. Slater & Michael Stohl (Eds.), *Current perspectives on international terrorism*. London: Macmillan Press.

Cristal, Moty. (2006). Negotiating under the Cross : The story of the forty day siege of the Church of Nativity. In I. William Zartman, *Negotiating with Terrorists* (pp. 103–130). Leiden, The Netherlands: Martinus Nijhoff Publishers.

De Dreu, Carsten K. (1995). Coercive power and concession making in bilateral negotiation. *Journal of Conflict Resolution, 39*, 646–670.

Dolnik, Adam, & Pilch, Richard. (2006). The Moscow theater hostage crisis: The perpetrators, their tactics, and the Russian response. In I. William Zartman, *Negotiating with terrorists* (pp. 131–164). Leiden, The Netherlands: Martinus Nijhoff Publishers.

Donohue, William A. (1998). Managing equivocality and relational paradox in the Oslo Peace Negotiations. *Journal of Language and Social Psychology, 17*, 72–96.

Donohue, William A., & Hoobler, Gregory. D. (2002). Relational frames and their ethical implications in international negotiation: An analysis based on the Oslo II negotiations. *International Negotiation, 7*, 143–167.

Donohue, William A., Kaufmann, Gary, Smith, Richard, & Ramesh, Clospet. (1991). Crisis bargaining: A framework for understanding intense conflict. *International Journal of Group Tensions, 21*, 133–154.

Donohue, William A., Ramesh, Clospet, & Borchgrevink, Carl. (1991). Crisis bargaining: Tracking relational paradox in hostage negotiation. *International Journal of Conflict Management, 2*, 257–274.

Donohue, William A., & Roberto, Anthony J. (1993). Relational development as negotiated order in hostage negotiation. *Human Communication Research, 20*, 175–198.

Donohue, William A., & Taylor, Paul J. (2006). Testing Relational Order Theory in hostage negotiation. Paper presented to the International Association for Conflict Management.

Donohue, William A., & Taylor, Paul J. (2004). Testing the role effect in terrorist negotiations. *International Negotiation, 8*(3) 85–105.

Faure, Guy O. (2006). Negotiating with terrorists: The hostage case. In I. William Zartman, *Negotiating with terrorists* (pp. 25–50). Leiden, The Netherlands: Martinus Nijhoff Publishers.

Giebels, Ellen, de Dreu, Carsten K.W., & Van de Vliert, Evert. (2000). Interdependence in negotiation: Effects of exit options and social motive on distributive and integrative negotiation. *European Journal of Social Psychology, 30*, 255–272.

Glaser, Barry G., & Strauss, Anselm L. (1967). *The discovery of grounded theory: Strategies for qualitative research*. Chicago: Aldine.

Hammer, Mitchell R., & Rogan, Randall G. (1997). Negotiation models in crisis situations: The value of a communication-based approach. In Randall Rogan, Mitchell Hammer, & Clinton Van Zandt, *Dynamic Processes of Crisis Negotiation* (pp. 9–24). Westport, CT: Praeger.

Harik, Judith P. (2004). *Hezbollah: The Changing Face of Terrorism*. London: I.B. Tauris.

Hayes, Richard E. (1988). *Models of Structure and Process of Terrorist Groups: Decision-Making Processes*. Vienna: VA: Evidence Based Research.

Hayes, Richard E. (2002). Negotiations with terrorists. In Victor Kremenyuk (Ed.), *International negotiation* (pp. 416–430). San Francisco, CA: Jossey-Bass.

Hayes, Richard E., Kaminski, Stacey R., & Beres, Steven M. (2003). Negotiating the non-negotiable: Dealing with absolutist terrorists. *International Negotiation, 8*, 9–24.

Hoffman, Bruce. (1999). *Inside Terrorism*. New York: Columbia University Press.

Holsti, Ole R. (1969). *Content Analysis for the Social Sciences and Humanities*. Reading, MA: Addison-Wesley.

Krippendorff, Klaus. (1980). *Content Analysis: An Introduction to its Methodology*. Beverly Hills, CA: Sage.

McMains, Michael J., & Mullins, Wayman C. (2001). *Crisis Negotiations: Managing Critical Incidents and Hostage Situations in Law Enforcement and Corrections* (2nd ed.). Cincinnati, OH: Anderson.

Mickolus, Edward F. (1980). *Transnational Terrorism: A Chronology of Events, 1968–1979*. London: Aldwych Press.

Mickolus, Edward F. (1993). *Terrorism 1988–1991: A Chronology of Events and a Selectively Annotated Bibliography*. Westport, CT: Greenwood Press.

Mickolus, Edward F., & Simmons, Susan L. (1997). *Terrorism 1992–1995: A Chronology of Events and a Selectively Annotated Bibliography*. Westport, CT: Greenwood Press.

Mickolus, Edward F., Sandler Todd, & Murdock, Jean M. (1989). *International Terrorism in the 1980s* (vol. 2, 1984–1987). Ames, IO: Iowa State University Press.

Miron, M.S., & Goldstein, Arnold P. (1979). *Hostage*. New York: Pergamon.

Muir, William Ker. (1977). *Police: Streetcorner Politicians*. Chicago: University of Chicago Press.

Noesner, Gary W., & Webster, Michael. (1997). Crisis intervention: Using active listening skills in negotiations. *FBI Law Enforcement Bulletin, 66*, 13–19.

Post, Jerrold M., Ruby, Keven G., & Shaw, Eric D. (2002). The radical group in context 2: Identification of critical elements in the analysis of risk for terrorism by radical group type. *Studies in Conflict and Terrorism, 25*, 101–126.

Reich, Walter. (1998). *Origins of Terrorism: Psychologies, Ideologies, Theologies, States of Mind*. Washington, DC: Woodrow Wilson Center Press.

Rogan, Randall G., Hammer, Mitchell R., & Van Zandt, Clinton R. (1997). *Dynamic Processes of Crisis Negotiation*. Westport, CT: Praeger.

Russell, Charles A., Banker, Leon J., & Miller, Bowman H. (1979). Out-inventing the terrorist. In Yonah Alexander, David Carlton, & Paul Wilkinson (Eds.), *Terrorism: Theory and Practice* (pp. 3–42). Boulder, CO: Westview.

Shelling, Thomas C. (1956). An essay on bargaining. *The American Economic Review, 46*, 281–306.

Silke, Andrew (2003). Becoming a terrorist. In Andrew Silke (Ed.), *Terrorists, Victims and Society: Psychological Perspectives on Terrorism and its Consequences* (pp. 29–53). Chichester, UK: Wiley.

Strauss, Anselm (1978). *Negotiations: Varieties, Contexts, Processes, and Social Order*. San Francisco: Jossey-Bass.

Taylor, Paul. J. (2002). A cylindrical model of communication behavior in crisis negotiations. *Human Communication Research, 28*, 7–48.

Taylor, Paul J., & Donald, Ian. J. (2004). The structure of communication behavior in simulated and actual crisis negotiations. *Human Communication Research, 30*, 443–478.

Taylor, Paul. J., & Thomas, Sally (2005). Linguistic style matching and negotiation outcome. Paper presented to the International Association for Conflict Management.

Van Kleef, Gerben A., de Dreu, Carsten. K.W., & Manstead, A.S.R. (2004). The interpersonal effects of emotions in negotiations: A motivated information processing approach. *Journal of Personality and Social Psychology, 87*, 510–528.

Vecchi, Gregory M., Van Hasselt, Vincent B., & Romano, Stephen J. (2005). Crisis (hostage) negotiation: Current strategies and issues in high-risk conflict resolution. *Aggression and Violent Behavior, 10*, 533–551.

Victoroff, Jeff (2005). The mind of the terrorist: A review and critique of psychological approaches. *The Journal of Conflict Resolution, 49*, 3–42.

Wagner, Richard V. (2006). Terrorism: A peace psychological analysis. *Journal of Social Issues, 62*, 155–171.

Wilson, Margaret A. (2000). Toward a model of terrorist behavior in hostage-taking incidents. *Journal of Conflict Resolution, 44*, 403–424.

Winter, David. G. (1991). Measuring personality at a distance: Development of an integrated system for scoring motives in running text. In A.J. Stewart, J.M. Healy, Jr., & D.J. Ozer (Eds.), *Perspectives in Personality: Approaches to Understanding Lives* (pp. 59–89). London: Jessica Kingsley.

Wright, Robert G. (2003). No outside entrances— A decade after Waco: Reassessing crisis negotiations at Mount Carmel in light of new government disclosures. *Nova Religio, 7*, 101–110.

Zartman, I. William (2006). Negotiating with terrorists: Introduction. In I. William Zartman, *Negotiating With Terrorists* (pp. 1–8). Leiden, The Netherlands: Martinus Nijhoff Publishers.

23

Media and Conflict Resolution

Eytan Gilboa

Interest in the media's roles in conflict and conflict resolution has been increasingly growing in the last fifteen years (Gilboa, 2000a, 2002a). Most studies, however, have focused on the often negative contributions of the media to the escalation and violence phases of conflict. Scholars have paid much less attention to conflict resolution and reconciliation. The interest in the media effects on conflicts stem from technological innovations in mass communication, primarily in proliferation of global television news networks and the Internet. The global networks can broadcast live from almost any place on the globe to any other place. Websites and weblogs provide state and non-state actors, as well as individuals, with endless opportunities to exchange and debate events and processes both inside and outside political entities (Bollier, 2003; Larson, 2004). The Internet can penetrate any national boundaries, even those of the most closed and authoritarian societies.

Commentators and scholars invented the term "CNN effect" to describe how dominant global television coverage has become in world affairs, especially in acute international conflicts. The term implies that television coverage forces policy makers to take actions they otherwise would not have taken (Gilboa, 2005a; Robinson, 2002). It means that the media determine the national interest and usurp policymaking from elected and appointed officials. Scholars and practitioners have also noticed how the media, particularly radio, was instrumental in fomenting conflict and violence in places such as Rwanda and Bosnia (Buric, 2000; Kellow & Steeves, 1998; Temple-Raston, 2005), and concluded that roles can be converted into positive contributions to conflict resolution. Experts in conflict resolution have been very optimistic and enthusiastic about these contributions (Howard, 2003; Reljic, 2004; Melone, Terzis, & Beleli, 2002). They have designed and established many media programs in conflict regions, wrote manuals for journalists both in the developed and the underdeveloped world, organized conferences, and wrote books, reports and surveys (Hieber, 2001; International Media Support, 2003; Ukpabi, 2001; Walton, 2004).

Early studies of actual and potential contributions of the media to conflict resolution focused on the Cold War, arms races, international negotiation and images of the enemy (Arno & Dissanayake, 1984; Bruck, 1989; Davison, 1974; Korzenny & Ting-Toomey,

1990; Roach, 1993). "Peace journalism" prescribes certain roles for the media in international conflicts (Galtung, 1998, 2002; Lynch, 2002; McGoldrick & Lynch, 2000), but this approach focused more on war and violence. It compared and contrasted "war journalism" with "peace journalism," heavily criticizing the first and passionately advocating the second. Peace journalism has been very controversial because it touches on sensitive nerves of professional journalism norms such as objectivity, impartiality and balance (Hanitzsch, 2004; Seib, 2002).

Scholars and practitioners have used many terms, concepts, approaches, theories and models to describe and analyze effects of the modern media on conflict resolution. Many of these terms and approaches are highly vague or even confusing. One popular example is "peace building" which is too general and imprecise. The same applies to "peace operations" or "peacemaking." This work adheres to the organizing concept of this volume: conflict resolution. Most writers divide conflict into three phases: pre-conflict, conflict and post-conflict. The emphasis in this framework is on conflict, the pre- and post-phases are defined only by a time factor. In this context, conflict is equated with violence and conflict resolution is equated with negotiations and may appear at each phase.

This work views conflict resolution as a distinctive phase in the dynamic development of conflict. Scholars and practitioners have interchangeably employed different terms to describe media effects such as intervention, roles and coverage. Coverage is different from the other functions. It refers to the media output: newspapers or broadcasts. Coverage includes reports but also opinions on current events and processes. Roles refer to various activities other than coverage, such as performing confidence-building measures or mediation, and to values and standards that should determine coverage (Gilboa, 2000a, 2002b). This work explores both coverage and roles but the emphasis is on roles.

The chapter presents what we know about the media's roles in conflict resolution, what we need to know, and how we should fill the gaps in existing knowledge. It includes three parts. The first presents and analyzes various typologies of media intervention in conflict resolution and media coverage. The second part presents an analysis of positive and negative media contributions to several critical areas of conflict resolution, including signaling and communication, confidence building and destruction, mediation, and promoting and cultivating negotiations and agreements. The last part offers a new framework for future research and practice based on integration of theories and approaches from the fields of communication and conflict studies.

TYPOLOGIES OF MEDIA INTERVENTION AND COVERAGE

Many scholars and practitioners have tended to view the media's roles in conflict resolution as an intervention, usually of a third party. Intervention means liberating and reforming the local media and creating political, social and economic conditions favorable for media-sponsored conflict resolution activities. Third parties include governmental agencies, such as the US Agency for International Development, international organizations such as the UN and NGOs such as the Search for Common Ground. They all developed and experimented with many media projects designed to promote conflict resolution and reconciliation.

Most of the projects were designed to strengthen the local media or establish peace-oriented radio and television stations and programs. NGOs and foundations have been the most active.[1] Geelen (2002, p. 46) identified 32 media projects widely distributed around the world, in Africa, South East Asia, the Balkans, Eastern Europe, the CIS, South America, South Asia and the Middle East. The proliferation of projects required a theoretical and empirical effort to study and evaluate them. Media coverage of conflict resolution, especially of international negotiation, has been a constant issue for debate and analysis both inside the communities of scholars and practitioners and among them. Framing has been a major issue in research about coverage. This section offers typologies of media projects and of coverage and framing.

Media intervention

Several scholars and practitioners have constructed typologies to identify different types of media intervention (Table 23.1). Curtis (2000, pp. 142–143) suggested four types of intervention: The first, improving the media environment, is designed to reform existing media systems, eliminate hate media and create security for journalists. The second provides audiences with information about peace-building activities. The third is more proactive and utilizes specific programming to directly affect reconciliation and dialogues. The last type, building media institutions and practices, is designed to achieve long-term goals including training schools for journalists; encouraging indigenous media-focused NGOs, and establishing communication policies intended to disseminate diverse views and ideas.

Curtis used the conflicts in Rwanda and Bosnia to illustrate the utility of her typology. She investigated Radio Agatashya, independent regional radio broadcasting for Rwandan refugees, and the Media Experts Commission and the Open Broadcasting Network established in Bosnia. Curtis didn't systematically apply her framework and the results of her investigation are mixed and problematic. She acknowledged that implementation of one type of intervention may contradict another one. For example, providing valuable information on refugees driven out of their homes through violence on Radio Agatashya contradicted the need to promote reconciliation among all the groups

engaged in the civil war. This is an excellent observation but Curtis didn't say how this dilemma could be resolved.

Howard (2002, pp. 10–11) distinguished among five types of interventions by goals and methods. His first, *rudimentary journalism training,* is designed to challenge government controlled media systems, especially in non-democratic societies. It seeks to educate journalists about the basic norms of free media including impartiality, accuracy and balance. The second type, *responsible journalism development*, is deigned to develop more advanced journalism skills in areas such as investigative and exploratory journalism. The goal is to make society responsive to conflict resolution. The third type, *transitional journalism development*, is intended to create self-awareness among journalists about conflict resolution roles they should perform in society. The idea is to convert journalists from being just objective observers to serve as active participants in the promotion of conflict resolution. The fourth type, *proactive media-based intervention*, refers to outside intervention to counter hate media or propaganda. This intervention is usually associated with peace-keeping forces or activities of NGOs. The last type, *intended outcome programming*, is designed to transform attitudes and promote reconciliation via specific media and contents.

Howard's typology is somewhat confusing and too simplistic Howard, Rolt, Van de Veen & Verhoeven (2003) employed this typology to classify, analyze and evaluate various media projects pursued around the world, mostly since the early 1990s. Table 23.2 reveals the limits of Howard's typology. Too many projects appear in more then one type of intervention. All the projects in Type 1 also appear in Type 2 and all

Table 23.1 Typologies of media intervention

Curtis (2000)	Howard (2002)	Frohardt & Temin (2003)
1. Improving the immediate media environment	1. Rudimentary journalism training	1. Structural
2. Informing and educating the public	2. Responsible journalism development	2. Content-specific
3. Promoting societal reconciliation	3. Transitional journalism development	3. Entertainment-oriented
4. Building media institutions	4. Proactive media intervention	4. Aggressive
	5. Intended outcome programming	

Table 23.2   Media projects by types of intervention

Type of Intervention	Project	Location
1. Rudimentary journalism training	Philippine Investigative Journalism*	Philippine
	IREX's Promedia Program*	Central & East Europe
	Open Society Institute Network Media Program*	Central & East Europe
	Internews Central Asia*	Tajikistan
	IMPACS Cambodia Journalists Training*	Cambodia
	Reseau Liberte*	Kosovo, Vietnam, Africa
	OSCE Mission Kosovo*	Kosovo, Bosnia
2. Responsible journalism development	Radio Netherlands, Africa Office**	Benin
	Open Asia Television	Central Asia
3. Transitional journalism development	Media for Peace	Columbia
	Center for Conflict Resolution	Uganda
	Studio Ijambo**	Burundi
	Radio Blue Sky	Kosovo
	Reporting for Peace	Indonesia
4. Proactive media intervention	Radio Soap Opera for Peace***	Senegal
	Arusha Video Project***	Rwanda
	Operation Spear	Balkans
	UNTAC Radio***	Cambodia
	New Home, New Life***	Afghanistan
5. Intended outcome programming	Talking Drum Studio	Liberia, Sierra Leone
	Nashe Maalo	Macedonia
	Radio Okapi	DR Congo

*   Also Type 2
**   Also Types 4 and 5
***   Also Type 5
Adapted from Howard, R., Rolt, F., Van de Veen, H., & Verhoeven, J. (2003).

but one project in Type 4 also appear in Type 5. One project, "Radio Netherlands Africa Office," was described as performing Types 2, 4 and 5. Type 3 is highly problematic and contradicts goals of the first two types. Type 4 is confusing because it isn't clear whether media intervention is accompanied by a peacekeeping force, or the other way around. Given the results of this application and classification exercise, it would have been more useful to amalgamate Types 1 and 2 and Types 4 and 5. In addition, it isn't sufficiently clear whether the typology is based on a hierarchy of interventions that may move from a basic to a more advanced level. While the first three types may constitute a hierarchical system, moving from basic to more sophisticated intervention, the last two may be activated at any point in time. In addition, it isn't clear which type of media, local or foreign, should be used for the various interventions. Howard argued that all the types may appear in all his phases of conflict:

pre-conflict, conflict and post-conflict, but it would have been much more useful to match specific interventions with different phases of conflict.

Frohardt and Temin (2003) suggested four types of media intervention in conflict regions: *structural, content-specific, entertainment-oriented,* and *aggressive.* They are designed to reform the media in conflict regions and make them stronger, more independent and more resistant to government pressure and manipulations. The first type includes the strengthening of independent media, such as the strengthening of the anti-government Serbian radio station B92 during the Bosnia conflict; developing journalist competence, working with the legislature and the judiciary to protect free speech and independent media; promoting diversity in the journalist corps and media ownership and media monitoring.

Content-specific interventions include "repersonalization" and "issue-oriented training." Repersonalization calls for the portraying of people mostly as individuals. Pioneered by Internews, *Spacebridges* is an example of this strategy as it allowed individuals from communities in conflict, such as Muslim, Serb, and Croat refugees from Bosnia, to conduct personal dialogues with each other over a live video feed. Issue-oriented training involves training of journalists on how to report on sensitive and explosive issues in a manner that would help, rather than hinder, conflict resolution. Entertainment-oriented programming is based on the assumption that all types of programs, not just news and documentaries, should be used to manage and resolve conflicts. These may include soap operas for adults and programs for children designed to encourage dialogue and discourage hate and violence. The last type of intervention, the aggressive one, is intended to combat media abuses in the prevention and violent phases of conflict, and is much less relevant to conflict resolution. Aggressive interventions include the building of alternative sources of information, such as external radio and television stations, and jamming of hate media.

A comparative analysis of the intervention typologies yields both similarities and differences.[2] Curtis' *improving the immediate media environment* is similar to Howard's *rudimentary journalism training* and to Frohardt and Temin's *structural* intervention. Curtis, however, distinguished between short- (Type 1) and long-term programs (Type 4) to reform the local media, but the other typologies don't recognize a time dimension. Curtis' Type 1 intervention may include Frohardt and Temin's Type 4. Howard suggested three different interventions for creating media systems responsive to the requirements of conflict resolution while the other two typologies suggested only one type of this intervention.

All the typologies confused goals and means. In just a three-year period, three authors suggested three different typologies using very different terms and characteristics, and instead of building and expanding on one promising typology, they have ignored each other. It would have been more useful to adopt one clearly defined and explained typology of media intervention and systematically apply it. The main problem with the media projects isn't just confusing terminology and unclear goals and means. Very few scholarly studies have been conducted on the actual results of media intervention, and most of them focused on projects in Africa (Hagos, 2001; Mbaine, 2006; Ojo, 2003). The studies reveal mixed results but there isn't sufficient accumulation to determine which strategies and programs are the most effective and which fail to produce even minimal results.

Media coverage

Theoretical studies and simulation experiments as well as practical experience suggest that secret talks, particularly between enemies, increase negotiating flexibility and the willingness to make necessary concessions in order to reach agreements (Druckman, 1995; Druckman & Druckman, 1996; Kelman, 1997, pp. 189–190; Pruitt, 1997, p. 246). Policy makers and diplomats prefer secret diplomacy because of the nature of international negotiation and the immunity from political cost in case of failure. Negotiations to resolve difficult international conflicts entail long and hard bargaining. They move in stages from the initial presentation of tough opening demands, through the making of often painful and risky concessions, to a final compromise based on reciprocal concessions of both sides. Diplomats believe that premature disclosure of initial negotiating positions and tactics, and of the potential to make concessions, expose them to pressure from both the other side's negotiators and their own domestic opinion. Such stressful conditions could end negotiations prematurely or hamper diplomacy with unnecessary long discussions, resulting in less effective agreements (Eban, 1998).

Gilboa (2000b) developed three conceptual models to analyze media coverage of international negotiations: *Secret Diplomacy, Closed-Door Diplomacy, and Open Diplomacy*. They are based on the degree to which diplomatic negotiations are exposed to the media and public opinion. In the *Secret Diplomacy* model, the media and the public are totally excluded from negotiations and there is no media coverage of any kind. In *Closed-Door Diplomacy*, they are partially excluded and media coverage is narrowly confined to mostly technical issues such as who negotiates with whom, where and when. In the *Open Diplomacy* model, negotiations are much more open to the media and coverage is more extensive. Three main variables determine the ability of policy makers to implement each of these models: purpose, legitimacy, and controllability. Purpose refers to the goals of the sides in a negotiation process. Legitimacy refers to recognition and acceptance of a negotiation process by the public on the basis of moral, ideological or political criteria. Controllability refers to means negotiators employ to control media access and coverage of international negotiation.

In the *Secret Diplomacy Model*, officials prevent any coverage of negotiation and exercise full control over media access when they negotiate a major transformation in relations with enemies and expect to make significant controversial concessions with overwhelming effects. In the information age, it has been much more difficult to keep negotiations secret, especially at the highest levels of government. Officials and diplomats, however, have found innovative ways to shield critical negotiations from the public eye (Gilboa, 1998a). In 1971, Kissinger pursued secret diplomacy with China, designed to revolutionize the relations between the two powers. In 1977 and 1993, Israel employed secret negotiations with Egypt and the PLO respectively, to achieve a breakthrough in hostile and violent relations. Other cases of secret negotiations include the post-Falklands negotiations between Britain and Argentina, the peace process in Northern Ireland, and the "2 plus 4" (the two German states and the United States, the Soviet Union, Britain, and France) discussions over the unification of Germany.

In the *Open Diplomacy Model*, negotiations are readily accessible to the media and to public scrutiny and debate. It is characterized by extensive and direct media coverage of international negotiations. In this model, negotiators frequently conduct official press conferences, hold briefings, grant interviews, and even allow reporters access to conference rooms. Officials use this model primarily in three situations: when they negotiate with friendly or neutral actors to improve or maintain existing relations; after a breakthrough in relations, when they think that sufficient trust had been achieved and there is no need to conduct secret negotiations; and when they wish to achieve secondary results. Sometimes international actors enter negotiations for reasons other than conflict resolution such as satisfying a third actor, improving image and reputation, gaining time, getting immediate rewards, deceiving enemies and rivals, and obtaining valuable information (Iklè, 1964, pp. 43–58). By definition, open diplomacy is the best model to achieve such secondary results. Many policy makers and scholars believe, for example, that since 2003, Iran has conducted talks on its nuclear programs with a group representing the EU (the UK, France and Germany) solely to gain time for a concealed effort to acquire nuclear weapons.

Closed-Door Diplomacy is the most interesting model. It stands between secret and open diplomacy but is much closer to the secret model. The actors in this model typically include a mediator and parties to a conflict who had decided to seek conflict resolution through peaceful means, have gone through several rounds of negotiation and made progress, but have failed to reach an agreement. In Closed-Door Diplomacy, the media cover only technical aspects. They are aware of the dates when negotiations are scheduled to begin, where the talks will be conducted, and the identity and ranks of the participants. Once the actual negotiations begin, a news blackout is drawn over the talks with only limited information being provided about the actual progress and results. This way, the participants are effectively isolated from their respective domestic public opinions, from opposition forces, pressure groups, other states, international organizations and transnational actors, as long as the negotiations continue. US administrations used Close-Door Diplomacy in difficult conflicts in the Middle East and the Balkans, including the 1978 Camp David conference with the leaders of Israel and Egypt and the 1995 Dayton, Ohio talks between the leaders of Serbia, Bosnia and Croatia.

Much of the literature on media coverage of conflict and conflict resolution is based on various assumptions about media effects. The communication literature is rich in theories and models of media effects such as agenda-setting and framing, but both scholars and practitioners in conflict resolution rarely employ them, and very few studies integrate framing with concepts and theories from conflict resolution. "To frame is to select some aspects of a perceived reality and make them more salient in a communication text, in such a way as to promote a particular problem definition, causal interpretation, moral evaluation, and/or treatment recommendation" (Entman, 1993, p. 52). According to Reese (2001), "Frames are *organizing principles* that are socially *shared* and *persistent* over time, that work *symbolically* to meaningfully *structure* the social world" (p. 11). Contrary to popular myth, the media is only one actor in the framing process. Politicians, policy makers, elites, interest groups, foreign leaders all try to win public acceptance of their framing. The media participate in the framing contest but leaders have much more influence on the final outcome (Entman, 2004, pp. 2–22).

Very few scholars have conducted research on framing of conflict resolution. Shinar (2000) investigated "peace talk" in conflict resolution processes in the Middle East and Northern Ireland. He found that in these two cases, peace was framed in a war discourse and therefore coverage didn't help the process. In another study, Shinar (2002) found that the Israeli and the Western media wrongly framed the Oslo peace process through "the reconciliation/end-of-the conflict" model, while the correct one should have been the "conflict management"

model. Kempf (2002) used an interesting methodology to decode framing of escalation and de-escalation of the conflict in Bosnia.

Framing may provide valuable information about the readiness of the sides to pursue serious conflict resolution. Zartman (2000) has developed the "ripeness concept" to determine whether parties to a conflict have the needed motivation to reach an agreement. Ripeness may emerge in two main situations: when the sides feel that they have reached a "Mutually Hurting Stalemate" or a "Mutually Enhancing Opportunity." The first situation "pushes" parties to move from conflict management to conflict resolution, while the second "pulls" them towards resolution. Donohue and Hoobler (2002) have suggested that public exchanges by policy makers and negotiators via the media during negotiations may reveal critical information about the Mutually Enhancing Opportunity dimension of ripeness. To investigate their interesting hypotheses, they combined "relational order theory" from psychology, "ripeness" from conflict studies and "framing" from communication. Donohue and Hoobler applied the integrated approach, "relational ripeness" to the Oslo I and Oslo II Israeli–Palestinian negotiations. Their findings are significant because they help to better understand how relational messages evolve, and what they reveal about the social and political context in which negotiations occur. This study also demonstrates the value of integrative multi-disciplinary research. It moves several steps ahead of merely studying framing, because it places the results within theoretical contexts of both conflict studies and psychology.

MEDIA AND CONFLICT RESOLUTION FUNCTIONS

The media perform several functions in conflict resolution, known mostly as "media diplomacy" and "media-broker diplomacy" (Cohen, 1986; Gilboa, 1998b, 2002b, 2002c, 2005b). Politicians and policy makers use the media to advance negotiations, build confidence, and cultivate public support for negotiations and agreements. The media also function as an independent actor, initiating and facilitating negotiations and conducting mediation. The media can both help or hinder the pursuance of these functions. This section combines and integrates approaches from conflict and communication theories in the areas of signaling and communication, mediation, confidence building and destruction, and promoting and cultivating negotiations and agreements.

Signaling and communication

In the absence of direct channels of communication, or when one side is unsure about how the other would react to conditions for negotiations or to proposals for conflict resolution, officials use the media, with or without attribution, to send signals and messages to leaders of rival states and non-state actors. Using the media for signaling purposes has been known for many years (Jönsson, 1996). Using the media without attribution to sources is particularly efficient when policy makers wish to fly a "trial balloon." They can avoid embarrassment and disassociate themselves from an idea that may receive a negative response. Leaders use reliable third parties to secretly explore intentions of the other side, but sometimes they simultaneously use the media to support the secret exchanges and to further indicate their serious intentions.

After the 1973 Arab–Israeli war, Secretary of State Henry Kissinger mediated between Israel and the two attacking Arab states: Egypt and Syria. He pursed this effort through "shuttle diplomacy" and highly sophisticated use of the reporters accompanying him on his plane. He employed the media for signaling, communication and pressure on policy makers of all the sides. He often gave senior diplomatic correspondents aboard his plane background reports, information, and leaks, mostly intended to signal to the sides his expectations of the next visit. This way he extracted concessions from the negotiating parties and broke deadlocks (Isaacson, 1992).

During grave international crises, or when all diplomatic channels are severed, the media provide the only channel for communication and negotiation between the rival actors. During the first phase of the 1979–1981 Iranian hostage crisis, the United States communicated with the terrorists holding the hostages exclusively through the media (Larson, 1986). A similar case occurred in the 1985 hijacking of a TWA jetliner to Beirut (Gilboa, 1990). Sparre (2001) and Spencer (2004) argued that the parties to the conflict in Northern Ireland conducted dialogues and exchanged messages through the media because formal negotiations among them were neither possible nor desirable. The media dialogue helped the sides keep the peace process alive and exchange significant messages.

In recent years, leaders have been using global communication more frequently than traditional diplomatic channels to deliver messages intended to alter an image or to open a new page. US State Department spokesperson Nicholas Burns (1996) admitted: "We use the briefings to send messages to foreign governments about our foreign policy. For example, I sometimes read carefully calibrated statements to communicate with the governments with which we have no diplomatic relations: Iraq, Iran, Libya and North Korea" (pp. 12–13). Leaders in other parts of the world employ the same technique. For example, in January 1998, the newly elected Iranian President Mohammed Khatami chose CNN to send a conciliatory message to the United States (Associated Press, 1998). Sometimes attitudes toward journalists of the other side send an important signal. When Syrian leaders excluded Israeli journalists from press conferences on Israeli–Syrian negotiations, they undermined confidence in the Syrian intentions, while allowing them to participate and ask questions built confidence (Gilboa, 2002c, pp. 198–199).

Mediation

Occasionally, the media function as an independent actor, initiating and facilitating negotiations. While not new, international mediation by journalists seems to have been expanding in recent years. Larson (1988) observed: "television provides an interactive channel for diplomacy which is instantaneous or timely and in which journalists frequently assume an equal role with officials in the diplomatic dialogue" (p.'43). Gurevitch (1991) referred to journalists who directly intervene in diplomacy as "international political brokers" (pp. 187–188). Graber (2002, p. 171) said they became "surrogates for public officials" by actively participating in an evolving situation, such as a diplomatic impasse.

Theories of international negotiation may help place the mediation roles of journalists in a proper context by emphasizing the significance of "pre-negotiation" stages, the role of "third parties," and "track-two diplomacy" (Zartman & Rasmussen, 1997). During the pre-negotiation stage, the sides explore the advantages and shortcomings of a specific negotiation process and make a decision—based on information received from the other party and domestic and external considerations—on whether or not they should enter formal negotiations (Saunders, 2001). At this stage, mediators attempt to persuade leaders to replace confrontation and violence with a commitment to peaceful resolution and negotiations. Frequently, parties to a conflict are unable to begin direct formal negotiations and need a third party to help. Third parties can be formal representatives of superpowers, neutral states, international organizations or just ordinary individuals (Hampson, 2001). Third parties are particularly helpful in the pre-negotiation stage.

While "track-one diplomacy" refers to government-to-government, formal, and official interaction between representatives of sovereign states, "track-two diplomacy" refers to unofficial negotiators or mediators and informal forms of negotiation (McDonald & Bendahmane, 1995; Volkan, 1991). At first, track-two diplomacy described only contacts and negotiations at the people-to-people level, but later was expanded to include negotiations involving peoples and governments. Gilboa (2005b) suggested that it is useful to view journalists acting independently as third parties, pursuing track-two diplomacy, particularly in pre-negotiation stages, and used the term "media-broker diplomacy" to describe this role. Journalists primarily pursue this function when they temporarily become mediators and specifically help parties to begin official negotiation.

A journalist may initiate mediation or may be asked by one or more parties to pursue it. In this model, journalists talk to the two sides, transmit relevant information, and suggest detailed procedures, proposals, and ideas that may advance official negotiations. This format was seen in Walter Cronkite's mediation in 1977 between Egyptian President Anwar Sadat and Israeli Prime Minister Menachem Begin; in the attempt of the British correspondent Patrick Seale in 2000 to break the deadlock in Israeli–Syrian negotiations; and the attempt in 2002 of Russian reporter Anna Politkovskaya to mediate between the Russian government and Chechen terrorists who held 700 hostages at the Moscow Theater (Gilboa, 2002c; 2005b). The primary professional mission of journalists is to uncover events, not to conceal them. Yet journalists have been engaged as mediators in secret negotiations (Gilboa, 1998a). The most well-known case is the mediation of John Scali (1995), diplomatic correspondent for ABC News, during the 1962 Cuban missile crisis. The Soviets selected him because he was known for his fair reporting and close ties with policy makers in Washington.

Confidence building and destruction

In the critical pre-negotiation phase, journalists can unofficially promote and facilitate interaction among conflicted parties, and can improve communication and increase mutual understanding. The goal is to convince the sides that they should seriously consider negotiation as the preferred method for resolving their conflict. This role is more likely to happen when there is no formal third party helping enemies to engage in conflict resolution. It typically occurs when representatives of rival sides are brought together on air to discuss the issues dividing them. A well-known and respected journalist associated with a highly regarded program has a better chance of successfully performing this role. This function was seen in a series of special programs Ted Koppel broadcasted on *Nightline,* in 1988 and 2000, on the Palestinian–Israeli conflict, and in 1988 on the conflict in South Africa (Koppel & Gibson, 1996); the role of Thomas Friedman of *The New York Times* in initiating and promoting the 2002 Saudi Arabia plan for Arab–Israeli peace; and the role of Michael Gonzalez of *The Wall Street Journal* in 2003 in initiating and promoting a European alliance with the United States before the war in Iraq began (Gilboa, 2005b, pp. 106–111).

The media may intentionally or unintentionally destroy confidence as well. The typical example would be media coverage of violence and terrorism used by organizations opposing conflict resolution (Cohen-Almagor, 2005). Media coverage of spectacular terrorist events usually turns into a disaster marathon (Katz & Liebes, 2007). It occurs when the broadcast media, particularly television, suspend regular scheduling and keep repeating many times the pictures of death and destruction caused by terrorist attacks and bombing. The continuing broadcast, which sometimes lasts for a few days, raises doubts about peace prospects and the value of negotiations. Disaster marathon plays right into the hands of the terrorists who wish to gain wide publicity for their agenda and stands. Israeli television coverage of horrific homicide bombing carried out in Israeli cities by Hamas and Islamic Jihad, two terrorist Palestinian organizations opposing peace with Israel, was blamed for undermining confidence in Israeli–Palestinian negotiations. Disaster marathon, however, reveals a difficult professional dilemma. The media employ news value criteria in covering events, and by these standards devote considerable attention to terrorist attacks. The dilemma represents a collision between two principles: values and standards of coverage versus providing a stage to vicious terrorists and opponents and peace.

The thought of journalists pursing mediation and confidence-building measures is indeed intriguing. If parties to a conflict cannot make progress on their own, and if no third parties are around, why should journalists be prevented from conducting mediation and constructive diplomacy? The frequent counterargument is that journalists are supposed to cover events, not create them. Gurevitch (1991) noted that "the active participation of journalists in the events they presumably 'cover' is often achieved at the cost of sacrificing traditional journalistic norms, such as editorial control" (p. 187). The journalists decide which actors, perspectives, and parts of the story to include and which to ignore. Furthermore, historically, journalists who have become players in a negotiation process have not suspended their professional reporting and coverage of the process. In fact, they have become players due to their professional standing and work. Therefore, journalists must be extremely cautious in using their profession to mediate in international conflicts, as should be policy makers who employ them for this purpose.

Promoting agreements

The media, particularly television, may contribute to reconciliation through media events—spectacular celebrations of peace agreements. The media contribution is particularly critical in situations where the respective societies are highly suspicious of each other and have been educated for years to believe that the other side is only interested in violence and war. Media events are broadcast live, organized outside the media, pre-planned, and presented with reverence and ceremony (Dayan & Katz, 1992). Live coverage of media events interrupts scheduled broadcasting and attracts wide audiences around the world. Diplomatic media events include summit meetings between rival powers, such as the United States and the

Soviet Union during the Cold War, and celebrations of peace agreements signed between former enemies. Media events can be used at the onset of negotiations to build confidence and facilitate negotiations, or at the end of negotiations to mobilize public support for reconciliation. The reconciliation effect of media events gained vivid expression in chapters of US–USSR "summit diplomacy" and in Arab–Israeli negotiations.

Gorbachev's summits with Presidents Reagan and Bush demonstrate how the two superpowers became adept at exploiting the media in the transition from the Cold War to the post-Cold War era. Their summits, above all, reflected the dramatic changes in superpower relations (Negrine, 1996). The climactic Gorbachev–Bush summit held in Washington in May 1990 officially ended the Cold War. Reagan used the summits to legitimize the dramatic shift in his attitudes toward the Soviet Union, branded as "the evil empire" at the beginning of his presidency.

Media events became increasingly popular and were frequently used in Arab–Israeli reconciliation efforts (Gilboa, 2002c, pp. 204–207). These include Sadat's historic visit to Jerusalem in November 1977 and the signing ceremonies of the Israeli–Egyptian Peace Treaty of March 1979, the PLO–Israel Declaration of Principles of September 1993, and the Israeli–Jordanian Peace Treaty of October 1994. Leaders consider media events to be an effective tool in building confidence and mobilizing domestic and global public support for difficult peacemaking processes and reconciliation. According to the typology of media events suggested by Dayan and Katz, the US–Soviet summit meetings and the Arab–Israeli media events belong to the category of conquests where a great leader, such as Gorbachev or Sadat, was able to overcome decades of hatred, conflict, and war and replace them with negotiations, cooperation, and peace.

Long and Brecke (2003) employed the term *reconciliation events* (p. 6) to assess reconciliation in civil and international conflicts. These are defined as turning points leading to improving relations and lessening the chance of a recurrence of violence. Reconciliation events include the following elements: direct physical contact or proximity between opponents, usually at a senior level; a public ceremony accompanied by substantial publicity or media attention that relays the event to the wider national society; and ritualistic or symbolic behavior that indicates the parties consider the dispute resolved and that more amicable relations are expected to follow. The authors argued that in both civil and international conflicts, reconciliation events are a valid proxy indicator of reconciliation. They offered two models of reconciliation: a forgiveness psychological model and a signaling rational choice model. The first is more useful in explaining reconciliation in civil conflicts, while the second is more useful in explaining reconciliation in international conflicts. The signaling model predicts that resumption of conflict after conflict resolution becomes less likely when reconciliation events are "part of a costly, novel, voluntary, and irrevocable concession in a negotiated bargain" (p. 3).

A reconciliation event in a civil conflict would be a peace agreement such as the 1992 Accords of Chapultepec signed between the government of El Salvador and the leftist guerrilla organization Farabundo Marti Front for National Liberation; or the establishment in 1995 of the Truce and Reconciliation Commission in South Africa. A reconciliation event in international conflicts would be a framework for peace such as the 1978 Israeli–Egyptian Camp David accords; the restoration of full diplomatic relations such as Great Britain and Argentina accomplished in 1990; or a formal peace agreement such as the agreement Vietnam and Cambodia signed in 1991. Long and Brecke concluded that emotion played a significant role in reconciliation, and that reconciliation events were associated with reductions in international conflict, de-escalated violence, and restored order. The problem with this study is the concept of a reconciliation event. The authors offered a highly simplistic definition of reconciliation and were probably unaware of the theory of media events that is very relevant for their study (Dayan & Katz, 1992). Despite these limitations, their study offers a media-dependent instrument that may help forecast chances for reconciliation in international conflict.

Analysis of media or reconciliation events reveals advantages as well as shortcomings. They certainly confirm legitimacy on negotiations and help to mobilize public support for agreements. On the other hand, by definition, media events have to be spectacular thereby creating high expectations for rapid and efficient progress toward peace. But as recent Arab–Israeli peace processes demonstrate, even following breakthroughs, difficult and long negotiations are needed to conclude agreements. The gap between the promise of media events and the actual results could create disappointments and confusion. Media events are not always successful, as was the case in the 1991 Arab–Israeli Madrid conference, and such ploys become far less effective when employed too frequently and the groundbreaking effect becomes diluted (Liebes & Katz, 1997). Recently, Katz and Liebes (2007) argued that traumatic events such as the 9/11 terror attacks in the USA, recent wars and natural disasters have upstaged peace ceremonies. Disasters took over because innovations in communication technologies have scattered audiences and taken the novelty from live broadcasting. Conflict resolution requires great visionary leaders and so far in this century they are in short supply. In retrospect, in several cases, the positive effects of media events have been short-lived. Yet in theory they provide enough time for great leaders to move forward beyond the point of no return in conflict resolution processes.

A FRAMEWORK FOR RESEARCH AND PRACTICE

The preceding survey and analysis of approaches to research on media and conflict resolution reveal several fundamental weaknesses. The lacks of collaboration among scholars and practitioners and of multi-disciplinary tools for analysis have been responsible for the slow advancement of knowledge. The first step to close the gap could be an effort to construct one basic framework for analysis of both theoretical and practical approaches and projects. This effort should be based on careful integration of models and theories from the fields of both communication and conflict resolution. This section suggests a new comprehensive framework for analysis, which is based on several significant distinctions among types and phases of conflict and types, levels and functions of the media.

Types of conflict

Since the end of the Cold War, the nature and level of international conflicts have changed considerably (Crocker, Hampson, & Aall, 2001). Until the end of the Cold War, most conflicts occurred between and among states, but afterward they mostly occurred at the intrastate or global levels. Ethnic and civil wars erupted in Yugoslavia and the former Soviet Union and they also exploded in Africa, in places such as Rwanda, Somalia, Sudan and Liberia. At the other end, the September 11 terrorist attacks on New York and Washington by Islamic fundamentalists, and similar subsequent attacks in Great Britain, Spain, Kenya, Indonesia, Bali, Turkey, Tunisia, Saudi Arabia, and Egypt, as well as the US-led wars in Afghanistan and Iraq, represent conflict at the global level. The "clash of civilizations" theory and debates about the economic and social consequences of globalization also deal with conflict at the global level (Barber, 1995; Huntington, 1996; Nye, 2004).

Contemporary conflicts generated analytical distinctions among different kinds and levels of violence. Even during the Cold War, protracted limited violence, exemplified primarily in terrorism and guerilla warfare, and not large-scale conventional wars, have dominated international relations. Consequently, scholars have distinguished between *High Intensity Conflict* (HIC), where violence is characterized by major wars, and

Low Intensity Conflict (LIC), where violence is characterized by much more limited and irregular uses of force. Luttwak (2002) coined a post-modern term—"post-heroic war"—to describe the essence of LIC. Media coverage of LIC is extremely crucial because the main goal of the sides engaged in this type of conflict is to alter the enemy's perception (Sowers, 2005). A conflict in a particular region may be moving across time from one type of conflict to another. For example, in 2003, the USA fought a full-scale war in Iraq, but since then has been engaged in LIC. Given the basic different characteristics of the two types of conflict, their resolution may require different approaches. Consequently, media intervention and coverage in the resolution of LIC may present different challenges and dilemmas.

Phases of conflict

Many scholars and practitioners distinguished among three highly simplistic phases of conflict: pre-conflict, conflict, and post-conflict (Howard, 2002; Spurk, 2002) or pre-violence, violence and post-violence. I think that we need meaningful concepts and not just time frames to describe the pre- and post-conflict phases, and I suggest distinguishing among four stages of conflict based on a critical condition and a principal intervention goal: onset prevention, escalation management, de-escalation resolution and termination reconciliation (Gilboa, 2006, pp. 599–601, 2007). Each phase has distinctive characteristics and ends in specific outcomes. Only the last two phases are relevant to this work. I suggest that the post-conflict or post-violence phase should be divided into two separate stages: resolution and reconciliation. The difference between the two stems from the significant distinction Galtung (1969) made between "negative peace" and "positive peace." Negative peace refers only to the absence of violence, while positive peace refers to the building of new relations in many relevant areas between former enemies, including open borders, trade, tourism, and cultural ties. Other scholars made a similar

distinction between "conflict resolution" and "conflict transformation" (Lederach, 1995, 1997). In the resolution phase, leaders attempt to negotiate an agreement to end violence. If they reach a formal agreement, it may end violence and facilitate transformation; if they do not, they may resume violence or create a stalemate. According to Lederach, conflict transformation usually involves transforming perceptions of issues, actions, and other people or groups; the way conflict is expressed; and it must take place both at the personal and the systemic level.

The distinctions between resolution and transformation of conflicts are based on the assumption that even if the sides reach a peace agreement, it is only an agreement between leaders, not between peoples, and it has to be fully implemented and respected over time. Therefore, in the reconciliation stage, the parties attempt to move from negative peace to positive peace. They try to fully engage their respective peoples and transform relations from hostility to amicability. Väyrynen (1999) raised questions about the meaning of transformation and placed the concept in a different context. To him, transformation means a major change in a principal element of a conflict including actors, issues, and rules, and therefore it may occur at any phase. He even argued that transformation must happen before resolution becomes possible. Given this approach and the different meanings applied to transformation, I searched for an alternative concept. The options were "peace building" and "reconciliation." Several scholars equate the two (Jeong, 2002; Paris, 2004), but others (Howard, 2002; Lederach, 2005; Spurk, 2002) use peace building as a general concept. I prefer "reconciliation" because it best captures the essence of the last stage in conflict resolution (Bar-Siman-Tov, 2004; Brown & Poremski, 2005; Rothstein, 1999).

Types of media

Any analysis of the media roles in conflict resolution must address both the traditional media (newspapers, television and radio) and the new media. Very little research has been conducted on the functions of the new media. When analyzing the media roles, it is also necessary to distinguish among different types and levels of media. In many studies, authors write about "the media," but they often mean the Western media. "Global" often refers to the ability of media outlets to reach global audiences or to networks claiming to represent a truly world perspective devoid of any national, ethnic or cultural bias. The hybrid "Glocal" refers to media that deal with local or national issues but are capable of reaching audiences around the world such as the Internet.

I suggest distinguishing among five levels of media by geopolitical criteria: local, national, regional, international, and global. Local media include newspapers, television, and radio stations operating in a town, a city, or a district. National media include newspapers and electronic media operating within the boundaries of nation-states. Regional media operate in a region defined by history, culture, tradition, values, language, or religion. Examples of regional media include the Dubai-based Al-Arabia that broadcast primarily to the Middle-East, and the South African Broadcasting Corporation that serves Africa. International media include broadcast and print media used or sponsored by states to operate across international borders. International media include the Voice of America, BBC World, Qatar's based Al-Jazeera, France 24, the Russian Vesti-TV and the Iranian Press TV. The global media include privately owned commercial television networks such as CNN International; and print media such as the *International Herald Tribune* and *The Economist*.

Both the international and the global media reach global audiences, but the international media present news and commentary from the perspective of a particular state, while the global media have no such official allegiance. It is also interesting to note that both CNN and the BBC operate two separate broadcasting systems: CNN International is a global network while CNN-US is national, and BBC World is an international network while BBC-UK is national. The global networks don't broadcast respectively in the USA and the UK. There are significant differences in approach and content between the national, the international and the global broadcasting of the same network, but very little research has been conducted to explore how wide the differences are and what their implications are. Al-Jazeera is a unique case because it was established and is subsidized by the Emir of Qatar (Powers & Gilboa, 2007). It is extremely important to distinguish between the local and the national media in conflict regions and external media that operate outside these regions.

Media functions

The functional theory is a classic communication theory anchored in sociological system theory, which views institutions, including the media, as performing roles designed to meet the needs of individuals and societies. The functional theory paved the way to several approaches and techniques in modern communication research including media effects, uses and gratifications, agenda-setting, framing, priming, cultivation theory and the spiral of silence theory. Several scholars have even described the functional theory as a paradigm—a master theory in control of most research in mass communication (McQuail, 2000). Application of functionalism to mass communication developed over time through several stages. Lasswell (1948) first suggested three media functions: surveillance of the environment (news coverage); correlation of the parts of society (interpretation of news and information, commentary, and editorial opinion); and transmission of culture (history, values, religion, language, etc.). Wright (1960) added a fourth function: entertainment. He also distinguished between functions and dysfunctions, and constructed a framework for functional analysis. McQuail (1987) added a fifth function, mobilization: the "campaigning for societal objectives in the sphere of politics, war, economic development, work, and sometimes religion" (p. 71).

Wright's important distinction between functions and dysfunctions is very pertinent to this study. Most approaches to media intervention in conflict resolution have ignored unintended consequences, both positive and negative. The media may provide useful information to citizens who could be motivated to act against their own interests and the interests of their community. For example, the purpose of reporting on financial difficulties of a bank is positive, or functional—warning bank customers of a threat to their accounts—but the result could be dysfunctional if all of them went to the bank, liquidated their assets, and drove the bank to bankruptcy. Application of the Wright formula suggests that even if the media are sincerely interested in positive contribution to conflict resolution, the results may backfire. Media-initiated negotiations could be functional, if coverage helps to build wide public support for the process, but if opposition forces prevail, the coverage could be dysfunctional. In addition, functions and dysfunctions may vary for each of the five basic media functions, all of which are relevant to the study of media intervention in conflict resolution. Even entertainment may include implicit or explicit messages that may either help or hinder efforts to effectively deal with conflict resolution and reconciliation.

Substantial research is needed to explore functions and dysfunctions for different types of conflict and media.

The framework

Figure 23.1 describes the proposed framework for analysis. It shows how research can be organized to explore positive and negative contributions of the media by the five media functions and the two stages of conflict resolution. Other possible dimensions include the two types of conflict: HIC and LIC; the two types of media, traditional and new: newspaper, television, radio and the Internet; and the five levels of media: local, national, regional, international and global. The proposed framework is flexible and allows partial or selective applications. Researchers do not necessarily need to apply the whole framework to all the phases, dimensions and variables. They may choose to investigate all the five functions in one stage; or one function, such as news, across the two phases; or they can focus on one function in one phase, such as interpretation in conflict resolution. They may apply the basic framework to each of the three other dimensions. For example, one could investigate the functions and dysfunctions of news in the new media or in the local media.

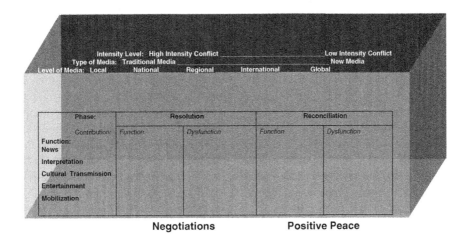

Figure 23.1   Conflict resolution and reconciliation: A framework for analysis

CONCLUSIONS

This work demonstrates that the media serve both as a tool in the hands of policy makers and negotiators, and as an independent actor pursuing their own interest and agenda. The many media projects in conflict regions show how the media can be used to advance conflict resolution. Contributions to specific functions such as confidence building and mediation demonstrate the media's independent role. The media, however, can both help and hinder conflict resolution. It can contribute to confidence building but also to confidence destruction, and both could be pursued intentionally or unintentionally. In general, practitioners and scholars have highly exaggerated the actual and potential media contribution to conflict resolution.

This work reveals substantial gaps in knowledge, practice and research on the media's roles in conflict resolution. The gaps exist at several levels and areas. Experts and practitioners in conflict resolution have often ignored relevant knowledge in communication, while communication scholars and practitioners have often ignored the relevant literature on conflict resolution. Scholars in both conflict studies and communication have often ignored the contributions of practitioners. Several scholars and practitioners in the same field have even ignored each other. The local and national media are much more significant because they directly affect the evolution and development of conflict resolution. Yet while most practitioners have designed programs for the local and the national media, most scholars have paid much more attention to the Western and the global media.

Most approaches to the media's roles in conflict resolution suffer from structural, theoretical and methodological weaknesses. Practitioners have been very optimistic about the potential contributions of the media to conflict resolution, and consequently have initiated and created many interesting media projects in conflict regions. They have ignored, however, relevant research on media effects that don't support many of their assumptions. For example, ideas about media intervention are based on the assumption of powerful, casual and linear media effects. "Media effects," however, is a major field of research in communication and the findings reveal more limitations than power and influence (Hanitzsch, 2004). Media intervention considers the audience as a single aggregate of dispersed individuals, but communication theory has identified pluralistic audiences with different characteristics. Media intervention assumes that publishers and journalists, especially at the local media level, can disregard the interests of their specific audiences, but communication theory suggests that this assumption is unnatural and economically impossible. Moreover, the media intervention approaches place responsibility on the media to resolve and transform conflicts, but communication theory does not recognize this role, and sociological system theory places responsibility for these functions on political institutions and leaders.

Another weakness is the emphasis on normative assertions. Scholars and practitioners mostly write about the roles the media *should* play and much less about the roles the media actually do. Not enough empirical scholarly studies have been conducted on media and conflict resolution. Evaluative research should be an integral part of any media project designed to promote conflict resolution. Scientific progress requires much more collaboration among scholars and practitioners from all the relevant disciplines. Conflict resolution practitioners should consult communication theories and models, particularly on media effects, and scholars should focus much more on empirical studies.

Researchers have employed many different theories, methods, and concepts to analyze potential and actual media contributions to conflict resolution. Future research, however, has to be much more systematic and cumulative. An effective approach requires a multidisciplinary and multi-dimensional framework that could explore the media's roles in conflict resolution and reconciliation through several identical or similar categories. The proposed multi-disciplinary and multi-dimensional framework combines and integrates communication and conflict theories and could be a first step in the right direction. The framework is very comprehensive and requires prioritizing of research. The first priority is to investigate functions and dysfunctions of the local media and the next one is to focus on the new media. Systematic application of the framework to case studies at different levels may help to promote badly needed knowledge and understanding of the various ways the media are influencing conflict resolution.

NOTES

1 Canada: *IMPACS: The Institute for Media, Policy and Civil Society, Communications Initiative;* Denmark: *International Media Support (IMS)*; Ghana: *Media Foundation for West Africa;* Namibia: *Media Institute for Southern Africa;* Switzerland: *The Hirondelle Foundation, Media Action International, Institute for Media, Peace and Security*; United Kingdom: *Institute for War and Peace Reporting, Panos Institute International, Reporting the World;* United States: *InterNews Network, Search for Common Ground, International Research and Exchanges Board.*

2 Rolt (2005) offered a specific confusing and unnecessary typology for non-news media initiatives. It is confusing because it lumps together contents, format and distribution, and it is unnecessary because all the general intervention typologies include under different headings all his proposed types of non-news media initiatives.

REFERENCES

Arno, A., & Dissanayake, W. (Eds.). (1984). *The news media in national and international conflict.* Boulder, CO: Westview.

Associated Press. (1998). Iranian president sends U.S. message. *International Herald Tribune,* January 8, 1.

Barber, B. (1995). *Jihad vs. McWorld.* New York: Times Books.

Bar-Siman-Tov, Y. (Ed.). (2004). *From conflict resolution to reconciliation.* New York: Oxford University Press.

Bollier, D. (2003). *People/ networks/ power: Communication technologies and the new international politics.* Washington, DC: The Aspen Institute, Communications & Society Program.

Brown, A., & Poremski, K. (Eds.). (2005). *Roads to reconciliation: Conflict and dialogue in the twenty-first century.* Armonk, NY: Sharpe.

Bruck, P. (1989). Strategies for peace, strategies for news research. *Journal of Communication, 39,* 108–129.

Buric, A. (2000). The media: War and peace in Bosnia. In A. Davis (Ed.), *Regional media in conflict: Case studies in local war reporting* (pp. 64–99). London: Institute for War and Peace Reporting.

Burns, N. (1996). Talking to the world about American foreign policy. *Harvard International Journal of Press/Politic, 1,* 10–14.

Cohen, Y. (1986). *Media diplomacy.* London: Frank Cass.

Cohen-Almagor, R. (2005). Media coverage of acts of terrorism: Troubling episodes and suggested guidelines. *Canadian Journal of Communication, 30,* 383–409.

Crocker, C., Hampson, F.O., & Aall, P. (Eds.). (2001). *Turbulent peace: The challenges of managing international conflict.* Washington, DC: United States Institute of Peace Press.

Curtis, D. (2000). Broadcasting peace: An analysis of local media post-conflict peace-building projects in Rwanda and Bosnia. *Canadian Journal of Development Studies, XXI,* 141–155.

Davison, W. P. (1974). *Mass communication and conflict resolution.* New York: Praeger.

Dayan, D., & Katz, E. (1992). *Media events: The live broadcasting of history.* Cambridge, MA: Harvard University Press.

Donohue, W., & Hoobler, G. (2002). Relational ripeness in the Oslo I and Oslo II Israeli–Palestinian negotiations. In E. Gilboa (Ed.), *Media and conflict: Framing issues, making policy, shaping opinions* (pp. 65–88). Ardsley, NY: Transnational Publishers.

Druckman, D. (1995). Situational levers of position change: Further explorations. *Annals of the American Academy of Political and Social Science, 542,* 61–80.

Druckman, D., & Druckman, J. (1996). Visibility and negotiating flexibility. *Journal of Social Psychology, 136,* 117–120.

Eban, A. (1998). *Diplomacy for the next century.* New Haven and London: Yale University Press.

Entman, R. (1993). Framing: Toward clarification of a fractured paradigm. *Journal of Communication, 43,* 51–58.

Entman, R. (2004). *Projections of power: Framing news, public opinion, and U.S. foreign policy.* Chicago: The University of Chicago Press.

Frohardt, M., & Temin, J. (2003). *Use and abuse of media in vulnerable societies.* Washington,

DC: United States Institute of Peace, Special Report, No. 110.

Galtung, J. (1969). Violence, peace, and peace research. *Journal of Peace Research, 6,* 167–191.

Galtung, J. (1998). High road, low road: Charting the course for peace journalism. *Track Two, 7.* Retrieved May 12, 2002, from ccrweb.ccr.uct.ac.za/two7_4/po7_highroad lowroad.html

Galtung, J. (2002). Peace journalism – a challenge. In W. Kempf & H. Luostarinen (Eds.), *Journalism and the new world order: Studying war and the media* (pp. 259–272). Göteborg, Sweden: Nordicom.

Geelen, M. (Ed.). (2002). *The role of the media in conflict prevention, conflict management and peacebuilding.* Amsterdam: The Ministry of Foreign Affairs and the Netherlands Association of Journalists.

Gilboa, E. (1990). Effects of televised presidential addresses on public opinion: President Reagan and terrorism in the Middle East. *Presidential Studies Quarterly, XX,* 43–53.

Gilboa, E. (1998a). Secret diplomacy in the television age. *Gazette, 60,* 211–225.

Gilboa, E. (1998b). Media diplomacy: Conceptual divergence and applications. *Harvard International Journal of Press/Politics, 3,* 56–75.

Gilboa, E. (2000a). Mass communication and diplomacy: A theoretical framework. *Communication Theory, 10,* 275–309.

Gilboa, E. (2000b). Media coverage of international negotiation: A taxonomy of levels and effects. *International Negotiation, 5,* 543–568.

Gilboa, E. (Ed.). (2002a). *Media and conflict: Framing issues, making policy, shaping opinions.* Ardsley, NY: Transnational Publishers.

Gilboa, E. (2002b). Global communication and foreign policy. *Journal of Communication, 52,* 731–748.

Gilboa, E. (2002c). Media diplomacy in the Arab-Israeli conflict. In E. Gilboa (Ed.), *Media and conflict: Framing issues, making policy, shaping opinions* (pp. 193–211). Ardsley, NY: Transnational Publishers.

Gilboa, E. (2005a). The CNN Effect: The search for a communication theory of international relations. *Political Communication, 22,* 27–44.

Gilboa, E. (2005b). Media-broker diplomacy: When journalists become mediators. *Critical Studies in Media Communication, 22,* 99–120.

Gilboa, E. (2006). Media and international conflict. In J. Oetzel, & S. Ting-Toomey (Eds.), *The SAGE Handbook of Conflict Communication: Integrating Theory, Research, and Practice* (pp. 595–626). Thousand Oaks, CA: Sage Publications.

Gilboa, E. (2007). Media and international conflict: A multidisciplinary approach. *Journal of Dispute Resolution,* Vol. 2007 (1), 229–237.

Graber, D. (2002). *Mass media and American politics* (6th edn). Washington, DC: Congressional Quarterly Press.

Gurevitch, M. (1991). The globalization of electronic journalism. In J. Curran & M. Gurevitch (Eds.), *Mass media and society* (pp. 178–193). London: Edward Arnold.

Hagos, A. (2001). *Media intervention in peacebuilding in Burundi: The Studio Ijambo experience and impact.* Washington, DC: Agency for International Development.

Hampson, F.O. (2001). Parent, midwife, or accidental executioner? The role of third parties in ending violent conflict. In C. Crocker, F.O. Hampson, & P. Aall (Eds.), *Turbulent peace: The challenges of managing international conflict* (pp. 387–406). Washington, DC: United States Institute of Peace Press.

Hanitzsch, T. (2004). Journalists as peacekeeping force? Peace journalism and mass communication theory. *Journalism Studies, 5,* 483–495.

Hieber, L. (2001). *Lifeline media: Reaching populations in crisis. A guide to developing media projects in conflict situations.* Geneva: Media Action International.

Howard, R. (2002). *An operational framework for media and peacebuilding.* Vancouver, BC: Institute for Media, Policy, and Civil Society.

Howard, R. (2003). *Conflict sensitive journalism.* Vancouver, BC: Institute for Media, Policy, and Civil Society.

Howard, R., Rolt, F., Van de Veen, H., & Verhoeven, J. (2003). *The power of the media: A handbook for peacebuilders.* Utrecht, Netherlands: European Centre for Conflict Prevention.

Huntington, S. (1996). *The clash of civilizations and the remaking of world order.* New York: Simon and Schuster.

Iklè, C. (1964). *How nations negotiate.* New York: Praeger.

International Media Support. (2003). *Media and peace in Sudan: Options for immediate action.* Copenhagen, Denmark: International Media Support.

Isaacson, W. (1992). *Kissinger: A biography.* New York: Simon and Schuster.

Jeong, H. (Ed). (2002). *Approaches to peacebuilding.* New York: Palgrave.

Jönsson, C. (1996). Diplomatic signaling in the television age. *Harvard International Journal of Press/Politics, 1,* 24–40.

Katz, E., & Liebes, T. (2007). "No more peace": How disasters, terror and war have upstaged media events. *International Journal of Communication, 1,* 157–166.

Kellow, C., & Steeves, L.H. (1998). The role of radio in the Rwandan genocide. *Journal of Communication, 48,* 107–128.

Kelman, H. (1997). Some determinants of the Oslo breakthrough. *International Negotiation, 2*, 183–194.

Kempf, W. (2002). Escalating and deescalating aspects in the coverage of the Bosnia conflict: A comparative study. In W. Kempf & H. Luostarinen (Eds.), *Journalism and the new world order: Studying war and the media* (pp. 227–255). Göteborg, Sweden: Nordicom.

Koppel, T., & Gibson, K. (1996). *Nightline: history in the making and the making of television.* New York: Times Books.

Korzenny, F., & Ting-Toomey, S. (Eds.). (1990). *Communicating for peace: Diplomacy and negotiation.* London: Sage.

Larson, J. (1986). Television and U.S. foreign policy: The case of the Iran hostage crisis. *Journal of Communication, 36,* 108–130.

Larson, J. (1988). *Global television and foreign policy.* New York: Foreign Policy Association, Headline Series, No. 283.

Larson, J. (2004). *The Internet and foreign policy.* New York: Foreign Policy Association, Headline Series, No. 325.

Lasswell, H. (1948). The structure and function of communication in society. In L. Bryson (Ed.), *The communication of ideas* (pp. 37–51). New York: Harper.

Lederach, J.P. (1995). *Preparing for peace: Conflict transformation across cultures.* Syracuse, NY: Syracuse University Press.

Lederach, J.P. (1997). *Building peace: Sustainable reconciliation in divided societies.* Washington, DC: United States Institute of Peace Press.

Lederach, J.P. (2005). *The moral imagination: The art and soul of building peace.* New York: Oxford University Press.

Liebes, T., & Katz, E. (1997). Staging peace: Televised ceremonies of reconciliation. *The Communication Review, 2,* 235–257.

Long, W., & Brecke, P. (2003). *War and reconciliation: Reason and emotion in conflict resolution.* Cambridge, MA: MIT Press.

Luttwak, E. (2002). *Strategy: The logic of war and peace.* Cambridge, MA: Harvard University Press.

Lynch, J. (2002). *Reporting the World.* Taplow, UK: Conflict and Peace Forums.

Mbaine, A. (Ed.). (2006). *Media in situations of conflict: Roles, challenges and responsibilities.* East Lansing, MI: Michigan University Press.

McDonald, J. Jr., & Bendahmane, D. (Eds.). (1995). *Conflict resolution: Track two diplomacy.* Washington, DC: Institute for Multi-Track Diplomacy.

McGoldrick, A., & Lynch, J. (2000). *Peace journalism: How to do it?* Retrieved June 29, 2004, from www.transcend.org/pjmanual.htm

McQuail, D. (1987). *Mass communication theory: An introduction* (2nd edn.) London: Sage.

McQuail, D. (2000). *McQuail's mass communication theory.* London: Sage.

Melone, S., Terzis, G., & Beleli, O. (2002). *Using the media for conflict transformation: The Common Ground experience.* Berlin: Berghof Research Center for Constructive Conflict Management.

Negrine, R. (1996). *The communication of politics.* London: Sage.

Nye, J. (2004). *Power in the global information age: From realism to globalization.* London: Routledge.

Ojo, E. (2003). The mass media and the challenges of sustainable democratic values in Nigeria: Possibilities and limitations. *Media, Culture & Society, 25,* 821–840.

Paris, R. (2004). *At war's end: Building peace after civil conflict.* Cambridge: Cambridge University Press.

Powers, S., & Gilboa, E. (2007). The public diplomacy of Al-Jazeera. In P. Seib (Ed.), *New media and the new Middle East* (pp. 53–80). New York: Palgrave.

Pruitt, D. (1997). Ripeness theory and the Oslo talks. *International Negotiation, 2,* 237–250.

Reese, S. (2001). Prologue—framing public life: A bridging model for media research. In S. Reese, O. Gandy, Jr., & A. Grant (Eds.), *Framing public life: Perspectives on media and our understanding of the social world* (pp. 7–31). Mahwah, NJ: Lawrence Erlbaum.

Reljic, D. (2004). *The news media and the transformation of ethnopolitical conflicts.* Berlin: Berghof Research Center for Constructive Conflict Management.

Roach, C. (Ed.). (1993). *Communication and culture in war and peace.* London: Sage.

Robinson, P. (2002). *The CNN effect: The myth of news, foreign policy and intervention.* London & New York: Routledge.

Rolt, F. (2005). *Reaching hearts and minds. People building peace.* Utrecht, Netherlands: European Center for Conflict Prevention.

Rothstein, R. (Ed.). (1999). *After the peace: Resistance and reconciliation.* Boulder, CO: Lynne Rienner.

Saunders, H. (2001). Prenegotiation and circumnegotiation: Arenas of the multilevel peace process. In C. Crocker, F.O. Hampson, & P. Aall (Eds.), *Turbulent peace: The challenges of managing international conflict* (pp. 483–496). Washington, DC: United States Institute of Peace Press.

Scali, J. (1995). Backstage mediation in the Cuban missile crisis. In J. McDonald, Jr., & D. Bendahmane (Eds.), *Conflict resolution: Track two diplomacy* (pp. 93–102). Washington, DC: Institute for Multi-Track Diplomacy.

Seib, P. (2002). *The global journalist: News and conscience in a world of conflict.* Lanham, MD: Rowman & Littlefield.

Shinar, D. (2000). Media diplomacy and peace talk: The Middle East and Northern Ireland. *Gazette, 62,* 83–97.

Shinar, D. (2002). Cultural conflict in the Middle East: The media as peacemakers. In E. Gilboa (Ed.), *Media and conflict: Framing issues, making policy, shaping opinions* (pp. 281–294). Ardsley, NY: Transnational Publishers.

Sowers, T. (2005). *Media coverage of low intensity conflict.* Paper presented at the annual meeting of the Southern Political Science Association, New Orleans.

Sparre, K. (2001). Megaphone diplomacy in the Northern Irish peace process: Squaring the circle by talking to terrorists through journalists. *Harvard International Journal of Press/Politics, 6,* 88–104.

Spencer, G. (2004). The impact of television news on the Northern Ireland peace process. *Media, Culture & Society, 26,* 602–623.

Spurk, C. (2002). *Media and peacebuilding: Concepts, actors, and challenges.* Bern, Switzerland: Swisspeace, Working paper, 1/2002.

Temple-Raston, D. (2005). *Justice on the grass: Three Rwandan journalists, their trial for war crimes and a nation's quest for redemption.* New York: The Free Press.

Ukpabi, C. (Ed.) (2001). *Handbook on journalism ethics: African case studies.* Kaapstad: Media Institute Southern Africa (MISA).

Väyrynen, R. (1999). From conflict resolution to conflict transformation: A critical review. In H-W. Jong (Ed.), *The new agenda for peace research* (pp. 135–160). Brookfield, VT: Ashgate.

Volkan, V. (1991). Official and unofficial diplomacy: An overview. In V. Volkan, J. Montville, & D. Julius (Eds.), *The psychodynamics of international relationships.* Vol. II Unofficial diplomacy at work, (pp. 1–16). Lexington, MA: Lexington Books.

Walton, F. (2004). *In service of truth and the common good: The impact of media on global peace and conflict.* Washington, DC: The Aspen Institute, Communications & Society Program.

Wright, C. (1960). Functional analysis and mass communication. *Public Opinion Quarterly, 24,* 605–620.

Zartman, I.W. (2000). Ripeness: The hurting stalemate and beyond. In P.C. Stern & D. Druckman (Eds.), *International conflict resolution after the Cold War* (pp. 225–250). Washington, DC: National Academy Press.

Zartman, I.W., & Rasmussen, J.L. (Eds.) (1997). *Peacemaking in international conflict: Methods and techniques.* Washington, DC: United States Institute of Peace Press.

Democracy and Conflict Resolution

David Kinsella and David L. Rousseau

Democratic political processes regulate competition among groups with conflicting preferences. Although much of the competition occurs peacefully within existing political institutions, democratic practices can also facilitate the resolution of intense conflict when the political system is challenged from within by groups fighting against the established government, and when it is challenged from without and on the brink of interstate war. This chapter provides an overview of the scholarly literature linking democracy to peace and conflict resolution, including pertinent theoretical propositions and the balance of evidence generated by empirical researchers. The promise of peace associated with civil liberty, political openness, and the foreign policies of democratic states has long figured into the writings of moral and political philosophers, perhaps most notably in Immanuel Kant's essay *Perpetual Peace*, published in 1795. But the burgeoning academic literature in recent decades is largely the product of social scientific research, much (but not all) of which is built upon the analysis of

large quantitative data sets. Our primary focus, then, is what social science, and in particular political science, tells us about the relationship between democracy, conflict resolution, and peace between and within states.

DEMOCRACY AND CONFLICT BETWEEN STATES

The realist school of thought in international relations, which greatly influenced both scholarship and policy-making during the cold war, maintains that state behavior is primarily driven by the balance of power among rivals in the international system (Morgenthau 1948; Waltz 1979; Mearsheimer 2001). Realists assume that states resemble unitary rational actors in pursuit of a single overriding objective: survival and security in an anarchic system. The strenuous demands of the international system lead all states to behave in a similar fashion regardless of their particular political institutions, economic structure, ideological orientation, or leadership quality. Specifically, realists typically predict that states will balance power (e.g. increase defense spending or conclude alliances) against all stronger states because they represent a threat to the survival of the state. Under similar circumstances, democracies behave no differently than autocracies.

This realist position came under increasing scrutiny beginning in the 1980s. Doyle (1983, 1986), for example, compiled a list of liberal societies and interstate wars during the nineteenth and twentieth centuries and found that no two democracies had engaged in a full-scale war. He concluded that "liberal states have created a separate peace, as Kant argued they would, and have also discovered liberal reasons for aggression, as he feared they might" (Doyle 1986: 1151). Rummel (1983, 1985) came to a similar conclusion after subjecting the proposition to somewhat more systematic testing. Path-breaking work by Doyle and Rummel triggered an avalanche of empirical and theoretical investigations into what is now referred to as "the democratic peace." According to Levy (1988), the democratic peace is the closest thing to an empirical law found in the study of international relations.

Some of the earliest research examined the characteristics of democratic governments and societies that shape the state's general foreign policy orientation and behavior. The argument that democratic states are more peaceful in their relations with all states, no matter how they are governed, is known as the *monadic* version of the democratic peace proposition. While there is empirical evidence to support this argument, it is not as robust as the evidence accumulated in support of the *dyadic* democratic peace proposition, which focuses on the interaction between two democratic states. Most recently, scholars have begun to examine *systemic* versions of the democratic peace in which the proportion of democracies in the international system influences the perceived legitimacy of democratic institutions and the use of military force in international society.

Thus, scholars have attempted to explain the democratic peace using a series of related arguments, which identify causal mechanisms operating at different levels of analysis. It has been difficult to distinguish the relative explanatory power of these competing arguments because data sets constructed to test arguments at one level of analysis are often not appropriate for testing arguments at other levels. However, progress in both theoretical development and empirical analysis has reduced this problem in recent years (e.g. Bennett and Stam 2000, 2004; Rousseau 2005). The following review of democratic peace theory and research is organized according to the main causal mechanisms identified in the academic literature.

Democratic norms and conflict resolution

Many explanations of the democratic peace emphasize the socialization of political leaders within their domestic political environments (Dixon 1993, 1994; Maoz and Russett 1993; Russett 1993; Huth and Allee 2002). This argument has two parts. First, democratic political elites have risen to positions of leadership within a political system that emphasizes compromise and non-violence. Conflicts of interest in democracies are usually resolved through negotiation and log-rolling. Losing a political battle does not result in the loss of political rights or exclusion from future political competition. Moreover, coercion and violence are not considered legitimate means for resolving conflicts. Conversely, political leaders in nondemocratic states are socialized in an environment in which politics is more akin to a zero-sum game in which rivals and those on the losing end of political struggles are regularly removed from the game. Coercion and violence are more widely accepted as legitimate means for resolving political conflicts. In general, political leaders in autocracies are more likely to impose decisions rather than compromise when dealing with the opposition.

Second, the argument assumes that domestic political norms are externalized by decision makers when they become embroiled in international disputes. Presidents and prime ministers approach conflicts of interest in the international environment in much the same way they approach conflicts in the domestic environment, and with conflict-resolution skills honed by their domestic political experiences. Compared to their counterparts in authoritarian regimes, democratic leaders are more likely to seek negotiation, mediation, or arbitration (Dixon 1994; Raymond 1994). Their approach to international conflict resolution reduces the likelihood that an international dispute will escalate into a militarized crisis and war.

The strong version of the norms argument holds that democratic leaders externalize peaceful practices of conflict resolution in their interactions with all types of regimes. In contrast to this monadic claim, those who emphasize the dyadic nature of the democratic peace argue that although all decision makers are inclined to externalize domestic practices of dispute resolution when dealing with interstate conflicts, this externalization is *conditional* for democratic decision makers. Democratic leaders externalize their domestic norms only if they expect similar behavior from their foreign counterparts. Because democratic decision makers expect that choices by other democratic leaders are also shaped by norms of peaceful conflict resolution, there is little risk in an attempting to resolve their conflict in accordance with these shared norms. Conversely, because democracies expect nondemocratic states to externalize coercive and uncompromising norms of conflict resolution, they adopt similar strategies when dealing with these opponents. The argument therefore assumes that a democratic state's behavior is conditioned upon the expected behavior of its opponent and that the opponent's regime type informs this expectation.

A related argument highlights the importance of identity formation. Some have suggested that peace between democracies is a function of a common social identity (Risse-Kappen 1995; Hopf 1998, 2002; Kahl 1998/99). Social identities are bundles of shared values, beliefs, attitudes, norms, and roles that are used to draw boundaries between in-group and out-groups. Members of one's own group are viewed as less threatening than members of other groups. If democratic polities use democratic values and norms to define the in-group, the actions and capabilities of other democracies are then viewed as less threatening. Their shared identity will reduce the likelihood that either party will resort to violence to resolve a political dispute. Although realists discount the importance of ideational factors in world politics, liberals and constructivists have long maintained that a shared sense of identity partly accounts for lower levels of international conflict. While liberals tend to focus on a shared liberal identity, constructivists believe that many types of shared identity may reduce interstate conflict. Risse-Kappen (1995), for example, argues that a shared sense of identity among democratic states, and not simply their concern with the balance of power, explains decision making within the North Atlantic Treaty Organization. Laboratory experiments have also demonstrated that shared cultural beliefs and experiences can decrease intersubjective threat perceptions (Mintz and Geva 1993; Rousseau 2006).

Explanations for both the monadic and dyadic versions of the democratic peace imply that as the number of democracies in the international system increase, the number of interstate wars will fall. However, the literature also identifies causal processes operating at the systemic level. As democratic practices spread globally—that is, as they become internalized by more societies and are reflected in public policy-making—the international system is increasingly "saturated" with democratic culture and norms of peaceful conflict resolution. In an international society in which democratic practice is so commonly viewed as legitimate and effective, the methods of conflict resolution employed by democratic states have a greater probability of being reflected in the behavior of nondemocratic states as well. When viewing the international system as a whole, then, we should observe fewer interstate conflicts. Testing arguments operating at the systemic level of analysis is difficult; a correlation between two variables at the systemic level (e.g. number of wars and the percentage of nondemocracies) may be expected even if the causal relationships are limited to those hypothesized for the monadic and dyadic versions of the democratic peace (Rousseau and Kim 2005; Gartzke and Weisiger 2006). Problems of inference notwithstanding, statistical analyses of the systemic normative argument have provided some support for the system-level claim (Gleditsch and Hegre 1997; Crescenzi and Enterline 1999; McLaughlin et al. 1999; Kadera et al. 2003).

Democratic institutions and restraint

Another class of explanations for the democratic peace highlights the institutions of democratic governance, broadly defined, and the domestic political costs of using force (e.g. Morgan and Campbell 1991; Morgan and Schwebach 1992). Decisions to use military force are choices made by leaders based largely on calculations of political costs and benefits. Foreign policy decisions can have costly domestic political repercussions. The expenditure of resources and loss of human life often mobilize opposition groups or fracture ruling coalitions (Mueller 1973; Cotton 1987; Bueno de Mesquita and Siverson 1995). Compared to leaders in other political systems, democratic decision makers are more sensitive to these potential domestic costs, and this constrains their behavior when interacting with nondemocratic states. The monadic version of the institutional argument posits that democratic institutional constraints make leaders less likely to initiate war regardless of the regime type of their opponent. Recent social scientific research has produced evidence supporting this stronger version of the democratic peace hypothesis (Huth and Allee 2002; Bennett and Stam 2004; Rousseau 2005).

The nature of political institutions can have a bearing on the credibility of signals sent during an international crisis. Fearon (1994, 1995) argues that in a world of complete information, decision makers can determine each side's expected value for war—the ends sought and the likelihood of achieving them while suffering the costs of armed combat. In such a world, war would be rare; if each side's aims were known, along with the price each was willing to pay in blood and treasure, it would always be possible to strike a bargain acceptable to all without actually having to suffer the costs of war. Unfortunately, we live in a world of incomplete information. A government's willingness to use force is usually private information, and leaders may have an incentive to exaggerate or otherwise misrepresent their resolve in order to strike a better bargain. In this context of incomplete information, signals of resolve are more credible when leaders are likely to pay higher domestic audience costs for bluffing, and democracies are political systems in which audience costs are highest. Moreover, the openness of political debate in democracies provides information to foreign opponents. When the political opposition in a democracy lines up behind the executive during an international confrontation, this is a powerful signal that because the party in power will pay high political costs for backing down, the executive is probably not bluffing (Schultz 1998, 1999, 2001).

Another institutional argument derives from a game theoretic model of political survival developed by Bueno de Mesquita et al. (1999, 2003). Public policies, both domestic and foreign, yield a mix of public and private goods. Public goods, of course, are available to the entire society, whereas private goods can be allocated as leaders see fit. Political systems vary in terms of the proportion of society involved in the selection of political leaders (the selectorate), and the proportion of the selectorate whose support is required to maintain one's position of power or, in the case of a challenger, to unseat the current leader (the winning coalition). Democratic states have large selectorates and large winning coalitions. Autocratic states may have large selectorates, too, when elections have high voter turnouts but are nevertheless rigged, but they always have small winning coalitions. Political survival in a democracy therefore requires that goods, public and private, be distributed among a larger winning coalition than is the case in an autocracy. Public goods serve that purpose well in a democracy because they go to all, while the value of private goods diminishes due to the larger number of recipients. In an autocracy, however, private goods are relatively more important to the leader's political survival because they are distributed among a smaller constituency.

Bueno de Mesquita and his colleagues argue that successful public policies generate the public goods that democratic leaders need in order to stay in office. Autocratic leaders prefer that their policies succeed, but the consequences of policy failure for political survival are not dire as long as the leader has access to resources that can be distributed as private goods to a small winning coalition. What are the implications for the democratic peace? With higher political costs of policy failure, democratic leaders avoid international contests unless they are confident of victory. And once they become involved in a crisis or war, democrats try harder to win. Contests with other democratic states of similar capabilities are to be avoided for this reason, but democratic states are not so disinclined to avoid confronting autocratic states, whose leaders have less to lose politically by backing down. The model does suggest, however, that stronger democracies also face fewer disincentives when confronting weaker democracies; the stronger state is likely to succeed no matter how hard the weaker one tries, and policy success is what counts for political survival.

Democratic political institutions often influence foreign policy decision making in particular ways regardless of the regime type of the opponent. But given a set of institutional constraints, the leaders of democratic states may well behave differently depending on whether or not their opponents are believed to be similarly constrained. For example, Bueno de Mesquita and Lalman (1992) propose a three-part institutional explanation for the dyadic democratic peace. First, the international system is assumed to consist of hawkish states (leaders are uncompromising and predisposed to use force to resolve disputes) and dovish states (leaders are prone to compromise and use strategies of reciprocation). At the same time, there is some uncertainty surrounding which strategy will be adopted by any particular state. Second, domestic institutional structures reduce (but do not eliminate) this uncertainty by signaling a state's most likely strategy. Due to the potential domestic costs of using force, decision makers believe that democracies are more likely than nondemocracies to adopt dovish strategies. Third, when a democracy confronts another democracy, each expects a negotiated outcome and the exercise of restraint when contemplating the use of force. But when an autocracy confronts a democracy, a hawkish leader expects to encounter a dovish one and is likely to exploit the situation. In such a situation, the dove feels compelled to adopt the aggressive strategy of the hawk and may initiate conflict in order to preempt an expected attack. The logic of the argument is dyadic: democratic states pursue strategies involving compromise and nonviolence only when dealing with other democratic states.

Another institutional explanation for the dyadic character of the democratic peace focuses on the difficulty of mobilizing popular support for the use of force. According to Maoz and Russett (1993), the inclusiveness of democratic regimes hinders their ability to rapidly mobilize societal groups in support of military action. Authoritarian regimes, with constituencies spanning a much narrower range of the political spectrum, can more quickly reach the necessary consensus on the use of force. When a dispute emerges between two democratic states, the slow process of mobilization in both states creates opportunities for the resolution of the conflict through noncoercive means. However, when a conflict arises between a democratic state and an authoritarian state, rapid mobilization by the latter forces democratic leaders to find ways to work around normal political processes. That is, the emergency situation encourages the democratic state to adopt the tactics of its nondemocratic opponent.

Critics of the democratic peace thesis

In addition to the studies discussed above, there is considerable additional social scientific research that supports one or more of the propositions contained in democratic peace theory, especially as concerns dyadic peace (see, e.g., Maoz and Abdolali 1989; Bremer 1993; Rousseau et al. 1996; Rasler and Thompson 2001; Russett and Oneal 2001; Dixon and Senese 2002; Peceny et al. 2002). But despite the impressive body of evidence, the academic literature includes many studies that aim to refute the democratic peace proposition in part or in whole. Some of the most noteworthy research focuses on the purported risks to peace presented by democratizing states.

While acknowledging that mature democracies rarely fight each other, Mansfield and Snyder (1995, 2002a, 2002b) have argued that the process of democratic reform may actually increase the probability of war. Their empirical findings, based on both qualitative and quantitative analyses, have been read not only as partly refuting democratic peace theory, but also as calling into question the wisdom of efforts to promote democracy in other countries, a cornerstone of Western foreign policy following the end of the Cold War. If the *condition* of being democratic decreases the probability of violent conflict, how could the *process* of becoming more democratic have the opposite effect? Mansfield and Snyder propose that transitional regimes experiencing high level of political mobilization together with weak institution controls are often tempted to incite external conflict. The intense political competition ushered in by the disintegration of the previous authoritarian government leads elites and would-be leaders to identify

issues that can be used to build broad popular coalitions.

The issues that tend to be exploited by elites, according to Mansfield and Snyder, are those that can become the basis for a "belligerent nationalist coalition." The old elite, including the military establishment, often seek to define themselves as the guardians of the nationalist cause, reminding the populace of the dangers they collectively face. Newly emerging interest groups are also inclined to seize on such issues as group leaders feel compelled to assert their nationalist credentials as a means of unifying the fragmented interests bubbling to the surface in an unstable political environment. While the masses may not be particularly war-prone at the start of this process, sustained appeals to nationalism from across the political spectrum can quickly create a belligerent popular mood. The intensification of this mood can trigger "blow-back," a situation in which the leadership feels compelled to behave aggressively having become trapped by their own demagoguery. In their initial research on wars during the nineteenth and twentieth centuries, Mansfield and Snyder (1995, 8) found "that democratizing states—those that have recently undergone regime change in a democratic direction—are much more war-prone than states that have undergone no regime change, and are somewhat more war-prone than those that have undergone a change in an autocratic direction."

Analyses by Mansfield and Snyder have been challenged on a number of methodological grounds (Enterline 1996, 1998; Weede 1996; Wolf 1996; Thompson and Tucker 1997), and other empirical investigations into the war-inducing effects of democratization report evidence at odds with theirs (Gleditsch and Ward 2000; Russett and Oneal 2001; Oneal, Russett, and Berbaum 2003; Bennett and Stam 2004; Rousseau 2005). Mansfield and Snyder have responded to these critiques in various ways, but their most recent work has included a closer examination of the position of transitioning states along the autocracy–democracy spectrum and its implication for becoming involved in militarized disputes or wars. They have generally concluded that the probability of conflict is increased when autocratic states make incomplete democratic transitions, but not when they make complete transitions. Nor do partially democratic regimes appear dangerous when they are undergoing transitions to full democracy (Mansfield and Snyder 2005).

In challenging some of the core assumptions and arguments of realist theory, it is not surprising that the democratic peace research program has itself come under attack from various angles. Gowa (1999), for instance, argues that the democratic peace is spurious, that it is a function not of democratic governance and conflict resolution but security considerations within the Western alliance in its opposition to the Soviet bloc after World War II. Democratic peace researchers have responded to this and other criticisms on realist grounds by controlling for a number of factors that feature in realist explanations of war and peace, including geography, alliance, the balance of military capabilities, and nuclear armament. They have also controlled for other liberal factors, like wealth, trade, and participation in international organizations. Efforts to model the liberal determinants of peace alongside realist ones have demonstrated that evidence for the democratic peace is quite robust (e.g. Russett and Oneal 2001; Kinsella and Russett 2002; Kim and Rousseau 2005; Rousseau 2005).

Other critics point to the difficulties of measuring democracy, an exceedingly complex social scientific construct. These difficulties led early exploratory research to opt for dichotomous measures of regime type (e.g. Doyle 1986), but the majority of later studies have employed the democracy and autocracy scales developed by the Polity Project (see Marshall and Jaggers 2002). Although indices constructed from the Polity scales have a number of important strengths, they are rough measures and are often insensitive to small but important changes in domestic power configurations. Democratic peace researchers have typically responded to

such objections by modifying their measures and retesting their propositions. Rousseau (2005), for example, finds strong support for both the monadic and dyadic democratic peace propositions using new measures and data for institutional constraint.

A more fundamental objection to the measurement of democracy in the democratic peace literature is leveled by Oren (1995, 2003). Polities can be measured along numerous dimensions, and social scientific practice at any given moment reflects the identity evaluation and threat perceptions prevailing during that historical period. Oren argues that in the case of social science research in the United States, the features of democracy considered most important are those that the American political system shares with the political systems of friendly states, while those features it shares with its enemies tend to be downplayed. Oren's claim, therefore, is that the democratic peace is an artifact of a built-in bias of the social scientific community. This is a provocative critique to be sure, though one that has so far not prompted much reaction among democratic peace researchers.

The theoretical underpinnings of the democratic peace project have also been scrutinized. There is a lack of agreement within the research community regarding the exact causal mechanisms responsible for the empirical regularities that are routinely observed. While we know that democracies do not fight other democracies, we are not sure which of the many causal mechanisms is behind the pattern, or which have the most influence in different contexts. Others have examined the logic of both the normative and institutional explanations discussed above, arguing that those explanations imply even more pacific behavior on the part of democratic states than what democratic peace researchers are able to show (Rosato 2003). To some extent, these critiques replay earlier objections to the challenges posed to realist theory. What they have not done, however, is undermine the democratic peace proposition, the research program supporting it, or the implication that the spread of democratic forms of governance enhance the prospects for the resolution of conflicts between states (Ray 2003; Chernoff 2004; Kinsella 2005).

DEMOCRACY AND CONFLICT WITHIN STATES

In the political science literature, the term "democratic peace" almost always refers to the extraordinary infrequency of war and other forms of violent conflict between democratic states, as well as the body of theory and research explaining it. Much less extensive, but rapidly expanding in recent years, is the social scientific literature on civil war which addresses directly the relationship between democratic governance and the outbreak or resolution of violent domestic conflict. The role of democracy in mitigating (or possibly exacerbating) conflict within states needs to be understood against the backdrop of competing theories of rebellion and civil war (see Sambanis 2002).

Early work by political scientists derived from the fairly intuitive notion that people rebel when they feel deprived in some way. Deprivation and discontent breed anger, which may be combined with military means to provide the genesis for armed insurgency against the state. Feelings of deprivation are not necessarily based on objective conditions; they are relative to conditions that people believe they deserve but have been denied, due either to discrimination or incapacity on the part of the government (Davies 1962; Gurr 1970; Tilly 1978). Grievances against the government or other groups within society can be related to political conditions, economic conditions, or both.

More recent work, including research by economists, starts by observing that social discontent is seemingly ubiquitous and that demand-side explanations of civil war fail to account for the far less common occurrence of civil war. Among the many societies that are home to especially aggrieved groups, what distinguishes relatively stable societies from those experiencing civil war, according to this perspective, are the impediments to

collective action, which limit the supply of rebels willing to undertake the hardships and risks of armed insurgency (Lichbach 1995). The expected utility of rebellion is higher when poor economic circumstances reduce opportunity costs, when the reach of central government authority is constricted, and when geographic and economic conditions (like rough terrain and the availability of lootable resources) are conducive to armed insurgency (Ross 1999; Collier 2000; Reno 2000; Fearon and Laitin 2003; Collier and Hoeffler 2004).

Grievance and political openness

The role of democracy figures most prominently in political theories of internal conflict. Democratic governments are less likely to curtail individual liberties and are more likely to grant equal protection under the law; the absence of such rights and freedoms is frequently a source of resentment on the part of disadvantaged groups within nondemocratic societies. Where grievances do exist in democratic societies, the openness of the political system allows group discontent to be expressed nonviolently, including by way of confrontational but nevertheless lawful means like strikes and protests (Eckstein and Gurr 1975; Diamond 1999). Disadvantaged and oppressed groups in nondemocratic societies have relatively few alternatives short of open rebellion against the state. The proposition that democracies are at lower risk of civil war and other forms of mass internal violence has received some empirical support (e.g. Rummel 1995; Gurr 2000), but this finding is not as robust as the evidence for the democratic peace between states (Hegre and Sambanis 2006).

Supply side explanations found in many economic theories of civil war tend to downplay the significance of democracy because political rights and freedoms are assumed to bear upon the degree of grievance and discontent found within societies, factors judged to be of secondary importance. However, the extent that political systems vary in terms of the inclusiveness of popular representation pertains also to the opportunity cost of rebellion. The decision to pursue extralegal means to redress grievances is a decision to forego the opportunities available within the political system. Autocratic systems, of course, are not very inclusive and the interests of disaffected groups are less likely to be represented in the policy-making process. But even among democratic states, inclusiveness varies and there is some evidence to suggest that proportional representation systems, in which even disaffected groups may occupy seats in parliament, have a lower probability of experiencing civil war than majoritarian systems, which tend to marginalize smaller groups when their interests do not correspond to those of the median voter (Reynal-Querol 2002).

One possible reason for divergent expectations regarding the role of democratic governance in reducing the probability of civil war is that theory and research on the question has not paid enough attention to the different types of civil wars and rebellions that societies experience. The factors explaining ethnic and nonethnic civil wars are not exactly the same. Ethnic civil wars pit ethnic communities against the state (and its supporters) and are fought over communal status within society. Nonethnic civil wars, like revolutionary wars, are fought over ideological or class-based disputes rather than identity issues. While economic theories of civil war see the opportunity costs of rebellion primarily in terms of economic opportunities, ethnicity and identity-based grievances are often unrelated to economic deprivation (see, for example, Rothchild 1997; Arnson and Zartman 2005). A distinguishing feature of ethnic civil war, according to Sambanis (2001), is resentment at the absence of civil rights and freedoms, discrimination in the adjudication of disputes between societal groups, and the lack of political representation or regional autonomy. These sorts of grievances emerge less often in democratic political systems, and Sambanis shows evidence that ethnic civil wars are indeed unlikely to occur in democratic societies. He also finds that if a state has

democratic neighbors, it is less likely to become embroiled in an internal ethnic conflict. Hostilities often spill over national borders and weak democratic institutions increase the risk that disaffected ethnic groups in adjacent states will take up arms against their own governments.

The suppression of dissent is a defining feature of closed political systems. Therefore, for any given level of grievance (and other factors contributing to armed rebellion), we would expect authoritarian states to experience fewer civil wars than states with more open political systems. That is, the most democratic societies face few rebellions because the level of grievance is generally lower; group conflict is more often resolved nonviolently, even if sometimes contentiously. But the most authoritarian societies may also face few rebellions, despite a higher level of grievance, because group conflict tends to be suppressed by the state. This parabolic relationship between political openness and civil war is one that has been repeatedly reported in the empirical literature (e.g. Muller and Weede 1990; Ellingsen 2000; Hegre et al. 2001).

Where does this leave partially democratic states? The literature does indeed suggest that these are the societies most likely to experience serious internal conflict. When political rights and freedoms are not fully respected, grievances emerge within disadvantaged groups. Although partially democratic systems, just like fully democratic systems, may permit the mobilization of groups whose interests are at odds with the policies pursued by the government, they are also quicker to repress protests, strikes, and other forms of civil disobedience, thereby inflaming discontent and resentment even as they close off opportunities for groups to redress their grievances. When a regime combines the permissive elements of democracy with the repressive elements of autocracy, the risks of violent domestic conflict are at their highest.

In many cases, partly free societies are also those undergoing political change. The argument linking civil violence to the transition from authoritarian to democratic rule is associated with the work of Samuel Huntington (1968, 1991), among others, and is the starting point for the contention, discussed above, that democratizing states are more likely to become involved in interstate conflicts. The collapse of autocratic institutions encourages groups to mobilize and compete for control of government policy and positions of authority. Yet this surge in political activity is difficult to channel in constructive directions due to the weakness of participatory political institutions and the underdeveloped state of democratic norms. In this fluid environment, groups often turn against the fragile authority of the central government. Their resentments stoked further by opportunistic leaders, this group hostility can become violent to the point of armed rebellion (Snyder 2000; Kaufman 2001).

Hegre et al. (2001) show that both of these factors—the institutional inconsistencies characteristic of partially democratic political systems and the volatility and opportunism associated with political change—are correlated with a higher probability of civil war. They estimate that partially democratic societies are four times as likely to descend into civil war as are complete democracies. Societies undergoing a regime change, whether in the democratic or autocratic direction, are at higher risk of civil war than stable political systems, and remain at higher risk for five years after the regime change. Although the findings suggest civil war is more common in partially democratic societies than in societies with autocratic governments, other studies have shown that autocratic governments are more likely than democracies to experience regime transitions (e.g. Gates et al. 2006). Thus, while democratization may bring a greater risk of domestic conflict, if democratic political institutions are fully consolidated, the new regime is at the lowest risk of civil war, due both to its institutional features and to its durability as a political system.

The impact of political openness and political change on the occurrence of civil war is called into question by some researchers

because they posit that economic opportunity costs are a more important consideration than either group grievances or the opportunity costs of redressing those grievances through democratic institutions. When controlling for the level of economic development, the residual effects of such political factors should be minimal (Fearon and Laitin 2003; Collier and Hoeffler 2004). Although the empirical evidence linking an increased risk of civil war to incomplete democratization is robust (Hegre and Sambanis 2006), more research is probably needed on economic development and democratic governance as mutually reinforcing mechanisms of domestic conflict resolution. Evidence suggests the peace between democratic states is strongest when those states are also economically developed (e.g. Mousseau 2000; Mousseau et al. 2003), and a similar dynamic may operate at the domestic level (Hegre 2003).

Settlement and peace-building

The conditions most conducive to preventing the outbreak of civil war are related to those most conducive to peace settlements and the reestablishment of political stability in the wake of civil war. The power of the central government must be consolidated, its legitimacy must be established or enhanced by allowing previously excluded groups access to the policy-making process, and sufficient economic resources must be mustered and allocated to support the peace-building process. The creation of each of these conditions may be assisted in various ways by external actors (Zartman 1995; Regan 2000). Intergovernmental organizations, for example, especially those composed mainly of democratic states, have been effective in facilitating peace-building processes within both member and nonmember states (Pevehouse 2005; Pevehouse and Russett 2006). In the case of extremely destructive civil wars, and especially those in which group hatreds are acute and communal violence never far below the surface, real peace may not be possible in the near term. Political stability may require the establishment of a central government that rules with an iron fist rather than wide consent. However, draconian solutions of this sort fall outside the liberal paradigm guiding peace-building efforts since the end of the Cold War (Paris 1997).

Given the secondary role played by political practices and institutions in economic theories of civil war, relatively little attention has been devoted to questions of peace settlement and post-war reconstruction beyond highlighting the need to transform war economies (e.g. Pugh and Cooper 2004). An exception is Wantchekon's (2004) game theoretic analysis of "warlord democracy." Wantchekon considers an interaction involving three players: two warring factions (warlords) and the citizenry. Each warring faction seeks political power and the economic benefits that come with it. While the civil war is in progress, each expropriates the wealth of a subset of the citizenry they control as well as mineral wealth of the territory they occupy. The interests of the citizenry depend on their affiliation with the contending warlords. Those who support one or the other enjoy both the warlord's protection and the full economic benefit of their labors and investments. Those who support neither receive no protection and the return on their economic activities is subject to expropriation. A continued state of belligerency, with its continued expropriation of wealth, encourages unaffiliated citizens to invest less, which diminishes the warlords' take. Wantchekon suggests that both warlords may expect to do better by disarming and choosing democracy. In this case, each campaigns for the citizens' vote by proposing a tax rate, and the electoral competition brings promised tax rates down to the point where expected government revenue equals the warlord's take under conditions of continued belligerency. Because the legal tax rate is to be applied to the economic activities of the entire citizenry, it is lower than what is applied to the smaller population under each warring faction's control during belligerency. The winning faction's total take will be improved relative to the status quo, because citizens will now be investing more, and as long as both factions

estimate that they have a reasonable chance of winning forthcoming elections—which Wantchekon shows need not be greater than one-half—democracy is the rational choice (Wantchekon and Neeman 2002; see also Przeworski 1999).

This notion of warlord democracy stands in contrast to the argument that political order in the aftermath of social upheaval may require authoritarian rule, or at least a substantial measure of illiberalism (e.g. Huntington 1968; Zakaria 2003). Still, although even those who once profited from civil war may benefit from a system of democratic governance, getting there is rarely a simple matter. Several studies have pointed to the difficulty of post-civil war political reform and the fragility of democratic institutions when the wounds of communal conflict are fresh and the process of national reconciliation is in its infancy. Power-sharing arrangements can be essential elements in bringing warring factions to a settlement by assuring the representation of group interests in policymaking and state-building (Walter 2002; Hartzell and Hoddie 2003). But members of a governing cartel of group elites may resist the consolidation of more participatory political reforms as hard-won gains become jeopardized by the uncertainties of the democratic process (Rothchild and Roeder 2005). Majoritarian solutions have a mediocre track record in pluralistic societies plagued by suspicion and hostility; the absence of guarantees leave minorities understandably fearful of demagoguery and democratic tyranny.

In some post-conflict environments, there is such a thing as too much democracy too fast. Stable democracy provides mechanisms for the peaceful resolution of social conflict, but democratic governance (like market capitalism) is inherently competitive. Electoral competition, perhaps more than any other single institution, is emblematic of the democratic process, which is why the holding of elections after peace settlements have been reached is so often taken as an indication that a previously dysfunctional polity has made a successful political transition. In a pluralistic setting, however, electoral competition may encourage candidates for office to distinguish the interests of their constituents from those of other groups, and even to exaggerate them, reinforcing the perceived group differences that fed the violent conflict from which society just emerged. This does not mean that elections should necessarily give way to other, less participatory forms of political representation, like power sharing, but it does mean that electoral rules need to be designed so that candidates are compelled to seek support from outside their own factions. Extremist appeals should not pay on election day. It may also mean that elections cannot be rushed, that they should be delayed until such time as violent passions have subsided, warring factions have been disarmed, and the social infrastructure has resumed its basic functions.

The danger, of course, is that the difficulties associated with peace-building and state-building will become a justification for delaying indefinitely democratic consolidation. In the contemporary scholarly literature, there is a near-consensus that democratic political reform is a necessary component of peace-building after civil war, at least once a modicum of post-conflict stabilization has been achieved. Those critical of prevailing practices of "liberal peace-building" usually do not question the ultimate aim, but rather the rate at which the political process is opened up to societal forces or the design of representative institutions in the near term (e.g. Paris 1997, 2004; Fukuyama 2005; Barnett 2006).

CONCLUSION: PUSHING DEMOCRACY TO ACHIEVE PEACE

Social science theory and research has established a strong connection between democracy and conflict resolution between and within states. As an empirical matter, the peace among democratically governed states is almost universally accepted. Although related claims and counterclaims— concerning, for example, the general peacefulness of democratic states or the dangers posed by democratizing states—continue to be debated, the core dyadic proposition remains beyond dispute. Democratic peace theory still has its detractors, primarily within the realist school of thought, but the theory continues to be developed and is becoming increasingly formalized within the rational choice framework. Empirical evidence linking democracy to civil peace and conflict resolution is not as robust, but it is accumulating. More research is also needed to help disentangle the pacifying effects of democracy from the effects of economic development, and to establish which types of democratic practices and institutions make for enduring peace and stability in the aftermath of civil war. The continued application of formal models will advance theory in this area as well.

Whatever questions remain, it is clear that democratic governance is generally conducive to the resolution of both civil and international conflict. The policy implications also seem clear: the spread of democracy is good for international society as a whole, for the security of democratic states in particular, and for the peoples residing in war-torn regions of the globe. It has, of course, been the policy of the democratic major powers, and especially the United States, to promote democratic reform worldwide—a policy that predates the recent accumulation of social scientific research linking democracy to domestic and international peace (e.g. Carothers 1999; Ikenberry 2000). Yet the end of the Cold War and the dissipation of the major ideological challenge to representative democracy and market capitalism brought with it a greater willingness to discuss the use of military force as a means of toppling authoritarian regimes, with the expectation that democratization, while good for those liberated from tyrannical rule, also generates positive externalities for regional and international security. Again, military intervention with the purpose (among others) of pushing democratic reform is not new, but in the United States at least, a renewed confidence in American power and the universality of democratic aspirations has encouraged some to be more forthright in recommending the use of military means to accelerate the historical forces driving the spread of democracy (Fukuyama 2006).

As discussed above, most of the reservations in the scholarly literature concerning the connection between democracy and peaceful conflict resolution turn on the social upheaval sometimes associated with democratic transitions. There are other reservations, however. Aside from the irony that democracy, and therefore peace, might be promoted at gunpoint, the efficacy of "democratic imperialism" (Kristol and Kagan 2000; Kurtz 2003) has been called into question. Although there is some statistical evidence linking US military intervention to the democratization of target states (e.g. Meernik 1996; Peceny 1999), when looking at the specific cases of US interventions intended (wholly or in part) to contribute to the creation or consolidation of democratic regimes, fewer than half succeeded. And democratization was almost never the by-product of US interventions undertaken for purposes other than regime change (Russett 2005; Pickering and Peceny 2006). The success rate for military interventions by Britain and France is even worse. Furthermore, there is little evidence that imposing democratic reforms on a state in an otherwise nondemocratic region will serve to encourage democratization elsewhere in the region (Enterline and Greig 2005).

These and other studies of intervention recognize that the promotion of democracy is rarely the sole purpose of military action by the US or other democratic major powers. When democratic reforms prove difficult—usually they do—and threaten the intervener's other policy aims, the intervening government's own electoral survival normally dictates that democratization be abandoned altogether or that it be limited to mainly symbolic reforms, even rigged elections (Bueno de Mesquita and Downs 2006). Multilateral operations like those mounted by the United Nations, the more forceful ones included, seem to have a better track record than unilateral interventions. But peace-building and democratization are never easy, particularly after civil wars in societies divided along ethnic or religious lines (on the determinants of success, see Doyle and Sambanis 2006). And even when military intervention is likely to succeed in bringing about a democratic transition and stable peace, it must be weighed against the direct costs in blood and treasure, as well as the opportunity costs of foregoing alternative peaceful methods of conflict resolution.

NOTE

1 Our thanks to the editors and to Bruce Russett for comments on an earlier draft of this chapter.

REFERENCES

Arnson, Cynthia J., and I William Zartman, eds. 2005. *Rethinking the Economics of War: The Intersection of Need, Creed, and Greed.* Baltimore, MD: Johns Hopkins University Press.

Barnett, Michael. 2006. "Building a Republican Peace: Stabilizing States after War." *International Security* 30(4): 87–112.

Bennett, D. Scott, and Allan C. Stam. 2000. "Research Design and Estimator Choices in the Analysis of Interstate Disputes." *Journal of Conflict Resolution* 44(5): 653–85.

Bennett, D. Scott, and Allan C. Stam. 2004. *The Behavioral Origins of War.* Ann Arbor: University of Michigan Press.

Bremer, Stuart A. 1993. "Democracy and Militarized Interstate Conflict, 1816–1965." *International Interactions* 18(3): 231–49.

Bueno de Mesquita, Bruce, and George W. Downs. 2006. "Intervention and Democracy." *International Organization* 60(3): 627–49.

Bueno de Mesquita, Bruce, and David Lalman. 1992. *War and Reason.* New Haven, CT: Yale University Press.

Bueno de Mesquita, Bruce, James D. Morrow, Randolph M. Siverson, and Alastair Smith. 1999. "An Institutional Explanation of the Democratic Peace." *American Political Science Review* 93(4): 791–807.

Bueno de Mesquita, Bruce, and Randolph M. Siverson. 1995. "War and the Survival of Political Leaders: A Comparative Analysis of Regime Type and Accountability." *American Political Science Review* 89(4): 841–55.

Bueno de Mesquita, Bruce, Alastair Smith, Randolph M. Siverson, and James D. Morrow. 2003. *The Logic of Political Survival*. Cambridge, MA: MIT Press.

Carothers, Thomas. 1999. *Aiding Democracy Abroad: The Learning Curve*. Washington, DC: Carnegie Endowment.

Chernoff, Fred. 2004. "The Study of Democratic Peace and Progress in International Relations." *International Studies Review* 6: 49–77.

Collier, Paul. 2000. "Rebellion as Quasi-Criminal Activity." *Journal of Conflict Resolution* 44(6): 839–53.

Collier, Paul, and Anke Hoeffler. 2004. "Greed and Grievance in Civil War." *Oxford Economic Papers* 56: 563–95.

Cotton, Timothy Y. 1987. "War and American Democracy." *Journal of Conflict Resolution* 30(4): 616–35.

Crescenzi, Mark J. C., and Andrew J. Enterline. 1999. "Ripples from the Waves? A Systemic, Time-Series Analysis of Democracy, Democratization, and Interstate War." *Journal of Peace Research* 36(1): 75–94.

Davies, James C. 1962. "Toward a Theory of Revolution." *American Sociological Review* 27: 5–19.

Diamond, Larry. 1999. *Developing Democracy: Toward Consolidation*. Baltimore, MD: Johns Hopkins University Press.

Dixon, William J. 1993. "Democracy and the Management of International Conflict." *Journal of Conflict Resolution* 37(1): 42–68.

Dixon, William J. 1994. "Democracy and the Peaceful Settlement of International Conflict." *American Political Science Review* 88(1): 14–32.

Dixon, William J., and Paul D. Senese. 2002. "Democracy, Disputes, and Negotiated Settlements." *Journal of Conflict Resolution* 46(4): 547–71.

Doyle, Michael W. 1983. "Kant, Liberal Legacies, and Foreign Affairs," parts 1 and 2. *Philosophy and Public Affairs* 12(3/4): 205–35, 323–53.

Doyle, Michael W. 1986. "Liberalism and World Politics." *American Political Science Review* 80(4): 1151–69.

Doyle, Michael W., and Nicholas Sambanis. 2006. *Making War and Building Peace: United Nations Peace Operations*. Princeton, NJ: Princeton University Press.

Eckstein, Harry, and Ted Robert Gurr. 1975. *Patterns of Authority: A Structural Basis for Political Inquiry*. New York: John Wiley.

Ellingsen, Tanja. 2000. "Colorful Community or Ethnic Witches' Brew: Multiethnicity and Domestic Conflict During and After the Cold War." *Journal of Conflict Resolution* 44(2): 228–49.

Enterline, Andrew J. 1996. "Driving While Democratizing (DWD)." *International Security* 20: 183–96.

Enterline, Andrew J. 1998. "Regime Changes, Geographic Neighborhoods, and Interstate. Conflict, 1816–1992." *Journal of Conflict Resolution* 42: 804–29.

Enterline, Andrew J., and J. Michael Greig. 2005. "Beacons of Hope? The Impact of Imposed Democracy on Regional Peace, Democracy and Prosperity." *Journal of Politics* 67(4): 175–98.

Fearon, James D. 1994. "Domestic Political Audiences and the Escalation of International Disputes." *American Political Science Review* 88(3): 577–92.

Fearon, James D. 1995. "Rationalist Explanations for War." *International Organization* 49(3): 379–414.

Fearon, James D., and David D. Laitin. 2003. "Ethnicity, Insurgency, and Civil War." *American Political Science Review* 97: 75–90.

Fukuyama, Francis. 2005. "'Stateness' First." *Journal of Democracy* 16(1): 84–88.

Fukuyama, Francis. 2006. *America at the Crossroads: Democracy, Power, and the Neoconservative Legacy*. New Haven, CT: Yale University Press.

Gartzke, Erik, and Alex Weisiger. 2006. "Development, Difference, and Democratic Duplicity as Determinants of the Systemic Liberal Peace." Unpublished manuscript.

Gates, Scott, Håvard Hegre, Mark P. Jones, and Håvard Strand. 2006. "Institutional Inconsistency and Political Instability: The Duration of Polities." *American Journal of Political Science* 50(4): 893–908.

Gleditsch, Kristian S., and Michael D. Ward. 2000. "War and Peace in Space and Time: The Role of Democratization." *International Studies Quarterly* 44(1): 1–29.

Gleditsch, Nils Petter, and Håvard Hegre. 1997. "Peace and Democracy: Three Levels of Analysis." *Journal of Conflict Resolution* 41(2): 283–310.

Gowa, Joanne. 1999. *Ballots and Bullets: The Elusive Democratic Peace*. Princeton, NJ: Princeton University Press.

Gurr, Ted Robert. 1970. *Why Men Rebel*. Princeton, NJ: Princeton University Press.

Gurr, Ted Robert. 2000. *People Versus States: Minorities at Risk in the New Century*. Washington, DC: United States Institute of Peace.

Hartzell, Caroline, and Matthew Hoddie. 2003. "Institutionalizing Peace: Power Sharing and Post-Civil War Conflict Management." *American Journal of Political Science* 47(2): 318–32.

Hegre, Håvard. 2003. "Disentangling Democracy and Development as Determinants of Armed Conflict." Paper presented at the annual meeting of the International Studies Association, February 26 – March 1, Portland, OR.

Hegre, Håvard, Tanja Ellingsen, Scott Gates, and Nils Petter Gleditsch. 2001. "Toward a Democratic Civil Peace? Democracy, Political Change, and Civil War, 1816–1992." *American Political Science Review* 95(1): 33–48.

Hegre, Håvard, and Nicholas Sambanis. 2006. "Sensitivity Analysis of Empirical Results on Civil War Onset." *Journal of Conflict Resolution* 50(4): 508–35.

Hopf, Ted. 1998. "The Promise of Constructivism in International Relations Theory." *International Security* 23: 171–200.

Hopf, Ted. 2002. *Constructing Allies at Home: Identities and Interests in Soviet and Russian Foreign Policy, 1955–99.* Ithaca, NY: Cornell University Press.

Huntington, Samuel P. 1968. *Political Order in Changing Societies.* New Haven, CT: Yale University Press.

Huntington, Samuel P. 1991. *The Third Wave: Democratization in the Late Twentieth Century.* Norman: University of Oklahoma Press.

Huth, Paul K., and Todd L. Allee. 2002. *The Democratic Peace and Territorial Conflict in the Twentieth Century.* Cambridge: Cambridge University Press.

Ikenberry, G. John. 2000. "America's Liberal Grand Strategy: Democracy and National Security in the Post-War Era." In *American Democracy Promotion: Impulses, Strategies, and Impacts*, ed. Michael Cox, G. John Ikenberry, and Takashi Inoguchi. New York: Oxford University Press.

Kadera, Kelly M., Mark J.C. Crescenzi, and Megan L. Shannon. 2003. "Democratic Survival, Peace, and War in the International System." *American Journal of Political Science* 47(2): 23–47.

Kahl, Colin H. 1998/99. "Constructing a Separate Peace: Constructivism, Collective Liberal Identity, and Democratic Peace." *Security Studies* 8(2): 94–119.

Kant, Immanuel. 1971 [1795]. "Perpetual Peace: A Philosophical Essay." In *Kant: Political Writings*, 2nd edn, ed. Hans Reiss. Cambridge: Cambridge University Press.

Kaufman, Stuart J. 2001. *Modern Hatreds: The Symbolic Politics of Ethnic War.* Ithaca, NY: Cornell University Press.

Kim, Hyung Min, and David L. Rousseau. 2005. "The Classical Liberals Were Half Right (or Half Wrong): New Tests of the Liberal Peace, 1960–88." *Journal of Peace Research* 42(5): 523–43.

Kinsella, David. 2005. "No Rest for the Democratic Peace." *American Political Science Review* 99(3): 453–57.

Kinsella, David, and Bruce Russett. 2002. "Conflict Emergence and Escalation in Interactive International Dyads." *Journal of Politics* 64(4): 1045–68.

Kristol, William, and Robert Kagan. 2000. *Present Dangers: Crisis and Opportunity in American Foreign and Defense Policy.* San Francisco: Encounter.

Kurtz, Stanley. 2003. "Democratic Imperialism: A Blueprint." *Policy Review* 118: 3–21.

Levy, Jack S. 1988. "Domestic Politics and War." In *The Origin and Prevention of Major Wars*, ed. Robert I. Rotberg and Theodore K. Rabb. Cambridge: Cambridge University Press.

Lichbach, Mark Irving. 1995. *The Rebel's Dilemma.* Ann Arbor: University of Michigan Press.

Mansfield, Edward, and Jack Snyder. 1995. "Democratization and the Danger of War." *International Security* 20(1): 5–38.

Mansfield, Edward, and Jack Snyder. 2002a. "Incomplete Democratization and the Outbreak of Military Disputes." *International Studies Quarterly* 46: 529–49.

Mansfield, Edward, and Jack Snyder. 2002b. "Democratic Transitions, Institutional Strength, and War." *International Organization* 56(2): 297–337.

Mansfield, Edward, and Jack Snyder. 2005. *Electing to Fight: Why Emerging Democracies Go To War.* Cambridge, MA: MIT Press.

Marshall, Monty G., and Keith Jaggers. 2002. "Polity IV Project: Dataset Users Manual." Available at www.cidcm.umd.edu/inscr/polity

Maoz, Zeev, and Bruce Russett. 1993. "Normative and Structural Causes of Democratic Peace, 1946–1986." *American Political Science Review* 87(3): 624–38.

Maoz, Zeev, and Nasrin Abdolali. 1989. "Regime Type and International Conflict." *Journal of Conflict Resolution* 33(1): 3–35.

McLaughlin, Sara, Scott Gates, and Håvard Hegre. 1999. "Evolution in Democracy—War Dynamics." *Journal of Conflict Resolution* 43(6): 771–92.

Mearsheimer, John J. 2001. *The Tragedy of Great Power Politics.* New York: W. W. Norton.

Meernik, James. 1996. "United States Military Intervention and the Promotion of Democracy." *Journal of Peace Research* 33: 391–402

Mintz, Alex, and Nehemia Geva. 1993. "Why Don't Democracies Fight Each Other? An Experimental Study." *Journal of Conflict Resolution* 37/3 (September): 484–503.

Morgan, T. Clifton, and Sally H. Campbell. 1991. "Domestic Structure, Decisional Constraints, and War." *Journal of Conflict Resolution* 35(2): 187–211.

Morgan, T. Clifton, and Valerie L. Schwebach. 1992. "Take Two Democracies and Call Me in the Morning: A Prescription for Peace?" *International Interactions* 17(4): 305–20.

Morgenthau, Hans. 1948. *Politics Among Nations: The Struggle for Power and Peace.* New York: Knopf.

Mousseau, Michael. 2000. "Market Prosperity, Democratic Consolidation, and Democratic Peace." *Journal of Conflict Resolution* 44(4): 472–507.

Mousseau, Michael, Håvard Hegre, and John Oneal. 2003. "How the Wealth of Nations Conditions the Liberal Peace." *European Journal of International Relations* 9(2): 277–314.

Mueller, John E. 1973. *War, Presidents, and Public Opinion*. Lanham, MD: University Press of America.

Muller, Edward N., and Erich Weede. 1990. "Cross-National Variation in Political Violence: A Rational Action Approach." *Journal of Conflict Resolution* 34(4): 624–51.

Oneal, John R., Bruce Russett, and Michael L. Berbaum. 2003. "Causes of Peace: Democracy, Independence, and International Organizations, 1885–1992." *International Studies Quarterly* 47(3): 371–93.

Oren, Ido. 1995. "The Subjectivity of the 'Democratic' Peace: Changing US Perceptions of Imperial Germany." *International Security* 20(2): 147–84.

Oren, Ido. 2003. *Our Enemies and US: America's Rivalries and the Making of Political Science*. Ithaca, NY: Cornell University Press.

Paris, Roland. 1997. "Peacebuilding and the Limits of Liberal Internationalism." *International Security* 22(2): 54–89.

Paris, Roland. 2004. At *War's End: Building Peace after Civil Conflict*. New York: Cambridge University Press.

Peceny, Mark. 1999. *Democracy at the Point of Bayonets*. University Park: Pennsylvania University Press.

Peceny, Mark, Caroline C. Beer, and Shannon Sanchex-Terry. 2002. "Dictatorial Peace?" *American Political Science Review* 96(1): 15–26.

Pevehouse, Jon C. 2005. *Democracy from Above: Regional Organizations and Democratization*. Cambridge: Cambridge University Press.

Pevehouse, Jon C., and Bruce Russett. 2006. "Democratic Intergovernmental Organizations Promote Peace." *International Organization* 60(4): 969–1000.

Pickering, Jeffrey, and Mark Peceny. 2006. "Forging Democracy at Gunpoint." *International Studies Quarterly* 50(3): 539–59.

Przeworski, Adam. 1999. "Minimalist Conception of Democracy: A Defense." In *Democracy's Value*, ed. Ian Shapiro and Casiano Hacker-Cordon. Cambridge: Cambridge University Press.

Pugh, Michael and Neil Cooper, with Jonathan Goodhand. 2004. *War Economies in a Regional Context: Challenges of Transformation*. Boulder, CO: Lynne Rienner.

Rasler, Karen, and William R. Thompson. 2001. "Rivalries and the Democratic Peace in the Major Power System." *Journal of Peace Research* 38(6): 659–83.

Ray, James Lee. 2003. "A Lakatosian View of the Democratic Peace Research Program." In *Progress in International Relations Theory: Appraising the Field*, ed. Colin Elman and Meriam Fendius Elman. Cambridge, MA: MIT Press.

Raymond, Gregory A. 1994. "Democracies, Disputes, and Third-Party Intermediaries." *Journal of Conflict Resolution* 38(1): 24–42.

Regan, Patrick M. 2000. *Civil Wars and Foreign Powers: Outside Intervention in Intrastate Conflict*. Ann Arbor: University of Michigan Press.

Reno, William. 2000. "Shadow States and the Political Economy of Civil Wars." In *Greed and Grievance: Economic Agendas in Civil Wars*, ed. Mats Berdal and David M. Malone. Boulder, CO: Lynne Rienner.

Reynal-Querol, Marta. 2002. "Political Systems, Stability and Civil War." *Defence and Peace Economics* 13(6): 465–83.

Risse-Kappen, Thomas. 1995. *Cooperation Among Democracies: The European Influence on U.S. Foreign Policy*. Princeton, NJ: Princeton University Press.

Rosato, Sebastian. 2003. "The Flawed Logic of Democratic Peace Theory." *American Political Science Review* 97(4): 585–602.

Ross, Michael L. 1999. "The Political Economy of the Resource Curse." *World Politics* 51: 297–322.

Rothchild, Donald. 1997. *Managing Ethnic Conflict in Africa: Pressures and Incentives for Cooperation*. Washington, DC: Brookings Institution Press.

Rothchild, Donald, and Philip G. Roeder. 2005. "Power Sharing as an Impediment to Peace and Democracy." In *Sustainable Peace: Power and Democracy After Civil Wars*, ed. Philip G. Roeder and Donald Rothchild. Ithaca, NY: Cornell University Press.

Rousseau, David L. 2005. *Democracy and War: Institutions, Norms, and the Evolution of International Conflict*. Stanford, CA: Stanford University Press.

Rousseau, David L. 2006. *Identifying Threats and Threatening Identities: The Social Construction of Realism and Liberalism*. Stanford, CA: Stanford University Press.

Rousseau, David L., and Hyung Min Kim. 2005. "The Reciprocal Relationship Between Military Conflict and Political Development." Paper presented at the annual meeting of the American Political Science Association, Washington, DC, August.

Rousseau, David L., Christopher Gelpi, Dan Reiter, and Paul Huth. 1996. "Assessing the Dyadic Nature of the Democratic Peace, 1918–1988." *American Political Science Review* 90(3): 512–33.

Rummel, R.J. 1983. "Libertarianism and International Violence." *Journal of Conflict Resolution* 27(1):27–72.

Rummel, R.J. 1985. "Libertarian Propositions on Violence Within and Between Nations: A Test Against Published Research Results." *Journal of Conflict Resolution* 29: 419–55.

Rummel, R.J. 1995. "Democracy, Power, Genocide, and Mass Murder." *Journal of Conflict Resolution* 39(1): 3–26.

Russett, Bruce 1993. *Grasping the Democratic Peace: Principles for a Post-Cold War World*. Princeton, NJ: Princeton University Press.

Russett, Bruce. 2005. "Bushwhacking the Democratic Peace." *International Studies Perspectives* 6(4): 395–408.

Russett, Bruce, and John R. Oneal. 2001. *Triangulating Peace: Democracy, Interdependence, and International Organizations*. New York: W. W. Norton.

Sambanis, Nicholas. 2001. "Do Ethnic and Nonethnic Civil Wars Have the Same Causes?" *Journal of Conflict Resolution* 45(3): 259–82.

Sambanis, Nicholas. 2002. "A Review of Recent Advances and Future Directions in the Quantitative Literature on Civil Wars. *Defence and Peace Economics* 13(3): 215–43.

Schultz, Kenneth A. 1998. "Domestic Opposition and Signaling in International Crises." *American Political Science Review* 92(4): 829–44.

Schultz, Kenneth A. 1999. "Do Democratic Institutions Constrain or Inform? Contrasting Two Institutional Perspectives on Democracy and War." *International Organization* 53(2): 233–66.

Schultz, Kenneth A. 2001. *Democracy and Coercive Diplomacy*. Oxford: Oxford University Press.

Snyder, Jack. 2000. *From Voting to Violence: Democratization and Nationalist Conflict*. New York: W. W. Norton.

Thompson, William R., and Richard Tucker. 1997. "A Tale of Two Democratic Peace Critiques." *Journal of Conflict Resolution* 41(3): 428–54.

Tilly, Charles. 1978. *From Mobilization to Revolution*. Reading, MA: Addison-Wesley.

Walter, Barbara F. 2002. *Committing to Peace: The Successful Settlement of Civil Wars*. Princeton, NJ: Princeton University Press.

Waltz, Kenneth N. 1979. *Theory of International Politics*. Reading, MA: Addison-Wesley.

Wantchekon, Leonard. 2004. "The Paradox of Warlord Democracy: A Theoretical Investigation." *American Political Science Review* 98(1): 17–33.

Wantchekon, Leonard, and Zvika Neeman. 2002. "A Theory of Post-Civil War Democratization." *Journal of Theoretical Politics* 14: 439–64.

Weede, Erich. 1996. "Correspondence: Democratization and the Danger of War." *International Security* 20(4): 180–83.

Wolf, Reinhard. 1996. "Correspondence: Democratization and the Danger of War." *International Security* 20(4): 176–80.

Zakaria, Fareed. 2003. *The Future of Freedom: Illiberalism at Home and Abroad*. New York: W. W. Norton.

Zartman, I. William. 1995. "Putting Things back Together." In *Collapsed States: The Disintegration and Restoration of Legitimate Authority*, ed. I. William Zartman. Boulder, CO: Lynne Rienner.

25

Why Mediation Matters: Ending Intractable Conflicts[1]

Chester A. Crocker, Fen Osler Hampson, and Pamela Aall

As the 21st century began, many hoped that it would be a less violent one than the 20th, the most violent century in history (Licklider 2005). With the fall of the Berlin Wall in 1990, a decade of peacemaking helped end a large number of conflicts in Africa, Latin America, Europe, and Asia. In El Salvador, Guatemala, Mozambique, Namibia, and Cambodia, violent conflicts yielded to negotiated peace agreements. There is now compelling statistical evidence that the high watermark of global conflicts came just as the Cold War was ending. Since then, there has been a steady decline, not just in the number of intrastate wars, but also in their lethality as measured by the number of victims of these conflicts. These statistics also reveal surprising news about interstate conflict—specifically, that the number of interstate wars has remained at relatively low, if consistent, levels since World War II (Gurr 2000, 2007; Mack 2005).

Even so, many of the world's conflicts have proven resilient to any kind of settlement or resolution. In the Middle East, in spite of almost five decades of peacemaking by the United States and other third parties, the conflict between Israelis and Palestinians has continued. Outbreaks of violence and terrorism have hardened public opinion on both sides. In Sri Lanka, despite repeated efforts at mediation by Norwegian interlocutors, the conflict between the Sinhalese-dominated government and the Tamil insurgency shows few signs of abating. In Africa, the long-awaited signing of a peace agreement between the government and the Sudan People Liberation Movement has been overshadowed by a continued high level of violence in Darfur. And longstanding insurgencies in Thailand and the Philippines pose a continuing threat to political stability in these countries.

The conflicts of the 20th century, which have spilled over into the 21st, have been called many things: "intractable," "protracted," "self-sustaining," "deep rooted," or the product of "ancient hatreds." Much intellectual and scholarly effort has been devoted to studying their origins, causes, and their consequences. Many of these conflicts—though obviously not all—have also been the subject of prolonged and sustained international efforts to end them, including diplomacy, mediation, military intervention, peacekeeping, humanitarian and development assistance, and other kinds of intervention. However, they have proven to be extraordinarily resilient to any kind of settlement or resolution.

Many scholars, analysts, and practitioners have grappled with the definition of intractability (Azar 1986; Burton 1987; Pruitt & Olczak 1995; Coleman 2000; Kriesberg 2003; Pruitt & Kim 2004). Some scholars question the concept on the grounds that there are few "long wars" in the recent history of international relations as measured by the number of battle-related deaths. Intractable conflicts, however, are conflicts that generally tend to experience episodic but recurring bouts of violence and appear to be highly resistant—though not necessarily impossible—to resolve through a process of negotiated settlement or peacemaking.[1] They are also conflicts where the main targets of violence are often civilians and/or the military forces of the state. Terrorist attacks are often the preferred means of violence in these conflicts, even though such attacks typically tend to accompany armed insurgencies by guerrilla forces or other kinds of freedom fighters. And even if violence is on the decline or has disappeared completely, intractable conflicts may exist in a suspended state of animation because they refuse to yield to negotiated efforts to secure a more lasting political settlement. In these kinds of situations—what we refer to as "frozen" or abeyant intractable conflicts—the potential for a renewed outbreak of violence exists (Kriesberg 2005).

For the purposes of discussion, we propose a very broad definition: intractable conflicts are conflicts that have persisted over time and refused to yield to efforts—either by the direct parties, or, more often, with third-party assistance—to arrive at a political settlement. Their resistance to a settlement may appear to derive from a single cause or principal ingredient, but closer examination usually points to multiple causes and many contributing factors. Intractable conflicts are also conflicts in which armed parties enjoy relative autonomy to pursue their unilateral objectives free from considerations of cost and risk. They are not accountable to anyone.

Whatever conditions lie behind the dispute, intractable conflicts share a common characteristic: they defy settlement because leaders believe their objectives are irreconcilable and they have a greater interest in maintaining the status quo—which may be violent—than considering their political alternatives. In other words, these local decision-makers seek to resist or prevent the emergence of politics as the arena for settling their differences. Although all intractable conflicts share this characteristic, the actual level of violence and the potential for an escalation of military hostilities may vary from one setting to another. Sri Lanka continues to experience high levels of violence—usually terrorist-based—while Cyprus has not seen violence for many decades even though a political settlement has remained elusive. And the Middle East shows that levels of violence can escalate, de-escalate, and re-escalate over the lifetime of a conflict.

Another important point: if we confine our examination to the last 10 years we would believe that intractable conflicts are largely intrastate—that is to say, they take place within the borders of a state. There are, nonetheless, many conflicts that are essentially interstate disputes where the parties are—or consider themselves to be—"sovereign" entities. This distinction between inter- and intrastate conflict breaks down when contested sovereignty, or the refusal of one (or more) parties to recognize the sovereign claims of the other side, lies at the heart of the dispute. Further, the intrastate–interstate distinction or dichotomy can be extremely artificial because many so-called "intrastate" or "civil" conflicts involve external actors, including regional neighbors, who not only try to manipulate the conflict for their own ends, but may also be actively involved in the fighting itself. The actual line between "civil" and "interstate" disputes is a blurry one indeed.

Some intractable conflicts are hot conflict zones, like the Sudan or Israel–Palestine. Violence is a more or less endemic feature of these conflicts even though the actual level of violence may be intermittent, sporadic, or even seasonal (dry seasons, for example, are good for launching conventional military offensives against insurgents). Such conflicts may be stalemated because they have not reached that plateau—what William Zartman (1986, 1989, 2000) calls a mutually hurting stalemate—where the costs of a political set-tlement are appreciably lower (and recognized to be so) than the military and political costs of continued fighting. They therefore elude the moment of ripeness, that is the moment when all of the parties are seriously interested in exploring their political options and finally commit themselves to resolving their differences through negotiation rather than force of arms.

Abeyant intractable conflicts share a common characteristic with active intractable conflicts: they are not ripe because the parties themselves have not experienced the full and direct costs of a mutually hurting stale-mate. They differ, however, in crucial ways. Abeyant intractable conflicts are conflicts in which violence is suspended or "frozen" (i.e. they have gone into remission), usually because a third party is willing and capable of guaranteeing the terms of a negotiated cease-fire—a cease-fire that may also include the broad outlines of a political settlement, for example as in the case of Cyprus. When outsiders freeze a conflict through providing the means to check violence and keep peace, they save lives and manage the problem, prevent it from spreading and limit damage, but they may also, perversely, sustain the underlying polarity and delay political solutions. In this situation, outsiders become indispensable and their eventual departure presents a security dilemma for local parties, as there is real potential for escalation if those third-party security guarantees are withdrawn.

CAUSES OF INTRACTABILITY

Intractability has many causes. As we argue below, those factors that contributed to the outbreak of a conflict typically recede into the background while other factors, such as the vested interests of war profiteers and political opportunists who benefit from the conflict's continuation, move to the foreground of the identifiable "causes" of intractability. There are also "bad neighbor-hood" effects that contribute to a conflict's intractability, especially in the case of buffer states that sit between rival regional powers and groupings.

Geography and geopolitics may promote intractability. Some states lie on the border-line line between larger civilizations—Sudan between black and Arab Africa, and Kashmir between large Islamic and Hindu states. In other cases, neighboring wars may engulf a conflict, holding it captive to a resolution of the larger war, as Burundi's conflict was engulfed by the war in neighboring Congo. And many so-called "internal" patterns of enmity and amity are shaped by regional power distributions and specific factors such as border disputes, ethnic diasporas, ideo-logical alignments, and neighboring states whose interests are served by continuing conflict, as illustrated by a number of conflicts in the former Soviet Union: South Ossetia, Abkhazia, Transnistria, and Nagorno-Karabakh.

Deep-seated identity and grievance issues as well as a considerable amount of war profiteering by representatives of one group or another are frequent characteristics of intractable conflicts. The conflict in Sri Lanka has endured for 60 years, and pits the majority Sinhalese against a sizable minority group, the Tamils. These groups are divided by ethnicity, religion and language, and grievances in this conflict are deep around each of these frac-tures. In many cases, these identity conflicts are manipulated by political entrepreneurs—or what Michael Brown (1996, p. 575) calls "bad leaders"— who inflame latent or overt differences in order to build their own powerbase. President Charles Taylor, who fomented civil war in his own Liberia as well as neighboring Sierra Leone, and now stands accused of war crimes by the Special Court for Sierra Leone, is one example of a political agency entrepreneur. President Slobodan Milosevic, head of Serbia during the Balkans conflict, whipped up anti-Muslim hatred as a means of consolidating his hold on his own country—and on Serbs through the Balkans area.

Poverty and the denial of basic human needs are seen by some as key sources of conflict. While there are examples throughout history of conflict erupting because of the denial of economic needs—the French Revolution for one—there are also a number of examples of countries that have endured poverty without falling into conflict. However, the extent to which the basic needs of certain groups in society are systematically denied and/or discriminated against by those in power can lay the seeds for conflict, especially if there is no legitimate way to channel those grievances through the political process (Stewart & Brown 2007). In other cases, however, it is not internal instability that feeds intractability, but rather a kind of stasis that develops around the fighting. For instance, a stable and tolerable stalemate makes it easy for sides to settle into comfortable accommodation with persistent warfare that sustains power bases. Continued war does not jeopardize either side's core constituency, even though those who suffer and pay the price for continued fighting—especially the civilian targets—are disenfranchised in every sense. The long war in Angola was sustained because the government had access to oil revenues and the rebels profited from an illegal trade in diamonds. This access to a steady stream of resources created a stalemate in which neither side was hurt sufficiently by the conflict to want to give it up.

Avarice of predatory warlords who profit from the political economy of violence through arms sales, smuggling, and other illicit commercial practices and transactions is another important factor in intractable conflict settings. As Paul Collier (2000, 2007; Collier et al., 2003) and others argue, it is clear that "conflict pays" in monetary as well as political terms. And the dividends are such that those who are the chief beneficiaries of the war economy may have strong economic incentives to keep the conflict boiling. The recent film about "blood diamonds" has highlighted the role that this mineral played in funding the civil war in Sierra Leone, but it also happens with other resources—drugs in Colombia, and small weapons all over the world.

Polarized, zero-sum notions of identity can also produce intractability. The situation between Israelis and Palestinians shows us that conflicts which continue over long periods lead to the accumulation of grievances incorporated into each party's version of history. Each side sees itself as a victim, and creates or reinterprets key cultural and religious symbols that perpetuate both the sense of resentment and the conflict. In intractable conflicts, violence enters the everyday world of thousands of people and becomes a way of life. Conflict becomes institutionalized as vested interests rise in keeping the conflict going. Violence becomes the norm as parties become wedded to a logic and culture of revenge. Young people grow up in a conflict and know no other way of life. And as a population becomes inured to conflict, the hope that it will end recedes.

Failures in earlier peacemaking efforts can also result in the promotion by the parties of mutually exclusive basic requirements and preconditions for negotiations. These basic requirements may mask a fundamental unwillingness to negotiate, as both parties know that you cannot satisfy the requirements of one side without contradicting the basic requirement of the other side. For instance, in many internal conflicts, the underdog insurgents keep the ability to continue the struggle as a trump card, resisting all attempts at disarmament or demobilization before a political agreement has been reached. The government on the other hand often insists that disarmament or demobilization are necessary preconditions for talks to begin. The Basque conflict still endures after almost 40 years despite strong support in the Basque region for its settlement, precisely because the separatist group ETA will not renounce the use of violence—the only card this marginalized group still holds. Without this renunciation, however, it will be very difficult for a Spanish government to stay in power if it does engage in talks. This pattern reoccurs in intractable conflicts elsewhere, leading to procedural and substantive standoffs as one side says that it needs a signed agreement in order to stop fighting, and the other refuses to talk until violence ceases. In some cases, both sides may be posturing, because they view any movement to the negotiating table as a dangerously risky zero-sum game.

Local decision-makers who see their battle as a zero-sum game may resist or prevent the emergence of politics as the arena for settling their differences because, for them, what their opponent gains, they lose. Resistance to a settlement may appear to derive from a single cause or principal ingredient, but closer examination usually points to multiple causes and many contributing factors. Nevertheless, intractable conflicts share a common characteristic: they defy settlement because leaders believe their objectives are fundamentally irreconcilable and parties have more interest in the ongoing war than in any known alternative state of being.

In sum, the sources of intractability are not the same as the original causes of the conflict. No matter what issues formed the foundation for the initial conflict, a number of other elements will come into the mix to augment or even supplant the original disputes. Wars over time create new issues and agendas that were not present at the outset, including the way each side treats the other. The conflict in Kashmir is part of a larger set of bilateral conflict issues that have divided India and Pakistan since their joint emergence from the British Empire in the 1940s. Now, that agenda includes nuclear risk reduction and targeting/weaponization programs, trade/travel issues, other border issues, regional rivalries, and above all the two countries' identity dispute between Muslim homeland Pakistan and secular India. The bilateral issue agenda has ballooned with the passage of time, so that today Kashmir is much more deeply embedded in polarized issues than it was in the late 1940s.

OPTIONS FOR SETTLEMENT

As discussed at greater length below, one option for settlement of intractable conflicts is to *let the conflict settle itself*: that is, to abstain from intervention and hope that the sides either come to their own compromise or that one side wins. The problem with "just saying no" to intervention is that the premises are weak. Warring parties may get tired and more sober. They may even get more realistic about the prospects for winning an outright victory. But even when the "false optimism" that may prompt decisions to start fighting is long gone (Blainey 1988), these conditions do not necessarily translate into a settlement: as we have seen, intractability includes dimensions that aggravate and add incrementally to the initial sources or roots of the problem. As for outright victories, there appear to be fewer of these in today's world, even when one side is far stronger than the other in purely military terms.

A second approach for dealing with intractable cases is *conflict management*. Typically, this involves freezing the conflict, through a negotiated and durable cease-fire and the subsequent, long-term deployment of outside forces. Conflict management may be the best option among bad alternatives. In Cyprus and the Balkans, conflict management has helped quell the violence and allowed time and changing circumstance to moderate political passions in the hope that new forms of political accommodation can develop. This process is not necessarily linear, because violence can erupt again unless a capable third-party peacemaker simultaneously supports an ongoing negotiating process and demonstrates a real commitment to achieving a negotiated result. Intractable conflicts do not necessarily subside if they are simply managed below the boil for some years. After the Simla agreement (Thornton & Bokhari 1988), the conflict in Kashmir was managed—in the sense that there was little direct fighting—for eighteen years and yet violent conflict broke out again in the mid-1990s. Unless something is done during quiet times to ripen a conflict, the passage of time alone will not make the conflict easier to solve and may make resolution harder as new issues, agendas, grievances, and levels of bitterness set in.

Peaceful settlement by means of *mediation and conflict resolution* is the third option for handling intractable conflicts. Here, one of the central challenges is not only to wean the parties from their "addiction" to violence, but also to change incentive structures so the parties see that there are real, concrete gains to be realized by ending violence. Negotiated settlement, in other words, has to be made more attractive than continued fighting to those who are in control of the decision-making. Mediators need to acquire resources of leverage and influence in order to address the parties' interests, objective needs, vulnerabilities, insecurities, fears, and their sense of "sunk costs" in the conflict to date.

At the same time, intractable conflicts are not just battles of interest, but also battles of wills, beliefs, values, and subjective needs. There are critical psychological elements of intractable conflict that cannot be left unattended or ignored by third parties. Powerful actors are sometimes capable of deciphering and responding to such conflict dimensions. Official mediators with experience of intractable conflicts may become expert at learning the parties "political requirements" for going to settlement. Often, however, various unofficial intermediaries have played a key role in addressing the "subjective" dimensions of the conflict, including such issues as identity, survival, and the demonization of the other side. Informal dialogue and communication that deal with deep-rooted fears and perceptions are often key to changing attitudes and the hostile images warring parties have of each other. The solution may lie in what Harold Saunders in a later chapter calls a process and pattern of "circum-negotiation"—working in

the wider community to supplement and reinforce so-called track-one diplomacy by *creating a supportive political climate and constituency for peacemaking*.

These latter options do not exist in hermetically sealed, separate compartments. To illustrate, negotiated solutions to conflicts mediated by powerful actors may depend upon reaching down to their constituencies and enabling decision-makers to build support for compromise, at least on those issues where compromise is possible. Or, to take another example, it may take many years of protracted third-party efforts to move decision-makers—and their publics—to a different place where the idea of reconciliation and compromise is less easily dismissed. Conflict management—that is, suppression or control of a conflict—can under the right circumstances become a way station on the road to eventual resolution or even transformation. Powerful third parties will require the staying power to see the task through, as well as the imagination to recognize the limits of managing the manifestations of conflict; in the end, they may need to engage and eventually hand off to local civil society and non-official third-party actors in building peace (Lederach 1998, 2007).

WHEN TO MEDIATE IN INTRACTABLE CONFLICTS

Any analysis of mediating intractable conflicts must start by asking why third parties should engage at all (given that prior failure is a hallmark of intractability). A related challenge is to determine when they should seek to engage in an intractable conflict—and when they should not. In considering these issues, one can contrast engagement with its philosophic opposite, namely, to wait for the outright victory of one side. Victory, it might be argued, may provide greater future stability than a mediated compromise that risks breaking down over issues that never quite get resolved. Despite short-term humanitarian and ethical problems with "letting nature take its course," there may be both ethical and prudential factors in favor of doing so in the longer term.

However, this line of reasoning depends on assessments of what "nature's course" really is. It is sometimes argued that war is akin to a forest fire in that it continues to burn until all available fuel has been consumed. Fuel, in the case of conflicts, takes the form of internally and externally derived resources (human, financial, operational) to support the war effort. In this analysis, letting a conflict burn itself out may be the most practical option and may eliminate future emergencies and disasters (Luttwak 2001). But there are other sides to this coin. First, in the modern era, most conflicts do not seem to follow this script, in part because the forces of globalization and the disappearance of the Cold War restraints make it much easier than before for underdogs to acquire tangible resources and political support. Modern wars have a tendency to continue, to sputter on or to recur rather than lead to lopsided victories. Second, in doing so, intractable conflicts do not get better, easier, clearer, or more amenable to ultimate resolution. On the contrary, there are ample examples—in places such as Colombia, Uganda, Cote d'Ivoire, Lebanon, and Kashmir—of conflicts that get more deeply impacted by layers of local, regional, and international issues and rivalries. In one analysis, conflicts may migrate from initial roots in societal grievances or neighboring rivalries into struggles based on competing "creeds" or identities. Over time, wars may also acquire a hard crust of vested interests in the form of organizational or personal "greed" factors that make them almost immune to political settlement procedures (Arnson & Zartman 2005).

Finally, intractability and state failure appear to be closely associated, one feeding from and encouraging the other. The argument against intervening in intractable cases needs to take into account the potential consequences of abstention, including the ill effects of conflict spread, conflict metamorphosis, and the broader consequences for regional and international order of conflict spawned by or within failing states (Patrick 2006).

This analysis does not argue that third parties should reflexively engage whenever they perceive an intractable conflict; however, there are clearly certain criteria or conditions that should serve as warnings to a potential third party not to engage or to engage only after rigorous tests. These conditions relate to (a) the mediator's capacity and motives and (b) the status of the conflict and the nature of the parties' behavior. Starting with the mediator, it is harmful to propose or offer mediation if the mediator is not "ready" or equipped to undertake the task. Being "ready" has a number of political, operational, and other components that ought to be the object of serious reflection before a proposal is made (Crocker, Hampson & Aall 2003). It is also inappropriate to offer to mediate in order simply to be included in a photo opportunity or to be seen "doing something" without a serious intent to engage in the hard work of peacemaking. Another circumstance in which mediation may be inappropriate is when the prospective mediator is too closely aligned with one party or too directly involved in the conflict to be capable of meeting the minimum conditions of a balanced engagement. This is not to say that a mediator must be "impartial" to be effective, but that the mediator needs to be capable politically of pressing and influencing both sides toward a settlement.

Turning to the second set of criteria, a mediator should hesitate or decline involvement when a viable negotiating framework and mechanism already exists, and a new initiative could damage or destabilize this existing peace process. To do otherwise is poor tradecraft and only plays into the hands of parties engaged in "forum shopping" or other counterproductive games. Similarly, mediation may not be the right answer when the prospective mediator is eager to acquire a peacemaking role, but the parties themselves do not demonstrate any serious intention to explore a political solution. In such circumstances, the mediator needs to test parties' motives and avoid pleading for the assignment. The mediator should be cautious about engaging when it would play into the hands of a dominant conflict party, legitimizing actions that may cross the line of acceptable conduct. The best response in some conflict situations, in other words, may be police action, coercive diplomacy, or benign neglect, rather than mediation. There may also be intermediate steps or stages during the prenegotiation phase when the third party is best advised to undertake activities aimed at "ripening" the conflict through traditional diplomatic means or— for a non-official actor—through engagement aimed at affecting political constituencies or influential elites.

To state these ideas in a more positive manner, we assert that mediation may be the appropriate response when (a) the conflict parties know they need help and are ready at least to explore alternatives to continued fighting, (b) the mediator is "ready" and has significant links to or history with the conflict and relevant assets of leverage or influence, (c) the mediator is prepared to commit to a substantive engagement in order to shape events and not just be seen to be "doing something," (d) a change of circumstances within the conflict or its environs offers the prospect of gaining entry and subsequent traction with the parties, and/or (e) mediation offers a possible method of containing or managing a conflict that might otherwise escalate or spread geographically.

HOW TO MEDIATE INTRACTABLE CONFLICTS

Effective mediation in intractable cases is about good strategy. Designing a good mediation strategy in any conflict, intractable or not, involves first and foremost conducting a thorough analysis of the history and nature of the conflict: parties, power balances among the parties, issues, positions and interests, sources of leverage, the external context, potential entry points. It is important that potential mediators maintain a watching brief over the conflict and get ready to engage should an opportunity emerge. These opportunities may appear as a result of leadership changes, an escalation in the level of violence

that fundamentally alters public perceptions and discredits the "warring" status quo, or a change in regional or global power balances that signals to the warring parties that various external actors recognize they have a changing stake or set of interests in the conflict. This watching brief should include a constant calculation of the costs—to the mediator (and his or her supporting institution) as well as the parties—of action and inaction.

Mediated interventions must be attuned to the specific dynamics or phases of conflicts. During the course of a conflict, the nature of the conflict may change in terms of the level of violence, the willingness of affected constituencies to seek a negotiated way out of the conflict, the degree to which perceptions are hardened (or are immutable), the degree to which "external" regional or global players are engaged in the conflict, and the level of weariness of the affected populace with continued violence. Given these changing conditions, different bargaining and negotiation strategies may be called for at different phases or stages of these conflicts. For instance, if a conflict is escalating and shows dangers of spilling over its traditional boundaries, third-party intervention may focus on controlling or preventing the conflict from further escalation. These mediated interventions may be diplomatic or they may include some coercive elements, such as the threat or use of sanctions or military deployment, to persuade or push parties to de-escalate. Global norms, such as those regarding human rights and genocide, can affect third-party propensities to intervene with military means as a prelude to formal mediation. If, on the other hand, a conflict has entered a stage of exhaustion, when parties have lost their will to fight but cannot seem to move to negotiations, the mediator may take a more facilitative approach to peacemaking, passing messages between the parties and/or providing a neutral forum where the parties can meet (Kriesberg & Thorson 1991; Lund 1997).

It often takes a special kind of leadership to take advantage of the opportunities that emerge due to a shift in the tectonic plates of the global (or regional) geopolitical system or a change in the local landscape. The search for peace is not an automatic reaction to a change; in fact, there usually is a great resistance to change among the current leaders of the conflict. Consequently, an important role that third parties play is to mentor new leaders and foster the emergence of new elites that are more open to the idea of negotiated settlement. This new leadership may be even more necessary to the implementation stage, as it is very rare that a "struggle politician" can make the transition from military leader to advocate of reconciliation.

At the same time, mediators must continue to work with the existing leadership, helping it to come to terms with the enormous personal, political, and social risks that moving toward peace entails. Ending intractable conflicts demands a quantum leap in terms of leadership requirements, both for the warring parties and for the mediator. Here, it is important that a wide range of outside institutions support the mediation process. Tangible support in the form of incentives to the parties to settle— for instance, promises of trade, aid, and other material resources—would be very helpful in these circumstances. But the kind of support that is critical to the process is intangible—for example the absence of dissenting voices from the mediator's home institution and unified international support for the mediation effort and for keeping the process moving forward.

Good mediation strategy also has to be complemented by effective mediation tactics. When a negotiation process has gone stale or reached a dead end, mediators may have to change their negotiating tactics. In these circumstances, mediators typically have to secure new sources of leverage over the parties or change the perceptions about the costs and benefits of those who have become too comfortable with the status quo. They sometimes have to reframe issues and create (or identify) new options for parties who are stuck in a rut.

Creating and implementing a careful plan is essential to the effectiveness of all outside interventions into conflicts, whether they have gone on for years or for just a few months.

However, intractable conflicts also require the mediator to deal with the outcomes of the conflict's duration, especially in cases in which there have been multiple efforts to resolve it. Intractable conflicts suffer from negotiation roadblocks and discredited solutions. If parties have engaged in negotiation at various times over a long conflict—as was the case in the North–South conflict in Sudan— it is likely that the parties have considered a variety of possible resolutions. The mediator has to deal with the parties' assumptions that they already know everything the other side has to offer, and therefore talks are a waste of time. A salient solution to the conflict may no longer be available if it has already been tried on the parties once or more and has become discredited because of its failure to help parties reach a negotiated settlement. Here, the challenge for the mediator is not so much of trying to invent something new as it is to resurrect discredited formulas and/or to keep them alive for the time when the parties are serious about getting back to the negotiating table. The challenge, in other words, may be less about the parameters for designing the eventual settlement than about how to get there.

Intractable conflicts tend to take over the societies they affect. They permeate all societal institutions—politics, economics, the media, religion, education—and dominate the political and social discourse. No one escapes from their impact, even in conflicts where the level of violence is low, as was the case in Northern Ireland, or confined to specific areas, as in Sri Lanka. The conflict shapes the way that people see their world and often determines the borders of that world. In any conflict, dealing with the "other," is always an issue. Enmity, particularly once violence has broken out, is difficult to turn to any other kind of relationship, which is the reason that arriving at reconciliation may take decades. But in the case of intractable conflicts, that enmity enters deep into people's daily lives. And it is often augmented by isolation, as channels for communication are cut off. The Turkish and Greek Cypriots were cut off from each other for 29 years, until the borders were opened in 2003. Israelis and Palestinians are now separated by a wall. Even in Northern Ireland, where Catholics and Protestants shared territory, they lived in carefully segregated neighborhoods and sent their children to separate schools.

This level of infiltration provides the mediator with a set of challenges that is difficult to meet alone. The mediator is often most effective in creating and nurturing the negotiating space between the warring parties, identifying issues and possible areas of agreement. Reaching out throughout society will take the cooperation of the combatants' leadership, and will take collaboration among all of the institutions that can play a constructive role in changing popular attitudes—civil society, the news media, prominent figures, the arts. In order to reach out to these sectors, mediators in intractable conflicts need to work with third-party institutions that have access to them, like development agencies and international NGOs. These third-party organizations need to work together to form a constituency for peace in the larger society, as discussed by Saunders in this volume, so that if and when political leaders reach a settlement, it is not overturned by a society that has been excluded from the process.

WHO SHOULD MEDIATE INTRACTABLE CONFLICTS?

To ask who should mediate implies that there is a long line of potential candidates that are capable of stepping into the role and willing to do so. Historically, it has been more often the case that conflicts were allowed to burn on without outside interference as long as they did not destabilize large regions or threaten the interests of major powers. The international community ignored both the conditions that led to violent conflict and the violent conflict itself for a variety of reasons. Among the strongest was the tradition of respect for national sovereignty and the strong prohibition against interfering in the internal affairs of an independent state. Over the past 15 years, however,

this prohibition has weakened as states and international institutions have been forced to recognize the horrendous human toll of unresolved conflicts. The result has been increased interest in mediation among both official and non-official organizations.

The 2005 *Human Security Report*, working from data derived from the UN Department of Political Affairs (DPA), notes that UN preventive diplomacy initiatives rose from one to six between 1990 and 2002, while UN mediation, facilitation, and good offices efforts rose from four to 15 over the same period (Mack 2005, p. 153). Fifteen years ago, it was rare for a non-official organization to become involved in mediation; today, there are many examples of NGOs playing principal roles in preparing for or assisting talks: the Carter Center in the 1999 agreement between Uganda and Sudan, the Community of Sant'Egidio in the Mozambique settlement, the Henri Dunant Centre for Humanitarian Dialogue and the Conflict Management Initiative in Aceh. At the same time, powerful states have been active in mediating protracted conflicts, as the USA has done in the Middle East and smaller states—Norway in Sri Lanka, for instance—have entered into the field as well.

The involvement of different kinds of institutions—states, international organizations, NGOs—in peacemaking in intractable conflicts raises the question of whether one set of institutions is best suited for mediating in long-term conflict. In other words, in situations where the parties are thoroughly entrenched in their positions, can only the most powerful actors, using their sticks and carrots, move the parties to negotiation? Or is reaching peace in these circumstances a result of moral authority of the international community, available only through the UN, African Union, and other intergovernmental organizations? Or are individual peacemakers and respected non-official organizations the best suited to making peace in intractable conflicts?

In comparing the activities of organizations that could mediate intractable conflicts, a distinction that is often made is in their ability, or lack thereof, to employ the tools of power in mediation to persuade parties to a conflict to talk rather than fight. In this regard, governments, especially large governments, have quite a lot of power, international organizations have less, and the general perception is that non-official organizations have next to none. However, in trying to address multilayered intractable conflicts, the response may also need to be multilayered. Official organizations, such as the UN or a powerful state, can offer incentives and disincentives—like aid, trade, threats of sanctions or military action—to make the parties to the conflict more amenable to negotiation. However, there are also contributions that non-official organizations can make to bolster the official process, especially by building support for peace in the larger community.

The level of violence may dictate when one set of institutions is more appropriate than others. When violence is low, parties may be open to interventions by a wide range of mediators. At this stage, one of the main challenges is to establish direct communication between the parties. Here, various non-governmental actors and scholar/practitioners may enjoy a comparative advantage because they can help to establish informal channels of communication without compromising the interests of the parties or formally committing them to a politically risky course of action. As the parties begin to grasp how much they will have to compromise in a negotiated settlement, however, these third parties will face an uphill struggle keeping the negotiations on course. Mediation efforts at this level should therefore be directed at "lengthening the shadow of the future" by dramatizing the long-term costs of violence to the parties if negotiations fail. Ideally, they should also be directed at changing the attitudes of the parties by creating domestic constituencies that are supportive of negotiation and political as opposed to military options.

When the threat of violence is high or increasing, mediators' leverage is limited because the parties continue to believe that they can gain more from continued fighting than they can through negotiation. Intractable conflicts are often caught at this stage, and mediators who exercise reward and coercive power will likely have to be brought into the formal negotiating process—exercising what is sometimes called "mediation with muscle." Absent of these externally induced incentives, parties will have little incentive to stay at the table and may, in fact, be willing to escalate the conflict in the hope of achieving their objectives.

Generally, these mediators with muscles are powerful states, and are engaged in mediation in pursuit of a national or foreign policy interest. The result is often a bias toward one of the conflict parties, which introduces a set of complications into the mediator–conflict party equation. The "bias-sometimes-helps" thesis is an important and widely understood element in the international mediation literature (Touval & Zartman 2007). But the proposition rests on the core assumption that bias helps only if the third party enjoys some freedom of maneuver during the actual negotiation process. In many intractable disputes, the third party faces very strong, internal, domestic political pressure—from groups that are allied, or see themselves as allied, to the parties in the conflict—which constricts its own negotiating options. The North–South conflict in Sudan provides an interesting example. For many years, a number of US and European church groups threw their support to the Christian and animist south and effectively barred or constrained official communication with Khartoum. But when the United States decided finally to engage, these same groups gave the US-led effort some added leverage through their support of the president's envoy, former senator John Danforth.

This raises the interesting if rather sensitive subject of the suitability of large, unruly, open democratic systems to play a primary mediating role in places where there are diaspora or political linkages that outweigh the need for a balanced effort to mediate in the national interest. It is also true that in other intractable conflict cases—for instance, Cyprus, Northern Ireland, and Sudan— serving administrations have been very conscious of the impact of their intermediary efforts on relations with particular domestic constituencies. The presence or absence of such domestic pressures may also help to explain why countries—Norway, for example—that do not have large immigrant populations or diaspora communities sometimes may enjoy certain comparative advantages in playing intermediary roles, especially when less intrusive kinds of bargaining strategies are warranted.

Determining who should mediate depends on many factors, including the parties' preference, availability of appropriate candidates, the willingness of the mediator's home institution or the international community to support the effort. It is important to recognize that poor or weak tradecraft by third-party interveners has the potential to exacerbate the problem and further deepen an intractable conflict. To the extent that some intractable conflicts are not of high priority for some mediators (and the countries they represent), a tepid or halfhearted negotiated intervention may be only marginally better than none. The international community has also started to acknowledge that mediation can be taught, and that the requisite preparation and skills can be honed in advance. The UN's Department of Political Affairs DPA has set itself the tasks of recruiting the best available envoys and mediators, nurturing future professionals in the field, serving as a focal point of interaction with other mediation efforts, stepping up administrative and logistical support for UN envoys, and similar goals. The centerpiece of the new thrust is the creation in late 2005 of the Mediation Support Unit to serve as a "central repository for peacemaking experience and to act as a clearing house for lessons learned and best practices ... [while also undertaking] to coordinate training for mediators and provide them with advice on UN standards and operating procedures." Other institutions, including the US Institute of Peace, are developing teaching and training programs to prepare not only official mediators, but also NGO and military staff to play constructive intermediary roles at many levels of intractable conflicts.

Prolonged conflicts need mediation by a set of skilled mediators from diverse institutions working in concert. They may also require a multiple track mediation strategy that is directed at both elites and various factions and groups within civil society, that is, a series of simultaneous mediated interventions by governmental and non-governmental mediators that engage different groups in the conflict (UN 2008). A prolonged conflict is unlikely to be fully settled unless the wider public is brought along; when this is ignored, the leaders and mediators run the risk of losing popular support for the process.

It is important to recognize that a competitive dimension has emerged as the field of mediation has developed. The problem of how to reap the benefits of composite, layered, or sequenced peacemaking while, at the same time, to avoid the negative side effects of "multiparty mediation" is a serious one. It cannot be wished away by generalized appeals for "coherence". When a conflict becomes crowded with mediators seeking to play a role, it tells us several things. First, it typically means there could be trouble ahead: when mediators are unable to organize themselves with a sense of common purpose, it suggests that there are different "outside" views about how the conflict should be resolved. In addition, it may indicate that the conflict has "attracted" would-be mediators who have a wide range of political, bureaucratic, institutional, or financial incentives to become role players—and to be seen doing so. The problem can become acute in the absence of an external "gatekeeper," such as an international or regional body with the stature to impose some measure of order on the proceedings. The mediation field does not have any obvious self-regulating mechanism—that is, unless major actors care enough to cooperate for common purpose and identify a lead actor or mediating group to organize and conduct the process. This is eventually what happened in the case of the North–South conflict in Sudan where the Intergovernmental Authority on Development (IGAD), a subregional body, and its critically important external parties (the USA, UK, Norway, and, at certain points,

Switzerland and Italy) worked coherently to bring about the 2005 Comprehensive Peace Agreement (Morrison & de Waal 2005).

CONCLUSION

Intractable conflicts are hard to mediate. But because they are hard, persistent, embedded, and enduring, this does not mean that they are impossible to deal with and resistant to any and all kinds of negotiated solutions. When third parties engage in peacemaking— helping parties to recalculate the costs and benefits of continuing the fight, assisting parties to reframe the issues, nurturing a state of ripeness, developing friends of the process to help in implementation, working in the larger society to develop a vision of an alternative future, or bringing a forgotten conflict to the world's attention—they are putting pressure directly on the sources of intractability: the deeply ingrained attitudes and modes of behavior of the parties and the conditions that have allowed the conflict to continue unchecked. There is evidence to confirm that highlyskilled, multilayered, persistent third-party assistance is a necessary component of effective peace processes in intractable conflicts.

NOTES

1 As the *Beyond Intractability.org* project notes, "Intractability" is a controversial concept, which means different things to different people. Some people …dislike the term, as they see it as too negative: intractable conflicts are impossible to resolve, they say, so people think they are not worth dealing with …[Others believe, however, that] there is a set of conflicts out there that are hard to deal with. 'Protracted.' 'Destructive.' 'Deep-rooted.' 'Resolution-resistant.' 'Intransigent'. 'Gridlocked.' 'Identity-based.' 'Needs based.' 'Complex.' 'Difficult.' 'Malignant.' 'Enduring' …. As we see it, intractable conflicts are those that lie at the frontier of the field—the conflicts that stubbornly seem to elude *resolution*, even when the best available techniques are applied. Examples abound: abortion, homosexual rights, and race relations in the United States; and the Israeli—Palestinian problem, Sri Lanka , and Kashmir (among many others) abroad. These conflicts are

not hopeless, and they most certainly are worth dealing with. But they are very different from more tractable conflicts, such as most labor-management conflicts, some family conflicts, many workplace conflicts and even many international conflicts that can be successfully resolved through negotiation or mediation. Intractable conflicts need a different, more multi-faceted, and more prolonged approach." http://(www.beyondintractability.org/essay/meaning_intractability/?nid=1003)

REFERENCES

Arnson, Cynthia & Zartman I. William 2005. *Rethinking the Economics of War: The Intersection of Need, Creed and Greed*. Washington, DC: Woodrow Wilson International Center for Scholars Press.

Axelrod, Robert 1984. *The Evolution of Cooperation*. New York: Basic Books.

Azar, Edward E. 1986. "Protracted International Conflicts: Ten Propositions," in Edward E. Azar and John W. Burton, eds., *International Conflict Resolution: Theory and Practice*. Brighton, UK: Wheatsheaf Books.

Blainey, Geoffrey 1988. *The Causes of War*, 3rd edn. New York: The Free Press.

Brown, Michael E. 1996. "The Causes and Regional Dimensions of Internal Conflict," in Michael E. Brown, ed., *The International Dimensions of Internal Conflict*. Cambridge, MA: MIT Press.

Burton, John 1987. *Resolving Deep-rooted Conflict: A Handbook*. Lanham, MD: University Press of America.

Collier, Paul 2000. "Doing Well Out of War: An Economic Perspective," in Mats Berdal and David M. Malone, eds., *Greed and Grievance: Economic Agendas in Civil Wars*. Boulder, CO: Lynne Rienner; Ottawa: International Development Research Centre.

—— 2007. "Economic Causes of Civil Conflict and Their Implications for Policy," in Chester A. Crocker, Fen Osler Hampson, and Pamela Aall, eds., *Leashing the Dogs of War: Conflict Management in a Divided Word*. Washington, DC: United States Institute of Peace Press.

Collier, Paul; Lani Elliott, Hagard Hegre, Martha Reynal-Querol, Anke Hoeffler and Nicholas Sambanis, 2003. *Breaking the conflict Trap: Civil War and Development Policy*. New York, Oxford University Press.

Coleman, Peter 2000. "Intractable Conflict," in Morton Deutsch and Peter T. Coleman, eds., *The Handbook of Conflict Resolution: Theory and Practice*. San Francisco: Jossey-Bass.

Crocker, Chester A., Hampson, Fen Olsen, and Aall, Pamela 2003. "Ready for Prime Time: The Who, When and Why of International Mediation," *Negotiation Journal* XIX 155–167.

—— eds. 1999. *Herding Cats: Multiparty Mediation in a Complex World*. Washington, DC: US Institute of Peace Press.

—— eds. 2004. *Taming Intractable Conflicts: Mediation in the Hardest Cases*. Washington, DC: US Institute of Peace Press.

—— eds. 2005. *Grasping the Nettle: Analyzing Cases of Intractable* Conflict. Washington, DC: US Institute of Peace Press.

—— eds. 2007. *Leashing the Dogs of War: Conflict Management in a Divided World*. Washington, DC: US Institute of Peace Press.

Gurr, Ted Robert 2000. *Peoples versus States: Minorities at Risk in the New Century*. Washington, DC: United States Institute of Peace Press.

—— 2007. "Minorities and Nationalists: Managing Ethnopolitical Conflict in the New Century," in Chester A. Crocker, Fen Olsen Hampson, and Pamela Aall, eds., *Turbulent Peace*: The Challenges of Managing International Conflict.

Kriesberg, Louis 2003. *Constructive Conflicts: From Escalation to Resolution,* 2nd edn. Lanham, MD: Rowman and Littlefield.

—— 2005. "Nature, Dynamics, and Phases of Intractability," in Chester A. Crocker, Fen Olsen Hampson, and Pamela Aall, eds., *Grasping the Nettle: Analyzing Cases of Intractable Conflict*. Washington, DC: US Institute of Peace Press.

—— and Thorson, Stuart J. eds. 1991. *Timing the De-escalation of International Conflicts*. Syracuse: Syracuse University Press.

Lederach, John Paul 1996. *Preparing for Peace: Conflict Transformation Across Cultures*. Syracuse: Syracuse University Press.

—— *Building Peace*

—— 2005. "Civil Society and Reconciliation," in Chester A. Crocker, Fen Olsen Hampson, and Pamela Aall, eds., *Turbulent Peace*.

Licklider, Roy 2005. "Comparative Studies of Long Wars," in Chester A. Crocker, Fen Olsen Hampson, and Pamela Aall, eds., *Grasping the Nettle: Analyzing Cases of Intractable Conflict*. Washington, DC: US Institute of Peace Press.

Lund, Michael 1997. *Preventing Violent Conflicts: A Strategy for Preventive Diplomacy* Washington, DC: United States Institute of Peace Press.

Luttwak, Edward N. 2007. "The Curse of Inconclusive Intervention," in Chester A. Crocker,

Fen Olsen Hampson, and Pamela Aall, eds., *Turbulent Peace*.

Mack, Andrew 2005. *Human Security Report 2005: War and Peace in the 21st Century*. British Columbia, Canada: Human Security Center, available at www.humansecurityreport.info/content/view/28/63/

Morrison, J. Stephen and Alex de Waal. 2004. " Can Sudan Escape its Intractability?" *In Grasping the Nettle*.

Patrick, Stewart 2006. "Weak States and Global Threats: Fact or Fiction?" in *The Washington Quarterly*, XXIX 2: (Spring).

Pruitt, Dean G. and Olczak, P. "Beyond Hope: Approaches to Resolving Seemingly Intractable Conflict," in B. B. Bunker and Jeffrey Z. Rubin, eds., *Conflict, Cooperation and Justice: Essays Inspired by the work of Morton Deutsh*. San Fransisco Jossey-Bass.

Pruitt, Dean G. and Kim, Sung Hee 2004. *Social Conflict: Escalation, Stalemate, Settlement*. New York: McGraw-Hill.

Stewart, Frances and Brown, Graham 2007. "Motivations for Conflict: Groups and Individuals," in Chester A. Crocker, Fen Olsen Hampson, and Pamela Aall, eds., *Leashing the Dogs of War: Conflict Management in a Divided World*. Washington, DC: US Institute of Peace Press.

Thornton, Thomas Perry and Bokhari, Imtiaz 1988. *The Simla Agreement*. Foreign Policy Institute, The Johns Hopkins University.

Touval, Saadia and Zartman, I. William 2007. "International Mediation in Post-Cold War Era," in Chester A. Crocker, Fen Olsen Hampson, and Pamela Aall, eds., *Turbulent Peace*, Washington, DC. United States Institute of Peace Press.

United Nations Department of Political Affairs' "Peacemaking" website, available at www.un.org/Depts/dpa/peace.html

Zartman, I. William 1986. "Ripening Conflict, Ripe Moment, Formula, and Mediation," in Diane Bendahmane and John MacDonald, eds., *Perspectives on Negotiation*. Washington, DC: Foreign Service Institute.

—— 1989. *Ripe for Resolution: Conflict and Intervention in Africa*. New York: Oxford University Press.

—— 2000. "Ripeness: The Hurting Stalemate and Beyond," in Paul Stern and Daniel Druckman, eds., *International Conflict Resolution after the Cold War*. National Academy Press.

26

Culture and Conflict Resolution

Guy Olivier Faure

Our world is facing a new situation in history with its technological development. It has considerably brought men closer to each other, suppressed distances, shortened transportation time, and increased opportunities for communicating and interacting. With the development of Third World economies, the multiplication of foreign investments, and the huge growth of exchanges, the world economy has gone one step further in achieving a higher degree of integration. Even countries that were for so long out of the global trend are now strongly part of this movement. As a consequence, opportunities for conflicts and for negotiation dramatically increase and intercultural encounters are multiplied. Concerns for the common heritage of our planet, such as scarce resource management and threats to the environment, nuclear proliferation, natural disasters, danger of wars, also contribute to getting people of all countries to meet and seek solutions.

With the modern media and the growing interdependence between nations, the visibility of national cultures has been considerably increased. In turn, two contrasting trends could be considered: either this interdependence will lead to relationships transcending the bounds of culture or to people becoming more sensitive towards the differentiating effects of cultures.

Understanding a negotiation is to apprehend the sense that actors attach to their actions and the significance they give to what they observe. Many events that take place in a negotiation cannot be explained by a theory such as that of rational choice because from one culture to another, rationality is developed through different ways and processes, sometimes integrating intangible interests, turning intercultural negotiation into a very complex process.

The current intellectual challenge is to grasp in its functional aspect the quicksilver concept of culture and to analyze under which circumstances it becomes a causal variable. Then, the subsequent point is to shed light on how and with what consequences this happens. In addition, the encounter between two or more cultures takes research to another level of complexity: what may come out of this uncertain chemistry, of this "correlation of cultures"?

This query on the role of culture and its distinctive effects may bear another fruit than mere knowledge. It could help to build predictive instruments concerning negotiators' behaviors and provide means for a better control of the conflict resolution process and subsequently of its outcome.

WHAT IS CULTURE?

The concept of culture is vague, general, carrying several meanings and elusive, giving birth to a host of assumptions. Edouard Herriot, a French writer and politician, has defined culture as *what remains when one has forgotten everything*. This paradoxical proposition captures one of the most salient properties of culture: the fact that it is not a matter of substance but a way of thinking or acting of which the individual is usually unaware. If one wants to be more specific on the topic, culture could be defined as "a set of shared and enduring meanings, values, and beliefs that characterize national, ethnic, or other groups and orient their behavior" (Faure and Rubin, 1993).

Culture may be understood as a system of widely accepted beliefs and assumptions that are transmitted from one generation to the next through a learning process. They pertain to people and their interaction, the relationship between them and their environment, how they deal most effectively with their environments given their available resources (Trompenaars, 1993). As mentioned by Ross (1997b), "culture is a framework for organizing the world, for locating the self and others in it, for making sense of the actions and interpreting motives of others." Herskovitz (1995) considers culture as the "human-made part of the environment," where man left its print on nature. Triandis (1994) distinguishes between "subjective culture" made of categories, norms, roles, and values, the underlying grammar for interpreting messages and "objective culture," regrouping human products such as tools, chairs, and airplanes.

Clearly, people are constrained both by reality and by their perception of reality. They tend to act according to beliefs and values provided by their culture. "The role of culture is to answer questions even before they are raised," observes a French sociologist (Akoun, 1989). Thus, common sense is typically a cultural product. Culture is also expressed through the way human beings consider nature, space, time, or major events of one's life. However, culture cannot just be defined as a computer's software for it does not only provide orientations for action but meanings and contributes to establish, assert, and preserve identity. "Culture is a distinct group construct. Individuals have personalities; groups have cultures," underline Adair and Brett (2004). From a short-term perspective, culture can be viewed as a kind of structural component, conditioning human behavior and leaving an enduring print on people. Culture is constantly in flux and from a long-term perspective, it is a dynamic social phenomenon that provides changes over time through integration of new values and disqualification of former major values.

Culture leads to specific behaviors but also and chiefly to differing modes of thinking. Researchers from the University of Michigan, Nisbett and Masuda have shown evidence of opposed modes in their cognitive approach by the Americans and Japanese. The latter start from the context and give a great importance to it. By contrast, Americans move directly toward what seems to them most significant, the interaction itself. The Chinese intellectual approach appears as holistic and based on empirical evidence, whereas Western thinking is analytical and lies on abstract logic. Thus, linear thinking with its rules of univocal relations of causation and the definition of conceptual categories is not a universal way of understanding but is a typically Western approach.

Hall (1976) divides cultures into two clusters, high versus low context, according to the importance people give to the environment in collecting data, interpreting signals, and acting. The Chinese or Japanese belong to *high context* societies, resorting more for instance to indirect action and implicit expressions, whereas Westerners are parts of *low context* societies where action is far more direct, and their expressions more explicit. People who belong to each of these societies find substantial difficulties in decoding the messages and behaviors of the other or making the right assumption about what is behind them.

Hofstede (1980; 2001) distinguishes five basic dimensions of culture that may be used to classify the behavior of negotiators. One dimension concerns the *power distance* between actors, which expresses the willingness of people to accept hierarchical differences. Another measure is the tendency to *avoid uncertainty*, which is narrowly related to stress, stability, and the desire for rule enforcement. A third dimension, *individualism*, deals with the relationship between the individual and the collectivity. The last dimension, *masculinity*, relates to ambition defined as the desire to achieve success (for instance, in business), to be the best, and to earn more. This is opposed to the feminine pole, which means taking a more modest stance, a relation-oriented attitude, and a care for giving support, for nurturing. The last dimension, *time frame*, opposes long-term and short-term orientations in goals. The behavior of social actors such as negotiators may be ranked in each of these categories. In a comparative mode, national cultural profiles may be characterized with the help of these indicators.

Language is a cultural output that may help to apprehend how cultural factors influence social action. A basic function of language is to structure reality and organize experience. Language provides categories to seize and express what is perceived and to turn it into thinking. Any particular language has its own set of categories to interpret reality. These categories may considerably differ from one society to another.

National ethnic cultures strongly contribute to shaping what is usually referred to as a "national negotiating style" by combining their own influence with that of history, and of the political system. Subcultures such as family culture, religious culture, gender culture, or corporate culture may also influence negotiation behavior by providing

their own norms of conduct, symbols, and meanings.

Cultures are not homogenous, monolithic. They aggregate elements coming from the environmental conditions, and from history. The rationale of a culture is extremely difficult to discern. It is far from being a coherent and stable system of values but rather a "bundle of cultural norms" that are subject to "dialectic tension" (Janosik, 1987). The outcome of the cultural management of these tensions may vary according to time and people. Thus, Blaker (1977) distinguishes between two very different domestic ideals of conflict resolution within the Japanese culture, the "harmonious cooperation" and the "warrior ethic." Both ideals are rather incompatible but at the same time they are strongly embedded in the Japanese tradition. According to circumstances, one or the other can be legitimate. These tensions between values provide some internal dynamics for change and, as a consequence, the related behaviors become much less predictable than they appear in the Hofstede model. In the same fashion, French culture has always been articulated around conflicting values such as liberty and equality. According to the period, one or the other would dominate, eliciting a change in priorities. This variation on the scale of preferences can be viewed as an indicator of the cultural dynamics.

HOW CULTURE INFLUENCES CONFLICT RESOLUTION

During the time of British rule over India, a dispute arose between the British authorities and the King of Bhutan over the Bhutanese having whisked off some English people. To make his point stronger, the King of Bhutan, the "Dragon ruler," threatened the British with having to face a "divine force of twelve angry gods" who were, in addition, "very ferocious ghosts." If it was possibly taken as a joke on one side, it was the most serious statement that could be made in Bhutanese culture.

In other traditional societies such as in Africa, China, and elsewhere, unusual parties to Westerners such as evil spirits, or ancestors coming back from the dead, may join in the conflict resolution process (Faure, 2000a). Thus, culture may clearly come in unexpectedly, confirming the observation from Faure and Rubin: "What is it that cannot quite be seen but follows us around constantly? [...] The answer [...] is culture" (Faure and Rubin, 1993: XI). A Westerner may realize that his way of eating is not universal the day he is in China and has only a pair of chopsticks to eat his rice. A fish does not know it lives in the water until it is taken out of the water, as the old saying goes. What is often observed is that culture's effect on negotiation is subtle and this subtlety, however, does not really reduce the importance of culture but only makes it less visible (Faure and Rubin, 1993). The subtle influence of culture has to be grasped in an organized way to disclose some of its content. Culture does not need to have a visible impact, or to be consciously perceived to be influential.

Negotiating is a multidimensional activity and the overall orientation adopted by an actor to achieve his goal is a strategy. Strategic choices are led by interests and values, which, in turn, relate to culture. A negotiator may rely on legal norms to solve a conflict, or on the relational dimension, or on the affective dimension, or on intuition, or on force, or on mediation. The process can be defined as the core of the negotiation, the interaction between the actors. This interaction is made up of moves or tactics of all kinds designed to exchange information, to create new options or divide a resource and trade off concessions. These actions are value-related and what can be seen as legitimate in one culture can be totally rejected in another culture. For instance, not sticking to one's word or deceiving the other party about a deadline can be viewed from very different angles.

Culture may impact conflict resolution processes at four different levels: behaviors, beliefs, cognition, and identity. *Behaviors*, the more visible level, concern the way to play in selecting a range of acceptable behaviors and defensible arguments. In some cultures, action will be direct, conflict widely

accepted and problems met head on; in others, action will be indirect, conflict not openly acknowledged and problems only dealt with through allusions. Russians, for instance, tend to negotiate from a position of strength and do not mind resorting to aggressive tactics such as threats, whereas the Japanese are highly reluctant to directly confront the counterpart (Kimura, 1980). Tactics such as "take it or leave it" or issuing direct threats are part of the American culture. The Asian-Pacific cultures would better be illustrated by the use, for instance, of the "salami tactic" (nibbling) or just keeping silent and not answering.

Power distribution may be in some cases very unequal and culture tends to legitimize some types of situational power such as those linked to resources, position, status, age, role and to disavow others. In China, a business negotiation is always conceived as an unbalanced situation. It is not the foreigner who sells to his Chinese counterpart but the Chinaman who buys from the foreigner. Thus, in the Chinese view, the buyer has a strong bargaining position and it is quite legitimate for the most powerful to impose his own views. If the foreign seller treats the Chinese as an equal, he will be viewed as arrogant (Fang, 1999; Faure, 1999a). In the former USSR, the Party could not be wrong. In traditional African villages, in a discussion, the eldest always has the final word. Such a priori judgments will influence the whole process by weighting strongly on negotiators' behaviors.

Being polite is in some cultures more important than telling the truth. Bluffing, issuing threats can be seen in some societies as some of the very many means available to the negotiator. In other societies, it is a sufficient reason for breaking off the whole relationship. A list of 15 tactics considered as "dirty tricks" in the North American culture has been established by Adler (1986), drawing upon Fisher & Ury (1981). Some of them would never be understood as dirty tricks in the Chinese culture but rather as common practice. For instance, "too little eye contact" does not mean in China the launching of psychological warfare but simply a polite and modest attitude, which is the sign of a good education. Similarly, the absence of a private place to talk does not mean that the Chinese negotiator is trying to put his foreign counterpart in a stressful situation. In the Chinese culture, there is very little privacy and a negotiation is a rather public discussion, as is much of the life of people in professional settings.

A number of publications address the behavioral aspects of negotiation emphasizing cultural differences under the heading of "negotiating styles" (Binnendijk, 1987; Cogan, 2003; Fang, 1999; Fisher, 1980; Graham and Sano, 1984; Smyser, 2002; Snyder, 1999; Solomon, 1999; Wittes, 2005). Some tend to describe the typical ways in which negotiators behave when they are, for instance, Latin American, Japanese, Chinese, or Arab. Conclusions are sometimes drawn in terms of advice for the practitioner such as "do not call your Chinese counterpart by his first name," "while sitting in a tent, do not show the sole of your shoes to your Arab counterpart," "do not give a slap on the shoulder of your Japanese counterpart to show him sympathy," "when you meet a Latin-American negotiator, do not suggest getting to work before getting well acquainted." These rather anecdotal observations may sometimes be useful to the businessman in an unfamiliar place but bear limitations, as they do not really help to understand the culture of the counterpart across the table, the carpet, or the tent. Sometimes, they tend to feed an excessively homogeneous and stereotyped representation of the counterpart, thus conditioning behaviors through selective perceptions of reality, and finally generating self-fulfilling prophecies.

Communication is another major component of the conflict resolution process. All negotiations depend on effective communication, which means that both parties should interpret messages similarly. When communication is indirect, its content ambiguous, and the related feedback scarce, negotiation requires a lot of decoding from the participants. Culture and context provide, then, the two main keys to an accurate

perception of signals sent by the other party. Differences do not only lie in what is said but in how it is said and also in the social context of the discussions. For instance, drawing conclusions from a field study on US/Japanese negotiations, Graham (1993: 139) observes, "Americans are unable to read Japanese expressions and wrongly describe the Japanese as expressionless."

The significance of the Japanese smile is an interesting case with which to illustrate the complexity of the task, and at the same time its necessity, because from an objective data one can derive opposite conclusions. A Japanese smile can be perceived as a mask of politeness, an opaque wall behind which one observes the other. It can express cooperation or denial, joy or anger, certainty or total ignorance, trust or distrust, pleasure or embarrassment. Only some knowledge of the Japanese culture and the reference to the current context of the smile may enable one to get access to its real meaning.

Communication may play an important role in the domain of constructive ambiguity as illustrated by the Hainan incident (2001). A collision near the Chinese island of Hainan between a US surveillance aircraft and a Chinese fighter jet led to the death of the Chinese pilot. Meanwhile, the US plane had to make an emergency landing on Chinese ground. The Chinese authorities demanded recognition of full responsibility and deep apologies that the US government was not willing to give. After 11 days of fruitless discussions, the USA offered a letter understood on their side as simply stating how sorry they were for the death of the Chinese pilot and for the landing without authorization. The letter was written only in English. On the Chinese side, it was translated as a letter of apologies. Semantic ambiguity and linguistic flexibility were essential tools to bring the conflict to an end.

The second level, that of *beliefs*, puts forth a set of values coming from the cultural background of the negotiator. These values, stating what is desirable and what is not, operate as instrumental goals and directly orient the behavior of the actors. For instance, the Chinese culture favors harmony and this has a clear influence on negotiation practices such as face-saving, indirect action, collective concern, and relational orientation (Faure, 1999b). Adair and Brett (2004: 163) suggest a model based on an East–West distinction in negotiation with respect to beliefs, goals, and norms. Negotiators from the East (Japan, China) tend to frame negotiation as a relationship. They look for trust built through indirect information sharing and affective influence. Westerners (USA, Germany) tend to frame negotiation as a distribution of resources. They look for joint gains enacted through direct information exchange and rational influence behaviors.

As mentioned in the introduction to this handbook, conflicts over values are much more difficult to solve than conflicts of interest. If only national cultures were at play, as a set of shared values, culture would generate a highly predictable pattern of nego-tiating behavior. With the corporate culture and the professional culture, the assumption of homogeneity looses its relevance and common values become more difficult to discern. In turn, combined with personality variables within strategic behaviors, the final attitude would become much less predictable, if ever.

Ethics are also brought into the interaction by the negotiators themselves. The cultural line drawn between what should not be done, or tolerated, varies from one culture to another. In some cultures, people easily resort to means of action such as lies, deception, or bribes that are considered as absolutely unacceptable by other cultures. To come to an agreement, parties normally have to meet some norm of fairness in their final offer. Perceived fairness can be closely linked with cultural differences (Roth et al., 1991). Behind such a concept, one can find different, sometimes conflicting, principles of justice strongly correlated with social values. Some cultures would favor equality of concessions or gains as a basic norm of fairness; others would, for instance, prefer imbalanced gains distributed according to the specific needs of each party.

Cognition bears upon the definition of conflict and the conflict resolution paradigm that is dominant in a given culture. Cognition relates to ways of perceiving, understanding, conceiving what is at stake in a conflict: goods, money, power, technology, status, face concerns, etc. Cognitive obstacles and biases are sources of misperception, often the cause of failure in reaching an agreement (Jönsson, 1990). Cognition also relates to how the negotiation is perceived in itself, the nature of the game that the actors are playing: a strength test, a relationship, a search for justice, a palabra, a game of seduction, a construction exercise, a human adventure, etc. Cognition also concerns what one party knows about the other party. What are the driving perceptions operating: stereotypes, historical memory, past personal experiences, etc.? Stereotyping by bringing together various traits reduces cognitive complexity to simple terms, easier to handle during the preparation of the negotiation. Selective perceptions, attribution, perpetu-ate stereotypes, strengthen pre-notions and assumptions.

For Americans, negotiation is mainly a give and take exercise, but for the Japanese, it is far from being so and, in any case, much more of a relationship (Kimura, 1980: 65). How negotiators frame the situation and deal with it is influenced by their own culture. For instance, will a set of issues be viewed as a list of items to be discussed sequentially as Americans do, or will it be seen as a system of interconnected elements to be approached in a holistic way as the Japanese do (Graham & Sano, 1984: 29)?

Cross-cultural differences in the perception of time may also affect the conflict resolution process. In the West, time is conceived as a commodity that has a cost and should be used with parsimony. In contrast, in the Orient, time is often viewed as an unlimited resource like the air everyone breathes. As a consequence, time pressure will have very little effect on oriental negotiation behavior. As it has been said by a Chinese negotiator to his Western counterpart who was pushing him to quickly come to an agreement: "China has been able to do without your technology for 5000 years. We can wait for a few more years."

The way to consider conflict as normal, acceptable, unavoidable, or pathological leads people to deal differently with it. If people are used to living in tense contexts where aggressiveness often bursts, they will be much less disturbed than people who experience a much quieter life, such as in the case of a situation in which the counterpart becomes highly emotional. In doing business in Japan, what is viewed as a conflictual negotiation by the Japanese may not be seen as such by Americans. Similarly, what American negotiators often see as a delaying device can simply be for the Japanese the time needed to get to know the other party better. One of the major obstacles in joint venture negotiations in China, as shown by Faure (2000c), comes from the fact that both parties do not conceive the issues at stake and even the negotiation process itself in an identical way. Often, there is little compatibility between both views, thus leading to an agreement based on a huge misunderstanding.

Studies in chronometrics show that the way people organize and react to time varies according to cultures. Time is not an objective contextual component in which all events happen but a way to organize them (Macduff, 2006). Brislin and Kim (2003) distinguish between flexibility of time and the pace of time. The first category includes punctuality, and the polychronic/monochronic distinction. The category of pace encompasses patience/impatience, orientation to past, present, future, and perceptions about the efficient use of time. These various components of time may play a role at the negotiation table as they also vary considerably from one culture to another.

Views of time may strongly vary according to cultures. For instance, in discussions with government representatives of Canada with First Nation People on land claims, the latter tend to see time as stretching forward and back, binding them in relationship with several generations in both directions (LeBaron and Grundison, 1993).

Perception is constructed in the way that one perceives what he expects to perceive through selecting information that fits his learned categories. Using English in negotiating has some influence on the negotiation process. With its construction of subject–predicate, Kimmel (2000) underlines that English creates a world of objects that act or are acted on with fixed relationships between things and their attributes. It creates a causal world of actors–actions–results (Stewart, 1987). Other ways of thinking are judged as wrong or inferior or, at best, weird.

Culture may also influence how the parties interpret the outcome that has been attained. In some societies, an agreement is a final decision carved in marble that has to be strictly implemented. In others, an agreement is a written paper that was valid the day it was signed and which may be modified if the external conditions prevailing at the time of the signing have changed. For the Chinese, for instance, signing a contract is not closing a deal but substantiating a relationship at a certain stage of a long-term process.

The general approach to conflict resolution is clearly conditioned by actors' culture. To the Cartesian–analytical approach implemented in the West can be opposed by the holistic approach shared by the Chinese and Japanese. The first approach aims to split the problem into subsets and solve the difficulties as and when required; the second tends to assess the entire situation and learn how to accommodate the relative influence of the many forces involved (Redding, 1990). Within the whole problem, language, a basic cultural product, is a major instrument in cognitive activities. Problems can only be defined within existing categories as has already been emphasized. As commonly said, "if your only tool is a hammer, then every problem is a nail." Labeling is, thus, a major cultural activity that conditions and, to some extent, structures social action. Culture may also influence the method negotiators use in order to reach an agreement Kolb and Faure, 1994. Some cultures, such as the French or the German, favor a deductive approach, looking first for acceptable principles, and then applying them to concrete issues. Other cultures, such as the American, would rather adopt an inductive approach, dealing pragmatically with encountered difficulties, and underlying principles may only become discernible in the end (Salacuse, 1991).

Identity is the fourth level of intervention, the deepest, the most sensitive and the most difficult to deal with. Through symbols, for instance, we produce meanings and enact our identity. Identity addresses queries on the conception of the self, of responsibility, accountability to the group, to history, to future generations. Issues of honor mentioned in the introduction to this book are classified as one of the basic types of conflict issues (D'Neil, 1999; Mitchell, 1981). The Palestinian–Israeli conflict does not have only to do with sharing land, sovereignty, and division of scarce resources, such as water, but includes identity issues through acknowledgement and representation (Lowi and Rothman, 1993).

In international relations, we may identify by nationality, ethnic background, profession, religion, organization, ideological creeds, and many more sources. The point then is not to betray oneself by letting the whole reference group be attacked, humiliated, insulted. In some cultures, even a shopkeeper may feel offended if a client does not start bargaining before buying. People may be humiliated if they feel they are not treated adequately because of what they are, their origin, or their gender. It may also work the other way round and some people may expect to be treated better than others because they are perceived as different, for instance, when being upgraded on a long-haul flight. Identity can undergo negotiated change. Negotiation is construction, evolution of images, beliefs, perceptions, values as illustrated by Mezran (2007) on Magribi identities or by Zartman (2001).

When identity is not built by differentiation but mainly through opposition to the other party, any change likely to improve the conditions for a settlement may appear as a betrayal. Modifying the elements that comprise one's identity is a denial of oneself and can be viewed, at the symbolic level, as a destructive attempt. Fundamental core values such as national identity and national sovereignty (Salacuse, 1993) can easily, when challenged, turn a negotiation into a merciless fight. Difficult to grasp, highly complex to manipulate, extremely costly to restore, identity aspects remain the untouchable core of culture.

ASSESSING THE IMPORTANCE OF CULTURE IN CONFLICT RESOLUTION

Culture permeates all components of conflict resolution such as the understanding of the problem, the choice of a strategy, and the handling of the process. However, cultural awareness, if necessary, is not enough to solve the conflict. Going beyond this methodological postulate, some of the well-known literature on negotiation and conflict resolution such as *The Art and Science of Negotiation* (Raiffa, 1982) or *Getting to Yes* (Fisher and Ury, 1981) simply ignores culture. It is in itself an implicit judgment on how unimportant this dimension is for these authors. When considering explicit critical views on the relevance of culture as a causal variable, Zartman observes that it is often used as a convenient residual category to explain negative outcomes when nothing else works (Zartman, 1993). It also has the advantage of not putting into question the ability of the negotiator himself in case of failure.

Avruch (1998) discusses this issue in contrasting two basic views on culture in conflict resolution. On the one hand, we have Burton (1987) who considers culture as unimportant because all humans have similar needs which are nonnegotiable and which humans strive to fulfill. On the other hand, we have Lederach (1995) who sees culture as providing the logic by which people reason. Kimmel, addressing cultural awareness, ascribes the cause of the phenomenon of minimization of the importance of culture to the fact that people tend to believe that basic patterns of behavior are universal because "all adult humans are in some ways basically alike" (Kimmel,

2000: 162). Thus, Americans typically believe that everyone is basically alike and that people have the same essential needs as they have. Then, differences among people are believed to be individual, not cultural. This assumption is denounced by Kissinger (in *Diplomacy*, 1994) as "crusading universalism," when referring to the US underlying political culture in foreign affairs (Wanis, 2005: 125).

A skeptic such as Zartman (1993: 17), considering the current state of research on international negotiation, regards the understanding of its effects on the process as "tautological, [...] and its role in the process basically epiphenomenal." Culture tends to be defined tautologically. When culture is related to independent variables, these variables end up being cultural too. If, for instance, social structure is claimed to determine culture, at the same time, it is a cultural product. The view according to which culture has a real but feeble influence is also advocated by Gulliver (1979: 64). Culture mainly colors behavioral expressions of a strategic nature.

Basing their findings on case studies, Faure and Rubin (1993) observe that in time of crisis, when stakes are high, tensions exacerbated by culture may matter the most. The Middle East case provides a classic example of such a situation. Lempereur and Colson (2004) observe that experimental works tend to show that the results reached by a pair of negotiators of the same culture are rather identical whatever the culture is. This would lead to conclude that no culture is more effective than another in solving problems. However, a reservation could be brought up in the very concept of value creation. In addition, outcomes reached by pairs of different cultures are lower than those obtained by pairs of homogenous cultures. The difficulty in intercultural settings appears in a clear way, thus demonstrating the importance of culture.

In fact, as underlined by Elgström (1994), while raising the issue of the "internal validity" of culture as the relevant determinant, it is extremely difficult to precisely assess the relative influence of each major variable operating in the negotiation process. Outcomes can also be determined by other variables such as structural or process variables and it would not make sense to turn culture into the unique explanatory variable of a whole and often complex process. As shown by Druckman et al. (1976) in a study of bargaining behavior of Indians, Argentineans and Americans, culture does matter in determining behavior but other factors such as age, gender, and environment also play an important role, paving the way to multicausal models. The cultural component of a negotiation situation enters in a game of mutual influences with other components such as the structural and the strategic dimensions. The reality of a situation is never made of totally distinct, autonomous categories and its ultimate rationale borrows from the various interactions happening among these three dimensions.

Structural aspects are, for instance, widely conditioned by the social culture. Thus, legal frameworks and administrative ways of intervention are influenced by values and habits related to the culture in which they are embedded. Similarly, strategic behaviors are part of a range of choices narrowed by the possibilities offered by the law of the country and by the social norms to which actors abide. Thus, not any kind of move is allowed in a negotiation, and a number of "rules of the game" should be followed, reducing accordingly the margin of maneuver of the negotiators (Faure et al., 2000). In the same way, all that is culturally conceivable is not strategically feasible because of the nature of the interaction (common project or division of a resource) and the goals that are targeted reduce the field of what is possible. Lastly, from another angle, the strategic component, when often repeated or in the process of institutionalization, generates culture through the new norms that are set up.

As pointed out by Weiss (1999: 69), in a letter to the editor concerning an article he published on "culturally responsive strategies" (1994), Fukushima, discussing negotiations with Americans, has suggested three variables that "may be much more important than cultural familiarity: the purpose and context of the negotiation; the position of the counterpart in his or her organization; and the general disposition of the counterpart to negotiating with Americans."

Although quite open to the possible importance of the cultural dimension, Elgström (1994: 295) insists on the danger of having behaviors "ascribed to cultural factors, while, in fact, action is prescribed by the distribution of power, that is a structural phenomenon." For instance, he draws from his own research that Tanzanian negotiators seldom rejected an offer of foreign aid but not in the same way, as Japanese negotiators would hesitate to give a flat "no" as an answer. It should rather be attributed to the weakness of the Tanzanian bargaining position (Elgström, 1990).

Ross (1997) provides explanations for the very limited role conceited to culture by political scientists. One reason is simply the risk of transforming hopes for a rigorous analysis into "just so" accounts. Culture also offers a political discourse masking more serious differences dividing groups. Finally, employing the concept of culture may lead one to involve oneself in a series of controversies already deeply dividing anthropologists, such as relativism, the importance of searching for generalizations, the possibility of comparison and the role of psychological mechanisms in cultural explanations.

Another stream of critics with, for instance, Winham (1980), tend to emphasize the limited number of situations in which culture matters. In complex, multilateral, and highly professionalized negotiations, national cultures lose their importance or even relevance as explanatory factors. A strong objection to the importance of culture in negotiation and conflict resolution is raised by a number of psychologists who tend to consider that individual variables are by far the most important, and that personality is the leading force in the interaction process. The answers to this can only be found in real case studies and might even provide a different answer each time. In addition, and this restriction cannot be easily lifted, it is sometimes very difficult to draw a line between cultural variables and personality variables. If we consider, for instance, risk-taking behavior,

it may belong to both sets and only a specific investigation within a case study will enable the researcher to draw an accurate conclusion.

CURRENT RESEARCH ON CULTURAL ISSUES IN CONFLICT RESOLUTION

The first systematic observations made on culture as an object of study per se goes back to the founders of modern anthropology such as Tylor (1871), Linton (1936), and Benedict (1934). However, cross-cultural approaches providing concepts for comparing cultures only took place with Hall (1976), then Hofstede (1980). Further on, Hofstede refined and expanded his theory. New comparative research-finding appeared with Hampden-Turner and Trompenaars (2000) aiming to build cross-cultural competences. Exploring meaning-making, they define five axes along which people may position themselves: universalist/particularist, specific/diffuse, inner directed/outer directed, synchronous/sequential in using time.

Establishing systematic comparison between cultures is a much more difficult task than it could appear a priori because behind the same words, there can be very different realities. For instance, the Chinese concept of negotiation does not strictly overlap with the Anglo-Saxon concept (Faure, 1995a). The Chinese concept refers to a situation of conflict while the Anglo-Saxon concept is much wider and includes any type of divergence. This observation also applies to negotiation exercises and simulations, for a cooperative game in one culture can be viewed as a competitive game in another culture. Cooperation and competition correspond to semantic sets that vary according to cultures. As a consequence, experimental subjects will understand the implicit rules of the game differently. Then, comparing performances will not be totally relevant and the conclusions drawn can be strongly biased.

Research on international negotiation is also influenced by the cultural conditions of its development. Ways of looking at objects and ideas are culturalized, framed by given concepts and contemporary problematiques. Are the scientific means we possess today adapted to identically study a negotiation carried out in Manhattan and in Timbuktu? One cannot be fully positive about this issue.

The current bulk of research on cultural issues in conflict resolution is predominantly North American and demonstrates very little interest in non-US literature on the subject (Dupont, 1994). Again, culture comes into the picture to influence researchers on negotiation behaviors as well as negotiators' behaviors. As underlined by Weiss (1995), bodies of work on negotiation have developed outside the USA, for example in France, The Netherlands, Sweden, Argentina, and Russia. Indigenous research on international negotiation has even been carried out in unexpected places, such as Nepal or China (Faure, 1995c).

Research on international negotiation focusing on cultural variables or integrating cultural components in its models and paradigms has been very recently started and is still largely in the making. Four main streams of investigation can be distinguished: national negotiation styles, case studies, experimental psychology on specific variables, and comparative/integrated approaches.

National negotiating styles refer to negotiation practices as observed within diplomatic activities or business discussions. The Chinese negotiator is a strong object of interest (Fang, 1999; Faure, 1998, 1999a, 2000b, 2000c; Frankenstein, 1986; Kirkbride et al., 1991; Pye, 1982; Solomon, 1999). The Japanese negotiator has also raised considerable interest for US research (Blaker, 1977; Graham, 1993). Using a set of common characteristics, Casse (1982), then Weiss and Stripp (1985, 1998), compared six cultures putting the emphasis on negotiation conception, cultural predisposition and typical ways of acting for each negotiator. Salacuse (1991), directly addressing the negotiation activity, identifies ten factors that strongly characterize negotiating styles, each of them consisting of two opposite poles such as negotiating

goals (contract vs relationship), global attitude (win-win vs win-lose), time sensitivity (high vs low), and emotionalism (high vs low).

A second approach has been based on *case studies* done in domains such as diplomacy (Cohen, 1991; Dupont, 1993; Elgström, 1992; Jönsson, 1979; Kimura, 1980; Smyser, 2002; Snyder, 1999; Wittes, 2005), business (Blaker, Giarra and Vogel, 2002; Chen, 1999; Faure, 1998; Li, 1999), anthropology (Gulliver, 1979), and environmental issues (Sjöstedt, 2003). The purpose is to draw analysis contributing to a better understanding of the mechanisms used in these different situations to solve a difficult problem.

A third category of research concerns social psychology and resorts to *experimental settings*. The point is to know to which extent a pre-selected variable plays a role in a built-up negotiation situation. Among the representatives of this approach are Jehn and Weldon (1997), Adair and Brett (2004), Leung (1997), Graham, Mintu and Rodgers (1994); Graham (1983, 1984, 1993); and Kirkbride, Tang and Westwood (1991).

A fourth stream aims by various means, such as comparative methods, to draw observations and conclusions of a more general reaching. Among those *integrative attempts* can be mentioned anthropological-oriented works (Avruch, 1998; Faure, 2003; Nader and Todd, 1978; Zartman, 2001). Other scholars have drawn their findings from materials from international business (Salacuse, 1991; Weiss, 1993), or from putting into perspective several types of investigations (Faure and Rubin, 1993; Fisher, 1980; Kimmel, 2000; Wanis, 2005). For instance, Salacuse (1991) divides the negotiation process into three phases, each of them having a particular objective and a specific rationale. Similarly, Cohen (1991) scrutinizes the impact of different negotiation styles during various stages of the conflict resolution process.

DEBATED ISSUES

An important debate relates to the very object of the research: the strategic or the cognitive dimension of the conflict. Both are essential for developing knowledge but now the cognitive approach tends to be of a growing importance in current research (Avruch, 1998; Faure, 2003). The point is to grasp images, representations, and conceptions, which is what will organize the understanding that the actor has of the situation and his motivations and which will as a consequence influence his behavior. Thus, there is an evolution in research from the strategic approach inherited from Morgenthau, based on objective criteria in terms of cost benefits, to a system of interpretation inherited from the Weberian tradition which puts the emphasis on the meaning that actors give to their actions. Lederach (1995) insists on the fact that culture provides the logic by which people reason, and thus define problems and deal with them.

A number of researchers contend that most of the conflicts grounded in cultural differences are about definition and perception of social reality (Avruch, 1998; Kimmel, 2000). Ross (1997b) argues, "The most widely cited weakness of rational choice theory is its inattention to context specific interests and cross-cultural differences in how interests are conceptualized." The importance of the language used in international meetings is emphasized by Kimmel (2000). With its grammatical construction of subject–predicate, "English creates a world of objects with fixed relations between things and their attributes. English speakers think of a causal world of actors–actions–results" (Stewart, 1987). Attitudes by themselves do not give a clear idea about real intentions unless understood through the cultural prism. Jehn and Weldon (1997), while studying conflict handling in China, observe that, for instance, an attitude expressing a care for avoiding conflict in one culture, such as keeping silent, can be viewed as aggressive in another culture.

On the concept of culture

The concept itself raises problems as culture is, according to Weiss, "neither consistently nor adequately defined" (1999: 70). Anthropologists such as Kroeber and Kluckhohn (1963) have collected more than 160 different definitions of culture. Weiss also observes that authors such as Avruch and Black (1991), and Poortinga and Hendriks (1989) have picked up on very different uses of the term culture. Janosik (1987) has identified four basic approaches, each one related to a specific understanding of the concept and its whereabouts. The first, culture as learned behavior, refers to what people do rather than what they think. The second defines it as shared values; the third views culture as a bundle of components "in tension" with each other; while the fourth contends that culture has to be approached within a context (personal, social) to fully reach its meaningful aspects. Studying culture within negotiation raises an important point about the nature of negotiation. Should negotiation be simply viewed as "a communication process to resolve some matter over which parties are in conflict," as stated by Adair and Brett (2004: 158)?

Zartman (1993) contends also that culture, viewed as a sum of behavioral traits of a collectivity, remains a vague concept, a "cultural basket," and even a "ghost" whose significance is never clearly defined. For this author, culturalists do not seriously substantiate their assertions and, in no case, "relate distinct behavior in a common process to independent cultural traits" (1993: 18). Zartman underlines the difficulty in identifying the cultural roots of a negotiator, as each person belongs at the same time to a national culture, possibly an ethnic one, a religious system of values, a professional one, a family one, and an organizational one. Relying excessively on such a tool as culture runs the risk of stereotyping the counterpart, thus reducing the potential for creativity in devising a solution (see Zartman in this book).

On methodology

In the domain of international relations, Ross (1997a) observes that political scientists are simply reluctant to resort to concepts such as culture. He provides an explanation by pointing out that for them, culture violates canons of methodological individualism while raising serious unit of analysis problems for which there are no easy answers. For those who go beyond this reservation, other essential questions are asked. Should research still focus on "national character" as it has been done since early anthropological studies, or should it be limited to "negotiating styles" as suggested by Avruch (1998: 31)? Taking an opposite stance, Adair and Brett (2004: 159) resort to "national boundaries to identify cultures, because national boundaries define institutional bound, and as a result provide an objective way to distinguish cultural groups."

Most of what we know about cultural styles in conflict resolution is based on observations made in individuals' and groups' practices in intracultural negotiations. We should not take for granted that in intercultural negotiations, behaviors should be alike (Frances, 1991; Weiss, 1987). How representative of a group is an individual? How much of the norms of his or her social group has he or she internalized? Knowing the cultural norms of a group does not always help to predict the behavior of one of its members, which reduces the usefulness of national taxonomies such as "Chinese negotiators tend to do that and that in such a situation ..." In international negotiations, there is a tendency to overestimate the homogeneity of the out-group (Jönsson, 1990), which introduces a bias when compared with reality. If "no negotiator is a cultural robot" as stated by Salacuse (1993, 201), if the range of options he or she can take at some stage of the conflict resolution process is too wide, there is no room for predictability.

Grasping the attitude of the parties during the conflict resolution process with an objective and universal tool is another challenge. What is essential is not so much the behaviors as such but the meanings they carry in the minds of their authors. Does the simple fact of never objecting to an offer in a negotiation imply a positive attitude? An objective observation does not guarantee the scientific quality of what has been found.

Should similar tools be used to investigate an analytical culture such as the Western one and a holistic culture such as the Chinese? Until now, research has only implemented analytical approaches, which ultimately lead to try to understand a culture exclusively through the lenses of another. Are, for instance, Western personality constructs relevant in a Chinese context? This is a question that requires digging deeper in this domain (Liu, Friedman and Chi, 2002).

"Emic" aspects of culture are what make a culture unique as opposed to "etic" aspects, being what provides ground for comparisons. Emics are especially of interest to the social anthropologist and etics to the cross-cultural psychologist. Research tends to resort to etic measurements of emic constructs, for instance, social distance in various societies. However, the basis of social distance is often an emic attribute such as tribe, religion, social group, nationality. Then, what is used as an indicator in one culture to measure social distance may not make sense in another culture. For instance, asking an American if "he would mind having a Turk touch his earthenware," which is a question that only makes sense in India (Triandis, 1994, p. 72). In fact, research should go in an opposite direction and use emic measurements of etic constructs by first building separately parallel scales by members of each culture and only afterward compare and standardize them.

What experimentalists often call negotiators are not negotiators but students who are asked to negotiate in an artificial setting. Thus, the findings when any should not be labeled, for instance, US negotiators vs Brazilian negotiators but US students vs Brazilian students, put in an artificial negotiation situation. Clearly, these experiments do not have much in common with the work of diplomats or business people dealing with international issues.

NEW AREAS FOR RESEARCH

Reviewing what has been achieved and considering what should still be done,

Faure (2002) concluded that future research on the complex links that culture keeps with negotiation should be articulated around four main perspectives:

- The shift from a comparative focus to an intercultural investigation;
- A stronger concern for interpreting contradictions within any cultural set;
- A better connection between the cognitive aspect and the behavioral dimension;
- A clearer positioning of the cultural dimension with regard to the strategic dimension.

Comparative approaches, taxonomic studies describing a negotiation and approaches drawn from anthropology exploring negotiation styles have clear merits but also obvious limitations. Other types of queries are taking place. Another type of approach, still largely to come, consists in bringing the focus on the chemistry resulting from the interaction between two cultures. If the point were not to predict some kind of outcome, at least it would be most important to introduce some understanding of what happens in this complex interaction with such an uncertain result. Work has been done in this area with French–German relations after World War II (Demorgon et al., 2003). Weiss (1994b) has proposed a range of eight cultural strategies among which the negotiator may choose according to the parties' level of familiarity with each other's culture. Among them are: to employ an agent, to adapt to the counterpart's script, to induce the counterpart to follow one's own script or to transcend either home culture by improvising a new script ("effect symphony").

More investigation is needed on topics such as the problem of within-culture variation, for instance, at the negotiation table within each party. If a negotiation lasts long enough, it may allow or even trigger significant evolutions in terms of values, beliefs, and perceptions.

Another query addresses the topic of universality. Are there universals in conflict resolution approaches such as not only concepts but also rationales, and resolution methods that allow going beyond the uniqueness of a situation?

The recurring question on the possible influence of culture, which is aporetic, should be replaced, as suggested by Faure and Rubin (1993: 229), by a more relevant type of enquiry on the special conditions or circumstances under which culture matters. This question has been addressed on the issue of power, especially when the power relation is imbalanced. Cohen (1991) contends that culture has limited effects "in any situation in which force majeure can be involved, when the weaker has no choice but to comply with the will of the strongest." Thus, power trumps cultural issues. However, even the neo-realists consider that in the case of protracted conflicts such as dealing with identity, or ethnicity, even large power discrepancies do not matter very much. The debate remains open. What has to be kept in mind for future research is to go further in exploring the circumstances within which the cultural dimension plays or does not play a role in taking into account contextual, organizational, strategic variables as well as the type of stake.

Nonverbal communication should also have far more importance than is often the case, as it is essential in high context cultures where indirect approaches and face saving are prerequisites for maintaining harmony between the parties to the dispute.

The role of identity in conflict resolution has not been explored enough although useful attempts have been carried out (Faure and Rubin, 1993; Freshman, 2005; Zartman, 2001). The assumption of a fixed identity also often prevails, which runs counter to realistic research (Freshman, 2005: 102). Identity beliefs are too often treated as obstacles and have not been given a fair status in explaining processes of conflict resolution and outcomes. Economists, for instance, tend to put them in the same category as emotions, just hampering rational agreements. Another direction for research would be to see in which situations culture could be used as an "enabler" of conflict management practices, as suggested by Wanis-St John (2005).

When considering the three main types of activity people resort to in conflict resolution: concession-convergence, compensation, and transformation, it would be most useful to do research on the influence of culture on each of the logics related to these activities. Are values, beliefs, norms, and conceptions influential? If so, how and what are the outcomes?

FROM THEORY TO PRACTICE

Application of research findings in real world situations is far from being satisfactory. The very weak relation between theory and practice has several causes. Researchers sometimes formulate their analysis in a language that is so far from what practitioners may expect for an effective communication that they are simply not read. Findings are sometimes so scattered and the passage from the descriptive–explanatory level to the normative–prescriptive level appears extremely difficult, although considerable efforts have been made in this domain with the PIN books (see Faure and Rubin, 1993; Sjöstedt, 2003).

Practitioners in action, pressured by deadlines, do not always have enough time and motivation to read full books whose content applicable to their needs may be tenuous. Confronted with the urgent necessities of their task, they may also realize that cultures are far more complex and much less homogeneous than the model offered by current taxonomies. Negotiators' culture aggregates a number of variables and de facto combines several cultures. It may thus be quite a challenge to make an effective use of what has been learned about one type of national negotiating style. In addition, if knowing the language of the counterpart is important, it is far from being sufficient to grasp the whole of the complexities of a culture in a conflict situation. And, finally, culture evolves throughout time, making behaviors sometimes still very difficult to predict when coming to practice at the negotiation table.

The most important opportunity for transferring knowledge into practice is done through training. Intercultural training programs have developed tremendously in these last decades, especially with the globalization process. However, very few address substantive issues directly related to conflict resolution or mediation. They rather deal with cultural self-awareness and focus on cultural assumptions that have been unconsciously internalized. They may also deal with the cultural assumptions that exist in the group sitting at the other side of the negotiation table. However, not much has been beyond knowing and understanding each other's perspectives. Questions about what to do and how to do it are still very much in need of answers.

The basic hypothesis on which intercultural training workshops rely is simply that they can provide the participants with skills for modifying their psycho-cultural interpretations, and for developing new metaphors allowing parties to view each other differently (Avruch, 1998; Ross, 1997a). Wanis-St John (2005: 129) suggests that parties should "move toward ethno-relative approaches" and once they have recognized their own cultural preferences, and understood others, they should be able to build bridges between them. In intercultural negotiation, the maxim "do unto others as you would have them do unto you" does not apply as soon as we abandon the universalistic assumption.

One of the most important practical uses of cultural differences is in creativity to seek new options when confronted with a problem. Each culture has a specific range of capabilities for innovating. As both ranges do not strictly overlap, the resulting range is wider than any of the one culture range, thus broadening the scope of possible options.

When the point in a negotiation is to bridge the cultural gap, in order to operate effectively, Salacuse (1999: 233) suggests several ways:

- Learn about the other side's culture.
- Do not stereotype. Treat people as individuals, not as cultural robots.

- Bridge the gap using the other side's culture to identify and build a relationship.
- Use one's own culture, helping the other to become more familiar with it.
- Combine elements from both cultures in an integrative cultural blend.
- Resort to a third culture if, for instance, both sides have studied or lived in a common country.

Culture may also be strategically instrumentalized by shrewd negotiators. A clever Chinese negotiator may, for instance, make his foreign counterpart believe that he is acting according to social habits and traditions, when in fact he is playing with these strategically. The foreign negotiator has to carefully assess which one is the driving force behind the Chinese behavior and to this purpose find significant indicators.

When one knows enough about the culture of the other, the subsequent question is what to do. The advice of "when in Rome do as the Romans" may not be either always feasible or effective (Weiss, 1994a&b). It is far from being obvious that when in China, a Western negotiator is expected to behave like a Chinese person. Such behavior may raise more questions than answers and end up confusing the other party.

A number of practice-oriented books have been published such as Foster (1992), Moran and Stripp (1991), and Salacuse (1991), giving clues and advice about what to do while negotiating in some specific circumstances. Research has also provided some useful conclusions that can be used by practitioners to foresee what could happen when negotiating. Elgström (1994: 295) points out the following observations:

- The degree of dissimilarity between negotiating parties makes culture exert more impact (Cohen, 1987: 75).
- Culturally caused misunderstandings are more prevalent in new relationships than between parties that have been meeting on a regular basis (Elgström, 1990).
- When essential interests are at stake, culture has less opportunity to influence the negotiation process (Cohen, 1987: 76).

Other useful findings show that the role of culture is correlated with the intensity of the conflict. As conflict increases, so does the role of culture (Faure and Rubin, 1993: 216). Complex, multilateral, long-lasting negotiations (such as the WTO) leave less room for cultural influences than one-shot, bilateral encounters (Winham, 1980).

Considerable efforts have been made to grasp and explain mechanisms that conduct a particular culture to solve conflict among its members (Faure, 2003; Gulliver, 1979; Nader and Todd, 1978; Zartman, 2000). However, knowing that there are still something like 8000 cultures remaining in the world, and that the speed of extinction is such that after a generation there might be only a few hundred left, it is more than urgent to investigate these societies to get a better understanding of the basic process of conflict resolution in its multiple expressions.

REFERENCES

Adair W. and Brett J. (2004). Culture and Negotiation Processes. In Gelfand M.J. and Brett J., The Handbook of Negotiation and Culture. Stanford University Press.

Adler N. (1986). International Dimensions of Organizational Behavior. Boston, Kent Publishing.

Akoun A. (1989). L'illusion Sociale. Paris, PUF.

Avruch K. (1998). Culture and Conflict Resolution. Washington, DC, United States Institute of Peace Press.

Avruch K. and Black P.W. (1991). The Culture Question and Conflict Resolution. Peace and Change, 16, 1, 22–45.

Benedict R. (1934). *Patterns of Culture*. Boston: Houghton Mifflin.

Binnendijk H. (1987). National Negotiating Styles. Washington, DC, US Department of State.

Blaker M. (1977). Japanese International Negotiating Style. New York, Columbia University Press.

Blaker M., Giarra P. and Vogel E. (2002). Case Studies in Japanese Behavior. Washington, DC, US Institute of Peace Press.

Brislin R. and Kim E. (2003). 'Cultural diversity in people's understanding and uses of time', *Applied Psychology*, volume 52, July 2003.

Burton J. (1987). Resolving Deep-Rooted Conflict: A Handbook. Lanham, MD and London: University Press of America.

Carnevale P. and Radhakrishnan P. (1994). Group Endowment and the Theory of Collectivism. University of Illinois at Urbana-Champaign, Department of Psychology.

Casse P. (1982). Training for the Multicultural Manager. Washington, DC, Society of Intercultural Education, Training, and Research.

Chen D. (1999) Three-dimensional Chinese Rationales in Negotiation. In Kolb D., Negotiation Eclectics. Cambridge, MA, PON Books.

Cogan C. (2003) French Negotiating Behavior: Dealing with la Grande Nation. Washington, DC, United States Institute of Peace Press.

Cohen R. (1987) International Communication: An Intercultural Approach. Cooperation and Conflict, 22, 1, 63–80.

Cohen R. (1991) Negotiating across Cultures: Communication Obstacles in International Diplomacy. Washington, DC, US Institute of Peace Press.

Cohen R. (1993). An Advocate's View. In Faure G.O. and Rubin J., Culture and Negotiation. Newbury Park, CA, Sage.

Demorgon J., Lipiansky E.-M. Muller B. and H. Nicklas (2003). Dynamiques interculturelles pour l'Europe. Paris, Anthropos.

Deng F. (1993). Northern and Southern Sudan: the Nile. In Faure G.O. and Rubin J., Culture and Negotiation. Newbury Park, CA, Sage.

Druckman D. et al. (1976). Cultural Differences in Bargaining Behavior: India, Argentina, and the U.S. *Journal of Conflict Resolution*, 20, 3.

Dupont C. (1993). Switzerland, France, Germany, the Netherlands: the Rhine. In Faure G.O. and Rubin J., Culture and Negotiation. Newbury Park, CA, Sage.

Dupont C. (1994). La négociation: conduite, théorie, applications. Paris, Dalloz.

Elgström O. (1990). Norms, Culture, and Cognitive Problems in Foreign Aid Negotiations. Negotiation Journal, 6, 2.

Elgström O. (1992). Foreign Aid Negotiations. Aldershot, Avebury.

ElgstrÖM O. (1994). National Culture and International Negotiations. Cooperation and Conflict, 29, 3.

Fang T. (1999). Chinese Business Negotiating Style. Thousand Oaks, Sage.

Faure G.O. (1995a). Conflict Formulation: The Cross Cultural Challenge. In Bunker B. and Rubin J. (eds), Conflict, Cooperation, and Justice. San Francisco, Jossey- Bass.

Faure G.O. (1995c). Research on Negotiation in China. PIN Points, Laxenburg, Austria, 8.

Faure G.O. (1998). Negotiation: the Chinese concept. Negotiation Journal, 14, 1.

Faure G.O. (1999a). The Cultural Dimension of Negotiation: The Chinese Case. Group Decision and Negotiation, Kluwer Academic Publishers, 9, 3.

Faure G.O. (1999b). L'approche chinoise de la négociation: stratégies et stratagèmes. Gérer et Comprendre, Annales des Mines, Juin, 36–48.

Faure G.O. (2000a) Traditional Conflict Management in Africa and China. In Zartman I.W., Traditional Cures for Modern Conflicts : African Conflict Medicine. Boulder, CO, Lynne Rienner.

Faure G.O. (2000b). Joint Ventures in China and their Negotiation, in Kremenyuk V. and Sjöstedt G., International Economic Negotiation. Cheltenham, UK, Edward Elgar.

Faure G.O. (2000c). Negotiation for Setting up Joint Ventures in China. International Negotiation, 5, 1.

Faure G.O. (2002). Negotiation: The Cultural Dimension. In International Negotiations: Analysis, Approaches, Issues, Kremenyuk (ed.), V. San Francisco, CA.

Faure G.O. (2003). How People Negotiate. Dordrecht, Kluwer Academic Publishers.

Faure G.O. and Rubin J. (eds) (1993). Culture and Negotiation. Newbury Park, CA, Sage.

Faure G.O., Mermet L., Touzard H., and Dupont C. (2000). La négociation: situations et problématiques. Paris, Editions Dunod.

Fisher G. (1980). International Negotiations: A Cross-cultural Perspective. Yarmouth, ME, Intercultural Press.

Fisher R. and Ury W. (1981). Getting to Yes: Negotiating Agreements without Giving in. Boston, Houghton Mifflin.

Foster D.A. (1992). Bargaining across Borders. New York, McGraw-Hill.

Frances J.N.P. (1991). When in Rome: The Effects of Cultural Adaptation on Intercultural Business Negotiations. *Journal of International Business Studies*, 22, 403–428.

Frankenstein J. (1986). Trends in Chinese Business Practices: Changes in the Beijing Wind. California Management Review, 29, 1.

Freshman C. (2005). Identity, Beliefs, Emotions, and Negotiation Success. In Moffitt M. and Bordone R., The Handbook of Dispute Resolution. Harvard, PON, Harvard Law School.

Gauthey F. (1995). Au-delà de la malédiction de Babel. A.N.D.C.P. Personnel, 360, Mai.

Graham J. (1983). Brazilian, Japanese, and American Business Negotiations. *Journal of International Business Studies*, Spring/Summer.

Graham J. (1984). A Comparison of Japanese and American Business Negotiations. *International Journal of Research in Marketing*, 1.

Graham J. (1993). The Japanese Negotiating Style: Characteristics of a Distinct Approach. *Negotiation Journal*, 9, 2, April.

Graham J., Mintu A., and Rodgers W. (1994). Explorations of Negotiation Behavior in Ten Foreign Cultures Using a Model Developed in the United States. Management Science, 40, 1.

Graham J. and Sano Y. (1984). Smart Bargaining: Doing Business with the Japanese. Cambridge, MA, Ballinger.

Gulliver P.H. (1979). Disputes and Negotiation: A Cross-cultural Perspective. New York, Academic Press.

Hall E. (1976). Beyond Culture. New York, Doubleday.

Herskovitz M.J. (1955). Cultural Anthropology. New York, Knopf.

Hofstede G. (1980). Culture's Consequences. Beverly Hills, CA, Sage.

Hofstede G. (1989). Cultural Predictors of National Negotiating Styles. In Mautner-Markhof F. (ed.), Processes of International Negotiation. Boulder, CO, Westview.

Hofstede G. (2001). Culture's Consequences: Comparing Values, Behaviors, Institutions, and Organizations across Nations, 2nd edn. Thousand Oaks, CA, Sage.

Huntington S. (1987). The goals of development. In Weiner M. and Huntington S. (eds), Understanding Political Development. Boston, Little Brown.

Janosik R. (1987). Rethinking the Culture-Negotiation Link. *Negotiation Journal*, 3.

Jehn K.A. and Weldon E. (1997). Management Attitudes toward Conflict: Cross-cultural Differences in Resolution Styles. *Journal of International Management*, 3, 4, 291–321.

Jönsson C. (1979). Soviet Bargaining Behavior: The Nuclear Test Ban Case. New York, Columbia University Press.

Jönsson C. (1990). Communication in International Bargaining. London, Pinter.

Kimmel P. (2000). Culture and Conflict. In Deutsch M. and Coleman P., Handbook of Conflict Resolution: Theory and Practice. San Francisco, Jossey- Bass.

Kimura H. (1980). Soviet and Japanese Negotiation Behavior: The Spring 1977 Fisheries Talks. Orbis, 24, 1.

Kirkbride P., Tang S. and Westwood R. (1991). Chinese Conflict Preferences and Negotiating Behavior: Cultural and Psychological Influences. Organization Studies, 12, 3, 365–386.

Kissinger H. (1994). Diplomacy. New York, Simon and Schuster.

Kolb D. and Faure G.O. (1994). Organizational Theory: The Interface of Structure, Culture, Procedures and Negotiation Process. In Zartman I.W., International Multilateral Negotiation. San Francisco, Jossey- Bass.

Kroeber A. and Kluckhohn C. (1963). Culture: A Critical Review of Concepts and Definitions. New York, Random House.

LeBaron M. and Grundison B. (1993). *Conflict and Culture: Research in Five Communities in British Columbia*. Victoria, British Columbia: University of Victoria.

Lederach J.P. (1995). Preparing for Peace: Conflict Transformation Across Cultures. Syracuse, Syracuse University Press.

Lempereur A. et Colson A. (2004). *Méthode de négociation*, Paris, Dunod.

Leung K. (1997) Negotiation and Award Allocation Across Cultures. In Earley P.C. and Erez M., New Perspectives on International Industrial/Organizational Psychology. San Francisco, Jossey-Bass.

Li X. (1999). Chinese-Dutch Business Negotiations. Amsterdam, Rodopi.

Linton R. (1936) *The Study of Man.* Appleton-Century, New York.

Liu L., Friedman R., and Chi S. (2002). Negotiating in Different Cultures: Are Western Personality Dimensions Relevant in Chinese Culture? Paper submitted at the 15th Annual Conference of the International Association for Conflict Management.

Lowi M. and Rothman J. (1993). Arabs and Israelis: The Jordan River. In Faure G.O. & Rubin J., Culture and Negotiation. Newbury Park, CA, Sage.

Macduff I. (2006). 'Your Pace or Mine? Culture, Time, and Negotiation', *Negotiation Journal* 22 (1), 31–45.

Mezran K. (2007). Negotiation and Construction of National Identities. Boston, MA, Martin Nijhoff.

Moran R.T. and Stripp W.G. (1991). Dynamics of Successful International Business Negotiations. Houston, Gulf.

Nader L. and Todd H.F. (1978). The Disputing Process: Law in Ten Societies. New York, Columbia University Press.

O'Neill B. (1999). *Symbols, Honor and War.* Ann Arbor, MI: University of Michigan Press.

Poortinga Y.H. and Hendriks E.C. (1989). Culture as a Factor in International Negotiations: A Proposed Research Project from a Psychological Perspective. In Mautner-Markhof F., Processes of International Negotiation. Boulder, CO, Westview Press.

Pye L. (1982). Chinese Commercial Negotiating Style. Cambridge, Oelgeschlager, Gunn and Hain.

Raiffa H. (1982). The Art and Science of Negotiation. Cambridge, MA, Harvard University Press.

Redding G. (1990). The Spirit of Chinese Capitalism. Berlin, De Gruyter.

Ross M.H. (1997a). The Relevance of Culture for the Study of Political Psychology and Ethnic Conflict. Political Psychology, 2, 299–326.

Ross M.H. (1997b) Culture and Identity in Comparative Political Analysis. In Lichbach M. and Zuckerman A. (eds), Comparative Politics: Rationality, Culture, and Structure. Cambridge University Press.

Roth A. et al. (1991). Bargaining and Market Behavior in Jerusalem, Ljubljana, Pittsburgh, and Tokyo: An Experimental Study. American Economic Review, 81.

Salacuse J. (1993). Implications for Practitioners. In Faure G.O. & Rubin J., Culture and Negotiation. Newbury Park, CA, Sage.

Salacuse J. (1999). Intercultural Negotiation in International Business. Group Decision and Negotiation, Kluwer Academic Publishers, 9, 3.

Shakun M. (1999). An Esd Computer Culture for Intercultural Problem Solving and Negotiation. Group Decision and Negotiation, 8, 3.

Sjöstedt G. (2003). Professional Cultures in International Negotiation: Bridge or Rift? Lanham, Boulder.

Smyser W.R. (2002). How Germans Negotiate. Washington, DC, United States Institute of Peace Press.

Snyder S. (1999). North Korean Negotiating Behavior. Washington, DC, United States Institute of Peace Press.

Solomon R. (1999). Chinese Negotiating Behavior. Washington, DC, United States Institute of Peace Press.

Stewart E.C. (1987). The Primordial Roots of Being. Zygon, 22, 87–107.

Triandis H.C. (1994). Culture and Social Behavior. New York, McGraw-Hill.

Trompenaars F. (1993) Riding the Waves of Culture: Understanding Cultural Diversity in Business. London, The Economist Books.

Trompenaars F. and Hampden-Turner C. (2000). *Building Cross-Cultural Competence: How to Create Wealth from Conflicting Values.* Yale University Press.

Tylor E.B. (1971) *Primitive Culture: Researches into the Development of Mythology, Philosophy, Religion.* London: John Murray.

Wanis-St John A. (2005). Cultural Pathways in Negotiation and Conflict Management. In Moffitt M. and Bordone R., The Handbook of Dispute Resolution. Harvard, Pon, Harvard Law School.

Weiss S.E. (1987). Negotiation and Culture: Some Thoughts on Models, Ghosts, and Options. National Institute of Dispute Resolution. Newsletter, Washington, NIDR.

Weiss S.E. (1993). Analysis of Complex Negotiations in International Business: The RBC Perspective. Organization Science, 4, 2.

Weiss S.E. (1994a). Negotiating with "Romans": Part 1. Sloan Management Review, 35, 2, 51–61.

Weiss S.E. (1994b). Negotiating with "Romans": Part 2. Sloan Management Review, 35, 3, 85–99.

Weiss S.E. (1995). International Business Negotiations Research: Bricks, Mortar, and Prospects. In Punnett B. and Shenkar O., Handbook on International Management Research. Blackwell Publishers.

Weiss S. (1994) *Sloan Management Review*, Spring, pp. 85–99.

Weiss S. (1999). Opening a Dialogue on Negotiation and Culture: A "Believer" Considers Skeptics' Views. In Kolb D., Negotiation Eclectics. Cambridge, MA, Pon Books.

Weiss S. and Stripp W. (1985). Negotiating with Foreign Business Persons. Working Paper 85–6, New York University Graduate School of Business Administration.

Weiss S. and Stripp W. (1998). Negotiating with Foreign Business Persons: An Introduction for Americans with Propositions on Six Cultures. In Niemeier S., Campbell C.P., and Dirven R. (eds), The Cultural Context in Business Communication (pp. 51–118). Amsterdam: John Benjamins Publishing Company.

Winham G.R. (1980). International Negotiation in an Age of Transition. *International Journal*, 35, 1–20.

Wittes T.C. (2005). How Israelis and Palestinians Negotiate. Washington, DC, United States Institute of Peace Press.

Zartman I.W. (1993). A Skeptic's View. In Faure G.O. & Rubin J., Culture and Negotiation. Newbury Park, CA, Sage.

Zartman I.W. (2001). Negotiating Identity: From Metaphor to Process. International Negotiation, 2.

Zartman I.W. and Faure G.O. (2005). Escalation and Negotiation in International Conflicts. Cambridge University Press.

27

Peacekeeping and Beyond

Paul F. Diehl

Scholarly work on peacekeeping and related concerns has undergone a number of transitions, roughly paralleling changes and developments in the practice of peace operations on the global stage. Practitioners provided the first systematic analysis of peacekeeping operations, with scholars joining the enterprise relatively late. Single case studies have given way to large N research, some of which are now data based. The exclusive focus on traditional peacekeeping operations has evolved to a consideration of a broader set of peace operations. Among the constants, however, are the focus on explaining mission effectiveness (even as such success is ill-defined) and the largely atheoretical character of the studies.

This chapter reviews the major concerns and findings associated with peacekeeping research, with special attention to what scholarly research can tell us about peacekeeping and where significant gaps still remain. A note on terminology is appropriate at the outset. 'Peacekeeping' will be used throughout the chapter to designate a wide range of peace operations, recognizing that there are significant variations among them and that different labels are frequently used; indeed, a section below discusses some definitional differences. Distinctions are made, however, when theoretical arguments or empirical findings are applicable to only a subset of operations, such as peace-building ones.

THE STUDY OF PEACE OBSERVATION AND PEACEKEEPING: A FIRST CUT

The term 'peacekeeping' first became common around the time most analysts pinpoint to be the first peacekeeping operation – the United Nations Emergency Force (UNEF I) in 1956, deployed as a part of defusing the Suez Crisis. Nevertheless, there were a number of precursors to peacekeeping operations, most notably what are referred to as peace observation missions; such operations generally involved a small number of unarmed personnel, who would report back to the authorizing organization on whichever matters (e.g. plebiscites, cease-fires) were contained in the mandate. Some scholarly attention was paid to such operations, but it was largely embedded in broader studies of the sponsoring organizations, such as the League of Nations. These (e.g. Barros, 1968) were largely historical accounts of the operations, with attention directed primarily to the authorization, budgets, and results of individual missions. The most comprehensive compilation of information on these missions is found in Wainhouse (1966), who reports on 40-plus operations over the period since the founding of the League of Nations through the early 1960s. Although he mixes different kinds of missions (early observer mission with enforcement actions in Korea and a peacekeeping operation in Cyprus), this study is definitive for detailing the bases of the disputes that preceded the operations, the politics surrounding the authorization of the missions, and ultimately a brief evaluation of each operation. Yet this classic and other works that are of the same era and before are primarily useful as secondary sources for researchers interested in particular operations.

The first true peacekeeping studies would not appear until peacekeeping as a strategy became more common in the early 1960s, but even then, such works shared significant limitations with their precursors, even as they became more numerous. Most notably, almost every one of the early works on peacekeeping was an idiographic, single case study. These include analyses of peacekeeping operations in the Middle East, Cyprus, and the Congo most notably (e.g. Frye, 1957; Rosner, 1963; Carnall, 1965; Lefever, 1967; Abi-Saab, 1978; House, 1978). Such works are excellent sources for understanding the backgrounds to the relevant crises as well as the UN authorization and implementation processes; for the latter, Security Council records and UN documents are the primary reference bases.

The purposes of these works were not so much to understand peacekeeping as a general phenomenon, but to provide thick description and understanding of the case at hand. All of these studies contain an evaluation of the successes and failures associated with each mission, although few, if any, contain any specific criteria for those evaluations. Generalizations beyond the case at hand are sometimes offered, but it is not clear to what extent they may be applicable beyond that context. In accounting for operational dynamics or outcomes, such studies focused heavily on macro-level factors, particularly those related to the authorizing organization; for example, the clarity of the mandate and adequate resources were frequently cited as key concerns.

A related set of peacekeeping analyses in this same era comes from UN personnel, professional military officers, or organizations that train peacekeepers and conduct operations. These studies are aptly characterized by Paris (2000) as focused almost exclusively on policy issues, rather than on theoretical concerns. Most are dedicated to 'lessons learned,' a term repeatedly used in the literature. The goal of these analyses is to derive guidelines and policy prescriptions from past peacekeeping operations so as to improve the performance of future operations. Not surprisingly, virtually all of these prescriptions are those at the micro or operational level. These are the elements most familiar to the authors as well as those most subject to policy adaptation. Accordingly, these studies focus on doctrinal issues, problems in command and control of troops, coordination of multinational units, and tactical aspects of peacekeeping. Memoirs or reflections of former peacekeeping commanders (e.g. Bull, 1973; Allan, 1996) tend to be particularly narrow, indicative of the scope of their experiences, whereas those authored by UN personnel (e.g. Rikhye, 1984) or private organizations, such as the International Peace Academy (e.g. International Peace Academy, 1984), reflect a greater breadth of operational concerns and any guidelines tend to be drawn from a wider set of peacekeeping experiences.

What can be gleaned from this practitioner literature? At one level, there are a number of practical guidelines on how to conduct a peacekeeping operation, and some significant convergence on those basic principles. Nevertheless, there are two notable limitations. First, if most of the precepts in these studies were adopted, they would likely affect the efficiency of the operation, rather than determine the ultimate success or failure of those missions. As noted below, those factors that seem to have the greatest impact on peace operations are not necessarily the ones directly under the control of military commanders. Second, the shelf-life of the conclusions drawn in many of these studies is questionable; this goes beyond serious issues involving the validity of personal observations drawn by a single individual with dubious standards of evidence, considerably below those in scholarly analyses. The transportability of conclusions depends on the similarity of the mission examined and those in the future. This is a questionable assumption even across missions in the same historical era (e.g. the UN operation in Cyprus was quite different than the one in the Congo). Yet, peace operations have changed dramatically in size, mission, rules of engagement, and deployment context, such that it is doubtful that lessons drawn from early traditional operations are at all appropriate for contemporary operations.

Over the last several decades, peacekeeping research has changed significantly, with substantially greater attention given to conceptual, theoretical, and empirical issues.

CONCEPTUAL DEVELOPMENTS

Relatively new fields of study must first identify and define the core concepts around which research will center. In the case of war, the conceptual components and operational measures of that term are now relatively well accepted, but that was not the case in earlier decades when international conflict research was in its nascent stage. With respect to peacekeeping, there is still some considerable debate on what kind of phenomena fall under its rubric, a problem compounded by shifts in the actual practice of peace operations. In addition, considerable debate has centered on definitions of success and failure; this is more than a semantic concern as most peacekeeping research has been dedicated to understanding the conditions for success. Thus, two prerequisites for empirical research on peacekeeping are identifying what falls within that domain as well defining the

most important dependent variable in such analyses: success.

Definitions and taxonomies

Peacekeeping analyses are notorious for their conceptual muddles. It is common for the terms peacekeeping, peace-building, peace enforcement, peacemaking, and a host of other terms to be used interchangeably. Indeed, the United Nations website (www. un.org/Depts/dpko/dpko/index.asp) labels a broad set of operations over its history as 'peacekeeping,' implying similar attributes. Even when distinctions are made, there is not necessarily agreement among scholars and practitioners on the conceptual components of a given term. Much of the problem is attributable to the metamorphosis of peace operations since the late 1980s. Prior to that, peacekeeping (now what is commonly referred to as traditional or cold war peacekeeping) consisted of lightly armed troops whose primary purpose was to separate combatants, following a cease-fire, but usually prior to final conflict resolution. Such operations were based on the so-called 'holy trinity': host state consent, impartiality, and minimum use of force (Bellamy and Williams, 2005a). That is, peacekeeping troops were only deployed when a host state gave its permission, the deployment was not intended to favor one combatant over another, and the force operated under very restrictive rules of engagement. Most operations resembled these elements (with a few exceptions – see the UN operation in the Congo) during the Cold War, and this definition served to distinguish peacekeeping from military intervention.[1] This conceptual definition quickly became obsolete as host state consent, impartiality, and use of force became variables along a continuum rather than defining conditions for peace operations.

How does one sort out the different terms and components that make up the broad category of peace operations? A useful place to begin is in the definitions put forward by the then UN Secretary-General

Boutros Boutros-Ghali (1995), the standard or baseline conceptualization of peacekeeping-related definitions used by scholars and policymakers. Beyond a traditional conception of peacekeeping, Boutros Ghali distinguishes it from two other forms of UN intervention: preventive diplomacy and peacemaking. Preventive diplomacy is 'action to prevent disputes from arising between parties,' whereas peacemaking is 'action to bring hostile parties to agreement.' The use of peace forces is only one possible strategy for these two approaches, and in practice, peace soldiers have rarely (e.g. preventive UN forces in Macedonia) been used in these fashions. More notable is the difference between peacekeeping and peace-building.

Boutros-Ghali speaks of 'peace-building' as the 'creation of a new environment,' not merely the cessation of hostilities facilitated by traditional peacekeeping. Although by no means a clear consensus in the literature, there are a series of characteristics or dimensions by which peace-building can be compared with other concepts, most notably traditional peacekeeping.

The first dimension concerns the goal(s) of peace-building. Most seem to agree with Boutros-Ghali (1995) that, minimally, the purpose of peace-building is to prevent the recurrence of conflict. Yet there is some disagreement over whether this idea of 'negative peace' (the absence of violent conflict) should be extended to include elements of 'positive peace,' including reconciliation, value transformation, and justice concerns. Virtually all differences in conceptualizations of peace-building can be traced back to disagreements on this point.

The second dimension of peace-building includes the strategies and accompanying activities designed to achieve the goal(s). Not surprisingly, these vary somewhat according to whether one pursues goals broader than preventing conflict recurrence or not. A minimalist strategy of preventing conflict recurrence adopts strategies consistent with conflict management. Thus, some peace-building activities include disarming warring parties, destroying weapons, and training indigenous security personnel. Facilitating elections, repatriating refugees, and strengthening government institutions are peace-building activities consistent with this minimalist strategy (see Boutros-Ghali, 1995 for these and other examples). A broader conception of peace-building leads to somewhat different strategies and sets of activities. Some (Cockell, 2000; Doyle and Sambanis, 2000; Cousens, 2001) see peace-building as addressing the 'root causes of conflict.' Minimalists expect conflict to occur, but desire to manage it peacefully. In contrast, the maximalist strategy does not merely promote management, but *conflict resolution* as well (for a broad list of activities, see Cockell, 2000; Ramsbottom, 2000; Newman and Schnabel, 2002).

A third dimension concerns the timing of such activities. Most conceptions of peace-building envision its activities to occur following some type of peace settlement between warring parties. This is in contrast to other peace operations. Preventive diplomacy and its accompanying actions are supposed to be put in place *before* significant levels of violence occur. Peace enforcement takes place in the context of ongoing armed conflict. Traditional peacekeepers are usually deployed after the cessation of violence, but prior to any peace settlement (hence their primary roles are as cease-fire monitors). Peace-building then takes places *after* prevention failed, *after* traditional peacekeeping (if it occurred), and *after* peacemaking.

A fourth dimension is the context in which peace-building should be carried out. Boutros-Ghali (1995) envisions that peace-building could occur following either interstate or intrastate conflict; he also notes some activities appropriate to each context. De facto, however, most of the discussion of peace-building has assumed that it would be employed in a civil context, following an intrastate war, significant ethnic conflict, or even in a failed state (see Maley, Sampford, and Thakur, 2003). In practice, we should recognize that the distinctions between intrastate and interstate conflict break down when neighboring states intervene in civil conflicts, best illustrated by the Congo war starting in the 1990s.

The fifth and final dimension is the actors that will carry out the peace-building actions. As Pugh (2000) notes, peace-building seems to assume that external actors will play a significant, if not exclusive, role in this enterprise. Again, an examination of the strategy and activities would not seem to preclude local actors, and indeed some elements (e.g. truth and reconciliation commissions) may be more successful when external actors are not the driving forces. Also implicit in the peace-building notion is that such actors will act in an impartial fashion for the greater good of the society, exercising some moral authority rather than pursuing private interests. Normatively, most regard peace-building as an altruistic enterprise, but as Pugh (2000) argues, such conceptions may still promote particular ideologies (e.g. democracy, neo-capitalism, and the like – see also Paris, 2004 for an elaboration).

Even accepting these conceptualizations does not mean that each type of peace operation is completely different or that even those in the same category are homogenous. Thus, a number of scholars have devised taxonomies that go beyond conceptual distinctions to indicate variation on other dimensions. Among the first and most notable was that put forward by James (1990). Using a broad conception of peacekeeping and reviewing all operations prior to 1990, he classified them in four categories according to the relationship of the conflict to surrounding states. 'Backyard problems' were those that took place within the sphere of a major power. 'Clubhouse troubles' occur when a group of states organize an operation to deal with an 'in-group' problem. 'Neighborhood quarrels' are those conflicts that do not fall into the first two categories and largely remain localized, but do not reach the level of 'dangerous crossroads,' which are those conflicts most prone to escalation and the greater involvement of external parties. Talentino (2004) divided peace-building operations into three categories: limited, extensive, and nation-building. She seems to make such distinctions

based on the operation's enforcement powers, scope of reform activities, timing of deployment, and degree of control over the local government machinery.

Actual operations may include missions that fall into multiple categories and missions sometimes mutate over their lifetimes. Thus, Diehl, Druckman, and Wall (1998) sought to measure the degrees of difference between missions. Unlike previous work, their taxonomy was tied to a broader theoretical framework derived from the scholarly literature on conflict management and resolution. They examined 16 different peace missions across 12 different dimensions suggested by those literatures and peacekeeping experts. The net result was an identification of four distinct clusters, scaled using traditional peacekeeping as a reference point: passive monitoring, damage limitation, restoring civil society, and coercive missions respectively.

The studies above were explicit attempts to conceptualize peacekeeping operations and their variants. Yet, a large set of studies implicitly engaged in classification exercises as they attempted to delineate the evolution of peace operations over time. Various scholars (Wiseman, 1987; James, 1990; Goulding, 1993; Segal, 1995; Malone and Wermester, 2000; Schmidl, 2000; Jakobsen, 2002; Bellamy, Williams, and Griffin, 2004; and Talentino, 2004) have divided peacekeeping history into different periods or epochs, largely according to the kinds of missions performed and thereby implicitly make conceptual distinctions between those missions. These treatments differ in a number of ways, but there is some general agreement. First, most treat the creation of the first traditional peacekeeping operation as *sui generis*, a significant break with past practice. There is also a notable break around 1988 or 1989, when peacekeeping operations increase dramatically in number and take on new missions. The terms 'new' (Ratner, 1995) or 'second-generation' (Mackinlay and Chopra, 1992) peacekeeping are among the labels used to describe these operations; in fact, their commonality is more that they differ from traditional missions rather than that they share substantial attributes among themselves.

Success and failure

As noted below, a plurality of peacekeeping studies focus on the conditions for success in those missions and attempt to draw lessons for future operations. From a research standpoint then, it is perhaps surprising that relatively little attention is given to defining what is meant by success. The abundance of attention is given to the independent variables in studies, and considerably less (if any at all) is given to the dependent variable. Most often, scholars delve into the reasons an operation succeeded or failed without detailing how that judgment was reached. Sometimes, the operational criteria are implicit in the discussions of the alleged influences, but explicit *a priori* conceptualizations of success and operational indicators are relatively rare.

Determining what constitutes success or failure is a prerequisite for building knowledge about the factors associated with those conditions. Yet, there is considerable disagreement among even those scholars that have broached the subject matter (for a range of views, see Druckman and Stern, 1997). Beyond normative preferences, there are several concerns that make it difficult to find a consensus. First, when conceptualizing peacekeeping success, the question arises: success for whom? Although rarely addressed directly, there are several sets of stakeholders in peace operations, each of which might generate different ideas on success: the international community, the main protagonist states or groups, the local population, and the states contributing soldiers (Durch in Druckman and Stern, 1997). Although each stakeholder may share some common interests (e.g. limiting violence), their interests are not completely coterminous. For example, a contributing state may have as one of its goals limiting casualties to its soldiers. Succeeding in that goal, however, may necessitate actions that undermine the international community's goal of human rights protection for the

threatened population. Thus, there needs to be a clearer specification of whose success is assessed and recognition that different factors may affect success in multiple ways across stakeholders.

Second, defining success will vary according to whether one adopts a short versus long-term perspective (Weiss, 1994; Bellamy and Williams, 2005b). Success may be conceptualized as achievement of goals that occur during the course of a peace operation or in some time frame immediately following the withdrawal of the peacekeeping force. An example of the former is alleviation of starvation and improvement of medical conditions during a humanitarian operation; an example of the latter is the absence of violent conflict for several years following the operation (e.g. Enterline and Kang, 2003; Doyle and Sambanis, 2006). These are certainly valid conceptions and ones most amenable to the needs of policymakers. Yet, we know that a longer-term perspective, however, often leads to a different assessment of an operation's success or failure. For example, various peacekeeping efforts in East Timor were almost universally considered a success in the immediate aftermath, only to prompt a reassessment when violence and instability returned in 2006. As with different stakeholders, there may be significant differences in the predictor and outcome variables for short- and long-term success. With respect to the latter, two problems arise. An initial problem is specifying how long a window should be considered in assessing peacekeeping outcomes. Given path dependency and other effects, peacekeeping may have consequences that extend for decades. Yet, extraordinarily long time frames make it impossible to assess ongoing and recently concluded operations (Bellamy and Williams, 2005b). Furthermore, the longer the time period that passes between the end of the operation and the assessment, the more difficult it will be to draw causal conclusions about the impact of the operation; intervening forces are likely to have as great or greater impact as the peace operations on future conditions.

A third consideration is developing a baseline against which to assess peacekeeping's effects. Some suggest that peacekeeping be compared to a situation in which no action was taken by the international community (e.g. Durch in Druckman and Stern, 1997). Related to this standard is one in which the conditions prior to deployment are compared to those during and following the operation (e.g. Kaysen and Rathjens, 1995; Heemskerk and Weller, 2002). This standard has the advantage of 'normalizing' the baseline, as moderate levels of violence during peacekeeping may be considered progress in some contexts (e.g. deployment during full-scale civil war), but backsliding in others (e.g. deployment following a cease-fire). Yet, decision makers' choices are rarely between just peacekeeping and inaction (Diehl, 1994). Some scholars suggest that analysts consider opportunity costs imposed by the choice of peacekeeping (Ratner in Druckman and Stern, 1997). Problems with this standard, however, are that it requires an adequate specification of alternative policies and then an accurate counter-factual analysis of what would have happened if other alternatives had been selected. Needless to say, neither of these steps is straightforward and the validity of such efforts would be difficult to determine. Still others suggest comparing effectiveness across peacekeeping operations (Ratner, 1995; Stiles and McDonald, 1992, refer to this as a trend-based assessment), but this generates only comparative assessments of what may be dissimilar operations and provides no absolute assessment baseline.

Not surprisingly, most analysts advocate using guidelines provided in the operation's mandate, the authorizing document (e.g. Security Council resolution) provided by the organization carrying out the mission (e.g. Durch, 1993; Ratner, 1995; Bratt, 1996; O'Neill and Rees, 2005; Bellamy and Williams, 2005b). Mandates often contain specific tasks to be completed or benchmarks that should be reached. In this way, the comparison is made to a given standard specific to the mission; presumably the mandate was created with reference to extant conditions,

but not necessarily. There may be standards created related to election supervision, troop withdrawal and disarmament, the creation of civil society institutions, and human rights among many others. Particular conceptions and indicators are far too numerous to list here. In one sense, this is appropriate as a particular mission is only judged according to the task with which it was assigned. On the other hand, there are a number of drawbacks associated with using mandates to define success. First, the mandates given operations are the products of political deliberation and compromise, and the result is that they are frequently vague. There is much room for debate on the scope and detail of the operation's mission; this alone makes it difficult to assess whether the designs of the mandate have been achieved (Diehl in Druckman and Stern, 1997). Second, mandates may be inflexible in the face of changing conflict conditions, and thus what peacekeepers are attempting to do may no longer reflect the standards present in the mandate (Bellamy and Williams, 2005b). Third, 'mandate clarity' is associated with peacekeeping success, making the whole use of mandates in evaluations endogenous (Diehl in Druckman and Stern, 1997).

Regardless of mission or the phase of conflict in which the peacekeeping operation is deployed, there are some generic standards for success applicable to all missions. Perhaps the most common one in the literature is conflict abatement (e.g. Diehl, 1994; Bratt, 1996; Welch, 2000; Fortna, 2004a, 2004b; Mullenbach, 2006; Pushkina, 2006). All peacekeeping operations are supposed to discourage violent conflict (e.g. renewed war, organized crime), a prerequisite for any other mission that might be performed. Somewhat less common, although still prominent, is conflict containment; this involves preventing the conflict from expanding to include additional internal actors, neighboring states, or major powers (Weinberger, 1983; Allan, 1996; Bratt, 1996; Jett, 2000; Ofuatey-Kodjoe, 2002; O'Neill and Rees, 2005; Pushkina, 2006). Finally, many analysts assign peacekeepers the role of creating an environment suitable for conflict resolution (Diehl, 1994; Allan, 1996; O'Neill and Rees, 2005). Yet, this would seem applicable only to those operations deployed prior to a peace agreement.

Even as the conceptual development of peacekeeping success has improved, operational indicators for those concepts have lagged behind. There are few data sets devoted exclusively to peace operations, and therefore to the extent that scholars use operational indicators, they are borrowed from conflict studies in general. Thus, it is not surprising that a popular measure of conflict abatement is the 'duration of peace,' the number of months or years from the time of peacekeeping deployment to the onset of renewed war or violence (e.g. Fortna, 2004a, 2004b; Mullenbach, 2006)

Theoretical frameworks

Peacekeeping research has historically been atheoretical or at best has involved what has been called 'problem-solving' theory (Bellamy, 2004), the practical concern with developing strategies for conflict management and resolution. Much of this was a conscious choice as authors focused on improving peacekeeping performance. It was also the case that peacekeeping did not centrally fit into the Cold War or traditional military strategies, the centerpieces of most theorizing in international relations (Pugh, 2003). Yet, even as these efforts were attempts to build generalizations, these were largely empirical generalizations with little or no attempt to provide broad theoretical explanations. Diehl (1994) was perhaps the first to identify potential variables that influence peacekeeping success and then systematically test propositions across multiple cases. Although some theoretical logic underlay each of those factors, there was not an integrated model or theoretical argument tying these disparate elements together.

For over a decade, several scholars (Fetherston, 1994a, 2000; Paris, 2000; Pugh, 2003) have lamented the lack of theory in peacekeeping analyses, but progress has been remarkably slow. Some theoretical

efforts aspired to create a 'theory of peacekeeping,' attempts at mid-level theory. Fetherston (1994a; 1994b) adopted a contingency framework, derived from studies of conflict management, and based on the assumption that conflicts have subjective and objective elements. The central point is that different techniques of conflict management, including peacekeeping, can be utilized to deal with different objective and subjective aspects of conflict. Success in this framework is designated as the achievement of 'positive' peace, along a number of security and social dimensions. Ultimately, this provides a normative framework upon which to analyze peacekeeping rather than a theory of peacekeeping per se. Somewhat similarly, Diehl, Druckman, and Wall (1998) adopt a framework from the conflict management literature, the distributive–integrative bargaining distinction developed by Walton and McKersie (1965). Yet, this again is more a heuristic, for taxonomical purposes in their analyses, rather than a well articulated theoretical argument. Tethering peacekeeping studies to those in conflict management has the advantage of being able to draw upon an extensive and well-developed body of research and ideas, although no scholar has yet brought this application to fruition.

A number of other works have provided scholars with suggested theoretical approaches, pointing the way to theoretical development, but stopping short of actual theory. Because peacekeeping research has always had a strong normative element, it is not surprising that suggested avenues for peacekeeping theory have emphasized this aspect. Critical theory approaches (Bellamy, 2004; Pugh, 2004) reject an objectivist view of global politics and peacekeeping (see Bellamy, 2004 for a comparison), and adopt the normative position that peace operations should promote human security and emancipation. Critical theory analysts often focus on how peace operations may be designed and executed to support the interests of the hegemon or leading states in the international system (Fetherston, 2000;

Pugh, 2004; see also Gibbs, 1997, for a discussion), an effect that is to be resisted according to these theorists. Similarly, postmodern approaches such as that by Debrix (1999) also emphasize the subjectivist aspects of peacekeeping that are said to serve an unjust world order. Critical theory and related approaches have the advantages of raising fundamental questions about peacekeeping that would largely be ignored outside of this framework. Most peacekeeping analyses are myopic, focused only on the immediate and local effects of the operations. A critical theory framework forces scholars to inquire whose interests are served by the missions and what effects those operations have on the prevailing global order. One drawback, however, is that the normative orientation is not necessarily compatible with validating a theoretical argument through value-free social-science testing.

Much of critical theory responds to contention that peacekeeping is a component of the liberal world order. Liberalization (i.e. open markets, democracy) is supposed to be the remedy for armed conflict, a normative proposition as much or more than a theoretical one. Paris (2004) studies peace-building in the aftermath of civil conflicts from the liberal perspective, and assesses the extent to which peace-building serves those interests. Once again, this is a framework that leads the researcher to pose certain questions, rather than necessarily being a model or theory that provides answers to those questions.

Some of the most promising theoretical works on peacekeeping have not been those seeking to construct original theory. Instead, the modal approach has been to use extant theory to inform us about one element of peacekeeping operations, rather than as an attempt to build a theory of peacekeeping or to provide a comprehensive explanation for peacekeeping. In this vein, there have been a number of different theoretical applications to peacekeeping, reflecting the range of theoretical approaches in the international relations discipline.

Realist theory has traditionally considered actions of international organizations as epiphenomena, largely reflective of major states' interests. Using a realist lense on peacekeeping, Neack (1995) explores whether states contribute troops to peacekeeping operations for self-interested (consistent with realist motives) or more altruistic reasons. Consistent with state foreign policy behavior as the unit of analysis, Sandler and his colleagues (Khanna, Sandler, and Shimizu, 1998; Shimizu and Sandler, 2002) have analyzed peacekeeping contributions from a public goods perspective. The authors argue that peacekeeping is a public good, and the theory of those goods can give us insights into the willingness of states to contribute to those efforts, as well as their propensity to 'free ride' on others.

Rational choice models have also been applied to peacekeeping (Smith and Stam, 2003). Such models often view war as an information problem, and the imposition of peacekeeping troops may interrupt the flow of information during warfare that would permit the warring parties to reach a settlement. Yet once a settlement is reached, peacekeepers may provide the credible commitment to guarantee implementation, allowing parties to overcome one of the key barriers to peace in the long run identified by rational choice theorists.

Peacekeeping has also drawn the attention of liberalism theorists, most notably those concerned with the so-called democratic peace. Lebovic (2004) looks at whether the level of democracy of a country makes it more likely to contribute troops to UN peacekeeping operations; he reports a strong positive relationship between democracy and peacekeeping contributions in post-Cold War operations.

Finally, constructivist approaches to peacekeeping include a broad range of issues, including identifying different kinds of discourse involved in the authorization and conduct of peacekeeping operations (Neack and Knudson, 1999). Most prominent, however, have been general theoretical approaches to international organizations in which peacekeeping operations are an important application. For example, Barnett and Finnemore (2004) use a sociological variant of constructivism to posit that the UN bureaucracy can exercise significant autonomy (quite in contrast to realist conceptions) on international organization actions, including peacekeeping.

EMPIRICAL PATTERNS

The deployment of peacekeepers

Most research has taken peacekeeping operations as a given, with little or no consideration of when such operations are deployed. Beyond some research design concerns with the absence of control group comparisons (e.g. cases without peacekeeping), scholars ignored the fact that the conflicts that experience peacekeeping will ultimately influence any assessment of the operations' utility as a conflict management tool. It is unlikely that peacekeeping operations are sent to a random set of conflicts (i.e. in scholarly parlance, there are 'selection effects'); if peacekeeping missions are sent only to the most intractable conflicts, then it would not be surprising for them to experience a high failure rate. This concern was ignored for years in peacekeeping research, and only a few studies have inquired about the conditions for peacekeeping deployment.

Several scholars (De Jonge Oudraat, 1996; Gibbs, 1997) have asserted that the national interests of the major power states determine where peacekeepers are sent (for a critique of this position, see Andersson, 2000; Jakobsen, 1996). Yet, there have been few systematic studies that test such assertions. Mullenbach (2005) argues that international-level factors, rather than state-level ones, best account for decisions for third-party actors to create peacekeeping missions. Specifically, he notes that peacekeeping is less likely when the target state has an alliance with a major power or is a major power itself. In contrast, peacekeeping missions are more likely to form when there was prior major power intervention or involvement by the UN or a regional organization.

Other scholars focus on conditions associated with the conflict to explain mission onset. Gilligan and Stedman (2003) examine post-Cold War civil conflicts and conclude that peacekeeping operations are more likely to be deployed in high severity and protracted conflicts, but less likely in states with large government armies. This study is perhaps most important for what the authors did *not* find, dispelling many myths about peacekeeping. There was no evidence that peacekeeping was more likely in secessionist conflicts, non-democracies, former colonies of UN Security Council members, or states with high primary commodity exports. Similarly, Fortna (2004a) identifies a number of factors *not* associated with peacekeeping operations, including identity conflicts, among others. Yet, she makes an important distinction between different kinds of peacekeeping missions (consent vs. enforcement based), the organizing agencies of the operations (UN vs. other), and temporal changes (Cold War vs. post-Cold War). Controlling for these distinctions, Fortna finds that various factors that have clear or no effects in the aggregate (e.g. government army size, war severity, and democracy) actually have context-specific impacts. Nevertheless, Fortna still concludes that consent-based peacekeeping does tend to be sent to the most difficult cases. Thus, peacekeepers are sent to conflicts in which it will be hard to be successful. The great bulk of studies on peacekeeping have been dedicated to assessing if, and under what conditions, peacekeeping has any effects.

Does peacekeeping make a difference?

There are essentially two sets of empirical analysis on peacekeeping outcomes. By far, the less common but perhaps the most important are those that assess the impact of peacekeeping on conflict processes. Typically, these measure peacekeeping's effects vis-à-vis other important factors and consider both cases with peacekeeping, as well as control groups' conflicts without peacekeeping deployment. In contrast are numerous studies that look at only peacekeeping cases and judge what elements lead to success or failure.

The focus and findings of peacekeeping studies depend heavily on which kinds of operations are chosen for study and what kinds of missions are assessed. In perhaps the only systematic study of its kind, Greig and Diehl (2005) examine the impact of peacekeepers on peacemaking, or the likelihood that disputants will sign a peace agreement. There is considerable disagreement over whether this should even be expected of peacekeeping forces (Johansen, 1994), but early work in the field (Diehl, 1994) debated whether peacekeeping actually inhibited conflict resolution. Analyses of this proposition tended to rely almost exclusively on a single case: Cyprus (Sambanis, 1999). Greig and Diehl (2005) examined a range of interstate rivalries and civil wars since 1945 and concluded first that the presence of peacekeepers actually made direct negotiation and third-party mediation *less* likely, although the effect was stronger for interstate conflict than civil wars. Furthermore, when mediation and negotiation did occur under the auspices of peacekeeping, the protagonists were less likely to reach an agreement. Thus, peacekeeping may actually inhibit final conflict resolution, and peacekeeping operations often had a greater effect on these processes than any other factor examined. Greig and Diehl (2005) argue that peacekeepers lessen the chance of a hurting stalemate by stopping the fighting and by limiting the flow of information about capabilities and possible settlement terms that comes from active fighting. They conclude by suggesting that there is a tradeoff between peacekeeping and peacemaking.

To what extent does peacekeeping actually help to keep the peace? In a series of studies, Fortna (2003, 2004a, 2004b) demonstrates that peacekeeping lengthens the time for the reemergence of war, especially in the post-Cold War era, and even across different types of peace operations (observer, traditional, and multidimensional peacekeeping). Peace is more durable when peacekeepers are present.

Fortna (2004b) attributes such success to a number of factors. She contends that the peacekeepers make attacks more difficult, take away the element of surprise, and raise the international costs of aggression. Among parties that desire peace, peacekeepers mitigate the security dilemma, signal mutual intentions for a peaceful resolution, and lessen the likelihood of accidents or minor engagements that could escalate. It is difficult to test these causal mechanisms directly, although the observed aggregate effects of conflict reduction are consistent with them.

Another set of studies concentrate on peace-building, looking at the impact of peacekeeping operations on a broad set of outcomes beyond the limitation of violence. Doyle and Sambanis (2000) explored the aftermath of civil wars to look at the conditions under which states were able to move toward democracy and avoid further conflict. Among other factors, the presence of UN peacekeepers was found to have a positive impact.

Overall, the empirical results demonstrate that peacekeeping operations do have an impact on conflictual relationships, even when controlling for other factors. Most of the time, this is positive as peacekeeping forces consistently are able to deter or otherwise inhibit the renewal of conflict. Peacekeepers are also valuable in peace-building activities. Yet, more systematic evidence also exists that peacekeeping may actually lessen the likelihood of conflict management attempts, as well as lessen their success rate when such diplomatic efforts do occur. Unfortunately, many of these findings are based on statistical analysis in which peacekeeping is merely a dichotomous variable (peacekeeping/no peacekeeping), with only a few studies going a step farther in breaking down mission types. Such studies go a long way in establishing general effects of peacekeeping operations. Yet, we know that some peacekeeping operations are more successful than others, and simple analyses will not be able to detect (1) which characteristics of such operations enhance or limit their impact and (2) what conditions interact with peacekeeping operations to produce differential impacts. Some clues to these concerns are found in analyses of peacekeeping success.

The correlates of peacekeeping success

If the studies in the previous section have the weakness of only looking at peacekeeping as a dichotomous variable, studies of peacekeeping success have the advantage of examining specific peacekeeping characteristics and conditions very closely. Yet, most of the studies in this section look only at deployed operations, with no controls for conflicts that do not experience peacekeeping. Nevertheless, there is a wide body of literature that seeks to develop 'lessons learned,' effectively presenting findings on the conditions for peacekeeping success.

To some extent, what scholars find as correlates of peacekeeping success depends on where they look. Practitioners and former military officers have regularly identified a series of factors at the operational level (e.g. Skogmo, 1989). These include the clarity of the mandate, the resources provided for the operation, and a variety of concerns associated with training. Many of these findings are suspect because they are based on the biased and personal experiences of the observers as applied to unsystematic conceptions of peacekeeping success. One might surmise that they are better understood as indicative of the elements that affect the efficiency of a peacekeeping operation, rather than primary determinants of its overall success. Even when some aspects are relevant in a broader sense, they are merely indicators of some broader processes; for example, problems with mandate clarity or resources are merely indicators or manifestations of the lack of consensus within the organizing coalition or major powers in the regional or international system.

Among the numerous assessments of peacekeeping and across different conceptions of success, there is some consensus on what factors are associated with peacekeeping success. With respect to traditional

peacekeeping operations and its relatives, scholars note several factors related to the operation itself, although above the tactical level. Certainly, mandate clarity is mentioned, but as noted above this may only be a surrogate for the underlying support (political and material), or lack thereof, for the mission. More important is the geographic elements of a mission (Diehl, 1994). Peacekeeping missions are most successful when deployed so as to detect cease-fire violations adequately, be relatively invulnerable to attack, and clearly separate the combatants.

Most of the other factors identified by analysts have concerned the behavior of actors and the conditions associated with the conflict. The cooperation of the primary disputants (Bratt, 1997; Jett, 2000; MacQueen, 2002) is thought to be critical for peacekeeping success. Yet, such claims run the risk of a tautology: if peacekeeping success is defined by the lack of violence by the disputants, then lack of violence by the disputants cannot be considered a causal factor. Existing research has not clearly specified when and why disputants would choose to abandon a cease-fire and undermine the peacekeeping operation.

Beyond the primary disputants, most relevant are the actions of neighboring states or interested major powers. Third-party states can influence the success of a peacekeeping operation in several ways (Urquhart, 1983). Most obviously, they can directly intervene militarily in the conflict, causing a renewal of the fighting or jeopardizing the safety and mission of the peacekeeping operation. More subtly, they might supply arms and other assistance to one of the disputants (or to a subnational actor — see below) that serves to undermine the peacekeeping force's ability to limit violence. They might also bring diplomatic pressure to bear on one of the actors, such that the actor is more or less disposed to support the peacekeeping presence (Diehl, 1994; Bratt, 1997; Jett, 2000). Third-party states might also have an indirect influence on the peacekeeping operation by virtue of their relationship to the primary disputants in other contexts.

Conflict between a third-party state and one of the disputants over issues related or unrelated to the conflict in question can heighten tension in the area. The new conflict could spill over and poison the cease-fire between the primary disputants. Most dangerous would be a situation in which a primary disputant is aligned with a third-party state that becomes involved in a militarized conflict with the other primary disputant. In that case, the primary disputants are often dragged into renewed conflict by virtue of competing alignment patterns. Third parties have the potential to play either a positive or negative role in the performance of peacekeeping operations. One suspects, however, that the latter is more likely. There are potentially more ways to complicate a peacekeeping operation than to assist it. Furthermore, a third-party state that supports a peacekeeping operation will likely stay out of the conflict, whereas in opposition it will tend to take a more active role.

The exception may be the major power states, especially the remaining superpower, the United States (Bratt, 1997; MacQueen, 2002). Major powers have the military capacity and political influence to prod recalcitrant disputants to cooperate with the peacekeeping force. Yet, for most peace missions, that major power must act impartially even if it is aligned with one of the protagonists. Major powers can also play an important supplemental role, providing critical political support within the organizing agency and contributing money, logistical support, and other forms of help to the peacekeeping operation.

Third-party states are not the only relevant actors, as many peacekeeping deployments are subject to the actions of subnational actors (e.g. see Norton, 1991). These include ethnic groups, competing political movements, and terrorist organizations. The behavior of these groups could be especially important when peacekeeping forces are thrust into areas of internal instability (Diehl, 1994; Bratt, 1997; Jett, 2000). In some cases, subnational actors may actually control larger geographic areas than the recognized government. Unlike third-party states, however, subnational actors

affect peacekeeping operations primarily by direct actions of support or opposition. Their cooperation could be crucial in fostering a minimum level of violence in the area of deployment.

Overall, the key concerns with respect to third-party cooperation are their (1) preferences and interests and (2) the resources they command (Diehl, 2000). If the peacekeeping operation does not serve the interests of third parties, this is likely to generate opposition to the force. Yet, this opposition alone is not sufficient to jeopardize peacekeeping success. Third parties must have significant resources that could be brought to bear upon the peacekeeping mission. Such resources include political influence with key actors and the local population in the area of peacekeeping deployment. The ability to intervene militarily or supply weaponry to those opposed to the operation may also be critical.

Generally, it seems clear that peacekeeping operations experience more problems in conflicts that have an internal conflict component as compared to those purely between two or more states (Diehl, 1994; Wesley, 1997; Jett, 2000). There appear to be several explanations. First, civil conflicts often involve more than two identifiable groups in conflict; by definition, an internationalized civil war involves more than two actors. In contrast, interstate disputes have been overwhelmingly dyadic. Thus, as the number of actors in the dispute increases so does the likelihood that one or more of them will object to the cease-fire and the provisions for the deployment of the peacekeeping forces; they may take military action against other actors or the peacekeeping forces. Beyond the difficulty of aggregating multiple preferences in support of a peacekeeping operation, the geographic requirements (found to be significant above) are different in a civil conflict than an interstate one. Civil instability may mean that several groups are operating in different parts of the country. This could necessitate that the peacekeeping operation covers a broader territory, opening up the possibility of more violent incidents. Furthermore, unlike an identifiable international border or cease-fire line, it may be impossible to demarcate a line or area that separates the many sides in the conflict. Being from the same state and often not wearing military uniforms (indeed, sometimes not being traditional military or paramilitary units at all), participants in a civil conflict are hard to identify, much less to separate when they occupy the same geographic area. Interstate disputants can more easily be identified and separated across internationally recognized borders or militarily defined cease-fire lines. Civil conflict may be quite dangerous to peacekeeping and the situation more difficult to control. James (1994: 17) notes that in civil conflict, 'Arms are likely to be in the hands of groups who may be unskilled in their use, lack tight discipline, and probably engage in guerrilla tactics. Light arms are also likely to be kept in individual homes, and may be widely distributed.' These conditions open the peacekeepers up to sniper fire and other problems, as well as making it virtually impossible to secure a given area fully. The international response to civil conflicts, or at least that of UN peacekeepers, has been inappropriate and has undermined effectiveness (Wesley, 1997). UN planners have misread many of the situations and the traditional peacekeeping strategies have not easily translated into the civil conflict context.

Peacekeepers have also been judged to be more effective in the later phases of conflict than in earlier ones (Diehl, 1994; Bratt, 1997; Jett, 2000; MacQueen, 2002). There has only been one operation in the previolence phase (UN operation in Macedonia), and therefore no basis yet for generalizations. Yet, research indicates that peacekeepers have problems during active hostilities as they do not have the equipment or mandate to carry out what are essentially enforcement missions (Boulden, 2001). Peacekeepers are given credit for conflict abatement in the post–cease fire, pre-settlement phase. Yet, the consensus seems to be that peacekeeping is most effective in a fourth conflict phase; after the disputants have signed a peace agreement (not merely a cease-fire) and the peacekeeping force is charged with assisting in the implementation

of that agreement. Deployment in that phase gets the operation out of the peacemaking dilemma identified by Greig and Diehl (2005) and increases the likelihood of cooperation from relevant parties.

Deployment in the final phase of conflict may increase the chances of success, but it does not guarantee it. Many of the missions in this phase are peace-building ones, and prominent research has helped identify when such missions are likely to be successful. Peace-building is a long-term process and it is difficult to identify correlates of success for a process that is still incomplete in most cases. Paris (2004) is critical of the way that peace-building strategies have been implemented. He decries the world community's attempts to build democracy and stability too quickly and without adequate resources. He also thinks that the domestic institutions need to be properly strengthened before peace-building can succeed. This is suggestive that there may be prerequisites for success that are directly outside the control of the peace-building operation itself. The war-proneness of democratizing states (Mansfield and Snyder, 2005) is also a condition that seems to complicate any attempts at peace-building.

Doyle and Sambanis (2006) considered peace-building in the aftermath of a large sample of civil wars. They conclude that a UN mission is a virtual prerequisite for some peace-building success; even under the best of other conditions (even with low levels of hostility), UN intervention is needed unless high levels of local capacity are present. UN missions usually produce results superior to those in which UN action is absent, but success may be elusive under conditions of high hostility and a legacy of significant casualties. In general, peacebuilding is also negatively affected by ethic cleavages, large numbers of factions, and low initial development levels. As with some of the factors associated with success in traditional missions, these are contextual factors largely out of the control of the peacekeeping operation.

Another looming concern is the effect of the organizing agency on the effectiveness of the operation. Regional organizations have recently taken on greater peacekeeping roles, and the relative effectiveness of those operations vis-à-vis those managed by the United Nations is a theoretical and policy concern. It is difficult to generalize on this given the wide variation in capabilities and peacekeeping scenarios across different regional organizations. Nevertheless, there are a number of hypothesized advantages to regional operations, such as greater consensus and support and restraint of third-party states. Similarly, some purported disadvantages, relative to UN operations, including problems with regional hegemons, meeting external threats, and inadequate resources, may outweigh such advantages (see Diehl, 1994; Bellamy and Williams, 2005b). There is not yet, however, a definitive study that systematically compares UN and regional effectiveness (nor hybrid operations).

FUTURE RESEARCH DIRECTIONS

Relative to other subjects in the conflict management field, peacekeeping research is a relatively recent focus and accordingly it is also relatively underdeveloped. Nevertheless, the rise in the number and frequency of peace operations in the world has attracted the attention of many scholars, who now examine these phenomena in a more systematic fashion. As one looks to the future, and assuming a continuing relevance for peacekeeping, there are several directions that would move the study of peacekeeping forward.

Most obviously, greater attention to theoretical concerns is a prerequisite for progress. The easiest path would be to exploit existing theoretical approaches at least in the short run, but this is unlikely to produce a broad understanding of peacekeeping in the long run. At best, it can illuminate various pieces without revealing the whole picture. Accordingly, attempts at mid-range theory may be the best strategy. Such a result must include theory that can account for when peacekeepers are deployed and what kinds of impact they have in an integrated explanation.

The construction of theoretical arguments will need to be followed by empirical validation on more than the single case that dominates the headlines of the day. Unfortunately, much of current peacekeeping research is inadequate. A survey of the articles appearing in the journal *International Peacekeeping* since its inception finds most are not concerned with theory and focus only a single country's peacekeeping policies or a single peacekeeping operation. Instead, scholars need to draw generalizations across a broad set of operations. Yet, they need to be equally sensitive to variations across missions and that different models may be needed to understand different missions. To carry out such research, scholars must construct data sets dealing with peacekeeping and its relevant characteristics in particular. Using current data sets on conflicts has some significant limitations. First, this leads to using only simplified peacekeeping variables (peacekeeping vs. no peacekeeping or categories of operations) as these data sets do not include any information on the operations. Second, these data sets are designed for time-series analyses, but peacekeeping operations and their outcomes show limited variation on a year-to-year basis and must be analyzed in the aggregate. This means gathering data on peacekeeping operations as the units of analysis.

How does one decide whether peacekeeping missions differ or what variables might be collected in a data-gathering effort? It comes back to good theorizing, which will guide the way. Without effective theorizing, peacekeeping research will remain in its nascent stage, and policy relevant conclusions will continue to be drawn on limited and probably misleading grounds.

NOTES

1 Many analyses did not make a distinction between observation and traditional peacekeeping. The former was very similar to the latter, but often consisted of a smaller force, did not necessarily perform an interposition function, and usually consisted of unarmed personnel.

REFERENCES

Abi-Saab, George (1978) *The United Nations Operation in the Congo*. London: Oxford University Press.

Allan, James H. (1996) *Peacekeeping: Outspoken Observations by a Field Officer*. Westport, CT: Praeger Publishers.

Andersson, Andreas (2000) 'Democracies and UN peacekeeping operations, 1990–1996', *International Peacekeeping*, 7: 1–22.

Barnett, Michael. and Finnemore, Martha (2004) *Rules for the World*. Ithaca, NY: Cornell University Press.

Barros, James (1968) *The Aaland Islands Question: Its Settlement by the League of Nations*. New Haven: Yale University Press.

Bellamy, Alex J. (2004) 'The "next stage" in peace operations theory?', *International Peacekeeping*, 11(1): 17–38.

Bellamy, Alex J., Williams, Paul and Griffin, Stuart (2004) *Understanding Peacekeeping*. Cambridge: Polity Press.

Bellamy, Alex J. and Williams, Paul (2005a) 'Introduction: Thinking anew about peace operations', in Alex J. Bellamy (ed.), *Operations and Global Order*. London: Routledge. pp. 1–15.

Bellamy, Alex J. and Williams, Paul (2005b) 'Who's keeping the peace? Regionalization and contemporary peace operations', *International Security*, 29(4): 157–95.

Boulden, Jane (2001) *Peace Enforcement: The United Nations Experience in Congo, Somalia, and Bosnia*. Westport, CT: Praeger.

Boutros-Ghali, Boutros (1995) *An Agenda for Peace*. 2nd edn. New York: United Nations.

Bratt, Duane (1996) 'Assessing the success of UN peacekeeping operations', *International Peacekeeping*, 3(4): 64–81.

Bratt, Duane (1997) 'Explaining peacekeeping performance: The UN in internal conflicts', *International Peacekeeping*, 4(3): 45–70.

Bull, Odd (1973) *War and Peace in the Middle East: The Experiences and Views of a UN Observer*. Boulder, CO: Westview Press.

Carnall, Geoffrey (1965) *To Keep the Peace: The United Nations Peace Force*. London: Peace News.

Cockell, John (2000) 'Conceptualising peacebuilding: Human security and sustainable peace', in Michael Pugh (ed.), *Regeneration of War-Torn Societies*. London: Macmillan. pp. 15–37.

Cousens, Elizabeth (2001) 'Introduction', in Elizabeth Cousens and Chetan Kumar (eds), *Peacebuilding as Politics: Cultivating Peace in Fragile Societies*. Boulder: Lynne Rienner Publishers. pp. 1–20.

Debrix, Francois (1999) *Re-Envisioning Peacekeeping: The United Nations and the Mobilization of Ideology*. MN: University of Minnesota Press.

De Jonge Oudraat, Chantal (1996) 'The United Nations and Internal Conflict', in Michael Brown (ed.), *International Dimensions of Internal Conflicts*. Cambridge, MA: MIT Press.

Diehl, Paul F. (1994) *International Peacekeeping*. Revised edn. Baltimore, MD: Johns Hopkins University Press.

Diehl, Paul F. (2000) 'Forks in the road: Theoretical and policy concerns for 21st century peacekeeping', *Global Society*, 14: 337–60.

Diehl, Paul F., Druckman, Daniel and Wall, James (1998) 'International peacekeeping and conflict resolution: A taxonomic analysis with implications', *Journal of Conflict Resolution*, 42: 33–55.

Doyle, Michael and Sambanis, Nicholas (2000) 'International peacebuilding: A theoretical and quantitative analysis', *American Political Science Review*, 94: 779–802.

Doyle, Michael W. and Sambanis, Nicholas (2006) *Making War and Building Peace: United Nations Peace Operations*. Princeton: Princeton University Press.

Druckman, Daniel and Stern, Paul C. (1997) 'The forum: Evaluating peacekeeping missions', *Mershon International Studies Review*, 41(1): 151–65.

Durch, William J. (2003) 'Peace and stability operations in Afghanistan: Requirements and force options.' Presentation from the Henry L. Stimson Center, June 28.

Enterline, Andrew and Kang, Seonjou (2003) 'Stopping the killing sooner? Assessing the success of United Nations peacekeeping in civil wars', paper presented at the Peace Science Society annual meeting, Arizona.

Fetherston, A. Betts (1994a) 'Putting the peace back into peacekeeping: Theory must inform practice', *International Peacekeeping*, 1(1): 3–29.

Fetherston, A. Betts (1994b) *Towards a Theory of United Nations Peacekeeping*. London: Macmillan Press Ltd.

Fetherston, A. Betts (2000) 'Peacekeeping, conflict resolution and peacebuilding: A reconsideration of theoretical frameworks', *International Peacekeeping*, 7(1): 190–218.

Fortna, Virginia Page (2003) 'Inside and out: Peacekeeping and the duration of peace after civil and interstate wars', *International Studies Review*, 5(4): 97–114.

Fortna, Virginia Page (2004a) 'Does peacekeeping keep peace? International intervention and the duration of peace after civil war', *International Studies Quarterly*, 48: 269–92.

Fortna, Virginia Page (2004b) 'Interstate peacekeeping: Causal mechanism and empirical effects', *World Politics*, 481–519.

Frye, William (1957) *A United Nations Peace Force.* New York: Oceana.

Gibbs, David (1997) 'Is peacekeeping a new form of imperialism?' *International Peacekeeping,* 4: 122–28.

Gilligan, Michael and Stedman, Stephen (2003) Where do the peacekeepers go? With *International Studies Review,* 5(4): 37–54

Greig, J. Michael and Diehl, Paul F. (2005) 'The peacekeeping–peacemaking dilemma', *International Studies Quarterly,* 49: 621–45.

Goulding, Marak (1993) 'The evolution of United Nations peacekeeping', *International Affairs,* 69: 451–64.

Heemskerk, Renske and Weller, Evelien (2002) *Best of Intentions? Designing the Mandate: The United Nations Peace Missions in Cambodia and Bosnia-Herzegovina.* University of Amsterdam.

House, Arthur (1978) *The UN in the Congo.* Washington, DC: University Press of America.

International Peace Academy (1984) *Peacekeeper's Handbook.* New York: Pergamon.

Jakobsen, Peter Viggo (1996) 'National interest, humanitarianism or CNN: What triggers UN peace enforcement after the Cold War?', *Journal of Peace Research,* 33: 205–15.

Jakobsen, Peter Viggo (2002) 'The transformation of United Nations peace operations in the 1990s: Adding globalization to the conventional "end of the Cold War explanation"', *Cooperation and Conflict,* 37: 267–82.

James, Alan (1990) *Peacekeeping in International Politics.* London: Macmillan.

James, Alan (1994) 'The Congo controversies', *International Peacekeeping,* 1: 44–58.

Jett, Dennis C. (2000) *Why Peacekeeping Fails.* New York: St Martin's Press.

Johansen, Robert (1994) 'UN peacekeeping: How should we measure success?' *Mershon International Studies Review,* 38(2): 307–10.

Kaysen, Carl and Rathjens, George (1995) *Peace Operations by the United Nations: The Case for a Volunteer UN Military Force.* Committee on International Security Studies, American Academy of Arts and Sciences, Cambridge, MA.

Khanna, Jyoti, Sandler, Todd and Shimizu, Hirofumi (1998) 'Sharing the financial burden for UN and NATO peacekeeping, 1976–1996', *Journal of Conflict Resolution,* 42(2): 176–95.

Lebovic, James (2004) 'Democracies and United Nations peace operations after the Cold War', *Journal of Conflict Resolution,* 48: 910–36.

Lefever, Ernest (1967) *Uncertain Mandate: Politics of the UN Congo Operation.* Baltimore, MD: Johns Hopkins University Press.

Mackinlay, John and Chopra, Jarat (1992) 'Second generation multinational operations', *Washington Quarterly,* 15: 113–31.

MacQueen, Norrie (2002) *United Nations Peacekeeping in Africa since 1960.* London: Pearson Education.

Maley, William, Sampford, Charles and Thakur, Ramesh (eds) (2003) *From Civil Strife to Civil Society: Civil and Military Responsibilities in Disrupted States.* Tokyo: United Nations Press.

Malone, David and Wermester, Karen (2000) 'Boom or bust?: The changing nature of UN peacekeeping', *International Peacekeeping,* 7: 37–54.

Mansfield, Edward D. and Snyder, Jack (2005) *Electing to Fight: Why Emerging Democracies Go to War (BCSIA Studies in International Security).* Cambridge: MIT Press.

Mullenbach, Mark J. (2005) 'Deciding to keep peace: An analysis of international influences on the establishment of third-party peacekeeping missions', *International Studies Quarterly,* 49: 529–56.

Mullenbach, Mark J. (2006) 'Reconstructing strife-torn societies: Third-party peacebuilding in intrastate disputes', in T.D. Mason and J.D. Meernik (eds), *Conflict Prevention and Peacebuilding in Post-War Societies.* London: Taylor and Francis. pp. 53–80.

Neack, Laura (1995) 'UN peace-keeping: In the interest of community or self?', *Journal of Peace Research,* 32: 181–96.

Neack, Laura and Knudson, Roger (1999) 'The multiple meanings and purposes of peacekeeping in Cyprus', *International Politics,* 36: 465–502.

Newman, Edward and Schnabel, Albrecht (eds) (2002) 'Recovering from civil conflict: Reconciliation, peace and development', *International Peacekeeping,* 9, special issue.

Norton, Augustus Richard (1991) 'The demise of the MNF', in Anthony McDermott and Kjell Skjelsbaek (eds), *Peacebuilding as Politics: The Multinational Force in Beirut, 1982–1984.* Miami: Florida International University Press. pp. 80–94.

O'Neill, John Terrence and Rees, Nicholas (2005) *United Nations Peacekeeping in the Post Cold War Era.* New York: Routledge.

Ofuatey-Kodjoe, W. (2002) 'The impact of peacekeeping on target sales: Lessons from the Liberian experience', in R.R. Laremont (ed.), *The Causes of War and the Consequences of Peacekeeping in Africa.* Portsmouth, NJ: Heinemann Publishers. pp. 118–42.

Paris, Roland (1997) 'Peacebuilding and the limits of liberal institutionalism', *International Security,* 22: 54–89.

Paris, Roland (2000) 'Broadening the study of peace operations', *International Studies Review,* 2: 27–44.

Paris, Roland (2004) *At War's End: Building Peace After Civil Conflict.* Cambridge: Cambridge University Press.

Pugh, Michael (2000) 'Introduction: The ownership of regeneration and peacebuilding', in M. Pugh (ed.), *Regeneration of War Torn Societies.* London: Macmillan. pp. 1–12.

Pugh, Michael (2003) 'Peacekeeping and IR theory: Phantom of the opera?', *International Peacekeeping,* 10(4): 104–12.

Pugh, Michael (2004) 'Peacekeeping and critical theory', *International Peacekeeping,* 11(1): 39–58.

Pushkina, Darya (2006) 'A recipe for success? Ingredients of a successful peacekeeping mission', *International Peacekeeping,* 13(2): 133–49.

Ramsbottom, Oliver (2000) 'Reflections on UN post-settlement peacebuilding', *International Peacekeeping,* 7: 167–89.

Ratner, Steven R. (1995) *The New UN Peacekeeping.* New York: St Martin's Press.

Rikhye, Indar Jit (1984) *The Theory and Practice of International Peacekeeping.* New York: St Martin's Press.

Rosner, Gabriella (1963) *The United Nations Emergency Force.* New York: Columbia University Press.

Sambanis, Nicholas (1999) 'The UN operation in Cyprus: A new look at the peacekeeping–peacemaking relationship', *International Peacekeeping,* 6(1): 79–108.

Schmidl, E.A. (2000) 'The evolution of peace operations from the nineteenth century', in E.A. Schmidl (ed.), *Peace Operations between Peace and War.* London: Frank Cass.

Segal, David (1995) 'Five phases of United Nations peacekeeping: An evolutionary typology', *Journal of Political and Military Sociology,* 22: 65–79.

Shimizu, Hirofumi and Sandler, Todd (2002) 'Peacebuilding and burden sharing, 1994–2000', *Journal of Peace Research,* 39(6): 651–68.

Skogmo, Bjorn (1989) *UNIFIL: International Peacekeeping in Lebanon, 1978–1988.* Boulder: Lynne Rienner.

Smith, Alastair and Stam, Alan (2003) 'Mediation and peacekeeping in random walk model of civil and interstate war', *International Studies Review,* 5: 115–35.

Stiles, Kendall W. and McDonald, Maryellen (1992) 'After consensus, what? Performance criteria for the UN in the post-Cold War era', *Journal of Peace Research,* 29(3): 299–311.

Talentino, Andrea (2004) 'One step forward, one step back?: The development of peacebuilding as concept and strategy', *Journal of Conflict Studies,* 24(2): 33–61.

Urquhart, Brian (1983) 'Peacekeeping: A view from the operational center', in Henry Wiseman (ed.), *Peacekeeping: Appraisals and Proposals.* New York: Pergamon. pp. 161–74.

Wainhouse, David (1966) *International Peace Observation: A History and Forecast.* Baltimore, MD: Johns Hopkins University Press.

Walton, Richard E. and McKersie, Robert (1965) *A Behavioral Theory of Labor Negotiation.* New York: McGraw-Hill.

Wambaugh, Sara (1970) *The Saar Plebiscite.* Cambridge: Harvard University Press.

Weinberger, Naomi Joy (1983) 'Peacekeeping operations in Lebanon', *The Middle East Journal,* 47(3): 341–69.

Weiss, Thomas G. (1994) 'The United Nations and civil wars', *The Washington Quarterly,* 17(4): 139–59.

Welch, C. David (2000) 'Peacekeeping: The US, the UN and regional players.' Speech at the Meridian International Center on Peacekeeping, October 18.

Wesley, Michael (1997) *Casualties of the New World Order: The Causes of Failure of UN Missions to Civil Wars.* New York: St Martin's Press.

Wiseman, Henry (1987) 'The United Nations and international peacekeeping: A comparative analysis', in United Nations Institute for Training and Peace Research, *The United Nations and the Maintenance of International Peace and Security.* Dordrecht: Martinus Nijhoff. pp. 263–333.

28

Reconciliation as a Peace-Building Process: Scope and Limits[1]

Valerie Rosoux

For decades, political thinkers and official representatives have been reluctant to consider reconciliation as a relevant concept in their field. Because of the religious connotation of the term, they have generally regarded reconciliation as a spiritual process limited to interpersonal relationships. Since the end of the Cold War, more and more specialists in history, philosophy, psychology, sociology, criminology, international relations and political science pay attention to what is designated as "probably the most important condition" for maintaining a stable peace (Bar-Siman-Tov, 2000: 237). However, reconciliation appears as an "undertheorized phenomenon" (Long and Brecke, 2003: 147), a "controversial and rather obscure" notion (Forsberg, 2003: 73) or even a "rather crude analytical tool" (Hermann, 2004: 40–41). Therefore, it seems crucial to question the scope and limits of reconciliation as a peace-building process.

The purpose of this chapter is neither to overcome all the shortcomings of this concept, nor to define it once and for all. It is rather to present a survey of the field of studies and issues related to reconciliation after wars and mass atrocities. Numerous scholars try to analyze how former adversaries can put the past into a manageable perspective so that it no longer blocks the development of a cooperative relationship. In this regard, two major examples are often considered: the Franco-German case and the South African case. The first one concerns a process of rapprochement after several international conflicts while the second depicts the situation of a divided society. Despite the uniqueness of each situation and the basic distinctions between international and internal processes of reconciliation, these two examples make it possible to highlight some common mechanisms.

The analysis is divided into three parts. The first one examines the various conceptions of reconciliation as a political process. The second attempts to delineate to what extent it can be appropriate to refer to the notion of reconciliation as a strategy of conflict transformation. To do so, it will emphasize the fact that at the end of an international or intercommunity conflict, the real question is not whether or not the adversarial relationship should be transformed – but rather how and when such an exercise should take place. The third and final part stresses the main limits of the concept of reconciliation when applied to the societal – and not personal – level.

WALKING AMONG DEFINITIONS

Despite its increasing use, reconciliation appears as a polysemic concept. So far, there is no consensus about the necessary conditions for it. For some, reconciliation requires above all the establishment of order based on a negotiated settlement or a cease-fire. In this view, reconciliation refers to any "mutually conciliatory accommodation between former protagonists" (Long and Brecke, 2003: 1). Beside this pragmatic vision, others call attention to the "transcendent" nature of a far more demanding process requiring truth, mercy, justice and peace (Lederach, 1997). Between these two conceptions, most of the scholars underline different and sometimes competing definitions of the concept. Let us take a couple of examples to illustrate this variety of tones. For some, the core element of reconciliation is *trust* (Govier and Verwoerd, 2002; Amstutz, 2005; Nadler and Liviatan, 2006). In this line, Marrow suggests that reconciliation "is reestablishment of friendship that can inspire sufficient trust across the traditional split" (1999: 132). For another group of scholars, the key element is *truth*. In this view, reconciliation allows us to face "unwelcome truths in order to harmonize incommensurable world views so that inevitable and continuing conflicts and differences stand at least within a single universe of comprehensibility" (Asmal *et al.*, 1997: 46). Yet, other voices claim

that the essence of reconciliation is a psychological process of transformation leading ultimately to an *identity* change (Bar-Tal and Bennink, 2004; Kelman, 2004).

Beyond this variety, three main approaches to political reconciliation can be distinguished: structural, social–psychological and spiritual ones. The first approach gives priority to security, economic interdependence and political cooperation between parties (Kacowicz, 2000). The second underlines the cognitive and emotional aspects of the process of rapprochement between former adversaries (Bar-Siman-Tov, 2004). The third one accentuates a process of collective healing based on the rehabilitation of both victims and offenders (Tutu, 1999). The structural approach generally deals with the interests and the issues at stake, whereas the two others concentrate on the relationships between parties.

(1) Structures and Institutions – After the cessation of violent acts, parties in conflict can establish mutually accepted structural and institutional mechanisms to reduce the general perception of threat and to resolve any possible disagreement. When the former belligerents live in different states, these mechanisms can take the form of confidence-building measures like exchanging representatives in various political, economic and cultural spheres; maintaining formal and regular channels of communication and consultation between public officials; developing joint institutions and organizations to stimulate economic and political interdependence; reducing tensions by disarmament, demobilization of military forces, demilitarization of territories. The Franco-German case illustrates the effectiveness of such structural measures. Six years after the end of World War II, an economic union for coal and steel production was created; in 1963, Charles de Gaulle and Konrad Adenauer signed the Elysee Treaty which institutionalized regular meetings between foreign, defense and education ministers; in 1988, the Franco-German Council was established and in 1995, joint military units were formed (Ackermann, 1994). When adversaries live together in one single state, structural measures mainly concern institutional reforms. Their purpose is to integrate all the groups in a democratic system, to restore human and civil rights and to favor a fair redistribution of wealth.

(2) Relationships – Although some structural changes can be implemented relatively quickly after the end of a conflict, the transformation of relationships does not occur in the same way. Studies dedicated to this slow and arduous process are interconnected but their vision of the transformation process is diverging. Cognitive and social–psychological approaches analyse what they call a "deep change" in the public's psychological repertoire. This evolution results from a reciprocal process of adjustments of beliefs, attitudes, motivations and emotions shared by the majority of society members (Bar-Tal and Bennink, 2004: 17). The so-called spiritual approaches go a step further by asserting that reconciliation attempts to lead to forgiveness for the adversary's misdeeds (Shriver, 1995; Lederach, 1998; Staub, 2000; Philpott, 2006). However, as we will see, there is no consensus about the appropriateness of forgiveness in international relations.

This classification could easily be challenged[2]. The picture to describe is so rich that there are many ways to do it. Since the aim of this chapter is not to settle the issue from a theoretical point of view, we will not get involved in an academic debate about labels and categorizations. The main point to keep in mind at that stage is that even though structural measures are critical to establish a basic level of trust, they are likely not sufficient to resolve protracted conflicts (Wilmer, 1998: 93). A reconciliation process obviously implies the transformation of relationships between former opponents. The dramatic statement of Egyptian President Anwar al-Sadat before the Israeli Knesset on 29 November 1977 highlights the necessity to reconfigurate relationships between parties: "Yet there remains another wall. This wall constitutes a psychological barrier between us, a barrier of suspicion […] of rejection […] of fear […] of deception […] a barrier of distorted interpretation of every event and statement. Today, through my visit to you, I ask why don't we stretch out our hands with faith and sincerity so that together we might destroy this barrier?" (quoted by Maoz, 2004: 228). Here is probably the core of the issue. How do you launch a process of "reframing" in order to encompass the majority of individuals affected by the conflict? Or, to put it in a metaphorical way,

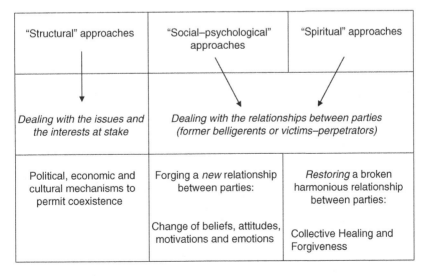

"Structural" approaches	"Social–psychological" approaches	"Spiritual" approaches
Dealing with the issues and the interests at stake	Dealing with the relationships between parties (former belligerents or victims–perpetrators)	
Political, economic and cultural mechanisms to permit coexistence	Forging a *new* relationship between parties: Change of beliefs, attitudes, motivations and emotions	*Restoring* a broken harmonious relationship between parties: Collective Healing and Forgiveness

Figure 28.1

how do you "demobilize" the minds (Horne *et al.*, 2002; Pouligny *et al.*, 2007: 5)?

HOW DO YOU "DEMOBILIZE" THE MINDS?

Although many scholars describe reconciliation as a succession of stages, this section does not talk about the issue in terms of strict sequence. The process of reconciliation is not a linear one. At each stage, a relapse back into violent means of dealing with conflicts is possible. Furthermore, the stages that are stressed in the literature (joint projects, cultural exchanges, truth telling, mutual acknowledgement, apology, justice, reparation, forgiveness...) do not always follow after each other in any set order. Thus, rather than directly skimming through a list of specific techniques and ingredients for lasting reconciliation, this section suggests a focus firstly on two historical cases that are often qualified as "exemplary".

Reconciliation as a historical possibility

The Franco-German case is fascinating because it makes it possible to examine a process of interstate rapprochement from a long perspective. The South African case enlightens an internal reconciliation process that results from a negotiation between the main parties in presence, and not a military victory of one of them (as is the case after World War II). The two cases show that the motives for reconciliation can be both pragmatic and moral. They also reveal that the outcomes of the so-called reconciliation process could be questioned in many ways.

The Franco-German case

The process undergone by France and Germany since the end of World War II demonstrates that "yesterday's hereditary enemies" may become "determined friends" (de Gaulle, 1970: 428–9). For more than a century and a half, the incessant reminder of past confrontations created entrenched

positions on either side of the Rhine. These perceptions gave rise to belligerent discourses calling for the crushing of the ancestral enemy. However, in the immediate post-war years, French and German politicians and private citizens deliberately sought to influence the public opinion to support a process of reconciliation between the two countries. This rapprochement proceeded in "waves" (Grosser, 1967: 6). The first wave was that of a small minority of pioneers. Among them, historians from both countries quickly engaged in the arduous task of revising textbooks and national histories. Their objective was to critically scrutinize the myths of a "hereditary enmity" between France and Germany. The second wave was constituted by the "Europeanists". In 1950, Jean Monnet and Robert Schuman launched the project of the European Coal and Steel Community to integrate Germany into the Western camp. The third wave occurred under de Gaulle and Adenauer. In 1958, both leaders officially put an end to the calls for mutual destruction. This decision was not a matter of altruism; it directly corresponded to French and German national interests. France and Germany each needed the other, as Adenauer and de Gaulle readily recognized. In September 1962, Chancellor Adenauer said, "Thank God, the interest of France coincides with the interest of Germany". President de Gaulle explained later that "it is clear that our interests meet and will meet more and more. Germany needs us as much as we need it" (Peyrefitte, 1994). The configuration of the broader international system was also decisive for stimulating reconciliation. Among the political, economic, and security considerations that promoted this process, four were particularly significant: the complete and radical character of Germany's defeat (and therefore its need for political rehabilitation and return of sovereignty), the process of building the European community, the existence of a common enemy (the USSR), and the external – mostly American – support for a rapprochement.

Between 1958 and 1962, de Gaulle and Adenauer undertook considerable efforts to persuade the public of the necessity of a Franco-German rapprochement. They carried out frequent trips on both sides of the Rhine to help their populations overcome preconceived ideas and fears rooted in past events. As a result, this process progressively affected all levels of society. The Elysee Treaty of 1963 made the Franco-German rapprochement durable, thanks to a double linkage: the requirements for regular consultation and the promotion of interaction on a "people-to-people" level. The *institutional* mechanisms provided for by the Elysee Treaty and supplemented in 1988 have created a structure of constant dialogue through semestrial meetings of Head of State, foreign and technical ministers' consultations as well as joint councils in all fields. On the *people-to-people* level, the Franco-German relationship has reached an unmatched level of intensity. Polls show that Germany is considered to be France's "best friend" by the population. Over 1800 towns are concerned by twin-cities programs. More than five million youth have been involved in various student exchange programs. The existence of a jointly operated TV network – ARTE – is but another example. In the trade field, each country is the other's most important partner (Gardner-Feldman, 1999).

Since the Elysee Treaty, the authorities of the two states have systematically tried to avoid being locked into memories that are strictly national. They recognized that national perceptions overlap and have to be considered as mutually dependent. The purpose was to develop a "common language" capable of encompassing the two nations' conflict-ridden past. Former French Prime Minister Lionel Jospin summed up this process: memory should be considered not as "a way to awaken ancient sufferings" but as "a tool allowing people to make peace with the past, without forgetting previous wounds" (1999). Such a method implies a more complex approach to otherness. Leaders of both sides no longer describe the two nations as possessing identities that are totally heterogeneous and independent. Instead, they depict them as peoples who are bound together

by links derived from history and who have committed actions causing mutual wounds. The purpose is not to impose a vision about past and present realities. It is rather to iron out the conditions for the "cohabitation" of diverging experiences.

The official meaning given to the battle of Verdun is an outstanding example of this kind of transformation. The number of victims – a quarter of a million young soldiers – added to the ruthless nature of the combats created fearful remembrances in the consciences on both territories. As early as 1916, a patriotic representation of the combats was being elaborated, separately, in France and in Germany. On the French side, Verdun witnessed the glory, the heroism and the victorious spirit of the French combatants. On the other side of the Rhine, it was quickly recovered by the national–socialist ideology. Four decades later, the Franco-German rapprochement paved the way for a new interpretation to be given to this event. Verdun became a symbol with a similar meaning to all combatants – French *and* Germans. The memories were not presented any longer as national and separate. They were rather unified as a result of the reconciliation which had occurred: the soldiers which combated in the opposite camps were then gathered in a common tribute. This reinterpretation was given a symbolic expression when François Mitterrand and Helmut Kohl stood hand in hand in front of the Ossuary of Douaumont (France).

The effort which is realized to integrate national memories does not imply that events will be given a uniform representation on both sides in the future. Integration does not bring about plurality to be set aside. In fact, it supposes that a form of disagreement may be accepted to a certain extent. One may speak, in that regard, of a reasonable disagreement, which appears to be admitted by the parties (Dwyer, 1999; Schapp, 2005). In that sense, what is often called a "work of memory" remains a process concerning *memories* – that concept being then used in a plural form. Yet such an evolution does not develop directly and spontaneously, but only emerges gradually and painstakingly. The work of memory that has been undertaken by French and German authorities takes root in deep divergences. Identifying and softening these divergences is a more realistic goal than eliminating them. Even in the Franco-German case, which is often qualified as remarkable, reconciliation appears as an open-ended process. Although the first Franco-German commission of historians already met in 1950, the last textbook written by French and German historians has only recently been published (Geiss and Le Quintrec, 2007). According to Chancellor Gerhard Schröder, such a common work remains necessary because of the persistence of "memory misunderstandings" between the two nations (Jospin and Schröder, 1999). One could add that, despite this historical rapprochement, Franco-German relations have been subject to a series of crises and strains, which can easily reopen profound scars. In this regard, the reconciliation process is never totally irreversible.

The South African case

The negotiations that made possible the transition from apartheid were based explicitly on the need to acknowledge "gray zones" that occurred in the past. In 1995, the preamble to the new South African Constitution opened with a striking statement of this sensibility. It rejected retribution and called for past injustices to be addressed "on the basis that there is a need for understanding but not for vengeance, a need for reparation but not for retaliation". To do so, the Truth and Reconciliation Commission (TRC) was set up by the South African parliament. Its objective was to investigate human rights violations during the apartheid era between 1960 and 1994. Anglican Archbishop Desmond Tutu chaired the 17-member body. Aside from its frequently described shortcomings, the TRC had at least one merit. It opened the floor to victims of each side and gave them a chance to tell their story. The hope was that the process of talking would somehow alleviate the sufferings endured in silence for so long. As President Nelson Mandela said, "South

African people must remember their dreadful past in order to be able to deal with it, to forgive when it is necessary, but never to forget" (Mandela, 1999). In the same vein, Desmond Tutu asserted: "There is no future without forgiveness, but to forgive, one must know what happened. In order not to repeat what happened to others, we must remember" (1999).

To turn the page of apartheid, a deliberate link was made between the proceedings of the TRC and the granting of amnesty. In order to obtain amnesty, an offender had to apply to the TRC, participate in its hearings, and meet with its requirements, including the requirement of full disclosure. This restorative justice aimed at achieving the healing and restoration of all concerned – of victims in the first place, but also of offenders, their families and the larger community (van Ness, 1993: 259). The ultimate purpose of this initiative was not to punish offenders, but to reintegrate them into the community and to repair damaged communal bonds (Tutu, 2000: 59–60).

Nevertheless, it would be naive to be too optimistic regarding these objectives. The TRC was above all shaped by political constraints and more particularly by the balance of power between the parties. The issue of amnesty for human rights offenders was decided by a political deal between the outgoing political elite (the National Party) and the African National Congress (ANC). In other words, the TRC was a compromise solution forced on the country by the fact that those who had power were not going to surrender it without guarantees that they would not be prosecuted after stepping down. This background is typical of a general pattern. As Wilson has shown, the area of justice in transition is the one in which leaders are most likely to reach a deal over the heads of ordinary people, and *ipso facto* the one in which civil groups are usually the least effective in shaping the course of the talks (2001: 198–200). However, in South Africa, human rights organizations played a certain role once the political settlement was struck between the two main political parties.

They did a great deal of lobbying between the passage of the interim constitution and the National Unity and Reconciliation Act in 1995. Consequently, they prevented a blanket amnesty and had a significant impact in framing the terms of the commission.

At the end of the day, the TRC faced criticisms and led to controversies and disputes. The fundamental objection was that it has sacrificed the rights of victims and survivors and their legitimate need for justice. The pretended healing effect of the TRC indeed varied considerably from one set of victims to another. To cite an example, Churchill Mxenge, the brother of an assassinated activist, Griffiths Mxenge, objected: "Unless justice is done, it's difficult for any person to think of forgiving" (quoted by Rosenberg, 1996: 88). This statement recalls that the national process of moving forward and making amends rarely coincides with individual processes. On a purely psychological level, for a survivor to react in an overly forgiving way toward perpetrators, or to simply let bygones be bygones, is highly improbable in the short term. Yet, for all its obvious imperfections, the TRC performs the crucial task of acknowledgement of the victim's loss.

In 2003, the TRC issued its final report and warned against any granting of blanket amnesty for perpetrators, arguing that it would "undermine the commission's work". The report also recommended that $348 million in reparations be paid to more than 21,000 victims of apartheid, urging businesses to contribute along with the government. Nowadays, thousands of people are still waiting for reparations. Continuing disparities in wealth, housing, education, and health between blacks and whites indicate that the process of reconciliation still involves a lot of hard work. In the long run, the challenge is immense since it is to create a society within which the chances of the recurrence of the kinds of gross violations of human rights that occurred in the past are reduced to a minimum. Nonetheless, the disintegration of the South African state through racial conflict is unlikely in the foreseeable future.

Reconciliation as a set of patterns

These examples are rich but they cannot be transformed in a model that could be generalized to other cases. To demonstrate it, let us stress one characteristic of the two chosen cases: the nearly universal condemnation of the Nazi regime and of the apartheid regime. This crucial element is indeed far from being common. In most of the cases, one of the main resistances to launch a reconciliation process lies in the extreme difficulty associated with deciding who the perpetrators and the victims were. This specific feature shows the inappropriateness of any normative model in that matter. Having said that, we cannot deny that there are common experiences that people go through across different contexts if they are involved in violent conflict. From that viewpoint, three main questions can be taken into account to understand how former adversaries try to restore a clear line between the past and the future: *how* (a), *who* (b) and *when* (c).

(a) How? A triple process of reassessment

In a reflection on coexistence after a violent past, Michael Ignatieff distinguishes two meanings of reconciliation: it can firstly be seen as an emotional meeting of hearts and minds, while, in a much more political sense, it means "accepting the world as it actually is, instead of fighting or opposing it" (Ignatieff, 2003: 326). Since the purpose of this chapter is to focus on political – and not individual – reconciliation, this second meaning merits to be taken into deeper consideration. How do you understand this process of "accepting the world as it is"? With which reality (which realities) should one be reconciled? In his analysis, partly based on the South African case, Ignatieff gives the two following examples: for many whites, to be reconciled meant acknowledging the majority rule while for many black victims, it meant accepting the fact that their individual desire for revenge would never be achieved.

Beyond these examples, we can consider that this process of acceptance basically implies a triple form of reassessment: reassessment of the representation that each party has about the other; reassessment of the self-image; reassessment of the common past.

"Reframing" the other and self-reflection.

In deep-rooted, protracted conflicts, nearly institutionalized images of the enemy prevail and dominate perceptions. The other side is frequently described as having evil intentions, low morality and inferior traits. Negation of the other as human being becomes a central element of each party's identity. A sense of mutual vulnerability leads indeed each side to fear that by recognizing the other's identity, it is denying its own. As Kelman has noted, "each side seems concerned, then – perhaps at an unconscious level – that acceptance of the other's nationhood would undermine the moral basis of its own claims. In sum, fulfilment of the other's national identity is perceived by each side as equivalent to the destruction of its own identity. Thus, neither side can be expected to make a move to accept the other unless and until it develops a sense of assurance that its own existence is secure" (1978: 170–171). Moreover, as long as the other is demonized, each party can avoid seeing itself in the role of victimizer (Kelman, 1999).

Accordingly, it is not surprising that the recognition of the rival does not occur in the twinkling of an eye. As long as losses have not been mourned, groups are unable to alter their positions and to develop the kind of empathy that many see as necessary for settling bitter conflicts (White, 1984; Volkan, 1988; Halpern and Weinstein, 2004). The consideration of the other as he is, and not any longer as one would like him to be, requires both a change of attitudes – from backward-looking attitudes to forward-looking attitudes (Zartman and Kremenyuk, 2005) – and a change of perceptions that are only conceivable when coexistence appears to be an absolute necessity for each party. In this condition, the impact of a dehumanization of the enemy can only be gradually mitigated by

the pursuit of common goals and the establishment of personal relationships between parties. Such a structural and relational transformation tends to enrich the image of the other in personalizing the members of the rival group, in separating the wrongdoer from the wrong which has been committed and – when it is appropriate – in perceiving the former enemy as a victim of the conflict as well (Bar-Tal, 2000).

In an ultimate phase, reconciliation reflects a shift in attention from blaming the other to taking responsibility for its own attitudes. Though, the journey from a "victimhood psychology" (based on group memory of violent aggression and injustices in the past decades or even centuries) to the status of "actor" is long and demanding (Montville, 2001: 132). During the conflict, groups tend to view themselves in a one-sided way involving self-glorification and self-praise, ignoring any information that might shed negative light on the group. In acknowledging the past in its complexity, each party has the feeling that it could lead to a weakening of its core identity. Kelman shows that it is just the opposite: such a self-reflection actually implies a strengthening, rather than a weakening, of each party's identity (2004: 121).

Confronting history.

Coming to terms with the past implies the reexamination of historical narratives and the revaluation of national myths, on each side of the conflict. As Richard Jackson shows in his chapter on constructivism, discursive structures that underpin violence and conflict can be deconstructed – at least to some extent. However, the "recreation of the record of the past" (Zartman and Kremenyuk, 2005: 300) cannot be undertaken immediately upon the cessation of hostilities. Many case studies show that leaders firstly opted for partial amnesia. The early phases of the reconciliation process do indeed entail powerful resistances within the population. Therefore, some "willful ignorance" may seem appropriate (Bargal and Sivan 2004: 144). However, this choice does probably not put into question the need, in the long run, for coping directly with the past (Krondorfer, 1995).

At this stage, the question is probably not to wonder whether one should remember *or* forget, but how to remember *and* forget in order to move forward (Garton Ash, 2003: 415). In this respect, scholars generally agree that an adjustment regarding diverging interpretations of the past may function as a long-term confidence-building measure. For example, Tambiah (1986) suggests that peacemaking in Sri Lanka must involve the deconstruction of historical accounts of ethnic origins, differences, and traditions. This, he says, will permit the two communities of the country to understand better their many common experiences and not to limit their attention to those experiences that divide them. Similarly, Philipps (2001) asserts that in German/East–Central European relations, official statements of mutual apologies have been central for reconciliation to take a public face. In the Balkans, the executive director of the Balkan Trust for Democracy in Belgrade, Ivan Vejvoda, asserts that "reconciliation cannot be achieved without a committed and sustained effort to shed as much light as possible" on the most uncomfortable episodes of the past (Magarditsch, 2005: 172).

In this view, each party is supposed to take responsibility for the past pain. Except in cases of radical asymmetry (such as genocides, mass killing or crimes against humanity), violent conflicts generally lead to grievances and victims on each side. Nonetheless, public acknowledgement of the crimes (by the perpetrators to the victims or surviving relatives; or by the representatives of the state in the name of which the crimes were committed) remains an immense challenge on the ground, the main difficulty being that each party usually perceives itself as the victim and the other side as being responsible to initiate the process of making accounts for past wrongdoings (Nadler, 2002). In spite of that, historical cases show that this situation of pluralistic, and even contradictory, visions of the past can progressively be overcome (Barsalou and Baxter, 2007).

As various analysts have pointed out, "reconciliatory events" (such as public ceremonies between senior representatives from each side) can have a real impact on the relations between former adversaries (Kelman, 1991; Volkan, 1998; Bargal and Sivan, 2004: 125). To prove it, scholars stress the rational, and not only emotive, dimensions of the process. From a game theoretical point of view, reconciliation events can be seen as costly signals that manifest the commitment for improving relations. This is particularly true when initiatives are costly, unexpected, unambiguous and made unilaterally (Long and Brecke, 2003: 21–22). This point can be illustrated by statements of Sadat during his visit to Jerusalem. Although it would be naive to overestimate the impact of Sadat's words on Israeli public opinion, it is likely that his explicit understanding of the suffering endured by the Jews throughout centuries had a real significance in the minds (Montville 2001: 137).

In the same line, symbolic gestures like formal or informal apology, visits to the location of atrocities, legal acts or any concrete step of compensation can constitute "turning points" in the interaction between former rivals. During the last decade, official representatives in several regions of the world have admitted responsibility for past discriminatory practices through a critical investigation into their national past. In the case of the Czech–German Declaration on Mutual Relations and Their Future Development, signed in January 1997, apologies were mutual. In this document, Germany accepted responsibility for the events of World War II and expressed regret for the sufferings and wrongs wrought against the Czech people. The Czech Republic expressed remorse for the sufferings and wrongs perpetrated against Germans expelled from the Sudetenland after the war.

This focus on the constructive impact of public acknowledgement of the past has to be nuanced by recent studies showing that, in the absence of a basic level of trust between parties, adversary's acknowledgement and even apologies are generally discounted as manipulative action. In such circumstances, they have no positive effects on willingness for reconciliation. On the contrary, in situations characterized by a high level of distrust (which is the case after protracted conflicts), it may even lower this willingness (Nadler and Liviatan, 2006). Knowing that the process of trust-building between former enemies is long and challenging, one should avoid any euphoria in that matter. Michael Lund's chapter on conflict prevention and the reflection of Fen Hampson, Chester Crocker and Pamela Aall on enmity and intractability are revealing in this regard (see Chapters 15 and 25).

(b) Who? A bottom-up and top-down process

Some scholars depict reconciliation as a process taking fundamental place between populations (Bar-On, 1996). Others highlight above all the role of national political leadership in launching the process (Bargal and Sivan, 2004). A central element of the bottom-up versus top-down tension is the conception of groups. At the local level, groups are described in terms of networks of individuals, each individual being a key vehicle of change. Improved interpersonal relations among community members are seen as the primary area for reconciliation work. Home-grown and grassroots initiatives are viewed as the key to success. In contrast, the top-down approach examines groups in more abstract terms as being composed of categories of identity that derive from national political divisions. In this sense, national intervention must first take place to create the conditions within which local dynamics can change (Van der Merwe, 2003: 113).

Beyond this tension, case studies indicate that the reconciliation process may begin either with the leaders or the grass roots. To be effective, this process must proceed bottom-up *and* top-down simultaneously. In other words, reconciliation requires both a political and a public momentum. Without political support "from above", the efforts of some individuals and/or groups will not be sufficient

to influence the whole population and to give clear signals to the other party. Conversely, without the support of the population, official discourses and public ceremonies are sterile and vain. The success of the reconciliation process depends to a large extent on the dissemination of the ideas associated with it among the grass roots. At the top level, statements and speeches, but also symbolic acts to manifest the change of attitudes towards the former enemy are revealed to be crucial (Bargal and Sivan, 2004: 128–143). Similarly, middle-level leaders, such as prominent figures in ethnic, religious, economic, academic, intellectual, cultural or artistic circles, play an important role to initiate and implement policies of reconciliation. In the same way, local leaders, businessmen, educators and many others may adhere to or resist the reconciliation process (Lederach, 1998).

Aside from the linkages between unofficial and official processes, a very important factor lies in the personal past of the respective leaders. Things will go more smoothly if the rapprochement is advocated by a person who has accomplished heroic actions against the enemy with whom reconciliation is being sought. This person then asks the population to undergo a transformation that he has undergone himself – that is, to overcome resentment towards the former enemy. For instance, the historical legitimacy of Charles de Gaulle probably helped the French people to change their views about the Germans. A similar point can be made with respect to Nelson Mandela in South Africa. This point is fundamental since the outcome of the process depends above all on popular support. For, even if a rapprochement seems necessary to the representatives of each party, it cannot be imposed by decree. The authorities can create a climate that encourages private steps towards reconciliation but they cannot force individual initiatives. At the most basic level, reconciliation is all about individuals.

In brief, the reconciliation process is substantially "home grown" rather than imposed from outside or under the tutelage of a more powerful third party or organization. Third parties and nongovernmental organizations play critical roles in encouraging and supporting each step of the process. But reconciliation cannot occur without the active efforts of each side's leaders and the support of the entire society or at least the majority of it.

(c) When? The ripeness question

One of the crucial issues to keep in mind is the ripeness question (Zartman, 2000): when is there any protagonist ripe to risk reconciliation efforts? Case studies indicate how essential time is where the objective is to change an adversarial relationship. Some events, particularly traumatic violations of human rights, can remain unexpressed for a period of time – a period that psychoanalysts often call "latent" (Weinrich 1999: 189). There does not appear to be any standard in this matter. However, one can reasonably think that the transformation of the representations that parties have of the other, of the past, and of themselves is an ongoing process that generally lasts for several generations. Such a process may not be imposed on a population that is still deeply hurt by stigmata of the past. As wounding often hinders any immediate rapprochement, one can probably postulate the following proposition: the shorter the delay between the conflict and the reconciliation process, the sharper the resistance within the population.

Even in the Franco-German case, the time factor turns out to be decisive. In this regard, it is worthwhile to underline the gap between official and social processes concerning the past. Officially, French and German authorities highlighted the necessity of facing the past a bit more than 10 years after the end of the war. Thus, they multiplied speeches, commemorations and symbolic gestures in order to take into consideration each other's past. By contrast, the systematic analysis of the activities organized in the broad field of education by the Deutsch-Französisches Jugendwerk/Office franco-allemand pour la Jeunesse from 1963 to 2001 shows that

painful questions of the past were not openly addressed before the early 1990s (Delori, 2002). This research leads to the conclusion that, in the framework of exchange programs, diverging interpretations of the past among nationals of the two sides were mostly ignored.

In the South African case, timing is a key variable as well. One of the main shortcomings of the TRC was precisely that reconciliation in such a frame was a questionable goal. Individual reconciliation has indeed a different time scale from that of any commission. Individual healing is a process paced by its own inner timing which cannot be pushed or programmed. In a few years, truth commissions could only create the conditions in which reconciliation might eventually occur (Garton Ash, 2003: 416). Accordingly, although the reconciliation process does not have any formal beginning and ending, it seems appropriate to conceive it as a – at least – two-stage process as per the following: first, a peaceful coexistence for pragmatic reasons (common involvement in institutional and economic frames), and then afterwards a potential transformation of beliefs and identities.

Useful distinctions

In the literature, the concept of reconciliation is often linked with the notions of truth, justice and forgiveness. This way to look at the picture is easily understandable. Each historical case shows that, on the ground, these mechanisms are deeply interconnected. Yet, at a theoretical level, the analysis is likely to gain in clarity if these processes are distinguished. One could argue that truth, justice and forgiveness greatly contribute to the establishment of a lasting peace. However, a linear correlation between these processes and reconciliation cannot simply be presumed. Therefore, we prefer not to consider them as preconditions of reconciliation (in the same way as, for instance, a security bargain that ensures safety on all sides). Hence, rather than encompassing the three notions under a very broad – and to some extent confusing – label of reconciliation, we suggest a deeper study of the articulation between them. To do so in a variety of contexts, more research drawing from a broad range of disciplines is needed. Let us simply shed light on some questions raised by these linkages.

(a) The need for justice

After a violent conflict, the expectations of victims in terms of justice are very high. Especially in horrendous situations like Rwanda, Yugoslavia, Cambodia and others, many consider that reconciliation is not appropriate because it is too soft on criminal conduct of offenders. According to many victims, there cannot be reconciliation without justice. In this respect, justice appears as one component of reconciliation (Kriesberg, 2004: 83). However, mutual relationship between justice and reconciliation can be disputed.

Actually, although frustrating for victims, incomplete justice sometimes appears as a practical necessity. In South Africa, for instance, the possibility of amnesty for apartheid killers directly resulted from the peace negotiation leading to the democratic transition. In Rwanda, to take another example, the prosecution of all the genocidaires was simply impossible. From April to July 1994, more than 800,000 people (Tutsis for the majority) were killed. One year later, the lack of staff and financial support was so striking that Rwandan authorities admitted that national courts would take more than a century to try all the suspects. In 2003, about 80,000 people accused of human rights crimes were packed into jail, often in insalubrious conditions, still waiting to come before the court. To face the concrete impossibility of any exemplar justice, various measures were taken: the liberation of 10,000 prisoners for health or age reasons, the increasing number of collective proceedings and the launching of a new version of a traditional conciliation procedure, called the *gacaga* system (Digneffe and Fierens, 2003). The Rwandan case illustrates a general question raised by Hannah Arendt: how do you exercise

justice after crimes "that one can neither punish, nor forgive" (1961: 307)?

In order to cope with that issue, some scholars consider that the central question in reconciliation is not whether justice is done, but rather how one goes about doing it in ways that can also promote peaceful coexistence between parties (Assefa, n.d.; Evenson, 2004). To favour such delicate coexistence, they call for a "restorative justice" – as opposed to "retributive justice". Whereas the aim of any criminal justice process is primarily to identify guilt and to administer the punishment required by the law, restorative justice tends to appease the bitterness and resentment that exist between the parties. To the partisans of this dynamic, the punishment of the offenders alone does not prevent them from continuing to hate the other side (Cobban, 2007). So, they seek to favour an environment where the offenders take the responsibility of acknowledging their offence and get motivated to change the relationship from destructive to constructive.

This focus on restorative justice shows the difficulty of defining the notion of justice. Does it encompass the whole range of ways to insure a "sense of justice", from trials, purges, truth commissions, opening of archives to symbolic acts of expiation, memorials and institutional reform (Teitel, 2000)? In terms of distinctions, is it not useful to differentiate what Zartman calls a "backward-looking notion of justice" as retribution and strict reparation, and a "forward-looking notion of justice" aimed at establishing a new relationship on the basis of equal respect between parties? In this sense, justice does not only concern the way to compensate victims as much as possible, but also – and even more – the necessity to revise the system in which parties are in relations, so that injustices perpetuated in the past would no longer be possible in the future (Zartman and Kremenyuk, 2005: 294). Distinctions of that type could be multiplied. Beyond debates referring to this notion (see Chapter 30 by Cecilia Albin in this book), it seems that justice is required in the aftermath of conflict, but that it can hardly provide the only basis for reconciliation.

(b) The search for truth

The concepts of truth and reconciliation have become closely associated with the implementation of truth commissions around the world. Beside the prominent South African case, truth commissions were created in countries as diverse as Croatia, Ghana, Morocco, Argentina, Nigeria, Central African Republic, Timor-Leste, Sierra Leone, Liberia, Peru, to name a few. In each of these cases, "truth-telling" processes emphasized reconciliation as a goal. The hope was that learning the truth would somehow convince citizens to put the past behind and move forward. The linkage between truth and reconciliation was so systematic that it has finally achieved the status of a "truism" (Borer, 2004: 21). Indeed, is there any evidence that truth is inherently a road to reconciliation?

So far, the thought that reconciliation requires truth is not plausible as a "general empirical rule" (Allen, 1999: 317). In this respect, the analysis of the South African case by James L. Gibson is telling. In a study dedicated to the TRC and its consequences on South African society, Gibson precisely focuses on the assertion that truth leads to reconciliation. Based on extensive surveys and social science analysis, his reflection concludes that the TRC did succeed in convincing a majority of South Africans that all sides were guilty of human rights violations and in turn suffered from violations. To him, this common interpretation of the apartheid era provides the basis for reconciliation. Nevertheless, it is striking that one of Gibson's measures of reconciliation, political tolerance, remains scarce in South African culture (2004).

Furthermore, even though some individual victims report experiencing feelings of "catharsis", a lot of them agree that feelings of anger and frustration have not diminished in the least. Given this ambivalent evidence, Allen asserts, "it is doubtful whether any general claims whatsoever can be made about the capacity of truth commissions to secure the claimed benefits, even for individuals" (Allen, 1999: 316).

Nobody can deny the fact that amnesia refuses victims the public acknowledgement of their pain and, therefore, can surely not contribute to reconciliation in the long run. Yet, in certain circumstances, the search for truth can be seen as undermining the fragile cooperation by holding on to the past instead of looking to the future. For that reason, the standard sequence of truth and reconciliation could be reversed. To illustrate it, Forsberg gives the example of the Finish civil war between reactionary Whites and revolutionary Reds in 1918 (2003: 74–75). United in 1939 against their common enemy, the Soviet Union, both parties waited more than one generation to know the truth about the civil war. This example shows that the parties involved in a process of reconciliation need to feel sufficiently secure before they can allow themselves to remember what shames them as well as what justifies them. And the achievement of such security may require a decade, a generation or even more, of silence.

In underlining the ambivalence of truth-telling processes (as a condition for reconciliation *and* as a potential impediment to achieve reconciliation), the purpose is neither to underevaluate the genuine need for knowing the truth of past violence, nor to suggest a relativistic view of the historical truth. It is to show that, even though seeking accuracy about the past and allowing victims to tell their stories are vital steps in the reconciliation process (Phelps, 2004), truth in itself does not bring reconciliation.

Once again, a major difficulty is the polysemic character of truth. A variety of meanings can be attributed to this notion, namely factual truth (searched by historians), personal truth (on the basis of each person's subjective experience), or even official truth (chosen narrative of the past). Regarding the process of rapprochement between former adversaries, the acknowledgement of the facts by all sides is as important as the revealing of the past (and probably even more so).

The clarification of contested historical events is a decisive step toward changing the relationship between protagonists. However, facts alone do not lead to the establishment of a shared vision. Yet, interpretation that the facts are given is one of the critical elements of any conflict resolution (Forsberg, 2003: 73). In this regard, subjective views of the past do not necessarily undermine the search for "truth". Intersubjective truth can only emerge if different accounts of the past are allowed to exist. That perspective does not lead to a relativistic stance that all the diverging, and sometimes contradictory, narratives of the same past are equally valid. Admittedly, *events* cannot be erased. One cannot undo what has been done, or pretend that what happened never occurred. However, the *meaning* that is attributed to past events is never fixed once and for all (Ricoeur, 2000: 496). After an international or intercommunity conflict, as it has been showed in the Franco-German case, it would be naïve to expect the establishment of a single, shared "truth". As Garton Ash notes, the purpose is not to have a single agreed version of the past, but to achieve "an agreed description of the basic factual landscape of the past" that could constitute the "factual framework within which the vital healthy and unending battle of interpretations must go on" (2003: 416–417).

(c) A contested forgiveness?

According to some scholars, the degree to which truth commissions contribute to long-term reconciliation is partly determined by whether perpetrators or state officials acknowledge and apologize for wrongs (Hayner, 2001: 252). That assertion leads to the examination of a third and last notion: forgiveness. In South Africa, the advocates of restorative justice emphasized a quasi-transcendental view of reconciliation ideally based on a perpetrator's repentance and a victim's forgiveness (Graybill and Lanegran, 2004: 6). In this particular context, forgiveness – originally related to the private and personal sphere – is used in a collective

and political sense. However, the linkage between forgiveness and reconciliation is controversial (Brudholm, 2006).

Firstly, the notion of forgiveness is far from being a crucial reference in all religions (Hermann, 2004: 45). Knowing that this term doesn't have a universal significance, can one consider forgiveness as a necessary condition for reconciliation? Secondly, the political use of forgiveness raises the sensitive question of a double delegation. Who can ask for it and who can grant it? On the one hand, people ask for forgiveness in the name of their late fathers. As descendants, they are not perpetrators themselves. On the other hand, survivors forgive in the name of the dead victims. However, an authentic apology can probably not be consigned and assumed by the principals without altering its meaning and its moral force (Tavuchis, 1991: 49). Moreover, strictly speaking, a state cannot forgive. In a collective frame, the reference to the concept of forgiveness can only be metaphorical. Many cases show the concrete limits of such a metaphor. Let us stress the reaction of the South African Joyce Mthimkulu towards those who had applied to the TRC for amnesty for their killing of her son: "They are not asking forgiveness from us, the people who have lost their loved ones. They are asking forgiveness from the government. They did not do nothing to the government. What they did, they did to us" (quoted by Biggar, 2003: 316). Similarly, various representatives of the Afghan civil society categorically refused the parliamentary project of an amnesty for groups suspected of perpetrating war crimes during a quarter-century of fighting. According to Afghanistan's highest body of Islamic clerics, parliament cannot issue a blanket amnesty because "only the victims of those crimes can forgive the perpetrators" (*The Boston Globe*, 11 March 2007).

These reactions show the importance of having in mind a clear distinction between interpersonal processes (micro level) and interstate or intercommunity processes (macro level). Since the representatives asking for "forgiveness" repudiate in general deeds done by other members of a nation, these acts can be associated with expressions of regret, rather than ones of remorse. They remain political acts of apology rather than individual acts of repentance. In this respect, the case of Milan Babic is an exception. Babic was the first President of the Republic of Serbian Krajina, a largely Serb-populated region that broke away from Croatia. Indicted for war crimes by the International Criminal Tribunal for the Former Yugoslavia in 2004, he admitted that he knowingly and intentionally participated in the campaign of persecutions against Croatians. Before sentencing, he solemnly apologized to the Croatian people: "I stand before this tribunal with a deep sense of shame and remorse. I allowed myself to participate in the persecution of the worst kind against people only because they were Croats, not Serbs". His words were unequivocal: "I ask my brother Croats to forgive us, their brother Serbs" (*Le Monde*, 10 March 2006).

Even in this case of political *and* personal apologies, another argument can be underlined. How do you measure the level of sincerity of official representatives? This point is critical since the absence of remorse by those who are perceived as the aggressors creates an overwhelming sense of injustice in the victims (Montville, 2001: 131). Words can be seen as easy to utter ("talk is cheap"). As a result, apologizers are often asked to demonstrate their sincerity with actions such as reparation payments. Yet, this issue raises supplementary questions (Torpey, 2003; Jewsiewicki, 2004; Colonomos, 2005). How do you compensate victims for the suffering that has been endured? Until when? How do you avoid a succession of unlimited demands? Furthermore, reparations are most likely to occur in situations where there is clearly a perpetrator and a victim, which is rarely the case in interstate or interethnic conflicts, in which each side sees itself as a victim of past injustices.

These arguments do not deny the potential impact of public acknowledgements and diplomatic apologies. But they highlight the useful clarification between the interpersonal frame (appropriate for forgiveness) and the political or collective frame (pertinent for public acknowledgements and diplomatic apologies). Beyond this clarification, the multiplication and the emotional resonance of official apologies merit questioning (Barkan and Karn, 2006). How do you interpret the increasing number of public acknowledgements? Do these official signs of repentance reveal the emergence of a new international morality based on a cosmopolitan conscience (Barkan, 2000)? Or do they result instead from a pragmatic calculation in an increasingly interdependent world (Cohen, 2004)?

PRACTICAL LIMITATIONS OF THE CONCEPT

Besides its theoretical volatility, the concept of reconciliation has practical shortcomings. In the field, this notion arouses a variety of reactions, from enthusiasm to irony and scorn. A first group of actors, mainly involved in NGOs, explicitly calls for reconciliation. In their view, reconciliation is much more than a concept: it is one of their goals. Still, the notion provokes strong resistances as well. Two types of rejection can be observed. The first one results from the attitude of many victims of past violations. The fear of being manipulated by the power and the call for justice explain their hostility against what they perceive as a new type of injunction. A second kind of resistance is expressed by those, especially within the diplomatic and political sphere, who consider this idea as *naive*. Irritated by its spiritual connotation, they regard it as useless and even sometimes counterproductive. To sum up, we could assume that reconciliation fails to promote the transformation of the conflict when it reveals itself to be a sparkling political program (1) or a miraculous formula (2).

Reconciliation as a political slogan

In the immediate aftermath of a violent conflict, victims or relatives of dead victims distrust the notion of reconciliation, especially if it is proclaimed as official policy. The gap between individual and political processes is obvious in the case of the mothers of the disappeared group in Argentina, *Madres de la Plaza de Mayo* (the mothers of the Plaza de Mayo), who still refuse compensation. At the official level, the need to reconcile is presented as a way to look forward. However, for victims, this "politics of reconciliation" is often perceived as a rhetorical argument that despises the sufferings endured in the past. In Rwanda, for instance, voices coming from all communities denounce what they call as the "ideology of reconciliation". Among them, Immaculée Mukarwego argues: "Reconciliation. This word became unbearable to me and to most of the survivors who I know. To me, it is even perfectly indecent after a genocide. [...] 'To reconcile', as it is written in the dictionary, consists in making people at odds agree again. [...] Do I have to consider that what happened in Rwanda between April and July 1994 is the product of a dispute, a quarrel, a disagreement and therefore that it would not be understandable not to reconcile? Do the people who use this word all the time realize that its meaning is fundamentally simplistic?" (*Le Soir*, 7 April 2004).

The resentment of a population deeply affected by a conflict seems inevitable. From a psychotherapeutic approach, resentment is seen as legitimate and even necessary to express self-respect (Murphy and Hampton, 1988; Montville, 1993: 120). One Rwandan survivor eager to let bygones be bygones and involved in reconciliation processes explained: "I took the time to hate everybody. It took me ten years. I needed this time for hatred. Now I can think about reconciliation". Though, such evolution does not constitute a rule in that matter. In other cases, those who suffered in the flesh or who lost their family circle keep the stigmata of the past tragedy during their whole life (Edkins, 2003: 230–232). The record of another Rwandan survivor manifests it: "This is not the end of the genocide that really stops a genocide, because inwardly genocide never stops" (Mujawayo and Belhaddad, 2004: 197). There is the same echo in the words

of Speciosa Mukayiranga: "The survivor remains inconsolable. He resigns himself but he remains in revolt and powerless. He does not know what to do, the social environment does not understand him, and he does not understand himself either" (Mukayiranga, 2004: 777). This feeling is also emphasized by Jean Améry (who was subject to torture during World War II). To him, "what happened really happened" and "the fact that this happened cannot be taken thoughtlessly"; "nothing is cicatrised, and the wound that was almost healed always reopens and suppurates" (1995: 17–20). These sentences indicate a tension that cannot be avoided when speaking about reconciliation: the legitimate need to look forward always has the risk of denying people damaged by life (Brudholm, 2008).

Reconciliation as a miraculous formula

Social resistances do not only limit the ambitions of official authorities. They also put into question the moralistic and somehow euphoric view adopted by some scholars and practitioners.

As has been underlined, reconciliation involves prolonged, deep and multifaceted processes. To be fruitful, these processes require the management of expectations in at least three different ways. First, a call for the restoration of a supposed "harmony" between former adversaries is doubtful. Reconciliation tends to create an environment in which differences, misunderstandings and conflicts can be negotiated and not purely eliminated (Schaap, 2005: 21; Gardner-Feldman, 2006). In the same sense, references to "healing" are understandable in a metaphorical sense, but the passage from an individual to a social group remains questionable anyway. How do you heal the wound of a society? Such an idealized and therapeutic conception obviously fails to be a realistic model of reconciliation (Hazan, 2006).

Second, practitioners involved in conflict transformation risk facing major difficulties if they present reconciliation as a "kit for stabilizing peace". Reconciliation as such does not constitute a normative model or a magical solution that can be applied to any conflict. Its scope, as well as its chances of success, depend on at least two main elements: the generation effect and the context of each specific case. Therefore, it would be vain and possibly detrimental to formulate general considerations without taking into account the potential perils of context-insensitive reconciliation attempts (Hermann, 2004: 49). From a philosophical point of view, one could even question the fact that reconciliation as such is to be sought. Once again, more research on cases where there is no formal reconciliation and more broadly, on potential negative consequences of reconciliation projects, could be highly valuable.

A third element can be stressed regarding outsiders such as international organizations or mediators: the essence of reconciliation is the voluntary initiative of the parties. The rapprochement between former enemies depends on the extent to which the international community facilitates the process and provides concrete assistance for pursuing it. Yet, the forces for change are primarily internal and cannot be coerced. In Kosovo, for instance, reconciliation between Serbs and Albanians is a key objective for the United Nations peace-consolidation mission which based its approach on the promotion of multiethnicity. However, the impossibility of reaching a negotiated agreement about the status of Kosovo shows that the reconciliation process can only be an endogenous one (Duclos, 2003). In Rwanda, the same comment can be made to European – and especially Belgian – officials. The notion of reconciliation seems to be unacceptable when it sounds like advice given by the former colonial authorities: "Coming from Europeans, this word [reconciliation] has incontestably a paternalist and contemptuous connotation since 'the Blacks' are perceived as children who are invited to make peace after a struggle" (Mugarwego, *Le Soir,* 7 April 2004). These remarks favour a "modest" picture of reconciliation (Dwyer, 1999). Rather than expecting a process that entails justice, forgiveness and harmony, it is

critical to adopt an opinion that is reasonable in terms of aims and in terms of timing.

In 2004, Hermann asserted that "at least for now the notion of reconciliation cannot serve as the key concept for cracking the enigma of peacemaking and peace stabilizing" (p. 40). It is indeed difficult to deny the ambiguity and shortcomings of reconciliation in the field of international relations. Numerous difficulties have been highlighted in this study. On the theoretical level, the lack of consensus about the meaning of reconciliation is a major challenge for scholars and practitioners. The variety of conceptions analyzed above is quite puzzling: seen as synonymous with peaceful coexistence for some, it appears as the panacea for others. At the practical level, there are two main ways to conceive of the notion of reconciliation: as a goal or as a process. As a goal, it often sounds like a rhetorical argument. It may even become a slogan or a kind of label ("politics of reconciliation") that is implicitly required by international donors. As a process, reconciliation reveals itself to be more effective. Rather than being a static end-state, it refers to a continuously evolving and developing quality of relationship. However, there is no consensus on the specific conditions, timing and sequences of reconciliation. So how do we conclude then?

This reflection focused on the following hypothesis: solving conflicts in a durable manner implies a gradual change of the representations that parties have about the other, about their past and about themselves – this means a crucial change in their identities. Such an evolution is likely to be a never-ending journey that involves both governments and civil society, marked by progress and setbacks. The development of trust after violent conflicts cannot be reduced to a rational choice in favour of the best option. It is not so much a question of method and technique as a way to articulate politics and emotions, interests and human relations (Saunders, 1999: 4–5). At the end of the day, the rehearsal of clashing past experiences depends on each person's ability to risk (see Harold Saunders' chapter on dialogue in this book). Speaking of individual attitudes, let us conclude with the opinion of Robert Antelme just after his return from the camp of Dachau, in 1945: "The same indignation that was expressed by Frenchmen against Nazi barbarity must now be expressed against the attitude of some Frenchmen. [...]. Far from taking revenge on us, the man who shoots down or hits a German prisoner actually insults us". "To think that a deportee could be delighted that some Germans in France are becoming themselves 'deportees', or even simply tolerate it, means that one did not understand anything of what has been lived over there" (2005: 10 and 17). One single opinion will clearly not "crack the enigma of peace stabilizing" but it can be an invitation to go on investigating. Although current lacunae in the literature can be seen as real brakes, they also provide a fascinating challenge.

NOTES

1 The author would like to thank Thomas Brudholm, Ariel Colonomos and Pierre Hassner for helpful comments and stimulating discussions.

2 Gardner-Feldman (1999) distinguishes philosophical-emotional and practical-material components of reconciliation. In the same line, Long and Brecke (2003) analyze two main models of reconciliation: a signalling model and a forgiveness model. Hermann (2004) discerns cognitive, emotional-spiritual and procedural aspects of reconciliation. Nadler (2002) puts an emphasis on socioemotional and instrumental reconciliation. Schaap (2005) emphasizes restorative and political reconciliation approaches. Galtung (2001) refers to no less than twelve different conceptions of reconciliation.

REFERENCES

Ackermann, Alice. 1994. "Reconciliation as a Peace-Building Process in Post-War Europe: The Franco-German case", *Peace and Change*, 19 (3): 229–250.

Allen, Jonathan. 1999. "Balancing Justice and Social Unity: Political Theory and the Idea of a Truth and Reconciliation Commission", *University of Toronto Law Journal*, 49 (3): 315–353.

Améry, Jean. 1995. *Par-delà le crime et le châtiment. Essai pour surmonter le mal*. Paris: Actes sud.

Amstutz, Mark. R. 2005. *The Healing of Nations. The Promise and Limits of Political Forgiveness*. Lanham: Rowman and Littlefield Publishers.

Antelme, Robert. 2005. *Vengeance?* Mayenne: Farrago.

Arendt, Hannah. 1961. *Condition de l'homme moderne*. Paris: Calmann-Lévy.

Asmal, Kader, Asmal, Louise and Roberts, Ronald S. 1997. *Reconciliation Through Truth: Reckoning of Apartheid's Criminal Governance*. Cape Town: David Philips.

Assefa, Hizkias. n.d. "The Meaning of Reconciliation", available at www.gppac.net/documents/pbp/part1/2_reconc.htm

Bargal, David and Sivan, Emmanuel. 2004. "Leadership and Reconciliation", in Y. Bar-Siman-Tov (ed.), *From Conflict Resolution to Reconciliation*. Oxford: Oxford University Press. pp. 125–147.

Barkan, Elazar. 2000. *The Guilt of Nations. Restitutions and Negotiating Historical Injustices*. New York and London: W.W. Norton and Company.

Barkan, Elazar and Karn, Alexander. (eds.). 2006. *Taking Wrongs Seriously. Apologies and Reconciliation*. Stanford: Stanford University Press.

Bar-On, Dan. 1996. *In Pursuit of Peace: A History of the Israeli Peace Movement*. Washington, DC: United States Institute of Peace.

Barsalou, Judy and Baxter, Victoria. 2007. "The Urge to Remember. The Role of Memorials in Social Reconstruction and Transitional Justice", *Stabilization and Reconstruction Series*, 5 (report of the United States Institute of Peace).

Bar-Siman-Tov, Yaacov. 2000. "Israel-Egypt Peace: Stable Peace?", in Arie M. Kacowicz, Yaacov Bar-Siman-Tov, Ole Elgaström, Magnus Jerneck (eds.), *Stable Peace among Nations*. Boulder: Rowman and Littlefield Publishers. pp. 220–238.

Bar-Siman-Tov, Yaacov. (ed.). 2004. *From Conflict Resolution to Reconciliation*. Oxford: Oxford University Press.

Bar-Tal, Daniel. 2000. "From Intractable Conflict Through Conflict Resolution to Reconciliation: Psychological Analysis", *Political Psychology*, 21: 351–365.

Bar-Tal, Daniel and Benninck, Gemma H. 2004. "The nature of reconciliation as an outcome and as a process", in Yaacov Bar-siman-Tov (ed.), *op. cit.*, pp. 11–38.

Biggar, Nigel (ed.). 2003. *Burying the Past. Making Peace and doing Justice after Civil Conflicts*. Washington: Georgetown University Press.

Borer, Tristan Anne. 2004. "Reconciling South Africa or South Africans? Cautionary Notes from the TRC", *African Studies Quarterly*, 8 (1): 19–38.

Brudholm, Thomas. 2006. "Revisiting Resentments: Jean Améry and the Dark Side of Forgiveness and Reconciliation", *Journal of Human Rights*, 5: 7–26.

Brudholm, Thomas. 2008. *Resentment's Virtue: Jean Amery and the Refusal to Forgive.* Philadelphia: Temple University Press.

Cobban, Helena. 2007. *Amnesty after Atrocity? Healing Nations After Genocide and War Crimes.* Boulder: Paradigm Publishers.

Cohen, Raymond. 2004. "Apology and Reconciliation in International Relations", in Yaacov Bar-Siman-Tov (ed.), *op cit.* pp. 177–195.

Colonomos, Ariel. 2005. *La morale dans les relations internationales.* Paris: Odile Jacob.

de Gaulle, Charles. 1970. *Discours et messages.* Paris: Plon.

Delori, Mathias. 2002. *Le travail de mémoire au sein de l'OFAJ (1963–2001).* Final dissertation, Institut d'Etudes Politiques de Grenoble.

Digneffe, Françoise and Fierens, Jacques. (ed.). 2003. *Justice et gacaca. L'expérience rwandaise et le génocide.* Namur: Presses universitaires de Namur.

Duclos, Nathalie. 2003. "Incertaine réconciliation au Kosovo", *Raisons politiques,* 9 (2): 141–159.

Dwyer, Susan. 1999. "Reconciliation for Realists", *Ethics and International Affairs,* 13: 81–98.

Edkins, Jenny. 2003. *Trauma and the Memory of Politics.* Cambridge: Cambridge University Press.

Evenson, Elizabeth M. 2004. "Truth and Justice in Sierra Leone: Coordination between Commission and The Court", *Columbia Law Review,* 104 (3): 730–767.

Forsberg, Tuomas. 2003. "The Philosophy and Practice of Dealing with the Past", in Nigel Biggar (ed.), *Burying the Past. Making Peace and doing Justice after Civil Conflicts.* Washington: Georgetown University Press. pp. 65–84.

Galtung, Johan. 2001. "After Violence, Reconstruction, Reconciliation, and Resolution", in Mohammed Abu-Nimer (ed.), *Reconciliation, Justice and Coexistence. Theory and Practice.* Lanham: Lexington Books. pp. 3–23.

Gardner-Feldman, Lily. 1999. "The Principle and Practice of 'Reconciliation' in German Foreign Policy/ Relations with France, Israel, Poland and Czech Republic", *International Affairs,* 75 (2): 333–356.

Gardner-Feldman, Lily. 2006. *Germany's External Reconciliation as a Defining Feature of Foreign Policy: Lessons for Japan?* Available at www.aicgs.org/analysis/c/lgf042806.aspx

Garton Ash, Timothy. 2003. "The Waters of Mesomnesia", in Anne-Marie Le Gloannec and Alexander Smolar (eds.), *Entre Kant et Kosovo. Etudes offertes à Pierre Hassner.* Paris: Presses de Sciences Po. pp. 405–419.

Geiss, Peter and Le Quintrec, Guillaume. 2007. *Histoire/Geschichte. L'Europe et le monde depuis 1945.* Paris: Nathan.

Gibson, James. L. 2004. *Overcoming Apartheid: Can Truth Reconcile a Divided Nation?* New York: Russell Sage Foundation.

Govier, Trudy and Verwoerd, Wilhelm. 2002. "Trust and the Problem of National Reconciliation", *Philosophy of the Social Sciences,* 32 (6): 178–205.

Graybill, Lyn and Lanegran, Kimberly. 2004. "Truth, Justice, and Reconciliation in Africa: Issues and Cases", *African Studies Quarterly,* 8 (1): 1–18. Available at www.africa.ufl.edu/asq/v8/v8i1a1.htm

Grosser, Alfred. 1967. *French Foreign Policy under de Gaulle.* Boston: Little Brown.

Halpern, Jodi and Weinstein, Harvey M. 2004. "Rehumanizing the Other: Empathy and Reconciliation", *Human Rights Quarterly,* 26 (3): 561–583.

Magarditsch, Hatschikjan, Reljic, Dusan and Sebek, Nenad. (eds.). 2005. *Disclosing Hidden History: Lustration in the Western Balkans. A Project Documentation.* Belgrade : Cicero. Available at www.lustration.net/pap_cfd.pdf

Hayner, Priscilla B. 2001. *Unspeakable Truths: Confronting State Terror and Atrocity.* New York: Routledge.

Hazan, Pierre. 2006. "Measuring the Impact of Punishment and Forgiveness: a Framework for evaluating Transitional Justice", *International Review of the Red Cross,* 88 (861): 19–47.

Hermann, Tamar S. 2004. "Reconciliation: Reflections on the Theoretical and Practical Utility of the Term", in Yaacov Bar-Siman-Tov (ed.), *op. cit.* pp. 39–60.

Horne, John. 2002. "Démobilisations culturelles après la Grande Guerre", *La revue 14–18 Aujourd'hui* (5): 41–157.

Ignatieff, Michael. 2003. "Afterword. Reflections on Coexistence", in Antonia Chayes, and Marta Minow (eds.), *Imagine Coexistence: Restoring Humanity after Violent Conflict.* San Francisco: Jossey-Bass. pp. 325–333.

Jewsiewicki, Bogumil. 2004. "Réparations, restitutions, réconciliations", *Cahiers d'études africaines,* 173–174: 7–24.

Jospin, Lionel and Schröder, Gerhard. 1999. "Memory and Identity", Genshagen, Sept. 24–25, www.doc.diplomatie.gouv.fr/BASIS/epic/www/doc/DDW?M=2&K=952270850&W=DATE+%3D+%2725.09.1999%27+ORDER+BY+DATE/Descend

Kacowicz, Arie M. and Bar-Siman-Tov, Yaacov. 2000. "Stable Peace: A Conceptual Framework", in Arie M. Kacowicz Yaacov Bar-Siman-Tov, Ole Elgaström, Magnus Jerneck (eds.), *Stable Peace among Nations.* Lanham: Rowman & Littlefield. pp. 11–35.

Kelman, Herbert C. 1978. "Israelis and Palestinians: Psychological Prerequisites for Mutual Acceptance", *International Security,* 3 (1): 162–186.

Kelman, Herbert C. 1991. "Interactive Problem-Solving: The Uses and Limits of a Therapeutic Model for the Resolution of International Conflicts", in V. Volkan, J. Montville and D. Julius (eds.), *The Psychodynamics of International Relationships*, vol. 2. Lexington, Mass.: Lexington Books. pp. 145–160.

Kelman, Herbert C. 1999. "Transforming the Relationship between Former Enemies. A Social-Psychological Analysis", in Robert L. Rothstein (ed.), *After the Peace. Resistance and Reconciliation*. London: Boulder. pp. 193–205.

Kelman, Herbert C. 2004. "Reconciliation as Identity Change: A Social Psychological Perspective", in Yaacov Bar-Siman-Tov (ed.), *op. cit.* pp. 111–124.

Kriesberg, Louis. 2004. "Comparing Reconciliation Actions within and between Countries", in Yaacov Bar-Siman-Tov (ed.), *op. cit.* pp. 81–110.

Krondorfer, Björn. 1995. *Remembrance and Reconciliation: Encounters Between Young Jews and Germans*. New Haven, Conn. : Yale University Press.

Lederach, John Paul. 1997. *Building Peace: Sustainable Reconciliation in Divided Societies*. Washington, DC: United States Institute of Peace Press.

Lederach, John Paul. 1998. "Beyond Violence: Building Sustainable Peace", in Eugene Weiner (ed.), *The Handbook of Interethnic Coexistence*. New York: Continuum. pp. 236–245.

Long, William J. and Brecke, Peter B. 2003. *War and Reconciliation. Reason and Emotion in Conflict Resolution*. Cambridge: The MIT Press.

Mandela, Nelson. 1999 "Pardonne, mais n'oublie pas", *Le Monde*, 7 août.

Maoz, Ifat. 2004. "Social-Cognitive Mechanisms in Reconciliation", in Yaacov Bar-Siman-Tov (ed.), *op. cit.* pp. 225–237.

Montville, Joseph. 1993. "The Healing Function in Political Conflict Resolution", in Dennis Sandole and Hugo van der Merve (eds.), *Conflict Resolution Theory and Practice: Integration and Application*. Manchester: Manchester University Press. pp. 112–127.

Montville, Joseph. 2001. "Justice and the Burdens of History", paper presented at the 24th conference of the International Society of Political Psychology, Cuernavaca, Mexico, 14–18 July.

Mujawayo, Esther and Belhaddad, Saouad. 2004. *Survivantes. Rwanda, histoire d'un génocide*. La Tour-d'Aigues: Éditions de l'Aube.

Mukayiranga, Speciosa. 2004. "Sentiments de rescapés", in Catherine Coquio (ed.), *L'Histoire trouée. Négation et témoignage*. Nantes, l'Atalante. pp. 776–785.

Murphy, Jeffrie G. and Hampton, Jean. (eds.). 1988. *Forgiveness and Mercy*. Cambridge: Cambridge University Press.

Nadler, Arie. 2002. "Post Resolution Processes: An Instrumental and Socio-emotional Route to Reconciliation", in Gavriel Salomon and Baruch Nevo (eds.), *Peace Education: The Concept, Principles and Practices around the World*. Mahwah, NJ: Lawrence Erlbaum. pp. 127–143.

Nadler, Arie and Liviatan, Ido. 2006. "Intergroup Reconciliation: Effects of Adversary's Expressions of Empathy, Responsibility, and Recipients' Trust", *Personality and Social Psychology Bulletin*, 32: 459–470.

Peyrefitte, Alain. 1994. *C'était de Gaulle*. Paris: Fayard.

Phelps, Teresa G. 2004. *Shattered Voices. Language, Violence and the Work of Truth Commissions*. Philadelphia: University of Pennsylvania Press.

Philipps, Ann. 2001. "The Politics of Reconciliation Revisited: Germany and East-Central Europe", *World Affairs*, 163 (4): 171–191.

Philpott, Daniel. (ed.) 2006. *Politics of Past Evil: Religion, Reconciliation, And the Dilemmas of Transitional Justice*. Chicago: University of Notre-Dame Press.

Pouligny, Béatrice, Chesterman, Simon and Schnabel, Albrecht. (eds.). 2007. *After Mass Crime. Rebuilding States and Communities*. New York: United Nations University.

Ricoeur, Paul. 2000. *La mémoire, l'histoire, l'oubli*. Paris: Le Seuil.

Rosenberg, Tina. 1996. "A Reporter at Large: Recovering from Apartheid", *New Yorker*, 18 November, p. 86.

Schapp, Andrew. 2005. *Political Reconciliation*. London : Routledge.

Saunders, Harold H. 1999. *A Public Peace Process*. New York: St Martin's Press.

Shriver, Donald. W. 1995. *An Ethic for Enemies: Forgiveness in Politics*. New York: Oxford University Press.

Staub, Ervin. 2000. "Genocide and Mass Killing: Origins, Prevention, Healing and Reconciliation", *Political Psychology*, 21: 367–82.

Tambiah, Stanley. 1986. *Sri-Lanka: Ethnic Fratricide and the Dismantling of Democracy*. London: Tauris.

Tavuchis, Nicholas. 1991. *Mea Culpa. A Sociology of Apology and Reconciliation*. Stanford: Stanford University Press.

Teitel, Ruti. 2000. *Transitional Justice*. Oxford: Oxford University Press.

Torpey, Jonh. (ed.). 2003. *Politics and the Past. On Repairing Historical Injustices*. Lanham: Roman & Littlefield Publishers.

Tutu, Desmund. 1999. *No Future without Forgiveness*. New York: Doubleday.

Tutu, Desmund. 2000. "Reconciliation in Post-Apartheid South Africa: Experience of the Truth Commission", in *The Art of Peace: Nobel Peace Laureates Discuss Human Rights, Conflict and Resolution*. Ithaca, NY: Snow Lion Publications.

Van der Merwe, Hugo. 2003. "National and Community Reconciliation. Competing Agendas in the South African Truth and Reconciliation Commission", in Nigel Biggar, *op. cit.* pp. 101–124.

Van Ness, Daniel. 1993. "New Wine and Old Wineskins: Four Challenges of Restorative Justice", *Criminal Law Forum*, 4 (2): 251–276.

Volkan, Vamik. 1988. *The Need to have Enemies and Allies. From Clinical Practice to International Relationships*. New York: Jason Aronson.

Volkan, Vamik. 1998. "The Tree Model: Psychopolitical Dialogues and the Promotion of Coexistence", in Eugene Weiner (ed.), *op. cit.* pp. 343–358.

Weinrich, Harald. 1999. *Léthé. Art et critique de l'oubli*. Paris: Fayard.

White, Ralph. 1984. *Fearful Warriors: A Psychological Profile of U.S.–Soviet Relations*. New York: Free Press.

Wilmer, Franke. 1998. "The Social Construction of Conflict Reconciliation in the Former Yugoslavia", *Social Justice*, 25 (4): 90–113.

Zartman, I. William. 2000. "Ripeness: The Hurting Stalemate and Beyond", in Paul Stern, and Daniel Druckman (eds.), *International Conflict Resolution after the Cold War*. Washington, DC: National Academy Press. pp. 225–250.

Zartman, I. William and Kremenyuk, Victor. (eds.). 2005. *Peace versus Justice. Negotiating Forward- and Backward-Looking Outcomes*. Lanham: Rowman & Littlefield Publishers.

29

Assessing Outcomes: Conflict Management and the Durability of Peace

Scott Sigmund Gartner and Molly M. Melin

Conflict management is as old as conflict itself. Yet, for years, scientific studies of conflict management lagged behind other areas of study in the field of international relations, such as conflict initiation, remaining mostly anecdotal. The conflict resolution process was shrouded in mystique since most actions were conducted behind closed doors and were highly confidential (Young 1967). Scholars were skeptical about the possibility of creating generalizations about conflict management and its outcomes (Meyer 1960; Simkin 1971). As a result, the activities involved in managing conflict and the outcomes of these efforts have only recently become a focus of systematic scholarship (Young 1967; Bercovitch and Gartner 2006a). As the scientific study of conflict resolution gained acceptance, scholars began to collect information about the occurrence of management and its characteristics. Driven by an increase in the availability of management

information and data, along with an increase in the practice of third-party conflict resolution, management efforts, especially mediation, have increasingly become a focus of systematic analysis (see Bercovitch 1997; Regan and Stam 2000; Greig 2005; Beardsley et al. 2006; Bercovitch and Gartner 2006a). These recent studies have dramatically improved our understanding of the management process and its impact on conflict resolution.

Conflict management typically results in one of two outcomes: an agreement or continued fighting. This chapter focuses on the management efforts that result in an agreement and examines the nature and duration of these settlements. We: (1) describe the conflict management process generally; (2) examine the theoretical approaches used to analyze conflict resolution and settlement duration; (3) compare descriptive statistics on agreement type and duration using a variety of different data sets and examine why they differ; (4) present brief vignettes of conflict management that highlight the issues and patterns presented; and (5) address future research by discussing the importance of understanding two crucial theoretical factors, selection and substitutability, which both currently limit our ability to move this promising research forward.

THE CONFLICT MANAGEMENT PROCESS

By conflict management, we mean any steps taken to help resolve a conflict peacefully, from bilateral negotiation to third-party mediation. Third-party managers include a variety of different types, including nation-states, state coalitions, regional or international organizations, and individuals (Dixon 1996). Conflict management efforts involve the interaction of various decisions by disputants and possibly intermediaries. These potential interactions are depicted in Figure 29.1.

As the schematic of the conflict management process in Figure 29.1 shows, a third party can offer to help or be invited to manage the conflict at any point in a conflict. If no third party is involved, then the disputants may fight or negotiate themselves. When a third party does become involved as a conflict manager, its actions may or may not lead to a settlement. Should no settlement be reached, the third party may either offer further management or discontinue involvement all together. Following the establishment of a settlement, the agreement may or may not be upheld. Although this chapter focuses on the final phase of the management process, dispute settlements are related to the behavior and results of earlier phases in the conflict management process.

ASSESSING CONFLICT MANAGEMENT OUTCOMES

Much of the existing scholarship defines successful conflict management as the establishment of an agreement. Similarly, it is common to assume the goal of a management effort is to resolve the conflict by making it "too costly for combatants to continue fighting"(Regan 1996, 341). However, concluding that a conflict management effort is successful necessitates having knowledge of the goal of the effort, which is especially problematic

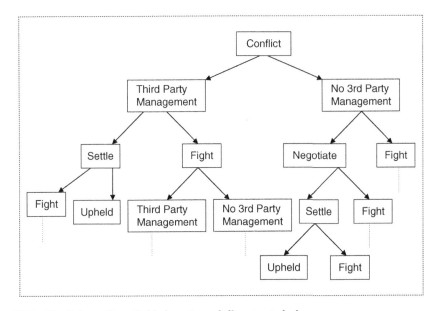

Figure 29.1   The interaction of third party and disputant choices

when third parties are involved. Territorial acquisition, regional stability, protection of interveners' diplomatic, economic, or military interests, ideology or the upholding of human rights are all possible goals of management activities (Pearson 1974). States frequently pursue more than one goal with their foreign policies (Morgan and Palmer 2000; Palmer and Morgan 2006). It is therefore necessary to disaggregate further the outcomes of conflict management to examine them critically.

Scholars have examined the type of agreement established as a way of further disaggregating conflict management outcomes. For example, achieving a ceasefire, however temporary and ill designed, may represent a successful and effective management effort (Bercovitch and Gartner 2006b). One can think of the numerous temporary ceasefires in the former Yugoslavia, each of which gave the parties the opportunity to feed the hungry and care for the wounded before fighting resumed. Achieving a limited agreement in a previously intractable conflict may be no less significant than the achievement of a full settlement in a more tractable dispute. Arguing that mediation is unsuccessful where it does not produce a full settlement thus represents a failure to appreciate the full complexity of conflict, the different outcomes that may bring a conflict to an end, and the decision processes underlying the entry or exit of a mediator.

Although a short ceasefire may represent relative progress, a truly effective management effort must allow peace to consolidate so that a political settlement takes root (Kissinger 1996). Many management efforts result in ceasefires that last only a few hours and do not enable true resolution. In the recent Yugoslavian case, there were 91 mediated settlements, almost half of which lasted one week or less (Gartner and Bercovitch 2006). Disputants may sign agreements without the intention of upholding them. Agreements such as ceasefires may actually be strategic – providing one side with an opportunity to improve its military position and fight longer. These realities suggest that effective conflict resolution involves "removing the causes as well as the manifestations of a conflict between parties and eliminating the sources of incompatibility in their position" which, represents "a long-term proposition"(Zartman 1997, 11). Examining how long peace agreements last after they are agreed upon, rather than focusing solely on whether an agreement was reached, provides a clearer understanding of the conflict management process and can help generate more effective prescriptions for resolving international disputes.

An agreement can provide a brief time period that allows for political changes to occur that lead to a permanent peace, or it can fail to address sufficiently the issues underlying the dispute and conflict can break out again. Change can only occur if there is a period of peace following an agreement. Agreements that last only a brief time fail to provide sufficient opportunity for effective political change since they fail to provide the political space necessary for new institutions and policies to gain traction and lead to lasting peace (Gartner and Bercovitch 2006). Thus, a critical aspect of the peace process is to "make it over the hump" and allow dispute settlements to take effect and alter the underlying political situation fueling the dispute. As the period immediately after a settlement is implemented poses a high risk of the return to conflict, Rothchild calls this period the "treacherous transition period"(2002, 3).

Almost half of all agreements fail to last two months (Gartner and Bercovitch 2006). These short-lived agreements failed to provide the "space" necessary for an agreement to shift political conditions (Rothchild 2002). While short-lived agreements clearly represent a failure of the agreement, they capture a different type of failure than if the terms of the settlement are implemented and conflict breaks out again. Both types of failure are important (Bercovitch and Gartner 2006b). Yet most studies ignore the problem of short-lived agreements, instead defining outcomes such that reemerging conflicts are new disputes.

Recent developments

In refining our approach to analyzing conflict management outcomes, some scholars focus less on the determinants of successful management and more on the durability of management outcomes. Only long-lasting agreements can truly allow for conflict resolution. Authors have begun to converge on two determinants of why agreements hold or fail (Gerner and Schrodt 2001; Fortna 2003b, 2004b; Bercovitch and Gartner 2006b). The first, what Fortna terms the baseline prospects for peace (called selection effects by Gartner and Bercovitch, and contextual effects by Gerner and Schrodt), are characteristics of the situation over which actors in the present have little control, such as the issue in dispute and history of the conflict. The second involves actors' deliberate attempts to enhance the durability of peace.

Baseline prospects for conflict resolution

Contextual variables distinguish *ex ante* the cases that are hard to terminate and likely to have a fragile settlement from those that are more amenable to settlement and likely to remain peaceful (Gerner and Schrodt 2001; Bercovitch and Gartner 2006b). These consist of situational or structural factors that exist at the time of an agreement. Examples include the outcome of the conflict, the number of disputants and their relationship, and the cost of the dispute. These variables capture the underlying factors that characterize a conflict and its attendant agreements; they do not represent a variable easily changed through conflict management.

The nature of the dispute, the issue involved, the dispute's intensity and violence, and the nature of the disputants affect the likelihood of a settlement having a short duration. Evidence suggests that agreements reached in conflicts over certain issues (e.g. territorial) are less likely to hold (Hensel 1994; Huth and Allee 2002). We must therefore consider the sources of the conflict carefully (see Vasquez and Valeriano in this volume; Gopin in this volume; Kinsella in this volume). Other studies have linked outcome

durability to power capabilities (Werner 1998, 1999; Dixon and Senese 2002; Quinn et al. 2006). Belligerents and third-party managers have little control over these contextual factors. At most, they can only make an effort to account for them and limit any negative effects they may have on the life of the agreement.

Proactive measures for conflict resolution

The second type of factors that determine the durability of a peace agreement are direct attempts to form a strong and lasting agreement (or process effects). Variables that directly influence the likelihood of a settlement also alter the latent mechanism that affects the duration of a settlement. These steps account for the problem that led to conflict and try to create a long-lasting settlement. Such measures include creating demilitarized zones to separate troops, monitoring by international observers, and third-party guarantees. Thus, the nature of the settlement and its resulting changes influence the likelihood of a settlement being short-lived. We break process effects into two parts: the method used to manage the conflict and the provisions within the agreement.

Conflict management method The nature of the conflict management process affects the durability of agreements. There are many methods used to manage conflict (Bercovitch and Regan 1999). The different methods of managing a conflict may work together, as more than one method is often used in the same conflict. The choice of strategies is dynamic and dependent upon the reaction of the disputants (Maoz and Terris 2006). *Negotiation* involves direct conflict management among the disputants without third-party assistance, whereby two parties seek a mutually acceptable agreement through compromise (see Zartman, in this volume). *Vocalization* involves public third-party appeals or demands for the disputants to negotiate, agree to a ceasefire, or withdraw troops and are common initial reactions of the international community to a dispute. *Economic sanctions* formalize intermediary demands by limiting financial interaction with the disputants. *Mediation* involves third-party assistance in finding a mutually acceptable agreement (see Bercovitch, in this volume). *Positive inducements* include economic and military aid, support in international organizations, and assistance with civil administration. These are the carrots of conflict management. *Adjudication* and *Arbitration* use the international legal system to manage the conflict by generating a binding decision to which the disputants must adhere (see Cede, in this volume). *Noncombatant troops* act as peacekeepers, humanitarian protectors, military observers, or help to clear minefields. Direct *Military Intervention* includes the use of troops across borders with the intent to stop an ongoing conflict (Holzgrefe and Keohane 2003). The method of management a third party employs has substantive implications for the outcome of the management effort and the durability of any settlement achieved (Regan 1996).

Third parties become involved in the disputes that are amongst the most difficult to resolve. These disputes are thus more likely to result in short-lived outcomes. However, this is because third parties get the tough cases, and not because third parties have a negative effect on agreements (Gartner and Bercovitch 2006). Rather, the presence of a third party as a guarantor actually increases the likelihood of an agreement, more than would otherwise be the case for these challenging, hard-to-resolve conflicts (Fortna 2004b). To understand fully the effects of third-party actions therefore requires that we control for the baseline prospects for peace and examine the entire management process (Bercovitch and Gartner 2006b; Melin et al. 2006).

Which third-party actions are the most effective in resolving conflicts? Only a few studies that compare third-party actions exist; Regan analyzes the success of third-party diplomatic, economic, and military efforts (Regan 1996). He finds that a mixed strategy is best for determining intervention success rather than a focus on just economic sanctions or military force. Frazier and Dixon examine the efficacy of different third-party actors

and conflict management techniques (2006). They find that international governmental organizations (IGOs) are the most effective in reaching a negotiated settlement. They also conclude that mediation is an effective technique to produce settlements but that military actions, such as peacekeeping, are more successful.

Agreement provisions   Mechanisms within the agreement can also promote peace by altering the incentive structures of the disputants to raise the cost of attack, reducing uncertainty about actions and intentions, and preventing accidents that could lead to war. Provisions made within agreements matter and can lessen the risk of further war. Precautions included in agreements, such as demilitarized zones, dispute resolution commissions, peacekeeping, and external guarantees, can establish a durable peace (Fortna 2004a; Greig and Diehl 2005). Note that there is an underappreciated negative effect: sometimes the factors that increase the likelihood of the disputing parties agreeing to a settlement, such as power sharing, can decrease the likely duration of that same agreement (Rothchild 2002).

The importance of third-party guarantors is a consistent theme in studies of peace durability. Hartzell, Hoddie, and Rothchild examine the stability of civil war settlements (2001). They control for situational characteristics, such as international system structure, nature of the previous regime, conflict duration, conflict issue, and conflict intensity. They find that territorial autonomy and third-party guarantors are important keys to establishing stability. This study was replicated by Pearson, Lounsbery, Walker, and Mann with a broader definition of conflict (2006). The results differ in that territorial autonomy is not as important, but third-party guarantors are still central for a durable peace.

The importance of third-party involvement and assurance is also a focus of Walter (2002), who argues that combatants must design credible guarantees on the terms of agreement for peace to take hold, which necessitates outside assistance. She confirms the critical nature of third-party security guarantees and the importance of effective power-sharing pacts, and finds that adversaries do, in fact, consider such factors in deciding whether to negotiate or fight. Peacekeeping efforts have also been shown to have important effects on the duration of peace in both interstate wars (Fortna 2003a; Smith and Stam 2003) and in intrastate wars (Doyle and Sambanis 2000; Hartzell et al. 2001). Scholars consistently find that while the involvement of third parties as conflict managers signals the difficulty of establishing a lasting peace due to the baseline characteristics of the conflict and disputants, the presence of third parties make it more likely that these agreements last than if no third party were present in the same case.

AGREEMENT DURATION

While few have studied agreement duration, the recent development of conflict management data provides a preliminary

picture of the nature of settlement durability and allows us to establish an understanding of the factors that lead to lasting peace. We provide, for the first time, an overview of the four most important data sets on conflict resolution and their associated summary statistics in Table 29.1. These data sets flow from very different conflict management research agendas and thus have fundamentally different approaches. The major differences between these data sets include: the actors considered as conflict managers, the actions identified as conflict management, and the measures of success. This variation clearly has implications for the results that will come from analysis on each of these data sets. A description of each data set and summary statistics for important agreement duration and outcome type measures are discussed below.

An agreement is only a "final" agreement *ex post*. *Ex ante*, an agreement's duration and permanence are unknown; seemingly weak treaties can be enduring, while settlements anticipated to be conclusive may fail

Table 29.1   Summary of conflict management data

Data Source	Definition of Success	Definition of Management	Definition of Conflict Manager
Third Party Interventions and Militarized Interstate Disputes	Short-term Outcome: Successful, Unsuccessful Long-term Outcome: Successful, Unsuccessful	Verbal, Diplomatic, Judicial, Administrative, Military	State, Coalition of States, IGO, NGO
International Crisis Behavior	Impact on Crises Abatement: Delayed, No Effect, Marginal Effect, Important Effect, Most Important Effect	Discussion, Fact-finding, Good offices, Condemnation, Call for action, Mediation, Arbitration, Adjudication, Sanctions, Observer group, Military force	Superpower, Regional or Security Organization, Global Organization
Ceasefires	No New COW War for the Dyad	Mediation, Guarantee	Sovereign States
International Conflict Management	Durability of Outcome: Less than 1 week, 1 week, 2 weeks, 3 weeks, 4 weeks, 5 weeks, 6 weeks, 7 weeks, 8 weeks + Management Outcome: Unsuccessful, Ceasefire, Partial Agreement, Full Settlement	Negotiation, Mediation, Arbitration, Referral to International Institution, Multilateral Conference	Individual, State, IGO, Regional Organization

almost immediately. It is critical to use data sets that include both brief agreements that fizzle and long-lasting agreements in order to develop an understanding of how conflict resolution efforts work. As a result, we do not include common conflict data sets like the *Correlates of War* and *Militarized Interstate Dispute* data, since they only identify so-called "final agreements" that are coded as such *ex post* once an agreement lasts long enough for renewed fighting to be considered a new dispute. This lack of inclusiveness is not a comment on these data sets' quality as conflict data, but addresses their utility as conflict management data sources.

The *International Conflict Management* (ICM) data set was compiled with a focus on international conflict management mechanisms, with the conflict management effort being the unit of analysis (Bercovitch 2000). The data define international conflict as an "organised and continuous militarized conflict, or a demonstration of intention to use military force involving at least one state" (Bercovitch 1998, 6). This definition yields 333 disputes from the 1945–2000 post-World War II period. Conflict management includes negotiation, mediation, arbitration, referral to international institutions, and multilateral conferences. Management represents the actions of individuals, states, and international and regional organizations, taken to resolve an international conflict. The data, described in Table 29.2, offer two methods for measuring conflict management outcomes. The first variable is a categorical measure of any agreement, which includes outcomes of unsuccessful, ceasefire, partial agreement, or full settlement (Bercovitch and Gartner 2006b). The second is the length of time the agreement lasts, ranging from under a week to over eight weeks (Gartner and Bercovitch 2006).

One sees that the distribution of the duration of outcomes shown in Table 29.2 is U-shaped. The most common outcome is those that last eight weeks or more, with 1042 observations in this category. The second most common category is those that end quickly, with 243

Table 29.2 Summary statistics for *International Conflict Management* outcome variables[1]

Durability of Intervention Outcome

Outcome Variable	Frequency	Percent
Less than 1 week	243	15.20
1 week	72	4.50
2 weeks	59	3.69
3 weeks	27	1.69
4 weeks	109	6.82
5 weeks	7	0.44
6 weeks	25	1.56
7 weeks	15	0.94
8 weeks or more	1042	65.17
Total	1599	100

Intervention Outcome

Offered only	242	4.84
Unsuccessful	2543	50.82
Ceasefire	394	7.87
Partial Agreement	1502	30.02
Full Settlement	323	6.45
Total	5004	100

[1] This includes totals from all actions defined by the ICM data set as management: negotiation, mediation, arbitration, referral to international institutions, and multilateral conferences.

agreements lasting less than one week. Those agreements in the middle number from seven observations (those agreements lasting five weeks) to 109 observations (those lasting four weeks). The range in this variation is at least partially due to the measurement of agreement durability being censored at eight weeks or more. However, the distribution also reveals the importance of considering variation in the life of an agreement, as many fail to last even a week.

There is also variation in the types of agreements established. Although most (2543 observations) management efforts are unsuccessful and do not lead to an agreement of any type, there is more variation than a dichotomous measure of successful or unsuccessful captures. Of those cases for which an agreement is established, many (1502 observations) are only partial agreements and very few (323 observations) result in full settlements.

Third Party Interventions and Militarized Interstate Disputes (TPI) data address 1178 interventions in MIDs from 1946 to 2000 (Frazier and Dixon 2005). It categorizes third-party intermediary actions into five categories: verbal expression, diplomatic approaches, judicial processes, administrative, and military. In addition to containing information on the methods of management, the data set includes information on the short-term and long-term outcomes of the management effort. It also identifies the third parties, which include states, coalitions of states, international governmental organizations, and nongovernmental organizations. The data are described in Table 29.3. Many (117) of the agreements that were successful in the short term were not successful in the long term.

International Crises Behavior (ICB) contain information on 334 international crises, 32 protracted conflicts, and 975 crisis actors from the end of World War I through 2002 identified by the International Crisis Behavior data project (Brecher and Wilkenfeld 1998). ICB data includes information on regional and global organizations and major powers that intervene, along with information on the dispute and the conflict. The ICB Data Viewer is an updated interactive version of the data and summaries originally published

as part of *A Study of Crisis* by Michael Brecher and Jonathan Wilkenfeld (1998). The ICB data include management actions by superpowers, great powers, regional, global, and security organizations. Actions include discussion without resolution, fact-finding, good offices, condemnation, call for action, mediation, arbitration, adjudication, sanctions, observer group, and emergency military forces. Outcomes from these efforts include: (1) whether the activity delayed the termination; (2) had no effect on the termination; (3) was an important contributor to the termination; or (4) was the most important contributor to termination of the conflict. The data are described in Table 29.4. Superpower involvement is the most likely factor to escalate a crisis (in 48 of the observations). Mediators, on the other hand, are frequently the most important contributors to resolving the crises.

The Ceasefires (CF) data contains information on 48 ceasefires in international wars from 1946 to 1998, each representing a dyadic ceasefire between principal belligerents in a Correlates of War interstate war (Fortna 2004b). Each case has multiple observations over time, running from the ceasefire or the end of the previous time period, until the end of the calendar year, a substantial change in agreement terms, or another war between the same belligerents, whichever comes first. These data include information on the ceasefires and how long they lasted, the situations between the belligerents at the time of the ceasefire, and changes over time, along with detailed information on the content of agreements. If the period does not end with a new COW war for the dyad, the agreement is considered successful. Third-party activities included in the data are mediation (third-party involvement as mediator of the ceasefire, exercising restraint, acting as patron for one side) and third-party guarantees (third party provides explicit or well-understood guarantee of peace). The data are described in Table 29.5. The majority of the observations do not include third-party involvement,

Table 29.3 Summary statistics for *Third Party Interventions and Militarized Interstate Disputes* outcome variables[1]

Short-Term Outcome of Intervention

Outcome Variable	Frequency	Percent
Successful	328	41.57
Inconclusive	25	3.17
Unsuccessful	387	49.05
Don't Know	49	6.12
Total	789	100

Long-Term Outcome of Intervention

Successful	211	26.74
Inconclusive	53	6.72
Unsuccessful	469	59.44
Don't Know	56	7.10
Total	789	100

[1] This includes all actions the TPI dataset defines as management: Verbal expression, diplomatic approaches, judicial processes, administrative, and military.

Table 29.4   Summary statistics for
***International Crisis Behavior* outcome**
variables[1]

Great Power Involvement Effect on Timing of Crisis
Abatement

Outcome Variable	Frequency	Percent
No GP activity	10	13.51
GP delayed termination	17	22.97
GP had no effect	12	16.22
GP more rapid termination	35	47.30
Missing	0	0
Total	74[2]	100

Superpower Involvement Effect on Timing of Crisis
Abatement

No SP activity	225	51.02
SP escalated crisis	37	8.39
SP had no effect	118	26.76
SP more rapid termination	58	13.15
Missing	3	.68
Total	441	100

Global Organization Involvement Effect on Timing of
Crisis Abatement

No GO activity	8	1.81
GO escalated crisis	212	48.07
GO had no effect	5	1.13
GO more rapid termination	151	34.24
Missing	65	14.74
Total	441	100

Regional Organization Involvement Effect on Timing of
Crisis Abatement

No RO activity	102	23.13
RO escalated crisis	171	38.78
RO had no effect	7	1.59
RO more rapid termination	108	24.49
Missing	53	12.02
Total	441	100

Mediator Involvement Effect on Timing of Crisis
Abatement

No Med activity	306	69.39
Med had no effect	28	6.35
Med escalated crisis	0	0
Med more rapid termination	98	22.22
Missing	9	2.04
Total	441	100

[1] This includes all actions the TPI dataset defines as management: Verbal expression, diplomatic approaches, judicial processes, administrative, and military.
[2] The raw total for great power involvement is different from the raw totals for other methods of involvement since this includes only cases before 1939.

and these bilateral cases are the most likely to return to conflict. No observations that included third-party guarantees returned to war.

Table 29.5   Summary statistics for the
***Ceasefires* outcome variables[1]**

	No Failure	Failure	Total
No Third Party	529	13	542
Mediation	274	8	282
Guarantee	52	0	52
Total	855	21	876

[1] This includes all actions the Ceasefire dataset defines as management: mediation (involvement as mediator of the ceasefire, exercising restraint, acting as patron for one side) and guarantee (provides guarantee of peace).

Variation on a theme

The variations in each data set have substantial implications for assessing conflict management outcomes. Figure 29.2 graphs the percent of successful management efforts by data set, using the strictest definition of success included in each data set, and employing a definition of conflict management that includes *any* type of third-party actions. We use percentages of successful management efforts to compare the data since each data set has different units of analysis.

The International Conflict Management data set (ICM) has by far the lowest percentage of successful management efforts (6.45% of observations are successful), where success is defined as establishing a full settlement. The International Crisis Behavior data (ICB) has the next strictest definition of successful management, where mediation is the most important factor in the timing of settlement duration (which is the case for 11% of the observations). The Third Party Interventions and Militarized Interstate Disputes data (TPI) find 26.74% of the management efforts included are successful in the long term. Finally, the Ceasefires data (CF) has the most liberal definition of success, with 97% of the agreements examined never failing.

This enormous variation in management outcome is a product of how the data sets define success, conflict, and management, along with the varied units of analyses and different time periods examined. Note that we are not arguing that one data set, or even that one approach or unit of analysis, is the "correct" one. Each of these research agendas,

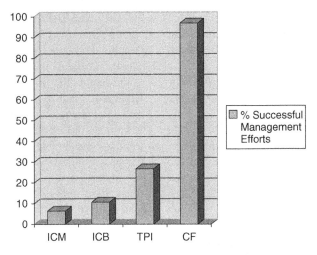

Figure 29.2   Overview of successful management efforts by data set

with their theories and data, provide a different and valuable perspective on the conflict management process. We are suggesting, however, that these data require scholars to: (1) recognize that no data set is the final word and keep in mind their varied approaches; (2) employ multiple data sets when possible; and (3) realize that these resources contribute to, and are the result of, a dramatic increase in the scientific study of dispute resolution (Bercovitch and Gartner 2006a).

Variations in durability: the breakup of Yugoslavia and the Egypt/Israeli conflict

The necessity of considering the longevity of an agreement in assessing the effectiveness of third-party management and understanding when a conflict is resolved is well-illustrated by the cases of the break-up of Yugoslavia and the conflict between Israel and Egypt. The war in the Balkans is one of the most common disputes found in the *International Conflict Management* data set, with 91 mediated settlements (Bercovitch and Gartner 2006b). In the Yugoslavian Civil War, over 35% of the settlements lasted less than one week and 14% lasted just one week. Many settlements were broken within 24 hours of coming to an agreement. Thirty-five percent of the

settlements lasted eight weeks or more. With almost half of all settlements lasting one week or less, this case illustrates the importance of analyzing the likelihood of a settlement being short-lived. Simply classifying any management effort that resulted in some sort of an agreement as "successful" would grossly misrepresent the effect that various conflict management efforts had on settling the dispute by lumping all of these agreements together – no matter how short-lived (for an analysis of Yugoslavian Civil War agreement duration, see Gartner and Bercovitch 2006).

The Yugoslavian conflict was mediated by the United Nations, the European Union, and the United States. Most of the settlement attempts before 1995 now appear largely ineffective. These agreements were followed by the more successful Dayton Peace Accords signed in December 1995, which is seen by some as a suboptimal compromise with a continued lack of resolution for many of the dispute's issues (Cousens 2002). The outcome of the Dayton agreement was a separation of the conflict parties through the dissolution of Yugoslavia. Although this settlement halted the violence, it did not resolve the conflict, as is seen by the renewed conflict and subsequent intervention in Kosovo. Some claim that the accords were unsuccessful at creating a durable peace because they did not provide an institutional framework, as was accomplished by the settlements in other ethnically divided societies such as South Africa and Northern Ireland (Greenberg et al. 2000).

The case of Yugoslavia, with multiple short-lived peace agreements, contrasts with the conflict settlement process involving *Israel* and *Egypt*. The treaty between Israel and Egypt was signed on March 26, 1979, following the 1978 Camp David Accords. The main features of the treaty were the mutual recognition of each country by the other, the cessation of the state of war that had existed since the 1948 Arab-Israeli War, and the withdrawal by Israel of its armed forces and civilians from the Sinai Peninsula which Israel had captured during the 1967 Six-Day War. The agreement notably made Egypt the first Arab country to recognize Israel officially (Jordan would follow suit in 1994). The peace treaty was signed after Egyptian President Anwar Sadat's landmark visit to Israel in 1978. Even after the Camp David agreements, a treaty was not certain since Egypt was under intense pressure from Arab countries not to sign a separate settlement.

A separate Israeli-US Memorandum of Agreement, concluded on the same day as the Camp David agreement between Israel and Egypt, lays out the US commitment to Israel in case the treaty is violated, the role of the UN and the future supply of military and economic aid to Israel. The United States also helped organize a peacekeeping mission along the Egyptian-Israeli border, which still maintains a rotating infantry task force. The treaty also created a Multi-National Force and Observers funded by Egypt, Israel, the United States, Germany, Japan, and Switzerland. The presence of third-party guarantors is an important determinant in the agreement's longevity. The groundbreaking peace paved the way for subsequent Israeli negotiations and treaties with Jordan and the Palestinians. Although relations between Cairo and Jerusalem have not been warm, they share what is considered a "cold peace" and the treaty between Israel and Egypt has lasted almost 20 years. All agree a cold peace is better than a hot war.

FUTURE RESEARCH

Despite both the recent theoretical and empirical improvement in our understanding of the factors that influence military dispute settlements and the dramatic increase in the employment of conflict management techniques, the conflict management literature still has considerable room for improvement. We focus on two directions for advancing our understanding of settlement durability: considering more effectively the roles of selection and substitutability in conflict management outcomes and, in particular, agreement duration.

Selection effects

Conflict management behavior is not random, but rather is the result of actors making strategic decisions based on their anticipation of the consequences resulting from those decisions. This strategic process affects why some conflicts are mediated in the first place (and some are not) and the outcomes of particular management activities and therefore must be taken into consideration in any study of conflict management.

> Outcomes ranging from the foreign policy of individual states to international phenomena such as war or cooperation cannot be understood apart from the strategic choices actors make and the interaction of those choices. (Lake and Powell 1999, 3)

Accepting that international outcomes result from the interaction of actors' purposeful choices requires that we acknowledge that this process creates selection effects (Fearon 2002; Reed 2002). Failing to study the expectations of decision makers introduces selection bias and can lead to incorrect inferences.

Selection effects mean that the population from which a dispute is drawn provides information about the likely outcome of that dispute and its attendant agreements. We identify three types of selection effects related to conflict management: entry effects, management method effects, and dispute effects.

Entry Effects: The first selection effect is a product of an actor's involvement as a manager. Third parties make strategic calculations about whether or not to become involved in a dispute, and belligerents make strategic decisions about whether or not a conflict manager is acceptable. We observe only those situations where conflict managers thought their actions were likely to have a desired outcome, resulting in a selection effect. Research must therefore consider not only the outcomes of conflict management effort, but also the reasons conflicts are managed by an outside party and those that are not managed.

Management Method Effects: The second selection effect is a consequence of actors' strategic choice of conflict management method. Actors have expectations about which methods of management will be the most effective. Intermediaries strategically choose their approach to managing a conflict according to how difficult they anticipate resolution will be while minimizing their costs and efforts. Since cases that merit more expensive methods of management are the most difficult to resolve, conflicts receiving such measures are less likely to reach a lasting resolution. Thus, because mediation is generally more costly than most other third-party resolution efforts, we can expect that the conflicts that merit mediation are, *ex ante*, comparatively more difficult to resolve.

Dispute Effects: The third selection effect results from the characteristics of the disputes that require outside assistance for resolution. Since the cases requiring outside involvement are the ones the disputants are unable to resolve themselves, managers are most likely to become involved in the conflicts that are difficult to resolve (Greig 2005; Bercovitch and Gartner 2006b). This is critical if the conditions that involved third parties in the first place also influence the effectiveness of the effort. That a third party becomes involved at all signals the likely effects of the effort, as third parties are less likely to generate a lasting resolution compared to cases in which

the disputants resolve the conflict themselves (Regan 2002).

Despite the necessity of considering the entire strategic process, many studies of conflict management focus solely on the characteristics of successful involvement and most authors focus on a single method of management (Frei 1976; Kleiboer 1996). For example, there is much debate surrounding the effectiveness of economic sanctions (Hufbauer and Schott 1983; Li 1993; Martin 1993; Weiss 1999). Similar debates exist in the military intervention literature (Regan 1996) and the vast mediation literature (Mack and Snyder 1957; Ott 1972; Pruitt 1981; Kleiboer 1996; Bercovitch 1998; Regan 2000). It remains unclear which management efforts are the most effective and why.

Recent work has begun to incorporate the role of selection in the duration of peace agreements. New studies have begun to examine: (1) the role of selection effects in mediated conflicts (Bercovitch and Gartner 2006b); (2) which actors are likely to act as mediators and which disputants accept third-party offers to mediate (Schmidt 2004); and (3) the supply and demand of mediation (Crescenzi et al. 2005; Beardsley 2006). Future research should follow this progress and examine the variation in the identity and method of outside involvement across conflicts and the results of this variation on the effectiveness of third-party management efforts.

Substitutability

The literatures on mediation, economic sanction, and military action have remained isolated from one another, despite the fact that they all address methods of dispute resolution. The complexities of foreign policy decision making require attention to issues of substitutability (Most and Starr 1984, 1989). Policymakers have a wide array of available options for approaching any range of policy issues, since any cause may have a number of effects and any effect can stem from several causes (Morgan and Palmer 2000). Different conflicts may lead to similar responses (as in mediation efforts by the USA with Israel and Egypt in the 1970s, by the Vatican in the Falkland conflict between Argentina and the UK in 1982, and by Congo with Burundi and Rwanda in 1966). In addition, there are multiple ways to respond to similar types of conflicts (as was the case of the UN observers sent in 1992 to Yugoslavia compared to the later NATO military intervention in Kosovo). Economic sanctions, diplomatic efforts, and military operations are substitutable foreign policy instruments potentially triggered in response to conflict.

Analysis of the complex decision process involved in choosing a response to conflict requires the inclusion of the various foreign policy instruments available to policymakers and is "essential" for the comparison of state policies (Palmer and Bhandari 2000, 6). Accounting for foreign policy substitutability captures some of the complexity of international relations omitted in much of the existing research and reflects intuition of how policy is made (Morgan and Palmer 2000). Research that fails to address the issue of substitutability in foreign policy risks producing inaccurate results and unconvincing conclusions (see also Most and Starr 1989).

> Focusing on only one [policy] would mean a failure to provide full coverage of the possible outcomes and lead to incomplete results that fail to cumulate (or even make sense when compared). The results would fail to capture the theory or model being tested (as only part was being tested). (Starr 2000, 129)

Management methods are rarely used in isolation, and yet they are treated as such in a majority of the existing literature. As a result, it remains unclear how methods of conflict management work together theoretically and in practice. If the outside party is truly interested in resolving the conflict, it will likely employ different tactics until the conflict is resolved. For example, the United States and European Union used economic sanctions, mediation, and eventually military intervention to help end the bloody conflict that arose during the breakup of Yugoslavia. Future research should build on the work

of authors who systematically evaluate the relative effectiveness of third-party conflict management techniques and recognize the existence of foreign policy substitutability in approaching conflict management (Dixon 1996; Regan 2000).

CONCLUSION

Signing a peace agreement does not mean that the conflict is resolved and there will be peace. The durations of peace agreements vary considerably, with some never taking hold and others lasting for centuries. Thus, the first order of business in examining conflict settlement duration is to recognize the variation in outcome duration. The second issue is to recognize that we can, and recently have begun to, study this variation in a systematic manner. Recent studies have developed an increasingly sophisticated understanding of the factors that lead to conflict resolution. Third, it would be easy to look at the variation in findings on settlement durability and type, however, and disagree with our assessments of scientific progress. There is significant variation in studies' conclusions about the factors that influence outcomes. It is critical to recognize, however, that much of the variation results from the employment of different data sets that have fundamentally different units of analyses, definitions of settlement, and analytical frameworks. Varied empirical measures help to make our collective research stronger, and it is not necessary to choose the "best" data set. It is necessary, however, to recognize this variation and to understand how it is likely to influence research results. Nevertheless, some of the variation in findings on settlement duration results from failure to appreciate the importance of both selection effects and policy substitutability. Future theories need to incorporate these processes directly.

Every war ends, but not every peace lasts. Blainey argues that theories of war should be theories of peace (1988). We think that theories of peace should also be theories of war – that is, scholars examining peace agreements and conflict resolution need to consider their fragility and durability and the factors that contribute to the resumption of conflict. This recognition will help to develop both a better theoretical understanding of the conflict resolution process and better conflict management practices.

REFERENCES

Beardsley, Kyle. 2006. "Not All Mediators are Created Equal: Choosing Who Mediates." Paper presented at Annual Meeting of the American Political Science Association, Washington, DC.

Beardsley, Kyle, David M. Quinn, Bidisha Biswas, and Jonathan Wilkenfeld. 2006. "Mediation Style and Crisis Outcomes." *Journal of Conflict Resolution* 50 (1): 58–86.

Bercovitch, Jacob. 1997. "Mediation in International Conflict: An Overview of Theory, a Review of Practice." In *Peacemaking in International Conflict: Methods and Techniques*, ed. W. Zartman and J.L. Rasmussen. Washington, DC: United States Institute of Peace Press.

——. 1998. "The Study of International Mediation: Empirical Research and the State of the Art." Paper presented at The Conference on Civilian Conflict Resolution, Castle Hunnigen.

——. 2000. "The International Conflict Management Dataset Codebook."

Bercovitch, Jacob, and Scott Sigmund Gartner. 2006a. "Empirical Studies in International Mediation: Introduction." *International Interactions* 32 (4): 319–328.

——. 2006b. "Is there Method in the Madness of Mediation? Some Lessons for Mediators from Quantitative Studies of Mediation." *International Interactions* 32 (4): 329–354.

Bercovitch, Jacob, and Patrick Regan. 1999. "The Structure of International Conflict Management: An Analysis of the Effects of Interactability and Mediation." *International Journal of Peace Studies* 4 (1).

Blainey, Geoffrey. 1988. *The Causes of War*. New York: Free Press.

Brecher, Michael, and Jonathan Wilkenfeld. 1998. *A Study of Crisis*. Ann Arbor: University of Michigan Press.

Cousens, Elizabeth M. 2002. "From Missed Opportunities to Overcompensation: Implementing the Dayton Agreement on Bosnia." In *Ending Civil Wars: The Implementation of Peace Agreements*, ed. E.M. Cousens, D.S. Rothchild and S.J. Stedman. Boulder: Lynne Rienner Publishers.

Crescenzi, Mark J.C., Kelly M. Kadera, Sara McLaughlin Mitchell, and Clayton L. Thyne. 2005. "A Supply Side Theory of Third Party Conflict Management." Paper presented at Annual Meeting of the International Studies Association, Honolulu, Hawaii.

Dixon, William J. 1996. "Third-Party Techniques for Preventing Conflict Escalation and Promoting Peaceful Settlement." *International Organization* 50 (4): 653–681.

Dixon, William J., and Paul D. Senese. 2002. "Democracy, Disputes, and Negotiated Settlements." *Journal of Conflict Resolution* 46 (4): 547–571.

Doyle, Michael W., and Nicholas Sambanis. 2000. "International Peacebuilding: A Theoretical and Quantitative Analysis." *American Political Science Review* 94 (4): 779–802.

Fearon, James D. 2002. "Selection Effects and Deterrence." *International Interactions* 28 (1): 5–30.

Fortna, Virginia Page. 2003a. "Inside and Out: Peacekeeping and the Duration of Peace after Civil and Interstate Wars." *International Studies Review* 5 (4): 97–114.

——. 2003b. "Scraps of Paper: Agreements and the Durability of Peace." *International Organization* 57: 337–372.

——. 2004a. "Interstate Peacekeeping: Causal Mechanisms and Empirical Effects." *World Politics* 56 (4): 481–519.

——. 2004b. *Peace Time: Ceasefire Agreements and the Durability of Peace*. Princeton, NJ: Princeton University Press.

Frazier, Derrick, and William J. Dixon. 2005. Third Party Intermediaries and Negotiated Settlements. Paper presented at Annual Meeting of the American Political Science Association, September 1–3, Washington, DC.

Frazier, Derrick V., and William J. Dixon. 2006. "Third Party Intermediaries and Negotiated Settlements, 1946–2000." *International Interactions* 32 (4): 385–408.

Frei, Daniel. 1976. "Conditions Affecting the Effectiveness of International Mediation." *Papers of the Peace Science Society International* 26: 67–84.

Gartner, Scott S., and Jacob Bercovitch. 2006. "Overcoming Obstacles to Peace: The Contribution of Mediation to Short-Lived Settlements." *International Studies Quarterly* 50: 819–840.

Gerner, Deborah J., and Philip A. Schrodt. 2001. "Analyzing the Dynamics of International Mediation Processes in the Middle East and the

Former Yugoslavia." Paper presented at International Studies Association, Chicago, Illinois.

Greenberg, Melanie C., John H. Barton, and Margaret E. McGuinness, eds. 2000. *Words over War: Mediation and Arbitration to Prevent Deadly Conflict.* Lanham, MD: Rowman and Littlefield.

Greig, J. Michael. 2005. "Stepping Into the Fray: When Do Mediators Mediate?" *American Journal of Political Science* 49 (2): 249–266.

Greig, J. Michael, and Paul F. Diehl. 2005. "The Peacekeeping-Peacemaking Dilemma." *International Studies Quarterly* 49 (4): 621–646.

Hartzell, Caroline, Mathew Hoddie, and Donald Rothchild. 2001. "Stabilizing the Peace After Civil War: An Investigation of Some Key Variables." *International Organization* 55 (1): 183–208.

Hensel, Paul R. 1994. "One Thing Leads to Another: Recurrent Disputes in Latin America." *Journal of Peace Research* 31 (3): 281–297.

Holzgrefe, J.L., and Robert O. Keohane, eds. 2003. *Humanitarian Intervention: Ethical, Legal, and Political Dilemmas.* New York: Cambridge University Press.

Hufbauer, G.C., and Jeffrey J. Schott. 1983. *Economic Sanctions in Support of Foreign Policy Goals.* Washington, DC: Institute for International Economics.

Huth, Paul K., and Todd L. Allee. 2002. *The Democratic Peace and Territorial Conflict in the Twentieth Century.* New York: Cambridge University Press.

Kissinger, Henry. 1996. "The New World Order." In *Managing Global Chaos: Sources of and Responses to International Conflict*, ed. C. A. Crocker, F. O. Hampson and P. Aall. Washington DC: United States Institute of Peace Press.

Kleiboer, Marieke. 1996. "Understanding Success and Failure of International Mediation." *Journal of Conflict Resolution* 40 (2): 360–389.

Lake, David A., and Robert Powell. 1999. "International Relations: A Strategic Choice Approach." In *Strategic Choice and International Relations*, ed. D. Lake and R. Powell. Princeton, NJ: Princeton University Press.

Li, Chien-pin. 1993. "The Effectiveness of Sanction Linkages: Issues and Actors." *International Studies Quarterly* 37 (3): 349–370.

Mack, Raymond, and Richard Snyder. 1957. "An Analysis of Social Conflict: Toward an Overview and Synthesis." *Journal of Conflict Resolution* 1: 212–248.

Maoz, Zeev, and Leslie G. Terris. 2006. "Credibility and Strategy in International Mediation." *International Interactions* 32 (4): 409–440.

Martin, Lisa L. 1993. "Credibility, Costs, and Institutions: Cooperation and Economic Sanctions." *World Politics* 45: 406–432.

Melin, Molly, Scott Sigmund Gartner, and Jacob Bercovitch. 2006. "Do Conflicts Matter? Analyzing Third Party Choice of Intervention in Conflicts." Paper presented at Annual Meeting of the American Political Science Association, Philadelphia, PA.

Meyer, Arthur. 1960. "Functions of the Mediator in Collective Bargaining." *Industrial and Labor Relations Review* 13 (June): 159–165.

Morgan, T. Clifton, and Glenn Palmer. 2000. "A Model of Foreign Policy Substitutability: Selecting the Right Tools for the Right Job(s)." *Journal of Conflict Resolution* 44 (1): 11–32.

Most, Benjamin A., and Harvey Starr. 1984. "International Relations Theory, Foreign Policy Substitutability, and 'Nice' Laws." *World Politics* 36 (3): 383–406.

———. 1989. *Inquiry, Logic, and International Politics.* Columbia: University of South Carolina Press.

Ott, M. 1972. "Mediation as a Method of Conflict Resolution." *International Organization* 26: 595–618.

Palmer, Glenn, and Archana Bhandari. 2000. "The Investigation of Substitutability in Foreign Policy." *Journal of Conflict Resolution* 44 (1): 3–10.

Palmer, Glenn, and Clifton T. Morgan. 2006. *A Theory of Foreign Policy.* Princeton: Princeton University Press.

Pearson, Frederic S. 1974. "Foreign Military Interventions and Domestic Disputes." *International Studies Quarterly* 18 (3): 259–289.

Pearson, Frederic S., Marie Olson Lounsbery, Scott Walker, and Sonja Mann. 2006. "Rethinking Models of Civil War Settlement." *International Interactions* 32 (2): 109–128.

Pruitt, Dean G. 1981. *Negotiator Behavior.* New York: Academic Press.

Quinn, David M., Jonathan Wilkenfeld, and Kathleen Smarick. 2006. "Power Play: Mediation in Symmetric and Asymmetric International Crises." *International Interactions* 32 (4): 441–470.

Reed, William. 2002. "Selection Effects and World Politics Research." *International Interactions* 28 (1): 1–4.

Regan, Patrick. 1996. "Conditions of Successful Third-Party Intervention in Intrastate Conflicts." *Journal of Conflict Resolution* 40 (2): 336–359.

———. 2000. "Substituting Policies During US Interventions in Internal Conflicts: A Little of This, a Little of That." *Journal of Conflict Resolution* 44 (1): 90–106.

———. 2002. "Third Party Interventions and the Duration of Interstate Conflict." *Journal of Conflict Resolution* 46 (1): 55–73.

Regan, Patrick, and Allan C. Stam. 2000. "In the Nick of Time: Conflict Management, Mediation Timing, and the Duration of Interstate Disputes." *International Studies Quarterly* 44 (2): 239–260.

Rothchild, Donald. 2002. "The Two-Phase Peace Implementation Process in Africa and its Implications for Democratization." *Politics and Economics* 59.

Schmidt, Holger. 2004. "Regime Type and Conflict Management by International Organizations: The Case of the UN, 1945–2001." Paper presented at Annual Meeting of the International Studies Association, Montreal, Canada.

Simkin, William E. 1971. *Mediation and the Dynamics of Collective Bargaining.* Washington, DC: Bureau of National Affairs.

Smith, Alastair, and Allan C. Stam. 2003. "Mediation and Peacekeeping in a Random Walk Model of Civil and Interstate War." *International Studies Review* 5 (4): 115–135.

Starr, Harvey. 2000. "Substitutability in Foreign Policy: Theoretically Central, Empirically Elusive." *Journal of Conflict Resolution* 44 (1): 128–138.

Walter, Barbara. 2002. *Committing to Peace: The Successful Settlement of Civil Wars.* Princeton, NJ: Princeton University Press.

Weiss, Thomas G. 1999. "Sanctions as a Foreign Policy Tool: Weighing Humanitarian Impulses." *Journal of Peace Research* 36 (5): 499–509.

Werner, Suzanne. 1998. "Negotiating the Terms of Settlement." *Journal of Conflict Resolution* 42 (3): 321–343.

———. 1999. "The Precarious Nature of Peace: Resolving the Issues, Enforcing the Settlement, and Renegotiating." *American Journal of Political Science* 43: 912–933.

Young, Oran R. 1967. *The Intermediaries: Third Parties in International Crises.* Princeton: Princeton University Press.

Zartman, I. William. 1997. "Introduction: Toward the Resolution of International Conflicts." In *Peacemaking in International Conflict,* ed. I.W. Zartman and J.L. Rasmussen. Washington, DC: United States Institute of Peace Press.

30

Peace vs. Justice – and Beyond

Cecilia Albin

How justice relates to conflict resolution and peace has become intensively debated by both scholars and practitioners. Is there a conflict or tension between justice and peace and, if so, when? Which of the two values should be prioritized, if and when both cannot be pursued or achieved? Although commonly phrased the "peace vs. justice" question, it encompasses in fact a range of approaches, some of which do not regard the two values as being in conflict. Thus, "peace vs. justice" has become an umbrella term for a debate with many different answers: to seek peace with justice (no peace without justice), peace first and justice later (justice follows from peace), justice first and peace later (peace follows from justice), and so on.

Traditionally, conflict managers have sought "pragmatically" to end violence and achieve peace. In this, there has been little concern about norms such as justice, although once peace is established it may well bring justice as well. Another set of approaches have regarded justice as a basic human need and injustice as a common root cause of

conflict, that must be addressed if peace is to result and endure (e.g. Burton, 1990). Here the peace vs. justice dichotomy is rejected as false and misleading, for the two values go hand in hand (Lederach, 1995; see also Galtung, 1969). The international community is at times portrayed as too narrowly focused on containing conflict in and stabilizing particular trouble areas, without working to reduce global inequities on which peace ultimately depends (Tschirgi, 2005).

The reality of war, high-profile justice issues and the pressing need for policy guidance have brought the debate into the international limelight. How justice relates to peace and conflict resolution, what these values mean and which is to be prioritized have been or remain controversial policy issues in conflicts around the world – among them Rwanda, South Africa, Israel-Palestine, Cambodia, Guatemala, El Salvador, Bosnia-Herzegovina and Northern Ireland. The many societies emerging from civil war and repressive rule have underscored that, in the task to build peace in the shadow of past gross human rights violations, moral principles stand side by side with political imperatives and strategic concerns. The recent literature on "transitional justice" often portrays this as a dilemma requiring difficult trade-offs between ethical standards and political strategy. For example, punishing severe justice violations may alienate actors who are also needed in building peace. Yet peace without justice may fail to gain public support and legitimacy and thus fall apart (e.g. Biggar, 2003). While taking on the peace vs. justice question with new intensity, research on post-conflict societies presents different conclusions on how the two values relate to each other and are to be balanced even when drawing on the same conflict cases. Crucial as the question is in that context, it is only one of several in which it arises.

THE CORE ARGUMENTS

This chapter engages with the peace vs. justice debate, particularly as found in the research literature to date, and relates it to conflict resolution in particular. In so doing, the aim is to take the debate further in several ways. Its framing of the key problem as being one monolithic value standing against the other is often misleading and simplistic. In many situations, particularly in a longer-term perspective, the issue is not whether peace or justice is to be chosen or prioritized, for both are clearly needed in some sense for conflict resolution and a durable settlement. The core questions are instead: What kind of justice and what kind of peace should be promoted (what steps should be taken)? How are the pursuits of these two values (the steps) best timed, sequenced and combined over time-that is, what kind of justice is to (can) be furthered in what stage of the process of conflict resolution and peace-building?

The work on addressing these questions is started in this chapter, with the development of some founding arguments. One is that the pursuit of justice does not categorically either undermine or promote peace. It can do, and does, both. We need to examine specific

contexts in order to get clearer on how they affect each other. In other words, it depends largely on *the contextual details*. Overall, the two values are not quite as contradictory as they are often portrayed to be.

One factor stressed here is *the importance of stages and timing* in examining how justice relates to peace. The chapter examines three stages of the peace-making process: the stages in which parties move from conflict to dialogue (pre-negotiation), and from negotiation to agreement, and the post-agreement and post-conflict phases of securing a durable peace. Each stage of the conflict resolution process raises its own issues and principles of justice which affect peace-making differently. We need to pay close attention to these particularities and variations, in order to learn how to best handle the peace-justice relationship. Moreover, the stages obviously affect each other and make it difficult to understand the fate of justice and peace within the confines of a single phase. For example, how justice issues were handled in the negotiation process (say, a process experienced as unjust) will affect the prospects of consolidating peace subsequently. If parties while negotiating arrive at a shared view of what justice means and requires, this will enhance the chances of reaching an agreement.

Another contextual factor is the particular justice issues and concepts involved. Some questions of justice are far more easily addressed and acted upon in a peace process than others. Put differently, *some principles or aspects of justice relax or even remove the tension with peace while others increase it.* Moreover, if parties hold compatible notions of justice, or are able to reconcile conflicting principles, this will obviously pave the way better for peace than if they do not. A third contextual factor is *the relations between parties, in particular the distribution of power* between them. It will often influence (but not alone determine) how far justice is taken into account, and whose claims are most heard. A common reason for the breakdown of peace negotiations, for example, is discrepancy between the most compelling justice principles and the distribution of power (Zartman et al., 1996): Justice argues for something which the prevailing (im-)balance of power resists or does not permit. The balance of forces among former opponents has shown to influence how far justice, in the sense of accountability for past human rights violations, is compatible with peace in soceities emerging from civil war (Sriram, 2004). A fourth factor is *the time-frame used*: Peace—for example, in the sense of an urgency to cease hostilities – may require compromise on justice in the short term, but not in a long-term perspective.

Of course, the peace vs. justice question is not new. Nor are the debates and controversies over it. They have deep roots, and many current arguments now put forward pick up on older traditions. The proponents of various "peace projects" in the 17th and 18th centuries clearly associated the avoidance of war and international order with important aspects of justice – such as the rule of law and its impartial application to all states, and collective decision-making within a federation of states from which nations would derive their rights (see Jacob, 1974). Most well-known among these is Immanuel Kant's proposal of 1795 for a "league of peace", which would be able to secure perpetual peace. This normative-legal tradition as an answer to the problems of international anarchy and war was reflected in the later design of the League of Nations and its successor, the United Nations. But both institutions set it off against another – that of entrusting major powers and a balance of power system with preserving peace and order. Classical realist theory of international relations, at its heyday in the 1950s and 1960s, often ignores the subject of international justice altogether (see Brown, 1997). Alternatively, it overtly rejects that peace, defined as the absence of force, is dependent upon justice in any meaningful sense: "Nothing substantive is said about the nature of the justice which presumably forms the indispensable concomitant of peace" (Osgood & Tucker, 1967, p. 221). In international political theory, Henley Bull's *The Anarchical Society* (1977)

is a classic pointing to both commonalities and differences with realist theory. Here order, maintained by a balance of power between states, is generally the most fundamental value to be prioritized when required over both justice and peace. Issues of justice which threaten order are best left closed. But order, whenever possible, should serve justice: normative principles help to govern inter-state relations.

The terms "peace" and "justice" refer to and imply widely different matters in the research literature. "Peace" is minimally freedom from overt violence and war, but to this is often added different requirements (including, in some instances, the achievement of justice in some sense). What "justice" entails and requires in turn, particularly in an international or global context, is diffuse or disputed. In this chapter, "peace" refers broadly to both *processes* of resolving conflict and promoting or maintaining peace (e.g. negotiation, conflict prevention, peace building), and *outcomes* (e.g. peace agreements, durable peace). "Justice" refers to general standards for allocating collective benefits, opportunities and burdens which may take many forms (Albin, 1993). Different types of justice concepts and principles (e.g. procedural vs. substantial, internal vs. external and impartial) which are commonly held and used are discussed, along with their implications for peace.[1]

FROM CONFLICT TO DIALOGUE

This initial phase of the conflict resolution process involves two basic steps. First, parties explore and decide individually and jointly whether to attempt to resolve their conflict by peaceful means, which in most cases means by negotiation. Secondly, they work to reach agreement on how the negotiations are to be conducted, for example, participants and any third parties, agenda issues, and venue. What justice issues arise then in this phase, and how do they affect the chances to get peace negotiations underway and to a successful conclusion? This is the least researched phase when it comes to justice and the peace vs. justice question: these issues are not addressed in major work on pre-negotiation (Gross Stein, 1989; Zartman & Berman, 1982).

On the first step, most conflicts involve justice issues of some kind. But there is enormous variation in terms of how amenable they are, and are seen to be, to peace-making. Earlier research demonstrates that justice is capable of triggering war (Welch, 1993), as well as the onset of negotiations. Justice issues linked to fundamental needs, values, rights or interests tend to be seen as exclusive (zero-sum) and non-negotiable, or at least very painful and costly to compromise upon. Whether this makes peace-making impossible or just difficult depends partly on how the conflict is approached. Basically, parties must come to regard their justice issues-their interpretation and the application of justice-as negotiable and negotiation as a desirable option. Unofficial dialogues and problem-solving workshops with people out-side government are discussed extensively in the literature as a necessary and effective means to address various deep-rooted needs, which includes justice, and prepare for formal negotiations (e.g. Kelman, 2000; Saunders, 2001). Also at play here is how far the parties need cooperation as a means to get the justice issues addressed, or need to reach an agreement at all. If both or all parties regard negotiation as the only reasonable hope to reduce injustice, this obviously facilitates. If only one party is dependent upon negotiation to restore justice for itself, or even to survive in any form, this creates an inequality which makes justice difficult to combine with peace-making. Negotiations may well get underway but justice, at least for or as defined by the most dependent party, will suffer. By contrast, justice issues connected to more peripheral interests lend themselves well to negotiation.

The second step – deciding on how the negotiations are to be conducted – raises a whole set of different justice and fairness issues. They usually concern three matters: participating parties, agenda-setting, and forum and rules for the negotiations (Albin, 2001). Who gets a seat at the bargaining table and on what terms obviously influences what issues and interests are subsequently taken into account. A general notion of fairness is that participation should be as representative and protective as possible of all key parties and interests involved. How this principle is best operationalized in practice, however, is rarely straightforward and sometimes controversial. The increase in intra-state conflicts and global problems means that government representatives of states are no longer considered the sole actors. In the areas of human rights and the environment, for example, this has often meant complementary involvement by non-governmental organizations in a variety of ad hoc roles. Agenda-setting raises justice and fairness issues for similar reasons. Each party naturally seeks to steer this activity in a way which takes good care of its own interests. In the end, a reasonably balanced agenda usually has to be created, however, which includes and ranks issues with respect for all parties' important concerns. Finally, unless they already have an obvious home, the forum and rules for the talks need to be established. Here, fairness is often associated with a neutral forum and site (or alternation between partisan ones) and prior agreement on modes of decision-making and other rules of the game.

How prominent or controversial justice is in this preparatory stage varies widely. Some conflicts fall within areas where for one reason or another it will not be an issue: negotiations may already be ongoing and well established and accepted in form and format, or there may be widely held norms and expectations governing the justice issues. Many multilateral talks on trade, the environment and arms proliferation have become institutionalized over the decades and are of this kind. Other conflicts fall outside of established tracks and the parties will need to work out an agreement on how, over what and by whom the talks are to be conducted. In sum, for justice to have a positive effect on peace-making in this stage, any important justice issues need to be resolved and usually with considerations of representativeness and balance. Otherwise, formal negotiations may never get underway or if they do, any resulting agreement may suffer later when it comes to implementation and compliance.

FROM NEGOTIATION TO AGREEMENT

This phase concerns the interaction between parties as they work to reach an agreement. It begins with the opening of official talks; proceeds through bargaining, problem-solving and concession-making; and ends with an agreement of some kind or/and disagreement (failure). The agreement may be procedural (e.g. to continue negotiations at a later stage), or substantial (e.g. a text setting out the terms for settling the conflict).

Most of the research literature on negotiation, particularly in international contexts, still either ignores or rejects the roles played by justice. Those studies which have been done on the subject tend to deal with isolated aspects, for example, the role of reciprocity in concession-making for reaching a successful outcome. More comprehensive work on the peace vs. justice question in this phase, further discussed below, is limited and the agreed conclusions are very few. It is here argued that justice and fairness play important roles in this phase, and this can either undermine or promote peace depending on the circumstances. Furthermore, the justice and fairness issues which arise and affect peace-making concern two basic matters. One is process fairness: how parties relate to and treat each other while negotiating, or the relational and process aspects of how an agreement or other outcome is reached. The other concerns outcome fairness or justice: what principles or notions of justice, if any, are to guide the terms of an agreement.

Process fairness

On the first matter, the specific ethical issues which often arise concern fair hearing, fair play and fair procedures (Albin, 2001). Fair hearing means that the process includes

or is representative of all parties to the conflict and their interests. It also means that all participating parties have a chance to put forward their cases and be heard, and their interests are considered seriously. Fair play means that the agreed or understood rules of the game are actually followed, and not broken or altered for individual gain. In addition, parties must be able to accept and reject proposals freely so that any agreement reached is voluntary. Coercive or imposed agreements may fail during the implementation phase, among other problems (e.g. Hampson, 1996).

The procedures concern the mechanisms used to arrive at an agreement, which may be explicit and specifically agreed (e.g. voting, single negotiating texts, divide-and-choose) or more diffuse and implicit (e.g. reciprocation of concessions). Unlike other ethical aspects, the negotiation process, reciprocity—that is, mutual responsiveness to each other's concessions—has been studied extensively by psychologists, sociologists and political scientists (see e.g. Parks & Komorita, 1998; Welch Larson, 1998). In the negotiation literature, it is widely recognized as both an ethical and an instrumental norm needed to move the process forward and reach an agreement. It is a fairness concept which influences whether and how far negotiators concede and accept a particular proposal. At times, it is more or less equalized with process fairness or justice (e.g. Zartman et al., 1996). By contrast, major philosophers and theories of justice respond differently: reciprocity is at once endorsed as a major principle of justice (Gauthier, 1986), accepted under certain conditions (Rawls, 1971), or rejected outright (Barry, 1995). Numerous academic studies on negotiation have over the years distinguished, conceptualized and labelled different patterns of reciprocity. They include equal concessions and equal sacrifices; tit-for-tat or matching; responsiveness to trend; and comparative responsiveness, meaning that each party makes concessions based on a comparison of its own and the other's tendencies to concede (Druckman & Bonoma, 1976). Comparative responsiveness was found to be the most practiced pattern of concession-making in a study covering six different international negotiations (Druckman & Harris, 1990).

What is thus portrayed is a quite specific kind of reciprocity, whereby one party's concession (its size and kind) is determined by the other's previous concession or series of concessions. Moreover, among various conditions, rough power equality is seen as required for or favors reciprocity in concession-making of this kind (e.g. Zartman, 1991). Although much remains to be learnt, this does not quite correspond to reality. Most major negotiations of international significance today are between parties whose relations are rather marked by inequalities of various kinds: in military capacity; political, diplomatic, and economic status and leverage; in responsibility for the problems under negotiations; and in resources and ability to contribute to or bear burdens resulting from a solution. Reciprocity remains a vitally important fairness concept and praxis. But what is mostly seen as fair and practiced is instead "diffuse reciprocity", whereby the emphasis is on crafting an agreement based on a reasonably balanced exchange of concessions. What is judged to be "reasonable" and "balanced" is not simply a comparison of the various parties' respective concessions and contributions. At least as important to take into account appears to be each party's relevant circumstances which may concern resources, entitlements and responsibility with regard to what is under negotiation. Each party is expected to reciprocate "enough" in view of both how far other parties have moved and its own capacity to afford concessions (Albin, 2001).

In sum, various aspects of process fairness go very well with peace-making and indeed promote it: a negotiation process perceived as fair will enhance the likelihood of an agreement being reached and implemented. The same arrangements may be accepted or rejected, depending on how parties feel about the process which produced them. The absence of fair hearing or fair play may well derail it. Similarly, if negotiators judge that their concessions are not sufficiently reciprocated, they may adopt more competitive tactics or withdraw from the process altogether. Diffuse reciprocity appears to be what is mostly expected. When practiced, it will facilitate peace-making, particularly between unequal parties. There is not enough systematic empirical evidence collected to demonstrate whether the fairness of the negotiation process also affects the long-term durability of agreements. It remains to be investigated whether judgments of the process (unless it is ongoing) remain important over time, or fade so that other factors, including possibly other fairness aspects such as the terms of the agreement, explain long-term durability.

Principles of outcome justice and peace-making

Achieving justice is rarely the sole or even primary objective of international negotiators. Yet what justice or fairness principles should guide in the terms of an agreement is an issue which always arises, more or less explicitly. The reasons are several. A negotiated agreement involves benefits and costs which must be allocated between parties in a reasonably balanced way. A single distributive principle seldom emerges on its own as the obvious one to use in complex international contexts: several principles— and several interpretations of them—tend to be applicable. Each principle leads to a different mix of benefits and burdens for parties, giving them different biases towards the range of possible allocation criteria.

There are two related aspects to the question of whether notions of outcome justice promote or undermine peace. The first concerns the particular concepts involved, which may be more or less easily combined with making peace. The second, discussed in the next section, concerns the compatibility of the justice notions held by parties. Starting with the concepts involved, three distinguishable types are *internal, external* and *impartial* criteria (Albin, 2001). The internal (contextual) approach is mostly procedural: it gives the concerned parties and the negotiation process the task of defining the substantial meaning of justice or fairness within that process. Just agreements are based on terms which the parties themselves have formulated and agreed to honor (Zartman, 1995; Zartman et al., 1996). These may or may not also draw on external principles of justice. But in the end parties choose for themselves. There are no particular independent requirements that the process or the agreement must fulfill, other than to deliver mutual gains to parties as rational benefit-seeking actors (Gauthier, 1986).

Impartial criteria, rooted in the philosophical literature, denote another procedural notion of justice: they indicate conditions which a process and an agreement must fulfill in order to be taken to be just and fair. While starting assumptions and specific requirements vary between approaches, they all place constraints on the pursuit of narrow self-interests and the use (abuse) of power and coercion. In John Rawls' renowned theory of "justice as fairness", parties, because of their selfishness, must define the substance of justice without knowing the effect on their own interests and position (Rawls, 1958, 1971). In Brian Barry's theory of justice as impartiality, by contrast, parties are motivated to be able to justify their behavior on grounds which others can accept as balanced and reasonable. Justice is what is agreed freely by parties, who are roughly equal in capacity to reject or veto a proposal. What is just elicits voluntary consent without the use of threats or rewards, and is also acceptable from a more general detached viewpoint (Barry, 1995).

External criteria here refer to well-recognized substantive principles of justice, whose general content is independent of particular contexts. A number of these are extensively discussed in the research literature, and often reflected in actual international negotiations, for example, the principles of equality, proportionality, compensatory justice and need (Albin, 2001; Deutsch, 1975; Pruitt, 1981).[2] What principles are most relevant for a specific problem and how they are to be interpreted need to be decided and agreed in negotiations. But each principle nonetheless has a basic meaning

with a limited number of possible applications, which constrain what justice can reasonably entail. Recent research addresses directly and in-depth how the peace versus justice question is handled in the process and outcome of negotiations. Here, "forward-looking" principles of justice are usefully distinguished from "backward-looking" ones (Zartman & Kremenyuk, 2005). Forward-looking notions are positive-sum and future-oriented: they turn their back on the past, and seek justice through and within the establishment of new cooperative relations based on mutual interests between parties. Backward-looking notions are zero-sum and seek justice retrospectively for past wrongdoings, rights and entitlements, for example, issues of accountability, compensation, reparations and punishment for earlier crimes.

Whether pursuing justice promotes or undermines peace thus depends in part on the particular concepts and principles involved. The contextual approach, by leaving the task of defining justice solely in the hands of the negotiating parties, is most easily combined with peace-making. The mere fact that something has been negotiated and agreed is the major, and sometimes a sufficient, indication that it is just. The impartial approach specifies requirements, and sometimes assumes motivations to behave justly, which best match negotiations between roughly equal parties. Negotiations between sharply unequal parties will not necessarily be entirely devoid of impartial justice, but they will rarely satisfy all the conditions commonly associated with this approach.[3] In this situation, pursuing "perfect justice" is indeed likely to make agreement, or even negotiation, impossible. The impact of external substantive criteria on peace processes will vary widely with the choice of particular principles and with the circumstances. An agreement based on equality may be hard to achieve when the parties are not equal to begin with. Compensatory justice requires identifying and motivating parties to provide a remedy for some inflicted harm. As for forward-looking vs. backward-looking notions, the former by definition are more easily combined with peace-making (when endorsed by parties). The latter supposedly prevent agreement from being reached or from being durable, as well as the achievement of justice. Based on wide-ranging case study research, Zartman concludes: "The record is striking. When parties base their position on a repetition of their past grievances, their past legalities, and their demands for reparations and punishment, negotiation is, in fact, war: an attempt to eliminate the other party by other means, not the search for a solution" (Zartman & Kremenyuk, 2005, p. 291).

While some factors have been discussed in the social-psychological and negotiation literatures (Albin, 1992; Zartman et al., 1996), research to date is far from mapping out fully what steers international negotiations in their choice of justice principle to apply. The most striking and often neglected reality in this regard, however, is that a single principle is rarely chosen: negotiators instead balance and combine different types of criteria (Young, 1994). Particularly in complex international cases, internal, impartial and external principles are frequently invoked to weigh all the pertinent factors when forging an agreement. A single standard can rarely capture the wide range of aspects to take into account. Examples of criteria which are often combined are mutual gain, proportionality and voluntary consent (absence of coercion). This has been found to serve both justice and peace: parties tend to regard the inclusion and balancing of different principles as an important element of justice in itself, and it certainly facilitates agreement in complex international talks (Albin, 2001).

The multiple roles of outcome justice in peace-making

The second aspect of whether notions of outcome justice promote or undermine peace concerns the compatibility (or not) of the notions held by parties. These notions may be the same or similar, they may be different but reconcilable, and they may be very far apart and irreconcilable. In each of these

cases, justice will take on a different role and affect the process and the outcome differently. Here again, it is impossible to argue generally that justice either promotes or undermines peace.

First, notions of outcome justice can play an instrumental role in negotiation and other peace-making efforts as external referents. This applies to situations in which the parties from the outset endorse the same or similar notions of a just solution. They have been extensively observed in the research literature, which refers to such shared notions as "focal points" which emerge as obvious and desirable to all parties (Schelling, 1960). They serve to coordinate expectations, guide the exchange of concessions, and decrease competitive behavior (Bartos, 1974; Deutsch, 1973). They thereby reduce the risks of disagreements and stalemates, and increase the likelihood of a timely and durable agreement being reached. Outcome fairness can certainly assume this facilitating role in international negotiations. The absence of great power inequalities is then important: parties are more likely to have similar notions of justice when they are roughly equal in relevant sources of power. In arms control negotiations during the Cold War, the USA and the Soviet Union as the sole nuclear powers were much directed by the expectation of agreements based on equality, such as equal ceilings or freezes and equal percentage reductions in existing arms arsenals.

This role of justice as an external referent is no longer the predominant one in negotiations of international significance. The existence of a shared notion at the start of the process has become unusual in these, whether, for instance, large-scale multilateral talks over global problems or internal negotiations to end civil war. A major reason is that the parties are typically marked by differences in resources, cultural norms, power and so on, and these shape their outlook on justice. Thus, the existence of divergent or even conflicting notions of justice at the outset is by far the most common situation. These instead become part of the dispute itself, and of any negotiations which get underway. What then happens to justice and the prospects for peace has been studied and discussed in recent work. Clearly, irreconcilable ideas of justice are disruptive: they can lead to violence and war and, if dialogue is not rejected entirely, to deadlock and breakdown in negotiations.

When parties with conflicting ideas of justice still attempt to reach an agreement, one of four routes is commonly chosen (Albin, 2001). First, parties can agree to redefine the problem and craft an agreement based on other considerations than justice. Secondly, they may agree on a procedure to settle their differences over the substance of a solution (e.g. arbitration). Thirdly, they may base an agreement mostly on one party's understanding of justice (e.g. that of the more powerful). Finally, as is often the case, parties may opt to balance and combine several principles which take account of their conflicting notions. This is a way of moving in the negotiation process from initially opposing concepts of justice, to a shared composite notion of what is just in a particular situation. When this succeeds, it increases satisfaction with the outcome and probably also the chances of a durable settlement. Research on the relationship between the handling of justice issues in the negotiation process or in its outcome, and the durability of international agreements, is new and has not yet yielded many definite conclusions.

A project led by Daniel Druckman and this author has so far provided evidence that incorporating principles of distributive justice into the terms of peace agreements contributes to their durability.

FROM AGREEMENT TO DURABLE PEACE

So far, the discussion has concerned how the peace vs. justice question plays out in moving from conflict to dialogue and from negotiation to an agreement. It will now turn to the question of justice and the longer-term durability of agreements and peace. First, the post-agreement tasks of securing implementation and compliance are considered. Next, the broader and longer-term imperative of durable peace is discussed.

After the agreement: justice in implementation and compliance

Recent research highlights the importance of continued negotiations after an agreement has been signed, to secure implementation and compliance (Spector & Zartman, 2003; Victor et al., 1998). This often determines whether an agreement on paper will remain just that, or actually result in an effective outcome. While some further negotiation is always needed after signature, international agreements in some areas (e.g. the global environment) appear to be particularly at risk of being stillborn. Very little research has, however, concerned itself with the role of justice and the peace vs. justice question in this phase. But important justice issues do arise in matters of implementation and compliance. Among them is the internationally well-established principle (legal and moral) concerning the obligation to honor and comply with freely negotiated agreements. These issues are, as reality demonstrates, perfectly capable of destroying entire peace agreements and peace processes.

First of all, one or more parties may not proceed with ratifying and implementing an agreement they have signed, or may delay doing so for a long time. There may be many reasons, more or less under their control. Complex legal or technical questions regarding ratification and enforcement may have to be resolved both within and between countries. Implementation may involve too great costs for some countries, for which the agreement itself does not provide cover. Domestic stakeholders, for example, in business or industry, may see their interests damaged by what has been agreed and may be strong enough to build barriers. Resistance to compromise on sovereign rights or lack of a sense of urgency are other reasons for agreements not being implemented (Susskind, 1994). Secondly, even if implemented, an agreement may be undermined with time by violations and failures to comply with obligations under it. Here lack of enforcement mechanisms and penalities, and insufficient incentives to comply, usually play a role. Sometimes states can avoid compliance and the costs it entails, and yet benefit from the agreement in much the same way as complying parties. With such free-riding, the costs are pushed over on other parties while the gains are retained. It is particularly tempting and therefore rampant when it comes to global public goods (e.g. a strong weapons non-proliferation regime, the global climate), the benefits of which are universally accessible and indivisible and cannot be denied to particular parties (Albin, 2003). Thirdly, parties which have by choice or not stood outside of the negotiation of the agreement may also choose to free-ride, or be capable of undermining it in other ways.

In all these cases, the legitimacy of the agreement will suffer. Powerful charges of injustice arise when parties do not honor agreements which they themselves have formulated and signed. In fact, they may be far more disruptive than feelings of injustice regarding the terms of the agreement itself. There are many international examples of this; among them, the negotiations between Israel and the PLO since 1993 and negotiations under the Nuclear Non-Proliferation Treaty, particularly since 1995. How far things can, and should, go before the agreement collapses depends on the circumstances, including costs of withdrawal for individual parties and the value of their alternatives. In one view of justice, the obligation to comply remains as long as the agreement is effective in serving its goals-and enough other parties also comply to make this possible (Barry, 1989). Whatever the particulars, justice in matters of implementation and compliance generally serves peace, while negligence of it or outright injustices will undermine peace.

After the war: transitional justice and peace

How can societies emerging from civil war and/or repressive rule deal with past injustices, and still move toward durable peace? Will attempts to redress past injustices promote or tear asunder the creation of a new peaceful (democratic) society? This is the context in which the peace vs. justice question has so far been most intensively debated, both in scholarship and policy-making. It has given rise to a large research literature, by now sharply divided over how to answer it. And it has made human rights activists collide with conflict managers over proper strategy in efforts to end devastating internal wars around the world (see Parlevliet, 2002). The apparent divisions result partly from focus on different aspects of justice and peace, and different time frames: behind the same labels, people talk in fact about different things which are not necessarily contradictory. But there are also genuine differences in the importance and priority attached to aspects of justice and peace, which remain unresolved.

"Transitional justice" here refers to the *norms* and *instruments* on the basis of which a society or new government, in transition from armed conflict and/or authoritarian rule, addresses past injustices committed in war or by the previous regime. At times, the term refers also to measures to prevent further atrocities and secure justice in the future; for example, through a new justice system (Call, 2004). It is about principles of justice, as well as the means used to act upon them. Depending on the context and the choice of the new government, transitional justice can entail a range of approaches (Elster, 2004): legal (e.g. the restoration of the rule of law), political, economic, administrative, psychological (e.g. reconciliation – see Rosoux's contribution to this volume), or a combination of these. The general goals of transitional justice are durable peace and/or stable democratic government. Often societies are in transition from both armed conflict and autocracy, and regard democratization as a pillar of a new peaceful order. No consensus exists, however, on a more specific set of goals or criteria which transitional justice should fulfill to be deemed successful and completed. Also discussed is whether this kind of justice, in principle and practice, reflects a political-pragmatic compromise on "real" justice in times of transition rather than its own type of justice.

Most debated is the question of what principle (and interpretation of it), and what instrument of transitional justice should be chosen under what conditions.[4] Different proposals are made in the literature, corresponding to the diversity of situations and approaches contained within the thinking and practice of transitional justice (e.g. Graybill & Lanegran, 2004; Kritz, 1995; O'Connor & Rausch, 2007). Two fundamental principles are retributive justice and restorative justice. The former holds that those responsible for past injustices (e.g. war crimes, human rights violations) should be held accountable and be punished. The focus is on the offenders and committed wrongdoings. The associated instruments are mostly legal, such as criminal trials in international or national courts and tribunals, and reform of the existing national judicial system. Restorative justice is about healing the wounds of and compensating the victims, and restoring relationships and reconciling communities involving former enemies. It involves measures such as truth commissions and truth telling, reparations and compensation, and acts of apology and forgiveness. One study distinguishes five types of approaches to transitional justice, drawing on wide-ranging case examples of democratization processes: criminal justice, historical justice, reparatory justice, administrative justice and constitutional justice (Teitel, 2000). In another study, focus is also on criminal justice, but with a different emphasis on vindication of the victim rather than punishment of the guilty (Biggar, 2001). Yet another holds that the restoration of justice after war must involve three elements: (re-)distributive justice, as a means to address causes of conflict; legal justice, as a means to deal with symptoms of conflict; and rectificatory (roughly retributive) justice, as a way to handle the consequences of conflict (Mani, 2002, 2005).

Of course, the debate is not only about the principles and meaning of transitional justice. Most of all, it is about strategy. One discussion is about how different principles and instruments of transitionary justice may in practice work against each other, for example those of retributive and restorative justice. Offenders must participate in various processes of restorative justice, but are of course unlikely to do so if at the same time tried and punished in the name of retributive justice (see Kauffman, 2005). Another set of findings suggest that mechanisms such as trials and international tribunals do not really promote reconciliation (Stover & Weinstein, 2004). The most relevant discussion here is exactly over the peace vs. justice question: what aspects of transitional justice are considered possible and prudent to pursue given political realities and the politics of peace-making and peace-building. There are essentially three overlapping answers given in the research literature to date.

One proposed answer is that peace comes first and must be prioritized: it can be or is best built without justice at least for an initial period of time. Peace—for example, the end of violence and internal conflict—is the basis for the success of other pursuits, and a precondition for achieving justice subsequently. Attempting to address justice issues first or together with peace issues is politically unrealistic and dangerous, and will lead to neither justice nor peace. Justice must follow after peace—or else it will undermine the achievement and durability of both peace and justice. Proponents of this approach stress the need for pragmatism, particularly in war-torn societies marked by political volatility and institutional weaknesses. In this context, attempting to punish those responsible for gross human rights violations, for example, may only lead to further crimes. One study holds that "a norm-governed political order must be based on a political bargain among contending groups ... on striking politically expedient bargains that create effective political coalitions to contain the power of potential perpetrators of abuses ... Amnesty—or simply ignoring past abuses—may be a necessary tool ... Once such deals are struck, institutions based on the rule of law become more feasible" (Snyder & Vinjamuri, 2003/04, p. 6). In arguing for pragmatism and the "logic of consequences", it examines the use and result of three approaches to the pursuit of justice and peace in 32 cases of civil wars from 1989 to 2003. Other research points out that the absence of provisions for justice, such as human rights, in a peace agreement does not inhibit their inclusion or role in subsequent laws (Putnam, 2002).

The second basic answer to the peace vs. justice question in post-war societies starts off from a different premise. Both justice and peace need to be pursued from the outset. While tensions between the two goals are recognized, choosing one over the other is not an option: peace cannot be restored or built and will not endure unless demands for justice are addressed (Mani, 2002, 2005). Current policies are typically short term and centered upon ending or containing violence, at the expense of issues essential to lasting peace such as the underlying causes of conflict (Tschirgi, 2005). Whether justice is the foundation from or through which peace follows varies, but clearly the two values are interlinked and not opposing. This becomes particularly clear when examining the long-term requirements of durable peace and stability, for example, in the legal justice area. In countries emerging from civil war, peace is impossible without the establishment and implementation of the rule of law. That involves a range of principles, institutions and processes concerned with various aspects of justice and accountability which, in one view, are most effective if established and implemented domestically by the concerned countries themselves (Kritz, 2001). One study highlights, with reference to the work of the International Criminal Tribunal for the former Yugoslavia, how criminal justice contributes to durable peace by punishing inhumane or unjust actions and deterring further atrocities (Akhavan, 1998). Another examines how and when justice can be reconciled with peace through various instruments, mostly associated with retributive and restorative justice (Biggar, 2001). Noting that most countries concerned are impoverished, yet another adds the importance of instruments of distributive justice to address socio-economic

inequalities as a cause of conflict (Mani, 2002).

The third answer regards certain aspects of justice as compatible with peace. These are often labelled "forward-looking" in seeking justice not retrospectively, but within future arrangements and institutions (Snyder & Vinjamuri, 2003/04; Zartman & Kremenyuk, 2005). Conversely, the pursuit of backward-looking notions of justice focusing on rectifying past wrongdoings are seen as detrimental to peace-building. Of course, the three different approaches here outlined overlap. For example, while in the first approach, justice is subordinated to or even eliminated by political constraints and calculations to a certain stage, it is not seen as dispensable in the long run: without justice, including the institutionalization of the rule of law and democracy, peace will not endure (e.g. Hampson, 1996). Thus, peace and justice are not even here, in the final analysis, opposing. The question is instead about timing and sequencing – when and how far each goal is best pursued so as to eventually fulfill both, given political circumstances.

CONCLUSION

This chapter has examined how justice relates to peace and peace-making, in different stages of the conflict resolution process. The research literature to date mostly examines the peace vs. justice dilemma within a single stage, and often frames the problem as being one monolithic value standing against the other. Much of the literature is specifically on post-conflict (transitional) societies faced with past injustices while attempting to build a durable peace. It has been argued here that the contextual details are decisive for how the two values relate to each other, and that it is impossible to say categorically that justice either undermines or promotes peace. It can do and does both, depending on the circumstances. Among the major factors are the phase of peace-making involved, the time-frame (short- or long-term), the particular concepts of justice at play and whether these are shared by parties, and the prevailing balance of forces between parties.

In many situations, particularly in a longer-term perspective, the issue is not whether peace or justice is to be chosen or prioritized for both are clearly needed in some sense. The core questions are instead: what kind of justice and what kind of peace should be promoted (what steps should be taken)? How are the pursuits of these two values (the steps) best timed, sequenced and combined over time— that is, what kind of justice is to (can) be furthered in what stage of the process of conflict resolution and peace-building?

Behind the "peace vs. justice" label thus lurks a web of different relationships and interactions between the two values. Many of these are still little researched and poorly understood. How far conflict resolvers should seek to achieve justice depends partly on what is politically wise and possible, but also on what is beneficial for long-term peace. The roles of justice in bringing parties into dialogue, and in peace processes and the terms of agreements, have been examined here. Yet we still possess relatively little systematic knowledge about, for instance, the importance of justice for durable peace in the long term.

Other questions concern in what sense and how both justice and peace are best promoted over time, rather than whether both are needed or which is to be prioritized. For example, there are many instruments of transitional justice. What makes a leader choose one instrument over another, and what instrument *should* she choose if stable peace is a prime concern? The actual effects and consequences in the field of the use of different mechanisms need to be better examined. These and other questions point perhaps foremost to the need for more empirical investigations, to fill the gaps and put to test propositions and assumptions found in both scholarship and policy.

NOTES

1 For a discussion of the concept of "just peace", see e.g. Allan & Keller (2006).

2 For a review of the literature on external principles of justice, see Albin (1992), pp. 41ff.

3 This is well discussed in Barry (1995). A particularly illustrative example is the Israel-PLO interim talks from 1993 and onwards (see Albin, 2001).

4 A comprehensive discussion of mechanisms available to achieve accountability for past human rights violations is found in Bassiouni (2002). On the use of reparations for historical injustices, see Torpey (2003).

REFERENCES

Akhavan, Payam. 1998. "Justice in the Hague, Peace in the Former Yugoslavia? A Commentary on the United Nations War Crimes Tribunal", *Human Rights Quarterly*, 20, 4: 737–816.

Albin, Cecilia. 1992. "Fairness Issues in Negotiation: Structure, Process, Procedures and Outcome". Working Paper 92–88, December. Laxenburg, Austria: International Institute for Applied Systems Analysis.

Albin, Cecilia. 1993. "The Role of Fairness in Negotiation", *Negotiation Journal*, 9, 3: 223–244.

Albin, Cecilia. 2001. *Justice and Fairness in International Negotiation*. Cambridge, UK: Cambridge University Press.

Albin, Cecilia. 2003. "Negotiating International Cooperation: Global Public Goods and Fairness", *Review of International Studies*, 29, 3: 365–385.

Allan, Pierre and Alexis Keller, eds. 2006. *What is a Just Peace?* Oxford: Oxford University Press.

Barry, Brian. 1989. "Can States be Moral?". In Brian Barry, *Democracy, Power and Justice. Essays in Political Theory*. Oxford: Clarendon Press.

Barry, Brian. 1995. *Justice as Impartiality*. Oxford: Clarendon Press.

Bartos, Otomar. 1974. *Process and Outcome of Negotiations*. New York: Columbia University Press.

Bassiouni, M. Cherif, ed. 2002. *Post-Conflict Justice*. Ardsley, New York: Transnational Publishers.

Biggar, Nigel. 2003. "Making Peace or Doing Justice: Must We Choose?". In Nigel Biggar, ed., *Burying the Past. Making Peace and Doing Justice after Civil Conflict*. Washington, DC: Georgetown University Press.

Brown, Chris. 1997. "Review Article: Theories of International Justice", *British Journal of Political Science*, 27, 2: 273–297.

Bull, Henley. 1977. *The Anarchical Society. A Study of Order in World Politics*. London: MacMillan Press.

Burton, John. 1990. *Conflict Resolution and Prevention*. New York: St Martins Press.

Call, Charles. 2004. "Is Transitional Justice Really Just?", *Brown Journal of World Affairs*, 11, 1: 101–113.

Deutsch, Morton. 1973. *The Resolution of Conflict: Constructive and Destructive Processes*. New Haven: Yale University Press.

Deutsch, Morton. 1975. "Equity, Equality, and Need: What Determines Which Value Will Be Used as the Basis of Distributive Justice?", *Journal of Social Issues*, 31, 3: 137–150.

Druckman, Daniel and Thomas V. Bonoma. 1976. "Determinants of Bargaining Behavior in a Bilateral Monopoly Situation II: Opponent's Concession Rate and Similarity", *Behavioral Science*, 21: 252–262.

Druckman, Daniel and Richard Harris. 1990. "Alternative Models of Responsiveness in International Negotiation", *Journal of Conflict Resolution*, 34, 2: 234–251.

Elster, Jon. 2004. *Closing the Books: Transitional Justice in Historical Perspective*. New York: Cambridge University Press.

Galtung, Johan. 1969. "Violence, Peace, and Peace Research", *Journal of Peace Research*, 6, 3: 167–191.

Gauthier, David. 1986. *Morals by Agreement*. Oxford: Clarendon Press.

Graybill, Lynn and Kimberly Lanegran. 2004. "Truth, Justice, and Reconciliation in Africa: Issues and Cases", *African Studies Quarterly*, 8, 1 (electronic journal).

Gross Stein, Janice, ed. 1989. *Getting to the Table: The Processes of International Prenegotiation*. Baltimore, MD: The Johns Hopkins University Press.

Hampson, Fen Osler. 1996. *Nurturing Peace: Why Peace Settlements Succeed or Fail*. Washington, DC: The United States Institute of Peace Press.

Jacob, M.C., ed. 1974. *Peace Projects of the Eighteenth Century*. New York: Garland.

Kauffman, Craig. 2005. "Transitional Justice in Guatemala: Linking the Past and the Future". Paper prepared for the International Studies Association South Conference, Miami, Florida, 3–5 November 2005.

Kelman, Herbert. 2000. "The Role of the Scholar-Practitioner in International Conflict Resolution", *International Studies Perspectives*, 1, 3: 273–287.

Kritz, Neil, ed. 1995. *Transitional Justice*. Volumes I-III. Washington, DC: United States Institute of Peace Press.

Kritz, Neil. 2001. "The Rule of Law in the Postconflict Phase: Building a Stable Peace". In Chester Crocker, Fen Olser Hampson and Pamela Aall, eds., *Turbulent Peace: The Challenges of Managing International Conflict*. Washington, DC: United States Institute of Peace Press.

Lederach, John Paul. 1995. *Preparing for Peace: Conflict Transformation Across Cultures*. Syracuse, New York: Syracuse University Press.

Mani, Rama. 2002. *Beyond Retribution: Seeking Justice in the Shadows of War*. Cambridge: Polity Press.

Mani, Rama. 2005. "Balancing Peace with Justice in the Aftermath of Violent Conflict", *Development*, 48, 3: 25–34.

O'Connor, Vivienne and Colette Rausch, eds. 2007. *Model Codes for Post-Conflict Criminal Justice*. Volume I: Model Criminal Code. Washington, DC: United States Institute of Peace Press.

Osgood, Robert and Robert Tucker. 1967. *Force, Order and Justice*. Baltimore, Maryland: The Johns Hopkins Press.

Parks, Craig and Samuel Komorita. 1998. "Reciprocity Research and Its Implications for the Negotiation Process", *International Negotiation*, 3, 2: 151–169.

Parlevliet, Michelle. 2002. "Bridging the Divide: Exploring the Relationship Between Human Rights and Conflict Management", *Track Two*, 11, 1: 8–43.

Pruitt, Dean. 1981. *Negotiation Behavior*. New York: Academic Press.

Putnam, Tonya. 2002. "Human rights and sustainable peace". In Stephen John Stedman, Donald Rothchild and Elizabeth Cousens, eds., *Ending Civil Wars: The Implementation of Peace Agreements*. Boulder, Colorado: Lynne Rienner Publishers.

Rawls, John. 1958. "Justice as Fairness", *Philosophical Review*, 67: 164–94.

Rawls, John. 1971. *A Theory of Justice*. Cambridge, Massachusetts: Harvard University Press.

Saunders, Harold H. 2001. *A Public Peace Process: Sustained Dialogue to Transform Racial and Ethnic Conflicts*. New York: Palgrave.

Schelling, Thomas. 1960. *The Strategy of Conflict*. Cambridge, Massachusetts: Harvard University Press.

Snyder, Jack and Leslie Vinjamuri. 2003/04. "Trials and Errors: Principle and Pragmatism in Strategies of International Justice", *International Security*, 28, 3: 5–44.

Spector, Bertram and I. William Zartman, eds. 2003. *Getting it Done: Postagreement Negotiation and International Regimes*. Washington, DC: United States Institute of Peace.

Sriram, Chandra Lekha. 2004. *Confronting Past Human Rights Violations: Justice vs. Peace in Times of Transition*. New York: Frank Cass.

Stover, Eric and Harvey Weinstein, eds. 2004. *My Neighbor, My Enemy: Justice and Community in the Aftermath of Ethnic Cleansing*. New York: Cambridge University Press.

Susskind, Lawrence. 1994. *Environmental Diplomacy, Negotiating More Effective Global Agreements.* Oxford and New York: Oxford University Press.

Teitel, Ruti. 2000. *Transitional Justice.* New York: Oxford University Press.

Torpey, John, ed. 2003. *Politics and the Past: On Repairing Historical Injustices.* Lanham, Maryland: Rowman & Littlefield Publishers.

Tschirgi, Necla. 2005. "Peacebuilding through Global Peace and Justice", *Development,* 48, 3: 50–56.

Victor, David, Kal Raustiala and Eugene Skolnikoff, eds. 1998. *The Implementation and Effectiveness of International Environmental Commitments.* Laxenburg, Austria: International Institute for Applied Systems Analysis.

Welch, David. 1993. *Justice and the Genesis of War.* Cambridge: Cambridge University Press.

Welch Larson, Deborah. 1998. "Exchange and Reciprocity in International Negotiations", *International Negotiation,* 3, 2: 121–138.

Young, Peyton. 1994. *Equity: In Theory and Practice.* Princeton, NJ: Princeton University Press.

Zartman, I. William. 1991. "The Structure of Negotiation". In Victor Kremenyuk, ed., *International Negotiation: Analysis, Approaches, Issues.* San Francisco: Jossey-Bass Publishers.

Zartman, I. William. 1995. "The Role of Justice in Global Security Negotiations", *American Behavioral Scientist,* 38, 6: 889–903.

Zartman, I. William and Maureen Berman. 1982. *The Practical Negotiator.* New Haven and London: Yale University Press.

Zartman, I. William, Daniel Druckman, Lloyd Jensen, Dean G. Pruilt, and H. Peyton Young, 1996. "Negotiation as a Search for Justice", *International Negotiation,* 1, 1: 79–98.

Zartman, I. William and Victor Kremenyuk. 2005. *Peace versus Justice: Negotiating Forward- and Backward-Looking Outcomes.* Lanham, Maryland: Rowman & Littlefield Publishers.

31

The Spread of Civil War[1]

Kristian Skrede Gleditsch

INTRODUCTION

Civil war has been by far the most common form of conflict in the international system since 1945.[2] Although interstate conflicts have been more lethal, in the sense that each single conflict on average generates a larger number of casualties, outbreaks of civil wars have been more frequent, and civil wars tend to be more persistent and more difficult to settle than interstate conflicts.[3] In addition to the direct fatalities as a result of acts of combat, civil wars have also created large indirect costs through economics losses, and often leave severe legacies in the countries affected, which threaten to undermine the future economic and political viability of affected countries (see e.g. Ashford and Huet-Vaughan 1997; Collier et al. 2003; Ghobarah, Huth and Russett 2003; Kang and Meernik 2005; Lopez and Wodon 2005; Plümper and Neumayer 2006). Indeed, Collier et al. (2003) argue that the long-term effects of civil war are so severe as to amount to "development in reverse". The salience of civil conflicts in the post-Cold War era has led to a great deal of interest in whether and how external efforts may help facilitate the resolving of such conflicts (see e.g. Hampson 1996; Stedman, Rothchild and Cousens 2002; Zartman 1995).

Although civil wars clearly pose very severe problems for the countries where conflict takes place, intrastate conflict has traditionally not been thought of as an "international" problem or security concern. Whereas relations between states have always been a central topic in the study of conflict, much of the academic research on civil war has treated conflict within countries primarily as a "domestic" or "internal" issue, where the causes and consequences of conflict have been assumed to be confined to the country where the conflict takes place. Researchers have related civil war to various domestic explanatory factors such as a country's income (e.g. Collier and Hoeffler 2004), state strength and factors determining the opportunities for insurgencies such as mountainous terrain (e.g. Fearon and Laitin 2003), or political instability (e.g. Hegre et al. 2001). However, there are many reasons to question whether such a "closed polity" approach – where individual states are treated as isolated units, unaffected by events and actors in other states – can be appropriate for understanding civil war and the full range of their consequences. Many researchers have pointed to how civil wars often display various transnational dimensions (e.g. Brown 1993, 1996; Gleditsch 2007; Salehyan and Gleditsch 2006). The actors involved in violent civil conflicts in a given state are often linked in various ways to actors in other states. These transnational linkages imply that we will often need to look beyond individual nation states to understand why conflicts turn violent and evolve in particular ways. Furthermore, the consequences of intrastate conflicts are not necessarily limited to the individual state where violence first occurs. Violence in civil wars often crosses national boundaries, and there is an increasing recognition that conflict in one state may spread and foster violence in other states, as well as generate conflict between nation states. Moreover, the consequences of civil war may spread and affect other states through externalities of conflict such as refugees and the economic impact of conflict in neighboring countries. This in turn implies that civil war is not merely a problem for the countries experiencing conflict, but can have wide ranging security implications for other states as well. If the risk of civil wars and the prospects for their settlement are influenced by transnational factors, conflict resolution efforts are unlikely to be effective unless they consider features beyond the individual country where conflict occurs. Furthermore, the fact that interest in the outcomes and consequences of conflict often extend beyond the original conflict locations can provide help in understanding the incentives and constraints for outside actors in engaging in conflict resolution efforts.

In this chapter, I review the existing literature on the international spread of civil war and the consequences of the spread of civil war for theories of conflict and the prospects for conflict resolution. Given the limited space available here, such a review must necessarily be selective. In particular, I will not able to give full justice to the extensive literature on the causes of civil wars and their consequences within states,

but will instead focus on their transnational implications and spread. To be explicit on terms, I here mean by the spread of civil war either how civil wars in one state can increase the risks of outbreaks of violence elsewhere or new conflicts involving other states, as well as conflict externalities or detrimental consequences generated by civil wars that are felt by states other than the country where the conflict initially breaks out. Since I am only focusing on the spread of ongoing civil violence, I will not discuss how international factors more generally may promote civil war, including, for example, how the global Cold War rivalry may have ignited civil wars, as seen in the Greek Civil War (e.g. Close 1993; O'Ballance 1966). Moreover, I will not cover what Lake and Rothchild (1998) call the escalation of civil wars to international actors, or cases where other states intervene on the side of government in a civil war, without the spread of the location of fighting to other states, as for example in Afghanistan (for an overview of when interventions in civil wars are more or less likely, see Regan 2000).[4]

I will first start with a brief overview of the main known empirical facts with respect to the tendency for civil conflicts to spread between states. I then proceed to discuss in more detail a series of broad classes of different forms of the spread of civil war and their consequences, with a particular focus on the mechanisms that may tie the presence of a civil war to the consequences for other states and actors. I first focus on mechanisms that may lead to the spread of new civil war onsets in other states, distinguishing between cases that involve specific transnational actors or issue linkages, and cases where conflict externalities and demonstration effects can promote conflict in unrelated conflict dyads. In addition to spread in terms of new cases of civil war onset, I will consider how civil wars may give rise to new forms of conflict involving other actors, such as interstate conflicts or transnational terrorism. Finally, I will discuss how civil wars can have pernicious consequences for states other than the country of origin, or the location where the conflict occurs. I will provide illustrative examples of each of the forms of spread and evidence supporting the plausibility of the postulated mechanisms in the existing literature. However, as most research on civil war has focused on their causes and consequences within states, there has been relatively little empirical research on the spread of civil war. Moreover, there are significant challenges in collecting data and analyzing the extent to which the particular forms of spread occur and their frequency. However, the mechanisms discussed are potentially important mechanisms than in principle can be evaluated more systematically, and I will discuss promising avenues for future data collection efforts and research projects.

THE CLUSTERING OF CIVIL WAR

It is well known that certain parts of the world have experienced more civil conflict than others, and many researchers have noted the existence of conflict clusters, or areas that experience a large number of conflicts at the same time (Buzan and Wæver 2003; Gleditsch 2002; Singer and Wildavsky 1996. For example, in the 1980s, Central America saw a large number of Marxist insurgencies, and later, in the 1990s, there were a large number of simultaneous or consecutive conflicts in the Great Lakes region of Africa. Figure 31.1 displays the geographical distribution of intrastate conflicts listed in the Uppsala Conflict Dataset (Gleditsch et al. 2002) over the period 1993–2003, as displayed by the *ViewConflicts* program (Rød 2003). Certain conflict clusters are clearly discernable, including Western Africa, the Caucasus, and the Balkans.

The conventional "closed polity" approach to comparative civil war studies would treat all of these conflicts of war as independent events, where each outbreak occurs in an independent manner, due to factors fully contained within each individual country. This assumption, however, contrasts sharply with much of the case-based discussion of civil wars in conflict-prone regions, which often

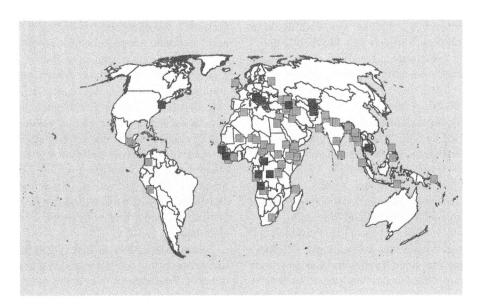

Figure 31.1   Location of armed conflicts, 1993–2003
Note: Location of intrastate conflicts (dark) and internationalized intrastate conflicts (light dots), 1993–2003, based on the Uppsala conflict data. Each dot corresponds to the geographical midpoint of a conflict assigned a unique ID, based on conflict incompatibility. See Gleditsch et al. (2002) for further details on the Uppsala conflict data.

emphasizes the importance of transnational linkages between conflicts and actors (e.g. Ardón 1998; Bye 1991; Collier and Sambanis 2005; McNulty 1999). Moreover, many statistical analyses have found that countries with neighboring states experiencing civil war appear to have a pronounced higher likelihood of violent conflict onset than other states (e.g. Esty et al. 1998; Gleditsch 2007; Salehyan and Gleditsch 2006; Sambanis 2001; Ward and Gleditsch 2002). Skeptics might wonder whether this seeming clustering in conflict is persuasive evidence for diffusion, since the domestic factors believed to influence the likelihood of civil war such as poor economic performance are also likely to cluster geographically (see e.g. Gleditsch 2002).[5] However, this spatial clustering in civil war holds even after considering other potential influences on civil war that may be spatially clustered, and has been replicated in many studies. Indeed, Hegre and Sambanis (2006) find that the positive impact of neighboring conflict on the risk of civil war is one of the few predictors in civil conflict studies that remains robust under many possible specifications.

Although the finding that conflict in a neighboring state increases the risk of conflict is not controversial by itself, there is little consensus on what it is about the presence of civil war in one state that increases the risk of civil conflict in another state. Most of the literature on the diffusion of conflict has focused on other forms of conflicts, such as interstate wars (e.g. Siverson and Starr 1991), urban riots (e.g. Midlarsky 1978; Myers 2000), general political protest, including non-violent actions such as demonstrations and strikes (e.g. Hill and Rothchild 1986; Reising 1999), or forms of one-sided violence against civilians such as lynching (e.g. Tolnay, Deane and Beck 1996), and has not been directly related to civil war *per se*. In the next section, I will consider possible mechanisms linking civil war in one state to an increased risk in other states. Much of the literature on the spread of civil war has been cast rather narrowly around direct conflict contagion and geographic proximity as a measure of the

opportunity for conflict to spread. Buhaug and Gleditsch (2008) find that the risk of civil war does not depend on measures of degrees of interaction opportunity such as length of shared borders, which suggests that particular ties between states are more important than just geographical closeness per se. Moreover, there are many ways other than through the actual onset of a civil war in another state whereby a civil war in one state may "spread" or influence other states. For example, civil wars may spread to forms of conflict other than civil war, and civil wars may have many detrimental consequences for other states even in cases where violence does not erupt. These forms of spread are discussed in subsequent sections.

Spread of civil conflict onset

Spread of conflict onset through transnational actor linkages

One of the most obvious mechanisms whereby conflicts may spread is through transnational linkages to actors in an ongoing civil war. The actors in civil wars often have a transnational presence. In particular, many civil wars revolve around peripheral ethnic groups who seek political concessions or secession from a nation state. Most ethnic groups are not confined to a single nation state, but often extend into other states. For example, about two-thirds of the ethnic groups included in the Minorities at Risk data set (Gurr 1993) are considered to have significant segments in other states. Individuals in a minority group may face similar grievances in many states, and decisions to resort to violence in one state are likely to be influenced by decisions made elsewhere.

Transnational ethnic linkages can influence the prospects for conflict onset in a number of ways. Transnational ethnic kin often contribute financially to insurgencies. Moreover, individuals from transnational communities often participate in insurgencies in other states. Hence, groups that can draw upon assets among diasporas can often mobilize resources far greater than would be expected from their size or influence. Groups with transnational linkages can furthermore often benefit from safe havens among communities in other states. Transnational bases of support in other states can greatly increase the fighting capacity of insurgencies that would otherwise be weak and ineffective. Although international borders are not necessarily difficult to cross in a military sense, their political status as markers of state sovereignty makes it politically more difficult for states to violate them (e.g. Salehyan forthcoming). Members of émigré communities often hold more extreme views than individuals in origin countries, and are less likely to be deterred by government repression, since these cannot as easily be targeted. Just as transnational linkages can influence initial onset, there are many factors that that can increase the potential of civil wars that involve groups with a transnational presence to spread between countries. Successful rebellion by group members in one state can often inspire members of the ethnic community in other states to resort to violence. If a group is already mobilized in one state, then it can count on access to arms and trained combatants in other states.

The cases of the Albanian communities in Kosovo and Macedonia illustrate the role that transnational ethnic ties may play in civil conflict onset and its spread. Although Albanians were a majority in the Kosovo region of Serbia, their political and cultural autonomy became severely repressed after Milošević revoked the province's auton-omy in 1989. Whereas the local Albanian leaders favored a non-violent strategy of confrontation, the more hard-line Kosovo Liberation Army (KLA) advocating violent struggle emerged in the late 1990s. The KLA was heavily dependent upon support from the Albanian émigré community, and recruited massively among Albanians outside the province. Moreover, the organization benefited from bases in Albania, where it could retreat and regroup under repression from the militarily much stronger Yugoslav Federal Army. Whereas the armed conflict in Kosovo ended after the NATO intervention,

the Albanian insurgency that broke out in 2001 in Macedonia can be seen as a continuation of the prior Kosovo insurgency, seeking to replicate the successful use of violence to gain political concessions in Macedonia. Although formally an independent organization, many of the combatants in the Albania National Liberation Army (NLA) in Macedonia had previously participated in the KLA uprising in Kosovo, and the NLA arose in the wake of the massive influx of Albanian refugees from Kosovo to Macedonia. The specific timing of the NLA insurgency is difficult to explain with reference only to events inside Macedonia proper. Although Albanians faced many grievances in Macedonia, the authorities had made significant concessions to the Albanian community prior to the outbreak and the government at the time included Albanian political parties.

The presence of such transnational ethnic linkages in many civil wars suggests that this is likely to be one of the important mechanisms underlying the spatial clustering in civil wars. However, it is difficult to assess more systematically to what extent such linkages influence resort to violence. Most analysis looks only at linkages in actual conflicts (e.g. Heraclides 1999; Salehyan, Gleditsch and Cunningham 2006), which does not allow us to assess how many potential opportunities for transnational support are *not* associated with onset. Buhaug and Gates (2002) find that civil wars are more likely to take place in border areas, but do not consider whether the actors involved have kin on the other side of an international boundary. Using country level data, Gleditsch (2007) finds that states with a larger number of transnational groups are more likely to experience conflict onset, but this does not directly answer whether the transnational communities with potential transnational support are more likely to rebel. At the group level, data from the Minorities at Risk (MAR) project suggest that ethnic groups with transnational kin support are much more likely to engage in rebellion (see Gurr 1993). However, there are a number of problems associated with using the MAR data here. The MAR data are organized around minorities in specific countries, and limited to minorities considered to be at risk.[6] Moreover, some of the groups identified cannot be considered cohesive actors, such as "Foreign Workers" in Switzerland or "Blacks/Asians" in the UK, and the labels used are not standardized across countries. This makes it difficult to analyze group linkages across state boundaries. New efforts to improve data on ethnicity and political exclusion will greatly facilitate new empirical research in this area (see Cederman, Rød and Weidmann 2006).

Spread of conflict onset through government alliances and rivalries

Alliances between peripheral groups and state governments are another form of transnational linkages that can induce the spread of conflict between states. Many insurgent groups count on support from the governments of other states. In some cases, insurgent groups and neighboring governments have shared ties, and support will often stem from sympathy for groups and a desire to see some concession for the group's objectives. However, state support for insurgencies in other states may also be motivated out of antipathy with the government of that state, or pecuniary motives from conflict rather than necessarily sympathy or links with insurgent groups per se. Government involvement in insurgencies in other countries can lead to competitive interventions, where states support insurgencies in rival countries to retaliate for intrusion in their own domestic affairs. Since the prospects for support and its reliability will depend upon who holds power in other states, changes in the coalitions that hold power in relevant countries will augur large changes in the resources that insurgent groups can mobilize.

Western Africa around the turn of the Millennium exemplifies such patterns of competitive interventions giving rise to new outbreaks of civil conflict as well as making civil wars more persistent. Former Liberian President Charles Taylor, for example—who himself rose to political prominence as a warlord in a civil war, operating from Côte d'Ivoire—had consistently poor relations with his neighbors, and is widely held to have supported insurgencies in other states in the region, including the Revolutionary United Front (RUF) in Sierra Leone and the Forces Démocratiques de Guinée rebels in Guinea.[7] Taylor's involvement in neighboring conflicts in turn brought about new anti-Taylor insurgencies in Liberia, allegedly supported by neighboring regimes seeking to retaliate for Taylor's intrusion in their internal affairs. The government of Guinea is believed to have backed Liberians United for Reconciliation and Democracy (LURD), while the Ivorian government allegedly backed the Movement for Democracy in Liberia (MODEL). By the end of 2003, the two movements had greatly reduced the Taylor government's control over Liberia, and Taylor eventually agreed to resign under international pressure. The Great Lakes Region of Africa in the late 1990s further illustrate how regional shocks and changes in political coalitions in other states influence the prospects for civil war outbreaks (see McNulty 1999). When the Tutsi-dominated Rwanda Patriotic Front seized control in Rwanda with the assistance of Uganda, many ethnic Hutus fled to refugee camps in neighboring Zaire. These refugee camps became dominated by the Hutu Interahamwe militias and former military personnel, who carried out several attacks against Rwandese territory. In retaliation, the government of Rwanda started to support a long-dormant Marxist insurgency in Zaire headed by Laurent Kabila, hoping to undermine the stability of Zaire and afford opportunities for Rwanda to directly intervene and limit the military threat emanating from the refugee camps. With the new outside support, Kabila defeated the Mobutu regime relatively easily, seizing the capital Kinshasa in May 1997.

These tendencies have been supported more generally in some empirical studies, albeit the measures used have often been somewhat indirect. Using democracy as a proxy for constraints and opportunities for intervention in the affairs of other states, Gleditsch (2007) and Sambanis (2001) find that states with less democratic neighbors are more likely to experience civil war onset. Salehyan (forthcoming) show that the risk of conflict onset is higher for states with neighboring rivals. Looking at ongoing conflicts, Akcinaroglu and Radziszewski (2005) find that rivalries tend to prolong war duration. Salehyan, Gleditsch, and Cunningham (2006) develop new indicators of assistance from states, including cases where such support is alleged, but not acknowledged. Their analysis indicates that support from other states tend to make civil conflicts more persistent, supporting the idea that outside support can make conflicts more difficult to resolve.

Spread of conflict through direct conflict contagion

So far, I have discussed how direct linkages between actors in an ongoing civil war and actors in other states can make new conflicts more likely. However, civil war in one country may also increase the risk of conflict in other states, even in the absence of any direct functional links between the actors involved or the issues at stake in the conflict. Conflict in one country may promote conflict onset in other states due to demonstration effects. Resort to violence by one group in one state by one group facing grievances can inspire other groups with grievances against a government to follow their lead, even in the absence of any direct contact. One the one hand, the success of others may promote violence, as groups are likely to emulate the strategies that have been successful in other countries. As a result, we would expect that politically successful insurgencies in one state could give rise to a bandwagon or series of copycat efforts in other states. On the other hand, the problems faced by others may also lead groups to resort to violence for defensive purposes in the wake of experiences from other states undergoing civil war. If actors observe severe repression carried out against a minority group in another state, they may come to believe that similar acts could occur in their own state. Expecting state repression and fearing that they may be at a disadvantage later, groups may be more likely to resort to mobilization and preemptive use of violence.

Demonstration or learning effects across states are difficult to assess directly, since we do not have any way of inferring to what extent decisions to rebel are made contingent on events in other states (see e.g. Kuran 1998). Hill et al. (1998) suggest one approach to study diffusion based on temporal contagion (see also Coleman 1964; Strang and Tuma 1993), but such methods have not yet been applied to the study of civil war. However, the history of anti-colonial movements, particular insurgent tactics, and conflicts within certain regions show temporal dynamics that are consistent with demonstration and learning effects across countries. The colonial struggle in Algeria against the French, for example, became a source of inspiration for movements in many other countries, including the PLO, who shifted to a strategy of guerrilla warfare as it came under control of the Fatah faction lead by Yasser Arafat. The radical Sionists's successful use of terrorism to obtain political concessions under the British Mandate in Palestine was later emulated by the Greek National Organization of Cypriot Fighters (EOAK) seeking independence from Britain. More recently, suicide bombing appears to have diffused and gained popularity based on its perceived success in other states (e.g. Enders and Sandler 2005; Pape 2003). Tull and Mehler (2005) argue that the proliferation of power-sharing agreements in efforts to end civil wars have encouraged insurgencies as the method for would-be-leaders to establish a claim on power. Finally, the end of the Cold War saw a number of outbreaks of civil conflict in the former Soviet Union, which are often seen as evidence of demonstration and emulation effects across conflicts and actors within the successor states.

The spread and availability of arms is another feature that can give rise to the spread of conflicts. Rebels require some military means to launch an insurgency against a state or to resist government forces. Whereas states – within some limitations – can purchase arms on the global markets, rebels have fewer avenues for purchasing weapons openly. Moreover, countries that experience or are considered at risk of civil war often become subject to international sanctions on the sale of weapons (e.g. Tierney 2005). This in turn creates opportunities for black market dealers to capitalize on the demand for weapons (see Brauer 2007). Civil war in another country may increase the risk of civil war by increasing the availability of arms, thereby lowering the costs to launching insurgencies (e.g. Collier and Hoeffler 2004). Since borders are often porous, neighboring countries may find it difficult to prevent arms from coming in from neighboring countries. Hence, all else equal, a higher availability of arms in neighboring states undergoing conflict should be expected to increase the risk of conflict in neighboring states through lowering the cost of launching insurgencies.

There has been relatively little empirical research on how arms availability influences the risk of conflict. Looking at official arms transfer data, Craft and Smaldone (2002, 2003) find that greater availability of arms increases the probability of conflict. Arms transfer data, however, record primarily sales to government, and are less suitable for addressing the issue of access to arms for insurgents, who often may be unable to by arms on the open market. Killicoat (2006) develops a new data set on Kalashnikov assault rifle prices to evaluate the link between the price of arms and conflict outbreaks. His results suggest that lower prices indeed are associated with a greater probability of conflict. Moreover, the price of arms vary strongly by measures of the effective trade barriers for illicit trade, which in turn suggests that civil wars in neighboring states combined with decreased ability to monitor cross border interactions can substantially increase the availability of cheap arms and heighten the risk of conflict.

Spread to interstate conflict and transnational terrorism

In addition to outbreaks of intrastate conflict in other states, civil war may also spread violence outside the boundaries of the state where the conflict occurs through promoting types of violence other than traditional intrastate conflicts.

There are many ways in which a civil war may give rise to a war between states. Just as the activities of civil wars are rarely fully confined within the boundary of a single country, they can often lead to conflict between the origin country and other affected parties. Civil wars often take place in border areas (e.g. Buhaug and Gates 2002), and rebels will often move across international borders to seek safety from government repression (e.g. Salehyan forthcoming). But although borders may afford rebels some degree of protection from government forces since governments face political problems in crossing into the territory of other sovereign states, border violations certainly can and do occur (see Gleditsch and Salehyan 2007). In some cases, military forces may pursue rebels into neighboring territory, or retaliate against rebel activities by aerial bombardment. In some cases, states have even invaded and occupied the territory of other states to deny rebels ground to operate and launch attacks from. Such activities are likely to generate strong protests from the country that sees its territorial sovereignty violated. In some cases, the response may extend beyond diplomatic protest and include militarized use of violence.

Civil wars may also give way to international wars due to the transnational linkages of the conflict actors, even in the absence of any direct border violations. The insurgent side in civil wars will often count on support from sympathetic governments. Such linkages between civil war actors and foreign governments may give rise to conflict between states in several ways. First, repression or abuses against the constituency of an insurgent group may lead an outside government to protest against the conflict host government, possibly backed up with threats of resorting to military force unless the government in the conflict country ceases to suppress the group in question. Second, actual intrusion or alleged support by outside governments for the insurgent side in a civil war government will often lead to protests from the conflict government, which may be backed up by threats or actual resort to military force. Finally, conflict may ensue due to the consequences of conflict for other states, including accidental bombings or refugee burdens imposed on neighboring states.

Many researchers have postulated that the international conflict behavior of states may be related to domestic conflict (e.g. Rummel 1963; Wilkenfeld 1968). However, most of this literature has focused on so-called diversionary conflict, where states are held to start conflict in order to distract attention from domestic discontent (e.g. Coser 1956; Hess and Orphanides 1995; Levy 1989), rather than the possibility that interstate conflict behavior may reflect responses to civil wars. Gleditsch and Salehyan (2007) find that the presence of a civil war almost doubles the likelihood that a country will find itself involved in a militarized interstate dispute (MID). Similarly, at the dyadic level, the odds of a MID increase by a factor of over 1.3 if one of the states involved find themselves at a civil war. Investigating the international security risks associated with particular linkages remain difficult, given the limited information in existing data sources. Salehyan (forthcoming) shows that tacit or explicit support for rebel organizations— particularly the provision of sanctuary— increases the probability of conflict between states, with external rebel bases yielding a particularly large effect. A number of studies have looked at how ethnic minority groups present in other states may predict to conflict with other states (e.g. Davis and Moore 1997; Woodwell 2004). However, these studies do not consider whether the ethnic relations are characterized by violent conflict, or how particular acts at the domestic level influence violence between states.

The lack of empirical research on possible linkages between intrastate and interstate conflict reflects a more general lack of attention to issues in the literature on international conflict (e.g. Diehl 1992). Much of the research on conflict between states simply blackboxes the specific issues over which conflict may arise, and instead looks at how characteristics of relations between states can influence the risk that disputes or crises will turn violent. Statistical models of the probability of conflict between states have tended to emphasize predictors of peace, such as joint democracy, rather than features making war likely (e.g. Fearon 1995; Oneal and Russett 2001). However, Gleditsch and Salehyan (2007) find that about a third of the disputes for which summaries are available in the new Militarized Interstate Dispute (MID) data seem to originate out of issues or conflicts within states. It is unreasonable to expect that one should be able to predict conflict between states well without attention to the potential issues over which conflict may arise, and many models of interstate conflict that focus exclusively on state-to-state relations such as power and trade simply may not have the relevant explanatory factors to identify where conflict is likely to occur.

Investigating the relationship between civil war and conflict between states has also been complicated by ambiguities in distinguishing between forms of conflict and the ways that this has been handled in existing data. For most conceptualizations, whether a given conflict should be considered interstate or intrastate will depend on the degree of involvement of other states on the rebel side. At the extreme end, a direct military intervention on the part of the insurgent side could turn a civil war into an interstate war. However, outside support to insurgents is rarely at a level where the insurgent side ceases to be a meaningful actor. Since a full military intervention is very costly, states often support insurgents in other ways, including military or financial support. Many existing data collection projects impose a strict and mutually exclusive separation between interstate or civil wars. However, such a sharp distinction is often quite difficult to draw in practice, especially when conflicts are treated as aggregate events. The Correlates of War project has, for example, changed its classification of the Kashmiri conflict between the interstate and intrastate categories, due to reevaluations of the extent of Pakistani involvement (see e.g. Gleditsch 2004). A better alternative to conceptualize conflict would be to recognize that a given issue may give rise to both intrastate or interstate events, and instead study linkages between the two by examining to what extent one type of interactions influence the other (see e.g. Gleditsch and Beardsley 2004; Goldstein and Pevehouse 1997).

Civil wars may also give rise to transnational violence by non-state actors, for example, in the form of transnational terrorism. Terrorism is often used as a tool in a civil war (e.g. Kalyvas 2004), but a civil war can also give rise to incidences of terrorism in other states. Individuals associated with insurgents in civil wars may carry out terrorist attacks against government interests in other states. Consider, for example, the Kurdish Worker Party (PKK), which has staged several attacks against Turkish embassies in Western European countries as part of their struggle for Kurdish autonomy. Moreover, terrorism as a tool in a civil war may give rise to demonstration effects and copy-cat activities in other conflicts. Furthermore, terrorist organizations often collaborate, and offer training and logistical support to other organizations. The Provisional Irish Republican Army (IRA), for example, is widely believed to have cooperated with other terrorist bodies such as armed factions of the Palestinian Liberation Organization (PLO), the Basque separatist organization ETA, and, most recently, the Columbian Armed Revolutionary Forces (FARC). Finally, civil war may give rise to increased international terrorism through its effects on countries undergoing conflict. Civil war can undermine the capacity of states experiencing conflict and lead to "failed states", unable to exercise effective control over its territory. There is considerable fear that terrorist organizations may take advantage of failed states to operate and carry out attacks elsewhere (see e.g. Rice 2003), although it is unclear to what extent this has actually happened.[8]

Spread of impact of civil war

In addition to outbreaks of violence in other states, civil war may also "spread" in the sense that the consequences of civil war may be felt severely in states other than the one where the actual fighting occurs. Civil war tends to have many externalities or negative consequences for neighboring states. Conflict tends to disrupt economic activities, and Bayer and Rupert (2004) find that bilateral trade is reduced by about a third. Since trade tends to be between neighboring countries, the effects of decline of trade are likely to be felt particularly hard in neighboring states, and severe trade interruptions can in turn undermine their economies' performance and growth rates. Civil war in one state may also destroy vital transport, communications, and infrastructure links for neighboring countries, which in turn can have negative economic consequences. Civil war can generate large refugee flows, and people with limited resources tend to flee to neighboring countries (e.g. Shellman and Moore 2006). Refugees can impose a substantial economic burden on the host country, and may give rise to political challenges with an increased risk of violence, especially in cases where refugees originate from countries undergoing armed conflict (Salehyan 2008; Salehyan and Gleditsch 2006). Finally, civil war can undermine health, not just in the country that experiences conflict, but often has pernicious consequences in adjacent countries that experience the fallout from conflict. Refugees are often forced to live in unsanitary conditions in refugee camps, which provide fertile grounds for the spread of infectious diseases (see Iqbal 2006). The ability of a neighboring country to respond adequately to the health and refugee challenges posed by civil conflicts may be further undermined by the economic consequences of the conflict.

Although there are a large number of empirical studies of the consequences of conflict, relatively few studies have examined empirically how civil war affects other potentially exposed countries. Sandler and

Murdoch (2004) examine the impact of civil wars on economic growth in neighboring countries in a neo-classical growth model, using a variety of measures of closeness to conflict to capture their spatial impact. Their results demonstrate a strong impact of civil war in nearby locations on growth. Although the magnitude of the estimated effects in their model depends on the number of neighbors and the share at war, the results suggest that the long-term impact of having a neighbor at war is about 30% of the consequences of a country itself being at war (pp. 143–5). Moore and Shellman (2004) consider a variety of measures of violence, and find that both government repression as well as dissident violence exert strong effects on the number of refugees emanating from a country (see also Davenport, Moore and Poe 2003; Schmeidl 1997). While resource-rich individuals can seek security in industrialized states, low resource refugees will typically end up in neighboring states with limited means to accommodate them. Brezis and Krugman (1996) examine the impact of large influxes of refugees, and conclude that the short-term economic challenges are considerable. Ghobarah, Huth, and Russett (2004) find a significant impact of conflicts in a neighboring state on health in terms of estimates of premature loss of life developed. Toole and Waldman (1993) document severe health problems among refugees in war-torn areas. Whereas countries that have experienced civil war sometimes receive aid for post-conflict reconstruction, such aid is rarely extended to neighbors who may have suffered extensively from civil conflicts.

Implications for conflict resolution

In this chapter, I have reviewed possible forms through which civil conflicts and their consequences may spread to other states. The occurrence of a civil war in one state is likely to increase the prospects that we will see civil war in neighboring states through transnational linkages between actors, alliances with other governments, and conflict contagion mechanisms. Moreover, civil wars can give

rise to conflicts between states, either due to border violations, responses to human rights violations in civil wars, or conflict over the consequences of civil war. Finally, civil wars can have many externalities or pernicious implications for neighboring countries, even when these themselves do not experience conflict onset. Although some of these mechanisms are more thoroughly examined and supported than others, they all attest to the fact that civil war is not a security problem limited to the country where a conflict first breaks out, but has many security implications for other countries as well.

Transnational factors have been underappreciated in the study of civil war, perhaps in part since they are more difficult to study systematically across a large number of cases than standard country attributes or profiles. This, however, should not blind us to the fact that countries are not isolated units, and how a wealth of communications and interactions connect individuals across national boundaries. Whereas most work on civil war has focused on features within a given country, researchers need to be sensitive to how the relations between groups at the domestic level can be influenced by outside actors and events in ways that make violence more likely. External forces can promote outbreak of conflict, even in cases that we would not normally consider strong candidates for civil conflict based exclusively on their domestic characteristics. Moreover, many transnational linkages can influence features often though as "domestic". For example, state strength and economic performance can be undermined by the negative consequences of war in other states (e.g. Easterly and Levine 1998). Furthermore, ethnic antagonisms are not static and entirely determined by a country's prior history as is sometimes assumed by the idea that conflicts are driven by "ancient hatreds" (e.g. Kaplan 1993), but the extent to which they become politicized may strongly reflect international influences (e.g. Kuran 1998). Moreover, we should be cautious in trying to impose a strict separation of civil war and interstate conflict, but recognize that intra and interstate conflict can emanate from related issues and often will take place at the same time. If the closed polity model is an inadequate analytic framework for understanding civil war, then it is also unlikely to provide a good basis for effective conflict resolution efforts.

Although there is a risk that civil wars may spread to other states, it is by no means inevitable that they will. In some cases, domestic factors in the exposed countries may help to reduce the risks of the spread of conflict. For example, a more responsive government may be able to accommodate potentially aggrieved groups, and prevent violent conflict. The many dire predictions that violence conflict would arise over the situation of the Hungarian minority in Romania in the late 1980s did not materialize, in part because the two governments realized that they had a severe potential problem on their hands, and therefore had strong incentives to cooperate and contain extremists (see Gartzke and Gleditsch 2006). Just as conflict may be contagious, then so can peace or cases where violent conflicts get settled or issues are solved in a non-violent manner. Saideman (1998) points to how demonstration effects do not necessarily instigate violence in other states, since groups or governments may draw inspiration from cases where conflicts are resolved or managed by means other than violence (see also Gleditsch 2002). Existing peace agreements or settlements in one conflict may be used as templates or focal points in negotiations, and can potentially make it easier to reach settlements in other conflicts (e.g. Schneckener 2002). Finally, states with better governance may be better able to address the externalities of conflict in other states. The case of Malawi, which received nearly 2 million refugees fleeing the conflict in Mozambique in the 1980s and 1990s, shows how concerted government efforts to integrate refugees and help in subsequent repatriation can mitigate the impact of refugees, even in a very poor society (see Salehyan and Gleditsch 2006). Many analyses of the consequences of conflict externalities such as health and immigration insist on how short-term challenges are not inevitably tied to poor long-term outcomes. Although meeting short-term challenges requires a considerable degree of resources that host states often may struggle to come up with, refugees can in the long run actually promise many valuable benefits for host countries (e.g. Brezis and Krugman 1996; Jacobsen 2002).

Conflict resolution studies are often particularly interested in what external parties may do in order to facilitate settlements among the main antagonist. Much of the research on civil war has focused on identifying conditions where intervention by other states can help decrease violence and promote settlement in civil conflicts (e.g. Doyle and Sambanis 2006; Regan 2000), for example, by making it more costly for parties to continue fighting or enforcing settlements in the wake of conflict or serving as independent monitors to verify compliance. However, although efforts to contain civil war within the country where they occur obviously are important, the potential for transnational spread of conflict and their detrimental consequences should not be overlooked, and the effectiveness of peace plans may be enhanced by taking into account other states in a region. If transnational links are important for the onset of a conflict or its continuation, then externally directed conflict resolution efforts are unlikely to be fully effective if exclusively targeted on changing the behaviors of the main conflict antagonist, and can be enhanced by also actively involving transnational constituents and external actors that can exert some influence over the conflict antagonists (e.g. Lyons 2006). For example, international involvement in the conflict in Macedonia, as well as the anticipated implications for relations with the European Union, appear to have helped ensure that the Albanian government adopt a cautious stance, not support the KLA, and contain extremists, which was important in preventing further escalation of the conflict (e.g. International Crisis Group 2004).

External parties can have an important role with regards to changing the incentives for actors to cooperate with settlements of disputes arising out of civil conflicts, as well as their opportunities to undermine them. In particular, researchers have noted that although formal agreements over contentions issues such as territory tend to be effective in preventing further conflict between states (Hensel et al. 2006), agreements have a much poorer record in interstate disputes that arise out of issues related to civil war or conflict within countries (Schultz 2007). One possible explanation for the relative lack of success of agreements in preventing recurrent disputes arising out of civil wars is that these agreements rely on compliance from parties that may be only partly under the control of state governments. In some cases, external parties may be able to influence the incentives of actors that the states themselves cannot control. For example, the United States could limit the ability of IRA supporters to raise resources among Irish émigré communities, over which the Irish Republic or the UK had little direct influence.

Taking the transnational features of civil conflicts into account may also help us better understand motives and constraints for outside involvement in efforts to control civil conflict and their implications for the optimal design and likely effectiveness of conflict resolution efforts. On the one hand, multilateral conflict resolution efforts should avoid too much involvement of certain external actors with particular vested interest in conflicts that could raise concerns among conflict antagonists and aggravate conflicts. Whereas certain neighboring states often may be suspected of having ties to conflict antagonists and their own agendas—for example, Serbia or Bulgaria would be a poor choice for leading a peacekeeping missing in Macedonia—devising peacekeeping forces composed of states outside the region in question can help ensure that forces are perceived as neutral by the main parties. However, other countries less affected by a conflict also have fewer private benefits from conflict resolution and may hence be less willing to finance such efforts (e.g. Shimizu and Sandler 2002). As such, the prospects for effective conflict resolution efforts may be increased when designed so as to combine a greater share in financing efforts by countries most likely to be affected, and therefore willing to take on additional costs, with leadership or a larger share of personnel and participants from countries that can help ensure impartiality.

The transnational dimensions of civil war also suggest that conflict resolution efforts often may be constructive even if it is not possible to directly target the main antagonist. In many cases, efforts to stop civil war through direct interventions in the conflict country may be difficult to enact, either because of a lack of demand (i.e. the parties involved in the conflict are unwilling to accept any outside intrusion) or a lack of supply (i.e. no outside body is willing to commit to peacemaking or peacekeeping efforts in the conflict), and the problematic aspects of the legitimacy of interventions into the affairs of sovereign states without their consent. In instances when policymakers have few means available for addressing conflicts in the country where they occur, efforts that can help sustain neighboring states from the challenges posed by the spill-over from a civil war may provide the best possible investment for decreasing the future risk of expanding war and minimizing the long-term impact on development from conflict. Moreover, strengthening governance and peace among neighbors may eventually help to foster efforts to settle conflict in the country where the conflict originates.

NOTES

1 I am grateful for comments from the editors, two anonymous reviewers, as well as participants at the workshop on this handbook at the Institute of Applied Systems Analysis, Laxenburg, Austria 30 June - 2 July 2007. This research was supported by grants from the US National Science Foundation (SES-0351670), the Carnegie Corporation, and the Research Council of Norway through its support for the Centre for the Study of Civil War. I am also grateful for travel support from the British Academy.

2 To be clear, by civil war I here mean a violent conflict over some incompatibility between at least two organized groups, of which one is a government and one is not a state, that generates some casualties as a direct result of fighting. Note that this excludes one-sided violence, where the victims are not an

organized group, inter-communal conflicts that do not involve a government, as well as non-violent forms of conflict such as demonstrations and strikes. For further discussion on different attempts to define civil war, see e.g. Sambanis, (2004).

3 For a systematic review of trends in conflict and the distribution of types of conflict in the Uppsala Armed Conflict Data (ACD), see Gleditsch et al. (2002) The ACD data are available at www.prio.no/cwp/armedconflict/. Pillar (1983) compares patterns of war termination by type of conflict, and shows that civil wars are far less likely to end in negotiated settlements. Lacina and Gleditsch (2005) examine trends in battle deaths, based on supplementary information for the ACD events available at www.prio.no/cscw/cross/battledeaths.

4 Most research on conflict follows the correlates of War project's distinction between *interstate* wars where both antagonists are independent nation states and *intrastate* or *extra-systemic* conflicts where nation states fight actors that are not states (e.g. Sarkees 2000; Small and Singer 1982). By these criteria, civil wars can become transformed into a new interstate dispute when foreign states intervene on the side of the opposition and directly confront the government. However, there can be considerable ambiguity over what is meant by states intervening on the side of the opposition and whether a given conflict should be considered interstate or intrastate, and the examples of transnational characteristics cited above suggest that imposing mutually exclusive categories may often generate misleading consequences. I will return to these issues later.

5 The problem that outcomes believed to reflect similar mechanisms operating within each unit may stem from diffusion between units was first noted by Galton (1889), hence the term "Galton's problem". However, the problem of inference runs the other way as well; studies of diffusion face an "inverse Galton's problem" in that similarity in outcomes could be due to the similarity of the units, rather than diffusion between units (see Gleditsch and Ward 2006).

6 Christin and Hug (2004) suggest that the MAR data suffer from selection biases in conflict studies, by only sampling groups on criteria related to conflict, and present empirical evidence suggesting that selection biases plague analyses based on the MAR data. Öberg (2002) supplements the MAR data with additional data on minorities not at risk, and reaches a less pessimistic conclusion regarding the potential selection biases.

7 Indeed, Taylor was in 2003 indicted by the UN Special Court for Sierra Leone for crimes against humanity for his involvement in the conflict in Sierra Leone (see Vines 2003).

8 Somalia is an often-cited example of the link between failed states and terrorism (e.g. International Crisis Group 2002). However, although the absence of an effective central government after the fall of Siad Barre has enabled Islamist groups to operate freely, most of their activities have been limited to Somalia, with the exception of one group (al-Itihaad al-Islami) that has attacked targets in the Ogaden region of Ethiopia.

REFERENCES

Akcinaroglu, Seden, and Elizabeth Radziszewski. 2005. "Expectations, Rivalries, and Civil War Duration". *International Interactions* 31 (4): 349–374.

Ardón, Patricia. 1998. *La Paz y los Conflictos en Centroamérica*. Guatemala City, London: CIDECA, OXFAM.

Ashford, Mary-Wynne, and Yolanda Huet-Vaughan. 1997. The Impact of War on Women. In *War and Public Health*, edited by Barry S. Levy and Victor W. Sidel. New York and Oxford: Oxford University Press.

Bayer, Resat, and Matt C. Rupert. 2004. "Effects of Civil Wars on International Trade, 1950–1992". *Journal of Peace Research* 41 (6): 699–713.

Brauer, Jurgen. 2007. Arms Industries, Arms Trade, and Developing Countries. In *Handbook of Defense Economics*, edited by Todd Sandler and Keith Hartley. Amster-dam: Elsevier.

Brezis, Elise S., and Paul R. Krugman. 1996. "Immigration, Investment, and Real Wages". *Journal of Population Economics* 9 (1): 83–93.

Brown, Michael E., ed. 1993. *Ethnic Conflict and International Security*. Princeton, NJ: Princeton University Press.

Brown, Michael E., ed. 1996. *The International Dimensions of Internal Conflict*. Cambridge, MA: MIT Press.

Buhaug, Halvard, and Scott Gates. 2002. "The Geography of Civil War". *Journal of Peace Research* 39 (4): 417–433.

Buhaug, Halvard, and Kristian Skrede Gleditsch. 2008. "Contagion or Confusion? Why Conflicts Cluster in Space". *International Studies Quarterly* 52 (2): 215–233.

Buzan, Barry, and Ole Wæver. 2003. *Regions and Powers: The Structure of International Security*. Cambridge: Cambridge University Press.

Bye, Vegard. 1991. *La Paz Prohibida: El Laberinto Centroamericano en la Década de los Ochenta*. San José, Costa Rica: Editorial Departamento Ecuménico de Investigaciones.

Cederman, Lars-Erik, Jan K. Rød, and Nils Weidmann. 2006. Geo-Referencing of Ethnic Groups: Creating a New Dataset. Paper presented at the Geographic Representations of War Network (GROW-NET) Workshop, Oslo, 10–11 February.

Christin, Thomas, and Simon Hug. 2004. Federalism and Conflict Resolution: Considering Selection Biases. Typescript, University of St Gallen.

Close, David H., ed. 1993. *The Greek Civil War, 1943–1950: Studies in Polarization*. London: Routledge.

Coleman, James S. 1964. *Introduction to Mathematical Sociology*. New York: Free Press.

Collier, Paul, Lani Elliott, Håvard Hegre, Anke Hoeffler, Marta Reynal-Querol, and Nicholas Sambanis. 2003. *Breaking the Conflict Trap: Civil War and Development Policy*. Oxford University Press and Washington, DC: World Bank, online at econ.worldbank.org/prr/CivilWarPRR/.

Collier, Paul, and Anke Hoeffler. 2004. "Greed and Grievance in Civil War". *Oxford Economic Papers* 56 (4): 663–595.

Collier, Paul, and Nicholas Sambanis, eds. 2005. *Understanding Civil War: Evidence and Analysis. Vol. 1, Africa*. Washington, DC: World Bank.

Coser, Lewis. 1956. *The Functions of Social Conflict*. London: Routledge.

Craft, Cassidy, and Joseph P. Smaldone. 2002. "The Arms Trade and the Incidence of Political Violence in sub-Saharan Africa, 1967–97". *Journal of Peace Research* 39 (6): 693–710.

Craft, Cassidy, and Joseph P. Smaldone. 2003. "Arms Imports in Sub-Saharan Africa: Predicting Conflict Involvement". *Defence and Peace Economics* 14 (1): 37–49.

Davenport, Christian A., Will H. Moore, and Steven C. Poe. 2003. "Sometimes You Just Have to Leave: Threat and Refugee Movements, 1964–1989". *International Interactions* 29 (1): 27–55.

Davis, David R., and Will H. Moore. 1997. "Ethnicity Matters: Transnational Ethnic Alliances and Foreign Policy Behavior". *International Studies Quarterly* 41 (1): 171–184.

Diehl, Paul F. 1992. "What are they Fighting for? The Importance of Issues in International Conflict Research". *Journal of Peace Research* 29: 333–344.

Doyle, Michael W., and Nicholas Sambanis. 2006. *Making War and Building Peace: United Nations Peace Operations*. Princeton, NJ: Princeton University Press.

Easterly, William, and Ross Levine. 1998. "Troubles with the Neighbours: Africa's Problem, Africa's Opportunity". *Journal of African Economies* 7 (1): 120–142.

Enders, Walter, and Todd Sandler. 2005. *The Political Economy of Terrorism*. Cambridge: Cambridge University Press.

Esty, Daniel C., Jack Goldstone, Ted Robert Gurr, Barbara Harff, Pamela T. Surko, Alan N. Unger, and Robert

Chen. 1998. The State Failure Project: Early Warning Research for US Foreign Policy Planning. In *Preventive Measures: Building Risk Assessment and Crisis Early Warning Systems*, edited by John L. Davies and Ted Robert Gurr. Boulder, CO and Totowa, NJ: Rowman and Littlefield.

Fearon, James D. 1995. "Rationalist Explanations for War". *International Organization* 49 (3): 379–414.

Fearon, James D., and David D. Laitin. 2003. "Ethnicity, Insurgency, and Civil War". *American Political Science Review* 97 (1): 75–90.

Galton, Francis. 1889. "Comment on E.B. Taylor 'On a Method of Investigating the Development of Institutions: Applied to Laws of Marriage and Descent'". *Journal of the Royal Anthropological Institute* 18: 268–9.

Gartzke, Erik A., and Kristian Skrede Gleditsch. 2006. "Identity and Conflict: Ties that Bind and Differences that Divide". *European Journal of International Relations* 12 (1): 53–87.

Ghobarah, Hazem Adam, Paul Huth, and Bruce Russett. 2004. "The Postwar Public Health Effects of Civil Conflict". *Social Science and Medicine* 59 (4): 869–884.

Ghobarah, Hazem Adam, Paul Huth, and Bruce M. Russett. 2003. "Civil Wars Kill and Maim People Long after the Shooting Stops". *American Political Science Review* 97 (2): 189–202.

Gleditsch, Kristian Skrede. 2002. *All International Politics is Local: The Diffusion of Conflict, Integration, and Democratization*. Ann Arbor, MI: University of Michi-gan Press.

Gleditsch, Kristian Skrede. 2004. "A Revised List of Wars Between and Within Independent States, 1816–2002". *International Interactions* 30 (4): 231–262.

Gleditsch, Kristian Skrede. 2007. "Transnational Dimensions of Civil War". *Journal of Peace Research* (3): 293–309.

Gleditsch, Kristian Skrede, and Kyle C. Beardsley. 2004. "Nosy Neighbors: Third Party Actors In Central American Conflicts". *Journal of Conflict Resolution* 46 (3): 379–402.

Gleditsch, Kristian Skrede, and Idean Salehyan. 2007. Civil Wars and Interstate Disputes. In *Making Sense of Civil War*, edited by Kaare Strøm and Magnus Öberg. London: Routledge.

Gleditsch, Kristian Skrede, and Michael D. Ward. 2006. "The Diffusion of Democracy and the International Context of Democratization". *International Organization* 60 (4): 911–933.

Gleditsch, Nils Petter, Peter Wallensteen, Mikael Eriksson, Margareta Sollenberg, and Håvard Strand. 2002. "Armed Conflict 1946–2001: A New

Dataset". *Journal of Peace Research* 39 (5): 615–637.

Goldstein, Joshua S., and Jon C. Pevehouse. 1997. "Reciprocity, Bullying, and International Cooperation: Time-Series Analysis of the Bosnia Conflict". *American Political Science Review* 91 (3): 515–530.

Gurr, Ted Robert. 1993. *Minorities at Risk: A Global View of Ethnopolitical Conflict.* Washington, DC: United States Institute of Peace Press.

Hampson, Fen Osler, ed. 1996. *Nurturing Peace: Why Peace Settlements Succeed or Fail.* Washington, DC: United States Institute of Peace.

Hegre, Håvard, Tanja Ellingsen, Scott Gates, and Nils Petter Gleditsch. 2001. "Toward a Democratic Civil Peace? Democracy, Political Change, and Civil War, 1816–1992". *American Political Science Review* 95: 33–48.

Hegre, Håvard, and Nicholas Sambanis. 2006. "Sensitivity Analysis of Empirical Results on the Causes of Civil War Onset". *Journal of Conflict Resolution* 50 (4): 508–535.

Hensel, Paul R., Sara McLaughlin Mitchell, Thomas E. Sowers II, and Clayton L. Thyne. 2006. Bones of Contention: Comparing Territorial, Maritime, and River Issues. Paper presented at the 2006 Annual Meeting of the American Political Science Association.

Heraclides, Alexis. 1999. "Secessionist Minorities and External Involvement". *International Organization* 44 (3): 341–378.

Hess, Gregory D., and Athanasios Orphanides. 1995. "War and Politics: An Economic, Rational Voter Framework". *American Economic Review* 85 (4): 828–846.

Hill, Stuart, and Don Rothchild. 1986. "Contagion of Political Conflict in Africa and the World". *Journal of Conflict Resolution* 30 (4): 716–735.

Hill, Stuart, Donald Rothchild, and Colin Cameron. 1998. Tactical Information and the Diffusion of Peaceful Protests. In *The International Spread of Ethnic Conflict: Fear, Diffusion, and Escalation,* edited by David A. Lake and Donald Rothchild. Princeton, NJ: Princeton University Press.

International Crisis Group. 2002. Somalia: Countering Terrorism in Failed States. Africa Report No. 45. Nairobi/Brussels: International Crisis Group.

International Crisis Group. 2004. Pan-Albanianism: How Big a Threat to Balkan Stability? ICG Europe Report No. 153.

Iqbal, Zaryab. 2006. "Health and Human Security: The Public Health Impact of Violent Conflict". *International Studies Quarterly* 50 (3): 631–649.

Jacobsen, Karen. 2002. "Can Refugees Benefit The State? Refugee Resources and African Statebuilding". *Journal of Modern African Studies* 40 (4): 577–596.

Kalyvas, Stathis. 2004. "The Paradox of Terrorism in Civil War". *Journal of Ethics* 8 (1): 97–138.

Kang, Seonjou, and James Meernik. 2005. "Civil War Destruction and the Prospects for Economic Growth". *Journal of Politics* 67 (1): 88–109.

Kaplan, Robert D. 1993. *Balkan Ghosts: A Journey Through History.* New York: St Martin's Press.

Killicoat, Phillip. 2006. Cheap Guns, More War? The Economics of Small Arms. Typescript, Department of Economics, Oxford University.

Kuran, Timur. 1998. Ethnic Dissimilation and its International Diffusion. In *The International Spread of Ethnic Conflict: Fear Diffusion, and Escalation,* edited by David A Lake and Donald Rothchild. Princeton, NJ: Princeton University Press.

Lacina, Bethany, and Nils Petter Gleditsch. 2005. "Monitoring Trends in Global Combat: A New Dataset of Battle Deaths". *European Journal of Population Studies* 21 (2–3): 145–166.

Lake, David A., and Donald Rothchild, eds. 1998. *The International Spread of Ethnic Conflict: Fear, Diffusion, and Escalation.* Princeton, NJ: Princeton University Press.

Levy, Jack S. 1989. The Diversionary Theory of War: A Critique. In *Handbook of War Studies,* edited by Manus I. Midlarsky. Ann Arbor, MI: University of Michigan Press.

Lopez, Humberto, and Quentin Wodon. 2005. "The Economic Impact of Armed Conflict in Rwanda". *Journal of African Economies* 14 (4): 586–602.

Lyons, Terrence. 2006. "Diasporas and Homeland Conflict". In *Globalization, Territoriality, and Conflict,* 111–129, edited by Miles Kahler and Barbara Walter. Cambridge: Cambridge University Press.

McNulty, Mel. 1999. "The Collapse of Zaire: Implosion, Revolution or External Sabotage?" *Journal of Modern African Studies* 37 (1): 53–82.

Midlarsky, Manus I. 1978. "Analyzing Diffusion and Contagion Effects: The Urban Disorders of the 1960s". *American Political Science Review* 72 (3): 996–1008.

Moore, Will H., and Stephen Shellman. 2004. "Fear of Persecution: Forced Migration, 1952–1995". *Journal of Conflict Resolution* 48 (5): 723–745.

Myers, Daniel J. 2000. "The Diffusion of Collective Violence: Infectiousness, Susceptibility, and Mass Media Networks". *American Journal of Sociology* 106 (1): 173–208.

O'Ballance, Edgar. 1966. *The Greek Civil War, 1944–1949.* London: Faber.

Öberg, Magnus. 2002. The Onset of Ethnic War as a Bargaining Process. Testing a Costly Signaling Model. Report No. 65, Department of Peace and Conflict Research, Uppsala University.

Oneal, John, and Bruce M. Russett. 2001. *Triangulating Peace: Democracy, Interdependence, and International Organizations*. New York: Norton.

Pape, Robert A. 2003. "The Strategic Logic of Suicide Terrorism". *American Political Science Review* 97 (3): 343–361.

Pillar, Paul R. 1983. *Negotiating Peace: War Termination as a Bargaining Process*. Princeton, NJ: Princeton University Press.

Plümper, Thomas, and Eric Neumayer. 2006. "The Unequal Burden of War: The Effect of Armed Conflict on the Gender Gap in Life Expectancy". *International Organization* 60 (3): 723–754.

Regan, Patrick M. 2000. *Civil Wars and Foreign Powers: Interventions and Intrastate Conflict*. Ann Arbor, MI: University of Michigan Press.

Reising, Uwe K.H. 1999. "United In Opposition? A Cross-national Time-Series Analysis of European Protest in Three Selected Countries, 1980–1995". *Journal Of Conflict Resolution* 43 (3): 317–342.

Rice, Susan E. 2003. The New National Security Strategy: Focus on Failed States. The Brookings Institution Policy Brief No. 116.

Rød, Jan Ketil. 2003. ViewConflicts: Software for Visualising Spatiotemporal Data on Armed Conflicts. Paper Presentation at the Joint Sessions of Workshops European Consortium for Political Research, Edinburgh, UK. 28 March–2 April, see also web page http://www.svt.ntnu.no/geo/forskning/konflikt/viewConflicts/general/papers/.

Rummel, Rudolph J. 1963. "Dimensions of Conflict Behavior Within and Between Nations". *General Systems* 8(1): 50.

Saideman, Stephen M. 1998. Is Pandora's Box Half-Empty or Half-Full? The Limited Virulence of Secession and the Domestic Sources of Disintegration. In *The International Spread of Ethnic Conflict: Fear, Diffusion, Escalation*, edited by David A. Lake and Donald Rothchild. Princeton, NJ: Princeton University Press.

Salehyan, Idean. 2005. Refugees, Climate Change, and Instability. Paper presented at the Human Security and Climate Change Conference, Asker, Norway 21–23 June, available at www.cicero.uio.no/humsec/papers/Salehyan.pdf.

Salehyan, Idean. 2006. Rebels Without Borders: State Boundaries, Transnational Opposition, and Civil Conflict. PhD Thesis, Department of Political Science, University of California, San Diego.

Salehyan, Idean. 2008. "From Climate Change to Conflict? No Consensus Yet". *Journal of Peace Research* 45 (3):315–326.

Salehyan, Idean. forthcoming. *Rebels without Borders: State Boundaries, Transnational Opposition, and Civil Conflict*. Ithaca, NY: Cornell University Press.

Salehyan, Idean, and Kristian Skrede Gleditsch. 2006. "Refugee Flows and the Spread of Civil War". *International Organization* 60 (2): 335–366.

Salehyan, Idean, Kristian Skrede Gleditsch, and David Cunningham. 2006. Transnational Linkages and Civil War Interactions. Typescript, Department of Government.

Sambanis, Nicholas. 2001. "Do Ethnic and Non-Ethnic Civil Wars Have the Same Causes? A Theoretical and Empirical Inquiry (Part 1)". *Journal of Conflict Resolution* 45 (3): 259–282.

Sambanis, Nicholas. 2004. "What is a Civil War? Conceptual and Empirical Complexities of an Operational Definition". *Journal of Conflict Resolution* 48 (6): 814–858.

Sandler, Todd, and James Murdoch. 2004. "Civil War and Economic Growth: Spatial Dispersion". *American Journal of Political Science* 48 (1): 138–151.

Sarkees, Meredith. 2000. "The Correlates of War Data on War: An Update to 1997". *Conflict Management and Peace Science* 18 (1): 123–144.

Schmeidl, Susanne. 1997. "Exploring the Causes of Forced Migration: A Pooled Time-Series Analysis, 1971–1990". *Social Science Quarterly* 78 (2): 284–308.

Schneckener, Ulrich. 2002. "Making Power-Sharing Work: Lessons from Successes and Failures in Ethnic Conflict Regulation". *Journal of Peace Research* 39 (2): 203–228.

Schultz, Kenneth A. 2007. The Enforcement Problem in Coercive Bargaining: Interstate Conflict over Rebel Support in Civil Wars. Typescript, Stanford University.

Shellman, Stephen, and Will H. Moore. 2006. "Refugee or Internally Displaced? To Where Should One Flee?" *Comparative Political Studies* 39 (5): 599–622.

Shimizu, Hirofumi, and Todd Sandler. 2002. "Peacekeeping and Burden-Sharing, 1994–2000". *Journal of Peace Research* 39 (6): 651–668.

Singer, Max, and Aaron Wildavsky. 1996. *The Real World Order: Zones of Peace/Zones of Turmoil*. Chatham, NJ: Chatham House.

Siverson, Randolph M., and Harvey Starr. 1991. *The Diffusion of War: A Study in Opportunity and Willingness*. Ann Arbor, MI: University of Michigan Press.

Small, Melvin, and David J. Singer. 1982. *Resort to Arms: International and Civil Wars, 1816–1980*. Beverly Hills, CA: Sage.

Stedman, Stephen John, Donald Rothchild, and Elizabeth M. Cousens, eds. 2002. *Ending Civil Wars: The Implementation of Peace Agreements*. Boulder, CO: Lynne Rienner.

Strang, David, and Nancy B. Tuma. 1993. "Spatial and Temporal Heterogeneity in Diffusion". *American Journal of Sociology* 99: 614–639.

Tierney, Dominic. 2005. "Irrelevant or Malevolent? UN Arms Embargoes in Civil Wars". *Review of International Studies* 31 (4): 645–664.

Tolnay, Stewart E., Glenn Deane, and Ellwood M. Beck. 1996. "Vicarious Violence: Spatial Effects On Southern Lynchings, 1890–1919". *American Journal of Sociology* 102 (3): 788–815.

Toole, M.J., and Ronald J. Waldman. 1993. "Refugees and Displaced Persons: War, Hunger, and Public Health". *Journal of the American Medical Association* 270 (5): 600–605.

Tull, D.M., and A. Mehler. 2005. "The Hidden Costs of Power-Sharing: Reproducing Insurgent Violence in Africa". *African Affairs* 104 (416): 375–398.

United Nations High Commissioner for Refugees. 2000. *The State of The World's Refugees: Fifty Years of Humanitarian Action*. New York: Oxford University Press.

Vines, Alex. 2003. "African Dictatorships: No Place to Hide". *World Today* 59 (10): 22–23.

Ward, Michael D., and Kristian Skrede Gleditsch. 2002. "Location, Location, Location: An MCMC Approach to Modeling the Spatial Context of War and Peace". *Political Analysis* 10: 244–260.

Wilkenfeld, Jonathan. 1968. "Domestic and Foreign Conflict Behavior of Nations". *Journal of Peace Research* 5: 56–69.

Woodwell, Doug. 2004. "Unwelcome Neighbors: Shared Ethnicity and International Conflict during the Cold War". *International Studies Quarterly* 48 (1): 197–223.

Zartman, I. William. 1995. *Elusive Peace: Negotiating an End to Civil War*. Washington, DC: Brooking.

32

Conflict Resolution and Human Rights: The State of the Art

Eileen F. Babbitt

Much of the political violence in today's world takes the form of civil war – clashes within states between identity groups who become arch enemies. Tragic examples in recent decades include the kind of internal wars that devastated Bosnia and Rwanda; that continue to rage in Iraq; and that threaten to flare up in many other countries in the Middle East, in Africa, in Asia.

As the world collectively struggles to address such conflicts, it has become clear that conflict resolution approaches aimed at simply stopping physical violence and loss of life are not enough. More systemic approaches are critically needed, not only to prevent violence but also to sustain peace agreements once they have been reached. To address today's wars, we have to create what Johann Galtung, writing 30 years ago, called "positive peace" (Galtung, 1969). This means confronting "structural" and "cultural" violence: the social, political, and economic conditions and the attitudes within a given

society that often lead to the use of physical violence. The integration of human rights principles into conflict resolution processes is a critical way to build pathways toward such positive peace.

The reasons for such an integration flow from the two theories that offer the most compelling explanations for what causes and sustains intra-state violence. The first theory, discussed by political scientists such as Ted Gurr, sees conflict as emerging when a group has a salient cultural identity and shares important collective grievances. Gurr argues that the mobilization to take political action stems from "a cultural group's shared grievances about unequal treatment and its desire to protect a valued identity" (Gurr, 1996: 63).

However, domestic political environments shape conflict as well. For example, conflict is much less likely to erupt in a democratic state that allows expression of grievances than in one whose government suppresses or ignores the claims of national groups. The risk of violent conflict is especially high in states making the transition to democracy, since coercive restraints on expression of identity are relaxed but the institutionalized means for their expression have not yet been consolidated (p. 69). Gurr also notes that the demands of ethnic groups are not always the same; some may be looking for access to existing political power, while others, for example in Quebec, seek to "exit," or secede from the current political structure and create an autonomous state.

An alternative theory, developed by Paul Collier, focuses entirely on economic elements and attaches little importance to objective ethnic grievances (Collier, 2000). Instead, Collier argues that although power differences and majority/minority relations within society may *sustain* conflict once it has begun, the issues of power that drive conflict are fundamentally about control of resources, especially primary exports. Furthermore, Collier states that objective grievances are usually not even a by-product of conflict, but are often generated by rebels to legitimize conflicts fueled by a desire to control resources. Thus, in his view, relations between minority and majority groups and power differentials play no significant role in causing conflict. In Collier's view, the potential sources of conflict (a desire for power and perceived identity-based grievances) are found in all societies, but the existence of war is predicated upon what he calls the *feasibility of predation:* the ability to use force to extort goods or money from their primary owners (Collier, 2000: 4). Thus, in determining whether overt conflict will erupt, issues such as political inequality and power imbalances are less important than the ability of rebel groups to "do well by war" and gain additional economic power through violent means.

Each of these theories places a different emphasis on the societal elements that may lead identity groups to an overt use of violence. Although the emphases are different, group identity and perceptions of discrimination are central in both: instrumental in Collier's theory, and motivational in Gurr's.

This is where the human rights agenda comes in, with two significant elements to enhance conflict resolution practice. The first is the development of international norms, to lay out clear standards of behavior to which international actors should be held accountable. As these standards are codified in international legal documents, they gain salience and legitimacy that can be used to enhance their persuasive power.

The second element of human rights practice is an outgrowth of the first: to affect the balance of power between governments and individuals, and more recently between governments and minority groups. Human rights norms cannot only constrain the power of states, but can also provide a source of leverage to identity groups who feel oppressed or victimized by discrimination.

From the perspective of those engaged in international conflict resolution, human rights become most salient when peace agreements are being negotiated. In practice, there is at least an implicit consensus among Track 1 mediators that human rights provisions should be included in the text of any peace agreement. Beyond that, the consensus unravels as to how, or even whether, to deal with human rights. This is particularly true of third-party processes such as mediation and facilitation, where impartiality is thought to be a key element of conflict resolution effectiveness.[1] This discussion will therefore focus on integrating human rights concerns into the work of third parties.

In order to explore the possibility of integrating human rights into third-party practice, we must delve into the potential role of law and norms in addressing intra-state conflicts – not from the perspective of an international lawyer but from the perspective of a conflict resolution practitioner. Just as is the case in US domestic mediation practice, my argument here is that international mediation and facilitation should more explicitly define themselves as operating in the "shadow of the law." This term was first coined by Robert Mnookin and Lewis Kornhauser in their 1979 study of US divorce mediation (Mnookin and Kornhauser, 1979: 950). Their argument is that the responsibility for constructing the agreement rests with the parties, but within the guidelines of existing legal norms and practice. It is therefore common in U.S. domestic mediation for the mediator to be quite familiar with the legal parameters of a particular case and to encourage the parties to take them into account in framing the terms of an agreement.

There are, however, many challenges to doing so in the international context. Before exploring these, it is important to note the similarities on which the conflict resolution and human rights fields rest.

SIMILARITIES BETWEEN CONFLICT RESOLUTION AND HUMAN RIGHTS

Both conflict resolution and human rights are social change movements, motivated by the desire to improve the human condition. They both operate from a set of normative principles that govern the practical work they do in the field, and it is from this basis of shared norms that synergy can develop between the two agendas at all levels within a given community.

Strengthening norms

There are many norms common to the human rights and conflict resolution approaches. The first is *participation*. From the human rights perspective, this involves an individual's ability to gain access to the political, economic, and social institutions of the country in which he/she lives, and not be barred from participating in such institutions because of race, religion, gender, or social class. The conflict resolution perspective coincides with this, and adds the importance of access to any ad hoc decision-making processes in which the individual or group is a stakeholder. Integration of these views presents no problems.

The second shared norm is *empowerment*. Empowerment through human rights comes as the rights themselves are enacted, that is, by having and claiming these rights,

people gain power over those who would oppress them. Looking through a conflict resolution lens, empowerment is a function of skill – for example, knowing how to negotiate effectively, build coalitions, create options for settlement, and mobilize one's constituency. These are complementary views, but under some circumstances may appear mutually exclusive. For example, a minority group adopting the human rights approach might choose to confront its state government, either non-violently or violently, to demand its rights. Using a conflict resolution approach, this same minority group would choose a more collaborative strategy, seeking to negotiate a deal rather than push its agenda by force. One could argue, however, that in order to negotiate effectively, a group must come to the table with sufficient leverage to strike an equitable deal; claiming its individual or group rights could be one way of obtaining such leverage. The non-violence strategy successfully adopted by the people of East Timor is a striking example of this (Stephan, 2006).

Equity is a third norm shared by those following the conflict resolution or human rights agendas. Both would argue that all human beings should be treated with respect, even those with whom we strongly disagree. From the human rights point of view, this includes equal access to due process, fair and impartial hearings, and protection from arbitrary arrest. From the conflict resolution standpoint, this also means making an effort to understand the needs and concerns of all sides, even of those who violate the rights of others. For both human rights and conflict resolution, equity does not mean the same as equality. Differences in resources (money, education, political power, property, etc.) still exist. The human rights agenda is much more explicit than that of conflict resolution in seeking equality as well as equity – and of confronting the power dynamics when resources are asymmetrical.

Finally, *security* (both physical and psychological) is a shared norm. Conflict resolution seeks to stop the use of violence in settling disagreements, transferring discussion to political and consensus-building forums. It also underscores the importance of addressing the basic human needs for identity and acknowledgment, as part of psychological security. Human rights seek to protect individuals from torture or other cruel and degrading punishment; prohibit slavery; and provide for freedom of conscience, religion, expression, and movement. Each addresses itself to a slightly different set of ways in which security can be undermined, but these are not mutually exclusive, and both would agree to the centrality of this array of issues.

Thus, the international conflict resolution agenda already shares many of the human rights norms, although not as vocally or visibly as their human rights counterparts. The challenge occurs, however, in how to translate these norms into practice. It is therefore important to investigate why conflict resolution practitioners shy away from the human rights agenda – as well as why the human rights world is skeptical of conflict resolution. The next sections of the chapter take on these questions.

CHALLENGES IN INTEGRATING THE INTERNATIONAL CONFLICT RESOLUTION AND HUMAN RIGHTS AGENDAS

Although we can identify key normative similarities between international conflict resolution and human rights, there are several major differences between them that have implications for conflict resolution theory and practice. The first is the way in which norm violators are treated. In human rights practice, violators of human rights norms are *prosecuted* through national or international courts and the human rights treaty bodies, or are *shunned and stigmatized* in keeping with the use of "naming and shaming" as a strategy for enforcement. There is a grave concern about appearing to reward bad behavior. In neutral third-party practice, however, violators of human rights norms are often *included* in discussions with both official and non-official third parties. Track 1 processes include

human rights violators because they are often the leaders who can "deliver" an agreement. Track 2 processes include such violators so the negotiators can better understand what is motivating their non-compliance and how they can be brought around to abiding by the norms. Neither Track 1 nor Track 2 processes place a high priority on confronting perpetrators over human rights violations.

A second major difference between conflict resolution and human rights is in their interpretations of "justice." In human rights terms, justice is connected to *state-level and individual accountability* for gross violations of human rights laws, and the remedy sought is primarily retributive in nature, for example, prosecution of individuals, political or economic sanctions against states.[2] For mediators, justice is more often defined as *fairness of a settlement in the eyes of the parties to the dispute*. Accountability mechanisms are only present if the parties agree to include them. To the extent that accountability is sought for criminal activity, Track 1 conflict resolution processes integrate accountability mechanisms for the future, in the form of provisions in negotiated peace agreements for enforcing human rights law, but do not routinely provide for retrospective punishment of individual perpetrators. Track 2 processes diverge even further by often embracing restorative rather than retributive justice.[3]

Finally, conflict resolution and human rights differ in their theories of social change. The human rights movement focuses on the creation of international norms, which in turn are intended to shape behaviors. The implicit assumption is that people should be held to moral imperatives of what is *right*, because these have been negotiated and agreed to in the Universal Declaration of Human Rights and its implementing Covenants.[4]

Conflict resolution practice has proceeded in a different way, by defining the means by which fair and sustainable results are achieved, and then seeking to demonstrate the power of those means in various Track 1 and Track 2 processes involving both governmental and non-governmental players.

Table 32.1 Key differences between conflict resolution and human rights

Issue	Human Rights	Conflict Resolution
Treatment of norms violators	Naming and shaming; no precedent for rewarding bad behavior; change behavior with "sticks" approach	Include violators in discussion, to learn their interests and change their behavior with "carrots" as well as "sticks." Change attitudes as well as behavior
Conception of justice	Individual accountability; punishment/retributive justice	Fairness in the eyes of the parties; restorative as well as retributive justice, to maintain relationships if possible
Theories of social change	Define the ends; design means to reach those ends	Define means; ends that emerge will be fair if the process is designed well and people are educated to use the process wisely

While some strong Track 1 mediators have very specific substantive goals for an agreement and impose those goals on the parties (e.g. the United States for the Dayton Accords), the majority of both Track 1 and Track 2 third parties believe that constructive change comes through a well-designed process of engagement and problem-solving. By facilitating such processes, and educating participants in how to develop strategies consistent with conflict resolution principles, these third parties hope to improve the quality and sustainability of relationships and agreements.

Therefore, both conflict resolution and human rights interventions seek behavior and attitude change, but by different procedural means. The human rights approach works primarily by imposing external norms (outside-in), whereas conflict resolution relies more on building consensus through non-adjudicatory means (inside-out).

WHY CONFLICT RESOLUTION PRACTITIONERS RESIST HUMAN RIGHTS

These various differences between the conflict resolution and human rights perspectives lead each side to reject the other's agenda fairly strongly. These dynamics deserve consideration, from both directions. From the conflict resolution perspective, the advocacy stance of human rights practitioners often leads them to frame their interactions in "distributive" or "zero-sum" terms.[5] Because

human rights advocates assume that states will not fully comply with their human rights treaty obligations and will find ways to justify non-compliance, these advocates feel they must adopt a hard-line position and show no willingness to compromise. They therefore take a position and refuse to budge, doing what negotiation specialists call *anchoring*, so that any compromise will come from the states, not from those advocating/monitoring human rights compliance. They basically adopt a non-negotiable position, and push on the government to meet their demands. In the view of negotiation specialists, however, such zero-sum bargaining strategies can be counter-productive, as they often lead to "hard bargaining" dynamics that produce deadlock rather than agreement.

Another concern from the conflict resolution perspective comes from depending exclusively on legal rules as a guiding principle for political and social order. The advantage of such legal rules is that they make standards more clear and visible and strengthen enforcement potential. The downside is that laws can become rigid and bureaucratic, losing both resilience and effectiveness. In addition, the institutions that administer the law can become overloaded, or can be perceived as biased against some identity groups. For example, the Alternative Dispute Resolution (ADR) movement in the United States was a means for increasing the "ownership" of agreements and parties' commitment to implementation as a balance to the slow, overburdened and impersonal court system.

However, in the USA, it also became very clear that some cases were better served by using the legal process: cases with important legal precedent, or with such great power asymmetry between the parties that the weaker party could be significantly harmed by engaging in negotiation without the "protection" of the law (e.g. cases of family mediation in which physical abuse was discovered and the case was referred on to legal experts). The challenge has been to establish guidance to negotiators and mediators that helps identify such cases. From the conflict resolution perspective, finding an effective balance between the protection and the rigidity of using legal rules is a key concern.

One final reason why the conflict resolution movement has been inconsistent about, and sometimes adamantly opposed to, embracing human rights as part of their theory and practice is their belief in the imperative of voluntary participation. That is, they strongly believe that parties will be more likely to act in good faith during negotiation and carry out the implementation of an agreement if these are accomplished without coercion from a third party. Data show that mediated agreements are more likely to "stick" than agreements that are adjudicated, because the parties themselves design the terms by which they are willing to settle.

One way to create an incentive for voluntary participation is through the perceived "impartiality" of any facilitator or mediator. Impartiality assures all of the parties to the conflict that their interests will be taken seriously in the negotiation process, and that the facilitator or mediator will not be unduly biased in communicating or attending to these interests. Without such perceived impartiality, parties in conflict are likely to opt out of a mediation or facilitation process – unless they are coerced into participation by a "mediator with muscle." A mediator with muscle can force parties to the table and even impose an agreement (as in the Dayton process for Bosnia), but then must maintain a continuing presence to be sure the parties implement the imposed settlement. For the most part,

conflict resolution practitioners try to avoid this, in order to maximize the possibility of the agreement being self-reinforcing.[6]

Conflict resolution practitioners are concerned that parties will never voluntarily submit to a process that calls their human rights record into question. The viability of negotiation is then threatened if one or more of the primary parties to the conflict refuse to participate. For example, when Lakhdar Brahimi, as the UN Special Representative to Afghanistan, negotiated with the Afghan "warlords" to conclude the 2002 Bonn Agreement, he was criticized by international human rights NGOs for not insisting upon accountability for their past abuses as part of the negotiations. His response to this criticism was to say that his job was to stop the violence first, and that accountability would follow later in the process (Sebenius, 2003). One can infer from this that Brahimi felt he could not get the warlords to participate or to come to agreement if each knew he would be judged for his past acts.

NGOs that conduct neutral third-party processes are even more concerned about this dilemma than their Track 1 counterparts. In their view, one of the most important credentials they bring to the conflict resolution process is impartiality; they provide a "safe" venue for conflicting parties to explore options and build better understanding precisely by *not* pressing the parties on specific issues. If an NGO does not offer that, it is worried that its presence would not be welcome or even tolerated by the conflicting parties.

Thus, although conflict resolution scholars and practitioners profess to be no less personally committed to human rights than the human rights activists themselves, they are also mindful of the ways in which it might limit their effectiveness as peacemakers.

WHY HUMAN RIGHTS ADVOCATES REJECT CONFLICT RESOLUTION

Likewise, human rights advocates have several strong reactions toward conflict resolution. The first objection is that conflict resolution work is driven by pragmatism, not principle. We often hear that "conflict resolution people only care about getting a settlement"[7] and that they have no normative framework guiding their actions. Two human rights concerns seem to lie behind this critique. The first is that no moral compass is being used to measure the appropriateness of an agreement. The human rights movement is built on a moral base, with the UDHR as a negotiated vision of a better world; from their perspective, all international activity that can do so should be furthering that moral vision. If the conflict resolution metric is "whatever the parties can live with," then unscrupulous leaders of any of the conflicting parties can fashion the text of an agreement to serve their personal interests, without a thought for their citizens or for the precedents it might set for the wider international community.

For example, the human rights view of the Bonn Agreement for Afghanistan, referred to just above, is that the negotiators lost out on the larger goal of creating a government based on the principles of fairness and rule of law, because they invited these "warlords" to the negotiating table in the interests of a pragmatic goal of ending the violence without holding them accountable for the harm they had caused (Niland, 2004: 72–3). It reflects the human rights belief that having a "moral imperative," even if it is not achieved, is a crucial aspiration in any society. This is seen to be in direct contrast to the conflict resolution view of these events, as discussed in the previous section.

A second human rights concern underlying the critique of pragmatism is that a process not framed by explicit moral norms runs the risk of allowing the powerful to dominate the weak. For example, this is an ongoing human rights concern in the negotiations between the Israeli government and the Palestinian leadership, in which Israel's military and political power appear to give it an edge in structuring the terms of any final agreement. Much of what motivates human rights declarations and treaties is protecting citizens from the power of the state – in effect, protecting the weak from abuses by the strong. If a conflict resolution actor, in the role of a mediator, does not address this power imbalance directly, and seek to rectify it in the context of any negotiation process, the human rights advocate will ask how the interests of the weak will be protected. If the interests of the weaker party must be compromised in order to keep the stronger party "at the table," how can the outcome of such a process be considered fair or just?

Thus, while conflict resolution and human rights share many key normative principles, conflict resolution practitioners who pay attention to human rights implement them in different ways than human rights advocates do. They strive to balance their role as a mediator or facilitator with their commitment to strengthening compliance with human rights norms – appropriately so. In doing so, however, they face challenges in addressing power asymmetries and social change. I will explore each of these cross-cutting issues in turn, as each must be handled carefully in an expanded conflict resolution agenda.

Power asymmetry

Both human rights and conflict resolution invoke principles of impartiality. However, the concept has completely different meanings for practitioners in each field. To a conflict resolution practitioner, impartiality requires even-handed treatment of all parties, regardless of their status or resources. For a human rights advocate, impartiality refers to the application of human rights norms, most of which are constructed to protect the weak individual from the abuses of the state or other potentially exploitative authorities. Thus, the human rights result does not appear impartial, but instead looks like (and often is) advocacy for one party over another. This presents a conundrum for the conflict resolution practitioner who recognizes that social justice requires creating a more level playing field, but who needs to maintain even-handedness to be credible.

However, as Crocker, Hampson, and Aall point out in their study of the use of Track 1 mediation in so-called "intractable" conflicts, such even-handedness does not mean passivity; in fact, it underscores the need for the mediator to apply pressure to *all* parties to keep the process moving toward settlement (Crocker et al., 2004: 95). This implies a different kind of impartiality – that of holding all parties' feet to the fire in whatever ways are necessary and possible.

From that framing of the Track 1 mediation role it is not a huge leap to imagine a similarly impartial application of human rights norms to all parties in a conflict. This is the decision that former UN Secretary General Kofi Annan made in instructing his special representatives not to waive accountability for genocide, war crimes, or crimes against humanity. This instruction is consistent not only with the UN Charter and the UDHR, but also with accountability mechanisms now enshrined in the mandate of the new International Criminal Court, created by a treaty with 139 signatories as of 31 December 2000.

In effect, the UN guidance on mediation is creating more salience for these specific norms, which enjoy at least the legalistic definition of universality. Although some would argue that this way of assessing universality is flawed because US and Western European values have superordinate power, particularly in the international bodies that created some of these treaties, the numbers of signatories to each treaty remain notable. One hundred and ninety one states ratified the UN Charter, more than 150 states have signed the UDHR, and 94 states have thus far ratified the ICC.[8] It is therefore arguable that parties to a conflict should not be surprised when mediators invoke these particular human rights principles.

The question then becomes whether there are other human rights norms that Track 1 mediators could invoke in an impartial way. Most peace agreements now include such provisions routinely, with both general reference to the foundational human rights treaties and specific provisions for the protection of rights that were abrogated in a particular conflict. In fact, for Track 1 mediators, there is no evidence that including human rights

provisions makes it more difficult to conclude a peace agreement (Hannum, 2005: 47). This implies that parties in intra-state conflicts now expect that international mediators will require such provisions, or that their future reputations in the international community will rest on their signaling their intention to abide by such norms.[9]

Conflict resolution NGOs engaging in Track 2 efforts face a harder problem. Impartiality is arguably their most important source of access into political negotiations. But, as the findings of a 2003 study of peace practices study clearly shows, most Track 2 work, while aspiring to have an impact on "peace writ large," in fact does not affect decision-making and structural change at the societal level.[10] Could this be, in part, because of the hesitancy to explicitly address power asymmetry and abuses of power by the more powerful parties? If so, how can Track 2 processes do this more effectively?

In his 2004 book entitled *Beyond Neutrality: Confronting the Crisis in Conflict Resolution*, Bernard Mayer raises this question as part of his critique of conflict resolution practice. He proposes that "… conflict resolution professionals have the potential to make a major difference if they can incorporate genuine advocacy into their work…When we serve as advocates, we can still think of ourselves as conflict specialists, bringing to our work the same insights, values, and skills that we may use as neutrals, and we can also urge our field to think of us in that way (Mayer, 2004: 117–119)."[11]

While I am not calling for non-official conflict resolution processes to deviate from their impartiality stance, I agree with Mayer's provocative statement that such processes must explore ways to include advocacy – not of a particular party, but of a set of social justice principles that are defined by human rights norms. At the very least, such organizations must engage in a conversation about the role of human rights in NGO work.

I would argue further that the conflict resolution community has a *responsibility* to incorporate human rights norms in cases of extreme power asymmetry. Human rights norms help address these asymmetries in two important ways. First, they help empower the weaker party—a norm that the conflict resolution community already endorses. By strengthening the salience of human rights norms, conflict resolution processes can achieve greater efficacy by giving a weaker party the support it might need to negotiate from a more equitable vantage point.

Second, human rights norms are important in reinforcing the notion that a state's sovereignty carries with it a responsibility to protect the civilians within its borders (Annan, 1999; Deng et al., 1996; International Development Research Center, 2001). This is reflected in the larger ongoing debate about humanitarian intervention: under what circumstances must the international community intervene when civilians are being abused by their own government? The conflict resolution community should not be absent from this discussion. Rather, it should consider when and how to invoke such responsibility in its dealing with state actors.

This brings us to the last aspect of the power equation: the importance of voluntary participation. How will conflict resolution experts get powerful parties to voluntarily participate in processes that bring human rights issues to the table? Again, the human rights approach of "naming and shaming" will not necessarily work in this context. For Track 1 mediators, a significant example of alternative strategies is provided by the OSCE High Commissioner on National Minorities, particularly as that role was developed by Max van der Stoel, the first High Commissioner. To fully understand this model of intervention requires knowledge of the political and institutional context within which the High Commissioner role has developed and will be explained more fully below.

In addition to confronting power asymmetry, strategy is a second issue of major concern for conflict resolution practitioners who wish to address human rights concerns.

Specifically, how does one catalyze a social change process that can bring about both peace *and* human rights?

Strategies for social change

Conflict resolution and human rights are both seeking to change the political culture in a given society. Conflict resolution processes are designed to move parties from destructive, violent ways of managing political differences to collaborative, constructive approaches. In addition, much of Track 2 conflict resolution is focused on changing attitudes as well – moving the parties from enmity to empathy. Human rights work also hopes to effect a transformation of political culture (Steiner, 2003: 781). From the human rights vantage point, this involves a move from a culture of impunity to a culture of accountability, one that values tolerance, individual dignity, and respect.

As the types of changes sought are different, the assumptions about how such changes can be catalyzed also vary significantly in the two approaches. Human rights are law-based, and change is created by invoking the ideals enshrined in the treaties and pushing states to meet these ideals. Although in practice human rights changes are recognized as being incremental (Steiner, 2003: 785)[12] the strategy to produce *any* change is to demand nothing less than the ideal. In conflict resolution, however, the means used to produce change are different: the design of processes to support a transformation of behavior and attitudes, thus opening up the possibilities for change to occur. This strategy is based on the belief that change cannot be imposed, but can only occur when the parties themselves decide that change is possible and beneficial.

The conventional wisdom is that these two strategies of change are antagonistic; that is, they cannot be used in pursuing opposing goals in the same context without undermining each other. This is especially thought to be true in post-settlement peace-building, where human rights and conflict resolution processes often clash. The disagreement between the two perspectives manifests itself most visibly in discussions about whether accountability should be pursued early in a peace-building process. From the human rights perspective, it is crucial to do so because it demonstrates an end to impunity and a commitment to the rule of law. For conflict resolution purposes, however, demands for accountability can interfere with short-term agreement-making and with the longer-term healing process that is necessary for groups to live together in peace. Human rights and conflict resolution thus follow two different strategies for change in this context, sometimes operating at odds with each other.

BREAKING NEW GROUND

In spite of these very real concerns and challenges, several Track 1 and Track 2 actors have begun to break new ground in combining human rights with conflict resolution work. What follows are examples of intergovernmental and non-governmental efforts to do just that. In all cases, the organization has made explicit its intention to capture the strengths inherent in both the conflict resolution and human rights perspectives.

Current approaches of the UN secretary general

At the UN in the early 1990s, the then Secretary General and his special representatives (SRSGs) found themselves confronted with situations in which parties to a conflict were willing to sign peace agreements that provided leaders with amnesty for crimes committed during the war. Alvaro de Soto, a former under-secretary general of the UN and an experienced mediator, reports the following:

> At the Secretariat, we began to wonder about the responsibility of a UN mediator or representative of the Secretary General in such situations.

We gathered a group composed largely of experienced negotiators – hard-nosed, reality based peacemakers – on the one hand, and representatives of human rights organizations and legal experts on the other. We discussed the issue for two and a half days for the purpose of seeing whether it was possible to reach an understanding between the two sides. Although we agreed it wasn't possible to legislate for all situations, we also agreed that it was important for any mediator acting on behalf of the Secretary General to make clear that the UN operated within a certain framework of law, and that the parties were expected to work within that framework as well. In other words, we need to draw bright lines and notify the parties that the UN could not be associated with a peace agreement that fell outside those lines – for example, by exonerating perpetrators of war crimes or crimes against humanity. If the parties decided to go ahead with such an agreement, the UN would take whatever action was appropriate to disassociate itself. This is the bare minimum. Ultimately we did draft guidelines, but we determined not to make them public because we feared that they would serve as a disincentive to parties otherwise interested in resorting to the UN for mediation (de Soto, 2004: 24–5) .

The UN Secretary General and his representatives found that their credibility was at risk when they became involved with agreements that did not explicitly deal with the accountability of individuals for the most heinous past crimes. They have therefore begun, even though not "on the record," to operate "in the shadow of the law," by refusing to be associated with agreements that fail to address the accountability question. In Sierra Leone, for example, this has resulted in the SRSG endorsing an agreement that provides national-level amnesty for criminal acts during the war, but that explicitly reserves the right of the international community to pursue international adjudication if the national mechanisms fail to act (O'Flaherty, forthcoming).

It is interesting to note, however, that the UN is still hedging its bets by not making these guidelines public, for fear of scaring parties away from mediation. This shows how powerful the countervailing norms are in international mediation and the limits on the leverage that third parties believe they can exercise.

OSCE High Commissioner on National Minorities[13]

The office of The High Commissioner on National Minorities (HCNM) of the Organization for Security and Cooperation in Europe (OSCE) was created by the OSCE in 1992 as a conflict prevention mechanism, in the wake of the escalating violence in the Balkans. The HCNM has worked well in many countries of Central and Eastern Europe to address the concerns of both governments and minority groups before such concerns have escalated to violent self-determination claims (Chigas, 1996).

Although nothing in the HCNM's mandate explicitly requires a normative framing for its work, its placement within the OSCE itself implicitly recognizes that human rights and minority rights principles are an integral component of this mechanism.[14] It is important to stress, however, that the High Commissioner was not conceived of as an advocate for minority groups; hence the title High Commissioner *on* rather than *for* National Minorities. This was done to preserve the idea of the HCNM as a security and conflict prevention mechanism, and also to assure the OSCE member states that the role was not to be an adversary of governments, but instead to advise both minority groups and governments on how to avoid escalatory confrontation. Thus, from the beginning, the HCNM was to integrate a rights-based and a conflict resolution-based approach. Its role has been described as that of a "normative mediator" (Ratner, 2000: 591) in that the High Commissioner has relied upon human rights conventions as a framework for the recommendations he makes to both governments and minority groups.

The HCNM's work in Romania shows how this integrated process operates. In the wake of Romanian independence from the Soviet Union and rising repression of its Hungarian minority, key issues for the Hungarians in Romania were language and education rights, and Hungarian participation in national politics (Horvath, 2002). The issue of minority-language use in public administration and education had sparked violent clashes in 1990 and threatened to again trigger crises in 1995 and 1998. Exacerbating this trend was increasing nationalist tendencies in the Romanian government, and the interest of the Hungarian Democratic Federation of Romania (UDMR) in regional autonomy (Kemp, 2001: 237–8).

Max Van der Stoel, a former Foreign Minister of the Netherlands who held the position of High Commissioner from its inception in 1992 until 2002, began visiting Romania in 1993 and continued working there throughout his 10-year term. He also visited Hungary, the "kin state" of the minority, helping to diffuse tensions created by Hungarian government support for the Hungarians in Romania. He began by encouraging the Romanian government to adopt legislation on minorities and education, and helped to expand the duties of the Advocate of the People, an ombuds position established by the 1991 Constitution. He later made specific legal recommendations for a Law on National Minorities, drawing from several OSCE, Council of Europe, and UN documents. When the Romanian government enacted a controversial Law on Education in 1995, he diffused the tension it created in a public statement simultaneously reassuring the Hungarian minority of the new possibilities that this opened for creative policy development and reminding the Government of its obligations "...pursuant to international standards" (Kemp, 2001: 238). Along with the non-governmental Foundation on Inter-Ethnic Relations, he provided seminars, training programs, and roundtable discussions on implementing minority rights, education opportunities for minorities, and OSCE procedures and legal frameworks on inter-ethnic relations (Horvath, 2002).

Finally, van der Stoel worked to improve relations between Romania and Hungary, diffusing their disagreement on the interpretation of group rights for minorities and paving the way for the 1996 signing of the Hungarian–Romanian Treaty of Friendship and Cooperation (Horvath, 2002). By 1997, Romania had also created a Department for the Protection of Ethnic Minorities, and representatives of the Hungarian minority first held ministerial posts in the government elected in November 1996 (Kemp, 2001: 239).

An in-depth analysis of this case, undertaken by The Centre for OSCE Research at the University of Hamburg, found that the High Commissioner played a critical role in diffusing crisis situations in 1995 (after the new education law) and in 1998 when the Hungarian political party threatened to leave the government. In both circumstances, he changed the frame of the debate and helped both sides see new possibilities.

NGO/Civil society efforts at integrating human rights into conflict resolution

NGOs can also play a significant role in demonstrating how conflict resolution and human rights can work together. However, it is difficult to systematically study the work of NGOs doing conflict resolution, as they are usually small, local, and hard to access. The Collaborative for Development Action, a US-based NGO, initiated a research project in 1999 intended to systematically collect information about the conflict resolution work of NGOs worldwide, which to date has been difficult to obtain other than through anecdotal means. The examples in this section are drawn from their database.[15]

Named "Reflecting on Peace Practice" (RPP), the research was designed as "an experience-based learning process that involves agencies whose programs attempt to prevent or mitigate violent conflict. Its purpose is to analyze experience at the individual program level across a broad range of agencies and contexts. Its goal is to improve the effectiveness of peace work ... [From] September 1999- to April 2001, RPP completed 26 field-based case studies of work in different areas of the world, in different conflicts and different stages of conflict. The cases examine what prompted people to undertake conflict work; what, how, and why

they did it; and what happened as a result of their efforts (and why).[16]

In reviewing these case studies as well as the RPP Issue Paper, "Balance and Trade-Offs between Working for Reduction of Violence or for Social Justice," one can group the international and local NGOs that say they do both human rights and conflict resolution into three categories. The first is the group that uses the terms "human rights" and "conflict resolution" in their titles and literature, but whose program activities are primarily one or the other. Their claims to address both sets of issues stem from their assertions that doing human rights work leads to peace, or that doing peace work protects human rights. Thus, by doing one, they believe they are implicitly doing the other (Anderson, 2001; Isaac, 2001; Zanduliet and Kriegman, 2001). It is not clear from the data available whether these assertions are accurate.

The second group is made up of those who, in trying to move into the justice arena, find that their "impartiality" is called into question and potentially compromises their conflict resolution credibility. They therefore choose to work either explicitly or implicitly *with* human rights organizations, either feeding the human rights advocates information about abuses they have observed in the context of their peacemaking work or following up on reported abuses by convening dialogue processes to confront the problem.[17] They present an interesting model of coordination between conflict resolution and human rights groups, rather than a change in conflict resolution theory and practice itself.

A third group of NGOs has found ways of integrating their conflict resolution and human rights work. While these do not necessarily serve as models, four examples are interesting because of the possibilities they represent.

First, a faith-based NGO in the Israeli Occupied Territories provides a visible "street presence" (the volunteers wear armbands to identify themselves) to monitor the treatment of the Palestinians living there, but also to engage in "conflict intensification" under some circumstances, on behalf of both sides, to make "hidden conflict more visible and open, for purposeful non-violent ends" (Fisher, 2000: 18). In their own words,

> The challenge…is to stand for justice, using conflict intensification judiciously and respectfully, while taking measures to prevent the demonization of "the other"…It involves taking a stand alongside victims – whether they be farmers who can no longer plow their land or bus-riders who no longer feel safe riding buses – while seeing the humanness in the perpetrators of harm, listening to them, taking measures to not allow one's statements or thinking to become prejudicial, and to constantly reach out in all directions (p. 19).

Second, an NGO in Sri Lanka is attempting to use a human rights issue – the protection of children – to bring together both Tamils and Sinhalese, believing that this is a common concern of both communities (Zanduliet and Kriegman, 2001: 23). Although the organization, as of 2001, had not been extremely effective in shaping concrete goals for the initiative, the notion of creating a shared normative vision for two contending societies is an intriguing one. Third, a coalition of faith-based organizations operating in Chiapas, Mexico, aims to help Mexican organizations promote peace there "by using its own presence to help protect nationals working for justice, peace, and human rights and by providing people outside of Mexico with information about the conflict" that is "not being disseminated through the press" (Levine, 2000: 12). It does this by providing a "witness" function for reporting actions taken by each side, and training in conflict transformation for all parties to the conflict. At the same time, it publishes quarterly bulletins extensively disseminated outside of Mexico as well as within the country, which discuss the human rights situation in the region but "… include the perspectives of all people involved in the events about which it is reporting. They have a reputation for unique evenhandedness in that regard."

A fourth approach, taken by International Alert of London, is to publicly proclaim its commitment to both human rights and conflict resolution. They have written an extensive Code of Conduct for their organization, available on their website, which explicitly details their support for human rights and humanitarian law while acknowledging that this is sometimes in tension with their primary aim of building trust and understanding (International Alert, 2004: 20). They see their role as "…principally that of supplementing and supporting those directly involved in the work of promoting and protecting human rights and humanitarian law and principles" (International Alert, 2004: 21) However, they are also engaged in advocacy work to ban land mines, control light weapons, and support vulnerable groups such as women and children. By "going public" with their combined set of conflict resolution and human rights principles, they create opportunities for quietly introducing these norms into their discussions with disputing parties. The key, according to the former secretary general of the organization, is to first build a trusting relationship with the parties, before the human rights issues are put on the table (Clements, 2005).

Undoubtedly, as the work of other conflict resolution NGOs comes to light, we will discover other powerful examples. The four NGO efforts discussed above suggest four possible ways that NGOS can explicitly add human rights norms to the conflict resolution agenda: (1) the "rhetoric" approach, in which a conflict resolution or human rights NGO explicitly states that its work is meant to address both sets of goals; (2) the "partnership" approach, where a conflict resolution NGO works closely with a human rights NGO; (3) the "parallel action" strategy, in which an NGO does both conflict resolution and human rights work separately but in the same context; and (4) the "integrated" approach, where human rights concerns are woven into the conflict resolution work.

Thus, both Track 1 and Track 2 actors are demonstrating not only that human rights norms and conflict resolution norms can coexist in the same organization, but also that the human rights norms can *support* the conflict resolution agenda in important ways.

AN AGENDA FOR CHANGE

The challenges in international politics have shifted in the last 15 years, as new countries and new identity groups have emerged from the collapse of the Soviet empire and the ending of the Cold War. Concurrently, and not entirely coincidentally, the conflict resolution movement has joined the human rights movement as a serious player in the efforts to produce constructive social change in an increasingly fragmented world. While pragmatism was effective in previous eras in order for "negative peace" to be established, we are learning through painful experience that this is not sufficient to keep violence at bay. We must now press for "positive peace" if we are to prevent societies from using violence to settle their differences, or sliding back into chaos after emerging from a brutal civil war. I've argued that one way to do that is for the international conflict resolution community to begin incorporating a more explicit human rights dimension in its work.

What, exactly, would such a shift require? First of all, it would mean a rethinking of basic assumptions. Conflict resolution practitioners who act as mediators or facilitators should not assume, as a default, that the inclusion of rights-based concerns is anathema to peace; there is no proof that this is the case. On the contrary, logic dictates that it could be just the opposite, especially in intra-state conflict in which human rights abuses have been either a cause or a consequence of the violence. In such cases, peace cannot be achieved unless the human rights dimensions of the problem are explicitly addressed.

Instead, third-party processes should substitute the default assumption that expanding the normative frame of peace-building is a good idea, and look for ways to do so. At the Track 1 level, the OSCE High Commissioner on National Minorities offers a provocative example of how this can work. It includes using compliance with human rights norms as an incentive, rather than only as a threat. As Max van der Stoel so ably demonstrated, there are numerous ways that governments can solve their internal problems by compliance with the norms rather than by the thwarting of them. A creative mediator can, and should, assist in framing alternatives for governments in this way, and should initiate that discussion if government representatives do not.

Track 1 mediators should also continue to clarify the limits of states' discretion in excusing the universally condemned crimes of genocide, war crimes, and crimes against humanity. Former United Nations Secretary General Kofi Annan did so explicitly in the guidance he gave to his special representatives. The International Criminal Court will assist in this as well, as its mandate calls for prosecution of these crimes.

For Track 2 conflict resolution actors, the agenda is slightly different. Without the leverage of the Track 1 mediators, Track 1½ and Track 2 third-party processes are more dependent, and effectively so, on the relationship that develops between the interveners and the parties to the conflict. Therefore, the framing of that relationship must include the human rights dimensions from its outset in the conflict assessment phase; this means assessing how human rights concerns are part of the problem and therefore have to be part of the solution.

Several NGOs mentioned earlier explicitly incorporate human rights concerns into their approach to conflict resolution, and other NGOs can draw on their examples. This could include a range of options, from simply stating human rights and social justice as a goal to integrating discussions about human rights concerns directly into conversations with the relevant parties. The first step, therefore, is for each Track 2 conflict resolution organization to reframe its mission statement to include its commitment to social justice and compliance with human rights norms.

In addition, NGOS can take on a more direct advocacy role in relation to their Track 1 counterparts, lobbying them to strengthen the official commitment to human rights and social justice. If *official* conflict resolution processes are more explicitly supportive of human rights norms, then the Track 2 processes that are set up to complement the official efforts can justifiably invoke these norms as well.[18]

Most importantly, those of us designing and implementing conflict resolution processes at all levels in intra-state conflicts cannot assume that human rights are "not our issue." They are key components of parties' interests and concerns, significant indicators of power asymmetry and sometimes power abuses, and often both a cause and a consequence of the conflicts we are trying to settle or transform. It is crucial that conflict resolution professionals know and understand the strengths and weaknesses of human rights norms, how these have been translated into international law, and the impacts such laws might have in a particular conflict. The question to answer is not if, but how, to use these norms in a constructive and appropriate way.

The strength of the combined conflict resolution/human rights agenda is a values-based structure *plus* a process for advancing it that takes into account the profound changes in attitude that are required to put such values into practice. The challenge for the conflict resolution professional is to embrace this agenda in order to make positive peace a reality.

NOTES

1 There is still debate in the international conflict resolution community about the centrality of impartiality to mediator effectiveness. See Zartman and Touval, 1996.

2 Retributive justice "...follows the principle: 'For your hurt [that you caused], we [the state] hurt [you] in return, but not necessarily in kind." (Shriver, quoted in Estrada-Hollenbeck, 2001: 68).

3 The view of restorative justice is that "The overarching aim of the criminal justice process should be to reconcile parties while repairing the injuries caused by crime. The criminal justice process should facilitate active participation by victims, offenders, and their communities. The government to the exclusion of others should not dominate it...(I)f there is no restoration of the social relationships that the conflict affected, true justice does not occur." Estrada-Hollenbeck, 2001: 74.

4 The International Covenant on Civil and Political Rights (ICCPR) and the International Covenant on Economic, Social, and Cultural Rights (ICESCR), each

ratified in 1976. In addition to these foundational documents, the human rights "corpus" includes many other documents: the Convention on the Prevention and Punishment of the Crime of Genocide (1948); the International Convention on the Elimination of All Forms of Racial Discrimination (1965); the Convention on the Elimination of All Forms of Discrimination against Women (1979); the Convention Against Torture and Other Cruel, Inhuman, or Degrading Treatment or Punishment (1984); the Convention on the Rights of the Child (1989); the European Convention for the Protection of Human Rights and Fundamental Freedoms (1953); the American Convention on Human Rights (1978); and the African Charter on Human and Peoples' Rights (1986). Finally, there are several treaties that pertain to the humanitarian laws of war (i.e. the four 1949 Geneva Conventions and the 1977 Protocols that expanded their reach), and various conventions adopted under the auspices of the International Labor Organization.

5 Distributive bargaining views all gains to the adversary as losses to oneself, and therefore the goal is not only to get as much as you can, but to do so at the other's expense. Hence the term "zero sum."

6 Coercive mediation, or mediation with muscle, is only possible if the third party has leverage it can use to change the calculation of disputing parties as to the costs and benefits of agreement. See Babbitt (1993) and Zartmen and Touval (2001).

7 Center for Human Rights and Conflict Resolution, Inaugural Conference, December 1, 2000. The Fletcher School of Law and Diplomacy, Tufts University.

8 As of May 3, 2004. See Human Rights Watch ([http://www.hrw.org/campaigns/icc/)] Accessed 4/2/2005.

9 For an interesting study on the impact of ratifying human rights treaties on state behavior, see Hathaway, 2002. A critique of Hathaway's findings can be found in Goodman and Jinks, 2003.

10 See Center for Development Action, Reflecting on Peace Practice Project http://www.cdainc.com/rpp/.

11 An early article by Susskind [Vermont Law Review] addressed the point in a slightly different way, arguing that mediators have the responsibility to raise the concerns of parties who are not represented at the negotiating table, often because they are not well organized or resourced enough to be "players." Mayer also acknowledges the important work of William Ury, in Ury's latest book *The Third Side*. Ury refers to the third-side role of "equalizer" as one in which a third-party intervener helps to mitigate a severe power imbalance by, for example, insisting that a high-power leader listen to a low-power groups' grievances. However, Mayer is going beyond even this role, exploring why and how conflict resolution specialists might work on the side of one party to a conflict.

12 785. Steiner refers to this as "progressive realization."

13 This section is taken from Babbitt (2006).

14 See OSCE Helsinki Final Act.

15 For information about CDA, see http://www.cdainc.com.

16 http://See www.cdainc.com/rpp/.

17 See "Balance and Tradeoffs between Working for Reduction of Violence or for Social Justice", available at www.cdainc.com/rpp/publications.php.

18 A concrete example of how the Track 1 and Track 2 actors might collaborate is provided by a meeting I attended in October 2001, held at the Rockefeller Foundation Conference Center in Bellagio, Italy. Sponsored by the Harvard Law School Human Rights Program and the International Centre for Ethnic Studies in Sri Lanka, it was designed as a discussion between professionals and scholars in human rights and conflict resolution about approaches to ethnic conflict and minority protection that could marry the two disciplines. Coming literally weeks after the September 11 attacks on the World Trade Center in the United States, the discussion took more than an academic view of how to address intergroup tensions and the grievances expressed by minority groups in relation to their governments. As part of the conversation, we created a possible set of principles to guide conflict resolution work in situations where human rights grievances are an issue. See Harvard Law School Human Rights Program (2004).

REFERENCES

Annan, K. (1999) "Two Concepts of Sovereignty", *The Economist* 18 September.

Anderson, M.B. (2001) "Extending the Humanitarian Mandate: Norwegian Church Aid's Decision to Institutionalize its Commitment to Peace." Collaborative for Development Action. Available from www.cdainc.com/rpp/publications.php.

Babbitt, E.F. (1993) "Beyond Neutrality: The Use of Leverage by Powerful States as Mediators in International Conflict". PhD dissertation, Massachusetts Institute of Technology.

Babbitt, E.F. (2006) "Mediating Rights-based Conflicts: Making Self-determination Negotiable", *International Negotiation* 11 (1): 185–208.

Babbitt, E.F. (forthcoming) *Principled Peace: Conflict Resolution and Human Rights in Intra-state Conflict.* Ann Arbor, MI: University of Michigan Press.

Clements, K. (2005) Interview, January 27. Former Secretary General of International Alert.

Collier, Paul (2000) "Economic Causes of Civil Conflict and their Implications for Policy". Washington, DC: World Bank.

Crocker, C.A., Hampson, F.O. and Aall, P. (2004) *Taming Intractable Conflicts: Mediation in the Hardest Cases.* Washington, DC: US Institute of Peace Press.

Deng, F. et al. (1996) *Sovereignty as Responsibility: Conflict Management in Africa.* Washington, DC: Brookings Institution.

De Soto, A. (2004) Quoted in "Ethnic Conflict, Minority Protection and Conflict Resolution: Human Rights Perspectives". Harvard Law School Human Rights Program, Cambridge, MA.

Estrada-Hollenbeck, M. (2001) "The Attainment of Justice, through Restoration not Litigation: The Subjective Road to Reconciliation", in M. Abu-Nimer (ed.), *Reconciliation, Justice and Co-existence: Theory and Practice.* Lanham, MD: Lexington Books.

Fisher, S. (2000) "Working with Conflict", in S.A. Lyke and J.G. Bock (eds), *Reflecting on the Christian Peacemaker Team in Hebron.* Collaborative for Development Action. Available from www.cdainc.com/rpp/publications.php.

Galtung, J. (1969) "Violence, Peace and Peace Research", *Journal of Peace Research* 6 (3).

Goodman, R. and Jinks, D. (2003) "Measuring the Effects of Human Rights Treaties", *European Journal of International Law* 14.

Gurr, T. (1996) "Minorities, Nationalists and Ethnopolitical Conflict", in C.A. Crocker, F.O. Hampson and P. Aall (eds), *Managing Global Chaos: Sources of and Responses to International Conflict.* Washington, DC: US Institute of Peace Press.

Hannum, H. (2005) "Human Rights in Conflict Resolution: The Role of the Office of the High Commissioner for Human Rights in UN Peacemaking and Peacebuilding." Medford, MA: The Center for Human Rights and Conflict Resolution, The Fletcher School of Law and Diplomacy, Tufts University.

Hathaway, O.A. (2002) "Do Human Rights Treaties Make a Difference?" *Yale Law Journal* 111.

International Alert (2004) *International Alert Code of Conduct. Appendix 1.* (p. 20). Available from www.international-alert.org/text/code_e.html (January 14).

International Development Research Center (2001) "The Responsibility to Protect: Report of the International Commission on Intervention and State Sovereignty". Ottawa, Canada: International Development Research Center.

Isaac, D. (2007) "Prio/Nansen Case Study: The Balkan Dialogue Project. Collaborative for Development Action." Available from www.cdainc.com/rpp/publications.php.

Levine, C. (2000) "International Service for Peace (Sipaz): Promoting Peace Building and Nonviolent

Conflict Transformation in Chiapas, Mexico." Collaborative for Development Action. Available from www.cdainc.com/rpp/publications.php.

Mayer, B.S. (2004) *Beyond Neutrality: Confronting the Crisis in Conflict Resolution.* San Francisco: Jossey-Bass.

Mnookin, R.H. and Kornhauser, L. (1979) "Bargaining in the Shadow of the Law: The Case of Divorce", *Yale Law Journal* 99: 950.

Niland, N. (2004) "Justice Postponed: The Marginalization of Human Rights in Afghanistan", in A. Donini, N. Niland and K. Wermester (eds), *Nation-building Unravelled? Aid, Peace and Justice in Afghanistan.* Bloomfield, CT: Kumarian Press.

O'Flaherty, M. (forthcoming) "Sierre Leone's Peace Process: The Role of the Human Rights Community", in E.F. Babbitt and E. Lutz (eds), *Human Rights and Conflict Resolution in Context.* Syracuse, NY: Syracuse University Press.

Sebenius, J. (2003) "Lakhdar Brahimi: Negotiating a New Government for Afghanistan". Program on Negotiation at Harvard Law School.

Steiner, H.J. (2003) "International Protection of Human Rights", in Malcolm D. Evans (ed.), *International Law.* Oxford: Oxford University Press.

Stephan, M. (1996) "Non-violent Action in Self-determination Disputes". PhD dissertation, The Fletcher School of Law and Diplomacy, Tufts University.

Zartman, I.W. and Touval, S. (1996) "International Mediation in the Post Cold War Era", in C.A. Crocker, F.O. Hampson and P. Aall (eds), *Managing Global Chaos: Sources of and Responses to International Conflict.* Washington, DC: US Institute of Peace Press.

Zanduliet, L. and Kriegman, O. (2001) "Unicef Sri Lanka: Children as Zones of Peace." Collaborative for Development Action. Available from www.cdainc.com/rpp/publications.php.

33

Resolution of Military Conflicts and Confrontations (Force and Arms Control)

Victor Kremenyuk

Military conflicts are considered, with all due grounds, among the most dangerous and intractable types of conflicts. We should remind ourselves that the possibility of using destructive weapons in such conflicts, inflicting human sacrifice, and destroying property and natural values tells enough of the bitterness and antagonism of these conflicts and of the hardships of their conduct. Usually, they can be either lost or won; other solutions so far were hardly attainable. Of course, there are political systems and political cultures which worship the use of violence and weapons and for them any military conflict is something "regular" and agreeable; but they are not what we consider a "normal" actor in international affairs. Even in the current highly controversial world, they are more an exclusion than a rule. But the most "normal" and "civilized" actors are also very often engaged in military conflicts and that raises an important question of how to solve them without necessarily going to war.

If nations go to war, then the solution to the conflict is decided by the results of the military showdown rather than by the considerations of reason and justice. And that is what is demanded by the current political imperative (Zartman and Kremenyuk, 2005).

International relations are full of military confrontations and military conflicts. Nations both go to war and prepare to do that, they either fight each other or threaten to do so (Sarkees, Wayman, and Singer, 2003). The difference between "conflicts" and "confrontations" is rather conditional: in this chapter, "conflicts" are treated as open hostilities ("hot wars") while "confrontations" as military conflicts short of direct showdown ("cold wars"). Both exist in contemporary international relations, though it is fair to acknowledge that the ratio is generally in favor of the cold wars. In each case, the major elements are practically the same: hostility, use of coercion, arms race and desire to achieve a position of power in order to impose a unilateral solution of the conflict, high instability and low predictability. At the same time, there is of course a difference: open hostilities are a major threat to world peace and the intervention of the UN is unavoidable with all the consequences, while confrontation short of war is considered a "private affair" which does not preclude any active outside intervention.

The real difference between the two is in the use of organized violence. In the case of confrontations, the use of military force is a political weapon strongly limited by the international law, rational considerations of security (avoidance of the retaliatory blow) and ethics (threat of unacceptable collateral damage). As a result, the cases of military confrontations are accompanied by strong written or unwritten "rules of prudence" (Allison, 1989) which prescribe a certain code of conduct of the adversaries which permits them to confront each other endlessly without a direct clash. In military conflicts, the use of force is going at full swing and the means which may limit its scope are the capabilities of economy, support of the population, availability of military reserves. The law of war and the position of the world community also play a role (Franck, 2007).

What makes both cases very similar is the use of violence and coercion as a means of the solution of the conflict (George, 1971). In the cases of hot wars, as well as in the cases of cold wars, the conflict develops not so much as a competition of different positions on the subject of the argument but mainly as a function of force capabilities and projection. No matter what the initial cause for the conflict (ideology, religion, borders, distribution of resources), the essence of it concentrates on the matters of the rivalry of military capabilities and all the aspects of it: arms race, military balance, ability to use force. The importance of the military component overshadows all other aspects and determines the state and the evolution of the conflict. And when the task of resolution is set, mostly it means the necessity to go back to the origins of the conflict where a

bifurcation (to use force or not) happened and to look there for a possible change of the strategy and other alternatives which may help either to avoid a conflict or to make it less destructive. Theoretically, it sounds simple but in practice it is almost impossible (Xenias, 2005).

THE METHOD: STEP BY STEP RESOLUTION

The guiding principle of Schelling's analysis of the strategy in conflict is the discovery of a permanently existing alternative which opens a possibility of choice on almost every stage of the development of the conflict (Schelling, 1960). Depending on the preferences of the actor, it is either a zero-sum or non-zero-sum game; going a bit further – it's a conflict or cooperation or a mixture. When a choice of a violent conflict strategy is considered preferable (because of the vast asymmetry in the capabilities of the two sides), then coercion is regarded as optimal for the interests of the stronger side as, for example, in the case of Israel in its conflict with the Arab states. But when there is no such clear advantage of one side over the other, the need to reconsider the past choices becomes urgent and accompanies the further evolution of the state of relations between the contenders. Theoretically, this need incorporates the possibility of a complete change of the strategy and the termination of the conflict (Axelrod, 1984).

In this sense, the development of the weapons of mass destruction (WMD) after World War II has significantly increased the stakes in a possible conflict between the nuclear states and opened up a new type of conflict strategy, that of deterrence and avoidance of the open hostilities. It has sharply increased the possible "cost" of the use of force and, thus, it has significantly contributed to the growth of doubts on the relevance of an open conflict as a solution to the disputed problem. This has changed the ratio between the attractiveness of the use of force (a promise of a "quick" and "decisive" solution) and reluctance to do so because of the expected losses. The strategy of the two nuclear superpowers, the Soviet Union and USA, has been split into two major parts: on the one hand, to seek for a possible strategic advantage (which could give a chance if not of a military victory at least of intimidation of the other side) and, on the other, to adhere to the "rules of prudence" in order to avoid an open hostility (George, Farley, and Dallin, 1988).

In the area of military conflicts, this situation has created a certain environment which has allowed the world to live for about 50 years without a major war (Vasquez, 2004). The two major adversaries were tied with the relationship of the Mutually Assured Destruction (MAD). They could threaten each other but did not risk going to war. Their allies and clients, being a part of their security arrangements, were not free to take steps which could engage them in military conflicts (with few exceptions, like the French war in Algeria or the British war in the Falkland Islands). In these matters, they had to follow the directives of the senior partner. The rest of the world, the so-called Third World, was more or less free to engage in military conflicts (and the arms sales policies of the superpowers seemingly encouraged it) but under the strict control of the UN Security Council where the same superpowers dominated. Besides, following their best intentions, the Soviet Union, USA and United Kingdom have concluded the Nonproliferation Treaty (NPT) in 1968, which has significantly reduced the searches for military advantage by smaller nations through the development of their individual nuclear weapons.

This system of inter- and intra-block mutual dependencies in the area of use of force has actively encouraged those who, due to different reasons (religious, moral, ethic, legal, etc.), objected to violence in principle. The huge losses of the nations in the two world wars in the 20th century, the advent of the weapons which could lead to even greater losses if used, the spread of conflicts among nations with the increase in number of independent states, the necessity to switch over at

least part of the resources from arms race to development – all this has greatly stimulated searches for alternative strategies in conflicts. It is understandable that conflicts happen and will continue to happen in the relations between sovereign states, but the legitimate question was: should they always develop as a military confrontation? Is the military force, even in the cases of definite advantage, the best solution? Doesn't social and intellectual progress open up opportunities for other than military solutions?

This was the beginning of conflict resolution thinking in the military area and the anti-violence considerations have played a significant role in its development (Franck, 2007). It has also prompted the spontaneous method of the resolution of military conflicts in this period. The efforts in this area had to follow the changes in the military capabilities of the nuclear powers and to respond to each of them with certain changes in the rules of conduct: partial or complete self-restraint (though complete self-restraint was more a dream than reality), parallel negotiated restraint, agreed limitations, cooperative efforts, joint endeavors. And that has contributed to the process of gradual resolution which led in the long run, step by step, to the end of the military stage of the conflict: from limitation to conflict stabilization, then to reduction of the conflict, and then to its resolution.

BEGINNINGS OF RESOLUTION: LIMITATION

Two sets of major factors have played an outstanding role in the limitation of the scope of violence and development of the military conflict resolution strategy. One is associated with the pressure of the international environment which included, first of all, the attitudes of the superpowers but also the role of the UN Security Council and General Assembly, the positions of individual nations, the interference of the Church and of numerous nongovernmental organizations (NGOs). The importance of this factor is in its legal nature and moral influence. The other factor was associated with the process of development of the military confrontation between the superpowers, not only because of their size and status but also because the evolution of their relationship has dominated in the military thinking, conflict analysis and in the assessment of the perspectives of the world system as such. The evolution of the relations between the big Twos has always attracted attention of other nations in the past (George, Farley, and Dallin, 1988). It is still important today when only one superpower is left (Krahman, 2005). The net result of the two factors was and is a strong tendency to limit the scope and frequency of the military conflicts, to put them under some sort of control and to look for alternatives.

There is a certain relationship between the birth, evolution and the end of any conflict. And from this point of view, it is appropriate and important to identify which decisions have produced the conflict and have led to its development. It may also help to understand why and how it lives and how it can be ended. As a classical example, some historians mention Barbara Tuchman's "Guns of August" at the beginning of WWI, in which she has given one of the best historical analyses of the interconnection between the decisions of the rivaling nations which lead in the long run to the outburst of the world crisis. This approach is also the basis for the so-called "decision making" theory of conflict analysis (Rapoport, 1960).

So, the problem of a resolution strategy is to understand which decisions, when and why, have played the role of a trigger and whether they can be reversed or changed or dismissed in order to redraft the path of the evolution of the military conflict. And the limitation of the conflict plays a certain role here because it reduces the intensity of the confrontation and thus gives a bigger chance to the factors which may contribute to the peaceful resolution of the conflict. Since a military conflict (and confrontation) is a case where the use of organized violence is the leading feature, it is understandable that it begins when, due to different reasons, non-violent evolution

of a conflict is considered irrelevant and a military action preferable. The state of the military capabilities and the hope for a victory, rather than justice and aspiration of a rational winning strategy, decide the outcome of the conflict: "when the cannons speak, the truth is silent" (Parsons, 2007). Both in the cases of "hot" and "cold" wars, the ability to use weapons is the major and practically the only factor which decides the evolution and the end of the conflict.

This simple and evident fact leaves at the same time an open and bleeding question as to whether this is the best possible solution and how long it will live. Evidently, the imposed solution may not be the best (as, for example, the enforced marriage can never bring happiness) and what will happen when the other side acquires more power (as did Russia under Putin)? The human experience has identified some cases when only a military solution is relevant, for example, in dealing with the dictatorial regimes (and from this point of view, President Bush's argument in favor of the attack of Saddam's Iraq because it was "a bloody dictatorship" has received a vast support) (Kremenyuk, 2004). But in many other cases, this is not so evident and that gives legitimate grounds for strong doubts and opposition to the use of force. It is even possible to state that very often the strategy of coercion with its bombasting rhetoric simply covers the intellectual and moral inability to find less belligerent and more promising ways to solve the conflict.

In the current conditions, something important has changed which gives us a chance to answer the hard questions on the relevance of coercion. First, the end of the Cold War between the Soviet Union and USA has produced legitimate aspirations of a similar peaceful end to other military conflicts and confrontations. Second, the ability of the two superpowers to overcome their differences (which at times seemed so important that their governments were ready to use all their arsenals to defend them) was regarded as their ability to enforce peaceful solutions on other conflicts, such as Nicaragua,

Afghanistan, Korea, India–Pakistan, Taiwan, Arab states–Israel, Cyprus, Bosnia and others. The growing attractiveness of non-violent solutions has changed significantly the whole attitude to the use of force as a political weapon. Suffice it to say that almost every government now has to develop a special argument in favor of the use of force once it decides to do it. Though the right to use force for the purposes of self defense is recognized by the UN Charter, still the nations are expected to give a profound explanation of their conflict behavior (something which was completely ignored by the US administration in the case of its attack on Iraq).

Two different views have been borne as a result. One concerned the centuries-old principle of the cost-benefit analysis of the use of force in a conflict. The spread of the WMD has introduced a totally new element into the understanding of this principle: use the threat of force as a tool of conflict management but don't use force as such because it is too destructive (George, 1971). And the desire by some nations to acquire WMD reveals that they see in this weapon the possibility of intimidating possible aggressors through the increase of the price of the use of power. The other raised the issue of whether there are means of conflict resolution which may adequately replace the military means. These two elements have contributed to the birth of the idea of changing the search for a violent solution to a non-violent one and, thus, of working out a conflict resolution strategy different from the military strategy. At that stage, the relevance of a conflict was not practically questioned; what was questioned was military violence as a means of conflict control.

It would be naive to expect that, once such conclusions were achieved, the force structures which existed for centuries and the whole historical tradition which was born because of the typical conduct of the nations will be immediately changed. Ideas of peaceful, non-violent solution of conflicts and confrontations only reflected the fact that very strong doubts have appeared about the efficiency of violent solutions and of the

necessity to introduce strong limitations to the use of force. The traditional anti-war and anti-militaristic position of those who always protested against the use of force was rather unexpectedly supported by the rational cold-blooded analysis of the consequences of the use of weapons in the current conditions. The adherents of the use of military force did not capitulate, though they had to take a defensive position. Instead, they suggested different means to circumvent the factor of the nuclear stalemate: "limited" wars, "low intensity" conflicts, "special" wars, wars "by proxy" and the like.

CONTROL AND MANAGEMENT

The general state of affairs in the conditions of the Cold War between the two nuclear giants, USA and USSR, has made it impossible to expect a decisive victory in almost any military conflict, not only in the direct war between them. The US failure in Vietnam (1965–1973) and the Soviet defeat in Afghanistan (1979–1988) have dramatically testified that, disregarding the tremendous military and technical asymmetry between the warring sides, the big powers could not hope for a military victory and political success. The same rule governed in other cases. Even in such a clear case as the Arab–Israeli wars of 1967, 1973, 1982 and others, when Israel demonstrated a strong military edge over any enemy among the Arab states, it was still not possible to transfer military successes into decisive political gains. This important conclusion has strengthened both very profound doubts on the relevance of the use of force generally and on the possibility of continuing the established policies in such areas as Korea, Taiwan, Cuba, Yugoslavia and finally in the relations between the superpowers.

The problem was split into two parts. One of them related to the cases of the open use of force. Here, the strategy of solution invented, as the reliable tool, the powers of the UN Security Council which can take decisions to stop fighting and to help the conflicting sides to freeze the military stage of the conflict. The technology for this type of development was not too sophisticated and its success depended mainly on the agreement of the superpowers, beginning with the Geneva Conferences of 1953 and 1954 where France, the UK, the USA and USSR together with China have succeeded in the termination of wars in Korea and Indochina. The UN Security Council helped to achieve a cease-fire in Kashmir, the Middle East, Congo, Balkans, East Timor and many other places All these efforts have played a role as a demonstration of a strong international capability to limit the scope of the open use of force and as a reminder of the preference for the search for peaceful solutions (McNamara, 1986).

There was a strong visible impact of this change on the concept and conduct of military conflicts. First, disregarding the official doctrines of "two and a half wars" shared by NATO and WTO during their confrontation in the years of the Cold War, in reality the idea to use WMD was completely reviewed: both sides agreed (Soviet–US Agreement on the Prevention of Nuclear War, 1973) not to use nuclear and other WMD against each other or against the third parties (George, Farley, and Dallin, 1988). Unfortunately, this rather important gain was not followed by similarly important agreements on the complete destruction of the nuclear weapons. They were left as something like a "guarantee" of the proper conduct of the other side but in reality played a provocative role in encouraging a partial proliferation: for example, India, Pakistan, North Korea and Iran.

Second, the ideas of "big wars" in Europe or in Asia were also completely revised. While officially they continued to be on the national security agendas of both global adversaries, in reality they planned to limit them and, to the extent possible, avoid them. The whole effort of reduction of the conventional weapons in Europe and of the confidence building measures (CBM) were introduced as elements of avoiding the risk of another major war in Europe and Asia (Langlois and Langlois, 2005). The outstanding role

here was attributed to intended lack of fixed rules of a possible transition from a conventional to nuclear conflict because of the existence of tactical weapons and the delegation of the authority to use it to regional commanders.

Third, as a result of these developments, the type of military planning and the general concept has significantly changed. The idea of using military means in a conflict was not dropped as such but was strongly conditioned by the time limits, theater borders and weapons capabilities. The ideas of a "blitzkrieg" have prevailed: orientation to a quick and decisive blow, massive use of air force against the centers of command, control, and communications, military reserves, depots and industrial centers, quick ground forces operations, extensive use of airborne and special forces and the like (Bracken, 1983).

All these developments have significantly limited the possible scope of military conflicts. Besides, though some measures were suggested to put a possible evolution of a military conflict to a higher level under firm control, they did not give a sense of a guarantee that any military conflict started as a "blitzkrieg" would inevitably be conducted within some rational limits. The idea of a limitation of the use of military force in case of open hostilities accompanied the development of the military doctrines of the leading nations up to the present. At the same time, it has put a stress on the necessity to develop an alternative: either freezing of a military conflict or the peaceful settlement of the cause which has given birth to this conflict.

The method of putting an end to open hostilities and to transfer a conflict into the stage of "searches for peace" is well known and widely used (Weeks, 1991). It helps to reduce the sphere of military conflicts and leaves aside only the cases when, due to different reasons, the nations do not adhere to the basics of the UN Charter. But what becomes extremely important is that without some established and acceptable technology of transforming cease-fire into the process of peaceful solution, the open hostilities simply become cold wars and thus continue for decades: for example, Korea, India–Pakistan, Arab–Israeli, Cyprus, USA–Cuba. So, the problem which appears as a result is two-fold: how to capitalize on the success of a cease-fire and promote a peaceful settlement and, second, how to work out a firm universal strategy of the resolution of military confrontation (Fortna, 2002).

From limitation to reduction

The cost-benefit analysis and the post-Hiroshima ethics have played an outstanding role in introducing the policy of limitation of the military conflict. Rather visible and tangible results of this policy were achieved through the bilateral US–Soviet agreements of the 1970s and 1980s. The UN Conference for Disarmament in Geneva has also played an important role. At least, a ban on the use of some lethal WMD (biological and chemical) was negotiated and the initial grounds for other possible arms limitations: land mines, missiles and launchers, most dangerous types of light weapons. It gave grounds to a whole set of international agreements on the international trade in arms. In an indirect way, this development has contributed to the limitation of military conflicts and confrontations. This stage of the development of ideas to limit military conflicts was conducted by the introduction of rules which were destined to reduce the destructive capabilities of military actions. This development was enhanced by some independent studies of the combatants/non-combatants ratio among the losses in military conflicts (e.g. SIPRI research reports on Vietnam) and had, as a purpose, the task of introducing the weapons which at least did not cause unnecessary sufferings to the victims of the conflict and reduced the collateral damage.

What is really important is that it, on the one hand, continued the noble tradition of the Hague Conferences of the early 20th centuries to limit the use of "non-human" weapons but, on the other hand, also had the idea of some sort of control over the conflicts. These ideas were developed by some non-governmental organizations (UN associations) and governmental agencies (US Arms Control and Disarmament Agency). In the conditions of the Cold War, this problem was understood and was almost automatically solved through mechanisms of the alliance relations. It has become more of a problem after the end of the Cold War when smaller nations felt they had some freedom in their choices, for example, the occupation of Kuwait by Saddam Hussein's forces in 1990.

The major focus of attention in the searches for the solution of military conflicts in the 1970s and 1980s was with the US–Soviet confrontation. An important fall-out of the Cuban missile crisis in 1962 was the conclusion of the necessity to build a system of "safety fuses" which could substantially reduce the possibility of risk in the military relations between the superpowers. The work began with the 1963 "Hot Line" agreement which has allowed the establishment of a reliable communication line between Moscow and Washington, and continued into the 1970s with the agreement on Prevention of Incidents at and over the High Seas (1972), agreement on Unauthorized Launches (also 1972), agreement on the Prevention of the Nuclear War (1973) and some others. This action has allowed both to put the risks of confrontation under control and to limit further uncontrolled evolution of the conflict, including its destructiveness (George, Farley, and Dallin, 1988).

The attempts to limit destructiveness of military conflicts very logically increased an interest in more substantial efforts to reduce violence in conflicts. The pressures were coming from two sides. On one side, it was the conclusion on the limits of coercion in the present world due to the nuclear stalemate and to the policy of active intervention by the international community. On the other, it was a strong position of the public on the use of weapons which were too destructive and did not increase the conflict settlement capabilities. The adherents of the idea of solving conflicts through non-coercive means rather than through the use of force have gathered a large audience worldwide, which observed both the failure of the USA in Vietnam and of the Soviet Union in Afghanistan and came to a legitimate conclusion that the use of force, while helpful and efficient in some cases (the Desert Storm operation by US forces in Kuwait in 1991), in other, and much more numerous, cases is not that effective and desirable.

As a result, ideas of violence reduction have become rather popular in the 1990s following the end of the Cold War. They were mainly transformed into various concepts of "peace enforcement" and "peace intervention" (associated with UN or NATO) in cases when violence in a conflict exceeded a tolerable level and hurt human feelings, for example, hostilities in Bosnia in 1994–1995 (Williams and Caldwell, 2006). This policy included, as a possibility, efforts to settle the conflict peacefully, as in the case of the Dayton agreement on Bosnia testifies. On the other hand, the events in former Yugoslavia, conflicts in the former USSR, and other cases of active use of violence, have indicated that some level of attrition was still indispensable for the military solution of local conflicts (e.g. the war in Yugoslavia in 1999) and it was too premature to speak about a profound re-appraisal of the role of violence in conflicts.

That has not compromised a more general idea of conflict reduction policy. The ideas of conflict reduction have become extremely helpful in developing the strategy of military conflict resolution in the 1990s (Zartman and Kremenyuk, 1995). Of course, they did not include, at least in the beginning, a hope for the reduction of conflict potential generally. More than that, they used both humanitarian aspirations and pragmatic considerations in an attempt to prove that military conflicts have lost a significant part of their rationality and policy relevance (Stern and Druckman, 2000). But at the same time, they accepted the idea that conflicts were still sometimes necessary for the solution of other issues, like humanitarian interventions (Kosovo), punishment of terrorism (Afghanistan) and destruction of dictatorial regimes (Iraq).

Conflict reduction, as a concept, should not be considered in isolation from the general trends in international relations in the late 1980s to early 1990s. It was too early at that time to speak about a possibility of moving to a much less volatile type of relationship. It was possible and desirable in the area of the alliance relationship where conflicts happened sometimes but generally were subject to special procedures and mechanisms which worked like automatic production lines and took the issues of the differences in interests and goals of the allies (Greece and Turkey, UK and Iceland, UK and Spain) as a subject for peaceful settlement. But in other cases, when conflicts happened between the neutrals or the adversaries, they could hardly be subjected to the same limitation policies forcefully.

It was in the period when, due to the reduction of tensions in the relations between global adversaries, the USA and USSR, the role of the UN had chances for proliferation (e.g. Gorbachev's speech at the UN General Assembly in December 1988) which had set in motion conflict reduction possibilities. The capabilities of UN mechanisms in the conflict reduction area were grossly exaggerated but nonetheless played a certain role in propagating ideas of reduction of tensions. In order to make reduction a policy in conflict settlement, some additional measures were needed.

From reduction to stabilization: arms control and military balance

High crisis instability of a military conflict is conditioned by the existence of a "surprise attack" strategy which is an important element of the "blitzkrieg" thinking (Betts, 1982). It may also develop in another type of the conflict scenarios, the "Sarajevo case" (pre-World War I) because it triggers a sequence of developments which cannot be checked by any of the participants. As a result, the conflict development as such, because of its complicated nature, low predictability (or even unpredictability), and its possible outbursts, contains a large element of instability which becomes another threat to participants. It is one thing when any of them uses a strategy of blackmail and demonstrative aggressiveness as a tool of keeping the other side in a state of stress and hopes to control the conflict through this behavior ("strategy of blackmail"), and totally the other when the state of the conflict itself becomes a threat (Nye, Allison, and Carnesale, 1988). A major task of any rational player in a military conflict is to keep the state of the conflict under control and not to give the other side a chance to overtake it. Or, as an alternative, the task is to establish a system of joint control over the state of the conflict and to deny to any third party the possibility of interfering.

Usually, each side in a conflict wants to acquire the means to control the state of the conflict. There are means to achieve that goal: acquisition of the position of power through development of a unilateral military advantage, imposition of some sort of unilateral "rules of conduct", creation of a biased friendly environment around the conflict, etc. Depending on the balance of forces in the conflict, this may either help indeed to acquire a unilateral capacity to control the state of the conflict, or, vice versa, to increase its instability and unpredictability: if both feel strong enough to counter a possible threat, it helps to stabilize; if the unilateral gain is regarded as destabilizing, the conflict becomes a source of danger itself. The important difference here is between the state of affairs when both sides individually try to keep the conflict under control and thus to stabilize it (what in reality very often leads to instability) and the state of affairs when they understand that they should do it together. A joint search for the stability of the conflict means a great step forward in the process of the conflict management and usually it comes together with the shared goal, first, to reduce the destructiveness of the conflict, and, second, to reduce the conflicting element of the relationship. When the dangers of confrontation are compared with the benefits of stability, very often the desire to continue the struggle becomes questioned (George, 1971).

The attempt to bring more stability into a military conflict usually begins with the problem of the military balance. This balance consists of two different but interrelated parts. On one hand, there are figures, the amount and the type of the weapons which each side may deploy and the resulting capacity to inflict damage on the other side. The methods of calculation of the offensive and defensive capabilities of the two sides (including the state of combat readiness) may be different but, taken together, they give a more or less clear picture of the military capacity of each side. And these capacities may be compared, thus giving the decision-makers the possibility of either considering the balance as a basis for stability or regarding it as a pre-condition for instability if the other side has an edge in some decisive areas (e.g. sophisticated weapons, air force, missiles, WMD, etc.).

On the other hand, there are military doctrines on each side and the level of training of their forces which can either make the existing weapons an asset or a liability. A good example of such a balance is the Arab–Israeli ratio in 1967 or 1973: large amounts of the Soviet-supplied weapons to Egypt and Syria have never balanced the high combat readiness and high level of training of the Israeli troops. So, the military balance in itself is not yet a universal tool to keep the stability of the conflict under control. In order to become one, it has to be activated through a joint effort on both sides (Nuclear Weapons Freeze and Arms Control, 1983).

The central position of the military balance in an adversarial relationship presents a good opportunity for the policy of stabilization of the conflict and of making it hibernate. At the same time, it cannot give a full guarantee of the stability and predictability due to the possibility of a technical or human error which may, even involuntarily, destroy the balance and trigger escalation of the hostility. So, to develop a comprehensive strategy of conflict stabilization, as another step on the way to resolution, several ideas on military balance should be probed (Carnesale and Haass, 1987).

The first is arms control and the second is risk limitation (or control) policy. Arms control is an old and trusted idea. It may, if appropriately used, give a chance not only to establish a balance of military capabilities between the adversaries but also to make this balance verifiable, durable and operational. Generally, arms control may be unilateral, bilateral or multilateral. A good example of a unilateral arms control may be Japan which after World War II adopted a constitution in which the Japanese have pledged not to use their military force for any operations abroad (now reconsidered) and to use them only for self-defense. Another case of unilateral arms control is the commitment of the nations-signatories to multilateral agreements not to acquire certain types of weapons, WMD or conventional, and thus to contribute to some sort of stability of the military situation. Generally, the possibilities of unilateral arms control are grossly understudied: the US decision not to develop the neutron bomb and parallel US and Soviet unilateral pledges to destroy tactical nuclear weapons are good examples of this type of policy.

But the main areas of arms control are bilateral or multilateral agreements which give the possibility of keeping a certain military balance between the signatories in order to avoid arms race. These agreements may be of the "hierarchical" or of the "horizontal" types. An example of the "hierarchical" type is the Washington Conference of 1922 which tired to establish and legitimize a certain ratio of the naval armaments between the participants, fixing the dominant positions of the stronger nations and "recognizing" the rights of the smaller nations for some amount of the armaments. It considered it necessary to include the naval race in a framework which could combine two things: a "right" of the big powers to the maximum level of the armaments (the principle which was delivered into the Non-Proliferation Treaty, 1968) and the "agreement" of the weaker players to adhere to the levels assigned to them by the big powers. The principles of the "hierarchical"

model of arms control, as is evident in NPT, are viable and can still be used in some cases. At least some elements of "hierarchical" arms control exist in the treaty on Conventional Forces in Europe (CFE).

An example of "horizontal" arms control is the case of Soviet–US agreements, mainly in the area of strategic weapons. It began with the mutual agreement on the dismissal of the anti-ballistic systems, continued into the limitation of the most destabilizing weapons and ended with the establishment of ceilings on the levels and types of the allowed weaponry. In 2002, it evolved into the Agreement on the further reduction of the strategic potentials of the USA and Russia. The strategic balance between the two has become "non-provocative" and verifiable: it has established certain unilateral and bilateral verification procedures and generally contributed to the stabilization of the confrontation. The US–Soviet arms control arrangements have played an outstanding role as a means both of limitation of the conflict and of the creation of pre-requisites for the movement toward the end of the confrontation. In the current situation, it helps to keep alive the elements of co-operation between the two nuclear superpowers.

At the same time, there are some serious changes in this area which demand a thorough consideration and some new approaches. After the abrogation of the Anti-Ballistic Missiles (ABM) treaty of 1972 by the Bush administration in 2003, there is a perspective of deployment of the global US ABM system which to a large extent may take over some of the functions of strategic arms control. It may hurt the positions of Russia since it continued to be loyal to the dead ABM treaty and has stopped the work on its own ABM with the exclusion of the sophisticated anti-aircraft weaponry. The nervous reaction of Moscow to the plans of the deployment of the US anti-missile facilities in Europe demonstrated that the value of the arms control agreements of the period of the end of the Cold War may be compromised (Krahman, 2005).

The importance of arms control in the strategic and other areas of the armaments (intermediate and tactical nuclear as well as conventional) was not only that it has created pre-conditions for the end of the Soviet–American confrontation in the late 1980s. It has given a rather reliable and promising tool for possible changes in other strategic nuclear dyads: USA–China, China–India, India–Pakistan. Disregarding the successes at the end of the Soviet–US Cold War, the state of relations in these areas has hardly changed the value of the "horizontal" arms control and is far from being exhausted.

Multilateral arms control usually includes arms limitations and commitments in different areas. The Conventional Armed Forces Agreement in Europe (1990) is an outstanding example of such a multilateral commitment which, at the time of coming into force, has helped greatly to stabilize the situation in Europe and to put an end to NATO–WTO confrontation (Ripsman, 2005). From this point of view, it is important to study further the fate of the CFE treaty which has already become a hostage of the US–Russian differences on the anti-missile defenses. Such important areas of arms control as nuclear-free zones in different parts of the world and other regional arrangements may become questioned if the idea of the conventional arms control in Europe falls victim to the differences in US–Russian relations. Limitation on the purchase and acquisition of some "provocative" types of weapons can also be regarded as cases of "horizontal" arms control, for example, the conventions on limitations and even the ban on the missile technologies transfer.

Arms control is dutifully considered a very effective means of reducing the level of military confrontation and making it more stable and controllable. The other element of the same policy is the risk reduction measures which were introduced by the two superpowers, the USA and USSR, in the aftermath of the Cuban missile crisis. One of the results of the assessment of the Cuban crisis was the conclusion of a high risk potential which accompanied the arms race between the two. As was mentioned, the risk was a result of a high probability of a technical

or human error in the huge and complicated system of the strategic confrontation. Under some conditions, the technical systems could fail (especially the long-range observation and early-warning systems), while in others, the human factor could become crucial (in a mocking form, note the scenario of Stanley Kubik's "Dr Strangelove").

Understandably, the cost of such a "failure" could be too high and absolutely unacceptable for both sides, given what they understood during the October days of 1962. And, as a result, the conflict strategy of both has been modified almost overnight: if before the Cuban crisis, the "massive retaliation" strategy was a main tool of the confrontation on both sides, one of the first lessons from the crisis was a change towards "stabilization" and "risk reduction", or "stabilization through risk reduction". It contained the establishment of a reliable communication between the two sides, agreement on the procedures if something like a new crisis would erupt, and negotiation on different possible scenarios of risk development.

All in all, it took almost a decade of intensive diplomatic effort for both superpowers to agree on the measures which could reduce the risks of confrontation and make the possibility of an inadvertent conflict much lower. Attempts to start a parallel track of arms control agreements, disregarding the conclusion of the Partial Test Ban Treaty (PTBT) in 1963, proved unsuccessful until the risk reduction phase was completed. The then leaders of both sides, US President Johnson and the Soviet Prime Minister Kosygin, at their historical meeting in Glassboro (October 1967), agreed that since negotiations on risk reduction were going at full speed (including US–Soviet joint efforts on the NPT), they could start planning for the beginning of the first substantial arms control negotiation of the strategic arms limitation (SALT) which began in 1969.

Neither risk reduction nor arms control brings an end to a military confrontation though they limit substantially the possibility of an outbreak of hostilities. But they open up a way toward a stable military balance between the adversaries and, thus, make it possible to think about a profound alternative to confrontation, especially if it threatens to exhaust the financial and economic resources of the sides. Further steps in the direction of resolution become possible in two ways. One, domestic, relates to serious measures of disarmament and reduction of the military expense. And this becomes one of the most difficult tasks because reconsideration of the policy in a confrontation includes changes in budget spending, in the appropriations policy, in military spending, in force deployment and other measures which may have hard consequences for the economic perspectives of the whole area, for the state of unemployment, and for the investment in research.

The other is associated with a complete reconsideration of the conflict strategy and of the relation toward the adversary (Blum, 2005). This means the necessity for a profound reassessment of the nature of threat and of its background which sometimes may be followed by critical consequences, as was the fate of the Soviet Union after the end of the Cold War. If a system of political, economic and social relations was built for the purposes of war, as was Stalin's Soviet Union or Hitler's Reich, then with the reduction of tensions and forthcoming resolution of the conflict, the danger of disintegration of that system becomes real. The best minds in Gorbachev's Soviet government never gave due consideration to that.

From stabilization to resolution

There is a vast gap between stability of the conflict and its resolution. It is even possible to say that once a conflict is stabilized (as, for example, Korea in 1953), the incentives for its resolution sometimes become much less powerful than when the conflict was a war (Zagar and Kilgour, 2006). But no conflict may be solved without prior stabilization which is simply a pre-requisite for resolution. So, the problem is: what should be done when a conflict is stabilized, in order to move forward and to work out a resolution strategy?

To begin with, here we come to one of the most crucial questions asked at the beginning of the chapter: what is a "solution" for a military conflict and confrontation? When it is an open hostility, the answer to this question is simple and unequivocal: an end of hostilities, a cease-fire. And in the absolute majority of cases, this is the first, and very often, only answer: all the efforts on the part of those who are responsible for the international security (UN Security Council, regional security arrangements, big nations) are applied to put an end to the war. Very often, the end of the hostilities is regarded as even more important than a possible solution to the heart of the conflict: for example, the pressure of the UN, US administration, EC and others on Israel during the last war in Lebanon was so strong that the Israeli government had to cut down its operations, though maybe a resolute destruction of the Hezbollah could be more helpful for the further evolution of the conflict. But in any case, when a military conflict or a war takes place, the purpose of the response to it is absolutely clear: to stop the fighting!

And the ideal case would be if the end of fighting could be transformed into the end of the conflict itself (Williams and Caldwell, 2006). In reality, that happens mainly when the fighting is finished with a resolute defeat of one side and a complete victory of the other, complete in the full sense of the word: capitulation of the losing side. Only in this case, as is evident from the history of the end of WWII, does the possibility appear of putting an end to the conflict. The USA has correctly learned the lessons of WWI and that is why President Roosevelt suggested, first, declaring capitulation of the Hitler regime as the main purpose of the war (the Casablanca conference of 1943) and, second, occupying the defeated Axis nations, in order to introduce such changes in their political and economic systems that they would never be allowed to become revenge seekers (the main sense of the Yalta and Potsdam conferences in 1945). This was a genuine and 100 percent excellent end to the conflict. Such ends do not happen often, though there were also successful cases of the

Taliban regime in Afghanistan and Saddam's regime in Iraq (Rose, 2005).

What about confrontations? Or about conflicts when the phase of the open hostilities is ended due to the pressure from the outside? And here, at least in theory, though there are some practical solutions, we come to two different strategies. One of them is concentrated mainly on a purely military aspect (disarmament), while the other goes much more deeply into the political area. The first resolution strategy is based on the cost-benefit analysis and uses as a starting point the assessment of the comparative evaluation: does the subject of the conflict deserve that much risk and expense? There is always the possibility of judging how much a positive end of the conflict may give to a nation and how much this nation should invest in the winning strategy.

It does not include such "non-material" values as prestige, influence, and glory but in general the level of the current knowledge gives the possibility of having a solid judgment on input–output ratio and its validity for the relevant strategy, including possible destruction and human losses if open hostilities happen. As a result, the decision-maker may always take a rational decision based on the comparison between expected gains and expected losses. And if the result is not in favor of the military strategy, there is the possibility of looking for a non-violent solution, following Lao Tse's advice: if you cannot afford a military solution, try non-military.

The other resolution strategy is much more complicated. If the adversary is not destroyed and has not capitulated and the confrontation is ended with the 0:0 score (even if the other side disintegrates after the end of the conflict, as did the Soviet Union), then the question is: how viable is this solution? Will it survive its success? The conflict resolution thinking in the area of military conflicts and confrontations usually ended at the stage of the peaceful settlement and never went further, while the cases of the US–North Korean, US–Vietnamese and Soviet/Russian–Afghani relations after the

end of hostilities showed that the end of hostilities does not mean the end of the underlying conflict. It continues in the form of a political confrontation which may one day resume the military dimension. All this was well known and did not cause much concern until the issue touched the nuclear powers.

Recent developments in the US–Russian relations raise one very important issue. Since the US–Soviet Cold War was ended without any "peace treaty", that is, a document which would frame the legal and political aspects of this event (maybe because of the disintegration of the Soviet Union, or maybe because no one cared about such "formalities"), both sides experienced certain hardships in formulating their vision of the future of their relations. It concerned the type of their relations, identification of their interests which could either correspond to the interests of the other side or, at least, do not deny them; it also needed to prescribe mechanisms and methods of solution for both old and new problems in their relations.

In wider terms, this case tells us that a solution to a military confrontation, contrary to open military conflicts, is a much more complicated case. It is not enough to stop fighting (if it goes on) and to agree to a cease-fire. It is not enough to agree on some disarmament and verification procedure. It is not even enough to work out confidence building measures and to adhere to them strictly. What is needed and is extremely important is to find out carefully which were the sources of the initial conflict, why it has brought both sides to a confrontation, what role was played by the military factors, whether military factors could bring a desirable solution to the confrontation and, finally, what should be done to ensure that in the future the partners will not go back to the trenches if the situation changes. Besides, there should also be some program of positive interaction, of co-operation. Otherwise, the efforts to leave the conflict behind may become pointless.

This subject becomes extremely important today. There is the problem of ending the US war in Iraq. There is the problem of ending military confrontations in areas which play the role of the sites of conflicts since the days of the Cold War (Korea, Indian subcontinent, the Middle East, Cyprus, Balkans). There is the problem of "rogue states" or, in other words, "axis of evil". There is Africa with its endless list of ethnic wars. There is a growing perspective of future conflicts between states in transformation, contenders for space and resources. In short, there is a whole agenda of possible military conflicts and this is the high time to work out acceptable procedures and means for the resolution and prevention of military conflicts.

REFERENCES

Axelrod, Robert (1984) *The Evolution of Cooperation.* New York: Basic Books

Betts, Richard K. (1982) *Surprise Attack: Lessons for Defense Planning.* Washington, DC: Brookings Institution.

Blum, Andrew (2005) "The Future of Conflict: Exploring the Use of Comparative Scenarios in Track II Peace Building", *International Studies Perspectives*, 6, 3, 342–57.

Bracken, Paul (1983) *The Command and Control of Nuclear Forces.* New Haven and London: Yale University Press.

Carnesale, Albert and Richard Haass, eds (1987) *Superpower Arms Control: Setting the Record Straight.* Cambridge, MA: Ballinger Publishing Co.

Fortna, Virginia P. (2002) "Inside and Out: Peacekeeping and the Duration of Peace after Civil and Interstate Wars", *International Studies Review*, 5, 4, 97–114.

Franck, Thomas (2005) "When Nations Collide, Must Law be Silent?", *Peace Review: A Journal of Social Justice*, 19, 2, 227–36.

George, Alexander (1971) *The Limits of Coercive Diplomacy: Laos, Cuba, Vietnam.* Boston: Little, Brown Publishing Co.

George, Alexander L., Philip J. Farley, and Alexander Dallin, eds (1988) *US–Soviet Security Cooperation: Achievements, Failures, Lessons.* New York and Oxford: Oxford University Press.

Krahman, Elke (2005) "American Hegemony or Global Governance? Competing Visions of International Security", *International Studies Review*, 7, 4, 531–46.

Kremenyuk, Victor (2006) *Mezhdunarodnye Konflikty: Problemy Upravlenia I Kontrolia (International Conflicts: Problems of Control and Management).* Moscow: Iskran Publishers.

Langlois, Jean-Pierre P., and Catherine C. Langlois (2005) "Fully Informed and On the Road to Ruin: The Perfect Failure of Asymmetric Deterrence", *International Studies Quarterly*, 49, 3, 503–28.

McNamara, Robert S. (1986) *Blundering Into Disaster: Surviving the First Century of the Nuclear Age.* New York: Pantheon Books.

Nuclear Weapons Freeze and Arms Control (1983) Proceedings of a Symposium held at the American Academy of Arts and Sciences, January 13–15.

Nye, Joseph S., Graham T. Allison and Albert Carnesale, eds (1988) *Fateful Visions: Avoiding Nuclear Catastrophe.* Cambridge, MA: Ballinger Publishing Co.

Parsons, Kenneth A. (2007) "Structural Violence and Power", *Peace Review: A Journal of Social Justice*, 19, 2, 173–82.

Rapoport, Anatol (1960) *Fights, Games and Debates.* Ann Arbor: University of Michigan Press.

Rose, Euclid A. (2005) "From a Punitive to a Bargaining Model of Sanctions: Lessons from Iraq", *International Studies Quarterly*, 49, 3, 459–80.

Ripsman, Norrin M. (2005) "Two Stages of Transition from a Region of War to a Region of Peace: Realist Transition and Liberal Endurance", *International Studies Quarterly*, 49, 4, 669–94.

Sarkees, Meredith, Frank Wayman, and David Singer, J. (2003) "Inter-State, Intra-State and Extra-State Wars: A Comprehensive Look at Their Distribution over Time, 1816–1997", *International Studies Quarterly*, 47, 1, 49–70.

Schelling, Thomas (1960) *The Strategy of Conflict.* Cambridge, MA: University of Harvard Press.

Vasquez, John A. (2004) "The Probability of War, 1816–1992", *International Studies Quarterly*, 48, 1, 1–28.

Weeks, John, ed. (1991) *Beyond Superpower Rivalry: Latin America and the Third World.* New York and London: New York University Press.

Williams, Robert E. and Dan Caldwell (2006) "Jus Post Bellum: Just War Theory and the Principles of Just Peace", *International Studies Perspective*, 7, 4, 309–20.

Woodwell, Douglas (2004) "Unwelcome Neighbors: Shared Ethnicity and International Conflict during the Cold War", *International Studies Quarterly*, 48, 1, 197–224.

Xenias, Anastasia (2005) "Can a Global Peace Last even if Achieved? Huntington and the Democratic Peace", *International Studies Review*, 7, 3, 357–86.

Zagar, Frank C. and D. Marc Kilgour (2007) "The Deterrence Versus Restraint Dilemma in Extended Deterrence", *International Studies Review*, 8, 4, 623–42.

Zartman, I. William, ed. (2001) *Preventive Negotiation: Avoiding Conflict Escalation.* Carnegie Commission on Preventing Deadly Conflicts. London, Boulder, New York, Toronto, and Oxford: Rowman and Littlefield Publishing Co.

Zartman, I. William and Victor Kremenyuk, eds (1995) *Cooperative Security: Reducing Third World Wars.* Syracuse, NY: University of Syracuse Press.

Zartman, I. William and Victor Kremenyuk, eds (2005) *Peace Versus Justice: Negotiating Forward- and Backward-Looking Outcomes.* London, Boulder, New York, Toronto, and Oxford: Rowman and Littlefield Publishing Co.

34

Training and Education

Paul Meerts

TRAINING RESOLUTE CONFLICT NEGOTIATORS

A chapter on training and education in conflict resolution can go three ways: either it gives us the state of the art in training and education (Hemery 2005), or it is a recommendation of how trainers should train and educate (Boomen 2001), or it is a tool for training (Mühlen 2005). This chapter aspires to fulfill all three options in the limited space available. But it will first look at the question of why, and to what extent, training is of use to enhance the effectiveness of 'conflict resolutionalists'. After this, an overview of the present situation in 'Trainingland' (Seminaristan) will be given. Thirdly, recommendations will follow, expanding on some earlier work of the author. Fourthly, this chapter will provide interested readers with a selected set of instruments to be used in training those who need to be resolute in conflict situations. It is a very specific set of tools, though one could also use other mechanisms. It is hypothesized that the educators know—or will find out

by themselves—how to use the exercises in this chapter, though limited assistance will be given through a short introduction to each instrument. The exercises themselves can be found in the Annex. The chosen modes of conflict management are international negotiation processes. Any other inroad might have been legitimate: facilitation, mediation, arbitration, adjudication or even warfare. For practical and ideological reasons, as this Handbook of Conflict Resolution also bears the seal of the Processes of International Negotiation (PIN) Project of the International Institute of Applied Systems Analysis (IIASA), international negotiation has been chosen as the focal point. It is postulated that negotiation is one of the most important and effective tools in prevention and resolution (Zartman 2001), and it is therefore useful to train conflict managers in the art and science of this process. An effective negotiator will be able to deal with conflicts in an efficient way. But what is an effective conflict manager/negotiator and what can training contribute? Can it make a difference?

THE VALUE OF TRAINING AND ITS LIMITATIONS

If negotiation is one of the main tools in conflict management, then the first question to be asked should be: can we learn to do better? If it is a skill (science), then we can learn to do better. If it is in-born (art), not much can be done. Is negotiation art or science? One might solve this problem by writing a book titled 'The Art and Science of Negotiation' (Raiffa 1982) as PIN's father has done, suggesting that negotiation in conflict resolution is both an art and a science. It may not be in-born, but at least the skill of effective negotiation behavior is fostered by culture (Faure 2003). In my own experience over the last three decades, negotiators can be trained to do better.

Impact of training

It is best seen in courses with a duration of several months. From 1967 till 1982, the Society of International Affairs of The Netherlands organized a 'Course on International Relations' (LBB) for young Dutch diplomats, navy officers, post-academic civil servants and post-graduate students. At the very start, a simulation exercise (NATO or EEC) was introduced as a tool to get more grip on substance (Lipschits 1971). This game started at the beginning of the six-month course, ran parallel to the regular lectures, and served as its one-week finale. Chaired by an experienced diplomat (a high level ambassador or a former Minister of Foreign Affairs), it focused on content, but nevertheless participants had to negotiate a common document or a full night— starting at eight o'clock in the evening, and finishing at eight o'clock the next morning. At the time the author of this chapter took responsibility (end of the 1970s), the course was down to three/four months. Nothing was done on training in negotiation. For five years, I watched ten courses struggling with the negotiation process, people being chaotic, non-procedural, non-relational, distributional, positional, inflexible and aggressive. Outcomes were meager or never came

about. Participants complained about lack of negotiation skills and lack of training. But in all those years, no trainers could be hired to do the job. This was partly because they were too expensive, and partly because commercial trainers were abundant but trainers on diplomatic negotiations were absent—at least on the continent of Europe.

In 1983, the Society merged with three other institutions into the Netherlands Institute of International Relations, 'Clingendael', and the training problem was tackled right away. Having more budget space as Director of Training and Education, I could invite expensive private sector negotiation trainers, work with them and share our public sector simulation games, thereby training Clingendael staff in interstate negotiation processes. This took some seven years and the effects on the course members of the LBB were amazing: more effective negotiation processes, better outcomes. Since the late 1980s, separate specific negotiation seminars were created and exported to diplomatic academies (Meerts 1992) outside The Netherlands. Diplomatic institutes were—and still are—in need of training in diplomatic skills like negotiation but lacked appropriate trainers and exercises. A special workbook was created to overcome the shortage of exercises in training negotiation techniques (Meerts 2007). The specific negotiation seminars were also used to update LBB alumni. LBB course members from the period 1983–1993 did better on average than those from the 1972–1982 period who had not been trained in negotiation techniques. These are observations by the author, however, and cannot be sustained by hard data. But other analyses about the potential contribution of training to resolve international conflict underscore the opinion that training does make a difference (Fisher 1997, 471–486).

Impact of culture

Another observation by the author is on the difference of behavior of students and professionals in regular seminars on international negotiation processes since 1989, delivered in some 80 countries around the world.

The duration of these seminars is limited to two to four days. Most 'seminarists' had never received any formal negotiation training before, and if so, they had been trained in the 'Harvard Mode'. The individual 'growth' of participants depends very much, I observed, on their cultural background. As culture is an even more ambivalent subject than negotiation (or processes in general—they are like water: you cannot easily grasp them but they are essentials in life), I will be careful here. Still, my observation in the past fifteen years has been that trainees from low-context cultures were more open to training than those from high-context cultures (Cohen 1991). At the same time, the learning curve went exactly the other way around. Participants from the Balkans, South-Caucasus and Central Asia did much better at the end of the seminar than those from Britain, Germany and France. One could postulate that students form open societies have less problem in absorbing the training sessions but at the same time, they already have an attitude fostering effective negotiation behavior, that is, the management of the process in such a way that it will result in a substantial—in most cases forward-looking (Zartman 2005)—outcome. Training did make a difference as they were more effective in dealing with the process at the end, than at the beginning of the seminar. But on average, they did not experience the attitudinal change I observed in diplomats from countries in the Middle East or Eastern Europe.

In other words, it is more rewarding to work with students and professionals from countries where give-and-take in the interstate sphere is less common, where concession-making is seen as loss-of-face. Losing is of course psychologically more difficult than winning, and this process can create entrapment situations destroying fruitful win/win processes. But as trust is more secured in—for example, European Union negotiations—diplomats from Western (and at a later stage Central) European countries were more easy on give-and-take than their brothers from the outskirts of the Union. That might be societal culture

or political culture. Some behavioral change occurred, but this was not a genuine 'Aha Erlebnis' as was the case with participants from high-context societies. This difference in training impact might also be linked to the fact that West Europeans—and Americans even more so—are used to modern training methodologies while they are relatively new for East Europeans.

These observations are even more interesting as diplomats and civil servants from South-Eastern Europe, South Caucasus and the Middle East are born in high-density bargaining societies. Their context is of an environment where negotiation is part of daily life. In Western Europe, that context withered away in the 19th century. Obviously, bargaining in the soukh is not perceived in the same way as haggling between states. This might have to do with the honor factor. The state should not be corrupted by concession making. Face-saving is essential, thereby concession making is not seen as a viable option. Therefore, negotiators-in-training of the high-context parts of the world will not use their inherent haggling skills to the extend they are capable of doing this, while others lack these skills but compensate for this with their ability to be more open to the process of trading concessions, diagnosing package deals where others don't want to see them. Training can therefore help negotiators form high-context cultures to change their perception in such a way that they feel concession-exchange between states can be legitimate. As soon as they are made aware of this, their reservoir of haggling skills will help them to become a much more effective bargainer on the international platform—maybe more effective then their low-context colleagues, but training is a prerequisite here.

STATE OF THE ART: PRACTITIONERS, RESEARCHERS AND TRAINERS

Entering the International Institute of Applied Systems Analysis for the second conference on international negotiation processes at the end of the 1980s, I wondered how anything substantial could come out of a conference with so many people from so many different backgrounds. Several things struck me at that time: first, the differences in thinking between East European (mainly Soviet) academicians and academics from Europe and the United States; second, the number of my fellow countrymen present, all of them unknown to me. It was at that moment that my present-day negotiation network, and hence the Dutch PIN Group, was created. But my most important observation was that practitioners, researchers and trainers do not communicate at the same level. Forget the fact that many researchers are also teachers of international negotiation at universities and that they use their discoveries of the 'secrets' of negotiation to enhance their students' insight—teaching is not training; teaching is about 'the literature'. And although simulation games are used to illustrate theory, teaching is still a far cry from real training.

Charismatic trainers

Trainers are—in the best-case scenario—capable of providing participants with experience of negotiation processes. However, unlike teachers/researchers, trainers are often unaware of the bulk of modern literature. They often copy something that has been copied from somebody else who once developed a practicum on the basis of academic insights. Trainers can be charismatic people who often know more about private-sector management than about negotiation and have the empathy to influence the thinking and framing of course members. They radiate strength. Participants will often remember their personalities many years afterward, but forget what they taught about negotiation.

One would expect a natural life-cycle to consist of practitioners helping researchers to understand the soul of the negotiation process and trainers using the insights from research to train effective (future) practitioners. One would expect a mutual understanding to grow, just as has happened within PIN over the past 20 years—that the three groups

would come together in joint forums. While there is somewhat more communality today, however, on average, the cleavages between practitioners, academics and trainers have not been bridged. Why? And what's the remedy?

Old-fashioned diplomats

First of all, many practitioners, especially those in the interstate negotiations arena—mainly diplomats—do not really believe that negotiation is a science. To many, especially the old-fashioned diplomats, it is an art: in-born, something that cannot be learned. One might hope for a change as time goes by, but for the moment, these senior diplomats hold the most important diplomatic posts and dominate the scene. Apart from their perception—and perception determines reality—they are often handicapped by not understanding their own behavior. They are effective diplomatic negotiators, but they are not really aware why. What am I doing in order to be effective? How are we negotiating? They are so caught up in their routine that they often do not have the ability to explain what—in their behavior—made them effective negotiators.

Losing face?

Frequently, practitioners have a certain *dédain* for negotiation research and academic education. They do not really believe in training as a tool for becoming a better negotiator. Of course, I am stereotyping here, but many negotiation practitioners do not want to waste time by conferring with academics. And they also do not want negotiation 'experts' looking into their kitchens, first because this might harm the 'national' interests of their country (secrecy of negotiation in order to maintain room for maneuver) and, second, because they might lose face if consultants observe that mistakes are being made and opportunities lost. We should keep in mind here that even diplomatic negotiators are human beings (sic!). They sometimes show emotions and nonverbal leaks (e.g. unconscious body language), and they do not want this to be revealed to the outside world. The principle of 'open covenants, openly arrived at' has never worked.

And then there is the problem that practitioners, that is, civil servants, are not by definition effective teachers. Actually, they are often boring and have a problem putting a message across to their audience. Of course, there are notable exceptions, but on the whole it is a bad idea to ask (former) ambassadors to teach negotiation. Their accounts of the past do not raise awareness; we need exercises to do that.

Simulation games

Even those ambassadors who are ready to work with simulations still pose problems for the training staff. They look too one-sidedly at the reality level of the games and criticize them for not being correct in detail. However, this kind of realism stops good simulation games from working smoothly. It creates unnecessary complications, hampering the dynamics of the exercise and thus causing participants to lose the plot. After all, good role play only works well if the substance and procedure of the simulation exercise are easy to understand and the process and implementation are complicated—and thus interesting. If the game is too realistic, course members will have problems experiencing the processes. Balancing reality and fiction is one of the major dilemmas in games designed for learning processes. This is the first 'reality dilemma'. The game must be realistic, but does not—and should not— need to fully mirror reality, for in that case the game will fail to accomplish what it is aiming for: training the (potential) international negotiator. In some cases, the dilemma can be resolved by writing a forward-looking case, reflecting future probabilities (Ebner and Yael 2005).

For academics and trainers, this poses a problem. Practitioners sometimes spoil simulation games by openly commenting in a negative way, undermining the legitimacy of academics and trainers and their exercises in the eyes of the students. More serious is the second 'reality dilemma' where practitioners do not allow researchers (and trainers) to observe real-time negotiations. Negotiation 'experts' are sometimes invited to watch bilateral negotiations, but in multilateral interstate bargaining especially, the closed session is the rule. The result of this is twofold. First, practitioners do not profit from the insights of negotiation research, and serious mistakes are made on matters like timing and trust, strategy and tactics, skills and styles— indeed, in many consultations, we know that obvious mistakes were made and that process experts would probably have noticed them and helped the process stay on track. Second, the practitioner's attitude seriously hampers academics and trainers: not being able to observe real negotiation processes means that alternative methods, such as observing mock communication and studying *mémoires* and other written accounts, have to be used to approximate the real processes. Interviews and surveys might help a bit, but interviewees have a tendency to leave out the things they did wrong and to stress their moments of glory.

Video and DVD

A good alternative to watching international negotiation processes would be to be able to videotape them. This has been done in some rare instances. One famous example is the tape *Space Between Words* from 1971 (sic!) on the negotiation process that created the United Nations Disaster Relief Organization (UNDRO), of which a simulation exercise will be found in this chapter. In general, there is a real need for more openness on the side of governments in order to help 'negotiationists' uncover the underlying forces and dynamics of the international negotiation process. There are many tapes revealing negotiation processes and actor behavior, but they are simulated proceedings. Negotiators are actors, and all these videos and DVDs focus on the private sector. Not being real and not being public-sector seriously limits their value as training tools.

Commercial trainers

The private sector is relatively more open. Researchers have been given the chance to observe and measure labor negotiations, for example, and some boast that they can prophesy the outcome of this kind of one-dimensional bargaining with 90 percent precision. But this does not help us much in the international sphere, where issues like sovereignty play a major role and where multilateral processes are abundant. An interesting question, of course, is why companies are (1) more open about having negotiations observed and (2) show more willingness to spend much more money on negotiation training than governments and international organizations. Money is the clue here. Firms are in real need of effective negotiators, as ineffective representatives can mean poor business results and therefore loss of revenue. It is no coincidence that real training devices on negotiation were developed in the private sector by commercial trainers long before diplomatic negotiation seminars were launched. At the author's (Clingendael) Institute in the early 1980s, we transformed the findings of private-sector seminars into public-sector practica. Interestingly enough, commercial trainers used these transformed concepts to train civil servants, to whom business workshops were of little interest, given the different nature of public-sector and private-sector negotiations caused—inter alia—by different stakeholders. In the meantime, the question is to what extent mixed seminars would be useful for training business people in their dealings with civil servants and vice versa.

Characters versus culture

For the same reason, business is also ready to invest in intercultural seminars, while governments often see this as unnecessary. Ministries of foreign affairs, in particular, feel that their diplomatic mores overarch cultural differences and that culture is therefore not a real factor in negotiation processes. Research done at Clingendael Institute showed that EU Council working group negotiators see characters, rather than culture, as an obstacle to negotiations. However, the research also showed that the Dutch ministries (transport, social welfare, agriculture) that do pay attention to building relationships with fellow ministries of other EU member states have had fewer problems with culture than those (notably the Ministry of Economic Affairs) that did not invest in networks: prioritizing on issues, neglecting people.

Second-hand knowledge

As has been stated, we also see an abyss between academics and trainers for several reasons. One reason might be that academics feel that trainers—especially those from private-sector companies—do not really deliver anything worthwhile. Their knowledge of the literature is often scarce, second-hand, and confined to pieces of 'academic' work that are long past their sell-by date—literature passed on to them by others who often translated it into relevant exercises. Trainers also have a problem understanding the more complicated academic findings and, even if they do understand, the complexity of the scientific findings often prevents their being transformed into practical tools. Trainers will thus have to create their own tools. And just as practitioners often do not believe in the value and relevance of the academic findings, so too the academics mistrust the added value and correctness of the training devices. Academic programs on negotiation analysis are on the whole very different from training modules and are judged by many trainers—and practitioners, by the way—to be too theoretical and therefore not applicable to the education of new practitioners.

Commerce

Academics go for substance, trainers for money. There are many exceptions to this 'rule', but the fact is that trainers are often in the service of a company—or self-employed—and train for a living. They find it just too costly to invest time in academic conferences and writing book chapters and articles, and they are always in a hurry so that training programs will often be 'routinized' into formats that can be applied to any situation. Tailor-made seminars are quite rare; seminars balancing good content and good exercises even more so. In other words, not-for-profit organizations play a beneficial role here, as they have the resources to do research and therefore to act as vanguard in the renewal of training and education materials.

On the other hand, commercial trainers are often more aware—and better educated in—modern training techniques that many academic teachers lack. Apart from this, there is something like being 'gifted'. In order to make the money they need, commercial trainers work on seminars that are attractive to trainees—not only by content, but foremost by method. Therefore, these trainers develop more advanced methods of training than academics, but they themselves have to be charismatic in order to lure institutions into sending their staff to their training outfits. Some natural gift is needed to create effective theatre as well as effective training.

Academia

It may be because of this perception of negotiation as a 'mere' technical tool that non–Anglo-Saxon universities are—with the exception of a few like Mannheim and the College of Europe in Bruges—not willing to accept negotiation research and teaching as a viable academic study. An academic branch of the study of international relations? In the Anglo-Saxon world, negotiation studies and training are increasingly accepted as a useful adjunct to political and other sciences—often in the context of *conflict studies*—but this is not so much the case in Europe, Asia, Africa and Latin America. As a study revealing one of the major vehicles of international politics, however, a study of and training in negotiation studies is worthwhile because of the importance of (future) practitioners and scientists knowing how to deal effectively with the issues affecting our world, and because it is one

way for a country to build a more effective international policy.

Continental universities might take a while before they will be aware of modern literature on international negotiation processes, before they will acknowledge negotiation as an integral part of their academic curriculum. This is partly due to a lack of knowledge, being unaware of academic progress made in the past 20 years. On the other hand, it is snobbism too. How could something connected to skill training be academic? In that sense, negotiation research is the victim of the success of negotiation training. The latter is better know than the first, being overshadowed by it. Some mathematicians are making progress in academia with their methodologies on negotiation processes. Probably because their scientific approach strengthens the perception of others that somebody who uses such complicated methods must be a true academician and therefore his/her subject true as well. It will take a while till international negotiation will be seen as an indispensable ingredient of international relations. But in Europe the time will come, as it did in North America.

Diplomacy

It is vital for diplomatic and other organizations around the world to have interstate negotiation on their agenda, and not just by asking (former) ambassadors to speak about it. That is why the International Institute for Applied Systems Analysis is supporting the Processes of International Negotiation Project: while comprehensive knowledge about issues is undeniably important, so too are the ways of implementing it. Processes are the roads to implementation, while master classes, workshops and seminars are vital in training the people who have to fulfill the policies of the countries and resolve the conflicts bewitching them. It is interesting to see that more and more commercial trainers explore the diplomatic market. In order to be successful, they are forced to research the diplomatic features of international negotiation processes and to develop simulation exercises that accommodate the needs of the diplomat and civil servant, rather than those of the salesman.

MODUS OPERANDI

How to train international negotiation in an effective way? The first question is of course about effectiveness. I would define effectiveness as the ability of the trainer/training to influence the trainee to the degree that he/she will be able to manage the negotiation in such a way that an optimal outcome will be reached. This might only be so if the trainee changes his/her perception and thereby behavior. There is a multitude of ways to approach training effectiveness. But as we have seen before, testing these concepts on their ability to change real-world behavior remains a major stumbling block (Wheeler 2006, 187–197).

Trainers

We have already discussed the importance of charisma and I would like to add the dimension of being skilled and knowledgeable. Skill is a prerequisite for any training, commercial or diplomatic. If a trainer does not know how to handle participants, effectiveness will be nil. Empathy is needed to understand the emotional problems trainees face in negotiation. Being well trained him/herself is imperative. But training in itself will not suffice. A certain measure of artistry is needed, and we discussed the importance of charisma. Talent is needed, as skill alone will not do. Artistry, by the way, will often be aligned to people whose field of interest lies in science, diplomacy or bureaucracy—not so to politicians, maybe.

Being knowledgeable that case negotiation processes are part of international politics is important. A trainer without in-depth insights into the mechanics and the issues of modern politics, diplomacy and bureaucracy cannot convince his students. In many regions in the world, this is not enough. Thorough historical knowledge is needed to understand the 'soul'

of the diplomats being trained, the context their countries are in and have been in. 'Where they come from' is as important as 'where they go to'. In order to deliver effective training for diplomats from Armenia and Azerbaijan, it is vital to be aware of the history and present situation of the relationships between these states and their people. No training can even begin to be effective, to have an impact, if underlying traumas and motives are misunderstood.

Trainers who look for advice on training might look at the work of Pierre Casse, the most charismatic trainer this author is acquainted with, who is even capable of putting participants in a trance without them being aware of it (Casse and Deol 1985). Another excellent charismatic trainer—Bob Weibel—did not really publish till now. The most specialized trainer for trainers is without doubt the man who calls himself 'Thiagi' (www.thiagi.com). His train-the-trainers workshops are famous and effective. He focuses on the creation of short exercises raising awareness among trainers and trainees. Recently, John Hemery reported on Seminars on Chairing and Negotiation for UK diplomats and civil servants who were trained in preparation of the UK EU Presidency (Hemery and Meerts 2006, 197–208), highlighting the methodology used by the trainers involved. As far as broader negotiation literature is concerned, one might take a look at research overviews provided by serious academic researchers (Jönsson 2000).

Trainees

For the trainee, it is of course important to be able to learn how to be a more effective conflict manager using negotiation as his or her tool. The level of language education, the native language, etc. will have a decisive impact on the question 'is the student fit for negotiation training'? But also his political and bureaucratic system is a factor. In some systems, it will be difficult for participants to be open enough to undergo the change needed for being a more effective negotiator. Sometimes this is subconscious: the student is not aware of his external and internal resistance to experience the negotiation process in a good manner. Sometimes trainees are well aware of these constraints but cannot participate freely as some of their colleagues are secret agents being there with the assignment to spy on their compatriots.

Once I watched a group of Iranian diplomats simulating a meeting of the United Nations Security Council. The first intervention came from a person playing the role of a French diplomat. He started his statement as Iranians have to do, honoring God. Another Iranian, representing the United States, raised objections saying this was not normal practice in UNSC. After an informal back-channel debate of 20 minutes, they decided to live up to reality, notwithstanding the danger of one of them reporting this to Teheran. On another occasion, Russian diplomatic students felt free enough to explain the unreliable behavior of the Russian representing the Russian Federation, by saying—I quote the Russian 'playing' the United States—that 'the Russians can never be trusted'. It takes a Russian to say it; I would not dare.

Trainees who want to know more about negotiation processes might turn to the work of Willem Mastenbroek (2002), Saner (2005), Nierenberg (1976), Karrass (1992) or the classics of Fisher and Ury. The Fisher and Ury book *Getting to Yes* (1991) set the trend for common problem solving and has been followed by a range of publications pondering on the same theme. Trainees should be aware of the cultural bias in these books. The approaches of Nierenberg, Karrass and Fisher and Ury are quite American, of Saner Swiss and of Mastenbroek Dutch. But this can be seen as an advantage: it helps the trainee to be critical. All books meant to take (potential) negotiators 'by-the-hand' are relevant for the context the author is working in, but might have serious defaults in Central and East Asia, Africa and Latin America.

Tools

Trainers have macro and micro tools. Macro tools are the seminars or workshops they deliver. In general, seminars on negotiation should not take too much time—professionals especially have limited time available. The rule of thumb for me: the longer the seminar, the lower the level of participants and vice versa. This implies that a training for junior diplomats can be longer than one for senior diplomats. It does not mean however that levels should not be mixed. It is my experience that mixed groups are very fruitful: young learns from old and vice versa—as young diplomats are fresh from university, the more experienced can learn from them as well. Another good mix is intercultural and/or interdepartmental. The less mix, the less dynamic and the less effective the seminar will be. Of course, the trainer will have to be the intermediary, avoiding misperceptions and miscommunications. This is very demanding and very rewarding. Apart from the level and the nature of participants, their number is a point in case. Small seminars foster more individual attention and are in general more apt for trainers with a psychological background. Political scientists might cater better for seminars with larger groups. And then there is the difference between seminars being part of large programs and those which can be seen as autonomous modules. The last ones are more fit for mid-career and senior professionals, the first for junior professionals and university students.

Micro tools are the exercises to be used in the context of seminars and workshops. In general, two kinds of exercises can be distinguished: short and long ones. Short exercises are often meant to prepare the longer ones and they will normally precede them (as an example, see the first exercise in the Annex). Not always: they can also be used as tools of illustration and debriefing for the more extended ones. Short exercises can be on bilateral negotiations, long exercises on multilateral. Short exercises can be self-assessing. Longer ones are often role plays or simulations. As we will see later on, in-between forms can be developed like the minilateral 'Pentagame' (the second exercise in the Annex). Another distinction can be made between role-play exercises based on interaction between people (Boskma and Van der Meer 1973; Meerts and Schalker 1986) and simulations through computer-interaction (Lipschits 1971), and a mix of the two (Kaufman 1998, 59–75). Other tools are, as said before, audio-visual ones—both to be used to monitor and debrief behavior, or to be used as an example of negotiation behavior reality. An example of the last form is the DVD 'Space between Words' used in the simulation 'United Nations Disaster Relief Organization' (the third exercise in the Annex). The next part of this chapter will provide trainers with an example of a program plus three exercises.

The exercises in this chapter are all developed by the author, but he has been inspired by others on this. In the world of training, everybody borrows from everybody (as is the case in the world of art). The main point is to note the source of origin, but the problem is that this is not always known. Resource and guidebooks for exercises are, for example: Lewicki et al. (1994), Karrass (2000), Donnay (2006) and Meerts (1994, 133–141). The most important source of cases is the archive of the Pew Charitable Trust. The Clingendael Institute has its own range of simulation games being available to outsiders on a case by case basis. These exercises have been created by the informal 'Clingendael International Negotiation Group' (CLING) in the past two decades.

EXERCISES: BI-, MINI- AND MULTILATERALS

The small set of exercises that follows can be used to deliver training sessions with a duration of two to three days, depending on the level of the instructor, his/her ability to interlace the 'course' through short lectures, introductions and—most important of all—thorough debriefings. The last element is without doubt the most difficult and by far the most important part of a training module. After all, learning by doing is the focal point, but drawing lessons is the aim of the whole undertaking. The teacher/trainer is the one

who helps participants to be conscious of their mistakes and the ways to prevent them in the future. Every student will have his/her own style in dealing with this. It is up to the game master—and to the player—to foster this style and to enhance its effectiveness.

The sequence of the set of exercises offered here is probably the best chronological order in which they can be used. The bilateral discloses some of the intricate drives in integrative bargaining, the minilateral deals with managing complexity and the full multilateral is ideal for teaching drafting, as well as confronting theory with practice. It should be stressed that there is no problem at all in changing the sequence if the reader feels that this suits her or his purposes in a better way. In some cases, the order is not important at all. For example, the minilateral exercise has been written in order to help participants to prepare better for the full fledged simulation exercises. It is therefore sequenced before the more substantial games. However, the author of this chapter nowadays uses this game after the more far reaching simex. This is because participants will get to better insights if they first muddle through and then structure their behavior through the minilateral.

Either way, it will work, and it is up to the reader to chose and ponder on it and use the system to create a tailor-made tool that suits his purposes better. All the exercises have been put together by staff members of the Netherlands Institute of International Relations 'Clingendael'. They are an integral part of the—unpublished—'Workbook on International Negotiation' (Meerts 2007). They can be applied freely by the readers of this handbook. More on exercises and how to use them can be found in *The Expert Negotiator* (Saner 2005).

Program

A regular program might start with a lecture by the trainer. The author of this chapter normally starts with a short introduction, sketching the evolution of the negotiation process as a tool in conflict resolution over the centuries, and stressing the interrelationship between warfare and negotiation (if war is politics by other means, then negotiation might be war by other means…), as well as the importance of building institutions around the processes in order to compensate for lack of trust.

But others, like the Swiss trainer Robert Weibel, prefer to throw the group in the pond right away. This can be a helpful method, especially with groups who are not used to working alone and are thereby forced to wake up immediately. The author will normally take an hour for a warming-up lecture, before he splashes participants into the process by asking them individually to define international negotiation as a tool in conflict resolution. In a second step, they are asked to form small groups which have to negotiate a common definition of the subject. In a third step, the trainer will debrief the negotiation process they just experienced. In a fourth step, he then analyses their outcomes with them. This procedure might take a full morning but can be abridged substantially.

The second half of the morning can be used to apply exercises on strategy and tactics, skills and styles. It can sometimes be more convenient, however, to use these short exercises as instruments to create voids between the more substantial games. This is again up to the reader. It is also up to her or him to add other dimensions to the seminar, like politics (Iklé 1987), procedure (Kaufmann 1996), culture (Hofstede 1980), and/or non-verbal behavior and leaks (Goodfield 1999). But the remaining time in the first morning can also be used to exercise the bilateral— a negotiation of the European Union (EU) with a central European country—shown in this chapter. The net playing time is 30 minutes, but with introduction, preparation and debriefing, at least a full hour is needed.

The minilateral (a Clingendael pentagame being remolded by Nato Defence College), being an internal negotiation of the North Atlantic Treaty Organization (NATO) on an external crisis, will take the full first afternoon. The net playing time is 90 to 120 minutes, but again with introduction–preparation–debriefing being added, three hours will be needed. It very much depends

on the size of the group. At Nato Defence College, some 80 people take part in the game. With eight parallel negotiations in teams of ten, time is quickly running out. But as said before, it is also possible to start right away with the full multilateral text exercise and use the minilateral on the third and last day as a means to take a closer look at managing multilateral complexity.

The full fledged simulation game in the United Nations (UNDRO) context will take a full day. This will consist of a three-hour morning session for introduction, preparation, plenary and a first round of exploration, and then three hours in the afternoon for a second round of exploration, drafting and debriefing. This can easily be stretched into the next morning, especially if the process is supplemented by a BBC videotape of the real negotiation process (1971), on which basis this simulation has been created (2004). The tape takes one hour net, but with analysis it might be two or three.

Bilateral exercise (see Annex Part I)

The bilateral exercise is about a conflict of interest between the European Union and the Central European State of Quarania, which have their own needs that might, or might not be, appeased. The question is not about enlargement of the EU, but the idea is to conclude a so-called 'Europe Agreement' on twelve (or less) issues between both actors. It is beneficial for both parties to trade some issues, but not all. They should keep commodities that are more valuable to them than to the other party, while they try to give goods that are less valuable than the ones they get in return. They can create any package they wish, trading two issues for one, or whatever, but it is not allowed to change sentences or value points, as they are fixed.

Through barter trade, both parties try to come to an agreement, thereby overcoming their conflicting positions. The European Union wants Quarania to release profits of EU investments in that country, to enlarge the landing rights for EU carriers in the Quaranian capital, to close the dangerous (in the eyes of the EU at least) Chernobyl type nuclear plant in the Quaranian city of Chozno, to have better access to the Quaranian market for EU industrial products and services, and to start a political dialogue on democracy and human rights. Quarania needs better access to the EU for its citizens, rural products and textiles, as well as technical, financial and managerial assistance (to help it in restructuring its bureaucracy). They cannot settle their conflicting interests through compromise—they have to do it through compensation, and package dealing.

Of course, different packages stand for different values. One package deal is maybe not as effective as another one. The problem is that the moment one deal has been concluded, another more valuable one might be blocked by this agreement. In other words, participants will learn that they have to be patient. They should not start to bargain right away, but explore extensively. And only if they have enough information (but participants should never show each other their value points) about the most effective combinations, then they might go into the bargaining phase.

It is easier for Quarania to do better, as the combinations are more transparent to them. They only need to deal on a few issues, while the EU has smaller margins on more issues. Both have 26 points as their bottom line (BATNA, resistance or reservation point). By exchange of all commodities, each will have 36 points, but they can do much better if they are selective about their agreements. Though it will always be win/win, odd combinations like 44 against 29 can occur. The exercise shows that negotiators matter: same starting positions, different outcomes.

Minilateral exercise
(see Annex Part II)

The minilateral is a negotiation between six NATO countries (represented by one person or by delegations of two or three) having to draft a common document on a crisis in the non-existing Mediterranean Muslim country of Janubia. Member states have different views on the developments over there, depending on their interests. The bigger these interests, the more careful they are in criticizing the Janubian government and the more willing they are to support it. NATO members far away from the scene are far more critical and others take an in-between position. The UK might be a fair chair here, but why not rotate the presidency every 15 minutes? This is a good exercise in combining fairness and the defense of interests! Participants then learn how to balance national and collective interests, maximizing and optimizing needs.

This short-track multilateral exercise (pentagame or in this example a hexagame, as septagame is also a possibility but more involved as countries create too much of a mess) teaches inter alia the management of multilateral complexity. Participants will learn that they will again have to explore extensively and intensively. It is vital to work in rounds. Rounds for exploring (opening game), for parking, so not deciding on issues but putting them aside on a waiting list (mid game), and rounds for agreements (end game). The construction is such that there will always be a country that has a problem with an issue. Therefore, a solution is impossible if packages are not seen and used. And in principle: the more decisions, the better the outcome. And we will not only compare the individual scores, but also those of parallel groups. Several 'NATOs' are competing with each other here, actors will often forget.

As more actors are involved, the complexity is difficult to handle. Where is common ground? Common ground is nowhere, unless negotiators are creative enough to construct it by combining issues. As in the bilateral, sentences and value points cannot be changed. The exercise is unique in the sense of linking a diplomatic text to priorities (value points). The issues are bracketed parts of a draft text, those elements where parties have conflicting interests. Participants deal with four baskets of issues here. In another exercise, in EU context instead of NATO grid, less countries deal with more issues. Trainers can use the idea of the exercise to create any matrix on any situation. Another minilateral is between the five permanent members of the Security Council on a crisis in the Mediterranean, while Clingendael also created an exercise in which the littoral states of the Caspian negotiate on the status of the Sea, demarcations, security, exploration, mineral resources, pipelines, maritime transport, fisheries, pollution, population, etc.

Participants might believe their only options are to choose one topic out of every basket, but if they think outside the box, they will see that more decisions can be taken within each basket. In the exercise shown below, in a meeting of six NATO countries, six decisions can be taken (at least, according to the game master). However, participants might perceive more decisions. They could perhaps state that immediate evacuation is the same thing as within two weeks and therefore both agreements can be concluded at the same time. Or they might defend the position that one can condemn the government on its human rights behavior, while still supporting it as the legitimate state structure of the country. And why not decide to mediate and ask France to do this on behalf of the North Atlantic Council? If the participants feel that these are defendable outcomes, why not? Negotiation is about situation is about perception. But in the end, your interests and the arguments you use are just tools you need in order to implement your mandate—not nice, but realistic.

Multilateral Exercise
(see Annex Part III)

The full fledged multilateral exercise shows participants the creative 'chaos' of multiparty/multi-issue negotiation. This game has been based on a negotiation in Ecosoc, the United Nations Council for Economic and Social Issues. This negotiation took place in Geneva in 1971 and has been taped by the BBC. Clingendael staff bracketed the real final outcome on the basis of this tape. The game master can compare the final outcome of the simulated game with the real text by noting that all words included in the final text are marked by a plus, and all skipped parts by a minus. In two cases, only part of the text between brackets has been accepted, while other parts have been left out. In note 14, only

the central part between brackets has been adopted in reality; in note 17, adequate is out and permanent is in. *Of course, the game master should take out the + and − if she/he uses the draft text for training purposes.*

The conflict in this exercise is between France and the United States. The USA at the time was much more multilaterally motivated than 30 years later. They wanted to interfere with the prerogatives of non-state actors like the Red Cross ('The League') and Unicef. These organizations played a dominant role in disaster relief and the USA, through the mouth of ambassador George Bush Sr. in his opening statement for Ecosoc, wanted to have more grip on the efforts of these and other non-governmental organizations. The USA promoted the role of the UN in this. They proposed to establish a strong UN organization called UNDRO: the United Nations Disaster Relief Organization. Its High Commissioner should have the power to mobilize, direct and coordinate relief actions in natural disasters.

The French, however, did not think that states should interfere too much in the autonomous policies of organizations like the Red Cross, Unicef, WHO, FAO, etc. One of their motives had been that they already had a lot of influence on these international organizations while they feared US pressure in relief activities. Knowing that they could not stop the USA, they tried to undermine the power of the organization that had to be created. France did not want the High Commissioner to direct ('diriger'), but to guide ('orienter'). They did not want UNDRO to be in New York but in Geneva, not with an independent director, not with a substantial staff, not with its own budget and not firmly within the UN. In the end, the word 'directed' was accepted in the official English text but it was agreed that the official French translation would be 'orienter'(sic!). The Americans won, but it was a Pyrrhus victory and UNDRO never flourished: a clear-cut example of a backward-looking outcome.

In this simulation, a working group is formed that has to draft a text on behalf of Ecosoc. Ambassador Bush is back in New York and Bernie Segorin, US ambassador in

Geneva, has to fulfil his mandate. Stuck as he is by the policy word 'direct', he tries to explain its content as coordination without changing the word direct: 'a traffic cop directs traffic, he does not drive all the vehicles'. The Brits do not like a strong UNDRO but they have to cosponsor the US proposals, as do the Peruvians and Indonesians, who would like to go even further ('instruct'). The French are supported by the Soviet representatives as well as the Red Cross and Unicef. The chair (UN Assistant Secretary-General Kitani (Kurdish Iraqi) takes a neutral position while Tunisia acts as friend-of-the chair. Decisions are taken by unanimity between the seven states, and the other actors can only try to influence these decisions, not block them. Delegations consist of more than one person. After a plenary session, the negotiations might take place in parallel sessions. The advantage is that the results of several groups can be compared with each other.

CONCLUSIONS

Why train conflict managers in international negotiation? Because training makes a difference (Fisher 1997, 471–486). Some will use their new skills to be more effective in managing the crisis through negotiation processes. Others will even change their behaviour in a more fundamental way. It has been observed in this chapter that public sector representatives from Western Europe will, on average, belong to category I, and those from Eastern Europe to category II. This might have to do with political and societal culture and the (non-)exposure to modern training techniques. The more rigid participants were in their approach to conflict management through negotiation, the more revolutionary their change in behavior, if this change materialized. Context has an impact on training results in two ways: the climate in the seminar and the political and societal environment negotiators came from.

What can be said about the present situation in the field of conflict resolution

and negotiation training? First of all, the old observation that practitioners should help researchers to understand negotiation processes while researchers should feed trainers with new insights is still valid but also unrealistic. The three categories do not seriously overlap, though there are exceptions, like the German ambassador to Uganda who is a trainer of German diplomats at the same time (Mühlen 2005). A flow between the categories is still absent and this hampers effective training of 'conflict resolvers', though efforts have recently been made to integrate resource persons in training seminars in a novel way. The laboratory will then be constructed around the practitioners who will be tied to strict rules to make them as student-relevant as possible (Ibbotson Groth and Glevoll 2007). Furthermore, continental Europe is still lagging behind the USA and the UK in elevating the discipline of negotiation processes to an academic level. This is an obstacle for serious training in conflict resolution through international negotiation at the professional stages of learning.

How can trainers best train their trainees? Is there any advice on training modes and tools? Although training is becoming more and more 'en vogue' and trainers are increasingly seen as important contributors to the enhancement of conflict management and negotiation skills, really effective train-the-trainers' facilities are relatively scarce. Trainees have more chances to experience laboratory situations, but ministries are still quite hesitant of prioritizing on training. To the contrary, companies are much more willing to invest in this development in human resources. Negotiation is still often seen as something one can learn by doing, notwithstanding the fact that mistakes can have devastating effects. Training tools are still relatively scarce in public-sector training that still has to borrow from the private sector. Academic publications providing tools are nearly non-existent. But progress is made and methods for evaluating exercises and simulations are being developed (Torney-Purta 1998, 77–97).

Where do we find the tools we need to train our trainees? Slowly but surely research findings can be used to upgrade training tools (Druckman and Robinson 1998, 7–38). This last chapter of the Sage Handbook on Conflict Resolution provides the reader with three types of exercises that can be used in training conflict managers through international negotiation processes. The given exercises are put in rank order from bilateral through minilateral to multilateral, according to growing complexity. These exercises and simulations, developed by the Clingendael Institute in The Hague, have been tested in over 80 countries around the world. It is up to the trainer or teacher to use them in the way he/she sees fit. It is up to her or him to use these games as a basis for other games or to create variants suitable for the context they are needed in. Prescriptions to trainers and teachers don't work, as they do not work for participants and trainees either. Experiencing the process and adapting to it is the key to effectiveness.

REFERENCES

Boomen, Bert van den, ed., 2001. *The Art of Effective Training: Handbook for Trainers*. Amsterdam: Alfred Mozer Foundation.

Boskma, Peter, and Van der Meer, Frans, 1974. *Simulaties van Internationale Betrekkingen*. Groningen: H.D. Tjeenk Willink.

Casse, Pierre, and Deol, Sander, 1985. *Managing Intercultural Negotiations*. Washington DC: Sietar International.

Cohen, Raymond, 1997. *Negotiating Across Cultures*, rev. edn. Washington DC: United States Institute of Peace Press.

Donnay, Arlette, 2006. 'Exercice de négociation bilatérale entre diplomates allemands et argentins', *Négociations*, 5. Liège : De Boeck.

Druckman, Daniel, and Robinson, Victor, 1998. 'From Research to Application: Utilizing Research Findings in Negotiation Training Programs', in Joyce P. Kaufman, ed., *International Negotiation*, Vol. 3, 1. The Hague: Kluwer Law International.

Ebner, Noam, and Efron, Yael, 2005. 'Using Tomorrow's Headlines for Today's Training: Creating Pseudo-reality in Conflict Resolution Simulation Games', *Negotiation Journal*, XXI, 3: 377–393.

Faure, Guy-Olivier, ed., 2003. *How People Negotiate: Resolving Disputes in Different Cultures*. Dordrecht: Kluwer Academic Publishers.

Fisher, Ronald, 1997. 'The Potential Contribution of Training to Resolving International Conflict', in Ronald J. Fisher, ed., *International Negotiation*, Vol. 2, 3. The Hague: Kluwer Law International.

Fisher, Roger, and Ury, William, with Patton, Bill, 1991. *Getting to Yes*, 2nd edn. New York: Penguin Books.

Goodfield, Barry A., 1999. *Insight and Action*. London: University of Westminster Press.

Hemery, John, 2005. 'Training for Public Diplomacy: An Evolutionary Perspective', in Jan Melissen, ed., *The New Public Diplomacy, Soft Power in International Relations*. Houndmills: Palgrave/Macmillan.

Hemery, John, and Meerts, Paul, 2006. 'Training for Chairing: A Practical Approach', in Jan Melissen, ed., *The Hague Journal of Diplomacy*, Vol. 1, 2. Leiden: Martinus Nijhoff Publishers.

Hofstede, Geert, 1980. *Culture's Consequences*. Beverly Hills: Sage Publishers.

Ibbotson Groth, Brian, and Glevoll, Solvi, 2007. 'A New Use of Practitioners in Teaching Negotiation', *Negotiation Journal*, XXIII, 2: 173–184. New York: Plenum Press.

Iklé, Fred, 1987. *How Nations Negotiate*. New York: Harper & Row.

Jönsson, Christer, 2000. *Bargaining, Negotiation and Diplomacy: A Research Overview*. Leicester: Discussion Papers of the Diplomatic Studies Programme, No. 63.

Karrass, Chester L., 2000. *Effective Negotiating: Workbook and Discussion Guide*. Beverly Hills: Karrass Ltd.

Kaufman, Joyce P., 1998. 'Using Simulation as a Tool to Teach About International Negotiation', in Joyce P. Kaufman, ed., *International Negotiation*, Vol. 3, 1. The Hague: Kluwer Law International.

Kaufmann, Johann, 1996. *Conference Diplomacy*. London: Macmillan Press.

Lewicki, Roy. J., Barry, B. and Saunders, D.M., 1994. *Negotiation*, 2 Vols, 2nd edn. Boston: McGraw-Hill/Irwin.

Lipschits, Ies, 1971. *Simulaties in de Internationale Politiek*. Deventer: Van Loghum Slaterus.

Mastenbroek, Willem, 2002. *Negotiating as Emotional Management*. Heemstede: Holland Business Publications.

Meerts, Paul W., 1991. *A Short Guide to Diplomatic Training*. The Hague: Clingendael Institute.

Meerts, Paul W., 1994. 'Simulating Topical Diplomatic Negotiations', in Roger Armstrong, Fred Percival and Danny Saunders, eds., *The Simulation and Gaming Yearbook, Vol. 2*. London: Sagset, Kogan Page Ltd.

Meerts, Paul W., 2002. 'Training of Negotiators', in Victor A. Kremenyuk, ed., *International Negotiation, Analysis, Approaches, Issues*. San Francisco: Jossey-Bass Publishers.

Meerts, Paul W., 2007. *Workbook on International Negotiation*, 16th edn. The Hague: Clingendael Institute.

Meerts, Paul W., and Schalker, Arnout, 1986. *Internationaal Overleg in Spelvorm*. The Hague: Clingendael Institute.

Mühlen, Alexander, 2005. *Internationales Verhandeln, Konfrontation Wettbewerb, Zusammenarbeit*. Münster: Lit Verlag.

Nierenberg, Gerald, 1976. *The Complete Negotiator*. New York: Nierenberg & Zeif Publishers.

Raiffa, Howard, 1982. *The Art & Science of Negotiation*. Cambridge MA: Harvard University Press.

Saner, Raymond, 2005. *The Expert Negotiator*. Leiden: Martinus Nijhoff Publishers.

Torney-Purta, Judith, 1998. 'Evaluating Programs Designed to Teach International Content and Negotiation Skills', in Joyce P. Kaufman, *International Negotiation*, Vol. 3, 1. The Hague: Kluwer Law International.

Wheeler, Michael, 2006. 'Is Teaching Negotiation Too Easy, Too Hard, or Both?', *Negotiation Journal*, XXII, 2: 187–197. New York: Plenum Press.

Zartman, I. William, 2001. 'Conclusion: Discounting the Cost', in I.W. Zartman, ed., *Preventive Negotiation, Avoiding Conflict Escalation*. Lanham: Rowman & Littlefield Publishers.

Zartman, I. William, and Kremenyuk, Victor, eds., 2005. *Peace versus Justice: Negotiating Forward- and Backward-Looking Outcomes*. Lanham: Rowman & Littlefield Publishers.

ANNEX

PART I

Bilateral Exercise 1: Integrated Negotiations about a trade and cooperation agreement between the European Union and Quarania

European Union

You will negotiate on behalf of the European Union with a government representative of Quarania about a new trade and cooperation agreement. You will try to reach a negotiated result that should be as positive as possible by exchanging concessions.

Below you will find two tables. The *upper* table contains a list of concessions that you may *give* to your opponent; the *lower* table contains concessions that you would like to *receive* from your opponent. Every concession has a certain value. This value is expressed by a number. A high number means that this concession is of great value to you. It is up to you to decide **how many** and **which** concessions you are willing to trade for concessions of Quarania, but try to maximize your final score!

You calculate your final score by adding up the concessions, if any, that you *did not give away* (in the upper table) to the concessions that you *actually received* (in the lower table).

Possible concession of the **European Union**:	Value to you
Better access to the EU market for agricultural products	3
Technical assistance for industrial technology transfer	4
Financial protocol (a 'soft' loan of 500 MEURO—another burden on the EU budget)	6
Special aid programme to restructure the Quaranian government	4
Abandoning of the import restrictions on textiles (southern EU member states have objections)	7
Generous visa policy for citizens of Quarania (Quarania only has a small population)	2
Subtotal of concessions that you did not give away:	(A)

Possible concession of **Quarania**:	Value to you
Release profits of EU investments (the only way to make worthwhile investments for EU companies)	8
Enlarging landing rights of EU carriers (the capital Tarbad has strategic position for flights to the Far East)	6
Closing of the nuclear plant at Chozno	5
Better market access for industrial EU products	3
Better market access for EU services	7
Political dialogue about democracy and human rights (one of the underlying conditions for this agreement is the democratic development of Quarania)	7
Subtotal of concessions that you received:	(B)

Final Score (A+B)

Bilateral Exercise 2: Integrated Negotiations about a trade and cooperation agreement between the European Union and Quarania

Quarania

You will negotiate on behalf of the Quaranian government with a representative of the European Union about a new trade and cooperation agreement. You will try to reach a negotiated result that should be as positive as possible by exchanging concessions.

Below you will find two tables. The *upper* table contains a list of concessions that

you may *give* to your opponent; the *lower* table contains concessions that you would like to *receive* from your opponent. Every concession has a certain value. This value is expressed by a number. A high number means that this concession is of great value to you. It is up to you to decide **how many** and **which** concessions you are willing to trade for concessions of the EU, but try to maximize your final score!

You calculate your final score by adding up the concessions, if any, that you *did not give away* (in the upper table) to the concessions that you *actually received* (in the lower table).

Possible concession of **Quarania**:	Value to you
Release profits of EU investors (reinvestment of profits is essential for the economic development of Quarania)	6
Enlarging landing rights of EU carriers on your national airport of Tarbad city	5
Closing of the nuclear plant at Chozno (most important supplier of energy)	4
Better market access for industrial EU products in Quarania	6
Better market access for EU services in Quarania	3
Political dialogue about democracy and human rights	2
Subtotal of concessions that you did not **give away:**	(A)
Possible concession of the **European Union**:	Value to you
Better access to the EU market for agricultural products (most important export sector)	2
Technical assistance for industrial technology transfer (however industry is hardly developed)	2
Financial protocol (a 'soft' loan of 500 MEURO—this support is crucial for your balance of payments)	10
Special aid programme for the restructuring of the Quaranian government services	8
Abandoning restrictions on textile import	5
Generous visa policy for citizens of Quarania (a lot of working migrants would like to move to the EU)	9
Subtotal of concessions that you received:	(B)
Final score (A+B)	

PART II

Minilateral exercise	France	Italy	Spain	UK	Denmark	Sweden	Common total
Evacuation of EU Citizens							
No decision is taken concerning evacuation	−20	−10	−5	−10	0	5	−40
The Council decides not to evacuate EU citizens	−30	−20	−15	−15	−5	0	−85
The Council decides that evacuation will take place immediately	30	30	20	20	5	−10	95
or within the next two weeks	10	10	10	5	5	15	55
or within the next month	5	5	5	0	10	20	45
Additionally, decides to have it protected by an ad hoc coalition led by France	10	5	−5	0	−5	0	5
or by EU Forces	−5	10	5	−10	−5	−5	−10
or by a NATO Combined Joint Task Force	−20	−10	10	15	10	−15	−10

(Continued)

Part II cont'd

Minilateral exercise	France	Italy	Spain	UK	Denmark	Sweden	Common total
Evacuation of EU Citizens							
Mediation in the Conflict							
No decision is taken about mediation	−10	−10	−5	−5	0	−5	−35
The Council decides to mediate in the conflict	15	10	5	−10	5	10	35
The Council allows France to mediate on its behalf	20	5	−5	−5	−5	−5	5
The Council asks the UN to mediate	−20	−15	0	10	10	5	−5
Humanitarian Aid							
No decision is taken about the delivery of humanitarian aid	−5	−5	−10	0	0	0	−20
The Council decides not to deliver humanitarian aid	−15	−15	−5	−5	−5	0	−45
The Council decides to deliver humanitarian aid, protected or not	15	15	15	15	10	5	75
Additionally, the Council decides to do so under military protection	10	10	10	5	5	−10	30
Council's Political Position							
Press release condemns all parties involved within the conflict	−5	−5	10	15	15	30	60
Press release condemns only the Janubian Government	−20	−20	0	10	10	−5	−25
Press release condemns only the IPP, the RIF and similar groups	15	15	0	−5	5	−10	20
Press release expresses support of the Janubian Government	30	30	−10	−15	−5	−15	15
Press release expresses neither support to nor condemnation of any of the parties	5	5	−5	0	0	0	5
National score in optimal solution (shaded cells)	75	65	55	45	35	25	300
Maximum national score (bold figures in table)	125	120	70	80	60	65	
Common result if national score is maximized	245	245	285	245	195	250	

PART III

Multilateral Exercise

Case: Negotiating the establishment of the United Nations Disaster Relief Organization (UNDRO)

Objective

The objective of this simulation exercise is to practice and sharpen multilateral negotiation skills and to analyse verbal and nonverbal negotiation behaviour.

Scenario

It is 21 July 1971. Recent natural disasters, such as the severe floods in Central Europe, droughts in Afghanistan and Western Africa, as well as earthquakes in the USSR, Turkey, Indonesia and Peru, have prompted the United Nations to consider its structural involvement in disaster relief operations. Many UN institutions, such as the United Nations Children's Fund (UNICEF), the Food and Agricultural Organization (FAO), the World Health Organization (WHO) and the United Nations Development Programme (UNDP) are in fact already working in this area, but their efforts are not well coordinated. Public opinion demands better coordination of relief efforts, as it does not want its (voluntary) funds to be wasted.

At the initiative of a number of disaster-stricken developing countries, the General Assembly of the UN requested the Secretary-General in 1969 to draft a comprehensive report on the possibilities of rationalizing and improving the work of the UN system in disaster relief operations. This report, which became available at the 3 July 1971 session of the Economic and Social Council (ECOSOC), emphasized the urgent need for improved organizational arrangements in the provision of assistance by and through the United Nations system.

The ambitious US Permanent Representative to the UN, George Bush, immediately followed up on the Secretary-General's report by calling for the establishment of a United Nations Disaster Relief Organization (UNDRO), that would 'mobilise, direct and coordinate' disaster relief efforts by UN institutions and non-governmental organizations such as the Red Cross. The staff of the US Permanent Representation to the UN at Geneva has been taking long hours in redrafting a resolution for adoption by the ECOSOC at its plenary session of 23 July, the day after tomorrow. Elements of this draft have been discussed in informal meetings with various member states, the UN Secretariat and other stakeholders.

Procedure

Before the crucial plenary session of 23 July, the draft resolution will be discussed in a **Special Working Group on Disaster Relief**, consisting of representatives of the United States (US), the United Kingdom (UK), France, the Union of Soviet Socialist Republics (USSR), Tunisia, Peru, Indonesia, the International Committee of the Red Cross (ICRC), the United Nations Children's Fund (UNICEF) and chaired by the UN Secretariat (UNS) in Geneva. **Consensus** is needed between the representatives of the member states; *UNICEF and the ICRC* can only try to *influence* their decisions (they have no voting power). The meeting takes place in formal and informal sessions. The objective of the meeting—and the responsibility of the chair— is to iron out preferably all of the differences of opinion concerning the mandate, function and status of UNDRO.

DRAFT RESOLUTION 15129(LI), as proposed by 13 powers, for consideration at Council meeting 1790 on 23 July 1971

The Economic and Social Council

Bearing in mind that throughout history, natural disasters and emergency situations have inflicted heavy loss of life and property, affecting every people and every country,

Aware of the varying needs of nations experiencing such disorders, which present new challenges for international cooperation,

Concerned over the ability of the international community to come to the aid of countries in a disaster situation,

Recalling General Assembly resolutions 2435(XXIII) of 19 December 1968 and 2717(XXV) of 15 December 1970 on assistance in cases of natural disaster,

Expressing appreciation for the Secretary-General's comprehensive report, and for its perceptive examination of all aspects of the question and taking note of the relevant passage in his statement to the Council on 5 July 1971,

Noting the study, annexed to the Secretary-General's report, on the legal status of disaster relief units made available through the United Nations,

Mindful of recent steps taken to improve evolving procedures in the United Nations system, voluntary agencies and individual Governments in the field of international disaster assistance,

Bearing in mind that assistance to meet the requests of the stricken countries without prejudice to their individual country programmes under the United Nations Development Programme can be an effective contribution to the rehabilitation and development of the stricken areas,

Bearing in mind also that the possible response of the International Bank for Reconstruction and Development and other credit organizations and development agencies to a request from the Governments concerned for complementary assistance for the stricken areas, without prejudice to the assistance provided by these organizations for the normal development programmes of the stricken countries, can be an important element in the reconstruction and development to the stricken areas,

Noting the competence of the United Nations and its agencies, [the United Nations Children's Fund, the United Nations High Commissioner for Refugees and the World Food Programme,][1] to render assistance in disasters and other emergency situations,

Noting further the key role which the resident representative of the United Nations Development Programme should play at the country level,

Recognizing the vital roles in international relief of [the International Red Cross and other][2] voluntary societies,

Recognizing further the necessity to ensure prompt, effective and efficient response to a Government's need for assistance at the time of a natural disaster or other emergency situation, that will bring to bear the resources of the United Nations, prospective donor countries, and voluntary agencies,

1) *Calls* on the Secretary-General to appoint a disaster relief coordinator, who would report directly to him, and who would be authorized, on behalf of the Secretary-General:

a) To [mobilize,][3] [instruct][4] [direct][5] [guide][6] and [co-ordinate][7] the relief activities of the various organizations of the United Nations system in response to a request for disaster assistance from a stricken State;

b) [To receive on behalf of the Secretary-General contributions offered to him for disaster relief assistance to be carried out by the United Nations, its agencies, and programmes, for particular emergency situations;][8]

c) To coordinate United Nations assistance with assistance given by intergovernmental and non-governmental organizations [in particular by the International Red Cross][9];

d) To assist the Government of the stricken State to assess relief and other needs and to evaluate the priority of these needs, to disseminate this information to prospective donors and others concerned; [and to serve as a clearing-house for assistance extended or planned by all sources of external aid;][10]

e) [To promote the study, prevention, control and prediction of natural disasters, including the collection and dissemination of information concerning technological developments;][11]

f) To assist in providing advice to Governments on predisaster planning in association with relevant voluntary organizations [particularly with the International Red Cross, and draw upon United Nations resources available for such a purpose][12];

g) To acquire and disseminate information relevant to planning and coordinating relief for disasters, including the improvement and establishment of stockpiles in disaster-prone areas, and to prepare suggestions to ensure the most effective use of available resources;

h) To phase out relief operations under his aegis as the stricken country moves into the stage of rehabilitation and reconstruction but to continue to interest himself, within the framework of his responsibilities for relief, in the activities of the United Nations agencies concerned with rehabilitation and reconstruction;

i) To prepare an annual report for the Secretary-General, to be submitted to the Economic and Social Council and the General Assembly;

2) *Recommends* that [the function of Disaster Relief Coordinator be implemented by the Under-Secretary-General for Economic and Social Affairs][13] [the Disaster Relief Coordinator be endowed with the title of High Commissioner, and appointed by the Secretary-General normally for a term of five years, at a level comparable to that of an Under-Secretary-General of the United Nations][14] [the disaster Relief Coordinator will be appointed by the Secretary-General normally for a term of three years, at a level comparable to that of Assistant Secretary-General][15];

3) *Recommends* that a [small][16] [adequate permanent][17] office be created in the United Nations system for disaster relief matters;

4) *Recommends* that this office be headed by the Disaster Relief Coordinator and located in [Geneva][18] [New York][19], [be a distinct element within the United Nations Secretariat,][20] and [be augmented as necessary by short-term secondment of personnel for individual emergencies][21] [be staffed within the limits of the current staff of the Secretariat][22];

5) *Requests* the Secretary-General to prepare a study for its fifty-third session, taking into account any relevant suggestions and the experience gained by the Disaster Relief Coordinator, on ways and means to enable the Disaster Relief Coordinator adequately to perform the functions entrusted to him under the present resolution;

6) *Further* endorses the plan for a roster of volunteers to be drawn from experienced staff members of the United Nations system and interested non-governmental organizations, who could be made available at very short notice;

7) *Recommends* that the Disaster Relief Coordinator should [maintain contact][23] [coordinate][24]

with the Governments of States Members of the United Nations and members of the specialized agencies and the International Atomic Energy Agency concerning available aid in emergency situations, such as food supplies, medicines, personnel, transportation and communications, as well as advice to countries in predisaster planning and preparedness;

8) *Invites* potential recipient Governments:

a) To establish disaster contingency plans [with appropriate assistance from the Disaster Relief Coordinator][25];

b) To appoint a single national disaster relief coordinator to facilitate the receipt of international aid in times of an emergency;

c) To establish stockpiles of emergency supplies such as tents, blankets, medicine and non-perishable food-stuffs;

d) To consider appropriate legislative or other measures to facilitate the receipt of aid, including overflight and landing rights and necessary privileges and immunities for relief units;

e) To improve national disaster warming systems;

9) *[Invites][26] [Requests][27]* potential donor Governments:

a) To respond promptly to any call by the Secretary-General or by the Disaster Relief Coordinator on his behalf;

b) To consider and to continue offering on a wider basis emergency assistance in disaster situations;

c) To inform the Disaster Relief Coordinator in advance about the facilities and services they might be in a position to provide immediately, including where possible relief units, logistical support and means of effective communications;

10) *Further [invites][28] [requests][29]* all organizations of the United Nations system and all other organizations involved to cooperate with the Disaster Relief Coordinator;

11) *Recommends* that the General Assembly at its 26 session endorse the foregoing proposals and recommendations.

United Nations Disaster Relief Organization (UNDRO): Individual Instructions

United Nations Secretariat (Assistant Secretary-General)

Your name is Ismat Kitani (Assistant Secretary-General of the UN, of Iraqi nationality). Your responsibility is to chair the meeting(s) in such a way that they result in a draft resolution acceptable to all Member States involved. This can mean abstention, but a negative vote kills the draft: the Member States have veto power on the issue. The non-governmental organizations and non-Member States have no vote but they are entitled to take part in the negotiations, trying to influence decision making of member states. Take a neutral stand, and act as mediator if needed. Use the corridors intensively, allow time for informal negotiations, and think of time management.

ICRC Representative (Non-governmental)

You are Henrik Beer of the International Committee of the League of the Red Cross. The idea of creating a competitor to the Red Cross in the cloak of a UN organization for disaster relief is a 'disaster' for the ICRC. Your board does not want this organization: it is an unnecessary duplication and it will only take funds from the ICRC. If you cannot stop the Americans on this, then try to weaken the mandate of UNDRO and its coordinator (director) as much as possible and prevent any voluntary funding; rather the UN should pay for UNDRO, if needed. Note: of the three keywords of Ambassador Bush (see scenario), the notion 'direct' is very problematic for the ICRC.

UNICEF Representative (Non-member State)

Your name is Henri Labouisse and you are representing the Children's Fund of the UN. You have severe doubts about the usefulness of a UN organization to fight the consequences of natural disasters. Too many actors are already active in the field. The main problem at the moment is to coordinate all the states and international organizations who want to send relief goods in case of a disaster. Yet another organization will only complicate matters and will compete with your funding resources. This should not happen! Of the three keywords of Ambassador Bush (see scenario), the word 'direct' is very problematic for UNICEF.

US Permanent Representative to the UN in Geneva (Ambassador)

You are Bernie Segorin and you represent the US position. Your country proposes the creation of UNDRO. It should be a new UN unit with its own, new budget and a firm mandate to enable it to act decisively in mobilizing, directing and coordinating all relief activities in the case of natural disasters. UNDRO stands for healthy competition with organizations like the ICRC and UNICEF which monopolize the present efforts to support stricken countries. This monopoly leads to waste of money in inflexible non-governmental bureaucracies. The coordinator of UNDRO—with the rank of High Commissioner speaking on behalf of the Secretary-General of the UN and firmly established within the UN system—should be as strong and influential as possible in order to overcome these bureaucratic obstacles. It is therefore instrumental to put UNDRO in New York, though this is open to negotiation. Note: the resolution must contain the three keywords mentioned by Ambassador Bush (see the 'scenario').

UK Permanent Representative (Ambassador)

Your name is Donal McCarthy, representing the United Kingdom. Her Majesty's government sees the importance of a disaster relief organization. It believes however that it should be enshrined in the UN system. The coordinator should have the title of High Commissioner and should have a semi-independent position. It sees the necessity of creating a new budget for UNDRO, but this could be limited as the staff can be partly recruited from the present UN secretariat. Voluntary funds should be used to

supplement the budget as much as possible in order to limit new UN spending. The mandate of UNDRO should be curtailed as you fear yet another bureaucracy if it becomes a policy-making unit instead of a mere implementation unit. However, you should not score at the detriment of your relationship with the USA. In the end, you will always have to agree with the Americans, though you try to undermine their position by having others criticize them.

French Permanent Representative (Ambassador)

Your name is Jean-Fernant Laurent, representative of the French Republic. Traditionally, France works through organizations like ICRC and UNICEF to help countries who are stricken by natural disasters. Furthermore, there is a strong bilateral French effort, especially in cases where francophone countries are victimized. The Americans now try to downgrade the French position in the area of disaster relief by proposing a new organization. Your task is to undermine the US efforts without damaging the French–US relationship too much. If UNDRO is unavoidable, then try to weaken its mandate and position as much as possible and try to keep it within your realm by putting it in Geneva, with a coordinator of a low rank, or a coordinator with a high rank who is doing the job on a part-time basis. He will only be active in case of disasters. As far as the UNDRO budget is concerned, you are against private voluntary funding as this might damage the funding possibilities of the ICRC. Note: of the three keywords mentioned by Ambassador Bush (see 'scenario'), the word 'direct' is problematic as it emphasizes too much that UNDRO should stand above, and not amongst, the disaster relief organizations. Try to keep this word out of the resolution or try to neutralize it as much as possible.

Soviet Permanent Representative (Ambassador)

Your name is Gleb Smirnov, representative of the Soviet Union. Why another UN organization? This will only cost money and the money will have to be paid by the member states. The USSR does not have a very strong economic position at the moment and you are instructed to limit UN spending as much as possible. You cannot, therefore, support the idea of creating UNDRO as a new, separate bureaucratic organization. But on the other hand, this case is not important enough for a Soviet veto. You might settle for an abstention if a majority in the Special Working Group decides on UNDRO as an autonomous body with its own director. As a compromise, you might support a disaster relief unit that is part and parcel of the present UN system in Geneva. Hereby, extra spending would be avoided as a part of the existing secretariat could do the work. The coordinator could be somebody with a high rank who does this as a side job, next to his main work elsewhere in the UN. Extra payment is not necessary. For the organization itself, one could also think of funding from private voluntary sources, in the way the ICRC has been funded up to now.

Tunisian Permanent Representative (Minister-Councillor)

Your country is in favour of creating a United Nations Disaster Relief Organization. UNDRO can be of great help for developing countries like Tunisia in case of natural disasters. You do not care too much about the format of UNDRO. It could be part of the UN family as a separate organization or its tasks could be given to an Under-Secretary-General of one of the existing bodies of the UN. Your special task in this negotiation is to support the chairman of the Special Working Group you are participating in. Together with him, you see to it that some kind of disaster relief facility will come into being. Keep in mind that the chairman in office of ECOSOC is the Tunisian diplomat. His Excellency Mr Idriss. He asked you to support the chair of the Working Group, the Assistant Secretary-General, Mr Kitani. But at the same time, your government instructed you not to undermine the Tunisian–French relationship by stepping too far away from the French position.

Peruvian Permanent Representative (Ambassador)

The government of Peru is one of those that took the initiative for the debates on the creation of a strong, autonomous UN organization called UNDRO. UNDRO should be able to instruct other UN and Non-Governmental Organizations in their dealings with natural disasters. UNDRO's Director should have the rank of Under-Secretary-General. His power over the other organizations must be expressed in his ability and his mandate to instruct the UN relief agencies and the NGOs like the Red Cross. If 'instruction' is unacceptable to the other negotiators in your Special Working group, then the UNDRO Director should at least have the mandate to 'mobilise, direct and coordinate' the relief activities. You can expect certain countries to be sceptical about the creation of UNDRO. The same is true for the established organizations in the field of disaster relief, for example, the Red Cross. Try to make sure that this promising initiative is not paralysed by these parties!

Indonesian Permanent Representative (Ambassador)

Together with the ambassador of Peru, you negotiate for a strong United Nations Disaster Relief Organization. UNDRO should have its own staff and its Director should be able to take the lead in relief activities. He can only do that if he has the power to steer the other relief agencies, both from the UN family and from the Non-Governmental side. It is a priority for a country like Indonesia, very vulnerable to natural disasters like earthquakes and floods—as well as man-made natural disasters like forest burnings—to have the best international coordination of relief activities one can imagine. You therefore welcome the speech of the US Permanent Representative to the United Nations, Ambassador Bush. UNDRO's Director should be endowed with the title of High Commissioner, have his own staff, and be appointed at the level of Under-Secretary-General.

NOTES

1 Proposed by UNICEF, supported by the Red Cross +

2 Proposed by the Red Cross, supported by UNICEF +

3 Proposed by the US, supported by the UK +

4 Proposed by Peru, supported by Indonesia −

5 Proposed by the US, supported by Peru +

6 Proposed by France, supported by the USSR −

7 Proposed by the US, supported by the UK +

8 Proposed by the US, supported by the UK +

9 Proposed by the US, supported by Indonesia and Peru −

10 Proposed by the US, supported by the UK +

11 Proposed by the USSR, supported by France +

12 Proposed by the France, supported by Tunisia +

13 Proposed by the USSR −

14 Proposed by the US − + −

15 Proposed by France −

16 Proposed by France, supported by the USSR +

17 Proposed by the US, supported by the UK − +

18 Proposed by the USSR, supported by France −

19 Proposed by the US, supported by the UK −

20 Proposed by the US, supported by Peru +

21 Proposed by the US +

22 Proposed by the USSR −

23 Proposed by France +

24 Proposed by the US −

25 Proposed by the US +

26 Proposed by France +

27 Proposed by the US −

28 Proposed by France +

29 Proposed by the US −

Conclusion: Emerging Problems in Theory and Practice

Jacob Bercovitch, Victor Kremenyuk,
and I. William Zartman

Perhaps more than most other handbook subjects, Conflict Resolution is an exciting field of intellectual attention, still in a state of development. It is of course exciting because it is so important to the maintenance of a better, safer world. The intellectual challenge is of immediate, practical import and its theory faces its ultimate test of practical value. Conflict resolution is not just a set of abstract ideas, it is a highly practical set of skills and behaviors. But it is also exciting because the field is still in its infancy, and so many advances remain to be made. It is a field that is truly interdisciplinary with many scholars and findings coming to the field from different branches of knowledge. What is known is for the greatest part relatively new knowledge, and every advance poses further challenges to discover newer knowledge. Conflict Resolution is a new and lively frontier of knowledge, and we have tried to capture this sense of intellectual adventure in the preceding chapters.

We have learned much about the sources and causes of conflict, how to respond to it, prevent it or resolve it, but there is much more we need to do, and many unanswered questions. One of the questions left unanswered in the theory and practice of Conflict Resolution so far, is: where to go from here? It is evident that Conflict Resolution is promising and deserves support. Also, it

is clear that with time, the CR approach will enjoy even more support because violent coercive solutions of conflicts become more and more expensive and the only viable alternative to it is a peaceful resolution. Weapons of mass destruction (WMD) have outlawed themselves in practice, except possibly at the hands of outlaws, and yet both interstate and intrastate conflict, often by the most primitive methods, has directly taken massive toll and indirectly destroyed and dehabilited entire societies (IRC 2001). The challenge is intensified.

Each of the four parts of this collection asks different questions and poses new directions for further research and for testing in practice. Part I, *History and Methods of Study*, shows Conflict Resolution to constitute a serious corrective to established patterns of studying international relations (IR) from a Realist or Institutional perspective only. The field began as "peace studies", a deliberate ideological challenge to foreign policy practice and to IR teaching. It has come a long way since then, picking up controlled comparisons in case studies, quantitative analysis, modeling, experimentation, social analysis, and multi-method research to add to diplomatic studies. Indeed, the variety of methodologies is so great that the opportunity for multimethod studies becomes more and more expansive. Today, methodologies old and new often tend to honker down in their approaches, defending themselves even more vigorously than their results, when they should be inviting cross-methodological testing and verification of those results. The first part of the book tries to capture this complexity and account for it, suggest the various ways conflict resolution can be studied, and shows how its findings impact so directly on our lives.

Methodologically and conceptually, this diversity has opened doors to new rooms of study. The Correlates of War (COW) project at the University of Michigan has produced a data bank used for testing many new propositions, but its presence calls for a brother bank of data on the Correlates of Peace (COP) (Telhami 2002). Other data banks have also been created (e.g. ICB, MID, ICM), and these indeed permit the analysis of different aspects of conflict, but more needs to be done if we are to understand how conflicts are or can be resolved. So there is a need, which we must all see as a challenge to meet, to develop better questions and data sources, so that better and more relevant answers can be sought (Bercovitch and Fretter 2007). Misleading results have been achieved through the use of proxies, which ignore the many steps that separate them from dynamic reality. Modeling too presents its challenge (Avenhaus and Zartman 2007). While models *of* negotiation are still seeking to catch up with actual practice at a meaningful depth of insight into process, models *for* negotiation have proven to be of great usefulness in illustrating proposed effect but are too little used, and models *in* negotiation such as for fair divisions and optimum packages have still to overcome the need for politics and ownership (Raiffa with Richardson and Metcalfe 2003). In a more standard direction, the controlled comparisons among case studies are fed new cases every day (or so). The methods we use to study conflict resolution affect the questions we ask, and the answers we get. The more aware we can be of that, the better will our practice of conflict resolution be.

Part II, *Issues and Sources of Conflict*, presents an exhaustive analysis of the issues, sources and causes that are associated with or produce conflict in the relations between individuals and groups. Many causes and sources are identified, but, in fact, the comprehensive knowledge that we have here only poses new questions for analysis. Territorial issues in conflict have been plumbed deep, but they still leave many questions unanswered when they move from political geography to psycho-geography: if sacred places are non-tradable items (Atran, Axelrod, and Davis 2007), how can they be made components of a positive-sum solution? Indeed, as the game theoretic presentation has shown, Chicken Dilemmas and Battles of the Sexes have two Nash equilibria, so how can collaborative situations be brought to a single joint and stable outcome? The dilemma is a clear example of the need for multi-method analysis.

Similarly, much has been done on the economic sources of conflict, even to the extent of purporting to elbow out other sources. But when in fact does general deprivation become reframed into terms of discrimination? Where do political entrepreneurs come from? And how can a country get out of the Conflict Trap (Collier et al. 2003), without falling back into the simplistic and millennial notion of structural causes, that underdevelopment is the cause and development is the cure to conflict? Beyond economics, current knowledge about conflict resolution faces the huge challenge of the future in handling ecological sources of existential threats of ever rising importance. More than ever, the answer lies in new and broader regimes that are increasingly difficult to negotiate but also increasingly difficult to enforce. Both aspects of conflict resolution—creation and enforcement—belong to the study of regimes that surged at one point in the past, then sagged, and demands revival in the future for its importance (Spector and Zartman 2003). And beyond that understanding lies the need to conceptualize the ever-growing net of ecological regimes that regulate international activity, themselves overlapping, contesting and conflicting with each other. Neither law nor politics know how to analyze, let alone manage, these conflicts.

Identity conflicts arise when one party's identity requires actions that impinge on another. This requirement can be internally focused or aggressive, either when one party's identity is only realized at the expense of another's or when one party feels the need to proselytize another. Or it can be externally driven or defensive, when one party feels itself to be under an existential threat. In all these cases, the operative trigger is subjective. It might be hypothesized that the more intense the identity feelings, the greater the chance for conflict with another party, but that does not solve the subjective problem. Which, when, and why – the eternal questions for social science analysis – compel us to push our research further.

Similarly, it is striking that the beginning of the new millennium faces a challenge to international relations from a mystical religious surge closer to the beginning of the previous millennium than to either the state-based, world-shrinking globalization or the positivist quantitativizing ways of studying it in the current era. Wars of religion and ideology were thought to be over, as History (as we knew it) was to be too, leaving both analysis and action unable to handle the new–old turn of conflict relations. This final challenge in the list of issues and sources of conflict reinforces at the highest level the fact that the field faces broad new questions, not only in the substance of its study but even in the procedures of its methodology, still seeking ways to grasp that substance.

Part III, *Methods of Managing Conflict*, deals with how parties in conflict or change agents from outside can do something to escape from an escalating and costly conflict. It begins with an account of the latest set of ideas on conflict resolution – conflict prevention. Launched at the UN by Dag Hammarskjöld and revived by Boutros Boutros Ghali, it almost immediately stumbled over its implications and never became an effective mandate. Yet prevention remains an aspiration for policy and an approach for research, elusive in both cases. Since conflict cannot be eliminated, only its escalation managed, resolved and transformed, prevention

depends on its existence, and faces the continual challenge of satisfying at the same time the needs and desires of the parties that gave rise to the conflict. Conflict management is the enemy of conflict resolution, as it removes the pressure to resolve, yet it is frequently the only means to reduce violence, a paradox that itself needs resolving.

For conflicts that cannot be prevented, the next tool of conflict resolution is negotiation, where some basic new opportunities appear. The new conflicts of the era pose questions about the assumptions of the negotiation process as developed, studied and practiced to date. Instead of a binary exercise between established parties, negotiation became increasingly a process of selecting parties, shaping awareness of interests, and arriving at an outcome that depends on the sides' faith in its implementation. Current theory and practice are not equipped to handle such a process. Nor – though they have dealt with questions of opening and process – have they addressed at all the subject of closure. In multilateral negotiation, so important to developing cooperation, the theory of coalition so basic to the process (and absent in bilateral negotiation) also demands to be revived and expanded beyond its earlier beginnings.

Mediation is more necessary than it should be and less frequently practiced than it could be. Conflicting parties need help, and are so engaged for ostensibly good reason that they cannot extract themselves from the costly conflict. The mediator is usually faced with the assumption that it knows the parties' interest in conflict vs. nonconflict better than they, and that it can help craft an agreement between conflicting demands of peace vs. justice. In so doing, the mediator draws on a limited supply of leverage, still not fully analyzed, to accomplish major transformations. The parties face the reentry problem of making their mediated behavior palatable to their home populations. Both theory and data are needed to analyze these problems and develop new knowledge useful to mediators and parties themselves.

Judicial methods of resolving conflict take ownership out of the hands of the parties and delegate it to a higher authority, much in the way that formal models *in* negotiation propose optimal solutions. But in the process of deciding guilt, the expanded international role of the judiciary under special courts and universal jurisdiction constitutes impediments to negotiated or mediated conflict management and resolution. Practice and research alike stand at the door to a solution to the paradox. Another paradox posed by evolving international law is the right to protect or sovereignty as responsibility, the duty imposed on stronger states to intervene in the affairs of weaker states to protect their population, in a reversal of the basis of the Westphalian system. But when that right is to be exercised remains deep in academic and diplomatic debate.

Similarly, the tool of dialog and the role of NGOs' Track 2 effects another penetration into the state sanctuary, held in the hands of actors who can go where states cannot. But the limits of this new activity are not yet clear, and neither are the measures of their success. The methods and the results are generally looser than standard negotiation and mediation, their purposes neither fully managing nor resolving, and their analysis and practice softer in the skills and processes involved. Yet the increasing penetrability of the state calls for increasingly sophisticated study and use of their methods and authorization of their agents.

Finally, the increasing prominence of international organizations (IOs) and non-governmental organizations (NGOs) on the global and regional levels brings to the fore a subject, like others above, caught in the cloud between their powers and their aspirations: working to provide leadership to the anarchic state system, yet dependent for its resources and authority on the very states they seek to control. The UN is weak to a fault, yet its very weakness keeps its members from enacting the reforms necessary to its strengthening (UN 2004). In some regions, such as Africa (with the AU) or Asia (with ASEAN), member states have enacted significant reforms, but their implementation has lagged. Between the two levels, the debate

over subsidiarity often adds to inactivity. Indeed, the biggest challenge to scholarship on the subject is not to fall off either side of the road into cynicism or idealism, while finding appropriate data and analysis of IO effects on conflict resolution.

The final part of the Handbook, Part IV, introduces *Current Features and Dilemmas in the study of Conflict Resolution*. Here the intellectual horizons of the field are stretched farther, and new issues and ideas that have a bearing on conflict and its reclusion are introduced. New forms of conflict, such as terrorism, and how best to respond to it, are discussed. Terrorism is a form of unregulated conflict where the parties' identities are not always certain, or are even obscured, and the means used to pursue objectives are at best indiscriminate. This form of conflict poses new challenges to all of us in the field and requires different approaches and methods, yet ultimately, we believe that even such conflicts can be negotiated and resolved.

Another element in the expanding Conflict Resolution context is the press and other media, which in the ostensible search for better information for a better informed public can come to play an important, but often disruptive, role in the search for solutions to violence and conflict. Both training and reconceptualization are called for. Interestingly, democracy plays a similar role. The line between informed public awareness and uninformed public participation in conflict and its resolution is often thin and porous. Democratization is often a context and source of conflict, even though democracy, once attained, is both a procedure for handling conflict and a condition for reducing it. New work is needed to smooth the passage from authoritarian to democratic stability.

Another issue that may have a major impact on conflict is culture. Indeed, some posit that any future conflict will be a conflict between cultures, not states or nations (Huntington, 1993). How does culture affect conflict resolution? How sensitive do we have to be to cultural differences? Does conflict resolution have the same resonance in different cultures? The Western tradition that is individually oriented is also one that encourages the belief that all conflicts and contradictions can be resolved. That is not necessarily the case with other traditions, and we must be aware of it as scholars – still primarily from the Western scientific communities – seek ways of understanding and producing resolution. We should also be aware of the increasing role of force and the control of force in the resolution of conflicts: when do backfires control and when do they become forest fires? We need to appreciate how and when force, arms control and measures short of war can be used, and to what extent they may help ameliorate a conflict situation or make it worse.

This part of the book also shows how in recent years the very concept of conflict resolution has been stretched. Traditionally, conflict resolution amounted to an attempt, successful or otherwise, between parties and/or outsiders to do something about their conflict, that is, to reach an agreement, reduce violence, and modify some aspects of their behavior. Yet, in fact, most of the conflicts that were apparently settled or resolved tended to reignite into violence within a few short years. As a result, the topic of durability arose as a subject of concern and of study, as research continues to identify the reasons why agreements last, or don't. We recognize the need for an extended approach to the issue of resolution. We now expect a genuine approach to conflict resolution to involve changing structural and attitudinal aspects of a relationship, not just its violent behavior. Thus, we talk about peace building, which is in effect a post-conflict resolution structural approach, and reconciliation, which is in effect a post-conflict resolution attitudinal approach, and posit these as the criteria for assessing whether a conflict is successfully resolved or not. Merely changing behavior is no longer sufficient. In the current complex and intermeshed environment, we need to tackle the sources as well as the manifestations of conflict. Peace and justice still elude a perfect reconciliation, human rights both impede and sustain resolution, and atonement and forgiveness vie for first place in a productive

sequence. As in many components of this field, the elements have been identified but their relationships need to be examined and more firmly established.

And at the same time, there is an accompanying need to teach the knowledge that is available and to train conflict managers in the field, no matter what their other professions are. Conflict Resolution is a universal calling, its technology still lags behind that of war, its heroes are still not as tall as generals in the public eyes, and any Nobel prizes won by its scholars have come from the discipline of economics. Yet, it does not have a Nobel Prize of its own, to whose laureates this book is dedicated. We need to strive for better knowledge about resolutions that achieve some degree of peace, but are also predicated on some notions of justice and equity. And that is a tall order indeed.

The other basic element is the power of morality. Realists who believed primarily in the power of the force for centuries ridiculed such religions as Christianity or Buddhism for their appeal to nonviolence, respect for human life, and belief in justice. The rules of conduct in conflict excluded any "weakness" and refer to human feeling as deviation from the normal, regular way of pursuing victory. Some compassion to the victims was allowed and tolerated only after the conflict was won. This was the ethics even of the crusade. The use of force was labeled *Ultima ratio regis*, the last resort of the kings. And in all these circumstances, the attempts to address the moral side of the violence in conflicts were bluntly ignored.

Something has changed with the advent of weapons of mass destruction. The innocent people, the population have become one of the targets of the strategy of coercion. Sovereignty, already porous, has become sovereignty as responsibility, subject to a Right to Protect. While in nondemocratic systems it has hardly changed the usual way of military planning and domestic repression, it has become a hard moral problem in democratic societies. It has become morally unacceptable for military and political leaders to acknowledge the fact of strategic planning in which innocent people were in advance identified as the "collateral damage". The mere fact that the notion of the "collateral damage" has appeared meant that there were some serious problems associated with the use of force even when the national security was at stake.

From this point of view, Conflict Resolution which promised a dignified outcome of conflict, which appealed also to human feelings, thus giving more support to those who abhorred the perspective of a conflict with millions dead, has appeared as an outcome. It has allowed all those who instinctively resisted the idea of a forced solution to enlist a weapon that could allow winning without defeating. It stands as a worthy lesson to analyze and pursue in the 21st century and beyond.

We began this volume with the question of what conflict resolution is, and whether all conflicts can be resolved. We have turned our attention to a myriad of issues, and offered the considered viewpoints of scholars, diplomats, and other practitioners. We have striven to provide an accurate and contemporaneous picture of where the field is at, and where it might be heading. We conclude this volume more than ever convinced that conflict resolution is not just possible or desirable in the current international environment. It is absolutely necessary. Resolving conflicts and making peace is no longer an option; it is an intellectual and practical skill that we must all possess.

REFERENCES

Bercovitch, Jacob and Judith Fretter. 2007. "Studying International Mediation: Developing Data Sets on Mediation, looking for Patterns and Searching for Answers". *International Negotiation* 12 (2): 145–173.

Index

CPSIA information can be obtained
at www.ICGtesting.com
Printed in the USA
BVOW08*2120180817

492498BV00005B/9/P